Dear West Customer:

West Academic Publishing has changed the look of its American Casebook Series®.

In keeping with our efforts to promote sustainability, we have replaced our former covers with book covers that are more environmentally friendly. Our casebooks will now be covered in a 100% renewable natural fiber. In addition, we have migrated to an ink supplier that favors vegetable-based materials, such as soy.

Using soy inks and natural fibers to print our textbooks reduces VOC emissions. Moreover, our primary paper supplier is certified by the Forest Stewardship Council, which is testament to our commitment to conservation and responsible business management.

The new cover design has migrated from the long-standing brown cover to a contemporary charcoal fabric cover with silver-stamped lettering and black accents. Please know that inside the cover, our books continue to provide the same trusted content that you've come to expect from West.

We've retained the ample margins that you have told us you appreciate in our texts while moving to a new, larger font, improving readability. We hope that you will find these books a pleasing addition to your bookshelf.

Another visible change is that you will no longer see the brand name Thomson West on our print products. With the recent merger of Thomson and Reuters, I am pleased to announce that books published under the West Academic Publishing imprint will once again display the West brand.

It will likely be several years before all of our casebooks are published with the new cover and interior design. We ask for your patience as the new covers are rolled out on new and revised books knowing that behind both the new and old covers, you will find the finest in legal education materials for teaching and learning.

Thank you for your continued patronage of the West brand, which is both rooted in history and forward looking towards future innovations in legal education. We invite you to be a part of our next evolution.

Best regards,

Louis H. Higgins
Editor in Chief, West Academic Publishing

CASES AND MATERIALS ON
JUVENILE JUSTICE ADMINISTRATION

Third Edition

■ ■ ■

By

Barry C. Feld

Centennial Professor of Law
University of Minnesota Law School

AMERICAN CASEBOOK SERIES®

WEST®

A Thomson Reuters business

Mat #40743266

© West, a Thomson business, 2000, 2004
© 2009 Thomson Reuters

> 610 Opperman Drive
> St. Paul, MN 55123
> 1–800–313–9378

Printed in the United States of America

ISBN: 978–0–314–19206–6

To my wife, Patricia, with love and gratitude

*

PREFACE

Young offenders constitute a significant part of the "crime problem." They pose difficult and interesting problems for youth policy and criminal justice policy—how do we respond when the child is a criminal and the criminal is a child? In the field of juvenile justice, states truly constitute "laboratories of experimentation." No single source of law governs juvenile courts. Rather, a combination of United States Supreme Court constitutional decisions, state court constitutional and non-constitutional decisions, statutes, juvenile court procedural rules, and administrative procedures govern different aspects of juvenile justice administration. As a consequence, states' laws and policies toward young offenders vary considerably. This Casebook will provide students with the background necessary to understand the policy issues that state statutes, court procedural rules, and federal and state judicial opinions address.

This Casebook focuses exclusively on the criminal and non-criminal misconduct of children that bring them within the jurisdiction of juvenile courts. It examines school, law enforcement, judicial, and administrative responses to youthful misconduct. It is designed for a two or three semester hour course, seminar, or clinic on young offenders and juvenile justice administration. It does not address child abuse, dependency and neglect, or juvenile or family courts' dependency processes. It deals with issues of "children's rights" only insofar as they relate to the processes of investigating and prosecuting juvenile offenders for delinquency and status-offenses. In the interests of readability, I have edited heavily the cases, statutes, and articles, and deleted most of the internal citations and footnotes of courts and commentators without indicating those omissions. Although I have tried to create a comprehensive, national casebook of materials on juvenile justice administration, every book can be improved. Please send any comments, suggestions, criticisms, or advice to feldx001@umn.edu or by mail: Barry Feld, University of Minnesota Law School, 229 19th Avenue South, Minneapolis, MN 55455.

Despite the Supreme Court's "Constitutional Domestication," juvenile courts primarily are statutory entities reflecting state legislative policy judgments. Three contending policy themes affect variations in juvenile justice administration: the legal and administrative consequences of regulating *children* rather than *adults*; the procedural and substantive implications of a justice system that nominally emphasizes *treatment* rather than *punishment*; and the tensions between *discretion* and *rules* that occur in a system that *treats children* rather than *punishes adults*. These materials provide a comparative perspective to enable students to analyze how different states grapple with similar issues of youth crime, justice administration, and public policy. Where states' policies diverge, the Casebook identifies different responses to the same problem to enable readers to understand the range of legal options. By studying the ways that different states answer crucial questions, students will become aware of the wider range of policy alternatives. By appreciating the assumptions and choices embedded in current law, as lawyers, they can better shape legal policies in the future. The materials lend themselves to two types of comparative analyses—similarities and differences between the juvenile and criminal justice systems, and among various states' juvenile justice systems. Despite the statutory nature of juvenile courts, I have designed these materials to provide a comprehensive national casebook. I strongly encourage teachers to supplement this casebook with materials from their state's juvenile code and leading cases to further enhance the comparative perspective.

I have taught a juvenile justice seminar and/or course from earlier editions of this casebook for a decade and I am grateful to a generation of students who helped me to refine them and bring them to fruition. Caroline Crenshaw, Class of 2009, and Ben Kaplan, Class of 2010, provided outstanding research assistance on this edition of the Casebook and responded to my outrageous research requests cheerfully, creatively, and comprehensively. Several distinguished juvenile justice colleagues generously took time from their busy schedules to review earlier versions of the First and Second Editions and made many thoughtful and helpful suggestions for continual improvement. I am very grateful to Professors Samuel Davis, Martin Gardner, Jeffrey Fagan, Martin Guggenheim, James Jacobs, Elizabeth Scott, Robert E. Shepherd, Jr., and Frank Zimring for their insightful comments and critiques. Perry Moriearty provided a thorough critique of this iteration of the casebook for which I'm very grateful. Of course, none of these colleagues bear any responsibility for my occasional failure to heed their wise counsel.

I have dedicated this book to my wife, Patricia Feld, my life partner of four decades and mother of my two wonderful children, Ari and Julia. I am grateful to Patricia beyond the capacity of words to express for the life that we share. Her support, encouragement, and patience have enabled me to grow professionally and personally and make every day of my life a joy and pleasure.

BARRY C. FELD

Effie, Minnesota
June 2009

ACKNOWLEDGEMENTS

American School Health Association for Ryoko Yamaguchi, et al., "Relationship Between Student Illicit Drug Use and School Drug–Testing Policies," 73 *Journal of School Health* 159 (copyright 2003, reprinted by permission).

Ballinger Press for The American Bar Association—Institute of Judicial Administration, *Juvenile Justice Standards Relating to Counsel for Private Parties* (copyright 1980, reprinted by permission).

Ballinger Press for The American Bar Association—Institute of Judicial Administration, *Juvenile Justice Standards Relating to Delinquency and Sanctions* (copyright 1980, reprinted by permission).

Ballinger Press for The American Bar Association—Institute of Judicial Administration, *Juvenile Justice Standards Relating to Dispositions* (copyright 1980, reprinted by permission).

Boston University for Barry Feld, "The Juvenile Court Meets the Principle of Offense: Punishment, Treatment, and the Difference It Makes," 68 *Boston University Law Review* 821 (copyright 1988, reprinted by permission of Boston University).

Brooklyn Law School for Linda F. Giardino, "Statutory Rhetoric: The Reality Behind Juvenile Justice Policies in America," 5 *Journal of Law & Policy* 223 (copyright 1996, reprinted by permission of Brooklyn Law School).

Dickinson School of Law for Donald J. Harris, "Due Process vs. Helping Kids in Trouble: Implementing the Right to Appeal from Adjudications of Delinquency in Pennsylvania," 98 *Dickinson Law Review* 209 (copyright 1998, reprinted by permission of Dickinson School of Law).

Fordham Law Review for Katherine Hunt Federle, "The Ethics of Empowerment: Rethinking the Role of Lawyers in Interviewing and Counseling the Child Client," 64 *Fordham Law Review* 1655 (copyright 1996, reprinted by permission).

Georgetown University Law Center for Richard Kay and Daniel Segal, "The Role of the Attorney in Juvenile Court Proceedings: A Non-Polar Approach," 61 *Georgetown Law Journal* 1401 (copyright 1973, reprinted by permission of the Georgetown University School of Law).

George Washington Law Review for Anne Proffitt Dupre, "Should Students Have Constitutional Rights? Keeping Order in the Public Schools," 65 *George Washington Law Review* 64 (copyright 1996, reprinted by permission of the George Washington Law Review).

William S. Hein & Co., Inc. for Elizabeth S. Lawton, *"Facilities Review Panel v. Coe*: The West Virginia Supreme Court of Appeals Adopts An Objective Approach to Deciding Pretrial Detention of Accused Juveniles," 95 *West Virginia Law Review* 505 (copyright 1993, reprinted by permission of William S. Hein & Co).

Hofstra University Law School for Barry C. Feld, "Competence, Culpability, and Punishment: Implications of *Atkins* for Executing and Sentencing Adolescents," 32 *Hofstra Law Review* 463 (copyright 2003, reprinted by permission of Hostra University Law Review).

Houghton and Mifflin Publishers for Robert M. Emerson, "Role Determinants in Juvenile Court," in Daniel Glaser, ed., *Handbook of Criminology* (copyright 1974, reprinted by permission).

Jefferson Law Book Company for Cynthia Kelly Conlon, "Urineschool: A study of the Impact of the *Earls* Decision on High School Random Drug Testing Policies," 32 *Journal of Law and Education* 297 (copyright 2003, reprinted by permission).

Joe Christensen, Inc. for Barry Feld, "Bad Law Makes Hard Cases: Reflections on Teen–Aged Axe–Murderers, Judicial Activism, and Legislative Default," 8 *Law & Inequality Journal* 1 (copyright 1990, reprinted by permission).

Kluwer Academic Publishers for Thomas Grisso, et al., "Juveniles' Competence to Stand Trial: A Comparison of Adolescents' and Adults' Capacities as Trial Defendants," 27 *Law and Human Behavior* 333 (copyright 2003, reprinted by permission of Kluwer Academic Publishers).

Minnesota Law Review Foundation for Barry Feld, "Race, Politics, and Juvenile Justice: The Warren Court and the Conservative 'Backlash'," 87 *Minnesota Law Review* 1447 (copyright 2003, reprinted by permission).

Minnesota Law Review Foundation for Barry Feld, "Violent Youth and Public Policy: A Case Study of Juvenile Justice Law Reform," 79 *Minnesota Law Review* 1011 (copyright 1995, reprinted by permission).

Minnesota Law Review Foundation for Barry Feld, "Criminalizing Juvenile Justice: Rules of Procedure for the Juvenile Court," 69 *Minnesota Law Review* 141 (copyright 1984, reprinted by permission).

Minnesota Law Review Foundation for Barry Feld, "Reference of Juvenile Offenders for Adult Prosecution: The Legislative Alternative to Asking Unanswerable Questions," 62 *Minnesota Law Review* 582 (copyright 1978, reprinted by permission).

National Academy Press for Joan McCord, Cathy Spatz Widom and Nancy Crowell, eds., *Juvenile Crime, Juvenile Justice* (copyright 2001, reprinted by permission of National Research Council and Institute of Medicine).

National Council of Juvenile and Family Court Judges for Leonard P. Edwards, "Confidentiality and the Juvenile and Family Courts," in 55 *Juve-*

nile & Family Court Judges Journal 1 (copyright 2004, reprinted by permission of National Council of Juvenile and Family Court Judges).

New York University Law Review for Lourdes M. Rosado, "Minors and the Fourth Amendments: How Juvenile Status Should Invoke Different Standards for Searches and Seizures on the Street," 71 *New York University Law Review* 762 (copyright 1996, reprinted by permission of the New York University Law Review).

New York University Law Review for Stuart C. Berman, "Student Fourth Amendment Rights: Defining the Scope of the T.L.O. School Search Exception," 66 *New York University Law Review* 1077 (copyright 1991, reprinted by permission of the New York University Law Review).

New York University Law Review for Martin Guggenheim, "The Right to be Represented But Not Heard: Reflections on Legal Representation for Children," 59 *New York University Law Review* 76 (copyright 1984, reprinted by permission).

North Carolina Law Review for Janet E. Ainsworth, "Re–Imaging Childhood and Reconstructing the Legal Order: The Case for Abolishing the Juvenile Court," 69 *North Carolina Law Review* 1083 (copyright 1991, reprinted by permission).

Northwestern University School of Law for Marcy Rasmussen Podkopacz and Barry C. Feld, "The Back–Door to Prison: Waiver Reform, 'Blended Sentencing,' and the Law of Unintended Consequences," 91 *Journal of Criminal Law and Criminology* 997 (copyright 2001, reprinted by permission of Northwestern University School of Law).

Northwestern University School of Law for Kent Roach, "Four Models of the Criminal Process," 89 *Journal of Criminal Law and Criminology* 617 (copyright 1999, reprinted by permission).

Northwestern University School of Law for Donna M. Bishop and Charles E. Frazier, "Race Effects in Juvenile Justice Decision–Making: Findings of a Statewide Analysis," 86 *Journal of Criminal Law and Criminology* 392 (copyright 1996, reprinted by permission of Northwestern University School of Law).

Northwestern University School of Law for Jeffrey Fagan and Martin Guggenheim, "Preventive Detention and the Judicial Prediction of Dangerousness of Juveniles: A Natural Experiment," 86 *Journal of Criminal Law and Criminology* 415 (copyright 1996, reprinted by permission of Northwestern University School of Law).

Northwestern University School of Law for Donna M. Bishop and Charles E. Frazier, "Gender Bias in Juvenile Justice Processing: Implications of the JJDP Act," 82 *Journal of Criminal Law and Criminology* 1182 (copyright 1992, reprinted by permission of Northwestern University School of Law).

Northwestern University School of Law for Robert O. Dawson, "The Future of Juvenile Justice: Is It Time to Abolish the System?," 81 *Journal of Criminal Law and Criminology* 136 (copyright 1990, printed by permission of Northwestern University School of Law).

Northwestern University School of Law for Barry Feld, "The Right to Counsel in Juvenile Court: An Empirical Study of When Lawyers Appear and the Difference They Make," 79 *Journal of Criminal Law and Criminology* 1185 (copyright 1989, reprinted by permission of Northwestern University School of Law).

Northwestern University School of Law for Barry Feld, "The Juvenile Court Meets the Principle of the Offense: Legislative Changes in Juvenile Waiver Statutes," 78 *Journal of Criminal Law and Criminology* 471 (copyright 1987, reprinted by permission of Northwestern University School of Law).

Office of Juvenile Justice and Delinquency Prevention for Charles Puzzanchera, Anne L. Stahl, Terrence A. Finnegan, Nancy Tierney, and Howard N. Snyder, *Juvenile Court Statistics 1999* (copyright 2003, reprinted by permission).

Office of Juvenile Justice and Delinquency Prevention for Howard Snyder, Melissa Sickmund & Eileen Poe–Yamagata, *Juvenile Offenders and Victims: 1997 Update on Violence* (copyright 1997, reprinted by permission).

Office of Juvenile Justice and Delinquency Prevention, Washington, D.C., U.S. Department of Justice for Patricia Torbet, Richard Gable, Hunter Hurst, IV, Imogene Montgomery, Linda Szymanski, and Douglas Thomas, *State Responses to Serious and Violent Juvenile Crime: Research Report* (copyright 1996, reprinted by permission).

Office of Juvenile Justice and Delinquency Prevention, Washington, D.C., U.S. Department of Justice for Howard Snyder and Melissa Sickmund, *Juvenile Offenders and Victims: 1999 National Report* (copyright 1999, reprinted by permission).

Office of Juvenile Justice and Delinquency Prevention, Washington, D.C., U.S. Department of Justice for Gordon Bazemore and Mark Umbreit, *Balanced and Restorative Justice: Program Summary* (copyright 1994, reprinted by permission).

Pearson Education, Publishers for David Matza, *Delinquency and Drift* (copyright 1964, reprinted by permission).

Sage Publications, Inc. for Mark W. Lipsey and David B. Wilson, "Effective Intervention for Serious Juvenile Offenders: A Synthesis of Research" in *Serious and Violent Juvenile Offenders: Risk Factors and Successful Interventions*, Rolf Loeber and David P. Farrington, eds. (copyright 1998, reprinted by permission).

Sage Publications, Inc. for Ira M. Schwartz, Linda Harris, and Laurie Levi, "The Jailing of Juveniles in Minnesota: A Case Study," 34 *Crime & Delinquency* (copyright 1988, reprinted by permission).

Sage Publications, Inc. for Kenneth Polk, "Juvenile Diversion: A Look at the Record," 36 *Crime and Delinquency* 648 (copyright 1984, reprinted by permission of Sage Publications, Inc.).

Sage Publications, Inc. for H. Ted Rubin, "The Emerging Prosecutor Dominance of the Juvenile Court Intake Process," 26 *Crime and Delinquency* 299 (copyright 1980, reprinted by permission).

Stanford Law School for Lois Weithorn, "Mental Hospitalization of Troublesome Youth: An Analysis of Skyrocketing Admission Rates," 40 *Stanford Law Review* 773 (copyright 1988, reprinted by permission of Stanford Law School).

Temple University School of Law for Paul Holland and Wallace J. Mlyniec, "Whatever Happened to the Right to Treatment?: The Modern Quest of a Historical Promise," 68 *Temple Law Review* 1791 (copyright 1995, reprinted by permission of Temple University School of Law).

University of California at Berkeley for Franklin E. Zimring, "The Common Thread: Diversion in Juvenile Justice," 88 *California Law Review* 2477 (copyright 2000, reprinted by permission of University of California Law Review).

University of California at Davis for Cheri Panzer, "Reducing Juvenile Recidivism Through Pre–Trial Diversion Programs: A Community's Involvement," 18 *Journal of Juvenile Law & Policy* 195 (copyright 1997, reprinted by permission of University of California at Davis).

University of California at Davis for Cesar C. Sarmiento, "Penal Code Section 26(1): A Rebuttable Presumption of a Juvenile's Incapacity to Commit a Crime—A Necessary Statute?," 12 *U. Cal. Davis. L. Rev.* 885 (copyright 1979, reprinted by permission of University of California at Davis).

University of California Los Angeles School of Law for John Braithwaite, "A Future Where Punishment is Marginalized: Realistic or Utopian?," 46 *UCLA Law Review* 1727 (copyright 1999, reprinted by permission).

University of California Press for Thomas Grisso, "Juveniles' Capacities to Wave *Miranda* Rights: An Empirical Analysis," 68 *California Law Review* 1162 (copyright 1980, reprinted by permission of the University of California Press).

The University of Chicago Press for Barry Feld, "Juvenile and Criminal Justice Systems' Responses to Youth Violence," 24 *Crime & Justice* 189 (copyright 1998, reprinted by permission of The University of Chicago Press).

University of Chicago Press for Richard J. Bonnie and Thomas Grisso, "Adjudicative Competence and Youthful Offenders," in Thomas Grisso and Robert Schwartz, eds., *Youth on Trial: A Developmental Perspective on Juvenile Justice* (copyright 2000, reprinted by permission of University of Chicago Press).

University of Chicago Press for Franklin E. Zimring and Jeffrey Fagan, "Transfer Policy and Law Reform," in Jeffrey Fagan and Franklin E. Zimring, eds., *The Changing Borders of Juvenile Justice: Transfer of Adolescents to the Criminal Court* (copyright 2000, reprinted by permission of The University of Chicago Press).

University of Chicago Press for Donna Bishop and Charles Frazier, "Consequences of Transfer," in Jeffrey Fagan and Franklin E. Zimring, eds.,

The Changing Borders of Juvenile Justice: Transfer of Adolescents to the Criminal Court (copyright 2000, reprinted by permission of The University of Chicago Press).

University of Chicago Press for Lynda Frost Clausel and Richard J. Bonnie, "Juvenile Justice on Appeal," in Jeffrey Fagan and Franklin E. Zimring, eds., *The Changing Borders of Juvenile Justice: Transfer of Adolescents to the Criminal Court* (copyright 2000, reprinted by permission of The University of Chicago Press).

University of Chicago Press for Gary L. Crippen, "Can the Courts Fairly Account for the Diminished Competence and Culpability of Juveniles," in Thomas Grisso and Robert Schwartz, eds., *Youth on Trial: A Developmental Perspective on Juvenile Justice* (copyright 2000, reprinted by permission of University of Chicago Press).

University of Cincinnati Law School for Irene Merker Rosenberg, *"Florida v. J.L.* and the Fourth Amendment Rights of Juvenile Delinquents," 69 *University of Cincinnati Law Review* 289 (copyright 2000, reprinted by permission of University of Cincinnati Law Review).

University of District of Columbia Law Review for Bart Lubow and Joseph B. Tulman, "The Unnecessary Detention of Children in the District of Columbia," *University of District of Columbia Law Review* IX (copyright 1995, reprinted by permission of University of District Columbia Law Review).

University of Florida Law Review for Mary Berkheiser, "The Fiction of Juvenile Right to Counsel: Waiver in the Juvenile Courts," 54 *Florida Law Review* 577 (copyright 2002, reprinted by permission of University of Florida School of Law).

The University of Iowa College of Law for William G. Buss, "The Fourth Amendment and Searches of Students in Public Schools," 59 *Iowa Law Review* 739 (copyright 1974, reprinted by permission of the University of Iowa College of Law).

University of Louisville, Ky., Children Rights Journal for Harry J. Rothgerber, Jr., "The Bootstrapping of Status Offenders: A Vicious Practice," 1 *J. U. L. Ky. Children, Rts. J.* 1 (copyright 1991, reprinted by permission).

University of Maryland School of Law for Ellen Marrus, "Best Interests Equal Zealous Advocacy: A Not So Radical View of Holistic Representation for Children Accused of Crime," 62 Maryland Law Review (copyright 2003, reprinted by permission of Maryland Law Review).

University of Michigan Law Review for "Public Right of Access to Juvenile Delinquency Hearings," 81 *Michigan Law Review* 1550 (copyright 1983, reprinted by permission of University of Michigan Law School).

University of San Francisco Law Review for Michael Dale, "Law Suits and Public Policy: The Role of Litigation in Correcting Conditions in Juvenile Detention Centers," 32 U.S.F. L. Rev. 675 (1998).

University of Texas Law School for Elizabeth S. Scott and Laurence Steinberg, "Blaming Youth," 81 *Texas Law Review* 799 (copyright 2003, reprinted by permission of University of Texas Law Review).

University of Texas School of Law for Irene Merker Rosenberg, "Public School Drug Testing," 33 *American Criminal Law Review* 349 (copyright 1996, reprinted by permission American Criminal Law Review).

Vanderbilt Law School for Julianne P. Sheffer, "Serious and Habitual Juvenile Offender Statutes: Reconciling Punishment and Rehabilitation Within the Juvenile Justice System," 48 *Vanderbilt Law Review* 479 (copyright 1995, reprinted by permission of Vanderbilt Law School).

Vanderbilt Law School for Martin Gardner, "Punishment and Juvenile Justice: A Conceptual Framework for Assessing Constitutional rights of Youthful Offenders," 35 *Vanderbilt Law Review* 719 (copyright 1982, reprinted by permission of Vanderbilt Law School).

Verity, Inc. for the Office of Juvenile Justice and Delinquency Prevention, "Curfew: An answer to Juvenile Delinquency and Victimization?," (copyright 1996, reprinted by permission).

Wake Forest University School of Law for Barry C. Feld, "The Constitutional Tension Between *Apprendi* and *McKeiver*: Sentence Enhancements Based on Delinquency Convictions and the Quality of Justice in Juvenile Courts," 38 Wake Forest Law Review 1111 (copyright 2003, reprinted by permission of Wake Forest University School of Law).

Wake Forest University School of Law for N. Lee Cooper, Patricia Puritz, and Wendy Shang, "Fulfilling the Promise of *In re Gault*: Advancing the Role of Lawyers for Children," 33 *Wake Forest Law Review* 651 (copyright 1998, reprinted by permission of Wake Forest University School of Law)

Wake Forest University School of Law for Martin Guggenheim and Randy Hertz, "Reflections on Judges, Juries, and Justice: Ensuring the Fairness of Juvenile Delinquency Trials," 33 *Wake Forest Law Review* 553 (copyright 1998, reprinted by permission of Wake Forest University School of Law).

Wake Forest University School of Law for Wayne A. Logan, "Proportionality and Punishment: Imposing Life Without Parole on Juveniles," 33 *Wake Forest Law Review* 689 (copyright 1998, reprinted by permission of Wake Forest University School of Law).

*

Summary of Contents

TABLE OF CONTENTS

TABLE OF CASES

The principal cases are in bold type. Cases cited or discussed in the text
are in roman type. References are to pages. Cases cited in principal
cases and within other quoted materials are not included.

TABLE OF STATUTES

CASES AND MATERIALS ON
JUVENILE JUSTICE
ADMINISTRATION

Third Edition

*

CHAPTER 1

INTRODUCTION

▪ ▪ ▪

How should the state respond when the child is a criminal and the criminal is a child? The answers involve considerations of youth policy and crime policy, both of which change over time. Until the early nineteenth century, the American legal system treated young people who violated the criminal law much as it did adult offenders. The classical criminal law recognized that the threat of sanctions could not deter those who did not know right from wrong and it excused from criminal liability the severely mentally ill and young children. Sanford J. Fox, *Responsibility in the Juvenile Court*, 11 Wm. & Mary L. Rev. 659 (1970). The common law's infancy defense provided the only criminal law doctrinal protection for youths. If courts found children criminally responsible, then they imposed the same sentences, including capital punishment, and committed them to the same penal facilities as they did adult criminals. A changing social construction of adolescence as a developmental stage distinct from adulthood and new sensibilities about children posed problems for the criminal justice system. Judges sometimes dismissed charges and juries occasionally acquitted young offenders to avoid imposing excessively harsh sentences. To avoid dismissals, nullification, and loss of formal social control over youths, in the early- to mid-nineteenth century, reformers in East Coast cities created the first age-segregated institutions for youth—Houses of Refuge. E.g. John Sutton, *Stubborn Children: Controlling Delinquency in the United States* (1988); Joseph Hawes, *Children in Urban Society: Juvenile Delinquency in Nineteenth–Century America* (1971). By mid-century, youth reformatories and institutions spread to rural and Midwestern regions of the country. Refuge managers received youths from a variety of sources—judicial commitments, overseers of the poor, local constables who apprehended homeless orphans, and parents who sought to control a disobedient child. David J. Rothman, *The Discovery of the Asylum* (1971).

Despite some institutional innovation, states continued to try and punish juveniles just like adults. At the end of the nineteenth century, these practices appalled Progressive reformers. They created the juvenile court as an informal welfare system and a diversionary alternative to the criminal process. Rather than punishing young offenders for their crimes, juvenile court judges made dispositions in the child's "best interests" and

1

the state functioned as *parens patriae*, as a surrogate parent. David J. Rothman, *Conscience and Convenience: The Asylum and Its Alternative in Progressive America* (1980). In 1967, the Supreme Court in *In re Gault*, 387 U.S. 1, 87 S.Ct. 1428, 18 L.Ed.2d 527 (1967), granted juveniles some constitutional procedural rights in delinquency hearings. In turn, *Gault* and subsequent due process decisions provided the impetus for states to modify juvenile courts' procedures, jurisdiction, and jurisprudence. Over the next three decades, judicial decisions and legislative amendments transformed the juvenile court from a nominally rehabilitative social welfare agency into a more criminal-like and punitive system for young offenders. The "baby boom" increase in youth crime that began in the 1960s and a sharp rise in urban youth homicide in the late–1980s and early–1990s provided political impetus to "get tough" on youth crime and led to harsher juvenile justice sentencing and transfer policies. More recently, research by developmental psychologists has demonstrated that children think and act differently from adults and reminded policy makers why states require a different type of justice system for juveniles than adults. This Chapter briefly examines juvenile courts' historical origins, "constitutional domestication," "get tough" era policies, and more recent, social science-based policy focus on how children differ from adults.

A. ORIGINS OF THE JUVENILE JUSTICE SYSTEM

Until the early nineteenth-century, the Anglo–American legal system treated young people who violated the criminal law much as it did other offenders. Before the Progressive reformers created the juvenile court, the common law infancy defense provided the only legal doctrine to protect young offenders charged with crimes. The infancy defense attempted to identify those offenders who lacked criminal responsibility and could not be blamed for their acts. The common law gradations reflected the intuitions of ancient Hebrews, Romans, and Muslims that "infants"— children incapable of speech—enjoyed immunity from criminal punishment because they lacked the ability to understand "right from wrong" necessary for criminally responsibility. The common law conclusively presumed that children less than seven years of age lacked criminal capacity; treated those fourteen years of age and older as fully responsible adults, and created a rebuttable presumption that those between seven and fourteen years of age lacked criminal capacity.

During the early nineteenth century, the social construction of *adolescence* as a developmental stage distinct from adulthood and new sensibilities about children began to pose problems for the criminal justice system. Nineteenth-century reformers began to create special institutions for youths to avoid subjecting them to criminal liability as adults or exempting them from legal control. In the early- to mid-nineteenth century, the first age-segregated youth institution, the House of Refuge, appeared in the cities of the east coast. By mid-century, reformatories and youth institutions spread to the rural and mid-western regions of the country. By the end of the century, the juvenile court appeared in Chicago, spread to other major urban centers, and completed the process of separating the system of social control of youths from adults.

The social history of the American juvenile court is an oft-told tale.* Changes in two cultural ideas—*childhood* and *social control*—that accompanied modernization and industrialization over a century ago led to the creation of the juvenile court. By the end of the nineteenth century, America began to change from a rural, agrarian society to an urban, industrial one. Modernization, urbanization, and immigration posed many social problems and a reform movement, the Progressives, emerged to address them. Progressives believed that benevolent state action guided by experts could alleviate social ills. They created a variety of public agencies to inculcate their middle-class values and to assimilate and "Americanize" immigrants and the poor to become virtuous citizens like themselves.

Changes in family structure and functions accompanied the economic transformation: families became more private, women's roles more domestic, and a newer view of childhood and adolescence as distinct developmental stages emerged.** Before the past two or three centuries, age provided neither the basis for a separate legal status nor for social segregation. People generally regarded young people as miniature adults, small versions of their parents. By the end of the nineteenth century, however, people increasingly viewed children as vulnerable, innocent, passive, and dependent beings who needed extended preparation for life. The newer vision of children altered traditional child-rearing practices and imposed a greater responsibility on parents to supervise their children's moral and social development. Many Progressive reform programs shared a child-centered theme; the juvenile court, child labor and welfare laws, and compulsory school attendance laws reflected and advanced the changing imagery of childhood.

Changes in ideological assumptions about the causes and control of crime inspired many Progressive criminal justice reforms. *See e.g.*, Frances Allen, "Legal Values and the Rehabilitative Ideal," in *The Borderland of Criminal Justice* (1964); Frances Allen, *The Decline of the Rehabilitative Ideal* (1981); David Rothman, *Conscience and Convenience, supra.* Although classical criminal law attributed crime to free-willed actors,

---

* *See e.g.*, Sanford Fox, "Juvenile Justice Reform: An Historical Perspective," 22 *Stan. L. Rev.* 1187 (1970); Anthony Platt, *The Childsavers: The Invention of Delinquency* (2nd ed. 1977); David Rothman, *Conscience and Convenience: The Asylum and Its Alternatives in Progressive America* (1980); Ellen Ryerson, *The Best–Laid Plans: America's Juvenile Court Experiment* (1978); Janet Ainsworth, "Re-imagining Childhood and Reconstructing the Legal Order: The Case for Abolishing the Juvenile Court," 69 *N.C.L.Rev.* 1083 (1991); Elizabeth J. Clapp, *Mothers of All Children: Women Reformers and the Rise of Juvenile Courts in Progressive Era America* (1998); Barry C. Feld, *Bad Kids: Race and the Transformation of the Juvenile Court* (1999); David Tanenhaus, *Juvenile Justice in the Making* (2004).

** *See e.g.*, Ainsworth, *Re-Imagining Childhood*, supra; Carl Degler, *At Odds: Women and the Family in American from the Revolution to the Present* (1980); Joseph Kett, *Rites of Passage: Adolescence in America 1790 to the Present* (1977); Sheila Rothman, *Woman's Proper Place: A History of Changing Ideals and Practices, 1870 to the Present* (1978).

positivist criminology regarded crime as determined rather than chosen. Criminology's attempt to identify the antecedent causes of criminal behavior reduced actors' moral responsibility and focused on reforming offenders rather than punishing them for their offenses. Applying medical analogies to the treatment of offenders, a growing class of social science professionals fostered the rehabilitative ideal. Whether their movement was in fact a humanitarian one to save poor and immigrant children or intended to expand social control over them, Progressive "child-savers" described juvenile courts as benign, non-punitive, and therapeutic.

Reflecting the changing social construction of adolescence, Progressive reformers viewed youthful autonomy as malign. Juvenile courts exercised jurisdiction over unruly children, reinforced parental authority and control, and allowed state intervention when parents were inadequate for the task. The legal doctrine of *parens patriae*, the State as parent, legitimated intervention. Juvenile court personnel used informal, discretionary procedures to diagnose the causes of and prescribe the cures for delinquency. By separating children from adults and providing a rehabilitative alternative to punishment, juvenile courts rejected the jurisprudence of the criminal law and its procedural safeguards such as juries and lawyers. Because the court's jurisdiction encompassed youths suffering from abuse, dependency, or neglect, as well as those charged with criminal offenses and noncriminal disobedience, reformers characterized proceedings as civil rather than criminal. Theoretically, a child's "best interests," background, and welfare guided dispositions. Because a youth's offense was only a symptom of her "real" needs, sentences were indeterminate, non-proportional, and could continue for the duration of minority.

ILLINOIS JUVENILE COURT ACT OF 1899

41st General Assembly Laws Regular Session (Illinois 1899).

An Act to regulate the treatment and control of dependent, neglected, and delinquent children.

Section 1. Be it enacted by the People of the State of Illinois, represented in the General Assembly: Definition. This act shall apply only to children under the age of 16 years not now or hereafter inmates of a State institution, or any training school for boys or industrial school for girls or some institution incorporated under the laws of this State ... For the purposes of this act the words dependent child and neglected child shall mean any child who for any reason is destitute or homeless or abandoned; or dependent upon the public for support; or has not proper parental care or guardianship; or who habitually begs or receives alms; or who is found living in any house of ill fame or with any vicious or disreputable person; or whose home, by reason of neglect, cruelty or depravity on the part of its parents, guardian or other person in whose care it may be, is an unfit place for such a child; and any child under the age of 8 years who is found peddling or selling any article or singing or playing any musical instrument upon the streets or giving any public entertainment. The words delinquent child shall include any child under the age of 16 years who violates any law of this State or any city or village ordinance. * * *

§ 2   *Jurisdiction.* The circuit and county courts of the several counties in this State shall have original jurisdiction in all cases coming within the terms of this act. In all trials under this act any person interested therein may demand a jury of six, or the judge of his own motion may order a jury of the same number, to try the case.

§ 3.   *Juvenile Court.* In counties having over 500,000 population the judges of the circuit court shall, at such times as they shall determine, designate one or more of their number whose duty it shall be to hear all cases coming under this act. A special court room, to be designated as the juvenile court room, shall be provided for the hearing of such cases, and the findings of the court shall be entered in a book or books to be kept for that purpose and known as the "Juvenile Record," and the court may, for convenience, be called the "Juvenile Court."

§ 4.   *Petition to the Court.* Any reputable person, being resident in the county, having knowledge of a child in his county who appears to be either neglected, dependent or delinquent, may file with the clerk of a court having jurisdiction in the matter a petition in writing, setting forth the facts, verified by affidavit. It shall be sufficient that the affidavit is upon information and belief.

§ 5.   *Summons.* Upon the filing of the petition a summons shall issue requiring the person having custody or control of the child, or with whom the child may be, to appear with the child at a place and time stated in the summons, which time shall be not less than 24 hours after service. The parents of the child * * * or its legal guardian * * * shall be notified of the proceedings, and in any case the judge may appoint some suitable person to act in behalf of the child. * * * [T]he court shall proceed to hear and dispose of the case in a summary manner. Pending the final disposition of any case the child may be retained in the possession of the person having the charge of same, or may be kept in some suitable place provided by the city or county authorities.

§ 6.   *Probation Officers.* The court shall have authority to appoint or designate one or more discreet persons of good character to serve as probation officers during the pleasure of the court; said probation officers to receive no compensation from the public treasury. In case a probation officer shall be appointed by any court, it shall be the duty of the clerk of the court * * * to notify the said probation officer in advance when any child is to be brought before the said court; it shall be the duty of the said probation officer to make such investigation as may be required by the court; to be present in court in order to represent the interests of the child when the case is heard; to furnish to the court such information and assistance as the judge may require; and to take such charge of any child before and after trial as may be directed by the court. * * *

§ 9.   *Disposition of Delinquent Children.* In the case of a delinquent child the court may continue the hearing from time to time, and may commit the child to the care and guardianship of a probation officer duly appointed by the court, and may allow said child to remain in its own home, subject to the visitation of the probation officer: such child to report to the probation officer as often as may be required and subject to be returned to the court for further proceedings, whenever such action may appear to be necessary; or the court may commit the child to the care and guardianship of the probation officer, to be placed in a suitable family home, subject to the friendly supervision of such probation officer; or it may authorize the said probation officer to board out the said child in some suitable family home, in case provision is made by voluntary contribution or otherwise for the payment of the board of such child, until a suitable provision may be made for the child in a home without such payment: or the court may commit the child, if a boy, to a training school for boys, or if a girl, to an industrial school for girls. Or, if the child is found guilty of any criminal offense, and the judge is of the opinion that the best interest require it, the court may commit the child to any institution within said county incorporated under the laws of this State for the care of delinquent children, or provided by a city for the care of such offenders, or may commit the child, if a boy over the age of ten years, to the State reformatory, or if a girl over the age of ten years, to the State Home for Juvenile Female Offenders. In no case shall a child be committed beyond his or her minority. A child committed to such an institution shall be subject to the control of the board of managers thereof, and the said board shall have power to parole such child on such conditions as it may prescribe, and the court shall, on the recommendation of the board, have power to discharge such child from custody whenever in the judgment of the court his or her reformation shall be complete; or the court may commit the child to the care and custody of some association that will receive it embracing in its objects the care of neglected and dependent children and that has been duly accredited as hereinafter provided.

§ 10. *Transfer From Justices and Police Magistrates.* When * * * a child under the age of 16 years is arrested with or without warrant, such child may, instead of being taken before a justice of the peace or police magistrate, be taken directly before such court; or if the child is taken before a justice of the peace or police magistrate, it shall be the duty of such justice of the peace or police magistrate to transfer the case to such court, and * * * the court may proceed to hear and dispose of the case in the same manner as if the child had been brought before the court upon petition as herein provided. * * *

§ 11. *Children Under Twelve Years Not To Be Committed to Jail.* No court or magistrate shall commit a child under twelve (12) years of age to a jail or police station, but if such child is unable to give bail it may be committed to the care of the sheriff, police officer or probation officer, who shall keep such children in some suitable placed provided by the city or county outside of the inclosure of any jail or police station. When any child shall be sentenced to confinement in any institution to which adult convicts are sentenced it shall be unlawful to confine such child in the same building with such adult convicts, or to confine such child in the same yard or inclosure with such adult convicts, or to bring such child into any yard or building in which adult convicts may be present. * * *

§ 21. *Construction of the Act.* This act shall be liberally construed, to the end that its purpose may be carried out, to wit: That the care, custody and discipline of a child shall approximate as nearly as may be that which should be given by its parents, and in all cases where it can properly be done the child be placed in an improved family home and become a member of the family by legal adoption or otherwise.

Approved April 21, 1899.

ILLINOIS JUVENILE COURT ACT
OF 1899, AS AMENDED 1907

45th General Assembly Laws, Regular Session (Illinois 1907).

An Act to amend [Illinois Juvenile Court Act of 1899]:

§ 2. [1]. That all persons under the age of twenty-one (21) years, shall, for purposes of this Act only, be considered wards of this State, and their persons shall be subject to the care, guardianship and control of the court as hereinafter provided. . . .

The words "delinquent child" shall mean any male child who while under the age of seventeen years or any female child who while under the age of eighteen years, violates any law of this State: or is incorrigible, or knowingly associates with thieves, vicious or immoral persons; or without just cause and without the consent of its parents, guardian or custodian absents itself from its home or place of abode, or is growing up in idleness or crime; or knowingly frequents a house of ill-repute; or knowingly frequents any policy shop or place where any gaming device is operated; or frequents any saloon or dram shop where intoxicating liquors are sold; or patronizes or visits any public pool room or bucket shop; or wanders about the streets in the night time without being on any lawful business or lawful occupation; or habitually wanders about any railroad yards or tracks or jumps or attempt to jump onto any moving train; or enters any car or engine without lawful authority; or uses vile, obscene, vulgar, profane or indecent language in any public place or about any school house; or is guilty of indecent or lascivious conduct; any child committing any of these acts herein mentioned shall be deemed a delinquent child and shall be cared for as such in the manner hereinafter provided.

A disposition of any child under this Act or any evidence given in such causes, shall not, in any civil, criminal or other cause or proceeding whatever in any court, be lawful or proper evidence against such child for any purposes whatever, except in subsequent cases against the same child under this Act. . . .

§ 9a. The court may in its discretion in any case of a delinquent child permit such child to be proceeded against in accordance with the laws that may be in force in this State governing the commission of crimes or violations of city, village, or town ordinance. In such case the petition filed under this Act shall be dismissed. . . .

Approved June 4, 1907.

Julian W. Mack, "The Juvenile Court," 23 *Harv. L. Rev.* 104 (1909), provides one of the earliest, most complete, and influential descriptions of the Progressive conception of the juvenile court reflected in the Illinois Juvenile Court Act:

The past decade marks a revolution in the attitude of the state toward its offending children. * * * The problem of the delinquent child, though juristically comparatively simple, is, in its social significance, of the greatest importance, for upon its wise solution depends the future of many of the rising generation. The legal questions, while not complicated, have, nevertheless, given rise to some discussion and to some slight dissent from the standpoint of constitutional law.

The first thought which suggests itself in connection with the juvenile court is, What is there distinctively new about it? We are familiar with the conception that the state is the higher or the ultimate parent of all of the dependents within its borders. We know that, whatever may have been the historical origin of the practice, for over two centuries, * * * the courts of chancery in England have exercised jurisdiction for the protection of the unfortunate child. * * *

Our common criminal law did not differentiate between the adult and the minor who had reached the age of criminal responsibility, seven at common law and in some of our states, ten in others, with a chance of escape up to twelve, if lacking in mental and moral maturity. The majesty and dignity of the state demanded vindication for infractions from both alike. The fundamental thought in our criminal jurisprudence was not, and in most jurisdictions is not, reformation of the criminal, but punishment; punishment as expiation for the wrong, punishment as a warning to other possible wrongdoers. The child was arrested, put into prison, indicted by the grand jury, tried by a petit jury, under all the forms and technicalities of our criminal law, with the aim of ascertaining whether it had done the specific act—nothing else—and if it had, then of visiting the punishment of the state upon it.

It is true that during the last century ameliorating influences mitigated the severity of the old regime; in the last fifty years our reformatories have played a great and very beneficent part in dealing with juvenile offenders. They supplanted the penitentiary. In them the endeavor was made, while punishing, to reform, to build up, to educate the prisoner so that when his time should have expired he could go out into the world capable at least of making an honest living. And in course of time, in some jurisdictions, the youths were separated from the older offenders even in stations, jails, and workhouses; but, nevertheless, generally in this country, the two classes were huddled together. The result of it all was that instead of the state's training its bad boys so as to make of them decent citizens, it permitted them to become the outlaws and outcasts of society;

it criminalized them by the very methods that it used in dealing with them. It did not aim to find out what the accused's history was, what his heredity, his environments, his associations; it did not ask how he had come to do the particular act which had brought him before the court. It put but one question, "Has he committed this crime?" It did not inquire, "What is the best thing to do for this lad?" It did not even punish him in a manner that would tend to improve him; the punishment was visited in proportion to the degree of wrongdoing evidenced by the single act; not by the needs of the boy, not by the needs of the state.

Today, however, the thinking public is putting another sort of question. Why is it not just and proper to treat these juvenile offenders, as we deal with the neglected children, as a wise and merciful father handles his own child whose errors are not discovered by the authorities? Why is it not the duty of the state, instead of asking merely whether a boy or a girl has committed a specific offense, to find out what he is, physically, mentally, morally, and then if it learns that he is treading the path that leads to criminality, to take him in charge, not so much to punish as to reform, not to degrade but to uplift, not to crush but to develop, not to make him a criminal but a worthy citizen.

And it is this thought—the thought that the child who has begun to go wrong, who is incorrigible, who has broken a law or an ordinance, is to be taken in hand by the state, not as an enemy but as a protector, as the ultimate guardian, because either the unwillingness or inability of the natural parents to guide it toward good citizenship has compelled the intervention of the public authorities; * * *

But in Illinois, and following the lead of Illinois, in most jurisdictions, the form of procedure is totally different and wisely so. It would seem to be obvious that, if the common law could fix the age of criminal responsibility at seven, and if the legislature could advance that age to ten or twelve, it can also raise it to sixteen or seventeen or eighteen, and that is what, in some measure, has been done. Under most of the juvenile-court laws a child under the designated age is to be proceeded against as a criminal only when in the judgment of the judge of the juvenile court, either as to any child, or in some states as to one over fourteen or over sixteen years of age, the interests of the state and of the child require that this be done. * * *

To get away from the notion that the child is to be dealt with as a criminal; to save it from the brand of criminality, the brand that sticks to it for life; to take it in hand and instead of first stigmatizing and then reforming it, to protect it from the stigma,—this is the work which is now being accomplished by dealing even with most of the delinquent children through the court that represents the *parens patriae* power of the state, the court of chancery. Proceedings are brought to have a guardian or representative of the state appointed to look after the child, to have the state intervene between the natural parent and the child because the child needs it, as evidenced by some of its acts, and because the parent is either unwilling or unable to train the child properly. * * *

If a child must be taken away from its home, if for the natural parental care that of the state is to be substituted, a real school, not a prison in disguise, must be provided. Whether the institutional life be only temporary until a foster home can be found, or for a longer period until the child can be restored to its own home or be given its complete freedom, the state must * * * in fulfilment of its moral obligation to the child, furnish the proper care. This cannot be done in one great building, with a single dormitory for all of the two or three or four hundred or more children, in which there will be no possibility of classification along the lines of age or degrees of delinquency, in which there will be no individualized attention. What is needed is a large area, preferably in the country,— because these children require the fresh air and contact with the soil even more than does the normal child,—laid out on the cottage plan, giving opportunity for family life, and in each cottage some good man and woman who will live with and for the children. Locks and bars and other indicia of prisons must be avoided; human love, supplemented by human interest and vigilance, must replace them. In such schools there must be opportunity for agricultural and industrial training, so that when the boys and girls come out, they will be fitted to do a man's or woman's work in the world, and not be merely a helpless lot, drifting aimlessly about. * * *

[T]aking a child away from its parents and sending it even to, an industrial school is, as far as possible, to be avoided; and * * * when it is allowed to return home, it must be under probation, subject to the guidance and friendly interest of the probation officer, the representative of the court. To raise the age of criminal responsibility from seven or ten to sixteen or eighteen, without providing for an efficient system of probation, would indeed be disastrous. Probation is, in fact, the keynote of juvenile-court legislation. * * * Wherever juvenile courts have been established, a system of probation has been provided for, and even where as yet the juvenile-court system has not been fully developed, some steps have been taken to substitute probation for imprisonment of juvenile offenders.

Most of the children who come before the court are, naturally, the children of the poor. In many cases the parents are foreigners, frequently unable to speak English, and without an understanding of American methods and views. What they need, more than anything else, is kindly assistance; and the aim of the court, in appointing a probation officer for the child, is to have the child and the parents feel, not so much the power, as the friendly interest of the state; to show them that the object of the court is to help them to train the child right; and therefore the probation officers must be men and women fitted for these tasks. * * *

The procedure and practice of the juvenile court is simple. In the first place the number of arrests is greatly decreased. The child and the parents are notified to appear in court, and unless the danger of escape is great, or the offense very serious, or the home totally unfit for the child, detention before hearing is unnecessary. Children are permitted to go on their own recognizance or that of their parents, or on giving bail. Probation officers should be and often are authorized to act in this respect. If, however, it becomes necessary to detain the children either before a hearing or pending a continuance, or even after the adjudication, before they can be admitted into the home or institution to which they are to be sent, they are no longer kept in prisons or jails, but in detention homes. In some states, the laws are mandatory that the local authorities provide such homes managed in accordance with the spirit of this legislation. These are feasible even in the smallest communities, inasmuch as the simplest kind of a building best meets the need.

The jurisdiction to hear the cases is generally granted to an existing court having full equity powers. In some cities, however, special courts have been provided, with judges devoting their entire time to this work. If these special courts can constitutionally be vested with full and complete chancery and criminal jurisdiction, much is to be said in favor of their establishment. In the large cities particularly the entire time of one judge may well be needed. It has been suggested from time to time that all of the judges of the municipal or special sessions courts be empowered to act in these cases, but while it would be valuable in metropolitan communities to have more than one detention home and court house, nevertheless it would seem to be even more important to have a single juvenile court judge. * * *

The personality of the judge is an all-important matter. * * * Because of the extent of his jurisdiction and the tremendous responsibility that it entails, it is * * * absolutely essential that he be a trained lawyer thoroughly imbued with the doctrine that ours is a "government of laws and not of men."

He must, however, be more than this. He must be a student of and deeply interested in the problems of philanthropy and child life, as well as a lover of children. He must be able to understand the boys' point of view and ideas of justice; he must be willing and patient enough to search out the underlying causes of the trouble and to formulate the plan by which, through the cooperation, ofttimes, of many agencies, the cure may be effected.

In some very important jurisdictions the vicious practice is indulged in of assigning a different judge to the juvenile-court work every month or every three months. It is impossible for these judges to gain the necessary experience or to devote the necessary time to the study of new problems. The service should under no circumstances be for less than one year, and preferably for a longer period. * * *

The problem for determination by the judge is not, Has this boy or girl committed a specific wrong, but What is he, how has he become what he is, and what had best be done in his interest and in the interest of the state to save him from a downward career. It is apparent at once that the ordinary legal evidence in a criminal court is not the sort of evidence to be heard in such a proceeding. A thorough investigation, usually made by the probation officer, will give the court much information bearing on the heredity and environment of the child. This, of course, will be supplemented in every possible way; but this alone is not enough. The physical and mental condition of the child must be known, for the relation between physical defects and criminality is very close. It is, therefore, of the utmost importance that there be attached to the court, as has been done in a few cities, a child study department, where every child, before hearing, shall be subjected to a thorough psycho-physical examination. In hundreds of cases the discovery and remedy of defective eyesight or hearing or some slight surgical operation will effectuate a complete change in the character of the lad.

The child who must be brought into court should, of course, be made to know that he is face to face with the power of the state, but he should at the same time, and more emphatically, be made to feel that he is the object of its care and solicitude. The ordinary trappings of the court-room are out of place in such hearings. The judge on a bench, looking down upon the boy standing at the bar, can never evoke a proper sympathetic spirit. Seated at a desk, with the child at his side, where he can on occasion put his arm around his shoulder and draw the lad to him, the judge, while losing none of his judicial dignity, will gain immensely in the effectiveness of his work. * * *

Valuable, however, as is the introduction of the juvenile court into our system of jurisprudence, valuable both in its effect upon the child, the parents, and the community at large, and in the great material saving to the state which the substitution of probation for imprisonment has brought about, nevertheless it is in no sense a cure-all. * * *

But more than this, the work of the juvenile court is, at the best, palliative, curative. The more important, indeed the vital thing, is to prevent the children from reaching that condition in which they have to be dealt with in any court, and we are not doing our duty to the children of today, the men and women of tomorrow, when we neglect to destroy the evils that are leading them into careers of delinquency, when we fail not merely to uproot the wrong, but to implant in place of it the positive good. * * *

Janet E. Ainsworth, "Re–Imagining Childhood and Reconstructing the Legal Order: The Case for Abolishing the Juvenile Court," 69 *N.C.L.Rev.* 1083 (1991), places the creation of the juvenile court in the larger context of the social construction of adolescence:

Juvenile courts exist in all fifty states of the United States and the District of Columbia, as well as in virtually all of the industrialized nations of the world. So ubiquitous is the institution of the juvenile court in the contemporary world that one easily might forget that it did not always exist. In fact, the juvenile court is a relatively recent invention. * * *

The choice of the word "invention" for this subheading is meant to be subtly jarring. After all, it is human creations which ordinarily are said to be "invented," whereas aspects of the natural world are said to be "discovered." By calling childhood an invention, I am suggesting that childhood is better seen as a social fact than as a biological one. * * * [T]he life-stage we call "childhood" is likewise a culturally and historically situated social construction. Of course, infants and young children are physiologically and psychologically different from older youths and adults; these differences undoubtedly persist across time and place. * * * Human biology may set the outside limits on our social definition of ourselves, but, since biological constructs are themselves human artifacts, social reality constrains what we imagine to be biological necessity as well.

Social definitions of reality determine which biological attributes will be considered authentic, meaningful, and constituent of identity, and which will be trivialized, ignored, suppressed, or even explicitly denied. * * *

Similarly, the socially constructed aspects of human life-stages such as childhood and adolescence far outweigh their invariant biological attributes. The number of stages into which an individual's life is divided and the essential qualities deemed characteristic of each stage in the life-cycle have varied over time and across cultures. Indeed, the very concept that human lives pass through life-stages with distinct characteristics has not always held the social and legal significance that it does in the contemporary West.

The definition of childhood—who is classified as a child, and what emotional, intellectual, and moral properties children are assumed to possess—has changed over time in response to changes in other facets of society. Historian Philippe Aries first pointed out the dramatic contrast between the modern Western conception of childhood and the conception held in the medieval European world. As he observed, "In medieval society, the idea of childhood did not exist. * * * [The] awareness of the particular nature of childhood * * * which distinguishes the child from the adult * * * was lacking." At that time, the primary age-based boundary was drawn between infancy, a time of physical dependence ending roughly at age seven, and full personhood. Those persons older than seven, especially those in the lower social classes, participated in the normal range of adult activities: they were apprenticed to begin their working lives, drank in taverns, shared the same games and amusements as adults, gambled, and were exposed to sexual behavior and jokes. Wearing the same kind of clothing, these young people even looked like adults. Not surprisingly, then, medieval art depicted them as miniature adults. In short, within the medieval world, the young were fully integrated members of the community. No one believed that young people were innocent beings who needed to be quarantined from a harsh adult world.

In later centuries, the period between the end of infancy and sexual maturity was redefined as a discrete stage in human development. Two seemingly contradictory strands of Western thought gave rise to this refiguration of childhood. On the one hand, the Calvinist doctrine of infant depravity characterized the young as inherently sinful and doomed to spiritual death absent coercive discipline by adults. In contrast, Enlightenment philosophy and the later romanticism of Rousseau saw children as innately innocent beings whose potential should be nurtured by parents without corrupting their natural goodness. What both of these conceptions of childhood shared, however, in contrast to the earlier medieval construction, was the belief that children are essentially *different* from adults and that one aspect of that difference is their intrinsic malleability.

The late nineteenth and early twentieth centuries saw an extension of this dramatic reconstruction of childhood. In the academy, experts dedicating their scholarship to the study of the child placed great emphasis on how inherently and essentially different children are from adults. The so-called "child-study" movement was predicated on the belief that childhood is composed of stages, each with characteristic emotions, capacities and needs. * * *

As this "child-study" movement gained momentum, prominent universities such as Harvard, Yale and Princeton rushed to set up departments of child development. In medicine, the perception of the uniqueness of childhood led to the birth of pediatrics and the founding of specialized children's hospitals. On the political front, Congress, in 1912, passed a federal bill to establish a special Children's Bureau within the Cabinet Department of Commerce and Labor.

At the same time that academic and governmental attention was focusing on childhood, the temporal contours of childhood were extended through the creation of a new stage of pre-adulthood—adolescence. Although the word "adolescence" was not actually invented during this period, the term rarely was used prior to the late nineteenth century, and little or no attention paid to any special characteristics that teenagers might have. By the turn of the century, the attributes of childhood were being applied to teenagers, who only a generation earlier would not have been distinguished from older adults. Since as children they were assumed to be vulnerable, malleable, and in need of adult guidance, training, and control before they could graduate to full personhood, adolescents now became targets of paternal adult attention. Compulsory school attendance laws, which earlier had been ignored in those few jurisdictions that enacted them, were passed in state legislatures and were increasingly enforced. Between 1900 and 1930, the number of high school graduates increased 600 percent. At the same time, legislatures promulgated child labor laws establishing a minimum age for workers, limiting the hours that could be worked, and regulating the conditions of employment. As a result, the number of people between the ages of ten and fifteen who were gainfully employed declined seventy-five percent from 1910 to 1930. The minimum age for marriage was raised to discourage early marrying. The consequences of this spate of law reform prolonged the economic dependence of adolescents, increased the amount of age stratification in society, and established a greater degree of formal social control over the young than had existed previously. * * *

Among all of the law reforms adopted during the Progressive Era to accommodate the new perception of the adolescent's nature and needs, the creation of the juvenile court undoubtedly ranks as the most far-reaching achievement. The rapidity with which the concept spread is striking. In 1899, Illinois passed the Juvenile Court Act, founding a juvenile system widely acknowledged at the time as the model for other states to follow. And follow they did; within twenty years all but three states had similar juvenile justice systems in place.

The desirability, even necessity, for a separate court system to address the problems of young people appeared obvious, given the newly emerging view of the adolescent as an immature creature in need of adult control. When parental control failed, the benevolent, if coercive, hand of the state could provide the corrective molding needed by the errant youth. By categorizing the adolescent as a sub-class of the child rather than as a type of adult, the Progressives fashioned a discrete juvenile justice system premised upon the belief that, like other children, adolescents are not morally accountable for their behavior. Thus, ordinary retributive punishment for the adolescent would be inappropriate. The Progressives treated lawbreaking by juveniles as a symptom justifying, in fact humanely requiring, state intervention to save them from a life of crime that might otherwise be their fate.

The allusion to medical treatment suggested by the word "symptom" is not accidental; the Progressives frequently compared social deviance to physical disease. Although Progressive ideology entertained an eclectic set of conflicting notions about the causes of deviant behavior, including physiological, genetic, and environmental theories, the belief that criminal behavior was caused by unwholesome environment, especially the baneful influence of squalid urban life, came to dominate correctional thinking. Juvenile misbehavior was seen as merely the overt manifestation of underlying social pathology. Like physical pathology, social pathology could not be ignored or the "disease" might progressively worsen. With proper diagnosis and treatment, however, social pathology was considered as susceptible to cure as physical ailments. Particularly in light of the supposedly malleable nature of juveniles, the Progressives exuded confidence in their ability to cure juvenile delinquency. * * *

To the advocates of the juvenile court, the essential difference between the moral and cognitive capacities of the juvenile and those of the adult did not serve merely to mitigate juvenile culpability for breaking the law, but to absolve the juvenile completely from criminal liability.

Juvenile court philosophy made no distinction between criminal and noncriminal behavior, as long as the behavior was considered deviant or inappropriate to the age of the juvenile. Behavior such as smoking, sexual activity, stubbornness, running away from home, swearing, and truancy could trigger juvenile court jurisdiction as validly as could breaking a criminal law. * * * The idea that the peculiar vulnerability of children justified state control over them was analogized to the well-established chancery court principle, *parens patriae,* which gave the state authority over parentless children. Invoking a chancery court pedigree for juvenile court jurisdiction, *the parens patriae* doctrine lent legitimacy to the new court system while it obscured the extent to which juvenile court marked an unprecedented expansion of state social control over adolescents.

Every aspect of the *parens patriae* juvenile court was designed to mold wayward youths into good citizens. The hallmark of the system was its disposition, individually tailored to address the needs and abilities of the juvenile in question. To that end, judges were given almost limitless discretion in crafting the disposition to facilitate whatever the judge thought would "cure" the youth. Juveniles could be put on probation until their majority, giving the juvenile court total control over every aspect of the probationer's life. If the juvenile was incarcerated in a juvenile detention facility, the commitment would be for an indeterminate period, because the judge could not perfectly predict in advance the amenability of the youth to rehabilitative treatment. Once rehabilitated, the youth would be released from further court control, regardless of the seriousness of the offense that gave rise to juvenile court jurisdiction, because the court's basis for its disposition was treatment, not punitive sanction. Indeed, the juvenile court judge could, at least in theory, discharge the juvenile offender immediately after the dispositional hearing if the judge believed that the youth had no need for court-monitored treatment or services, even if the juvenile had committed a serious offense.

Some states deliberately eliminated the usual procedural formalities of criminal adjudication from juvenile court. These formalities were considered both unnecessary and undesirable: unnecessary because the role of the court was not to adjudicate guilt and punish, but to prescribe treatment; undesirable because informality itself was deemed a part of the rehabilitative process. For this reason, trial by jury was eliminated in most juvenile courts as irrelevant to the proper determination before the court, because the court was less concerned with factually determining whether the child had broken the law than with sensitively diagnosing and treating the child's social pathology. * * *

The object of what Judge Mack termed "not so much the power, as the friendly interest of the state" was invariably referred to as "the child," the "boy or girl" or "the lad." Calling teenaged lawbreakers "children" was not disingenuous rhetoric. Rather, it demonstrates that the social construction of adolescence as a species of childhood powerfully informed the ideology and practice of the *parens patriae* juvenile court. * * *

Notes

1) Houses of Refuge Historians trace many features of the Progressive juvenile court to the Houses of Refuge that emerged in eastern cities during the middle-third of the nineteenth century. The Refuge marked the first specialized institutions for the formal social control of youth and appeared in the larger, eastern urban centers, first in New York and Boston in 1825, and in Philadelphia in 1828, in conjunction with the first burst of industrialization, immigration and urbanization in America. Jacksonian-era reformers created Refuges and other asylums to respond to the specific problems and disorganization caused by social change and to provide examples of proper discipline to guide the community. Refuge legislation adopted three important legal innovations: a formal age-based distinction between juvenile and adult offenders and institutional separation; the use of indeterminate commitments; and a broadened authority to deal with young offenders and dependent, neglected, and incorrigible children. See, e.g., Harold Finestone, *Victims of Change: Juvenile Delinquents in American Society* (1976); Joseph Hawes, *Children in Urban Society: Juvenile Delinquency in Nineteenth Century America* (1971); Robert Mennel, *Thorns and Thistles: Juvenile Delinquents in the United States 1825–1940* (1973); Robert Pickett, *House of Refuge: Origins of Juvenile Reform in New York State 1815–1857* (1969); David Rothman, *The Discovery of the Asylum: Social Order and Disorder in the New Republic* (1971).

In **Ex parte Crouse**, 4 Whart. 9 (1839), the father of Mary Ann Crouse challenged her commitment to the Philadelphia House of Refuge by a justice of the peace for being "an incorrigible or vicious female under the age of 18 years." The Chief Justice of the Pennsylvania Supreme Court, in a per curiam opinion, rejected the claim that her institutional commitment was punitive and thus unconstitutional without a jury trial:

> The object of the charity is reformation, by training its inmates to industry, by imbuing their minds with principles of morality and religion, by furnishing them with means to earn a living, and, above all, by separating them from the corrupting influence of improper associates. To this end may not the natural parents, when unequal to the task of education, or unworthy of it, be superseded by the parens patriae, or common guardian of the community? It is to be remembered that the public has a paramount interest in the virtue and knowledge of its members, and that, of strict right, the business of education belongs to it. That parents are ordinarily intrusted with it is because it can seldom be put into better hands; but, where they are incompetent or corrupt, what is there to prevent the public from withdrawing their faculties, held, as they obviously are, at its sufferance? The right of parental control is a natural, but not an unalienable, one. It is not excepted by the Declaration of Rights out of the subjects of ordinary legislation; and it consequently remains subject to the ordinary legislative power, which, if wantonly or inconveniently used, would soon be constitutionally restricted, but the competency of which, as the government is constituted, cannot be doubted. As to abridgment of indefeasible rights by confinement of the person, it is no more than what is born, to a greater or less extent, in every school; and we know of no natural right to exemption from restraints which conduce to an infant's welfare. Nor is there a doubt of the propriety of their application in the particular instance. The infant has been snatched from a course which must have ended in confirmed

depravity; and not only is the restraint of her person lawful, but it would be an act of extreme cruelty to release her from it. * * *

Analysts of juvenile courts attribute many of their characteristics to legal reforms associated with the earlier Refuges. "[L]egislation establishing the juvenile court in Chicago did no more than formalize long-standing practices for dealing with juveniles in Illinois. * * * [I]n almost every state the legal and ideological innovations typically associated with the juvenile court (e.g., the extension of legal control over noncriminal children, the denial of due process, and the legalization of the rehabilitative ideal) had occurred before the advent of children's courts, as a result of earlier legislation establishing juvenile reformatories." John Sutton, "Social Structure, Institutions, and the Legal Status of Children in the United States," 88 *Am.J.Soc.* 915, 917 (1983). *See also*, John Sutton, *Stubborn Children: Controlling Delinquency in the United States, 1640–1981* (1988).

The Illinois Juvenile Court Act of 1899, *supra* p. 4, responded to the Progressive's concern that the criminal justice system was inappropriate to deal with offending children. It created several alternatives to placing youths in adult facilities (§§ 9 and 11). It placed greater emphasis on schools and institutions to reform and protect children rather than to rely simply on incarceration (§ 9). It formally institutionalized the role of probation officers in dealing with youths in the community (§§ 6, 9). It also emphasized that the paramount concern of this new justice system was to be the welfare of the child (§ 21). Significantly, the 1907 amendments, p. 7, broadened the definition of "delinquent" (§ 2.1) beyond youths who committed crimes to include non-criminal misconduct or "status offenses".

2) Legal Approval of Juvenile Courts After States adopted juvenile court acts, appellate courts routinely affirmed their authority to try young offenders without providing criminal procedural safeguards and to commit them to institutions. In **Commonwealth v. Fisher**, 213 Pa. 48, 62 A. 198 (Pa. 1905), the juvenile challenged his commitment by the Philadelphia court of quarter sessions to the House of Refuge under authority of the juvenile court act of 1903:

> The objections of the appellant to the constitutionality of the [juvenile court] act, as presented by counsel, are: (a) Under its provisions the defendant was not taken into court by due process of law; (b) He was denied his right of trial before a jury on the charge of the felony for which he had been arrested; (c) The tribunal before which he appeared, and which heard the case and committed him to the House of Refuge, was an unconstitutional body, and without jurisdiction; (d) The act provides different punishments for the same offense by a classification of individuals according to age; * * *

> No new court is created by the act under consideration. In its title it is called an act to define the powers of an already existing and ancient court. In caring for the neglected or unfortunate children of the commonwealth, and in defining the powers to be exercised by that court in connection with these children, recognized by the state as its wards requiring its care and protection, jurisdiction is conferred upon that court as the appropriate one, and not upon a new one created by the act. The

court of quarter sessions is not simply a criminal court. The Constitution recognizes it, but says nothing as to its jurisdiction. * * * It is a mere convenient designation of the court of quarter sessions to call it, when caring for children, a "juvenile court"; but no such court, as an independent tribunal, is created. It is still the court of quarter sessions before which the proceedings are conducted, and though that court, in so conducting them, is to be known as the "juvenile court," the records are still those of the court of quarter sessions.

In pressing the objection that the appellant was not taken into custody by due process of law, the assumption, running through the entire argument of the appellant, is continued that the proceedings of the act of 1903 are of a criminal nature for the punishment of offenders for crimes committed, and that the appellant was so punished. But he was not, and he could not have been without due process of law; for the constitutional guaranty is that no one charged with a criminal offense shall be deprived of life, liberty, or property without due process of law. To save a child from becoming a criminal, or from continuing in a career of crime, to end in maturer years in public punishment and disgrace, the Legislature surely may provide for the salvation of such a child, if its parents or guardian be unable or unwilling to do so, by bringing it into one of the courts of the state without any process at all, for the purpose of subjecting it to the state's guardianship and protection. The natural parent needs no process to temporarily deprive his child of its liberty by confining it in his own home, to save it and to shield it from the consequences of persistence in a career of waywardness; nor is the state, when compelled, as parens patriae, to take the place of the father for the same purpose, required to adopt any process as a means of placing its hands upon the child to lead it into one of its courts. When the child gets there, and the court, with the power to save it, determines on its salvation, and not its punishment, it is immaterial how it got there. The act simply provides how children who ought to be saved may reach the court to be saved. * * *

The last reason to be noticed why the act should be declared unconstitutional is that it denies the appellant a trial by jury. Here again is the fallacy that he was tried by the court for any offense. "The right of trial by jury shall remain inviolate," are the words of the Bill of Rights, and no act of the Legislature can deny this right to any citizen, young or old, minor or adult, if he is to be tried for a crime against the commonwealth. But there was no trial for any crime here, and the act is operative only when there is to be no trial. The very purpose of the act is to prevent a trial, though, if the welfare of the public require that the minor should be tried, power to try it is not taken away from the court of quarter sessions; for the eleventh section expressly provides that nothing in the preceding sections "shall be in derogation of the powers of the courts of quarter sessions and oyer and terminer to try, upon an indictment, any delinquent child, who, in due course, may be brought to trial." This section was entirely unnecessary, for without it a delinquent child can be tried only by a jury for a crime charged; but, as already stated, the act is not for the trial of a child charged with a crime, but is mercifully to save it from such an ordeal, with the prison or penitentiary in its wake, if the child's own good and the best interests of the state justify such salvation. Whether the child deserves to be saved by the state is no more a question for a jury than whether the father, if able to save it, ought to save it. If the latter ought to save, but is powerless to do so, the former, by the act of 1903, undertakes the duty; and the Legislature, in directing how that duty is to be performed in a proper case, denies the child no right of a trial by a jury, for the simple reason that by the act it is not to be tried for anything. The court passes upon nothing but the propriety of an effort to save it, and, if a worthy subject for an effort of salvation, that effort is made in the way directed by the act. The act is but an exercise by the state of its supreme power over the welfare of its children, a power under which it can take a child from its father and let it go where it will, without committing it to any guardianship or any institution, if the welfare of the child, taking its age into consideration, can be thus best promoted. * * *

The proceeding is not one according to the course of the common law, in which the right of trial by jury is guarantied, but a mere statutory proceeding for the accomplishment of the protection of the helpless, which object was accomplished before the Constitution without the enjoyment of a jury trial. There is no restraint upon the natural liberty of children contemplated by such a law, none whatever, but rather the placing of them under the natural restraint, so far as practicable, that should be, but is not, exercised by parental authority. It is the mere conferring upon them that protection to which, under the circumstances, they are entitled as a matter of right. It is for their welfare and that of the community at large. The design is not punishment, nor the restraint imprisonment, any more than is the wholesome restraint which a parent exercises over his child. The severity in either case must necessarily be tempered to meet the necessities of the particular situation. There is no probability, in the proper administration of the law, of the child's liberty being unduly invaded. Every statute which is designed to give protection, care, and training to children, as a needed substitute for parental authority and performance of parental duty, is but a recognition of the duty of the state, as the legitimate guardian and protector of children where other guardianship fails. No constitutional right is violated, but one of the most important duties which organized society owes to its helpless members is performed, just in the measure that the law is framed with wisdom and is carefully administered. * * *

B. THE CONSTITUTIONAL DOMESTICATION OF THE JUVENILE COURT

The Supreme Court's decision in *In re Gault* mandated procedural safeguards in delinquency proceedings and focused initial judicial attention on whether the child committed an offense as a prerequisite to sentencing. In shifting the formal focus of juvenile courts from "real needs" to legal guilt, *Gault* reviewed the history of the juvenile court and identified two crucial disjunctions between juvenile justice rhetoric and reality: the theory versus practice of rehabilitation, and the differences between the criminal procedural safeguards afforded adult defendants and those available to juvenile delinquents.

IN RE GAULT

387 U.S. 1, 87 S.Ct. 1428, 18 L.Ed.2d 527 (1967).

[Portions of the opinion discussing specific procedural safeguards appear *infra* at p. 721]

MR. JUSTICE FORTAS delivered the opinion of the Court.

* * * From the inception of the juvenile court system, wide differences have been tolerated—indeed insisted upon—between the procedural rights accorded to adults and those of juveniles. In practically all jurisdictions, there are rights granted to adults which are withheld from juveniles. In addition to the specific problems involved in the present case, for example, it has been held that the juvenile is not entitled to bail, to indictment by grand jury, to a public trial or to trial by jury. It is frequent practice that rules governing the arrest and interrogation of adults by the police are not observed in the case of juveniles.

The history and theory underlying this development are well-known, but a recapitulation is necessary for purposes of this opinion. The Juvenile Court movement began in this country at the end of the last century. From the juvenile court statute adopted in Illinois in 1899, the system has spread to every State in the Union, the District of Columbia, and Puerto Rico. The constitutionality of juvenile court laws has been sustained in over 40 jurisdictions against a variety of attacks.

The early reformers were appalled by adult procedures and penalties, and by the fact that children could be given long prison sentences and mixed in jails with hardened criminals. They were profoundly convinced that society's duty to the child could not be confined by the concept of justice alone. They believed that society's role was not to ascertain whether the child was "guilty" or "innocent," but "What is he, how has he become what he is, and what had best be done in his interest and in the interest of the state to save him from a downward career." The child—essentially good, as they saw it—was to be made "to feel that he is the object of (the state's) care and solicitude," not that he was under arrest or on trial. The rules of criminal procedure were therefore altogether inapplicable. The apparent rigidities, technicalities, and harshness which they observed in both substantive and procedural criminal law were therefore to be discarded. The idea of crime and punishment was to be abandoned. The child was to be "treated" and "rehabilitated" and the procedures, from apprehension through institutionalization, were to be "clinical" rather than punitive.

These results were to be achieved, without coming to conceptual and constitutional grief, by insisting that the proceedings were not adversary, but that the state was proceeding as *parens patriae*. The Latin phrase proved to be a great help to those who sought to rationalize the exclusion of juveniles from the constitutional scheme; but its meaning is murky and its historic credentials are of dubious relevance. The phrase was taken from chancery practice, where, however, it was used to describe the power of the state to act *in loco parentis* for the purpose of protecting the property interests and the person of the child. But there is no trace of the doctrine in the history of criminal jurisprudence. At common law, children under seven were considered incapable of possessing criminal intent. Beyond that age, they were subjected to arrest, trial, and in theory to punishment like adult offenders. In these old days, the state was not deemed to have authority to accord them fewer procedural rights than adults.

The right of the state, as *parens patriae*, to deny to the child procedural rights available to his elders was elaborated by the assertion that a child, unlike an adult, has a right "not to liberty but to custody." He can be made to attorn to his parents, to go to school, etc. If his parents default in effectively performing their custodial functions—that is, if the child is "delinquent"—the state may intervene. In doing so, it does not deprive the child of any rights, because he has none. It merely provides the "custody" to which the child is entitled. On this basis, proceedings involving juveniles were described as "civil" not "criminal" and therefore not subject to the requirements which restrict the state when it seeks to deprive a person of his liberty.

Accordingly, the highest motives and most enlightened impulses led to a peculiar system for juveniles, unknown to our law in any comparable context. The constitutional and theoretical basis for this peculiar system is—to say the least—debatable. And in practice, * * * the results have not been entirely satisfactory. Juvenile Court history has again demonstrated that unbridled discretion, however benevolently motivated, is frequently a poor substitute for principle and procedure. In 1937, Dean Pound wrote: "The powers of the Star Chamber were a trifle in comparison with those of our juvenile courts * * *." The absence of substantive standards has not necessarily meant that children receive careful, compassionate, individualized treatment. The absence of procedural rules based upon constitutional principle has not always produced fair, efficient, and effective procedures. Departures from established principles of due process have frequently resulted not in enlightened procedure, but in arbitrariness. * * *

Failure to observe the fundamental requirements of due process has resulted in instances, which might have been avoided, of unfairness to individuals and inadequate or inaccurate findings of fact and unfortunate prescriptions of remedy. Due process of law is the primary and indispensable foundation of individual freedom. It is the basic and essential term in the social compact which defines the rights of the individual and delimits the powers which the state may exercise. * * * [T]he procedural rules which have been fashioned from the generality of due process are our best instruments for the distillation and evaluation of essential facts from the conflicting welter of data that life and our adversary methods present. It is these instruments of due process which enhance the possibility that truth will emerge from the confrontation of opposing versions and conflicting data. "Procedure is to law what 'scientific method' is to science."

It is claimed that juveniles obtain benefits from the special procedures applicable to them which more than offset the disadvantages of denial of the substance of normal due process. As we shall discuss, the observance of due process standards, intelligently and not ruthlessly administered, will not compel the States to abandon or displace any of the substantive benefits of the juvenile process. But it is important, we think, that the claimed benefits of the juvenile process should be candidly appraised. Neither sentiment nor folklore should cause us to shut our eyes, for example, to such startling findings as that reported in an exceptionally reliable study of repeaters or recidivism conducted by the Stanford Research Institute for the President's Commission on Crime in the District of Columbia. This Commission's Report states:

> "In fiscal 1966 approximately 66 percent of the 16– and 17–year–old juveniles referred to the court by the Youth Aid Division had been before the court previously. In 1965, 56 percent of those in the Receiving Home were repeaters. The SRI study revealed that 61 percent of the sample Juvenile Court referrals in 1965 had been previously referred at least once and that 42 percent had been referred at least twice before."

Certainly, these figures and the high crime rates among juveniles to which we have referred, could not lead us to conclude that the absence of constitutional protections reduces crime, or that the juvenile system, functioning free of constitutional inhibitions as it has largely done, is effective to reduce crime or rehabilitate offenders. We do not mean by this to denigrate the juvenile court process or to suggest that there are not aspects of the juvenile system relating to offenders which are valuable. But the features of the juvenile system which its proponents have asserted are of unique benefit will not be impaired by constitutional domestication. For example, the commendable principles relating to the processing and treatment of juveniles separately from adults are in no way involved or affected by the procedural issues under discussion. Further, we are told that one of the important benefits of the special juvenile court procedures is that they avoid classifying the juvenile as a "criminal." The juvenile offender is now classed as a "delinquent." There is, of course, no reason why this should not continue. It is disconcerting, however, that this term has come to involve only slightly less stigma than the term "criminal" applied to adults. It is also emphasized that in practically all jurisdictions, statutes provide that an adjudication of the child as a delinquent shall not operate as a civil disability or disqualify him for civil service appointment. There is no reason why the application of due process requirements should interfere with such provisions.

Beyond this, it is frequently said that juveniles are protected by the process from disclosure of their deviational behavior. As the Supreme Court of Arizona phrased it in the present case, the summary procedures of Juvenile Courts are sometimes defended by a statement that it is the law's policy "to hide youthful errors from the full gaze of the public and bury them in the graveyard of the forgotten past." This claim of secrecy, however, is more rhetoric than reality. Disclosure of court records is discretionary with the judge in most jurisdictions. Statutory restrictions almost invariably apply only to the court records, and even as to those the evidence is that many courts routinely furnish information to the FBI and the military, and on request to government agencies and even to private employers. Of more importance are police records. In most States the police keep a complete file of juvenile "police contacts" and have complete discretion as to disclosure of juvenile records. Police departments receive requests for information from the FBI and other law-enforcement agencies, the Armed Forces, and social service agencies, and most of them generally comply. Private employers word their application forms to produce information concerning juvenile arrests and court proceedings, and in some jurisdictions information concerning juvenile police contacts is furnished private employers as well as government agencies.

In any event, there is no reason why, consistently with due process, a State cannot continue if it deems it appropriate, to provide and to improve provision for the confidentiality of records of police contacts and court action relating to juveniles. * * *

Further, it is urged that the juvenile benefits from informal proceedings in the court. The early conception of the Juvenile Court proceeding was one in which a fatherly judge touched the heart and conscience of the erring youth by talking over his problems, by paternal advice and admonition, and in which, in extreme situations, benevolent and wise institutions of the State provided guidance and help "to save him from downward career." Then, as now, goodwill and compassion were admirably prevalent. But recent studies have, with surprising unanimity, entered sharp dissent as to the validity of this gentle conception. They suggest that the appearance as well as the actuality of fairness, impartiality and orderliness—in short, the essentials of due process—may be a more impressive and more therapeutic attitude so far as the juvenile is concerned. For example, in a recent study, the sociologists Wheeler and Cottrell observe that when the procedural laxness of the *"parens patriae"* attitude is followed by stern disciplining, the contrast may have an adverse effect upon the child, who feels that he has been deceived or enticed. They conclude as follows: "Unless appropriate due process of law is followed, even the juvenile who has violated the law may not feel that he is being fairly treated and may therefore resist the rehabilitative efforts of court personnel." Of course, it is not suggested that juvenile court judges should fail appropriately to take account, in their demeanor and conduct, of the emotional and psychological attitude of the juveniles with whom they are confronted. While due process requirements will, in some instances, introduce a degree of order and regularity to Juvenile Court proceedings to determine delinquency, and in contested cases will introduce some elements of the adversary system, nothing will require that the conception of the kindly juvenile judge be replaced by its opposite, nor do we here rule upon the question whether ordinary due process requirements must be observed with respect to hearings to determine the disposition of the delinquent child.

Ultimately, however, we confront the reality of that portion of the Juvenile Court process with which we deal in this case. A boy is charged with misconduct. The boy is committed to an institution where he may be restrained of liberty for years. It is of no constitutional consequence—and of limited practical meaning—that the institution to which he is committed is called an Industrial School. The fact of the matter is that, however euphemistic the title, a "receiving home" or an "industrial school" for juveniles is an institution of confinement in which the child is incarcerated for a greater or lesser time. His world becomes "a building with whitewashed walls, regimented routine and institutional hours * * *." Instead of mother and father and sisters and brothers and friends and classmates, his world is peopled by guards, custodians, state employees, and "delinquents" confined with him for anything from waywardness to rape and homicide.

In view of this, it would be extraordinary if our Constitution did not require the procedural regularity and the exercise of care implied in the phrase "due process." Under our Constitution, the condition of being a boy does not justify a kangaroo court. The traditional ideas of Juvenile Court procedure, indeed, contemplated that time would be available and care would be used to establish precisely what the juvenile did and why he did it—was it a prank of adolescence or a brutal act threatening serious consequences to himself or society unless corrected? Under traditional notions, one would assume that in a case like that of Gerald Gault, where the juvenile appears to have a home, a working mother and father, and an older brother, the Juvenile Judge would have made a careful inquiry and judgment as to the possibility that the boy could be disciplined and dealt with at home, despite his previous transgressions. Indeed, so far as appears in the record before us, except for some conversation with Gerald about his school work and his "wanting to go to * * * Grand Canyon with his father," the points to which the judge directed his attention were little different from those that would be involved in determining any charge of violation of a penal statute. The essential difference between Gerald's case and a normal criminal case is that safeguards available to adults were discarded in Gerald's case. The summary procedure as well as the long commitment was possible because Gerald was 15 years of age instead of over 18.

If Gerald had been over 18, he would not have been subject to Juvenile Court proceedings. For the particular offense immediately involved, the maximum punishment would have been a fine of $5 to $50, or imprisonment in jail for not more than two months. Instead, he was committed to custody for a maximum of six years. If he had been over 18 and had committed an offense to which such a sentence might apply, he would have been entitled to substantial rights under the Constitution of the United States as well as under Arizona's laws and constitution. The United States Constitution would guarantee him rights and protections with respect to arrest, search, and seizure, and pretrial interrogation. It would assure him of specific notice of the charges and adequate time to decide his course of action and to prepare his defense. He would be entitled to clear advice that he could be represented by counsel, and, at least if a felony were involved, the State would be required to provide counsel if his parents were unable to afford it. If the court acted on the basis of his confession, careful procedures would be required to assure its voluntariness. If the case went to trial, confrontation and opportunity for cross-examination would be guaranteed. So wide a gulf between the State's treatment of the adult and of the child requires a bridge sturdier than mere verbiage, and reasons more persuasive than cliche can provide. As Wheeler and Cottrell have put it, "The rhetoric of the juvenile court movement has developed without any necessarily close correspondence to the realities of court and institutional routines." * * .*

NOTES

1) The Constitutional Domestication of the Juvenile Court—A Brief Summary You may find three Supreme Court's Due Process decisions, infra: Gault, p. 721; In re Winship, p. 743; McKeiver v. Pennsylvania, p. 750. The following excerpt briefly summarizes their holdings and the constitutional framework of the contemporary juvenile court. **Barry C. Feld, "Race, Politics, and Juvenile Justice: The Warren Court and the Conservative 'Backlash,'" 87** *Minn.L.Rev.* **1447, 1481–94 (2003):**

From its Progressive origins until the early 1970s, the "Rehabilitative Ideal" and "penal-welfarism" defined the criminal and juvenile justice systems' policies and practices. The central tenets of the "Rehabilitative Ideal" include a focus on the individual offender, justice administration by clinical specialists and expert professionals, and welfare-oriented, indeterminate and discretionary decision-making practices. It presumes a general cultural agreement about the appropriate goals of change and the intervention strategies necessary to achieve them. Progressives believed that they could change people and that they knew how people should be changed. They felt that the new behavioral sciences provided them with the necessary tools to intervene and change people systematically. They assumed the virtues of their social order and the propriety of imposing their middle-class values on immigrants and the poor. They expected that social intervention, reform, and rising affluence eventually would reduce crime and asserted that the State had an affirmative responsibility to care for and control offenders.

Several forces combined in the 1960s to erode support for the "Rehabilitative Ideal." Left-wing critics of rehabilitation characterized penal programs as coercive instruments of social control that oppressed the poor and minorities. Liberals believed that treatment personnel's exercise of clinical discretion resulted in the unequal and disparate treatment of similarly situated offenders. Conservatives advocated "law and order" and favored punishment over rehabilitation in response to what they perceived as a breakdown of the social and legal order. They attributed crime and disorder to a permissive society and advocated firm discipline for the young, restoration of patriarchy in the family, respect for authority, and an end to the "coddling" of criminals. The combined critique of the rehabilitative model from the Left, Right, and Center produced a narrowing of sentencing factors—from individualized considerations of the offender to uniform and proportional sentences based on the nature of the offense. The critique also revived abandoned modes of public and political penal discourse about retribution and punishment, the expression of vengeful sentiments, and the imposition of draconian sanctions.

Despite occasional challenges and criticism of some aspects of juvenile justice, no sustained and systematic examination of the juvenile court occurred until the 1960s. The Supreme Court, encouraged by the persuasive critique of the "Rehabilitative Ideal," began the expansion of procedural safeguards to the juvenile court in *Kent v. United States*. Justice Fortas wrote that "the child receives the worst of both worlds: that he gets neither the protections accorded to adults nor the solicitous care and regenerative treatment postulated for children." Some procedural due process in judicial waiver hearings was therefore required.

The following year, in *In re Gault*, Fortas concluded that the entire juvenile justice process violated the Constitution and required a complete overhaul. *Gault* identified two crucial differences between juvenile justice rhetoric and reality: the theory versus the practice of "rehabilitation" and the differences between the procedural safeguards afforded adult criminal defendants and those available to juvenile delinquents. Although the Progressive juvenile court embraced a relationship of paternalism and informality, the Warren Court viewed the adversarial process and procedural safeguards as the appropriate way to structure the relationship between the individual and the State. Moreover, *Gault*'s "Due Process Revolution" demonstrated the link between procedure and substance, because once the Court required some procedural safeguards at trial, state laws and practices began to transform the juvenile court from the social welfare agency that the Progressives intended it to be into a formal legal institution. This "constitutional domestication" was the first step in the procedural and substantive convergence between the juvenile and the adult criminal justice systems. * * *

The Court concluded that, regardless of its therapeutic rhetoric, the reality of juvenile institutional confinement required "fundamentally fair" procedural safeguards. These protections included advance notice of charges, a fair and impartial hearing, the assistance of counsel, an opportunity to confront and cross-examine witnesses, and the privilege against self-incrimination. The Court limited its holding to the adjudicatory hearing at which the state determines that a child is delinquent. It asserted that adversarial procedural safeguards were essential in juvenile proceedings both to determine the truth—"factual accuracy"—and to preserve individual freedom by limiting the power of the state—"prevent governmental oppression"—and that its decision would not impair the juvenile court's ability to treat juveniles.

The Court based its holdings to grant delinquents the rights to notice, counsel, and confrontation on the generic notions of "fundamental fairness" required by Fourteenth Amendment due process rather than the specific requirements of the Sixth Amendment. The Court explicitly relied upon the Fifth Amendment, however, to provide juveniles the privilege against self-incrimination in delinquency proceedings. In granting delinquents the privilege against self-incrimination, *Gault* exemplified the dual functions that constitutional procedural safeguards perform in juvenile adjudications: assuring accurate fact finding and protecting against governmental oppression. *Gault* is an example of the Warren Court's general strategy of extending constitutional rights and using the adversary process to limit the State's coercive powers, to assure the regularity of law enforcement, and to reduce the need for constant judicial oversight.

In subsequent juvenile court "due process" decisions, the Court further elaborated on the criminal nature of delinquency proceedings. In *In re Winship*, the Court held that proof of delinquency must be established beyond a reasonable doubt, rather than by lower civil standards of proof. Because the Bill of Rights does not define the standard of proof in criminal cases, *Winship* first held that the Constitution requires proof beyond a reasonable doubt in adult criminal proceedings as a matter of "due process." The Court then extended the same standard of proof to juvenile proceedings for the same reason. According to *Winship*, preventing unwarranted convictions and limiting governmental power outweighed the dissent's concern that "criminalizing" the juvenile court would impair its therapeutic functions and erode the "differences between juvenile courts and traditional criminal courts." * * *

In *McKeiver v. Pennsylvania*, the Court declined to extend to juvenile hearings all of the procedural safeguards of adult criminal prosecutions. *McKeiver* held that the constitution did not require jury trials in state delinquency trials because "due process" required only "accurate factfinding," which a judge could provide as well as a jury. In concluding that due process required only accurate fact finding, however, the Court departed significantly from its prior emphasis on the dual rationales of accurate fact finding and protection against governmental oppression. In addition, *McKeiver* ignored the earlier analyses in *Gault* that applied the Fifth Amendment privilege against self-incrimination to prevent governmental oppression even though it might impede accurate fact finding. The *McKeiver* plurality, however, denied that delinquents required protection against governmental oppression, invoked the mythology of the paternalistic juvenile court judge, and rejected the concern that closed juvenile court hearings could prejudice the accuracy of fact finding. *McKeiver* emphasized the adverse impact that a constitutional right to jury trials would have on the informality, flexibility, and confidentiality of juvenile court proceedings.

Gault and its progeny precipitated a procedural revolution in the juvenile justice system that transformed its original Progressive conception as a social welfare agency. Progressive reformers intervened on the basis of the "real needs" of a child—her social circumstances, environment, and need for rehabilitation—and viewed formal proof of a crime as secondary. Although *McKeiver* declined to extend delinquents the right to a jury trial, *Gault* and *Winship* already had imported the adversarial model, attorneys, the privilege against self-incrimination, the criminal standard of proof, and the primacy of factual and legal guilt as a constitutional prerequisite to intervention. By adopting some criminal procedures to determine delinquency, the Court shifted the focus of the juvenile court from the Progressive emphasis on "real needs" to proof of criminal acts; it formalized the connection between criminal conduct and coercive intervention and effectively transformed juvenile proceedings into criminal prosecutions. Although the Court did not intend its "Due Process" decisions to obviate the juvenile court's rehabilitative agenda, in the aftermath of *Gault*, judicial, legislative, and administrative changes have fostered a procedural and substantive convergence with criminal courts. For most purposes, contemporary juvenile courts have become a wholly owned subsidiary of the criminal justice system. Providing a modicum of procedural justice legitimated greater punitiveness in juvenile courts because once states granted even a semblance of procedural justice, however inadequate, they more readily departed from a purely "rehabilitative" model of juvenile justice. It is an historical irony that concern about racial inequality provided the initial impetus for the Supreme Court's focus on procedural rights in states' juvenile justice systems, because it was the existence of those procedural rights that rationalized increasingly punitive penalties that fall most heavily on minority juvenile offenders.

C.   "GET TOUGH" POLICIES—1970s TO 1990s

The Supreme Court's "Due Process Revolution" coincided with a synergy of campus disorders, escalating baby-boom crime rates, and urban racial rebellions in the mid–1960s. National Republican politicians such as Barry Goldwater and Richard Nixon characterized these events as a crisis of "law and order," appealed to white southern voters' racial antipathy and resistance to school integration, and engineered a conservative backlash to foster a political realignment around issues of race and public policy. From the 1970s to the 1990s, conservative politicians used crime as a code word for race for electoral advantage, and advocated harsher, "get tough" crime policies that affected juvenile justice administration throughout the nation. In the mid–1980s, crack cocaine markets exploded in the inner cities, young drug dealers armed themselves, and rates of homicide among black youths escalated sharply. Increased urban violence accompanied the deindustrialization of the urban core and the emergence of the black underclass and provided political incentive to toughen responses to youth crime. Misgivings about the ability of juvenile courts either to rehabilitate violent offenders or to protect public safety bolstered policies to prosecute larger numbers of youths as adults. During this period, sensational news media coverage warned of a coming generation of "super-predators," put a black face on youth crime, and sustained political campaigns to "get tough" and to "crack down" on youth violence. News media coverage has systematically distorted reality by over-reporting violence crime and by overemphasizing the role of minority perpetrators in the commission of violent crime. The over-emphases on violence and race reinforce racial prejudices that, in turn, fuel harsher policies toward criminals. See Feld, "Race, Politics, and Juvenile Justice: The Warren Court and the Conservative Backlash," 87 *Minn. L. Rev.* 1447, 1523–1538 (2003).

Culminating in the late 1980s and early 1990s, almost every state enacted laws to simplify the transfer of youths to criminal courts or to require juvenile court judges to impose determinate or mandatory minimum sentences on those who remained within a more punitive juvenile system. Patricia Torbet, et al., *State Responses to Serious and Violent Juvenile Crime* (1996). Statutory changes in waiver laws used offense criteria to guide and limit judicial discretion, to give prosecutors greater charging authority, or automatically to exclude certain offenses from the jurisdiction of the juvenile court. Politicians' sound bites—"adult crime, adult time" or "old enough to do the crime, old enough to do the time"— exemplify the reformulation of adolescence and represent crime policies that provide no formal recognition of youthfulness in sentencing. Similar legislative changes affected the sentences that juvenile court judges imposed on delinquent offenders as well.

Barry C. Feld, "Race, Politics and Juvenile Justice: The Warren Court and the Conservative 'Backlash'," 87 *Minn. L. Rev.* at 1502–1523 (2003), summarizes the criminological and political context within which states enacted "get tough" law reforms:

By the early 1970s, urban riots, escalating rates of "baby boom" crime, dissatisfaction with the "treatment model" in penology, and the emerging "politics of crime" prompted calls for a return to classical principles of criminal law. Between 1964 and 1974, the number of homicides doubled, and produced a markedly more conservative public opinion about punishment and the response to crime. During this period, conservative politicians discovered the salience of "law and order" and other racially coded phrases as a way of describing social issues with racial implications. By the early 1970s, both liberal and conservative critics of rehabilitation and indeterminate sentencing began to swing the penal policy pendulum toward retribution, determinate sentences, and principles of "just deserts." Research on career criminals provided an empirical rationale for "selective incapacitation" and an additional reason to base sentencing decisions on the seriousness of offenses and criminal history rather than the characteristics of the offender. Evaluations of treatment effectiveness raised substantial doubts about clinicians' abilities to coerce behavioral changes, highlighted the subjectivity inherent in therapeutic justice, and called into question "what works" in correctional reform.

The shift of sentencing policy to emphasize offense criteria and the "just deserts" critique of rehabilitation produced strange philosophical and political bedfellows: liberals concerned about excessive discretion and discriminatory decisions, civil libertarians concerned about individual liberty and autonomy, and conservatives who denounced treatment as "soft on crime." Conservatives questioned the practical feasibility of rehabilitation and argued that indeterminate sentences released dangerous offenders who deserved lengthier sentences. Because liberals had criticized the failures of rehabilitation and indeterminate sentences as arbitrary and discriminatory criminal justice policies, they lacked a coherent alternative to conservative proposals to "crack down" on criminals. * * *

Doubts about the ability of juvenile courts either to rehabilitate chronic and violent young offenders or to protect public safety bolstered policies to "crack down" on youth crime and to prosecute larger numbers of youths as adults. In the 1980s and early 1990s, most states amended their juvenile codes either to simplify the transfer of young offenders to criminal courts, or to require juvenile court judges to impose longer, determinate, or mandatory sentences on those youths who remained within an increasingly punitive juvenile system. Both strategies de-emphasize rehabilitation and the circumstances of the offender, stress personal and justice system accountability and punishment, and base decisions on the seriousness of the present offense and prior record. Cumulatively, these changes reflect a fundamental inversion of juvenile justice jurisprudence and sentencing policies—from rehabilitation to retribution, from an emphasis on the offender to the seriousness of the offense, from a focus on a youth's "amenability to treatment" to punishment, and a transfer of sentencing discretion from the judicial to the legislative and executive branches.

Macro-structural, economic, and racial demographic changes that occurred in American cities during the 1970s and 1980s and the escalation in black youth homicide rates at the end of the 1980s facilitated the politics of crime that produced the "get-tough" juvenile justice policies of the early 1990s. * * * One factor contributing to "get tough" policies was the epidemic of crack cocaine, which spurred gun violence and youth homicides. * * * The proximate cause of "get tough" legislative changes was the success of conservative politicians who used crime as a "code word" to make racial appeals for electoral advantage. * * *

Starting in the early 1970s, the transition from an industrial to an information and service economy reduced job prospects for semi-skilled workers in the manufacturing sectors, and economic opportunities in the post-industrial city increasingly depended on skills and education. Moreover, because of differences in the timing of the "great migration," the experiences of urban Blacks differed from those of earlier European immigrants and placed them at a significant economic and structural disadvantage during the post-industrial transition. * * * Beginning in 1973, and for the first time since the post-World War II period of sustained growth, inflation-adjusted real hourly wages stagnated and then declined. * * * Moreover, the globalized economy and the overseas challenge to the domestic automobile and steel industries constituted a race-neutral development with profound racial consequences. Under the pressures of a globalizing economy, low-skill, entry-level jobs began to migrate overseas. * * *

During the post-World War II period, government highway, housing, and mortgage policies encouraged suburban expansion around urban centers. This spatially transformed many cities, and contributed to the growth of predominantly white suburbs around increasingly poor and minority urban cores. As black migration from the rural South to the urban North transformed the larger older cities, Whites simultaneously began to move from cities to the suburbs. Between the end of World War II and 1960, about one-third of all Blacks who had remained in the South migrated to other parts of the country; by 1960, the majority of all Blacks lived in central cities. Federal housing policies and interstate highway construction, combined with bank mortgage and real estate sales practices, spurred the growth of predominantly white suburbs ringing the poor and minority urban cores. In the 1950s and 1960s, urban renewal and highway construction disrupted and destroyed many urban black communities.

The isolation of Blacks in urban ghettos did not happen by chance or simply reflect their housing preferences. To the contrary, public policies and private institutional arrangements created racial segregation, and they continue to exacerbate the harmful consequences of concentrated poverty to the detriment of the economic and social welfare of black Americans. * * * Macro-structural economic changes associated with the post-industrial transition had a deleterious impact on urban minority residents. The greatest job losses occurred in those higher-paying, lower-skilled sectors of the manufacturing economy to which urban minorities previously had greatest access. Job growth occurred primarily in the suburbs and in those sectors of the information and service economies that required higher levels of education than most urban minority workers possessed. As a result of the economic, spatial, and racial reorganization of cities, an urban "underclass" living in concentrated poverty and in racial, social, and cultural isolation was created over several decades. * * *

By the end of the 1980s, the emergence of a black urban underclass, the introduction of crack cocaine into the inner cities, and the proliferation of guns among youths produced a sharp escalation in black youth homicide rates. The unique increase in black youth homicide provided the immediate political impetus to "get tough" and to "crack down" on youth crime. Because rates of offending vary by race, the political decision to "get tough" on youth violence effectively meant targeting young black men. The public perceives the "crime problem" and the juvenile court's clientele primarily as poor, urban black males. Politicians have manipulated and exploited these racially tinged perceptions for political advantage with demagogic pledges to "crack down" on youth crime, which has become a code word for harsher penalties for black males. * * *

The violent drug industry that crack cocaine spawned in large cities during the middle to late 1980s led to a dramatic increase in black youth homicide arrests involving guns. The low price of crack increased the numbers of buyers and weekly transactions, and thereby the number of sellers to accommodate the demand. Drug distribution attracted youths because they faced lower risks of severe penalties than adults, and because, especially for black males, they lacked alternative economic opportunities. Youths in the drug industry are likely to arm themselves for self-protection and take more risks than do adults. * * * Although guns constitute a "tool of the trade" in the drug industry, their proliferation within the wider youth population for self-defense and status also contributed to the escalation of homicides. The drug industry, in turn, contributed to the deterioration of urban neighborhoods by driving out stable families, undermining community leaders, weakening inhibitions against violence, and providing adolescents with attractive criminal role models.

Although "urban," "black," and "youth" each contribute to the prevalence of crime, the elevated black youth homicide rate reflects the pernicious intersection of all three. * * * Despite the structural determinants of youth crime, the intersections of race, guns, and homicide fanned the flames of public "panic" and fed the fire for a political "crack down" that led to the "get tough" reformulation of juvenile justice policies. By the early 1990s, the apparent randomness of gang violence and the disproportionate minority involvement in homicides had inflamed public fears. The substantial racial differences in rates of violent offenses had major implications for race-relations and the politics of crime. * * * [T]he increase in violent crime left the public vulnerable to "law and order" demagoguery. * * * [C]onservative politicians * * * demonized young people [as "Super-predators"] to muster support for "wars" on crime and drugs. They called for policies to transfer youths to criminal court. The success of these conservative politicians was made possible by sensationalized media coverage of the increase in gun homicide by young black males. This aided calls for a "crack down" on young offenders in general and violent minority offenders in particular.

Post-*Gault* Changes in Juvenile Justice Philosophy and Policy: 1960s–1990s. The following excerpt by **Howard Snyder and Melissa Sickmund,** *Juvenile Offenders and Victims: 2006 National Report* **96–97 (2006)** summarizes changes in juvenile justice policy over the past half century:

In the 1950's and 1960's, many came to question the ability of the juvenile court to succeed in rehabilitating delinquent youth. The treatment techniques available to juvenile justice professionals never reached the desired levels of effectiveness. Although the goal of rehabilitation through individualized justice—the basic philosophy of the juvenile justice system—was not in question, professionals were concerned about the growing number of juveniles, institutionalized indefinitely in the name of treatment.

In a series of decisions beginning in the 1960's, the U.S. Supreme Court required that juvenile courts become more formal—more like criminal courts. Formal hearings were now required in waiver situations, and delinquents facing possible confinement were given protection against self-incrimination and rights to receive notice of the charges against them, to present witnesses, to question witnesses, and to have an attorney. Proof "beyond a reasonable doubt" rather than merely "a preponderance of evidence" was now required for an adjudication. The Supreme Court, however, still held that there were enough "differences of substance between the criminal and juvenile courts ... to hold that a jury is not required in the latter."

Meanwhile Congress, in the Juvenile Delinquency Prevention and Control Act of 1968, recommended that children charged with noncriminal (status) offenses be handled outside the court system. A few years later, Congress passed the Juvenile Justice and Delinquency Prevention Act of 1974, which as a condition for State participation in the Formula Grants Program required deinstitutionalization of status offenders and non-offenders as well as the separation of juvenile delinquents from adult offenders. (In the 1980 amendments to the 1974 Act. Congress added a requirement that juveniles be removed from adult jail and lockup facilities.) Community-based programs, diversion, and deinstitutionalization became the banners of juvenile justice policy in the 1970's.

During the 1980's, the public perceived that serious juvenile crime was increasing and that the system was too lenient with offenders. Although there was substantial misperception regarding increases in juvenile crime, many States responded by passing more punitive laws. Some laws removed certain classes of offenders from the juvenile justice system and handled them as adult criminals in criminal court. Others required the juvenile justice system to be more like the criminal justice system and to treat certain classes of juvenile offenders as criminals but in juvenile court.

As a result, offenders charged with certain offenses are *excluded* from juvenile court jurisdiction or face *mandatory* or *automatic waiver to* criminal court. In some States, concurrent jurisdiction provisions give prosecutors the discretion to file certain juvenile cases directly in criminal court rather than juvenile court. In some States, some adjudicated juvenile offenders face *mandatory sentences.*

Five areas of change have emerged as States passed laws designed to crack down on juvenile crime. These laws generally involve expanded eligibility for criminal court processing and adult correctional sanctioning and reduced confidentiality protections for a subset of juvenile offenders. Between 1992 and 1997, all but three States changed laws in one or more of the following areas:

> Transfer provisions—Laws made it easier to transfer juvenile offenders from the juvenile justice system to the criminal justice system (45 States).

> Sentencing authority—Laws gave criminal and juvenile courts expanded sentencing options (31 States).

Confidentiality—Laws modified or removed traditional juvenile court confidentiality provisions by making records and proceedings more open (47 States).

In addition to these areas, there was change relating to:

Victims rights—Laws increased the role of victims of juvenile crime in the juvenile justice process (22 States).

Correctional programming—As a result of new transfer and sentencing laws, adult and juvenile correctional administrators developed new programs.

The 1980's and 1990's saw significant change in terms of treating more juvenile offenders as criminals. Recently, States have been attempting to strike a balance in their juvenile justice systems among system and offender accountability, offender competency development, and community protection. Juvenile code purpose clauses also incorporate restorative justice language (offenders repair the harm done to victims and communities and accept responsibility for their criminal actions).

"Get Tough" Law Reforms in the 1990s The following excerpt from **Patricia Torbet, et al.,** *State Responses to Serious and Violent Juvenile Crime* **xi–xvi (1996)**, summarizes changes in juvenile codes between 1992 and 1995 that legislatures enacted in response to increases in youth homicide rates in the late–1980s and early–1990s. Significantly, as the crime data in Chapter 2 report, beginning around 1994 and even before states implemented many of these legislative changes, youth crime rates began to drop precipitously and have continued to decline for the subsequent decade:

Nearly every State has taken legislative or executive action in response to escalating juvenile arrests for violent crime and public perceptions of a violent juvenile crime epidemic. These actions have significantly altered the legal response to violent or other serious juvenile crime in this country. In many States, changes have occurred in each legislative session since 1992, with more rapid and sweeping change occurring in 1995 and still more expected in 1996. This level of activity has occurred only three other times in our Nation's history; at the outset of the juvenile court movement at the turn of the century; following the U.S. Supreme Court's *Gault* decision in 1967; and with the enactment of the Juvenile Justice and Delinquency Prevention Act in 1974.

This reports documents the sea of change sweeping across the Nation in the handling of serious and violent juvenile offenders. All legislation enacted in 1992–1995 that targeted violent or other serious crimes by juveniles was analyzed to determine common themes and trends. * * * The report presents a compilation of these changes, an analysis of the direction of those changes and, where appropriate, a historical perspective highlighting instances where what is considered a recent change has, in fact, been around for some time in other States. Implications for policy and practice are offered as considerations for lawmakers and policymakers.

Five common themes emerged from the legislative analysis. Figure 1 identifies these themes as well as the general trend or direction of the changes adopted by States to respond to escalating serious crime by juveniles. The report is organized around each of these themes.

Figure 1

Themes and Trends in New Laws Targeting Violent or Other Serious Crime by Juveniles

Themes	Trends
Jurisdictional Authority	More serious and violent juvenile offenders are Being removed from the juvenile justice system in favor of criminal court prosecution
Judicial disposition/sentencing authority	More state legislatures are experimenting with new disposition/sentencing options
Correctional Programming	Correctional administrators are under pressure to develop programs as a result of new transfer and sentencing laws.
Confidentiality of juvenile court records and proceedings	Traditional confidentiality provisions are being revised in favor of more open proceedings and records.
Victims of juvenile crimes	Victims of juvenile crimes are being included as "active participants" in the juvenile justice process.

These trends represent both a reaction to the increasingly serious nature of juvenile crime and a fundamental shift in juvenile justice philosophy. Traditional notions of individualized dispositions based on the best interests of the juvenile are being diminished by interests in punishing criminal behavior. Inherent in many of the changes is the belief that serious and violent juvenile offenders must be held more accountable for their actions. Accountability is, in many instances, defined as punishment or a period of incarceration with less attention paid to the activities to be accomplished during that incarceration. Toward that end, dispositions are to be offense based rather than offender based, with the goal of punishment as opposed to rehabilitation.

The trend toward redefining the purpose of the juvenile justice system represents a fundamental philosophical departure, particularly in the handling of serious and violent juvenile offenders. This change in philosophy has resulted in dramatic shifts in the areas of jurisdiction, sentencing, correctional programming, confidentiality, and victims of crime. * * *

Chapter 2: Jurisdictional Authority

This theme refers to the potential for prosecuting a juvenile in criminal court and includes the mechanisms of judicial waiver, prosecutorial direct file, and statutory exclusion. Each mechanism establishes who has the authority to decide whether the juvenile or the criminal court will have jurisdiction over an alleged juvenile offender's case. Historically, the offender's age and current offense have been the criteria State legislatures established for determining eligibility for criminal prosecution.

The net result of the new laws has been to increase the potential for criminal justice prosecution and decrease the population eligible for juvenile court intervention. All States allow juveniles to be tried as adults in criminal court under certain circumstances. Since 1992, all but 10 States adopted or modified laws making it easier to prosecute juveniles in criminal court. Legislatures added significantly to the list of offenses now considered serious and/or lowered the age for which certain juveniles could be tried in criminal court. Some States require that juveniles with a particular offense history (a variation on the "three strikes" theme) be prosecuted in criminal court as well.

Legislatures also have increasingly enacted other provisions related to jurisdictional decisions, for example, "reverse waiver," "presumptive waiver," and "once waived/always waived."

Most of the changes in jurisdictional laws—and the change affecting the most juveniles—expand statutory exclusion provisions that automatically eliminate certain categories of juveniles from the juvenile court's original jurisdiction. Since 1992, 24 States added crimes to the list of excluded offenses, and 6 States lowered the age limit on some or all excluded offenses. In all, 36 States and the District of Columbia exclude certain categories of juveniles from juvenile court jurisdiction.

Implementation issues with respect to jurisdictional authority statutes include the following:

■ **Increased demands on court and prosecutor resources.** Criminal prosecutions require more prosecutor resources; three strikes statutes mean fewer pleas and more jury trials.

■ **Longer pretrial stays.** The increase in the number of transferred juveniles, the potential for appeals, and normal criminal justice processing delays mean that more juveniles are being detained for longer period of time in juvenile detention facilities or adult jails.

■ **Overcrowding and programming problems.** Juvenile detention facilities are not programmed for lengthy pretrial stays or while awaiting placement; jails do not provide educational or other services typically available in juvenile detention.

■ **Lack of guidelines or reporting requirements for prosecutors.** Unlike statewide reporting requirements for courts, there are no such requirements for prosecutorial decisions, nor are there guidelines for making decisions.

■ **Procedural issues related to habitual offender statutes.** New three strikes and you're an adult statutes are in vogue; however, juveniles may have been denied some protections that are accorded to adult defendants in criminal court such as the right to counsel.

Chapter 3: Judicial Disposition/Sentencing Authority

This theme refers to the dispositions or sentencing options available to judges for a juvenile adjudicated or convicted of a serious or violent offense. New laws have had a dramatic impact on sentencing practices, including (1) the imposition of mandatory minimum sentences; (2) the extension of juvenile court jurisdiction beyond the age of majority; and (3) the imposition of "blended sentences" that mix both juvenile and adult sanctions.

Since 1992, legislatures in 13 States and the District of Columbia have added or modified statutes that provide for a mandatory minimum period of incarceration for juveniles convicted of certain violent or other serious crimes.

Extended jurisdiction statutes allow the juvenile court judge to commit a juvenile to a State juvenile institution beyond the age of a juvenile court's jurisdiction, typically age 18. New laws have extended the court's continuing jurisdiction to age 21, or to age 25 in a few States.

"Blended sentencing" refers to the imposition of juvenile and/or adult correctional sanctions. Five basic models of blended sentencing have emerged in recent legislation. Each of the models applies to a subset of alleged juvenile offenders specified by statute, usually defined by age and a serious or violent offense. In three of the models, the juvenile court retains responsibility for adjudicating the case. In the remaining two models, the criminal court has jurisdiction for trying the case. The models also represent the imposition of either "exclusive" sanctioning (either juvenile or adult sanctions), "inclusive" sanctioning (both juvenile and adult sanctions), or "contiguous" sanctioning (first juvenile, then adult sanctions). By the end of the 1995 legislative session, 16 States had enacted some form of blended sentencing statute.

Blended sentencing models in which the juvenile court retains jurisdiction mandate either real consequences or strong incentives to encourage juveniles to access the opportunities available to them in the juvenile justice framework.

Implementation issues with respect to judicial disposition and sentencing include the following:

■ **Rights of juveniles.** Because many of the new sentencing options put juveniles at risk of adult sentences, rights of counsel and jury trial are critical.

■ **System ambivalence.** Blended sentencing options demonstrate ambivalence and a lack of resolve about what to do with serious and violent juvenile offenders on two fronts: transferring juveniles for whom the juvenile justice system is inadequate, and/or bolstering the resolves and the resources of the juvenile justice system to adequately address the needs of these very difficult offenders.

■ **System confusion.** Blended sentencing options create confusion among system actors: When is a juvenile a juvenile, and when is he considered an adult? This is an especially critical issue during processing and subsequent placement.

Chapter 4: Correctional Programming for Juveniles Who Commit Violent or Other Serious Offenses

This theme refers to the range of correctional programs available for juveniles convicted of violent or other serious crimes in either juvenile or criminal courts. Dramatic shifts have occurred in correctional programming due to an increased emphasis on protecting the public and holding offenders accountable for their actions. As a result, adult correctional systems are increasingly challenged to develop programming for younger and more vulnerable inmates. Juvenile correctional systems are increasingly being burdened with older, more violent juveniles.

Inquiries into correctional options for serious and violent juvenile offenders revealed a wide range of correction system responses, including:

■ **Straight adult incarceration.** Juveniles sentenced and incarcerated as adults with little differentiation in programming.

■ **Graduated incarceration.** Juveniles sentenced as adults but incarcerated in juvenile correctional facilities until they reach a certain age at which they may be transferred to adult facilities for the remainder of their sentences.

■ **Segregated incarceration.** Juveniles sentenced as adults but housed in separate facilities for younger adult offenders, occasionally with specialized programming.

■ **Youthful offenders.** Designating certain juveniles as youthful offenders with or without special programming or legal protections.

■ **Back to basics.** Enhanced juvenile corrections systems with a wide range of sanctions to hold juveniles accountable and to protect the public.

Implementation issues with respect to correctional programming include the following:

■ **Turf issues.** Some critics contend that had the juvenile justice system received the resources necessary to improve that system, they could have done as good a job or a better job, and at less cost.

■ **Funding/capacity issues.** Few States have a good plan for paying for changes, nor do they have a mechanism for implementing them.

■ **Programming issues.** Adult corrections departments are being asked to develop programs for a population they neither want nor have the expertise to address. Reform overlooks community corrections as a legitimate sanction for some serious and violent juvenile offenders.

Chapter 5: Confidentiality of Juvenile Court Records and Proceedings

This theme refers to how the juvenile justice system treats information about juveniles charged with or adjudicated for a violent or serious offense. Even though confidentiality issues have existed for decades, there has always been a presumption that juveniles needed to be protected from the full disclosure of their youthful indiscretions. However, as juvenile crime became more violent, community protection and the public's right to know have begun to displace confidentiality as a bedrock principle. Moreover, the need to share information across service delivery systems that see the same subset of juveniles is a concern.

Significant legislative activity has occurred with respect to the disclosure, use, and destruction of juvenile records and the openness of juvenile court proceedings. These trends represent a definitive shift in the use and management of information with notable impact on juvenile justice processing.

Since 1992, States have increasingly called for a presumption of open proceedings and the release of juvenile offenders' names, particularly if the offense was a serious or violent one.

Many States now open juvenile court records to school officials or require that schools be notified when a juvenile is taken into custody for a crime of violence or when a deadly weapon is used. Some States have lowered the age for which juvenile court records may be made publicly available.

Aside from disclosing or sharing information across systems for the purpose of better coordinating services, legislatures have made provisions in three other areas of juvenile records use: (1) centralized repositories, usually based on fingerprinting or photographing; (2) the criminal court's sue of a defendant's juvenile record; and (3) sex offender registration laws.

Historically, most legislatures have made specific provision for sealing or expunging juvenile court records. Since 1992, States have increased the number of years that must pass before sealing is allowed. In other States, if a juvenile has committed a violent or other serious felony, his juvenile record cannot be sealed or expunged.

Implementation issues with respect to confidentiality provisions include the following:

■ **Quality of records.** The quality and completeness of juvenile arrest and court records must be addressed, particularly when juvenile records are required to be a part of a central repository.

■ **Disclosure.** Reporting arrest information without a subsequent requirement to report adjudication outcomes may lead to unfair assumptions about a juvenile's behavior.

■ **Open proceedings.** Courtroom security and judicial authority to close proceedings to protect either the victim or the offender are concerns.
* * *

Chapter 8: Summary

The composite of change produced by recent legislative and executive actions includes the following:

■ **Change if everywhere.** Since 1992, 48 of the 51 State legislatures (including the District of Columbia) have made substantive changes to their laws targeting juveniles who commit violent or serious crimes.

■ **Change is consistent**. The nature of justice for a subset of juveniles now involves an increased eligibility for criminal, rather than juvenile, court processing and adult correctional sanctions. The underlying intent of change was to ease and support the State's decision to punish, hold accountable, and incarcerate for longer periods of time those juveniles who had, by instant offense or history, passed a threshold of tolerated "juvenile" criminal behavior.

■ **Decisionmaking roles are changing.** Either directly through prosecutorial direct filing or indirectly through the charging process in exclusion cases, the prosecutor has clearly emerged with an expanded role in justice system responses to serious and violent juvenile offenders. The juvenile court judge, in 1996, has significantly less authority to make decisions regarding the venue for, or the dispositional outcome of, cases involving violent or other serious crime than he or she did in 1992.

■ **Changes will impact minority juveniles.** Because minority juveniles are already over-represented in the crime categories targeted by new laws (e.g. serious and violent offenses, particularly those involving weapons, and juvenile with more extensive histories), these laws will have a disproportionate impact on minorities.

■ **Change involves secure placement.** With few exceptions, changes in sentencing and correctional programming options available to courts have been in the direction of increased incarceration of juveniles convicted of violent or other serious crimes without comparable attention to community corrections, including probation and aftercare.

■ **Change precedes capacity.** Legislative prescriptions for enhanced accountability for serious and violent juvenile offenders have, in many cases, anticipated resources and capacity that do not exist.

■ **Change is not tested.** In most instances, the reliance on changes that expand existing systems of criminal prosecution and adult corrections for serious and violent juvenile offenders has not been based on evidence that clearly demonstrates the efficacy of the intervention.

The violent criminal behavior of a relatively small proportion of juvenile offenders has created a public perception of rampant violent crime by juveniles and has prompted action by State legislatures and governors to get tough on crime. * * *

While most juvenile justice practitioners concede that some juvenile offenders should be treated as adults by virtue of the nature of their conduct, their prior delinquency, or their lack of amenability to treatment, there is widespread concern in the field over the consequences of treating significant numbers of juvenile offenders as adults.

Clearly, States have shifted the justice system's emphasis to holding juveniles accountable for the seriousness of their offenses. While some States appear to have incorporated that position into a balanced approach that includes protecting the public, restoring the community, and enhancing the offender's ability to function as a law-abiding, contributing member of society, many others have moved to a clear-cut punishment theme. In both instances, States are incarcerating more juvenile offenders for longer periods and redefining more of them as adults. It is not at all clear, however, that punishment is more certain, proportionate, longer, or more effective in the adult system for the entire population of juveniles being transferred. The significant policy issues over what to do about serious and violent juvenile offenders must be debated with the best outcome information available. The impact and consequences of such far-reaching changes in law and practice require that States study their actions. * * *

D. REASSESSING ADOLESCENT COMPETENCE AND CULPABILITY

Nearly a century after its creation, widespread public, policy-maker, and political dissatisfaction with the juvenile justice system produced contradictory impulses. Some politicians advocated "get tough" policies and criticized juvenile courts for failing to adopt harsher, retributive strategies to hold young offenders accountable and to treat them just like adults. Supporters of juvenile courts criticized them for failing to meet the needs of their clientele, many of whom suffered from psychological problems, educational deficits, poverty and abuse. They condemned the racial disparities in juvenile justice administration that produced disproportionate minority confinement. The general public perceived the juvenile justice system as incapable of rehabilitating offenders, reducing youth crime, or protecting the public safety.

Beginning in the mid–1990s, the John D. and Catherine T. MacArthur Foundation sponsored a Network on Adolescent Development and Juvenile Justice (ADJJ) to provide an evidence-based rationale for juvenile justice policy. http://www.adjj.org The ADJJ Network conducted interdisciplinary research to examine developmental differences between children and adults and to consider the implications of immaturity for structuring the juvenile justice system. The research program focused on three broad themes: adolescents' competence; culpability; and potential for change. Research on competence focused on how adolescents think and their decision-making capacities and how those limitations affect their ability to participate in the criminal or juvenile justice systems. Research on culpability focused on adolescents' criminal responsibility and their degree of deserved punishment and provides a rationale for categorical mitigation of sanctions for adolescents. Research on capacity to change examines the etiology of delinquency and the factors that promote youths' desistance from crime. The ADJJ Network has published a series of edited books and monographs and its research is encouraging a re-examination and amelioration of some of the harsher "get tough" policies enacted previously. The MacArthur Foundation is collaborating with policy makers in several states to implement developmentally appropriate juvenile justice policies.

NOTES

1) The following excerpt summarizes the research on adolescent culpability and provides a rationale to reconsider the recently enacted "get tough" juvenile justice policies. **MacArthur Foundation Research Network on Adolescent Development and Juvenile Justice, Less Guilty By Reason of Adolescence:**

In 2005, in a landmark decision[, *Roper v. Simmons*], the U.S. Supreme Court outlawed the death penalty for offenders who were younger than 18 when they committed their crimes. The ruling centered on the issue of culpability, or criminal blameworthiness. Unlike competence, which concerns an individual's ability to serve as a defendant during trial or adjudication, culpability turns on the offender's state of mind at the time of the offense, including factors that would mitigate, or lessen, the degree of responsibility.

The Court's ruling . . . ran counter to a nationwide trend toward harsher sentences for juveniles. Over the preceding decade, as serious crime rose and public safety became a focus of concern, legislators in virtually every state had enacted laws lowering the age at which juveniles could be tried and punished as adults for a broad range of crimes. This and other changes have resulted in the trial of more than 200,000 youths in the adult criminal system each year.

Proponents of the tougher laws argue that youths who have committed violent crimes need more than a slap on the wrist from a juvenile court. It is naïve, they say, to continue to rely on a juvenile system designed for a simpler era, when youths were getting into fistfights in the schoolyard; drugs, guns, and other serious crimes are adult offenses that demand adult punishment. Yet the premise of the juvenile justice system is that adolescents are different from adults, in ways that make them potentially less blameworthy than adults for their criminal acts.

The legal system has long held that criminal punishment should be based not only on the harm caused, but also on the blameworthiness of the offender. How blameworthy a person is for a crime depends on the circumstances of the crime and of the person committing it. Traditionally, the courts have considered several categories of mitigating factors when determining a defendant's culpability. These include:

- Impaired decision-making capacity, usually due to mental illness or disability,
- The circumstances of the crime—for example, whether it was committed under duress,
- The individual's personal character, which may suggest a low risk of continuing crime.

Such factors don't make a person exempt from punishment—rather, they indicate that the punishment should be less than it would be for others committing similar crimes, but under different circumstances.

Should developmental immaturity be added to the list of mitigating factors? Should juveniles, in general, be treated more leniently than adults? A major study by the Research Network on Adolescent Development and Juvenile Justice now provides strong evidence that the answer is yes.

The study of juvenile culpability was designed to provide scientific data on whether, in what ways, and at what ages adolescents differ from adults.

Many studies have shown that by the age of sixteen, adolescents' cognitive abilities—loosely, their intelligence or ability to reason—closely mirrors that of adults. But how people reason is only one influence on how they make decisions. In the real world, especially in high-pressure crime situations, judgments are made in the heat of the moment, often in the company of peers. In these situations, adolescents' other common traits—their short-sightedness, their impulsivity, their susceptibility to peer influence—can quickly undermine their decision-making capacity. * * *

Short–Sighted Decision–Making One important element of mature decision-making is a sense of the future consequences of an act. A variety of studies in which adolescents and adults are asked to envision themselves in the future have found that adults project their visions over a significantly longer time, suggesting much greater future orientation.

These findings are supported by data from the Network's culpability study. Adolescents characterized themselves as less likely to consider the future consequences of their actions than did adults. And when subjects in the study were presented with various choices measuring their preference for smaller, immediate rewards versus larger, longer-term rewards (for example, "Would you rather have $100 today or $1,000 a year from now?"), adolescents had a lower "tipping point"—the amount of money they would take to get it immediately as opposed to waiting.

How might these characteristics carry over into the real world? When weighing the long-term consequences of a crime, adolescents may simply be unable to see far enough into the future to make a good decision. Their lack of foresight, along with their tendency to pay more attention to immediate gratification than to long-term consequences, are among the factors that may lead them to make bad decisions.

Poor Impulse Control The Network's study also found that as individuals age, they become less impulsive and less likely to seek thrills; in fact, gains in these aspects of self-control continue well into early adulthood. This was evident in individuals' descriptions of themselves and on tasks designed to measure impulse control. On the "Tower of London" task, for example— where the goal is to solve a puzzle in as few moves as possible, with a wrong move requiring extra moves to undo it—adolescents took less time to consider their first move, jumping the gun before planning ahead.

Network research also suggests that adolescents are both less sensitive to risk and more sensitive to rewards—an attitude than can lead to greater risk-taking. The new data confirm and expand on earlier studies gauging attitudes toward risk, which found that adults spontaneously mention more potential risks than teens. Juveniles' tendency to pay more attention to the potential benefits of a risky decision than to its likely costs may contribute to their impulsivity in crime situations.

Vulnerability to Peer Pressure The law does not require exceptional bravery of citizens in the face of threats or other duress. A person who robs a bank with a gun in his back is not as blameworthy as another who willingly robs a bank; coercion and distress are mitigating factors. Adolescents, too, face coercion, but of a different sort.

Pressure from peers is keenly felt by teens. Peer influence can affect youths' decisions directly, as when adolescents are coerced to take risks they might otherwise avoid. More indirectly, youths' desire for peer approval, or their fear of rejection, may lead them to do things they might not otherwise do. In the Network's culpability study, individuals' reports of their vulnerability to peer pressure declined over the course of adolescence and young adulthood. Other Network research now underway is examining how adolescent risk-taking is "activated" by the presence of peers or by emotional arousal. For example, an earlier Network study, involving a computer car-driving task, showed that the mere presence of friends increased risk-taking in adolescents and college undergraduates, though not adults.

Although not every teen succumbs to peer pressures, some youths face more coercive situations than others. Many of those in the juvenile justice system live in tough neighborhoods, where losing face can be not only humiliating but dangerous. Capitulating in the face of a challenge can be a sign of weakness, inviting attack and continued persecution. To the extent that coercion or duress is a mitigating factor, the situations in which many juvenile crimes are committed should lessen their culpability.

Confirmation from Brain Studies Recent findings from neuroscience line up well with the Network's psychosocial research, showing that brain maturation is a process that continues through adolescence and into early adulthood. For example, there is good evidence that the brain systems that govern impulse control, planning, and thinking ahead are still developing well beyond age 18. There are also several studies indicating that the systems governing reward sensitivity are "amped up" at puberty, which would lead to an increase in sensation-seeking and in valuing benefits over risks. And there is emerging evidence that the brain systems that govern the processing of emotional and social information are affected by the hormonal changes of puberty in ways that make people more sensitive to the reactions of those around them—and thus more susceptible to the influence of peers.

Policy Implications: A Separate System for Young Offenders The scientific arguments do not say that adolescents cannot distinguish right from wrong, nor that they should be exempt from punishment. Rather, they point to the need to consider the developmental stage of adolescence as a mitigating factor when juveniles are facing criminal prosecution. The same factors that make youths ineligible to vote or to serve on a jury require us to treat them differently from adults when they commit crimes.

Some have argued that courts ought to assess defendants' maturity on a case-by-case basis, pointing to the fact that older adolescents, in particular, vary in their capacity for mature decision-making. But the tools needed to measure psychosocial maturity on an individual basis are not well developed, nor is it possible to distinguish reliably between mature and immature adolescents on the basis of brain images. Consequently, assessing maturity on an individual basis, as we do with other mitigating factors, is likely to produce many errors. However, the maturing process follows a similar pattern across virtually all teenagers. Therefore it is both logical and efficient to treat adolescents as a special legal category—and to refer the vast majority of offenders under the age of 18 to juvenile court, where they will be treated as responsible but less blameworthy, and where they will receive less punishment and more rehabilitation and treatment than typical adult offenders. The juvenile system does not excuse youths of their crimes; rather, it acknowledges the development stage and its role in the crimes committed, and punishes appropriately.

At the same time, any legal regime must pay attention to legitimate concerns about public safety. There will always be some youths—such as older, violent recidivists—who have exhausted the resources and patience of the juvenile justice system, and whose danger to the community warrants adjudication in criminal court. But these represent only a very small percentage of juvenile offenders. Trying and punishing youths as adults is an option that should be used sparingly.

Legislatures in several states have begun to reconsider the punitive laws enacted in recent decades. They have already recognized that prosecuting and punishing juveniles as adults carries high costs, for the youths and for their communities. Now we can offer lawmakers in all states a large body of research on which to build a more just and effective juvenile justice system.

2) Youthfulness and immaturity as rationale for a separate juvenile justice system The procedural and substantive convergence between juvenile and criminal courts described in *State Responses to Youth Violence*, supra pp. 35–42, has provoked discussion of contemporary rationale for a juvenile justice system. **Elizabeth S. Scott and Laurence Steinberg, "Blaming Youth," 81 *Tex. L. Rev.* 799, 835–838 (2003)** offer one justification for a separate youth justice system:

If, in fact, adolescent offenders are generally less culpable than their adult counterparts, how should the legal system recognize their diminished responsibility? At a structural level, the first important policy choice is whether immaturity should be considered on an individualized basis, as is typical of most other mitigating conditions, or as the basis for a separate category of young offenders. Traditional juvenile justice policy employed a categorical approach that continues in a diluted form in the contemporary juvenile court and correctional system. As the boundary between the juvenile and adult system breaks down, however, evaluation of immaturity as a mitigator increasingly takes place (if at all) on an individualized basis in a transfer hearing or at sentencing.

The uniqueness of immaturity as a mitigating condition argues for the adoption of (or renewed commitment to) a categorical approach in this context. Other mitigators—emotional disturbance and coercive external circumstances, for example—affect criminal choices with endless variety and idiosyncratic impact on behavior. Thus, individualized consideration of mitigation is appropriate when these phenomena are involved. In contrast, the capacities and processes associated with adolescence are characteristic of individuals in a relatively defined group, whose development follows a roughly prescribed course to maturity, and whose criminal choices are predictably affected in ways that mitigate culpability. Although individual variations exist within the age cohort of adolescence, coherent boundaries can delineate a minimum age for adult adjudication, as well as a period of years beyond this minimum when a strong presumption of reduced culpability operates to keep most youths in a separate system. The age boundary is justified if the presumption of immaturity can be applied confidently to most individuals in the group. This approach offers substantial efficiencies over one in which immaturity is assessed on a case-by-case basis, particularly since mitigation claims likely would be a part of every criminal adjudication involving a juvenile.

Adopting a mitigation framework does not mean that all youths are less mature than adults in their decisionmaking capacity or that all juveniles are unformed in their identity development. Some individuals exhibit mature judgment at an early age—although most of these youths are not offenders. For others, antisocial tendencies that begin in childhood continue in a stable pattern of criminal conduct that defines their adult characters. Adult punishment of mature youths might be fair if these individuals could be identified with some degree of certainty. But we currently lack the diagnostic tools to evaluate psycho-social maturity reliably on an individualized basis or to distinguish young career criminals from ordinary adolescents who, as adults, will repudiate their reckless experimentation. Litigating maturity on a case-by-case basis is likely to be an error-prone undertaking, with the outcomes determined by factors other than immaturity.

A developmentally-informed boundary constraining decisionmakers represents a collective pre-commitment to recognizing the mitigating character of youth in assigning blame. Otherwise, immaturity often may be ignored when the exigencies of a particular case engender a punitive response; indeed, it is likely to count as mitigating only when the youth otherwise presents a sympathetic case. This concern is critical, given the evidence that illegitimate racial and ethnic biases influence attitudes about the punishment of young offenders and that decisionmakers appear to discount the mitigating impact of immaturity in minority youths. The integrity and legitimacy of any individualized decisionmaking process is vulnerable to contamination from racist attitudes or from unconscious racial stereotyping that operates even among individuals who may lack overt prejudice. In the death penalty context, the

Supreme Court implicitly has recognized that categorical restrictions on individualized blaming judgments are sometimes necessary to safeguard against racism. Similarly, a structural boundary that hinders adult adjudication of young offenders is justified as a counterweight to this pernicious influence.

Categorical recognition of the mitigating impact of immaturity provides the conceptual framework for a separate justice system for juveniles but does not itself dictate a particular set of institutional arrangements. A variety of arrangements, including a systematic sentencing discount for young offenders in adult court, might satisfy the demands of proportionality. Ultimately, the case for a separate system rests on utilitarian considerations as well as on proportionality concerns. Because most young lawbreakers are "adolescent-limited" offenders, the social cost of youth crime will be minimized by policies that attend to the impact of punishment on the future lives and prospects of young offenders. The research suggests that a separate juvenile court and correctional system are more likely than the adult justice system to offer an environment in which youths can successfully "mature out" of their antisocial tendencies and to provide educational and job training programs to prepare young offenders for conventional adult roles. Thus, to a considerable extent, social welfare and fairness converge to support a separate juvenile justice system grounded in mitigation. * * *

Implementing a mitigation-based model of juvenile justice will require significant shifts in crime policy, but it will not require a radical overhaul of the juvenile justice system itself. Probably because of the scathing criticisms of its inadequacies, the juvenile system has undergone substantial change in the past generation, evolving toward one that increasingly emphasizes accountability and public protection. Although the public image of the modern juvenile court continues to be distorted by lingering echoes of the traditional rhetoric, delinquents under its jurisdiction are increasingly subject to proportionate punishment for their offenses. * * *

3) Diversion as rationale for a separate juvenile justice system
Even if juvenile courts increasingly resemble criminal courts and administer a form of punishment proportional to youths' diminished culpability, does another justification exist to maintain a separate justice system for children? Scott and Steinberg acknowledge that criminal courts formally could recognize youthfulness as a mitigating factor in sentencing based on the diminished responsibility of adolescents. Is the following excerpt consistent with Mack's original conception of the juvenile court? It provides a revisionist interpretation and an alternative rationale for a separate juvenile justice system. *Franklin E. Zimring*, **"The Common Thread: Diversion in Juvenile Justice,"** *88 Cal. L. Rev.* **2477 (2000):**

A central objective of those who created the juvenile court was to protect young delinquents from the destructive punishments of the criminal justice system. This promotion of juvenile court as a diversion from criminal justice is distinct from more ambitious programs of "child saving" intervention because avoiding harm can be achieved even if no effective crime prevention treatments are available. This essay shows diversion has been an important motive in juvenile justice from the beginning, and became the dominant purpose of a separate juvenile court after *In Re Gault* in 1967. The past thirty years have been the juvenile court's finest hour as a diversion project; the rate of juvenile incarceration has been stable, while incarceration of young adults has soared. * * *

A substantial step toward understanding both the institutional status and justifying rationale of the modern juvenile court is to revise our view of the original justifications of the new court for delinquent children. I think that two justifications existed from the start for creating a Juvenile Court, and I shall call these two different policies the diversionary and interventionist justifications for a separate children's court. The diversionary goal of the court was to save kids from the savagery of the criminal courts and prisons. The interventionist goal was to create programs that would rescue delinquents from crime and truancy. The diversionary justification for juvenile court was always the most important of the two rationales, and it remains so today.

In the foundational period of the Juvenile Court, when different groups formed coalitions for different reasons, and when many reformers had multiple reasons to support a new court, the diversionary critique of criminal court processing of minors was always stronger and more widely accepted than the interventionist vision of the court. When it much later became apparent that some elements of the interventionist justification were in conflict with both the realities of court function and with the principles of legality and proportionality, the diversionary rationale for the court emerged as the central explanation for the court's separate operation. These diversionary principles of juvenile justice are well suited both to a modern theory of adolescent development and to principles of procedural fairness and proportionality in legal response to youth crime. My goal in this Essay is to show both the continuity and coherence of the diversionary rationale for juvenile courts through the first 100 years of their history. * * *

Those who put their hopes in a new juvenile court to assume responsibility over young offenders had two reasons to assume the new court would be an improvement on the criminal processing of children. The first belief was that a child-centered juvenile court could avoid the many harms that criminal punishment visited on the young. The reformers found penalties unnecessarily harsh, and considered places of confinement to be schools for crime that corrupted the innocent and confirmed the redeemable in the path of chronic criminality. From this perspective, the first great virtue of the juvenile court was that it would not continue the destructive impact of the criminal justice system on children. This theory of justification for juvenile court, the diversionary rationale, argues that the new court could do good by simply doing less harm than the traditional criminal processes. * * *

The diversionary justification for juvenile court can easily be contrasted with the second justification for the new court: what I wish to call the interventionist rationale. While the diversionary approach promised the avoidance of the criminal court's harms, the interventionist argument emphasized the positive good that new programs administered by child welfare experts could achieve. A child-centered court was an opportunity to design positive programs that would simultaneously protect the community and cure the child. This was the notion of child saving that made the court's early justifications seem so extreme.

While the diversionary and interventionist justifications are conceptually quite distinct, there seems to have been little awareness at the court's founding that these two approaches to justifying the new court might conflict. The same people who believed in the diversionary virtues of a new court affirmed its interventionist potential as well. And because there was no contemporary awareness of potential conflict, the court's supporters did not have to choose between these separate but attractive rationales for the new institution.

But the diversionary rationale had several obvious advantages over an interventionist theory as a justification for an untested reform. In the first place, the new court could be counted on to achieve social good whether or not its treatment interventions worked. Avoiding the harms of the criminalization of children was a near-term benefit, whatever the programmatic potential of the new court's interventions might prove to be. A second advantage of a diversionary perspective is the way that doing less harm fit the shape and orientation of the new court's major tool, probation. Community supervision is rarely an heroic intervention; it does not take extensive power over the lives of young offenders when compared to jails, prisons, and work camps. It is also, in addition to its high moral principle, a method of responding to official delinquency that is relatively cheap. * * *

If the diversion of youth from the rigors of criminal punishment was a dominant motive for the new court, why does this justification not play a larger role in the historical accounts of the creation of the court? While diversionary motives dominate the contemporary accounts of the court's early years, these efforts to reduce the gratuitous harms of the criminal court do not receive much notice in the historical critiques of the court that appeared in the 1960s and 1970s.

Part of the reason later scholars give more account to the interventionist theory of juvenile justice is that such a claim was both novel and controversial, while child protective sentiments are so widely shared as to be without any singular importance at any particular historical moment. The pro-child sentiments that support diversion in 1899 do not set that era far off from 1940 or 1980. The claims of interventionist prowess are considered by contrast a striking historical artifact by the 1960s and 1970s, if not before.

Many accounts of the court's justifications were written by judges with a vested interest in expanding the powers and prestige of this new office; this fact provides another historical explanation for the inflated emphasis on interventionist dogma. Avoiding harm for children is a modest objective, indeed, when compared to the therapeutic rescue of those about to fall to the lower depths. * * *

Within the juvenile court, the major programmatic advantage was probation. * * * The emphasis on probation and community-based supervision fits nicely with a diversionary justification for juvenile courts. The job of the court is first not to harm the youth and then to attempt to help in community settings. This same programmatic emphasis does not mesh well with the romantic rhetoric of child saving. Probation is at its essence an incremental social control strategy, one that relies on the basic health and functionality of the subjects' community life. * * *

The other major increase in social control was the explicit extension of all juvenile court sanctions to non-criminal behavior such as disobedience to adults, truancy, and curfew. Clearly, the court was not extending jurisdiction in this direction in the name of diversion. But the same jurisprudence of childhood dependency that supported these powers for status offenders also was a foundation for keeping young offenders out of criminal courts. So there was no direct clash between status offender jurisdictions and diversion from criminal court for other developments. * * *

Only after two-thirds of the twentieth century had passed did the United States Supreme Court consider the procedural protections that due process required when accused delinquents were in jeopardy of secure confinement in state institutions. One important issue in *In re Gault*, the case that decided most of these issues in 1967, was the need for informality if the court was to achieve its child-saving mission. * * * Justice Fortas, writing the majority opinion, argued that there was no serious tension between the therapeutic intentions of the juvenile court and procedural protections for the accused who come before the court. * * *

For an informal and interventionist juvenile court, standards of proof and defense lawyers are a major drawback to identifying children in need and providing them with help. Due process is therefore a major handicap to achieving such an informal juvenile court. But if saving kids from the gratuitous harms inflicted by the criminal process is the aim, there is no inherent conflict between due process and the court's main beneficial functions.

The best illustration of the tension between due process and an interventionist court is the issue raised by the case of *In re Winship* in 1970. The state of New York allowed a petition alleging delinquency to be sustained in Juvenile Court if the state proved such facts by a preponderance of the evidence, the usual standard of proof in civil trials. The appellants, using *Gault* as authority, argued that delinquency could only be established by proof of its constituent facts beyond a reasonable doubt. The Supreme Court agreed with this conclusion.

But what is the justification for requiring proof beyond a reasonable doubt in criminal cases? The usual law day speech tells us that erroneous acquittals are less socially harmful than erroneous convictions: "It is better that ten guilty men go free than that one innocent man gets convicted!" However, if the Juvenile Court is there to help delinquents, it does not make sense to say "It is better that ten kids who need help do not get help than that one kid who does not need help is erroneously assisted!" If the dominant purpose of juvenile justice is forceful intervention for the child's own good, the rules in *Gault* and *Winship* were a decisive rejection of the juvenile court's jurisprudence.

Every aspect of due process protection is consistent with a diversionary theory of juvenile justice. If the principle benefit of juvenile court is that it keeps kids from the destructive impact of the criminal courts, this benefit may be provided whether or not the new court makes a formal sanctioning decision in a particular case. A high burden of proof or a children's lawyer will not cost the court its diversionary function.

The diversionary theory of juvenile justice also fits better with the portrait of the modern juvenile justice system that Justice Fortas presented in *Gault*. The recognition in cases such as *Gault* and *Winship* that terms such as "delinquent" carry stigma and that juvenile court sanctions may function as punishments poses no threat to the diversionary rationale. As long as the juvenile court can be seen as the lesser of evils, a diversionary view of the court is both sophisticated and pragmatic, and need not deny that punitive motives might color sanctioning decisions in the children's court.

The interventionist view of court processes was always more fragile because it required that interventions be characterized positively in order to justify the court's existence. To label as "punishment" what the juvenile court does to delinquents is to deny the truth of a central premise of the interventionist theory.

Viewed in this light, the majority opinion in *Gault* rejected one enduring rationale for a separate juvenile court and elevated a second theory to supremacy. The Juvenile Court that the United States Supreme Court approved was child protective chiefly by keeping kids out of prisons and jails. Such an institution could be parsimonious with its own punishments, restricting them to cases with strong evidence and fair procedures, without threatening its own substantive mission. The arrogance of unqualified judicial power was not necessary to this version of the court's purposes. * * *

Like many other American institutions, the juvenile court, itself just an experiment at the beginning of the century, has witnessed changes to its clientele, to its political and legal constituencies, and in its operations over the twentieth century. But the core concern of the court, "to prevent children from being treated as criminals," is just as clear in 1999 as in 1899. As the usual period of schooling and economic dependency in adolescence has lengthened over the twentieth century, the maximum age for juvenile court delinquency first drifted upward to the eighteenth birthday in most states, and then stayed at eighteen in most states, reflecting an age boundary close to the mode for high school graduation. The period of semi-autonomy that now spans most of the teen years is spent for the most part in the delinquency jurisdiction of juvenile courts. * * *

The announcement of due process requirements * * * was closely followed by the first major federal legislation designed to influence the substantive content of state juvenile justice policy by providing financial rewards to state systems that met the federal standards. The two major targets of the 1974 Juvenile Justice legislation fit quite comfortably under a traditional diversionary view of the court's objectives. The first push of the federal law was to remove minors from American jails and prisons. The protective segregation of children had been at the heart of the diversion agenda in 1899. While the original reformers would have been disturbed to find that seventy-five years of American history had not yet achieved this primitive reform, the continuing struggle to attain separate housing for kids in confinement was a purely diversionary reform in obvious accord with the original vision of the court.

So, too, was the second major objective of the 1974 legislation, the deinstitutionalization of status offenders. The saga of the status offender was one of the great failings of the interventionist theory of juvenile courts. In the original legislation, the noncriminal behaviors later to be called status offenses were simply additional behaviors that could justify a finding of delinquency as well as any placement that the juvenile court could order for a delinquent. Kids who ran away from home or were disobedient or truant could be committed to the same institutions as the juvenile burglar and auto thief.

There were two problems associated with secure institutional confinement for noncriminal misbehavior: It was grossly unfair and it was manifestly ineffectual. By 1974, nearly all in the youth welfare profession agreed on the need to scale back on this branch of the rehabilitative ideal. The direct conflict between not allowing the Juvenile Courts to order secure institutions for truants and an interventionist theory of the court is obvious, because the interventionist judge claimed broad power to do whatever the troubled child needed.

However, there is no necessary conflict between limits on the coercive interventions allowed for noncriminal behaviors and a diversionary theory of juvenile justice. Simply because reformers wish to keep adolescent law violators out of jail does not mean that the same observers support serious punishment for noncriminal kids. * * *

Perhaps the most dramatic evidence of the efficacy and importance of diversionary policies in modern juvenile justice is the sustained attack on the modern juvenile court by the political forces of law and order. At the federal level, Republican legislative majorities have been attempting to use federal financial incentives, pioneered in the Juvenile Justice and Delinquency Prevention Act of 1974, to push a series of standards designed to create more punitive sanctions within the delinquency jurisdiction of the juvenile court and easier transfers of serious juvenile offenders to criminal courts.

The rhetoric in support of this legislation uses new phrases such as "accountability" and "graduated sanctions" to describe the desired juvenile court outcomes. But the common enemy of the transfer policies and the harsher juvenile court punishments proposed in the legislation is a juvenile court tradition that seeks to avoid permanent stigma and disfiguring punishments of delinquents. The terms of reprobation aimed at the court by its critics on the right—terms such as "revolving door justice," "slap on the wrist," "Kiddie Court"—are an acknowledgment of the court's diversionary intent. To the extent that the attacks by its critics are based on empirical truth, those assaults pay tribute to the efficacy of a court that has been seeking to avoid the harshest outcomes for its caseload throughout the twentieth century.

But is there any truth to the rumor that juvenile courts protect delinquents from destructive punishments? * * * My best guess is that the protective impact of a diversionary juvenile court on sanctions for youth crime is largest when punitive policies are at their most dominant in criminal courts, in other words, in ages like the American present. * * * But the larger the punitive bite of the criminal court system becomes, the more likely it will be that a separate court for the youngest offenders takes some of the bite out of the state sanctions that juvenile offenders receive. * * *

The period 1971–1991 was not a typical interlude in the history of American crime policy. It was, instead, the period of the most substantial growth in the scale of imprisonment in the history of the Republic. Never was the pressure for confinement as consistent and substantial. Total confinement for the younger group [of juveniles aged 14–17] increased by 21% while the incarceration rate of young adults [aged 18–24] more than doubled. By 1991, the difference in incarceration rates for the two groups was more than 2 to 1, and this very substantial gap is one reason why those who had succeeded in radically altering punishments in criminal courts might have resented the stability in policy and outcome that occurred for younger offenders.

The pattern during the early 1990s is more complicated. The rate at which 14–to–17–year–olds were incarcerated grew almost as much in the four years after 1991 as it did in the two decades prior to 1991. For that reason, it may look like a significant shift toward toughness had finally taken hold. But the growth in young adult incarceration was much greater than in the younger age group, so that the gap between older juveniles and young adults actually widened in the early 1990s. * * *

These data suggest that the diversionary objective of the juvenile justice system insulated delinquents from the brunt of a high magnitude expansion in incarceration in the criminal justice system. * * * If diversion was an organizing principle of modern juvenile justice, then the Juvenile Courts were keeping their promises through the 1970s and 1980s in the United States.

Their consistent incarceration-limiting policy generated substantial political pressure on juvenile courts in the United States while the criminal justice system experienced two and one half decades of uninterrupted penal expansion. * * * [T]he flurry of legislative activity to create larger punishments for juvenile offenders [require a new explanation]. The usual account of juvenile crime legislation explains it as the concern of politicians and citizens with juvenile crime and violence. But the rate of serious juvenile violence has dropped steadily after 1994 and the attack on juvenile court has not let up. * * *

[T]he political forces that had produced extraordinary expansion through the rest of the penal system had been stymied in juvenile courts. In that sense, the under-eighteen population became the last significant battleground for the "get tough" orientation that had already permeated the rest of the peno-correctional system. The exceptional diversionary performance of American juvenile courts in the 1970s and 1980s rendered the system vulnerable to the same attacks that had succeeded decades before in criminal justice.

So the angry assaults on juvenile courts throughout the 1990s are a tribute to the efficacy of juvenile justice in protecting delinquents from the incarcerative explosion that had happened everywhere else. The largest irony of the 1990s from a diversionary standpoint is that the Juvenile Courts were under constant assault not because they had failed in their youth serving mission, but because they had succeeded in protecting their clientele from the new orthodoxy in crime control. * * *

E. CONCLUSION

Despite their benevolent rhetoric and aspirations, Progressive "child-savers" designed the juvenile court to discriminate—to "Americanize" immigrants, to control the poor, and to provide a coercive mechanism to distinguish between "our children" and "other people's children." Rothman, *Conscience and Convenience*. And, a century later, racial disparities and disproportionate minority confinement remains a characteristic feature of juvenile justice administration. Barry C. Feld, *Bad Kids: Race and the Transformation of the Juvenile Court* (1999) [hereinafter Feld, *Bad Kids*]; Darnell F. Hawkins and Kimberly Kempf–Leonard, *Our Children, Their Children: Confronting Racial and Ethnic Differences in American Juvenile Justice* (2005). Even prior to the recent "crack down" on juveniles, studies consistently reported racial disparities in juvenile court judges' waiver decisions. Judges are more likely to transfer minority youths than white youths to criminal court and the disparities are greatest for youths charged with violent and drug offenses. As a result of successive screening and differential processing of youths by race, the majority of juveniles transferred to criminal court and sentenced to prison are minority youths. Empirical evaluations of juvenile court sentencing practices also report that after controlling for offense variables, the individualized justice of juvenile courts consistently produces racial disparities in sentencing. The juvenile justice process entails a succession of decisions—intake, petition, detention, adjudication or waiver, and disposition—and the compound effects of even small disparities produces larger cumulative differences. In 1988, Congress amended the Juvenile Justice and Delinquency Prevention Act and required states that receive federal juvenile justice funds to assure equality of treatment on the basis of race and to examine what accounts for minority overrepresentation in detention facilities and institutions. Focusing on the sources of and appropriate policy responses to Disproportionate Minority Confinement (DMC) will be a recurring theme in these materials.

In their pursuit of the rehabilitative ideal, the Progressives situated the juvenile court on several legal and cultural fault-lines. They created binary conceptions for the juvenile and criminal justice systems: either child or adult; either determinism or freewill; either dependent or responsible; either treatment or punishment; either procedural informality or formality; either discretion or the rule of law. The past four decades have witnessed a significant shift from the former to the latter of each of these pairs as a result of *Gault* and its progeny. *Gault* precipitated a procedural revolution in the juvenile court system that unintentionally but inevitably transformed its original Progressive conception. Progressive reformers envisioned the commission of an offense as essentially secondary to a determination of the real needs of a child. They premised intervention on the need for rehabilitation rather than the crime committed. Although *McKeiver* refused to extend the right to a jury trial to juveniles, *Gault* and

Winship imported the adversarial model, the privilege against self-incrimination, the right to an attorney, the criminal standard of proof, and proof of factual and legal guilt as a constitutional prerequisite to intervention. By emphasizing criminal procedural regularity in delinquency hearings, *Gault* shifted the focus of delinquency hearings from a child's "real needs" to proof of legal guilt and formalized the connection between criminal conduct and coercive intervention. Providing a modicum of procedural justice also legitimated greater punitiveness in juvenile courts.

Over the next four decades, court decisions, statutory amendments, and administrative changes transformed the juvenile court from a social welfare agency into a scaled-down, second-class criminal court for young offenders. These trends included procedural, jurisdictional, and jurisprudential modifications of the juvenile court. In addition to the procedural convergence between juvenile and criminal courts, jurisdictional reforms diverted many noncriminal status offenders away from the juvenile court and transferred increasing numbers of serious young offenders to criminal court. Jurisprudential changes in juvenile court sentencing policies de-emphasize rehabilitation and focus increasingly on punishment of ordinary delinquents.

Two competing cultural and legal conceptions of young people facilitated juvenile courts' transformation from a social welfare agency into a penal organization. On the one hand, the law and culture view young people as innocent, vulnerable, fragile, and dependent *children* whom their parents and the state should protect and nurture. On the other hand, the law and culture perceive young people as vigorous, autonomous and responsible almost *adult-like* people from whose criminal behavior the public needs protection. The ambivalent and conflicted "jurisprudence of youth" enables policy makers selectively to manipulate the competing social constructs of *innocence* and *responsibility* to maximize the social control of young people. Over the past three decades, the intersections of race and crime have provided the impetus for juvenile justice policies to use these alternative constructs of youth to conduct a form of "criminological triage." At the "soft-end," juvenile court reforms have shifted non-criminal status offenders, primarily female and white, out of the juvenile justice system into a "hidden system" of social control in the private-sector mental health and chemical dependency industries. See Chapter 8. Diversion, deinstitutionalization, and "decriminalization" of status offenders have altered the role of juvenile courts as states removed status jurisdiction from their juvenile codes entirely, redefined it to avoid the stigma of crime/delinquency adjudications, and limited the dispositions noncriminal offenders can receive. At the "hard end," states transfer increasing numbers of youths, disproportionately minority, into the criminal justice system for prosecution as adults. See Chapter 6. As states narrow their jurisdiction at the "hard end" and at the "soft-end," the dispositions the remaining delinquents receive increasingly reflect the impact of the "justice model" and doctrines of criminal law in which principles of proportionality and determinacy based on the present offense and prior record, rather than the "best interests" of the child, dictate the length, location, and intensity of intervention. Finally, as the dispositions by the juvenile court increasingly subordinate the needs of the offender to the nature of the offense and traditional justifications for punishment, the formal procedural safeguards of the juvenile court increasingly resemble those of the adult criminal process.

Although *Gault* transformed the juvenile court from a welfare agency into a more legalistic one, a substantial gulf remains between the "law on the books" and the "law in action." States continue to manipulate the fluid concepts of children and adults, or treatment and punishment in order to maximize the social control of young people. On the one hand, almost all states use the adult standard of "knowing, intelligent, and voluntary waiver" under the "totality of the circumstances" to gauge juveniles' waivers of *Miranda* rights and their right to counsel, even though juveniles lack the legal competence of adults. See Chapters 3 and 6; Barry C. Feld, *Justice For Children: The Right To Counsel and the Juvenile Courts* (1993) [hereinafter Feld, *Justice for Children*]. On the other hand, even as juvenile courts have become more punitive, most states continue to deny juveniles access to jury trials and to other procedural rights guaranteed to adults. See Chapter 7. The recent developmental psychological research on adolescents' legal competence and criminal responsibility poses new challenges for the structure and administration of the juvenile justice system.

CHAPTER 2

JUVENILE COURT JURISDICTION AND JURISPRUDENCE

■ ■ ■

Juvenile courts are exclusively statutory entities. Young offenders enjoy no constitutional right to be tried in a juvenile court. However, once states choose to create juvenile courts, various constitutional limitations and requirements structure their administration. *In re Gault*, 387 U.S. 1, 87 S.Ct. 1428, 18 L.Ed.2d 527 (1967). Because juvenile courts exist solely as a matter of legislative grace, states' responses to the misconduct of children may vary considerably. As a matter of state legislative policy, juvenile courts may differ in their maximum age of jurisdiction, for example, seventeen, sixteen, or fifteen years of age, the types of offenses over which the courts exercise jurisdiction, and the lengths and types of dispositions or sanctions which they may impose.

Delinquency. States define juvenile court jurisdiction based upon a youth's age and conduct. The age of jurisdiction varies from state to state. Typically, the maximum age of juvenile court jurisdiction is seventeen years of age, i.e. an eighteen year old offender is an adult. Some states set the maximum age at sixteen or even fifteen years of age. Youths below the statutory maximum age normally will be treated as "juveniles." In most states, even though the age of juvenile court jurisdiction is defined in terms of a youth's age at the time of offense or misconduct, the dispositional authority of the court may extend beyond the age of majority. Thus, a youth who is adjudicated a "delinquent" may receive a juvenile court disposition or sentence that can continue until nineteen, twenty, twenty-one, or even twenty-five years of age.

In addition, juvenile court jurisdiction is based on conduct by children or toward children by others. The term "delinquency" subsumes conduct by a child which would be a crime, offense, or violation if committed by an adult. In most states, juvenile courts have original and exclusive jurisdiction over all criminal matters involving children, e.g. *Minn. Stat.* § 260.111 (1999). In other states, some serious offenses may be excluded from juvenile court jurisdiction, or juvenile and criminal courts may share concurrent jurisdiction over certain criminal matters, and prosecutors' charging decisions determine the forum. *See* Barry Feld, "The Juvenile Court Meets the Principle of the Offense: Legislative Changes in Juvenile

Waiver Statutes," 78 *J. Criminal Law & Criminology* 471 (1987); Howard Snyder and Melissa Sickmund, *Juvenile Offenders and Victims: 2006 National Report* (2006).

Non–Criminal Status Offenses. Juvenile courts also exercise jurisdiction over non-criminal misconduct by juveniles, the so-called "status offenses"—truancy, incorrigibility, run-away, consumption of alcohol, tobacco, curfew violations, or the like—that would not be criminal if engaged in by adults. " 'Status offense' means an act prohibited by law which would not be an offense if committed by an adult." *Va. Stat.* § 16.1–228 (1998). The existence of status jurisdiction, in whatever form, is an instance of regulating children under circumstances in which adults remain free from coercive state intervention. Until recent reforms, status offenses comprised one form of "delinquency." One reform has been to "decriminalize" status offenses by relabeling juveniles who engage in such conduct as Persons in Need of Services (PINS), or Children in Need of Protection and Services (CHIPS). Very young children who commit crimes also may fall within this non-criminal jurisdiction. With some limitations, most of the dispositions available for delinquents may also be used for status offenders. Section C of Chapter 2 examines the non-criminal jurisdiction of juvenile courts.

Dependency, Neglect, and Abuse. Juvenile courts also exercise jurisdiction on behalf of children to protect them from the conduct of others. Typically, legal definitions of abuse focus on physical, emotional, or moral harm inflicted upon children by their caretakers or others. For example, states define "child abuse" as "physical injury, mental or emotional injury, sexual abuse, sexual exploitation, sale or attempted sale or negligent treatment or maltreatment of a child by a parent, guardian or custodian who is responsible for the child's welfare, under circumstances which harm or threaten the health or welfare of the child." *W. Va. Stat.* § 49–1–3 (c) (1998). Abuse or neglect typically entail "fault" on the part of the caretaker, whereas dependency suggests "no fault," for example, when a child's welfare suffers as a result of circumstances or conditions beyond the control of the caretaker. *See generally*, Robert D. Goldstein, *Child Abuse and Neglect: Cases and Materials* (1999).

Family Courts. In some jurisdictions, unified family courts have replaced juvenile courts. The family court's jurisdiction includes not only delinquency, status, and dependency, abuse, and neglect matters, but also an array of family-related matters such as divorce proceedings, adoption, paternity suits, criminal prosecution for abuse or domestic violence, and the like. Like juvenile courts, family courts use a specialist judge assisted by social workers and other support and service personnel to address all the matters associated with families in distress. Proponents of family courts assert that combining all of the proceedings affecting children and families in one setting can contribute to efficient decision-making and the mobilization of resources dealing with the multiplicity of problems presented in troubled families.

NOTES

1) Statutes set age limits for juvenile court jurisdiction. The following excerpt summarizes the role of age in defining juvenile courts' delinquency jurisdiction and dispositional authority. **Howard Snyder and Melissa Sickmund,** *Juvenile Offenders and Victims: 2006 National Report* **103 (2006):**

Statutes set age limits for original jurisdiction of the juvenile court In most states, the juvenile court has original jurisdiction over all youth charged with a law violation who were younger than age 18 at the time of the offense, arrest, or referral to court. Since 1975, four states have changed their age criteria: Alabama raised its upper age from 15 to 16 in 1976 and to 17 in 1977; Wyoming lowered its upper age from 18 to 17 in 1993; and in 1996, New Hampshire and Wisconsin lowered their upper age from 17 to 16.

Oldest age for original juvenile court jurisdiction in delinquency matters, 2004:

Age	State
15	Connecticut, New York, North Carolina
16	Georgia, Illinois, Louisiana, Massachusetts, Michigan, Missouri, New Hampshire, South Carolina, Texas, Wisconsin
17	Alabama, Alaska, Arizona, Arkansas, California, Colorado, Delaware, District of Columbia, Florida, Hawaii, Idaho, Indiana, Iowa, Kansas, Kentucky, Maine, Maryland, Minnesota, Mississippi, Montana, Nebraska, Nevada, New Jersey, New Mexico, North Dakota, Ohio, Oklahoma, Oregon, Pennsylvania, Rhode Island, South Dakota, Tennessee, Utah, Vermont, Virginia, Washington, West Virginia, Wyoming

Many states have higher upper ages of juvenile court jurisdiction in status offense, abuse, neglect, or dependency matters—typically through age 20. In many states, the juvenile court has original jurisdiction over young adults who committed offenses while juveniles.

States often have statutory exceptions to basic age criteria. For example, many states exclude married or otherwise emancipated juveniles from juvenile court jurisdiction. Other exceptions, related to the youth's age, alleged offense, and/or prior court history, place certain youth under the original jurisdiction of the criminal court. In some states, a combination of the youth's age, offense, and prior record places the youth under the original jurisdiction of both the juvenile and criminal courts. In these states, the prosecutor has the authority to decide which court will initially handle the case.

As of the end of the 2004 legislative session, 16 states have statutes that set the lowest age of juvenile court delinquency jurisdiction. Other states rely on case law or common law. Children younger than a certain age are presumed to be incapable of criminal intent and, therefore, are exempt from prosecution and punishment.

Youngest age for original juvenile court jurisdiction in delinquency matters, 2004:

Age	State
6	North Carolina
7	Maryland, Massachusetts, New York
8	Arizona
10	Arkansas, Colorado, Kansas, Louisiana, Minnesota, Mississippi, Pennsylvania, South Dakota, Texas, Vermont, Wisconsin

Juvenile court authority over youth may extend beyond the upper age of original jurisdiction Through extended jurisdiction mechanisms, legislatures enable the court to provide sanctions and services for a duration of time that is in the best interests of the juvenile and the public, even for older juveniles who have reached the age at which original juvenile court jurisdiction ends.

As of the end of the 2004 legislative session, statutes in 34 states extend juvenile court jurisdiction in delinquency cases until the 21st birthday.

Oldest age over which the juvenile court may retain jurisdiction for disposition purposes in delinquency matters, 2004:

Age	State
18	Alaska, Iowa, Kentucky, Nebraska, Oklahoma, Tennessee
19	Mississippi, North Dakota
20	Alabama, Arizona*, Arkansas, Connecticut, Delaware, District of Columbia, Georgia, Idaho, Illinois, Indiana, Louisiana, Maine, Maryland, Massachusetts, Michigan, Minnesota, Missouri, Nevada**, New Hampshire, New Mexico, New York, North Carolina, Ohio, Pennsylvania, Rhode Island, South Carolina, South Dakota, Texas, Utah, Vermont, Virginia, Washington, West Virginia, Wyoming
21	Florida
22	Kansas
24	California, Montana, Oregon, Wisconsin
***	Colorado, Hawaii, New Jersey

Note: Extended jurisdiction may be restricted to certain offenses or juveniles.

*Arizona statute extends jurisdiction through age 20, but a 1979 state supreme court decision held that juvenile court jurisdiction terminates at age 18.

**Until the full term of the disposition order for sex offenders.

***Until the full term of the disposition order.

In some states, the juvenile court may impose adult correctional sanctions on certain adjudicated delinquents that extend the term of confinement well beyond the upper age of juvenile jurisdiction. Such sentencing options are included in the set of dispositional options known as blended sentencing.

2) Recent changes in juvenile court age jurisdiction. After earlier, ''get tough'' strategies to lower the age of juvenile court jurisdiction, several states have reconsidered their jurisdictional policies and raised the age of youths within the jurisdiction of juvenile courts. Connecticut, whose delinquency jurisdiction previously ended when a child attained the age of sixteen, extended its jurisdictional age to eighteen years, effective January 1, 2010. *See* Conn. Stat. § 46b–120 (2008) (permitting certain offenses involving 16–and 17–year olds to be adjudicated in juvenile courts).

North Carolina juvenile court jurisdiction currently ends at fifteen years of age. The legislature mandated its Sentencing and Policy Advisory Commission to study "youthful offenders" between sixteen and twenty-one years of age, to submit a report to the 2007 legislature, and to propose changes. H.B. 1723, Reg. Sess. at §§ 34.1, 34.2 (N.C. 2006). The Report recommended to raise the age of juvenile court jurisdiction from those under sixteen years of age to those under eighteen years of age and to create a "youthful offender" system for young adult offenders convicted in criminal courts of misdemeanors and low-level felonies. North Carolina Sentencing and Policy Advisory Commission, *Report on Study of Youthful Offenders Pursuant to Session Law 2006–248, Sections 34.1 and 34.2* (2007) *available at* http://www.nccourts.org/Courts/CRS/Councils/spac/Documents/yo_% 20finalreporttolegislature.pdf   In recommending that North Carolina join the other thirty-seven jurisdictions that set the age of jurisdiction at eighteen, the Commission emphasized that:

> the slow maturation process of juveniles and the concomitant need for society to allow for some second chances for this group while providing them with a balance of punishment and treatment in a separate and more rehabilitative system. A significant volume of scientific evidence on stages of human development points to immaturity and its effect on reduced criminal culpability in youth up to age 18 and beyond, well into their 20's. At least four areas of developmental immaturity may bear directly on the criminal culpability of youth: impaired risk perception, foreshortened time perspective, greater susceptibility to peer influence, and reduced capacity for behavioral controls. *Id.* at 8.

Because "kids are different," the Commission proposed that juveniles receive age-appropriate programs and rehabilitation to enhance "moral reasoning, problem solving, social skills, and impulse control" to enable them successfully to reintegrate into the community. Despite strong policy support and professional advocacy, the North Carolina legislature has resisted efforts to increase the jurisdictional age to eighteen years of age. See Tamar R. Birckhead, "North Carolina, Juvenile Court Jurisdiction, and the Resistance to Reform," 86 *N. Car. L. Rev.* 1443 (2008) (attributing resistance to legislative unwillingness to fund juvenile justice, objections of police and prosecutors to "coddling" young offenders, marginalization of the juvenile court by the bench and bar, and public indifference).

In addition to the successful reform in Connecticut, several other states currently are re-evaluating their jurisdictional age policies. *See* H. Ted Rubin, "Juvenile or Adult Jurisdiction? Age Changes in the States," Vol. 13, No. 6 *Juvenile Justice Update* 1 (December/January 2008), reporting on reform efforts to raise the age jurisdiction in Illinois, North Carolina, Wisconsin and New Hampshire.

A. JUVENILE CRIME AND JUVENILE JUSTICE ADMINISTRATION

As Chapter 1 indicated, the Progressives who created juvenile courts had greater ambitions than simply to prosecute children for their crimes. At the same time, however, states define the core of juvenile courts' delinquency jurisdiction based on a youth's commission of a criminal offense. The juvenile court's role as a "therapeutic" agency defined by a child's criminality is further complicated by public perceptions about youth crime. Based on media depictions and "get tough" political rhetoric, the public perceives juvenile crime as increasing, becoming more violent, directed at people rather than property, and victimizing the elderly, females, or strangers. Addressing issues of juvenile justice policy requires an appreciation of the nature of juvenile courts' caseloads, the characteristics of the youths who appear in juvenile courts, and the variability of juvenile justice administration.

The following excerpt from **Howard Snyder and Melissa Sickmund,** *Juvenile Offenders and Victims: 2006 National Report* **125, 128–133, 157–162, 171–176 (2006),** provides some basic information about the nature of juvenile crime, characteristics of delinquent offenders, and an introduction to juvenile justice administration:

IN 2003, LAW ENFORCEMENT AGENCIES REPORTED 2.2 MILLION ARRESTS
OF PERSONS UNDER AGE 18

The most serious charge in almost half of all juvenile arrests in 2003 was larceny-theft, simple assault, a drug abuse violation, disorderly conduct, or a liquor law violation

Most serious offense	2003 juvenile arrest estimates	Percent of total juvenile arrests					
		Female	Ages 16–17	White	Black	American Indian	Asian
Total	2,220,300	29%	68%	71%	27%	1%	2%
Violent Crime Index	92,300	18	67	53	45	1	1
Murder and non-negligent manslaughter	1,130	9	89	49	48	1	2
Forcible rape	4,240	2	63	64	33	2	1
Robbery	25,440	9	75	35	63	0	2
Aggravated assault	61,490	24	64	59	38	1	1
Property Crime Index	463,300	32	63	69	28	1	2
Burglary	85,100	12	65	71	26	1	1
Larceny-theft	325,600	39	62	70	27	1	2
Motor vehicle theft	44,500	17	75	56	40	1	2
Arson	8,200	12	39	81	17	1	1
Other (simple) assault	241,900	32	57	61	36	1	1
Forgery and counterfeiting	4,700	35	87	77	20	1	2
Fraud	8,100	33	82	66	32	1	1
Embezzlement	1,200	40	94	68	30	0	2
Stolen property (buying, receiving, possessing)	24,300	15	73	57	41	1	1
Vandalism	107,700	14	56	80	18	1	1
Weapons (carrying, possessing, etc.)	39,200	11	64	66	32	1	2
Prostitution and commercialized vice	1,400	69	86	51	47	0	1
Sex offense (except forcible rape and prostitution)	18,300	9	49	71	26	1	1
Drug abuse violation	197,100	16	83	72	26	1	1
Gambling	1,700	2	85	12	86	0	2
Offenses against family and children	7,000	39	65	77	20	2	2
Driving under the influence	21,000	20	98	94	4	2	1
Liquor laws	136,900	35	90	92	4	3	1
Drunkenness	17,600	23	87	89	8	2	1
Disorderly conduct	193,000	31	59	64	34	1	1
Vagrancy	2,300	25	75	62	37	1	1
All other offenses (except traffic)	379,800	27	72	74	23	1	2
Suspicion	1,500	24	74	66	33	1	0
Curfew and loitering law violation	136,500	30	71	68	30	1	1
Runaway	123,600	59	64	73	20	2	5
U.S. population ages 10–17	33,499,000	49	24	78	16	1	4

■ Females accounted for the majority of arrests for running away from home (59%) and prostitution and commercialized vice (69%).

■   Black youth, who accounted for 16% of the juvenile population in 2003, were involved in a disproportionate number of juvenile arrests for robbery (63%), murder (48%), motor vehicle theft (40%), and aggravated assault (38%).

Notes: UCR data do not distinguish the ethnic group Hispanic; Hispanics may be of any race. In 2003, 92% of Hispanics ages 10–17 were classified racially as white. National estimates of juvenile arrests were developed using FBI estimates of total arrests and juvenile arrest proportions in the reporting sample. Detail may not add to totals because of rounding.

Source: Authors' analyses of the FBI's Crime in the United States 2003.

Gender-specific factors influence juvenile arrest trends If juvenile males and females were contributing equally to an arrest trend, then the female proportion of juvenile arrests would remain constant. If, however, the female proportion changes, that means that the female arrest trend differs from the male trend—and any explanation of juvenile arrest trends must incorporate factors that affect males and females differently.

A major story in the last few years has been the rise in the proportion of females entering the juvenile justice system. In 1980, 20% of all juvenile arrests were female arrests; in 2003, this percentage had increased to 29%—with the majority of this growth since the early 1990s. The female proportion increased between 1980 and 2003 in juvenile arrests for Violent Crime Index offenses (from 10% to 18%) and for Property Crime Index offenses (from 19% to 32%); however, the female proportion of drug abuse violations arrests was the same in 1980 and 2003 (16%). This implies there were (1) different factors influencing the volume and/or nature of law-violating behaviors by male and female juveniles over this time period and/or (2) differential responses by law enforcement to these behaviors.

A closer look at violence trends points to possible explanations If juvenile females had simply become more violent, the female proportion of juvenile arrests would be expected to have increased for each violent crime. This did not occur. For example, the female proportion of juvenile arrests remained relatively constant between 1980 and 2003 for robbery (7% to 9%). The change that caused the Violent Crime Index proportion to increase between 1980 and 2003 was the increase in the female proportion of juvenile arrests for aggravated assault (from 15% to 24%). Similarly, a large increase was seen in the female proportion of juvenile arrests for simple assault (from 21% to 32%). To understand the relative increase in female arrests for violence, it is necessary to look for factors related primarily to assault.

One possible explanation for this pattern could be the changing response of law enforcement to domestic violence incidents. Domestic assaults represent a larger proportion of female violence than male violence. For example, analysis of the 2001 NIBRS data finds that 18% of aggravated assaults known to law enforcement committed by juvenile males were against family members or intimate partners, compared with 33% of aggravated assaults committed by juvenile females. Mandatory arrest laws for domestic violence, coupled with an increased willingness to report these crimes to authorities, would yield a greater increase in female than male arrests for assault, while having no effect on the other violent crimes. Thus, policy and social changes may be a stimulus for the increased proportion of juvenile female arrests.

The female proportion of arrests increased for many offenses When the female proportion of juvenile arrests remains constant over time, factors controlling this arrest trend are unrelated to gender. This pattern is seen in juvenile robbery and arson arrests from 1980 through 2003. Over this period, the female arrest proportions for some other offenses (e.g., murder, prostitution, and drug abuse violations) first declined and then increased back to earlier levels. However, for most other offenses (e.g., aggravated assault, simple assault, burglary, larceny-theft, motor vehicle theft, vandalism, weapons, liquor, and curfew/loitering law violations), the female proportions of juvenile arrests increased substantially over the 1980–2003 period.

In 2003, the juvenile violent crime arrest rate was lower than it was before its increase in the late 1980s

The juvenile violent crime arrest rate is at its lowest level in a generation Between 1980 and 1988, the juvenile Violent Crime Index arrest rate was essentially constant. The rate began to increase in 1989; by 1994, it was 61% above its 1988 level. This unsettling trend triggered speculation that the nature of juvenile offenders had changed and spurred state legislators to pass laws that made sanctioning youth in the adult justice system easier. After 1994, how ever, the juvenile Violent Crime Index arrest rate fell consistently for the next 9 years; by 2003, it had fallen below the levels of the early 1980s.

The female violent crime arrest rate remains relatively high In 1980, the male juvenile Violent Crime Index arrest rate was 8.3 times the female rate. With only a few exceptions, this gender disparity declined annually between 1980 and 2003, so that by 2003, the male rate was just 4.2 times the female rate. In the growth period between 1988 and 1994, the female rate increased more than the male rate (98% vs. 56%). The decline in the juvenile violent crime arrest rate between 1994 and 2003 was driven primarily by the male arrest rate, which fell more than the female rate (51% vs. 32%). The convergence in the male and female rates between 1980 and 2003 reflects an overall 26% decline in the male rate coupled with a 47% increase in the female rate.

Violent crime arrest rates declined more for black youth than other racial groups All racial groups experienced large increases in their juvenile Violent Crime Index arrest rate between 1988 and 1994—and large declines between 1994 and 2003. By 2003, the white juvenile Violent Crime Index arrest rate had returned to its 1988 level. In contrast, the 2003 rates for the other races were all below their 1988 levels: blacks (–35%), American Indian (–16%), and Asian (–23%).

The juvenile violent crime wave predicted by some in the mid–1990s has not occurred The extraordinary growth in juvenile arrests for murder between 1987 and 1993 caused some to say and many to believe that America's youth were out of control. The juvenile arrest rate for murder increased 110% over this period, and speculation was that the rate would continue to grow. However, the juvenile arrest rate for murder then declined, more quickly than it had increased, so that by 1998, the rate returned to the 1987 level. After 1998, the rate continued to decline; by 2003, the rate was about half of its level in 1987 and 77% below the peak year of 1993. In 2003, juvenile arrests for murder were at a 30–year low.

Juvenile murder arrest rates were at generational lows in 2003 During the period from 1980 to 2003, the male juvenile murder arrest rate averaged 12 times the female rate. The growth in the overall juvenile murder arrest rate between 1987 and 1993 was attributable to the large increase (117%) in the much larger male rate. However, during this period, the female rate also increased (36%), although this change had relatively little effect on the overall trend. Both the male and female rates fell substantially between 1993 and 2003 (78% and 62%, respectively). In 2003, both rates were at their lowest levels since at least 1980.

During the period from 1980 through 2003, the black juvenile murder arrest rate averaged more than 6 times the white rate, but their trends over the period were similar. Between 1987 and 1993, both the black rate and the white rate increased substantially (130% and 75%, respectively). Both rates then fell dramatically between 1993 and 2003, so that the 2003 juvenile murder arrest rate was far below the 1987 rate both black juveniles (–62%) and white juveniles (–43%). * * *

Juvenile courts handled 1.6 million delinquency cases in 2002—up from 1.1 million in 1985

Juvenile court caseloads have grown and changed In 2002, U.S. courts with juvenile jurisdiction handled an estimated 1.6 million cases in which the juvenile was charged with a delinquency offense—an offense for which an adult could be prosecuted in criminal court. Thus, U.S. juvenile courts handled more than 4,400 delinquency cases per day in 2002. In comparison, approximately 1,100 delinquency cases were processed daily in 1960.

Changes in the juvenile court delinquency caseload over the years have strained the courts' resources and programs. The volume of delinquency cases handled by juvenile courts rose 41% between 1985 and 2002. Courts were asked to respond not only to more cases but also to a different type of caseload—one with more person offense and drug cases.

Law enforcement refers most delinquency cases to court Delinquency and status offense cases are referred to juvenile courts by a number of different sources, including law enforcement agencies, social services agencies, victims, probation officers, schools, or parents.

Percent of cases referred by law enforcement agencies:

Offense	2002
Delinquency	82%
Person	87
Property	91
Drugs	90
Public order	61

Status offense (formal cases)	
Runaway	55%
Truancy	14
Ungovernability	30
Liquor	92

In 2002, 82% of delinquency cases were referred by law enforcement agencies. This proportion has changed little over the past two decades. Law enforcement agencies are generally much less likely to be the source of referral for formally handled status offense cases (involving offenses that are not crimes for adults) than delinquency cases. The exception is status liquor law violations (underage drinking and possession of alcohol).

Cases increased for males and females through the mid–1990s; since then cases have declined for males

Females account for a relatively small share of delinquency cases In 2002, juvenile courts handled more than 423,000 delinquency cases involving female juveniles—just over one-quarter of all delinquency cases handled in 2002. Females made up a fairly large share of cases in some offense categories—larceny-theft (38%), disorderly conduct (33%), simple assault (32%), and liquor law cases (32%). For other offense categories, the female share of the caseload was relatively small—violent sex offenses other than rape (5%), robbery (9%), burglary (10%), arson (13%), and weapons offenses (14%).

The female share of delinquency cases increased steadily from 1991 through 2002 The proportion of delinquency cases that involved females was 19% in 1991; by 2002, it had increased 7 percentage points to 26%. * * *

In 2002, male and female offense profiles were similar, but not as similar as they were in 1985. For both males and females, 2002 caseloads had smaller shares of property crimes and more person crimes than in 1985 Compared with offense profiles in 1985, both male and female delinquency caseloads had greater proportions of person offense cases in 2002. Both male and female caseloads saw substantial reductions in the proportion of cases that involved property crimes. Despite the reduction in the property crime share of delinquency cases, property cases were still the most common type of case for both males and females in 2002.

Compared with males, females had a greater proportion of person offense cases and a smaller proportion of drug offense cases in 2002. In 1985, the offense profiles for cases involving males and females differed less than in 2002.

A disproportionate number of delinquency cases involved black juveniles. In 2002, blacks constituted 16% of the juvenile population but 29% of the delinquency caseload Although a majority of delinquency cases handled in 2002 involved white youth (1,086,700 or 67%), a disproportionate number of cases involved blacks (473,100 or 29%), given their proportion of the juvenile population. In 2002, white youth made up 78% of the juvenile population (youth ages 10 through the upper age of juvenile court jurisdiction in each state), black youth 16%, and youth of other races 6%.

The racial profile of delinquency cases overall was essentially the same in 1985 and 2002, although some of the general offense categories had noticeable changes. The proportion of black juveniles changed from 23% in 1985 to 28% in 2002 for property cases and from 21% to 29% for public order cases.

Offense profiles for whites and blacks differed Delinquency caseloads for black juveniles contained a greater proportion of person offenses than did caseloads for white juveniles and those of other races. For all racial groups, property offenses accounted for the largest proportion of cases and drug offenses the smallest proportion. Compared with 1985, for all racial groups, person and public order offenses made up a larger share and property offenses a smaller share of delinquency cases in 2002.

In 2002, the disparity between rates for black youth and white youth was lowest for drug cases In 2002, case rates for black juveniles were substantially higher than rates for other juveniles in all offense categories, but the degree of disparity varied. The person offense case rate for black juveniles (28.2 per 1,000) was nearly 3 times the rate for white juveniles (9.5), the public order case rate for black juveniles (23.4) was more than 2 times the rate for white juveniles (11.4), and the property case rate for black juveniles (34.2) was nearly 2 times the rate for white juveniles (17.5).

In comparison, in 2002, the drug offense case rate for black juveniles (8.2) was less than 1.5 times the rate for white juveniles (6.0). Although the disparity between black and white drug case rates was relatively small in 2002, that was not always true. In fact, in 1991, the drug offense case rate for black juveniles was more than 5.5 times the rate for white juveniles. No other offense reached this extent of disparity between black and white case rates. * * *

The petitioned caseload increased 80% from 1985 to 2002 as formal case handling became more likely

In a formally processed case, petitioners ask the court to order sanctions Formal case handling involves the filing of a petition requesting that the court hold an adjudicatory or waiver hearing. Decision-makers (police, probation, intake, prosecutor, or other screening officer) may consider informal case handling if they believe that accountability and rehabilitation can be achieved without formal court intervention. Compared with informally handled (non-petitioned) cases, formally processed (petitioned) delinquency cases tend to involve more serious offenses, older juveniles, and juveniles with longer court histories.

If the court decides to handle the matter informally, the offender agrees to comply with one or more sanctions such as community service, victim restitution, or voluntary probation supervision. Informal cases are generally held open pending successful completion of the disposition. If the court's conditions are met, the charges are dismissed. If, however, the offender does not fulfill the conditions, the case is likely to be petitioned for formal processing.

The use of formal handling has increased In 1985, juvenile courts formally processed 45% of delinquency cases. By 2002, that proportion had increased to 58%. Cases in each of the four general offense categories were more likely to be handled formally in 2002 than in 1985.

In 2002, property offense cases were the least likely to be petitioned for formal handling, and drug cases were the most likely. In fact, from 1985 to 2002, drug offense cases went from least likely to most likely to be petitioned. The 61% petitioning rate for drug cases in 2002, however, was substantially lower than the peak rate of 68% in 1991. No other offense category experienced such an upsurge in petitioning between 1985 and 2002.

The proportion of petitioned cases increased from 1985–2002 for all demographic groups The likelihood of formal case processing increased from 1985 to 2002 for both males and females and for all races and ages. In 2002, as in 1985, courts petitioned a larger share of delinquency cases involving males than females. This was true for each of the general offense categories. Courts petitioned a larger share of delinquency cases involving blacks than whites or youth of other races.

From 1985 to 2002, the number of cases in which the youth was adjudicated delinquent rose 85%. Adjudication was more likely for some types of cases than others Youth were adjudicated delinquent in a smaller proportion of person offense cases than in cases involving other categories of offenses. This lower rate of adjudication in person offense cases may reflect, in part, reluctance to divert these cases from the formal juvenile justice system without a judge's review.

Adjudication rates also varied by gender, race, and age of the youth. The likelihood of adjudication in 2002 was somewhat less for females than for males. This was true across offense categories. Black youth were less likely to be adjudicated than were white youth or youth of other races. Cases involving youth age 15 or younger were slightly more likely to result in adjudication than cases involving older youth, although older youth had a greater share of cases waived to criminal court.

Offense profiles for petitioned and adjudicated cases show a shift away from property cases Compared with 1985, both petitioned and adjudicated cases had increased proportions of person, drug, and public order offenses in 2002. The 2002 offense profile for adjudicated cases was very similar to the profile for petitioned cases.

Most adjudicated delinquency cases result in residential placement or formal probation. Residential placement and formal probation caseloads saw a shift away from property cases Compared with 1985, both residential placement and formal probation cases had increased proportions of person, drug, and public order offenses in 2002. In 2002, cases ordered to residential placement had a greater share of person and public order cases and a smaller share of drug cases than cases ordered to formal probation.

Residential placement and probation caseloads increased between 1985 and 2002 The number of delinquency cases in which adjudicated youth were ordered out of the home to some form of residential placement rose 44% between 1985 and 2002, from 100,400 to 144,000. In comparison, the number of delinquency cases receiving formal probation as the most severe initial disposition following adjudication more than doubled from 1985 to 2002, from 189,600 to 385,400. The growth in formal probation cases was greater than the growth in delinquency cases at referral (41%) and adjudication (85%).

The number of adjudicated cases receiving other sanctions (e.g., community service, restitution) as their most severe disposition rose 140% from 1985 to 2002, from 35,400 to 85,000. However, the majority of cases resulting in other sanctions were handled informally.

Probation was more likely than residential placement. In 23% of adjudicated delinquency cases, the court ordered the youth to residential placement such as a training school, treatment center, boot camp, drug treatment or private placement facility, or group home. In 62% of adjudicated delinquency cases, probation was the most severe sanction ordered.

Once adjudicated, females were less likely than males, and white youth were less likely than black youth or youth of other races, to be ordered to residential placement. These demographic patterns in the use of residential placement and probation, however, do not control for criminal histories and other risk factors related to dispositional decisions and increased severity of sanctions.

Probation conditions are designed to control and rehabilitate Probation is the oldest and most widely used community-based corrections program. Probation is used both for first-time, low-risk offenders and as an alternative to institutional confinement for more serious offenders. During a period of probation supervision, a juvenile offender remains in the community and can continue normal activities such as school and work. However, the juvenile must comply with certain conditions.

Compliance with probation conditions may be voluntary: the youth agrees to conditions in lieu of for mal adjudication. Or compliance may be mandatory following adjudication: the youth is formally ordered to a term of probation and must comply with the conditions established by the court. Most (62%) juvenile probation dispositions in 2002 were formal (i.e., enacted under court order following adjudication).

In addition to being required to meet regularly with a probation officer, a juvenile assigned to probation may be ordered to adhere to a curfew, complete a specified period of community service, or pay restitution. More serious offenders may be placed on intensive supervision requiring more frequent contact with their probation officer and stricter conditions. Typically, probation can be revoked if the juvenile violates the conditions. If probation is revoked, the court may reconsider its disposition and impose stricter sanctions.

Black youth account for a disproportionate share of cases at all stages of case processing. The overrepresentation of black youth was greatest for person offense cases. At most stages of case processing, the share of white youth was greater for drug offenses than other offense categories. At all stages of the system, youth of other races made up 5% or less of the caseload. The proportion of cases that involved black youth was the same for adjudicated cases as for cases overall (29%). In fact, the racial profile of cases was similar at referral and adjudication for all offense categories. The largest proportion of black youth was found in detained and waived person offense cases, where black youth accounted for 41% of cases.

B. JUVENILE COURT DELINQUENCY JURISDICTION FOR CRIMINAL VIOLATIONS

Juvenile courts are exclusively statutory entities and states may define their jurisdiction in different ways. Every state defines its delinquency jurisdiction on the basis of age and criminal conduct. A legislature may establish the maximum jurisdictional age as seventeen, sixteen, or fifteen years of age, and confer original jurisdiction over all offenses that would be crimes if committed by an adult or it may exclude certain offenses from the juvenile court's jurisdiction. For example, Virginia defines a "delinquent child" as a person who, "prior to his eighteenth birthday," commits "an act designated a crime under the law of this Commonwealth, or an ordinance of any city, county, town or service district, or under federal law * * *." *Va. Stat.* § 16.1–228 (1998).

Other states may give juvenile and criminal courts concurrent jurisdiction over certain ages and offenses and allow prosecutors to select the jurisdictional forum. For example, in Nebraska the "juvenile court shall have concurrent original jurisdiction with the district court" and a prosecutor may choose whether a youth sixteen or seventeen years of age and charged with a felony will be tried in the juvenile or criminal justice system. *Neb. Stat.* § 43–247 (1998). In Chapter 6, we will consider more extensively the jurisdictional questions of who, how, and why states transfer youths from juvenile to criminal court for prosecution as adults.

West's Ann. Cal. Welf. & Inst. Code § 602. Minors violating laws defining crime; ward of court (2004):

(a) Except as provided in subdivision (b), any person who is under the age of 18 years when he or she violates any law of this state or of the United States or any ordinance of any city or county of this state defining crime other than an ordinance establishing a curfew based solely on age, is within the jurisdiction of the juvenile court, which may adjudge such person to be a ward of the court.

(b) Any person who is alleged, when he or she was 14 years of age or older, to have committed one of the following offenses shall be prosecuted under the general law in a court of criminal jurisdiction:

(1) Murder, ... if one of the [aggravating] circumstances ... is alleged by the prosecutor, and the prosecutor alleges that the minor personally killed the victim.

(2) The following sex offenses, if the prosecutor alleges that the minor personally committed the offense, and if the prosecutor alleges one of the circumstances enumerated in the One Strike law . . . applies:

(A) Rape, . . .

(B) Spousal rape, . . .

(C) Forcible sex offenses in concert with another, . . .

(D) Forcible lewd and lascivious acts on a child under the age of 14 years, . . .

(E) Forcible sexual penetration, . . .

(F) Sodomy or oral copulation . . . by force, violence, duress, menace, or fear of immediate and unlawful bodily injury on the victim or another person.

(G) Lewd and lascivious acts on a child under the age of 14 years, . . .

Minn. Stat. § 260B.007. Definitions (2004)

Subd. 3. Child. "Child" means an individual under 18 years of age and includes any minor alleged to have been delinquent or a juvenile traffic offender prior to having become 18 years of age.

Subd. 6. Delinquent child. (a) Except as otherwise provided in paragraph (b), "delinquent child" means a child:

(1) who has violated any state or local law, . . . ;

(2) who has violated a federal law or a law of another state and whose case has been referred to the juvenile court if the violation would be an act of delinquency if committed in this state or a crime or offense if committed by an adult;

(3) who has escaped from confinement to a state juvenile correctional facility after being committed to the custody of the commissioner of corrections; or

(4) who has escaped from confinement to a local juvenile correctional facility after being committed to the facility by the court.

(b) The term delinquent child does not include a child alleged to have committed murder in the first degree after becoming 16 years of age, but the term delinquent child does include a child alleged to have committed attempted murder in the first degree.

Minn.Stat. § 260C.007 Definitions (2004):

Subd. 6. Child in need of protection or services. "Child in need of protection or services" means a child who is in need of protection or services because the child: * * *

(12) has committed a delinquent act or a juvenile petty offense before becoming ten years old.

Minn.Stat. § 260B.101 Jurisdiction (2004)

Subdivision 1. Children who are delinquent. * * * [T]he juvenile court has original and exclusive jurisdiction in proceedings concerning any child who is alleged to be delinquent, a juvenile traffic offender, a juvenile petty offender, and in proceedings concerning any minor alleged to have been a delinquent, a juvenile petty offender, or a juvenile traffic offender prior to having become 18 years of age. The juvenile court shall deal with such a minor as it deals with any other child who is alleged to be delinquent or a juvenile traffic offender.

New York McKinney's Family Court Act § 301.2 Definitions (2004)

As used in this article, the following terms shall have the following meanings:

1.   "Juvenile delinquent" means a person over seven and less than sixteen years of age, who, having committed an act that would constitute a crime if committed by an adult, (a) is not criminally responsible for such conduct by reason of infancy, or (b) is the defendant in an action ordered removed from a criminal court to the family court pursuant to article seven hundred twenty-five of the criminal procedure law.

New York McKinney's Family Court Act § 302.1. Jurisdiction (2004)

1.   The family court has exclusive original jurisdiction over any proceeding to determine whether a person is a juvenile delinquent.

2.   In determining the jurisdiction of the court the age of such person at the time the delinquent act allegedly was committed is controlling.

1.   APPLICABILITY OF CRIMINAL LAW JURISPRUDENCE TO JUVENILE COURT PROCEEDINGS

Because states define their juvenile courts' jurisdiction based on a youth engaging in conduct that would be a crime if committed by an adult, questions arise as to whether the criminal law's jurisprudence also should carry over into the law of juvenile courts. For example, may a delinquent assert the common law infancy defense in order to defeat juvenile court's jurisdiction? May a delinquent seek acquittal on the grounds of insanity? May a juvenile court proceed against a youth who lack competency to stand trial? If the purpose of the juvenile court is to treat young offenders, then does classical criminal law jurisprudence developed in a justice system that seeks to punish presumptively responsible, free-will moral actors even apply? Issues of criminal law and jurisprudence arise because every state's definition of delinquency jurisdiction includes violations of criminal law. Because delinquency proceedings differ from criminal prosecutions, however, the following cases focus on the applicability and implications of criminal law doctrines for juvenile courts.

a. Availability of Common Law Infancy Defense

IN RE TYVONNE J.

211 Conn. 151, 558 A.2d 661 (1989).

GLASS, ASSOCIATE JUSTICE. In this case we decide whether the common law defense of infancy applies to juvenile delinquency proceedings. The respondent appealed to the Appellate Court from an adjudication of delinquency, claiming that the trial court erred in denying his motion for judgment of acquittal. * * * We find no error.

The relevant facts are not in dispute. * * * [Tyvonne, who was eight years old, found a small pistol. The following day he took the pistol to school and told another child about it. After school, Tyvonne and the victim argued over whether the pistol was real. Several children examined the pistol and decided that it was a toy. The victim challenged Tyvonne saying, "Shoot me, shoot me." Tyvonne exclaimed, "I'll show you it's real," pointed the pistol at the victim, and fired one shot, which struck and injured her. The state filed a delinquency petition arising from the shooting. The trial court ordered a psychological evaluation of the respondent. After the state completed its case, defense counsel made an oral motion for acquittal, claiming that the state had introduced no evidence to rebut the common law presumption that children between the ages of seven and fourteen lacked the capacity to commit a crime. The court reserved decision on the motion to acquit, but ordered an examination to determine Tyvonne's competency. Following the competency evaluation, the trial court denied the motion for acquittal. The trial court adjudicated Tyvonne delinquent based on a finding that he had committed assault in the second degree, ordered a preliminary investigation, and at the disposition hearing committed him to the department of children and youth services (DCYS) for a period not to exceed four years.]

On appeal, the respondent * * * asserts that Connecticut's juvenile justice legislation does not expressly or implicitly eliminate the common law infancy defense from delinquency proceedings. He further argues that because the original goals of rehabilitation and remediation in the juvenile justice system have not been attained, there is no justification for excluding the infancy defense from juvenile delinquency proceedings. Consequently, he claims, the trial court erred in not requiring the state to rebut the presumption that he was incapable of committing the offense underlying the delinquency adjudication. We are not persuaded.

The respondent argues that, even though the legislature may abolish common law rules, statutes in derogation of the common law must be strictly construed. He asserts that because the juvenile justice legislation is silent with respect to the common law infancy defense, the common law presumptions must apply to delinquency proceedings. The state argues, however, that Connecticut's juvenile justice legislation implicitly abolishes the defense and, further, that application of the defense in delinquency proceedings would frustrate the legislation's remedial objectives. * * *

"By the seventeenth century, the Roman classification of criminal responsibility became the basis of the English common-law approach, so that children under seven were incapable of committing a crime while those between seven and fourteen were presumed incapable. Such presumption however was rebuttable by strong and clear evidence. Those [fourteen and over] were subject to the same criminal laws as were adults." * * *

The common law defense of infancy, like the defense of insanity, differs from the criminal law's requirement of "mens rea" or criminal intent. The law recognized that while a child may have actually intended to perform a criminal act, children in general could not reasonably be presumed capable of differentiating right from wrong. The presumptions of incapacity were created to avoid punishing those who, because of age, could not appreciate the moral dimensions of their behavior, and for whom the threat of punishment would not act as a deterrent. Although a number of states have codified the common law rule by statute; there is no statutory infancy defense in Connecticut.

The concept of juvenile delinquency did not exist at common law. In most states, * * * legislation was enacted that rendered children under a certain age liable as "delinquents" for committing acts that, if committed by an adult, would be criminal. * * * Even though the Superior Court is Connecticut's trial court of general jurisdiction, and juvenile matters are heard in the Superior Court, juvenile proceedings are conducted separately from all other business of the Superior Court. Delinquency is defined in General Statutes § 46b–120 as follows: "[A] child may be found 'delinquent' (1) who has violated any federal or state law or municipal or local ordinance * * * or (2) who has violated any order of the superior court * * *." An important feature of the legislation since its inception is presently expressed in General Statutes § 46b–145, which provides: "No child shall be prosecuted for an offense before the superior court, nor shall the adjudication of such court that a child is delinquent in any case be deemed a conviction of crime * * *."

Shortly after the creation of the juvenile justice system, we addressed the issue whether a delinquency proceeding is tantamount to a criminal prosecution. In that case, we stated that "the Act [creating the juvenile justice system] * * * is not of a criminal nature. * * *" "The Act is but an exercise by the State of its * * * power over the welfare of its children," and a juvenile subjected to delinquency proceedings "[is] tried for no offense," but "[comes] under the operation of the law in order that he might not be tried for any offense." * * * [W]e have on several occasions recognized that * * * juvenile proceedings are fundamentally different from criminal proceedings.

The rehabilitative nature of our juvenile justice system is most saliently evidenced by the statutory provisions pertaining to the disposition of delinquent juveniles. * * * [T]he trial court may not render a disposition of the case of any delinquent child until the trial court receives from the probation officer assigned to the case a comprehensive background report on the child's characteristics, history and home life. The disposition of a child found delinquent for a serious juvenile offense may be made only after the court receives a complete evaluation of the child's physical and psychological health * * * [and] the trial court may place the juvenile "in the care of any institution or agency which is permitted by law to care for children, order the child to remain in his own home or in the custody of a relative or any other fit person subject to the supervision of the probation officer or withhold or suspend execution of any judgment." The court may also order the juvenile to perform public service or to make restitution when appropriate, provided that the child and his parent or guardian consent to such an order.

Significantly, commitment of the child to DCYS may be made only if the court finds that "its probation services or other services available to the court are not adequate for such child. * * * " Prior to any such commitment, however, the court must "consult with [DCYS] to determine the placement which will be in the best interest of such child." When the trial court determines that a commitment must be made, it may commit the child to DCYS for an indeterminate period not to exceed two years, or in the case of a child found delinquent for committing a serious juvenile offense, for an indeterminate period not to exceed four years. DCYS may petition for an extension of the commitment of a child originally committed for two years. An extension may not exceed an additional two years, and may only be ordered when, after a hearing, it is found to be in the best interests of the child.

Several other provisions of the General Statutes and the Practice Book delineate fundamental distinctions between delinquency and criminal proceedings. For example, Practice Book § 1034(1) provides that a juvenile delinquency hearing "shall not be conducted as a criminal trial; the proceedings shall be at all times as informal as the requirements of due process and fairness permit." Further, unlike the records of convicted criminals, the records of juvenile delinquency proceedings generally are confidential. * * *

It is clear from our analysis that the purpose of the comprehensive statutory treatment of "juvenile delinquents" is clinical and rehabilitative, rather than retributive or punitive. * * * "[T]he objective of juvenile court proceedings is to 'determin[e] the needs of the child and of society rather than adjudicat[e] criminal conduct. The objectives are to provide measures of guidance and rehabilitation . . . not to fix criminal responsibility, guilt and punishment.' Thus the child found delinquent is not perceived as a criminal guilty of one or more offenses, but rather as a child in need of guidance and rehabilitative services." In effect, the statutes regulating juvenile misconduct represent a system-wide displacement of the common law.

With the enactment of juvenile justice legislation nationwide, several courts have addressed the issue whether the infancy defense applies to delinquency proceedings. Most have held that, in the absence of legislation codifying or adopting the defense, incapacity is not a defense in delinquency proceedings. These courts observe that because a delinquency adjudication is not a criminal conviction, it is unnecessary to determine whether the juvenile understood the moral implications of his or her behavior. In addition, some decisions recognize that the defense would frustrate the remedial purposes of juvenile justice legislation.

Because Connecticut's juvenile justice system is designed to provide delinquent minors with guidance and rehabilitation, we agree with the courts that hold that the common law infancy defense, created to protect children from being punished as criminals, has no place in delinquency proceedings. We also agree that the legislature could decide that the infancy defense would unnecessarily interfere with the state's legitimate efforts to provide structured forms of guidance for children who have committed acts of delinquency. It could conclude that the defense inevitably would exclude those children most in need of guidance from a system designed to instill socially responsible behavior. To construe the legislature's silence as indicating an intent to preserve the infancy defense in delinquency proceedings is unwarranted in light of the legislation's obvious and singular remedial objectives. We are not persuaded that recognition of the defense would advance the interests of either the child or society.[9]

Relying on a number of decisions in other states, however, the respondent argues that the rehabilitative objectives of juvenile justice have become defunct, and cannot justify excluding the infancy defense from delinquency proceedings. Most of the decisions holding the infancy defense applicable to juvenile proceedings have been based on specific legislation adopting the defense, and therefore are irrelevant to the present case.

Some courts, however, have held that even absent pertinent legislation, the common law infancy defense applies to delinquency proceedings. These courts advance the notion that the United States Supreme Court decisions in *Kent v. United States*, *In re Gault*, and *In re Winship*, reflect the evolving reality that the true objectives of juvenile justice legislation are not rehabilitation and treatment, but accountability and punishment. * * *

The respondent does not argue that the United States Supreme Court's juvenile decisions require the common law incapacity defense in delinquency proceedings as a matter of fundamental constitutional fairness. Nor does he suggest that the exclusion of the incapacity defense introduces procedural arbitrariness. Instead, the respondent gleans from those cases the proposition that since the juvenile justice system punishes rather than rehabilitates, there is no good reason not to recognize incapac-

---

9. Nothing in this opinion should be construed to deter the legislature from considering the desirability of a floor for such juvenile proceedings in recognition of the fact that the clinical and rehabilitative needs of a four or eight year old are different from those of a fourteen or fifteen year old.

ity as a defense. We are not persuaded, however, that *Kent* and *Gault* warrant the proposition that the respondent discerns.

We acknowledge that the United States Supreme Court has opined that the rehabilitative goals of the various state juvenile courts have often not been attained. The court has made it quite clear that states may not deny juveniles fundamental due process rights simply by labeling delinquency proceedings "civil," or by asserting that the purpose of delinquency proceedings is rehabilitative. Thus, the *parens patriae* doctrine does not support inroads on basic constitutional guarantees simply because a state claims that its juvenile justice system is "rehabilitative" rather than "punitive." The United States Supreme Court, however, has expressly refused to hold that the rehabilitative goals of the various systems of juvenile justice may under no circumstances justify appropriate differential treatment of a child adjudicated a delinquent. Further, the court has never suggested that such differential treatment, based on the juvenile justice systems' fundamentally nonpunitive objectives, is intrinsically illegitimate. * * *

We do not discern in *Kent* and its progeny an abandonment of the rehabilitative focus of juvenile justice. The respondent has not presented us with any grounds for concluding that the rehabilitative objectives of Connecticut's juvenile justice system are contradicted in practice. We therefore decline to adopt the somewhat cynical view expressed by some writers that the ideals of the juvenile justice system are now bankrupt, and have necessarily succumbed to the corrosive effects of institutionalization.

Further, we are not persuaded by the respondent's argument that the statutory treatment of juveniles who commit "serious juvenile offenses" requires a conclusion that there is no genuine difference between juvenile and criminal proceedings. The four year maximum commitment term for serious juvenile offenders * * * certainly contemplates the possibility of a serious restriction on the juvenile's liberty. But as we have already observed, any commitment order must be predicated on a determination that other options not involving commitment are inadequate to address the child's needs. In addition, placement of the child in a program or facility must be based on the child's best interests. We cannot infer from these provisions a legislative intent to inflict retribution on the serious juvenile offender. * * *

There is no error. In this opinion the other Justices concurred.

b.   Immaturity and Infancy Defense in Juvenile Court

IN RE GLADYS R.

1 Cal.3d 855, 83 Cal.Rptr. 671, 464 P.2d 127 (1970).

TOBRINER, JUSTICE. Gladys R., a 12–year–old girl, appeals from a judgment declaring her a ward of the court and committing her to the custody of the probation officer for private institutional placement. For the reasons we shall point out, the court committed reversible error in reviewing the social study report before the jurisdictional hearing. We also conclude that the juvenile court should consider whether a child appreciates the wrongfulness of her conduct in determining whether the child should be declared a ward under section 602[1] of the Welfare and Institutions Code (Pen.Code, § 26). * * *

As we have stated, section 602 provides that any minor who violates "any law of this State," that defines crime, comes under the jurisdiction of the juvenile court. We shall point out that in order to become a ward of the court under that section, clear proof must show that a child under the age of 14 years at the time of committing the act appreciated its wrongfulness. This conclusion follows from the statutory postulate that the jurisdiction of the court must rest upon a violation of a law that defines crime and from the further statutory requirement of Penal Code section 26, subdivision One,[10] that, by definition, a child under the age of 14 years does not commit a crime in the absence of clear proof that he "knew its wrongfulness."

A ruling that a child could be committed to the juvenile court under section 602, in the absence of such clear proof, would compel the disregard of section 26 or the assumption of its repeal. Indeed, the Welfare and Institutions Code provides that the juvenile courts exercise exclusive jurisdiction over all minors under the age of 16; these children cannot otherwise be tried as criminal offenders. Hence, if section 26 pertains at all to a definition of criminal conduct it must apply to proceedings under section 602 which, in turn, covers "[a]ny person under the age of 21 years who violates any law of this State * * *."

We cannot presume the repeal of section 26 by implication; the decisions clearly establish the contrary presumption. We have said that "To overcome the presumption the two acts must be irreconcilable, clearly repugnant, and so inconsistent that the two cannot have concurrent operation. The courts are bound, if possible, to maintain the integrity of both statutes if the two may stand together."

In enacting section 602 of the Welfare and Institutions Code, the Legislature must have considered the pre-existing section 26; that section constituted practically the only special provision for children in the entire legal system. Section 26 did not lie at the periphery of the statutory scheme, bearing only tangentially upon juvenile offenders. Necessarily confronted with the section, the Legislature must have intended in its

---

1. Welfare and Institutions Code section 602 reads: "Any person under the age of 21 years who violates any law of this State * * * defining crime * * * is within the jurisdiction of the juvenile court, which may adjudge such person to be a ward of the court." References hereinafter to section 602, without mention of any code, are to the quoted section.

10. "All persons are capable of committing crimes except those belonging to the following classes: One—Children under the age of fourteen, in the absence of clear proof that at the time of committing the act charged against them, they knew its wrongfulness." (Pen.Code § 26, subd. One.) References hereinafter to section 26, without mention of any code, are to the quoted section.

later enactment of section 602 a definition of crime consistent with the older section. If the Legislature had intended to repeal section 26 or to sever it from section 602, it could have done so expressly. Yet the legislative history of the present California Juvenile Court Law, of which section 602 forms a part, indicates no such intent. In fact, the commission that drafted the present law refers to the necessity of "respectable proof of the jurisdictional facts" for the institution of proceedings under section 602 for the violation of "serious crimes against persons and property."

Section 26 accords with the historical treatment of juveniles, deriving from the early common law that children under the age of seven could not be held responsible for criminal conduct. Between the ages of seven and fourteen the common law rebuttably presumed children incapable of criminal acts, unless the particular child possessed the requisite age and experience to understand the wrongfulness of his act. California likewise rebuttably presumes all minors under the age of 14 incapable of committing a crime, but does not totally exclude any child from criminal responsibility. Section 26 embodies a venerable truth, which is no less true for its extreme age, that a young child cannot be held to the same standard of criminal responsibility as his more experienced elders. A juvenile court must therefore consider a child's age, experience, and understanding in determining whether he would be capable of committing conduct proscribed by section 602. * * *

Furthermore, section 26 provides the kind of fundamental protection to children charged under section 602 which this court should not lightly discard. Section 602 is clearly distinguishable from sections 600 and 601 with respect to the consequences of their operation upon the child: upon the application of section 602, commitment of the youth to the custody of the California Youth Authority becomes far more likely. Section 600 concerns dependent children who need care because of home conditions or medical deficiencies.[18] Section 601 covers delinquent children whose acts fall short of criminal conduct.[19] Section 602 pertains to minors who have violated a court order or a criminal law.

If a juvenile court finds a lack of clear proof that a child under 14 years at the time of committing the act possessed knowledge of its

---

18. Section 600. "Any person under the age of 21 years who comes within any of the following descriptions is within the jurisdiction of the juvenile court which may adjudge such person to be a dependent child of the court: (a) Who is in need of proper and effective parental care or control and has no parent or guardian, or has no parent or guardian willing to exercise or capable of exercising such care or control, or has no parent or guardian actually exercising such care or control. (b) Who is destitute, or who is not provided with the necessities of life, or who is not provided with a home or suitable place of abode, or whose home is an unfit place for him by reason of neglect, cruelty, or depravity of either of his parents, or of his guardian or other person in whose custody or care he is. (c) Who is physically dangerous to the public because of a mental or physical deficiency, disorder or abnormality." (Welf. & Inst. Code, § 600.)

19. Section 601. "Any person under the age of 21 years who persistently or habitually refuses to obey the reasonable and proper orders or directions of his parents, guardian, custodian or school authorities, or who is beyond the control of such person, or any person who is a habitual truant from school within the meaning of any law of this State, or who from any cause is in danger of leading an idle, dissolute, lewd, or immoral life, is within the jurisdiction of the juvenile court which may adjudge such person to be a ward of the court." (Welf. & Inst.Code, § 601.)

wrongfulness under sections 602 and 26, the court might well declare the child a ward under section 600 or 601. These latter provisions carry far less severe consequences for the liberty and life of the child. After all, it is the purpose of the Welfare and Institutions Code to "insure that the rights or physical, mental or moral welfare of children are not violated or threatened by their present circumstances or environment." Strong policy reasons cast doubt upon the placement of a child who is unable to appreciate the wrongfulness of his conduct with an institution where he will come into contact with many youths who are well versed in criminality.[22] To argue that we should trust entirely to the discretion of the juvenile court in this matter does not justify a ruling that section 26 is inapplicable to the definition of crime within section 602. We cannot condone a decision which would both misinterpret the statute and expose the child to consequences possibly disastrous to himself and society as a whole.

Other sections may possibly be invoked to provide for a wardship for this child with no injurious potentials. Section 601 provides that a child who disobeys the lawful orders of his parents or school authorities, who is beyond the control of such persons, or who is in danger of leading an immoral life may be adjudged a ward of the court. Section 601 might clearly cover younger children who lacked the age or experience to understand the wrongfulness of their conduct. It the juvenile court considers section 601 inappropriate for the particular child, he may be covered by the even broader provisions of section 600.

Section 602 should apply only to those who are over 14 and may be presumed to understand the wrongfulness of their acts and to those under the age of 14 who clearly appreciate the wrongfulness of their conduct. In the instant case we are confronted with a 12–year–old girl of the social and mental age of a 7–year–old. Section 26 stands to protect her and other young people like her from the harsh strictures of section 602. Only if the age, experience, knowledge, and conduct of the child demonstrate by clear proof that he has violated a criminal law should he be declared a ward of the court under section 602. * * *

[O]ver the past centuries our society has attained a stage of relative sophistication in which it recognizes that antisocial conduct in most cases stems from psychological motivation in the individual that cannot be segregated into the easy categories of "criminal" or "noncriminal." It would be particularly undesirable for a juvenile court, arbitrarily, without analysis of the child's appreciation of the "wrongfulness" of her conduct, to hold this emotionally disturbed child of 12 years guilty of criminal conduct. To reach that result we would, in our judgment, be compelled to

22. The Attorney General expresses some concern that if section 26 prevents a child from being brought under the supervision of the juvenile court under section 602 "it is quite possible that no other juvenile proceedings could be initiated other than under section 602, where the act amounts to something proscribed by the Penal Code." But as we observed in *In re Dennis M.*: "Indeed, the youth's alleged crime may often be only the latest or most overt symptom of an underlying behavioral or personality disorder which could equally well warrant a declaration of wardship pursuant to other provisions of the Code."

misread the pertinent statutes, to disregard even our presently inadequate knowledge of psychology, and to retreat to an approach which pre-dates the early common law.

The judgment is reversed and the case is remanded to the Santa Clara County Superior Court, sitting as a juvenile court, for further proceedings consistent with this opinion.

BURKE, JUSTICE (concurring and dissenting.) I concur with the majority opinion except the portion which holds that in order for a minor under 14 to be within the jurisdiction of the juvenile court under Welfare and Institutions Code section 602 there must be "clear proof" that the minor at the time of committing the crime knew of its wrongfulness (Pen.Code, § 26, subd. One). With respect to that portion I dissent.

Proceedings in the juvenile court are conducted for the protection and benefit of minors and not to prosecute them as law violators.[2] It is unreasonable to believe that the Legislature intended Penal Code section 26, subdivision One, to apply in a proceeding instituted for the minor's benefit and which seeks to determine whether the minor comes within the terms of section 602. Application of that subdivision in such juvenile court proceedings could result in excluding some minors who are in dire need of the care and guidance afforded by the Juvenile Court Law from receiving those benefits. It appears likely that the very minors so excluded would be those in greater need of receiving such care than others more sophisticated who plainly knew that their acts were wrongful.

The majority state, "If a juvenile court finds a lack of clear proof that a child under 14 years at the time of committing the act possessed knowledge of its wrongfulness under sections 602 and 26, the court might well declare the child a ward under Welfare and Institutions Code sections 600 or 601." The quoted statement, however, fails to give adequate consideration to the fact that many children who violate a law defining a crime may not be found to come within either section 600 or 601. Under the majority position such children will be deprived of the attention they need in order to become law-abiding citizens. For example, a 12–year–old boy on one occasion exhibits a loaded gun in a threatening manner in the presence of another, and the evidence does not show his conduct was the result of "a mental or physical deficiency, disorder, or abnormality,". A 13–year–old girl has possession of marijuana. A 13–year–old boy on one occasion commits statutory rape, with a willing 13–year–old girl in a private place, or goes joyriding or commit petty theft. In none of the foregoing instances is there "clear proof" that the minor at the time of

---

2. Section 502 reads: "The purpose of this chapter [the Arnold Kennick Juvenile Court law] is to secure for each minor under the jurisdiction of the juvenile court such care and guidance, preferably in his own home, as will serve the spiritual, emotional, mental, and physical welfare of the minor and the best interests of the State; to preserve and strengthen the minor's family ties whenever possible, removing him from the custody of his parents only when his welfare or safety and protection of the public cannot be adequately safeguarded without removal; and, when the minor is removed from his own family, to secure for him custody, care, and discipline as nearly as possible equivalent to that which should have been given by his parents. This chapter shall be liberally construed to carry out these purposes."

committing the crime had knowledge of its wrongfulness. In the foregoing instances some juvenile courts might conclude that the minor did not come within either section 600 or 601, and additional proof to bring the minor within section 600 or 601 might not be available.

It is implicit in the above quoted statement of the majority that knowledge of the wrongfulness of the act is not required for an adjudication that a minor under 14 is a person described by section 601. A minor may be adjudicated to come within section 601 where he has persistently refused to obey the reasonable and proper orders of school authorities. It would have been anomalous had the Legislature required knowledge of the wrongfulness of his act by a minor under 14 who committed a serious crime in order for the court to have jurisdiction under one section and not to have required it for a relatively lesser transgression under another. The welfare of the child and the best interests of society manifestly would make jurisdiction of the former child more imperative than jurisdiction over the latter child. Although one difference exists with respect to the disposition that may be made of a minor found to come within section 601 and a minor found to come within section 602, otherwise the same dispositions are authorized for both such minors and both may be ordered confined, for example, in a juvenile home.

The common law rebuttable presumption of lack of criminal capacity of a child between 7 and 14 has been regarded as inapplicable in juvenile court proceedings. The cited cases reasoned that juvenile court proceedings are not criminal in nature and are not instituted to punish the child for any offense but rather have the purpose of providing for the child's welfare. In this state the Legislature has specifically provided that a juvenile court proceeding shall not be deemed a criminal proceeding. * * *

The majority also note that "Section 602 is clearly distinguishable from sections 600 and 601 with respect to the consequences of their operation upon the child: upon the application of section 602, commitment of the youth to the custody of the California Youth Authority becomes far more likely." However, the Welfare and Institutions Code places restrictions on such a commitment, and where such a commitment is authorized it is only one of several possible alternatives. Under the circumstances the fact that Youth Authority commitment may be an alternative available for a minor found to be a person described by section 602 should not preclude holding subdivision One of section 26 is inapplicable in a juvenile court proceeding under section 602. * * *

Subdivision *Three* of Penal Code section 26 (insanity) has been held applicable in a juvenile court proceeding to determine whether a minor is a person described by section 602, but it does not follow that subdivision *One* of section 26 is likewise applicable in such a proceeding. Permitting the defense of insanity in such a proceeding does not deprive the minor of needed care, whereas holding subdivision One of section 26 applicable in such a proceeding can, as we have seen, deprive minors of needed care.

For the reasons above stated I would uphold the position of the Attorney General that subdivision One of section 26 is inapplicable in a juvenile court proceeding to determine whether a minor comes within section 602.

NOTES

1) Infancy and Juvenile Court Andrew M. Carter, *Age Matters: The Case for a Constitutionalized Infancy Defense*, 54 U. Kansas L. Rev. 687, 721 (2006), reports that "The issue of whether the infancy defense had any role to play in juvenile proceedings arose fairly quickly, and the decisions have almost uniformly resolved against recognition of the infancy defense in juvenile proceedings. Most of the decisions rest on the premise that the rehabilitative ideal and *parens patriae* doctrine upon which the juvenile court was founded are based, first and foremost, on the notion that the child is being helped not punished. As one of the early [1915] decisions explained, 'proceedings in the juvenile court are not criminal in their nature, and not instituted to punish the child for any offense. The purpose and end of such proceedings is to provide for the welfare of the child and to remove him from unpropitious surroundings.' Once criminal culpability and punishment were removed from the equation, the courts generally concluded that the capacity to form criminal intent—to know right from wrong—became irrelevant and the infancy defense, therefore, inapposite." Lara A. Bazelon, *Exploding the Superpredator Myth: Why Infancy is the Preadolescent's Best Defense in Juvenile Court*, 75 N.Y.U.L.Rev. 159, 162 (2000) describes three rationales courts use to deny juveniles the infancy defense in delinquency proceedings. "The Rehabilitation Theory dismisses the infancy defense as irrelevant in a civil and rehabilitative legal forum. The Procedural Policing Theory asserts that procedural safeguards for juveniles, mandated since the late 1960s by the United States Supreme Court, have made capacity findings an unnecessary additional protection. The Demarcation Theory claims that while a child's state of mind at the time of the offense is critical to a finding of guilt, a child's capacity to attach meaning and consequences to that offense is not."

The majority of appellate courts that have considered the continued vitality of the infancy defense have followed the rationale of *Tyvonne J.* and concluded that the juvenile court system supercedes it. In the absence of legislation codifying or adopting the defense, an immaturity or infancy defense is not available in juvenile court delinquency proceedings. *See e.g., Jennings v. State*, 384 So.2d 104 (Ala.1980); *Gammons v. Berlat*, 144 Ariz. 148, 696 P.2d 700 (1985); *State v. D.H.*, 340 So.2d 1163 (Fla.1976); *In re Michael*, 423 A.2d 1180, 1183 (R.I.1981) ("Once one accepts the principle that a finding of delinquency or waywardness in a juvenile proceeding is not the equivalent of finding that the juvenile has committed a crime, there is no necessity of a finding that the juvenile had such maturity that he or she knew what he or she was doing was wrong. A juvenile is delinquent * * * not because the juvenile has committed a crime, but because the juvenile has committed an act that would be a crime if committed by a person not a juvenile and because the juvenile requires 'such care, guidance and control as will serve the child's welfare and the best interests of the state.' "); *G.J.I. v.*

State, 778 P.2d 485, 487 (Okl.Cr.App. 1989) (juvenile has not "explained what would be accomplished by acknowledging this antiquated defense in a modern juvenile proceeding"). These courts conclude that because a delinquency adjudication is not a criminal conviction, it is unnecessary to determine whether the juvenile understood the moral implication of the behavior. Moreover, recognizing the defense could frustrate the remedial purposes of juvenile justice.

Sanford J. Fox, "Responsibility in the Juvenile Court," 11 *William and Mary Law Review* 659 at 671 (1970), questions the *Gladys R.* majority's reasoning. "If there is anything to the supposition that legislative supporters of the original juvenile court law were genuinely concerned with helping children in trouble, then it makes little sense to attribute to them the simultaneous intent to insulate these same children from the help by means of a § 26(1) defense. Those legislators would hardly have thought of the helping facilities, such as reform schools, as being of the same repressive and punitive nature that the majority of the court seems to assume them to be. It is difficult to avoid concluding that the matter of legislative intent is little more than a crutch to support the policy decision the court had arrived at through other means." What is the majority's policy decision to which Fox refers?

Cesar C. Sarmiento, "Penal Code Section 26(1): Rebuttable Presumption of a Juvenile's Incapacity to Commit a Crime—A Necessary Statute?," 12 *U. Cal. Davis. L. Rev.* 885, 889–90 (1979) contends that "[S]ection 26(1) is obsolete. Under the common law criminal system, the fact that courts punished children and adults alike, made the presumption regarding capacity a necessary safeguard. Today, however, the criminal justice system treats adults and children separately. The state deals with juvenile offenders under the age of eighteen exclusively within the juvenile system absent extraordinary circumstances to warrant transferring the offender to the adult criminal system. * * * The reason for this dual system is identical to the reason for the common law presumption of incapacity incorporated in Section 26(1): the criminal system should base punishment on culpability and since children are less mature than adults, they should receive different treatment. Using separate courts permits the juvenile system to provide treatment more suitable to juveniles. For example, juvenile delinquents are not subject to the same penal institutions as adults; a juvenile court hearing is informal and non-criminal in nature; a juvenile delinquent is not subject to capital punishment; and the public is excluded from the juvenile court proceeding." Similarly, Andrew Walkover, "The Infancy Defense in the New Juvenile Court," 31 *U.C.L.A.L. Rev.* 503, 516–571 (1984), observes that "[b]ecause *parens patriae* theory depends on the notion that the child is being helped and thus is not being tried for a crime and punished as a criminal, there was no need to determine whether the child had the capacity to act in a culpable fashion. Indeed, assertion of the defense could be viewed as wrongfully precluding treatment for those very children most susceptible to the benefits of intervention, children who had committed wrongs without a clear sense of the wrongfulness of their acts."

A few states follow *Gladys R.* and recognize the availability of an infancy defense that may defeat juvenile court jurisdiction. Those that find the infancy defense applicable to juvenile proceedings base their decisions on specific legislation adopting the defense, *e.g. State v. Q.D.*, 102 Wash.2d 19, 685 P.2d 557 (1984), or on a judicial determination that the true purpose of juvenile courts is not rehabilitation and treatment, but accountability and punishment, *e.g. In re William A.*, 313 Md. 690, 548 A.2d 130, 133 (1988) ("* * * [J]uvenile statutes typically require, for a delinquency adjudication, that the child commit an act which constitutes a crime if committed by an adult, and if the child lacks capacity to have the requisite mens rea for a particular crime, he has not committed an act amounting to a crime.")

2) Infancy and Problems of Proof The Supreme Court of Washington in *State v. J.P.S.*, 135 Wash.2d 34, 954 P.2d 894, 896–897 (1998), discussed how the state may rebut the statutory presumption that children older than eight years but younger than twelve-years-of age lacked criminal capacity. "[T]he State has the burden to rebut the presumption of incapacity by clear and convincing evidence. * * * The legal test is whether J.P.S. had knowledge of the wrongfulness of the act at the time he committed the offense and not that he realized it was wrong after the fact. Capacity must be found to exist separate from any mental element of the offense. Capacity is not an element of the crime; rather it is a general determination that the child understood the act and its wrongfulness. * * * The following factors may be relevant in determining whether a child knew the act he or she committed was wrong: (1) the nature of the crime; (2) the child's age and maturity; (3) whether the child showed a desire for secrecy; (4) whether the child admonished the victim not to tell; (5) prior conduct similar to that charged; (6) any consequences that attached to the conduct; and (7) acknowledgment that the behavior was wrong and could lead to detention. Also relevant is testimony from those acquainted with the child and the testimony of experts. A child's age, maturity, experience, and understanding may all be relevant in deciding if a given child had knowledge of the act's wrongfulness at the time it was committed."

Should it matter whether or not a youth intends to do harm? Isn't it sufficient that eight-year-old Tyvonne brought a pistol to school? Or, that a youth hurt someone or took their property? Of what relevance is Oliver Wendell Holmes' famous dictum that "even a dog can tell the difference between being stumbled over and being kicked" to the question of whether or not juveniles should enjoy the infancy defense?

3) Academic Commentary Unlike the majority of state courts, most academic commentators argue that state law should allow delinquents to assert an infancy defense. *See e.g.,* James C. Weissman, "Toward an Integrated Theory of Delinquency Responsibility," 60 *Denver Law Journal* 486 (1983); Andrew Walkover, "The Infancy Defense in the New Juvenile Court," 31 *U. C. L. A. Law Review* 503 (1984); Sanford J. Fox, "Responsibility in the Juvenile Court," 11 *William and Mary Law Review* 659 (1970); Francis Barry McCarthy, "The Role of the Concept of Responsibility in Juvenile Delinquency Proceedings," 10 *U. Michigan J. Law Reform* 181 (1977). Some conclude that the distinctions between rehabilitative treatment in a juvenile court and punishment in a criminal court are insufficient to justify denial of the defense. Others contend that even rehabilitative treatment still constitutes coercive interference with liberty.

4) Criminal Court Sentences of Juveniles If a youth fourteen years of age or older knows "right from wrong," that is, possesses the requisite *mens rea*, then at common law, a court could find a juvenile just as criminally responsible as any adult offender facing the same charges. In the *mens rea*-as-capacity formulation, if one is criminally responsible for making blameworthy choices, then one deserves the same punishment as any other criminal actor making comparable choices. *Mens rea* as a criminal law grading principle is characteristically binary; it is either present or not. In theory, no special doctrinal protections operate for youths older than fourteen who are tried in criminal courts absent some "diminished responsibility" doctrine. Peter Arenella, "The Diminished Capacity and Diminished Responsibility Defenses: Two Children of a Doomed Marriage," 77 *Columbia Law Rev.* 827 (1977); Stephen Morse, "Undiminished Confusion in Diminished Capacity," 75 *J. Crim. L. & Criminology* 1 (1984). If most youths "know right from wrong" by age fourteen, what justifies extending immunity from criminal consequences to ages sixteen, seventeen, or eighteen, rather than the common law rebuttable ages of seven to fourteen? In short, why a separate juvenile court? And if the rationale of reduced culpability apply to older juveniles, then why do criminal courts disregard "youthfulness as a mitigating factor" when they convict and sentence transferred juveniles.

The issues of criminal capacity have special importance for youths older than fourteen years of age. Waiver of juveniles to criminal courts for sentencing as adults implicates legal and cultural understandings of juveniles' criminal responsibility. As we explore more fully in Chapter 6, waiver laws that exclude even young offenders from juvenile court jurisdiction exposes some youths to life without parole sentences for crimes they committed at thirteen or fourteen years of age. Such draconian sentences challenge the social construction of adolescence and the idea that juveniles are less criminally responsible than adults.

The Minnesota Supreme Court in **State v. Mitchell**, 577 N.W.2d 481 (Minn.1998), addressed the constitutionality of sentencing a 15–year–old child to life imprisonment without the possibility of parole for 30 years:

> The Supreme Court has held that life imprisonment without the possibility of parole for cocaine possession is not cruel and unusual. *Michigan v. Harmelin*, (1991). Further, the Supreme Court has concluded that it is cruel and unusual punishment to sentence a 15–year–old to death. *Thompson v. Oklahoma* (1988) (plurality).

> We have repeatedly made clear that "[t]he severity of criminal sanctions is a legislative concern. A lawmaking body is equipped to weigh the policy considerations involved and determine what sanctions, if any, serve the interests of the people it represents." In this case, the legislature has determined that a person convicted of first-degree murder is to receive a mandatory life sentence with a minimum of 30 years. Once the juvenile court has waived jurisdiction, the state is to "proceed with the case as if the jurisdiction of the juvenile court had never attached." Further, the sentencing guidelines provide that sentences apply with the same presumptive force to a child who has been certified as an adult as they would to one who was 18 or older at the time of the crime.

Nevertheless, a legislatively-mandated punishment cannot stand if it is cruel or unusual in violation of the Minnesota Constitution.

Generally, when determining whether a punishment is cruel or unusual, this court focuses on the proportionality of the crime to the punishment. The Supreme Court, in deciding whether punishment is cruel and unusual, asks if the punishment comports with the "evolving standards of decency that mark the progress of a maturing society." Evolving standards of decency were crucial in *Thompson v. Oklahoma*, when the Court found that the execution of a 15–year–old is "now generally abhorrent to the conscience of the community." * * *

[W]e must analyze whether such a sentence [of mandatory life imprisonment] as applied to a 15–year–old child is unusual. Only one federal court has addressed the specific issue of whether it is cruel and unusual punishment under the federal constitution to sentence a 15–year–old to life imprisonment without the possibility of parole. * * * [In] *Harris v. Wright*, [see p. 677, *infra*], the Ninth Circuit Court of Appeals examined the issue across the country. The *Harris* court cited to the defendant's brief which stated that there are two states with statutes that explicitly preclude mandatory adult sentences for children below the age of 16, two states where the high courts have prohibited mandatory life sentences for children, 26 states which do not punish anyone with mandatory life sentences without the possibility of parole, and at least 21 states that do sentence 15–year–old children to life imprisonment without the possibility of parole. The court used this information to conclude that no consensus exists among the states, and thus such a sentence does not offend evolving standards of decency nationwide. * * *

Unless there is a fundamental right at issue, judicial scrutiny of state legislation under substantive due process is not exacting. This court has held that no person, regardless of age, has the right to a juvenile disposition. Likewise, there is no fundamental right to have age considered in adult sentencing. When there is no fundamental right at issue, substantive due process requires only that a statute "not be arbitrary or capricious or, stated another way, that [it] be a reasonable means to a permissive object." We have held that the automatic certification of a 16–year–old indicted for first-degree murder without a hearing did not violate substantive due process. We have also held that a mandatory life sentence for first-degree murder does not violate substantive due process, even though such a sentence does not allow the district court to consider mitigating factors. * * *

[W]e would prefer that the legislature provide the courts with the option to treat children differently than adults. * * * [W]e find no constitutional violation in the child's sentence, but we are sympathetic to the concern expressed by the district court judge who sentenced Mitchell when he stated that there should have been a "middle ground." * * * Because he was certified as an adult, Mitchell must serve a mandatory minimum of 30 years, and may serve up to a life term in prison.

Chapter 6 examines in greater depth the issues associated with youths transferred to criminal courts for trial and sentencing as adults.

5) Developmental Psychology and Adolescent Criminal Responsibility: What Do Kids Know and When Do they Know It? Developmental psychological research sponsored by the MacArthur Foundation provides a scientific foundation for distinctions between how adolescents and adults think based on differences in maturity of judgment, temperance, attitudes toward risk, and the like. *See e.g.*, Elizabeth Scott, N. Dickon Reppucci, and Jennifer L. Woolard, "Evaluating Adolescent Decision Making in Legal Contexts," 19 *Law and Human Behavior* 221 (1995); Elizabeth Scott, "Judgment and Reasoning in Adolescent Decision-making," 37 *Villanova Law Review* 1607 (1992); Lawrence Steinberg and Elizabeth Cauffman, "Maturity of Judgment in Adolescence: Psychosocial Factors in Adolescent Decision-making, 20 *Law and Human Behavior*" 249 (1996); Elizabeth Cauffman and Laurence Steinberg, "The Cognitive and Affective Influences on Adolescent Decision–Making," 68 *Temple L. Rev.* 1763 (1995); Elizabeth S. Scott and Thomas Grisso, "The Evolution of Adolescence: A Developmental Perspective on Juvenile Justice Reform," 88 *J. Crim. L. & Criminology* 137 (1997); Elizabeth S. Scott and Laurence Steinberg, *Rethinking Juvenile Justice* (2008).

The following excerpt from **Elizabeth S. Scott and Laurence Steinberg, "Blaming Youth," 81** *Tex. L. Rev.* **799, 801, 811–821, 829–35 (2003),** summarizes developmental psychological research on adolescent reasoning and maturity of judgment:

Using the tools of developmental psychology, we examine two important dimensions of adolescence that distinguish this group from adults in ways that are important to criminal culpability. First, the scientific evidence indicates that teens are simply less competent decision-makers than adults, largely because typical features of adolescent psycho-social development contribute to immature judgment. Adolescent capacities for autonomous choice, self-management, risk perception and calculation of future consequences are deficient as compared to those of adults, and these traits influence decision-making in ways that can lead to risky conduct. Second, adolescence is a developmental period in which personal identity and character are in flux, and begin to take shape through a process of exploration and experimentation. Youthful involvement in crime is often a part of this process, and, as such, it reflects the values and preferences of a transitory stage, rather than those of an individual with a settled identity. Most young law violators do not become adult criminals, because their youthful choices are shaped by factors and processes that are peculiar to (and characteristic of) adolescence. * * *

Adolescent decision-making capacity is diminished as compared to adults due to psycho-social immaturity. At the same time, the scientific evidence suggests that most young lawbreakers are "ordinary" persons (and quite different from typical adult criminals) in that normal developmental forces drive their criminal conduct. This is important in two ways. First, ordinary adolescents are more vulnerable than are adults to exogenous pressures that can lead to criminal conduct. Further, an important source of mitigation in criminal law—evidence that the criminal act did not derive from bad moral character—is as applicable to youths as to upstanding adults who act aberrantly. * * *

In order to construct a modern juvenile justice framework, we first examine the attributes of childhood and adolescence that distinguish young offenders from their adult counterparts in ways that are relevant to their criminal choices. Scientists who study adolescence view this stage as a bridge between childhood and adulthood—a period during which various decision-making capacities develop, although not at a uniform rate. By mid-adolescence, cognitive capacities for reasoning and understanding are probably close to those of adults, although teens are likely less skilled in using these capacities to make real-life decisions. In psycho-social development, however, teens mature more slowly. This contributes to what in common parlance would be called immature judgment—the tendency of adolescents to make choices that may be harmful to themselves or others. The ways in which psycho-social factors influence decision-making and the kinds of choices adolescents make depend, in part, on the social context in which they find themselves. Adolescence is also a stage of individuation and identity formation, processes closely linked to psycho-social development. Individuals do not develop a coherent sense of identity until young adulthood, and adolescence is characterized by exploration, experimentation, and fluctuations in self-image. This movement from a fluid and embryonic sense of identity to one that is more stable and well-developed includes developments in the realms of morality, values, and beliefs.

In this Part, we examine the dimensions of psychological and social development that provide the basis of our claim that adolescent involvement in crime differs from that of adults in ways that are important to assessments of culpability. First, several features of cognitive and psycho-social development in adolescence undermine competent decision-making and distinguish youths from adults. Second, the relationship between psycho-social development and the forming of personal identity in adolescence is important to understanding unique features of youthful criminal activity. Our analysis explains that typical adolescent criminal conduct is qualitatively different from that of adults because it is driven by developmental forces that are constitutive of this developmental stage.

A. *Cognitive and Psycho–Social Development*

Understanding and Reasoning.—The most familiar factors related to decision-making capacity are reasoning and understanding, basic elements of cognitive development. These capacities increase through childhood into adolescence; thus, pre-adolescents and younger teens differ substantially from adults in their cognitive abilities (although there is great variability among individuals). These developments, described in rich detail by Jean Piaget and subsequent researchers in cognitive development, are undergirded by increases in specific and general knowledge gained through education and experience, and by improvements in basic information-processing skills, including attention, short-and long-term memory, and organization.

By mid-adolescence, tentative scientific evidence supports the claim that adolescents' capacities for understanding and reasoning in making decisions roughly approximate those of adults. These findings from laboratory studies are only modestly useful, however, in understanding how youths compare to adults in making choices that have salience to their lives or that are presented in stressful unstructured settings (such as the street) in which decision-makers must rely on personal experience and knowledge. For these reasons, it remains uncertain whether adolescent cognitive capacity—as it affects choices relevant to criminal conduct—is comparable to that of adults.

Judgment Factors in Decision-making.—Psycho-social development proceeds more slowly than cognitive development. As a consequence, even when adolescent cognitive capacities approximate those of adults, youthful decision-making may still differ due to immature judgment. The psycho-social factors most relevant to differences in judgment include: (a) peer orientation, (b) attitudes toward and perception of risk, (c) temporal perspective, and (d) capacity for self-management. While cognitive capacities shape the process of decision-making, immature judgment can affect outcomes because these developmental factors influence adolescent values and preferences that drive the cost-benefit calculus in the making of choices.

Substantial research evidence supports the conventional wisdom that teens are more responsive to peer influence than are adults. Susceptibility to peer influence increases between childhood and early adolescence as adolescents begin to individuate from parental control. This susceptibility peaks around age fourteen and declines slowly during the high-school years. Peer influence affects adolescent judgment both directly and indirectly. In some contexts, adolescents might make choices in response to direct peer pressure. More indirectly, adolescents' desire for peer approval (and fear of rejection) affects their choices, even without direct coercion. Finally, peers may provide models for behavior that adolescents believe will assist them to accomplish their own ends.

Future orientation, the capacity and inclination to project events into the future, may also influence judgment, since it will affect the extent to which individuals consider the long-term consequences of their actions in making choices. Over an extended period between childhood and young adulthood, individuals become more future-oriented. Adolescents tend to discount the future more than adults do, and to weigh more heavily short-term consequences of decisions—both risks and benefits—in making choices. There are several plausible explanations for this age gap in future orientation. First, owing to cognitive limitations in their ability to think hypothetically, adolescents simply may be less able than adults to think about events that have not yet occurred (i.e., events that may occur sometime in the future). Second, adolescents' weaker future orientation may reflect their more limited life experience. For adolescents, a consequence five years in the future may seem very remote, while a short-term consequence may be valued disproportionately due to its immediacy.

Research evidence also suggests that adolescents differ from adults in their perception of, and attitude toward, risk. It is well established that adolescents and young adults generally take more health and safety risks than do older adults by engaging more frequently in behaviors such as unprotected sex, drunk driving, and criminal conduct. Moreover, a synergy likely exists between adolescent peer orientation and risk-taking; considerable evidence indicates that people generally make riskier decisions in groups than they do alone. In general, adolescents are less risk-averse than adults, generally weighing rewards more heavily than risks in making choices. In part, this may be due to limits on youthful time perspective; taking risks is more costly for those who focus on the future. Finally, adolescents may have different values and goals than do adults, leading them to calculate risks and rewards differently. For example, the danger of risk-taking could constitute a reward for an adolescent but a cost to an adult.

The widely held stereotype that adolescents are more impulsive than adults is supported by the relatively sparse research on developmental changes in impulsivity and self-management over the course of adolescence. In general, studies show gradual but steady increases in individuals' capacity for self-direction throughout the adolescent years, with gains continuing through the final years of high school. Impulsivity, as a general trait, increases between middle adolescence and early adulthood and declines there-after, as does sensation-seeking. Research also indicates that adolescents have more rapid and more extreme mood swings (both positive and negative) than adults, although the connection between moodiness and impulsivity is not clear. While more research is needed, the available evidence supports the notion that adolescents may have more difficulty regulating their moods, impulses, and behaviors than do adults.

Although most of the developmental research on cognitive and psycho-social functioning involves psychological studies, mounting evidence suggests that some of the differences between adults and adolescents have an organic dimension. Research on brain development, although in its early stages, indicates that regions of the brain implicated in processes of long-term planning, regulation of emotion, impulse control, and the evaluation of risk and reward continue to mature over the course of adolescence, and perhaps well into young adulthood. At puberty, changes in the limbic system—a part of the brain that is central in the processing and regulation of emotion—may stimulate adolescents to seek higher levels of novelty and to take more risks; these changes may also contribute to increased emotionality and vulnerability to stress. At the same time, patterns of development in the prefrontal cortex, which is active during the performance of complicated tasks involving plan-ning and decision-making, suggest that these higher-order cognitive capacities may be immature well into middle adolescence. One scientist has likened the psychological consequences of brain development in adolescence to "starting the engines without a skilled driver."

For most adolescents, the characteristic developmental influences on decision-making will change in predictable ways. As the typical adolescent matures into adulthood, he becomes a more experienced and competent decision-maker; susceptibility to peer influence attenuates, risk perception improves, risk averseness increases, time perspective expands to focus more on long-term consequences, and self-management improves. These develop-ments lead to changes in values and preferences. As adolescents become adults, they are likely to make different choices from their youthful selves, choices that reflect more mature judgment. * * *

[U]nlike adult criminals, adolescents usually commit crimes with peers, although the precise mechanisms by which peer orientation shapes criminal behavior are not well understood. Researchers have also linked desistance from crime in late adolescence to improved future orientation and to changing patterns of peer relationships. * * * As a general proposition, teens are inclined to engage in risky behaviors that reflect their immaturity of judgment. It seems very likely that the psycho-social influences shaping adolescents' decision-making in other settings contribute to their choices about criminal activity as well.

     2. *Psycho–Social Development in Social Context.*—The psycho-social factors that influence decision-making are an important component of youthful criminal choices. Whether teens become involved in crime, and what crimes they commit depend on other ingredients as well, including opportunity and social context. Adolescent peer orientation makes youths who live in high-crime neighborhoods susceptible to powerful pressures to join in criminal activity, and compliance may be more typical than resistance. * * * [S]trong social norms within urban adolescent male subcultures prescribe a set of attitudes and behaviors that often lead to violent crime. Moreover, avoiding confrontation when challenged by a rival results in a loss of social status and ostracism by peer affiliates, which in itself can create vulnerability to physical attack. * * * [O]rdinary youths in poor urban neighborhoods face coercive peer pressure and sometimes tangible threats that propel them to get involved in crime while making extrication difficult.

     The coercive impact of social context is exacerbated because adolescents are subject to legal and practical restrictions on their ability to escape these criminogenic settings. Financially dependent on their parents or guardians and subject to their legal authority, adolescents cannot escape their homes, schools, and neighborhoods. At least until age sixteen, a web of legal restrictions on their liberty prevents adolescents from doing what we might expect of an adult in the same context—move to another location in which the pressures to offend are lessened. Because adolescents lack legal and practical autonomy, they are in a real sense trapped in whatever social setting they occupy and are more restricted in their capacity to avoid coercive criminogenic influences than are adults.

B. The Formation of Personal Identity and Experimentation in Crime

     The emergence of personal identity is an important developmental function of adolescence, and one in which the aspects of psycho-social development discussed earlier play a key role. During this period, youths begin to separate from their parents and take steps toward an autonomous personhood. Developmental psychologists describe two interrelated processes: individuation (the process of establishing autonomy from one's parents), and identity development (the process of creating a coherent and integrated sense of self). A predictable developmental sequence can be described. Most pre-adolescents strive to please their parents and other adults by complying with their wishes and parroting adult beliefs and values. During early and middle adolescence, youths individuate from parents, a process that can involve a certain amount of risky behavior reflecting rebellion and a shift in orientation from parents to peers. By late adolescence, individuation is complete, autonomy from both parental and peer influence is achieved, and the individual is well on the way toward the establishment of personal identity.

Adolescence has often been described as a period of "identity crisis"—an ongoing struggle to achieve self-definition. According to developmental theory, the process of identity development is a lengthy one that involves considerable exploration and experimentation with different behaviors and identity "elements." These elements include both superficial characteristics, such as style of dress, appearance, or manner of speaking, and deeper phenomena, such as personality traits, attitudes, values, and beliefs. As the individual experiments, she gauges the reactions of others as well as her own satisfaction, and through a process of trial and error, over time selects and integrates the identity elements of a realized self. Not surprisingly, given adolescent risk preferences (perhaps combined with rebellion against parental values in the course of individuation), identity experimentation often involves risky, illegal, or dangerous activities—alcohol use, drug use, unsafe sex, delinquent conduct, and the like. For most teens, this experimentation is fleeting; it ceases with maturity as identity becomes settled. Only a relatively small proportion of adolescents who experiment in risky or illegal activities develop entrenched patterns of problem behavior that persist into adulthood. Thus, predicting the development of relatively more permanent and enduring traits on the basis of risky behavior patterns observed in adolescence is an uncertain business. * * *

This account of identity development in adolescence informs our understanding of patterns of criminal conduct among teens. Criminal behavior is rare in childhood and early adolescence. Onset typically occurs during a period in which adolescents separate from parents and parental influence, and become more focused on peers. The incidence of antisocial behavior increases through age sixteen and declines sharply from age seventeen onward. Most teenage males engage in some criminal activity; indeed, psychologist Terrie Moffitt describes it as "a normal part of teen life." However, only a small group of young offenders will persist in a life of crime. Based on these patterns, Moffitt offers a taxonomy of adolescent antisocial conduct, in which typical teenage lawbreakers are described as "adolescence-limited" offenders, while a much smaller group are described as "life-course-persistent" offenders. Most youths in the first group have little notable history of antisocial conduct in childhood, and, predictably, in late adolescence or early adulthood, they will "mature out" of their inclination to get involved in criminal activity. * * *

The upshot is that the criminal conduct of most young wrongdoers is quite different from that of typical adult criminals. It is fair to assume that most adults who engage in criminal conduct act upon subjectively defined preferences and values, and that their choices can fairly be charged to deficient moral character. This cannot fairly be said of the crimes of typical juvenile actors, whose choices, while unfortunate, are shaped by development factors that are constitutive of adolescence. To be sure, some adolescents may be in the early stages of developing a criminal identity and reprehensible moral character traits—Moffitt's "life-course-persistent" offenders—but most are not. The criminal choices of typical young offenders differ from those of adults, not only because the choice, qua choice, is deficient as the product of immature judgment, but also because the adolescent's criminal act does not express the actor's bad character. * * *

The differences that distinguish adolescents from adults are more subtle—mitigating, but not exculpatory. Most obviously, cognitive and psychosocial immaturity undermines youthful decision-making in ways that reduce culpability. Moreover, due to their immaturity, adolescents may be more vulnerable to coercive pressures than are adults. Finally because their criminal acts are influenced by normal developmental processes, typical adolescent law breakers are different from fully responsible adults whose crimes are assumed to be the product of bad moral character. Thus, young offenders are less culpable than adults because of their diminished capacity; but they are also appropriately identified with actors who succumb to coercive pressures or who demonstrate that their criminal acts were out of character, and who are less culpable because their responses are those of ordinary persons. * * *

Adolescent offenders indeed are different from the rest of us, but they (or most of them) are also ordinary persons—although not ordinary adults. This is not to say, of course, that all adolescents will commit crimes, or that those who do are without blame. It is to say, however, that those whom psychologists call normative adolescents may well succumb to the extraordinary pressures of a criminogenic social context. Beyond this, the typical adolescent can be distinguished from most criminals and aligned with ordinary persons whose crimes deserve less than full punishment, because his wrongful act does not derive from attitudes and values that are part of his continuing identity as a person; in other words, his crime is not an expression of bad character. Here again, immature youths are not like ordinary adults—fully realized selves who have internalized the law's values. Instead, adolescent crime is a costly manifestation of influences and processes that are characteristic of a discrete stage in human development. If we consider youthful culpability against the predicted responses of an "ordinary adolescent," the mitigating character of immaturity becomes clear. * * *

[A]dolescents in high crime neighborhoods are subject both to unique social pressures that induce them to join in criminal activity and to restrictions on their freedom that tangibly limit their ability to escape. These restrictions are constitutive of a well-defined legal status resulting from youthful dependency that substantially limits autonomy. Beyond this, ordinary adolescents lack the life skills and psycho-social capacities that would allow them to escape the extraordinary circumstances present in these social contexts. Indeed, ordinary adults might well succumb to the pressures. These circumstances are similar in kind to those involved in claims of duress, provocation, necessity, or domination by co-defendants, and appropriately are deemed mitigating of culpability. When adolescents cross the line to legal adulthood, the formal disabilities of youth are lifted; young adults can avoid the situational pressures they face by removing themselves from the criminogenic setting. Moreover, normal maturation enables individuals to cope with circumstances that are overwhelming in adolescence. Thus, adults have no claim of situational mitigation on the ground that they are restricted to a social setting in which avoiding crime is difficult.

The framework we employ for analyzing the culpability of juveniles in response to extraordinary circumstances uses as a baseline the reactions of ordinary adolescents. Under the conventional standard, criminal conduct is less culpable if an ordinary ("reasonable") person, with a typical set of adult psychological and moral capacities, might be led to respond similarly when subjected to the same unusual pressures as the wrongdoer. Yet, this baseline can be criticized for failing to accommodate responses to external pressures that are reasonable for adolescents. The psychological attributes that normal adolescents bring to their experience increase the challenges they face in responding to crime-inducing social contexts. The baseline adjustment clarifies that many adolescents responding to external circumstances, like ordinary adults who claim situational mitigation, can explain their criminal choices in terms of exogenous pressures rather than individual moral deficiency. * * *

The conclusion that blameworthiness decreases when actors can negate the inference that their bad acts reflect bad moral character has a broader importance in assessing the culpability of typical young offenders. * * * The criminal choice of the typical adolescent cannot be evaluated by comparing it to his previously established good character, because his personal identity and his character have not yet stabilized. Yet, like the adult actor who establishes mitigation, it can be said that the adolescent's harmful act does not express his bad character; indeed, it does not manifest "character" at all, but something else—in this case, developmental immaturity. Most youths will outgrow their inclination to get involved in crime and mature into persons who do not reject the law's values.

2. CRIMINAL LAW JURISPRUDENCE: INSANITY DEFENSE AND COMPETENCY DETERMINATIONS IN JUVENILE COURTS

"The mental health of a juvenile is relevant to a number of issues in a delinquency proceeding. The juvenile or family court judge, for example, may wish to know about prior mental health treatment, the youth's social and emotional maturity, the school placement or special needs of the juvenile, and any other indications of a mental disorder, either currently or at the time of the offense. The juvenile's mental health may affect the court's judgment on appropriateness of transfer to adult court or various dispositional placements. It may also influence the juvenile's ability to waive certain pretrial rights such as the right to remain silent during custodial interrogation, capacity to assist the lawyer or to participate in the defense of the charges, ability to make decisions about trial rights, and even responsibility for the delinquent behavior." Lynda E. Frost and Robert E. Shepherd, Jr., "Mental Health Issues in Juvenile Delinquency Proceedings," 11 *Criminal Justice* 52 (Fall, 1996). In particular, a juvenile's mental health may affect the ability of the court to adjudicate a youth delinquent—the insanity defense—or even to conduct a trial—competency to stand trial.

a. Insanity

COMMONWEALTH v. CHATMAN

260 Va. 562, 538 S.E.2d 304 (Va. 2000).

KINSER, JUSTICE. In this appeal, we address a question of first impression in this Commonwealth, whether a 13–year–old juvenile has either a constitutional or statutory right to assert an insanity defense at the adjudicatory phase of a juvenile delinquency proceeding. Because we conclude that a juvenile does not have that right in such proceedings under either the Due Process Clause of the Fourteenth Amendment or the statutes of this Commonwealth, we will reverse the judgment of the Court of Appeals holding that the availability of the insanity defense in such juvenile proceedings is essential to due process. * * *

In the circuit court, Chatman moved for a psychiatric evaluation to determine whether he was insane at the time of the offense. In support of his motion, Chatman asserted that he "has a long history of mental illness and seeks a psychiatric evaluation to establish an insanity defense." He alleged that on the day of the offense, a medical doctor examined him and opined that Chatman displayed homicidal ideations. Chatman further alleged that a licensed clinical psychologist evaluated him two days after the offense and diagnosed a "Schizophreniform Disorder."

At a hearing on Chatman's motion, the Commonwealth did not contest that Chatman's alleged mental problems would entitle him to a psychiatric evaluation to determine his sanity at the time of the offense if he were an adult. However, the Commonwealth argued that, as a 13–year–old juvenile, Chatman had neither a due process right under the Fourteenth Amendment of the Constitution of the United States nor a statutory right to assert an insanity defense at the adjudicatory phase of a juvenile delinquency proceeding. The circuit court agreed with the Commonwealth and denied the motion. After a bench trial, [the court found the defendant delinquent].

Chatman then petitioned the Court of Appeals for an appeal from the circuit court's judgment. * * * The Court of Appeals acknowledged that the provisions of the Code pertaining to the juvenile and domestic relations district courts do not expressly provide for or prohibit an insanity defense by a juvenile at an adjudicatory hearing. However, the court found "no reasonable basis for concluding that an insanity defense is unavailable to a juvenile at a proceeding to adjudicate him or her delinquent as it would be to an adult defendant in a criminal trial." The Court of Appeals concluded that "the right to assert an insanity defense is an essential of 'due process and fair treatment' which is required at a juvenile delinquency adjudication."

The Commonwealth petitioned the Court of Appeals for rehearing and also requested a rehearing en banc. The Court of Appeals denied both petitions, and we awarded the Commonwealth this appeal. * * *

Although the Court of Appeals based its decision on the Due Process Clause of the Fourteenth Amendment, the Commonwealth argues that Chatman has neither a constitutional nor a statutory right to raise an insanity defense. These are the two sources upon which Chatman relies to assert that he has such a right. Consequently, we will address the arguments *seriatim.*

In Virginia, we have recognized the defense of insanity as set forth in *M'Naghten's Case.* Under the *M'Naghten* definition, an accused must establish that he or she did not know the difference between right and wrong, or that he or she did not understand the nature and consequences of the acts in question. If a defendant relies on the defense of insanity, the burden rests on the defendant "to prove to the satisfaction of the jury" that he or she was insane at the time of the offense.

Chatman asserts that he has a right under the Due Process Clause of the Fourteenth Amendment to assert this insanity defense. Relying on the decisions of the Supreme Court in *In re Gault,* and *In re Winship,* Chatman argues that "the right to present an insanity defense goes to fundamental due process fairness and is not one of those rights that can be withheld from him."

The Commonwealth, however, disagrees and argues that, since the Constitution does not require states to recognize an insanity defense for adults charged with committing criminal acts, *see Medina v. California,* (1992), *Powell v. Texas,* (1968), it follows that a juvenile likewise does not have a right under the Due Process Clause to assert such a defense in a delinquency proceeding. The Commonwealth contends that, even if the insanity defense were constitutionally guaranteed in adult criminal trials, the right to raise the defense would nonetheless still not apply in juvenile delinquency proceedings. Continuing, the Commonwealth asserts that, in contrast to those rights that were afforded to juveniles in *Gault* and *Winship,* the insanity defense is not fundamental to the factfinding process because sanity, unlike *mens rea,* is not an element of the offense. We agree with the Commonwealth's position.

The question in *Powell* was whether a conviction for public drunkenness violates the Cruel and Unusual Punishment Clause of the Eighth Amendment. In analyzing that question, the plurality's opinion addressed the role of the states vis-a-vis the Supreme Court in developing common law concepts to assess an individual's accountability for criminal acts:
* * *

> Nothing could be less fruitful than for this Court to be impelled into defining some sort of insanity test in constitutional terms.... If a person in the 'condition' of being a chronic alcoholic cannot be criminally punished as a constitutional matter for being drunk in public, it would seem to follow that a person who contends that, in terms of one test, 'his unlawful act was the product of mental disease or mental defect,' would state an issue of constitutional dimension with regard to his criminal responsibility had he been tried under

some different and perhaps lesser standard, *e.g.,* the right-wrong test of *M'Naghten's Case.*

Twenty-four years later in *Medina,* the view expressed in *Powell* concerning the role of the states in developing certain doctrines was expressed more succinctly with regard to the insanity defense. The Court in *Medina* stated, "while the Due Process Clause affords an incompetent defendant the right not to be tried, we have not said that the Constitution requires the States to recognize the insanity defense."[3]

The Court of Appeals did not discuss the decisions in *Powell* or *Medina.* Nor did it acknowledge the fact that the Supreme Court has never held that the Due Process Clause requires states to recognize the defense of insanity for an adult accused of committing a crime. * * * Neither the Court of Appeals nor Chatman has explained why a 13–year-old juvenile should be granted a right under the Due Process Clause in a proceeding to adjudicate delinquency when that right is not constitutionally mandated for adults in criminal proceedings to adjudicate their guilt or innocence.[4]

The plurality in *Powell* recognized the difficulties in elevating the opportunity to assert an insanity defense to a right of constitutional dimensions. Not all states that allow a defendant to raise an insanity defense utilize the *M'Naghten* test for insanity. Thus, if due process includes the right to assert the defense of insanity, the Supreme Court would "be impelled into defining some sort of insanity test in constitutional terms." But, as the plurality said, "formulating a constitutional rule would reduce, if not eliminate, [the] fruitful experimentation [with different standards], and freeze the developing productive dialogue between law and psychiatry into a rigid constitutional mold."

Thus, we conclude that the Court of Appeals erred in holding that the circuit court violated Chatman's due process rights when it denied his motion for a psychiatric evaluation, thereby preventing him from asserting an insanity defense at the adjudicatory proceeding on the petition charging Chatman with delinquency.

Having disposed of Chatman's constitutional claim, we now turn to his argument that he also has a statutory right to raise an insanity defense. * * *

We begin the statutory analysis by reviewing the provisions of the Code pertaining to the adjudication and disposition of a 13–year-old juvenile charged with delinquency. A "[d]elinquent child" is defined as "a child who has committed a delinquent act." A "[d]elinquent act" is "an

---

3. However, the Supreme Court has held that an incompetent defendant has a right under the Due Process Clause not to be tried. *Drope v. Missouri,* (1975); *Pate v. Robinson,* (1966). The General Assembly has established a procedure to determine if a juvenile is unable to understand the pending proceedings or to assist an attorney in a defense.

4. The fact that the General Assembly has created a statutory mechanism for an adult to assert an insanity defense in a criminal proceeding does not transform the insanity defense into a constitutional right for either adults or juveniles. Chatman has not argued that he has a right under the Equal Protection Clause to raise an insanity defense.

act designated a crime under the law of this Commonwealth...." When a juvenile is found to be delinquent, the juvenile court or the circuit court has several available options with regard to making "orders of disposition for [the juvenile's] supervision, care and rehabilitation." One of those options, which is relevant to the present case, is to commit a juvenile who has been adjudicated delinquent to an appropriate hospital ... when the court "reasonably believes" that the juvenile is mentally ill. The court's authority ... is, however, predicated upon a finding of delinquency. * * *

Notably, in contrast to the specific statutory provisions dealing with a juvenile's incompetence to stand trial, the Code does not contain any provision allowing the use of an insanity defense at the adjudicatory phase of a delinquency proceeding. Instead, the General Assembly elected to make a juvenile's mental illness or insanity a factor to be considered during disposition *after* the juvenile had been adjudicated delinquent. * * *

Nevertheless, Chatman contends that the provisions * * * should be interpreted as applying to juveniles during an adjudication of delinquency. In response, the Commonwealth points out that, under the provisions pertaining to the disposition of persons acquitted by reason of insanity, it is possible to have an indeterminate period of commitment for inpatient treatment. Because of this possibility, the Commonwealth reasons that those provisions cannot apply to juveniles because the juvenile and domestic relations district courts do not have jurisdiction over a juvenile beyond the juvenile's 21st birthday. We agree with the Commonwealth.

When a defendant is acquitted by reason of insanity at the time of the offense, the court must place the acquittee in the temporary custody of the Commissioner of Mental Health for an evaluation to determine whether that acquittee can be released or requires commitment. If an acquittee is mentally ill and in need of inpatient hospitalization, the court must commit the acquittee. When an acquittee is committed for inpatient hospitalization, the committing court must conduct periodic assessments of the confined acquittee's continuing need for such treatment. As the Commonwealth points out, the provisions of the Code dealing with the disposition of persons acquitted by reason of insanity do not, however, limit the length of time that an acquittee can be confined for inpatient treatment. Thus, it is conceivable that an acquittee could be confined for inpatient treatment for many years or for the remainder of his or her life, if the acquittee continues to be mentally ill and in need of inpatient treatment.

However, the juvenile and domestic relations district courts retain jurisdiction over a juvenile only until that juvenile attains the age of 21 years. Thus, if the statutory scheme governing the disposition of persons acquitted by reason of insanity were available to a 13–year–old juvenile, that scheme's indeterminate period of commitment for inpatient hospitalization could run afoul of the limited duration of the juvenile and domestic relations district courts' jurisdiction. If the General Assembly had intended for a juvenile such as Chatman to assert an insanity defense * * *, we believe that it would have resolved this conflict. Thus, we conclude that Chatman does not have a statutory right to raise the defense of insanity at the adjudicatory phase of his delinquency proceeding.

For these reasons, we will reverse the judgment of the Court of Appeals and reinstate the judgment of the circuit court adjudicating Chatman to be delinquent.

K<small>OONTZ</small>, J<small>USTICE</small>, dissenting. Today a majority of this Court permits Christopher Chatman, a 13–year–old juvenile who well may not have known the difference between right and wrong or not have understood the nature and consequences of his act, to be adjudicated a delinquent. * * * The majority permits this child to be adjudicated and committed by the trial court because it concludes that a 13–year–old child does not have a right to assert an insanity defense at the adjudicatory phase of a juvenile delinquency proceeding under either the Due Process Clause of the Fourteenth Amendment or the statutes of this Commonwealth. The majority permits this child to be so treated even though it acknowledges that this Court has recognized the defense of insanity for adults, under the so-called M'Naghten Rule, since 1871. * * *

The Court of Appeals properly noted that "the * * * [the juvenile code] does not expressly provide for or prohibit an insanity defense at either an adjudicatory hearing in [juvenile] court or in an appeal to the circuit court upon a finding of delinquency." After referencing the various statutes that provide the mechanism for a criminal defendant to raise and prove an insanity defense * * * the Court of Appeals found "no reasonable basis for concluding that an insanity defense is unavailable to a juvenile at a proceeding to adjudicate him or her delinquent as it would be to an adult defendant in a criminal trial." The Court further concluded that "the right to assert an insanity defense is an essential of 'due process and fair treatment' which is required at a juvenile delinquency adjudication." The Court expressly noted that because Chatman was not yet 14 years of age at the time the charged offense was committed, he could not have been tried as an adult in the circuit court. Finally, the Court also noted that it expressed no opinion regarding Chatman's disposition in the event he were to be found not guilty by reason of insanity.

Upon appeal to this Court, the majority carefully limits its holding to apply only to a juvenile under age 14. Undoubtedly this is so because under the pertinent statutory scheme age 14 is the critical age in determining whether a juvenile may be tried as an adult and under certain circumstances sentenced to incarceration as an adult. The apparent significance of making this careful distinction in the majority's analysis between age 13 and age 14 is that presumably there would be no question that when a juvenile 14 years old or older is tried as an adult, such a juvenile would have the same right as an adult to assert a defense of insanity to the charged offense.

The majority concludes that "the General Assembly elected to make a juvenile's mental illness or insanity a factor to be considered during the [dispositional phase and] *after* the juvenile had been adjudicated delinquent." This statute, however, specifically addresses a case where the juvenile court "reasonably believes" that a juvenile "*is* mentally ill or mentally retarded." Clearly this statute addresses the court's dispositional options with regard to a juvenile's mental condition *at the time of the proceeding;* the insanity defense, in sharp contrast, addresses the juvenile's mental condition *at the time the charged offense was committed.* Thus, under the majority's analysis, where a 13–year–old juvenile is proven to be insane at the time he or she committed the charged offense, but not mentally ill at the time of the adjudicatory hearing regarding that offense, that juvenile may nevertheless be adjudicated a delinquent. Surely there can be no such offense as being delinquent by reason of being insane.

The United States Supreme Court's statement that "while the Due Process Clause affords an incompetent defendant the right not to be tried . . ., we have not said that the Constitution requires the States to recognize the insanity defense," *Medina v. California,* is not dispositive of the issue whether a 13–year–old juvenile has the right to assert that defense in this Commonwealth. Under well-established principles, that holding does not prevent this Commonwealth from extending the right to assert the insanity defense both to adults and to all juveniles as a matter of state law. And in doing so, the Commonwealth is free, for purposes of state law, to find that "fundamental fairness" requires that both adults and juveniles be permitted to assert this defense. In my view, the General Assembly, relying upon this Court's long recognition of the insanity defense without express limitation to the age of the accused, also has not limited or restricted this defense to cases involving adults charged with criminal acts.

The pertinent statutes * * * provide the mechanism for a criminal defendant to raise and prove an insanity defense. The right to assert that defense, however, arises from this Court's recognition of that right as a matter of the common law of this Commonwealth unless otherwise limited or restricted by statute. Code implicitly acknowledges the right for a juvenile to assert the insanity defense in the adjudicatory phase of the juvenile court proceeding. The statute provides, in pertinent part, that "[i]n *any case* in which *a person* charged with a crime intends . . . to put in issue his insanity at the time of the crime charged . . . he, or his counsel, shall give notice in writing to the attorney for the Commonwealth. . . ." The broad language in this statute does not limit its application to proceedings involving adult defendants. A juvenile, even one 13 years old, is "a person." * * * In addition, because the insanity defense has been recognized as a part of the common law of this Commonwealth and has been deeply engrained in the practice of criminal law here since 1871, we can assume that the General Assembly intended "fair treatment" for both adults and juveniles * * * and, thus, used the term "person" in this statute to accomplish that purpose.

Admittedly, it is mere speculation as to whether Chatman could successfully establish his insanity at the time of the charged offense. * * * There is, however, a significant difference between the existence of the right for the juvenile to assert an insanity defense on the one hand, and, on the other, in what manner the juvenile court upon acquitting the juvenile by reason of his or her insanity would apply the statutory provisions for the treatment of a person so acquitted.

The answer to the "conflict" which the majority perceives in this statutory scheme, in my view, is that the acquitted juvenile would remain committed until his or her 21st birthday only if he or she remained mentally ill. Upon reaching his or her 21st birthday the acquitted juvenile would have to be released absent any further action by the Commonwealth. In that regard, nothing would prohibit the Commissioner of Mental Health into whose custody the juvenile was originally committed, to file a petition in the appropriate court to have the person recommitted. * * *

For these reasons, in my view, the Court of Appeals properly determined that Chatman was entitled to a mental health evaluation in anticipation of asserting an insanity defense. Accordingly, I would affirm the judgment of the Court of Appeals.

NOTES

1) Constitutional or Statutory Right to an Insanity Defense In contrast with *Chatham*, the Louisiana Supreme Court in *In the Interest of Causey*, 363 So.2d 472 (La.1978), concluded that the "right" to an "insanity defense" is a "fundamental" one:

> [W]e granted certiorari to determine whether a juvenile has a right to plead not guilty by reason of insanity. * * * There is no statutory right to plead not guilty by reason of insanity in a Louisiana juvenile proceeding, since such proceedings are conducted as civil proceedings, with certain enumerated differences. We hold, however, that the due process guaranties of the Fourteenth Amendment to the United States Constitution, and of Article I, Section 2 of the Louisiana Constitution, require that a juvenile be granted this right. * * *
>
> The insanity defense, and the underlying notion that an accused must understand the nature of his acts in order to be criminally responsible (the *Mens rea* concept), are deeply rooted in our legal tradition and philosophy. We deem it clear * * * that the due process-fundamental fairness concepts of our state and federal constitutions would be violated, at least in adult prosecutions for crimes requiring intent, if an accused were denied the right to plead the insanity defense.
>
> However, not every constitutional right guaranteed to adults by the concept of fundamental fairness is automatically guaranteed to juveniles. The United States Supreme Court has undertaken a case-by-case analysis

of juvenile proceedings, making not only the historical inquiry into whether the rights asserted were part of fundamental fairness, but also a functional analysis of whether giving the particular right in question to the juvenile defendant would interfere with any of the beneficial aspects of a juvenile proceeding. Only those rights that are both "fundamental" and "essential," in that they perform a function too important to sacrifice in favor of the benefits theoretically afforded by a civil-style juvenile proceeding, have been held to be required in such proceedings. * * *

The availability of some procedure for differentiating between those who are culpably responsible for their act and those who are merely ill is, as we have seen, a part of "fundamental fairness." Moreover, it is hard to see that any important aim of the juvenile system is thwarted by affording such a distinction to the mentally ill juvenile.

The function of the insanity plea is much more akin to that of the burden of proof imposed on juvenile proceedings in *Winship*, than of the jury trial involved in *McKeiver* and *Dino*. An insanity defense, like a high burden of proof, will generically spell the difference between conviction and acquittal. * * * The right to plead insanity, absent some other effective means of distinguishing mental illness from moral culpability, is also fundamental. There is no compelling reason to deny either of these constitutional rights to juveniles charged with conduct that would be serious crimes if committed by adults. * * *

See generally, Emily S. Pollock, "Those Crazy Kids: Providing the Insanity Defense in Juvenile Court," 85 *Minn.L.Rev.* 2041 (2001) (analyzing the rationale for and availability of the insanity defense in juvenile court).

2) Finding of Insanity Affects Disposition Some courts have found that applicable juvenile court statutes require them to recognize the defense, *e.g. In re Winburn*, 32 Wis.2d 152, 145 N.W.2d 178 (1966). Absent a statutory requirement, however, other courts have concluded that the insanity defense does not bar an adjudication of delinquency, but a juvenile's mental disability does limit the nature of the disposition that may be imposed. In *In re H.C.*, 106 N.J.Super. 583, 256 A.2d 322, 328–29 (Juv. & Dom.Rel.1969), the Court held that

> if an adjudication of delinquency, even in the face of proof of insanity, could lead to treatment and other rehabilitative measures, the result would * * * promote the best interests of the juvenile and favorably reflect the fundamental concept of the juvenile court. * * * [The "insanity defense"] must impose a limitation upon the dispositionary aspect of juvenile matters. Again, the ruling is simply that insanity is no defense to adjudication. But I also hold that a juvenile who has been adjudicated delinquent based upon an anti-social act committed while insane under the *M'Naghten* rule cannot be subjected to penal sanctions. * * * If an adult may avoid penal sanctions—i.e., incarceration in prison or reformatory because of mental disease—a child with the same affliction cannot be treated more harshly because he is a juvenile. * * * [P]sychiatric testimony * * * compel the conclusion that a residential treatment facility is essential for H.C.

The legislature subsequently overruled the result in *H.C., N.J. Stat. Ann* § 2A:4A–40 (West 1995), and provided juveniles with a statutory right to an insanity defense. *In re R.G.W.*, 135 N.J.Super. 125, 342 A.2d 869 (1975).

However, other courts endorse the judicial rationale of *H.C.* For example, in **Matter of C.W.M.**, 407 A.2d 617, 622–623 (D.C.Ct.App.1979), the Court rejected the juvenile's constitutional challenge to a statute that prohibited the child from raising the insanity defense to a charge of delinquency:

> [U]nlike a criminal trial a juvenile fact-finding hearing does not result in a determination of criminal responsibility. Nor is the succeeding dispositional hearing intended to result in the imposition of any penal sanction on the child. Rather, the purpose is to determine the treatment required to rehabilitate him. Accordingly, the insanity defense would be superfluous in a juvenile delinquency proceeding. * * * We recognize that although the juvenile justice system is not intended to impose penal sanctions, the Family Division frequently orders forms of rehabilitation that a child might regard as punishment. We also recognized that an insanity acquittee, because morally blameless, may not be subject to any form of punishment. Of course, * * * an adjudication of delinquency does not result in the imposition of any penal sanction. * * * Nevertheless we deem it to be an indispensable element of fundamental fairness that a mentally ill child offender be accorded the same opportunity for psychiatric treatment and ultimate release as a similarly situated adult. * * * We conclude that the statutes and rules regulating juvenile delinquency proceedings in the District of Columbia presently provide adequate means of ensuring that any mentally ill child offender receives care and treatment similar to that provided for mentally ill criminal defendants. * * * We hold that the [Family] Division *must* consider, at the dispositional hearing the mental health of the child at the time of the offense, as well as at the time of such hearing.

If the theory of the juvenile court is that all delinquency dispositions are rehabilitative, or at least non-penal, does *HC* or *C.M.W.* provide any practical protections for juveniles? How is a "residential treatment facility" different from a juvenile institution or training school? How do they differ from penal sanctions? Don't all involve a loss of liberty? Many more juvenile cases raise an infancy defense than raise an insanity defense? If you represented a mentally ill twelve-year-old juvenile, which defense would you assert and why?

B. COMPETENCY

An adult criminal defendant must have "sufficient present ability to consult with his lawyer with a reasonable degree of rationale understanding [and have a] rational as well as factual understanding of the proceedings against him," *Dusky v. United States*, 362 U.S. 402, 402, 80 S.Ct. 788, 4 L.Ed.2d 824 (1960), and have the capacity "to assist in preparing his defense." *Drope v. Missouri*, 420 U.S. 162, 171, 95 S.Ct. 896, 43 L.Ed.2d 103 (1975). About half the states address juveniles' competency in their statutes or case law and conclude that delinquents have a fundamental right not to be tried while incompetent. *See e.g., Fla.Stat.Ann.* § 985.223 (West 1998) (incompetency in juvenile delinquency cases); *Kansas Stat.*

Ann. § 38–1637 (1997) (proceedings to determine competency); *In the Interest of S.H.*, 220 Ga.App. 569, 469 S.E.2d 810 (1996) (providing juveniles with procedural rights in delinquency proceedings would be meaningless if defendant was not capable of exercising them); *State v. E.C.*, 83 Wash.App. 523, 922 P.2d 152 (1996) (granting juvenile courts greater latitude in handling incompetent juveniles, if that is necessary to meet the needs of the juvenile offender); *Dandoy v. Superior Court*, 127 Ariz. 184, 619 P.2d 12 (1980) ("It appears that the determination of mental competency of a juvenile for trial is one of those instances where the procedure followed in adult prosecution must be applied to juvenile cases"). *But see, G.J.I. v. State*, 778 P.2d 485, 487 (Okla.Crim.App. 1989) (because delinquency proceedings are rehabilitative and not criminal, legislature intended for juvenile courts to adjudicate delinquents regardless of juvenile's mental state.)

GOLDEN v. STATE

341 Ark. 963, 21 S.W.3d 801 (Ark. 2000).

W.H. "Dub" Arnold, Chief Justice. This case involves the issues of whether a juvenile defendant has a right to have his competency to proceed determined prior to adjudication and, further, whether a juvenile has a right to assert the defense of insanity. We hold that a juvenile does have a due process right to have his competency determined prior to adjudication and, as such, reverse the trial court on this point. However, we hold that neither due process nor equal protection affords a juvenile the right to an insanity defense and, therefore, affirm the trial court on these issues.

On March 24, 1998, appellant Andrew Golden and Mitchell Johnson opened fire on their classmates at Westside Elementary School in Jonesboro, Arkansas. One teacher and four students were killed, and one teacher and nine students were wounded. At the time of the shootings, appellant Andrew Golden was eleven years old. * * *

We agree with appellant only as to his first point on appeal and hold that a juvenile does have a due process right to have his competency determined prior to adjudication; as such, we reverse the trial court on this point * * *

A. Competency to Stand Trial

The law is clear that defendants in criminal cases have a fundamental right not to stand trial while incompetent. This right protects criminal defendants' fundamental interests in their own liberty by ensuring that they are able to participate in their defense in an effort to avoid conviction and incarceration. In regard to juvenile proceedings, while the Arkansas Juvenile Code seems to presume that a defendant being tried in juvenile court is incompetent to some degree, particularly one who is under the age of fourteen, there was no statutory provision for juveniles at the time of appellant's hearing affording juveniles the same fundamental liberty interests as adults where the issue of competency is concerned.[5]

Although this issue is one of first impression in Arkansas, the United States Supreme Court held, in the case of *In re Gault* that while proceedings in a juvenile court need not conform with *all* the requirements of a criminal trial, primarily because of the special nature of the proceedings, essential requirements of due process and fair treatment must be met. The Court, in *Gault,* specifically acknowledged a juvenile's right to constitutionally adequate notice, the right against self-incrimination, and the right to cross-examine witnesses; further, the Court explicitly held that a juvenile must be afforded the right to counsel during these proceedings. Logically, this right to counsel means little if the juvenile is unaware of the proceedings or unable to communicate with counsel due to a psychological or developmental disability. Therefore, applying *Gault,* we hold that a juvenile *must* be allowed to assert incompetency and have his competency determined prior to adjudication. As such, we reverse the trial court on this point. * * *

LAVENSKI R. SMITH, JUSTICE, dissenting. I would affirm the trial court's denial of a competency hearing. I do so because the distinctions that exist between juvenile court proceedings and adult criminal proceedings are substantial and are rationally based upon the differences between adults and children. Although according a juvenile the right to a competency hearing appears equitable, it is, I submit, unwise. It reflects the continued erosion of all distinction between juvenile court and adult criminal courts. This erosion could ultimately lead to the irrelevance of juvenile codes in general.

Juveniles do not have a fundamental due process right to not be deprived of their liberty as a result of a hearing during which they were incompetent. The State's *parens patriae* interest, under proper circumstances subordinates the child's liberty interest. A juvenile has a liberty interest, which the U.S. Supreme Court describes as "substantial," but of which they also state that "that interest must be qualified by the recognition that juveniles, unlike adults, are always in some form of custody." The U.S. Supreme Court in this same opinion also states, "Children by definition are not assumed to have the capacity to take care of themselves. They are assumed to be subject to the control of their parents, and if parental control falters, the State must play its role as *parens patriae.*" * * *

[J]uveniles will not be competent in the sense adults would be, because they are assumed not to have the capacity to take care of themselves. In fact, the juvenile proceedings are designed to accomplish its

---

5. Although it may not be applied retroactively, it should be noted that when the General Assembly amended the juvenile code in 1999, it added an entire section on competency. The new language provides for a determination of capacity to stand trial for juveniles charged with certain crimes (capital murder being one of them). Further, it properly provides for an "age appropriate" capacity standard to apply to juveniles, which is different than that of adults.

ends without regard to the juvenile's competence because its absence is presumed. * * *

Because the U.S. Supreme Court speaks of a "legitimate State objective," the applicable test is the "rational basis test." That test is whether there is any rational basis connected to a legitimate State purpose. The statute may not be arbitrary or capricious. I would hold that there is a rational basis for the juvenile code not providing for competency hearings in juvenile cases. Therefore, I respectfully dissent.

NOTES

1) Adjudicative Competence and Adolescent Development On the issue of juveniles' competency in delinquency or criminal proceedings, *see* Vance L. Cowden and Geoffrey R. McKee, "Competency to Stand Trial in Juvenile Delinquency Proceedings–Cognitive Maturity and the Attorney–Client Relationship," 33 *Univ. of Louisville J. Family Law* 629 (1994) (judges neglect competency issues because juvenile courts adhere to therapeutic, rather than adversarial, model. "Because the best interests of the child and treatment are the goals of this non-adversarial system, is it not logical for the participants to view the mental or physical condition of the accused as simply factors to be considered in determining the appropriate treatment?" However, of 144 youths referred for competency evaluation, only one-fifth of youths younger than 13 years of age and only about one-half of 13 year olds were found competent as compared with about 80–90 percent of adults evaluated)." *See generally*, Thomas Grisso, "Juveniles' Competence to Stand Trial: New Questions for an Era of Punitive Juvenile Justice Reform," in *Rethinking Assessment, Competency and Sentencing for a Harsher Era of Juvenile Justice*, edited by Patricia Puritz (Washington, D.C.: American Bar Association 1997); T. Grisso, M. Miller & B. Sales, "Competency to Stand Trial in Juvenile Court," 10 *Int. J. Psychiatry and Law* 1 (1987); Thomas Grisso, "Juvenile Competency to Stand Trial," 12 *Criminal Justice* 4 (Fall, 1997); Richard Barnum and Thomas Grisso, "Competence to Stand Trial in Juvenile Court in Massachusetts: Issues of Therapeutic Jurisprudence," 20 *N. E. J. Criminal and Civil Confinement* 321 (1994); Richard Redding and Lynda Frost, "Adjudicative Competence in the Modern Juvenile Court," 9 *Va. J. Social Pol'y & L.* 353 (2002); Deborah K. Cooper, "Juveniles' Understanding of Trial–Related Information: Are they Competent Defendants?," 15 *Behavioral Sci. & Law* 167, 177–178 (1997) (" * * * [F]ar more children at all ages did not have this level of understanding. * * * [T]he presumption that the 16–year–olds would perform substantially better than the 3 younger age groups was not borne out. * * * [I]t appears that children are functioning differently from adults within the court system, and do not have an understanding of the legal process necessary for competence to stand trial, even after their factual understanding is significantly and substantially increased by educational training.").

As juvenile courts have become more formal and punitive, analysts increasingly question the competence of juveniles to function in such setting. The John D. and Catherine T. MacArthur Foundation funded a series of research projects on mental health, adolescent development and the juvenile justice system. *See e.g.* Thomas Grisso and Robert G. Schwartz, eds., *Youth on Trial: A Developmental Perspective on Juvenile Justice* (Chicago: University of Chicago Press 2000). **Richard J. Bonnie and Thomas Grisso, "Adjudicative Competence and Youthful Offenders," in Grisso and Schwartz, *Youth on Trial* at 76**, argue that adjudicative competence requires assessment of a defendant's capacity to: "1) understand the charges and the basic elements of the adversary system (understanding), 2) appreciate one's situation as a defendant in a criminal prosecution (appreciation), and 3) relate pertinent information to counsel concerning the facts of the case (reasoning)." The legislative trend to transfer more and younger juveniles to criminal court for prosecution as adults raises questions about the impact of developmental capacity on their competency to stand trial. "Some youths, especially those who are nearer to the minimum age for waiver to criminal court, may have significant deficits in competence-related abilities due not to mental disorder but to developmental immaturity.* * * [E]ven if their formal capacities for understanding and reasoning are adequately developed, the psychological context in which they perceive the legal process, or in which they weigh the consequences of their choices in that process, may affect their decisions in ways that are developmentally linked. * * * This tendency could lead them to make choices in the adjudicative process (about waiver of important rights or pleading, for example) that do not reflect the values that they would bring to bear on the judgment a few short years later when they become adults." Id. at 87–88.

A study of adjudicative competence compared the performance of adolescents in detention facilities and community settings with those of young adults in jails and in the community. The MacArthur Foundation research reported that youths aged fifteen and younger performed significantly more poorly than did young adults. **Thomas Grisso, et al., "Juveniles' Competence to Stand Trial: A Comparison of Adolescents' and Adults' Capacities as Trial Defendants," 27 *Law and Human Behavior* 333, 357 (2003).**

> [J]uveniles aged 15 and younger are significantly more likely than older adolescents and young adults to be impaired in ways that compromise their ability to serve as competent defendants in a criminal proceeding. "Using a variety of competency assessment tools, the research found that a greater proportion youths below sixteen years of age manifested a level of impairment consistent with that of persons found incompetent to stand trial. Compared with the young adults, adolescents also tended to make poorer choices about plea agreements that reflected a greater tendency to comply with authority and psycho-social immaturity." Adolescents are more likely than young adults to make choices that reflect a propensity to comply with authority figures such as confessing to the police rather than remaining silent or accepting a prosecutor's offer of a plea. In addition, when being interrogated by the police, consulting with an attorney, or evaluating a plea agreement, younger adolescents are less likely, or perhaps less able, than others to recognize the risks inherent in the various choices they face or to consider the long-term, and not merely the immediate, consequences of their legal decisions.

Grisso, et al., discuss the policy implications of developmental immaturity on adjudicative competence in both the criminal and juvenile justice systems:

[T]he same due process constraints that prohibit the adjudication of mentally ill and mentally retarded defendants who do not understand the process they face or cannot assist their attorneys also apply to juveniles who are incompetent because of immaturity alone. The standard announced by the Supreme Court in *Dusky v. United States* (1960) is a functional test, and functionally it should make no difference whether the source of the defendant's incompetency is mental illness or immaturity. This study confronts policy makers and courts with an uncomfortable reality. * * *

Most obvious, perhaps, are the policy and practical implications for the adjudication of youths in adult criminal court. * * * When youths are charged directly in criminal court, the proper mechanism might be a requirement that an evaluation and determination of competence to stand trial would automatically precede the adjudication. The optimal age boundary for an automatic inquiry into competence is not obvious. * * * It does seem clear, however, that at some minimal age, the risk of incompetence is so great that a determination should always be a predicate to adjudication in adult court. * * * The findings of the study may also be relevant to the legislative determination of the minimum age for adjudication of youths in adult court. Many jurisdictions have set the age bar very low for adult prosecution of youths for serious crimes, usually without consideration of the likelihood that many youths of the specified minimum age may be incompetent. * * *

The findings of the study should also focus attention on the issue of competence to stand trial in juvenile court delinquency proceedings. Many states extend the competence requirement to juvenile court adjudications, but most focus on mental illness and disability as the sources of incapacity. An important consideration in expanding the doctrinal framework to include incompetence as a result of immaturity is whether the competence standard applied in juvenile court should be less demanding than that applied in adult criminal court. This is important because the standard for competence in juvenile court will determine whether youths adjudicated incompetent as adults can be tried as juveniles. If a less demanding standard operates in juvenile court proceedings, many younger defendants who lack the capacity to be adjudicated as adults can be tried in this venue. Otherwise, the question of how to respond to these immature defendants presents a daunting challenge.

We believe that a more relaxed competence standard in juvenile court is compatible with the demands of constitutional due process. The Supreme Court has made it clear that the requirements of due process in delinquency proceedings are not identical to those that regulate criminal trials (*McKeiver v. Pennsylvania*, 1971). The justification for a separate juvenile court rests in part on the fact that it is not an exact replica of criminal court. If juvenile court jurisdiction ends when the minor reaches adulthood (an important "if"), then the stakes of a delinquency proceeding are not as high as those faced by a youth charged with a felony in adult court. Under these conditions, no constitutional bar would restrict the use of a more relaxed standard of adjudicative competence in juvenile court. *Id*. at 358–360.

2) Competency Procedures In finding a juvenile's right to a competency determination, the Court *In the Matter of W.A.F.*, 573 A.2d 1264, 1267 (D.C.App.1990), explained that "The first function served by the adult competency requirement and the *Dusky* standard is to assure that the person charged with violating the law is able to prepare a defense, in order to increase the accuracy of the factual and guilt determinations. No less a need exists for a youth in juvenile delinquency proceedings. The condition precedent for the court's ordering of a rehabilitative disposition in a juvenile delinquency proceeding is a factual determination that the juvenile has violated a provision of the criminal law. Even if all the parties to a juvenile delinquency proceeding share the goal of finding a disposition in the child's best interests, and the proceedings may be less adversarial than adult prosecution, such proceedings clearly present an opportunity for factual disputes* * * Consequently, we find no inconsistency between the goals of the juvenile system * * * and the basic principle that the accuracy of the fact finding determination—and the accused's own minimal contribution thereto— is part of the fundamental fairness inherent in due process."

Contrast the rationale of *W.A.F.*, with the reasoning of the Indiana Supreme Court in **In re K.G.**, 808 N.E.2d 631 (Ind. 2004), which held that juveniles have a constitutional right to a competency determination, but declined to use the adult competency statute:

> The trial court proceeded under the adult competency statute. * * * The State contends here, as it did before the Court of Appeals, that the trial court's reliance on the adult competency statute was improper because the juvenile code provides procedures that permit a court to make competency determinations for children and place them in treatment centers when necessary. The Court of Appeals rejected this argument, concluding (1) juveniles have a constitutional right to have their competency determined before they are subjected to delinquency proceedings, and (2) because the juvenile code provides no procedure for determining the competency of children, the adult competency statute applies. * * * Principles of fundamental fairness require that this right be afforded in juvenile proceedings. Thus, we summarily affirm the opinion of the Court of Appeals on this issue. We disagree with our colleagues, however, on the applicability of the adult competency statute. * * *

> Indiana Code section 31–32–1–1 provides, "If a child is alleged to be a delinquent child, the procedures governing criminal trials apply in all matters not covered by the juvenile law." It is true that the juvenile code does not provide an explicit procedure for handling juvenile competency issues. Nonetheless, in construing a statute our main objective is to determine, give effect to, and implement the intent of the legislature. As a matter of statutory interpretation, and considering the history and purpose underlying the juvenile code, we do not believe the Legislature intended that the adult competency statute should apply to juveniles.

The policy of this State and the purpose of our juvenile code are to "ensure that children within the juvenile justice system are treated as persons in need of care, protection, treatment, and rehabilitation." * * * Under the juvenile code, the juvenile court acts not only as adjudicator of legal responsibility but also as administrator of probation, detention, and many related child and family social service programs. * * * In essence the code affords juvenile courts a degree of discretion and flexibility, unparalleled in the criminal code, to address the needs of children and to act in their best interests. That flexibility is severely compromised by resorting to the procedures set forth in the adult competency statute when resolving questions concerning juvenile competency. More specifically, the statute mandates that where a defendant is found to be incompetent to stand trial, the trial court "*shall ... order* the defendant committed to the division of mental health and addiction, to be confined by the division in an appropriate psychiatric institution." There certainly are occasions where it may not be in the child's best interest to be committed to the division of mental health. * * * In addition to the lack of adequate facilities or programs, because of the physical location of these state run facilities, a juvenile committed to the division of mental health under the auspices of the adult competency statute could be confined in an institution hundreds of miles from home and family. This could not have been the intent of the Legislature. Even in the context of a child found to be delinquent, the trial court is prohibited from placing the child in a facility outside of the child's county of residence "unless placement of the child in a comparable facility with adequate services located in the child's county of residence is unavailable or the child's county of residence does not have an appropriate comparable facility with adequate services." In our view no less is required for juveniles only alleged to be delinquent.

This is not to say that a juvenile court is prohibited from entering an order committing a child found to be incompetent to an appropriate facility operated by the department of mental health. We merely hold that the adult competency statute is not the proper vehicle to accomplish this end. Rather we believe Indiana Code Section 31–32–12–1 is sufficient to the task.[1] If narrowly construed the statute allows for the examination

1. 1The statute provides:

If the procedures under IC 31–32–13 are followed, the juvenile court may authorize mental or physical examinations or treatment under the following circumstances:

(1) If the court has not authorized the filing of a petition but a physician certifies that an emergency exists, the court:

(A) may order medical or physical examination or treatment of the child; and

(B) may order the child detained in a health care facility while the emergency exists.

(2) If the court has not authorized the filing of a petition but a physician certifies that continued medical care is necessary to protect the child after the emergency has passed, the court:

(A) may order medical services for a reasonable length of time; and

(B) may order the child detained while medical services are provided.

(3) If the court has authorized the filing of a petition alleging that a child is a delinquent child or a child in need of services, the court may order examination of the child to provide information for the dispositional hearing. The court may also order medical examinations and treatment of the child under any circumstances otherwise permitted by this section.

and treatment of children under only three circumstances: (1) before the filing of a delinquency or CHINS petition, if an emergency exists, the court may order an examination or treatment; (2) after the filing of a delinquency or CHINS petition, the court may order an examination of the child to provide information for the dispositional hearing; and (3) after a child has been adjudicated a delinquent or CHINS, the court may order examination or treatment as a part of the dispositional decree. This is the view advanced by Marion County on behalf of the juveniles in this case and to which the Court of Appeals agreed.

Viewed slightly differently, however, the statute is more comprehensive. More specifically the statute provides "[t]he court may also order medical examinations and treatment of the child under any circumstances otherwise permitted by this section." Although the statute does not specifically mention "competency," given a juvenile court's flexibility in addressing the needs of children and acting in their best interest, we conclude that this statute allows for the examination and/or treatment of a child after a delinquency petition has been filed in order to determine the child's competency. * * *

3) Fla.R.Juv.P. Rule 8.095 Procedure When Child Believed to Be Incompetent or Insane. (a) Incompetency At Time of Adjudicatory Hearing * * *

(1) *Motion.* (A) A written motion for examination of the child made by counsel for the child shall contain * * * reasonable grounds to believe that the child is incompetent to proceed. To the extent that it does not invade the lawyer-client privilege, the motion shall contain a recital of the specific observations of and conversations with the child that have formed the basis for the motion.

(B) A written motion for examination of the child made by counsel for the state shall contain * * * on reasonable grounds to believe the child is incompetent to proceed and shall include a recital of the specific facts that have formed the basis for the motion, including a recitation of the observations of and statements of the child that have caused the state to file the motion.

(2) *Setting Hearing.* If at any time prior to or during the adjudicatory hearing * * * the court has reasonable grounds to believe the child * * * may be incompetent to proceed with an adjudicatory hearing, the court on its own motion or motion of counsel for the child or the state shall immediately stay the proceedings and fix a time for a hearing for the determination of the child's mental condition.

(3) *Child Found Competent to Proceed.* If at the hearing * * * the child is found to be competent to proceed with an adjudicatory hearing, the court shall enter an order so finding and proceed accordingly.

(4) *Child Found Incompetent to Proceed.* If at the hearing * * * the child is found to be incompetent to proceed, the child must be adjudicated incompe-

---

(4) After a child has been adjudicated a delinquent child or a child in need of services, the court may order examinations and treatment under IC 31–34–20 or IC 31–37–19.

tent to proceed and may be involuntarily committed as provided by law to the Department of Children and Family Services for treatment * * *

(c) Appointment of Expert Witnesses; Detention of Child for Examination.

(1) When a question has been raised concerning the sanity or competency of the child * * * the court may on its own motion, and shall on motion of the state or the child, appoint no more than 3, nor fewer than 2, disinterested qualified experts to examine the child as to competency or sanity of the child * * *. Attorneys for the state and the child may be present at the examination. * * * Other competent evidence may be introduced at the hearing. The appointment of experts by the court shall not preclude the state or the child from calling other expert witnesses to testify at the adjudicatory hearing* * *or at the hearing to determine the mental condition of the child.* * *

(d) Competence to Proceed; Scope of Examination and Report.

(1) *Examination by Experts.* On appointment by the court, the experts shall examine the child with respect to the issue of competence to proceed as specified by the court in its order appointing the experts.

(A) The experts first shall consider factors related to whether the child meets the criteria for competence to proceed; that is, whether the child has sufficient present ability to consult with counsel with a reasonable degree of rational understanding and whether the child has a rational and factual understanding of the present proceedings.

(B) In considering the competence of the child to proceed, the examining experts shall consider and include in their reports the child's capacity to:

(i) appreciate the charges or allegations against the child;

(ii) appreciate the range and nature of possible penalties that may be imposed in the proceedings against the child, if applicable;

(iii) understand the adversary nature of the legal process;

(iv) disclose to counsel facts pertinent to the proceedings at issue;

(v) display appropriate courtroom behavior; and

(vi) testify relevantly.

The experts also may consider any other factors they deem to be relevant.

(C) Any report concluding that a child is not competent must include the basis for the competency determination. * * *

(2) *Treatment Recommendations.* If the experts find that the child is incompetent to proceed, they shall report on any recommended treatment for the child to attain competence to proceed. A recommendation as to whether residential or nonresidential treatment or training is required must be included. * * *

(5) *Limited Use of Competency Evidence.*

(A) * * * [A]ny information elicited during a hearing on competency to proceed or commitment held under this rule, shall be used only in determining the mental competency to proceed, the commitment of the child, or other treatment of the child.

Tate v. State, 864 So.2d 44 (Fla.App. 4 Dist. 2003), involved the highly-publicized case of a twelve year old juvenile convicted as an adult of first-degree murder for brutal "wrestling" injuries inflicted on a six-year-old girl and who received a mandatory sentence to life in prison. On appeal, the Court found that the trial judge violated defendant's due process rights by failing to order, *sua sponte*, pretrial and post-trial competency evaluations, and reversed and remanded for further proceedings:

> The question we resolve, here, is whether, due to his extremely young age and lack of previous exposure to the judicial system, a competency evaluation was constitutionally mandated to determine whether Tate had sufficient present ability to consult with his lawyer with a reasonable degree of rational understanding and whether he had a rational, as well as factual, understanding of the proceedings against him. We conclude that it was. * * *

> [A neuropsychologist] testified that Tate had a mental delay of about three to four years, "which means that Lionel has an age equivalent of nine or ten years old." It is undisputed that Tate's IQ is approximately 90. * * * [A] child psychiatrist testified that Tate had the social maturity of a six–year–old and delays in inferential thinking. * * * [D]efense counsel wanted to reveal what led him to believe that Tate was not competent during trial, but was apparently precluded from doing so [by Tate's mother's unwillingness to allow him to waive attorney-client privilege]. * * *

> We also recognize that competency hearings are not, per se, mandated simply because a child is tried as an adult. However, in light of Tate's age, the facts developed pre-trial and post-trial, and his lack of previous exposure to the judicial system, a competency hearing should have been held, particularly given the complexity of the legal proceedings and the fact that he was denied * * * a waiver hearing to determine whether the child should be tried as an adult. * * *

> Even if a child of Tate's age is deemed to have the capacity to understand less serious charges, or common place juvenile court proceedings, it cannot be determined, absent a hearing, whether Tate could meet competency standards incident to facing a first-degree murder charge involving profound decisions regarding strategy, whether to make disclosures, intelligently analyze plea offers, and consider waiving important rights.

> The record reflects that questions regarding Tate's competency were not lurking subtly in the background, but were readily apparent, as his immaturity and developmental delays were very much at the heart of the defense. It is also alleged that his I.Q. of 90 or 91 means that 75% of children his age scored higher, and that he had significant mental delays. * * * [W]e conclude that it was error to fail to, sua sponte, order a competency hearing pre-trial and, in any event, to deny the post-trial request for a competency hearing.

> In light of the fact based professional doubts expressed post-trial concerning Tate's competency, Tate was entitled to a complete evaluation and hearing at that time, if for no other reason than to clarify the record,

notwithstanding that the trial court may have been correct in concluding that Tate's demeanor and disinterest did not necessarily mean that he did not understand the proceedings and that his incompetency was not previously raised despite defense counsel's continuing access to professional help. * * *

Upon remand, Tate is entitled to a new trial because a hearing at this late date to determine the present competency of a maturing adolescent cannot adequately retroactively protect his rights. * * * At a minimum, under the circumstances of this case, the court had an obligation to ensure that the juvenile defendant, who was less than the age of fourteen, with known disabilities raised in his defense and who faced mandatory life imprisonment, was competent to understand the plea offer and the ramifications thereof, and understood the defense being raised and the state's evidence to refute the defense position, so as to ensure that Tate could effectively assist in his defense.

The prospect of mandatory life without parole for a crime committed by a twelve-year old youth of dubious competency generated considerable scholarly commentary. See e.g., Steven Bell, "Tate v. State: Highlighting the Need for a Mandatory Competency Hearing," 28 Nova L. Rev. 575 (2004); Michael J. Dale, "Making Sense of the Lionel Tate Case," 28 Nova L. Rev. 467 (2004); Joseph Yalon, "Constitutional Right to a Competence Hearing," 26 J. Juv. L. 127 (2006).

4) Different Standards for Competence in Juvenile and Adult Proceedings Grisso, et al., *Juvenile's Competence*, *supra*, Note 1, p. 110 suggests that a more relaxed competency standard may be appropriate in juvenile court than in criminal court. See e.g. *In re Bailey*, 150 Ohio App.3d 664, 782 N.E.2d 1177, 1180 (2 Dist. 2002), noting that "There is authority to support a juvenile court's finding that while a child may be incompetent to stand trial in adult court, he or she may nevertheless be competent to enter an admission and stand for adjudication in juvenile court, because of the differences in the complexities in adult criminal proceedings versus juvenile proceedings. A juvenile court can properly consider those differences in determining whether a child is competent to enter an admission * * * because that statutory standard must be assessed in light of juvenile, rather than adult, norms."

Elizabeth S. Scott and Thomas Grisso, "Developmental Incompetence, Due Process, and Juvenile Justice Policy," 83 *N.C.L.Rev.* **793 (2005),** argue for a relaxed standard of competence in juvenile delinquency proceedings:

* * * At a minimum, the research on adolescent development and adjudicative competence challenges courts to consider incompetence claims based on immaturity along with those caused by mental illness and disability. We will argue, however, that the features that distinguish incompetence based on immaturity from the more familiar variations make this simple doctrinal response inadequate. The incorporation of a developmental competence requirement into youth crime regulation necessitates more extensive institutional and doctrinal adjustments, if substantial disruption of criminal and juvenile proceedings is to be avoided. Most importantly, the adoption of dual

standards of competence is necessary if juvenile delinquency proceedings are to serve as default dispositions for youths found incompetent in criminal courts; generally, this is the key to avoiding an institutional crisis under which large numbers of incompetent youths cannot be adjudicated in either court. We argue that youths who are incompetent under the *Dusky* standard can be subject to a relaxed competence standard in juvenile court without violating constitutional norms so long as the dispositions to which they are subject are different in purpose and punitiveness from criminal sentences. * * *

The application of dual competence standards in criminal and delinquency proceedings is important for another reason; it is the means to avoid profound disruption of juvenile delinquency proceedings. Although few thirteen-year-olds are subject to criminal charges, many face adjudication in juvenile court. The research evidence suggests that evenhanded application of adult competence criteria may well result in the disqualification of a substantial percentage of youngsters from adjudication in any court. This outcome is jarring in light of uncontroversial premises of juvenile court jurisdiction; few would challenge the appropriateness of delinquency proceedings for younger teens. Thus, as a policy matter, a strong case can be made for a relaxed juvenile court competence standard under which immature youths could be tried in delinquency proceedings, even though they are incompetent to stand trial under adult criteria. * * *

The question that we address is not whether delinquency proceedings are subject to the competence requirement at all—we take that to be settled—but whether the application of a relaxed standard in this setting (requiring less competence than is required in a criminal proceeding) can satisfy the demands of due process. As a purely conceptual matter, the adoption of dual standards is quite feasible because competence, unlike many procedural protections is largely a continuous rather than binary construct. * * * [T]he legal boundary between competence and incompetence is located along a continuum by legal authorities on the basis of a mix of policy concerns. * * * The upshot for our purposes is that the competence thresholds for delinquency and criminal proceedings can be fixed at different locations on the basis different policy demands.

This, of course, does not resolve the question of whether dual standards satisfy the mandate of due process. The Supreme Court has emphasized that the Constitution does not require the wholesale incorporation of adult procedural rights into delinquency proceedings. * * * First, the Court has emphasized that a procedural safeguard that is likely to be "disruptive of the unique nature of the juvenile process" and to dilute its beneficial aspects may not be required in juvenile court. * * * However, this deference rests on the assumption that a juvenile delinquency proceeding is different from a criminal trial in ways that serve the interests of youths facing charges in juvenile court. This qualifying condition is important to our analysis, leading us to conclude that, regardless of its disruptive impact, a relaxed juvenile court competence standard is constitutionally sufficient only if delinquency proceedings promote the welfare of youths who do not meet the adult standard. Finally, the Court has focused on whether a contested procedural safeguard is important for accurate factfinding in the adjudication of criminal charges. We extend this concern to examine whether a relaxed juvenile court competence standard adequately satisfies the purposes of the competence requirement as applied in this setting.

As to the first consideration about the disruptiveness of the proposed procedure, * * * serious disruption of delinquency proceedings is likely to follow if a uniform competence standard is applied in criminal and juvenile courts and that this can be avoided by adopting a relaxed standard. First, juvenile courts that apply the adult standard are likely to be burdened with a flood of petitions for competence evaluations and hearings, resulting in a major diversion of financial and human resources to a process that most would agree should have limited importance in this legal setting. Also, if many younger defendants are found incompetent under the adult standard, government efforts to protect the public from youth crime, to hold young offenders accountable, and to provide them with rehabilitative services will be undermined. As we have argued, a doctrinal regime under which many younger teens—particularly those charged with serious crimes—might be immune from prosecution probably would be rejected as unacceptable, and ultimately, would undermine the legitimacy of the juvenile court. Under a tailored juvenile court standard, this procedural safeguard can function to exclude only those youths whose extreme immaturity makes even juvenile court adjudication inappropriate.

Although the potentially disruptive impact of a uniform competence standard seems clear, the constitutional adequacy of a dual-standards regime also depends on whether delinquency proceedings differ substantially from criminal proceedings, such that the more protective adult standard is not mandated in this setting. * * * A relaxed competence standard will meet this second condition of "distinctiveness" if delinquency proceedings are different from criminal trials in two important dimensions. The first concerns the severity of punishment and its impact on the future lives of young offenders. Juvenile court sanctions, especially for serious crimes, must be of shorter duration than those imposed on adult criminals. Moreover, dispositions should be completed within a self-contained juvenile correctional system, such that they do not extend into adulthood or affect adult status or opportunities. The traditional juvenile justice system was characterized by dispositions more lenient than the adult system, and contemporary regimes can be evaluated along this dimension as well. If the dispositional differences are insufficient in this regard, the adult standard must be applied.

The distinctiveness condition also requires that the purposes of delinquency proceedings must be broader than those of criminal proceedings and must include consideration of the welfare of young offenders. Today, to be sure, criminal and delinquency proceedings both aim to punish offenders, deter crime and protect public safety through the incapacitation of dangerous persons. However, the juvenile system, traditionally at least, also has been committed to treatment and to offering dispositions that enhance the likelihood that delinquent youths will become productive adults. This distinction from the adult justice system is important in the justification of a relaxed competence standard in delinquency proceedings.

The upshot of our analysis is that whether a juvenile court adjudication is sufficiently different from a criminal trial to justify relaxing the constitutionally required competence standard depends in part on institutional features defining the juvenile justice system and its purposes. If youths facing adjudication in juvenile court are subject to dispositions that are more lenient than criminal punishment and that are aimed (in part) at promoting youth welfare, then the stakes they face are lower than (and different from) those facing criminal defendants and the need for adult procedural safeguards to protect their interests is less compelling. Under these conditions, a relaxed standard in delinquency proceedings may be justified, given the disruptive impact on delinquency proceedings of applying a uniform standard. On the other hand, if juvenile proceedings and criminal trials are alike in their consequences and purposes, then accused youths should receive the same protections as criminal defendants.

Assuming the institutional preconditions are met (for now), a relaxed standard will meet the mandate of fundamental fairness only if it also satisfies the underlying purposes of the criminal competence requirement—the promotion of dignity, accuracy, and defendant participation. Under the competence criteria that we endorse, a youth facing a delinquency proceeding must have a basic understanding of the charges and proceeding and of her position as defendant in that proceeding, and the capacity to communicate with her attorney. This standard accommodates the developmental incapacities that might leave many youths incompetent to be tried as adults, while at the same time requiring basic comprehension of the delinquency proceeding, its meaning, and consequences. * * *

In a regime of dual standards, very few youths will be in the category of defendants who cannot be adjudicated in juvenile proceedings due to their incompetence. Of this small group, some may attain competence in a reasonable period through training, and most of the rest will be subject to dispositions that assure that they receive adequate supervision and useful remedial services. Thus, dealing with this group creates little threat of systemic crisis, in sharp contrast to the potential disruption of both juvenile and criminal proceedings that is likely to occur under a uniform standard. * * *

Compare the reasoning of the Minnesota Court of Appeals, CRIPPEN, Judge, **In the Matter of the WELFARE OF D.D.N.**, 582 N.W.2d 278 (Mn. Ct. Ap. 1998), with the arguments made by Scott and Grisso, "Developmental Incompetence, Due Process, and Juvenile Justice Policy," *supra*. With which position do you agree and why?

> * * * The briefs of the parties allude to an expanding body of research and reporting on the diminished capacity of adolescents to assist their own interests at various stages in the prosecution of their alleged offenses. The prosecuting attorney points to the scholarly opinion in this literature that, notwithstanding evidence of the diminished capacity of adolescent offenders to participate in court proceedings, a relaxed standard of competency might be justified in proceedings where the court will make a rehabilitative disposition. But in Minnesota, a lower standard for juvenile competency is precluded both by the supreme court's juvenile justice rules and by that court's earlier decision.

Minnesota rules of court relating to juvenile and adult competency hold children and adults to the same competency standard. Minn.R.Juv.P. 20.01, subd. 1(B), which sets the standard for juvenile competency, states:

A child shall not be permitted to enter a plea or be tried or sentenced for any offense if the child lacks sufficient ability to:

(1) consult with a reasonable degree of rational understanding with defense counsel; or

(2) understand the proceedings or participate in the defense due to mental illness or mental deficiency.

The adult competency standard similarly defines competency as the ability to consult with counsel and to understand the nature of the proceeding. This similarity of standards is also dictated by *In re Welfare of S.W.T.*, (Minn. 1979), in which the Minnesota Supreme Court (prior to the enactment of the juvenile competency rule) applied the adult standard in determining the competency of a child. Here, the prosecuting attorney argues that the availability of shorter-term sanctions and the rehabilitative nature of those dispositions may justify a lower level of competency. But this argument overlooks the reality that rehabilitative sanctions can and do involve a major loss of a child's liberties.

The Georgia Court of Appeals, also addressing the issue of competency of juveniles, pointed directly to the liberty interests of the child that are at risk in a proceeding leading to a rehabilitative disposition. In *In re S.H.*, (1996), the court held that the juvenile court had violated S.H.'s due process rights by adjudicating him a delinquent when it had also found that the 12–year–old was incompetent to stand trial. The court found that, although juvenile proceedings emphasize rehabilitation, thereby sparing "the child some of the collateral consequences of a criminal conviction," both "juvenile and criminal proceedings may result in a significant loss of liberty." Principles of fundamental fairness, therefore, require that juveniles be afforded the same protection against being tried while incompetent as adults.

The prosecutor's argument also overlooks the fact that, although rehabilitation eliminates retribution and deterrence of others, it does not always eliminate punishment. The juvenile court's dispositions must be rehabilitative and tied to the needs of and opportunities for the child, but these laws do not prohibit "a rational, punitive disposition, one where the record shows that correction or rehabilitation of the child reasonably cannot be achieved without a penalty."

A determination of competency, even in the context of juvenile adjudicatory proceedings, is a fundamental right. Because of this and because dispositions in juvenile proceedings, including rehabilitative dispositions, may involve both punishment and a substantial loss of liberty, the level of competence required to permit a child's participation in juvenile court proceedings can be no less than the competence demanded for trial or sentencing of an adult. Children, like adults, must be able "to

understand the nature of the proceedings against [them] and to participate in [their] own defense."[2]

3. PUNISHMENT, TREATMENT, AND SENTENCING JUVENILES

As a matter of state policy, laws may classify children differently than
adults, and states may prescribe treatment rather than punishment for
offenders. If states choose to treat youths as juveniles rather than to
punish them as adults, to what extent do criminal law sentencing principles like determinacy, proportionality, or the length of the adult criminal
term limit the lengths of juvenile dispositions? How do children differ
from adults, or treatment differ from punishment so as to justify the
differences in lengths of juveniles' sentences?

The following excerpt, **Martin R. Gardner, "Punishment and
Juvenile Justice: A Conceptual Framework for Assessing Constitutional Rights of Youthful Offenders," 35 *Vand.L.Rev.* 791, 815–
818, 833 (1982)**, describes some of the conceptual differences between
treatment and punishment that provide the foundation for a separate
system of juvenile justice. It also provides a very useful analytical framework for examining the question whether juvenile courts treat or punish
youths:

Therapeutic dispositions, like preventive detentions, sometimes display punitive characteristics. Involuntary therapy often entails not only a
stigma to the patient and severe restrictions of his liberty, but also painful
and unpleasant treatment. Despite its similarly to punishment, however,
therapy is a concept analytically distinct from punishment. * * * [C]om-
mentators have provided valuable insights into this distinction by describing therapy as purposeful behavior toward another person that is intended
to alter that person's condition in a manner beneficial to him. This
purportedly beneficial behavior is always subject to revision upon a
showing that a different mode of behavior would produce more beneficial
results, or that a change in the person's condition has eliminated the need
for further therapy.

Examination of the role of offensive conduct illustrates the essential
difference between coercive therapy and punishment. The distinction is
similar to that between preventive detention and punishment. In cases of
punishment, the state imposes restraints upon persons because they have
committed offenses. Cases of therapy, however, do not involve necessarily
a relation between the restraints imposed upon the person and his past
conduct. Therapy—like preventive detention and unlike punishment—is a
forward-looking response to a person's present undesirable status. Unlike

---

2. We also note appellant's observation that, when making a competency determination, the
court should consider not only the child's ability to consult with counsel and understand the
judicial proceeding but also the child's age as a measure of his capacity. Researchers confirm the
characteristics of youth that bear on a person's competency. But these factors, immaturity,
developmental delays, and emotional disorders unique to age, are measured in the assessment of
competency, without attempting to give weight to age alone as a measure of the condition.

preventive detention, which merely incapacitates, therapy seeks to alleviate the undesirable status condition. * * *

The Supreme Court's approach to defining punishment includes the following three characteristics. First, * * * the Court will use its definitional approach to assess all claims of governmental punishment, regardless of whether the claim presents a direct constitutional attack upon a specified statute * * * or an allegation that the restraints constitute nonstatutorily imposed punishments. Second, * * * the Court consistently has focused upon the intent of the alleged punisher as an essential element to determine the presence or absence of punishment. Last, the Court does not seem to alter its definition of punishment to fit the particular constitutional problem at issue. Substantive and procedural constitutional rights are included in the same punishment analysis. * * *

Courts may discern punitive purposes from either the express words or actions of the alleged punisher or from independent inquiries into the possible functions of an allegedly punitive sanction. When the state imposes restraints that suspiciously resemble punishment, courts may infer a punitive purpose if the restraints are unreasonably harsh in relation to the articulated nonpenal objectives. Punishment is a concept analytically distinct from regulation, preventive detention, and therapy. Regulation is the imposition of sanctions to control future conduct without necessarily attending to anyone's past wrongdoing. Preventive detention is the purposeful restriction of liberty of a person, who because of his present status, may pose a danger. Unlike punishment, which is generally determinate—that is knowable in kind and duration at the time the triggering offense is committed—preventive detention is indeterminate—that is, unknowable in duration at the time of imposition. Therapy is the alteration of a person's undesirable physical or mental condition in a manner beneficial to the person until the undesirable condition no longer exists. Therapy is characteristically indeterminate because its effectiveness is generally unknown in advance. * * *

The Court's cases from *Gault* to *Breed* demonstrate clearly that the juvenile justice system reflects a mixture of therapeutic and punitive concerns. To the extent that the system is punitive, important constitutional consequences follow. Yet, apart from misleading reliance upon the effect theory, the Court's juvenile cases provide no definition of punishment—much less a standard for distinguishing punishment from therapy. * * *

IN RE ERIC J.

25 Cal.3d 522, 159 Cal.Rptr. 317, 601 P.2d 549 (1979).

CLARK, JUSTICE. ERIC J., a minor, appeals from an order continuing his juvenile court wardship and committing him to the Youth Authority after findings he committed burglary and was in contempt of court for violating conditions of an earlier order granting probation. The maximum term for which he might be confined was determined to be three and one-half years three years for the burglary and six months for the misdemeanor contempt. The commitment order must be modified to recite that appellant's maximum term is three years, two months, and that he is to receive forty-six days credit for time in custody prior to commitment. As modified, the judgment will be affirmed. * * *

Relying on *People v. Olivas* (1976), appellant contends Welfare and Institutions Code section 726 denies him equal protection of the laws by providing that the maximum term of confinement for a juvenile is the longest term imposable upon an adult for the same offense, without the necessity of finding circumstances in aggravation of the crime justifying imposition of the upper term as is required in adult criminal procedure by Penal Code section 1170, subdivision (b).

Section 726, subdivision (c), of the Welfare and Institutions Code provides in relevant part: "In any case in which the minor is removed from the physical custody of his parent or guardian as the result of an order of wardship made pursuant to Section 602, the order shall specify that the minor may not be held in physical confinement for a period in excess of the maximum term of imprisonment which could be imposed upon an adult convicted of the offense or offenses which brought or continued the minor under the jurisdiction of the juvenile court. As used in this section and in Section 731, 'maximum term of imprisonment' means the longest of the three time periods set forth in paragraph (2) of subdivision (a) of Section 1170 of the Penal Code, but without the need to follow the provisions of subdivision (b) of Section 1170 of the Penal Code or to consider time for good behavior or participation pursuant to Sections 2930, 2931, and 2932 of the Penal Code, plus enhancements which must be proven if pled."

Section 1170, subdivision (b), of the Penal Code provides: "When a judgment of imprisonment is to be imposed and the statute specifies three possible terms, the court shall order imposition of the middle term, unless there are circumstances in aggravation or mitigation of the crime. At least four days prior to the time set for imposition of judgment either party may submit a statement in aggravation or mitigation to dispute facts in the record or the probation officer's report, or to present additional facts. In determining whether there are circumstances that justify imposition of the upper or lower term, the court may consider the record in the case, the probation officer's report, other reports including reports received pursuant to Section 1203.03 and statements in aggravation or mitigation submitted by the prosecution or the defendant, and any further evidence introduced at the sentencing hearing. The court shall set forth on the record the facts and reasons for imposing the upper or lower term. * * * "

Appellant was found to have committed burglary. Because the court failed to find the degree of the offense, it is deemed to be of the second degree. Second degree burglary is punishable "by imprisonment in the county jail not exceeding one year or in the state prison." Where it is not otherwise specified, the term for an offense punishable by imprisonment in a state prison is "16 months, or two or three years." Pursuant to Welfare and Institutions Code section 726, subdivision (c), the maximum term for which appellant might be confined for the burglary was determined to be three years. He contends that, in the absence of any finding of aggravation, it is a denial of equal protection of the law not to set the maximum at two years.

In *People v. Olivas*, this court held that section 1770 of the Welfare and Institutions Code violated the equal protection clauses of the California and United States Constitutions insofar as it permitted misdemeanants between the ages of 16 and 21 to be committed to the Youth Authority for a term potentially longer than the maximum jail term which might have been imposed for the same offense if committed by a person over the age of 21 years. We emphasized that youthful misdemeanants committed pursuant to section 1731.5 "have been prosecuted as *adults*, adjudged by the same standards which apply to *any competent adult*, and convicted as adults *in adult courts.*" "We are not confronted," we stressed, "by a situation in which a juvenile adjudged *under the Juvenile Court Law as a juvenile* contends that his term of involuntary confinement may exceed that which might have been imposed on an adult or juvenile who committed the identical unlawful act and was thereafter convicted *in the criminal courts*. Since that situation is not before us, we reserve consideration of the issue should it arise in some future case and we express no opinion on the merits of such a contention."

The situation not before us in *Olivas* is presented here. Appellant was adjudged under Juvenile Court Law as a juvenile. Pursuant to Welfare and Institutions Code section 726, subdivision (c), the maximum term for which he might be confined for the burglary was automatically set at three years. An adult or juvenile convicted in the criminal courts of committing the identical unlawful act could not, without a finding of aggravating circumstances, be imprisoned more than two years.

Despite this disparity, appellant has not been denied equal protection of the laws. The first prerequisite to a meritorious claim under the equal protection clause is a showing that the state has adopted a classification that affects two or more *similarly situated* groups in an unequal manner. Adults convicted in the criminal courts and sentenced to prison and youths adjudged wards of the juvenile courts and committed to the Youth Authority are not "similarly situated."

For purposes of this discussion, the most significant difference between minors and adults is that "[t]he liberty interest of a minor is qualitatively different than that of an adult, being subject both to reasonable regulation by the state to an extent not permissible with adults, and to an even greater extent to the control of the minor's parents unless 'it appears that the parental decisions will jeopardize the health or safety of the child or have a potential for significant social burdens.'" When the minor must be removed from the custody of his parents for his own welfare or for the safety and protection of the public, the state assuming the parents' role, the state also assumes the parents' authority to limit the minor's freedom of action.

" 'The concept of the equal protection of the laws compels recognition of the proposition that persons similarly situated with respect to the legitimate purpose of the law receive like treatment.' " The state does not have the same purpose in sentencing adults to prison that it has in committing minors to the Youth Authority. Adults convicted in the criminal courts are sentenced to prison as punishment while minors adjudged wards of the juvenile courts are committed to the Youth Authority for the purposes of treatment and rehabilitation.

This distinction has been significantly sharpened recently. Under the Indeterminate Sentence Law, which was the system under review in *Olivas*, the purposes of imprisonment were deterrence, isolation and rehabilitation. Not the least of these was rehabilitation. "It is generally recognized by the courts and by modern penologists that the purpose of the indeterminate sentence law, like other modern laws in relation to the administration of the criminal law, is to mitigate the punishment which would otherwise be imposed upon the offender. These laws place emphasis upon the reformation of the offender. They seek to make the punishment fit the criminal rather than the crime."

The enactment of the Uniform Determinate Sentencing Act marked a significant change in the penal philosophy of this state regarding adult offenders. "The Legislature finds and declares that the purpose of imprisonment for crime is punishment. This purpose is best served by terms proportionate to the seriousness of the offense with provision for uniformity in the sentences of offenders committing the same offense under similar circumstances. The Legislature further finds and declares that the elimination of disparity and the provision of uniformity of sentences can best be achieved by determinate sentences fixed by statute in proportion to the seriousness of the offense as determined by the Legislature to be imposed by the court with specified discretion."

There has been no like revolution in society's attitude toward juvenile offenders. It is still true that "[j]uvenile commitment proceedings are designed for the purposes of rehabilitation and treatment, not punishment." Therefore, Juvenile Court Law continues to provide for indeterminate terms, with provision for parole as soon as appropriate.

In *Olivas* this court objected that "(t)here has been no showing made that youthful offenders necessarily require longer periods of confinement for rehabilitative purposes than older adults." No such objection is appropriate here since under the Determinate Sentencing Act rehabilitation is no longer the standard for term fixing. * * *

In conclusion, because minors and adults are not "similarly situated" with respect to their interest in liberty, and because minors adjudged wards of the juvenile courts and committed to the Youth Authority and adults convicted in the criminal courts and sentenced to prison are not confined for the same purposes, Welfare and Institutions Code section 726 does not deny minors equal protection of the laws. * * *

NOTES

1) Another Equal Protection Rationale In *Smith v. State*, 444 S.W.2d 941 (Tex. Ct. Civ. App. 1969), the juvenile court judge committed a fifteen-year-old delinquent to the State training school for an indeterminate period not extending beyond his twenty-first birthday. The juvenile complained that he faced possible confinement for a period of almost five years for carrying a switch-blade knife whereas an adult convicted of the same offense could not be confined for more than one year. The Court rejected his claim that the "difference in the authorized period of confinement solely because of his tender years denies him the equal protection of the laws." In upholding, the longer, indeterminate disposition, the Court noted:

> Where a class is selected for differential treatment, the pertinent inquiry concerns the existence of some reasonable nexus between the classification adopted and a valid governmental objective. A classification is invulnerable to an "equal protection" attack if it is reasonable, and a classification is reasonable if it includes all persons who are similarly situated with respect to the law. * * * [A] statute will be upheld if any state of facts may reasonably be conceived which would sustain the rationality of the classification. This standard assigns to the Legislature the primary responsibility for evaluating the relevant facts and results in a judicial tolerance of a rather loose relationship between the classifying trait and the legislative purpose, without inquiring whether the social benefits resulting from the statute are important enough to justify the burdens imposed upon the affected class. Perhaps the most important practical effect of this method of inquiring into the reasonableness of a classification is that it places upon the person attacking the statute the burden of demonstrating that the classification is utterly lacking in rational justification. * * *

> The purpose of our statutes relating to the handling of youthful offenders is, as in other states having juvenile court systems, the education, treatment and rehabilitation of the child, rather than retributive punishment.[13] The emphasis on training and rehabilitation, rather than punishment, is underscored by the declaration that juvenile proceedings are civil, rather than criminal, in nature. Instead of a complaint or indictment we have a "petition." * * *

---

13. "The purpose of this Act is to secure for each child * * * such care, guidance and control, preferably in his own home, as will serve the child's welfare and the best interest of the state; and when such child is removed from his own family, to secure for him custody, care and discipline as nearly as possible equivalent to that which should have been given him by his parents." Art. 2338–1, § 1. "The purpose of this Act is * * * to provide a program of constructive training aimed at rehabilitation and reestablishment in society of children adjudged delinquent by the courts of this state and committed to the Texas Youth Council, and to provide active parole supervision for such delinquent children until officially discharged from custody of the Texas Youth Council." Art. 5143d, § 1. The purpose of the training schools, "and of all education, work, training, discipline, recreation, and other activities carried on in the schools and other facilities shall be to restore and build up the self-respect and self-reliance of the children and youth lodged therein to qualify them for good citizenship and honorable employment." Id., § 21.

Since the purpose of the legislation is to salvage youthful offenders, it requires no straining of the judicial imagination to find the existence of a reasonable relationship between the legislative purpose and the use of age as the classifying trait. It is indisputably the province of the Legislature to determine the manner in which various offenders will be treated, and if the difference in treatment is founded upon an arguably rational basis, the legislative decision is determinative. The Legislature could reasonably have concluded that children, as a class, should be subject to indefinite periods of confinement, not to extend beyond their twenty-first birthday, in order to insure sufficient time to accord the child sufficient treatment of the type required for his effective rehabilitation. This conclusion might be based on physiological and psychological differences between children and adults, the types of crimes committed by children, their relation to the criminal world, their unique susceptibility to rehabilitation, and their reaction, as a class, to confinement and discipline, as well as reformative treatment. It is true that some or all of these conclusions are based on sociological, psychological and penological theories which are not universally agreed on among so-called social scientists, but the fact that eminent scholars believe such theories to be valid prevents us from branding them as palpably irrational.

Since appellant has produced no data refuting the legislative conclusion that children who engage in deviant conduct require a different type and manner of confinement than do adult criminals, the presumption of validity with which the permissive method of review shields the statute remains unpierced. * * *

If the purpose of permitting longer periods of detention for children was to punish youthful offenders more severely than adult criminals, the application of a strict standard of review would seem justified. But where the legislative purpose is to benefit the affected class, a less strict standard would seem proper. We are familiar with the literature reflecting disillusionment concerning the practical administration of the rehabilitative ideal, and the burgeoning literature of criticism of the juvenile system in this country. But, as the Texas Supreme Court pointed out only a few days ago, "while we must accept as true much of the dismal picture painted in *Gault* as to the abuses of the juvenile system, we cannot condemn out of hand the Texas Youth Council, the juvenile judges, and other trained people working in this field. The policy of the juvenile laws has been fixed by the Texas Legislature; and we conceive it to be our duty to uphold the spirit of that law * * *."

The purpose of our juvenile laws is benign, rather than invidious. Whether the law is actually beneficial to the affected class is a question which is not susceptible of easy judicial determination. The determination of the beneficial effects of our system depends, at least in part, on complicated factual judgments of whether our juvenile program helps or impedes the salvation of child offenders. It is not necessary, in this case, to hold that the required judgment is of the sort that should be left to the political processes. But we do hold that, in the absence of at least some data indicating that the legislative promise of treatment rather than punishment is not, in fact, being kept, we should not attempt, by a reasoning process alone, to determine whether the promised benefits are, in fact, being accorded to juvenile offenders. * * * But the record before us is bare of any indication that the promise of treatment and rehabilitation has been broken, and that the legislative declaration of purpose is no more than cant and hypocrisy used to justify what is essentially a system that does no more than provide longer terms of imprisonment for children.

What evidence could Smith produce to demonstrate that "the promise of treatment and rehabilitation has been broken"? How would a judge know whether a youth is receiving treatment or punishment?

2) Juvenile Dispositions Exceed Length of Adult Criminal Sentences In *In the Interest of J.K. v. State*, 68 Wis.2d 426, 431, 228 N.W.2d 713, 715–716 (Wis. 1975), the Wisconsin Supreme Court rationalized a juvenile's indeterminate sentence for a period longer than that authorized for an adult because a juvenile's institutional placement was not the equivalent of incarceration as an adult. The Court rejected the delinquent's claim that equated "institutional placement under the Children's Code with incarceration of an adult offender under the Criminal Code. Such exact and complete analogizing of proceedings in the children's court with proceedings in the criminal courts was early rejected by this court. * * * If the state legislature were to eliminate incarceration as an appropriate penalty for the adult crime of possession of LSD, that would not limit or change the right of a juvenile court judge to place an adjudged delinquent found to have possessed LSD, in the custody of the state department until the age of 18. * * * Such commitment of a juvenile is not for the purpose of penalty or punishment, but for the purpose of effecting a result that will serve the best interests of the child, its parents and the public."

3) The Benefits of Being Sentenced to a Longer Term as a Juvenile In *In re Interest of A.M.H.*, 233 Neb. 610, 447 N.W.2d 40 (Neb.1989), the judge ordered a juvenile confined in an institution until she reached the age of 19, a possible term of a year and a half, whereas an adult convicted of the same offense could be incarcerated for no more than three months. Despite the differences in sentence lengths, the Nebraska Supreme Court rejected the juvenile's equal protection claim:

Equal protection guarantees that similar persons will be dealt with similarly by the government. When examining a claim of deprivation of equal protection, the first inquiry is whether the statute discriminates among those who are similarly situated. [The difference in sentences] does not deny equal protection to juveniles * * * because such juvenile offenders are not similarly situated to adult offenders inasmuch as an institutional placement of a minor is not to be equated with the incarceration of an adult offender. * * *

We do not find adult offenders and juveniles adjudicated delinquent to be "similarly circumstanced" * * * The Juvenile Court Act has a legitimate and salutary goal, "to provide for the rehabilitation of delinquent minors at a stage before they have embarked upon the commission of substantive criminal offenses." * * * The primary purpose of the Act is remedial and preventive rather than punitive.* * * To this end the juvenile court acts as *parens patriae* * * * and the court and its allied agencies must be enabled to give the minor the care and guidance the Act is designed to provide. * * * As the indeterminate sentencing scheme of the Act is considered to play a useful role in achieving this goal and is applied similarly to all juveniles declared to be delinquent, it meets constitutional standards. * * * We note further that the Act offers unique benefits and favorable treatment to juvenile offenders which are not available to adult offenders. A juvenile may at any time apply to the court for a change in custodianship from the Department of Corrections or for restoration to the custody of his parents * * * and the court must terminate its wardship of a minor * * * if at any time it finds the best interests of the minor and the public no longer require it to be continued. * * * In addition to this continuous opportunity to seek early release, the juvenile incurs no criminal record and is not disqualified from subsequently holding public office or receiving any license other than, in an appropriate case, one relating to the operation of motor vehicles. * * * There is also special provision for the confinement of minors, who, if under 17 years of age, may not be incarcerated with adult criminal offenders * * *.

4) Children vs. Adults or Treatment vs. Punishment Did the court in *Eric J.*, p. 123, reject his equal protection claims because children differ from adults and therefore the legislature may classify offenders on the basis of age? In what ways does *Smith*, p. 127 suggest that young people differ from adults that justifies longer terms for youths? Or, did those courts base their equal protection analyses on the differences between *treatment* as a juvenile and *punishment* as an adult? How can a court determine whether the state is treating or punishing a juvenile confined in an institution for committing an offense? *See e.g.*, Barry C. Feld, "The Juvenile Court Meets the Principle of Offense: Punishment, Treatment, and the Difference it Makes," 68 *B.U.L.Rev.* 821 (1988). Or, did the court base its equal protection distinctions on the differences between juveniles' and adults' liberty interests? As we will see in Chapter 5, *Schall v. Martin*, the United States Supreme Court observed that juveniles are not entitled to "liberty, but to custody."

5) The Purpose of Juvenile Court Intervention In *Smith*, the Court emphasized the purpose of the Texas juvenile court legislation. How does a Court know the purpose of legislation? Forty-two states' juvenile codes contain a statement of legislative purpose or similar preamble. Since the late–1970s, however, at least ten states—almost one-quarter of those with legislative purpose statement in their juvenile law statutes—have redefined the purpose of their juvenile courts. *See* Feld, "Punishment, Treatment, and the Difference it Makes," *supra* note 4. These purpose clause amendments downplay the role of rehabilitation in the child's "best interest" and acknowledge the importance of public safety, punishment, and individual accountability in the juvenile justice system. One of the distinguishing characteristics of these purposes clause amendments is that "in many jurisdictions accountability and punishment have emerged among the express purposes of juvenile justice statutes." Andrew Walkover, "The Infancy Defense in the New Juvenile Court," 31 *UCLA L.Rev.* 503 at 528 (1984).

States have redefined the purpose of their juvenile courts to include the following objectives: "correct juveniles for their acts of delinquency," *Ark. Stat.Ann.* § 9–27–302(b)(2) (1987); "protect society * * * [while] recognizing that the application of sanctions which are consistent with the seriousness of the offense is appropriate in all cases," *Fla.Stat.Ann.* § 39.001(2)(a) (West Supp. 1988); "render appropriate punishment to offenders," *Haw.Rev.Stat.* § 571–1 (1985); "protect the public by enforcing the legal obligations children have to society," *Ind.Code Ann.* § 31–6–1–1 (Burns 1980); "protect the community against those acts of its citizens which are harmful to others and * * * reduce the incidence of delinquent behavior," *Va. Code Ann.* § 16.1–227 (1988); and "reduce the rate of juvenile delinquency and * * * provide a system for the rehabilitation or detention of juvenile delinquents and the protection of the welfare of the general public," *W.Va.Code* § 49–1–1(a) (1986). *See generally,* Linda F. Giardino, "Statutory Rhetoric: The Reality Behind Juvenile Justice Policies in America," 5 *Journal of Law and Policy* 223 (1996).

Since the courts decided *Smith* and *Eric J.*, both Texas and California have amended the purpose clauses of their juvenile codes. *See* Chapter 8, *infra* at 927–28. In Texas, the purpose is now to "protect the welfare of the community and to * * * control the commission of unlawful acts by children" and "consistent with the protection of the public and public safety * * * to promote the concept of *punishment* for criminal acts," *Tex. Fam. Code Ann.* § 51.01 (2) (Vernon 1998). In California, the purpose is now to "provide for the protection and safety of the public," *Cal.Wel. & Inst. Code* § 202 (West Supp. 1998). The California preamble also authorizes "punishment that is consistent with the rehabilitative objectives," insists that " '[p]unishment,' for the purposes of this chapter, does not include retribution," and charges juvenile courts to "consider safety and protection of the public" as well as the "best interests of the minor" when judges make their sentencing decisions, *Cal. Welf. & Inst. Code* § 202 (West Supp. 1988). Would either of these amended purpose clauses have affected the courts' analyses or the outcomes in *Smith* or *Eric J.*? We will consider these legislative changes in juvenile code purpose clauses further in Chapter 8 when we revisit the distinctions between "treatment" as a juvenile and "punishment" as an adult.

6) Punishment or Treatment In *Eric J.*, the Court noted that "juvenile commitment proceedings are designed for the purposes of rehabilitation and treatment, not punishment." Analyzing juvenile courts' sentencing statutes and dispositional practices provides another indicator of the punitive or therapeutic purposes of juvenile court dispositions. When a statute bases a delinquent's sentence on the characteristics of the past offense, the judge usually imposes a determinate and proportional sentence with a penal goal of retribution or deterrence. When a judge bases the disposition on the characteristics of the offender, however, she typically imposes a sentence that is indeterminate and non-proportional with a goal of rehabilitation or incapacitation. The theory that correctional administrators will release an offender only when she has been "rehabilitated" underlies indeterminate sentencing. When judges individualize youth's sentences, theoretically they only consider the offense for diagnostic purposes and as an indicator the child's "real needs," *See* Barry C. Feld, "The Juvenile Court Meets the Principle of

Offense: Punishment, Treatment, and the Difference it Makes," 68 *B.U.L.Rev.* 821, 847–879 (1988), who analyzes the shift in juvenile court sentencing legislation from indeterminate, non-proportional, and offender-oriented dispositions to determinate, proportional, and offense-based dispositions. *See also,* Julianne P. Sheffer, "Serious and Habitual Juvenile Offender Statutes: Reconciling Punishment and Rehabilitation Within the Juvenile Justice System," 48 *Vand. L. Rev.* 479 (1995). If a state imposes determinate sentences on a juvenile based on the seriousness of the present offense and prior record, would that affect the court's analysis in *Eric J.*? Again, we will reconsider these issues in Chapter 8 when we examine the dispositions that juvenile court judges impose on delinquents.

C. NON–CRIMINAL MISCONDUCT— STATUS OFFENSES

Progressive reformers envisioned "childhood" as a period of vulnerability and dependency. They viewed adolescence as a period of preparation for adulthood and regarded certain "adult-like" activities as inimical to children's long-term development. Anthony Platt, *The Childsavers: The Invention of Delinquency* (2nd ed., 1977). Families and schools bore primary responsibility to socialize, supervise, and control young people. Progressives viewed young people as nested within these primary socializing agencies, re-enforced their dependency within them, and regarded their autonomy from them as threatening to themselves and the community. If a young person "escaped" from this overlapping network of supervision, then she literally was "out of control." The juvenile court provided an organizational mechanism to regulate children, to re-enforce the authority of the other social institutions that controlled children, and to oversee the adequacy of their families' supervision. Recall, the original definition of a delinquent child in the Illinois Juvenile Court Act of 1899 included only those youths who violated the law. *Supra*, p. 4. However, the 1907 amendment to the Act, broadened the scope of jurisdiction of the juvenile court to encompass not only those youths who violated the law, but also those who were incorrigible, growing up in idleness, frequenting unsavory environs, and the like. *Supra*, p. 7.

The Progressives conceived of the juvenile court as a benign substitute for parental inadequacy, as *parens patriae*, and included status offenses in its definition of delinquency so that public authorities could respond to vulnerable children at risk and their ineffective families. John Sutton, *Stubborn Children: Controlling Delinquency in the United States* (1988). Part of the juvenile court's mission included enforcing other peoples' rules about childhood, for example, parental discipline or school regulations. Virtually all of the behaviors subsumed in the status jurisdiction represent efforts either to reinforce the authority of the primary socializing agencies, to reinstate controls over youths, or to enforce the norms of childhood. Because "incorrigible," "stubborn," or run-away children threatened parental control, juvenile courts intervened to reinforce parents' authority. When truant children "escaped" from or threatened the control of schools, juvenile court intervened to reassert schools' dominion. Youthful behavior such as "waywardness," "immorality," alcohol consumption, or sexual experimentation posed a threat to a youth's long-term development, offended Progressives' sensibilities about the nature of children, offended the normative construction of childhood, and thus constituted adult activities forbidden to young people.

The essential characteristic of status offenses are behavior in which adults may engage but which the state prohibits for young people simply because of their age, that is, their "status" as children. Lee Teitelbaum, "Status Offenses and Status Offenders," in *A Century of Juvenile Justice* 159–60 (M. Rosenheim, F. Zimring, D. Tanenhaus, and B. Dohrn, eds., 2002), notes that status offenses are wrongful only because the child is a minor. Being a child—a legal minor—is a status that one occupies without regard to conduct or choice and which subjects those who occupy that status to special restrictions by the juvenile court. Juvenile courts' status offense jurisdiction encompasses several types of violations. Some status offenses are "proscriptive rules (of the "thou shalt not" variety) that apply only to young people, such as laws prohibiting those under some specified age from using alcohol or being on the streets past a certain hour." Other status offenses entail violations of "prescriptive rules." These rules require children to do something affirmative—to obey their parents' orders, to attend school, and the like. Children who violate these rules may be deemed "incorrigible" or "unruly," or truant. A third type of regulation concerns children who are "wayward" or "growing up in idleness or crime." These generic catch-all prohibitions apply to children may not have violated a specific proscription applicable to minors or disobeyed parental rules, but who appear to be in circumstances in which they have or may do something wrong. Juvenile courts' jurisdiction over status offenses authorizes states to regulate children's behaviors much more extensively than comparable conduct by adults. To that extent, juvenile courts' status jurisdiction implicates children's rights, the differences between young people and adults, and the functions of families.

A full-blown exploration of "children's rights" is beyond the scope of these materials or a juvenile justice and delinquency course. *See e.g.* Joseph Hawes, *The Children's Rights Movement: A History of Advocacy and Protection* (1991); David Archard, *Children: Rights and Childhood* (1993); Martha Minow, *Making All the Difference: Inclusion, Exclusion, and American Law* (1990). Suffice it to say, because of the dependent status of children, young people's "rights" or claims to autonomy implicate the interests of the child, the parent, and the state, and the balance of interests and authority among the three. "A certain tension has always existed in American law, both public and private, between the competing values of protection or autonomy for children. How should decision making authority be allocated between child and parent, and equally important, how should that same power be allocated between parent and state? Essentially, the question is 'Who decides what is best for the child?' " Samuel M. Davis, Elizabeth S. Scott, Walter Wadlington, and Charles H. Whitebread, *Children in the Legal System* 1 (4th Ed., 2009).

NOTES

1) Characteristics of Status Offenses The following excerpt from **Howard Snyder and Melissa Sickmund,** *Juvenile Offenders and Victims: 2006 National Report* **106–107, 191–192 (2006)** summarizes some of the characteristics of and court responses to status offenders:

Status offense and delinquency case processing differ. A delinquent offense is an act committed by a juvenile for which an adult could be prosecuted in criminal court. There are, however, behaviors that are law violations only for juveniles and/or young adults because of their status. These "status offenses" may include behaviors such as running away from home, truancy, alcohol possession or use, ungovernability, and curfew violations.

In many ways, the processing of status offense cases parallels that of delinquency cases. Not all states, however, consider all of these behaviors to be law violations. Many states view such behaviors as indicators that the child is in need of supervision. These states handle status offense matters more like dependency cases than delinquency cases, responding to the behaviors by providing social services.

Although many status offenders enter the juvenile justice system through law enforcement, in many states, the initial official contact is a child welfare agency. About half of all status offense cases referred to juvenile court come from law enforcement.

The federal Juvenile Justice and Delinquency Prevention Act states that jurisdiction shall not hold status offenders in secure juvenile facilities for detention or placement. This policy has been labeled deinstitutionalization of status offenders. There is an exception to the general policy: a status offender may be confined in a secure juvenile facility if he or she has violated a valid court order, such as a probation order requiring the youth to attend school and observe a curfew. * * *

The formal status offense caseload differs substantially from the delinquency caseload. What are status offenses? Status offenses are behaviors that are law violations only if committed by a person of juvenile status. Such behaviors include running away from home, ungovernability (being beyond the control of parents or guardians), truancy, and underage drinking (which also applies to young adults through age 20). A number of other behaviors may be considered status offenses (e.g., curfew violations, tobacco offenses), but they are not detailed in these analyses.

In many jurisdictions, agencies other than juvenile courts are responsible for handling status offense cases. In some communities, for example, family crisis units, county attorneys, and social services agencies have assumed this responsibility. If status offense cases are referred to juvenile court, the court may divert some of these youths away from the formal justice system to other agencies for service rather than filing a petition for formal processing. The analyses presented here are based on juvenile court data and are, thus, limited to cases petition to court for formal processing between 1985 and 2002.

Of petitioned status offense cases handled by juvenile courts between 1985 and 2002 involving charges of truancy or liquor law violations, running away from home, or ungovernability, the most common were truancy violations (34%) followed by liquor law violations (30%), running away (19%), and ungovernability (17%).

Females account for most run-away cases A major difference between delinquency and status offense cases is the large proportion of status cases that involve females.

Percent of petitioned status offense cases involving females, 1985–2002

Offense	Female Proportion
Runaway	61%
Truancy	46
Ungovernability	46
Liquor	30

The juvenile court ordered probation in most adjudicated status offense cases From 1985 through 2002, among adjudicated runaway, truancy, ungovernability, and liquor law violation cases, formal probation was the most likely disposition. Some cases resulted in out-of-home (residential placement), and some (primarily liquor cases) resulted in other sanctions such as fines, community service, restitution, or referrals to other agencies for services. The remaining few were released with no additional sanctions.

Percent of petitioned status offense cases involving females, 1985–2002

Offense	Residential placement	Formal probation
Runaway	27%	61%
Truancy	11	78
Ungovernability	26	66
Liquor	8	57

2) Statutes Defining Status Offenses Consider the following statutory formulations of juvenile court jurisdiction over non-criminal misconduct. Which of these provisions provides the most guidance to children, their parents, and the juvenile court judge enforcing them? As you reflect on your own adolescence, could the state have applied any of these provisions to your conduct?

Cal. Welf. & Inst. Code § 601 (West 1998). Minors habitually disobedient or truant

(a) Any person under the age of 18 years who persistently or habitually refuses to obey the reasonable and proper orders or directions of his or her parents, guardian, or custodian, or who is beyond the control of that person, or who is under the age of 18 years when he or she violated any ordinance of any city or county of this state establishing a curfew based solely on age is within the jurisdiction of the juvenile court which may adjudge the minor to be a ward of the court.

(b) If a minor has four or more truancies within one school year * * * or a school attendance review board or probation officer determines that the available public and private services are insufficient or inappropriate to correct the habitual truancy of the minor, or to correct the minor's persistent or habitual refusal to obey the reasonable and proper orders or directions of school authorities, * * * the minor is then within the jurisdiction of the juvenile court which may adjudge the minor to be a ward of the court. However, * * * no minor who is adjudged a ward of the court pursuant solely to this subdivision shall be removed from the custody of the parent or guardian except during school hours.

Minn. Stat. § 260.015 Definitions (1997)

Subd. 19. Habitual truant. "Habitual truant" means a child under the age of 16 years who is absent from attendance at school without lawful excuse for seven school days if the child is in elementary school or for one or more class periods on seven school days if the child is in middle school, junior high school, or high school.

Subd. 20. Runaway. "Runaway" means an unmarried child under the age of 18 years who is absent from the home of a parent or other lawful placement without the consent of the parent, guardian, or lawful custodian.

Subd. 21. Juvenile petty offender; juvenile petty offense. (a) "Juvenile petty offense" includes a juvenile alcohol offense, a juvenile controlled substance offense, * * * or a violation of a local ordinance, which by its terms prohibits conduct by a child under the age of 18 years which would be lawful conduct if committed by an adult.

(b) Except as otherwise provided in paragraph (c), "juvenile petty offense" also includes an offense that would be a misdemeanor if committed by an adult.

(c) "Juvenile petty offense" does not include any of the following:

(1) a misdemeanor-level violation of [certain violent offenses];

(2) a major traffic offense or an adult court traffic offense * * *;

(3) a misdemeanor-level offense committed by a child whom the juvenile court previously has found to have committed a misdemeanor, gross misdemeanor, or felony offense; or

(4) a misdemeanor-level offense committed by a child whom the juvenile court has found to have committed a misdemeanor-level juvenile petty offense on two or more prior occasions, unless the county attorney designates the child on the petition as a juvenile petty offender notwithstanding this prior record. * * *

Subd. 22. Juvenile alcohol offense. "Juvenile alcohol offense" means a violation by a child of any provision of [the alcohol code] or an equivalent local ordinance.

Subd. 23. Juvenile controlled substance offense. "Juvenile controlled substance offense" means a violation by a child * * * with respect to a small amount of marijuana or an equivalent local ordinance.

Ohio Stat. § 2151.022 (West 1998): As used in this chapter, "unruly child" includes any of the following:

(A) Any child who does not subject himself or herself to the reasonable control of his or her parents, teachers, guardian, or custodian, by reason of being wayward or habitually disobedient;

(B) Who is an habitual truant from home or school;

(C) Any child who so deports himself or herself as to injure or endanger his or her health or morals or the health or morals of others;

(D) Who attempts to enter the marriage relation in any state without the consent of his parents, custodian, legal guardian, or other legal authority;

(E) Any child who is found in a disreputable place, visits or patronizes a place prohibited by law, or associates with vagrant, vicious, criminal, notorious, or immoral persons;

(F) Any child who engages in an occupation prohibited by law or is in a situation dangerous to life or limb or injurious to his or her health or morals or the health or morals of others;

(G) Who has violated a law * * * that is applicable only to a child.

South Carolina Code § 20–7–6605 (8) (1999). "Status offense" means any offense which would not be a misdemeanor or felony if committed by an adult, including, but not limited to, incorrigibility or beyond the control of parents, truancy, running away, playing or loitering in a billiard room, playing a pinball machine or gaining admission to a theater by false identification.

How many of these "status offense" provisions have adult analogies? What, if anything, does a state do about adults who engage in these prohibited behaviors? Why are these behaviors subject to control when engaged in by children? Which statutes better defines the appropriate bases for state intervention? The following materials illustrate states' efforts to define the problematic "status" of childhood and autonomy, and explore some of the legal and policy issues embedded in regulating non-criminal misconduct. As the cases of *E.S.G.* and *S.S.* illustrate, sometimes parents invoke the authority of the state as an ally to enable parents to reassert control over "wayward" and "immoral" children. On the other hand, as the materials on curfew illustrate, sometimes the state may assert authority over children's autonomy and either restrict or re-enforce parents' child-rearing preferences.

S. S. AND L. B. v. STATE

299 A.2d 560 (Me.1973).

POMEROY, JUSTICE. [Juveniles challenged validity of their adjudication for the status offense of "living in circumstances of manifest danger of falling into habits of vice or immorality." They contended that the statute violated the Due Process Clause of the Fourteenth Amendment because it was unconstitutionally vague; violated Due Process Clause because the conduct on which the Juvenile Court based its judgment would not have been a criminal offense of committed by an adult; and violated Equal Protection Clause because the juveniles' conduct would not have been a criminal offense if committed by an adult.]

The petition alleged in each case the juvenile was "living in circumstances of manifest danger of falling into habits of vice or immorality." No other material circumstances of the cases are presented in the record before us. We are not informed by the record exactly what conduct of the juveniles was alleged in the petitions as supporting the conclusory allegation. Suffice it to say the cases as presented to this Court raise no issue as to the legal sufficiency of the petitions.

We are confronted then with a facial attack on the constitutionality of 15 M.R.S.A. 2552 insofar as it purports to give jurisdiction to juvenile courts to treat as a juvenile offender, a juvenile whose conduct is described therein as "living in circumstances of manifest danger of falling into habits of vice or immorality." * * *

The petitioners here clearly equate due process requirements in juvenile proceedings with the well established due process requirements of criminal proceedings. With this contention we do not agree.

The petitioners further argue that because a juvenile proceeding can result in restrictions upon a juvenile's liberty or even his loss of liberty, the conclusion is compelled that the due process requirements of criminal prosecution must apply. We answer this by saying it is not every loss of liberty which gives rise to an application of the standards of due process required in criminal proceedings. Just as the natural parent may constitutionally place limitation on the child's freedom of locomotion and may substitute the will and judgment of the parent for that of the child and thus constrain the child's will for his own protection, so also may the State in the exercise of its parens patriae guardianship. The juvenile proceeding is not a criminal proceeding. Its purpose is not punishment. "The basic and primary idea of the legislature is salvation, not punishment."

It, therefore, follows that the due process requirements of the Constitution must be equated to this sui generis proceeding and not to a criminal proceeding.

The statute with which we are here concerned calls for the protective facilities of the State to come into play whenever a juvenile, as defined by the Act, commits an offense and whenever the conduct of the juvenile is such that he or she is living in circumstances of manifest danger of falling into habits of vice or immorality. The statute does not relate to a status. By its express terms it relates to conduct of the juvenile. It treats with a class of persons, i.e., a person under the age of 17 in whom the State has asserted a special protective interest with constitutional validity.

The statute is unconstitutionally vague on its face even if the strictest standard applicable to criminal proceedings were to be followed only if when considering this limited class of persons, i.e., persons under the age of 17, men and women of common intelligence can only guess as to its meaning. * * * If no standard of conduct is specified at all, legislation is unconstitutionally vague. It is valid legislation, however, if it requires a person to conform his conduct to an imprecise but comprehensible normative standard.

We conclude that when applied to this class, the language of the statute is sufficiently definite to withstand constitutional attack on grounds of vagueness.

The meaning of the reference phrase becomes clear when one considers the history and purpose of our juvenile laws. The basic purpose of affording juveniles special treatment is that the State as *parens patriae* has a duty to avoid giving children criminal records and, insofar as possible, prepare the child to cope with life and not become a criminal in his adult years.

The Legislature accords special treatment to those juveniles whose conduct would be criminal if done by an adult, and based on the predictive concept, offers its preventive and corrective facilities to those juveniles whose conduct, if unchanged, is likely to become criminal when the child becomes an adult. Thus, the conduct of a juvenile which constitutes living in circumstances of manifest danger of falling into habits of vice or immorality means conduct of the juvenile while living in circumstances which make it clear that if such conduct is continued, there is manifest danger of falling into habits of criminal conduct-such conduct being considered vice and immorality.

The terms vice or immorality mean those vices and those immoral acts which are defined by statute as criminal and the constituent elements of which are clearly described in the statute and in the case law interpreting the statute or by common law definition.

Stated simply, the judgment which must be made by the juvenile judge is: On the basis of the allegations of the petition and the facts presented in support thereof, has the juvenile demonstrated a pattern of conduct which manifests or makes clear to all reasonable men that if persisted in and not changed, there is real danger that the conduct will, when the child becomes an adult, bring about violation of the criminal statutes? * * *

The petitioners' complaint that there is denial of equal protection of the law because the conduct sufficient to bring the juvenile within the ambit of the juvenile statute would not have been a criminal offense, if committed by an adult, is answered by pointing out that the child is not charged with criminal conduct. The statute merely provides that the protective custody of the State shall come into play whenever there is conduct manifesting a danger that if persisted in, it will become criminal when the child becomes an adult.

Much of the petitioners' brief is dedicated to an attempt to demonstrate that the predictive system has failed and as Mr. Justice Fortas said in *Gault*, the child winds up with the worst of two worlds. We concede that the statistics cited in *Gault* make a powerful case for the conclusion that the juvenile offender system has been neither well funded nor well administered. Despite this impressive documentation, our faith in the soundness of the predictive system is not shaken. We think no reasonable man would shoot a sound horse because his saddle stirrup needs repairs. The only alternative it seems to us would be to take what Mr. Justice Blackmun described as the easy way and to flatly hold the full scope of rights constitutionally assured for the adult accused in criminal proceedings are to be imposed on this State's juvenile proceedings. This would be overlooking the difference in substance as well as procedure in the two. In fact, the criteria for determining due process requirements of non-criminal proceedings by the State are the same for children as for adults.

We fear, should deviant children be diverted to the criminal processes, great social harm would result.

By the Act of 1854 and by the Act of 1931, Maine embarked upon a humanitarian program designed to save deviant children from a life of adult lawlessness. To make the program feasible it required children to give up some rights they had formerly enjoyed when they were treated through the criminal process. * * *

To divert children back into the stream of criminal process would surely result in restoration of all the constitutional safeguards accorded adult criminals, but we fear it would have the effect of diverting public attitudes from the humanitarian goal of providing a helping hand to the deviant young.[6] * * * The time may come when we are disabused of our belief that the potential for growth inherent in the juvenile system cannot be ignored. * * *

This facial attack on this statute must fail. The entry must be, Writ of Habeas Corpus denied in both cases.

---

6. A theme of paternalism and benign motivation permeates the history and present posture of the juvenile system. This requires special comment of a cautionary nature. It is not the motivation of the State in this area which justifies the application of non-criminal standards of due process, but it is, rather, recognition of the Legislature's right to establish a separate and non-criminal system for juveniles. The Court is not and must not be beguiled by the commendable intentions of the State but must, because of them, all the more diligently scrutinize the separate system established to insure that it contains the safeguards necessary to protect the rights of the individual juvenile from abuse. As Justice Brandeis said, dissenting in *Olmstead v. United States*, (1927) "Experience should teach us to be most on our guard to protect liberty when the government's purposes are beneficent. * * * The greatest dangers to liberty lurk in insidious encroachment by men of zeal, well-meaning but without understanding." A similar idea was expressed by two dissenting justices in *Wyman v. James*, (1971). (Marshall and Brennan, JJ., dissenting): "A paternalistic notion that a complaining citizen's constitutional rights can be violated so long as the State is somehow helping him is alien to our Nation's philosophy." These words of caution must be considered in evaluating the holding in the instant case and in dealing with future problems which arise out of the juvenile system.

DUFRESNE, CHIEF JUSTICE (dissenting).

* * * The reported issue is, whether 15 M.R.S.A. § 2552 prohibiting the following conduct of juveniles—"living in circumstances of manifest danger of falling into habits of vice or immorality"—is facially unconstitutional on the ground of vagueness. The Maine Juvenile Act is no different from most of the statutes on the subject in the various states. In certain aspects, the Act is very specific in that it makes it an offense for a juvenile to commit any of the offenses made criminal when committed by adults, plus habitual truancy and repetitive desertion of one's home without just cause, but, then, in an effort to vest a broad discretion in the Juvenile Court, the Legislature extends the definition of a juvenile offense to include an open-ended general concept of offensive conduct such as "behaving in an incorrigible or indecent and lascivious manner", "knowingly and willfully associating with vicious, criminal or grossly immoral people" and "living in circumstances of manifest danger of falling into habits of vice or immorality." We are only concerned with the last portion of the statute.

The "void for vagueness" doctrine, applicable to test the constitutionality of any statutory provision, requires that a statute be sufficiently certain and definite in meaning to afford a reasonable degree of guidance as to just what constitutes the conduct required or prohibited to all involved in its application, to the persons whose activity the statute attempts to regulate, to the courts who must decide rights or obligations under it, and, in the criminal and juvenile sectors, to the police who are charged with its enforcement. Stated otherwise, the rule is that "a statute which either forbids or requires the doing of an act in terms so vague that men of common intelligence must necessarily guess at its meaning and differ as to its application violates the first essential of due process." * * *

Reasonable precision in the definition of proscribed conduct for juveniles should occupy a position of the highest order in the scheme of constitutional values, equally so with similar reasonable particularity in the definition of prohibited adult criminal activity. A juvenile's forfeiture of his liberty for committing a juvenile offense is just as weighty on the scales of justice in terms of due process of law as an adult's loss of liberty for conviction of crime. Statutory vagueness in legislation regulating juvenile conduct under penalty of State wardship is equally abhorrent under considerations of fair play, if not more so, as uncertainty in criminal statutes may be to the adult world. Definitional uncertainty in a juvenile offense statute is an open invitation to virtually unfettered administration by the police and arbitrary judicial adjudication by the courts. It lends itself to an unconstitutional delegation of legislative power to the juvenile judge by permitting him to decide without reasonable legislative standards what the law is in each case. It makes for unequal dispensation of justice. All persons are entitled to be informed as to what the State commands or forbids. * * *

It is contended that the Maine Juvenile Act, in defining juvenile offenses in terms of "living in circumstances of manifest danger of falling into habits of vice or immorality" is unconstitutionally vague and violative of due process, because it imposes a loss of liberty upon the status or mode of life of the juvenile. It is true that, according to Webster's definitions of "living", the term may refer to the "state" of a person, to the "fact of being" in circumstances of manifest danger of falling into habits of vice or immorality. On the other hand, it could refer to the concept of "producing * * * action" which brings about such circumstances. Construing the statute in the light of the benevolent purposes of the juvenile legislation, I do ascribe to the Legislature an intent to proscribe active conduct and not to penalize a juvenile's status as such acquired by the pursuit of a certain pattern of living. Thus, the Act in this area would pass constitutional requirements, provided the definition of the juvenile offense in its totality furnishes the necessary intelligible standards to guide the child, his parents, the police and the courts. * * *

It is within the legislative domain to prohibit juvenile conduct conducive to future criminality. The Legislature may pass laws designed to protect minor children against a life of delinquency and determine in its wisdom what activities involve danger that a child will become a hazard either to himself or to society. The State may, to protect its interest in the proper operation, control and discipline of the family unit, pass legislation tending to insure the existence of harmonious relations between family members, and between the family unit and the rest of the public society, to the extent of making it a crime or a juvenile offense for juveniles persistently to disobey reasonable and lawful parental commands. But, all such laws, designed to suppress crime in the future through preventive conviction and incarceration in the case of adults or preventive adjudication of delinquency and wardship when juveniles are involved, as desirable as they may be to combat crime or juvenile delinquency, cannot be achieved through techniques that trample on constitutional rights. The rule of law implies equality and justice in application which cannot exist when legislation provides no reasonable standard to determine prohibited conduct. * * *

I believe that the Due Process Clause of the Fourteenth Amendment establishes a sphere of personal liberty for every individual, and this includes juveniles, subject to reasonable intrusions by the State in furtherance of legitimate state interests. A juvenile has a constitutional right to freedom from being state institutionalized except for justifiable state action in furtherance of a legitimate public interest but, even then, the State's exercise of power must be energized, and deployed within proper constitutional strictures, one of which is that the statute defining the State's right to interfere must provide reasonable standards to guarantee against arbitrary and unequal application of the law. * * *

The concept of juveniles found "living in circumstances of manifest danger of falling into habits of vice or immorality" is not of recent vintage. * * * We must, therefore, approach the construction of the reference statute having in mind that the Legislature was thinking in terms of modes of life in juveniles mostly characterized by idleness and vagrancy which were then philosophically considered fertile soil of future criminality. Far from the minds of our Legislators was the modern precision of constitutional due process espoused by the *Gault*, *Winship* and *McKeiver* decisions. * * *

The youth of this State are entitled to know what conduct will jeopardize their right to live at home and force them into a State institution. The application of due process requirements to the statute defining juvenile offenses will in no way affect the informality, flexibility, or speed of the juvenile hearing, except that it will protect the child against the uncontrolled subjective discretion of well-meaning officials. Instead of being disruptive of the juvenile process, compliance with fair notice requirements will advance the basic philosophy, idealism and purposes of the system.

It is conceded that the language of the statute—"habits" of vice or "immorality"—, when used in their unbridled connotation, fails to meet that degree of specificity which due process enjoins on legislative enactments purporting to regulate conduct the violation of which subjects the individual to the loss of his liberties. * * * The concept of morality, and the same would be true of its near-synonym "vice", has occupied men of extraordinary intelligence for centuries, without notable progress (among even philosophers and theologians) toward a common understanding. Certainly, the present generation has a much different conception of the term from that entertained by past generations. A legislative directive addressed to children couched in terms so broad that men of extraordinary intelligence cannot agree as to meaning must perforce be constitutionally deficient for vagueness. * * *

[By judicial fiat, the majority interprets the statute] as a pattern of conduct which manifests or makes clear to all reasonable men that if persisted in and not changed, there is real danger that the conduct will, when the child becomes an adult, bring about violation of the criminal statutes.

Such a definition creates as much confusion and ambiguity as it attempts to resolve. First, it seems to require proof of active conduct, whether of commission or omission, not of a criminal nature in itself— (violation of any criminal statute is a juvenile offense). Secondly, the conduct need not be misconduct—(eating as a glutton might be precursory to a life of thievery). Thirdly, there must be more than one act or omission, since the definition speaks of a pattern of conduct. Fourthly, the repeated conduct must be of such a nature that all reasonable men would conclude that if persisted in and not changed, there would exist a real danger when the child becomes an adult (in the near or distant future depending on the age of the child at the time) that because of such conduct he will violate the criminal laws. The new definition fails to delineate with sufficient precision the nature of the conduct which will activate the statute. The standards set up are so encompassing as to encourage arbitrary and discriminatory enforcement of the law and to force compliance with different life-styles deemed appropriate by the

respective judges before whom the juvenile may be compelled to appear.
* * *

On the merits, I would declare the section of the statute at issue unconstitutional and would set aside the original adjudication of a juvenile offense in each case and order the respective petitioners released from their commitment and detention under it, since I conclude it gives insufficient notice to youth as to the reach of the law, provides law enforcement officers with no clear guide for evaluation of prohibited juvenile conduct, and offers the judge inadequate standards for inclusion and exclusion in the dispensation of even justice. It is impermissibly vague.

NOTES

1) Judicial Rejection of "Void for Vagueness" Challenges Courts exhibit little patience with juveniles' claims that "incorrigibility" and "immorality" statutes fail to provide them with adequate notice or punish them for their "status" as children. "It is not feasible for a statute to specify the instances in which a child might be out of control of his parents * * * in a self-destructive manner. Spelling out every prohibited act or omission is not required if the general terms are understandable. * * * Children of ordinary understanding know that they must obey their parents or those persons lawfully standing in a parent's place. Therefore, the phrase 'beyond the control and power of his parents' gives fundamentally fair notice to the child of a pattern of behavior that might cause him or her to be considered incorrigible." *In re Jackson*, 6 Wash.App. 962, 965, 497 P.2d 259, 261 (1972). In *Blondheim v. State*, 84 Wash.2d 874, 880, 529 P.2d 1096, 1101 (Wash. 1975), the Court observed that "Although incorrigibility is a condition or state of being, one acquires such a 'status' only by reason of one's conduct or a pattern of behavior proscribed by the statute. An incorrigible child is one 'who is beyond the control and power of his parents * * *.' The statute does not relate to a true 'status.' Rather, it related to a course of conduct or the nature of the child which places it beyond the lawfully exercised control or lawfully exercised power of its parents, guardian, or custodian. * * * The 'status' of being incorrigible was established by proof of the facts alleged in the petition. But, it was not the 'status' of being incorrigible for which petition was given a suspended commitment and placed on probation. Rather, it was her conduct which placed her beyond the lawfully exercised control or power of her mother, that led to her being found incorrigible, and, thus, resulted in the suspended commitment."

Other jurisdictions label their "status" offenders as "Children in Need of Supervision" or CINS. *E.g., La. Stat. Ann.–R.S.* § 13:1569 (15) (1975). Courts summarily reject "void for vagueness" challenges to those CINS statutes as well. "[T]he intent of the legislature is to provide for judicial supervision of certain class of children who are engaging in conduct which is detrimental to their development and well-being in lieu of affixing the stigma of delinquency on such children upon adjudication. * * * A detailed listing of every type of behavior falling within the purview of a 'child in need of supervision' is unrealistic. A cursory attempt to define all types of behavior injurious to a child with mathematical precision makes the reason for granting broad and general jurisdiction obvious. The state's interest in protecting the physical, moral or mental well-being of children under seventeen years of age is at the heart of the juvenile act." *In re Tina Marie Gras*, 337 So.2d 641, 644–45 (La. Ct. App. 1976). Similarly, the court in *District of Columbia v. B.J.R.*, 332 A.2d 58, 60–61 (D.C.Ct.App.1975), observed that "Children of ordinary understanding know that to repeatedly abscond from home in defiance of the lawful commands of one's parent is a rather drastic form of disobedience that may well precipitate some disciplinary or punitive action. * * * [L]anguage limitations are particularly acute for the draftsmen of juvenile laws designed to implement the broad social policy of reinforcing parents in carrying out their responsibility to support and promote the welfare of their children. To enable parents to carry out this legal obligation, the law gives them the authority to control their children through the giving of reasonable and lawful commands. The CINS statute reinforces this authority and may be invoked when children repeatedly refuse to recognize their obligation to obey such commands."

In **E. S. G. v. State**, 447 S.W.2d 225 (Tex. Ct. Civ. App. 1969), appellant's mother enlisted the juvenile court to deal with her fourteen-year-old daughter over whom she had lost control. E.S.G. remained away from her home for days at a time, lived with a girl reputed by her mother to be a prostitute, and with whom she hung around at the Bus Station and other public places. After E.S.G. had been absent from home for over a week, her mother and a police officer located her in a downtown transient apartment only partially dressed and with a young adult male. The juvenile court adjudged E.S.G. delinquent and committed her to the State Training School for Girls for an indefinite term not to extend beyond her twenty-first birthday. E.S.G. appealed and challenged the validity of the "status offense" statute:

> BARROW, C.J.: The finding of delinquency is based on Sec. 3(f) of said Act, which defines a delinquent child as one who "habitually so deports himself as to injure or endanger the morals or health of himself or others." The question presented here is whether this portion of the statute is unconstitutionally vague. * * *

> The relatively comprehensive word "morals" is one which conveys concrete impressions to the ordinary person. Such word is in constant use in popular parlance, and this word or words of similar import are used in the statutes of most States to define behavior illegal for a child. In thirty-three States a child can be found delinquent if he is guilty of immoral conduct, and the various States' definitions of immoral conduct are all somewhat similar to Sec. 3(f). The obvious reason for granting such broad and general jurisdiction is seen when one makes even a cursory attempt to define all the types and patterns of behavior and conduct injurious to a child. The need to correct habits and patterns of behavior which are injurious to the health or morals of the child goes to the very heart of our Juvenile Act. The judge in this case observed that most girls who came before said court were charged with violation of this section.

It is not questioned that appellant was engaged in a course of conduct injurious to her morals, if not her health. Nor could it be questioned that this fourteen-year-old girl understood that such conduct was injurious to her morals. Even her attorney recognized that her parents had lost control and that the girl desperately needed supervision. * * *

The use of words such as "morals" is not confined to our Juvenile Act. * * * [T]he Court [has] said: "(These) terms (general welfare, health, peace, morals and safety of the people, and sense of decency) have a well-accepted and understood meaning 'Other States have reached a similar result.' * * * "The use of words of general meaning is the essence of our code system. Thus, in a sphere so vital to the community as the welfare of its youth, the words used in a statute designed to enable the Legislature to come to grips effectively with the problems of juvenile delinquency should be upheld where their frequent use in penal statutes gives assurance that they are understood by men of ordinary intelligence."

It is conceded that Sec. 3(f), supra, defines a delinquent child in general terms. However, the petition filed under same must allege the specific acts or conduct which brings the child within the prohibited behavior. This protects the rights of the child in the adjudicatory stage of the proceedings. We do not believe that the section in question is unconstitutionally vague. * * *

CADENA, Justice (dissenting): The Texas Juvenile Act, is typical of almost every statute on the subject in that, after defining the term "delinquent child" in rather specific language relating to conduct violative of penal statutes and ordinances, it vests broad discretion in the Juvenile Court by extending the definition to include any child who "habitually so deports himself as to injure or endanger the morals or health of himself or others" or who "habitually associates with vicious and immoral persons." In this case, the petition filed by the State alleged that appellant had habitually so conducted herself as to endanger "the morals or health of herself and others," without specifying whether the facts alleged in the petition constituted a threat to appellant's morals or health, or to the morals or health of others. * * *

The vagueness doctrine requires that a statute be sufficiently clear to give notice of the conduct required or prohibited to those whose activity the statute attempts to regulate. A judgment that a particular statute does not provide the required certainty or definiteness is seldom, if ever, a completely objective conclusion.* * *

Appellant here was found guilty of "habitually" engaging in conduct calculated to "injure" or "endanger" the "morals" or "health" of herself or of others. The principal source of uncertainty in the statute probably results from the use of the word "morals," a term involving an appeal to judgment and requiring determination of questions of degree, although, perhaps to a lesser extent, the words "habitually," "injure" and "danger" are also classifiable as ductile terms. The difficulty with terms such as "morals" is that they have no external "object-referent."

Where the equilibrium between the individual's claim of freedom and society's demands upon him is left to be struck *ad hoc* on the basis of subjective evaluations, the case law furnishes no reliable guide to the application of the requirement of definiteness. * * *

The consistent failure of courts to attempt to define language of the type now before us merely points up the fact that such language has no objective meaning in the sense of contrast with merely individual opinion or preference. If a statute is, in reality, not vague, the result would be that, after the decision in the particular case, the statute is sufficiently clear and precise to enable men of common intelligence and understanding to determine what is prohibited and what is permissible. * * * It is no answer to a vagueness attack to say that language is definite and certain while confessing a complete inability to express what the language means.

In any event, cases where judges profess to understand perfectly the meaning of such terms as "morals" are instances where the statutory language is directed to adults. Here, a directive addressed to children is couched in terms which have been the source of controversy among theologians, philosophers and judges for centuries. It is one thing to say that a judge, drawing upon his experience and knowledge of the law and of "meanings" attached to nebulous terms at common law, should understand what is moral and what is not. It is another thing to expect a child of ten or, as in this case, of fourteen, to understand the meaning of words which judges are unable to define while assuring us that the language is "perfectly clear." * * *

The application of less strict constitutional standards to juvenile proceedings has sometimes been justified by distinguishing between proceedings, such as criminal cases, where the adjudication relates to past conduct, and those cases, such as juvenile cases, where the purpose of the inquiry is to determine a present or future condition. The distinction is, at best, illusory. All conduct determinations can be, by the careful choice of language, transformed into condition determinations. The inquiry can always be focused, not on the defendant's past conduct, but on a condition of which such misdeeds are probative. The danger in resting a particular decision on the conduct-condition dichotomy is that a court can achieve a result substantially the same as that flowing from the criminal-civil distinction rejected in *Gault.* * * *

The provision on which the State relies in this case is typically vague and all-encompassing, especially when administered with the informality which is typical of the juvenile court. It establishes the judge or jury as the arbiter of the behavior and morals of every child. The situation is ripe for overreaching, for imposition of the judge's or jury's own code of youthful conduct. Such provisions easily become a means of enforcing conformity. For example, today, most adults seem to associate long hair with immoral conduct, except, perhaps, in the case of their own children, in which instance it is regarded as nothing more than an unsettling and transitory adolescent foible. The provision in question is vague enough to allow almost any child, given compromising circumstances, to be caught up in the jurisdictional net of the juvenile court.

Provisions such as those found in Section 3(f) lack a common meaning; they are not derived from fixed, or even reasonably fixed, criteria; they allow labeling a child as a "delinquent" even where it is clear that his actions are reasonably normal responses to highly provocative or intolerable situations. The statute, lacking reasonable standards, is "susceptible of sweeping and improper application," and it furnishes a convenient tool for use against particular persons or groups who incur official displeasure. Nor is there any overriding need for such vagueness. In the case of appellant, a sufficiently clear warning could have been formulated by the Legislature without calling in the English faculty of a university. All that had to be done was to state that a child who ran away from home was in need of the State's "protection." Such direct statutory language would authorize the commitment of more than a majority of the girls who have been committed to a state training school.

Our Legislature, perhaps, has the power to make the jurisdiction of the juvenile court depend upon unexamined assumptions that certain conduct is a precursor to delinquency. I do not accept the explanation that we cannot adequately protect our youth without vesting the courts with power to make their findings of jurisdiction dependent on subjective definitions.

2) The Gendered Administration of Status Offenses Both *S.S. and L.B.* and *E.S.G.* involved the commitment of female offenders to delinquency institutions for non-criminal misconduct. Snyder and Sickmund, *National Report, supra* note 1, p. 134, reported that states are proportionally more likely to deal with girls as status offenders than as delinquents. As the cases illustrate, states traditionally treated status offenses as a form of delinquency, and detained and incarcerated status delinquents in the same institutions as criminal delinquents even though they had committed no crimes. Parental referrals often overloaded juvenile courts with intra-family disputes, diverted scarce resources from other tasks and exacerbated rather than ameliorated family conflict. R. Hale Andrews, Jr., & Andrew H. Cohn, "Ungovernability: The Unjustifiable Jurisdiction," 83 *Yale L.J.* 1383 (1974). The cases also illustrate that the status jurisdiction raises legal issues of "void for vagueness," equal protection, and procedural justice. Juveniles charged with status offenses typically enjoyed fewer procedural rights than youths charged with criminal delinquency, for example, the burden of proof. *See e.g.* Erin M. Smith, "In a Child's Best Interest: Juvenile Status Offenders Deserve Procedural Due Process," 10 *Law and Inequality* 253 (1992). Status offense legislation granted judges broad discretion to prevent unruliness or immorality from ripening into criminality, and intervention often reflected individual judges' values and prejudices. The exercise of standardless discretion to regulate noncriminal misconduct often had a disproportionate impact on poor, minority, and female juveniles. Meda Chesney–Lind, "Judicial Paternalism and the Female Status Offender: Training Women to Know Their Place," 23 *Crime & Delinquency* 121 (1977); Meda Chesney–Lind and Randall Shelden, *Girls, Delinquency, and Juvenile Justice* (2nd ed. 1997).

While the notion of helping "troubled" children is inherently attractive, commentators and policy groups have criticized extensively the definition and administration of status jurisdiction in the post-*Gault* decades. Legislative recognition that juvenile courts often failed to realize their benevolent purposes has led to a strategic retrenchment of juvenile courts' jurisdiction over non-criminal misconduct such as "immorality" or "incorrigibility," behavior that would not be a crime if committed by an adult. In the 1970s, critics objected that juvenile courts' status jurisdiction treated non-criminal offenders indiscriminately like criminal delinquents, disabled families and other sources of referral through one-sided intervention, and posed insuperable legal issues for the court. *See* H. Ted Rubin, *Juvenile Justice: Policy, Practice, and Law* (2d ed. 1985) (states traditionally treated status offenses as a form of delinquency, detained and confined status delinquents in the same institutions as criminal delinquents); Joel F. Handler & Julie Zatz, *Neither Angels nor Thieves: Studies in Deinstitutionilization of Status Offenders* (1982); Al Katz & Lee E. Teitelbaum, "PINS Jurisdiction, the Vagueness Doctrine, and the Rule of Law," 53 *Ind. L.J.* 1 (1978) (concluding that judges exercise of standardless discretion to regulate noncriminal misconduct had a disproportionate impact on female juveniles); Meda Chesney–Lind, "Girls and Status Offenses: Is Juvenile Justice Still Sexist?," 20 *Crim. Just. Abstract* 144 (1988).

As we will see in Chapters 4, 5, and 8, judicial and legislative disillusionment with juvenile courts' responses to noncriminal youths led to diversion, deinstitutionalization, and decriminalization reforms that have removed much of the "soft" end of juvenile court clientele. Malcolm W. Klein, "Deinstitutionalization and Diversion of Juvenile Offenders: A Litany of Impediments," 1 *Crime & Just.* 145 (1979) (implementation of diversion reforms and their possible "net-widening" effects). The Federal Juvenile Justice and Delinquency Prevention Act (JJDPA) of 1974, 42 *U.S.C.* § 5633(a)(12)(A) (1995), required states to begin a process of removing noncriminal offenders from secure detention and correctional facilities, and provided the impetus to deinstitutionalize status offenders. Although the number of status offenders in secure detention facilities and institutions declined by the mid–1980s, juvenile courts confined only a small proportion of status offenders in secure institutions and most remain eligible for commitment to "forestry camps" and other medium security facilities. John Sutton, *Stubborn Children* (1988). Moreover, amendments to the Federal Juvenile Justice and Delinquency Prevention Act in 1980 weakened even the restrictions on secure confinement; status offenders who run away from non-secure placements or violated court orders may be charged with contempt of court, a delinquent act, and incarcerated. 42 *U.S.C.* § 5633(a)(12)(A) (1983); Jan Costello and Nancy Worthington, "Incarcerating Status Offenders: Attempts to Circumvent the Juvenile Justice and Delinquency Prevention Act," 16 *Harvard Civil Rights–Civil Liberties L. Rev.* 41 (1981); Ira Schwartz, Martha Steketee, and Victoria Schneider, "Federal Juvenile Justice Policy and the Incarceration of Girls," 36 *Crime and Delinquency* 503 (1990). The use of the contempt power to "bootstrap" status offenders into delinquents remain an important continuing source of gender bias in juvenile justice administration. Donna Bishop and Charles Frazier, "Gender Bias in Juvenile Justice Processing: The Implications of the JJDP Act," 82 *Journal of Criminal Law and Crim.* 1162 (1992); Cheryl Dalby, "Gender Bias Toward Status Offenders: A Paternalistic Agenda Carried Out Through the JJDPA," 12 *L. & Inequality* 429 (1994). Finally, deinstitutionalization also provided the impetus to transfer many middle-class, white, and female youths whom the juvenile justice system formerly handled as status offenders into the private sector system of mental health and chemical dependency treatment and confinement. See, e.g., Ira M. Schwartz, *(In)Justice for Juveniles* (1989); Lois A. Weithorn, "Mental Hospitalization of Troublesome Youth: An Analysis of Skyrocketing Admission Rates," 40 *Stan. L. Rev.* 773 (1988).

These legislative and judicial reforms represent a strategic withdrawal from "child saving," an acknowledgment of the limited utility of coercive intervention to provide for child welfare, a reduced role in enforcing normative concepts of childhood, and a diminished prevention mission. Despite the decline of the broad "morality" status jurisdiction, efforts to regulate specific aspects of the non-criminal conduct of children persist in many guises, for example, truancy, curfew, tobacco and alcohol consumption, and the like. We will encounter issues associated with status offenses when we consider diversion in Chapter 4, detention in Chapter 5, procedural safeguards in Chapter 7, and dispositions in Chapter 8.

3) Judicial Resolution of Domestic Discord: Problem Parents bring their fourteen-year-old daughter, Pamela, to juvenile court and file a petition alleging that she is an "unruly child." At the hearing, the parents testify that Pamela refuses to obey their reasonable commands, dates a seventeen-year-old youth of whom they strongly disapprove, stays out late, lies to them when confronted about her behavior, constitutes a negative influence on her younger siblings, and they no longer want her in the home. They disbelieve her promises to be good in the future and will not permit her to return home until the court has "taught her a lesson." Given the statutory definition of status jurisdiction, how should a juvenile court judge respond? *In re William S.*, 120 Misc.2d 790, 466 N.Y.S.2d 914 (1983); *In re Jacqueline Jackson*, 6 Wash.App. 962, 497 P.2d 259 (Wash. Ct. App., 1972) (failed regularly to attend school classes, did not inform parents of whereabouts and remained away from home at night). Should the judge be able to place Pamela in a detention center to "teach her a lesson"? In a non-secure, shelter-care facility? What if, when her parents return the next day, she refuses to return home with them and vows to run-away? How should the court respond then? *In re Snyder's Welfare*, 85 Wash.2d 182, 532 P.2d 278 (1975) (placing daughter in foster home on probation and ordering her and her parents to seek counseling to reconcile relationship). What if counseling is unsuccessful? In the absence of status jurisdiction, how would or should families resolve intra-family disputes? Should young people be allowed to "divorce" their parents? If they do, what happens to them?

1. CURFEW: AN OFFENSE FOR CHILDREN ONLY

Juvenile curfews provide a rich example of laws and policies for children for which no direct adult analogues exist. When young people challenge the validity of legislative restrictions on their freedom and autonomy, what standard of review should courts use and why? Does a youth have a "fundamental right" to autonomy? Does classification on the basis of age constitute a "suspect class"? What is the "compelling state interest" in imposing a curfew? How should a state "narrowly tailor its regulations" to achieve this interest? What types of data and justifications should judges require when they review the validity of curfew laws? How should courts balance the respective interests of juveniles, their parents, and states in limiting youth's autonomy?

QUTB v. BARTLETT

11 F.3d 488 (5th Cir.1993).

JOLLY, CIRCUIT JUDGE: This appeal presents a challenge to the constitutionality of a nocturnal juvenile curfew ordinance enacted by Dallas, Texas. The ordinance makes it a misdemeanor for persons under the age of seventeen to use the city streets or to be present at other public places within the city between certain hours. Several plaintiffs brought suit against the city to strike down the ordinance. The district court ruled for the plaintiffs, holding that the ordinance violated both the United States and the Texas Constitutions, and permanently enjoined enforcement of the ordinance. The city appeals. Because we conclude that this ordinance does not violate the United States or Texas Constitutions, we reverse the district court.

On June 12, 1991, in response to citizens' demands for protection of the city's youth, the Dallas City Council enacted a juvenile curfew ordinance. This ordinance prohibits persons under seventeen years of age from remaining in a public place or establishment from 11 p.m. until 6 a.m. on week nights, and from 12 midnight until 6 a.m. on weekends. As defined by the ordinance, a "public place" is any place to which the public or a substantial group of the public has access, and includes streets, highways, and the common areas of schools, hospitals, apartment houses, office buildings, transport facilities, and shops. "Establishment" is defined as "any privately-owned place of business operated for a profit to which the public is invited, including but not limited to any place of amusement or entertainment."

Although the ordinance restricts the hours when minors are allowed in public areas, the ordinance also contains a number of exceptions, or defenses. A person under the age of seventeen in a public place during curfew hours does not violate the ordinance if he or she is accompanied by a parent or guardian, or is on an errand for a parent or guardian. Likewise, minors would be allowed in public places if they are in a motor vehicle traveling to or from a place of employment, or if they are involved in employment related activities. Affected minors could attend school, religious, or civic organizational functions—or generally exercise their First Amendment speech and associational rights—without violating the ordinance. Nor is it a violation to engage in interstate travel, or remain on a sidewalk in front of the minor's home, or the home of a neighbor. And finally, the ordinance places no restrictions on a minor's ability to move about during curfew hours in the case of an emergency. A minor violates the curfew if he or she remains in any public place or on the premises of any establishment during curfew hours, and if the minors' activities are not exempted from coverage. If a minor is apparently violating the ordinance, the ordinance requires police officers to ask the age of the apparent offender, and to inquire into the reasons for being in a public place during curfew hours before taking any enforcement action. An officer may issue a citation or arrest the apparent offender only if the officer reasonably believes that the person has violated the ordinance and that no defenses apply. If convicted, an offending party is subject to a fine not to exceed $500.00 for each separate offense.

Like minors who have violated the offense, a parent of a minor, or an owner, operator, or employee of a business establishment is also subject to a fine not to exceed $500 for each separate offense. A parent or guardian of a minor violates the ordinance if he or she knowingly permits, or by insufficient control allows, a minor child to remain in any public place or on the premises of any establishment during curfew hours. An owner, operator, or employee of a business establishment commits an offense by knowingly allowing a minor to remain upon the premises of the establishment during curfew hours.

On July 3, 1991, two weeks after the ordinance was enacted, Elizabeth Qutb and three other parents filed suit—both individually and as next friends of their teenage children—seeking a temporary restraining order and a permanent injunction against the enforcement of the juvenile curfew ordinance on the basis that the ordinance is unconstitutional.[4] The district court certified the plaintiffs as a class that consisted of two subclasses: persons under the age of seventeen, and parents of persons under the age of seventeen. * * * [T]he district court held that the curfew impermissibly restricted minors' First Amendment right to associate, and that it created classifications that could not withstand constitutional scrutiny. Accordingly, the district court permanently enjoined enforcement of the curfew, and the city now appeals.

We review de novo the district court's conclusions of constitutional law. The minor plaintiffs argue, inter alia, that the curfew ordinance violates the Equal Protection Clause of the Fourteenth Amendment. The Equal Protection Clause "is essentially a direction that all persons similarly situated should be treated alike." Only if the challenged government action classifies or distinguishes between two or more relevant groups must we conduct an equal protection inquiry. Here, it is clear that the curfew ordinance distinguishes between classes of individuals on the basis on age, treating those persons under the age of seventeen differently from

---

4. Before the district court, the plaintiffs asserted several grounds for holding the ordinance unconstitutional. First, they argued that the ordinance impermissibly restricts First Amendment rights of free speech and free association. They also contended that the ordinance violates the Fourth and Fourteenth Amendment right against unreasonable searches and seizures, and that the ordinance divests them of their Fifth and Fourteenth Amendment rights to a presumption of innocence, proof beyond a reasonable doubt, and freedom against self-incrimination. Plaintiffs further maintained that the ordinance violates the equal protection clause, and implicates fundamental liberty and privacy interests protected by the due process clause of the Fourteenth Amendment. Finally, plaintiffs argued that the ordinance is vague and overly broad.

those persons age seventeen and older. Because the curfew ordinance distinguishes between two groups, we must analyze the curfew ordinance under the Equal Protection Clause.

Under the Equal Protection analysis, we apply different standards of review depending upon the right or classification involved. If a classification disadvantages a "suspect class" or impinges upon a "fundamental right," the ordinance is subject to strict scrutiny. Under the strict scrutiny standard, we accord the classification no presumption of constitutionality. Instead, we ask whether the classification promotes a compelling governmental interest and, if so, whether the ordinance is narrowly tailored such that there are no less restrictive means available to effectuate the desired end. In this case, no one has argued, and correctly so, that a classification based on age is a suspect classification. *See Gregory v. Ashcroft*, 501 U.S. 452, 470, 111 S.Ct. 2395, 2406, 115 L.Ed.2d 410 (1991) (holding that age is not a suspect class). The minor plaintiffs, however, have argued that the curfew ordinance impinges upon their "fundamental right" to move about freely in public. For purposes of our analysis, we assume without deciding that the right to move about freely is a fundamental right. We are mindful, however, that this ordinance is directed solely at the activities of juveniles and, under certain circumstances, minors may be treated differently from adults.[6]

Because we assume that the curfew impinges upon a fundamental right, we will now subject the ordinance to strict scrutiny review. As stated earlier, to survive strict scrutiny, a classification created by the ordinance must promote a compelling governmental interest, and it must be narrowly tailored to achieve this interest. The city's stated interest in enacting the ordinance is to reduce juvenile crime and victimization, while promoting juvenile safety and well-being. The Supreme Court has recognized that the state "has a strong and legitimate interest in the welfare of its young citizens, whose immaturity, inexperience, and lack of judgment may sometimes impair their ability to exercise their rights wisely." In this case, the plaintiffs concede and the district court held that the state's interest in this case is compelling. Given the fact that the state's interest is elevated by the minority status of the affected persons, we have no difficulty agreeing with the parties and with the district court.

In the light of the state's compelling interest in increasing juvenile safety and decreasing juvenile crime, we must now determine whether the curfew ordinance is narrowly tailored to achieve that interest. The district court held that the city "totally failed to establish that the Ordinance's

---

6. In *Bellotti v. Baird*, the Court recognized that there were three reasons that allows a court to treat the rights of minors differently from rights of adults: the peculiar vulnerability of children; their inability to make critical decisions in an informed, mature manner; and the importance of the parental role in child rearing. *Bellotti v. Baird*. This analysis affects the balancing between of the state's interest against the interests of the minor when determining whether the state's interest is compelling. However, given the fact that the parties and the district court all agree that the interest of the state in this instance is compelling, it is unnecessary to conduct a full *Bellotti* analysis.

classification between minors and non-minors is narrowly tailored to achieve the stated goals of the curfew." We disagree.

To be narrowly tailored, there must be a nexus between the stated government interest and the classification created by the ordinance. This test "ensures that the means chosen 'fit' this compelling goal so closely that there is little or no possibility that the motive for the classification was illegitimate * * *."

The articulated purpose of the curfew ordinance enacted by the city of Dallas is to protect juveniles from harm, and to reduce juvenile crime and violence occurring in the city. The ordinance's distinction based upon age furthers these objectives. Before the district court, the city presented the following statistical information: 1. Juvenile crime increases proportionally with age between ten years old and sixteen years old. 2. In 1989, Dallas recorded 5,160 juvenile arrests, while in 1990 there were 5,425 juvenile arrests. In 1990 there were forty murders, ninety-one sex offenses, 233 robberies, and 230 aggravated assaults committed by juveniles. From January 1991 through April 1991, juveniles were arrested for twenty-one murders, thirty sex offenses, 128 robberies, 107 aggravated assaults, and 1,042 crimes against property. 3. Murders are most likely to occur between 10:00 p.m. and 1:00 a.m. and most likely to occur in apartments and apartment parking lots and streets and highways. 4. Aggravated assaults are most likely to occur between 11:00 p.m. and 1:00 a.m. 5. Rapes are most likely to occur between 1:00 a.m. and 3:00 a.m. and sixteen percent of rapes occur on public streets and highways. 6. Thirty-one percent of robberies occur on streets and highways. Although the city was unable to provide precise data concerning the number of juveniles who commit crimes during the curfew hours, or the number of juvenile victims of crimes committed during the curfew, the city nonetheless provided sufficient data to demonstrate that the classification created by the ordinance "fits" the state's compelling interest.

Furthermore, we are convinced that this curfew ordinance also employs the least restrictive means of accomplishing its goals. The ordinance contains various "defenses" that allow affected minors to remain in public areas during curfew hours. Although the district court concluded that "[i]t is what the Ordinance restricts * * * and not what it exempts that matters the most," it is clear to us that neither the restrictions of the curfew ordinance nor its defenses can be viewed in isolation from each other; the ordinance can be examined fairly only when the defenses are considered as a part of the whole. To be sure, the defenses are the most important consideration in determining whether this ordinance is narrowly tailored. * * *

With the ordinance before us today, the city of Dallas has created a nocturnal juvenile curfew that satisfies strict scrutiny. By including the defenses to a violation of the ordinance, the city has enacted a narrowly drawn ordinance that allows the city to meet its stated goals[8] while

8. According to the city, its goals in enacting the ordinance are to (1) reduce the number of juvenile crime victims; (2) reduce injury accidents involving juveniles; (3) reduce additional time

respecting the rights of the affected minors. As the city points out, a juvenile may move about freely in Dallas if accompanied by a parent or a guardian, or a person at least eighteen years of age who is authorized by a parent or guardian to have custody of the minor. If the juvenile is traveling interstate, returning from a school-sponsored function, a civic organization-sponsored function, or a religious function, or going home after work, the ordinance does not apply. If the juvenile is on an errand for his or her parent or guardian, the ordinance does not apply. If the juvenile is involved in an emergency, the ordinance does not apply. If the juvenile is on a sidewalk in front of his or her home or the home of a neighbor, the ordinance does not apply. Most notably, if the juvenile is exercising his or her First Amendment rights, the curfew ordinance does not apply.

Against the ordinance's an [sic] expansive list of defenses, the district court attempted to provide examples of activities with which the curfew ordinance would interfere. The district court suggested the example of "a midnight basketball league aimed solely at keeping juveniles off of the streets" to demonstrate that participation in legitimate desirable activities would violate the ordinance unless the activities were officially organized, sponsored, or supervised by the city, a school, a civic association, or some "other entity." In its effort to demonstrate that the ordinance was overly broad, the district court referred to concerts, movies, plays, study groups, or church activities that may extend past curfew hours. The district court finally noted that "every juvenile in the city could be arrested and fined up to $500.00 upon conviction if he or she merely sought to take an innocent stroll or 'gaze at the stars from a public park.'"

With due respect to the able district court, we are convinced that upon examination its analysis collapses. It is true, of course, that the curfew ordinance would restrict some late-night activities of juveniles; if indeed it did not, then there would be no purpose in enacting it. But when balanced with the compelling interest sought to be addressed—protecting juveniles and preventing juvenile crime—the impositions are minor. The district court failed to observe that none of the activities it listed are restricted if the juvenile is accompanied by a parent or a guardian. Even if the child is unaccompanied by a parent or a guardian, we can presume that most events such as a "midnight basketball league" or a church youth group outing ordinarily would be organized, sponsored or supervised by an adult or an organization, and these are exceptions to the curfew. Although it is true that in some situations unaccompanied juve-

---

for officers in the field; (4) provide additional options for dealing with gang problems; (5) reduce juvenile peer pressure to stay out late; and (6) assist parents in the control of their children. The aim of the ordinance is to deter criminal conduct involving juveniles as well as penalize those individuals who violate it. However, the city states that its intent is not to penalize every youth found in public during curfew hours, but to use the ordinance as a tool to help address other criminal activity problems that involve or may potentially involve juveniles. The curfew ordinance provides an officer with reasonable suspicion to approach gangs to determine if any of them are juveniles. According to the city, the curfew ordinance can help address Dallas's gang problem because gang members often congregate in public and set up an environment where criminal activities take place, such as drive-by shootings, fights, and "turf" disputes.

niles may be forced to attend early evening features of a movie or leave a play or concert before its conclusion, this imposition is ameliorated by several of the ordinance's defenses so that the juvenile is not deprived of actually attending such cultural and entertainment opportunities. Furthermore, a juvenile can take an "innocent stroll" and stare at the stars until 11:00 on week-nights and until 12:00 midnight on weekends; indeed, a juvenile may stare at the stars all night long from the front sidewalk of his or her home or the home of a neighbor. Thus, after carefully examining the juvenile curfew ordinance enacted by the city of Dallas, we conclude that it is narrowly tailored to address the city's compelling interest and any burden this ordinance places upon minors' constitutional rights will be minimal.[9]

In addition to the claims presented by the minor plaintiffs, the parental plaintiffs argue that the curfew ordinance violates their fundamental right of privacy because it dictates the manner in which their children must be raised. Although we recognize that a parent's right to rear their children without undue governmental interference is a fundamental component of due process, we are convinced that this ordinance presents only a minimal intrusion into the parents' rights. In fact, the only aspect of parenting that this ordinance bears upon is the parents' right to allow the minor to remain in public places, unaccompanied by a parent or guardian or other authorized person, during the hours restricted by the curfew ordinance. Because of the broad exemptions included in the curfew ordinance, the parent retains the right to make decisions regarding his or her child in all other areas: the parent may allow the minor to remain in public so long as the minor is accompanied by a parent or guardian, or a person at least eighteen years of age who is authorized by a parent or guardian to have custody of the minor. The parent may allow the minor to attend all activities organized by groups such as church groups, civic organizations, schools, or the city of Dallas. The parent may still allow the child to hold a job, to perform an errand for the parent, and to seek help in emergency situations.

In this case, the parents have failed to convince us that the ordinance will impermissibly impinge on their rights as parents. The parents' only "evidence" to support their argument is the testimony of the mother of one of the plaintiffs that her daughter would soon be going to college, and the curfew ordinance—applying only between 11 p.m. and 6 a.m.—would

---

9. The minor plaintiffs argued and the district court held that the minors' first amendment rights of association are also impermissibly impinged upon by the curfew ordinance. We disagree. First, it is questionable whether a fundamental right of association is implicated. The Supreme Court has held that there is no "generalized right of social association," and, that seems to be precisely the type of association we are primarily concerned with in this case. Even in those instances when minors may, for example, associate for political or religious reasons, the majority of those situations will be exempted under one of the defenses to the curfew ordinance. In any event, we have determined that this curfew ordinance satisfies strict scrutiny, and any negligible burden on the individual's right to associate is outweighed by the compelling interests of the state. We have also considered the minor plaintiffs' Equal Protection argument in the light of the Texas Constitution. We find nothing and we have been pointed to no authority—other than an unrelated defamation case—that warrants a different treatment of this issue under the state constitution.

somehow deprive her daughter of the opportunity to learn to manage her time and make decisions before going away to college. Certainly this testimony is insufficient to support the district court's finding that the ordinance unconstitutionally infringed the liberty and privacy interests of parents.

In conclusion, we find that the state has demonstrated that the curfew ordinance furthers a compelling state interest, i.e., protecting juveniles from crime on the streets. We further conclude that the ordinance is narrowly tailored to achieve this compelling state interest. Accordingly, we hold that the nocturnal juvenile curfew ordinance enacted by the city of Dallas is constitutional.

The judgment of the district court is therefore REVERSED.

NOTES

1) Strict or Intermediate Scrutiny and the Characterization of Juveniles' Rights and Interests Appellate courts differ as to whether to use strict or intermediate scrutiny when evaluating juveniles' equal protection challenges to curfew statutes. They reach different outcomes depending on how they characterize the protected interest at stake. For example, courts respond more favorably to juveniles' First Amendment claims than they do to general assertions of a liberty interest. In **Nunez v. City of San Diego**, 114 F.3d 935, 950 (9th Cir. 1997), the court used a "strict scrutiny" analysis and invalidated the San Diego juvenile curfew ordinance because it unduly restricted minors' legitimate First Amendment rights:

> Minors, like adults, have a fundamental right to freedom of expression. Expression includes speech and expressive conduct. Thus, a facial First Amendment challenge to an ordinance can be brought against regulation of "spoken words" or where a statute by its terms regulates the time, place and manner of expressive or communicative conduct. Not every ordinance that burdens expressive conduct implicates the First Amendment, however. The Supreme Court has said that where the facial challenge involves conduct rather than speech itself, the ordinance's overbreadth "must not only be real, but substantial as well, judged in relation to [its] plainly legitimate sweep." Thus, generally applicable regulations of conduct implicate the First Amendment only if they (1) impose a disproportionate burden on those engaged in First Amendment activities; or (2) constitute governmental regulation of conduct with an expressive element. * * *

> San Diego's curfew ordinance restricts access to any and all public forums. * * * [T]he San Diego ordinance significantly restricts expression in all forums for one-third of each day.

> San Diego's broader restriction prohibits conduct that is a necessary precursor to most public expression—thus qualifying as conduct "commonly associated with" expression. * * * [T]he San Diego curfew ordinance has an integral effect on the ability of minors to express themselves. Thus, the San Diego ordinance "is directed narrowly and

specifically at expression or conduct commonly associated with expression." * * *

Having concluded a First Amendment facial challenge is permissible, we apply the traditional three-part test to determine whether the ordinance is a reasonable time, place, and manner restriction: (1) it must be content neutral; (2) it must be narrowly tailored to a significant government interest; and (3) it must leave open ample alternative channels for legitimate expression. It is undisputed that the regulation is content neutral. Plaintiffs contend that ordinance fails the other two prongs of the test.

For First Amendment purposes, the physical and psychological well-being of minors is a compelling government interest. Thus, the ordinance must be narrowly tailored to achieve that interest. We hold the ordinance is not narrowly tailored because it does not sufficiently exempt legitimate First Amendment activities from the curfew. The City argues in its brief that "a broad First Amendment expression exception would effectively reduce a curfew ordinance to a useless device." This admission destroys an argument that the City narrowly tailored its ordinance to serve its compelling interest in minors' well-being while imposing only a minimal burden on their First Amendment rights. The City did not create a robust, or even minimal, First Amendment exception to permit minors to express themselves during curfew hours without the supervision of a parent or guardian, apparently preferring instead to have no First Amendment exception at all. This is not narrow tailoring. We therefore need not reach the question of whether the ordinance leaves open adequate alternative channels of expression. The ordinance is not a reasonable time, place, and manner restriction under the First Amendment. * * *

In **Schleifer v. City of Charlottesville**, 159 F.3d 843 at 847, 851 (4th Cir.1998), the Fourth Circuit Court of Appeals used an "intermediate scrutiny" approach and upheld the constitutionality of a juvenile curfew ordinance for the City of Charlottesville:

First, children do possess at least qualified rights, so an ordinance which restricts their liberty to the extent that this one does should be subject to more than rational basis review. Second, because children do not possess the same rights as adults, the ordinance should be subject to less than the strictest level of scrutiny. We thus believe intermediate scrutiny to be the most appropriate level of review and must determine whether the ordinance is "substantially related" to "important" governmental interests. We also conclude, however, that the ordinance survives constitutional attack under either a substantial or a compelling state interest standard. The narrow means chosen by the City in the ordinance serve strong and indeed compelling public needs.

The text of the Charlottesville curfew ordinance identifies three legislative purposes: (1) to reduce juvenile violence and crime within the city; (2) to protect juveniles themselves from being swept up in unlawful drug activities and from becoming prey to older perpetrators of crime; and (3) to strengthen parental responsibility for children. These enumerated purposes represent important and compelling governmental interests.

The Charlottesville ordinance carefully mirrors the Dallas curfew ordinance that the Fifth Circuit found to satisfy strict scrutiny in *Qutb*. Like the Charlottesville ordinance, the Dallas curfew covered fewer hours than San Diego's and affected minors under the age of seventeen, not eighteen. In addition to exceptions for employment and emergencies and when a minor is in the presence of a parent or guardian, the curfew at issue in *Qutb* included a broad exception for sponsored activities, a First Amendment exception, an exception for being outside on the sidewalk adjacent to the minor's home, and an exception for interstate travel. * * * This curfew, with its narrow scope and comprehensive list of exceptions, represents the least restrictive means to advance Charlottesville's compelling interests. Thus, it would survive even strict scrutiny if that were the appropriate standard of review.

The dissent in **Schleifer v. City of Charlottesville**, 159 F.3d 843 at 862–65 (4th Cir. 1998), argued for a "strict scrutiny" analysis:

Why are the federal constitutional rights of persons who are defined as minors under state law different from those of adults? The answer is that a minor's constitutional rights are basically the same as those of adults, but in certain situations there may be "significant state interest[s] * * * that [are] not present in the case of an adult" that will support a broader authority to regulate minors. When these interests justify regulation, they do so not because a minor's constitutional rights are always inferior to those of an adult but rather because the government's specific interests as regards minors are sometimes sufficient to allow a regulation to survive strict scrutiny. Accordingly, I would hold that the "fundamental rights" of minors are no less fundamental than those of adults and, thus, must be protected with the same vigor under a strict scrutiny analysis. * * * The majority would apply intermediate scrutiny in all cases involving minors, even those in which the government has no justification specific to minors for infringing upon their fundamental rights. In the latter situation the governmental interest in regulating minors under the majority's approach is identical to its interest in regulating adults. Yet the rights of minors could still be treated differently because their "fundamental" rights are not protected with strict scrutiny review. * * * The majority's holding, therefore, allows a minor to be deprived of constitutional rights when a similar deprivation would be constitutionally intolerable for adults, even though the state lacks any reason for different treatment. This result cannot be justified and essentially creates a second-class citizenship for all persons under the age of majority. For these persons, federal constitutional rights will "mature and come into being magically only when [they] attain[ ] the state-defined age of majority. * * * "

In **Hutchins v. District of Columbia**, 188 F.3d 531 (D.C.Cir.1999) the District of Columbia Court of Appeals en banc upheld the validity of the curfew enacted in the District of Columbia using an "intermediate scrutiny" analysis:

We think that juveniles do not have a fundamental right to be on the streets at night without adult supervision. The Supreme Court has already rejected the idea that juveniles have a right to "come and go at will" because "juveniles, unlike adults, are always in some form of custody," and we see no reason why the asserted right here would fare any better. That the rights of juveniles are not necessarily coextensive with those of adults is undisputed, and "unemancipated minors lack some of the most fundamental rights of self-determination—including even the right of liberty in its narrow sense, i.e., the right to come and go at will." * * * Not only is it anomalous to say that juveniles have a right to be unsupervised when they are always in some form of custody, but the recognition of such a right would fly in the face of the state's well-established powers of parens patriae in preserving and promoting the welfare of children. The state's authority over children's activities is unquestionably broader than that over like actions of adults. And it would be inconsistent to find a fundamental right here, when the Court has concluded that the state may intrude upon the "freedom" of juveniles in a variety of similar circumstances without implicating fundamental rights, and can do so in far more intrusive ways than is contemplated here. * * *

Even if juveniles themselves lack a fundamental right of movement, appellees claim that parents have a fundamental, substantive due process right to direct and control their children's upbringing and that such a right is abridged by the curfew. * * * [I]nsofar as a parent can be thought to have a fundamental right, as against the state, in the upbringing of his or her children, that right is focused on the parents' control of the home and the parents' interest in controlling, if he or she wishes, the formal education of children. It does not extend to a parent's right to unilaterally determine when and if children will be on the streets—certainly at night. That is not among the "intimate family decisions" encompassed by such a right.

Even if the curfew implicated fundamental rights of children or their parents, it would survive heightened scrutiny. * * * Considering children's rights first, we agree that constitutional rights do not instantaneously appear only when juveniles reach the age of majority. Still, children's rights are not coextensive with those of adults. So "although children generally are protected by the same constitutional guarantees * * * as are adults, the State is entitled to adjust its legal system to account for children's vulnerability" by exercising broader authority over their activities. This means, at minimum, that a lesser degree of scrutiny is appropriate when evaluating restrictions on minors' activities where their unique vulnerability, immaturity, and need for parental guidance warrant increased state oversight. * * * [S]omething less than strict scrutiny—intermediate scrutiny—would be appropriate here. Not only can juveniles be thought to be more vulnerable to harm during curfew hours than adults, but they are less able to make mature decisions in the face of peer pressure, and are more in need of parental supervision during curfew hours.

To withstand intermediate scrutiny, the curfew must be "substantially related" (rather than narrowly tailored) to the achievement of "important" (rather than compelling) government interests. The asserted government interest here is to protect the welfare of minors by reducing the likelihood that minors will perpetrate or become victims of crime and by promoting parental responsibility. * * * [T]here can be no serious dispute that protecting the welfare of minors by reducing juvenile crime and victimization is an important government interest. * * *

In judging the closeness of the relationship between the means chosen (the curfew), and the government's interest, we see three interrelated concepts: the factual premises upon which the legislature based its decision, the logical connection the remedy has to those premises, and the scope of the remedy employed. * * *

Assuming * * * that the fundamental rights of parents are implicated by curfews, we also conclude that this curfew passes intermediate scrutiny because it is carefully fashioned much more to enhance parental authority than to challenge it. * * * The curfew's defenses allow the parents almost total discretion over their children's activities during curfew hours. There are no restrictions whatsoever on a juvenile's activities if the juvenile is accompanied by a parent, guardian, or an adult over the age of 21 authorized by the parent to supervise the juvenile. * * * Together with the defenses provided for employment and emergencies, parents retain ample authority to exercise parental control. Since the curfew generously accommodates parental rights, preserving parental discretion to direct the upbringing of their children, it does not unconstitutionally infringe on such rights. * * *

Four judges dissented in *Hutchins* from the majority's intermediate scrutiny analysis and objected that the factual premises upon which the majority relied failed to establish the necessary "substantial relationship" between the juvenile crime problem and the District's curfew remedy:

All members of the court agree that a test at least as rigorous as intermediate scrutiny would be proper for evaluating burdens on minors' fundamental right to freedom of movement. * * * Even when the court assumes that the curfew burdens a fundamental right to movement, it fails to conform its application of intermediate scrutiny to Supreme Court instruction and example demonstrating that the proper judicial role requires attention to the evidence on which the legislature relies in intruding upon a fundamental right. When properly applied, intermediate scrutiny reveals that key elements of the curfew—age and time—are insufficiently tailored to address the problem of juvenile crime and victimization that confronted the legislature. By ignoring evidence that almost half of juvenile crime is committed by persons not covered by the curfew, and that most of that crime occurs at hours not within the curfew, the legislature has failed to demonstrate, on this record, the requisite fit between the problem and the chosen solution. * * *

When a minor's fundamental right to movement is at issue, intermediate rather than strict scrutiny is most appropriate. The essence of intermediate scrutiny, as distinct from rational basis review, is that the government must tailor its burden to relatively specific and important ends and justify incidents of the law that exceed or depart from those ends. Tailoring is particularly important when the rights of minors are at stake, inasmuch as substantial discrepancies between the treatment of adults and minors have often turned on unsubstantiated assumptions rather than persuasive evidence. * * *

[I]n the absence of a record warranting deference[,] the curfew does not survive the heightened scrutiny that accompanies the burdens it places on minors' right to free movement. * * *

2) Curfews, Police Discretion, and the Fourth Amendment. The court in *Qutb*, p. 154, n. 8, noted that curfew ordinances provide "a tool to help address other criminal activity problems that involve or may potentially involve juveniles. The curfew ordinance provides an officer with reasonable suspicion to approach gangs to determine if any of them are juveniles." In **Waters v. Barry**, 711 F.Supp. 1125 (D.D.C.1989), the court invalidated an earlier version of the District of Columbia's curfew ordinance as a violation of equal protection. However, the court rejected the claim that the curfew authority violated juveniles' Fourth Amendment right to be free from unreasonable searches and seizures:

[A]s the very language of the Fourth Amendment provides, a right to be free from such intrusions exists only so long as there is not probable cause to believe that an offense has been committed. Here, the District has attempted to criminalize the public presence of juveniles during the curfew hours. Were they not otherwise unconstitutional, the proscriptions of the Act would provide, in fact, valid substantive references for determining the presence or absence of probable cause in a given case. Although the purported crime is utterly simple—nocturnal, public youth—that simplicity causes the type of proof required to justify a search or seizure to be similarly uncomplex. Thus, were a police officer to reasonably conclude that an individual looked "young"—that he or she looked like a minor—the officer would have "probable cause" to believe that the individual was engaged in an illegal act, i.e., being on the streets during the curfew period. If the individual could not prove that he or she was over 18, or that he or she fell within one of the Act's other exceptions, the officer would be entitled to place the individual under arrest. So long as the officer could reasonably have believed that the individual looked "young," the search, seizure or arrest would take place on the basis of probable cause and no Fourth Amendment violation would occur. * * *

As *Qutb* and *Waters* clearly recognize, juvenile curfews give police broad discretion to engage in "pretextual stops" of those youths who look "young." In *Whren v. United States*, 517 U.S. 806, 116 S.Ct. 1769, 135 L.Ed.2d 89 (1996), the Supreme Court held that as long as a police officer had an "objective" basis for her behavior, for example, "reasonable suspicion" or "probable cause" of any law violation, the Court would not examine the officer's "subjective motivation" or what enforcement decision a "reasonable" police officer might have made under similar circumstances absent an ulterior motive. "Subjective intentions play no role in ordinary, probable-cause Fourth

Amendment analysis." Thus, *Whren* provides many opportunities for the pretextual use of curfew violations for other law enforcement purposes. *See e.g.,* Brian J. Lester, "Is It Too Late for Juvenile Curfews? *Qutb* Logic and the Constitution," 25 Hostra L. Rev. 665, 695–6 (1996), who notes that "A prextual stop occurs when the police, using a legal justification such as a minor infraction of the law, 'make[s] a stop in order to search a person or place, or to interrogate a person, for an unrelated serious crime for which they do not have the reasonable suspicion necessary to support a stop.' The evil of pretextual stops is the unlimited power and discretion it gives to police officers to make arrests and searches based upon minor offenses. * * * [U]nder a legal pretext, the police can use the curfew as a reason to approach a juvenile that they suspect is engaged in a serious crime. The justification for approaching is legitimate, but the officer's actual motivation is a pretext. If the juvenile is out past the curfew, an arrest might result in a search and discovery of contraband. The selective enforcement of the curfew to search particular people can result in discrimination."

Debra Livingston, "Gang Loitering, the Court, and Some Realism About Police Patrol," 1999 *S. Ct. Rev.* 141, 171 notes that "it is perverse that vagueness decisions supposedly emanating from a concern with the potential for arbitrary police enforcement may well have tilted localities in the direction of enacting curfews as opposed to gang loitering, disorderly conduct, or other similar public order laws. Curfews may or may not be a better way of reducing crime and improving the quality of life in public spaces, but there is little to suggest that curfews are preferable from the standpoint of limiting the opportunity for arbitrary and discriminatory police enforcement. At least within the hours of their operation, curfews may have the practical effect of authorizing police to approach and detain any person who appears young enough to trigger their prohibitions. * * * Curfews, moreover, are often enacted as 'quick-fix' solutions to concerns about community violence—and without consideration of the police resources needed to enforce them even-handedly. Such laws may not be vague, but the manner in which they are (or are not) employed can in practice still subject a large number of people to spotty, erratic—and even arbitrary—enforcement efforts."

3) Juvenile Crime Rates and the Rational Basis of Curfews The peak time of arrests of juveniles for violent crimes occurs at 3 p.m., and more than one-third of all juvenile arrests for violence occur between 3 p.m. and 6 p.m. "Violent crimes committed by juveniles peak at the close of the school day and decline throughout the evening hours. By contrast with juveniles, the number of violent crimes committed by adults increases from early morning through midnight." Howard Snyder and Melissa Sickmund, *Juvenile Offenders and Victims* 48 (1995). Between 8 p.m. and 6 a.m., police arrest larger proportions of adults than juveniles for violent offenses. What are the implications of these findings for the court's analysis in *Qutb*?

Howard Snyder, "Time of Day Juveniles are Most Likely to Commit Violent Crime Index Offenses," (September 1998); adapted from Melissa Sickmund, Howard Snyder, Eileen Poe–Yamagata, *Juvenile Offenders and Victims: 1997 Update on Violence*. Reports differences in the times at which juveniles and adults commit violent crimes:

Violent Crime Index offending peaks after school for juveniles. About half of the days in a year are school days. The other days fall in summer months, on weekends, and on holidays. Even though school days are half of all days, 57% of violent crimes committed by juveniles occur on school days. In fact, 1 of every 5 violent crimes committed by juveniles occurs in the four hours following the end of the school day (i.e., between 2 p.m. and 6 p.m.).

On nonschool days the incidence of juvenile violence increases through the afternoon and early evening hours, peaking between 8 p.m. and 10 p.m. Temporal patterns of adult violence do not vary between school and nonschool days. Adult violence increases through the afternoon and evening hours, peaking around 11 p.m.

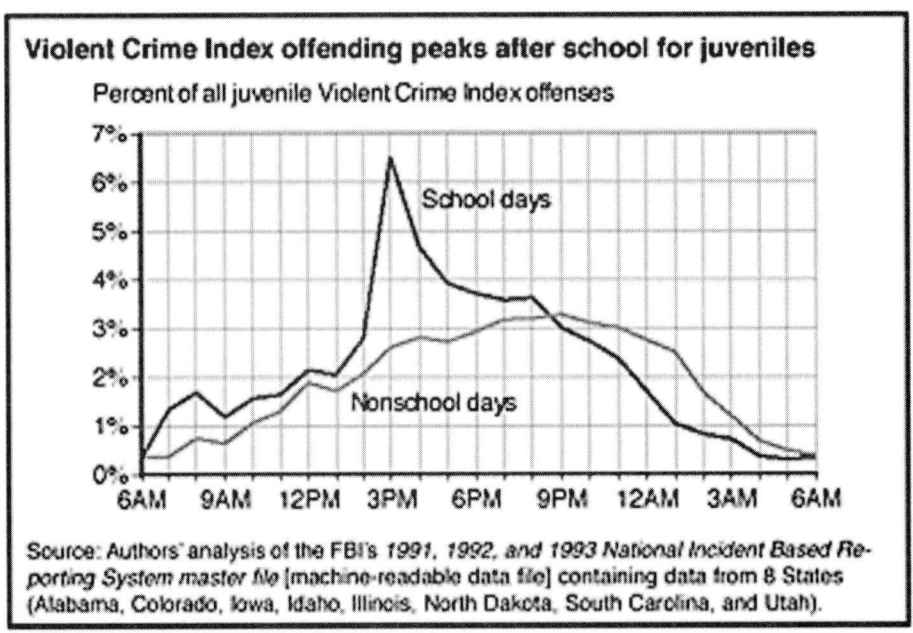

In *Schleifer v. City of Charlottesville*, 159 F.3d 843 at 847, 851 (4th Cir.1998), the court considered and rejected the argument that the curfew did not cover the times when juveniles committed most of their crimes:

> Plaintiffs also dispute the effectiveness of the curfew in reducing juvenile crime. They say that the real problem of juvenile crime is not at night, but in the after school hours. Plaintiffs make much of a report entitled *Juvenile Offenders and Victims: 1996 Update on Violence*, which asserts that only seventeen percent of violent juvenile crime occurs during typical curfew hours, while twenty-two percent happens between 2:00 p.m. and 6:00 p.m. on school days. The City responds that the lower rate of late-night crime may reflect the fact that several of the South Carolina cities in the study actually had late-night curfews in effect. And with respect to conditions in Charlottesville before the curfew, City police officers and Charlottesville's Commonwealth's Attorney confirmed that

the most serious crimes committed by juveniles occurred during curfew hours. Further, the City Council considered evidence that juvenile offenses occurring in Charlottesville between 11:00 p.m. and 6:00 a.m. increased by thirty-eight percent during 1995 and a further ten percent during 1996. Thus the City had reason to believe that, in both volume and severity, nighttime juvenile crime was a serious, growing problem in Charlottesville. * * * Fundamentally, however, this dispute about the desirability or ultimate efficacy of a curfew is a political debate, not a judicial one. If local communities conclude that curfews are ineffective in reducing crime, too onerous to enforce, or too intrusive on the liberties of minors, then they are free to discontinue them. Yet local legislative bodies are entitled to draw their conclusions in light of experience with a curfew's operation, and not have their efforts at reducing juvenile violence shut down by a court before they even have a chance to make a difference.

4) *Bellotti v. Baird* and Juvenile Curfews–Another Framework for Constitutional Analysis The courts in *Qutb*, p. 153, fn. 6, referred to the Supreme Court's decision in *Belotti v. Baird* in their analyses of juvenile curfews. In *Bellotti v. Baird*, 443 U.S. 622, 99 S.Ct. 3035, 61 L.Ed.2d 797 (1979), a plurality of the Supreme Court articulated a general framework for determining when the state may give less deference to the constitutional rights of minors than to those of adults. The *Belotti* plurality noted three factors which may justify differential treatment in a given case: (1) "the peculiar vulnerability of children"; (2) "their inability to make crucial decisions in an informed, mature manner"; and (3) "the importance of the parental role in child rearing." However, the court in *Qutb* did not undertake a full *Belotti* analysis to determine whether the city's disparate treatment was warranted because the parties conceded the existence of a compelling state interest. *See generally*, Brian J. Lester, "Is It Too Late for Juvenile Curfews? *Qutb* Logic and the Constitution," 25 Hofstra L. Rev. 665, 683 (1996), criticizing *Qutb* for bypassing a full *Belloti* analysis. "The mere fact that a compelling state interest exists should not carry as much weight as it did in the *Qutb* court's analysis. Courts can use a concession by all parties as to the existence of a compelling state interest to assist in balancing the factors, but it does not give courts the authority to bypass the balancing of the factors. A *Belotti* analysis still should be performed to determine if a significant state interest not present in the case of adults is applicable to children."

In ***Waters v. Barry***, 711 F.Supp. 1125 (D.D.C.1989), in contrast with *Qutb*, the court applied the *Belotti* factors in its analysis of a District of Columbia juvenile curfew invalidated prior to the one upheld in *Hutchins*, and concluded that they did not justify special restrictions on young people:

> As to the first factor, it is obvious that the plague afflicting the District poses no peculiar danger to children; those thousands of the District's juveniles who engage in wholly legitimate nocturnal activities are no more endangered in the current climate than are the District's adults. The violence is ubiquitous; it afflicts all of us. The Court therefore sees no reason to place a peculiar burden upon the constitutional rights of children, particularly when to do so would involve the deprivation of so much that may be valuable.

The second factor is juveniles' "inability to make critical decisions in an informed, mature manner." The *Bellotti* Court elaborated: in certain situations, the state may "limit the freedom of children to choose for themselves in the making of important, affirmative choices with potentially serious consequences." In this Court's view, the decision to either stay inside or roam at night simply does not present the type of profound decision which *Bellotti* would leave to the state. A decision to leave the house at night does not ineluctably lead to nighttime violence; in all but the exceptional case, nocturnal activities, even by juveniles, will not have "serious consequences." * * *

The final *Bellotti* factor is the importance of the parental role in child-rearing. The District's curfew rests upon the implicit assumption that the traditional family unit, in which parents exercise control over their children's activities, has dissolved in many areas of this city. The Court has no doubt that such an assumption may be accurate with respect to many of this city's "families." Nevertheless, this assumption ignores the many thousands of the District's families for whom the ideal of family unity and parental control still lives. As to these families, struggling against the pressures of modern life, the Act gracelessly arrogates unto itself and to the police the precious rights of parenthood. Rather than furthering the parental role in child-rearing, the Court views the Act as frustrating the parental role in the vast majority of the District's families.

5) Academic Commentary on Juvenile Curfew Ordinances A report by the Office of Juvenile Justice and Delinquency Prevention, *Curfew: An Answer to Juvenile Delinquency and Victimization?* (1996), summarizes the current scope of curfew laws:

Traditionally, the determination of a minor's curfew has been considered to be a family issue, within the parental purview, rather than a matter to be determined by government. Nevertheless, public curfews have been enacted and enforced throughout the Nation's history in reaction to increased juvenile delinquency, decreased parental supervision, and other social trends. Recent increases in juvenile crime and victimization have prompted local communities in many States to once again consider evening curfews (e.g. from 11 p.m. to 6 a.m. on school days and from midnight to 6 a.m. on non-school days) as a viable means to enhance the safety of the community and its children. * * * In a recent study of curfew ordinances in the 200 largest U.S. cities (population of 100,000 or greater in 1992), Ruefle and Reynolds found a dramatic surge in curfew legislation during the first half of the 1990's. Of the 200 cities surveyed, 93 (47 percent) had curfews in effect on January 1, 1990. Between January 1990 and the spring of 1995, an additional 53 of these 200 cities (27 percent) enacted juvenile curfew ordinances, bringing the total of those with curfew laws to 146 (73 percent). During the same period, 37 of the 93 cities with an existing curfew ordinance revised that legislation.

See also, William Ruefle and Kenneth Mike Reynolds, "Curfews and delinquency in Major American Cities," 41 *Crime & Delinq.* 347, 353–54 (1995) (juvenile curfew ordinances exists in 77% of major American cities, and 44% of those cities enacted their curfews after 1989).

The recent spate of curfew ordinances and their judicial challenges have generated extensive legal commentary and analyses. *See e.g.* Kevin Siebert, "Nocturnal Juvenile Curfew Ordinances: The Fifth Circuit 'Narrowly Tailors' a Dallas Ordinance, But Will Similar Ordinances Encounter the Same Interpretation," 73 *Washington U. L. Q.* 1711 (1995); Katherine Hunt Federle, "Children, Curfews, and the Constitution," 73 *Washington U. L. Q.* 1315, 1367 (1995) ("In the context of juvenile curfew laws, the incapacities of children and their concomitant need to be protected from themselves and others permit the state to restrict the activities of children in ways that are impermissible in the case of adults."); Michael Jordan, "From the Constitutionality of Juvenile Curfew Ordinances to a Children's Agenda for the 1990s: Is It Really a Simple Matter of Supporting Family Values and Recognizing Fundamental Rights," 5 *St. Thomas L. Rev.* 389 (1993); Susan Horowitz, "A Search for Constitutional Standards: Judicial Review of Juvenile Curfew Ordinances," 24 *Columbia J. Law and Social Problems* 381 (1991); Tona Trollinger, "The Juvenile Curfew: Unconstitutional Imprisonment," 4 *Wm. & Mary Bill Rts. J.* 949 (1996); Susan L. Freitas, "After Midnight: The Constitutional Status of Juvenile Curfew Ordinances in California," 24 *Hastings Const.L.Q.* 219 (1996); Gregory Z. Chen, "Youth Curfews and the Trilogy of Parent, Child, and State Relations," 72 *N.Y.U.L.Rev.* 131 (1997).

CHAPTER 3

POLICE AND JUVENILES: PRE-TRIAL CRIMINAL PROCEDURE

■ ■ ■

This chapter is not intended to replicate the coverage of the standard course on criminal procedure, for example, to teach the details of Fourth Amendment search and seizure law or of Fifth Amendment interrogation doctrines. Rather, it assumes that the adult constitutional criminal procedural framework generally applies to law enforcement practices involving juveniles. The various materials then examine how states modify their criminal procedures when they apply them to children rather than to adults or because they pursue benevolent and therapeutic purposes rather than punitive ones. If juveniles always are in somebody's custody—parents, schools, or other caretakers—then how does that affect the "reasonableness" of their expectations of privacy when police or other custodians search them? If juveniles are less mature and responsible than adults, then how should the law accommodate youths' developmental limitations in their dealings with police? Questions of juveniles' competence and capacity recur when they consent to a search or waive their *Miranda* rights and agree to police interrogation. Should legal doctrines treat juveniles essentially like adults, or should they provide them with greater protections to compensate for their immaturity and vulnerability? If children pose special problems of social control in certain contexts, for example, in schools, then how should the legal order modify criminal procedures to accommodate those special institutional needs?

A. FOURTH AMENDMENT CRIMINAL PROCEDURE AND JUVENILE JUSTICE

To implement the jurisdiction of the juvenile court, statutes authorize police to take youths into custody—to arrest—who violate criminal laws or commit status offenses. In most states, police may exercise their discretion and issue a citation in lieu of arrest for minor offenses. If they take a youth into custody, then they may transport the youth to the police station, to the police juvenile division, or to a juvenile detention facility. Pursuant to an arrest, police may conduct a search incident to arrest of the person and the area under their immediate control, and may finger-print the person. Thus, when police took nine-year-old Latrice Branch into custody for throwing acorns at a neighbor's window—destruction of prop-erty—"Standard operating procedures require that any time an officer transports an individual, whether adult or juvenile, to the police station in a squad car, that individual must be handcuffed." *Branch v. McGeeney*, 123 Md.App. 330, 718 A.2d 631 (Ct. Spec. App. 1998). The materials in this section explore the extent to which states' law and policy modify the criminal procedures applicable to adults when they apply them to chil-dren.

How do the following statutes differ in the authority they give to police officers when they take a youth into custody? When should police take a youth into custody? What should they do with them after they have taken them into custody?

Vernons Texas Code Ann., Family Code § 52.01. Taking into Custody; Issuance of Warning Notice (2004):

(a) A child may be taken into custody:

(1) pursuant to an order of the juvenile court * * *;

(2) pursuant to the laws of arrest;

(3) by a law-enforcement officer, including a school district peace officer * * *, if there is probable cause to believe that the child has engaged in:

(A) conduct that violates a penal law of this state or a penal ordi-nance of any political subdivision of this state;

(B) delinquent conduct or conduct indicating a need for supervision; or

(C) conduct that violates a condition of probation imposed by the juvenile court;

(4) by a probation officer if there is probable cause to believe that the child has violated a condition of probation imposed by the juvenile court; * * *

(b) The taking of a child into custody is not an arrest except for the purpose of determining the validity of taking him into custody or the validity of a search under the laws and constitution of this state or of the United States.

M.S.A. § 260B.175 Taking child into custody (2004)

Subdivision 1. Immediate custody. No child may be taken into immediate custody except: (a) With an order issued by the court * * *, or by a warrant * * *;

(b) In accordance with the laws relating to arrests; or

(c) By a peace officer or probation or parole officer when it is reasonably believed that the child has violated the terms of probation, parole, or other field supervision.

Subd. 2. Not an arrest. The taking of a child into custody under the provisions of this section shall not be considered an arrest. * * *

Subd. 4. Protective pat-down search of child authorized. (a) A peace officer who takes a child of any age or gender into custody * * * is authorized to perform a protective pat-down search of the child in order to protect the officer's safety.

(b) A peace officer also may perform a protective pat-down search of a child in order to protect the officer's safety in circumstances where the officer does not intend to take the child into custody, if this section authorizes the officer to take the child into custody.

(c) Evidence discovered in the course of a lawful search under this section is admissible.

NOTE

If a police officer takes a juvenile into custody "in accordance with the laws relating to arrests," why do the statutes provide that taking a child into custody "shall not be considered an arrest"? How does M.S.A. § 260B.175 Subd. 4 affect our understanding of custody?

1. PROBABLE CAUSE AND JUVENILE JUSTICE

LANES v. STATE

767 S.W.2d 789 (Tex. Ct. Crim. App. 1989).

WHITE, JUDGE. Appellant, a juvenile certified for trial as an adult * * * [was] convicted of burglary of a habitation. Punishment was assessed at twenty years imprisonment.

The Ninth Court of Appeals affirmed the conviction holding inter alia, that a fingerprint order, issued pursuant to Section 51.15, V.T.C.A., Family Code, provided sufficient probable cause to arrest and fingerprint a juvenile.* Appellant petitioned this Court for discretionary review arguing that, independent of the Sec. 51.15, *supra*, probable cause requirement to fingerprint a child, Article I, Section 9 of the Texas Constitution and the Fourth and Fourteenth Amendments of the United States Constitution require probable cause to arrest a child in order to obtain his fingerprints. Because this raises a question of first impression, i.e., whether the probable cause requirement of Art. I, Sec. 9 and the Fourth Amendment applies in full force to a juvenile arrest,[3] we granted appellant's petition. After having carefully considered the issues, we now hold that it does.

* [Ed. VTCA § 51.15 provides that "a child may not be photographed or fingerprinted without consent of the juvenile court unless the child is taken into custody or referred to the juvenile court for conduct that constitutes a felony or a misdemeanor punishable by confinement in jail."]

3. We use the term "arrest" advisedly. The arrest of a child is often labeled as merely "detainment" or "protective custody." In the instant context, however, we find it appropriate to dispense with such euphemistic nomenclature. Such a position comports with Section 52.01(b), V.T.C.A., Family Code, which states, "[t]he taking of a child into custody is not an arrest except

The facts of the case can be simply stated. Pursuant to a consent order from the juvenile court authorizing the taking of appellant's fingerprints, a police officer arrested appellant at his high school, transported him to the police station and took his fingerprints.[4] The trial court as well as the Court of Appeals found that this order provided sufficient authority for an arrest. We disagree.

The issue presented is whether the probable cause requisite of Art. I, Sec. 9 of the Texas Constitution and the Fourth Amendment of the U.S. Constitution, applicable to the states through the Fourteenth, applies to the arrest of a child.[5] This precise issue has not been decided by our Court or the U.S. Supreme Court. It has, however, long been settled that the Fourth Amendment is, to some undetermined extent, applicable to juvenile proceedings. This rule was best expressed in the seminal opinion on juvenile rights—*In re Gault*. The *Gault* Court stated, "[n]either the Fourteenth Amendment nor the Bill of Rights is for adults alone." * * *

In order to determine whether and to what degree each protection extended to juvenile proceedings, the Supreme Court seemed to utilize a comparative analysis wherein the purposes and goals of the juvenile system were compared to the particular right being asserted. The Court balanced the function that a constitutional or procedural right served against its impact or degree of impairment on the unique processes of the juvenile court and then factored in consideration of the degree of realistic success the juvenile system had obtained. Because this balancing test constitutes a neutral, pragmatic analysis of all protective intentions involved, we find it valid and now adopt it as our own.

Application of such an analysis to the instant facts initially requires an exploration of the specific purposes of both the juvenile system and the constitutional right being asserted. The purposes of the Texas juvenile system have remained basically the same as they were at its inception.

for the purpose of determining the validity of taking him into custody * * * under the laws of and constitution of this state or of the United States."

4. The record does not reflect whether appellant was released or detained following fingerprinting; however, the arrest of appellant at school in order to take him to the police station constitutes a seizure sufficient to invoke Art. I, Sec. 9 and Fourth Amendment protections.

5. While in many instances Texas law is merely coextensive with Federal law, the Texas Legislature has made evident its intent to give greater protections to its juveniles through enactment of the Texas Family Code. In Title 3 of the Code, Texas has statutorily enacted greater protections under state law than currently received under the Federal Constitution. For example, *McKeiver v. Pennsylvania*, denies juveniles the Federal Due Process guarantee of a jury trial whereas V.T.C.A., Family Code Sec. 54.03(c) requires a jury trial in delinquency proceedings. The Texas Family Code also extends to juveniles guarantees on which the U.S. Supreme Court has not yet ruled. For example, V.T.C.A., Family Code Sec. 54.03(e), excludes illegally seized evidence from trial and also prohibits an adjudication of delinquency founded only upon either uncorroborated accomplice testimony or the child's out-of-court statement. Therefore, although the protections offered by Art. I, sec. 9 and the Fourth Amendment are identical, our extension of the probable cause requirement inherent in both is based upon the particular and more protective purposes and policies of the Texas juvenile system. Consequently, although we rule on both Federal and State questions, we find it more appropriate to base our holding primarily on State constitutional grounds. We do, however, heavily rely on Fourth Amendment precedent since Texas has adopted such as authoritative of Art. I, sec. 9 protections.

Conveniently, the specific intent of the Texas juvenile scheme * * * states,

This title shall be construed to effectuate the following public purposes:

(1) to provide for the care, the protection, and the wholesome moral, mental, and physical development of children coming within its provisions;

(2) to protect the welfare of the community and to control the commission of unlawful acts by children;

(3) consistent with the protection of the public interest, to remove from children committing unlawful acts the taint of criminality and the consequences of criminal behavior and to substitute a program of treatment, training, and rehabilitation;

(4) to achieve the foregoing purposes in a family environment whenever possible, separating the child from his parents only when necessary for his welfare or in the interest of public safety and when a child is removed from his family, to give him the care that should be provided by parents; and

(5) to provide a simple judicial procedure through which the provisions of this title are executed and enforced and in which the parties are assured a fair hearing and their constitutional and other legal rights recognized and enforced.

Additionally, Section 54.04(c), V.T.C.A., Family Code, requires that even after a finding of guilt, a child cannot be sentenced or detained unless the court further finds that he is in need of rehabilitation or that the protection of the public or the child requires such. If the court does not so find, it must immediately release the child. Thus, as statutorily evidenced, rehabilitation and child protection remain as the pervasive and uniform themes of the Texas juvenile system.

Article I, sec. 9 and the Fourth Amendment are also protection attentive entities. Art. I, sec. 9 requires that the "people be secure in their persons * * * from all unreasonable seizures and searches" and the Fourth Amendment requires: "[t]he right of the people to be secure in their persons * * * against unreasonable searches and seizures, shall not be violated." The purpose of these two provisions is the same—to safeguard the privacy and security of individuals against arbitrary governmental invasions. * * *

The requirement of probable cause has historically been the stalwart enforcer of these privacy protections. Probable Cause is defined as that evidence which is sufficient to warrant a reasonable and prudent person in believing that a particular person has committed or is committing an offense. This requisite for a warrantless arrest protects individuals from being at the complete mercy of an officer's arbitrary caprice and prevents oppressive or prejudicial use of the power to arrest, while, at the same time, providing for community protection through valid law enforcement.

Thus, the probable cause requisite safeguards citizens from rash and unreasonable interferences of privacy and from unfounded charges of crime.

With these basic purposes of the juvenile system and the probable cause requirement in mind, we now turn to compare the ramifications involved in enforcement of the two. One of the fundamental goals of the juvenile system is rehabilitation. Essential to a rehabilitative environment is the proper attitudinal setting. Children have the strongest sense of justice—a product of youth, energy, and innocence. Such an inherent sense of justice, however, is fragile and can easily be turned to cynicism, helplessness, disillusionment and disrespect. Not only would such an attitude be contra-rehabilitative, but it could breed dissention [sic] and reactionary criminal behavior.

A child arrested without valid reason by a seemingly all-powerful and challengeless exercise of police power would instantly intuit the injustice and react accordingly. Even a juvenile who has violated the law but is unfairly arrested will feel deceived and thus resist any rehabilitative efforts. Inherent in youth is a malleable nature, and example can be the most formidable teacher. We must institutionalize justice in order to engender it among our youth. Affording a child the essentials of basic human dignity and announcing a respect for their autonomy through the extension of constitutional privacy protections can only further these efforts.

Other important goals of the Texas juvenile scheme include protection of the community and the child. * * * The community need not be protected from a child who has presumptively not committed an offense. Nor does a child need to be protected from himself when he is not in trouble. Thus, requiring probable cause can only help to prevent such erroneous and unnecessary arrests.

The Texas juvenile system also seeks to avoid the taint of criminality in order to prevent recidivism and promote rehabilitation. The best method of avoiding attachment of a criminal taint is keeping the child completely out of the system. * * * Requiring probable cause to arrest a child can only serve to reduce the risk that innocent youths will be so erroneously stigmatized.

An almost unavoidable consequence of arrest is detention. Pre-trial detention can be extremely destructive to a child's life and act as the determinative factor toward recidivism. The impressionability of juveniles can make even the most minimal experience of incarceration extremely injurious, and such injury is compounded where confinement is unfounded. All too quickly juveniles subjected to detention come to view society at large as "oppressive" and "hostile" and to "regard themselves as irremediably 'delinquent.'" * * * Such negative self-labeling is clearly counter-rehabilitative and can easily lead to self-fulfilling prophecy. It seems appropriate to require some probable cause evidence of wrongdoing before subjecting a child to the possibility of such detriment.

Further, the disruption that detention causes in a child's everyday life runs counter to any rehabilitative efforts. If the child is attending school, a week's absence while in detention would undoubtedly cause him to fall behind in his work thus enhancing disillusionment and contributing to the possibility that he will drop out. Further, if employed, the child's absence from work could cause loss of employment which further entangles him in a downward spiral. Lack of education and a poor employment record—two major causes of recidivism—can only serve to perpetuate delinquency. An arresting officer makes the first and, thus, most important decision of whether the child will be arrested and introduced into a system plagued with such negative possibilities. Such a momentous and determinative decision should at least be based on facts sufficient to sustain a reasonable belief that an offense was being or had been committed.

A further purpose of the juvenile system is preservation of the family environment either at home or, when detention is a necessity, to perpetuate a family-type atmosphere in the detention facility. Obviously, the optimal method of family preservation is keeping the family intact. By requiring some evidence of wrongdoing before disrupting the family and removing the child can only further this goal.

The old adage that a child, by virtue of his age, has no right to freedom but only a right to custody since he is presumably under constant parental control, does not withstand scrutiny or application in the instant context. Assuredly, a child is or should be under constant parental authority, but this comprises an entirely different form of custody than that of State detention. No one seriously argues anymore that State custody in any way approximates the family environment. * * * To require probable cause prior to placement of a juvenile in such an institutional setting can only serve to prevent erroneous disruption and destruction of the family environment.

The foregoing discussion renders the conclusion that the purposes of the Texas juvenile system and the probable cause requirement of Art. I, sec. 9 are in harmony. The limitations imposed by these two protective entities do not conflict or undermine one another, but rather accommodate and enhance the goals sought by both. Probable cause protects the sanctity of personal freedom through the prevention of unnecessary arrests. The juvenile system was designed to protect and rehabilitate children. We in no way see how imposing a probable cause requirement will deter juvenile courts from pursuing its ameliorative goals. * * *

Based on the foregoing analysis, we now extend the probable cause requirement of Art. I, sec. 9 and the Fourth Amendment to juvenile proceedings. * * * [I]mposition of a probable cause requirement will not severely limit or disrupt proper law enforcement since it is not an ultra-restrictive requirement. Rather, it was purposely designed as a realistic, practical, and workable determination to be based upon the "totality of the circumstances" presented. * * *

The probable cause requirement rests on the principal that a true balance between an individual—whether youth or adult—and the government depends on the recognition and respect of "the right to be let alone—the most comprehensive of rights and the right most valued by civilized men." Today we are proudly able to afford such a right to juveniles.

Application of this law to the instant facts requires reversal. Appellant was arrested pursuant to a fingerprint consent order issued under Sec. 51.15, *supra*. * * *

It is agreed that the officers had authority to fingerprint appellant pursuant to the 51.15 consent order; however, this order in no way conferred authority to arrest. At a suppression hearing, the State carries the burden of either producing a warrant and supporting affidavit or establishing evidentiary facts sufficient to show probable cause. In the instant case the State did not come forward with a warrant, but only introduced the fingerprint consent form. The State and the Court of Appeals seem to argue that this form takes the place of an arrest warrant, thus shifting the burden of proof back to appellant. This argument does not withstand scrutiny. The bare-bones fingerprint consent order neither facially confers authority to arrest nor evinces any factual probable cause basis. Further, there is nothing on the face of the order which exhibits any judicial intent to authorize an arrest. Having none of the protective characteristics or purposes of a warrant, this order simply cannot take the place of such.

Without a warrant, the State carried the burden of establishing the validity of the arrest. This burden the State wholly failed to carry. At the suppression hearing, the judge who issued the order did not testify and no facts were elicited concerning probable cause. Thus we find that appellant's fingerprints were taken during an illegal juvenile arrest which was not founded on probable cause. Because the only direct evidence linking appellant to the scene of the crime was his fingerprints, we cannot say beyond a reasonable doubt that their introduction made no contribution to the verdict. Consequently, we reverse the holding of the Court of Appeals and remand this cause to the trial court. * * *

NOTES

1) **Fingerprinting Suspects** In *Davis v. Mississippi*, 394 U.S. 721, 727, 89 S.Ct. 1394, 22 L.Ed.2d 676 (1969), the U.S. Supreme Court noted that "because of the unique nature of the fingerprinting process, such detentions might, under narrowly defined circumstances, be found to comply with the Fourth Amendment even though there is no probable cause in the traditional sense." In *Hayes v. Florida*, 470 U.S. 811, 814, 105 S.Ct. 1643, 1646, 84 L.Ed.2d 705 (1985), the Court suppressed the defendant's fingerprints obtained when "there was no probable cause to arrest, no consent to the journey to the police station, and no judicial authorization for such a detention for fingerprinting purposes." However, *Hayes* reiterated that "a brief detention

in the field for the purpose of fingerprinting, where there is only reasonable suspicion" could be permissible. 470 U.S. at 816, 105 S.Ct. at 1647. "[T]he Fourth Amendment would permit seizures for the purpose of fingerprinting, if there is reasonable suspicion that the suspect has committed a criminal act, if there is a reasonable basis for believing that fingerprinting will establish or negate the suspect's connection with that crime, and if the procedure is carried out with dispatch." 470 U.S. at 817, 105 S.Ct. at 1647.

2) Fingerprinting Juveniles Does the following Ohio statute, which authorizes police to fingerprint a juvenile taken into custody for a felony or with the consent of a juvenile court judge, satisfy the constitutional requirements of *Davis* and *Hayes*?:

Ohio Rev. Code Ann. § 2151.313 (West 1999). Fingerprinting or Photographing Child in an Investigation (A)(1) Except as provided in division (A)(2) of this section, * * * no child shall be fingerprinted or photographed in the investigation of any violation of law without the consent of the juvenile judge.

(2) Subject to division (A)(3) of this section, a law enforcement officer may fingerprint and photograph a child without the consent of the juvenile judge when the child is arrested or otherwise taken into custody for the commission of an act that would be an offense * * * if committed by an adult, and there is probable cause to believe that the child may have been involved in the commission of the act. A law enforcement officer who takes fingerprints or photographs of a child * * * immediately shall inform the juvenile court that the fingerprints or photographs were taken and shall provide the court with the identity of the child, the number of fingerprints and photographs taken, and the name and address of each person who has custody and control of the fingerprints or photographs or copies of the fingerprints or photographs.

(3) This section does not apply to a child to whom either of the following applies:

(a) The child has been arrested or otherwise taken into custody for committing, or has been adjudicated a delinquent child for committing, an act that would be a felony if committed by an adult or has been convicted of or pleaded guilty to committing a felony.

(b) There is probable cause to believe that the child may have committed an act that would be a felony if committed by an adult. * * *

In *In re Order Requiring Fingerprinting of a Juvenile*, 42 Ohio St.3d 124, 537 N.E.2d 1286 (Oh., 1989), the Ohio Supreme Court relied upon the dicta in *Davis* and *Hayes* to authorize detention of a juvenile for fingerprinting without probable cause. While the U.S. Supreme Court invalidated Davis' fingerprints because the police confined him in jail overnight for questioning and arrested him as one of twenty suspects in a police dragnet, the Ohio Court noted that the statute, *Ohio Rev. Code* § 2151.313, was limited in scope, purpose, and duration to taking the youth to the police station solely for fingerprinting. The court emphasized that the juvenile court judge protected the youth's interests because § 2151.313 provides that "no child shall be fingerprinted or photographed in the investigation of any violation of law without the consent of the juvenile judge." The dissent objected that the fingerprint order is in the nature of a warrant which must be supported by a judicial determination of probable cause. "Otherwise, the order would amount to a slip of paper devoid of foundation similar to a warrant issued upon less than probable cause. The fact that it was issued by a judicial officer would not alter this conclusion." 42 Ohio St.3d at 129, 537 N.E.2d at 1291. Is judicial oversight the equivalent protection of Fourth Amendment probable cause? *See* Karen R. Koehler, "Civil Procedure: Ohio Forgoes Probable Cause on Orders for Obtaining Non-testimonial Evidence From a Juvenile," 15 *U. Dayton L. Rev.* 289 (1990).

   3) Applicability of Fourth Amendment to Juveniles On the Street Lourdes M. Rosado, "Minors and the Fourth Amendments: How Juvenile Status Should Invoke Different Standards for Searches and Seizures on the Street," 71 *N.Y.U.L.Rev.* 762, 775 (1996), argues that "juveniles are entitled to the same effective level of Fourth Amendment protection as adults in the context of searches and seizures on the street and that providing them with such equivalent protection requires greater safeguards. * * * [However,] the Supreme Court has held that it is constitutional to extend *fewer* safeguards to juveniles. The Court has been somewhat willing to relax the usual constitutional safeguards in environments that are specifically structured to ensure the well-being of minors. * * * " Rosado argues that in the context of consent searches and "stops" that result from submission to inherent authority, children stand on a different developmental footing than adults and therefore require *more* protections than adults from unreasonable searches and seizes. "[A]s a society we have chosen to protect juveniles from their own immaturity in a variety of contexts. Adults are allowed to make 'poor' choices because second-guessing their choices would unacceptably undermine their autonomy; an adult's 'poor' choices are assumed to reflect the adult's subjective preferences. By contrast, a juvenile's poor choices are seen as the product of the developmental factors * * * and it is assumed that the youth will 'outgrow' these choices and make different ones as an adult. * * * [T]he Fourth Amendment can extend the same level of protection to juveniles as it does to adults only if these differences are taken into account." *Id.* at 795.

2. TAKING JUVENILES INTO CUSTODY

IN RE JAIME P.
40 Cal.4th 128, 51 Cal.Rptr.3d 430, 146 P.3d 965 (Cal. 2006).

CHIN, J.

   In this case, we consider the continued vitality of *In re Tyrell J.* upholding a warrantless search of a juvenile probationer by an officer who lacked reasonable suspicion of any criminal activity and was unaware that the juvenile had consented to such a search as a condition of his probation. We conclude that developments subsequent to *Tyrell J.*, including the recent high court decision in *Samson v. California* (2006), (*Samson*), our own decision in *People v. Sanders* (2003) (*Sanders*), and lower court cases and scholarly comment critical of *Tyrell J.*, have convinced us that it should be overruled. * * *

[On April 27, 2004, Fairfield Police Officer Moody detained Jaime P. and three other youths after he observed the driver of the car turn corners without signaling and then pull over to the curb, again without signaling. The State conceded that under state traffic laws, these violations would not have justified a vehicle stop. Moody pulled in behind the car and detained and questioned two passengers who got out of the car. At the suppression hearing, he testified that he questioned them because a nearby home had been the target of gang violence. After a backup officer arrived, Moody questioned the driver, Jaime P., and a passenger who had remained seated in the car. Jaime P. said he did not have a driver's license. While talking to Jaime P., Moody saw a box of ammunition in plain view on the front floor. Moody ordered Jaime P. and the passenger out of the car and pat-searched all four youths. He determined that none of them had a valid driver's license and called a tow truck to remove the car. An inventory search of the vehicle revealed a loaded .44–caliber handgun beneath the rear passenger seat.]

* * * [T]he juvenile court denied minor's motion to suppress the firearm, relying upon minor's probation search condition to justify the officer's action. The record shows minor was on probation with the condition, among others, that he submit his person and property, including his vehicle and residence, to a warrantless search and seizure by any peace officer at any time, with or without probable cause. * * * [M]inor contended on appeal that the juvenile court erred by denying his motion to suppress. * * * We will reverse.

Does a juvenile's probationary search condition justify an otherwise illegal search and seizure if the officers conducting the search are then unaware that the juvenile is on probation and subject to the search condition? Our decision in *Tyrell J.*, held that the officers' prior knowledge of the probation condition was not necessary in a juvenile case. We reasoned, in part, that "imposing a strict requirement that the searching officer must always have advance knowledge of the search condition would be inconsistent with the special needs of the juvenile probation scheme. That scheme embraces a goal of rehabilitating youngsters who have transgressed the law, a goal that is arguably stronger than in the adult context.... [T]he condition of probation permitting police ... to conduct warrantless searches is imposed by the juvenile court to serve the important goal of deterring future misconduct." We also relied upon the reduced expectation of privacy that probationers, as a general matter, hold, and reasoned that suppressing the evidence under the circumstances presented would not further the purpose of the exclusionary rule.

We recently considered whether prior knowledge of a search condition is required to uphold an otherwise unlawful search of the residence of an adult parolee, concluding the search "may not be justified by the circumstance that the suspect was subject to a search condition of which the law enforcement officers were unaware when the search was conducted." This is so, we reasoned, because "whether a search is reasonable must be determined based upon the circumstances known to the officer when the search is conducted." *Sanders* explained that the "primary purpose of the exclusionary rule [is] to deter police misconduct" and that to admit evidence seized during a search that the officer had no reason to believe was lawful, merely because a search condition had been imposed, "would legitimize unlawful police conduct." * * *

As noted, *Tyrell J.* justified its holding on three broad grounds: (1) "the special needs of the juvenile probation scheme"; (2) "the important goal of deterring future misconduct"; and (3) the reduced expectation of privacy that probationers, as a general matter, hold. In combination, these three factors convinced us that suppressing the evidence under the circumstances presented in that case would not further the purpose of the exclusionary rule. But our subsequent decision in demonstrate that these grounds may no longer be entitled to much weight.

In *Sanders*, we relied on *In re Martinez* and its "rule that whether a search is reasonable must be determined based upon the circumstances known to the officer when the search is conducted and is consistent with the primary purpose of the exclusionary rule-to deter police misconduct." An officer acting in reliance on a search condition may act reasonably, even in the absence of any particularized suspicion of criminal activity, and such a search does not violate the suspect's reasonable expectation of privacy.

With respect to the reasonable expectation of privacy of one subject to a search condition, *Sanders* observed that "[a] parolee's expectation of privacy certainly is diminished, but it is not eliminated," and "whether the parolee has a reasonable expectation of privacy is inextricably linked to whether the search was reasonable." *Sanders* continued by observing that despite a "diminished expectation of privacy" held by one subject to a search condition, the search cannot be justified if the officer is unaware of the condition. Thus, in *Sander*'s view, despite being subject to a search condition, a person retains a reasonable expectation the officers will not undertake a random search supported by neither reasonable suspicion of criminal activity nor advance knowledge of the search condition.

As for deterrence of criminal acts, *Sanders* reviewed the decision in *United States v. Knights* (2001) (*Knights*), allowing a search of an adult probationer's house by an officer aware of the suspect's search condition. *Sanders* observed that *Knights* would not extend to the situation in *Sanders*, stating "[b]ut if an officer is unaware that a suspect is on probation and subject to a search condition, the search is not justified by the state's interest in supervising probationers or by the concern that probationers are more likely to commit criminal acts." As the dissent in *Tyrell J.* observed, requiring the officers be aware of the search condition would not itself affect the goal of deterrence: The very existence of a probation search condition, whether for adults or juveniles, should deter further criminal acts, and that deterrent effect would not be eroded merely by requiring that searching officers be aware of that condition.

What of *Tyrell J.*'s reliance on "the special needs of the juvenile probation scheme"? In *Sanders*, we left open the question whether such special needs indeed exist and would justify *Tyrell J.*'s holding. Justice Kennard's dissent in *Tyrell J.*, doubted the validity of the majority's reliance on such special needs, observing that in that case, as here, the search was conducted by a police officer acting without knowledge of the search condition, rather than by a probation officer having an ongoing supervisory relationship with the probationer, whose welfare he or she sought to promote. In other words, the dissent questioned whether the special needs of the juvenile probation scheme could be promoted by allowing a police search not premised on prior knowledge of that condition. * * *

In the present case, the People initially insisted that because minor supposedly lacked a reasonable expectation of privacy, he was not "searched" in the constitutional sense. But, as the Attorney General later conceded, the People's major premise is incorrect, because under both *Sanders* and *Tyrell J.*, a search condition may diminish, but does not entirely preclude, a reasonable expectation of privacy, i.e., a reasonable expectation that officers will not undertake a random search supported by neither evidence of criminal activity nor advance knowledge of the search condition. This reasoning would apply with equal force to juvenile or adult probationers.

Indeed, the high court's decision in *Samson* reinforces *Sander*'s view that persons on probation or parole who are subject to a search condition nonetheless retain some residual expectation of privacy. *Samson* involved a parolee search conducted by officers aware of the parolee's consent-to-search condition, and held that, applying the usual " 'totality of the circumstances' " test to determine reasonableness, the Fourth Amendment did not prohibit such officers from conducting a suspicionless search of the parolee. *Samson* reasoned that parolees have a greatly reduced expectation of privacy by reason of their parolee status and their consent to warrantless searches. * * *

But under *Samson*, both parolees and probationers retain some expectation of privacy, albeit a reduced one. Indeed, *Samson* noted that "parolees have fewer expectations of privacy than probationers, because parole is more akin to imprisonment than probation is to imprisonment." This reasoning severely undercuts *Tyrell J.*'s conclusion that juvenile probationers who are subject to a search condition have no reasonable expectation of privacy whatever. * * *

Responding to the question whether a search by an officer unaware of a probation condition would promote the special needs of the juvenile probation system, the People simply claim that the *Tyrell J.* rule would discourage criminal behavior by juvenile probationers who know they may be searched at any time. In *Sanders*, we rejected a similar "deterrence" justification for searching adult parolees or probationers. We stated that "if an officer is unaware that a suspect is on probation and subject to a search condition, the search is not justified by the state's interest in supervising probationers or by the concern that probationers are more likely to commit criminal acts." * * *

[T]he very existence of a probation search condition, whether for adults or juveniles, should amply deter further criminal acts, and that deterrent effect would not be eroded merely by requiring that searching officers be aware of that condition. If there are other "special needs" of the juvenile probation system that would be undermined by the rule we propose, the People do not identify them, nor do we discern any. * * * For the foregoing reasons, we overrule *In re Tyrell J.* and reverse the judgment * * *.

BAXTER, J., Dissenting.

In finding the juvenile court erroneously denied suppression of the loaded firearm found in the juvenile probationer's car, the majority adopts the rule that, when an officer detains a juvenile driving on a public street, without advance knowledge that the juvenile is subject to a search and seizure condition of probation but with a mistaken belief that a traffic violation has occurred, any contraband subsequently found in the car must be suppressed, notwithstanding the juvenile's greatly reduced expectation of privacy due to the probation condition and other circumstances surrounding the detention and subsequent search. * * *

In re Tyrell J. upheld the admission of evidence obtained through the warrantless search of a juvenile by a police officer who was unaware of the juvenile's probation search condition at the time of the search. In doing so, *Tyrell J.* stated categorically that a minor subject to a probation condition allowing warrantless searches has "no reasonable expectation of privacy" over contraband on his person. Today the majority overrules *Tyrell J.* by adopting a different rule that, without exception, the absence of advance officer knowledge of a juvenile's probation search condition compels exclusion of the fruits of a suspicionless detention and subsequent search of the juvenile probationer's car. Recent Fourth Amendment decisions, however, make it apparent that both categorical approaches are wrong. * * *

With regard to the degree to which a search is intrusive, there was no dispute that the juvenile in *Tyrell J.*, like the juvenile here, was on probation under the lawfully imposed condition that he submit his person and property to warrantless search by any peace officer, with or without probable cause, and there appeared no reason to doubt the juvenile had been clearly informed of this condition. *Tyrell J.*'s observation that a juvenile probationer subject to a valid search condition "has a greatly reduced expectation of privacy" over his or her person or property is very similar to the United States Supreme Court's conclusion that the existence of a probation search condition is a "salient circumstance" that "significantly diminish[es]" the probationer's "reasonable expectation of privacy." * * *

As for the degree to which a warrantless search of a juvenile probationer is " 'needed for the promotion of legitimate governmental interests' ", there is no doubt the governmental interests at stake in the probation context are legitimate and well established. * * * "On the one hand is the hope that he will successfully complete probation and be integrated back into the community. On the other is the concern, quite justified, that he will be more likely to engage in criminal conduct than an ordinary member of the community." * * *

Additionally, this case involves the special needs of juvenile probation, which " 'is not an act of leniency, but is a final order made in the minor's best interest.' " As Justice Werdegar keenly observes, "[t]he purposes and goals of juvenile proceedings are manifestly different from criminal proceedings involving adults." "Unlike a prison sentence and subsequent period of parole imposed on the adult offender, '[t]he process of the juvenile court involves determination of the needs of the child and society, provision for guidance and treatment for the juvenile, and protection of the child from punishment and stigma.' " Accordingly, a juvenile has no choice whether or not to accept a condition of probation that subjects him to a warrantless search, for "[i]t would be inconsistent with the juvenile court's determination of the best manner in which to facilitate rehabilitation of a minor if [the minor] could ... elect to forgo home placement on probation and instead choose detention at the California Youth Authority." * * *

Applying the proper analysis to the facts of this case, I conclude the detention of the juvenile and the warrantless search of his vehicle were reasonable within the contemplation of the Fourth Amendment, despite the officer's lack of knowledge of the juvenile's probation search condition. * * *

I agree *Tyrell J.* should be disapproved to the extent it concludes that a juvenile subject to a valid search and seizure condition of probation has no reasonable expectation of privacy. * * * [T]he reasonableness of a search depends on the totality of the circumstances. Under that analysis, a juvenile who is subject to a valid search condition has privacy expectations that are greatly reduced but not eliminated, and the existence of a valid search condition is significant but not necessarily controlling on the question of reasonableness. * * *

[D]espite the officer's ignorance of the juvenile's probation search condition, I would find that the traffic stop and subsequent inventory search of the car did not violate the juvenile's rights under the Fourth Amendment, and would hold that the loaded firearm evidence was admissible in juvenile court.

NOTE

1) **Suppression of Evidence** The juveniles in *Lanes v. State* and *Jaime P.* challenged the validity of the police custody by moving to suppress the evidence obtained as a result of the search conducted pursuant to their detention. Although the United States Supreme Court has not directly decided

whether the exclusionary remedy is available to delinquents in juvenile court for violations of their Fourth Amendment rights, *see New Jersey v. T.L.O.*, *infra* and pp. 189, 191, the Court in *Florida v. J.L.*, 529 U.S. 266, 120 S.Ct. 1375, 146 L.Ed.2d 254 (2000), unanimously held that an anonymous tip that a young black man wearing a plaid shirt who would be found in a particular location would be carrying a gun did not justify a stop-and-frisk. In holding that the information lacked sufficient "indicia of reliability" and failed to provide "reasonable suspicion," the Court reinstated the decision by the trial judge and the Florida Supreme Court to suppress the evidence against the juvenile. Irene Merker Rosenberg, "*Florida v. J.L.* and the Fourth Amendment Rights of Juvenile Delinquents: Peekaboo!," 69 *U. Cin. L.Rev.* 289, 294–95 (2000) interprets the Court's decision in *J.L.* as implicitly finding that juveniles are entitled to the same Fourth Amendment protections as adults outside of the school context, including an exclusionary remedy:

> The issue before the Court was, in effect if not form, whether to suppress the evidence obtained by the police during a frisk that is unlawful. The Court nonetheless framed the question as one of substance rather than remedy. * * * [I]t was unnecessary for the Court to decide whether the exclusionary rule applies to juveniles as a matter of federal law since in Florida that right is granted by statute. Indeed, all states seem to have either explicitly or implicitly determined that the exclusionary rule applies at least to non-school searches of minors by police officers. That would mean that the *J.L.* Court is finding a substantive violation of the Federal Constitution that will be remedied by state law. * * * In *T.L.O.* * * *, the Court may well have been assuming without stating that police searches of minors, at least out of school, would be governed by the usual Fourth Amendment standard. * * * The Court clearly understood that J.L. was a juvenile and that, by making its ruling in such a context, it was holding that the federal constitutional standard for frisks is the same for adults and children, at least with respect to police frisks outside of the public schools.

3. SEARCHES INCIDENT TO CUSTODY

IN THE MATTER OF Z.M.

337 Mont. 278, 160 P.3d 490 (Mt. 2007).

JUSTICE W. WILLIAM LEAPHART delivered the Opinion of the Court.

[Z.M.'s mother called the high school liaison officer to report that Z.M., her fourteen-year-old son, had not returned home the previous night. She asked authorities to pick up Z.M. and contact her if they found him. The school resource officer told Officer Bache to keep a lookout for Z.M. Later that morning, Bache spotted Z.M. and D.O. walking in town. When he stopped to talk to them, he smelled the odor of alcohol and asked them if they had been drinking. They told him they had been drinking the night before. When Bache asked them why they were not in school, they told him that they were not going to go to school. Bache told them that because he could smell alcohol, he would take them into custody. Before he put them in his car, Bache noticed that Z.M.'s shirt was bulky and he heard a clanking sound in D.O.'s pockets. He asked them what they had in their pockets. Z.M. removed a bottle of vodka from his sweatshirt pocket and D.O. produced bottles of liquor. Bache had the boys turn their pockets inside out, which revealed money. Bache said that it is standard practice to have persons empty their pockets before they get into the police car. Subsequent investigation linked the alcohol and cash to a bowling alley burglary. The juvenile court denied Z.M.'s motion to suppress the evidence and Z.M. pled guilty.]

Pursuant to § 41–5–321(1), MCA, of the Youth Court Act, a person under the age of eighteen years may be taken into custody by a law enforcement officer pursuant to a lawful arrest for violation of the law. Taking a youth into custody is "not an arrest except for the purpose of determining the validity of the taking under the constitution of Montana or the United States." Since Z.M. has argued that his being taken into custody was unconstitutional, we will treat the taking as an arrest for the purpose of determining whether the taking was valid.

A search without a warrant is per se unreasonable. However, when a lawful arrest is made, a police officer may "reasonably search the person arrested and the area immediately within his reach in order to locate any weapons the person might use or any evidence that might otherwise be destroyed."

Z.M. concedes that Bache had a right to stop Z.M. in order to tell him he needed to go home or contact his mother. Z.M. argues that Bache had no right to proceed beyond this point because there was no evidence Z.M. was engaged in criminal behavior. In response to Z.M.'s motion to suppress, the State argued that Bache was allowed to make the stop and take the youths into custody based on the community caretaker doctrine and probable cause.

The Youth Court concluded that based on the community caretaker doctrine, Bache was justified in stopping the youths. When Bache then smelled alcohol on the youths, he was justified in taking them to the police station for their safety. Finally, the court concluded Bache, for his own safety, was justified in determining what the youths had in their pockets prior to putting the youths in the police car.

When Bache stopped and talked to Z.M., he knew that Z.M. was truant, which was the basis for the stop. Z.M. concedes this was a reasonable basis to stop Z.M. While talking to the boys, Bache smelled alcohol, which was objective data from which Bache, a trained officer, could infer the underage boys had been drinking. A person under the age of twenty-one years old is prohibited from possessing or consuming an intoxicating substance. Bache thus had a particularized suspicion that Z.M. consumed or possessed alcohol in violation of the law. Bache stepped out of the car and approached Z.M. and D.O., at which time he confirmed that both boys smelled of alcohol. * * * Bache also noticed the bulge in Z.M.'s front pocket.

Based on the fact that Bache smelled alcohol on Z.M., Bache's particularized suspicion that Z.M. had been drinking developed into probable cause to believe that Z.M. committed the offense of consuming or possessing alcohol. Because MIP [Minor in Possession] is a nonjailable offense, the question, then, is whether the circumstances surrounding the stop, including concern for Z.M.'s safety or the public's safety, required immediate arrest. Bache had determined that Z.M. had been drinking. Bache was concerned Z.M. could obtain more alcohol and continue drinking. * * * Z.M. was only fourteen years old. Bache knew that Z.M. had been missing from home overnight and was truant from school with no intent to return. Further, in taking custody of Z.M., Bache was acting at the request of both Z.M.'s mother and the school's resource officer that he be picked up when found. These circumstances warranted immediate arrest. Thus, it was reasonable for Bache to take Z.M. into custody for the youth's safety. * * *

[W]e conclude that Z.M. was taken into custody, and for the purposes of our constitutional analysis, an arrest occurred at this point. * * * [B]ecause Bache made a lawful arrest, he was entitled to search Z.M. and the area within his reach to locate weapons or evidence. In this case, Bache found the money and a bottle of alcohol.

We affirm the court's denial of Z.M.'s motion to suppress the money and alcohol on the basis that Bache had probable cause to make an arrest, including circumstances requiring immediate arrest, and thus it was constitutionally permissible for Bache to take Z.M. into custody. * * * Further, it was reasonable for Bache to conduct a search incident to that taking. * * *

NOTES

1) **Search Incident to Custody** State statutes authorize police to conduct a "search incident to custody" when officers arrest a youth for a "status offense":

Minnesota Stat. Ann. § 260C.175. Taking child into custody (2004).

Subd. 1. Immediate custody. No child may be taken into immediate custody except: * * *

(b) by a peace officer:

(1) when a child has run away from a parent, guardian, or custodian, or when the peace officer reasonably believes the child has run away from a parent, guardian, or custodian; or

(2) when a child is found in surroundings or conditions which endanger the child's health or welfare or which such peace officer reasonably believes will endanger the child's health or welfare. * * *

(c) by a peace officer or probation or parole officer when it is reasonably believed that the child has violated the terms of probation, parole, or other field supervision; * * *.

Subd. 3. Protective pat-down search of child authorized. (a) A peace officer who takes a child of any age or gender into custody under the provisions of this section is authorized to perform a protective pat-down search of the child in order to protect the officer's safety.

(b) A peace officer also may perform a protective pat-down search of a child in order to protect the officer's safety in circumstances where the officer does not intend to take the child into custody, if this section authorizes the officer to take the child into custody.

(c) Evidence discovered in the course of a lawful search under this section is admissible.

2) Rationale of Search Incident to Custody In *In re Adrian B.*, 11 Neb.App. 656, 658 N.W.2d 722 (2003), school officials contacted Officer Puckett and told her that Adrian B., who was not a student at that school and whom Puckett knew was on runaway status, was in the counselor's office. Puckett testified that during three years as a school resource officer, she had had more than 90 contacts with Adrian, knew that he did not comply with rules or obey authority figures and that he was a runaway. She also testified that she had no reason to believe that he was armed or dangerous or carrying a weapon. Upon entering the counselor's office, Puckett regarded Adrian as in custody and not free to leave. She searched his coat and found marijuana and rolling papers. The Court of Appeals upheld officers' authority to conduct a search incident to taking a juvenile into temporary custody for a non-criminal violation:

> In Nebraska, one of the stated purposes of our juvenile code is "[t]o assure the rights of all juveniles to care and protection and a safe and stable living environment and to development of their capacities for a healthy personality, physical well-being, and useful citizenship and to protect the public interest." It follows that the provisions of [the custody statute] which allow peace officers to take juveniles into temporary custody under certain circumstances are in place to protect both the juvenile and the public interest.

> Allowing a search incident to temporary detention of a juvenile after the juvenile is taken into temporary custody protects the juvenile, law enforcement officers, and others with whom the juvenile may come into contact. Further, denying law enforcement officers the authority to conduct searches of juveniles being taken into temporary custody would require officers to take unnecessary risks in the performance of their duties. Therefore, we hold that when a juvenile is taken into temporary custody * * * the peace officer may conduct a search incident to temporary detention. * * * Pursuant to a lawful custodial arrest, law enforcement officers may conduct a warrantless search of the person arrested and of the immediately surrounding area in order to remove any weapons that the arrestee may use to resist arrest or effect an escape and in order to prevent the concealment or destruction of evidence. We find that this law is equally applicable to searches incident to the lawful temporary detention of juveniles. * * *

The court in *In the Interests of J.G.*, 227 N.J.Super. 324, 547 A.2d 336 (Ch. 1988), offered several justifications to uphold the "search incident to custody" that a police officer conducted of a runaway juvenile that yielded marijuana for which the state subsequently prosecuted him as a delinquent. "The search was lawful inasmuch as it was incident to the custodial detention of the juvenile. * * * The juvenile's conduct constitutes a status offense. Nevertheless, an officer still has authority to detain a juvenile whether for juvenile delinquency or as a status offender. * * * When a person is arrested, the arresting officer may search the person arrested and seize any weapons or evidence found on the person's body to prevent destruction or concealment thereof. * * * The taking into custody of a juvenile is analogous to the arrest of an adult. An adult arrest is for the protection of society from an alleged dangerous person. Taking a juvenile into custody is for the purpose of protecting the juvenile's health, morals and well being. When a juvenile is taken into custody, *Chimel* reasoning applies and a search incident to detention is proper. * * *[S]ince the officer had the authority to detain the juvenile, the officer also had the authority to search the juvenile under the inventory search theory in *Illinois v. Lafayette*. * * * Based on the lawful detention, the juvenile's possessions could have been inventorily searched at the station house and the greenish vegetation would have been uncovered anyway * * * under the doctrine of inevitable discovery."

   3) Probable Cause of Status Offense Violation Of what must a police officer have "probable cause" in order to take a juvenile into custody for a "status offense"? *See In re Mark Anthony G.*, 169 A.D.2d 89, 571 N.Y.S.2d 481 (A.D. 1 Dept. 1991) (youthful appearance, late hour, and presence alone at location, vague answers, inconsistent responses, and inability to produce any identification provided basis for detention as a "runaway" and "pat down").

   For what is a police officer "searching" when she conducts a frisk incident to taking a youth into custody? In *In re Terrence G.*, 109 A.D.2d 440, 492 N.Y.S.2d 365 (A.D. 1 Dept. 1985), police detained a juvenile under a "runaway statute" in an area known to be a national gathering place for runaways, i.e. Port Authority—Times' Square area, and notorious for its high incidence of criminal activity by armed juvenile runaways. The court ruled that the officer could legally conduct the "pat down" search that revealed a gun. "Nothing in the noncriminal appellation of this detention serves to obliterate the dangers of the 'in-custody' situation. Here, the circumstances of respondent's detention, coupled with the particularly high duty of protection owed him and other detainees by the runaway statutes, were more than ample justification for the pat down. * * * The police officers who detained respondent * * * were clearly charged with effectuating the State's '*parens patriae* interest in preserving and promoting the welfare of the child.' " *Id*. at 370.

B.   SEARCHING JUVENILES: SCHOOLS AND "SPECIAL NEEDS"

   A principal gets a tip (usually from a student informer) about a student marijuana user. He opens the student's locker with a pass key and goes through the pockets of the jacket hanging inside. Marijuana is found and is turned over to the police. As a result the student is processed through the juvenile justice system, where he files a motion to suppress the evidence obtained from the search. The motion is denied, the student is adjudicated a delinquent. * * * There are variations on the theme—a vice-principal instead of the principal; a search of the student's person rather than his locker; heroin or amphetamines rather than marijuana; earlier involvement of police officers.

William G. Buss, "The Fourth Amendment and Searches of Students in Public Schools," 59 *Iowa L. Rev.* 739, 739 (1974).

When seventeen-year-old Jane Smith, a resident of Smalltown U.S.A., drove * * * into the parking lot of Building X, police officers with drug-sniffing canines were examining a nearby vehicle. Before entering the red-brick building, Jane had to pass through a metal detector. Walking down Building X's hallway, she encountered a security guard on patrol. Soon after, Jane overheard officials ordering someone to undress so that they could conduct a search for contraband. Finally, after passing a bulletin board sign announcing upcoming drug tests, Jane reached her destination. Perhaps surprisingly, Building X is neither a police station nor a maximum security prison, but rather the American schoolhouse of the 1990s.

Stuart C. Berman, "Student Fourth Amendment Rights: Defining the Scope of the *T.L.O.* School—Search Exception," 66 *N.Y.U. L. Rev.* 1077, 1077 (1991).

As a result of compulsory school attendance laws, large groups of young people congregate in schools. School officials' concerns about maintaining order, promoting a suitable educational environment, and controlling guns, drugs, and violence often may conflict with students' Fourth Amendment privacy interests. School searches occur frequently and many students report searches of their persons, purses, jackets, backpacks, or lockers. Young people are subject to school rules which do not apply to adults, and the potential for state infringement of young people's privacy is much greater than the risks of law enforcement confronting adults. However, because of their more extensive regulation, do young people have the same "reasonable expectation of privacy" as adults, and is "society prepared to recognize as objectively reasonable" their claims of privacy generally and especially in schools? Should young people in a school setting be subject to different Fourth Amendment requirements than adult citizens on the street or in their workplace? What are the competing interests? How might they be balanced "reasonably"?

Prior to *T.L.O.*, schools officials and courts developed a variety of rationales to justify searches of student's person and locker, *e.g.* school administrators acted as "private citizens," hence their searches entailed no state action; school officials acted *in loco parentis* under delegated authority from the students' parents; the character and needs of public schools created a special relationship that justifies special rules for searches of students' person and locker; students consented expressly or implicitly or the school administrator provided third-party consent. *See generally* William G. Buss, "The Fourth Amendment and Searches of Students in Public Schools," 59 *Iowa L. Rev.* 739 (1974), for pre-*T.L.O.* analyses.

1. SEARCHING JUVENILES IN SCHOOL

NEW JERSEY v. T.L.O.

469 U.S. 325, 105 S.Ct. 733, 83 L.Ed.2d 720 (1985).

JUSTICE WHITE delivered the opinion of the Court. We granted certiorari in this case to examine the appropriateness of the exclusionary rule as a remedy for searches carried out in violation of the Fourth Amendment by public school authorities. Our consideration of the proper application of the Fourth Amendment to the public schools, however, has led us to conclude that the search that gave rise to the case now before us did not violate the Fourth Amendment. Accordingly, we here address only the questions of the proper standard for assessing the legality of searches conducted by public school officials and the application of that standard to the facts of this case.

[On March 7, 1980, a teacher at Piscataway High School in Middlesex County, N.J., discovered two girls smoking in a lavatory. T.L.O., one of the two girls, was a 14–year–old high school freshman. Smoking in the lavatory violated a school rule and the teacher took the two girls to the Principal's office. Assistant Vice Principal Theodore Choplick questioned them and T.L.O.'s companion admitted that she had violated the rule. T.L.O., however, denied that she had smoked in the lavatory and claimed that she did not smoke at all. Choplick asked T.L.O. to come into his private office and demanded to see her purse. He opened her purse, found a pack of cigarettes which he removed from the purse, and held the cigarettes in front of her and confronted her for lying to him. As he reached the purse for cigarettes, Choplick also noticed a package of cigarette rolling papers. In his experience, Choplick associated possession of rolling papers with the use of marihuana. He suspected that a closer examination of the purse might yield further evidence of drug use and he searched the purse thoroughly. The search revealed a small amount of marihuana, a pipe, a number of empty plastic bags, a substantial quantity of money in one-dollar bills, an index card that appeared to list of students who owed T.L.O. money, and two letters that implicated T.L.O. in marihuana dealing. Choplick notified T.L.O.'s mother and the police, and turned the evidence over to the police. At the request of the police, T.L.O.'s mother took her daughter to police headquarters, where T.L.O. confessed that she had been selling marihuana at the high school. The State brought delinquency charges against T.L.O. based on the confession and the evidence seized by Choplick.[1] T.L.O. contended that Choplick's

---

1. T.L.O. also received a 3–day suspension from school for smoking cigarettes in a nonsmoking area and a 7–day suspension for possession of marihuana. On T.L.O.'s motion, the Superior

search of her purse violated the Fourth Amendment, moved to suppress the evidence he found and her confession, which the allegedly unlawful search also tainted. The Juvenile Court denied the motion to suppress. The court concluded that Choplick conducted a reasonable search. His initial decision to open the purse was justified by his well-founded suspicion that T.L.O. had violated the rule forbidding smoking in the lavatory. Once he opened the purse, he saw evidence of marihuana violations in plain view which justified a thorough search to determine the nature and extent of T.L.O.'s drug-related activities. The juvenile court denied T.L.O.'s motion to suppress, found her delinquent, and sentenced her to a year's probation.]

T.L.O. appealed the Fourth Amendment ruling, and the Supreme Court of New Jersey reversed the judgment of the Appellate Division and ordered the suppression of the evidence found in T.L.O.'s purse.

The New Jersey Supreme Court agreed with the lower courts that the Fourth Amendment applies to searches conducted by school officials. The court also rejected the State of New Jersey's argument that the exclusionary rule should not be employed to prevent the use in juvenile proceedings of evidence unlawfully seized by school officials. Declining to consider whether applying the rule to the fruits of searches by school officials would have any deterrent value, the court held simply that the precedents of this Court establish that "if an official search violates constitutional rights, the evidence is not admissible in criminal proceedings."

With respect to the question of the legality of the search before it, the court agreed with the Juvenile Court that a warrantless search by a school official does not violate the Fourth Amendment so long as the official "has reasonable grounds to believe that a student possesses evidence of illegal activity or activity that would interfere with school discipline and order." However, the court, with two justices dissenting, sharply disagreed with the Juvenile Court's conclusion that the search of the purse was reasonable. According to the majority, the contents of T.L.O.'s purse had no bearing on the accusation against T.L.O., for possession of cigarettes (as opposed to smoking them in the lavatory) did not violate school rules, and a mere desire for evidence that would impeach T.L.O.'s claim that she did not smoke cigarettes could not justify the search. Moreover, even if a reasonable suspicion that T.L.O. had cigarettes in her purse would justify a search, Mr. Choplick had no such suspicion, as no one had furnished him with any specific information that there were cigarettes in the purse. Finally, leaving aside the question whether Mr. Choplick was justified in opening the purse, the court held that the evidence of drug use that he saw inside did not justify the extensive "rummaging" through T.L.O.'s papers and effects that followed.

Court of New Jersey, Chancery Division, set aside the 7–day suspension on the ground that it was based on evidence seized in violation of the Fourth Amendment. The Board of Education apparently did not appeal the decision of the Chancery Division.

We granted the State of New Jersey's petition for certiorari. Although the State had argued in the Supreme Court of New Jersey that the search of T.L.O.'s purse did not violate the Fourth Amendment, the petition for certiorari raised only the question whether the exclusionary rule should operate to bar consideration in juvenile delinquency proceedings of evidence unlawfully seized by a school official without the involvement of law enforcement officers. When this case was first argued last Term, the State conceded for the purpose of argument that the standard devised by the New Jersey Supreme Court for determining the legality of school searches was appropriate and that the court had correctly applied that standard; the State contended only that the remedial purposes of the exclusionary rule were not well served by applying it to searches conducted by public authorities not primarily engaged in law enforcement.

Although we originally granted certiorari to decide the issue of the appropriate remedy in juvenile court proceedings for unlawful school searches, our doubts regarding the wisdom of deciding that question in isolation from the broader question of what limits, if any, the Fourth Amendment places on the activities of school authorities prompted us to order reargument on that question.[2] Having heard argument on the legality of the search of T.L.O.'s purse, we are satisfied that the search did not violate the Fourth Amendment.[3]

In determining whether the search at issue in this case violated the Fourth Amendment, we are faced initially with the question whether that

---

2. State and federal courts considering these questions have struggled to accommodate the interests protected by the Fourth Amendment and the interest of the States in providing a safe environment conducive to education in the public schools. Some courts have resolved the tension between these interests by giving full force to one or the other side of the balance. Thus, in a number of cases courts have held that school officials conducting in-school searches of students are private parties acting *in loco parentis* and are therefore not subject to the constraints of the Fourth Amendment. At least one court has held, on the other hand, that the Fourth Amendment applies in full to in-school searches by school officials and that a search conducted without probable cause is unreasonable; others have held or suggested that the probable-cause standard is applicable at least where the police are involved in a search; or where the search is highly intrusive.

The majority of courts that have addressed the issue of the Fourth Amendment in the schools have, like the Supreme Court of New Jersey in this case, reached a middle position: the Fourth Amendment applies to searches conducted by school authorities, but the special needs of the school environment require assessment of the legality of such searches against a standard less exacting than that of probable cause. These courts have, by and large, upheld warrantless searches by school authorities provided that they are supported by a reasonable suspicion that the search will uncover evidence of an infraction of school disciplinary rules or a violation of the law.

Although few have considered the matter, courts have also split over whether the exclusionary rule is an appropriate remedy for Fourth Amendment violations committed by school authorities. The Georgia courts have held that although the Fourth Amendment applies to the schools, the exclusionary rule does not. Other jurisdictions have applied the rule to exclude the fruits of unlawful school searches from criminal trials and delinquency proceedings.

3. In holding that the search of T.L.O.'s purse did not violate the Fourth Amendment, we do not implicitly determine that the exclusionary rule applies to the fruits of unlawful searches conducted by school authorities. The question whether evidence should be excluded from a criminal proceeding involves two discrete inquiries: whether the evidence was seized in violation of the Fourth Amendment, and whether the exclusionary rule is the appropriate remedy for the violation. Neither question is logically antecedent to the other, for a negative answer to either question is sufficient to dispose of the case. Thus, our determination that the search at issue in this case did not violate the Fourth Amendment implies no particular resolution of the question of the applicability of the exclusionary rule.

Amendment's prohibition on unreasonable searches and seizures applies to searches conducted by public school officials. We hold that it does.

It is now beyond dispute that "the Federal Constitution, by virtue of the Fourteenth Amendment, prohibits unreasonable searches and seizures by state officers." Equally indisputable is the proposition that the Fourteenth Amendment protects the rights of students against encroachment by public school officials * * *.

These two propositions—that the Fourth Amendment applies to the States through the Fourteenth Amendment, and that the actions of public school officials are subject to the limits placed on state action by the Fourteenth Amendment—might appear sufficient to answer the suggestion that the Fourth Amendment does not proscribe unreasonable searches by school officials. On reargument, however, the State of New Jersey has argued that the history of the Fourth Amendment indicates that the Amendment was intended to regulate only searches and seizures carried out by law enforcement officers; accordingly, although public school officials are concededly state agents for purposes of the Fourteenth Amendment, the Fourth Amendment creates no rights enforceable against them.[4] * * *

[T]his Court has never limited the Amendment's prohibition on unreasonable searches and seizures to operations conducted by the police. Rather, the Court has long spoken of the Fourth Amendment's strictures as restraints imposed upon "governmental action"—that is, "upon the activities of sovereign authority." Accordingly, we have held the Fourth Amendment applicable to the activities of civil as well as criminal authorities: building inspectors, Occupational Safety and Health Act inspectors, and even firemen entering privately owned premises to battle a fire, are all subject to the restraints imposed by the Fourth Amendment. * * *

We have held school officials subject to the commands of the First Amendment, and the Due Process Clause of the Fourteenth Amendment. If school authorities are state actors for purposes of the constitutional guarantees of freedom of expression and due process, it is difficult to understand why they should be deemed to be exercising parental rather than public authority when conducting searches of their students. More generally, the Court has recognized that "the concept of parental delegation" as a source of school authority is not entirely "consonant with compulsory education laws." Today's public school officials do not merely exercise authority voluntarily conferred on them by individual parents; rather, they act in furtherance of publicly mandated educational and disciplinary policies. In carrying out searches and other disciplinary functions pursuant to such policies, school officials act as representatives of the State, not merely as surrogates for the parents, and they cannot claim the parents' immunity from the strictures of the Fourth Amendment.

---

4. Cf. *Ingraham v. Wright,* 430 U.S. 651 (1977) (holding that the Eighth Amendment's prohibition of cruel and unusual punishment applies only to punishments imposed after criminal convictions and hence does not apply to the punishment of schoolchildren by public school officials).

To hold that the Fourth Amendment applies to searches conducted by school authorities is only to begin the inquiry into the standards governing such searches. Although the underlying command of the Fourth Amendment is always that searches and seizures be reasonable, what is reasonable depends on the context within which a search takes place. The determination of the standard of reasonableness governing any specific class of searches requires "balancing the need to search against the invasion which the search entails." On one side of the balance are arrayed the individual's legitimate expectations of privacy and personal security; on the other, the government's need for effective methods to deal with breaches of public order.

We have recognized that even a limited search of the person is a substantial invasion of privacy. *Terry v. Ohio*, (1967). We have also recognized that searches of closed items of personal luggage are intrusions on protected privacy interests, for "the Fourth Amendment provides protection to the owner of every container that conceals its contents from plain view." *United States v. Ross*, (1982). A search of a child's person or of a closed purse or other bag carried on her person,[5] no less than a similar search carried out on an adult, is undoubtedly a severe violation of subjective expectations of privacy.

Of course, the Fourth Amendment does not protect subjective expectations of privacy that are unreasonable or otherwise "illegitimate." To receive the protection of the Fourth Amendment, an expectation of privacy must be one that society is "prepared to recognize as legitimate." The State of New Jersey has argued that because of the pervasive supervision to which children in the schools are necessarily subject, a child has virtually no legitimate expectation of privacy in articles of personal property "unnecessarily" carried into a school. This argument has two factual premises: (1) the fundamental incompatibility of expectations of privacy with the maintenance of a sound educational environment; and (2) the minimal interest of the child in bringing any items of personal property into the school. Both premises are severely flawed.

Although this Court may take notice of the difficulty of maintaining discipline in the public schools today, the situation is not so dire that students in the schools may claim no legitimate expectations of privacy. We have recently recognized that the need to maintain order in a prison is such that prisoners retain no legitimate expectations of privacy in their cells, but it goes almost without saying that "[t]he prisoner and the

---

5. We do not address the question, not presented by this case, whether a schoolchild has a legitimate expectation of privacy in lockers, desks, or other school property provided for the storage of school supplies. Nor do we express any opinion on the standards (if any) governing searches of such areas by school officials or by other public authorities acting at the request of school officials. Compare *Zamora v. Pomeroy*, (C.A.10 1981) ("Inasmuch as the school had assumed joint control of the locker it cannot be successfully maintained that the school did not have a right to inspect it"), and *People v. Overton*, (1969) (deciding that school administrators have power to consent to search of a student's locker), with *State v. Engerud*, (1983) ("We are satisfied that in the context of this case the student had an expectation of privacy in the contents of his locker * * *. For the four years of high school, the school locker is a home away from home. In it the student stores the kind of personal 'effects' protected by the Fourth Amendment.").

schoolchild stand in wholly different circumstances, separated by the harsh facts of criminal conviction and incarceration." We are not yet ready to hold that the schools and the prisons need be equated for purposes of the Fourth Amendment.

Nor does the State's suggestion that children have no legitimate need to bring personal property into the schools seem well anchored in reality. Students at a minimum must bring to school not only the supplies needed for their studies, but also keys, money, and the necessaries of personal hygiene and grooming. In addition, students may carry on their persons or in purses or wallets such nondisruptive yet highly personal items as photographs, letters, and diaries. Finally, students may have perfectly legitimate reasons to carry with them articles of property needed in connection with extracurricular or recreational activities. In short, school-children may find it necessary to carry with them a variety of legitimate, noncontraband items, and there is no reason to conclude that they have necessarily waived all rights to privacy in such items merely by bringing them onto school grounds.

Against the child's interest in privacy must be set the substantial interest of teachers and administrators in maintaining discipline in the classroom and on school grounds. Maintaining order in the classroom has never been easy, but in recent years, school disorder has often taken particularly ugly forms: drug use and violent crime in the schools have become major social problems. Even in schools that have been spared the most severe disciplinary problems, the preservation of order and a proper educational environment requires close supervision of schoolchildren, as well as the enforcement of rules against conduct that would be perfectly permissible if undertaken by an adult. "Events calling for discipline are frequent occurrences and sometimes require immediate, effective action." Accordingly, we have recognized that maintaining security and order in the schools requires a certain degree of flexibility in school disciplinary procedures, and we have respected the value of preserving the informality of the student-teacher relationship.

How, then, should we strike the balance between the schoolchild's legitimate expectations of privacy and the school's equally legitimate need to maintain an environment in which learning can take place? It is evident that the school setting requires some easing of the restrictions to which searches by public authorities are ordinarily subject. The warrant require-ment, in particular, is unsuited to the school environment: requiring a teacher to obtain a warrant before searching a child suspected of an infraction of school rules (or of the criminal law) would unduly interfere with the maintenance of the swift and informal disciplinary procedures needed in the schools. Just as we have in other cases dispensed with the warrant requirement when "the burden of obtaining a warrant is likely to frustrate the governmental purpose behind the search," we hold today that school officials need not obtain a warrant before searching a student who is under their authority.

The school setting also requires some modification of the level of suspicion of illicit activity needed to justify a search. Ordinarily, a search—even one that may permissibly be carried out without a warrant—must be based upon "probable cause" to believe that a violation of the law has occurred. However, "probable cause" is not an irreducible requirement of a valid search. The fundamental command of the Fourth Amendment is that searches and seizures be reasonable, and although "both the concept of probable cause and the requirement of a warrant bear on the reasonableness of a search, * * * in certain limited circumstances neither is required." Thus, we have in a number of cases recognized the legality of searches and seizures based on suspicions that, although "reasonable," do not rise to the level of probable cause. Where a careful balancing of governmental and private interests suggests that the public interest is best served by a Fourth Amendment standard of reasonableness that stops short of probable cause, we have not hesitated to adopt such a standard.

We join the majority of courts that have examined this issue in concluding that the accommodation of the privacy interests of schoolchildren with the substantial need of teachers and administrators for freedom to maintain order in the schools does not require strict adherence to the requirement that searches be based on probable cause to believe that the subject of the search has violated or is violating the law. Rather, the legality of a search of a student should depend simply on the reasonableness, under all the circumstances, of the search. Determining the reasonableness of any search involves a twofold inquiry: first, one must consider "whether the * * * action was justified at its inception,"; second, one must determine whether the search as actually conducted "was reasonably related in scope to the circumstances which justified the interference in the first place,". Under ordinary circumstances, a search of a student by a teacher or other school official[7] will be "justified at its inception" when there are reasonable grounds for suspecting that the search will turn up evidence that the student has violated or is violating either the law or the rules of the school.[8] Such a search will be permissible in its scope when the measures adopted are reasonably related to the objectives of the

---

7. We here consider only searches carried out by school authorities acting alone and on their own authority. This case does not present the question of the appropriate standard for assessing the legality of searches conducted by school officials in conjunction with or at the behest of law enforcement agencies, and we express no opinion on that question. Cf. *Picha v. Wielgos*, (N.D.Ill.1976) (holding probable-cause standard applicable to searches involving the police).

8. We do not decide whether individualized suspicion is an essential element of the reasonableness standard we adopt for searches by school authorities. In other contexts, however, we have held that although "some quantum of individualized suspicion is usually a prerequisite to a constitutional search or seizure[,] * * * the Fourth Amendment imposes no irreducible requirement of such suspicion." Exceptions to the requirement of individualized suspicion are generally appropriate only where the privacy interests implicated by a search are minimal and where "other safeguards" are available "to assure that the individual's reasonable expectation of privacy is not 'subject to the discretion of the official in the field.' " Because the search of T.L.O.'s purse was based upon an individualized suspicion that she had violated school rules, we need not consider the circumstances that might justify school authorities in conducting searches unsupported by individualized suspicion.

search and not excessively intrusive in light of the age and sex of the student and the nature of the infraction.[9]

This standard will, we trust, neither unduly burden the efforts of school authorities to maintain order in their schools nor authorize unrestrained intrusions upon the privacy of schoolchildren. By focusing attention on the question of reasonableness, the standard will spare teachers and school administrators the necessity of schooling themselves in the niceties of probable cause and permit them to regulate their conduct according to the dictates of reason and common sense. At the same time, the reasonableness standard should ensure that the interests of students will be invaded no more than is necessary to achieve the legitimate end of preserving order in the schools.

There remains the question of the legality of the search in this case. We recognize that the "reasonable grounds" standard applied by the New Jersey Supreme Court in its consideration of this question is not substantially different from the standard that we have adopted today. Nonetheless, we believe that the New Jersey court's application of that standard to strike down the search of T.L.O.'s purse reflects a somewhat crabbed notion of reasonableness. Our review of the facts surrounding the search leads us to conclude that the search was in no sense unreasonable for Fourth Amendment purposes. * * *

The New Jersey Supreme Court pointed to two grounds for its holding that the search for cigarettes was unreasonable. First, the court observed that possession of cigarettes was not in itself illegal or a violation of school rules. Because the contents of T.L.O.'s purse would therefore have "no direct bearing on the infraction" of which she was accused (smoking in a lavatory where smoking was prohibited), there was no reason to search her purse. Second, even assuming that a search of T.L.O.'s purse might under some circumstances be reasonable in light of the accusation made against T.L.O., the New Jersey court concluded that Mr. Choplick in this particular case had no reasonable grounds to suspect that T.L.O. had cigarettes in her purse. At best, according to the court, Mr. Choplick had "a good hunch."

Both these conclusions are implausible. T.L.O. had been accused of smoking, and had denied the accusation in the strongest possible terms

---

9. Our reference to the nature of the infraction is not intended as an endorsement of Justice Stevens' suggestion that some rules regarding student conduct are by nature too "trivial" to justify a search based upon reasonable suspicion. We are unwilling to adopt a standard under which the legality of a search is dependent upon a judge's evaluation of the relative importance of various school rules. The maintenance of discipline in the schools requires not only that students be restrained from assaulting one another, abusing drugs and alcohol, and committing other crimes, but also that students conform themselves to the standards of conduct prescribed by school authorities. We have "repeatedly emphasized the need for affirming the comprehensive authority of the States and of school officials, consistent with fundamental constitutional safeguards, to prescribe and control conduct in the schools." The promulgation of a rule forbidding specified conduct presumably reflects a judgment on the part of school officials that such conduct is destructive of school order or of a proper educational environment. Absent any suggestion that the rule violates some substantive constitutional guarantee, the courts should, as a general matter, defer to that judgment and refrain from attempting to distinguish between rules that are important to the preservation of order in the schools and rules that are not.

when she stated that she did not smoke at all. Surely it cannot be said that under these circumstances, T.L.O.'s possession of cigarettes would be irrelevant to the charges against her or to her response to those charges. T.L.O.'s possession of cigarettes, once it was discovered, would both corroborate the report that she had been smoking and undermine the credibility of her defense to the charge of smoking. * * * The relevance of T.L.O.'s possession of cigarettes to the question whether she had been smoking and to the credibility of her denial that she smoked supplied the necessary "nexus" between the item searched for and the infraction under investigation. Thus, if Mr. Choplick in fact had a reasonable suspicion that T.L.O. had cigarettes in her purse, the search was justified despite the fact that the cigarettes, if found, would constitute "mere evidence" of a violation.

Of course, the New Jersey Supreme Court also held that Mr. Choplick had no reasonable suspicion that the purse would contain cigarettes. This conclusion is puzzling. A teacher had reported that T.L.O. was smoking in the lavatory. Certainly this report gave Mr. Choplick reason to suspect that T.L.O. was carrying cigarettes with her; and if she did have cigarettes, her purse was the obvious place in which to find them. * * * [T]he requirement of reasonable suspicion is not a requirement of absolute certainty: "sufficient probability, not certainty, is the touchstone of reasonableness under the Fourth Amendment * * *." Because the hypothesis that T.L.O. was carrying cigarettes in her purse was itself not unreasonable, it is irrelevant that other hypotheses were also consistent with the teacher's accusation. Accordingly, it cannot be said that Mr. Choplick acted unreasonably when he examined T.L.O.'s purse to see if it contained cigarettes.

Our conclusion that Mr. Choplick's decision to open T.L.O.'s purse was reasonable brings us to the question of the further search for marihuana once the pack of cigarettes was located. The suspicion upon which the search for marihuana was founded was provided when Mr. Choplick observed a package of rolling papers in the purse as he removed the pack of cigarettes. Although T.L.O. does not dispute the reasonableness of Mr. Choplick's belief that the rolling papers indicated the presence of marihuana, she does contend that the scope of the search Mr. Choplick conducted exceeded permissible bounds when he seized and read certain letters that implicated T.L.O. in drug dealing. This argument, too, is unpersuasive. The discovery of the rolling papers concededly gave rise to a reasonable suspicion that T.L.O. was carrying marihuana as well as cigarettes in her purse. This suspicion justified further exploration of T.L.O.'s purse, which turned up more evidence of drug-related activities: a pipe, a number of plastic bags of the type commonly used to store marihuana, a small quantity of marihuana, and a fairly substantial amount of money. Under these circumstances, it was not unreasonable to extend the search to a separate zippered compartment of the purse; and when a search of that compartment revealed an index card containing a list of "people who owe me money" as well as two letters, the inference that T.L.O. was involved in marihuana trafficking was substantial enough to justify Mr. Choplick in examining the letters to determine whether they contained any further evidence. In short, we cannot conclude that the search for marihuana was unreasonable in any respect.

Because the search resulting in the discovery of the evidence of marihuana dealing by T.L.O. was reasonable, the New Jersey Supreme Court's decision to exclude that evidence from T.L.O.'s juvenile delinquency proceedings on Fourth Amendment grounds was erroneous. Accordingly, the judgment of the Supreme Court of New Jersey is

Reversed.

JUSTICE POWELL, with whom JUSTICE O'CONNOR joins, concurring.

I agree with the Court's decision, and generally with its opinion. I would place greater emphasis, however, on the special characteristics of elementary and secondary schools that make it unnecessary to afford students the same constitutional protections granted adults and juveniles in a nonschool setting.

In any realistic sense, students within the school environment have a lesser expectation of privacy than members of the population generally. They spend the school hours in close association with each other, both in the classroom and during recreation periods. The students in a particular class often know each other and their teachers quite well. Of necessity, teachers have a degree of familiarity with, and authority over, their students that is unparalleled except perhaps in the relationship between parent and child. It is simply unrealistic to think that students have the same subjective expectation of privacy as the population generally. But for purposes of deciding this case, I can assume that children in school—no less than adults—have privacy interests that society is prepared to recognize as legitimate. * * *

The special relationship between teacher and student also distinguishes the setting within which schoolchildren operate. Law enforcement officers function as adversaries of criminal suspects. These officers have the responsibility to investigate criminal activity, to locate and arrest those who violate our laws, and to facilitate the charging and bringing of such persons to trial. Rarely does this type of adversarial relationship exist between school authorities and pupils. Instead, there is a commonality of interests between teachers and their pupils. The attitude of the typical teacher is one of personal responsibility for the student's welfare as well as for his education.

The primary duty of school officials and teachers, as the Court states, is the education and training of young people. A State has a compelling interest in assuring that the schools meet this responsibility. Without first establishing discipline and maintaining order, teachers cannot begin to educate their students. And apart from education, the school has the obligation to protect pupils from mistreatment by other children, and also to protect teachers themselves from violence by the few students whose conduct in recent years has prompted national concern. For me, it would be unreasonable and at odds with history to argue that the full panoply of constitutional rules applies with the same force and effect in the schoolhouse as it does in the enforcement of criminal laws. * * *

JUSTICE BLACKMUN, concurring in the judgment.

I join the judgment of the Court and agree with much that is said in its opinion. I write separately, however, because I believe the Court omits a crucial step in its analysis of whether a school search must be based upon probable-cause. The Court correctly states that we have recognized limited exceptions to the probable-cause requirement "[w]here a careful balancing of governmental and private interests suggests that the public interest is best served" by a lesser standard. I believe that we have used such a balancing test, rather than strictly applying the Fourth Amendment's Warrant and Probable–Cause Clause, only when we were confronted with "a special law enforcement need for greater flexibility." * * * Only in those exceptional circumstances in which special needs, beyond the normal need for law enforcement, make the warrant and probable-cause requirement impracticable, is a court entitled to substitute its balancing of interests for that of the Framers. * * *

The Court's implication that the balancing test is the rule rather than the exception is troubling for me because it is unnecessary in this case. The elementary and secondary school setting presents a special need for flexibility justifying a departure from the balance struck by the Framers. * * * The special need for an immediate response to behavior that threatens either the safety of schoolchildren and teachers or the educational process itself justifies the Court in excepting school searches from the warrant and probable-cause requirement, and in applying a standard determined by balancing the relevant interests. I agree with the standard the Court has announced, and with its application of the standard to the facts of this case. I therefore concur in its judgment.

JUSTICE BRENNAN, with whom JUSTICE MARSHALL joins, concurring in part and dissenting in part.

* * * Teachers, like all other government officials, must conform their conduct to the Fourth Amendment's protections of personal privacy and personal security. * * * [T]his principle is of particular importance when applied to schoolteachers, for children learn as much by example as by exposition. It would be incongruous and futile to charge teachers with the task of imbuing their students with an understanding of our system of constitutional democracy, while at the same time immunizing those same teachers from the need to respect constitutional protections.

I do not, however, otherwise join the Court's opinion. Today's decision sanctions school officials to conduct full-scale searches on a "reasonableness" standard whose only definite content is that it is *not* the same test as the "probable cause" standard found in the text of the Fourth Amendment. In adopting this unclear, unprecedented, and unnecessary departure from generally applicable Fourth Amendment standards, the Court carves out a broad exception to standards that this Court has developed over years of considering Fourth Amendment problems. Its decision is supported neither by precedent nor even by a fair application of the "balancing test" it proclaims in this very opinion.

Three basic principles underly this Court's Fourth Amendment jurisprudence. First, warrantless searches are *per se* unreasonable, subject only to a few specifically delineated and well-recognized exceptions. Second, full-scale searches—whether conducted in accordance with the warrant requirement or pursuant to one of its exceptions—are "reasonable" in Fourth Amendment terms only on a showing of probable cause to believe that a crime has been committed and that evidence of the crime will be found in the place to be searched. Third, categories of intrusions that are substantially less intrusive than full-scale searches or seizures may be justifiable in accordance with a balancing test even absent a warrant or probable cause, provided that the balancing test used gives sufficient weight to the privacy interests that will be infringed. * * *

I agree that schoolteachers or principals, when not acting as agents of law enforcement authorities, generally may conduct a search of their students' belongings without first obtaining a warrant. * * * [S]chool searches may justifiably be held to that extent to constitute an exception to the Fourth Amendment's warrant requirement. * * *

To require a showing of some extraordinary governmental interest before dispensing with the warrant requirement is not to undervalue society's need to apprehend violators of the criminal law. * * *

In this case, such extraordinary governmental interests do exist and are sufficient to justify an exception to the warrant requirement. Students are necessarily confined for most of the schoolday in close proximity to each other and to the school staff. I agree with the Court that we can take judicial notice of the serious problems of drugs and violence that plague our schools. * * * A teacher or principal could neither carry out essential teaching functions nor adequately protect students' safety if required to wait for a warrant before conducting a necessary search.

I emphatically disagree with the Court's decision to cast aside the constitutional probable-cause standard when assessing the constitutional validity of a schoolhouse search. The Court's decision jettisons the probable-cause standard—the only standard that finds support in the text of the Fourth Amendment—on the basis of its Rohrschach-like "balancing test." Use of such a "balancing test" to determine the standard for evaluating the validity of a full-scale search represents a sizable innovation in Fourth Amendment analysis. This innovation finds support neither in precedent nor policy and portends a dangerous weakening of the purpose of the Fourth Amendment to protect the privacy and security of our citizens. * * *

An unbroken line of cases in this Court have held that probable cause is a prerequisite for a full-scale search. * * * [T]he provisions of the Warrant Clause—a warrant and probable cause—provide the yardstick against which official searches and seizures are to be measured. The Fourth Amendment neither requires nor authorizes the conceptual free-for-all that ensues when an unguided balancing test is used to assess specific categories of searches. If the search in question is more than a minimally intrusive *Terry* stop, the constitutional probable-cause standard determines its validity. * * *

Considerations of the deepest significance for the freedom of our citizens counsel strict adherence to the principle that no search may be conducted where the official is not in possession of probable cause—that is, where the official does not know of "facts and circumstances [that] warrant a prudent man in believing that the offense has been committed." * * * [I]t was designed in addition to grant the individual a zone of privacy whose protections could be breached only where the "reasonable" requirements of the probable-cause standard were met. * * * That right protects the privacy and security of the individual unless the authorities can cross a specific threshold of need, designated by the term "probable cause." I cannot agree with the Court's assertions today that a "balancing test" can replace the constitutional threshold with one that is more convenient for those enforcing the laws but less protective of the citizens' liberty; the Fourth Amendment's protections should not be defaced by "a balancing process that overwhelms the individual's protection against unwarranted official intrusion by a governmental interest said to justify the search and seizure."

I thus do not accept the majority's premise that "[t]o hold that the Fourth Amendment applies to searches conducted by school authorities is only to begin the inquiry into the standards governing such searches." For me, the finding that the Fourth Amendment applies, coupled with the observation that what is at issue is a full-scale search, is the end of the inquiry. But even if I believed that a "balancing test" appropriately replaces the judgment of the Framers of the Fourth Amendment, I would nonetheless object to the cursory and shortsighted "test" that the Court employs to justify its predictable weakening of Fourth Amendment protections. In particular, the test employed by the Court vastly overstates the social costs that a probable-cause standard entails and, though it plausibly articulates the serious privacy interests at stake, inexplicably fails to accord them adequate weight in striking the balance.

The Court begins to articulate its "balancing test" by observing that "the government's need for effective methods to deal with breaches of public order" is to be weighed on one side of the balance. Of course, this is not correct. It is not the government's need for effective enforcement methods that should weigh in the balance, for ordinary Fourth Amendment standards—including probable cause—may well permit methods for maintaining the public order that are perfectly effective. If that were the case, the governmental interest in having effective standards would carry no weight at all as a justification for departing from the probable-cause standard. Rather, it is the costs of applying probable cause as opposed to applying some lesser standard that should be weighed on the government's side.

In order to tote up the costs of applying the probable-cause standard, it is thus necessary first to take into account the nature and content of that standard, and the likelihood that it would hamper achievement of the goal—vital not just to "teachers and administrators,"—of maintaining an effective educational setting in the public schools. * * *

Two Terms ago, in *Illinois v. Gates*, this Court expounded at some length its view of the probable-cause standard. Among the adjectives used to describe the standard were "practical," "fluid," "flexible," "easily applied," and "nontechnical." The probable-cause standard was to be seen as a "commonsense" test whose application depended on an evaluation of the "totality of the circumstances." * * *

[A]fter *Gates*, I would have thought that there could be no doubt that this "nontechnical," "practical," and "easily applied" concept was eminently serviceable in a context like a school, where teachers require the flexibility to respond quickly and decisively to emergencies. * * *

On my view, the presence of the word "unreasonable" in the text of the Fourth Amendment does not grant a shifting majority of this Court the authority to answer *all* Fourth Amendment questions by consulting its momentary vision of the social good. Full-scale searches unaccompanied by probable cause violate the Fourth Amendment. I do not pretend that our traditional Fourth Amendment doctrine automatically answers all of the difficult legal questions that occasionally arise. I do contend, however, that this Court has an obligation to provide some coherent framework to resolve such questions on the basis of more than a conclusory recitation of the results of a "balancing test." The Fourth Amendment itself supplies that framework and, because the Court today fails to heed its message, I must respectfully dissent.

JUSTICE STEVENS, with whom JUSTICE MARSHALL joins, and with whom JUSTICE BRENNAN joins as to Part I, concurring in part and dissenting in part.

* * * The search of a young woman's purse by a school administrator is a serious invasion of her legitimate expectations of privacy. A purse "is a common repository for one's personal effects and therefore is inevitably associated with the expectation of privacy." * * * In order to evaluate the reasonableness of such searches, "it is necessary 'first to focus upon the governmental interest which allegedly justifies official intrusion upon the constitutionally protected interests of the private citizen,' for there is 'no ready test for determining reasonableness other than by balancing the need to search [or seize] against the invasion which the search [or seizure] entails.'" * * *

But the majority's statement of the standard for evaluating the reasonableness of such searches is not suitably adapted to that end. The majority holds that "a search of a student by a teacher or other school official will be 'justified at its inception' when there are reasonable grounds for suspecting that the search will turn up evidence *that the student has violated or is violating* either the law or *the rules of the school*." This standard will permit teachers and school administrators to search students when they suspect that the search will reveal evidence of even the most trivial school regulation or precatory guideline for student behavior. The Court's standard for deciding whether a search is justified "at its inception" treats all violations of the rules of the school as though they were fungible. For the Court, a search for curlers and sunglasses in order to enforce the school dress code is apparently just as important as a search for evidence of heroin addiction or violent gang activity.

The majority, however, does not contend that school administrators have a compelling need to search students in order to achieve optimum enforcement of minor school regulations. To the contrary, when minor violations are involved, there is every indication that the informal school disciplinary process, with only minimum requirements of due process, can function effectively without the power to search for enough evidence to prove a criminal case. In arguing that teachers and school administrators need the power to search students based on a lessened standard, the United States as *amicus curiae* relies heavily on empirical evidence of a contemporary crisis of violence and unlawful behavior that is seriously undermining the process of education in American schools. A standard better attuned to this concern would permit teachers and school administrators to search a student when they have reason to believe that the search will uncover *evidence that the student is violating the law or engaging in conduct that is seriously disruptive of school order, or the educational process.*

This standard is properly directed at "[t]he sole justification for the [warrantless] search." In addition, a standard that varies the extent of the permissible intrusion with the gravity of the suspected offense is also more consistent with common-law experience and this Court's precedent. Criminal law has traditionally recognized a distinction between essentially regulatory offenses and serious violations of the peace, and graduated the response of the criminal justice system depending on the character of the violation. The application of a similar distinction in evaluating the reasonableness of warrantless searches and seizures "is not a novel idea." * * *

The logic of distinguishing between minor and serious offenses in evaluating the reasonableness of school searches is almost too clear for argument. In order to justify the serious intrusion on the persons and privacy of young people that New Jersey asks this Court to approve, the State must identify "some real immediate and serious consequences." While school administrators have entirely legitimate reasons for adopting school regulations and guidelines for student behavior, the authorization of searches to enforce them "displays a shocking lack of all sense of proportion."

The majority offers weak deference to these principles of balance and decency by announcing that school searches will only be reasonable in scope "when the measures adopted are reasonably related to the objectives of the search and not excessively intrusive in light of the age and sex of the student *and the nature of the infraction*." The majority offers no explanation why a two-part standard is necessary to evaluate the reasonableness of the ordinary school search. Significantly, in the balance of its opinion the Court pretermits any discussion of the nature of T.L.O.'s infraction of the "no smoking" rule.

The "rider" to the Court's standard for evaluating the reasonableness of the initial intrusion apparently is the Court's perception that its standard is overly generous and does not, by itself, achieve a fair balance between the administrator's right to search and the student's reasonable expectations of privacy. The Court's standard for evaluating the "scope" of reasonable school searches is obviously designed to prohibit physically intrusive searches of students by persons of the opposite sex for relatively minor offenses. The Court's effort to establish a standard that is, at once, clear enough to allow searches to be upheld in nearly every case, and flexible enough to prohibit obviously unreasonable intrusions of young adults' privacy only creates uncertainty in the extent of its resolve to prohibit the latter. Moreover, the majority's application of its standard in this case—to permit a male administrator to rummage through the purse of a female high school student in order to obtain evidence that she was smoking in a bathroom—raises grave doubts in my mind whether its effort will be effective. Unlike the Court, I believe the nature of the suspected infraction is a matter of first importance in deciding whether *any* invasion of privacy is permissible.

The Court embraces the standard applied by the New Jersey Supreme Court as equivalent to its own, and then deprecates the state court's application of the standard as reflecting "a somewhat crabbed notion of reasonableness." There is no mystery, however, in the state court's finding that the search in this case was unconstitutional; the decision below was not based on a manipulation of reasonable suspicion, but on the trivial character of the activity that promoted the official search. * * * [T]he state court's opinion focuses on the character of the rule infraction that is to be the object of the search.

In the view of the state court, there is a quite obvious and material difference between a search for evidence relating to violent or disruptive activity, and a search for evidence of a smoking rule violation. * * *

I respectfully dissent.

NOTES

1) Application of *T.L.O.*'s "Reasonableness" Standard Since *T.L.O.*, nearly every court examining a school-search has applied the *T.L.O.* framework broadly to uphold virtually all types of school searches. *See e.g.*

Williams by Williams v. Ellington, *936 F.2d 881 (6th Cir.1991);* Cason v. Cook, *810 F.2d 188 (1987);* James v. Unified Sch. Dist. No. 512, *899 F.Supp. 530 (D.Kan.1995);* Thompson v. Carthage School District, *87 F.3d 979 (8th Cir. 1996). In assessing "reasonableness," courts focus on the prohibited object sought and give school officials greater deference when they search for drugs or weapons than when they conduct a school-wide search for Magic Markers.* See People v. Alexander B., *220 Cal.App.3d 1572, 270 Cal.Rptr. 342 (1990);* Burnham v. West, *681 F.Supp. 1160 (E.D.Va.1987). In assessing the quantity of information necessary to support "reasonable suspicion," school officials may receive tips from teachers or school personnel, from students, from anonymous callers or writers, from sniffer dogs, or from electronic detection devices. When they receive tips, "Absent information that a particular student informant may be untrustworthy, school officials may ordinarily accept at face value the information they supply."* In re South Carolina v. State, *583 So.2d 188, 192 (1991). School officials also may rely on anonymous tips that provide specific details if the allegation is plausible because of conditions at the school.* See Martens v. Dist. No. 220, *620 F.Supp. 29 (N.D.Il.1985).*

2) Academic Reaction to *T.L.O.* Academic commentators have been less favorable to the *T.L.O.* analysis and suggest narrower interpretations of its holding. *See generally* Irene Rosenberg, *"New Jersey v. T.L.O.:* Of Children and Smokescreens," 19 *Fam.L.Q.* 311 (1985); Note, *"New Jersey v. T.L.O.:* The Supreme Court Severely Limits School Children's Fourth Amendment Rights When Being Searched by Public School Officials," 13 *Pepperdine L.Rev.* 87 (1985); Note, "School Searches under the Fourth Amendment: *New Jersey v. T.L.O.,"* 72 *Cornell. L.Rev.* 368 (1987); Note, *"New Jersey v. T.L.O.:* Qualified Fourth Amendment Rights for Public School Students," 64 *Or. L. Rev.* 727 (1989). Stuart Berman, "Student Fourth Amendment Rights: Defining the Scope of the *T.L.O.* School–Search Exception," 66 *N.Y.U.L.Rev.* 1077 (1991) suggests that the balancing of student and school interests varies with the context of the search and identifies different constellations of interests for the schoolhouse search; vehicle searches in the school parking lot; and searches conducted off-campus during extra-curricular activities.

3) *T.L.O.*'s Unanswered Questions—Applicability of Exclusionary Rule *T.L.O.* left many questions unanswered. Initially, the parties briefed *T.L.O.* on the question whether the exclusionary rule applied to school searches. Because the Court upheld the reasonableness of the search, it had no occasion to decide whether evidence illegally obtained must be excluded either from school disciplinary proceedings or in juvenile courts. *See T.L.O., supra* 191 fn. 3.

Exclusionary Rule in Juvenile Court Delinquency Hearings. Irene Merker Rosenberg, "A Door Left Open: Applicability of Fourth Amendment Exclusionary Rule to Juvenile Court Delinquency Hearings," 24 Am. J. Crim. L. 29, 58 (1996) notes that "A substantial majority of states has decided, explicitly or implicitly, that the exclusionary rule applies to delinquency proceedings." State courts consistently hold that the exclusionary rule does apply in juvenile delinquency prosecutions. *See, e.g., In re William G.,* 40 Cal.3d 550, 221 Cal.Rptr. 118, 709 P.2d 1287, 1298 (1985); *Interest of L.L.,* 90 Wis.2d 585, 280 N.W.2d 343, 347 (1979); *State v. Doe,* 93 N.M. 143, 597 P.2d

1183, 1186 (1979); *In re Marsh*, 40 Ill.2d 53, 237 N.E.2d 529, 531 (1968) ("the exclusionary rules required by the Fourth Amendment's prohibition against illegal search and seizures are applicable to proceedings under the Juvenile Court Act."); *In re Montrail M.*, 87 Md.App. 420, 434, 589 A.2d 1318 (Md. Ct. Spec. App. 1991) (Fourth Amendment's "twin goals of enabling the judiciary to avoid the taint of partnership in official lawlessness and of assuring the people * * * that the government would not profit from its lawless behavior" are as pertinent to juvenile delinquency proceedings as they are to criminal proceedings).

Exclusionary Rule in School Disciplinary Proceedings Most state courts have held that the exclusionary rule does not apply to school search cases even when school officials seize the evidence illegally. *E.g., In re Lance W.*, 37 Cal.3d 873, 210 Cal.Rptr. 631, 694 P.2d 744 (1985). Explaining the reluctance to apply the exclusionary rule in school disciplinary proceedings, Irene Merker Rosenberg, "A Door Left Open: Applicability of Fourth Amendment Exclusionary Rule to Juvenile Court Delinquency Hearings," 24 Am. J. Crim. L. 29, 42–43 (1996), argues that "with respect to searches by school authorities, we start with the premise that the officials in question are not police officers, a threshold factor strongly militating against application of the exclusionary rule. Combined with this powerful consideration is the uncertainty of the deterrent impact of the exclusionary rule on school officials. Add to the hopper the Court's inclination to give school personnel broad latitude in dealing with student misconduct, even when administrators have themselves exceeded permissible bounds. In these circumstances, the prospects for application of the exclusionary rule seem rather dim." The court in **Thompson v. Carthage School District**, 87 F.3d 979 (8th Cir. 1996), rationalized the denial of an exclusionary remedy in school proceedings:

> The judicially-created exclusionary rule precludes admission of unlawfully seized evidence in criminal trials. In the complex and turbulent history of the rule, the Court never has applied it to exclude evidence from a civil proceeding, federal or state. * * * The Court's 'framework' for deciding whether the exclusionary rule applies in a particular civil proceeding is to analyze whether the likely benefit of excluding illegally obtained evidence outweighs the societal costs of exclusion.

> The societal costs of applying the rule in school disciplinary proceedings are very high. For example, the exclusionary rule might bar a high school from expelling a student who confessed to killing a classmate on campus if his confession was not preceded by *Miranda* warnings. * * * To the extent the exclusionary rule prevents the disciplining of students who disrupt education or endanger other students, it frustrates the critical governmental function of educating and protecting children.

> Moreover, "maintaining security and order in the schools requires a certain degree of flexibility in school disciplinary procedures." Application of the exclusionary rule would require suppression hearing-like inquiries inconsistent with the demands of school discipline. * * *

> The benefit of the exclusionary rule depends upon whether it would effectively deter Fourth Amendment violations. * * * [S]chool officials both conducted the search and imposed the student discipline. Knowing

that evidence they illegally seize will be excluded at any subsequent disciplinary proceeding would likely have a strong deterrent effect. * * * School officials, on the other hand, are not law enforcement officers. They do not have an adversarial relationship with students. "Instead, there is a commonality of interests between teachers and their pupils. The attitude of the typical teacher is one of personal responsibility for the student's welfare as well as for his education." Moreover, children's legitimate expectations of privacy are somewhat limited at school * * *

In these circumstances, we conclude that there is little need for the exclusionary rule's likely deterrent effect. Indeed, we see some risk that application of the rule would deter educators from undertaking disciplinary proceedings that are needed to keep the schools safe and to control student misbehavior. In any event, any deterrence benefit would not begin to outweigh the high societal costs of imposing the rule.

D. Shayne Jones, "Application of the 'Exclusionary Rule' to Bar Use of Illegally Seized Evidence in Civil School Disciplinary Proceedings," 52 *J. Urban and Contemporary Law* 375, 397 (1997), criticized *Thompson* because it allows school officials to "trample on the substantive rights of students under the Fourth Amendment, knowing that even evidence which is seized illegally can be admitted to suspend or expel a student." On the other hand, some courts have applied the exclusionary rule to bar the use of evidence in school disciplinary proceedings because it provides the only viable remedy for students whose rights the school administrators have violated. *See, e.g.,* **Jones v. Latexo Independent School District**, 499 F.Supp. 223 (E.D. Tex. 1980), where the court held that:

> Having obtained evidence against the plaintiffs by means of an unconstitutional search, the defendants could not use that evidence as a justification for imposing punishment. Although criminal proceedings were never instituted against the students, the Fourth Amendment protects citizens against unreasonable invasions of privacy by government officials in the civil area as well. * * *

The primary vehicle for enforcing the strictures of the fourth amendment in our legal system is the "exclusionary rule," which prevents the use of unconstitutionally obtained evidence by the government in subsequent proceedings. While the exclusionary rule is most often employed in criminal cases, it has been resorted to on numerous occasions to redress fourth amendment violations in a variety of civil contexts as well.

In a case comparable on its facts to this one, Chief Judge Fox of the Western District of Michigan refused to allow a state college to rely upon the fruits of an unlawful search of student rooms to discipline those students occupying rooms where contraband was found. "If there were no exclusionary rule in this case," Judge Fox pointed out, "(school) authorities would have no incentive to respect the privacy of its students." He observed that students rarely have the means to pursue protracted damage actions to protect their rights and that school officials acting in good faith would, in any event, be immune from liability for damages. * * * Judge Fox concluded that in such circumstances "the exclusionary rule remains the only possible deterrent, the only effective way to positively encourage respect for the constitutional guarantee."

4) *T.L.O.***'s Unanswered Questions—Individualized Suspicion.** In any sufficiently large group of students, a statistical probability exists that someone will possess contraband. Does *T.L.O.*'s "reasonable suspicion" standard require "individualized suspicion" or just a "generalized probability"? *See T.L.O.*, *supra* p. 195 at fn. 8 ("We do not decide whether individualized suspicion is an essential element of the reasonableness standard we adopt for searches by school authorities.") Consider the following facts:

> The school bus driver told the high school principal that there were fresh cuts on seats of her bus. Concerned that a knife or other cutting weapon was on the school grounds, the principal decided to search all male students in grades six to twelve. After the search began, a student told the principal that there was a gun at the school that morning. Principal and a teacher brought each class of students to the teacher's classroom, and ordered them to remove their jackets, shoes, and socks, empty their pockets, and place these items on large tables. Principal then checked the students for concealed weapons with a metal detector. Teacher patted down a student if the metal detector sounded, as it often did because of the metal brads on the students' blue jeans. Principal also patted the students' coats and removed any objects he could feel in the coat pockets. Thompson was a ninth grade student whom neither the principal nor teacher had reason to suspect had cut the school bus seats or brought a weapon to school that morning. Teacher searched Thompson's coat pocket and found a used book of matches, a match box, and a cigarette package. The match box contained "a white substance" which tests determined to be crack cocaine.

Was the search "reasonable" under *T.L.O.*'s "reasonable suspicion" standard? *See Thompson v. Carthage School District*, 87 F.3d 979 (8th Cir. 1996). *See generally* Martin R. Gardner, "Student Privacy in the Wake of *T.L.O.*: An Appeal for an Individualized Suspicion Requirement for Valid Searches and Seizures in the Schools," 22 Ga. L. Rev. 897, 926 (1988); Myron Schreck, "The Fourth Amendment in the Public Schools: Issues in the 1990s and Beyond," 25 Urban Lawyer 117 (1993).

Teachers on previous extra-curricular band trips found that students had smuggled liquor along in their luggage. Could the school reasonably search all students' luggage as a prerequisite to boarding the bus for a required concert? *See Kuehn v. Renton School Dist. No. 403*, 103 Wash.2d 594, 694 P.2d 1078 (1985) ("To meet the reasonable belief standard, it was necessary for the school officials to have some basis for believing that drugs or alcohol would be found in the luggage of each individual student searched."); *Horton v. Goose Creek Indep. Sch. Dist.*, 690 F.2d 470 (5th Cir. 1982) (requiring individualized suspicion under reasonable belief standard).

In *Desilets v. Clearview Regional Board of Education*, 265 N.J.Super. 370, 627 A.2d 667 (N.J. Super. A.D. 1993), the court upheld a nondiscretionary search of the hand luggage of all students participating in a field trip. The court recalled "the rich opportunity for mischief which the field trip provides to some students. The need for close supervision in the schoolhouse is intensified on field trips where opportunities abound to elude the watchful eyes of chaperones. Administrators and teachers have a duty to protect students from the misbehavior of other students. In the context of a field trip, we add to that burden the duty to protect the general population from student mischief. * * * The deterrent effect of the board's search policy advances the legitimate interest of the school administrators in preventing students from taking contraband, in the broadest sense of the word, on field trips."

Metal Detector Screening in Public Schools Violence, the threat of violence and weapons are a fact of life in many schools. Magnetometers, or metal detectors, have become standard equipment in airports and public buildings, such as courthouses. May schools install metal detectors to limit the introduction of weapons at schools? Does requiring all students to walk through a metal detector constitute a search for Fourth Amendment purposes that requires "reasonable suspicion" or "individualized suspicion"? In *In re F.B.*, 442 Pa.Super. 216, 658 A.2d 1378 (1995), the court found that individualized suspicion was not required for metal detector screening at a Philadelphia high school because of the high rate of violence and the minimal intrusion caused by metal detector screening. In *People v. Pruitt*, 278 Ill. App.3d 194, 214 Ill.Dec. 974, 662 N.E.2d 540 (Ill. App. 1 Dist. 1996), the court ruled that metal detector screening satisfied the Fourth Amendment reasonableness test established in *T.L.O.* because the action was justified at its inception by the reality of violence in the school, and school officials conducted the search in a manner reasonably related in scope to the circumstances that justified it. See e.g., Eugene C. Bjorklun, "Using Metal Detectors in the Public Schools: Some Legal Issues," 111 Educ. Law. Rep. 1 (1996); Michael Ferraraccio, "Metal Detectors in the Public Schools: Fourth Amendment Concerns," 28 J. L. & Educ. 209, 224–29 (1999) (arguing that schools' use of metal detectors to conduct suspicionless searches violates students' Fourth Amendment rights);

5) ***T.L.O.*'s Unanswered Questions—Reasonable Expectation of Privacy in Lockers and Desks** Another question that *T.L.O.* did not answer was whether students have a "reasonable expectation of privacy" in their "lockers, desks, or other school property provided for the storage of school supplies." See *T.L.O.*, *supra* p. 193 at n. 5. Some courts note *T.L.O.*'s language—"schoolchildren may find it necessary to carry with them a variety of legitimate, noncontraband items, and there is no reasons to conclude that they have necessarily waived all rights to privacy in such items merely by bringing them onto school grounds"—and find that students have a reasonable expectation of privacy in their school lockers. See *e.g., In re S.C.*, 583 So.2d 188 (Miss.1991); *State v. Joseph T.*, 175 W.Va. 598, 336 S.E.2d 728 (1985); *Commonwealth v. Cass*, 446 Pa.Super. 66, 666 A.2d 313 (1995) (expectation of privacy in school locker); *In re Dumas*, 357 Pa.Super. 294, 515 A.2d 984 (1986) (applying *T.L.O.* standards to searches of lockers). What is the legal significance of finding that a student has a reasonable expectation of privacy in her locker?

How would the following statute affect a student's "reasonable expectation of privacy":

Minn. Stat. § 127.47. School locker policy (1998).

Subd. 1. Policy. It is the policy of the state of Minnesota that:

School lockers are the property of the school district. At no time does the school district relinquish its exclusive control of lockers provided for the convenience of students. Inspection of the interior of lockers may be conducted by school authorities for any reason at any time, without notice, without student consent, and without a search warrant. The personal possessions of students within a school locker may be searched only when school authorities have a reasonable suspicion that the search will uncover evidence of a violation of law or school rules. As soon as practicable after the search of a student's personal possessions, the school authorities must provide notice of the search to students whose lockers were searched unless disclosure would impede an ongoing investigation by police or school officials.

Subd. 2. Dissemination. The locker policy must be disseminated to parents and students in the way that other policies of general application to students are disseminated. A copy of the policy must be provided to a student the first time after the policy is effective that the student is given the use of a locker.

See, e.g., Zamora v. Pomeroy, 639 F.2d 662 (10th Cir. 1981) (concluding that school had joint control of locker and enjoyed right to inspect it); *In the Interest of Isiah B.*, 176 Wis.2d 639, 500 N.W.2d 637 (1993) (holding that random search of student's locker was justified because school had policy allowing for searches of lockers for any reason). Like the Minnesota statute, *supra*, a number of states' law simply states that students have no reasonable expectation of privacy in their lockers, which remain under the exclusive control of the school and subject to search without any justification. *See, e.g., Alaska Stat.* §§ 14.03.105, 14.45.190 (Michie 1998); *Conn. Gen. Stat.* § 54–33n (1997); *Fla. Stat. Ch.* 232.256 (1997); Iowa Code § 808A.2 (1997); *N.J. Stat. Ann.* § 18A:36–19.2 (West 1997); *Va. Code Ann.* § 22.1–277.01:2 (Michie 1998). Although the statutes authorize school officials to open the lockers, do they need "reasonable suspicion" in order to feel coats, squeeze back-packs, or open briefcases or other closed containers within the locker?

What may a school official do about the contents of a student's jacket or backpack stored within the locker? May the school official squeeze the containers and "plain feel" their contents? *See Minnesota v. Dickerson*, 508 U.S. 366, 113 S.Ct. 2130, 124 L.Ed.2d 334 (1993) (stating that officer's "squeezing, sliding and otherwise manipulating the outside of the defendant's pocket" after determining no weapon was present constituted a search in violation of *Terry*); *In the Interest of Dumas*, 357 Pa.Super. 294, 515 A.2d 984, 985 (1986) ("We are unable to conclude that a student would have an expectation of privacy in a purse or jacket which the student takes to school but would lose that expectation of privacy merely by placing the purse or jacket in school locker provided to the student for storage of personal items.")

In **State v. Jones**, 666 N.W.2d 142 (IA 2003), the Iowa Supreme Court analyzed students' expectation of privacy in their lockers. In *Jones*, school administrators attempted to complete an annual pre-winter break clean-out of students' lockers. Officials asked students to report to their locker at an assigned time to open it for inspection of its contents. The purpose of the clean-out was to ensure the health and safety of students and staff, to remove excessive trash and food, to retrieve overdue library books, and to find weapons and controlled substances. Although 80% of students reported to their lockers at their designated time, a sizeable minority, including Jones, did not. Two aides opened the lockers that had not been inspected. Jones' lockers contained a blue nylon coat hanging on a hook. One aide manipulated the coat and discovered a small bag of marijuana in an outside pocket. The school principal and aides removed Jones from his classroom, escorted him to his locker, and then removed the coat from the locker. Jones grabbed the coat, struck the principal across the arms, broke free and ran away. The principal gave chase, captured and held Jones until the police arrived. The police retrieved the bag of marijuana from the coat:

> [I]t is significant in this case that the search of Jones' locker occurred on school grounds. * * * [W]e must consider three factors: (1) "the nature of the privacy interest allegedly compromised" by the search, (2) "the character of the intrusion imposed by the [search] [p]olicy," and (3) "the nature and immediacy of the [school's] concerns and the efficacy of the [search] [p]olicy in meeting them." * * *

> In assessing the nature of the privacy interest in this case, it is imperative to remember this controversy arose within the school context "where the State is responsible for maintaining discipline, health, and safety." This reality has led the Court to acknowledge that "[s]ecuring order in the school environment sometimes requires that students be subjected to greater controls than those appropriate for adults." Although this may be the case, we do not believe it can be said that students have no expectation of privacy in a school setting, particularly in a location such as a locker. * * *

> However, the Court [in *T.L.O.*] specifically avoided answering the question of whether a student "has a legitimate expectation of privacy in lockers, desks, or other school property provided for the storage of school supplies." Likely due in part to the absence of an authoritative statement on this issue, various courts considering it have produced a divergence of opinion. Some courts have concluded that there is no expectation of privacy in a student locker, particularly in situations in which there exists a school or state regulation specifically disclaiming any privacy right. Other courts have concluded that a student does have a legitimate expectation of privacy in the contents of a school locker, even if a school or state regulation exists. In this case, both Muscatine school district policy and state law clearly contemplate and regulate searches of school lockers. Nevertheless, we believe Jones maintained a legitimate expectation of privacy in the contents of his locker.

> *T.L.O.* involved the search of a student's purse, but a student's locker presents a similar island of privacy in an otherwise public school. Numerous permissible items of a private nature are secreted away within a locker on a daily basis with the expectation that those items will remain private. * * * [S]chool policy effectively presumes this to be the case and protects this interest: in those situations in which the school seeks to search a locker, the school's rules contemplate the presence of the student

or at least a "waiver" of the student's opportunity to be present and supervising the search. Moreover, the school rules and state law related to search and seizure in schools are premised on a presumption of privacy; such legislation would likely be unnecessary if no expectation of privacy existed in the first place. Each of these factors indicates a broad societal recognition of a legitimate expectation of privacy in a school locker. Accordingly, we conclude that a student such as Jones has a measure of privacy in the contents of his locker.

We must next "consider the character of the intrusion imposed by the [search] [p]olicy." * * * [W]e believe the locker search was not overly intrusive, especially in light of the underlying governmental interest and broader purpose of the search. * * *

While it is possible that there would have been alternative ways to check the coat's contents, constitutional search and seizure provisions do not require the least intrusive action possible. Instead, they require a measure of "reasonableness, under all the circumstances." Under this standard, we conclude the search of the contents of Jones' locker was not overly intrusive. * * *

Although students are not stripped of constitutional protections in the school context, those protections must be balanced against the necessity of maintaining a controlled and disciplined environment in which the education of all students can be achieved. Thus, while students maintain a legitimate expectation of privacy in the contents of their school locker, that privacy may be impinged upon for reasonable activities by the school in furtherance of its duty to maintain a proper educational environment. * * *

6) *T.L.O.*'s Unanswered Questions—Excessively Intrusive In *T.L.O.*, the Court noted that a search must not be "excessively intrusive in light of the age and sex of the student and the nature of the infraction." *See T.L.O.*, *supra* p. 196 at fn. 9 and accompanying text. Why are those factors relevant to determining the justifiable scope of a search? In *T.L.O.*, a male principal searched the purse of a fourteen-year-old female student for evidence of a non-criminal rule violation. What type of search might be "excessively intrusive"?

7) *T.L.O.*'s Unanswered Questions—Non-school Student Searches What is the scope of *T.L.O.* with respect to non-classroom searches? Do school officials need a warrant or traditional search probable cause to search for drugs in a student's automobile parked in the school parking lot? *See e.g. State v. Slattery*, 56 Wash.App. 820, 787 P.2d 932, rev. denied, 114 Wash.2d 1015, 791 P.2d 534 (1990); *In re P.E.A.*, 754 P.2d 382 (Colo.1988); Note, "Fourth Amendment Protection in the School Environment: The Colorado Supreme Court's Application of the Reasonable Suspicion Standard in *State v. P.E.A.*," 61 *U. Colo. L. Rev.* 153 (1990).

8) *T.L.O.*'s Unanswered Questions—School Searches in Conjunction with or at the Behest of Law Enforcement The Court in *T.L.O.* noted that the case only raised the issue of searched conducted exclusively by school authorities acting alone and on their own authority. *See T.L.O.*, *supra* p. 195 at fn. 7. In **People v. Dilworth**, 169 Ill.2d 195, 661 N.E.2d 310, 214

SEC. B   SEARCHING JUVENILES: SCHOOLS & "SPECIAL NEEDS"   **213**

Ill.Dec. 456 (Ill. 1996), the Illinois Supreme Court considered whether to apply a "probable cause" or "reasonable suspicion" standard to school searches conducted by a police liaison officer, Ruettiger, employed by the local police department rather than a school employee. The liaison officer's primary purpose at the school was to prevent criminal activity and, if he discovered criminal activity, to arrest the offender and to transport him or her to the police station. Chief Justice BILANDIC, writing for the majority:

> [W]e must determine whether the proper fourth amendment standard to apply in this case is the less stringent reasonable suspicion standard for searches of students by school officials or the general standard of probable cause. Defendant insists that because Ruettiger was a police officer, he was required to have probable cause. * * *

> Decisions filed after *T.L.O.* that involve police officers in school settings can generally be grouped into three categories: (1) those where school officials initiate a search or where police involvement is minimal, (2) those involving school police or liaison officers acting on their own authority, and (3) those where outside police officers initiate a search. Where school officials initiate the search or police involvement is minimal, most courts have held that the reasonable suspicion test obtains. The same is true in cases involving school police or liaison officers acting on their own authority. However, where outside police officers initiate a search, or where school officials act at the behest of law enforcement agencies, the probable cause standard has been applied.

> In the present case, the record shows that Detective Ruettiger was a liaison police officer on staff at the Alternate School, which is a high school for students with behavioral disorders. * * * Given this scenario, this case is best characterized as involving a liaison police officer conducting a search on his own initiative and authority, in furtherance of the school's attempt to maintain a proper educational environment. We hold that the reasonable suspicion standard applies under these facts. * * *

> Our holding in this case also comports with *Vernonia School District 47J v. Acton.* There, the United States Supreme Court utilized a three-prong test for determining whether special needs beyond normal law enforcement require a departure from the usual fourth amendment standard of probable cause and a warrant. The competing interests of the individual and the State were balanced by an examination of the following: (1) the nature of the privacy interest upon which the search intrudes, (2) the character of the search, and (3) the nature and immediacy of the governmental concern at issue, and the efficacy of the means for meeting it.

> An analysis of each of these three factors supports our holding that reasonable suspicion, not probable cause, is the proper fourth amendment standard to be applied in this case. As to the first factor, the nature of the privacy interest upon which the search intrudes, it must be remembered that we are dealing with schoolchildren here. * * *

> The second factor is the character of the search. The intrusion complained of in this case is the seizure and search of defendant's flashlight by a school liaison officer. Of utmost significance, the liaison

officer had an individualized suspicion that defendant's flashlight contained drugs. He confirmed his suspicion by searching only that flashlight. Thus, we find this search as conducted to be minimally intrusive.

The final factor—the nature and immediacy of the governmental concern at issue, and the efficacy of the means for meeting it—also weighs in favor of the reasonable suspicion standard here. There is no doubt that the State has a compelling interest in providing a proper educational environment for students, which includes maintaining its schools free from the ravages of drugs. As to the efficacy of the means for meeting this interest, it is relevant that the search at issue took place at an alternate school for students with behavioral disorders. In order to maintain a proper educational environment at this particular school, school officials found it necessary to have a full-time police liaison as a member of its staff. The liaison officer assisted teachers and school officials with the difficult job of preserving order in this school.

In sum, our consideration of the three *Vernonia* factors supports our application of the reasonable suspicion standard in the case at bar. * * *

Justice NICKELS, dissenting. I respectfully dissent. I cannot agree with the majority that a police officer whose self-stated primary duty is to investigate and prevent criminal activity may search a student on school grounds on a lesser fourth amendment standard than probable cause merely because the police officer is permanently assigned to the school and is listed in the student handbook as a member of the school staff. * * *

The majority takes the position that for the purposes of the fourth amendment, Ruettiger is a school official similar to a teacher or principal. However, Ruettiger is a police officer. He is employed by the City of Joliet police department and is assigned to patrol the Alternate School grounds as a police liaison officer. Ruettiger's self-stated primary duty at the school is to investigate and prevent criminal activity. * * *

The fact that Ruettiger was a police officer, and acted as one in seizing and searching defendant's flashlight, is clear from the record. After observing and questioning defendant in the hallway, Ruettiger seized and searched defendant's flashlight because he suspected it contained drugs. After finding cocaine, Ruettiger chased and captured defendant, arrested him, placed him in custody, handcuffed him, placed him in the squad car, and took him down to the investigative division of the Joliet police station. There, Ruettiger handcuffed defendant to a wall, read him his *Miranda* rights, and interrogated him. These were the acts of a police officer, not a school official. * * *

All Federal and State decisions reviewed indicate that police officers, including police liaison officers, are required to have probable cause to search a student if they are significantly involved in the search. This was the law prior to *T.L.O.*, and has also been the law after *T.L.O.* * * *

Although several decisions have allowed student searches under the reasonable suspicion standard where police have participated in the search, these decisions have stressed that police involvement in the searches was minimal.

The majority attempts to find support for its holding by stating that the reasonable suspicion standard applies in those cases "involving school police or liaison officers." * * *

School police also have duties that are significantly more limited than police liaison officers, such as Ruettiger. * * * [T]he duties of the school police officer there "entailed quelling disturbances and generally carrying out the various school policies applicable to her job assignment." * * * In contrast to school police, Ruettiger's primary duty at the school was that of any police officer, to investigate and prevent criminal activity, arresting those he found violating the law. Unlike "school police," Ruettiger's duties were not limited in any manner. * * *

The distinction between school police and police liaison officers is significant because every case involving police liaison officers has indicated that probable cause is required if the officer acts on his own initiative, as Ruettiger did here. * * *

In sum, not one case involving a police search of a student at school, including cases involving police liaison officers, supports the majority's conclusion. In fact, every authority available has rejected the majority's view. * * * The result is that this court has for the first time in a long line of cases departed from the overwhelming view that police officers, even liaison police officers, are required to have probable cause to search a student on school grounds when instigating and carrying out a search. * * *

NOTE

As the majority and dissenting opinions in *Dilworth* indicate, "no clear case law exists as to whether SROs [School Resource Officers] should be held to a probable cause standard, as are regular police officers, or whether they should be allowed to operate under the lesser reasonableness standard, as are school administrators." Andrea G. Bough, "Searches and Seizures in Schools: Should Reasonable Suspicion or Probable Cause Apply to School Resource/Liaison Officers?," 67 *UMKC L. Rev.* 543 544 (1999). Some courts have reasoned that because the SRO is assigned to the school to assist school officials to maintain a safe and proper educational environment that reasonable suspicion is the appropriate standard *when* the officer conducts the search in conjunction with or at the behest of school officials. For example, if reasonable suspicion exists that a student has brought a weapon to school, it is better for a professional officer to conduct the search than an untrained teacher or school official. See e.g. *Ex Rel. Angelia D.B.*, 211 Wis.2d 140, 564 N.W.2d 682, 690 (1997). On the other hand, analysts observe that the increased and heightened presence of law enforcement officers in public schools and the convergence between school disciplinary practices and law enforcement strategies should require school liaison officers to adhere to traditional law enforcement and probable cause requirements. See Michael Pinard, "From the Classroom to the Courtroom: Reassessing Fourth Amendment Standards in Public School Searches Involving Law Enforcement Authorities," 45 *Arizona L. Rev.* 1067, 1079 (2003), who argues that "[T]he increased interdependency between school officials and law enforcement authorities * * * has greatly altered the methodologies and philosophies of school discipline processes. Most significantly, it has led to increased use of the juvenile and criminal justice systems to monitor and punish a broadened array of student conduct. As a result, there is a widening gulf between the more expansive use of law enforcement personnel in school discipline, along with the broadened categories of behaviors that could potentially introduce students to the criminal justice system, and the narrow (and narrowing) protections afforded students under the Fourth Amendment."

2.   DRUG DETECTION IN SCHOOLS

What are the implications of *T.L.O.* for generalized or individualized searches for drugs in schools? Can school officials employ "canine-partners" to develop reasonable suspicion or individualized suspicion to search? Can school officials require students to submit to mandatory and/or random drug-testing programs?

DOE v. RENFROW

475 F.Supp. 1012 (N.D.Ind.1979).

SHARP, DISTRICT JUDGE. This action was initiated in a complaint filed by several named plaintiffs protesting certain procedures conducted by officials of the Highland, Crown Point and Merrillville, Indiana school systems. Those named plaintiffs alleged that search activities conducted by certain school officials assisted by local police officers violated the plaintiffs' rights secured by the Fourth and Fourteenth Amendments to the Constitution. * * *

The school community of Highland has, among several elementary schools, a Junior and Senior High School. Both these campuses are located on the same site. The school buildings are adjacent to one another and the approximately 2,780 students of both schools share common facilities located in the buildings. * * *

[Beginning in the fall of 1978, school officials recorded twenty-one instances in which students were found in possession of drugs, drug paraphernalia or alcohol, or under the influence of drugs; thirteen incidents of those twenty-one incidents occurred within four weeks prior to the search; during that time school administrators received daily reports from faculty, students and parents about drug use at the Junior and Senior High Schools. School officials, teachers, and students became concerned about the negative impact that drug use in the school was having on the educational environment. Students using drugs disrupted classrooms and other students' opportunity to learn. Peer pressure favored drug use on campus, and students, faculty and administrators suffered a loss of morale.]

To combat what was perceived as an increasingly alarming drug problem within the school system, members of the Highland Town School District Board suggested the use of properly trained dogs to search for drugs within the school building. * * * [T]he school administrators informed the police officers that they intended to conduct an investigation within the school buildings using canine units to detect and remove any narcotics or narcotic paraphernalia. * * * The school officials insisted, and the police agreed, that no criminal investigations would occur as a result of any evidence recovered during the school investigation. The school officials did intend, however, to bring any necessary disciplinary actions against students found in possession of contraband.

On March 23, 1979, a school wide drug inspection was conducted by the administrators of the Highland School System with the assistance of the Highland Police Department and volunteer canine units trained in marijuana detection. The inspection occurred in both the Junior and Senior High School campuses and began during the first period class. Teachers were informed of the inspection that morning by means of a sealed note upon their classroom desks. Each classroom teacher was instructed to keep their students in the first period class and to have them perform their customary work. A canine team visited each classroom in both the Junior and Senior High School buildings. Each team consisted of a school administrator or teacher, a dog and its handler and a uniformed police officer. * * * Students were instructed to sit quietly in their seats with their hands and any purses to be placed upon their desk tops while the dog handler introduced the dog and led it up and down the desk aisles. The canine teams spent approximately five minutes in each room. No incidents of disruption occurred in the classrooms because of the presence of the dogs or the teams. The entire investigation lasted approximately two and one-half hours during which time students wishing to use the washrooms were allowed to leave the classroom with an escort of the same sex to the washroom door. * * * Uniformed police officers and school administrators were present in the halls during the entire investigation. * * * During the inspection, a dog alerted to a particular student on approximately fifty occasions. After each alert, the student was asked to empty his or her pockets or purse. A body search was conducted with respect to eleven students because the dog continued to alert after the student had emptied pockets or purse. Plaintiff Doe was one of those students to which a dog continued to alert after she emptied her pockets. She was quietly escorted to a nurse's station in the Junior High School and was asked to remain in the waiting room. Upon being asked to enter the inner office, two women introduced themselves to the plaintiff. One was a friend of the plaintiff's mother. Plaintiff was asked if she had ever used marijuana to which she answered she had not. She was then asked to remove her clothing. She was permitted to turn her back to the two women while she was disrobing. Upon removal, her clothing was briefly examined, her hair was lifted to determine if any substances were hidden in it, and she was immediately permitted to dress. No marijuana or other drugs were found in plaintiff's possession, although it was later discovered that plaintiff had been playing with one of her dogs that morning of the search and that dog was in heat.

As a result of the investigation seventeen students were found in possession of drugs; twelve of those students withdrew voluntarily from school and three students were expelled * * * [and] two students were suspended by the administration because they were found to be in possession of drug paraphernalia.

This Court is specifically confronted with the following issues: (1) whether the investigative procedure used by the school officials with the assistance of law enforcement officers, for the sole and exclusive purpose of furthering a valid educational goal of eliminating drug use within the school, was a seizure and search under the Fourth Amendment; (2) whether the use of dogs to detect marijuana and marijuana paraphernalia in the classroom was, standing alone, a search under the Fourth Amendment; (3) whether the admitted search of a student's clothing upon the continued alert of a trained drug detecting canine was violative of rights protected by the Fourth Amendment; and (4) whether the nude body search conducted solely upon the basis of a trained drug detecting canine's alert violated the plaintiff's right to be free from unreasonable search and seizure. * * *

Considering first plaintiff's contention that the investigation * * * constituted a mass detention and deprivation of freedom in violation of the Fourth Amendment, this Court finds the assertion to be without merit. Plaintiff, as well as other students, is subject to the daily routine of class attendance in an educational environment. During an eight hour day, students must move from room to room, attending classes designated by the administration and taught by teachers hired by the school system. * * * Such a regulation of a student's movement in no way denies that person any constitutionally guaranteed right. On the morning in question all students were given an opportunity to perform their usual classroom schedule for an extra 1 and ½ periods. Except for the five minute interval when the canine unit entered the room, plaintiff and all other students were exposed only to a longer than normal first period class. Such an extended period had been experienced at other times during convocations and school assemblies.

School officials maintain the discretion and authority for scheduling all student activities each school day. * * * Therefore, this Court finds no seizure of the plaintiff or other students within the Senior and Junior High School prior to any alert by the trained dogs.

Turning next to the search aspect of the Fourth Amendment, the issue becomes whether the activity of the defendants on the morning in question prior to any alert by the trained dogs was a search and, if so, whether the search, although warrantless, was reasonable. This Court finds for the reasons stated below that entry by the school officials into each classroom for five minutes was not a search contemplated by the

Fourth Amendment but, rather, was a justified action taken in accordance with the *In loco parentis* doctrine. * * * Finally, for purposes of this section, the sniffing of a trained narcotic detecting canine is not a search. Since no search was performed up until the time the dogs alerted, no warrant was necessary for the initial observation by the school officials.

There is no question as to the right and, indeed, the duty of school officials to maintain an educationally sound environment within the school. * * * Maintaining an educationally productive atmosphere within the school rests upon the school administrator certain heavy responsibilities. One of these is that of providing an environment free from activities harmful to the educational function and to the individual students. Drug use within the school became an activity the school administrator wished to eliminate. It cannot be denied that each of the school administrators possessed the authority to enter a classroom on the day in question in order to prevent the use of illicit drugs. Acting alone, each school administrator could have unquestionably surveyed a classroom to prevent drug use. Because those administrators now acted with assistance from a uniformed officer does not change their function. The officers were merely aiding in the inspection, at the request of the school administrators. Their presence does not change the actions of the school official from that of supervision *in loco parentis* to that of an unwarranted search. * * *

Nor does this court believe the presence of the dog unit within the classroom changes the nature of the observation. Again, the trainer and dog were in the rooms at the request and with the permission of the school administrators. The dog acted merely as an aide to the school administrator in detecting the scent of marijuana. The dog handler interpreted the actions of the dog for the benefit of the school administrator. Bringing these nonschool personnel into the classroom to aid the school administrators in their observation for drug abuse is, of itself, not a search. Students are exposed to various intrusions into their classroom environment. The presence of the canine team for several minutes was a minimal intrusion at best and not so serious as to invoke the protections of the Fourth Amendment.

Plaintiff, however, contends that the walking up the aisles and the sniffing of the dog constituted a search within the meaning of the Fourth Amendment and, as such, it was not based upon probable cause and was therefore in violation of her constitutionally protected rights. Plaintiff's assertion misreads the present state of the law concerning the use of drug detecting canines. * * *

Although the subject of using drug detecting canines has not been specifically addressed in this circuit, it has been analyzed in other courts. * * * A common thread that runs through * * * [the] cases was the fact that the law enforcement officers had previous independent information or "tips" concerning the whereabouts of the drugs that were later sniffed out by the dogs.

Turning to this case, the evidence shows the school administrators had compiled an extensive list of previous incidents of drug use within the school. In twenty school days before the investigation, thirteen incidents were reported where students were found either to be in possession of drugs or drug paraphernalia or under the influence of drugs or alcohol. * * * The use of the canine units was decided upon only after the upsurge in drug use at the schools. The school officials, therefore, had outside independent evidence indicating drug abuse within the school. Use of the dogs to detect where those drugs were located was not unreasonable under the circumstances. * * *

Also considered as a factor in the above cited dog-sniffing cases was the absence of any normal or justifiable expectation of privacy with respect to the objects searched. Although each of those cases dealt with the search of objects rather than of persons, as in this case, the same test of reasonableness applies. As the Supreme Court of the United States stated in *Katz v. United States*, the Fourth Amendment protections are the protections of people not places. The *Katz* Court held that police action which intrudes upon and invades an individual's justifiable expectation of privacy constitutes a search within the meaning of the Fourth Amendment. This Court first distinguishes *Katz* from this case on the basis that this is not a police action and second, that the students did not have a justifiable expectation of privacy that would preclude a school administrator from sniffing the air around the desks with the aid of a trained drug detecting canine. The use of the dog in this operation was an aid to the school administrator and as such its use is not considered a search. Moreover, plaintiff as well as other students in a public school, does not fall within the meaning of *Katz* because of the very nature of public school education. Any expectation of privacy necessarily diminishes in light of a student's constant supervision while in school. Because of the constant interaction among students, faculty and school administrators, a public school student cannot be said to enjoy any absolute expectation of privacy while in the classroom setting.

This is not to indicate that one attending public schools sheds his or her constitutional rights upon entering the school house doors; such is obviously not the case. However, in matters concerning the reasonable exercise of supervision and authority by school officials, this Court recognizes that a certain balancing occurs between an individual student's rights and the school administrator's need to protect all students and the educational process. A reasonable right to inspection is necessary to the school's performance of its duty to provide an educational environment. * * *

Moreover, the procedure of bringing the trained dogs into each classroom was planned so as to cause only a few minutes interruption. All students were treated similarly up until an alert by one of the dogs. No student was treated with any malice nor was the operation planned in a way so as to embarrass any particular student. Weighing the minimal intrusion against the school's need to rid itself of the drug problem, the actions of the school officials leading up to an alert by one of the dogs was reasonable and not a search for purposes of the Fourth Amendment. Up until the trained dogs indicated the presence of marijuana, no violation of any basic Fourth Amendment rights occurred.

When a dog alerted to the plaintiff, she was ordered by a police officer to empty her pockets onto the desk under the supervision of a school administrator. She contends that this violated her constitutional right to be secure against unreasonable search and seizure. * * *

In conducting the pocket search, as well as the other searches in question, the school officials clearly were not concerned with the discovery of evidence to be used in criminal prosecutions, but rather were concerned solely with the elimination of drug trafficking within the schools. It cannot be disputed that the school's interest in maintaining the safety, health and education of its students justified its grappling with the grave, even lethal, threat of drug abuse. The pocket search was conducted in furtherance of the school's legitimate interest in eliminating drug trafficking within the school. * * *

[S]o long as a school is pursuing those legitimate interests which are the source of its *in loco parentis* status, "maintaining the order, discipline, safety, supervision, and education of the students within the school", it is the general rule that the Fourth Amendment allows a warrantless intrusion into the student's sphere of privacy, if and only if the school has reasonable cause to believe that the student has violated or is violating school policies.

The pocket search was an invasion of the sphere of privacy which the Fourth Amendment protects; it was a search. But the alert of the dog constituted reasonable cause to believe that the plaintiff was concealing narcotics. Having that requisite reasonable cause to believe that the plaintiff was concealing narcotics, the defendants did not violate the plaintiff's Fourth Amendment rights by ordering her to empty her pockets onto the desk. By conducting the pocket search, the school officials did not violate the plaintiff's right to be secure against unreasonable search and seizure.

Plaintiff further alleges that being subjected to the nude search that morning violated her right against unreasonable search and seizure. It was only upon a continued alert of the trained canine that the school officials based their decision to search the plaintiff. This Court must focus upon the reasonableness of the search to determine its constitutionality. Upon doing so, this Court holds that conducting a nude search of a student solely upon the continued alert of a trained drug-detecting canine is unreasonable even under the lesser "reasonable cause to believe" standard.

Subjecting a student to a nude search is more than just the mild inconvenience of a pocket search, rather, it is an intrusion into an individual's basic justifiable expectation of privacy. Before such a search can be performed, the school administrators must articulate some facts that provide a reasonable cause to believe the student possesses the contraband sought. The continued alert by the trained canine alone is insufficient to justify such a search because the animal reacts only to the scent or odor of the marijuana plant, not the substance itself. * * *

Factors considered important when determining the reasonableness of a student search are: (1) the student's age; (2) the student's history and record in school; (3) the seriousness and prevalence of the problem to which the search is directed; and (4) the exigency requiring an immediate warrantless search.

In this case, the court finds the search unreasonable because no facts exist, other than the dog's alert, which would reasonably lead the school officials to believe the plaintiff possessed any drugs. Therefore, the nude search of plaintiff was unlawful because it did violate her Fourth Amendment right against an unreasonable search and seizure. * * *

It is this Court's finding that no such Fourth Amendment probable cause can be found in this record as to the body search of the only individual plaintiff remaining in this case. To be sure, the question may be close when the situation is frozen as of the time the search took place. However, this Court has serious reservations as to whether there were sufficient facts to justify a full body search of this plaintiff at the time it was conducted. * * *

It is settled case law that school officials possess a qualified immunity with respect to acts performed within the course of their duties. That immunity exists if the official acts in good faith and not in ignorance or disregard of settled indisputable principles of law. * * *

The defendant school administrators acted in good faith and with a regard for the welfare and health of the plaintiff. Her search was conducted in an atmosphere designed to reduce to a minimum any apprehension or embarrassment. Moreover, the law in the area of student searches in public schools is obviously unsettled as suggested by the diversity of the theories and results in the cases cited here. This Court will not charge school officials with "predicting the future course of constitutional law." Therefore, this Court finds that the defendant school officials are immune from liability arising out of the search and are entitled to summary judgment on the issue of monetary damages.

NOTES

1) Canine Sniffs as Searches—Intrusion on a Reasonable Expectation of Privacy In *United States v. Place*, 462 U.S. 696, 103 S.Ct. 2637, 77 L.Ed.2d 110 (1983), the U.S. Supreme Court held that a 90 minute detention of Place's bags in order to arrange for a "canine sniff" was overly long and constituted more than a temporary detention under *Terry v. Ohio*. In *dicta*, however, a plurality of the Court made the following observation about the uses of canine partners:

A "canine sniff" by a well-trained narcotics detection dog, however, does not require opening the luggage. It does not expose noncontraband items that otherwise would remain hidden from public view, as does, for example, an officer's rummaging through the contents of the luggage. Thus, the manner in which information is obtained through this investigative technique is much less intrusive than a typical search. Moreover, the sniff discloses only the presence or absence of narcotics, a contraband item. Thus, despite the fact that the sniff tells the authorities something about the contents of the luggage, the information obtained is limited. This limited disclosure also ensures that the owner of the property is not subjected to the embarrassment and inconvenience entailed in less discriminate and more intrusive investigative methods.

In these respects, the canine sniff is *sui generis*. We are aware of no other investigative procedure that is so limited both in the manner in which the information is obtained and in the content of the information revealed by the procedure. Therefore, we conclude that the particular course of investigation that the agents intended to pursue here—exposure of respondent's luggage, which was located in a public place, to a trained canine—did not constitute a "search" within the meaning of the Fourth Amendment.

In **Illinois v. Caballes**, 543 U.S. 405, 125 S.Ct. 834, 160 L.Ed.2d 842 (2005), the Court upheld a dog-sniff of a car stopped by a State Trooper for speeding. While the officer who stopped Caballes was writing a warning ticket, a second Trooper arrived on the scene and walked a narcotics dog around the car parked on the shoulder of the road. Based on the dog's alert, the officers searched the trunk, found marijuana, and arrested Caballes. The entire incident lasted less than 10 minutes and the use of the dog did not prolong the traffic encounter. The Illinois Supreme Court concluded that because the canine sniff was performed without any " 'specific and articulable facts' " to suggest drug activity, the use of the dog "unjustifiably enlarg[ed] the scope of a routine traffic stop into a drug investigation." Justice Stevens delivered the opinion of the Court which reversed the Illinois Supreme Court and reinstated Caballes' conviction:

> The question on which we granted certiorari is narrow: "Whether the Fourth Amendment requires reasonable, articulable suspicion to justify using a drug-detection dog to sniff a vehicle during a legitimate traffic stop." Thus, we proceed on the assumption that the officer conducting the dog sniff had no information about respondent except that he had been stopped for speeding; accordingly, we have omitted any reference to facts about respondent that might have triggered a modicum of suspicion. * * *

> In our view, conducting a dog sniff would not change the character of a traffic stop that is lawful at its inception and otherwise executed in a reasonable manner, unless the dog sniff itself infringed respondent's constitutionally protected interest in privacy. Our cases hold that it did not.

> Official conduct that does not "compromise any legitimate interest in privacy" is not a search subject to the Fourth Amendment. We have held that any interest in possessing contraband cannot be deemed "legitimate," and thus, governmental conduct that *only* reveals the possession

of contraband "compromises no legitimate privacy interest." This is because the expectation "that certain facts will not come to the attention of the authorities" is not the same as an interest in "privacy that society is prepared to consider reasonable." In *United States v. Place* (1983), *supra*, we treated a canine sniff by a well-trained narcotics-detection dog as *"sui generis"* because it "discloses only the presence or absence of narcotics, a contraband item." Respondent likewise concedes that "drug sniffs are designed, and if properly conducted are generally likely, to reveal only the presence of contraband." Although respondent argues that the error rates, particularly the existence of false positives, call into question the premise that drug-detection dogs alert only to contraband, the record contains no evidence or findings that support his argument. * * *

Accordingly, the use of a well-trained narcotics-detection dog—one that "does not expose non-contraband items that otherwise would remain hidden from public view,"—during a lawful traffic stop, generally does not implicate legitimate privacy interests. In this case, the dog sniff was performed on the exterior of respondent's car while he was lawfully seized for a traffic violation. Any intrusion on respondent's privacy expectations does not rise to the level of a constitutionally cognizable infringement.

This conclusion is entirely consistent with our recent decision that the use of a thermal-imaging device to detect the growth of marijuana in a home constituted an unlawful search. *Kyllo v. United States* (2001). Critical to that decision was the fact that the device was capable of detecting lawful activity—in that case, intimate details in a home, such as "at what hour each night the lady of the house takes her daily sauna and bath." The legitimate expectation that information about perfectly lawful activity will remain private is categorically distinguishable from respondent's hopes or expectations concerning the non-detection of contraband in the trunk of his car. A dog sniff conducted during a concededly lawful traffic stop that reveals no information other than the location of a substance that no individual has any right to possess does not violate the Fourth Amendment. * * *

Justice Souter, dissenting.

I would hold that using the dog for the purposes of determining the presence of marijuana in the car's trunk was a search unauthorized as an incident of the speeding stop and unjustified on any other ground. * * * In *United States v. Place*, we categorized the sniff of the narcotics-seeking dog as *"sui generis"* under the Fourth Amendment and held it was not a search. The classification rests not only upon the limited nature of the intrusion, but on a further premise that experience has shown to be untenable, the assumption that trained sniffing dogs do not err. What we have learned about the fallibility of dogs in the years since *Place* was decided would itself be reason to call for reconsidering *Place's* decision against treating the intentional use of a trained dog as a search. The portent of this very case, however, adds insistence to the call, for an uncritical adherence to *Place* would render the Fourth Amendment indifferent to suspicionless and indiscriminate sweeps of cars in parking garages and pedestrians on sidewalks; if a sniff is not preceded by a seizure subject to Fourth Amendment notice, it escapes Fourth Amendment review entirely unless it is treated as a search. We should not wait for these developments to occur before rethinking *Place's* analysis, which invites such untoward consequences.

At the heart both of *Place* and the Court's opinion today is the proposition that sniffs by a trained dog are *sui generis* because a reaction by the dog in going alert is a response to nothing but the presence of contraband. Hence, the argument goes, because the sniff can only reveal the presence of items devoid of any legal use, the sniff "does not implicate legitimate privacy interests" and is not to be treated as a search.

The infallible dog, however, is a creature of legal fiction. * * * [T]heir supposed infallibility is belied by judicial opinions describing well-trained animals sniffing and alerting with less than perfect accuracy, whether owing to errors by their handlers, the limitations of the dogs themselves, or even the pervasive contamination of currency by cocaine. * * * In practical terms, the evidence is clear that the dog that alerts hundreds of times will be wrong dozens of times.

Once the dog's fallibility is recognized, however, that ends the justification claimed in *Place* for treating the sniff as *sui generis* under the Fourth Amendment: the sniff alert does not necessarily signal hidden contraband, and opening the container or enclosed space whose emanations the dog has sensed will not necessarily reveal contraband or any other evidence of crime. * * * Thus in practice the government's use of a trained narcotics dog functions as a limited search to reveal undisclosed facts about private enclosures, to be used to justify a further and complete search of the enclosed area. And given the fallibility of the dog, the sniff is the first step in a process that may disclose "intimate details" without revealing contraband, just as a thermal-imaging device might do, as described in *Kyllo v. United States*.[3]

It makes sense, then, to treat a sniff as the search that it amounts to in practice, and to rely on the body of our Fourth Amendment cases, including *Kyllo*, in deciding whether such a search is reasonable. As a general proposition, using a dog to sniff for drugs is subject to the rule that the object of enforcing criminal laws does not, without more, justify suspicionless Fourth Amendment intrusions. Since the police claim to have had no particular suspicion that Caballes was violating any drug

---

3. *Kyllo* was concerned with whether a search occurred when the police used a thermal-imaging device on a house to detect heat emanations associated with high-powered marijuana-growing lamps. In concluding that using the device was a search, the Court stressed that the "Government [may not] us[e] a device ... to explore details of the home that would previously have been unknowable without physical intrusion." Any difference between the dwelling in *Kyllo* and the trunk of the car here may go to the issue of the reasonableness of the respective searches, but it has no bearing on the question of search or no search. Nor is it significant that *Kyllo's* imaging device would disclose personal details immediately, whereas they would be revealed only in the further step of opening the enclosed space following the dog's alert reaction; in practical terms the same values protected by the Fourth Amendment are at stake in each case. The justifications required by the Fourth Amendment may or may not differ as between the two practices, but if constitutional scrutiny is in order for the imager, it is in order for the dog.

law, this sniff search must stand or fall on its being ancillary to the traffic stop that led up to it. * * *

The Court today does not go so far as to say explicitly that sniff searches by dogs trained to sense contraband always get a free pass under the Fourth Amendment, since it reserves judgment on the constitutional significance of sniffs assumed to be more intrusive than a dog's walk around a stopped car. For this reason, I do not take the Court * * * as actually signaling recognition of a broad authority to conduct suspicion-less sniffs for drugs in any parked car, about which Justice Ginsburg is rightly concerned, or on the person of any pedestrian minding his own business on a sidewalk. But the Court's stated reasoning provides no apparent stopping point short of such excesses. For the sake of providing a workable framework to analyze cases on facts like these, which are certain to come along, I would treat the dog sniff as the familiar search it is in fact, subject to scrutiny under the Fourth Amendment.

Justice Ginsburg, with whom Justice Souter joins, dissenting.

* * * The unwarranted and nonconsensual expansion of the seizure here from a routine traffic stop to a drug investigation broadened the scope of the investigation in a manner that, in my judgment, runs afoul of the Fourth Amendment. * * * In my view, the Court diminishes the Fourth Amendment's force by abandoning the second *Terry* inquiry (was the police action "reasonably related in scope to the circumstances [justifiying] the [initial] interference"). A drug-detection dog is an intimi-dating animal. Injecting such an animal into a routine traffic stop changes the character of the encounter between the police and the motorist. The stop becomes broader, more adversarial, and (in at least some cases) longer. * * * Today's decision ... clears the way for suspi-cionless, dog-accompanied drug sweeps of parked cars along sidewalks and in parking lots. Nor would motorists have constitutional grounds for complaint should police with dogs, stationed at long traffic lights, circle cars waiting for the red signal to turn green. * * *

2) Canine "Sniffs"—People vs. Property Wayne LaFave, *Search and Seizure: A Treatise on the Fourth Amendment § 2.2(f)* at 373–74 (1987) contends that canine sniffs of persons involve a significantly greater intrusion than sniffs of luggage or cars. A canine sniff of a person "is embarrassing, overbearing and harassing, and thus should be subject to Fourth Amendment constraints." Similarly, Arnold H. Loewy notes that "the very act of being subject to a body sniff by a German shepherd may be offensive at best or harrowing at worst." Arnold H. Loewy, "The Fourth Amendment as a Device for Protecting the Innocent," 81 *Mich. L. Rev.* 1229 (1983).

The relative paucity of "people-sniffing" cases, viewed in conjunction with the abundance of cases challenging dog sniffs of luggage and cars, suggests that dog sniffs of people are a rarely used police procedure outside of the school context. May school officials confine students in a classroom and expose them to a narcotics detection dog? Are there Fourth Amendment differences between a dog sniffing people and sniffing their effects, e.g. backpacks, purses, or briefcases? If the dog signals the presence of contraband on the person or in the container, does that constitute reasonable suspicion for a more intrusive search of the person under *T.L.O.*? Does a canine sniff constitute probable cause for a complete search of the person? How extensively and intensively may authorities search without a warrant based on the information provided by a "well-trained narcotics detection dog"? The Court in ***Horton v. Goose Creek Ind. School District***, 690 F.2d 470, 478–79 (5th Cir. 1982), on facts similar to those in *Doe v. Renfrow*, observed that:

> the intensive smelling of people, even if done by dogs is indecent and demeaning. Most persons in our society deliberately attempt not to expose the odors emanating from their bodies to public smell. * * * Intentional close proximity sniffing of the person is offensive whether the sniffer be canine or human. One can imagine the embarrassment which a young adolescent, already self-conscious about his or her body, might experience when a dog, being handled by a representative of the school administration, enters the classroom specifically for the purpose of sniffing the air around his or her person.

> We need only look at the record in the case to see how a dog's sniffing technique—*i.e.*, sniffing around each child, putting his nose *on* the child and scratching and manifesting other signs of excitement in the case of an alert—is intrusive. * * * [T]he dogs put their noses 'up against' the persons they are investigating. * * * [W]e hold that sniffing by dogs of the students' persons in the manner involved in this case is a search within the purview of the fourth amendment.

Note, "The Constitutionality of Canine Searches in the Classroom," 71 *J. Crim. L. & Criminology* 39 (1980); Martin R. Gardner, "Sniffing for Drugs in the Classroom—Perspectives on Fourth Amendment Scope," 74 *N.W. U.L.Rev.* 803 (1980).

3) Canine Sniffs of Students Unlike the Court's decision in *Place* which involved luggage or in *Caballes* which involved an automobile, the court in *Doe v. Renfrow* approved the canine "sniff" of a person. Should a canine sniff of a student in school require some threshold individualized justification such as reasonable suspicion or even probable cause? In **Commonwealth v. Martin**, 534 Pa. 136, 626 A.2d 556 (Pa. 1993), the Pennsylvania Supreme Court analyzed the validity of "dog sniff" searches of the person:

> In *Commonwealth v. Johnston*, we held that use of a trained dog to sniff for the presence of drugs was, under * * * the Pennsylvania Constitution, a search. The search in *Johnston* concerned a storage locker, a place, and we specifically indicated "We are not called upon to decide in this case whether the same rules we have established today apply to a canine search of a person instead of a place." * * *

> The rules set down in *Johnston* were that in order for police to conduct a canine search of a place, they must be able to articulate reasonable grounds for believing that drugs may be present in the place they seek to test; and they must be lawfully present in the place where the canine sniff is conducted. The first question in this case is whether these rules also apply to a canine search of a person. * * *

> Although the federal courts do not consider a canine sniff search a "search" for Fourth Amendment purposes, we held in *Johnston* that a

canine sniff is a search under * * * the Pennsylvania Constitution, but because it involves a minimal intrusion and is directed to a compelling state interest in eradicating illegal trafficking in drugs, the sniff search may be carried out on the basis of an articulated "reasonable suspicion," not probable cause. We saw this as a constitutional middle ground between requiring probable cause to believe that a crime has been or is being committed or that contraband or evidence of a crime will be discovered, and requiring nothing at all before police would be permitted to conduct a sniff search.

This middle ground approach was acceptable in *Johnston* because police intrusion was minimal, because the intrusion was directed solely at contraband drugs, and because much of the law enforcement utility of drug detection dogs would be lost if full-blown warrant procedures were required. In this case, however, the search is that of a person, not a place, and accordingly, we believe that different interests are implicated. * * * [A]lthough privacy may relate both to property and to one's person, an invasion of one's person is, in the usual case, a more severe intrusion on one's privacy interest than an invasion of one's property.

Because the search in this case involved Martin's person, we believe that in addition to being lawfully in place at the time of the search, the police must have probable cause to believe that a canine search of a person will produce contraband or evidence of a crime. Reasonable suspicion of criminal activity will not suffice. Moreover, because the intrusion concerns the person, we also hold that once the police have probable cause and a sniff search has been conducted pursuant to that probable cause, before any search, beyond that permitted by *Terry v. Ohio*, may be conducted (patting down outer garments to check for weapons upon reasonable suspicion that the suspect may be armed), the police must secure a search warrant and they may detain the suspect for a reasonable time while the warrant is sought.

We are mindful that government has a compelling interest in eliminating the flow of illegal drugs into our society, and we do not seek to frustrate the effort to rid society of this scourge. But all things are not permissible even in the pursuit of a compelling state interest. The Constitution does not cease to exist merely because the government's interest is compelling. A police state does not arise whenever crime gets out of hand. * * * As we stated in *Johnston*, a free society cannot remain free if police may use drug detection dogs or any other crime detection device without restraint. * * *

In the absence of a clear Supreme Court holding on the issue, lower courts are divided on the question whether it is reasonable for school administrators or police to use canine partners to sniff-out drugs in school especially when the handlers direct the dog at students rather than their personal property. In **B.C. v. Plumas Unified School District**, 192 F.3d 1260 (9th Cir. 1999), a high school student brought a § 1983 action against school officials and law enforcement officers alleging that a dog sniff at school violated his Fourth Amendment right to be free from unreasonable searches and seizures. School officials required students to pass a deputy sheriff and a

SEC. B   SEARCHING JUVENILES: SCHOOLS & "SPECIAL NEEDS"   229

drug-sniffing dog stationed outside the classroom door. School officials then ordered the students to wait outside the classroom while the dog sniffed backpacks, jackets, and other belongings which the students left in the room. The Court of Appeals held that the dog sniff of the person was Fourth Amendment search and that a suspicionless dog sniff search of student was unreasonable in the circumstances:

A "search" occurs when an expectation of privacy that society is prepared to consider reasonable is infringed. The Supreme Court has held that the use of a trained canine to sniff unattended luggage is not a search within the meaning of the Fourth Amendment. But neither the Supreme Court nor the Ninth Circuit has addressed the issue whether a dog sniff of a person is a search.... [T]he level of intrusiveness is greater when the dog is permitted to sniff a person than when a dog sniffs unattended luggage ... [U]nder *Place* and *Jacobsen,* the level of intrusiveness of an investigative technique is critical to whether the actions of government officials constitute a search.

Only the Fifth and Seventh Circuits have directly addressed the question whether a dog sniff of a student's person is a search.... In *Horton,* the Fifth Circuit noted that " 'the intensive smelling of people, even if done by dogs, [is] indecent and demeaning' " and held that the sniffing by dogs of students was a search. The Fifth Circuit in *Horton* considered and expressly rejected the approach taken by the Seventh Circuit in *Doe v. Renfrow,* ... [on] facts nearly identical to those of *Horton.* But the court in *Renfrow* upheld the district court's ruling that a dog sniff of students is not a search.

We agree with the Fifth Circuit that "close proximity sniffing of the person is offensive whether the sniffer be canine or human." Because we believe that the dog sniff at issue in this case infringed B.C.'s reasonable expectation of privacy, we hold that it constitutes a search.

Having determined that a search occurred, we must determine whether the search was constitutional. The constitutionality of a search is measured by its reasonableness in the circumstances. "To be reasonable under the Fourth Amendment, a search must ordinarily be based on individualized suspicion of wrongdoing." School officials here admit that they had no "individualized suspicion of wrongdoing" by any student.

Despite this lack of any individualized suspicion, a suspicionless search may be reasonable " '[i]n limited circumstances, where [1] the privacy interests implicated by the search are minimal, *and* [2] where an important governmental interest furthered by the intrusion would be placed in jeopardy by a requirement of individualized suspicion.' " Moreover, the second part of the test requires *both* the existence of an " 'important governmental interest furthered by the intrusion' " *and* that this interest would be " 'placed in jeopardy by a requirement of individualized suspicion.' " * * *

While students have " 'a lesser expectation of privacy than members of the population generally'," they nonetheless retain an expectation of privacy when they enter the school grounds. Moreover, the district court found that the dog sniff was "highly intrusive" for the following reasons.

First, "the body and its odors are highly personal." Noting that dogs " 'often engender irrational fear'," the district court further explained that the fact "[t]hat search was sudden and unannounced add[ed] to its potentially distressing, and thus invasive, character." In addition, the "search was completely involuntary." Thus, we conclude that the Quincy High School students' privacy interests were not minimal.

Having considered the students' privacy interests, we turn to the government's interest in conducting such a search. There can be no dispute that deterring drug use by students is an important—if not a compelling—governmental interest. But the record here does not disclose that there was any drug crisis or even a drug problem at Quincy High in May 1996. In the absence of a drug problem or crisis at Quincy High, the government's important interest in deterring student drug use would not have been " 'placed in jeopardy by a requirement of individualized suspicion.' " We therefore conclude that the random and suspicionless dog sniff search of B.C. was unreasonable in the circumstances. * * *

4) Canine sniffs of students' cars in the school parking lot. Recall **Note 8, p. 212** and the standard for searches conducted by police officers at the behest of school officials. And consider the implications of Justices Souter's and Ginsburg's dissents in *Caballes, supra,* when police conduct a dog sniff of students' cars in the school parking lot. **Myers v. State (Indiana)**, 839 N.E.2d 1154 (Ind. 2005). A high school student charged with possessing a firearm on school property filed a motion to suppress the evidence resulting from a search of his car in the school parking lot. The trial judge denied his motion to suppress and a sharply divided Indiana Supreme Court affirmed the denial.

Dickson, Justice.

* * * Following an evidentiary hearing, the trial court denied the motion with a detailed order that included specific findings of fact, among which were the following:

1. This matter arises from a narcotic drug dog sweep conducted at the Austin High School on December 12, 2002. As a result of the sweep the Defendant's automobile was searched and a firearm was seized from the vehicle. * * *

4. ... [T]he evidence was that the Austin High School was a closed campus, and therefore Defendant was not free to leave school at any time he desired. The facts, herein, show that ... the vehicle [was] no longer "inherently mobile" and that to require that a Police Officer obtain a search warrant would not have been unreasonable.

5. The actual search of the vehicle was made herein not by a Police Officer but by a School Official. * * * The evidence, while indicating that the Police participated in the sweep, the record does not contain evidence that the police coerced, dominated or directed the actions of the School. Rather it was the School who determined that the sweep would take place, where the sweep was to be conducted, and the range of time in which the sweep was to be conducted, further it was the School who did any search after the dog had alerted to a locker or vehicle....

6.   Having determined that the School Officials herein did not act as agents of the Police, * * * [t]he Court, here, finds that the action of the School Officials in conducting the search of the Defendant's vehicle was not unreasonable under the circumstances. . . .

Acknowledging that school officials are subject to a less demanding constitutional standard for student searches and seizures than that applied to law enforcement officials, the defendant contends that such relaxed standards should not apply here due to substantial police involvement. He urges that the challenged actions were a police search, not a school search; that the use of police narcotic drug dogs at his particular vehicle was not supported by reasonable particularized suspicion; and that the resulting warrantless search of his vehicle was not justified by his consent or by the automobile exception to the warrant requirement. * * *

With respect to his claim that the dog sniff was unconstitutional, the defendant concedes that such dog sniffs are not "searches" requiring probable cause under the Fourth Amendment to the United States Constitution, but he contends that canine sniff activities must be supported by reasonable individualized suspicion. The defendant argues that the sniff test in this case lacked individualized reasonable suspicion, and thus the evidence should be suppressed.

The United States Supreme Court has recently addressed "[w]hether the Fourth Amendment requires reasonable, articulable suspicion to justify using a drug-detection dog to sniff a vehicle during a legitimate traffic stop." *Illinois v. Caballes,* [*supra*]. The Supreme Court observed that the dog sniff was performed on the exterior of a car and held that "[a]ny intrusion on respondent's privacy expectations does not rise to the level of a constitutionally cognizable infringement." Noting the absence of any contention that the traffic stop involved an unreasonable detention, the Court concluded: "A dog sniff conducted during a concededly lawful traffic stop that reveals no information other than the location of a substance that no individual has any right to possess does not violate the Fourth Amendment." * * *

In the present case, the defendant's car was subjected to the narcotics dog sniff test as it was parked and unoccupied and the defendant was in school. In light of *Caballes,* we reject the defendant's claim that reasonable individualized suspicion was required by the federal constitution before officials could use a trained narcotics-detection dog to sniff the outside of the defendant's unoccupied motor vehicle.

The defendant's other contention is that the warrantless search of his vehicle was not justified by the automobile exception to the general rule that a warrant is required for a search. * * * Resolution of this challenge requires consideration of whether the search of the defendant's vehicle is governed by the less demanding constitutional standard for searches and seizures conducted by school officials. * * *

The defendant argues that the warrantless search of his vehicle resulted from the substantial involvement of police with school officials and thus amounted to a constitutionally unreasonable search and seizure.

The defendant maintains that, because the police involvement in the search here was substantial, rather than minimal, the relaxed constitutional standard set out in *T.L.O.* is inapplicable, and that the warrant requirement should be fully applicable to prohibit the challenged search.

Although in *T.L.O.* the United States Supreme Court clearly relaxed the Fourth Amendment standard for school officials searching students, it expressly left open the appropriate standard for determining the legality of searches "conducted by school officials in conjunction with or at the behest of law enforcement agencies...." *T.L.O.* In the face of this open question, many lower courts have identified standards for three different possible scenarios of police involvement in searches of students in schools: (1) where school officials initiate the search or police involvement is minimal, the reasonableness standard is applied; (2) where the search is conducted by the school resource officer on his or her own initiative to further educationally related goals, the reasonableness standard is applied; and (3) where "outside" police officers initiate the search of a student for investigative purposes, the probable cause and warrant requirements are applied. [Ed. See p. 212, Note 8, *supra*] We find this approach and analysis persuasive. Thus, where a search is initiated and conducted by school officials alone, or where school officials initiate a search and police involvement is minimal, the reasonableness standard is applicable. And the ordinary warrant requirement will apply where "outside" police officers initiate, or are predominantly involved in, a school search of a student or student property for police investigative purposes.

The trial court determined as a matter of historical fact that the school officials, not the police, conducted the searches and that the police only assisted the school officials. The decision to conduct the sweep was made by the school and, although the time and date of the sweep was determined by the police, it was within a range of dates determined by the school; the areas to be searched were determined by the school; and the actual search was conducted by school officials. Because these facts from the record support the trial court's finding that the school initiated and conducted the search and sought only supporting police resources such as trained narcotics dogs that were not available to the school, we find that the propriety of the vehicle search under the Fourth Amendment is governed by the reasonableness test, not the warrant requirement. * * *

We conclude ... that the search was reasonable from its inception because it was conducted after an alert by a police narcotics dog. Furthermore, the search as conducted was reasonably related in scope because the school officials limited their searches to those areas upon which the dogs alerted. The vehicle search by school officials was thus reasonable.

Because reasonable suspicion is not required for a canine narcotics sniff of the exterior of an automobile that does not involve an unreasonable detention of a person, and because the search was predominantly initiated and conducted by the school officials of Austin High School and was reasonable, we affirm the trial court's denial of the defendant's motion to suppress the firearm seized from the defendant's vehicle as a result of the search.

Sullivan, Justice, dissenting.

I respectfully dissent. * * * In my view, this search, even though authorized by the school board as a general matter more than a year prior to its occurring and even though an assistant principal examined the vehicle, cannot be said to have been, using the Court's own test, "conducted by the school resource officer on his or her own initiative to further educationally related goals." The descent of officers upon the school from four separate police departments without any advance notice and their vehicle-by-vehicle search of the cars in the parking lot, it seems to me, constituted a search, again using the Court's test, "where 'outside' police officers [had] initiate[d] the search" for "investigative purposes." As such, under the Court's own formulation, the probable cause and warrant requirements applied.

I also respectfully disagree on the applicability of *Illinois v. Caballes* as precedent in this case. At issue in *Caballes* was whether a dog sniff itself infringed upon Caballes's constitutionally protected privacy interest during a traffic stop that was lawful at its inception and otherwise executed in a reasonable manner. Caballes had been stopped on a highway based on probable cause and there is nothing in the opinion to suggest that the dog sniff would not have violated the Fourth Amendment but for the concededly lawful traffic stop. (The *Caballes* opinion also suggests that the sniff was valid only with respect to drug contraband; that it would not have extended to the weapon discovered here.) Here, of course, the defendant was not the subject of lawful detention—or any detention at all—at the time of the dog sniff. His situation is much more like that of the defendant in *City of Indianapolis v. Edmond* (2000). In that familiar case, the Court held that the use of dog sniffs as part of brief, standardized, discretionless, automobiles stops violated the Fourth Amendment.

Rucker, Justice, dissenting.

The United States Supreme Court has determined that under limited circumstances a sniff test by a trained narcotics dog is not a search within the meaning of Fourth Amendment. And there is authority for the proposition that an alert by a trained narcotics dog may be enough to establish probable cause.

Taken together these cases seem to stand for the proposition that: (i) no warrant is required in the first instance for the use of a trained narcotics dog, and (ii) once the dog alerts to the presence of narcotics, probable cause has been established either to obtain a warrant or search pursuant to an exception. The question presented in this case however is one step removed, namely: whether something less than probable cause, i.e., reasonable articulable suspicion of criminal activity, is required before a narcotics dog may be used to conduct a sniff test. * * *

It appears to me that the Supreme Court's emphasis on dog sniffs in the context of traffic stops was deliberate. The Court could have said, as the majority says in this case, that the dog sniff was justified solely because the car was "parked and unoccupied." But it did not. In my view the majority's position here expands the use of drug sniffing dogs to a variety of contexts not specifically sanctioned by the *Caballes* court. Indeed, in a dissenting opinion Justice Souter made a similar point. Although complaining that the Court's stated reasoning "provides no apparent stopping point," Justice Souter pointed out that he did not believe the Court's was "actually signaling recognition of a broad authority to conduct suspicionless sniffs for drugs in any parked car ... or on the person of any pedestrian minding his own business on a sidewalk."

In essence, we are writing on a clean slate. Or perhaps, more precisely, *Caballes* leaves open the question of whether, in contexts other than traffic stops, the use of a drug-sniffing dog requires reasonable articulable suspicion of criminal activity. * * * Unlike the majority I am unwilling to expand the reach of *Caballes* beyond that which the Court itself articulated. Rather, it appears to me that the use of a dog's keen sense of smell to detect the presence of contraband within a car parked in a parking lot is a Fourth Amendment intrusion, albeit a limited one. I would hold therefore that before an officer may subject a vehicle, lawfully parked in a parking lot, to a canine sniff, the officer must first have at least a reasonable articulable suspicion that a crime is being committed. Otherwise such an intrusion is constitutionally impermissible. Because the officer in this case had no suspicion of criminal activity of any kind, the use of the drug-sniffing dog was in violation of the Fourth Amendment.

I also disagree with the majority's view that the search of Myers' vehicle was justified by the less demanding constitutional standard for searches and seizures conducted by school officials. * * * [S]ince *T.L.O.*, courts have taken a variety of approaches in determining whether *T.L.O.*'s reasonable suspicion standard applies or whether probable cause is required when police are involved in searches of students in school.

Here, the majority has sided with those jurisdictions holding that where "police involvement is minimal," the *T.L.O.* reasonableness standard applies. First, it is my view that the police involvement in this case was far more pervasive than the majority suggests. But more importantly the majority's view is inconsistent with a key underlying tenet of the "special needs" cases. Namely, the evidence obtained was not used or intended to be used for criminal law enforcement purposes. * * *

In this case, precisely because the school's drug prevention and detection policy was intended to (and did in fact) result in the seizure of evidence for law enforcement purposes, the traditional probable cause requirement was not waived. Indeed I endorse the view expressed by the Florida Court of Appeals: "where a law enforcement officer directs, participates or acquiesces in a search conducted by school officials, the officer must have probable cause for that search, even though the school officials acting alone are treated ... to a lesser constitutional standard...."

In sum, I am of the opinion that the seizure of the handgun in this case cannot be justified on the grounds proposed by the majority. I therefore dissent and would reverse the trial court's denial of Myers' motion to suppress.

5) Strip Searches and Nude Searches In *Doe*, the dog's alert ultimately led to the student's strip-search. Under *T.L.O.*, a court must decide whether school officials conducted a search "reasonably related in scope to the circumstances which justified the interference in the first place." If school officials possess reasonable suspicion that a student possesses drugs or is under the influence of drugs, may they conduct a strip search? A nude search? Following *T.L.O.*, courts find strip-searches valid when based on "reasonable suspicion." *See e.g., Cornfield v. Consolidated High School District No. 230*, 991 F.2d 1316 (7th Cir.1993) (deciding that school officials had strong reason to believe that plaintiff was hiding drugs in the crotch of his pants when they took him to locker room, and told him to remove pants but allowed him to put on gym uniform during search); *Widener v. Frye*, 809 F.Supp. 35 (S.D.Ohio 1992) (school officials detected odor of marijuana, observed student acting in a lethargic manner, taken into private office and told to remove jeans but not undergarments); *Williams v. Ellington*, 936 F.2d 881 (6th Cir.1991) (deciding that school officials had reason to believe female student was using drugs when they took student into private office where, in the presence of a female secretary, she removed her shirt, shoes and socks and lowered her jeans to her knees). *But see, Oliver v. McClung*, 919 F.Supp. 1206 (N.D. Indiana) (holding that strip search of seventh grade girls in an effort to recover stolen $4.50 was unreasonable under the circumstances); *State ex rel. Galford v. Mark Anthony B.*, 189 W.Va. 538, 433 S.E.2d 41, 48–49 (1993) (deciding that strip search of student to find money missing from teacher's purse was excessively intrusive and unreasonable in scope—"At some point, a line must be drawn which imposes limits upon how intrusive a student search can be. We certainly cannot imagine ever condoning a search that is any more physically intrusive than the one now before us."); *Jenkins v. Talladega City Board of Education*, 115 F.3d 821 (11th Cir. 1997) (holding that teachers who twice conducted strip search of two eight-year-old girls in attempt to locate allegedly missing $7 protected by qualified immunity because they should not have known that search was unreasonable). *See generally* Colleen J. Berry, "Students 'Stripped' of Their Constitutional Rights," 23 *So. Ill. U.L.J.* 223 (1998) (criticizing application of qualified immunity to protect teachers who conducted clearly "unreasonable" strip-search); Rosemary Spellman, "Strip Search of Juveniles and the Fourth Amendment: A Delicate Balance of Protection and Privacy," 22 J. Juv. L. 159 (2001) (noting that schools conduct strip searches based on concerns about school violence and drug use).

Scott A. Gartner, "Strip Searches of Students: What Johnny Really Learned At School and How Local School Boards Can Help Solve the Problem," 70 *So. Cal. L. Rev.* 921 (1997), summarizes and cites numerous examples of strip searches of students taking place in public schools. "By permitting school officials to exercise virtually unbridled discretion in the area of student searches, the Court has effectively given to teachers the same rights of search given to prison guards." *Id.* at 931. *See also* Steven F. Shatz, Molly Donovan, and Jeanne Hong, "The Strip Search of Children and the

Fourth Amendment," 26 *U.S.F.L. Rev.* 1, 39 (1991) ("Government officials who strip search a person without his or her consent commit one of the greatest intrusions possible on that person. When the victim of the search is a child, the experience may well cause serious psychological harm. * * * School officials should not be permitted to strip search any child without a warrant or consent, except in the case of a genuine emergency."); David C. Blickenstaff, "Strip Searches of Public School Students: Can *New Jersey v. T.L.O.* Solve the Problem?", 99 *Dick. L. Rev.* 1 (1994) (arguing that strip searches require justifications of probable cause, seriousness, and "imminent threat to safety or health").

Because of the intrusiveness of strip searches on students' privacy, should courts require more than reasonable suspicion, for example, probable cause? Rosemary Spellman, "Strip Search of Juveniles and the Fourth Amendment: A Delicate Balance of Protection and Privacy," 22 J. Juvenile L. 159, 172 (2001–2) ("any search of a school age child or adolescent has a greater impact than would the same search of an adult because the development of a sense of privacy is critical to a child's maturation."). Should the nature of the governmental interests or the seriousness of the violation limit strip searches? See e.g. Spellman, supra at 173 ("school officials must weigh the danger of the student's alleged conduct against the need to protect him or her from the humiliation and other emotional harms such a search produces."). Recall Justice Stevens' dissent in *T.L.O.*, where he asserted that the "governmental interest which allegedly justified official intrusion" should bear heavily on the reasonableness of the search. Because drugs and money are the items most readily hidden in private areas, are suspicions of theft or drug offenses sufficiently "compelling"?

6) Sufficiency of a student tip to furnish reasonable suspicion for strip searches Savana Redding and her parent brought a § 1983 action against the school district and school administrators for a strip search based on a tip provided by another student, Marissa, that Savana brought ibuprofen to school in violation of school rules. Based on Marissa's uncorroborated information, school officials took Redding to the nurse's office where she removed her clothes, pulled out her bra and exposed her breasts, and pulled her underwear out at the crotch and exposed her pelvic area. The search did not produce any pills. After unsatisfactory meetings with the school administrators, Savana's parents brought suit against the school district. Defendants' motion for summary judgment asserted that the strip search did not violate Savana's Fourth Amendment rights. The district court accepted that contention and ruled for defendants. It found that the need to locate the ibuprofen was sufficiently urgent that the strip search was "reasonably related" to the search's objective and was not "excessively intrusive." A divided panel, 2–1, upheld the grant of summary judgment because "the strong interest" in protecting students from prescription drugs outweighed the intrusion caused by a search conducted in a "reasonable manner." The dissent objected that the strip search failed to meet constitutional muster because it "was unreasonable to force Savana, a thirteen-year-old girl, to expose her breasts and pubic area to school officials" while they searched for ibuprofen. The divided *en banc* court in **Redding v. Safford Unified School Dist. No.1**, 531 F.3d

1071 (C.A.9, 2008), considered the sufficiency of student tips to justify intrusive searches and Wardlaw, Judge, found the search unreasonable:

> On the basis of an uncorroborated tip from the culpable eighth grader, public middle school officials searched futilely for prescription-strength ibuprofen by strip-searching thirteen-year-old honor student Savana Redding. We conclude that the school officials violated Savana's Fourth Amendment right to be free from unreasonable search and seizure. The strip search of Savana was neither "justified at its inception," nor, as a grossly intrusive search of a middle school girl to locate pills with the potency of two over-the-counter Advil capsules, "reasonably related in scope to the circumstances" giving rise to its initiation. * * *

> The crucial link—indeed, the only link—between Savana and the ibuprofen was Marissa's statement upon being caught with the pills that the ibuprofen (and the blame) was not hers, but rather was Savana's. * * * [O]n the sole basis of Marissa's attempt to shift the school officials' focus off herself and onto Savana, and without additional questioning or investigation, Wilson directed his assistant and the school nurse to require a thirteen-year-old to disrobe. * * *

> The Court [in *T.L.O.*] set forth a twofold inquiry to gauge reasonableness: "[F]irst, one must consider 'whether the ... action was justified at its inception;' second, one must determine whether the search as actually conducted 'was reasonably related in scope to the circumstances which justified the interference in the first place.' " The Court further held that a search will be permissible in its scope "when the measures adopted are reasonably related to the objectives of the search and not excessively intrusive in light of the age and sex of the student and the nature of the infraction." The Court crafted this test to "neither unduly burden the efforts of school authorities to maintain order in their schools nor authorize unrestrained intrusions upon the privacy of school children." * * *

> Nowhere does the *T.L.O.* Court tell us to accord school officials' judgments unblinking deference. Nor does *T.L.O.* provide blanket approval of strip searches of thirteen-year-olds remotely rumored to have had Advil merely because of a generalized drug problem. Rather, the Court made it clear that while it did not require school officials to apply a probable cause standard to a purse search, it plainly required them to act "according to the dictates of reason and common sense." As discussed below, the public school officials who strip searched Savana acted contrary to all reason and common sense as they trampled over her legitimate and substantial interests in privacy and security of her person. * * *

> Let there be no doubt: the Safford school officials conducted a strip search of Savana. * * * Savana did not have to be completely naked for the school officials to have strip searched her. * * * Savana was required by the public school officials to disrobe and expose the parts of her body underneath her underwear so that school officials could potentially find ibuprofen. The term may unsettle the sensibilities of our dissenting

colleagues; however, the accuracy of the designation merely cements the intrusiveness of what occurred. * * *

"Under ordinary circumstances, a search of a student by a teacher or other school official will be 'justified at its inception' when there are reasonable grounds for suspecting that the search will turn up evidence that the student has violated or is violating either the law or the rules of the school." Reasonableness, of course, depends on context. We agree with the Seventh Circuit that *T.L.O.* requires that "as the intrusiveness of the search of a student intensifies, so too does the standard of Fourth Amendment reasonableness. What may constitute reasonable suspicion for a search of a locker or even a pocket or pocketbook may fall well short of reasonableness for a nude search."[1] * * * "Although *T.L.O.* held that reasonable suspicion is the governing standard, the reasonableness of the suspicion is informed by the very intrusive nature of a strip search, requiring for its justification a high level of suspicion."

Here, as in *T.L.O.*, the school officials engaged in two related searches: first, a search of Savana's backpack and her pockets, which does not give rise to the claims in the complaint, and second, a strip search, which forms the basis of the complaint. * * * The causal link permitting the vice principal [in *T.L.O.*] to proceed from his first, less intrusive search to a second, more thorough search—the discovery of cigarettes and rolling papers—is entirely absent here. * * * Absent the sort of physical evidence found in *T.L.O.*, the primary purported justification for the strip search was Marissa's statement that Savana had given her the ibuprofen that she was caught with in violation of the school's rule. This self-serving statement, which shifted the culpability for bringing the pills to school from Marissa to Savana, does not justify initiating a highly invasive strip search of a student who bore no other connection to the pills in question. We do not treat all informants' tips as equal in their reliability. Rather, "[w]hen a court is considering whether an informant's tip is sufficient to support a finding of probable cause or reasonable suspicion, the court must employ a 'totality-of-the-circumstances approach' that takes into consideration the informant's 'veracity' or 'reliability' and his 'basis of knowledge.'" For good reason, we are most suspicious of those self-exculpatory tips that might unload potential punishment on a third party. Our concerns are heightened when the informant is a frightened eighth grader caught red-handed by a principal. This is particularly so when the student implicates another who has not previously been tied to the contraband and, more generally, has no disciplinary history whatsoever at the school. More succinctly, the self-serving statement of a cornered teenager facing significant punishment does not meet the heavy burden necessary to justify a search accurately described * * * as "de-meaning, dehumanizing, undignified, humiliating, terrifying, unpleasant [and] embarrassing."

At a minimum, Assistant Principal Wilson should have conducted additional investigation to corroborate Marissa's "tip" before directing

---

1. Notably, at least seven states—including two in this Circuit—have concluded that strip searches of school children are *never* permissible for *any* reason.

Savana into the nurse's office for disrobing. *See Williams by Willians v. Ellington* (6th Cir. 1991) ("While there is concern that students will be motivated by malice and falsely implicate other students in wrongdoing, that type of situation would be analogous to the anonymous tip. Because the tip lacks reliability, school officials would be required to further investigate the matter before a search or seizure would be warranted."); *Phaneuf v. Fraiken* (2006) ("While the uncorroborated tip no doubt justified additional inquiry and investigation by school officials, we are not convinced that it justified a step as intrusive as a strip search."). This need for further investigation is particularly heightened here because the initial tip provided no information as to whether Savana currently possessed ibuprofen pills or was hiding them in a place where a strip search would reveal them. * * *

Nor was the strip search "reasonably related in scope to the circumstances which justified the interference in the first place." The scope of a search is permissible only if "the measures adopted are reasonably related to the objectives of the search and *not excessively intrusive in light of the age and sex of the student and the nature of the infraction.*" Here, the public school authorities adopted a disproportionately extreme measure to search a thirteen-year-old girl for violating a school rule prohibiting possession of prescription and over-the-counter drugs. We conclude the strip search was not reasonably related to the search for ibuprofen, as the most logical places where the pills might have been found had already been searched to no avail, and no information pointed to the conclusion that the pills were hidden under her panties or bra. * * * Common sense informs us that directing a thirteen-year-old girl to remove her clothes, partially revealing her breasts and pelvic area, for allegedly possessing ibuprofen, an infraction that poses an imminent danger to no one, and which could be handled by keeping her in the principal's office until a parent arrived or simply sending her home, was excessively intrusive.

Along with our sister circuits, we have long recognized the psychological trauma intrinsic to a strip search. "The feelings of humiliation and degradation associated with forcibly exposing one's nude body to strangers for visual inspection is beyond dispute." As the Tenth Circuit has explained, "[t]he experience of disrobing and exposing one's self for visual inspection by a stranger clothed with the uniform and authority of the state ... can only be seen as thoroughly degrading and frightening." That Savana's search took place in a nurse's office in front of two women does not remove the sting of the procedure.

These concerns, pressing and legitimate when strip searches are conducted on adults in prison, are magnified when strip searches are performed on school children. * * * As adolescents enter puberty, "they become more conscious of their bodies and self-conscious about them. Consequently, the potential for a search to cause embarrassment and humiliation increases as children grow older." "[N]o one would seriously dispute that a nude search of a child is traumatic." * * *

And all this to find prescription-strength ibuprofen pills. We reject Safford's effort to lump together these run-of-the-mill anti-inflammatory pills with the evocative term "prescription drugs," in a knowing effort to shield an imprudent strip search of a young girl behind a larger war against drugs. * * * Nothing in the record provides any evidence that the school officials were concerned in this case about controlled substances violative of state or federal law. No legal decision cited to us or that we could find permitted a strip search to discover substances regularly available over the counter at any convenience store throughout the United States. And contrary to any suggestion that finding the ibuprofen was an urgent matter to avoid a parade of horribles, even if Savana had possessed the ibuprofen pills, any danger they posed was neutralized once school officials seized Savana and held her in the assistant principal's office. Savana had no means at that point to distribute the pills, and whatever immediately threatening activity the school may have perceived by the alleged possession of prescription-strength ibuprofen had been thwarted. The school officials had only to send Savana home for the afternoon to prevent the rumored lunchtime distribution from taking place—assuming she in fact possessed the pills on her person. The lack of any immediate danger to students only further diminishes the initial minimal nature of the alleged infraction of bringing ibuprofen onto campus. * * *

As the Seventh Circuit reasoned, * * * "a highly intrusive search in response to a minor infraction would ... not comport with the sliding scale advocated by the Supreme Court in *T.L.O.*" Here, we have exactly such a scenario with the important additional variable that the subject of the search was a thirteen-year-old pubescent girl. Approving such a strip search would eviscerate the Supreme Court's stated goal of developing a standard that "ensure[s] that the interests of students will be invaded no more than is necessary to achieve the legitimate end of preserving order in the schools." We therefore conclude that the strip search was impermissible in scope. The Safford public school officials violated Savana's Fourth Amendment rights. * * *

7) Students' "Reasonable Expectation of Privacy" of Freedom from Video Camera Surveillance in the Locker Room The 6th Circuit Court of Appeals in **Brannum v. Overton County School Bd., 516 F.3d 489 (C.A.6 (Tenn.) 2008),** confronted another question involving students' "reasonable expectations of privacy" in the school setting. In an effort to improve security at Livingston Middle School (LMS), the Overton County School Board installed video surveillance equipment throughout the school including in the boys' and girls' locker rooms. The cameras transmitted images to a computer terminal in Assistant Principal Jolley's office where they were displayed and stored on the computer's hard drive. The images were also accessible via remote internet connection and accessed ninety-eight different times during the five months the system was operational. During a girls' basketball game at LMS, visiting team members noticed the camera in the girls' locker room and told their coach. Although the LMS Principal Beatty assured the coach that the camera was not activated, the camera had recorded images of the team members in their undergarments when they changed their clothes. The visiting coach reported the camera to her school principal who, in turn, contacted the Overton School superintendent. The superintendent accessed the security system from his home and stated that the videotapes of the 10 to 14 year old girls contained "nothing more than images of a few bras and panties." School employees removed the locker room cameras later that day. Thirty-four students sued various officials of the school under 42 U.S.C. § 1983, alleging that the school authorities violated their constitutional right to privacy by installing and operating video surveillance equipment in the boys' and girls' locker rooms and by viewing and retaining the recorded images.

RYAN, Circuit Judge: * * * The students argue that their constitutionally protected right to privacy encompasses the right not to be videotaped while dressing and undressing in school athletic locker rooms—a place specifically designated by the school authorities for such intimate, personal activity. * * * We conclude that the privacy right involved here is one protected by the Fourth Amendment's guarantee against unreasonable searches, and that in this case, the defendants violated the students' rights under the amendment. * * *

The standards for testing the constitutionality of searches in the public school setting depend, to considerable extent, on the context: * * * First, we consider whether the state action—the installation of the cameras— "was justified at its inception"; and second, whether the search—here the videotaped surveillance—"as actually conducted 'was reasonably related in scope to the circumstances which justified the [surveillance/search] in the first place.' "

A student search is justified in its inception when there are reasonable grounds for suspecting that the search will garner evidence that a student has violated or is violating the law or the rules of the school, or is in imminent danger of injury on school premises. In this case, the policy of setting up video surveillance equipment throughout the school was instituted for the sake of increasing security, which is an appropriate and common sense purpose and not one subject to our judicial veto. * * *

A search—and there can be no dispute that videotaping students in a school locker room is a search under the Fourth Amendment—is "permissible in its scope when the measures adopted are reasonably related to the objectives of the search and not excessively intrusive in light of the age and sex of the student and the nature of the infraction." It is a matter of balancing the scope and the manner in which the search is conducted in light of the students' reasonable expectations of privacy, the nature of the intrusion, and the severity of the school officials' need in enacting such policies, including particularly, any history of injurious behavior that could reasonably suggest the need for the challenged intrusion. * * *

[E]ven in locker rooms, students retain "a significant privacy interest in their unclothed bodies." Unlike the situation in *Vernonia*, where the students and their parents were well aware that participation in school sports was conditioned on the students submitting to the drug testing policies, neither the students nor their parents in this case were aware of the video surveillance in the locker rooms, to say nothing of the videotaping. Further, while the Court in *Vernonia* pointed out the lower level of privacy typically associated with school locker rooms, we are satisfied that students using the LMS locker rooms could reasonably expect that no one, especially the school administrators, would videotape them, without their knowledge, in various states of undress while they changed their clothes for an athletic activity.

Video surveillance is inherently intrusive. * * * [T]he school officials wholly failed to institute any policies designed to protect the privacy of the students and did not even advise the students or their parents that students were being videotaped. * * * We believe that the scope of the secret surveillance in this case, like the strip search in *Beard*, significantly invaded the students' reasonable expectations of privacy. * * *

One measure of reasonableness is the congruence or incongruence of the policy to be served (student safety), and the means adopted to serve it. Surveillance of school hallways and other areas in which students mingle in the normal course of student life is one thing; camera surveillance of students dressing and undressing in the locker room—a place specifically set aside to offer privacy—is quite another. The two do not stand on equal footing.

Stated differently, the surveillance methodology employed, in particular the installation and operation of the cameras in the locker rooms, in order to be reasonable in its scope, must be congruent to the need for such a search in order to serve the policy goal of school safety and security. There is nothing whatsoever in this record to indicate that the defendants entertained any concerns about student safety or security in the locker rooms that would reasonably justify the installation of the cameras to record all the activities there. The defendants do not claim that any misconduct occurred in these areas in the past or that the plan to install the surveillance equipment in the school locker rooms was adopted because of any reasonable suspicion of wrongful activity or injurious behavior in the future. * * *

Given the universal understanding among middle school age children in this country that a school locker room is a place of heightened privacy, we believe placing cameras in such a way so as to view the children dressing and undressing in a locker room is incongruent to any demonstrated necessity, and wholly disproportionate to the claimed policy goal of assuring increased school security, especially when there is no history of any threat to security in the locker rooms. * * *

Under the qualified immunity doctrine, public officials cannot be held liable for violating a person's constitutional rights unless the right was clearly established at the time of the alleged improper conduct. * * * The policy of the law is that governmental administrative officials are sometimes "given a pass" for violating a citizen's constitutional rights because, if it were otherwise, government officials would be undesirably inhibited in exercising the broad discretion given them to carry out their duties wisely, effectively, and without fear of personal liability if they make a mistake that injures someone.

The "pass" does not extend, however, to violating a constitutional right that is "clearly established" and of which the violator is, or ought to have been, aware. * * * Some personal liberties are so fundamental to human dignity as to need no specific explication in our Constitution in order to ensure their protection against government invasion. Surreptitiously videotaping the plaintiffs in various states of undress is plainly among them. Stated differently, and more specifically, a person of ordinary common sense, to say nothing of professional school administrators, would know without need for specific instruction from a federal court, that teenagers have an inherent personal dignity, a sense of decency and self-respect, and a sensitivity about their bodily privacy that are at the core of their personal liberty and that are grossly offended by their being surreptitiously videotaped while changing their clothes in a school locker room. * * *

8) School Officials' Qualified Immunity In **Harlow v. Fitzgerald**, 457 U.S. 800, 102 S.Ct. 2727, 73 L.Ed.2d 396 (1982), the United States Supreme Court clarified the standard courts should use when assessing the liability of public officials, such as school administrators, for violations of citizens' constitutional rights:

> For executive officials in general, * * * qualified immunity represents the norm. * * * [T]he recognition of a qualified immunity defense for high executives reflected an attempt to balance competing values: not only the importance of a damages remedy to protect the rights of citizens, but also "the need to protect officials who are required to exercise their discretion and the related public interest in encouraging the vigorous exercise of official authority." * * *

> The resolution of immunity questions inherently requires a balance between the evils inevitable in any available alternative. In situations of abuse of office, an action for damages may offer the only realistic avenue for vindication of constitutional guarantees. It is this recognition that has required the denial of absolute immunity to most public officers. At the same time, however, it cannot be disputed seriously that claims frequently run against the innocent as well as the guilty—at a cost not only to the defendant officials, but to society as a whole. These social costs include the expenses of litigation, the diversion of official energy from pressing public issues, and the deterrence of able citizens from acceptance of public office. Finally, there is the danger that fear of being sued will "dampen the ardor of all but the most resolute, or the most irresponsible [public officials], in the unflinching discharge of their duties." * * *

> We therefore hold that government officials performing discretionary functions generally are shielded from liability for civil damages insofar as their conduct does not violate clearly established statutory or constitutional rights of which a reasonable person would have known. * * *

As *Harlow* indicates, the qualified immunity doctrine protects governmental officials performing discretionary functions from suit for damages under 42 U.S.C. § 1983 if their conduct did not violate clearly established rights of which a reasonable official would have known at the time of the conduct. *Burnham v. West*, 681 F.Supp. 1169, 1173 (E. D. Va. 1988) ("Liability for damages for every action which is found subsequently to have been violative of a student's constitutional rights and to have caused compensable injury would unfairly impose upon the school decision maker the burden of mistakes made in good faith in the course of exercising his discretion within the scope of his official duties.") The court in **B.C. v. Plumas Unified School District**, 192 F.3d 1260 (9th Cir. 1999), held that school officials are entitled to a qualified immunity defense if their conduct does not violate clearly established statutory or constitutional rights of which a reasonable person would have known:

> A right is "clearly established" if "the contours of [that] right [are] sufficiently clear that a reasonable official would understand that what he is doing violates that right." "To show that the right in question here was clearly established, [plaintiff] need not establish that [defendants'] 'behavior had been previously declared unconstitutional, only that the unlawfulness was apparent in light of preexisting law." "If the only reasonable conclusion from binding authority [was] that the disputed right existed, even if no case had specifically so declared, [defendants] would be on notice of the right and [they] would not be qualifiedly immune if they acted to offend it."

> When the dog sniff in this case occurred, it was not clearly established that the use of dogs to sniff students in a school setting constituted a search. As such, the unlawfulness of defendants' conduct "in light of preexisting law," was not "apparent." Therefore, each of defendants could "have believed that [his] conduct was lawful." Accordingly, we conclude that all defendants in their individual capacities are entitled to qualified immunity. * * *

PROBLEM

After the conflicting rulings in *Doe, Horton, Caballes, Redding, Beard*, and *B.C.*, what would you advise a school official to do if she asked you about conducting a suspicionless dog-sniff of students at a school with a moderate drug-problem? No significant drug problem? What should she do if the dog alerted to a particular student? If she conducted the canine sniff or a more intrusive search based on the dog's alert, would she be entitled to qualified immunity? Reconsider the liability of the school officials in *Doe* for the nude search after *Harlow*? Based on what you now know about school searches, would their conduct "violate clearly established statutory or constitutional rights of which a reasonable person would have known"? *See e.g. Doe v. Renfrow*, 631 F.2d 91 (7th Cir.1980) ("It does not require a constitutional scholar to conclude that a nude search of a thirteen-year-old child is an invasion of constitutional rights of some magnitude. * * * Apart from any constitutional readings and rulings, simple common sense would indicate that the conduct of the school officials in permitting such a nude search was not only unlawful but outrageous under 'settled indisputable principles of law.' "). In light of the inherent imprecision of *T.L.O.*'s reasonable suspicion standard and the additional latitude provided by a "good faith" and "objective reasonableness" inquiry, how often will a school official who conducts an unreasonable search be found liable for violating students' constitutional rights? In light of school officials' qualified immunity and good faith defense, does a student subjected to an invalid strip search have any effective remedy? See e.g., Spellman, *Strip Searches of Juveniles, supra*, note 4 at 177, who argues that

> Parents may be hesitant to file suit while their children are still students under the control of the offending school personnel. In fact, the fear of intimidation and reprisal would seem even greater in the school context due to the continuing interaction between teacher and student. Furthermore, parents may not realize that their children's constitutional rights have been violated and that they have any legal recourse, particularly if the child never communicates the incident to the parents. Finally, like police officers, school teachers and administrators also enjoy a qualified immunity from damages for claims of constitutional violations in actions undertaken in good faith. As a result, because the law on student strip searches is still unsettled, a teacher could successfully defend on the grounds that although the search turned out to be illegal, the teacher acted in good faith at the time.

3. DRUG–TESTING STUDENTS

Are there other types of *sui generis*, non-intrusive searches that school officials can perform without a warrant, probable cause, or even reasonable suspicion? Should the epidemic of drug abuse by young people, coupled with drugs' adverse impact on concentration, memory, and school performance, and the associated problems of discipline and disruption allow school authorities to create programs to detect and reduce drug use by students?

VERNONIA SCHOOL DISTRICT 47J v. ACTON
515 U.S. 646, 115 S.Ct. 2386, 132 L.Ed.2d 564 (1995).

JUSTICE SCALIA delivered the opinion of the Court.

The Student Athlete Drug Policy adopted by School District 47J in the town of Vernonia, Oregon, authorizes random urinalysis drug testing of students who participate in the District's school athletics programs. * * * [Petitioner School District operates one high school and three grade schools in the logging community of Vernonia, Oregon, where school sports play a prominent role in the town's life, and student athletes are admired. In the mid-to-late 1980's, school officials observed a sharp increase in drug use, disciplinary problems, and classroom disruptions. Student athletes appeared to be the leaders of the drug culture.] This caused the District's administrators particular concern, since drug use increases the risk of sports-related injury. Expert testimony at the trial confirmed the deleterious effects of drugs on motivation, memory, judgment, reaction, coordination, and performance. The high school football and wrestling coach witnessed a severe sternum injury suffered by a wrestler, and various omissions of safety procedures and misexecutions by football players, all attributable in his belief to the effects of drug use.

Initially, the District responded to the drug problem by offering special classes, speakers, and presentations designed to deter drug use. It even brought in a specially trained dog to detect drugs, but the drug problem persisted. * * * District officials began considering a drug-testing program. They held a parent "input night" to discuss the proposed Student Athlete Drug Policy (Policy), and the parents in attendance gave their unanimous approval. The school board approved the Policy for implementation in the fall of 1989. Its expressed purpose is to prevent student athletes from using drugs, to protect their health and safety, and to provide drug users with assistance programs.

The Policy applies to all students participating in interscholastic athletics. Students wishing to play sports must sign a form consenting to the testing and must obtain the written consent of their parents. Athletes are tested at the beginning of the season for their sport. In addition, once each week of the season the names of the athletes are placed in a "pool" from which a student, with the supervision of two adults, blindly draws the names of 10% of the athletes for random testing. Those selected are notified and tested that same day, if possible. The student to be tested completes a specimen control form which bears an assigned number. Prescription medications that the student is taking must be identified by providing a copy of the prescription or a doctor's authorization. The student then enters an empty locker room accompanied by an adult monitor of the same sex. Each boy selected produces a sample at a urinal, remaining fully clothed with his back to the monitor, who stands approximately 12 to 15 feet behind the student. * * * Girls produce samples in an enclosed bathroom stall, so that they can be heard but not observed. After the sample is produced, it is given to the monitor, who checks it for temperature and tampering and then transfers it to a vial.

The samples are sent to an independent laboratory, which routinely tests them for amphetamines, cocaine, and marijuana. Other drugs, such as LSD, may be screened at the request of the District, but the identity of a particular student does not determine which drugs will be tested. The laboratory's procedures are 99.94% accurate. The District follows strict procedures regarding the chain of custody and access to test results. * * * Only the superintendent, principals, vice-principals, and athletic directors have access to test results, and the results are not kept for more than one year.

If a sample tests positive, a second test is administered as soon as possible to confirm the result. If the second test is negative, no further action is taken. If the second test is positive, the athlete's parents are notified, and the school principal convenes a meeting with the student and his parents, at which the student is given the option of (1) participating for six weeks in an assistance program that includes weekly urinalysis, or (2) suffering suspension from athletics for the remainder of the current season and the next athletic season. The student is then retested prior to the start of the next athletic season for which he or she is eligible. The Policy states that a second offense results in automatic imposition of option (2); a third offense in suspension for the remainder of the current season and the next two athletic seasons.

In the fall of 1991, respondent James Acton, then a seventh-grader, signed up to play football at one of the District's grade schools. He was denied participation, however, because he and his parents refused to sign the testing consent forms. The Actons filed suit, seeking declaratory and injunctive relief from enforcement of the Policy on the grounds that it violated the Fourth and Fourteenth Amendments to the United States Constitution and Article I, § 9, of the Oregon Constitution. After a bench trial, the District Court entered an order denying the claims on the merits and dismissing the action. The United States Court of Appeals for the Ninth Circuit reversed, holding that the Policy violated both the Fourth and Fourteenth Amendments and Article I, § 9, of the Oregon Constitution. We granted certiorari.

The Fourth Amendment to the United States Constitution provides that the Federal Government shall not violate "[t]he right of the people to be secure in their persons, houses, papers, and effects, against unreasonable searches and seizures." * * * We have held that the Fourteenth Amendment extends this constitutional guarantee to searches and seizures by state officers, including public school officials. In *Skinner v. Railway Labor Executives' Assn.*, we held that state-compelled collection and testing of urine, such as that required by the Student Athlete Drug Policy, constitutes a "search" subject to the demands of the Fourth Amendment. As the text of the Fourth Amendment indicates, the ultimate measure of the constitutionality of a governmental search is "reasonableness." At least in a case such as this, where there was no clear practice, either approving or disapproving the type of search at issue, at the time the constitutional provision was enacted, whether a particular search meets the reasonableness standard " 'is judged by balancing its intrusion on the individual's Fourth Amendment interests against its promotion of legitimate governmental interests.' " * * * A search unsupported by probable cause can be constitutional, we have said, "when special needs, beyond the normal need for law enforcement, make the warrant and probable-cause requirement impracticable."

We have found such "special needs" to exist in the public-school context. There, the warrant requirement "would unduly interfere with the maintenance of the swift and informal disciplinary procedures [that are] needed," and "strict adherence to the requirement that searches be based upon probable cause" would undercut "the substantial need of teachers and administrators for freedom to maintain order in the schools." The school search we approved in *T.L.O.*, while not based on probable cause, was based on individualized suspicion of wrongdoing. As we explicitly acknowledged, however, " 'the Fourth Amendment imposes no irreducible requirement of such suspicion' ". We have upheld suspicionless searches and seizures to conduct drug testing of railroad personnel involved in train accidents; to conduct random drug testing of federal customs officers who carry arms or are involved in drug interdiction; and to maintain automobile checkpoints looking for illegal immigrants and contraband, and drunk drivers.

The first factor to be considered is the nature of the privacy interest upon which the search here at issue intrudes. The Fourth Amendment does not protect all subjective expectations of privacy, but only those that society recognizes as "legitimate." What expectations are legitimate varies, of course, with context, depending, for example, upon whether the individual asserting the privacy interest is at home, at work, in a car, or in a public park. In addition, the legitimacy of certain privacy expectations vis-á-vis the State may depend upon the individual's legal relationship with the State. * * * Central, in our view, to the present case is the fact that the subjects of the Policy are (1) children, who (2) have been committed to the temporary custody of the State as schoolmaster.

Traditionally at common law, and still today, unemancipated minors lack some of the most fundamental rights of self-determination—including even the right of liberty in its narrow sense, i.e., the right to come and go at will. They are subject, even as to their physical freedom, to the control of their parents or guardians. When parents place minor children in private schools for their education, the teachers and administrators of those schools stand *in loco parentis* over the children entrusted to them. * * *

In *T.L.O.* we rejected the notion that public schools, like private schools, exercise only parental power over their students, which of course is not subject to constitutional constraints. Such a view of things, we said, "is not entirely 'consonant with compulsory education laws,'", and is inconsistent with our prior decisions treating school officials as state actors for purposes of the Due Process and Free Speech Clauses. But while denying that the State's power over schoolchildren is formally no more than the delegated power of their parents, *T.L.O.* did not deny, but indeed emphasized, that the nature of that power is custodial and tutelary, permitting a degree of supervision and control that could not be exercised over free adults. "[A] proper educational environment requires close supervision of schoolchildren, as well as the enforcement of rules against conduct that would be perfectly permissible if undertaken by an adult." While we do not, of course, suggest that public schools as a general matter have such a degree of control over children as to give rise to a constitutional "duty to protect," we have acknowledged that for many purposes "school authorities ac[t] *in loco parentis*," with the power and indeed the duty to "inculcate the habits and manners of civility". Thus, while children assuredly do not "shed their constitutional rights * * * at the schoolhouse gate," the nature of those rights is what is appropriate for children in school. * * * Fourth Amendment rights, no less than First and Fourteenth Amendment rights, are different in public schools than elsewhere; the "reasonableness" inquiry cannot disregard the schools' custodial and tutelary responsibility for children. For their own good and that of their classmates, public school children are routinely required to submit to various physical examinations, and to be vaccinated against various diseases. * * * Particularly with regard to medical examinations and procedures, therefore, "students within the school environment have a lesser expectation of privacy than members of the population generally."

Legitimate privacy expectations are even less with regard to student athletes. School sports are not for the bashful. They require "suiting up" before each practice or event, and showering and changing afterwards. Public school locker rooms, the usual sites for these activities, are not notable for the privacy they afford. The locker rooms in Vernonia are typical: no individual dressing rooms are provided; shower heads are lined up along a wall, unseparated by any sort of partition or curtain; not even all the toilet stalls have doors. As the United States Court of Appeals for the Seventh Circuit has noted, there is "an element of 'communal undress' inherent in athletic participation".

There is an additional respect in which school athletes have a reduced expectation of privacy. By choosing to "go out for the team," they voluntarily subject themselves to a degree of regulation even higher than that imposed on students generally. * * * Somewhat like adults who choose to participate in a "closely regulated industry," students who voluntarily participate in school athletics have reason to expect intrusions upon normal rights and privileges, including privacy.

Having considered the scope of the legitimate expectation of privacy at issue here, we turn next to the character of the intrusion that is complained of. We recognized in *Skinner* that collecting the samples for urinalysis intrudes upon "an excretory function traditionally shielded by great privacy." We noted, however, that the degree of intrusion depends upon the manner in which production of the urine sample is monitored. Under the District's Policy, male students produce samples at a urinal along a wall. They remain fully clothed and are only observed from behind, if at all. Female students produce samples in an enclosed stall, with a female monitor standing outside listening only for sounds of tampering. These conditions are nearly identical to those typically encountered in public restrooms, which men, women, and especially school children use daily. Under such conditions, the privacy interests compromised by the process of obtaining the urine sample are in our view negligible.

The other privacy-invasive aspect of urinalysis is, of course, the information it discloses concerning the state of the subject's body, and the materials he has ingested. In this regard it is significant that the tests at issue here look only for drugs, and not for whether the student is, for example, epileptic, pregnant, or diabetic. Moreover, the drugs for which the samples are screened are standard, and do not vary according to the identity of the student. And finally, the results of the tests are disclosed only to a limited class of school personnel who have a need to know; and they are not turned over to law enforcement authorities or used for any internal disciplinary function.

Respondents argue, however, that the District's Policy is in fact more intrusive than this suggests, because it requires the students, if they are to avoid sanctions for a falsely positive test, to identify in advance prescription medications they are taking. We agree that this raises some cause for concern * * * [but we conclude] that the invasion of privacy was not significant.

Finally, we turn to consider the nature and immediacy of the governmental concern at issue here, and the efficacy of this means for meeting it. In both *Skinner* and *Von Raab*, we characterized the government interest motivating the search as "compelling." Relying on these cases, the District Court held that because the District's program also called for drug testing in the absence of individualized suspicion, the District "must demonstrate a 'compelling need' for the program." The Court of Appeals appears to have agreed with this view. It is a mistake, however, to think that the phrase "compelling state interest," in the Fourth Amendment context, describes a fixed, minimum quantum of governmental concern, so that one can dispose of a case by answering in isolation the question: Is there a compelling state interest here? Rather, the phrase describes an interest which appears important enough to justify the particular search at hand, in light of other factors which show the search to be relatively intrusive upon a genuine expectation of privacy. Whether that relatively high degree of government concern is necessary in this case or not, we think it is met.

That the nature of the concern is important—indeed, perhaps compelling—can hardly be doubted. Deterring drug use by our Nation's schoolchildren is at least as important as enhancing efficient enforcement of the Nation's laws against the importation of drugs, which was the governmental concern in *Von Raab*, or deterring drug use by engineers and trainmen, which was the governmental concern in *Skinner*. School years are the time when the physical, psychological, and addictive effects of drugs are most severe. * * * And of course the effects of a drug-infested school are visited not just upon the users, but upon the entire student body and faculty, as the educational process is disrupted. * * * Finally, it must not be lost sight of that this program is directed more narrowly to drug use by school athletes, where the risk of immediate physical harm to the drug user or those with whom he is playing his sport is particularly high. Apart from psychological effects, which include impairment of judgment, slow reaction time, and a lessening of the perception of pain, the particular drugs screened by the District's Policy have been demonstrated to pose substantial physical risks to athletes. * * *

As for the immediacy of the District's concerns: We are not inclined to question—indeed, we could not possibly find clearly erroneous—the District Court's conclusion that "a large segment of the student body, particularly those involved in interscholastic athletics, was in a state of rebellion," that "[d]isciplinary actions had reached 'epidemic proportions,'" and that "the rebellion was being fueled by alcohol and drug abuse as well as by the student's misperceptions about the drug culture." * * * As to the efficacy of this means for addressing the problem: It seems to us self-evident that a drug problem largely fueled by the "role model" effect of athletes' drug use, and of particular danger to athletes, is effectively addressed by making sure that athletes do not use drugs. Respondents argue that a "less intrusive means to the same end" was available, namely, "drug testing on suspicion of drug use." We have repeatedly refused to declare that only the "least intrusive" search practicable can be reasonable under the Fourth Amendment. Respondents' alternative entails substantial difficulties—if it is indeed practicable at all. It may be impracticable, for one thing, simply because the parents who are willing to accept random drug testing for athletes are not willing to accept accusatory drug testing for all students, which transforms the process into a badge of shame. Respondents' proposal brings the risk that teachers will impose testing arbitrarily upon troublesome but not drug-likely students. It generates the expense of defending lawsuits that charge such arbitrary imposition, or that simply demand greater process before accusatory drug testing is imposed. And not least of all, it adds to the ever-expanding diversionary duties of schoolteachers the new function of spotting and bringing to account drug abuse, a task for which they are ill prepared, and which is not readily compatible with their vocation. * * * In many respects, we think, testing based on "suspicion" of drug use would not be better, but worse.

Taking into account all the factors we have considered above—the decreased expectation of privacy, the relative unobtrusiveness of the search, and the severity of the need met by the search we conclude Vernonia's Policy is reasonable and hence constitutional.

We caution against the assumption that suspicionless drug testing will readily pass constitutional muster in other contexts. The most significant element in this case is the first we discussed: that the Policy was undertaken in furtherance of the government's responsibilities, under a public school system, as guardian and tutor of children entrusted to its care. * * * [W]hen the government acts as guardian and tutor the relevant question is whether the search is one that a reasonable guardian and tutor might undertake. Given the findings of need made by the District Court, we conclude that in the present case it is. * * *

We therefore vacate the judgment, and remand the case to the Court of Appeals for further proceedings consistent with this opinion.

It is so ordered.

JUSTICE GINSBURG, concurring. The Court constantly observes that the School District's drug-testing policy applies only to students who voluntarily participate in interscholastic athletics. * * * Correspondingly, the most severe sanction allowed under the District's policy is suspension from extracurricular athletic programs. I comprehend the Court's opinion as reserving the question whether the District, on no more than the showing made here, constitutionally could impose routine drug testing not only on those seeking to engage with others in team sports, but on all students required to attend school. * * *

JUSTICE O'CONNOR, with whom JUSTICE STEVENS and JUSTICE SOUTER join, dissenting. The population of our Nation's public schools, grades 7 through 12, numbers around 18 million. By the reasoning of today's decision, the millions of these students who participate in interscholastic sports, an overwhelming majority of whom have given school officials no reason whatsoever to suspect they use drugs at school, are open to an intrusive bodily search. In justifying this result, the Court dispenses with a requirement of individualized suspicion on considered policy grounds. First, it explains that precisely because every student athlete is being tested, there is no concern that school officials might act arbitrarily in choosing who to test. Second, a broad-based search regime, the Court reasons, dilutes the accusatory nature of the search. In making these policy arguments, of course, the Court sidesteps powerful, countervailing privacy concerns. Blanket searches, because they can involve "thousands or millions" of searches, "pos[e] a greater threat to liberty" than do suspicion-based ones, which "affec[t] one person at a time". Searches based on individualized suspicion also afford potential targets considerable control over whether they will, in fact, be searched because a person can avoid such a search by not acting in an objectively suspicious way. And given that the surest way to avoid acting suspiciously is to avoid the underlying wrongdoing, the costs of such a regime, one would think, are minimal.

But whether a blanket search is "better" than a regime based on individualized suspicion is not a debate in which we should engage. In my view, it is not open to judges or government officials to decide on policy grounds which is better and which is worse. For most of our constitutional history, mass, suspicionless searches have been generally considered per se unreasonable within the meaning of the Fourth Amendment. And we have allowed exceptions in recent years only where it has been clear that a suspicion-based regime would be ineffectual. Because that is not the case here, I dissent. * * *

Perhaps most telling of all, as reflected in the text of the Warrant Clause, the particular way the Framers chose to curb the abuses of general warrants—and by implication, all general searches—was not to impose a novel "evenhandedness" requirement; it was to retain the individualized suspicion requirement contained in the typical general warrant, but to make that requirement meaningful and enforceable, for instance, by raising the required level of individualized suspicion to objective probable cause. * * *

The view that mass, suspicionless searches, however evenhanded, are generally unreasonable remains inviolate in the criminal law enforcement context. * * * It is worth noting in this regard that state-compelled, state-monitored collection and testing of urine, while perhaps not the most intrusive of searches, is still "particularly destructive of privacy and offensive to personal dignity." We have not hesitated to treat monitored bowel movements as highly intrusive (even in the special border search context). * * * And certainly monitored urination combined with urine testing is more intrusive than some personal searches we have said trigger Fourth Amendment protections in the past. Finally, the collection and testing of urine is, of course, a search of a person, one of only four categories of suspect searches the Constitution mentions by name. * * *

Outside the criminal context, however, in response to the exigencies of modern life, our cases have upheld several evenhanded blanket searches, including some that are more than minimally intrusive, after balancing the invasion of privacy against the government's strong need. Most of these cases, of course, are distinguishable insofar as they involved searches either not of a personally intrusive nature, such as searches of closely regulated businesses, or arising in unique contexts such as prisons. * * *

In any event, in many of the cases that can be distinguished on the grounds suggested above and, more important, in all of the cases that cannot, we upheld the suspicionless search only after first recognizing the Fourth Amendment's longstanding preference for a suspicion-based search regime, and then pointing to sound reasons why such a regime would likely be ineffectual under the unusual circumstances presented. * * * "In limited circumstances, where the privacy interests implicated by the search are minimal, and where an important governmental interest furthered by the intrusion would be placed in jeopardy by a requirement of individualized suspicion, a search may be reasonable despite the absence of such suspicion." The obvious negative implication of this reasoning is that, if such an individualized suspicion requirement would not place the government's objectives in jeopardy, the requirement should not be forsaken. * * *

As an initial matter, I have serious doubts whether the Court is right * * * that a suspicion-based regime will lead to the testing of "troublesome but not drug-likely" students, [because] the required level of suspicion in the school context is objectively reasonable suspicion. * * * Moreover, any distress arising from what turns out to be a false accusation can be minimized by keeping the entire process confidential.

For another thing, the District's concern for the adversarial nature of a suspicion-based regime (which appears to extend even to those who are rightly accused) seems to ignore the fact that such a regime would not exist in a vacuum. Schools already have adversarial, disciplinary schemes that require teachers and administrators in many areas besides drug use to investigate student wrongdoing (often by means of accusatory searches); to make determinations about whether the wrongdoing occurred; and to impose punishment. To such a scheme, suspicion-based drug testing would be only a minor addition. * * * The high number of disciplinary referrals in the record in this case illustrates the District's robust scheme in action. * * *

But having misconstrued the fundamental role of the individualized suspicion requirement in Fourth Amendment analysis, the Court never seriously engages the practicality of such a requirement in the instant case. And that failure is crucial because nowhere is it less clear that an individualized suspicion requirement would be ineffectual than in the school context. In most schools, the entire pool of potential search targets—students—is under constant supervision by teachers and administrators and coaches, be it in classrooms, hallways, or locker rooms.

The record here indicates that the Vernonia schools are no exception. The great irony of this case is that most (though not all) of the evidence the District introduced to justify its suspicionless drug-testing program consisted of first-or second-hand stories of particular, identifiable students acting in ways that plainly gave rise to reasonable suspicion of in-school drug use and thus that would have justified a drug-related search under our *T.L.O.* decision. * * *

I do not believe that suspicionless drug testing is justified on these facts. But even if I agreed that some such testing were reasonable here, I see two other Fourth Amendment flaws in the District's program. First, and most serious, there is virtually no evidence in the record of a drug problem at the Washington Grade School, which includes the 7th and 8th grades, and which Acton attended when this litigation began. * * *

Second, even as to the high school, I find unreasonable the school's choice of student athletes as the class to subject to suspicionless testing—a choice that appears to have been driven more by a belief in what would pass constitutional muster, (indicating that the original program was targeted at students involved in any extracurricular activity), than by a belief in what was required to meet the District's principal disciplinary concern. * * *

On this record, then, it seems to me that the far more reasonable choice would have been to focus on the class of students found to have violated published school rules against severe disruption in class and around campus, disruption that had a strong nexus to drug use. * * * Such a choice would share two of the virtues of a suspicion-based regime: testing dramatically fewer students, tens as against hundreds, and giving students control, through their behavior, over the likelihood that they would be tested. Moreover, there would be a reduced concern for the accusatory nature of the search, because the Court's feared "badge of shame" would already exist, due to the antecedent accusation and finding of severe disruption. * * *

Having reviewed the record here, I cannot avoid the conclusion that the District's suspicionless policy of testing all student-athletes sweeps too broadly, and too imprecisely, to be reasonable under the Fourth Amendment.

NOTES

1) ***Skinner* and *Von Raab* as the Rationale of *Vernonia*** In *Skinner v. Railway Labor Executives' Association*, 489 U.S. 602, 109 S.Ct. 1402, 103 L.Ed.2d 639 (1989), the Supreme Court ruled that Federal Railroad Administration regulations requiring drug and alcohol testing of railroad employees involved in accidents without a warrant or reasonable suspicion were "reason-

able" under the Fourth Amendment because of the compelling governmental interest in assuring security in "safety-sensitive tasks" and the balance of public and private interests involved. "The Government's interest in regulating the conduct of railroad employees to ensure safety, like its supervision of probationers or regulated industries, or its operations of a government office, school, or prison, likewise presents 'special needs' beyond normal law enforcement that may justify departures from the usual warrant and probable cause requirements." *Id.* at 1414. By contrast, "the expectations of privacy of covered employees are diminished by reason of their participation in an industry that is regulated pervasively to ensure safety, a goal dependent, in substantial part, on the health and fitness of covered employees." *Id.* at 1418. Finally, "the government interest in testing without a showing of individualized suspicion is compelling. Employees subject to the tests discharge duties fraught with such risks of injury to others that even a momentary lapse of attention can have disastrous consequences." *Id.* at 1419.

In *National Treasury Employees Union v. Von Raab*, 489 U.S. 656, 109 S.Ct. 1384, 103 L.Ed.2d 685 (1989), the Supreme Court upheld the United States Customs Service employee drug testing program which did not require a warrant or individualized suspicion when employees applied for promotion to positions involving interdiction of illegal drugs or which required them to carry firearms. In addition to noting the compelling governmental interest in detecting drug use among customs employees, the Court also noted that " 'operational realities of the workplace' may render entirely reasonable certain work-related intrusions by supervisors that might be viewed as unreasonable in other contexts." *Id.* at 1393–94. "[T]he government has a compelling interest in ensuring that front-line interdiction personnel are physically fit, and have unimpeachable integrity and judgment." *Id.* at 1393. The Court noted that just as military personnel are subject to intrusive inquiries into their physical fitness and employees of the U.S. Mint expect routine personal searches when they leave the workplace, customs officials have a "diminished expectation of privacy." "[E]mployees involved in drug interdiction reasonably should expect effective inquiry into their fitness and probity. Much the same is true of employees who are required to carry firearms. Because successful performance of their duties depends uniquely on their judgment and dexterity, these employees cannot reasonably expect to keep from the Service personal information that bears directly on their fitness." *Id.* at 1394.

How do the analyses in *Skinner* and *Von Raab* affect the reasonableness of suspicionless urinalyses for students? What interests are the drug test in *Skinner* and *Von Raab* designed to vindicate? In *Acton*? May a school district require all students to take a "Comprehensive Medical Examination" to "identify the existence of any physical defects, illnesses, or communicable diseases?" Because the school district routinely collects urine samples as part of the physical examination to identify other illnesses, may it also analyze the samples to identify any drug and alcohol use by the pupils? Why or why not? Suppose the school district argues that alcohol and drug use/abuse are an illness? *See Odenheim v. Carlstadt–East Rutherford Regional School District*, 211 N.J.Super. 54, 510 A.2d 709 (Ch. 1985); *Anable v. Ford*, 653 F.Supp. 22 (W.D. Ark. 1985); *Schaill v. Tippecanoe County School Corporation*, 864 F.2d

1309 (7th Cir. 1988). *See* Paul Gillow, "Compulsory Urinalysis of Public School Students: An Unconstitutional Search and Seizure," 18 *Colum. Human Rights L. Rev.* 111 (1986). Reconsider Justice Powell's concurrence in *T.L.O.* on students' expectations of privacy? What is a student athlete's "expectation of privacy" where there is an "element of 'communal undress' inherent in athletic programs," where physical exams are a common prerequisite to participation, and where professional and collegiate athletes are subject to drug testing?

2) Scope of *Vernonia* and Application to Students in Other Extra-curricular Activities The majority in *Acton* emphasized that the school directed its suspicionless-search "more narrowly to drug use by school athletes, where the risk of immediate physical harm to the drug user or those with whom he is playing his sport is particularly high." This also provided the basis for Justice Ginsburg's concurrence in *Acton*. For several years, the question remained whether a school district could implement a broader random testing program that placed students participating in all extracurricular activities into the drug testing pool, for example, those who participate in debate, chess club, and dramatics or who wish to attend a school dance. The Supreme Court gave its answer in **Board of Education of Independent School District No. 92 of Pottawatomie County v. Earls**, 536 U.S. 822, 122 S.Ct. 2559, 153 L.Ed.2d 735 (2002), in which Justice THOMAS delivered the 5–4 opinion of the Court:

The Student Activities Drug Testing Policy * * * requires all students who participate in competitive extracurricular activities—[such as the Academic Team, Future Farmers of America, Future Homemakers of America, band, choir, pom-pom, cheerleading, and athletics]—to submit to drug testing. Because this Policy reasonably serves the School District's important interest in detecting and preventing drug use among its students, we hold that it is constitutional. * * *

Under the Policy, students are required to take a drug test before participating in an extracurricular activity, must submit to random drug testing while participating in that activity, and must agree to be tested at any time upon reasonable suspicion. The urinalysis tests are designed to detect only the use of illegal drugs, including amphetamines, marijuana, cocaine, opiates, and barbituates, not medical conditions or the presence of authorized prescription medications. * * *

In *Vernonia,* this Court held that the suspicionless drug testing of athletes was constitutional. The Court, however, did not simply authorize all school drug testing, but rather conducted a fact-specific balancing of the intrusion on the children's Fourth Amendment rights against the promotion of legitimate governmental interests. Applying the principles of *Vernonia* to the somewhat different facts of this case, we conclude that Tecumseh's Policy is also constitutional.

We first consider the nature of the privacy interest allegedly compromised by the drug testing. As in *Vernonia,* the context of the public school environment serves as the backdrop for the analysis of the privacy interest at stake and the reasonableness of the drug testing policy in general.

A student's privacy interest is limited in a public school environment where the State is responsible for maintaining discipline, health, and safety. Schoolchildren are routinely required to submit to physical examinations and vaccinations against disease. * * * Securing order in the school environment sometimes requires that students be subjected to greater controls than those appropriate for adults.

Respondents argue that because children participating in nonathletic extracurricular activities are not subject to regular physicals and communal undress, they have a stronger expectation of privacy than the athletes tested in *Vernonia.* This distinction, however, was not essential to our decision in *Vernonia,* which depended primarily upon the school's custodial responsibility and authority.

In any event, students who participate in competitive extracurricular activities voluntarily subject themselves to many of the same intrusions on their privacy as do athletes. Some of these clubs and activities require occasional off-campus travel and communal undress. All of them have their own rules and requirements for participating students that do not apply to the student body as a whole. * * * This regulation of extracurricular activities further diminishes the expectation of privacy among schoolchildren. We therefore conclude that the students affected by this Policy have a limited expectation of privacy.

Next, we consider the character of the intrusion imposed by the Policy. Urination is "an excretory function traditionally shielded by great privacy." But the "degree of intrusion" on one's privacy caused by collecting a urine sample "depends upon the manner in which production of the urine sample is monitored." * * * This procedure is virtually identical to that reviewed in *Vernonia,* except that it additionally protects privacy by allowing male students to produce their samples behind a closed stall. Given that we considered the method of collection in *Vernonia* a "negligible" intrusion, the method here is even less problematic. * * *

Moreover, the test results are not turned over to any law enforcement authority. Nor do the test results here lead to the imposition of discipline or have any academic consequences. Rather, the only consequence of a failed drug test is to limit the student's privilege of participating in extracurricular activities. Indeed, a student may test positive for drugs twice and still be allowed to participate in extracurricular activities. * * * Given the minimally intrusive nature of the sample collection and the limited uses to which the test results are put, we conclude that the invasion of students' privacy is not significant.

Finally, this Court must consider the nature and immediacy of the government's concerns and the efficacy of the Policy in meeting them. This Court has already articulated in detail the importance of the governmental concern in preventing drug use by schoolchildren. The drug abuse problem among our Nation's youth has hardly abated since *Vernonia* was decided in 1995. * * * Indeed, the nationwide drug epidemic makes the war against drugs a pressing concern in every school.

Additionally, the School District in this case has presented specific evidence of drug use at Tecumseh schools. * * * We decline to second-guess the finding of the District Court that "[v]iewing the evidence as a whole, it cannot be reasonably disputed that the [School District] was faced with a 'drug problem' when it adopted the Policy." * * *

Furthermore, this Court has not required a particularized or pervasive drug problem before allowing the government to conduct suspicionless drug testing. For instance, in *Von Raab* the Court upheld the drug testing of customs officials on a purely preventive basis, without any documented history of drug use by such officials. * * * Likewise, the need to prevent and deter the substantial harm of childhood drug use provides the necessary immediacy for a school testing policy. Indeed, it would make little sense to require a school district to wait for a substantial portion of its students to begin using drugs before it was allowed to institute a drug testing program designed to deter drug use. * * *

Respondents also argue that the testing of nonathletes does not implicate any safety concerns, and that safety is a "crucial factor" in applying the special needs framework. They contend that there must be "surpassing safety interests," or "extraordinary safety and national security hazards," in order to override the usual protections of the Fourth Amendment. Respondents are correct that safety factors into the special needs analysis, but the safety interest furthered by drug testing is undoubtedly substantial for all children, athletes and nonathletes alike. We know all too well that drug use carries a variety of health risks for children, including death from overdose.

We also reject respondents' argument that drug testing must presumptively be based upon an individualized reasonable suspicion of wrongdoing because such a testing regime would be less intrusive. In this context, the Fourth Amendment does not require a finding of individualized suspicion and we decline to impose such a requirement on schools attempting to prevent and detect drug use by students. Moreover, we question whether testing based on individualized suspicion in fact would be less intrusive. Such a regime would place an additional burden on public school teachers who are already tasked with the difficult job of maintaining order and discipline. A program of individualized suspicion might unfairly target members of unpopular groups. The fear of lawsuits resulting from such targeted searches may chill enforcement of the program, rendering it ineffective in combating drug use. * * *

Finally, we find that testing students who participate in extracurricular activities is a reasonably effective means of addressing the School District's legitimate concerns in preventing, deterring, and detecting drug use. * * * [W]e hold only that Tecumseh's Policy is a reasonable means of furthering the School District's important interest in preventing and deterring drug use among its schoolchildren. Accordingly, we reverse the judgment of the Court of Appeals.

Justice GINSBURG, with whom Justice STEVENS, JUSTICE O'CONNOR, and JUSTICE SOUTER join, dissenting. Seven years ago, in *Vernonia School Dist. 47J v. Acton*, this Court determined that a school district's policy of randomly testing the urine of its student athletes for illicit drugs did not violate the Fourth Amendment. In so ruling, the Court emphasized that drug use "increase[d] the risk of sports-related injury" and that Vernonia's athletes were the "leaders" of an aggressive local "drug culture" that had reached " 'epidemic proportions.' " Today, the Court relies upon *Vernonia* to permit a school district with a drug problem its superintendent repeatedly described as "not ... major," to test the urine of an academic team member solely by reason of her participation in a nonathletic, competitive extracurricular activity—participation associated with neither special dangers from, nor particular predilections for, drug use. * * * The particular testing program upheld today is not reasonable, it is capricious, even perverse: Petitioners' policy targets for testing a student population least likely to be at risk from illicit drugs and their damaging effects. I therefore dissent. * * *

The *Vernonia* Court concluded that a public school district facing a disruptive and explosive drug abuse problem sparked by members of its athletic teams had "special needs" that justified suspicionless testing of district athletes as a condition of their athletic participation.

This case presents circumstances dispositively different from those of *Vernonia.* True, as the Court stresses, Tecumseh students participating in competitive extracurricular activities other than athletics share two relevant characteristics with the athletes of *Vernonia.* First, both groups attend public schools. * * * Concern for student health and safety is basic to the school's caretaking, and it is undeniable that "drug use carries a variety of health risks for children, including death from overdose."

Those risks, however, are present for *all* schoolchildren. *Vernonia* cannot be read to endorse invasive and suspicionless drug testing of all students upon any evidence of drug use, solely because drugs jeopardize the life and health of those who use them. Many children, like many adults, engage in dangerous activities on their own time; that the children are enrolled in school scarcely allows government to monitor all such activities. If a student has a reasonable subjective expectation of privacy in the personal items she brings to school, surely she has a similar expectation regarding the chemical composition of her urine. Had the *Vernonia* Court agreed that public school attendance, in and of itself, permitted the State to test each student's blood or urine for drugs, the opinion in *Vernonia* could have saved many words.

The second commonality to which the Court points is the voluntary character of both interscholastic athletics and other competitive extracurricular activities. * * * Students "volunteer" for extracurricular pursuits in the same way they might volunteer for honors classes: They subject themselves to additional requirements, but they do so in order to take full advantage of the education offered them.

Voluntary participation in athletics has a distinctly different dimension: Schools regulate student athletes discretely because competitive school sports by their nature require communal undress and, more important, expose students to physical risks that schools have a duty to mitigate. For the very reason that schools cannot offer a program of competitive athletics without intimately affecting the privacy of students, *Vernonia* reasonably analogized school athletes to "adults who choose to participate in a closely regulated industry." * * *

Not only did the Vernonia and Tecumseh districts confront drug problems of distinctly different magnitudes, they also chose different solutions: Vernonia limited its policy to athletes; Tecumseh indiscriminately subjected to testing all participants in competitive extracurricular activities. * * * Notwithstanding nightmarish images of out-of-control flatware, livestock run amok, and colliding tubas disturbing the peace and quiet of Tecumseh, the great majority of students the School District seeks to test in truth are engaged in activities that are not safety sensitive to an unusual degree. There is a difference between imperfect tailoring and no tailoring at all. * * *

Nationwide, students who participate in extracurricular activities are significantly less likely to develop substance abuse problems than are their less-involved peers. Even if students might be deterred from drug use in order to preserve their extracurricular eligibility, it is at least as likely that other students might forgo their extracurricular involvement in order to avoid detection of their drug use. Tecumseh's policy thus falls short doubly if deterrence is its aim: It invades the privacy of students who need deterrence least, and risks steering students at greatest risk for substance abuse away from extracurricular involvement that potentially may palliate drug problems.

To summarize, this case resembles *Vernonia* only in that the School Districts in both cases conditioned engagement in activities outside the obligatory curriculum on random subjection to urinalysis. The defining characteristics of the two programs, however, are entirely dissimilar. The Vernonia district sought to test a subpopulation of students distinguished by their reduced expectation of privacy, their special susceptibility to drug-related injury, and their heavy involvement with drug use. The Tecumseh district seeks to test a much larger population associated with none of these factors. It does so, moreover, without carefully safeguarding student confidentiality and without regard to the program's untoward effects. A program so sweeping is not sheltered by *Vernonia;* its unreasonable reach renders it impermissible under the Fourth Amendment. * * *

3) Lower Court Reservations about *Vernonia* and *Earls* In **York v. Wahkiakum School District No. 200**, 163 Wash.2d 297, 178 P.3d 995 (WA 2008), the Washington Supreme Court interpreted a provision of the state constitution—"No person shall be disturbed in his private affairs, or his home invaded, without authority of law." Wash. Const. art. I, § 7—to give student athletes greater protection than that which the Court in *Vernonia* and *Earls* granted under the Fourth Amendment. The *York* Court's analysis considered whether the state's action to require a urine sample disturbed his privacy and whether the law justified the intrusion. Notwithstanding student athletes' greater regulation and reduced privacy in the locker room, *York* viewed collecting urine samples to be a significant intrusion on students' privacy. *York* rejected the state's legal justification that school conditions posed unique circumstances and declined to adopt *Vernonia*'s "special needs" exception in its interpretation of the state constitution. The Court feared that the "special needs" exception would provide no basis on which "to draw a principled line permitting drug testing only student athletes. If we were to allow random drug testing here, what prevents school districts from either later drug testing students participating in any extracurricular activities, as federal courts now allow, or testing the entire student population?"

In **Theodore v. Delaware Valley School Dist.**, 575 Pa. 321, 836 A.2d 76 (Pa.,2003), the Pennsylvania Supreme Court interpreted Article I., § 8 of the state constitution to require a more particularized showing by the school district of the need to conduct random drug-tests. The court noted that "the unique policy concerns safeguarding the individual right to privacy in Pennsylvania bring a greater degree of scrutiny to all searches where the protection of Article I, Section 8 is invoked" and that it "mandate[s] greater scrutiny in the school environment." The Court's state constitutional test in the school environment balances four factors: (1) the students' privacy interests, (2) the nature of the intrusion created by the search, (3) notice, and (4) the overall purpose to be achieved by the search and the immediate reasons prompting the decision to conduct the actual search. Examining those factors, *Theodore* noted "First, since the students' privacy rights here—rights which were rather summarily dismissed by *Earls*—have greater meaning under Article I, Section 8, the testing authorized by the District cannot be viewed as a trivial incursion on privacy." While acknowledging the need to combat and deter drugs, the court also analyzed the efficacy and reasonableness of selecting the targeted students for testing. "Although we do not for a moment downplay the seriousness of student use of drugs and alcohol, in this post-Columbine High School era otherwise-undetected alcohol and drug use by some students does not present the same sort of immediate and serious danger that is presented when students introduce weapons into schools. But, even if it did, the over- and under-inclusive means chosen by the District are not likely to accomplish the objective." The court concluded that "the suspicionless search policy at issue has not been supported by sufficient proof that there is an actual drug problem in the Delaware Valley School District; by individualized proof that the targeted students are at all likely to be part of whatever drug problem may (or may not) exist; or by reasonable proof that the policy actually addresses whatever drug problem may exist."

4) Efficacy of Drug–Testing as a Drug–Use Prevention Strategy Although the school administrators in *Vernonia* and *Earls* and some Supreme Court justices apparently believe that random drug-testing will prevent student drug use, whether such strategies actually reduce drug use is an empirical question. **Ryoko Yamaguchi, Lloyd D. Johnston, Patrick M. O'Malley, "Relationship Between Student Illicit Drug Use and School Drug–Testing Policies," 73 *J. School Health* 159 (2003),** used data on adolescent drug-use from self-administered questionnaires given to nationally representative samples of students in grades 8, 10, and 12, and obtained information on school characteristics including drug-testing policies from school administrators, and analyzed trends between 1998 and 2001. They reported that

> In the "war on drugs," schools employed a variety of mechanisms for enforcing zero-tolerance policies, including drug testing, metal detectors,

closed circuit cameras, and sniff dogs. These policies and procedures are often justified as necessary to ensure a safe, drug-free learning environment. However, drug testing can be costly for schools. A single standard drug test to detect marijuana, tobacco, cocaine, heroin, opiates, amphetamines, barbiturates, and tranquilizers can range from $14 to $30 per test, while a test for steroid use costs $100 per test. * * *

Few studies have examined the effectiveness and utility of drug testing. For example, though students in athletics and extracurricular activities may have the lowest reported drug use rates, the legal cases of *Earls* in 2002 and *Vernonia* in 1995 support the legality of schools to target these students. In addition, initiation of a school drug-testing policy usually results from an identified drug problem at a school, but little evaluation has been conducted to determine if the drug-testing policy effectively reduces the drug problem in school. In fact, some legal analysts suggest that a drug-testing policy actually may increase the problem of drugs in schools. * * *

The study addressed the following research questions: What percentage of schools employs a drug-testing policy? Which students are tested for drugs in these schools? On what basis are students tested for drugs in schools? How do characteristics of a school and its student body relate to drug testing? What relationship exists between student drug use and school drug testing. * * *

[F]rom 1998 through 2001 * * * drug testing was employed in a relatively small number of schools. Across the four years, 18.14% of schools reported using drug tests of any kind * * *.

Among groups of students drug tested during 1999–2001, students suspected of using drugs were most likely to be tested, with 14.04% of school testing such students * * * for cause and suspicion.

From 1999–2001, drug testing of students in extra curricular activities occurred in only 2.28% of schools * * *. From 1999–2001, drug testing of student athletes occurred in only 4.93% of schools * * *.

Among schools that reported any form of drug testing, the most common reason was for cause or suspicion. Across the four years, 14.15% of schools * * * tested due to cause or suspicion. * * * [S]ignificantly more high schools (22.74% * * *) reported drug testing than did middle schools (8% * * *). Similarly, socioeconomic status (SES) of schools had significant differences in drug testing, where high and low socioeconomic schools reported more drug testing (20.16% and 21.50% schools, respectively) than schools in the middle-SES category (13.20%). School size had significant differences, where large schools reported more drug testing than small schools (22.65% and 14.22% schools, respectively). In a multivariate analysis, school level and school size remained significant, while SES did not, as a predictor of drug testing. * * *

Does drug testing prevent or inhibit student drug use? Members of the Supreme Court appear to believe it does. However, among the eighth-, 10th-, and 12th-grade students surveyed in this study, school drug testing was not associated with either the prevalence or the frequency of student marijuana use, or of other illicit drug use. Nor was drug testing of athletes associated with lower-than-average marijuana and other illicit drug use by high school male athletes. * * *

In addition to effectiveness, other issues should be weighed by policy makers * * * including cost-effectiveness, false positives through poor training and handling, and alienation and resistance from students. * * *

While lack of effectiveness of drug testing is not definitive, results suggest that drug testing in schools may not provide a panacea for reducing student drug use that some (including some on the Supreme Court) had hoped. Research has shown that the strongest predictor of student drug use is students' attitudes toward drug use and perceptions of peer use. To prevent harmful student behaviors such as drug use, school policies that address these key values, attitudes, and perceptions may prove more important in drug prevention than drug testing.

Another study surveyed school principals' reactions to *Earls* and the school characteristics that influenced their decision whether or not to adopt random drug testing of students. **Cynthia Kelly Conlon, "Urineschool: A Study of the Impact of the *Earls* Decision on High School Random Drug Testing Policies," 32 *J. Law & Education* 297 (2003).** The principals who declined to implement random drug testing emphasized "the difficulty of getting support from all members of the community (especially student support), cost, and the problems with preserving confidentiality and maintaining student trust." *Id.* at 309. Conlon examined the relationship between "school functioning"—level of parental contact, instructional expenditures per pupil, chronic truancy rate, and average ACT score—and principals' decision whether or not to adopt a random drug testing policy. She reported that

In wealthy districts with high-functioning schools, parents are paying high property taxes and expecting an excellent education for their children. These parents are involved in their schools and make their views known about policies such as random drug testing. According to the principals, these parents don't want to subject their children to testing that they perceive could have negative consequences. * * * [T]hese parents have the political clout to control policy in their districts and block efforts to institute random drug testing. They also have the political savvy to make sure that the principals who are hired reflect their views * * *.

In districts with the "troubled" schools, with few financial resources and serious truancy problems and academic achievement issues, there is not enough political energy to institute random drug testing. * * * [P]arents are not involved enough in the school to have the clout to oppose such a policy, but the school has other more pressing priorities and a principal with a different agenda. * * *

The "mixed" schools are functioning adequately to serve the students. They are in the mid-range for spending and ACT scores but levels of parental contact vary. It is in these schools that the political power to institute random drug testing may tip in favor of the principals. All three of the schools that have random drug testing fall into this group * * *. In these less-wealthy districts, it may be that parents have less time to become involved in policy-making at the schools, giving the principal the freedom to pursue his own agenda with the school board. * * *

[T]he school's reaction is a function of a complex relationship among the parents, the principal and the school board. In wealthy districts, parents wield more political power and exert control over both the principal and the school board. * * *

In poorer districts with lower levels of parental contact, the principal may have more power but limited financial and human resources, making it hard to implement random drug testing. It is in the mid-level districts, where schools have adequate funding but parents are not as involved, that principals who support random drug testing have the political maneuverability to make it happen.

The most significant finding of all, however, may be that principals are making policy in the absence of data to show that random drug testing actually deters student drug use. Although intuition may suggest that testing will be a deterrent, little research has been conducted to find out if this is so. * * *

5) Academic Commentary on *Vernonia* and *Earls* Most legal analysts strongly criticized *Acton* and *Earls*. *See, e.g.,* **Irene Merker Rosenberg, "Public School Drug Testing: The Impact of *Acton*," 33 *Am. Crim. L. Rev.* 349, 377–78 (1996)**:

Such reflection might take into account that implementation of a school drug deterrence and detection program should turn not only on efficacy but also on the effect on the student's autonomy and sense of bodily integrity, their sense of fairness, and the limits of governmental power. It is not only children's bodies but also their minds and emotions that are affected by programs of this sort.

The *Acton* court, however, engaged in no such fine-tuned consideration. In a case purporting to balance governmental and individual interests and the intrusion on the latter, because the individual was a child, his interest was deemed minimal and his parents' interest nonexistent. * * * On the other hand, the competing governmental interest talismanically invoked the objective of deterring drug use in the public schools, an irresistible combination of law and order with protection of children's health. When the majority refused to offset that interest through any meaningful analysis of the need for and plausibility of Fourth Amendment constraints, such as an individualized suspicion standard, the result was preordained.

See also Carla E. Laszewski, "Gone to Pot: Student Athletes' Fourth Amendment Rights After *Vernonia School District 47J v. Acton*," 40 *St.Louis U.L.J.* 575, 610 (1996) ("While the decision directly pertains to student athletes, the possibility of wider application both in and out of the school setting exists. The Court finds all students have a decreased expectation of privacy in school. That fact coupled with the Court's preference for suspicionless testing because of the 'badge of shame' associated with a suspicion-based testing procedure, suggests other students could be subject to suspicionless testing."); Michael D.

Mosser, "Random Drug–Testing High School Student Athletes in *Vernonia School District 47J v. Acton*: Is the War on Drugs a Losing Battle for the Fourth Amendment?," 17 *Whittier L. Rev.* 527 (1996) (random drug-testing constitutes appropriate policy as confined to student athletes); Samantha Elizabeth Shutler, "Random, Suspicionless Drug Testing of High School Athletes: *Vernonia Sch. Dist. 47J v. Acton*," 86 *J.Crim.L. & Criminology* 1265, 1265 (1996) ("[T]he Supreme Court overstepped the boundaries of the Fourth Amendment in two ways: first, by finding the interest of the Vernonia District in promulgating the drug testing to be 'compelling' given the paucity of the evidence of athletes using drugs; and second, by holding that student athletes have diminished privacy expectations solely due to the structure and requirements of the athletic program.").

Commentators on *Earls* noted that nothing in the Court's holding preclude requiring mandatory random testing of all high school students. See e.g. Marcus Raymond, "Drug Testing Those Crazy Chess Club Kids: The Supreme Court Turns Away from the One Clear Path in the Maze of Special Needs Jurisprudence in *Board of Education v. Earls*," 22 *St. L. U. Public L. Rev.* 559, 589 (2003) ("[I]nstead of affirming the context-based approach used in *Vernonia* that limited drug testing to student athletes, the Court changed the context by redefining the relationship between the student and the school, leading to the allowance of drug testing students as a class. By doing so, the Court has laid the framework for a future in which all students may be forced to submit to drug tests."); Irene Merker Rosenberg, "The Public Schools Have a 'Special Need' for Their Students' Urine," 31 *Hofstra L. Rev.* 303, 315 (2002) ("[S]pecial safety concerns relating to the target group is largely irrelevant. The health of all children seems to be what is important, no matter how unstrenuous the activities in which they engage. Quarterbacks and chess club members are equal in that regard and if so, it is no small leap from that to all students, whether involved in extracurricular activities or not. After all, students could be injured during gym class or while running past each other in the halls.").

Not every commentator criticized *Vernonia*. In a thoughtful analysis of the Supreme Court's conflicted jurisprudence of education and the power of school authorities, **Anne Proffitt Dupre, "Should Students Have Constitutional Rights? Keeping Order in the Public Schools," 65 *Geo. Wash.L.Rev.* 49 at 64–70, 104–105 (1996)**, argues that the Court correctly decided *Acton* as part of a broader agenda to re-establish public authority. "By defining the nature of school power, the *Acton* Court has taken a step toward both practical and theoretical public school reform that may result in less court intervention in the day-to-day life of the classroom. The Court has defined school power such that schools possess the power of a custodian or guardian. The school power continuum, at least for Fourth Amendment purposes, has shifted to the parent end and, if some of the language in *Acton* is taken literally, may even have shifted back to *in loco parentis* power. * * * And the Court certainly has signaled to the nation that it has confidence in the public schools and educators to deal with yet another social issue: the war on drugs. * * * " Is the *in loco parentis* relationship between students and schools really the appropriate analogy or the equivalent of that of parents with their children? How many parents subject their children to random drug-testing or strip-searches?

C. CONSENT SEARCHES, "VOLUNTARINESS," AND YOUTHFULNESS

In *Schneckloth v. Bustamonte*, 412 U.S. 218, 93 S.Ct. 2041, 36 L.Ed.2d 854 (1973), the United States Supreme Court held that the standard by which to gauge the validity of a person's consent to a search was whether it was "voluntary" under the "totality of the circumstances." However, the Court did not define "voluntariness" as a "knowing choice among alternatives," but rather as a decision made in the absence of coercion. " '[V]oluntariness' has reflected an accommodation of the complex of values implicated in police questioning of a suspect. At one end of the spectrum is the acknowledged need for police questioning as a tool for the effective enforcement of criminal laws. * * * At the other end of the spectrum is the set of values reflecting society's deeply felt belief that the criminal law cannot be used as an instrument of unfairness, and that the possibility of unfair and even brutal police tactics poses a real and serious treat to civilized notions of justice." *Id.* at 224–25. The Court drew on cases assessing the "voluntariness" of a confession to inform its assessment of the "voluntariness" of a consent to search. The Court emphasized that "voluntariness" was a fact question that the Court should evaluate under the "totality of the circumstances," including factors such as "the charactcristics of the accused[,] * * * the youth of the accused, or his lack of education." *Id.* at 226. However, unlike a relinquishment of "trial rights" which requires a showing that the waiver was *"knowing, intelligent, and voluntary,"* a consent to search only need be "voluntarily given, and not the result of duress or coercion, express or implied. Voluntariness is a question of fact to be determined from all of the circumstances, and while the subject's knowledge of a right to refuse is a factor to be taken into account, the prosecution is not required to demonstrate such knowledge as a prerequisite to establishing a voluntary consent." *Id.* at 248–49.

Consent searches, as well as the materials in the next section about interrogating juveniles, raise the question of how the legal system should accommodate "youthfulness" in the justice process. Should the justice system treat juveniles like adults and use the same "totality of the circumstances" approach in assessing the validity of their decisions to relinquish legal rights, or should it provide special procedural protections to protect young people from their own immaturity and vulnerability? As you will see, courts generally decline to treat youthfulness as a categorical disability that precludes a voluntary consent or that requires additional procedural safeguards. For example, in *In re Jermaine*, 399 Pa.Super. 503, 582 A.2d 1058 (Super. Ct. Pa. 1990), the court noted that "The fact that the juvenile was sixteen and one-half years old at the time of the search, moreover, did not prevent her from giving voluntary consent to a search of her bag. 'Although age is one element to acknowledge in ascertaining when consent was given willingly, minority status alone does not prevent one from giving consent.' " *Id.* at 1064.

We will explore the issues of juveniles' competence to waive rights more fully in the context of interrogating juveniles, where legislatures and courts have grappled more extensively with the question of "what do kids know and when do they know it?" *See generally*, Lourdes M. Rosado, "Minors and the Fourth Amendment: How Juvenile Status Should Invoke Different Standards for Searches and Seizures on the Street," 71 *N.Y.U. L. Rev.* 762 (1996), who proposes that "[t]he court would apply a 'youthful' totality of the circumstances analysis in all cases, including those in which minors were advised that they could refuse consent, and they nevertheless agreed to the search. As the juvenile-confession case law informs us, a prior warning should be a necessary—although not sufficient—condition for a finding that consent to a search was voluntarily given, absent evidence that the juvenile knew he had the right to refuse consent. To assess the circumstances objectively through the eyes of the teenager, the court must take into account that a minor, as compared to an adult, would be more likely to think that he could not refuse the police officer and less likely to understand the implications of consenting." *Id.* at 791.

IN RE J.M.

619 A.2d 497 (D.C. Ct. App. 1992).

FARRELL, ASSOCIATE JUDGE. On reconsideration by the court en banc, we have decided to remand this case for explicit findings by the trial judge with respect to the key factual issue presented, namely, the bearing of appellant's age—fourteen at the time of his arrest—upon the voluntariness of his consent to the search of his person.

Appellant was adjudicated delinquent based upon a finding that he had possessed cocaine with intent to distribute it. Prior to trial, he moved to suppress the cocaine on grounds that it had been seized from him in violation of the Fourth Amendment. At the hearing on the motion, the facts established were essentially as follows. On October 31, 1989, Detective Donald Zattau and a team of Metropolitan Police officers were at the Greyhound–Trailways bus station in Northeast Washington, D.C. Their assignment was to question, and presumably search if they had cause or obtained consent, passengers arriving in or passing through Washington from New York City. At about 2:30 a.m. a bus arrived from New York en route to Wilmington, North Carolina. After the driver announced a ten-minute rest stop, Detective Zattau and two other officers boarded the bus dressed in civilian attire. Using the bus speaker system, Zattau announced their identity and purpose, explaining that they were part of a drug interdiction group that interviewed passengers arriving from New York because it was a "source supply of drugs," and in the past they had found that drugs were transported by bus passengers. After questioning other passengers, Zattau approached J.M., who was seated three-quarters of the way to the rear next to a window.

The detective introduced himself and, in a conversational voice, asked J.M.'s point of origin and destination and if he could see his bus ticket; he also asked if J.M. had heard the announcement over the speaker system, to which the youth replied that he had and understood it. Zattau asked if J.M. was carrying drugs or weapons, and when J.M. replied no, the detective asked if he could search the bag J.M. was carrying with him. J.M. consented, and the search revealed nothing. Zattau then asked if J.M. had drugs or weapons on his person; when J.M. said no, the officer asked if he would mind if he patted him down. In response J.M. turned toward the officer and raised his arms while still seated. Zattau patted him down and felt a hard object on his right side next to his rib cage. He lifted the shirt and discovered a plastic bag containing crack cocaine taped to J.M.'s body. J.M. was arrested.

J.M. testified that he was fourteen years old at the time of his arrest and fifteen at the time of the trial one and a half months later. He lived in Brooklyn, New York, and attended ninth grade. He acknowledged that he had consented to the search of his bag because he knew it contained nothing illegal and feared that if he did not consent, the police would become suspicious and investigate. He denied, however, that he had given Zattau permission to frisk him, asserting that the officer "just started patting me down." He made no effort to stop the frisk because if he had done so, the officers "would have got[ten] more suspicious at me."

In justifying the search, the government did not claim that Detective Zattau had reason to suspect appellant of a crime, but instead argued that * * * he had freely consented to the pat-down. Appellant, by contrast, argued * * * that under the totality of the circumstances his consent to the search was involuntary because he was fourteen years old at the time and "was traveling alone[,] and certainly under those circumstances, alone, black, barely a teenaged youth, would feel pressure when the police came up to him."

The trial judge denied the motion to suppress. He found, first, that J.M. had not been seized within the meaning of the Fourth Amendment merely because he was approached and questioned, and his consent to a search obtained. * * * The judge further credited Zattau's testimony that he had asked for and received J.M.'s permission before patting him down, and found that the consent was voluntary. * * * [W]hile concluding that J.M. had consented in order "to deflect suspicion from himself," the judge did not link this conclusion to any express findings about J.M.'s maturity or sophistication for his age, as shown by his conduct at the time of the search or his testimony and demeanor at the hearing. The judge did recognize that, even in the case of adults, "in these types of encounters * * * there is an inherent authority, obviously, that the officer carries with him when he is conducting this kind of an interview and asking to search a bag," but found that this authority had not coerced J.M. into consenting against his will. * * *

When the police patted him down, there unquestionably was a search of his person, which the government seeks to justify on the ground that he voluntarily consented. When the issue is voluntariness of a consent, "characteristics of the accused" become relevant, and may even be decisive. Among the factors *Schneckloth* cited as significant are "the youth of the accused; his lack of education; or his low intelligence"; and related to these may be "the lack of any advice to the accused of his constitutional rights." "[A]ccount must be taken of subtly coercive police questions, as well as the possibly vulnerable subjective state of the person who consents."

The factor in this case that has troubled the court—the division from the beginning, a majority of the entire court more recently—is the effect of appellant's age and maturity (or lack thereof) on his ability to consent voluntarily to the detective's request to frisk his body. We conclude that it is a factor critical to "the nature of [J.M.'s] subjective understanding" of his rights, and hence the validity of his consent under *Schneckloth*. But we also conclude that we cannot review the trial court's determination of consent on the basis of the findings addressing this factor so far. * * *

Sitting as the court *en banc*, we conclude that what the division correctly identified as the special vulnerability of juveniles to intimidation by figures of authority does not justify a presumptive rule invalidating consents by juveniles. *Schneckloth* emphasized that the issue of consent involves "analyzing all the circumstances of an individual consent," and this "careful sifting of the unique facts and circumstances of each case," is incompatible with isolating any "single controlling criterion" such as age and imbuing it with presumptively decisive weight in the consent analysis. * * * [I]t seems to us almost self-evident that a trial judge deciding the issue of consent by a youth must be sensitive to the heightened danger of coercion in this setting. Correspondingly, our own responsibilities as a reviewing court permit us to require that in such cases the trial judge make explicit findings on the record concerning the effect of age and relative immaturity on the voluntariness of the defendant's consent. These findings (which need not be in writing) are particularly necessary when it is conceded, as in this case, that the youth was not told he could withhold consent. * * *

We have no doubt that the experienced trial judge in this case, assigned specially to the juvenile court, was familiar with the law of seizure and consent under the Fourth Amendment and the need to consider "the setting in which the [police] conduct occurr[ed]," including the fact of J.M.'s youth. Nonetheless, we cannot properly discharge our review function on the basis of the findings apparent on the record. The judge, although aware J.M. was under fifteen at the time of the search, did not discuss this fact in explaining why the youth had voluntarily consented to the search. He did explain, after hearing testimony from Detective

Zattau and J.M., that J.M. had acceded to the request "to deflect suspicion from himself" in the hope of avoiding detection. * * * A desire to "deflect suspicion" from oneself by feigning cooperation may reveal sophistication and knowledge even by a fourteen-year-old, particularly one trusted to ferry a large amount of drugs by interstate transportation. But it may also reflect merely a belief by an inexperienced youth rightly conditioned, like most young people, to obey authority that a search will be conducted regardless of his consent—so that his only real "choice" is to pretend cooperation. Which of these hypotheses fits J.M.'s apparent cooperation must depend on an explicit evaluation of his maturity and knowledge in all the circumstances, including as one factor the failure of the police to tell him he could refuse consent. * * *

We hold that appellant was not seized prior to the conduct of the pat-down search, but remand on the issue of consent. In doing so, we reaffirm our recognition of the special ability of the trial court to decide issues of fact, including demeanor and credibility, and our willingness to defer to its judgment "where the facts admit of more than one interpretation." But this deference imposes an equal duty on the trial court to deal expressly and thoroughly with the significance of age before finding that a juvenile has consented to a search. We accordingly remand this case to the trial court for further consideration of that issue.

So ordered.

MACK, SENIOR JUDGE, dissenting, but concurring in the order of remand. * * * With the issue of consent still open, however, I want to go on record as agreeing with my colleagues that, on remand, the trial court must consider J.M.'s youth. Moreover, to speak the "unspeakable," the trial court should also consider the fact that J.M. was a fourteen year old *black* youth who had no previous involvement with the criminal justice system and who had not been advised that he could walk away or refuse to answer. * * *

When the government seeks to rely upon consent to justify the lawfulness of a search, the government bears the burden of proving that the consent was, in fact, freely and voluntarily given. Voluntariness is a question of fact to be determined from the totality of *all* the circumstances, including the characteristics of the accused, the details of the interrogation, and the failure to advise the accused of his constitutional rights. * * * Voluntariness traditionally has taken into account, *inter alia*, such evidence as a suspect's minimal schooling, low intelligence and lack of effective warnings to a suspect of his rights. Moreover, personal characteristics of the accused such as age, sex, race and even widowhood have been worth noting in the assessment of coercion. * * *

Whether the courts speak of it or not, race is a factor that has for many years engendered distrust between black males and law enforcement personnel. America's history in large measure may be responsible for this phenomenon; it is painful to remember the era when some local sheriffs, deputies, jailers, policemen and prominent citizens cooperated with purveyors of mob violence to provide punishment for blacks accused of crime. Even today, arrest statistics suggest, whatever the causes of crime, a litany of fear and distrust. Sadly, in the interest of protecting the public, these statistics can be used negatively to justify unequal treatment and thus engender hostility. To the extent that a "drug courier profile" (alluded to by the dissenting justices in *Florida v. Bostick*) might embrace race, it becomes circular exercise in institutionalized stereotyping. Our very diversity has always produced stereotyping which in turn has produced statistical data, which in turn has produced stereotyping. This in turn makes it difficult for our courts to apply meaningful legal standards consistent with our Constitution. I respectfully venture to suggest that no reasonable innocent black male (with any knowledge of American history) would feel free to ignore or walk away from a drug interdicting team. I would also suggest that if this hypothetical man was neither innocent nor reasonable, and armed, the lives of innocent people might be endangered in the close confines of a bus.

The trial court was right when it suggested that J.M. would have consented to anything. The issue, however, is whether that consent was voluntary. In determining the voluntariness of J.M.'s consent, I would factor into the totality of the circumstances the relevant characteristics of age and race, as well as the fact that appellant was not told that he was free to decline to consent to the search. I concur in remand.

NOTE

Parental Consent to Search Unlike adults, who may control their own private living arrangements, children necessarily must live with their parents or other legal guardians. In *United States v. Matlock*, 415 U.S. 164, 94 S.Ct. 988, 39 L.Ed.2d 242 (1974), the Supreme Court upheld the authority of other people to give third-party consent to a search based on their "common authority" over the premises. Thus, parents may allow police to search the home and their child's room based on either parents' right to control their child or their exercise of control over the premises. *In re Robert H.*, 78 Cal. Ap. 3d 894, 78 Cal.App.3d 894, 144 Cal.Rptr. 565 (1978). Consent based on parents' authority will prevail when the child is absent and, perhaps, even when the child is present and objects to the search. *See e.g.*, *In re Tariq A–R–Y*, 347 Md. 484, 701 A.2d 691, 692 (1997), holding that "a parent of an unemancipated minor can consent to a search of his or her child's personal belonging left in the common area of their home, over the child's objection." In *In re C.M.B. v. State*, 594 So.2d 695, 701 (Ala. Crim. App. 1991), the court held that because C.M.B. "had no legitimate expectation of privacy in his mother's bedroom where the gun was found," he lacked standing to challenge the search or to object to the validity of his mother's consent to the search. In *In re Salyer*, 44 Ill.App.3d 854, 859, 3 Ill.Dec. 648, 358 N.E.2d 1333, 1336–37 (1977), the court held that a mother may consent to the search of her 15–year–old son's room even though he kept his room locked with a combination lock on the outside and an inside lock and the mother had to knock to gain admittance to his room. "We believe that there is implicit in the rights and duties imposed upon a parent, the right to exert parental authority and control over a minor son's surroundings and that such implied right to control obviously includes a room in the home of the mother. We also conclude that the mother had at least common authority as to the room occupied by her 15–year–old child. * * * We therefore conclude that in view of the age of the child involved, the mother had the right to waive the requirement of a search warrant of a room in her house occupied by her minor child. * * *"

D. POLICE INTERROGATION OF JUVENILES

The legal issues surrounding interrogation of juveniles implicate both the punitive or rehabilitative roles of juvenile courts, and the developmental competence of children as opposed to adults. Recall from Julian Mack, "The Juvenile Court," *supra,* the Progressive reformers envisioned a non-adversarial juvenile courts in which judges presided as "benevolent fathers" and who thought it "best to try to persuade the child to bare his soul." *See also* Francis Barry McCarthy, "Pre–Adjudicatory Rights in Juvenile Court: An Historical and Constitutional Analysis," 42 *U. Pitt. L. Rev.* 457, 485 (1981). If, as many religions' teachings hold, confession is "good for the soul," then why are police interrogation and juvenile court judges' colloquies with juveniles so problematic?

The United States Supreme Court long has recognized that a youth's age and inexperience may affect the validity of waivers of constitutional rights and the voluntariness of confessions. Long before *Gault,* the Court instructed trial judges to be particularly sensitive to the dangers of unreliability and unfairness in the interrogation of juveniles. In **Haley v. Ohio**, 332 U.S. 596, 68 S.Ct. 302, 92 L.Ed. 224 (1948), police interrogated a fifteen-year-old "lad" in relays beginning shortly after midnight, denied him access to counsel, and confronted him with confessions of co-defendants before he finally confessed at five o'clock a.m. The Supreme Court reversed his conviction, ruling that a confession obtained under these circumstances was "involuntary":

> What transpired would make us pause for careful inquiry if a mature man was involved. And when, as here, a mere child—an easy victim of the law—is before us, special care in scrutinizing the record must be used. Age 15 is a tender and difficult age for a boy of any race. He cannot be judged by the more exacting standards of maturity. That which would leave a man cold and unimpressed can overawe and overwhelm a lad in his early teens. This is the period of great instability which the crisis of adolescence produces. * * * [W]e cannot believe that a lad of tender years is a match for the police in such a contest. He needs counsel and support if he is not to become the victim first of fear, then of panic. * * *

> The age of petitioner, the hours when he was grilled, the duration of his quizzing, the fact that he had no friend or counsel to advise him, the callous attitude of the police toward his rights combine to con-

vince us that this was a confession wrung from a child by means which the law should not sanction. *Id.* at 599–601.

In **Gallegos v. Colorado**, 370 U.S. 49, 82 S.Ct. 1209, 8 L.Ed.2d 325 (1962), the police extracted a confession from "a child of 14." The Court reiterated that the youth of the accused is a special circumstance that may affect the voluntariness of a confession and re-emphasized the vulnerability of youth:

> But a 14–year–old boy, no matter how sophisticated, is unlikely to have any conception of what will confront him when he is made accessible only to the police. * * * [W]e deal with a person who is not equal to the police in knowledge and understanding of the consequences of the questions and answers being recorded and who is unable to know how to protect his own interests or how to get the benefits of his constitutional rights. * * *

> A lawyer or an adult relative or friend could have given the petitioner the protection which his own immaturity could not. Adult advice would have put him on a less unequal footing with his interrogators. Without some adult protection against this inequality, a 14–year–old boy would not be able to know, let alone assert, such constitutional rights as he had. *Id.* at 54.

In both *Gallegos* and *Haley*, the Supreme Court considered the admissibility of confessions made by juveniles, employed the "voluntariness" test, and concluded that youthfulness was a "special circumstance" that required close judicial scrutiny. The Court's primary concern focused on the special vulnerability of children, the reliability of juveniles' confessions, and the accuracy of the fact-finding process.

In **In re Gault**, 387 U.S. 1, 87 S.Ct. 1428, 18 L.Ed.2d 527 (1967), the Court repeated that "admissions and confessions of juveniles require special caution," *id.* at 45, and suggested that "[e]ven greater protection might be required where juveniles are involved, since their immaturity and greater vulnerability place them at a greater disadvantage in their dealings with police." *Id.* at 55. Thus, the Court long had recognized that youths are not the equals of adults in the interrogation room and that they require greater procedural safeguards than adults, such as the presence of counsel, to compensate for their vulnerability and susceptibility to coercive influences. Although *Gault* recognized that the Fifth Amendment contributed to accurate fact finding and reliable confessions, the Court emphasized that it also functioned to reduce governmental oppression and to maintain a proper balance between the individual and the state:

> The privilege against self-incrimination is, of course, related to the question of the safeguards necessary to assure that admissions or confessions are reasonably trustworthy, that they are not mere fruits of fear or coercion, but are reliable expressions of the truth. The roots of the privilege are, however, far deeper. They tap the basic stream of religious and political principle because the privilege reflects the

limits of the individual's attornment to the state and—in a philosophical sense—insists upon the equality of the individual and the state. In other words, the privilege has a broader and deeper thrust than the rule which prevents the use of confessions which are the product of coercion because coercion is thought to carry with it the danger of unreliability. One of its purposes is to prevent the state, whether by force or by psychological domination, from overcoming the mind and will of the person under investigation and depriving him of the freedom to decide whether to assist the state in securing his conviction. *Id.* at 47.

The *Gault* Court cited *Miranda v. Arizona*, 384 U.S. 436, 86 S.Ct. 1602, 16 L.Ed.2d 694 (1966), as authority for the assertion that persons, even juveniles, cannot be compelled to testify against themselves. *Gault*, 387 U.S. at 50 n. 87, 56 n. 97. *Miranda* rights attach whenever an accused is in custody and questioned, and the privilege against self-incrimination is thereby threatened by the inherent coercion of custodial interrogation. The Supreme Court required police to administer the now-familiar *Miranda* warning as a prelude to "custodial interrogation" because "such an interrogation environment is created for no purpose other than to subjugate the individual to the will of his examiner. This atmosphere carries its own badge of intimidation. To be sure, this is not physical intimidation, but it is equally destructive of human dignity. The current practice of incommunicado interrogation is at odds with one of our Nation's most cherished principles—that the individual may not be compelled to incriminate himself. Unless adequate protective devices are employed to dispel the compulsion inherent in custodial surroundings, no statements obtained from the defendant can truly be the product of his free choice." *Miranda*, 384 U.S. at 457–58. Presumably *Gault* extends those same *Miranda* rights to juveniles even though the *Gault* decision concerned only delinquents' rights at the adjudicatory hearing. Although the Supreme Court has never explicitly held that *Miranda* applies to juvenile proceedings, the Court in *Fare v. Michael C.*, 442 U.S. 707 at 717 n. 4, 99 S.Ct. 2560, 61 L.Ed.2d 197 (1979), "assume[d] without deciding that the *Miranda* principles were fully applicable to the present [juvenile] proceedings."

The Supreme Court in *Haley*, *Gallegos*, and *Gault* recognized the special vulnerability of youth but did not explore fully the legal policies that states might adopt to accommodate the fact of youthfulness in the police interrogation environment. The following materials illustrate three alternative policy strategies available to protect juveniles during interrogation—judicial review of a juvenile's waiver of *Miranda* rights under the "totality of the circumstances," a "parental presence" *per se* requirement, or consultation with counsel. In evaluating the three alternatives, consider the extent to which the policies differ in their assessments of the competence of children versus adults, the role of treatment versus punishment, the value of discretion versus rules, and protecting the juvenile versus protecting society. Are juveniles the functional equals of adults when police interrogate them? In what ways do they differ? If juveniles are not the equals of adults, then how should the law accommodate the vulnerability and immaturity of young people?

1. *MIRANDA* WAIVERS AND THE "TOTALITY OF THE CIRCUMSTANCES" TEST

FARE v. MICHAEL C.
442 U.S. 707, 99 S.Ct. 2560, 61 L.Ed.2d 197 (1979).

MR. JUSTICE BLACKMUN delivered the opinion of the Court.

In *Miranda v. Arizona*, this Court established certain procedural safeguards designed to protect the rights of an accused, under the Fifth and Fourteenth Amendments, to be free from compelled self-incrimination during custodial interrogation. The Court specified, among other things, that if the accused indicates in any manner that he wishes to remain silent or to consult an attorney, interrogation must cease, and any statement obtained from him during interrogation thereafter may not be admitted against him at his trial.

In this case, the State of California, in the person of its acting chief probation officer, attacks the conclusion of the Supreme Court of California that a juvenile's request, made while undergoing custodial interrogation, to see his *probation officer* is *per se* an invocation of the juvenile's Fifth Amendment rights as pronounced in *Miranda*. * * *

Respondent Michael C. was implicated in the murder of Robert Yeager. * * * On the basis of this information, * * * police took respondent into custody at approximately 6:30 p.m. on February 4. Respondent then was 16 ½ years old and on probation to the Juvenile Court. He had been on probation since the age of 12. Approximately one year earlier he had served a term in a youth corrections camp under the supervision of the Juvenile Court. He had a record of several previous offenses, including burglary of guns and purse snatching, stretching back over several years.

Upon respondent's arrival at the * * * station house two police officers began to interrogate him. The officers and respondent were the only persons in the room during the interrogation. The conversation was tape-recorded. One of the officers initiated the interview by informing respondent that he had been brought in for questioning in relation to a murder. The officer fully advised respondent of his *Miranda* rights. The following exchange then occurred, as set out in the opinion of the California Supreme Court:

Q.   * * *. Do you understand all of these rights as I have explained them to you?

A.   Yeah.

Q.   Okay, do you wish to give up your right to remain silent and talk to us about this murder?

A. What murder? I don't know about no murder.

Q. I'll explain to you which one it is if you want to talk to us about it.

A. Yeah, I might talk to you.

Q. Do you want to give up your right to have an attorney present here while we talk about it?

A. *Can I have my probation officer here?*

Q. Well I can't get a hold of your probation officer right now. You have the right to an attorney.

A. How I know you guys won't pull no police officer in and tell me he's an attorney?

Q. Huh?

A. [How I know you guys won't pull no police officer in and tell me he's an attorney?]

Q. Your probation officer is Mr. Christiansen.

A. Yeah.

Q. Well I'm not going to call Mr. Christiansen tonight. There's a good chance we can talk to him later, but I'm not going to call him right now. If you want to talk to us without an attorney present, you can. If you don't want to, you don't have to. But if you want to say something, you can, and if you don't want to say something you don't have to. That's your right. You understand that right?

A. Yeah.

Q. Okay, will you talk to us without an attorney present?

A. Yeah I want to talk to you."

Respondent thereupon proceeded to answer questions put to him by the officers. He made statements and drew sketches that incriminated him in the Yeager murder. * * *

Respondent thereupon moved to suppress the statements and sketches he gave the police during the interrogation. He alleged that the statements had been obtained in violation of *Miranda* in that his request to see his probation officer at the outset of the questioning constituted an invocation of his Fifth Amendment right to remain silent, just as if he had requested the assistance of an attorney. Accordingly, respondent argued that since the interrogation did not cease until he had a chance to confer with his probation officer, the statements and sketches could not be admitted against him in the Juvenile Court proceedings. In so arguing, respondent relied by analogy on the decision in *People v. Burton*, where the Supreme Court of California had held that a minor's request, made during custodial interrogation, to see his parents constituted an invocation of the minor's Fifth Amendment rights.

In support of his suppression motion, respondent called his probation officer, Charles P. Christiansen, as a witness. Christiansen testified that he had instructed respondent that if at any time he had "a concern with his family," or ever had "a police contact," he should get in touch with his probation officer immediately. The witness stated that, on a previous occasion, when respondent had had a police contact and had failed to communicate with Christiansen, the probation officer had reprimanded him. This testimony, respondent argued, indicated that when he asked for his probation officer, he was in fact asserting his right to remain silent in the face of further questioning.

In a ruling from the bench, the court denied the motion to suppress. It held that the question whether respondent had waived his right to remain silent was one of fact to be determined on a case-by-case basis, and that the facts of this case showed a "clear waiver" by respondent of that right. The court observed that the transcript of the interrogation revealed that respondent specifically had told the officers that he would talk with them, and that this waiver had come at the outset of the interrogation and not after prolonged questioning. The court noted that respondent was a "16 and a half year old minor who has been through the court system before, has been to [probation] camp, has a probation officer, [and is not] a young, naive minor with no experience with the courts." Accordingly, it found that on the facts of the case respondent had waived his Fifth Amendment rights, notwithstanding the request to see his probation officer.

On appeal, the Supreme Court of California * * * held that respondent's "request to see his probation officer at the commencement of interrogation negated any possible willingness on his part to discuss his case with the police [and] thereby invoked his Fifth Amendment privilege." The court based this conclusion on its view that, because of the juvenile court system's emphasis on the relationship between a probation officer and the probationer, the officer was "a trusted guardian figure who exercises the authority of the state as *parens patriae* and whose duty it is to implement the protective and rehabilitative powers of the juvenile court." As a consequence, the court found that a minor's request for his probation officer was the same as a request to see his parents during interrogation, and thus under the rule of *Burton* constituted an invocation of the minor's Fifth Amendment rights.

The fact that the probation officer also served as a peace officer, and, whenever a proceeding against a juvenile was contemplated, was charged with a duty to file a petition alleging that the minor had committed an offense, did not alter, in the court's view, the fact that the officer in the eyes of the juvenile was a trusted guardian figure to whom the minor normally would turn for help when in trouble with the police. Relying on *Burton*, the court ruled that it would unduly restrict *Miranda* to limit its reach in a case involving a minor to a request by the minor for an attorney, since it would be " 'fatuous to assume that a minor in custody will be in a position to call an attorney for assistance and it is unrealistic to attribute no significance to his call for help from the only person to whom he normally looks—a parent or guardian.' " The court dismissed the concern expressed by the State that a request for a probation officer could not be distinguished from a request for one's football coach, music teacher, or clergyman on the ground that the probation officer, unlike those other figures in the juvenile's life, was charged by statute to represent the interests of the juvenile.

The court accordingly held that the probation officer would act to protect the minor's Fifth Amendment rights in precisely the way an attorney would act if called for by the accused. In so holding, the court found the request for a probation officer to be a *per se* invocation of Fifth Amendment rights in the same way the request for an attorney was found in *Miranda* to be, regardless of what the interrogation otherwise might reveal. * * * The court went on to conclude that since the State had not met its "burden of proving that a minor who requests to see his probation officer does not intend to assert his Fifth Amendment privilege," the trial court should not have admitted the confessions obtained after respondent had requested his probation officer. * * *

The rule the Court established in *Miranda* is clear. In order to be able to use statements obtained during custodial interrogation of the accused, the State must warn the accused prior to such questioning of his right to remain silent and of his right to have counsel, retained or appointed, present during interrogation. "Once [such] warnings have been given, the subsequent procedure is clear."

> "If the individual indicates in any manner, at any time prior to or during questioning, that he wishes to remain silent, the interrogation must cease. At this point he has shown that he intends to exercise his Fifth Amendment privilege; any statement taken after the person invokes his privilege cannot be other than the product of compulsion, subtle or otherwise. * * * If the individual states that he wants an attorney, the interrogation must cease until an attorney is present. At that time, the individual must have an opportunity to confer with the attorney and to have him present during any subsequent questioning. If the individual cannot obtain an attorney and he indicates that he wants one before speaking to police, they must respect his decision to remain silent."

Any statements obtained during custodial interrogation conducted in violation of these rules may not be admitted against the accused, at least during the State's case in chief.

Whatever the defects, if any, of this relatively rigid requirement that interrogation must cease upon the accused's request for an attorney, *Miranda*'s holding has the virtue of informing police and prosecutors with specificity as to what they may do in conducting custodial interrogation, and of informing courts under what circumstances statements obtained during such interrogation are not admissible. This gain in specificity, which benefits the accused and the State alike, has been thought to outweigh the burdens that the decision in *Miranda* imposes on law enforcement agencies and the courts by requiring the suppression of trustworthy and highly probative evidence even though the confession might be voluntary under traditional Fifth Amendment analysis.

The California court in this case, however, significantly has extended this rule by providing that a request by a juvenile for his probation officer has the same effect as a request for an attorney. * * *

The rule in *Miranda*, however, was based on this Court's perception that the lawyer occupies a critical position in our legal system because of his unique ability to protect the Fifth Amendment rights of a client undergoing custodial interrogation. Because of this special ability of the lawyer to help the client preserve his Fifth Amendment rights once the client becomes enmeshed in the adversary process, the Court found that "the right to have counsel present at the interrogation is indispensable to the protection of the Fifth Amendment privilege under the system" established by the Court. Moreover, the lawyer's presence helps guard against overreaching by the police and ensures that any statements actually obtained are accurately transcribed for presentation into evidence.

The *per se* aspect of *Miranda* was thus based on the unique role the lawyer plays in the adversary system of criminal justice in this country. Whether it is a minor or an adult who stands accused, the lawyer is the one person to whom society as a whole looks as the protector of the legal rights of that person in his dealings with the police and the courts. For this reason, the Court fashioned in *Miranda* the rigid rule that an accused's request for an attorney is *per se* an invocation of his Fifth Amendment rights, requiring that all interrogation cease.

A probation officer is not in the same posture with regard to either the accused or the system of justice as a whole. Often he is not trained in the law, and so is not in a position to advise the accused as to his legal rights. Neither is he a trained advocate, skilled in the representation of the interests of his client before both police and courts. He does not assume the power to act on behalf of his client by virtue of his status as adviser, nor are the communications of the accused to the probation officer shielded by the lawyer-client privilege.

Moreover, the probation officer is the employee of the State which seeks to prosecute the alleged offender. He is a peace officer, and as such is allied, to a greater or lesser extent, with his fellow peace officers. He owes an obligation to the State, notwithstanding the obligation he may also owe the juvenile under his supervision. In most cases, the probation officer is duty bound to report wrongdoing by the juvenile when it comes to his attention, even if by communication from the juvenile himself. Indeed, when this case arose, the probation officer had the responsibility for filing the petition alleging wrongdoing by the juvenile and seeking to have him taken into the custody of the Juvenile Court. It was respondent's probation officer who filed the petition against him, and it is the acting chief of probation for the State of California, a probation officer, who is petitioner in this Court today.[5]

In these circumstances, it cannot be said that the probation officer is able to offer the type of independent advice that an accused would expect from a lawyer retained or assigned to assist him during questioning. Indeed, the probation officer's duty to his employer in many, if not most, cases would conflict sharply with the interests of the juvenile. For where an attorney might well advise his client to remain silent in the face of interrogation by the police, and in doing so would be "exercising [his] good professional judgment * * * to protect to the extent of his ability the rights of his client," a probation officer would be bound to advise his charge to cooperate with the police. * * *

By the same token, a lawyer is able to protect his client's rights by learning the extent, if any, of the client's involvement in the crime under investigation, and advising his client accordingly. To facilitate this, the law rightly protects the communications between client and attorney from discovery. We doubt, however, that similar protection will be afforded the communications between the probation officer and the minor. Indeed, we doubt that a probation officer, consistent with his responsibilities to the public and his profession, could withhold from the police or the courts facts made known to him by the juvenile implicating the juvenile in the crime under investigation.

We thus believe it clear that the probation officer is not in a position to offer the type of legal assistance necessary to protect the Fifth Amendment rights of an accused undergoing custodial interrogation that a lawyer can offer. The Court in *Miranda* recognized that "the attorney plays a vital role in the administration of criminal justice under our

---

5. When this case arose, a California statute provided that a proceeding in juvenile court to declare a minor a ward of the court was to be commenced by the filing of a petition by a probation officer. This provision since has been amended to provide that most such petitions are to be filed by the prosecuting attorney. Respondent argues that, whatever the status of the probation officer as a peace officer at the time this case arose, the amendment * * * indicates that in the future a probation officer is not to be viewed as a legal adversary of the accused juvenile. Consequently, respondent believes that any holding of this Court with regard to respondent's 1976 request for a probation officer will be mere dictum with regard to a juvenile's similar request today.

We disagree. The fact that a California probation officer in 1976 was responsible for initiating a complaint is only one factor in our analysis. The fact remains that a probation officer does not fulfill the role in our system of criminal justice that an attorney does, regardless of whether he acts merely as a counselor or has significant law enforcement duties. And in California, as in many States, the other duties of a probation officer are incompatible with the view that he may act as a counselor to a juvenile accused of crime. The very California statute that imposes upon the probation officer the duty to represent the interests of the juvenile also provides: "It shall be the duty of the probation officer to prepare for every hearing [of criminal charges against a juvenile] a social study of the minor, containing such matters as may be relevant to a proper disposition of the case."

Similarly, a probation officer is required, upon the order of the juvenile court or the Youth Authority, to investigate the circumstances surrounding the charge against the minor and to file written reports and recommendations. And a probation officer in California continues to have the powers and authority of a peace officer in connection with any violation of a criminal statute that is discovered by the probation officer in the course of his probation activities. The duties of a peace officer, like the investigative and reporting duties of probation officers, are incompatible with the role of legal adviser to a juvenile accused of crime.

Constitution." It is this pivotal role of legal counsel that justifies the *per se* rule established in *Miranda*, and that distinguishes the request for counsel from the request for a probation officer, a clergyman, or a close friend. A probation officer simply is not necessary, in the way an attorney is, for the protection of the legal rights of the accused, juvenile or adult. He is significantly handicapped by the position he occupies in the juvenile system from serving as an effective protector of the rights of a juvenile suspected of a crime.

The California Supreme Court, however, found that the close relationship between juveniles and their probation officers compelled the conclusion that a probation officer, for purposes of *Miranda*, was sufficiently like a lawyer to justify extension of the *per se* rule. The fact that a relationship of trust and cooperation between a probation officer and a juvenile might exist, however, does not indicate that the probation officer is capable of rendering effective legal advice sufficient to protect the juvenile's rights during interrogation by the police, or of providing the other services rendered by a lawyer. * * *

Similarly, the fact that the State has created a statutory duty on the part of the probation officer to protect the interests of the juvenile does not render the probation officer any more capable of rendering legal assistance to the juvenile or of protecting his legal rights, especially in light of the fact that the State has also legislated a duty on the part of the officer to report wrongdoing by the juvenile and serve the ends of the juvenile court system. The State cannot transmute the relationship between probation officer and juvenile offender into the type of relationship between attorney and client that was essential to the holding of *Miranda* simply by legislating an amorphous "duty to advise and care for the juvenile defendant." Though such a statutory duty might serve to distinguish to some degree the probation officer from the coach and the clergyman, it does not justify the extension of *Miranda* to requests to see probation officers. If it did, the State could expand the class of persons covered by the *Miranda per se* rule simply by creating a duty to care for the juvenile on the part of other persons, regardless of whether the logic of *Miranda* would justify that extension.

Nor do we believe that a request by a juvenile to speak with his probation officer constitutes a *per se* request to remain silent. As indicated, since a probation officer does not fulfill the important role in protecting the rights of the accused juvenile that an attorney plays, we decline to find that the request for the probation officer is tantamount to the request for an attorney. And there is nothing inherent in the request for a probation officer that requires us to find that a juvenile's request to see one necessarily constitutes an expression of the juvenile's right to remain silent. * * *

We hold, therefore, that it was error to find that the request by respondent to speak with his probation officer *per se* constituted an invocation of respondent's Fifth Amendment right to be free from compelled self-incrimination. It therefore was also error to hold that because the police did not then cease interrogating respondent the statements he made during interrogation should have been suppressed. * * *

Miranda further recognized that after the required warnings are given the accused, "[i]f the interrogation continues without the presence of an attorney and a statement is taken, a heavy burden rests on the government to demonstrate that the defendant knowingly and intelligently waived his privilege against self-incrimination and his right to retained or appointed counsel." * * * [T]he question whether the accused waived his rights "is not one of form, but rather whether the defendant in fact knowingly and voluntarily waived the rights delineated in the *Miranda* case." Thus, the determination whether statements obtained during custodial interrogation are admissible against the accused is to be made upon an inquiry into the totality of the circumstances surrounding the interrogation, to ascertain whether the accused in fact knowingly and voluntarily decided to forgo his rights to remain silent and to have the assistance of counsel.

This totality-of-the-circumstances approach is adequate to determine whether there has been a waiver even where interrogation of juveniles is involved. We discern no persuasive reasons why any other approach is required where the question is whether a juvenile has waived his rights, as opposed to whether an adult has done so. The totality approach permits—indeed, it mandates—inquiry into all the circumstances surrounding the interrogation. This includes evaluation of the juvenile's age, experience, education, background, and intelligence, and into whether he has the capacity to understand the warnings given him, the nature of his Fifth Amendment rights, and the consequences of waiving those rights.

Courts repeatedly must deal with these issues of waiver with regard to a broad variety of constitutional rights. There is no reason to assume that such courts—especially juvenile courts, with their special expertise in this area—will be unable to apply the totality-of-the-circumstances analysis so as to take into account those special concerns that are present when young persons, often with limited experience and education and with immature judgment, are involved. Where the age and experience of a juvenile indicate that his request for his probation officer or his parents is, in fact, an invocation of his right to remain silent, the totality approach will allow the court the necessary flexibility to take this into account in making a waiver determination. At the same time, that approach refrains from imposing rigid restraints on police and courts in dealing with an experienced older juvenile with an extensive prior record who knowingly and intelligently waives his Fifth Amendment rights and voluntarily consents to interrogation.

In this case, we conclude that the California Supreme Court should have determined the issue of waiver on the basis of all the circumstances surrounding the interrogation of respondent. The Juvenile Court found that under this approach, respondent in fact had waived his Fifth Amendment rights and consented to interrogation by the police after his request to see his probation officer was denied. Given its view of the case, of course, the California Supreme Court did not consider this issue, though it did hold that the State had failed to prove that, notwithstanding respondent's request to see his probation officer, respondent had not intended to invoke his Fifth Amendment rights.

We feel that the conclusion of the Juvenile Court was correct. The transcript of the interrogation reveals that the police officers conducting the interrogation took care to ensure that respondent understood his rights. * * *

Further, no special factors indicate that respondent was unable to understand the nature of his actions. He was a 16½–year–old juvenile with considerable experience with the police. He had a record of several arrests. He had served time in a youth camp, and he had been on probation for several years. He was under the full-time supervision of probation authorities. There is no indication that he was of insufficient intelligence to understand the rights he was waiving, or what the consequences of that waiver would be. He was not worn down by improper interrogation tactics or lengthy questioning or by trickery or deceit. * * *

We hold, in short, that the California Supreme Court erred in finding that a juvenile's request for his probation officer was a *per se* invocation of that juvenile's Fifth Amendment rights under *Miranda*. We conclude, rather, that whether the statements obtained during subsequent interrogation of a juvenile who has asked to see his probation officer, but who has not asked to consult an attorney or expressly asserted his right to remain silent, are admissible on the basis of waiver remains a question to be resolved on the totality of the circumstances surrounding the interrogation. On the basis of the record in this case, we hold that the Juvenile Court's findings that respondent voluntarily and knowingly waived his rights and consented to continued interrogation, and that the statements obtained from him were voluntary, were proper, and that the admission of those statements in the proceeding against respondent in Juvenile Court was correct.

The judgment of the Supreme Court of California is reversed, and the case is remanded for further proceedings not inconsistent with this opinion.

It is so ordered.

MR. JUSTICE MARSHALL, with whom MR. JUSTICE BRENNAN and MR. JUSTICE STEVENS join, dissenting. In *Miranda v. Arizona*, , this Court sought to ensure that the inherently coercive pressures of custodial interrogation would not vitiate a suspect's privilege against self-incrimination. Noting that these pressures "can operate very quickly to overbear the will of one merely made aware of his privilege," the Court held:

"If [a suspect in custody] indicates in any manner, at any time prior to or during questioning, that he wishes to remain silent, the interrogation must cease. At this point he has shown that he intends to exercise his Fifth Amendment privilege; any statement taken after the person invokes his privilege cannot be other than the product of compulsion, subtle or otherwise. * * * If the individual states that he wants an attorney, the interrogation must cease until an attorney is present.''

As this Court has consistently recognized, the coerciveness of the custodial setting is of heightened concern where, as here, a juvenile is under investigation. * * *

It is therefore critical in the present context that we construe *Miranda*'s prophylactic requirements broadly to accomplish their intended purpose—"dispel[ling] the compulsion inherent in custodial surroundings." To effectuate this purpose, the Court must ensure that the "protective device" of legal counsel be readily available, and that any intimation of a desire to preclude questioning be scrupulously honored. Thus, I believe *Miranda* requires that interrogation cease whenever a juvenile requests an adult who is obligated to represent his interests. Such a request, in my judgment, constitutes both an attempt to obtain advice and a general invocation of the right to silence. For, as the California Supreme Court recognized, " '[i]t is fatuous to assume that a minor in custody will be in a position to call an attorney for assistance,' " or that he will trust the police to obtain a lawyer for him.[1] A juvenile in these circumstances will likely turn to his parents, or another adult responsible for his welfare, as the only means of securing legal counsel. Moreover, a request for such adult assistance is surely inconsistent with a present desire to speak freely. Requiring a strict verbal formula to invoke the protections of *Miranda* would "protect the knowledgeable accused from stationhouse coercion while abandoning the young person who knows no more than to ask for the * * * person he trusts."

On my reading of *Miranda*, a California juvenile's request for his probation officer should be treated as a *per se* assertion of Fifth Amendment rights. The California Supreme Court determined that probation officers have a statutory duty to represent minors' interests and, indeed, are "trusted guardian figure[s]" to whom a juvenile would likely turn for assistance. In addition, the court found, probation officers are particularly well suited to assist a juvenile "on such matters as to whether or not he should obtain an attorney" and "how to conduct himself with police." Hence, a juvenile's request for a probation officer may frequently be an attempt to secure protection from the coercive aspects of custodial questioning. * * *

Thus, given the role of probation officers under California law, a juvenile's request to see his officer may reflect a desire for precisely the kind of assistance *Miranda* guarantees an accused before he waives his

---

1. The facts of the instant case are illustrative. When the police offered to obtain an attorney for respondent, he replied: "How I know you guys won't pull no police officer in and tell me he's an attorney?" Significantly, the police made no attempt to allay that concern.

Fifth Amendment rights. At the very least, such a request signals a desire to remain silent until contact with the officer is made. Because the Court's contrary determination withdraws the safeguards of *Miranda* from those most in need of protection, I respectfully dissent.

MR. JUSTICE POWELL, dissenting. Although I agree with the Court that the Supreme Court of California misconstrued *Miranda v. Arizona,,* I would not reverse the California court's judgment. This Court repeatedly has recognized that "the greatest care" must be taken to assure that an alleged confession of a juvenile was voluntary. Respondent was a young person, 16 years old at the time of his arrest and the subsequent prolonged interrogation at the stationhouse. Although respondent had had prior brushes with the law, and was under supervision by a probation officer, the taped transcript of his interrogation—as well as his testimony at the suppression hearing—demonstrates that he was immature, emotional, and uneducated, and therefore was likely to be vulnerable to the skillful, two-on-one, repetitive style of interrogation to which he was subjected. * * * It is clear that the interrogating police did not exercise "the greatest care" to assure that respondent's "admission was voluntary." In the absence of counsel, and having refused to call the probation officer, they nevertheless engaged in protracted interrogation.

Although I view the case as close, I am not satisfied that this particular 16–year–old boy, in this particular situation, was subjected to a fair interrogation free from inherently coercive circumstances. For these reasons, I would affirm the judgment of the Supreme Court of California.

NOTES

1) If Custody + Interrogation = *Miranda* warning, then what is the effect of youthfulness and inexperience on determining juveniles' custody status? In **Yarborough v. Alvarado,** 541 U.S. 652, 124 S.Ct. 2140, 158 L.Ed.2d 938 (2004), police investigated Michael Alvarado for his role in a robbery and homicide. About one month after the crime, Sheriff's detective Cheryl Comstock contacted Alvarado's mother at work and told her that police needed to speak to her son. Although Alvarado's parents brought him to the station, Comstock denied their request to be present during the interview and they waited in the lobby while she questioned him. Alvarado was 17–years–old, had no criminal history, and had never been questioned by the police. Comstock conducted the interview which lasted about two hours. Alvarado did not sign a statement indicating that he participated voluntarily in the interview, nor did he receive a *Miranda* warning. Comstock expressed disbelief at Alvarado's initial account of his activities the night of the murder. Well into the course of the interrogation and after Alvarado started making incriminating statements, Comstock made comments that implied that Alvarado would go home at the end of the interview. The statement he made during the two-hour interrogation provided the primary basis for Alvarado's conviction of second degree murder and his sentence of 15–years to life. Alvarado claimed his age was a relevant "custody" factor in the *Miranda* analysis to decide whether "a reasonable person under the circumstances in which Alvarado was questioned would have felt free to leave." The trial court held that Alvarado was not in custody during the interview, so Comstock was not required to give him a *Miranda* warning. After exhausting his state appeals, Alvarado filed a petition for habeas corpus and the Ninth Circuit reversed and held that the state court erred in failing to account of a youth's age and inexperience when evaluating whether a reasonable person in his position would have felt free to leave:

KENNEDY, J., delivered the opinion of the Court, in which REHN-QUIST, C. J., and O'CONNOR, SCALIA, and THOMAS, JJ., joined. * * * *Miranda* itself held that preinterrogation warnings are required in the context of custodial interrogations given "the compulsion inherent in custodial surroundings." The Court explained that "custodial interroga-tion" meant "questioning initiated by law enforcement officers after a person has been taken into custody or otherwise deprived of his freedom of action in any significant way." * * *

After *Miranda,* the Court first applied the custody test in *Oregon v. Mathiason.* In *Mathiason,* a police officer contacted the suspect after a burglary victim identified him. The officer arranged to meet the suspect at a nearby police station. At the outset of the questioning, the officer stated his belief that the suspect was involved in the burglary but that he was not under arrest. During the 30–minute interview, the suspect admitted his guilt. He was then allowed to leave. The Court held that the questioning was not custodial because there was "no indication that the questioning took place in a context where [the suspect's] freedom to depart was restricted in any way." The Court noted that the suspect had come voluntarily to the police station, that he was informed that he was not under arrest, and that he was allowed to leave at the end of the interview. * * *

Our more recent cases instruct that custody must be determined based on a how a reasonable person in the suspect's situation would perceive his circumstances. In *Berkemer v. McCarty,* a police officer stopped a suspected drunk driver and asked him some questions. * * * The Court held the traffic stop noncustodial despite the officer's intent to arrest because he had not communicated that intent to the driver. "A policeman's unarticulated plan has no bearing on the question whether a suspect was 'in custody' at a particular time," the Court explained. "[T]he only relevant inquiry is how a reasonable man in the suspect's position would have understood his situation." * * *

Stansbury v. California, confirmed this analytical framework. *Stans-bury* explained that "the initial determination of custody depends on the objective circumstances of the interrogation, not on the subjective views harbored by either the interrogating officers or the person being ques-tioned." Courts must examine "all of the circumstances surrounding the interrogation" and determine "how a reasonable person in the position of the individual being questioned would gauge the breadth of his or her freedom of action."

Finally, in *Thompson v. Keohane,* the Court offered the following description of the *Miranda* custody test:

"Two discrete inquiries are essential to the determination: first, what were the circumstances surrounding the interrogation; and second, given those circumstances, would a reasonable person have felt he or she was not at liberty to terminate the interrogation and leave. Once the scene is set and the players' lines and actions are reconstructed, the court must apply an objective test to resolve the ultimate inquiry: was there a formal arrest or restraint on freedom of movement of the degree associated with a formal arrest." * * *

[W]e conclude that the state court's application of our clearly established law was reasonable. * * * [I]t can be said that fair-minded jurists could disagree over whether Alvarado was in custody. On one hand, certain facts weigh against a finding that Alvarado was in custody. The police did not transport Alvarado to the station or require him to appear at a particular time. They did not threaten him or suggest he would be placed under arrest. Alvarado's parents remained in the lobby during the interview, suggesting that the interview would be brief. In fact, according to trial counsel for Alvarado, he and his parents were told that the interview was " 'not going to be long.' " During the interview, Comstock focused on * * * [Alvarado's co-offender and] appealed to his interest in telling the truth and being helpful to a police officer. In addition, Comstock twice asked Alvarado if he wanted to take a break. At the end of the interview, Alvarado went home. All of these objective facts are consistent with an interrogation environment in which a reasonable person would have felt free to terminate the interview and leave. Indeed, a number of the facts echo those of *Mathiason,* a *per curiam* summary reversal in which we found it "clear from these facts" that the suspect was not in custody.

Other facts point in the opposite direction. Comstock interviewed Alvarado at the police station. The interview lasted two hours, four times longer than the 30–minute interview in *Mathiason.* Unlike the officer in *Mathiason,* Comstock did not tell Alvarado that he was free to leave. Alvarado was brought to the police station by his legal guardians rather than arriving on his own accord, making the extent of his control over his presence unclear. Counsel for Alvarado alleges that Alvarado's parents asked to be present at the interview but were rebuffed, a fact that—if known to Alvarado—might reasonably have led someone in Alvarado's position to feel more restricted than otherwise. These facts weigh in favor of the view that Alvarado was in custody.

These differing indications lead us to hold that the state court's application of our custody standard was reasonable. * * *

The Court of Appeals reached the opposite result by placing considerable reliance on Alvarado's age and inexperience with law enforcement. Our Court has not stated that a suspect's age or experience is relevant to the *Miranda* custody analysis, and counsel for Alvarado did not press the importance of either factor on direct appeal or in habeas proceedings. According to the Court of Appeals, however, our Court's emphasis on juvenile status in other contexts demanded consideration of Alvarado's age and inexperience here. The Court of Appeals viewed the state court's failure to "extend a clearly established legal principle [of the relevance of juvenile status] to a new context" as objectively unreasonable in this case, requiring issuance of the writ. * * *

Our opinions applying the *Miranda* custody test have not mentioned the suspect's age, much less mandated its consideration. The only indications in the Court's opinions relevant to a suspect's experience with law enforcement have rejected reliance on such factors.

There is an important conceptual difference between the *Miranda* custody test and the line of cases from other contexts considering age and experience. The *Miranda* custody inquiry is an objective test. As we stated in *Keohane,* "[o]nce the scene is set and the players' lines and actions are reconstructed, the court must apply an objective test to resolve the ultimate inquiry." The objective test furthers "the clarity of [*Miranda*'s] rule," ensuring that the police do not need "to make guesses as to [the circumstances] at issue before deciding how they may interrogate the suspect." To be sure, the line between permissible objective facts and impermissible subjective experiences can be indistinct in some cases. It is possible to subsume a subjective factor into an objective test by making the latter more specific in its formulation. Thus the Court of Appeals styled its inquiry as an objective test by considering what a "reasonable 17–year–old, with no prior history of arrest or police interviews" would perceive.

At the same time, the objective *Miranda* custody inquiry could reasonably be viewed as different from doctrinal tests that depend on the actual mindset of a particular suspect, where we do consider a suspect's age and experience. For example, the voluntariness of a statement is often said to depend on whether "the defendant's will was overborne," a question that logically can depend on "the characteristics of the accused." The characteristics of the accused can include the suspect's age, education, and intelligence, as well as a suspect's prior experience with law enforcement. In concluding that there was "no principled reason" why such factors should not also apply to the *Miranda* custody inquiry, the Court of Appeals ignored the argument that the custody inquiry states an objective rule designed to give clear guidance to the police, while consideration of a suspect's individual characteristics—including his age—could be viewed as creating a subjective inquiry. For these reasons, the state court's failure to consider Alvarado's age does not provide a proper basis for finding that the state court's decision was an unreasonable application of clearly established law. * * *

The state court considered the proper factors and reached a reasonable conclusion. The judgment of the Court of Appeals is

Reversed.

Justice O'CONNOR, concurring. I join the opinion of the Court, but write separately to express an additional reason for reversal. There may be cases in which a suspect's age will be relevant to the "custody" inquiry under *Miranda v. Arizona.* In this case, however, Alvarado was almost 18 years old at the time of his interview. It is difficult to expect police to recognize that a suspect is a juvenile when he is so close to the age of majority. Even when police do know a suspect's age, it may be difficult for them to ascertain what bearing it has on the likelihood that the suspect would feel free to leave. That is especially true here; 17½–year–olds vary widely in their reactions to police questioning, and many can be expected to behave as adults. Given these difficulties, I agree that the state court's decision in this case cannot be called an unreasonable application of federal law simply because it failed explicitly to mention Alvarado's age.

Justice BREYER with whom Justice STEVENS, Justice SOURTER, and Justice GINSBURG join, dissenting. In my view, Michael Alvarado clearly was "in custody" when the police questioned him (without *Miranda* warnings) about the murder. * * * Would a "reasonable person" in Alvarado's "position" have felt he was "at liberty to terminate the interrogation and leave"? A court must answer this question in light of "all of the circumstances surrounding the interrogation." And the obvious answer here is "no." * * *

What reasonable person in the circumstances—brought to a police station by his parents at police request, put in a small interrogation room, questioned for a solid two hours, and confronted with claims that there is strong evidence that he participated in a serious crime, could have thought to himself, "Well, anytime I want to leave I can just get up and walk out"? If the person harbored any doubts, would he still think he might be free to leave once he recalls that the police officer has just refused to let his parents remain with him during questioning? Would he still think that he, rather than the officer, controls the situation? * * *

The facts to which the majority points make clear what the police did *not* do, for example, come to Alvarado's house, tell him he was under arrest, handcuff him, place him in a locked cell, threaten him, or tell him explicitly that he was not free to leave. But what is important here is what the police *did* do—namely, have Alvarado's parents bring him to the station, put him with a single officer in a small room, keep his parents out, let him know that he was a suspect, and question him for two hours. These latter facts compel a single conclusion: A reasonable person in Alvarado's circumstances would *not* have felt free to terminate the interrogation and leave.

What about Alvarado's youth? The fact that Alvarado was 17 helps to show that he was unlikely to have felt free to ignore his parents' request to come to the station. And a 17–year–old is more likely than, say, a 35–year–old, to take a police officer's assertion of authority to keep parents outside the room as an assertion of authority to keep their child inside as well. * * *

Our cases do instruct lower courts to apply a "reasonable person" standard. But the "reasonable person" standard does not require a court to pretend that Alvarado was a 35–year–old with aging parents whose middle-aged children do what their parents ask only out of respect. Nor does it say that a court should pretend that Alvarado was the statistically determined "average person"—a working, married, 35–year–old white female with a high school degree.

Rather, the precise legal definition of "reasonable person" may, depending on legal context, appropriately account for certain personal characteristics. In negligence suits, for example, the question is what would a "reasonable person" do " 'under the same or similar circumstances.' " In answering that question, courts enjoy "latitude" and may make "allowance not only for external facts, but sometimes for certain characteristics of the actor himself," including physical disability, youth, or advanced age. This allowance makes sense in light of the tort standard's recognized purpose: deterrence. Given that purpose, why pretend that a child is an adult or that a blind man can see?

In the present context, that of *Miranda*'s "in custody" inquiry, the law has introduced the concept of a "reasonable person" to avoid judicial inquiry into subjective states of mind, and to focus the inquiry instead upon objective circumstances that are known to both the officer and the suspect and that are likely relevant to the way a person would understand his situation. * * *

In this case, Alvarado's youth is an objective circumstance that was known to the police. It is not a special quality, but rather a widely shared characteristic that generates commonsense conclusions about behavior and perception. To focus on the circumstance of age in a case like this does not complicate the "in custody" inquiry. And to say that courts should ignore widely shared, objective characteristics, like age, on the ground that only a (large) *minority* of the population possesses them would produce absurd results, the present instance being a case in point. * * *

Our cases also make clear that to determine how a suspect would have "gaug[ed]" his "freedom of movement," a court must carefully examine "all of the circumstances surrounding the interrogation," including, for example, how long the interrogation lasted (brief and routine or protracted?); how the suspect came to be questioned (voluntarily or against his will?); where the questioning took place (at a police station or in public?); and what the officer communicated to the individual during the interrogation (that he was a suspect? that he was under arrest? that he was free to leave at will?). In the present case, every one of these factors argues—and argues strongly—that Alvarado was in custody for *Miranda* purposes when the police questioned him.

Common sense, and an understanding of the law's basic purpose in this area, are enough to make clear that Alvarado's age—an objective, widely shared characteristic about which the police plainly knew—is also relevant to the inquiry. Unless one is prepared to pretend that Alvarado is someone he is not, a middle-aged gentleman, well-versed in police practices, it seems to me clear that the California courts made a serious mistake. I agree with the Ninth Circuit's similar conclusions. Consequently, I dissent.

2) The Court's *Miranda* doctrine and Police Interrogation of Juveniles In other cases interpreting *Miranda*, the Supreme Court in *Moran v. Burbine*, 475 U.S. 412 at 421, 106 S.Ct. 1135, 89 L.Ed.2d 410 (1986), clarified that a valid waiver required both "voluntariness" and a "knowing and intelligent" awareness of the right relinquished. According to *Moran*, a waiver of rights has two distinct elements—"voluntary in the sense that it was the product of a free and deliberate choice rather than intimidation, coercion, or deception," and that it was "made with a full awareness of both the nature of the right being abandoned and the consequences of the decision to abandon it." In *Moran*, police denied the defendant's attorney access to her client and did not inform the defendant that his lawyer wanted to speak with him. The Court opined that circumstances occurring outside of the presence of the defendant could not affect the validity of his decision to waive his rights. "Only if the 'totality of the circumstances surrounding the interrogation' reveal both an *uncoerced choice* and the requisite *level of comprehension* may a court properly conclude that the *Miranda* rights have been waived." *Id.* at 421 (emphasis added). However, courts interpret *comprehension* to mean only an understanding and awareness of the contents of the *Miranda*-warning rights themselves, for example, a right not to speak and to have counsel present, rather than an appreciation of the ramifications and legal consequences of a waiver. *See People v. Cheatham*, 453 Mich. 1 at 29, 551 N.W.2d 355 at 367 (Mich. 1996) ("[T]he test is not whether [the defendant] made an intelligent decision in the sense that it was wise or smart * * * but whether his decision was made with the full understanding that he need say nothing at all"). A youth's minimal awareness that police would not compel him to talk, but would use his statements against him would constitute an adequate understanding of the right to remain silent. *E.g., People v. Bernasco*, 138 Ill.2d 349, 150 Ill.Dec. 155, 562 N.E.2d 958, 964 (1990) (concluding that for *Miranda* purposes, intelligent knowledge "means the ability to understand the very words used in the warnings. It need not mean the ability to understand far-reaching legal and strategic effects of waiving one's rights, or to appreciate how widely or deeply an interrogation may probe, or to withstand the influence of stress or fancy"); *State v. Knights*, 482 A.2d 436 (Me.1984).

In *Colorado v. Connelly*, 479 U.S. 157, 107 S.Ct. 515, 93 L.Ed.2d 473 (1986), the Supreme Court held that absent police coercion, a defendant's mental state alone would not render a confession involuntary. "While a defendant's mental condition may be a significant factor in determining the 'voluntariness' of a confession, this factor alone does not justify a conclusion that the mental condition, apart from its relation to any alleged coercion by police, should dispose of the voluntariness issue." *Id.* at 164. *Connelly* emphasized that a "voluntariness" inquiry properly focused on police conduct, rather than the subjective susceptibility of the defendant. Thus, courts' assessments of *Miranda* waivers—"knowing, intelligent, and voluntary under the totality of the circumstances"—should focus narrowly on the suspect's awareness of and ability to comprehend the *Miranda* warnings and coercive police conduct that deprives her of the freedom to choose to exercise or to waive those rights.

Despite *Fare*'s suggestion that a juvenile only needs to indicate in "any manner" his or her desire to invoke the *Miranda* protections, the Supreme Court has held that police must cease interrogation only after a defendant clearly has "unambiguously invoked" his *Miranda* rights. *Davis v. United States*, 512 U.S. 452, 114 S.Ct. 2350, 129 L.Ed.2d 362 (1994) (holding that police have no obligation to stop interrogation until defendant makes an unambiguous or unequivocal request for counsel and police have no obligation to seek a clarification of an ambiguous reference to counsel). Thus, *Fare*, *Moran*, *Connelly*, and *Davis* put the burden on a youth affirmatively to invoke her *Miranda* rights clearly, unequivocally, and with adult-like technical precision before the Court will require police to honor her assertion of rights.

The *Fare* Court held that a child's request to speak with someone other than an attorney comprised simply one of many factors affecting the validity of a *Miranda* waiver, and expressly declined to give children greater procedural protection than adults. *See* Irene Merker Rosenberg, "The Constitutional Rights of Children Charged with Crime: Proposal for a Return to the Not So Distant Past," 27 *U.C.L.A. L. Rev.* 656 (1980); Francis Barry McCarthy, "Pre–Adjudicatory Rights in Juvenile Court: An Historical and Constitutional Analysis," 42 *U. Pitt. L. Rev.* 457 (1981); Barry C. Feld, "Criminalizing Juvenile Justice: Rules of Procedure for the Juvenile Court," 69 *Minn. L.Rev.* 141 (1984). *Fare* insisted that children invoke their legal rights with adult-like technical precision and denied that young people were inherently incapable of validly waiving their constitutional rights. The Court rejected the view that "adult and child are members of binary, dichotomous categories whose inherently differing cognitive capacities justify separate waiver rules." Janet E. Ainsworth, "Re–Imagining Childhood and Reconstructing the Legal Order: The Case for Abolishing the Juvenile Court," 69 *N.C. L. Rev.*, 1083 at 1116 (1991). By endorsing the adult waiver standard, the Court rejected the view that developmental or psychological differences between juveniles and adults justified or required different rules or special procedural protections. *See* Thomas Grisso, *Juveniles' Waivers of Rights: Legal and Psychological Competence* 209 (1981).

3) *Fare* in Theory and in Practice The vast majority of states follow *Fare,* use the adult "totality of the circumstances" test to evaluate juveniles' assertions or waivers of rights, and allow juveniles to waive *Miranda* and other constitutional rights. *See, e.g., Quick v. State*, 599 P.2d 712 (Alaska 1979) (deciding that juvenile may waive *Miranda* rights without consulting parent or other adult); *Carter v. State*, 697 So.2d 529, 533–34 (Fla. App. 1 Dist.1997) (affirming "totality" approach and upholding trial court exclusion of "Grisso Test" used to measure juvenile's ability to comprehend *Miranda* warnings); *Dutil v. State*, 93 Wash.2d 84, 606 P.2d 269 (Wash. 1980) (declining to adopt per se rule requiring presence of parent, guardian or counsel); *State v. Bobo*, 65 Ohio App.3d 685, 585 N.E.2d 429, 432–32 (Ohio Ct. App. 1989) (applying "totality test and holding that parental presence is 'only one factor in the totality of the circumstances' "). As the California Supreme Court held in the leading case of *People v. Lara*, 67 Cal.2d 365, 377, 62 Cal.Rptr. 586, 432 P.2d 202, 215 (Cal. 1967), *cert. denied*, 392 U.S. 945 (1968), "a minor has the capacity to make a voluntary confession, even of capital offenses, without the presence or consent of counsel or other responsible adult, and the admissibility of such a confession depends not on his age alone but on a combination of that factor with such other circumstances as his intelligence, education, experience, and ability to comprehend the meaning and effect of his statement."

Judges typically focus on characteristics of the juvenile, such as age, education, and I.Q., and on circumstances surrounding the interrogation, such as methods and length of the questioning, when they evaluate the validity of any waivers or the admissibility of any statement. *See, e.g., West v. United States*, 399 F.2d 467, 469 (5th Cir. 1968); *People v. Lara*, 67 Cal.2d 365, 367–77, 62 Cal.Rptr. 586, 432 P.2d 202, 217–18 (1967). Several leading cases have suggested extensive lists of factors for trial judges to consider when they assess the validity of juveniles' waiver decisions—age, education, physical condition, presence of or opportunity to consult with parent or other adult, length of interrogation, method of interrogation, knowledge of the charges, subsequent repudiation of the statement, understanding of the warnings given, warning of possible transfer to criminal court, and the like. *See e.g., Fare v. Michael C.*, 442 U.S. at 725; *State v. Benoit*, 126 N.H. 6, 15, 490 A.2d 295, 302 (1985); *Riley v. State*, 237 Ga. 124, 226 S.E.2d 922, 926 (1976); *State v. Williams*, 535 N.W.2d 277 at 287 (Minn. 1995) (declaring that factors to be considered under the totality-of-the-circumstances test include the juvenile's age, maturity, intelligence, education, prior criminal experience, any physical deprivations during the interrogation, the presence or absence of parents, the length and legality of the detention, the lack of or adequacy of warnings, and the nature of the interrogation).

While appellate courts have identified many relevant factors that bear on judges' assessments of "voluntariness," they do not assign controlling weight to any particular element and instead remit the weighing of different factors to the unfettered discretion of the trial court. A survey of juvenile waiver decisions between 1948 and 1979 concluded that no single factor determined the validity of a waiver because courts typically cited constellations of variables in conjunction with one another to justify their decisions. Thomas Grisso, "Juveniles' Capacities to Waive *Miranda* Rights: An Empirical Analysis," 68 *Cal. L. Rev.* 1134, 1138 (1980), notes that "There is no case law, however, which suggests how to evaluate all the considerations systematically. The manner in which the factors are weighed and combined has always been a matter of judicial discretion." Without clear-cut rules to protect children who lack the maturity or knowledge of adults, the "totality" approach leaves judges' discretion virtually unlimited and unreviewable.

When judges actually apply the "totality" test, they exclude only the most egregiously obtained confessions and then only on a haphazard basis. *See, e.g.,* Feld, *Criminalizing Juvenile Justice, supra* note 2, at 176; *In re W.C.*, 167 Ill.2d 307, 212 Ill.Dec. 563, 657 N.E.2d 908 (Ill. 1995) (upholding validity of waiver by thirteen-year old who was "illiterate and moderately retarded with an IQ of 48 * * * the equivalent developmentally of a six-to seven-year old"). A few courts closely scrutinize youths' *awareness* of the meaning of *Miranda* rights. In *People v. Bernasco*, 150 Ill.Dec. 155, 138 Ill.2d 349, 562 N.E.2d 958 (1990), the Court described the type of awareness required for a valid *Miranda* waiver as "being cognizant at all times of the State's intention to use [one's] statements to secure a conviction, and of the fact that one can stand mute and request a lawyer." The Court further stated that:

> If intelligent knowledge in the *Miranda* context means anything, it means the ability to *understand the very words used in the warnings*. It need not mean the ability to understand far-reaching legal and strategic effects of

waiving one's rights, or to appreciate how widely or deeply an interroga- tion may probe, or to withstand the influence of stress or fancy; *but to waive rights intelligently and knowingly, one must at least understand basically what those rights encompass and minimally what their waiver will entail. Id.* at 964. (Emphasis added)

The Court invalidated the confession made by a 17–year–old youth with subnormal intelligence, no prior police experience, and a 9th grade education because he did not have a "normal ability to understand questions and concepts." *Id.* at 964.

However, most courts tend to apply the "totality" standard very conser- vatively. Courts routinely find valid *Miranda* waivers when police testify that they advised a juvenile of her rights and she answered "yes" when asked if she understood them. *See* Wallace J. Mlyniec, "A Judge's Ethical Dilemma: Assessing a Child's Capacity to Choose," 64 *Fordham L. Rev.* 1873, 1902 (1996) (stating that at hearings to determine admissibility of statements, "police officers frequently relate that they read the *Miranda* warnings and that the child agreed to talk"). Even overtly coercive police interrogation techniques and a youth's very young age or mental deficiencies do not prevent trial judges from finding and appellate courts from upholding a waiver as "voluntary." *See e.g. W.M. v. State*, 585 So.2d 979 (Fla. 4th Dist. Ct. App. 1991). Appellate courts do not substitute their own evaluations of facts for those of a trial judge unless they find the trial judge's ruling to be "clearly erroneous," an "abuse of discretion," or without substantial support in the record. As a result, courts often uphold trial judges' decisions based on extreme facts. According to a dissenting judge in *W.M.*, the majority held that

a 10–year old boy with an I.Q. of 69 or 70, who had been placed by school authorities in a learning disability program and was described by one of his teachers as having difficulty understanding directions, who had no prior record with the police, who was crying and upset when taken into custody, and who was then held by police for nearly 6 hours * * * without any non-accusatorial adult present, could in the end knowingly and voluntarily confess to nearly every unsolved burglary on the police blotter.

Courts readily admit the confessions of illiterate, mentally retarded juveniles with IQs in the 60s, whom psychologist witnesses characterize as incapable of abstract reasoning. *See, e.g., People v. Cheatham*, 453 Mich. 1,36, 551 N.W.2d 355, 370 (Mich. 1996) (upholding waiver by an intellectually limited, illiterate juvenile with an IQ of 62 because "[l]ow mental ability in and of itself is insufficient to establish that a defendant did not understand his rights"); *State v. Cleary*, 161 Vt. 403, 641 A.2d 102 (Vt. 1994) (upholding waiver by juvenile with only a limited ability to read or write and an IQ of 65). *See e.g.*, Kevin P. Weis, "Confessions of Mentally Retarded Juveniles and the Validity of Miranda Rights Waiver," 37 *Brandeis L.J.* 117, 126 (1998), who notes that "Several characteristics common to the mentally retarded and juveniles tend to predispose members of these groups to waive their rights in a manner inconsistent with the requirements of voluntary, knowing, and intelligent waiver. Furthermore, these same characteristics may lead to in- creased incidence of false confessions, at least with respect to the mentally retarded. * * * Such traits, however, are common enough to conclude that it would be prudent to enact safeguards to ensure valid, trustworthy waivers and confessions are obtained."

Fare accepted police interrogation as a legitimate law enforcement tool, posited coerciveness as a fact question in each case, declined to unduly restrict law enforcement with bright-lines, and provided police with considerable latitude to exploit youths' vulnerability. Susceptibility to interrogation, in turn, adversely affects youths' subsequent dispositions. Juvenile court judges appear to sentence more severely youths who admit their criminal involvement than those who deny it. *See* R. Barry Ruback and Paula J. Vardaman, "Decision Making in Delinquency Cases: The Role of Race and Juveniles' Admission/Denial of Crime," 21 *Law & Human Behavior* 47 (1997).

4) What Do Kids Know and When Do They Know It? Can a typical juvenile make a "knowing, intelligent, and voluntary" waiver decision? Does a youth possess the developmental capacity to understand and waive constitutional rights? Empirical studies that evaluate juveniles' comprehension of their *Miranda* rights indicate that most juveniles who receive a *Miranda* warning may not understand the language, much less the legal concepts, well enough to waive their constitutional rights in a "knowing and intelligent" manner. Professor Thomas Grisso conducted tests to determine whether juveniles could paraphrase the words in the *Miranda* warning, whether they could define six critical words in the *Miranda* warning such as "attorney," "consult" and "appoint," and whether they could give correct true-false answers to twelve re-wordings of the *Miranda* warnings. *See* Thomas Grisso, "Juveniles' Capacities to Waive *Miranda* Rights: An Empirical Analysis," 68 *Cal. L. Rev.* 1134 (1980) [hereinafter *Juveniles' Capacities to Waive*]; Thomas Grisso, *Juveniles' Waivers of Rights: Legal and Psychological Competence* (1981) [hereinafter *Juveniles' Waivers of Rights*]; Thomas Grisso, "Juveniles' Consent in Delinquency Proceedings," in *Children's Competence to Consent* (Gary B. Melton, Gerald P. Koocher, and Michael J. Saks, eds., New York: Plenum Press 1983).

Grisso and his colleagues administered structured interviews, designed by a panel of psychologists and lawyers, to three samples of juvenile subjects, and to two samples of adult subjects, and compared the juveniles' performances with the adult norms. Most juveniles who received the warnings did not understand them well enough to waive their constitutional rights "knowingly and intelligently." Only 20.9% of the juveniles, as compared with 42.3% of the adults, demonstrated adequate understanding of the four components of a *Miranda* warning, while 55.3% of juveniles as contrasted with 23.1% of the adults exhibited no comprehension of at least one of the four warnings. Grisso, *Juveniles' Capacities to Waive, supra* at 1153–54. An earlier study found that over 90% of the juveniles whom police interrogated waived their rights, that an equal number did not understand the rights they waived, and that even a simplified version of the language in the *Miranda* warning failed to cure these defects. Bruce A. Ferguson and Alan C. Douglas, "A Study of Juvenile Waiver," 7 *San Diego L. Rev.* 39, 53 (1970).

Juveniles most frequently misunderstood the *Miranda* advisory that they had the right to consult with an attorney and to have one present during interrogation. Younger juveniles exhibited even greater difficulties understanding their rights. "As a class, juveniles younger than fifteen years of age failed to meet both the absolute and relative (adult norm) standards for comprehension * * *. The vast majority of these juveniles misunderstood at least one of the four standard *Miranda* statements, and compared with adults, demonstrated significantly poorer comprehension of the nature and significance of the *Miranda* rights." Grisso, *Juveniles' Capacities to Waive, supra* at 1160. Although "juveniles younger than fifteen manifest significantly poorer comprehension than adults of comparable intelligence," the level of comprehension exhibited by youths sixteen and older, although comparable to that of adults, left much to be desired. *Id.* at 1157.

A replication of Grisso's research in Canada reported that very few juveniles fully understood their warnings and that the youths who lacked comprehension waived their rights more readily. "[I]t seems likely that many if not most juveniles who are asked by the police to waive their rights do not have sufficient understanding to be competent to waive them." Rona Abramovitch, Karen Higgins–Biss, and Stephen Biss, "Young Persons' Comprehension of waivers in Criminal Proceedings," 35 *Canadian J. Criminology* 309, 320 (1993). Another study reported that youths interpreted the warning that "anything can and will be used against you in a court of law" to mean that "any disrespectful words directed toward police would be reported to the judge." *Novak v. Commonwealth*, 20 Va.App. 373, 457 S.E.2d 402 (Va. Ct. App.1995); Ellen R. Fulmer, "*Novak v. Commonwealth*: Are Virginia Courts Providing a Special Protection to Virginia's Juvenile Defendants," 30 *U. Rich. L. Rev.* 935, 955 (1996) (quoting Brief of Amicus Curiae on Behalf of Youth Advocacy Clinic and Mental Disabilities Clinic, University of Richmond Law School). A study of urban, black high school students who participated in a year-long "Street Law" course reported that education about *Miranda* rights did not improve students' understanding or comprehension of the content of a *Miranda* warning in ways that would enable them to take meaningful advantage of their rights. *See* Chevon M. Wall and Mary Furlong, "Comprehension of *Miranda* Rights by Urban Adolescents with Law–Related Education," 56 *Psych. Rep.* 359 (1985).

Moreover, research conducted under laboratory conditions may fail to capture adequately the individual characteristics, social context, and stressful coercive conditions associated with actual police interrogation. Responses to hypothetical questions propounded by social scientists in a relaxed atmosphere do not replicate adequately the conditions created by police who "can be gentle or tough, can explain the rights well or poorly, and in many ways can exert varying amounts of pressure to comply." Abramovitch, *Young Persons' Comprehension, supra* at 319; Grisso, *Juveniles' Consent in Delinquency Proceedings, supra* at 139. Typically, delinquents come from lower income households and may possess less verbal skills or capacity to understand legal abstractions than the middle-class youths who participated in these studies. Moreover, children from poorer and ethnic-minority backgrounds often express doubt that law enforcement officials will not punish them for exercising their legal rights. *See* Gary B. Melton, "Taking *Gault* Seriously: Toward a New Juvenile Court," 68 *Neb. L. Rev.* 146 (1989).

Immaturity, inexperience, and lower verbal competence than adults render youths especially vulnerable to police interrogation tactics.

Youths' social status relative to adult authority figures such as police also render them more susceptible than adults to the coercive pressures of interrogation. Children's greater dependence upon adults and societal expectations of youthful obedience to authority also make youths more vulnerable to police interrogation techniques. Most people believe that answering the police in a respectful and cooperative manner will benefit them, at least in the short run. Inexperienced youths may waive their rights and talk in the short-sighted and unrealistic belief that their interrogation will end more quickly and secure their release.

Many people from traditionally disempowered communities, such as females, African–Americans, and youth, pragmatically use indirect patterns of speech in order to avoid conflict in their dealings with authority figures. Janet E. Ainsworth, "In a Different Register: The Pragmatics of Powerlessness in Police Interrogation," 103 *Yale L.J.* 259 (1993). People with lower social status than their interrogators typically respond more passively, "talk" more readily, acquiesce to police suggestions more easily, and speak less assertively or aggressively. Edwin Driver, "Confessions and the Social Psychology of Coercion," 82 *Harvard L. Rev.* 42, 56 (1968). Thus, *Fare*'s requirement that youths invoke *Miranda* rights clearly, unambiguously, directly and with adult-like precision runs contrary to developmental psychological research findings about adolescent competence and to the normal and predictable social reactions and verbal styles of most delinquents subjected to custodial interrogation.

Lack of comprehension by minors raises questions about the adequacy of the *Miranda* warning as a safeguard. Empirical research suggests that juveniles simply are not as linguistically competent as adults to waive their rights, testify, or even understand the legal process. *See e.g.*, Karen Saywitz, Carol Jaenicke, and Lorinda Camparo, "Children's Knowledge of Legal Terminology," 14 *Law & Human Behavior* 523 (1990); Trudie Smith, "Law Talk: Juveniles' Understanding of Legal Language," 13 J. Crim. Just. 339 (1985); Regina M. Huerter and Bonnie E. Saltzman, "What Do 'They' Think? The Delinquency Court Process in Colorado as Viewed By the Youth," 69 *Den. U. L. Rev.* 345 (1992). Would the problems of waivers of rights be resolved if police gave *Miranda* warnings in a "simplified fashion"? *See State v. Benoit*, 126 N.H. 6, 490 A.2d 295 at 297–98 (N.H. 1985) where the "the record established that the interrogating officer read the defendant his rights from the standard adult *Miranda* form. The officer did not explain any of the rights, nor did he discuss [with the fifteen year old] * * * the possibility of his being tried as an adult for armed robbery." The New Hampshire Supreme Court concluded that before a juvenile could be deemed to have validly waived fundamental rights, "he or she must be informed, in language understandable to a child, of his or her rights." *Id.* at 304.

5) Juvenile False Confessions Critics of the "totality of the circumstances" test question whether a typical juvenile subjected to the inherent coercion of custodial interrogation ever can make a "knowing, intelligent, and voluntary" of rights. *See generally* Larry E. Holtz, "*Miranda* in a Juvenile

Setting: A Child's Right to Silence," 78 *J. Crim. L. & Criminology* 534 (1987); Comment, "The Judicial Response to Juvenile Confessions: An Examination of the *Per Se* Rule," 17 *Duq. L. Rev.* 659 (1978). **Steven A. Drizin and Richard A. Leo, "The Problem of False Confessions in the Post–DNA World," 82 *N. Car. L. Rev.* 891 (2004)** noted the special vulnerability of juveniles and their susceptibility to give false confessions when confronted with standard police interrogation techniques. They studied 125 cases DNA-exonerations, many of which included proven false confessions, and which involved a disproportionate number of juveniles:

> Consistent with previous research, juveniles, defined as persons under the age of eighteen, are over-represented in our sample of false confessions. In fact, juveniles comprise approximately one-third (33%) of our sample. More than half of the juvenile false confessors in our sample are ages fifteen and under (22/40), suggesting that children of this age group may be especially vulnerable to the pressures of interrogation and the possibility of false confession. At the same time, the vast majority of juvenile false confessors in our sample (33/40) are ages fourteen to seventeen, the age range at which many alleged juvenile offenders are tried as adults. * * *

> There are good reasons why juveniles may be more vulnerable to police pressure during interrogations. Juveniles are, of course, less mature than adults and have less life experience on which to draw. As a result, they tend to be more naïve and more easily intimidated by police power, persuasion, or coercion. They are thus less equipped to cope with stressful police interrogation and less likely to possess the psychological resources to resist the pressures of accusatorial police questioning. As a result, juveniles tend to be more ready to confess in response to police interrogation, especially coercive interrogation. * * *

> When one looks beyond the juveniles in our sample, however, it is clear that an age bias persists. Most false confessions in our sample come from the young. * * * To the extent that our sample is representative, this suggests that suspect's age is strongly correlated with the likelihood of eliciting a false confession. * * *

> One of the most troubling findings in our study concerns the number of young children who falsely confessed to serious crimes they did not commit. In our sample, we found seven children under the age of fourteen who were the victims of interrogation-induced confessions. * * *

> There are forty false confessions in this Article's database from suspects who were under the age of eighteen at the time they confessed. Precisely why these young people falsely confessed is not always clear. In most of the false confessions, we do not have audiotapes or videotapes of the interrogations, making it difficult to ascertain whether a particular police tactic triggered the false confession. In the absence of such research, we must rely on the juvenile confessor's account of why he confessed and the particular tactics used by police which triggered or contributed to the false confession. Although we do not have explanations in every case, one of the most common reasons cited by teenage false

confessors is the belief that by confessing, they would be able to go home.
* * *

Another trend which emerges from our database is the number of cases in which more than one defendant falsely confesses to the same brutal crime. There are thirty-eight cases in our database in which this phenomenon has occurred. This represents more than 30% of our sample. Of the thirty-eight cases involving multiple false confessions, nineteen, or 50% of these confessions, involve juveniles. Although the Central Park Jogger case contains the highest number of false confessions in a single case with five, there are several cases in our database with four false confessions, three cases with three, and numerous others with two."
* * *

[I]nterrogators need to receive specialized training in how to interrogate persons with developmental disabilities and juveniles, two subgroups of suspects who appear to be particularly vulnerable to falsely confessing when police apply psychological interrogation techniques to them. * * * Because juvenile suspects share many of the same characteristics as the developmentally disabled, notably their eagerness to comply with adult authority figures, impulsivity, immature judgment, and inability to recognize and weigh risks in decision-making, and appear to be at a greater risk of falsely confessing when subjected to psychological interrogation techniques, the same protections should be afforded to juveniles. In fact, in the wake of the Ryan Harris case and several other false confessions involving children and teenagers in Chicago, Illinois enacted a law requiring that all children under age thirteen be provided access to attorneys before their interrogations in murder and sex offense cases. Moreover, the Cook County State's Attorney's Office convened the Juvenile Court Competency Commission, a panel of experts from many disciplines, including child development specialists, child psychiatrists and psychologists, service providers, law enforcement personnel, prosecutors, judges, defenders, disability advocates, and educators, to study the ability of young people to understand and meaningfully participate in the interrogation process and court proceedings. The Commission recommended even broader reforms, including barring the State from using any uncounseled statements against children under age seventeen in any proceedings in which children face potential adult punishments, a requirement that the entire custodial interrogation of juveniles charged with felonies be videotaped, and that more effective procedures be developed to ensure that a minor's parent or guardian is present during police questioning. * * *

6) An empirical study of what kids know and their competence to exercise *Miranda* rights. Professor Barry C. Feld published two articles that provide the first empirical study of police interrogation of juveniles. See Barry C. Feld, "Juveniles Competence to Exercise Miranda Rights: An Empirical Study of Policy and Practice," 91 *Minn.L.Rev.* 26 (2006); "Police Interrogation of Juveniles: An Empirical Study of Policy and Practice," 97 *J. Crim. L. & Criminology* 219 (2006). The Minnesota Supreme Court in *State v. Scales* (1994) required police to record all interrogations of criminal suspects including juveniles. In Minnesota, trials of youths sixteen-and seventeen-years

of age and charged with a felony-level offense are public proceedings. Feld
obtained 66 interrogation files—tapes or transcripts, police reports, juvenile
court filings, pre-sentence investigation reports and dispositions—of older
juveniles charged with serious crimes in one urban county. Unlike both
Grisso's laboratory studies of adolescent competence, supra Note 4, p. 295 and
Drizin and Leo's study which also found juveniles fifteen years of age and
younger to be particularly vulnerable, Feld's study focused on older adolescents whom Grisso reported function more or less on a par with adults. In
"Juveniles Competence to Exercise *Miranda* Rights," Feld reported
that:

> Police arrested the vast majority (88%) of juveniles prior to interro-
> gating them. In a few cases, a juvenile's parent initially brought her to
> the police station for an interview, and police arrested an additional 5% of
> those youths following questioning. A parent was actually present during
> only one interview, and police arrested and detained that juvenile at the
> conclusion of the questioning.

> When police took these youths into custody, they placed the vast
> majority (88%) in detention. However, police released about 5% of youths
> whom they had previously arrested and detained after they questioned
> them. Nearly two-thirds (66%) of the interviews occurred at juvenile
> detention centers or other correctional facilities. Police conducted almost
> one-third (30%) of the remaining interviews at police stations, sheriff's
> departments, or at the time of arrest. Police conducted only 5% of the
> interviews in non-custodial settings, such as the juveniles' homes or high
> schools. * * *

> Police interrogation manuals emphasize the importance of establish-
> ing and maintaining a positive relationship with a suspect as a prelude to
> obtaining a waiver from and questioning her. The timing and administra-
> tion of the *Miranda* warning itself provides officers with opportunities to
> build rapport and subtly to predispose the suspect to waive her rights and
> talk with police. For example, the Supreme Court's decisions in *Miranda*,
> *Rhode Island v. Innis*, and *Pennsylvania v. Muniz* allow police officers to
> ask suspects routine "booking questions" without first administering a
> *Miranda* warning. In the majority of cases (56%), police did not adminis-
> ter the *Miranda* warning immediately upon engaging a juvenile, but
> instead used their initial contact to build rapport while asking suspects
> neutral questions—name, age and date of birth, address and telephone
> number, grade in school, etc.—while completing the *Miranda* advisory
> form. Some officers used youths' responses to these "booking questions"
> as opportunities to engage in casual conversations unrelated to the
> subject of the interview to put the youths more at ease and to condition
> them to respond to questions. * * *

> Police and prosecutors may establish objectively that a juvenile
> understands her rights by administering the *Miranda* advisory and ob-
> taining an affirmative response. In the simplest version, the officer reads
> each of the rights to the youth, followed by the question "Do you
> understand that?" After the juvenile affirmatively acknowledges each
> warning "on the record," she then initials the form. In nearly half the

cases, the officer had the youth read out loud the final paragraph of the form, in which the juvenile stipulates to receiving the warnings, initials each right, and signs the form. Following administration of the *Miranda* warning, every juvenile purported to understand her rights. The fifty-three juveniles who ultimately waived their rights clearly and affirmatively indicated a willingness to do so. * * *

Eighty percent of the juveniles waived their *Miranda* rights. These rates are consistent with the high waiver rates reported by the Yale Law Journal–New Haven Study, Leo's California research, Cassell and Hayman's Salt Lake observations, Gudjonsson's British studies, and Grisso's earlier juvenile research. Juveniles charged with crimes against the person and firearms violations exhibited the highest rates of waivers, and those charged with property and drug crimes waived their rights somewhat less frequently.

The Supreme Court in *Fare* emphasized Michael C's prior contacts with police as one factor supporting the validity of his waiver under the "totality of the circumstances." Similarly, criminological research also indicates that a suspect's prior experience with law enforcement is an important factor associated with rates of *Miranda* waivers and invocations. Recall from Table 1 that 42% of these juveniles had one or more felony arrests prior to their current arrest. * * * [J]uveniles with prior felony arrests waived their rights at substantially lower rates (68%) than did those with fewer or less serious police contacts (89%). * * *

Feld's second article—**"Police Interrogation of Juveniles"**—reports on how police questioned the juveniles who waived their *Miranda* rights. Some of those findings include:

> After completing the *Miranda* formalities, in about one-fifth (17%) of cases, officers described their roles as neutral, objective fact finders trying to determine what happened, rather than as adversaries. They invoked their professional expertise, advised the youths that they could distinguish between suspects who lied or told the truth, and reassured them that they would not lie to or trick them. * * *

> Once officers secured a *Miranda* waiver, they commenced interrogation in earnest. Questions can take a variety of forms, so I initially examined simply how officers framed their questions. * * * [I]n every interrogation (100%) officers asked juveniles at least some open-ended queries that invited them to provide an account. In nearly half the cases (42%), they began interrogation with open-ended questions and asked the suspect to "tell her story." * * * Leading questions play a prominent role in studies of false confessions because they require suspects to adopt interrogators' incriminating premises or feed suspects "inside information" that only a guilty party would know. Police asked leading questions in only half (49%) of the interrogations, and such questions did not feature prominently in any case. Interrogators "echoed"—repeating back a phrase or the last few words of the suspect's previous reply—in about half (47%) the cases to invite further comment. * * *

> Police interrogators use a two-pronged strategy to overcome suspects' resistance and to enable them to admit responsibility. Maximization

techniques intimidate suspects and impress on them the futility of denial, while minimization techniques provide moral justifications or face-saving alternatives to enable them to confess. Police may overstate the seriousness of the crime or make exaggerated or false claims about the evidence. The Reid Method recommends asking emotionally-charged Behavioral Analysis Interview (BAI) questions to provoke reactions from suspects. Leo reported that detectives used several maximization tactics: confront suspects with real and false evidence; refuse to accept denials; accuse suspects of lying; identify inconsistencies in suspects' stories; and emphasize the implausibility of suspects' claims. * * *

[T]he more common maximization strategies officers used [included]: confronting juveniles with evidence; asking BAI questions; playing on their fears; calling them liars; and pointing out inconsistencies. Officers used maximization strategies in nine out of ten (89%) interrogations and asked an average of five (5.1) different types of questions in the interrogations in which they used them. In more than two-thirds of the cases (70%), police confronted juveniles with evidence—identification by witnesses, statements of co-defendants, physical evidence, or fingerprints—to emphasize the strength of their case. In about one-half or more of the cases, officers asked BAI questions (62%), accused suspects of lying (49%), pointed out inconsistencies in suspects' responses (45%), and urged them to tell the truth (45%). In more than one-third of interrogations, the officers disputed suspects' assertions (40%), played on their fears (36%), and emphasized the seriousness of their predicament (34%). * * *

[O]fficers used the same types of maximization strategies to manipulate and intimidate juveniles as Leo observed them employ with adults. As the frequency count indicates, officers used several different types of maximization tactics in the course of an interrogation. Although officers spoke firmly and directly with juveniles, they did not raise their voices or shout at juveniles on any of the tapes to which I listened. * * *

Minimization techniques provide face-saving excuses and moral justifications to induce a confession by minimizing the seriousness of the offense or blaming the victim or accomplices. Police used minimization techniques in about half of the cases (45%). Strategies police used in between one-third and one-half of the cases included: the use of scenarios or themes to reduce suspects' feelings of guilt (50%); expressions of empathy (42%); comments minimizing the seriousness of the crime (38%); offers to help (38%); and appeals to honor (33%).

Officers frequently appealed to suspects to tell the truth. In many instances, they offered to investigate further or to work on behalf of a truth-telling youth. They also predicted that prosecutors and judges would look more favorably on youths who admitted responsibility. * * *

[J]uveniles confessed and admitted all the elements of the offense in less than one-fifth of the cases (17%). However, they provided some statements of evidentiary value in about half (53%) of the cases, for example, admitting that they served as a "look out" during a robbery or participated with others during a burglary even if they did not personally steal property. In about one-third (30%) of the cases, juveniles denied criminal involvement or made no incriminating admissions. Leo's research reported that police obtained successful outcomes in about three-quarters (76%) of the cases in which suspects waived their *Miranda* rights, and the Yale–New Haven study reported that about two-thirds (64%) of interrogations produced incriminating evidence. * * *

Cooperative, polite, or remorseful juveniles gave incriminating statements far more often than did hostile, resistant, or belligerent youths. * * * [A]bout two-thirds of juveniles (70%) exhibited a cooperative demeanor, while one-third (30%) appeared resistant. The vast majority (86%) of cooperative juveniles confessed or made incriminating admissions, while a large majority (69%) of resistant juveniles did not provide useful admissions. The fact that nearly one-third of youths resisted the police and two-thirds of them did not incriminate themselves provides some evidence of juveniles' competence in the interrogation room. * * *

Almost all cases of proven false confessions involved lengthy interrogation. * * * Cases involving firearms presented the most striking feature affecting lengths of interrogations. Although police questioned only one-quarter (25%) of suspects for more than thirty minutes, they interrogated 60% of juveniles charged with primary firearms offenses for longer than thirty minutes. Because the number of cases in which a firearm violation was the primary charge was small, I compared the lengths of interrogation in all cases in which juveniles used guns—for example, armed robbery, aggravated assault, and firearms possession—with cases in which juveniles used other weapons—for example, knives, blunt instruments, and automobiles—or no weapons. Police concluded 89% of interrogations in cases in which juveniles did not use guns in thirty minutes or less. By contrast, police questioned nearly two-thirds (60%) of juveniles in all cases involving guns for more than thirty minutes. Guns provide an indicator of offense seriousness, and police questioned these juveniles more extensively and aggressively. * * *

Police interrogate suspects to elicit confessions or admissions. They also use suspects' answers to obtain leads to other evidence and witnesses, to identify codefendants, and the like. Obtaining collateral evidence appears to be a secondary and not especially productive purpose of interrogation. * * * Police obtained some additional evidence in 15% of cases. Most commonly (11%), juveniles identified or corroborated the identity of other participants in the crime. In some instances, police conducted photo line-ups and had juveniles identify their confederates. * * *

The similarities in waiver rates, interrogation tactics, and suspects' responses between these older delinquents and Leo's adults suggest that courts, legislatures, and police policymakers should regulate interrogation practices directly rather than provide special procedural protections for sixteen-and seventeen-year-old juveniles. Within the past decade, near-unanimity has emerged among policy groups and scholars to mandate recording of interrogations to reduce coercion, to minimize dangers of false confessions, and to increase the visibility and transparency of the process. Recording creates an objective record of testimonial evidence. It provides an independent basis by which to resolve credibility disputes between police and defendants about *Miranda* warnings, waivers, or statements. It reduces the risks of false confessions. A complete record enables the fact finder to determine whether a statement contains facts uniquely known to the perpetrator or whether police supplied those facts to the suspect during interrogation. Recording protects police from false claims of abuse, protects defendants whose credibility is compromised by being charged, and protects innocent suspects from false confessions and wrongful convictions. Recording enhances police professionalism and contributes to more effective investigations.

Police must record the entire investigation—all preliminary interviews and initial interrogations—rather than just a final statement. Only a complete record of every interaction can protect against a final "voluntary" statement that ratifies an earlier coerced statement or against a false confession in which suspects repeat back unique facts about the crime previously furnished by the police. * * *

Courts and legislatures should consider limiting the length of time that police may interrogate suspects. The Court long has recognized that very lengthy interrogations produce involuntary confessions. Although the Supreme Court consistently has avoided prescribing explicit time limits for *Terry* stops, detentions, or interrogations, state courts and legislatures possess the competency to do so. The majority of all interrogations in this study were surprisingly brief and police concluded three-quarters (75%) in less than thirty minutes. Moreover, the brevity of questioning observed here is consistent with every empirical study that report that police complete the vast majority of interrogations in less than sixty minutes. By contrast, prolonged interrogation—especially in conjunction with youthfulness, mental retardation, or other psychological vulnerabilities—is strongly associated with eliciting false confessions.

Obviously, this study does not lend itself to prescribing specific limits to the lengths of interrogation. However, courts should at least create a sliding-scale presumption that police coerced an involuntary confession as the length of interrogation increases. Police complete nearly all interrogations of juveniles and adults in less than one or two hours. By contrast, they extract the vast majority of false confessions only after interrogating suspects for six hours or longer; those time limits could frame the strength and length of the presumption. A recent review of 125 cases of proven false confession reported that questioning lasted less than six hours in 16% of cases, continued between six and twelve hours in one-third (34%) of cases, persisted for between twelve and twenty-four hours in another one-third of cases (39%), and continued from one to three days in the remaining 11% of cases. Based on the short duration of routine interrogation and the lengthy time associated with police-induced false confessions, some analysts contend that "[r]egardless of the interrogation practices employed, an interrogation should not be allowed to extend beyond some prescribed limit, say six hours." Because some suspects may confess falsely to terminate a seemingly-endless interrogation, police should advise them of the maximum length of permissible questioning as part of the *Miranda* warning. * * *

The Court's decisions in *Fare* and *Alvarado* treated juveniles as the functional equals of adults during interrogation. Over the past quarter-century, developmental psychological research consistently has emphasized adolescents' inability to understand or exercise *Miranda* rights and their lack of competence in legal proceedings. Recent research on false confessions further underscores the unique vulnerability of youth and reports that police obtained more than one-third (35%) of proven false confessions from suspects under the age of eighteen. * * *

The Court's rulings in juvenile interrogation cases—*Haley, Gallegos, Gault, Fare*, and *Alvarado*—excluded statements elicited from those fifteen years of age or younger and admitted those obtained from sixteen- and seventeen-year-old youths. This *de facto* functional line closely tracks developmental psychological research that reports juveniles fifteen years of age and younger lack the ability to exercise *Miranda* rights while older juveniles perform more or less on par with adults in the interrogation room.

Developmental psychologists report that older juveniles exhibit relatively adult-like competence, and this study corroborates that sixteen- and seventeen-year-old juveniles appear to understand and to exercise their *Miranda* rights the same way as do adults. This consistency inferentially bolsters their research findings that juveniles fifteen years of age and younger lack competence to exercise *Miranda* rights. If developmental psychologists are right about one aspect of adolescents' competence, then they are likely correct about the other as well. Accordingly, even if the *Miranda* framework is adequate for older adolescents, it may provide insufficient protection for younger juveniles. Courts and legislatures should formally adopt the functional line that the Court drew and that psychologists discern between the competencies of youths sixteen years of age and older and those fifteen years of age and younger, and provide additional protections for the more vulnerable children.

This study is also remarkably congruent with Leo's observations of police interrogation of adults. Once these juveniles waived their *Miranda* rights, police used the same strategies and tactics to question them. The officers seemed to work from the same standard script and use the same techniques—The Reid Method. These juveniles responded to those tactics, cooperated or resisted, and provided incriminating evidence at about the same rate as did adults. As in Leo's study, the police interrogated the vast majority of these juveniles for a relatively brief period of time. In short, the law treats juveniles just like adults, and police question them just as they do older suspects. * * *

7) Circumstances rendering juvenile confessions involuntary Drizin and Leo, *supra*, identified youthfulness, lengthy interrogation, and high-visibility crimes that create pressures on police to use coercive interrogation tactics as the typical context for many police-induced false confessions. Even after juveniles waive their *Miranda* rights, courts still must determine whether they gave their statement voluntarily. **Doody v. Schriro**, 548 F.3d 847 (C.A.9 (Ariz.), 2008), provides an unusual example of close judicial review of the voluntariness of a juvenile's confession obtained during investigation of a high-visibility crime in which police conducted a lengthy interrogation and used coercive tactics. On August 10, 1991, police discovered nine bodies in a Thai Buddhist temple outside Phoenix, Arizona. The "Temple Murders" sparked a massive investigation. Although police initially suspected other perpetrators, ballistics reports led to a rifle owned by Caratachea, which, in turn, led to Caratachea's seventeen-year-old roommate, Johnathan Doody. The Arizona trial court and court of appeals denied Doody's motion to suppress his statement, finding the *Miranda* warnings adequate and the confession voluntary. On federal habeas review, for which the standard of review requires a judicial finding that the state court rulings represent an "unreasonable application of clearly established federal law" or an unreasonable determination of facts, the court, per BERZON, Circuit Judge, found Doody's confession involuntary:

> Seventeen-year-old Johnathan Doody was interrogated overnight for twelve hours straight. When, after several hours, he fell silent and refused to answer the officers' questions, the officers persisted, asking dozens of questions, many over and over again, and telling him he had to answer them. * * *

> At 9:25 p.m., two police officers began an interview that did not end until 10:00 a.m. the following morning. The entire interview was audio-taped. Doody was not informed of the taping and was not aware of it. * * * Doody was offered food, drink, and bathroom breaks several times during the night, although he never accepted food. Other than two brief bathroom breaks in the morning hours, the interview went on continuously during the twelve hours. * * *

> The interrogation was initially conducted by Detectives Riley and Munley. Detective Riley began with a casual introduction:

> [S]ince we're in kind of a formal setting and things like that and because [Detective Munley's] a police officer and I'm a police officer and things like that, sometimes some of the questions that we get into are, are a little bit sensitive and things like that. And what I'd like to do is before we, we go into that is read something to you and, so that you understand some of the protections and things that, that you have. It's not meant to scare you or anything like that. Don't, don't take it out of context, okay.

> He asked Doody if he had heard of *Miranda* warnings; Doody responded that he had not. Detective Riley repeatedly assured Doody that the warnings were "not meant to scare you" and told him, "I don't want you to feel that because I'm reading this to you that we necessarily feel that you're responsible for anything. It's for your benefit, it's for your protection and for ours as well."

> Although Detective Riley used a "juvenile Miranda warnings" form,[2] he orally expanded upon the written form. * * * At the conclusion of each warning, Doody indicated that he understood and initialed the

---

2. In addition to the traditional *Miranda* warnings, this form also asks if the juvenile wants a parent or guardian present during questioning and warns that the juvenile's case may be handled by adult, rather than juvenile, court.

juvenile *Miranda* form. Doody agreed to speak to the officers without a parent or attorney present, and the interrogation commenced.

Detectives Riley and Munley began by asking Doody casual questions about his roommates and friends, including which of his friends and acquaintances owned guns. Doody immediately volunteered that [his roommate] owned a gun, but denied ever having borrowed or shot it. The officers then asked Doody about the temple murders, inquiring where he was at the time of the murders and when he learned of them. Doody readily answered the questions, stating that on the night of the murders he saw a movie with a friend and then went home. * * * Detective Riley again asked Doody about his whereabouts on the night of the murders and whether he knew anything about the murders other than what was in the news. Doody denied any knowledge. * * *

Detectives Riley and Munley both proceeded to lecture Doody on how important it was for him to tell them the truth, and, now becoming more specific, informed him they "kn[e]w that you were along with at least one other person when [Caratachea]'s rifle was borrowed." They then demanded that he tell them about the borrowing of Caratachea's rifle, using words that went beyond urging or imploring: "[I]t's so important for you, for you to tell us. I mean you have to tell us. You have to." * * *

Detectives Riley and Munley launched into several more monologues on how important it was for Doody to tell them the truth and how they knew he was not doing so. This time, however, they told Doody that Caratachea's rifle was the murder weapon. Doody * * * continued to deny involvement in or knowledge of the murders despite the officers' repeated questions and insistence that he knew more than he was telling them.

Undeterred by his denials, the officers pushed harder. For almost an hour, from about 1:50 a.m. to 2:45 a.m., Detectives Riley and Munley told Doody that the case was "busted wide open," that he had to protect himself from what others were saying about him by telling them the truth, and that he knew exactly what happened at the temple. In the few times Doody spoke during this period he denied any knowledge or involvement.

At around 2:45 a.m., Detectives Riley and Munley were joined by Detective Sinsabaugh * * * [and] [f]or over two hours, all three officers * * * began to barrage Doody with questions. Doody essentially stopped responding altogether. They asked him five times whose plan it was to go to the temple; Doody did not answer once. They asked fourteen times whether it was Caratachea's idea; Doody answered once—that he did not know. They asked twenty-five times whether Doody was at the temple; Doody did not answer once. During this entire sequence, lasting twenty minutes, Doody answered one out of forty-five questions. Framing the repetitious questioning were demands for answers: "You have to tell us," the officers told Doody, "We have to know; you have to let us know." And, frustrated by Doody's silence, one officer sharply directed him: "Answer, Jonathan, answer."

The officers next began asking a series of questions about whether Doody was keeping silent because someone had threatened him. Doody answered a few of these questions, but fell silent again when the officers returned to asking him—seven times without a response—whose idea it was to go to the temple. Doody remained silent this time for eight minutes, failing to respond to thirty questions in a row. In the face of Doody's silence, Detective Sinsabaugh warned him, "I'm gonna stay here until I get an answer," and directed: "You've got to answer me"; "Jon, answer me." * * * Many of Doody's answers during this time are whispers, barely audible on the tapes.

At about 3:30 a.m., Detective Sinsabaugh asked him ten times if he had been involved with the temple incident, directing him: "Answer me. Answer me, Jonathan. Jonathan, answer me. Answer me. What, what's the problem? Answer me, Jonathan." After Detective Sinsabaugh asked yet again if Doody had been involved, Doody finally responded, "Yes." More than six hours into the interrogation, after forty-five minutes of relentless questioning in the face of Doody's almost complete silence, this was the first statement Doody made linking himself to the murders.

For about a half hour after this one-word response, most of the officers' questions again went unanswered; what answers Doody gave were largely monosyllabic. Showing increasing impatience with his silence, Detective Sinsabaugh told him, "if it's gonna take you all night to tell me two little simple things, we're gonna have a problem." But Doody still remained silent when asked fourteen times whether Caratachea was involved. * * *

Shortly after 4:00 a.m.—six and one-half hours after the interrogation began, and without a single break in questioning—Doody began to talk about the temple murders in a narrative fashion. He told the officers that he, Garcia, Caratachea, a friend of Caratachea's named George, and one other person went to the temple for what he thought was a plan to test the temple's security system. * * * Throughout, Doody maintained that he never knew until the events unfolded that the plan involved robbery or murder.

The interrogation ended at about 10:00 a.m., over twelve hours after it began. For almost nine hours, the interrogation never paused; in the final three hours, Doody had only two short breaks to use the restroom. By the end, he was sobbing. * * *

Finally, Doody claims that his confession was coerced and thus involuntary, so its admission at trial violated his Fourteenth Amendment right to due process. He points particularly to his age—seventeen and one-half years old—and the corresponding susceptibility to pressure from authority figures that comes with youth. The interrogation lasted over twelve hours, through an entire night, without food or significant breaks. He had never been arrested or interrogated as a suspect before that night. His parents were not present; in fact, Doody maintains, the task force went to some length to ensure their absence. * * *

In short, Doody paints an overall picture of downplayed warnings, a softly induced waiver of rights, and conduct conveying the message that

Doody would not be left alone until he confessed, all targeted at an unsavvy, increasingly sleep-deprived teenager. * * *

This case requires us to consider the interplay between the *Miranda* and voluntariness analyses, an interplay which, on the facts before us, informs both analyses. We therefore begin by considering that interaction, and then proceed to discuss first the *Miranda* issues and then the voluntariness question.

Although generally viewed as distinct, the two doctrines originated from the same concerns. * * * Whereas the Fifth Amendment by its text safeguards the individual against being "compelled in any criminal case to be a witness against himself," the due process protection stems from the principle that "tactics for eliciting inculpatory statements must fall within the broad constitutional boundaries imposed by the Fourteenth Amendment's guarantee of fundamental fairness."

The due process protection is embodied in a voluntariness inquiry that asks " 'whether a defendant's will was overborne' " by looking at the " 'totality of all the surrounding circumstances.' " The assessment of the totality of the circumstances may include consideration of the length and location of the interrogation; evaluation of the maturity, education, physical and mental condition of the defendant; and determination of whether the defendant was properly advised of his *Miranda* rights. Thus, by its nature, the voluntariness inquiry requires a case-by-case assessment, leading courts to grapple with the application of voluntariness principles in a variety of circumstances. * * *

[A]lthough adequate *Miranda* warnings provide a measure of protection against coercion in custodial police interrogations, the protection actually provided in any given case depends on how effective the warnings as given and implemented were in conveying their layered messages. In our voluntariness analysis today, therefore, we consider the extent to which the *Miranda* warnings—although, as we first conclude, technically adequate—actually protected against a coerced confession. * * *

The *Miranda* warnings given to Doody did little actually to inform him, a seventeen-year-old who had never heard of *Miranda*, of the importance of his rights. The officers downplayed the relevance of the warnings, and their application to the current questioning. * * * The clear message underlying these comments was that Doody need not take the warnings seriously and should waive his rights. Thus, although each required warning was technically delivered correctly, one of *Miranda*'s primary purposes—"to make the individual more acutely aware that he is faced with a phase of the adversary system—that he is not in the presence of persons acting solely in his interest,"—was undermined. * * *

Here, the officers interspersed the warnings with statements downplaying their significance. But the essential rights were conveyed, and * * * the oral elaborations of which Doody complains were not affirmatively misleading. Thus, although we find it a close question, we cannot conclude that the state court's decision that the warnings were adequate was "objectively unreasonable." This conclusion only means that *Mi*-

randa's irrebuttable presumption of coercion may not be invoked. But the excessively casual delivery of *Miranda* warnings to a juvenile, seemingly designed to ensure that he would ignore the warnings and waive his rights, gives little comfort that Doody commenced the interrogation with an understanding of what was at stake. * * *

Later statements by the officers further undercut the purpose of the *Miranda* warnings. * * * Specifically, the officers explicitly and implicitly told Doody—an increasingly sleep-deprived juvenile—that he did not have the right to remain silent. About five hours into the interrogation, Doody essentially stopped answering the officers' questions. In the face of his silence, three officers took turns asking the same questions again and again, sometimes dozens of times in a row, and repeatedly told Doody that he "ha[d]" to answer their questions. * * *

In short, although the state court's conclusion that there was no *Miranda* violation was reasonable, the safety net that proper, serious *Miranda* warnings provide—that of informing a suspect of his rights and of the gravity of the situation—was quite weak in this case, prone to give way as a protection against an involuntary confession if conditions were otherwise conducive to such a confession. * * *

We now turn to the voluntariness inquiry. At the outset, we find it notable that the officers' long lectures on how important it was for Doody to tell them the truth, which included repeated statements that they "knew" his denials of involvement were not true, did not alone result in his confession. * * * Doody did not confess to any involvement in the temple murders until about 2:45 to 3:30 a.m., after Doody had been interrogated for several hours already, three officers subjected him to forty-five minutes of repeated, overwhelmingly unanswered questions, interspersed with commands that Doody "had" to answer. This timing alone strongly suggests that his will was overcome * * * by the officers' overall, interrelated, coercive messages that they would continue relentlessly questioning him until he told them what they wanted to hear, and that he would eventually have to do so. These messages were believable, given the officers' extraordinary persistence in the face of Doody's silence to that point, the number of hours the interrogation had already gone on, and Doody's inevitable fatigue at 2:45 to 3:30 in the morning. * * *

Compounding the troubling scenario in this case is Doody's particular vulnerability to the officers' tactics: his age—seventeen—and the length of the interrogation, more than twelve unbroken hours, embracing an entire night. * * * Doody's vulnerability because of his youth was enhanced by the fact that he had never been arrested before and, as he told the officers, had never heard of *Miranda* rights. And numerous cases recognize the coercive potential in unbroken hours of interrogation of a juvenile, particularly when they take place overnight.

Nor was Doody interrogated in the presence of any friendly adult. Instead, he faced interrogation, alone, by two, three, and four officers at a time. Even though Doody agreed at the outset to speak to the officers without his parents present, the absence of a friendly adult is a factor in assessing the voluntariness of a juvenile's confession. * * *

Indeed, the content of Doody's confession itself provides strong evidence that his will was overborne. * * * [F]acing the officers' refusal to stop questioning him until they received the answers they wanted, Doody succumbed by providing some information that was suggested by the officers' questions but that the state now concedes is not true. * * *

A juvenile was given *Miranda* warnings in a downplayed manner that ensured he would not take them seriously and would waive his rights. With only a flimsy version of the protection the *Miranda* warnings are designed to provide, he was then interrogated for more than twelve hours, overnight, almost entirely without pause and with no friendly adult present. He was told that he had to answer the officers' questions and that the interrogation would not end until he confessed. He was finally broken down by the ceaseless questioning of two, three, and four police officers, questioning that continued despite his frequent long stretches of silence. Under these circumstances, we conclude, he did not voluntarily confess. * * *

8) Mandatory recording as another strategy to assure the voluntariness of juveniles' *Miranda* Waivers and Statements In **In the Interest of Jerrell C.J.**, 283 Wis.2d 145, 699 N.W.2d 110 (WI. 2005), the Wisconsin Supreme Court considered the voluntariness of the juvenile's confession. Although the Court rejected the juvenile's request for a *per se* parental presence requirement, it invoked its supervisory power to require police electronically to record all custodial interrogation of juveniles that occurs at a place of detention. Bradley, J., provided the several rationales for the Court's exercise of its supervisory power:

The final issue we consider is whether to adopt a rule requiring the state to electronically record all juvenile interrogations. To date, two states, Alaska and Minnesota, have mandated an electronic recording requirement by court decision. *Stephan v. State* (Alaska 1985); *State v. Scales* (Minn. 1994). Jerrell urges this court to follow suit.

According to Jerrell, a rule requiring electronic recording would provide courts with the best evidence from which it can determine, under the totality of the circumstances, whether a juvenile's confession is voluntary. He views the rule as critical to the integrity of the fact-finding process, as it is difficult to accurately recreate weeks or months later in a courtroom what transpired in a lengthy interrogation like his.

Again, the State does not take issue with the merits of Jerrell's proposal, but instead questions the court's authority or exercise of authority in adopting it. Additionally, it expresses concern with the court mandating a certain law enforcement practice. The State therefore maintains that the debate over electronic recording should occur in legislative chambers.

We are not persuaded by the State's arguments. Here, Jerrell is not asking this court to regulate police practice. Rather, he is requesting a rule governing the admissibility of a juvenile's confession into evidence. This would not make it illegal for police to interrogate juveniles without a recording. Instead, it would render the unrecorded interrogations and any resultant written confession inadmissible as evidence in court.

Plainly, this court has authority to adopt rules governing the admissibility of evidence. * * * [T]his court can regulate the flow of evidence in state courts, including the nature of the evidence developed and presented by law enforcement. Today, we regulate the evidence of juvenile confessions resulting from custodial interrogations. Like the Minnesota Supreme Court in *Scales*, we do so pursuant to our supervisory authority.

Experiences in Minnesota, Alaska, and hundreds of other jurisdictions that now voluntarily record demonstrate that the benefits of such practice greatly outweigh the costs, both real and perceived. After surveying 238 law enforcement agencies nationwide, Thomas Sullivan, former United States Attorney for the Northern District of Illinois, observed that "[a] contemporaneous electronic record of suspect interviews has proven to be an efficient and powerful law enforcement tool. Audio is good, video is better.... Recordings prevent disputes about officers' conduct, the treatment of suspects and statements they made." See Thomas P. Sullivan, *Police Experiences with Recording Custodial Interrogations,*6 (Summer2004), at http://www.law.northwestern.edu/depts./clinic/wrongful/documents/SullivanReport.pdf. Like Sullivan, we agree that electronic recording is an efficient and powerful tool in the administration of justice. We highlight some of these advantages here.

First, a recording requirement will provide courts with a more accurate and reliable record of a juvenile's interrogation. This will eliminate conflicts in evidence that are attributable to flaws in human memory. It will also enable judges to conduct nuanced reviews to resolve admissibility issues.

Second, an accurate record will reduce the number of disputes over *Miranda* and voluntariness issues for juveniles. Currently, courts spend an inordinate amount of time and resources wrestling with such slippery matters. This case alone generated four days of hearings based on Jerrell's postdisposition claim that his confession was involuntary. All of these hearings and the entire appellate process might have been avoided if Jerrell's interrogation had been electronically recorded. Not surprisingly, the circuit court twice remarked that it wished it had a videotape of the interrogation.

Third, recording will protect the individual interest of police officers wrongfully accused of improper tactics. Suspects will be unable to contradict an objective record of the interrogation. This is because "viewers and listeners see and/or hear precisely what was said and done, including whether suspects were forthcoming or evasive, changed their version of events, and appeared sincere and innocent or deceitful and guilty."

Fourth, a recording requirement will enhance law enforcement interrogations of juveniles. Police report that "[r]ecordings permit detectives to focus on the suspect rather than taking copious notes of the interview. When officers later review the recordings they often observe inconsistencies and evasive conduct which they overlooked while the interview was in progress." Furthermore, "recordings deter officers who might be inclined to engage in improper tactics or misstate what was said or done by the suspect[.]"

Finally, such a rule will protect the rights of the accused. Without a contemporaneous record of the interrogation, judges are forced to rely on the recollections of interested parties to reconstruct what occurred. The result is often a credibility contest between law enforcement officials and the juvenile, which law enforcement officials invariably win. The existence of an objective, comprehensive, and reviewable record will safeguard juveniles' constitutional rights by making it possible for them to challenge misleading or false testimony.

These reasons have prompted the American Bar Association to unanimously adopt a resolution urging legislatures or courts to enact laws or rules "requiring videotaping of the entirety of custodial interrogations of crime suspects at police precincts, courthouses, detention centers, or other places where suspects are held for questioning, or, where videotaping is impractical, to require the audiotaping of such custodial interrogations[.]"

We are mindful that adopting the rule proposed by Jerrell will be met with some hesitation. However, we agree with the court of appeals that "it is time for Wisconsin to tackle the false confession issue" and "take appropriate action so that the youth of our state are protected from confessing to crimes they did not commit." We are convinced than an electronic recording requirement is a means to that end.

In 1994, the Minnesota Supreme Court in *Scales* exercised its "supervisory power to insure the fair administration of justice." It required electronic recording of all questioning "where feasible," and without exception "when questioning occurs at a place of detention." Today, we also exercise our supervisory power to insure the fair administration of justice. All custodial interrogation of juveniles in future cases shall be electronically recorded where feasible, and without exception when questioning occurs at a place of detention. Audiotaping is sufficient to satisfy our requirement; however, videotaping may provide an even more complete picture of what transpired during the interrogation. * * *

The Court in *Jerrell C. J.* relied on Alaska and Minnesota's positive experience with recording interrogations. For the past decade, virtually every legal analyst, criminologist, and policy group has advocated audio recording or videotaping interrogations to reduce coercion, to minimize the dangers of false confessions, and to make the process more visible and transparent. *See e.g.*, Richard A. Leo, *Impact of Miranda Revisited*, 86 J. Crim. L. & Criminology 621, 682 (1996) (arguing that "The use of audio or videotaping inside the interrogation room creates an objective record of police questioning to which all interested and potentially interested parties may appeal—police, suspects, prosecutors, defense attorneys, and juries—in the determination of truth and in judgments of fairness. The use of videotaping is thus the most viable legal intervention for resolving many of the antinomies of crime control and due process inherent in police interrogation of the accused in a democratic society."); Paul G. Cassell, *Protecting the Innocent from False Confessions and Lost Confessions—And From Miranda*, 88 J. Crim. L. & Criminology 497, 553 (1998) (arguing for videotaping interrogations unless suspect objects to recording and simultaneously loosening *Miranda* restrictions on questioning);

Lawrence Schlam, *Police Interrogation of Children and State Constitutions: Why Not Videotape the MTV Generation?*, 26 U. Tol. L. Rev. 901 (1995); Steven A. Drizin & Marissa J. Reich, *Heeding the Lessons of History: The Need for Mandatory Recording of Police Interrogations to Accurately Assess the Reliability and Voluntariness of Confessions*, 52 Drake L. Rev. 619 (2004); Welsh S. White, *False Confessions and the Constitution: Safeguards Against Untrustworthy Confessions*, 32 Harvard Civ. Rights–Civ. Liberties L. Rev. 106, 153 (1997) (arguing that recording interrogations enables courts to scrutinize police practices, deters police from using abusive interrogation methods, facilitates courts' judgments about the reliability and voluntariness of state- ments, and reduces reliance on untrustworthy confessions); Steven A. Drizin & Beth A. Colgan, *Let the Cameras Roll: Mandatory Videotaping of Interroga- tions Is the Solution to Illinois' Problem of False Confessions*, 32 Loyola U. Chicago L. J. 337 (2001) (describing impetus behind and politics of Illinois adoption of limited requirements to record interrogations); Lisa Lewis, "Re- thinking Miranda: Truth Lies, and Videotape," 43 *Gonzaga L. Rev.* 199 (2007).

9) "Dumbed–Down" *Miranda* warnings to protect juveniles Courts and commentators have proposed other safeguards, besides parental presence, to bolster protection of youths' *Miranda* rights. If juveniles' lack of understanding or comprehension confounds assessments of waiver decisions, then police could administer a "dumbed-down" version of a *Miranda* warning "in language understandable to a child." *State v. Benoit*, 126 N.H. 6, 490 A.2d 295, 304 (N.H. 1985); Larry E. Holtz, "*Miranda* In a Juvenile Setting: A Child's Right to silence," 78 *J. Crim. L. & Criminology* 534 (1987); National Advisory Committee for Juvenile Justice and Delinquency Prevention, *Stan- dards for the Administration of Juvenile Justice* § 2.247 (1980) (*Miranda* warnings administered and "explained in language understandable by the juvenile"). How should a court rule on the admissibility of a confession if a juvenile lies about her age and police fail to administer the "dumbed-down" version of the warning? See infra p. 334, Note 7.

10) *Miranda* Warnings in Schools Are there other settings besides police interrogation in the station-house for which *Miranda* warnings or other procedural safeguards should be used when adult authorities interrogate juveniles? Suppose in *T.L.O.*, Mr. Choplick had asked T.L.O. about her involvement in drug-trafficking and she made incriminating statements? Would or should those statements be admissible without a *Miranda* warning? *See, e.g.,* Goodwin, "The Fifth Amendment in Public Schools: A Rationale for its Application in Investigations and Disciplinary Proceedings," 28 *Wm. & Mary L. Rev.* 683, 705 (1987); Eleftheria Keans, "Student Interrogations by School Officials: Out with Agency Law and in with Constitutional Warnings," 27 *Boston C. Third World L. J.* 375 (2007). Does *Miranda*'s concerns about the "inherent coercion of custodial interrogation" apply to children ques- tioned by school authority figures? Most courts conclude that interrogation is "non-custodial" when it is "conducted by school officials in furtherance of their disciplinary duties." *Boynton v. Casey,* 543 F.Supp. 995 (D. Me. 1982). Where police are present and participate, or where the schools officials act as agents of law enforcement, a different result may obtain. *See In re Brendan H.*, 82 Misc.2d 1077, 372 N.Y.S.2d 473 (N.Y. Fam. Ct. 1975).

Again, consider the role of school liaison officers in the interrogation of juveniles, *supra* Note 212, p. 8. In **In the Matter of the Welfare of R.J.E.,** 630 N.W.2d 457 (Minn. Ct. App. 2001), a uniformed police officer, working as a liaison officer had two uniformed school security guards escort 15 year old R.J.E. from his classroom to the 10′ × 10′ office they shared. When they arrived at the office, one of the security guards searched R.J.E. The school social worker was also present so that there were four adults in the office with R.J.E., three of whom were in uniform. The door to the office was closed. The police officer started a tape recorder and questioned R.J.E. without giving a *Miranda* warning. They suspected R.J.E. of inappropriately touching a female student, e.g. criminal sexual conduct. The officer never told R.J.E. that he was free to leave or that he could decline to answer any questions. Although the officer testified that he would have allowed R.J.E. to leave the room had he asked, R.J.E. testified that he believed that either the police officer or one of the security guards would have prevented him from leaving. The interview lasted about 15 minutes. After the interview, the officer turned R.J.E. over to the vice-principal because "there are school sanctions as well" as criminal charges:

> The district court held that R.J.E. was not entitled to a *Miranda* warning because he was not in custody when police questioned him. * * * The state concedes that R.J.E. was interrogated, and therefore our task is to determine whether R.J.E. was in custody. We consider a suspect to be in custody if a reasonable person under the circumstances would believe that he or she was in police custody to the degree associated with formal arrest. *See In re Welfare of G.S.P.* (Minn.App.2000) ("The test is not whether a reasonable person under the circumstances would believe they were not free to leave, but whether a reasonable person under the circumstances would believe they were in police custody of the degree associated with formal arrest."). * * * In *G.S.P.,* an assistant principal and a school-liaison police officer removed a 12–year–old student from his classroom. The assistant principal and the police officer questioned G.S.P. in the assistant principal's office. The officer did not issue a *Miranda* warning, but he tape-recorded the questioning, which was done in the presence of three school officials. The officer did not tell G.S.P. that he was free to leave or could talk to his parents. Instead, the officer told G.S.P. that he had no choice but to answer the questions. We held that G.S.P. was in custody during his interrogation and was entitled to a Miranda warning.

> Key to our decision in *G.S.P.* was the fact that the police officer failed to inform G.S.P. that he was not under arrest or that he was free to leave. Here, the interrogating officer failed to inform R.J.E. that he was free to leave or that he was not under arrest. The *G.S.P.* court also determined that the officer's tape-recording of the interview was "strongly suggestive of a custodial interrogation." Similarly, the recording of the interview with R.J.E. suggests to us that the interrogation was custodial. The state asserts that a general obligation to appear before a police officer and answer questions truthfully does not convert an interview into a custodial interrogation. Nonetheless, where a "uniformed officer summons a juvenile from the classroom to the office and actively participates in the

questioning, the circumstances suggest the coercive influence associated with a formal arrest."

R.J.E.'s interrogation took place in a small room with the door closed; the police officer conducted the interrogation in the presence of two uniformed school security guards and a social worker; the police officer never informed R.J.E. that he could decline to answer questions or that he was free to leave; R.J.E. believed that he was not free to leave. Although the interrogation lasted only 15 minutes, R.J.E. was 15 years old and had no prior experience with questioning by police or school officials. R.J.E. reasonably believed that he was restrained to a degree equivalent to formal arrest. We conclude that in light of all the surrounding circumstances, R.J.E. was in custody when the officer interrogated him, and the district court should have suppressed R.J.E.'s incriminating statements.[6]

11) Warning Juveniles about the Possibility of Adult Criminal Prosecution If a juvenile confesses while under the jurisdiction of the juvenile court and subsequently a judge transfers the youth for criminal prosecution as an adult, may a prosecutor introduce the juvenile's confession against her? Could the informal, non-adversary nature of the juvenile justice system lull a youth into a false sense of security and elicit a confession? Should the police warn a youth about possible subsequent uses of any statements? Compare e.g., Harling v. United States, 295 F.2d 161 (D.C. Cir. 1961) (holding that any statement made while in police custody is inadmissible in a criminal prosecution following a transfer hearing); State v. Maloney, 102 Ariz. 495, 433 P.2d 625 (1967) (statement inadmissible unless juvenile and parents advised that criminal proceedings are a possibility); with State v. Gullings, 244 Or. 173, 416 P.2d 311 (1966) (stating that statement is admissible as long as elicited in an adversarial atmosphere); Mitchell v. State, 3 Tenn.Crim.App. 494, 464 S.W.2d 307 (Tenn. Crim. App. 1971) (holding that any statement obtained in compliance with Miranda is admissible in criminal prosecution).

In **State v. Ouk**, 516 N.W.2d 180 (Minn. 1994), the Minnesota Supreme Court noted that:

We have recognized that juvenile confessions must be carefully scrutinized to ensure that the confidential atmosphere of the juvenile court does not encourage a confession by a juvenile which might otherwise be withheld. In Loyd we suggested the safest method was for the interrogating officers to advise juveniles that adult criminal prosecution

6. Although only of persuasive value, we find a decision by the Washington Court of Appeals instructive. In Washington v. D.R., a 14–year–old boy was found to be in custody when he was interviewed by a police officer in the presence of the assistant principal and a school social worker. The interview took place in the assistant principal's office, and the boy was told that he did not have to answer questions, but he was not otherwise given Miranda warnings. The boy did not believe that he was free to leave. Over the course of the interview, the officer indicated that he knew the boy had committed a sexual offense. The Washington court framed the inquiry as "whether a 14–year–old in D.R.'s position would have 'reasonably supposed his freedom of action was curtailed' and concluded that D.R. was in custody during his interview 'in light of [the officer's] failure to inform him he was free to leave, D.R.'s youth, the naturally coercive nature of the school and principal's office environment for children of his age, and the obviously accusatory nature of the interrogation.'"

could result in order to protect juveniles from unknowing and unintelligent waivers of their constitutional rights, but we held that the failure to so advise does not necessarily invalidate an otherwise valid waiver of rights. * * *

Under *Loyd* a juvenile waiver may be deemed valid provided that awareness of potential criminal responsibility may be imputed to the interrogated juvenile. Awareness of potential criminal responsibility may be imputed to defendant. * * * It was foreseeable from the nature of his arrest and from the nature of the crime (four victims shot at point blank range) that this matter would not be disposed of in the juvenile court system. * * *

[This court declines] to overrule our holding in *Loyd* and to adopt a *per se* exclusionary rule which would bar the use of a juvenile's confession in a criminal prosecution for a felony where the juvenile is not warned about the possibility of adult prosecution. *See State v. Benoit*, (requiring juveniles to be advised of possibility of being tried as adult). While we adhere to our holding in *Loyd*, we again strongly encourage law enforcement officers to advise juveniles about the possibility of criminal prosecution as an adult whenever such prosecution is possible in order to protect juveniles from unknowing and unintelligent waivers of their constitutional rights. * * *

2. PARENTAL PRESENCE DURING JUVENILES' INTERROGATIONS

The "totality" approach endorsed in *Fare* gives trial judges broad discretion to consider a youth's immaturity, but imposes minimal interference with police investigative work. Most states allow juveniles to waive constitutional rights such as *Miranda* and the right to counsel without restriction or assistance, and to confront the power of the State alone and unaided. Thus, *Fare* employs a "liberationist" rather than a "protectionist" construction of adolescence, affirms adolescents' ability to make autonomous legal decisions without additional special procedures, treats juveniles effectively like adults, and enables police interrogators to take advantage of youths' manifest social-psychological limitations relative to adults.

States' laws recognize that younger people have different social and psychological competencies than adults and paternalistically impose a host of legal disabilities on children to protect them from their own limitations in contexts other than criminal law enforcement. For example, states limit youths' ability to enter contracts, convey property, marry, drink, drive, file a law suit, or even donate blood. *See e.g., Thompson v. Oklahoma*, 487 U.S. 815, 108 S.Ct. 2687, 101 L.Ed.2d 702 (1988). Some states recognize this developmental reality and restrict youths' ability to waive legal rights. Courts explain that special procedural safeguards at interrogation, such as the "interested adult" rule, are designed

to afford protection to juveniles * * * disadvantaged by the immaturity occasioned by their youth. The rationale underlying this *per se* rule is that the immaturity of the juvenile significantly affects both the ability of the juvenile to understand fully his or her rights and the susceptibility of the juvenile to the compelling atmosphere of police interrogation, and that special protections are thus required to protect the juvenile from incompetently waiving his or her rights. It is believed that the interested adult can remedy the shortcomings resulting from immaturity by providing advice to enhance the juvenile's understanding of his or her rights and by being present during custodial interrogation to protect the child from the compelling atmosphere of custodial interrogation. *State v. Benoit*, 126 N.H. 6, 15, 490 A.2d 295, 302 (N.H. 1985).

Other courts explain that "The law presumes different levels of responsibility for juveniles and adults and, realizing that juveniles frequently lack the capacity to appreciate the consequences of their actions, seeks to protect them from the possible consequences of their immaturity. Moreover, by providing the juvenile with the opportunity for meaningful consultation with an informed adult, these procedures prevent the warnings from becoming merely a ritualistic recitation wherein the effect of actual comprehension by the juvenile is ignored." *Commonwealth v. A Juvenile*, 389 Mass. 128 at 132, 449 N.E.2d 654 at 656 (Mass. 1983).

IN THE INTEREST OF JERRELL C.J.

283 Wis.2d 145, 699 N.W.2d 110 (WI. 2005).

CHIEF JUSTICE ABRAHAMSON, concurring:

I would adopt a per se rule excluding in-custody admissions from any child under the age of 16 who has not been given the opportunity to consult with a parent or interested adult. Here are my top 8 (interrelated and overlapping) reasons for adopting a per se rule:

Reason No. 1. A per se rule should be adopted because Wisconsin law enforcement officers have not heeded the warning this court issued 30 years ago in *Theriault v. State* (1974) that law enforcement's failure to call a juvenile's parents would be viewed as "strong evidence that coercive tactics were used to elicit the incriminating statements." In addition to our admonishment in *Theriault*, in 1981 a Milwaukee County circuit court "berated the [Milwaukee] police department for not notifying the defendant's parents in order to give them an opportunity to be present during the police questioning." As the present case demonstrates, the long-time practice of Milwaukee police officers to exclude parents from the interrogation of juveniles has continued. Despite *Theriault* and the Milwaukee County circuit court's admonishment, the practice of excluding parents during juvenile interrogation is apparently widespread throughout the state. * * *

Reason No. 2. A per se rule should be adopted because Wisconsin courts have not heeded this court's warning from *Theriault* that law enforcement's failure to call a juvenile's parents would be viewed as "strong evidence that coercive tactics were used to elicit incriminating statements." Courts have inconsistently applied the totality of circumstances test and have tended to haphazardly exclude only the most egregiously obtained confessions. A fair reading of the Wisconsin cases demonstrates that Wisconsin courts (including this court) do not consider law enforcement's failure to call a juvenile's parents or an interested adult as strong or even some evidence of coercive tactics. * * *

Reason No. 3. A per se rule should be adopted because juveniles do not have the decision-making capacity and understanding of adults. Emerging studies demonstrate that the area of the brain governing decision making and the weighing of risks and rewards continues to develop into the late teens and the early twenties. Further studies show that children under the age of 16 are less capable than adults of understanding their *Miranda* rights, have a propensity to confess to police, and are less capable than adults of making long range decisions. As the United States Supreme Court observed over 40 years ago, adult advice would put a juvenile "on a less unequal footing with his [or her] interrogators." * * *

Reason No. 4. A per se rule should be adopted to prevent false confessions. Although it is difficult for many of us to understand what leads an innocent person to confess to a crime, especially a serious felony, researchers have documented that false confessions are "a leading cause of the wrongful convictions of the innocent in America."

When used against vulnerable suspects, standard police interrogation techniques are especially apt to lead to false confessions. Juveniles and the mentally retarded are the most vulnerable to modern psychological interrogation techniques. It follows that juveniles "appear with some regularity in false confession cases." * * *

Given the limited mental abilities of juveniles and their heightened susceptibility to suggestion, a per se rule is needed to increase the likelihood that a guilty verdict will not be based on a false confession and be overturned on appeal. A per se rule thus fosters the fair administration of justice.

Reason No. 5. A per se rule should be adopted to protect parental and family values. One of the oldest fundamental liberty interests recognized by the U.S. Supreme Court is that of parents to direct the care, control, and upbringing of their children. This constitutional protection extends to parents' right to be consulted in decisions that have potentially traumatic and permanent consequences. * * *

Reason No. 6. A per se rule should be adopted because it comports with Wisconsin legislative policy evidenced in numerous statutes requiring parents or guardians to have a say in a variety of significant decisions affecting their children. * * *

Reason No. 7. A per se rule should be adopted because it has proven to function well in other states and in England. According to one commentator, thirteen states have adopted, by case law or legislative action, some form of a per se parental consultation rule. In 1998 the Kansas supreme court [in *B.M.B.*, p. 326, Note 3] reviewed court-imposed rules from Massachusetts, Missouri, New York, Indiana, Vermont, and Florida and adopted a per se rule.

Great Britain's Police and Criminal Evidence Act of 1984 details a Code of Practice for the Detention, Treatment, and Questioning of Persons by Police Officers, including those persons under 17 years of age. Juveniles must have an "appropriate adult" present during interrogation. * * * Once a child is taken into custody, authorities must inform this adult as soon as practicable. Police are required to inform the child that an adult is there to advise him or her, and that he or she has the right to consult with the adult privately at any time. During the interview, the police must advise the adult that the adult is not expected to function merely as an observer, but is present to advise the child, assure that the interview is properly and fairly conducted, and "facilitate communication" between the parties.

Reason No. 8. A per se rule should be adopted because such a rule is the right, just, and fair way to operate the Wisconsin judicial system. * * *

Wisconsin must do more than apply the "totality of the circumstances" rule to protect children and families and tackle the problem of false confessions. Mandating electronic recording of juvenile interrogations is a very important step, but it is only one step. I would have the court fashion a rule requiring the participation of an interested adult in the interrogation process of juveniles. Other jurisdictions provide good working models. Such a rule will provide desperately needed procedural safeguards to protect children and families and to ensure the validity of confessions and the sound administration of justice.

NOTES

1) Louisiana's experiment with parental presence requirement The Louisiana Supreme Court in **In the Interests of Dino,** 359 So.2d 586 (La.1978), reviewed the confession that police obtained from a thirteen-year-old juvenile without his parents' presence. As in *Alvarado*, Dino's mother brought her son to the police station, but was not asked if she wanted to be present when police interrogated him. Even if judged under the "totality of the circumstances," the court concluded that "the State has not carried its heavy burden in proving that young Dino was aware not only of his rights, but also of the consequences of foregoing them, that he knew he was faced with a phase of the adversary system, and that he was aware that he was not in the presence of persons acting solely in his interest." The court then observed that "exclusive use of the totality of circumstances test in relation to waivers by juveniles tends to mire the courts in a morass of speculation similar to that from which *Miranda* was designed to extricate them in adult cases." While recognizing that *Miranda* did not address "the special needs of juveniles confronted with police interrogation, the reasons given for making the warnings an absolute prerequisite to interrogation point up the need for an absolute requirement that juveniles not be permitted to waive constitutional rights on their own." The *Dino* court offered a number of reasons to adopt a *per se* requirement of parental presence and consultation as a prerequisite to the admissibility of statements obtained from juveniles:

> [T]he rights which a juvenile may waive before interrogation are so fundamental to our system of constitutional rule and the expedient of requiring the advice of a parent, counsel or adviser so relatively simple and well established as a safeguard against a juvenile's improvident judicial acts, that we should not pause to inquire in individual cases whether the juvenile could, on his own, understand and effectively exercise his rights. Assessments of how the "totality of the circumstances" affected a juvenile in a particular case can never be more than speculation. Furthermore, whatever the background of the juvenile interrogated, assistance of an adult acting in his interest is indispensable to overcome the pressures of the interrogation and to insure that the juvenile knows he is free to exercise his rights at that point in time.
>
> The presence of a parent, counsel, or other adult acting in the juvenile's interest at the interrogation may serve several significant subsidiary functions as well. If the juvenile decides to talk to his interrogators, the assistance of an adult can mitigate the dangers of untrustworthiness. With an adult acting in his interest present the likelihood that the police will practice coercion is reduced, and if coercion is nevertheless exercised the adult can testify to it in court. The presence of such an adult can also help to guarantee that the accused gives a fully accurate statement and that the statement is rightly reported by the prosecution at trial.
>
> Moreover, such a rule will relieve the police from having to make a subjective judgment in each case. As noted by the Indiana Supreme Court in *Lewis v. State*, (1972):
>
> > The authorities seeking to question a juvenile enter into an area of doubt and confusion when the child appears to waive his rights to counsel and against self-incrimination. They are faced with the possibility of taking a statement from him only to have a court later find that his age and the surrounding circumstances precluded the child from making a valid waiver. There are no concrete guidelines for the authorities to follow in order to insure what the waiver will be upheld. The police are forced to speculate as to whether the law will judge this accused juvenile on the same plane as an adult in regard to the waiver of his constitutional rights, or whether the court will take cognizance of the age of the child and apply different standards. * * * It is harmful to the system of criminal justice to require law enforcement authorities to second guess the courts in the area of constitutional rights. Clearly defined procedures should be established in areas which lend themselves to such standards in order to assure both efficient police procedure and protection of the important

constitutional rights of the accused. Age is one area which lends itself to clearly defined standards.

Although a majority of jurisdictions allow a juvenile to waive his privilege against incrimination and his right to counsel without mature guidance, a growing number of courts and scholars recognize that a more ascertainable assurance of a knowing and intelligent waiver of constitutional rights should precede juvenile interrogation.

The courts of Pennsylvania, Indiana and Georgia, for example, have recently concluded that the administering of *Miranda* warnings to a juvenile, without providing an opportunity to consult with a mature, informed individual concerned primarily with the interest of the juvenile, is inadequate to offset the disadvantage occasioned by youth. Moreover, the Pennsylvania Supreme Court has held that the impediment of immaturity can only be overcome where the record establishes that the youth had access to the advice of an attorney, parent or other interested adult, and that the consulted adult was informed as to the constitutional rights available to the minor and aware of the consequences that might follow the election to be made.

Some "sophisticated" juveniles, without the benefit of adult advice, may understand the serious consequences flowing from a waiver of constitutional rights. However, one empirical study indicates that a large percentage of juveniles are incapable of knowingly and intelligently waiving constitutional rights. In any event, it is the general policy of our law to protect all minors from the possible consequences of immaturity.

Because most juveniles are not mature enough to understand their rights and are not competent to exercise them, the concepts of fundamental fairness * * * require that juveniles not be permitted to waive constitutional rights on their own. For these reasons we hold that in order for the State to meet its heavy burden of demonstrating that a waiver is made knowingly and intelligently, it must affirmatively show that the juvenile engaged in a meaningful consultation with an attorney or an informed parent, guardian, or other adult interested in his welfare before he waived his right to counsel and privilege against self-incrimination.

Accordingly, the purported waiver by a juvenile must be adjudged ineffective upon the failure by the State to establish any of three prerequisites to waiver, viz., that the juvenile actually consulted with an attorney or an adult before waiver, that the attorney or adult consulted was interested in the welfare of the juvenile, or that, if an adult other than an attorney was consulted, the adult was fully advised of the rights of the juvenile. * * *

Two decades later, in **State v. Fernandez**, 712 So.2d 485 (La.1998), the Louisiana Supreme Court overruled *Dino*'s *per se* parental presence requirement and reinstated the "totality" approach. *Fernandez* addressed the three bases on which *Dino* relied to depart from the "totality" standard: (1) a perceived growing trend towards an interested adult standard; (2) empirical studies; and (3) the public policy of Louisiana to protect juveniles:

In *Dino*, the majority noted a "growing number" of courts moving towards an "interested adult" standard, which was the source of the *Dino* requirements. * * * During the two decades since *Dino* was decided, Pennsylvania has gone full circle and returned to the totality of the circumstances standard. The court first shifted from a *per se* rule to a rebuttable presumption, and then returned to a totality of the circumstances standard, reasoning:

> The per se * * * rule, in discarding the totality of circumstances test, negated the relevance of all those factors which should be and must be considered in deciding whether a confession was knowingly and voluntarily given. Instead, a prophylactic principle was adopted and applied which shunned the real issue of the voluntariness of a confession. * * * In overruling [the *per se* rule], we recognized the lack of wisdom in a rule which is overly paternalistic, unnecessarily protective and sacrifices too much of the interests of justice. * * *

Hence, the principal authority on which the majority relied in *Dino* has now been overruled.

Another ground cited in *Dino* for deviating from the totality of the circumstances standard was an empirical study that established the inability of juveniles in general to knowingly and intelligently waive their constitutional rights. The empirical evidence to date arguably continues to demonstrate that "most juveniles—simply by reason of their age and limited education—fail to comprehend the language traditionally employed in *Miranda* warnings and the concepts embodied in the warnings." Nonetheless, we conclude, as have the majority of other jurisdictions, that the needs of juveniles can be accommodated by the totality of the circumstances standard. * * *

The final ground cited in *Dino* was the general policy of Louisiana law to protect juveniles from the possible consequences of their immaturity. The treatment accorded juveniles has undergone a sharp shift in the twenty years since *Dino* was decided. * * *

On reconsideration of *Dino*, we conclude that the prophylactic requirements adopted in *Dino*, although probably serving the salutory purpose of improving police procedures during the time since their promulgation, were not constitutionally or statutorily required and were improvidently adopted by judicial decision.

Under a totality of circumstances standard, the special needs of juveniles can be accommodated in a manner that affords protection not only to juveniles, but also to the interests of society and of justice. Excluding an otherwise valid confession of guilt just because the accused was a few months away from achieving non-juvenile status is simply too high a price to pay for the arguable benefit of more easily administering a *per se* rule that neither the framers of the Constitution nor the redactors of the Code of Criminal Procedure considered necessary. * * * While law enforcement officers would do well to continue to follow the *Dino* procedure in order to insure the validity of a confession by a juvenile, a prophylactic rule imposing these requirements as an absolute standard is not appropriate.

2) Empirical Support for *Per Se* Rule *Fernandez* noted that the empirical evidence demonstrated that "most juveniles—simply by reason of their age and limited education—fail to comprehend the language traditionally employed in *Miranda* warnings and the concepts embodied in the warnings." Recall the research by Grisso and others on juveniles' understanding of and competence to waive constitutional rights, *supra* p. 295, Note 4. Recall, too, the developmental psychological research on juveniles' adjudicative competence, *supra* p. 109, Note 1. Juveniles' questionable competence derives from generic developmental limitations which affect their ability to communicate, to reason and understand, and to exercise judgment and make sound decisions. Research evaluating adolescents' and young adults' competence to participate in their trials found significant differences in understanding and judgment. Most youths younger than thirteen-or fourteen-years of age lacked even basic competence to understand or meaningfully to participate in their defense. *See*, Thomas Grisso, et al., "Juveniles' Competence to Stand Trial: A Comparison of Adolescents' and Adults' Capacities as Trial Defendants," 27 *Law and Human Behavior* 333, 357 (2003). Many youths younger than sixteen years of age lacked basic competence either to stand trial as adults or to make legal decisions, such as their waivers of constitutional rights, without the assistance of counsel, and many older youths exhibited substantial impairment. Moreover, youths' limited time-perspective, emphasis on short-term versus long-term consequences, and concerns about peer approval cause them to make immature decisions relative to those of adults. One recent study reported that

> approximately one fifth of 14– to 15–year–olds are as impaired in capacities relevant to adjudicative competence as are seriously mentally ill adults who would likely be considered incompetent to stand trial by clinicians who perform evaluations for courts. * * * Not surprisingly, juveniles of below-average intelligence are more likely than juveniles of average intelligence to be impaired in abilities relevant for competence to stand trial. Because a greater proportion of youths in the juvenile justice system than in the community are of below-average intelligence, the risk for incompetence to stand trial is therefore even greater. Grisso, *supra*, at p. 110.

Juveniles' diminished understanding of rights, confusion about trial processes, limited language skills, and inadequate decision-making abilities increase their vulnerability to interrogation tactics and their likelihood to give false confessions. Saul M. Kassin and Katherine L. Keichel, "The Social Psychology of False Confessions: Compliance, Internalization, and Confabulation," 7 *Psychol. Sci.* 125, 129 (1996); Lisa M. Krzewinski, "But I Didn't Do It: Protecting the Rights of Juveniles During Interrogation," 22 *Boston C. Third World L. J.* 355, 356 (2002) (questioning juveniles capacity to understand privilege against self-incrimination or to voluntarily give reliable statements). Juveniles are less able than adults to exercise their *Miranda* rights and exhibit a significant tendency to comply with authority, such as confessing to police.

Juveniles' lack of understanding and vulnerability to coercion raises questions about the adequacy of the *Miranda* warning as a procedural safeguard to prevent youths from giving unreliable or false confessions.

Deceptive interrogation techniques may be especially effective when employed against the young and inexperienced. See e.g., Laurie Magid, "Deceptive Police Interrogation Practices: How Far is Too Far?," 99 Mich. L. Rev. 1168, 1169 (2001) (noting that "*Miranda* offers suspects little protection from deceptive interrogation techniques."); Barbara Kaban and Ann E Tobey, "When Police Question Children: Are Protections Adequate?," J. Center Children & Courts 151, 158 (1999) ("Interrogation procedures designed for adults but used with children increase the likelihood of false confessions and may even undermine the integrity of the fact-finding process."); Welsh S. White, "False Confessions and the Constitution: Safeguards Against Untrustworthy Confessions," 32 *Harv. Civil Right–Civ. Lib. L.Rev.* 105, 118–21 (1997) (summarizing standard interrogation techniques especially likely to elicit false confessions from suspects with particular characteristics such as mental retardation and youth).

Interrogation tactics such as presenting false evidence, using leading questions, and encouraging suspects to adopt police interpretations make juveniles more susceptible to give false or inaccurate confessions than adults. *See* Thomas D. Lyon, "The New Wave in Children's Suggestibility Research: A Critique," 84 *Cornell L. Rev.* 1004, 1011 (1999); Marty Beyer, "Immaturity, Culpability and Competency in Juveniles: A Study of 17 Cases," 15 *Crim. Just.* 26, 29 (Summer 2000); Gerald B. Koocher, "Different Lenses: Psycholegal Perspectives on Children's Rights," 16 *Nova L. Rev.* 711, 716 (1992) (attributing children's compliance with police during interrogation to socialization to obey authority figures).

Stressful conditions may cause children to change their stories and actually to believe their distorted perception of the event. The coercive context of interrogation and youths' limited understanding and verbal skills render young offenders more likely to comply with authority, to acquiesce in police interpretations, to fill in gaps through fabrication, to tell police what they think they want to hear, and to give unreliable and false confessions. David S. Tanenhaus and Steven A. Drizin, " 'Owing to the Extreme Youth of the Accused': The Changing Legal Response to Juvenile Homicide," 92 *J. Crim.L. & Crim.* 641, 671–89 (2002) (summarizing three homicide interrogation cases leading to false confessions and demonstrating police use of leading questions, suggesting answers, and drafting confessions for very young offenders); Matthew B. Johnson & Ronald C. Hunt, "The Psycholegal Interface in Juvenile Assessment of Miranda," 18 *Am. J. Forensic Psychol.* 17, 24 (2000) (noting compliance as "tendency to go along with instructions and directions without actual acceptance of the premises.").

Immaturity and suggestibility increase the likelihood of false confessions. Saul M. Kassin, "The Psychology of Confession Evidence," 52 *Am. Psychologist* 221 (1997); Allison D. Redlich and Gail S. Goodman, "Taking Responsibility for An Act Not Committed: The Influence of Age and Suggestibility," 27 *Law & Human Beh.* 141 (2003) (describing research in which younger, more suggestible experimental subjects presented with false evidence were more likely to confess to wrong-doing). Youths are also less able than adults to think strategically or to appreciate the consequences of admissions and are more likely to assume responsibility out of a misguided feeling of loyalty to peers. Aggressive questioning by police further increases the likelihood of false confessions and instances abound of juveniles confessing to homicides and other serious crimes that they did not commit. Although younger offenders are at greatest risk, even older youths evidence a heightened risk of giving false confessions. Juveniles' lack of competence and vulnerability to coercive interrogation increases the risks of false confessions and erroneous convictions. Juveniles often confess falsely in the mistaken belief that doing so would enable them to go home. See e.g. Steven A. Drizin and Richard A. Leo, "The Problem of False Confessions in the Post–DNA World," 82 *N. Car. L. Rev.* 891, 969 (2004).

3) Parental Presence Protections for Younger Juveniles Some state courts recognize the peculiar developmental limitations of younger juveniles and adopt per se requirements for those below fourteen years of age. The Kansas Supreme Court **In the Matter of B.M.B.** 264 Kan. 417, 955 P.2d 1302 (Kansas 1998), considered the admissibility of a confession obtained from ten-year-old B.M.B. The trial court judge found that B.M.B. made a knowing, intelligent, and voluntary waiver of his *Miranda* rights under the "totality of the circumstances":

> We cannot ignore the immaturity and inexperience of a child under 14 years of age and the obvious disadvantage such a child has in confronting a custodial police interrogation. In such a case, we conclude that the totality of the circumstances is not sufficient to ensure that the child makes an intelligent and knowing waiver of his rights.

> In Kansas, we have long recognized that under the law, a juvenile is not to be treated the same as an adult. * * * The State acts as *parens patriae* for the best interests and welfare of the child. A per se rule of exclusion as to statements made by a juvenile under 14 years of age is consistent with the legislature's commitment to rehabilitation of the juvenile and in providing that juveniles under 14 years of age cannot be prosecuted as adults. We do not overrule the holding in *Young* but limit its application to a juvenile 14 years of age and older.

> We hold, therefore, that a juvenile under 14 years of age must be given an opportunity to consult with his or her parent, guardian, or attorney as to whether he or she will waive his or her rights to an attorney and against self-incrimination. Both the parent and juvenile shall be advised of the juvenile's right to an attorney and to remain silent. Absent such warning and consultation, a statement or confession cannot be used against the juvenile at a subsequent hearing or trial. * * *

In **State v. Presha**, 163 N.J. 304, 748 A.2d 1108 (N.J. 2000), the New Jersey Supreme Court considered the voluntariness and admissibility of a confession obtained from a seventeen-year-old juvenile whose mother was absent from the interrogation room when police questioned her son. Although *Presha* adhered to the "totality" approach for older juveniles, it emphasized that parental presence was a factor of great weight. And, it adopted a *per se* requirement of parental presence for younger juveniles:

> We hold that courts should consider the totality of circumstances when reviewing the admissibility of confessions by juveniles in custody. Moreover, courts should consider the absence of a parent or legal guardian from the interrogation area as a highly significant fact when deter-

mining whether the State has demonstrated that a juvenile's waiver of rights was knowing, intelligent, and voluntary. * * *

We note that a special circumstance exists when a juvenile is under the age of fourteen. We will apply a different standard in that context, namely, the adult's absence will render the young offender's statement inadmissible as a matter of law, unless the parent or legal guardian is truly unavailable. Regardless of the juvenile's age, law enforcement officers must use their best efforts to locate the adult before beginning the interrogation and should account for those efforts to the trial court's satisfaction. * * *

The role of a parent in the context of a juvenile interrogation takes on special significance. In that circumstance, the parent serves as advisor to the juvenile, someone who can offer a measure of support in the unfamiliar setting of the police station. Thus, we have emphasized that "[w]henever possible and especially in the case of young children no child should be interviewed except in the presence of his parents or guardian."

Earlier in our history, the State's mission in respect of juvenile offenders was predominately one of rehabilitation. Consistent with that purpose, the presence of a parent in the interrogation area served not only to protect the juvenile's interests but, as importantly, to ensure the truthfulness of any statements to the police.

Today, the juvenile process is different * * * [and] punishment has now joined rehabilitation as a component of the State's core mission with respect to juvenile offenders.

With the State's increased focus on the apprehension and prosecution of youthful offenders, the parent's role in an interrogation setting takes on new significance. When younger offenders are in custody, the parent serves as a buffer between the juvenile, who is entitled to certain protections, and the police, whose investigative function brings the officers necessarily in conflict with the juvenile's legal interests. Parents are in a position to assist juveniles in understanding their rights, acting intelligently in waiving those rights, and otherwise remaining calm in the face of an interrogation.

In view of the changing realities of the juvenile process and the important rights at stake, we reaffirm our belief that a parent or legal guardian should be present in the interrogation room, whenever possible. In respect of confessions by juveniles of any age, courts should consider the adult's absence as a highly significant factor among all other facts and circumstances. By "highly significant factor" we mean that courts should give that factor added weight when balancing it against all other factors. By elevating the significance of the adult's role in the overall balance, we are satisfied that the rights of juveniles will be protected in a manner consistent with constitutional guarantees and modern realities.

As we have suggested in prior cases, younger offenders present a special circumstance in the context of a police interrogation. In respect of a juvenile under the age of fourteen, we believe an evaluation of the totality of circumstances would be insufficient to assure the knowing, intelligent, and voluntary waiver of rights. Accordingly, when a parent or legal guardian is absent from an interrogation involving a juvenile that young, any confession resulting from the interrogation should be deemed inadmissible as a matter of law, unless the adult was unwilling to be present or truly unavailable. * * *

In other contexts, our State policy reflects the appropriateness of age fourteen as a dividing line. New Jersey statutes and court rules contain numerous provisions creating age-differential standards set at fourteen.

Regardless of the juvenile's age, police officers must use their best efforts to locate a parent or legal guardian before beginning the interrogation. Moreover, to sustain the admissibility of incriminating statements made outside of the adult's presence, prosecutors are required to show to the trial court's satisfaction, upon sufficient proofs, that they were unable to locate the adult. Such an additional showing has been implied by other court decisions; we have expressly noted it here for the sake of completeness. * * *

4) Police Exclusion of Parents from Child's Interrogation The Court in **State v. Presha**, 163 N.J. 304, 748 A.2d 1108 (N.J. 2000), addressed the separate question of the police practice of excluding parents from the interrogation room when they questioned a juvenile. Although *Presha* endorsed a "totality" approach for older youths, it characterized deliberate exclusion of parents as a strong factor militating against admissibility of any statement obtained from the child in their absence:

It is difficult for us to envision prosecutors successfully carrying their burdens in future cases in which there has been some deliberate exclusion of a juvenile's parent or legal guardian from the interrogation. However, because the proof in the present case is so compelling that defendant's will was not overborne and the police did not have the benefit of our direction at the time of the interrogation, we see no reason to disturb the judgments below. * * *

Defendant argues for a different result relying, in part, on *State v. Reed*. In *Reed*, the defendant's lawyer attempted to consult with his client while at the prosecutor's office, but was not permitted to communicate with or assist him either at the outset of or during questioning. Nor did police inform the defendant that his attorney was waiting to see him. We held that the suspect's waiver of his privilege against self-incrimination was invalid.

This case is different from that presented in *Reed*. In *Reed*, the police denied the defendant all access to his attorney, whereas here [Presha's mother] was present in the interrogation area before the start of questioning and agreed with her son that she should leave the area. In *Reed*, the police did not inform the defendant that his attorney was waiting to assist him, whereas here defendant knew his mother was on the premises and could have interrupted the interrogation at any time to speak with her.

Moreover, we based our decision in *Reed* on the attorney-client relationship, unique in the criminal justice system. We noted that "our holding is supported in large measure by the special and essential role lawyers play in realizing the purpose of the right against self-incrimination." * * *

A parent obviously enjoys a special relationship with the juvenile; however, the attorney, not the parent, is trained in the law and serves in a unique role as the juvenile's advocate. Because of the above distinctions, we decline to apply our holding in *Reed* to this appeal. * * * [T]he totality of circumstances standard as enunciated here will work as it should: namely, when there has been a deliberate exclusion of a parent or legal guardian from the interrogation room and the police thereafter obtain the juvenile's confession, that confession almost invariably will be suppressed. * * *

STEIN, J., concurring. * * * I believe that the Court errs when it declines to state unequivocally the consequences in future cases of the deliberate exclusion of parents who have not been present at all during their child's interrogation, and does not acknowledge the obvious connection between the exclusion of parents and the availability of a juvenile's right to counsel. The adoption of a bright-line rule rendering inadmissible those statements made by a juvenile whose parent has been deliberately excluded by the police from the interrogation room would be consistent with statutes and judicial decisions throughout the country. There should be no uncertainty within our State's law enforcement community that the same rule will apply in New Jersey's courts. * * *

Courts and legislatures nationwide generally have adopted one of two approaches in deciding whether to admit a minor's confession obtained subsequent to the deliberate exclusion of a parent. Under the first approach, which most states follow, courts consider the totality of the circumstances. Notably, all courts that have applied that standard to a case in which a parent was deliberately excluded have suppressed the confession. * * *

The second approach, which mandates that the State demonstrate that an interested adult was present during an interrogation, has been statutorily adopted in ten states. Those statutes render inadmissible any statement made during interrogation by a juvenile outside the presence of an interested adult and prohibit the waiver of the right to counsel by a juvenile unless that waiver is accompanied by a waiver of a parent or other interested adult. Those jurisdictions consistently have held that any statements made during custodial interrogation are inadmissible where a juvenile's parents are absent.

Eight other states statutorily require police to notify a minor's guardian or custodian immediately if a minor is taken into custody. Statements made by juveniles during custodial interrogation where law enforcement authorities have violated those statutes consistently are suppressed. The courts in those states presumably would also suppress statements made where a parent is deliberately excluded from the juvenile's interrogation. * * *

A survey of the law of both this State and those other states that have addressed the issue thus reveals a clear consensus favoring protection of juveniles' rights by requiring the presence and active participation of a parent or guardian during the interrogation of a juvenile. * * *

Moreover, the implementation of a bright-line rule that requires the suppression of statements made by a juvenile whose parents have been deliberately excluded from their child's interrogation would discourage police officers from preventing family contact. Such a rule is clear and practical. It explicitly defines limits within which police officials can work, better protects the rights of New Jersey's juveniles and decreases the likelihood that the police will attempt to evade that which the law requires.

The Court also neglects to accord adequate significance to the parents' role in assisting juveniles to vindicate their constitutional right to counsel. * * * A juvenile's right to the assistance of counsel is hollow indeed unless a parent is present to assist the juvenile in retaining and paying for a lawyer. In that context, the deliberate exclusion of parents from a juvenile's interrogation room is the *de facto* equivalent of a denial of the right to counsel. * * *

Although the Court today adopts a *per se* rule suppressing statements made by those under the age of fourteen whose parents are not present during interrogation, a sixteen-year-old juvenile is hardly in a better position to get counsel than is a thirteen-year-old. In the eyes of a juvenile, the request to consult a parent may be essentially equivalent to a request to consult an attorney. Most juveniles do not know how to engage a lawyer without the assistance of a parent. Juveniles typically have neither the financial wherewithal necessary to retain counsel nor the requisite knowledge of the appropriate steps to take to find a lawyer suitable to their needs. Police tactics that deliberately deprive juveniles of contact with their parents effectively deprive them of their right to counsel. * * *

5) Policy rationale of parental presence or consultation with an "Interested Adult" States that have experimented with alternative strategies to compensate for youths' special vulnerabilities during interrogation use concrete guidelines or *per se* rules to assure the validity of a juvenile's waiver of rights or confession. They typically require either the presence of an "interested adult," such as a parent, or consultation with an attorney. *See e.g., Commonwealth v. Smith*, 472 Pa. 492, 372 A.2d 797 (1977); *Lewis v. State*, 259 Ind. 431, 288 N.E.2d 138 (Ind. 1972); *Freeman v. Wilcox*, 119 Ga.App. 325, 167 S.E.2d 163 (1969); *People v. Saiz*, 620 P.2d 15 (Colo. 1980); *Commonwealth v. A Juvenile*, 389 Mass. 128, 449 N.E.2d 654, 657 (1983) (holding that in order to demonstrate knowing an intelligent waiver by a juvenile, Commonwealth must show that "a parent or interested adult was present, understood the warnings, and had the opportunity to explain his rights to the juvenile so that the juvenile understands the significance of these rights"). In *In re E.T.C.*, 141 Vt. 375, 378, 449 A.2d 937, 939 (1982), the Vermont Supreme Court held that the state constitution imposed three criteria to establish a valid waiver by a juvenile: the youth "must be given the opportunity to consult with an adult * * *; that adult must be one who is not only generally interested in the welfare of the juvenile but completely independent from and disassociated with the prosecution, e.g., a parent, legal guardian, or attorney representing the juvenile; and * * * the independent interested adult must be informed and be aware of the rights guaranteed to the juvenile." Several states provide the right to the presence of a parent or interested adult by statute. *See, e.g., Ind. Code* § 31–6–7–3(a)(1982).

The *per se* approach excludes any waiver of rights or confession made by a juvenile if the police failed to adhere to the required procedural safeguards. The *per se* approach presumes that most juveniles lack maturity or legal competence and hence require special safeguards to protect them from their own limitations. States use several variants of an "interested adult" *per se* strategy to provide juveniles with greater protections at interrogation than those afforded youths by *Miranda* and *Fare*. Some require police to inform the juvenile and the "interested adult" of the youth's *Miranda* rights, to provide them with an opportunity to consult, and demand both to consent to any subsequent waiver. *See e.g., Lewis v. State*, 259 Ind. 431, 439, 288 N.E.2d 138, 142 (Ind. 1972) (barring admissibility of confession unless both juvenile and "his parents or guardian were informed of his rights to an attorney, and to remain silent. Furthermore, the child must be given an opportunity to consult * * * as to whether or not he wishes to waive those rights."); *Commonwealth v. A Juvenile,* 389 Mass. at 134, 449 N.E.2d at 657 (holding that state must demonstrate that "a parent or interested adult was present, understood the warnings and had the opportunity to explain rights to the juvenile so that the juvenile understands the significance of waiver of rights.").

Some states require the actual presence of the "interested adult" at the interrogation and bar statements obtained after police warned both the juvenile and parent, provided them with an opportunity to consult, but then excluded the parent. *See Conn.Gen.Stat.* § 46b–137(a) (West Supp. 1986) which bars statements "unless made by such child *in the presence of his parent*" and after both were advised of their rights. Connecticut courts strictly have construed this "parental presence" provision and barred statements obtained when police separated the juvenile from her parent after warnings and an opportunity to consult. *See e.g. In re Robert M.*, 22 Conn.App. 53, 56–7, 576 A.2d 549 (1990).

Other states require a juvenile below the age of fourteen years actually to consult with an interested adult, but provide older juveniles only with an opportunity to consult with an interested adult as a prerequisite to a valid waiver. *See e.g., Commonwealth v. A Juvenile*, 389 Mass. 128, 449 N.E.2d 654, 657 (1983); *Commonwealth v. Berry*, 410 Mass. 31, 570 N.E.2d 1004 (1991). Several state's statutes also incorporate variations of these "interested adult" requirements. *See e.g. Colo. Rev. Stat.* § 19–2–210(1) (1996) (parent present at interrogation and advised of juvenile's *Miranda* rights); *Conn. Gen. Stat.* § 46b–137 (1981); *Ind. Code. Ann.* § 31–32–5–1 (West 1998) (waiver only with counsel or after "meaningful consultation" with and in the presence of parent or guardian who "has no interest adverse to the child"); *Mont.Code Ann.* § 41–5–303(2); *N.M. Stat. Ann.* § 32A–2–14(E) (F) (1987) (confessions by child under thirteen years of age inadmissible, rebuttable presumption of inadmissibility by any child thirteen or fourteen); *Okla. Stat. Tit.* 10, § 1109(a) (1981); *Tex. Fam. Code Ann.* § 51.09 (Vernon 1997) (waiver by child *and* attorney, *unless* juvenile previously presented to and received

Miranda warning from a magistrate); *W.Va. Code* § 49–5–2(*l*) (Supp. 1996) (statements by juvenile under fourteen years of age inadmissible unless made in parents' presence).

What does the juvenile's right to parental presence entail? Does a request to see a parent require the cessation of further questioning? *People v. Burton*, 6 Cal.3d 375, 99 Cal.Rptr. 1, 491 P.2d 793 (1971). Does the right to parental access include the right to consult with them in private or only to have them present during the actual interrogation? *Hall v. State*, 264 Ind. 448, 346 N.E.2d 584 (1976). Suppose that the juvenile does not desire to have his or her parent present, whose preference prevails? *See e.g.* Ind. Stat. § 31–32–5–2 (West 1998) ("the child may waive the child's right to meaningful consultation" if the child is informed of that right and knowingly and voluntarily waives it in the presence of the parents).

States that require consultation with an "interested adult" or parents' presence at interrogation offer a variety of rationales. They contend that these safeguards will mitigate the dangers of untrustworthiness, reduce coercive influences, and provide an independent witness who can testify about any coercive practices that police used. They assert that parental presence will assure the accuracy of any statements obtained, involve parents in the process at the initial stages, ensure that police fully advise and a juvenile actually understand those advisories, and relieve police of the burden of making judgments about a youth's competency. States that require parental presence at interrogation recognize that most juveniles lack the maturity to understand their rights and the competence to exercise or waive them without prior consulting with a knowledgeable adult. Proponents believe that parental presence reduces a juvenile's isolation and fear, and provides them with access to legal advice.

In order for parental presence to fulfill its intended purposes, states also require that the juvenile have an opportunity for "meaningful consultation" with her parent or guardian. "The meaningful consultation requirement * * * is an added protection afforded only to juveniles. This additional safeguard applicable to juvenile waivers may be satisfied by 'actual consultation of a meaningful nature or by the express opportunity for such consultation, which [may then be] forsaken in the presence of the proper authority by the juvenile, so long as the juvenile knowingly and voluntarily waives his constitutional rights.' " *Hickman v. State*, 654 N.E.2d 278, 281 (Ind. Ct. App. 1995). Typically, parental presence and an opportunity for parent and child to confer in private satisfy the requirement. "The consultation requirement is designed to afford the juvenile a stabilizing and comparatively relaxed atmosphere in which to make a serious decision that could affect the rest of his life. The requirement is satisfied if actual consultation occurs or if there is an express opportunity for consultation which is properly forsaken by the juvenile. * * * What is important is that the child and adult be aware of an understand the child's rights in order to discuss them intelligently." *Patton v. State*, 588 N.E.2d 494, 496 (Ind.1992).

6) Role of Parents at their Child's Interrogation Courts that require parental presence as a prerequisite to a juvenile's waiver of rights assume that parent and child share an identity of interests and that parents can adequately understand the legal situation and can function as effective advisors. Because a juvenile's privilege against self-incrimination is a personal right, can others, even parents, assert or waive it?

The presence of parents during interrogation may not provide the envisioned benefit for the child and may increase, rather than decrease, the coercive pressures on a youth. Parents' potential conflict of interest with the child, emotional reactions to their child's arrest, or their own intellectual or social limitations may prevent them from playing the supportive role envisioned. Court cases report many instances in which parents coerce their children to confess to the police. *See, e.g., Anglin v. State*, 259 So.2d 752 (Fla.Dist.Ct.App.1972) (reciting that mother repeatedly urged her fifteen-year-old boy "to tell the truth" or "she would clobber him," but the court concluded that "the motherly concern for * * * the basic precepts of morality are to be commended* * * [and there was no] threat or coercion on [her] part"); *In the Matter of C.P.*, 411 A.2d 643, 650 (D.C. Ct. App. 1980) (admitting juvenile's statement which was not the result of police interrogation, but rather of well-intentioned parental influence, when mother "told him to tell the truth. I kept telling him to tell the truth, more than once I know. * * * I just repeating to him to tell the truth, tell the man the truth, tell what happened."); *Commonwealth v. Philip S.*, 414 Mass. 804, 611 N.E.2d 226 (Mass. Sup. Jud. Ct. 1993) ("'[o]ur interested adult rule, which we conclude was satisfied in this case, is not violated because a parent fails to provide what, in hindsight and from a legal perspective, might have been optimum advice.'").

Research indicates that most parents did not directly advise their children about the waiver decision and that those that did almost always urged the child to waive his or her rights. Thomas Grisso, *Juveniles' Waiver of Rights: Legal and Psychological Competence* 187–200 (1981). Why would parents appear predisposed to aggravate rather than to mitigate coercive police pressures at interrogation and urge their children to waive the right to silence? Research on adults' ability to understand and intelligently exercise their own *Miranda* rights casts doubt upon even well-intentioned parents' competence to assist their children. Edwin D. Driver, "Confessions and the Social Psychology of Coercion," 82 *Harv.L.Rev.* 42, 59 (1968) ("even highly educated men may make incriminating admissions simply because they fail to comprehend the legal significance of their remarks"); Griffith & Ayres, "A Postscript to the Miranda Project: Interrogation of Draft Protesters," 77 *Yale L.J.* 300, 305–10 (1967) (arguing that even sophisticated subjects failed to understand the nature and function of their constitutional rights); Medalie, Zeitz & Alexander, "Custodial Police Interrogation in Our Nation's Capital: The Attempt to Implement Miranda," 66 *Mich. L. Rev.* 1347, 1372–75 (1968) ("ratings indicated that 15 percent of the eighty-five 'post-*Miranda* defendants' failed to understand the warning of the right to presence of counsel, and 24 percent failed to understand the warning of the right to appointed counsel"); Project, "Interrogations in New Haven. The Impact of Miranda," 76 *Yale L.J.* 1519, 1613 (1967) ("Warnings are not useless, but neither can they eliminate whatever 'inherently coercive atmosphere' the police station may have."); Richard A. Leo, "Inside the Interrogation Room: A Qualitative and Quantitative Analysis of Contemporary American Police Practices," 86 *J. Crim. L. & Criminology* 266 (1996).

Parents seldom have legal training and may not understand or appreciate the legal problems their child faces.

> The most serious objections to this [parental presence] alternative concern the ability of layman to provide effective assistance in a pre-interrogation setting. Commentators have observed that many parents do not care, and that "[o]ften the parents are, at best, only equal in capacity to the child and therefore poorly equipped to comprehend the complexities confronting them." * * * When [the] finding [of parents' attitudes towards juveniles' rights in interrogation] are coupled with those of the instant studies, which indicate that many adults do not themselves adequately understand their *Miranda* rights, the "interested adult" alternative becomes even less attractive. Thomas Grisso, "Juveniles' Capacities to Waiver *Miranda* Rights: An Empirical Analysis," 68 *Calif. L. Rev.* 1134 at 1163 (1980).

See also, Thomas Grisso & Ring, "Parents' Attitudes Toward Juvenile's Rights in Interrogation," 6 *Crim.Just. & Behav.* 211, 224 (1979) (citing studies that suggest "that parental guidance in such matters often is not an adequate substitute for the advice of trained legal counsel").

7) Effect of a Juvenile's Misrepresentation of Her Age on Police Compliance with a Parental Presence Requirement A Colorado statute provides that no juvenile's statements will be admissible in evidence unless a parental figure was present during the interrogation and advised of the juvenile's *Miranda* rights. In **Nicholas v. People**, 973 P.2d 1213 (Colo. 1999), the Colorado Supreme Court held that even when a youth repeatedly lied to the police about his age and thereby caused them to believe that he was an adult rather than a juvenile, the plain language of the statute barred the admission of the juvenile's statements as evidence against him:

> Our sole task, therefore, is to determine whether the trial court correctly ruled that because Nicholas lied about his age, he is not entitled to the protection of section 19–2–210.* * *

> Here, the plain language of the statute is clear and unambiguous. According to section 19–2–210(1), "[n]o statements or admissions of a juvenile" made during custodial interrogation "shall be admissible in evidence against such juvenile unless a parent, guardian, or legal or physical custodian of the juvenile was present at such interrogation" and both the juvenile and the parental figure were advised of the juvenile's *Miranda* rights. * * * The use of the term "shall" indicates that the rule is mandatory. Thus, according to the plain language of section 19–2–210, the presence of a parental figure during the *Miranda* advisement and interrogation of a juvenile is a precondition to the admissibility of that juvenile's statements. * * *

> The General Assembly did not provide for an exception for juveniles who lie about their age to the police and claim to be adults. Nor did the General Assembly enumerate an exception for cases in which the police reasonably but mistakenly believe that their suspect is an adult. * * *.

The plain language of this statutory mandate reflects the General Assembly's recognition that juveniles generally lack the capacity to make important legal decisions alone. Thus, the General Assembly adopted the parental presence rule to further its purpose of strengthening family ties and to guard against invalid waivers of important constitutional rights by minors acting without assistance. * * *

The understanding that juveniles have less capacity than adults and therefore need special assistance has its counterpart in civil law in Colorado. The General Assembly set eighteen as the minimum age of competence for people to independently enter into contracts, manage estates, and sue and be sued. * * * This rule of law retains its vitality even in cases where the minor has induced the other party to enter into the contract by misrepresenting the minor's age. * * * Thus, we view our application of the plain meaning of section 19–2–210 here as consistent with the way in which civil law protects juveniles from being bound by legal decisions they make, even when they lie about their age. * * *

Because the plain language of the statute is clear and unambiguous, our task is straightforward: to apply the statute as written, without second-guessing the legislature's policy judgments. * * * Thus, even though Nicholas repeatedly lied about his age to the police, his statements were inadmissible under the plain language of section 19–2–210. * * *

Federal courts reach a similar result interpreting the Federal Juvenile Delinquency Act which provides special procedural safeguards for juveniles. In **United States v. Juvenile Male,** 528 F.3d 1146 (C.A.9 (Cal.), 2008), the juvenile, R.P., told the officer he was 18 when he was in fact a juvenile. A check of records showed the juvenile had previous arrests and that the birth dates on those records indicated that he was still a juvenile. Although the government argued that it was not obligated to comply with the statute when the juvenile misrepresents his age and indicates that he is an adult, the court rejected that position:

Under the Juvenile Delinquency Act, juveniles are entitled to distinct procedural protections with regard to interrogation and arraignment. * * * Upon the arrest of a juvenile, the arresting officer must "immediately advise [the] juvenile of his legal rights, in language [that is] comprehensi[ble] to a juvenile." 18 U.S.C. § 5033. The arresting officer must also "notify the parents, guardian or custodian of the rights of the juvenile," and the juvenile must "be taken before a magistrate judge forthwith." * * *

We conclude that under the plain language of the statute, the determinative factor in the application of § 5033 is whether the arrestee is in fact a juvenile, regardless of whether he indicates that he is an adult. Because R.P. was * * * a juvenile at the time of his arrest, he was entitled to the protections of § 5033. * * * Section 5033 begins "*[w]henever* a juvenile is taken into custody. . . ." On its face, then, the statute does not allow for exceptions in situations in which an officer has no reason to know of an individual's juvenile status or in which the juvenile lies about his age. Instead it requires that its protections be provided "*[w]henever* a juvenile is taken into custody." * * *

Not only is there no evidence in this case that application of the unambiguous text of the statute will lead to a result in conflict with the intentions of Congress, there are a number of reasons Congress might have concluded that precisely such a bright line rule is preferable. * * * The legislative history of the JDA does, however, reflect that Congress meant substantially to increase the procedural safeguards available to juveniles immediately after their arrest. The JDA was intended, among other things, to "provide basic procedural rights for juveniles who come under Federal jurisdiction and to bring Federal procedures up to the standards set by various model acts, many state codes and court decisions." * * * [T]he Act was adopted in part in response to the Supreme Court's decision in *In re Gault*, in which the Court emphasized that juvenile delinquency proceedings "must measure up to the essentials of due process and fair treatment." *Gault* focused in particular on police interrogation of juveniles, noting that "the greatest care must be taken to assure that" any confessions obtained as a result of interrogation are not the "product of ignorance of rights or of adolescent fantasy, fright or despair." * * *

Given this emphasis on strong procedural protections, there are several reasons Congress might have believed that requiring the protections of § 5033 "[w]henever a juvenile is taken into custody" is preferable to a rule allowing for exceptions based on the information provided by the juvenile. As the Supreme Court has repeatedly emphasized, a child is less capable than an adult of understanding the consequences and seriousness of arrest and detention. * * * Congress could have believed that a juvenile should also not be able to waive the JDA interrogation protections by lying about his age. The very premise of the JDA, indeed, is that juveniles will often make choices—including the choice to appear to be adults when they are not—that are not in their own interest.

Congress might also have concluded that the practical consequences of a rule that permits of no exceptions are more desirable than the consequences of, for example, a rule that would require courts to determine what information was available to the arresting officer. The strict rule adopted by Congress should, as a practical matter, induce arresting officers initially to treat an arrestee as a juvenile if there is some basis for doing so-for example, the arrestee's appearance, information about past arrests, or some other indication. The bright-line rule builds in the likelihood that arresting officers will evaluate all the available information and, when in doubt, treat the arrestee as a juvenile. The result would be a de facto reasonable knowledge rule, while at the same time avoiding difficult post-hoc judicial line drawing concerning whether or not a sufficient quantity of evidence existed to trigger juvenile protections.

Finally, Congress may have concluded that compliance with the requirements of § 5033 is an effective way to determine quickly whether an individual is in fact a juvenile. Prompt notification of an individual's parents * * * should immediately reveal information confirming or refuting the individual's juvenile status. And bringing the individual before a magistrate judge promptly will allow the judge to make a determination as to juvenile status as quickly as possible. * * *

8) Parental Presence, Juvenile Interrogation, and Adult Criminal Prosecution Suppose police obtain a confession from a youth over whom the juvenile court has jurisdiction. Does the failure to allow the youth to consult with a parent bar the admissibility of the statement in a subsequent criminal prosecution? *Alabama Rules of Juvenile Procedure 11(B)* (1998) governs the rights of the child while being questioned in custody and provides that "Before the child is questioned about anything concerning the charge on which the child was arrested, the person asking the questions must inform the child of the following rights: * * * (4) That if the child's counsel, parent, or guardian is not present, then the child has the right to communicate with them, and that, if necessary, reasonable means will be provided for the child to do so." In **Anderson v. State**, 729 So.2d 900 (Ala. Crim. App. 1998), the court considered the applicability of Rule 11(B)(4) to a confession obtained from a juvenile who was "automatically" prosecuted as an adult because the legislature excluded the offense with which he was charged from the jurisdiction of the juvenile court:

> "In addition to the standard *Miranda* warnings, [subsection (4) mandates that] a juvenile must also be informed that he can communicate with a parent or guardian." This court has long recognized the importance of affording children the additional right in Rule 11(B)(4):
>
>> Informing the child of his right to communicate with a parent or guardian serves two important purposes. First, '[t]his simple warning will give the juvenile the opportunity to obtain the guidance necessary in order for him to evaluate his rights.' Secondly, the rule recognizes that 'the parent or guardian may be the conduit through which the juvenile secures an attorney.' "
>
> "The rationale of courts holding a child's request to see a parent equivalent to a request to see an attorney, * * * is that, while an adult in trouble normally requests an attorney's assistance, a child logically expresses his desire for help and his unwillingness to proceed alone by requesting a parent's presence. * * * [I]n the case of a child, the right to assistance of counsel is hollow unless a parent is present, for a parent is normally the child's only avenue through which to evaluate and exercise the right to counsel." " * * * [I]t is undisputed that Anderson was not informed that he had a right to communicate with his parent or guardian. * * * "

In denying Anderson's motion to suppress his statement, the trial court ruled that it was sufficient, for purposes of admissibility, that Anderson had been informed of and had waived the standard *Miranda* rights before giving the statement. In so ruling, the trial court accepted the state's argument that Rule 11(B)(4) did not apply to Anderson because of the enactment of § 12–15–34.1 * * * [which] automatically removes from the jurisdiction of the juvenile court a juvenile age 16 or over who is alleged to have committed any one of certain enumerated serious offenses. These offenders are now treated as adults. * * *

However, we cannot agree with the state that the rights granted to Anderson under Rule 11(B) were extinguished merely because he was alleged to have committed one of the serious offenses * * * which resulted in his automatic placement within the jurisdiction of the adult system. * * *

In *Ex parte Jackson*, the Alabama Supreme Court addressed the admissibility in an adult criminal prosecution of the custodial statement of a juvenile where the police, before obtaining the statement, had failed to inform the juvenile of his right * * * to consult with his parents. In holding that the juvenile's statement should have been suppressed in the criminal prosecution, the Supreme Court expressly rejected the state's argument that the trial court's determination that the juvenile was to be tried as an adult "cured" any error committed when the juvenile was not advised of his right to consult with his parents. The Supreme Court's holding in *Ex parte Jackson* made clear that the exclusionary rule is equally applicable whether the state seeks to admit a juvenile's custodial statement at a transfer hearing in the juvenile court, or at a criminal prosecution of the juvenile in the circuit court. Although a juvenile being tried in the circuit court may otherwise be treated as an adult, "[p]ublic policy, in addition to the constitutional requirements," supports the requirement that the juvenile be informed of his or her rights pursuant to Rule 11(B)(4).

Although Rule 11(B) is part of the Alabama Rules of Juvenile Procedure, "which govern the procedure for all matters in the juvenile court," it contains no limitation mandating its applicability only to proceedings in the juvenile court. Indeed, the holding in *Ex parte Jackson* clearly established that Rule 11(B) applies, in certain cases, to proceedings in the circuit court. * * * [T]his court has consistently recognized that the rights set forth in Rule 11(B), Ala.R.Juv.P., apply to juveniles regardless of which forum they may find themselves in—the juvenile court or the circuit court—and we have set aside convictions where custodial statements by juveniles obtained in violation of Rule 11(B)(4) were admitted in evidence at the criminal prosecutions of juveniles.

Although we have referred to "juveniles" heretofore in this opinion, properly speaking, Rule 11 provides for the "rights of the child." By its own terms, Rule 11(B) applies where a "child" is taken into custody and questioned by law enforcement authorities. The Alabama Rules of Juvenile Procedure do not define the term "child." However, that term is defined by statute as "[a]n individual under the age of 18, or under 19 years of age and before the juvenile court for a matter arising before that individual's 18th birthday." The rights set forth in Rule 11(B) belong to any person who is defined by statute as a "child" when taken into custody; those rights are not dependant upon the forum in which the child may ultimately be called upon to answer charges. * * *

[O]ur courts have consistently recognized that a juvenile "carries" certain rights as a child even after the juvenile has become subject to the procedures and penalties prescribed for adults. Moreover, surely a child accused of a serious offense, and therefore facing "automatic removal" to the jurisdiction of the circuit court for prosecution as an adult, has, when the child is facing custodial interrogation, at least as much need for parental guidance as a child accused of a less serious offense and who will be afforded a transfer hearing before any determination as to prosecution as an adult is made. * * *

By contrast, the Connecticut Supreme Court in **State v. Ledbetter**, 263 Conn. 1, 818 A.2d 1(Ct. 2003), considered the admissibility of a confession obtained from a juvenile and subsequently used against her in an adult criminal prosecution. Conn. Gen. Stat. § 46b–137(a) provides that "Any admission, confession or statement, written or oral, made by a child to a police officer or Juvenile Court official shall be inadmissible in any proceeding concerning the alleged delinquency of the child making such admission, confession or statement unless made by such child in the presence of his parent or parents or guardian and after the parent or parents or guardian and child have been advised" of the child's *Miranda* rights. The Supreme Court held that the parental presence statute is inapplicable inasmuch as its provisions pertain only to delinquency proceedings in juvenile court and not to prosecutions in criminal court:

> Under § 46b–137(a), unless a child's confession to the police is made in the presence of a parent or guardian after the parent or guardian and child have been advised of certain rights, that confession is "inadmissible in any proceeding concerning the alleged delinquency of the child...." By its express terms, therefore, § 46b–137(a) pertains only to proceedings that concern a child's *alleged delinquency*. [The delinquency statute] provides that "all proceedings concerning delinquent children" shall be heard in juvenile court. Thus, the defendant's confession would be subject to the protections of § 46b–137(a) if the state sought to introduce her confession in a proceeding involving the defendant's alleged delinquency in juvenile court.

> The defendant, however, was charged with class A and B felonies and, consequently, her case automatically was transferred from the juvenile court docket to the regular criminal docket in accordance with § 46b–127. The defendant, therefore, was tried as an adult in criminal court, not as a child in juvenile court. Consequently, the defendant's trial on felony murder and robbery charges properly cannot be characterized as a proceeding "*concerning the alleged delinquency*" of a child that falls within the purview of General Statutes § 46b–137(a). (Emphasis added.)

> Of course, the legislature was free to make § 46b–137(a) applicable to proceedings in criminal court as well as to proceedings in juvenile court. Indeed, the legislature could have extended the protections of § 46b–137(a) to criminal proceedings, if it had wished to do so, simply by omitting the limiting language contained in the statute. We can discern no reason, however, why the legislature would have used language expressly *restricting* the reach of § 46b–137 (a) to proceedings concerning delinquency if, as the defendant maintains, it had not intended to impose such a limitation.

> Furthermore, it is axiomatic that delinquency proceedings in juvenile court are fundamentally different from criminal proceedings. Indeed,

"adjudication as a juvenile rather than prosecution as an adult carries significant benefits, chief among which are a determination of delinquency rather than criminality; confidentiality; limitations with respect to sentencing; erasure of files; and isolation from the adult criminal population. * * * Just as the legislature has opted to grant certain important benefits to children accused of misconduct, so, too, has it chosen to except certain especially serious crimes from the juvenile system pursuant to § 46b–127." As reflected in the plain language of § 46b–137(a), the legislature also has determined that a child who is prosecuted criminally for committing one or more of those serious crimes shall not be entitled to the protections otherwise afforded children under § 46b–137(a). This legislative policy determination is a perfectly legitimate one because the legislature, in balancing competing considerations, reasonably could have concluded that, in light of the state's "valid and weighty interest in convicting the guilty"; a child's interest in receiving the protections of § 46b–137(a) is outweighed by the state's interest in using an otherwise admissible confession against that child in a criminal prosecution for the commission of a capital felony, class A or B felony or arson murder * * *.

3. RIGHT TO COUNSEL DURING INTERROGATION

Instead of relying on judges' discretionary review of the "totality of the circumstances" or parents' presence with a youth at interrogation, states could require the presence of an attorney and consultation with counsel prior to any juveniles' waiver of *Miranda* or the right to counsel. Waivers of *Miranda* rights and the right to counsel involve tactical and strategic considerations as well as an abstract awareness of the rights themselves. A *per se* requirement of consultation with counsel prior to any waiver of rights recognizes youths' immaturity, lack of experience with law enforcement, and provides the only effective means to protect their interests. Attorneys, rather than parents, possess the skills and training necessary to assist the child in the adversarial process.

IN THE INTEREST OF J.D.Z.

431 N.W.2d 272 (N.D. 1988).

ERICKSTAD, CHIEF JUSTICE. At a hearing before the juvenile court concerning a petition to declare J.D.Z. (hereinafter Joe, a pseudonym) to be a delinquent child, the court suppressed the confession of the minor child finding it was obtained in violation of his statutory and constitutional rights. The court ordered the petition to be dismissed and this appeal followed. We affirm.

[Someone vandalized a drilling rig truck and a Ditch Witch trencher. A "Crimestopper" tip identified J.D.Z. as a possible suspect or potential witness. Rummel, a Police Youth Bureau officer, decided to talk with Joe, a minor child, about the incident and went to the home of Joe, his mother, K.P. (hereinafter Karen), and his stepfather, B.P. (hereinafter Bob).]

All four sat down in the living room and Rummel began to question Joe. After a few initial questions, Rummel got the impression that Joe was not telling the truth and told him so.[1] Bob, the stepfather, also told Joe that he, too, knew Joe was not telling the truth. Rummel informed Joe that he was not under arrest and did not have to answer any questions. At that point Bob began asking Joe about the incident, stating that the questions would be answered and Joe would tell the truth because Bob wanted to get to the bottom of this.[2] It is at this point that Joe confessed

---

1. Hearing transcript at page 59:

"Q When you first told [Joe] what you were there for, what did you tell him?

"A I told him it was about the Plaza Del Toro and he said he knew. He understood what we were going to be talking about. * * *

"Q And then what did you tell [Joe]?

"A I told [Joe] that I didn't feel that he was telling the whole truth. I stated, you know, I don't think it is possible for you to see this young boy inside of the truck doing damage to the truck from a quarter of a mile.

"Q Okay, what happened next?

"A [Joe] became rather nervous and when he was talking to me he wouldn't talk to me he would talk to the floor and from previously in interviewing [Joe] I knew that he was not telling the whole truth at this point.

"Q Did you tell [Joe] that you felt that way?

"A Yes, I did."

2. Hearing transcript at page 61:

"A [Bob] then told [Joe] that he too knew that he was not telling the truth and he did want the truth from [Joe].

"Q At about this time then after [Bob] made that statement did you make any statements to [Joe] and [Bob] and [Karen]?

"A Yes, I informed them that he is not under arrest and he does not have to answer my questions.

"Q You recall telling them anything else?

"A No.

"Q Did [Bob] respond to that?

"A He stated that he will answer my questions and he will tell the truth because he wanted to get to the bottom of this.

"Q Those were [Bob's] exact words?

"A Yes.

"Q At this point you are sitting in the living room and you told [Joe] that he is not under arrest and he didn't have to answer any questions, is that correct?

"A Yes sir.

"Q And [Bob] stated we are going to get to the bottom of this?

"A Yes.

"Q Did you prompt or coach [Bob] in any way to make that statement?

"A No sir.

"Q After [Bob] made that statement that we are going to get to the bottom of this, did you ask any further questions?

"A I did later on. From that point [Bob] did most of the questioning. I took notes is what I did.

"Q Okay, so really at that particular point in time you weren't asking the question? [Bob] was?

"A Yes sir.

"Q Did you ask some questions?

"A Yes sir, I did ask some.

to having engaged in the vandalism of the vehicles together with another minor child. * * *

The district court suppressed the confession and found there was insufficient corroborating evidence to support the confession. The court said:

> The uncontroverted facts herein establish that the Respondent [Joe] had become the focus of the police investigation of the property damage crime. The Petitioner [Rummel] went to [Joe's] home for the express purpose of questioning [Joe] about the crime and [Joe's] involvement therein. Upon arrival, [Rummel] informed [Joe], a ten year old child, that [Joe] need not answer the [Rummel's] questions, but made no effort to ascertain [Joe's] comprehension of such advisement, failed to inform [Joe] of his constitutional and statutory rights pursuant to *Miranda v. Arizona*, and further failed to inform [Joe's] parents of the applicable rights.

> It is further clear that when [Rummel] received [Joe's] initial answer to [Rummel's] questions, [Rummel], from prior experience with [Joe], considered [Joe's] answers to be less than truthful, and in fact so stated. The questioning that continued, while propounded by the step father of [Joe], was accomplished in the presence of and for the purpose of furnishing information to [Rummel] concerning [Joe's] involvement in the alleged criminal activity.

> It is therefore the decision of this Court that the motion of [Joe] to suppress the confession of [Joe] as secured by [Rummel] is meritorious, that the confession was secured illegally in that [Rummel] failed to advise the minor child of his statutory and constitutional rights, failed to advise the parent of the minor child of the applicable statutory and constitutional rights, and that the interrogation that did occur was custodial in that the same occurred in the residence of the minor child and with the obvious presence of law enforcement authorities. * * *

The dispositive issue is whether or not Joe was denied the statutory right to counsel guaranteed by section 27–20–26, N.D.C.C. For if he was, it is immaterial whether or not he was denied a constitutional right. We find that Joe was denied this right and therefore the confession was properly suppressed. * * *

Section 27–20–26(1), N.D.C.C., provides a right to counsel under the Uniform Juvenile Court Act, and states in relevant part:

> [A] party is entitled to representation by legal counsel at all stages of any proceedings under this chapter and, if as a needy person he is unable to employ counsel, to have the court provide counsel for him.

"Q And after you explained, you made the statement that he was not under arrest and didn't have to answer any questions and [Bob] made his comments, what happened then?

"A [Bob] told him that he wanted the truth and then [Joe] stated that he was there."

* * * Counsel must be provided for a child not represented by his parent, guardian, or custodian.

We have recognized that the "stages of any proceedings" are not limited to those instances which take place in the courtroom but include circumstances in which an officer has focused his investigation on a particular suspect and is intent on gathering evidence, not merely investigating a complaint. * * *

In the instant case, the initial questions by Rummel to Joe about his knowledge of the incident may not constitute a stage of the proceedings. However, once Rummel became aware that Joe may have been personally involved in the vandalism, his line of questioning, and the investigation, focused on Joe. This focus, and the questions designed to elicit evidence of vandalism, caused the interview to become a "stage" of the "proceedings."[4] Before being asked any more questions, Joe was entitled to be advised of his right to counsel. * * * Rummel merely told Joe that he was not under arrest and that he did not have to answer any questions. No mention was made of his right to counsel.

Section 27–20–26, N.D.C.C., not only provides that a party is entitled to representation but specifically states: "Counsel *must* be provided for a child not represented by his parent, guardian, or custodian." [Emphasis added.] We have held that the mere presence of a parent does not constitute representation. * * *

While Joe's mother, Karen, and his mother's husband, Bob, were present during the questioning, we cannot say from the tenor of Bob's questions that he was representing Joe. We conclude that, under these particular circumstances, the mere presence of the parents during questioning by a police officer concerning an incident of vandalism in which their child is a suspect does not constitute representation of the interests of that minor child as contemplated by section 27–20–26, N.D.C.C. * * *

In light of the statutory guarantee of right to counsel provided by the Uniform Juvenile Court Act and our past decisions applying this guarantee, we conclude that Joe had the right to be represented when the investigation of Rummel began to focus on him. Here the mere presence of his mother and stepfather did not guarantee the representation intended by the Legislature. The State therefore had a mandatory duty to provide Joe with counsel before proceeding with further questioning. Because Joe was not represented when he confessed to involvement in the vandalism, that confession was obtained in violation of his statutory rights. The confession was properly suppressed by the juvenile court. We affirm.

---

4. We are utilizing this "focus" test as developed in our previous case law involving the Uniform Juvenile Court Act. In the context of adult criminal proceedings, we have decided that investigatory focus does not require the giving of the *Miranda* warnings. We concluded in *State v. Fields* that this Court has adopted a "custody" test for determining the application of *Miranda*. That conclusion, however, was in the context of adult criminal proceedings where we were considering the application of the *Miranda* warnings, not a statutory right to counsel under the Juvenile Court Act.

NOTES

1) Professional Support for Consultation With Counsel as a Prerequisite to Juveniles' Waivers of Rights *J.D.Z.* represents a third option to protect juveniles during interrogation, a *per se* rule that requires consultation with counsel and the presence of an attorney at every interrogation of a juvenile and prior to any waiver of the right to counsel. Since waivers of both *Miranda* rights and the right to counsel involve legal and strategic considerations as well as knowledge and understanding of rights and an appreciation of consequences, it is difficult to see how any other alternative could be as effective. A *per se* requirement of consultation with counsel prior to a waiver takes account of the immaturity of youths and their lack of experience in law enforcement situations. In addition, however, it recognizes that attorneys rather than parents possess the skills and training necessary to assist the child in the adversarial process.

Several professional groups have endorsed the appointment of and consultation with counsel as a prerequisite to any waiver of rights. The President's Commission on Law Enforcement and Administration of Justice recommended appointment of counsel for juveniles as a matter of course whenever the possibility of coercive state action existed. President's Commission on Law Enforcement and Administration of Justice, *The Challenge of Crime in a Free Society* 87 (1967). The National Advisory Committee Task Force on Juvenile Justice recommended that during police interrogation, states prohibit juveniles from "waiv[ing] the right against self-incrimination without the advice of counsel." National Advisory Committee on Criminal Justice Standards and Goals, *Report of the Task Force on Juvenile Justice and Delinquency Prevention* 212 (O.J.J.D.P., Washington, D.C.: 1976). The American Bar Association's Juvenile Justice Standards recommend that "[t]he right to counsel should attach as soon as the juvenile is taken into custody * * *, when a petition is filed * * *, or when the juvenile appears personally at an intake conference, whichever occurs first." American Bar Association–Institute of Judicial Administration, *Juvenile Justice Standards Relating to Pretrial Court Proceedings* 89 (Cambridge, MA: Ballinger, 1980). In addition, "[the juvenile] should have 'the effective assistance of counsel at all stages of the proceeding'" and this right to counsel should be mandatory and nonwaivable. *See also*, American Bar Association, Juvenile Justice Center, *A Call for Justice* (1995). The commentary to the Juvenile Justice Standards qualifies the absolute, nonwaivable nature of the right to counsel. "In recommending that the respondent's right to counsel in delinquency proceedings should be nonwaivable, this standard is not intended to foreclose absolutely the possibility of *pro se* representation by a juvenile." *Id.* at Standard 5.1 commentary at 93. The crucial issue for juveniles, as for adults, is whether such a waiver can occur "voluntarily and intelligently," particularly without prior consultation with counsel. It would be an extraordinary juvenile who should be able to persuade a court that he or she possesses sufficient maturity, competence, and legal sophistication to effect *pro se* representation and still obtain a fair trial.

2) Mandatory Consultation With Counsel Prior to Waivers Both the Juvenile Justice Standards and *Gault* and *Fare* recognize juveniles' need for legal counsel where a waiver of rights likely will affect subsequent proceedings. A few states require juveniles to be represented by an attorney at interrogation and bar youths from waiving the right to counsel without the written consent of a parent.

Iowa Stat. § 232.11. Right to assistance of counsel (West 1998)

1. A child shall have the right to be represented by counsel at the following stages of the proceedings within the jurisdiction of the juvenile court * * *:

> a. From the time the child is taken into custody for any alleged delinquent act that constitutes a serious or aggravated misdemeanor or felony * * * and during any questioning thereafter by a peace officer or probation officer. * * *

2. The child's right to be represented by counsel * * * shall not be waived by a child less than sixteen years of age without the written consent of the child's parent, guardian, or custodian. The waiver by a child who is at least sixteen years of age is valid only if a good faith effort has been made to notify the child's parent, guardian, or custodian that the child has been taken into custody and of the alleged delinquent act for which the child has been taken into custody, the location of the child, and the right of the parent, guardian, or custodian to visit and confer with the child.

In *In re J.A.N.*, 346 N.W.2d 495, 499 (Iowa 1984), the Iowa Supreme Court excluded the confession of a 14–year–old youth obtained in the absence of counsel or without parental consent. "The legislature has demanded that painstaking care must be taken to obtain parental consent before questioning a juvenile. The child can be expected to rely on the judgment of the consenting parent." In *State v. Walker*, 352 N.W.2d 239, 241–42 (Iowa 1984), the Iowa Supreme Court explained:

> Iowa's Juvenile Code implements and goes beyond the constitutional right to counsel provided for juveniles by explaining the stages of proceedings when a child may be represented, the effect of denial of the right to counsel on statements offered in evidence, and the specific methods by which police officers may obtain a waiver of the child's right to counsel. * * * [T]he statute distinguishes between juveniles less than sixteen years of age and juveniles, like defendant, who are at least sixteen. For children less than sixteen, the statute provides that no waiver of counsel is valid unless accompanied by the written consent of the parent. For the child who is at least sixteen years of age, the statute replaces written parental consent with the requirement that good faith efforts be made to notify the parent, guardian, or custodian and to provide the notified person with four explicit facts about the juvenile's circumstances. * * * The statute listed very specifically the four items of information which the officers must make a good faith effort to convey to the contacted parent. In enacting this statute, our legislature apparently believed that each part of the four part message would tend to impress upon a parent the importance of going to the side of the child and giving the child parental advice.

Should states have public defenders "on call" In order to assure the availability of counsel whom police could summon to the police station prior to any custodial interrogation of a juvenile?

An earlier version of the Texas Family Code, **Tex. Fam. Code Ann. § 51.09** (Vernon 1973) prohibited juveniles from waiving rights without assistance and concurrence of counsel:

> Unless a contrary intent clearly appears elsewhere in this title, any right granted to a child by this title or by the constitution or laws of this state or the United States may be waived in proceedings under this title if:
>
> (1) the waiver is made by the child and the attorney for the child;
>
> (2) the child and the attorney waiving the right are informed of and understand the right and the possible consequences of waiving it;
>
> (3) the waiver is voluntary; and
>
> (4) the waiver is made in writing or in court proceedings that are recorded.

See e.g. Robert Dawson, "Delinquent Children and Children in Need of Supervision: Draftsman's Comments to Title 3 of the Texas Family Code," 5 *Tex. Tech. L. Rev.* 509, 524–25 (1974); Comment, "Waiver of Constitutional Rights by a Juvenile Under the Texas Family Code: The 1975 Amendment to Section 51.09," 17 *S. Tex. L. J.* 301, 303 (1975). Because *Miranda* and *Gault* granted juveniles the constitutional right to the privilege against self-incrimination and to counsel, Texas courts ruled that Tex. Fam. Code § 51.09 prohibited interrogation without counsel. "[W]e hold that the privilege against self-incrimination may be waived by a juvenile only with concurrence of his attorney." *In re F.G.*, 511 S.W.2d 370, 374 (Tex. Civ. Ct. App. 1974). Similarly, in *In re S.E.B.*, 514 S.W.2d 948, 950–51 (Tex. Civ. Ct. App. 1974), the court emphasized the importance of counsel as a prerequisite to a valid waiver. "While it perhaps sound ridiculous to say that one must have an attorney in order to waive the right to an attorney, it must be remembered that the Legislature was taking every precaution to protect the rights of minors from those who might unintentionally or perhaps in some cases intentionally take advantage of one who is young, inexperienced and perhaps unable to exercise his constitutional rights until he finds it is too late to have those rights protected."

Legislative amendments in 1975 eliminated the requirement of assistance and concurrence of counsel and substituted instead a variation of the *Miranda* warning/waiver formula. The current version of **Tex. Fam. Code Ann. § 51.095** (West 1998) provides that "the statement of a child is admissible in evidence * * * if: (1) the statement is made in writing when the child is in a detention facility or other place of confinement or in the custody of an officer and: (A) the statement shows that the child has at some time before the making of the statement received from a magistrate a [*Miranda*] warning * * * "or "(5) the statement is made orally when the child is in a detention facility or other place of confinement or in the custody of an officer and the statement is recorded by an electronic recording device, including a device that records images * * *." Rather than insisting on the presence and concurrence of counsel, the Texas amendments allow juveniles to waive their

Miranda rights albeit with somewhat more elaborate procedural safeguards than those required by *Fare*.

3) Role of Counsel at Interrogation Affording mandatory, non-waivable counsel to juveniles during interrogation and at all court proceedings may not provide a panacea. Attorneys may not be capable of or committed to representing juvenile clients in an effective, adversarial manner. Organizational pressures to cooperate, judicial hostility toward adversarial litigants, role ambiguity created by the dual goals of rehabilitation and punishment, reluctance to help juveniles "beat a case," or an internalization of a court's treatment philosophy may compromise the role of counsel in juvenile court. *See* Abraham Blumberg, "The Practice of Law as A Confidence Game: Organizational Co-optation of a Profession," 1 *Law & Soc'y Rev.* 15, 19–20 (1967), described the co-optation of defense attorneys in the adult criminal process. Blumberg argues that certain institutional pressures and the need to maintain stable, cooperative relationships with other personnel and professionals in the system may be inconsistent with effective advocacy and an adversary position. Defense attorneys become involved in ongoing relations with prosecutors and judges and may depend on their cooperation. Similarly, prosecutors and the court depend on defense attorneys to cooperate in order to expedite a large volume of cases. The result is a system of informal relationships in which maintaining organizational stability may become more important than the representation of any given client. The same analysis has been applied to the role of attorneys in juvenile court.

Several studies report that juvenile court judges incarcerate juveniles who appear with counsel more frequently than they incarcerate juveniles who appear without counsel; private lawyers do not enhance juveniles' bargaining power or rights; and informal relationships in juvenile court influence judges to dispose of cases based on their personal feelings about counsel. Other studies have questioned whether lawyers can actually perform as adversaries in a system rooted in parens patriae and benevolent rehabilitation. *See generally*, Barry C. Feld, "The Right to Counsel In Juvenile Court: An Empirical Study of When Lawyers Appear and the Difference They Make," 79 *J. Crim. L. & Criminology* 1185 (1989); Barry C. Feld, *Justice for Children: The Right to Counsel and Juvenile Courts* (1993). We will examine the delivery of legal services and the role of counsel in juvenile courts extensively in Chapter 7.

4) Mandatory, Non-waivable Counsel at Interrogation: the Conundrum Mandatory, non-waivable appointment of counsel protects the rights of the juvenile and also helps the courts efficiently to handle cases and to assure that any decisions juvenile make truly are "knowing" and "intelligent." Clearly, a rule requiring courts to appoint counsel for juveniles prior to interrogation as well as throughout the process could substantially affect juvenile justice administration. The ability of police to obtain waivers from and interrogate youths likely would decrease. Indeed, courts decry the adverse effects that such procedural safeguards and *per se* rules would have on police interrogation and the efficient repression of crime, and share the "societal outrage against crime." Wallace J. Mlyniec, "A Judge's Ethical Dilemma: Assessing A Child's Capacity to Choose," 64 *Fordham L. Rev.* 1873 (1996) (stating that courts find most juvenile confessions to be knowing, intelligent and voluntary despite overwhelming research evidence to the contrary on juveniles' capacity to waive). "It is apparent most courts, required to deal pragmatically with an ever-mounting crime wave in which minors play a disproportionate role, have considered society's self-preservation interest in rejecting a blanket exclusion for juvenile confessions." *In re Thompson*, 241 N.W.2d 2, 5 (Iowa 1976). *See also State v. Francois* 197 So.2d 492, 495 (Fla. 1967) ("We feel, too, that 'self-confessed criminals should be punished, not liberated on the basis of dubious technicalities' even though they may be young.") As noted in *Dino* and *Fernandez*, *supra* p. 320, Note 1, the Pennsylvania Supreme Court abandoned its "interest adult" rule in favor of a "totality" approach, and observed that "protection of juveniles against the innate disadvantages associated with the immaturity of most youth may * * * be achieved in a manner that affords more adequate weight to the interests of society, and of justice." *Commonwealth v. Christmas*, 502 Pa. 218, 465 A.2d 989, 992 (Pa. 1983). Thus, most states categorically reject the only recognized and effective procedural safeguard to protect youths from their own vulnerability during interrogation and instead adopt a policy that functionally disadvantages youths.

Despite the adverse impact that the presence of counsel would have on police's ability to interrogate youths, however, *Gault* and *Miranda* already assure juveniles' access to counsel during interrogation and throughout the juvenile justice process if the youths know and are capable enough to request one. Only a youth who is ill-informed, inexperienced, or overwhelmed by the "inherent coercion of custodial interrogation" will cooperate with the police to her own detriment. Only an attorney can redress the imbalance between a vulnerable youth and the state. The issue is not one of entitlement, but rather the ease or difficulty with which courts find that juveniles waive their *Miranda* and counsel rights which, in turn, affects every other aspect of juvenile justice administration.

E. CONFIDENTIALITY AND PRE–TRIAL PROCEDURES: LINE–UPS, PHOTOGRAPHS, FINGERPRINTS, AND PUBLICITY

The Supreme Court in *In re Gault*, 387 U.S. 1 at 24–25, 87 S.Ct. 1428, 18 L.Ed.2d 527 (1967) noted that

[I]t is frequently said that juveniles are protected by the process from disclosure of their deviational behavior. * * * [T]he summary procedures of Juvenile Courts are sometimes defended by a statement that it is the law's policy to 'hide youthful errors from the full gaze of the public and bury them in the graveyard of the forgotten past.' This claim of secrecy, however, is more rhetoric than reality. Disclosure of [juvenile] court records is discretionary with the judge in most jurisdictions. Statutory restrictions almost invariably apply only to the court records, and even as to those the evidence is that many courts routinely furnish information to the FBI and the military, and on request to government agencies and even to private employers. Of more importance are police records. In most States the police keep a complete file of juvenile 'police contacts' and have complete discretion as to the disclosure of juvenile records. Police departments receive requests for information from the FBI and other law-enforcement agencies, the Armed Forces, and social service agencies, and most of them generally comply. Private employers word their application forms to produce information concerning juvenile arrests and court proceedings, and in some jurisdictions information concerning juvenile police contacts is furnished private employers as well as government agencies.

The Court in *United States v. Hall*, 452 F.Supp. 1008, 1010–13 (S.D.N.Y. 1977), noted that the Federal Youth Corrections Act, like the juvenile court, had as its goal "the rehabilitation of the young persons in this country who have made their first mistake, so to speak. * * * The evils of a criminal record are well known. The convicted are forever branded as untrustworthy members of society. Their job prospects are permanently compromised; they are often the subject of suspicion and mistrust. * * * [Sealing or expunging ensures] that the defendant no longer has a criminal 'record' and he can resume his life anew without the stigma of a conviction." However, the Court in *United States v. Johnson*, 28 F.3d 151, 155 (D.C. Cir. 1994) cautioned that "[w]hen yesterday's juvenile delinquent becomes today's adult criminal the reasons behind society's earlier forbearance disappear."

The range of identification procedures that may result in physical records is extensive. " 'Nontestimonial identification' means identification by fingerprints, palm prints, footprints, measurements, blood specimens, urine specimens, saliva samples, hair samples, or other reasonable physical examination, handwriting exemplars, voice samples, photographs, and lineups or similar identification procedures requiring the presence of a juvenile." N.C. Gen. Stat. § 7A–596 (Michie 1997).

Identification procedures—line-ups, photo arrays, and fingerprints—as well as the records of juvenile arrests and convictions, and pre-trial publicity raise several issues for juvenile justice administration. How should state policies balance public safety and the legitimate interests of law enforcement against the consequences for delinquents of subjecting them to routines criminal processing? Will the creation of records and dossiers permanently label and stigmatize youths and adversely affect their adult life chances?

Minnesota Rules of Juvenile Procedure Rule 5.06 (West 1998):

Subd. 1. Photographing. (A) Generally. A detained child may be photographed when the child is taken into custody in accordance with the laws relating to arrests. * * *

Subd. 2. Fingerprinting. (A) Generally. All children in custody alleged to have committed a felony may be fingerprinted without court order. Otherwise, a court order is required. * * *

Subd. 3. Line–Up. (A) Generally. A detained child may be placed in a line-up. A child may choose not to participate in a line-up which is not related to the matter for which the child is detained unless ordered by the court to appear in a line-up. * * *

(B) Right to Counsel During Line–Up for Child Alleged to be Delinquent. A child has the right to have counsel present when placed in a line-up related to a delinquent act for which the child has been taken into custody unless exigent circumstances exist such that providing counsel would unduly interfere with a prompt investigation of the crime. When a delinquency petition has been filed, counsel for the child shall be present for any line-up. Any identification evidence obtained without the presence of counsel shall be inadmissible, unless the line-up occurred before the filing of the petition and exigent circumstances existed preventing the presence of counsel. * * *

Comment—Rule 5

* * * Minn.R.Juv.P. 5.06, subd. 3 implements the policies of *U.S. v. Wade*, to provide the assistance of counsel to minimize the dangers of erroneous misidentification. Unlike the formalistic limitations imposed by *Kirby v. Illinois*, the rule recognizes that the dangers of unreliability, suggestibility, and error are inherent in all identification procedures. The rule attempts to balance the protection of a child from prejudicial misidentification with the State's interest in prompt investigation. A child who is in custody is entitled to have counsel present at a lineup, even prior to the filing of a delinquency petition, unless exigent circumstances exist and delay to provide counsel would unduly interfere with an expeditious investigation. Once an investigation proceeds beyond an immediate on-the-scene show-up, and especially once the child is in custody, there are no compelling law enforcement exigencies that offset the dangers of prejudice to the child. Since youth in custody already have a *Miranda* right to counsel, the delay involved in securing counsel will be a matter of hours at most and if conditions require immediate identification without even minimal delay or if counsel cannot be present within reasonable time, such exigent circumstances will justify proceeding without counsel.

1. PHOTOGRAPHS, FINGERPRINTS, AND OTHER RECORDS

Photographs

IN THE INTEREST OF M. B.

513 P.2d 230 (Colo. Ct. App. 1973).

* * * Prior to trial a hearing was held on a motion to suppress any identification of appellant by the complaining witness. The judge ruled that the photographic identification was inadmissible, but allowed an in-court identification by the complaining witness. The ruling was based

largely upon the complaining witness's testimony that he could identify the thief independently of the photographs. At trial, appellant was also identified in court by a waitress as the person who dined with the complaining witness on the night the theft occurred. * * *

Appellant next contends that the trial court erred by allowing the complaining witness to identify appellant in court because the identification was "tainted" by a prior improper photographic identification. We disagree. She makes a two-pronged attack on the propriety of the photographic identification. First, she argues that the photographic identification was improper because no attorney representing appellant was present. However, it is clear that no adversary judicial criminal proceeding had been initiated at that time, and, thus, the right to counsel had not yet arisen. Secondly, appellant contends the photographic identification was "impermissibly suggestive." The witness was presented with four photographs and only one other besides appellant's was of a girl of Hispanic ancestry. However, the officer who conducted the photographic identification testified that he used that mixture of photographs because they were the only ones he had in the appellant's age bracket. Moreover, all the subjects were about the same height and one of the Anglo girls appeared to be of Hispanic ancestry. There was no showing that any suggestive comments were made at the time the photographic identification was made. We note that the complaining witness had been in appellant's company for a considerable period of time on the evening the theft occurred. There was no "improper identification" made of appellant.

Judgment affirmed.

NOTES

1) Right to Counsel at Photo Display In *United States v. Ash*, 413 U.S. 300, 93 S.Ct. 2568, 37 L.Ed.2d 619 (1973), the United States Supreme Court held that a person whose photograph was used for purposes of identification did not have a constitutional right to have counsel present when those photographs were shown to a witness. Is that the only issue in *M.B.*?

2) Photos and the "Suspect Pool" Where did the police obtain the photograph of M.B. that they showed to the witness? If police take a youth into custody and fingerprint and photograph her, what should the state do with those records afterwards? What if the state either does not charge the youth with delinquency or the juvenile court eventually acquits or dismisses the charges against her?

Prosecutors introduce the "mug shot" photo array from which a witness initially identified a defendant to demonstrate the photos' fairness and lack of suggestibility and to bolster the witness' in-court identification of the juvenile. "The admissibility of mug shots is a question of degree. At one end of the spectrum, it is clear that when the photograph itself establishes that it was taken by the police in the context of a particular case, the photograph is inadmissible * * * because it tends to show the commission of an extraneous offense. * * * At the other end of the spectrum, it is also clear than when all marks identifying the picture as one taken by the police have been removed, the trial court does not err in admitting the photograph." *Araiza v. State*, 929 S.W.2d 552, 555 (Tex. Ct. App. 1996). In *Commonwealth v. Kent K.*, 427 Mass. 754, 757, 696 N.E.2d 511, 514 (1998), the witness identified the juvenile from an array of eight photographs. At the juvenile's jury trial, the detective who conducted the identification described the origins of the photographs shown to the witness. "The persons who have ever been arrested within the city of Boston from different suburbs. They're from the general geographic area around Boston, or anyone in the state, actually, anybody who's just been arrested in Boston." After the juvenile objected to the officer's testimony which indicated that he had been arrested previously for an unrelated offense, the judge instructed the jury that "a witness has taken the stand and has testified that the books that he used * * * contain photographs, all of which were people who were arrested at some time in the past. * * * I instruct you notwithstanding whatever you determine the evidence to be that if you determine that this juvenile might have been arrested in the past, that you are to disregard that completely. * * * I am telling you that that must be disregarded." In a delinquency bench trial, do juvenile court judges know the origins of photographs that police display to witnesses? How do they avoid the prejudice inherent in knowing a youth has been arrested previously?

Fingerprints

LANES v. STATE

[Chapter 3, *supra* p. 170].

NOTES

1) Fingerprinting Juveniles and the Creation of Permanent Records Fingerprinting juveniles raises juvenile justice policy issues in addition to the existence of probable cause or the procedures to obtain a court order. Because photographing and fingerprinting connote a criminal process that may stigmatize or self-label a youth, should states restrict the circumstances under which police subject juveniles to "routine booking procedures"? Once police create a dossier of photographs, fingerprints, and arrest reports, where should those documents be stored and who should have access to them? What types of restrictions should states place on the dissemination of this information to other law enforcement agencies, to juvenile and criminal courts, to social service agencies, and to schools?

Patricia Torbet, et al., *State Responses to Serious and Violent Juvenile Crime* **35—40 (1996)** describes changes in states' laws between 1992 and 1995 affecting the confidentiality of juvenile court records and proceedings:

[L]aw enforcement, child welfare, schools, and other youth-serving agencies see the same subset of juveniles under juvenile court jurisdiction. Accordingly, the need to share information across systems is apparent. As a result, we have seen a concerted effort to promote information-sharing partnerships among juvenile courts, probation departments, law enforcement, prosecutors, schools, and youth-serving agencies. The rationale for sharing information among system actors with a 'need to know' is a better coordinated and more efficient service delivery system that avoids duplication of services and better utilizes shrinking resources. The fundamental issue with respect to sharing juvenile records and opening proceedings is balancing the need to protect a juvenile's right to privacy with the need to assure the community's safety and provided needed services and supervision. * * *

Formerly private, juvenile court records are increasingly available to a wide variety of people. The 'need to know' argument requires proper disclosure of information among youth-service agencies. Many States open juvenile court records to school officials or require that schools be notified when a juvenile is taken into custody for all crimes of violence or crimes in which a deadly weapon is used. * * *

One of the most significant issues with regard to juvenile court and law enforcement records is the effective use of those records. Aside from disclosing or sharing information across systems for the purpose of better coordinating services, legislatures have made provision in four other areas of juvenile record use: centralized repositories/fingerprinting and photographing, targeting serious habitual offenders, criminal court use of defendant's juvenile record, and registration laws.

Statewide central repositories of criminal history records have existed for at least two decades. Central repositories can include adult records only, adult records separate from juvenile records, or adult and juvenile records combined. Centralized databases facilitate and support law enforcement operations. Police argue that juveniles mirror adults in their mobility; hence, juvenile records should be a part of adult criminal record data bases because they are essential for conducting statewide record checks. Those advocating separate databases for juvenile records are that once the distinction is lost between adult and juvenile records, it will also be lost in practice. Furthermore, it is argued that if juvenile records are not criminal records, they should not be used as such.

As of 1994, 27 States enacted laws authorizing establishment of a central record repository to hold juvenile arrest and/or court disposition records from throughout the state; 4 of these States * * * authorize a separate juvenile record center. Even when not available to the public, juvenile court records can become part of the State criminal record keeping system. In some States, a juvenile tried as an adult may have his criminal history record stored in the central repository. Fingerprints most often serve as the basis of the record. Forty-four States provide for a separate juvenile or adult criminal history repository, again usually based on fingerprints.

Proponents of fingerprinting argue that fingerprinting ensures accuracy in identifying a specific individual as the subject of a court disposition or arrest report. Forty-six States and the District of Columbia allow police to fingerprint juveniles who have been arrested, usually juveniles who have reached a specific age or have been arrested for felony offenses. * * * Forty-three states and the District of Columbia allow photographing of juveniles (mug shots for criminal history files) under certain circumstances.

Since 1992, quite a few States have expanded the conditions under which a juvenile may be fingerprinted or photographed. Many States also increased the ways that this information can be used. * * *

2) State Statutes Governing Fingerprinting of Juveniles The following statutes provide examples of different states' policies on the collection and dissemination of juveniles' records. How adequately do they respond to the conflicting policy concerns of protecting juveniles' confidentiality, facilitating effective law enforcement, and protecting the public?

Okla. Stat. Tit. 10 § 7307–1.6 (West 1998). Fingerprinting of persons under 18. The fingerprinting of persons under eighteen (18) years of age shall be as prescribed by law for the fingerprinting of adults, except as specified by the provisions of this section.

1.   When a child is detained or arrested in the course of an investigation of a criminal offense and:

a.   a comparison of the fingerprints of the child with fingerprints found during the investigation of the offense is negative, or

b.   a court finds that the child did not commit the alleged offense, all law enforcement records of the arrest and, if applicable, juvenile court and agency records shall be amended to reflect said facts immediately after the comparison or court finding;

2.   Fingerprints obtained pursuant to this section shall be retained in a central state depository and in a local depository maintained by a duly constituted law enforcement agency;

3.   Fingerprints obtained and maintained pursuant to this section may be used only by law enforcement officers for comparison purposes in connection with the investigation of a crime or to establish identity in instances of death, serious illness, runaways, or emergency. * * *

N.Y. Family Court Act § 306.1 (McKinney 1999). Fingerprinting of certain alleged juvenile delinquents. 1. Following the arrest of a child alleged to be a juvenile delinquent, or the filing of a delinquency petition involving a child who has not been arrested, the arresting officer or other appropriate police officer or agency shall take or cause to be taken fingerprints of such child if:

(a) the child is eleven years of age or older and the crime which is the subject of the arrest or which is charged in the petition constitutes a class A or B felony; or

(b) the child is thirteen years of age or older and the crime which is the subject of the arrest or which is charged in the petition constitutes a class C, D or E felony.

2.   Whenever fingerprints are required to be taken pursuant to subdivision one, the photograph and palmprints of the arrested child may also be taken. * * *

4. Upon the taking of fingerprints * * * the appropriate officer or agency shall, without unnecessary delay, forward such fingerprints to the division of criminal justice services and shall not retain such fingerprints or any copy thereof. Copies of photographs and palmprints taken pursuant to this section shall be kept confidential and only in the exclusive possession of such law enforcement agency, separate and apart from files of adults.

New Jersey Stat. 2A:4A–61 (West 1999). Fingerprint records; photographs of juveniles.

a.   Fingerprints of a juvenile may be taken only in the following circumstances:

(1) Where latent fingerprints are found during the investigation of an offense and a law enforcement officer has reason to believe that they are those of a juvenile, he may, with the consent of the court or juvenile and his parent or guardian fingerprint the juvenile for the purpose of comparison with the latent fingerprints. Fingerprint records taken pursuant to this paragraph may be retained by the department or agency taking them and shall be destroyed when the purpose for the taking of fingerprints has been fulfilled. * * *

Neb. Rev. Stat. § 43–252 (1998). Fingerprints; when authorized; disposition. * * * (3) The fingerprints of any juvenile shall not be sent to a state or federal depository by a law enforcement agency of this state unless: (a) The juvenile has been convicted of or adjudged to have committed a felony; (b) the juvenile has unlawfully terminated his or her commitment to a youth rehabilitation and treatment center; or (c) the juvenile is a runaway and a fingerprint check is needed for identification purposes to return the juvenile to his or her parent.

Conn. Gen. Stat. § 46b–133 (West 1998). Arrest of child. (a) * * * Whenever a child is arrested and charged with a crime, such child may be required to submit to the taking of his photograph, physical description and fingerprints. * * * [T]he photograph of any child arrested for the commission of a capital felony or class A felony may be disclosed to the public.

2.   PRE–TRIAL PUBLICITY

SMITH v. DAILY MAIL PUBLISHING CO.

443 U.S. 97, 99 S.Ct. 2667, 61 L.Ed.2d 399 (1979).

MR. CHIEF JUSTICE BURGER delivered the opinion of the Court. We granted certiorari to consider whether a West Virginia statute violates the First and Fourteenth Amendments of the United States Constitution by making it a crime for a newspaper to publish, without the written approval of the juvenile court, the name of any youth charged as a juvenile offender. * * *

The challenged West Virginia statute provides:

"[N]or shall the name of any child, in connection with any proceedings under this chapter, be published in any newspaper without a written order of the court...." W.Va.Code § 49–7–3 (1976). * * *

On February 9, 1978, a 15–year–old student was shot and killed at Hayes Junior High School in St. Albans, W. Va., a small community located about 13 miles outside of Charleston, W. Va. The alleged assailant, a 14–year–old classmate, was identified by seven different eyewitnesses and was arrested by police soon after the incident.

The Charleston Daily Mail and the Charleston Gazette, respondents here, learned of the shooting by monitoring routinely the police band radio frequency; they immediately dispatched reporters and photographers to the junior high school. The reporters for both papers obtained the name of the alleged assailant simply by asking various witnesses, the police, and an assistant prosecuting attorney who were at the school.

The staffs of both newspapers prepared articles for publication about the incident. The Daily Mail's first article appeared in its February 9 afternoon edition. The article did not mention the alleged attacker's name. The editorial decision to omit the name was made because of the statutory prohibition against publication without prior court approval.

The Gazette made a contrary editorial decision and published the juvenile's name and picture in an article about the shooting that appeared in the February 10 morning edition of the paper. In addition, the name of the alleged juvenile attacker was broadcast over at least three different radio stations on February 9 and 10. Since the information had become public knowledge, the Daily Mail decided to include the juvenile's name in an article in its afternoon paper on February 10.

On March 1, an indictment against the respondents was returned by a grand jury * * * [charging each newspaper with knowingly publishing the name of a youth involved in a juvenile proceeding in violation of the statute. Respondent-newspapers sought a writ of prohibition and alleged that the statute on which the prosecutor based the indictment violated the First and Fourteenth Amendments of the United States Constitution. The West Virginia Supreme Court of Appeals issued the writ of prohibition and held that the statute abridged the freedom of the press.] The court reasoned that the statute operated as a prior restraint on speech and that the State's interest in protecting the identity of the juvenile offender did not overcome the heavy presumption against the constitutionality of such prior restraints. * * *

Respondents urge this Court to hold that because § 49–7–3 requires court approval prior to publication of the juvenile's name it operates as a "prior restraint" on speech. * * * [R]espondents argue, the statute bears "a 'heavy presumption' against its constitutional validity." They claim that the State's interest in the anonymity of a juvenile offender is not sufficient to overcome that presumption.

Petitioners do not dispute that the statute amounts to a prior restraint on speech. Rather, they take the view that even if it is a prior restraint the statute is constitutional because of the significance of the State's interest in protecting the identity of juveniles. * * *

Whether we view the statute as a prior restraint or as a penal sanction for publishing lawfully obtained, truthful information is not dispositive because even the latter action requires the highest form of state interest to sustain its validity. Prior restraints have been accorded the most exacting scrutiny in previous cases. However, even when a state attempts to punish publication after the event it must nevertheless demonstrate that its punitive action was necessary to further the state interests asserted. * * *

[I]f a newspaper lawfully obtains truthful information about a matter of public significance then state officials may not constitutionally punish publication of the information, absent a need to further a state interest of the highest order. * * * Here respondents relied upon routine newspaper reporting techniques to ascertain the identity of the alleged assailant. * * * If the information is lawfully obtained, as it was here, the state may not punish its publication except when necessary to further an interest more substantial than is present here.

The sole interest advanced by the State to justify its criminal statute is to protect the anonymity of the juvenile offender. It is asserted that confidentiality will further his rehabilitation because publication of the name may encourage further antisocial conduct and also may cause the juvenile to lose future employment or suffer other consequences for this single offense. In *Davis v. Alaska*, similar arguments were advanced by the State to justify not permitting a criminal defendant to impeach a prosecution witness on the basis of his juvenile record. We said there that "[w]e do not and need not challenge the State's interest as a matter of its own policy in the administration of criminal justice to seek to preserve the anonymity of a juvenile offender." However, we concluded that the State's policy must be subordinated to the defendant's Sixth Amendment right of confrontation. The important rights created by the First Amendment must be considered along with the rights of defendants guaranteed by the Sixth Amendment. Therefore, the reasoning of *Davis* that the constitutional right must prevail over the state's interest in protecting juveniles applies with equal force here.

The magnitude of the State's interest in this statute is not sufficient to justify application of a criminal penalty to respondents. Moreover, the statute's approach does not satisfy constitutional requirements. The statute does not restrict the electronic media or any form of publication, except "newspapers," from printing the names of youths charged in a juvenile proceeding. In this very case, three radio stations announced the alleged assailant's name before the Daily Mail decided to publish it. Thus, even assuming the statute served a state interest of the highest order, it does not accomplish its stated purpose. * * *

Our holding in this case is narrow. There is no issue before us of unlawful press access to confidential judicial proceedings; there is no issue here of privacy or prejudicial pretrial publicity. At issue is simply the power of a state to punish the truthful publication of an alleged juvenile delinquent's name lawfully obtained by a newspaper. The asserted state interest cannot justify the statute's imposition of criminal sanctions on this type of publication. Accordingly, the judgment of the West Virginia Supreme Court of Appeals is

Affirmed.

MR. JUSTICE REHNQUIST, concurring in the judgment. The Court * * * concludes that the asserted state interest is not sufficient to justify punishment of publication of truthful, lawfully obtained information about a matter of public significance. So valued is the liberty of speech and of the press that there is a tendency in cases such as this to accept virtually any contention supported by a claim of interference with speech or the press.

I would resist that temptation. In my view, a State's interest in preserving the anonymity of its juvenile offenders—an interest that I consider to be, in the words of the Court, of the "highest order"—far outweighs any minimal interference with freedom of the press that a ban on publication of the youths' names entails.

It is a hallmark of our juvenile justice system in the United States that virtually from its inception at the end of the last century its proceedings have been conducted outside of the public's full gaze and the youths brought before our juvenile courts have been shielded from publicity. This insistence on confidentiality is born of a tender concern for the welfare of the child, to hide his youthful errors and " 'bury them in the graveyard of the forgotten past.' " The prohibition of publication of a juvenile's name is designed to protect the young person from the stigma of his misconduct and is rooted in the principle that a court concerned with juvenile affairs serves as a rehabilitative and protective agency of the State. Publication of the names of juvenile offenders may seriously impair the rehabilitative goals of the juvenile justice system and handicap the youths' prospects for adjustment in society and acceptance by the public. This exposure brings undue embarrassment to the families of youthful offenders and may cause the juvenile to lose employment opportunities or provide the hardcore delinquent the kind of attention he seeks, thereby encouraging him to commit further antisocial acts. Such publicity also renders nugatory States' expungement laws, for a potential employer or any other person can retrieve the information the States seek to "bury" simply by visiting the morgue of the local newspaper. The resultant widespread dissemination of a juvenile offender's name, therefore, may defeat the beneficent and rehabilitative purposes of a State's juvenile court system.

By contrast, a prohibition against publication of the names of youthful offenders represents only a minimal interference with freedom of the press. West Virginia's statute, like similar laws in other States, prohibits publication only of the name of the young person. The press is free to describe the details of the offense and inform the community of the proceedings against the juvenile. It is difficult to understand how publication of the youth's name is in any way necessary to performance of the press' "watchdog" role. In those rare instances where the press believes it is necessary to publish the juvenile's name, the West Virginia law, like the statutes of other States, permits the juvenile court judge to allow publication. The juvenile court judge, unlike the press, is capable of determining whether publishing the name of the particular young person will have a deleterious effect on his chances for rehabilitation and adjustment to society's norms.[2] * * *

Although I disagree with the Court that a state statute punishing publication of the identity of a juvenile offender can never serve an interest of the "highest order" and thus pass muster under the First Amendment, I agree with the Court that West Virginia's statute "does not accomplish its stated purpose." The West Virginia statute prohibits only newspapers from printing the names of youths charged in juvenile proceedings. Electronic media and other forms of publication can announce the young person's name with impunity. * * * This statute thus largely fails to achieve its purpose.

NOTES

1) Public's Interest in Identify of Juvenile Offenders How does prohibiting the Daily Mail from identifying the specific juvenile infringe on newspapers' watchdog function? What interest does the public have in knowing the identity of the particular juvenile?

2) Media Access to Closed Delinquency Proceedings If a public interest exists in publishing the identity of a juvenile, may the press insist on access to closed and confidential juvenile proceedings? We will explore in Chapter 7 the juvenile's right to a "public trial," the press' access to closed proceedings, and legislatures' efforts to balance protection of the juvenile and enhancing the visibility and accountability of the juvenile justice system. *See e.g. Minn. Stat. §* 260.155 Subd. 1(c) (West 1998) which provides that "The court shall open the hearings to the public in delinquency or extended jurisdiction juvenile proceedings where the child is alleged to have committed an offense or has been proven to have committed an offense that would be a felony if committed by an adult and the child was at least 16 years of age at the time of the offense * * *."

---

2. The Court relies on *Davis v. Alaska.* But *Davis,* which presented a clash between the interests of the State in affording anonymity to juvenile offenders and the defendant's Sixth Amendment right of confrontation, does not control the disposition of this case. In *Davis,* where the defendant's liberty was at stake, the Court stated that "[s]erious damage to the strength of the State's case would have been a real possibility had petitioner been allowed to pursue this line of inquiry [related to the juvenile offender's record]." The State also could have protected the youth from exposure by not using him to make out its case. By contrast, in this case the State took every step that was in its power to protect the juvenile's name, and the minimal interference with the freedom of the press caused by the ban on publication of the youth's name can hardly be compared with the possible deprivation of liberty involved in *Davis.* Because in each case we must carefully balance the interest of the State in pursuing its policy against the magnitude of the encroachment on the liberty of speech and of the press that the policy represents, it will not do simply to say, as the Court does, that the "important rights created by the First Amendment must be considered along with the rights of defendants guaranteed by the Sixth Amendment."

CHAPTER 4

PRELIMINARY SCREENING PROCEDURES: DIVERSION, INTAKE, AND THE FILING OF CHARGES

■ ■ ■

A number of individuals in the juvenile justice system make decisions that affect the welfare and processing of youths allegedly involved in criminal misconduct. Police officers who encounter youths may adjust a case informally on the street or at the station-house, divert it to a diversion program, or refer the youth to juvenile court intake for formal processing. Police also may make the initial decision whether to place a youth in a pretrial detention facility pending further review by a prosecutor or juvenile court judge. Probation officers in a juvenile court's intake-unit may refer a youth to the juvenile court for formal adjudication or may dispose of the case through informal supervision or diversion to a program run by the juvenile court or some other social services or community agency. Juvenile court intake workers and the juvenile court also review the case of any youth held in pretrial detention. Finally, even after formal adjudication, the juvenile court judge may choose from a wide array of dispositional alternatives ranging from continuing a case without a finding of delinquency, informal or formal probation, out-of-home placement, or commitment to a state training school.

Recent research indicates that the juvenile justice dispositional decision making process is a cumulative one; decisions made by the initial participants, for example, the police or juvenile court intake, affect the decisions made by subsequent participants, for example, juvenile court judges. Thus, assessing juvenile court sentencing practices requires familiarity with decisions made by other juvenile justice actors at other stages of the process who screen and winnow the cases that comprise the formal docket.

Several studies evaluate dispositional decision making by police officers in their initial encounters with juveniles and suggest that a youth's demeanor, her "impression management", as well as her offense affect police officers' exercises of discretion. If the police refer a case to juvenile court, typically an intake probation officer will screen it to decide whether to process the case formally or informally. Probation officers close or informally adjust about half of the cases referred to juvenile court intake. Over the past three decades, for example, the percentage of delinquency referrals resulting in the filing of formal delinquency petitions has ranged between about 41% and 57%. In 1999, 57% of referrals to juvenile courts resulted in the filing of formal petitions, the highest rate in decades. *See e.g.* Charles Puzzanchera, et al., *Juvenile Court Statistics 1999* 26 (2003). A child's social characteristics, family status, demeanor, or race, as well as the referral offenses, influence intake decision making and amplify racial and class disparities in processing youths referred to juvenile court. *See e.g.*, Donna M. Bishop and Charles E. Frazier, "Race Effects in Juvenile Justice Decision–Making: Findings of a Statewide Analysis," 86 *J. Crim. L. & Criminology* 392 (1996). As we will explore further in Chapter Five— detention—and Chapter Eight—sentencing—racial disparities in the processing of youths at each decision point have emerged as one of the central juvenile justice policy issues.

Following referral to juvenile court, either the local prosecuting authority or the juvenile court's probation or intake department make a screening decision whether to process a case formally or informally. These "gatekeepers" close many referrals at intake with some type of *informal disposition*: dismissal, counseling, warning, referral to another agency, community service, or probation. In about half of the cases, the prosecuting authority or a probation officer files a petition to formally initiate the juvenile court process. A petition compares legally with a prosecutor's filing of a complaint or information, or a grand jury's indictment in the adult criminal process. The relationship between the screening functions of a juvenile court's intake staff and the charging functions in the prosecuting attorney's office vary from state to state and county to county within a state.

Once the prosecutor or probation officer files a formal delinquency petition, the juvenile court arraigns the juvenile offender on the petition. Because the right to counsel attaches in juvenile court only after the prosecutor files a petition, a juvenile court judge typically appoints counsel to represent the juvenile beginning at this stage, if at all. As we will see in Chapter Five, for youths held in pretrial detention, the juvenile court also conducts a detention hearing to determine the youths' residential status pending further court processing. At the arraignment, a juvenile may admit or deny the allegations in the petition. For those youths held in detention, the court also makes a pretrial custody decision. For many youths, the detention hearing represents one of the most significant decisions that juvenile court judges make because the initial decision to detain also may affect the subsequent sentence. In many cases, juveniles admit the allegations of the petition at the arraignment and the court quickly disposes of their cases, often without the appointment of a defense attorney. In other cases, the juvenile court appoints a public defender or court appointed lawyer who confers briefly with the juvenile before the youth admits or denies the allegations in the petition. Like the adult criminal justice system, only a small fraction of delinquency cases actually result in formal, contested hearings or trials. As we will see in Chapter Seven, the procedural safeguards available to delinquents charged with criminal offenses differ in some important ways from those available to adult criminal defendants, most notably, the absence of a jury trial. As we will see in Chapter Eight, following a delinquency adjudication, the juvenile court judge possesses enormous discretion within which to impose a disposition. You may find a detailed description of the successive stages of juvenile justice decision-making—arrest, diversion, detention, formal petition, adjudication, disposition—in Joan McCord, Cathy Spatz Widom, and Nancy A. Crowell, Ed., *Juvenile Crime, Juvenile Justice* 162–200 (National Academy of Science, 2001).

The following "flow diagram" illustrates the formal stages of the juvenile justice process. It shows the winnowing and dispositions that occur at each step:

Delinquency Case Processing Overview, 2005

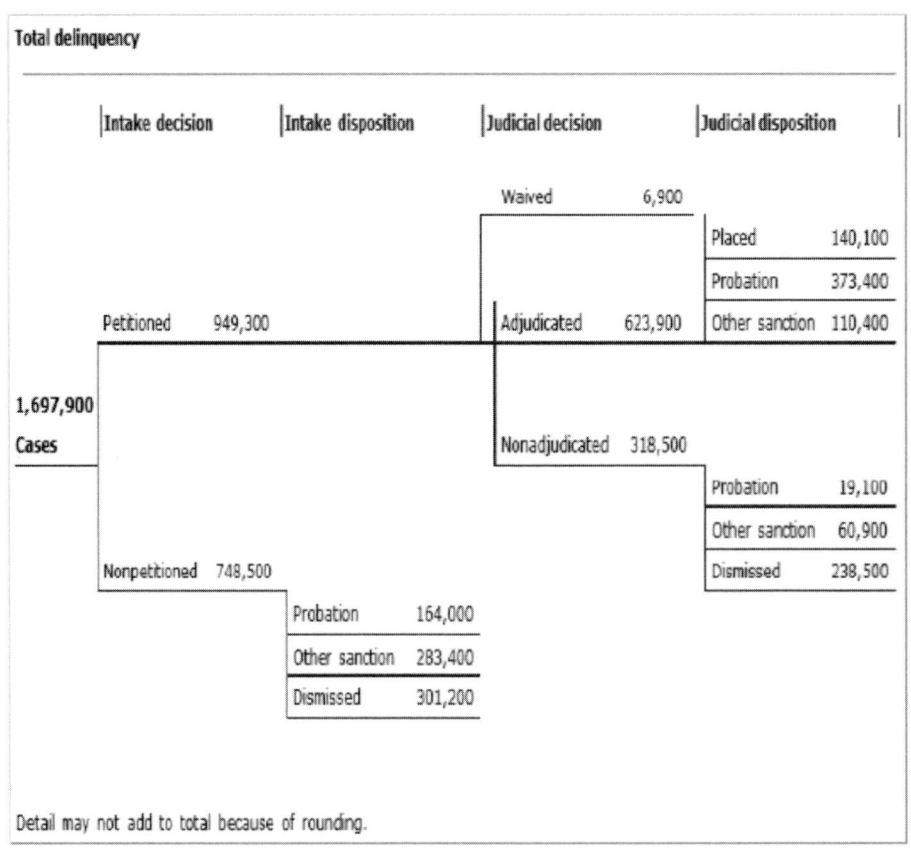

Source: *OJJDP Statistical Briefing Book*. Online. Available: http://ojjdp.ncjrs.gov/ojstatbb/court/JCSCF_Display.asp?ID=qa06601&year=2005&group=1&estimate=2. September 12, 2008.

Cases referred to juvenile court are first screened by an intake department (either within or outside the court). The intake department may decide to dismiss the case for lack of legal sufficiency or to resolve the matter formally (petitioned) or informally (nonpetitioned).

In 2005, 56% (949,300 of 1,697,900) of all delinquency cases disposed by juvenile courts were handled formally while 44% (748,500 of 1,697,900) were handled informally.

Among nonpetitioned cases, 40% (301,200 of 748,500) were dismissed at intake, often for lack of legal sufficiency. In the remaining cases (60%, or 447,400 of 748,500), youth voluntarily agreed to informal sanctions, including referral to a social service agency, informal probation, or the payment of fines or some form of voluntary restitution.

If the intake department decides that a case should be handled formally within the juvenile court, a petition is filed and the case is placed on the court calendar (or docket) for an adjudicatory hearing. On the other hand, the intake department may decide that a case should be removed from juvenile court and handled instead in criminal (adult) court. In these cases, a petition is usually filed in juvenile court requesting a waiver/transfer hearing, during which the juvenile court judge is asked to waive jurisdiction over the case.

In 2005, 66% (623,900 of 949,300 cases) of all formally processed delinquency cases resulted in the youth being adjudicated delinquent. In 34% (318,500 of 949,300) of these cases, the youth was not adjudicated and 1% (6,900 of 949,300) were judicially waived to criminal court.

At the disposition hearing, the juvenile court judge determines the most appropriate sanction, generally after reviewing a predisposition report prepared by the probation department. The range of options available to a court typically includes commitment to an institution; placement in a group or foster home or other residential facility; probation (either regular or intensive supervision); referral to an outside agency, day treatment, or mental health program; or imposition of a fine, community service, or restitution.

Youth in 22% (140,100 of 623,900) of adjudicated delinquency cases were placed in a residential facility. In another 60% (373,400 of 623,900) of these adjudicated cases, youth were placed on formal probation.

Racial Disparities in Juvenile Justice Case Processing Decision-making is cumulative and compounded, that is, earlier decisions affect subsequent ones and the effects of decisions compound over time. One of the most significant consequences of cumulative discretionary decisionmaking is the prevalence of racial disparities in the juvenile justice system. The National Academy of Science, **Joan McCord, Cathy Spatz Widom, and Nancy A. Crowell, Ed.,** *Juvenile Crime, Juvenile Justice* **231, 254, 257–58 (National Academy of Science, 2001)**, examined how initial decision-making contributes to racial disproportionality in the processing of minority juveniles and reported that:

> Although black youth represent approximately 15 percent of the U.S. population ages 10–17 in 1997, they represented 26 percent of all juvenile arrests, 30 percent of delinquency referrals to juvenile court, 45 percent of preadjudication decisions, 33 percent of petitioned delinquency cases, 46 percent of cases judicially waived to adult criminal court, and 40 percent of juveniles in public long-term institutions. Thus, the proportion of blacks under the supervision of the juvenile or adult criminal justice system is more than double their proportion in the general population. * * *

> Compound effects, even of small disparities, can produce larger differences. * * *

> Black juveniles are at greater risk than white juveniles of being arrested, charged for delinquency, and handled formally. They are not at greater risk, given formal handling, for being adjudicated delinquent or found guilty. Thus, at almost every stage in the juvenile justice process the racial disparity is clear, but not extreme. However, because the system operates cumulatively the risk is compounded and the end result is that black juveniles are three times as likely as white juveniles to end up in residential placement. * * *

A. INTAKE SCREENING AND DIVERSION OF JUVENILES—WHETHER TO REFER TO JUVENILE COURT

The 1965 President's Commission on Law Enforcement and Administration of Justice, *The Challenge of Crime in a Free Society* (1967) provided impetus for the United States Supreme Court decisions to reform juvenile justice procedures and practices. The Crime Commission critically examined many aspects of juvenile justice administration, acknowledged that "the great hopes originally held for the juvenile court have not been fulfilled", and made a number of recommendations that Supreme Court decisions later endorsed and state legislatures adopted. *Id*. at 80. The Crime Commission suggested that the juvenile court ultimately might evolve into a two-track system with separate criminal social control and social welfare functions. In such a system, public officials would divert and handle informally most minor delinquents and status offenders. President's Commission on Law Enforcement and Administration of Justice, *Task Force Report: Juvenile Delinquency and Youth Crime 2 (1967)*. "In place of the formal system, dispositional alternatives to adjudication must be developed for dealing with juveniles. * * * The range of conduct for which court intervention is authorized should be narrowed with greater emphasis upon consensual and informal means of meeting the problems of difficult children." Most juveniles commit trivial offenses, outgrow their delinquencies normally, and do no require formal intervention. "Labeling

Theory" in the 1960s and 1970s contended that official labels, such as delinquency, stigmatized youth and adversely affect the child's self-image and subsequent responses by police schools and community members. See e.g. Anne Rankin Mahoney, "The Effect of Labeling on Youths in the Juvenile Justice System: A Review of the Evidence," 8 *Law & Soc'y Rev.* 583 (1974). The Commission and others analysts recommended policies of "judicious non-intervention" or even "radical non-intervention" to avoid stigmatizing such juveniles. Beginning in the 1970s, the Crime Commission's recommendations led to judicial practices and legislative policies to divert less serious juvenile offenders from the juvenile court.

The Supreme Court's *Gault* decision increased the procedural formality and the administrative costs of processing all young offenders in juvenile courts and provided an additional impetus to address informally the cases of many juvenile "nuisances." Diversion programs constitute one reform strategy to minimize formal intervention and to provide supervision or services on an informal basis. Just as the original juvenile court diverted youths from adult criminal courts, theoretically diversion programs shift away from juvenile court youths who otherwise would enter that system. Proponents of diversion contend that it provides an efficient gate-keeping mechanism, constitutes the first-line of case-sorting and routing, and avoids stigmatizing or labeling some minor offenders. Diversion conserves scarce judicial resources and provides an informal means to respond to misbehavior that a formal system might otherwise ignore. It provides more efficient and flexible access to reintegrative community resources and rehabilitative services than a formal process. It also provides more efficient access to community-based intervention. The greater procedural formality associated with *Gault* subjects juvenile court decisions to some review and oversight. By contrast, police and intake gate-keepers continue to make low-visibility discretionary decisions on an informal basis.

Despite the theoretical rationale for handling youths outside the juvenile justice system, the materials that follow examine to what extent states have effectively implemented diversion reforms or instead converted them into an additional tool of social control that reaches further into the "normal" adolescent population. One concern of critics of diversion is that it "widens the net" of social control and "informally" treats youths to whom the juvenile justice system otherwise would not have responded. "[W]hen compared to youth who are not diverted and controlling for sociodemographic and legal variables such as offense severity and prior record, diverted youth experienced at least as much intrusiveness by the official juvenile justice system as did those youths who were not selected to be diverted. * * * In sum, the evidence is that this diversion projected failed to achieve appreciable success in limiting official intervention. Diverted youth in fact remained in the justice system longer than nondiverted youth." Charles E. Frazier and John K. Cochran, "Official Intervention, Diversion from the Juvenile Justice System, and Dynamics of Human Services Work: Effects of a Reform Goal Based on Labeling

Theory," 32 *Crime & Delinq.* 157, 172–73 (1986). Although voluntary participation and non-justice system implementation provided the original premises of diversion reform, to what extent have juvenile justice personnel implemented diversion programs consistently with those assumptions? Do diversion programs restrict themselves to youths who otherwise would enter the juvenile justice system or do they also encompass young people whom police previously might counsel, reprimand, and release if they had any police contacts at all? If program personnel can induce a youth to participate in a program by the threat of filing a petition, then is participation in a diversion program truly "voluntary"? Although the President's Crime Commission proposed to reduce juvenile courts' clientele, have diversion practices had the opposite effect of "widening the net of social control"? If diversion provides a useful gate-keeping tool and routing device for the juvenile court, then what standards or procedural safeguards, if any, should accompany the practice?

States structure the threshold screening and gate-keeping functions of their juvenile courts in various ways. In some jurisdictions, prosecutors decide whether to file a formal petition or to divert or adjust a juvenile's case informally. For example, *Arizona Juvenile Court Rules of Procedure* 2 (C) provides that "The county attorney, within its sole discretion, may designate for diversion or divert the prosecution of a juvenile accused of an incorrigible or a delinquent act to a community based alternative program or to a diversion program administered by the juvenile court."

More commonly, however, the juvenile court's probation officers conduct an intake screening at which they decide to divert, supervise informally, or refer juveniles to the prosecuting authority for the filing of a formal petition. State statutes or juvenile court rules of procedure specify with varying degrees of precision the types of cases to be handled informally or formally and the criteria probation staff should use to make these decisions. For example, **California Rules of Court, Rule 1404 (a)** (1999) mandates the presiding juvenile court judge, in cooperation with probation, welfare, the prosecuting attorney, law enforcement, and other agencies to establish an intake program to evaluate referrals and to pursue an appropriate course of action. Rule 1404 further provides:

(b) The intake program shall be designed to:

   (1) Provide for settlement at intake of:

      (A) Matters over which the juvenile court has no jurisdiction;

      (B) Matters in which there is insufficient evidence to support a petition; and

      (C) Matters which are suitable for referral to a nonjudicial agency or program available in the community;

   (2) Provide for a program of informal supervision of the child * * *; and

(3) Provide for the commencement of proceedings in the juvenile court only when necessary for the welfare of the child or protection of the public.

(c) The probation officer may and the social worker shall conduct an investigation and determine whether:

(1) The matter should be settled at intake by:

(A) Taking no action;

(B) Counseling the child and any others involved in the matter; or

(C) Referring the child and any others involved to other agencies and programs in the community;

(2) A program of informal supervision should be undertaken for not more than six months * * *; or

(3) A petition should be filed * * *, or the prosecuting attorney should be requested to file a petition * * *.

California Rules of Court, Rule 1405 (1999) provides the factors that intake staff should consider in making their screening decisions:

(a) In determining whether a matter * * * should be settled at intake, the social worker or probation officer shall consider:

(1) Whether there is sufficient evidence of a condition or conduct to bring the child within the jurisdiction of the court;

(2) If the alleged condition or conduct is not considered serious, whether the child has previously presented no significant problems in the home, school, or community;

(3) Whether the matter appears to have arisen from a temporary problem within the family which has been or can be resolved;

(4) Whether any agency or other resource in the community is better suited to serve the needs of the child, the parent or guardian, or both;

(5) The attitudes of the child and the parent or guardian;

(6) The age, maturity, and capabilities of the child;

(7) The dependency or delinquency history, if any, of the child;

(8) The recommendation, if any, of the referring party or agency;

(9) The attitudes of affected persons; and

(10) Any other circumstances that indicate that settling the matter at intake would be consistent with the welfare of the child and the protection of the public.

(b) In determining whether to undertake a program of informal supervision of a child, * * * the social worker or probation officer shall consider:

(1) If the condition or conduct is not considered serious, whether the child has had a problem in the home, school, or community which indicates that some supervision would be desirable;

(2) Whether the child and the parent or guardian seem able to resolve the matter with the assistance of the social worker or probation officer and without formal court action;

(3) Whether further observation or evaluation by the social worker or probation officer is needed before a decision can be reached; [and the factors listed in § 1405 (a) 5–10].

1. INTAKE DISPOSITION OF DELINQUENCY REFERRALS

Most states vest the preliminary screening authority in the juvenile court intake probation staff. *See e.g., Hawaii Rev. Stat.* § 571–31.2 (1998) ("The court or other designated agency * * * "); *Iowa Code Ann.* § 232.28 (West 1998) (intake officer of court shall consult with law enforcement, interview complainant, victim or witnesses, confer with child and parent, and, after consultation with county attorney when necessary, decide whether to file a petition). However, some jurisdictions require review by the prosecuting authority at the request of the complainant if court intake declines to file a delinquency petition. *See e.g.,* D.C. Code Ann. § 16–2305(c) (1998 Repl.) ("If the Director of Social Services has refused to recommend the filing of a delinquency or neglect petition, the Corporation Counsel, on request of the complainant, shall review the facts presented and shall prepare and file a petition if he believes such action is necessary to protect the community or the interests of the child. Any decision of the Corporation Counsel on whether to file a petition shall be final.")

The following excerpt from **H. Ted Rubin, "The Emerging Prosecutor Dominance of the Juvenile Court Intake Process," 26** *Crime and Delinquency* **at 302, 304 (1980)**, describes the traditional role of intake and some of the problems that screening cases by probation staff pose:

As a legal screening mechanism, intake is a means of ascertaining that there is a fit between the court's jurisdictional authority and the child's age and residence, the site of the offense, and the apparent evidentiary sufficiency for the particular offense alleged. The lack of fit of one of these legal elements should result in rejection of the case and the avoidance of unjustified hearings. Ascertaining another fit, the apparent need for formal court action, is an additional piece of the investigation. If there is no serious offense or repetitive pattern, informal resolution may be more functional than a judicial hearing. The judicial workload can be reserved for necessary cases, the formal juvenile record is averted, the threat can be made that the next time the youngster will be dealt with very seriously, and probation officer supervision caseloads can be maintained at more reasonable levels. The social facts are assessed here: child and family strengths or deficiencies across a wide social, psychological, educational, and economic terrain. Some cases are better served by external community agencies; sometimes such responses as payment of restitution to the victim can resolve a complaint satisfactorily. For some youngsters, the anxiety engendered by the police and intake process can be sufficient to convince them not to get into trouble again; for others, use of an informal probation period, which developed without statutory authorization but is now provided for in many current juvenile codes, accomplishes some of the same objectives as would be served by a formal petition. Furthermore, a substantial number of youngsters "short-stopped by intake" spend several nights in the local detention center or jail, a fact satisfying some officials wanting to see more than wrist slapping before these cases are dismissed. * * *

Historically, intake has been a review of legal and social factors, with the emphasis placed frequently on the latter dimensions. The legal facts * * * encompass the correlation between the offense facts and the required elements of the offense, the seriousness of the offense and the harm or damage done, the offense record and prior dispositions, and any present legal status (e.g., formal probation). The absence of legal training on the part of intake officers has placed them at a disadvantage in this respect; not infrequently they place the law in limbo in conducting the evaluation. This failure to conduct careful legal screening has often led to unrepresented youngsters' accepting terms of informal probation or later admitting to the offense before the judge without anyone's having scrutinized the legal sufficiency of the case. Competent evaluation of the legal correctness of police interrogation or search and seizure practices should not be expected of intake officers but should be accomplished before the imposition of coerced informal services and before the decision to file a case. The contention has grown that the legal evaluation role is one for the prosecutor. * * *

NOTES

1) Intake "Adjustment" In *Deshawn E. v. Safir*, 156 F.3d 340 (2d Cir., 1998), the court analyzed the administration of intake in New York:

> [T]he police "may take a child under the age of sixteen into custody without a warrant in cases in which [they] may arrest a person for a crime. * * * " After taking a child into custody, a police officer is directed to make "every reasonable effort" to notify the child's parent, guardian, or person legally responsible for the child's care that the minor has been taken into custody. After making reasonable efforts to notify the parent or guardian, the police have three options: (1) issue the minor an appearance ticket and release the child to the custody of his or her parent or guardian; (2) take the juvenile to Family Court or another authorized and suitable location or the child's residence for questioning; or (3) take the child to a juvenile detention facility.
>
> If the juvenile has been given an appearance ticket and released, the child must appear at Probation Services ("Probation") on a specified return date. Once the juvenile and parent or guardian appear, Probation conducts a preliminary conference to determine whether to file a delinquency proceeding or to "adjust" the case. Adjustment is a process in

which Probation meets informally with the juvenile and his or her parent or guardian to resolve the possible charges without the filing of a delinquency petition. At the preliminary conference, Probation is required to advise juveniles that they can participate in the adjustment process, and to notify each juvenile about certain rights with regard to the adjustment process. Juveniles must then agree to participate in the adjustment process.

All statements made by juveniles during the preliminary conference and adjustment process are confidential. Probation cannot communicate to the Presentment Agency, the agency with responsibility for filing a juvenile delinquency petition, any statement made to it by the juvenile, and no statement made by the juvenile during the adjustment process can be "admitted into evidence at a fact-finding hearing or * * * at any time prior to a conviction." Juveniles are not assigned or entitled to counsel during the adjustment proceedings, but a child may retain private counsel. After the preliminary conference, Probation determines whether a case is suitable for the adjustment process. If adjustment is successful, no delinquency petition is filed. If a case is not successfully adjusted the case is referred to the Presentment Agency and a delinquency proceeding may be commenced. * * *

2. INTAKE AND DIVERSION

As the flow-diagram and *Deshawn E.* indicate, probation officers adjust or handle many cases informally. One of the most common forms of adjustment is to divert or refer a juvenile to another agency or to place the juvenile under informal supervision by the juvenile court. Recall, *Zimring*, "The Common Thread: Diversion in Juvenile Justice," *supra* pp. 48–54 argued that Progressive Reformers created the juvenile court as a diversion from the criminal justice system. If that unstated premise is true, then why do we need a diversion from that diversion? Are there costs, as well as benefits, to diverting and handling juveniles' cases informally? The following excerpts by **Kenneth Polk, "Juvenile Diversion: A Look at the Record," 30** *Crime and Delinquency* **648–659 (1984)**, reviews some of the issues associated with diversion:

What are the accomplishments of juvenile diversion? In their recent review, Binder and Geis provide a spirited and provocative defense of diversion, noting that many of those finding fault with the concept base their observations on "polemical and ideological conclusions lacking a firm anchorage in fact." In their attempt to "rehabilitate the record of diversion," Binder and Geis express dismay at the fact that the response to diversion seems to be "inconsistent with the actual record." Their conclusion is that the criticisms of diversion originate in the personal motivations of sociologists and are the result of disciplinary narrowness, distrust of the police, and overidentification with the underdog.

That there have been questions raised about the success of diversion, and that the strongest of these seem to come from sociologists, cannot be disputed. Is it possible, however, that the source of these questions resides not so much in the motivations of sociologists, but in the record of diversion itself? A brief review of some of the empirical work on diversion may help to clarify and give shape to the features of the debate opened up by Binder and Geis.

A starting point for many analyses of diversion consists of assessing the outcomes of diversion in terms of its impact on subsequent delinquency. What is that record? It is clearly mixed. There are many studies which show that diversion is successful in reducing subsequent deviance. These results are at least equally balanced, however, by findings of no impact. One of the most methodologically rigorous evaluations of diversion concluded that: "The hypothesis that diversion leads to lower rates of subsequent delinquent behavior than traditional processing was not supported." In their review of several California diversion programs * * * the programs

> were found to have no measurable effect on the self-report delinquency, the attitudes, the family relations, or the minor misbehavior of their clients. Nor did they have a measurable effect on the official delinquency of their clients over a six-month or twelve-month follow-up period.

In their evaluation of several programs in Wisconsin, after making comparisons of records of subsequent delinquency between diversion and control clients, it was concluded * * * that "none of the comparisons resulted in a significant difference being demonstrated." Similarly, in a review of the outcomes of one diversion program it was concluded that "no strong inference can be made" * * * that diversion "had a significant impact on youths' subsequent delinquent behavior"; although it should be noted that this investigation did find consistent positive results on self-report measures of delinquency.

Even more important for the present argument, however, are indications of diversion as having harmful effects. In one analysis of a police diversion program, it was concluded that diversion served to aggravate rather than to deter recidivism. * * * [R]eceiving service, regardless of whether the intervention was in a traditional justice setting or in the diversion agency, resulted in higher levels of perceived labeling and self-report delinquency. * * * [A]lthough persons who were diverted had lower rates of recidivism than was true for persons who received a court petition, their rates were also higher than those released outright without any form of service. * * *

A major feature of the defense of diversion provided by Binder and Geis is their rejection of the concern that diversion may result in a widening of the net of juvenile justice. Their position seems based in the following propositions:

1. Diversion is beneficial in the sense that many or most clients are helped through the services provided by diversion programs.

2. Because diversion is helpful, then the proposition that doing nothing, rather than doing something, is unacceptable. Being precise, Binder and Geis find the argument that it is more desirable to ignore deviant behavior than to seek remedial help in diversion "a dubious proposition at best and a downright harmful one at worst."

3. Diversion programs in most cases are voluntary because "offenders and their families may refuse services without consequences."

4. When coercion is present, we are reminded that coercion has essentially been invited by the offender's choice of behavior. "If he or she wished to retain maximum freedom of choice, it would have been prudent either to have abstained from the earlier behavior or not to have gotten caught at it."

5. Because there is actual offense behavior at issue, then some form of social control is desirable and probably inevitable. There is nothing pernicious about social control in the view of Binder and Geis because it consists not simply of law, but of etiquette, norms, regulations, customs and ethics, and takes place in the home, street, school, or family. * * *

For Binder and Geis, given these premises, diversion becomes a reasonable and responsible form of expanding the devices of social control available to a community for coping with adolescent offense behavior and is worthy of an energetic defense. Because diversion is an effective, voluntary, and appropriate response to delinquent behavior, they find no merit in the concern that net-widening may result from diversion, observing instead:

> The phrase "widening the net" is, of course, employed pejoratively, with the intent to evoke an emotional response. It conjures up visions of a mesh net that is thrown over thrashing victims, incapacitating them as they flail about, desperately seeking to avoid captivity. The net is maneuvered by "agents of social control," another image provoking term, this one carrying a Nazi-like connotation. Both terms are employed for purposes of propaganda rather than to enlighten.

Unfortunately, however vivid the imagery, a case rejecting the net-widening argument is built by Binder and Geis which avoids reference to the empirical record. The first two premises are challenged by the evidence of the impact of diversion on subsequent behavior as cited above. If further research confirms either that diversion has no impact or that it is harmful, then the assumption that it is better to do something (in the form of diversion) than to do nothing becomes unsupportable.

Evidence exists which also raises questions about the voluntary nature of diversion services. Early in the development of diversion, Klapmuts cautioned that if being referred to the diversion program was backed by a threat of referral to court, then the allegedly nonpunitive agency in reality becomes an extension of the justice system and the diversion is a legal fiction. After reviewing the practices of a few diversion programs, Nejelski warned that: "there is a danger that diversion will become a means of expanding coercive intervention in the lives of children and families without proper concern for their rights." A national survey of over 300 youth service bureaus (YSBs), which included more intensive site analyses and interviews with 27 of the diversion agencies, provides some empirical support for such concerns:

> Data from our field visits suggest that diversionary referrals from court intake and courts to YSBs essentially facilitate deferred prosecution: generally are contingent upon admission of guilt without the advice of counsel; that "voluntary agreements" or consent decrees are obtained under coercive circumstances which vitiate the meaning of voluntariness; that throughout the diversionary and referral process the youth inhabits a legal limbo which increases his vulnerability to subsequent punishment for offenses previously committed, and which is a much more subtle and pernicious problem than double jeopardy.

A further problem in the viewpoint of Binder and Geis is their undifferentiated view of the sources of social control. In its original intent, as should be clear from the term "diversion," there was a recognition that control within the juvenile justice system should be sharply differentiated from other forms of social control. The basic assumed thrust of diversion would be to shift responsibility and intervention for some individuals who had entered juvenile justice processing outside of that system into some form of nonjustice, community alternative.

A major concern of many of the researchers who write about net-widening is the question of whether this is, in fact, what diversion programs accomplish. Is diversion serving as a process for moving young persons who have "penetrated" the justice network outward and away from that system, or has it become a device for incorporating a whole new class of clients inside an expanding justice system? Some have questioned whether it is offense behavior at all that brings clients to diversion agencies, pointing out that the attributes of diversion referrals (age, sex, reason for referral) suggest that a population quite different from delinquent offenders is being tapped by diversion programs. From his analysis of evaluations and descriptions of over 50 diversion programs, Klein was able to comment that:

> The cooptation of the diversion movement by law enforcement leaves the rather sour conclusion that not only have the purposes of diversion been perverted but, moreover, police power has been extended over youths and types of behavior not previously subjected to control.

Perhaps because the discipline makes them more sensitive to the organizational level of analysis, sociologists then become concerned with two issues. One, does the record of diversion show that responsibility for handling of cases is being shifted away from the justice system? When the data indicate that the programs are controlled by justice agencies, that referrals are coming from rather than to schools, families, and other community resources, and that the cases are those that would not under ordinary circumstances come to the attention of justice authorities, then diversion may be functioning in quite a different way than its originators intended and the term would imply.

Second, if clients come to diversion agencies for help with personal and social problems far removed from offense behavior, and if the diversion agency is part of the justice system, then, whatever the motivation, young persons are coming under the control of the justice system for behavior that, prior to the introduction of diversion, would not have led to such control.

The concern for net-widening is, in short, a concern about whether diversion is meeting its original goal of deflecting cases away from juvenile justice processing. A solid, data-grounded argument can be made which suggests that this goal is not being met, and that instead the juvenile justice system, under the banner of diversion, is taking on both more cases and expanded functions. It is not a question of whether services should be available for young persons, but one of where those services should be located. The underlying theory of diversion is that both the individuals served and the community itself would be better off if more of the responsibility for youth behavior were shifted to the community and away from juvenile justice. Is it really inappropriate to discuss an apparent inconsistency between what was planned and what resulted when the inconsistency is revealed by data and evidence? * * *

Alder and Polk * * * examine such propositions as: diversion clients are more likely to be female than are clients at other points of formal justice processing; the female clients are being referred to diversion programs disproportionately for the same kinds of behaviors (status offenses) that have provoked concern for sexism within the juvenile justice system; diversion programs may be expanding their network of social control; and finally, diversion may increase the probability of further deviance (and, thus, subsequent formal contact with the juvenile justice system). Literature and extensive data are presented to substantiate these points. Alder and Polk warn, however, that the data are not completely consistent with each point of their argument. They are forced to rely on secondary analysis, and data on some key points of a more complete argument chain are not available. Accordingly, they alert the reader to the conjectural nature of the argument. They then observe that if the above observations are accurate (and at least some data are available to support each point), then a reasonable derivative conclusion is that diversion may represent a form of hidden sexism which results in an increase in the number of girls who ultimately come under the control of juvenile justice agencies. * * *

Study after study suggests that the programs are often run by, or closely connected to, the justice system, and that most of the clients are not offenders being referred outward, but are youngsters with a variety of personal problems far removed from offense behavior who are being referred into this system. The evidence suggests that a large proportion of the programs may be coercive rather than voluntary. The data on impact do not permit us at this time to reject the hypothesis that the services may be either of no benefit or even harmful to the clients experiencing the diversion program. Several bits of evidence can be woven together to suggest that unanticipated consequences of diversion may be occurring in terms of hidden sexist processes. * * *

NOTES

1) **Efficacy of Diversion.** Although diversion and informal adjustment allows juvenile courts more efficiently to administer their caseloads, social scientists continue to debate both the "net-widening" effect and the efficacy of diversion as a crime reduction strategy. See e.g. William L. Selke, "Diversion and Crime Prevention," 20 *Criminology* 395 (1982) (programs had little effect); Malcolm Klein, "Deinstitutionalization and diversion of juvenile offenders: a litany of impediments," 1 *Crime and Justice* 145 (1979) (failures of implementation, co-optation by law enforcement, and net-widening effect); Anne Larason Schneider, "Diverting Status Offenses from Juvenile Court Jurisdiction," 30 *Crime and Delinquency* 347, 357 (1984) (the availability of a "less stigmatizing alternative, combined with the continued possibility of referral to the juvenile justice system, seemingly has increased the total number of status offense incidents referred either to the official system or to the diversion alternative.").

A few studies report that diversion had a positive effect on reducing recidivism rates. *See e.g.*, Mark R. Pogrebin, Eric D. Poole, and Robert M. Regoli, "Constructing and Implementing a Model Juvenile Diversion Program," 15 *Youth & Soc'y* 305 (1984) (introduction of juvenile diversion project reduced recidivism among those handled informally). Other studies, however, report that diversion either had no effect, produced a negative effect, or subjected youths to more extensive social control. Bruce L. Berg, "Arbitrary Arbitration: Diverting Juveniles into the Justice System," 37 *Juv. & Fam. Ct. J.* 31 (1986); Tomas G. Blomberg, "Diversion's Disparate Results and Unresolved Questions: An Integrative Evaluation Perspective," 20 *J. Res. Crime & Delin.* 24 (1983); Kevin Minor, David Hartmann, and Sue Terry, "Predictors of Juvenile Court Actions and Recidivism," 43 *Crime and Delinquency* 328 (1997) ("the actions taken by the court (i.e., diversion vs. petition) had little bearing on the probability of recidivism. * * * Juveniles who were diverted in the first court action were not significantly more or less likely than those who were petitioned to experience a second court referral."). For example, Charles Frazier and John Cochran, "Official Intervention, Diversion from the Juvenile Justice System, and Dynamics of Human Services Work: Effects of a Reform Goal Based on Labeling Theory," 32 *Crime and Delinquency* 157, 172–73 (1986), report that "the diversion program under study did not succeed in limiting official intervention in the lives of diverted youth. When compared to youth who were not diverted and controlling for socio-demographic and legal variables such as offense severity and prior record, diverted youth experienced at least as much intrusiveness by the official juvenile justice system as did those youths who were not selected to be diverted. * * * Diverted youth in fact remained in the justice system longer than nondiverted youth."

The study by the National Academy of Sciences, Joan McCord, Cathy Spatz Widom, and Nancy A. Crowell, Ed., *Juvenile Crime, Juvenile Justice* 167–176 (National Academy of Science, 2001), reviewed the evaluations of diversion programs in juvenile justice and reported that:

> One concern that is often raised about diversion programs is that they may result in net widening which is "a phenomenon whereby a program is set up to divert youth away from an institutional placement or some other type of juvenile court disposition, but, instead, merely brings more youth into the juvenile justice system who previously would never have entered." A true diversion program takes only juveniles who would ordinarily be involved in the juvenile justice system and places them in an alternative program. * * *

> On balance, the research on diversion * * * suggests that some community-based intervention can serve the needs of many juvenile offenders without added danger to the community. There also may be advantages to keeping juveniles in a less restrictive setting. Well-structured and well-run programs with appropriate services have the potential for improving the lives of diverted juveniles and their families and maintaining community safety. * * *

B. DIVERSION TO WHAT? RESTORATIVE JUSTICE AND OTHER JUVENILE JUSTICE DISPOSITIONS

In recent years, public and political concerns about victims and damage to the community, and the perceived short-comings of traditional punitive or rehabilitative sanctions have influenced the development of new juvenile justice programs. One significant juvenile justice policy innovations is "Restorative Justice" which proposes an alternative conceptualization of the justice process. *See e.g.,* Lode Walgrave and Gordon Bazemore, eds., *Restorative Justice* (1998). Restorative justice draws on programs and justice system innovations from Europe, New Zealand, and Australia where experiments with alternatives to the traditional juvenile justice system have advanced further than in the United States. The following materials summarize the intellectual roots and recent history of restorative justice and provide some statutory examples of efforts to implement these programs. As you read the statutes, consider how faithfully and effectively they implement the theoretical framework described in the articles.

The Office of Juvenile Justice and Delinquency Prevention has sponsored "restorative justice" programs in the United States, and the following excerpt by **Gordon Bazemore and Mark Umbreit,** *Balanced and Restorative Justice: Program Summary* 1–8 (1994), summarizes the characteristics of restorative justice:

Overview

Frustrated by policy pendulum swings between treatment and retribution and by unclear and unrealistic public expectations, a growing number of judges, probation officers, prosecutors, and other juvenile justice professionals are embracing a new vision for juvenile justice. As a concrete mission, the balanced approach allows juvenile justice systems and agencies to improve their capacity to protect the community and ensure accountability of the offender and the system. It enables offenders to become competent and productive citizens. Restorative justice, the guiding philosophical framework for this vision, promotes maximum involvement of the victim, the offender, and the community in the justice process and presents a clear alternative to sanctions and intervention based on retributive or traditional treatment assumptions. Within the context of the restorative justice philosophy, the balanced approach mission helps juvenile justice systems become more responsive to the needs of victims, offenders, and the community.

The balanced approach mission—What's new about the balanced approach?

At first glance it might appear that the balanced approach mission is little more than an attempt to repackage the traditional treatment agenda of juvenile justice with an emphasis on accountability and public protection. For most juvenile justice agencies, however, the commitment to competency development, accountability, and community protection that the balanced approach requires necessitates significant changes. These changes involve new performance objectives; new priorities for intervention; and a new view of the role of offenders, victims, and the community in the justice process.

Performance objectives

Juvenile justice systems based on the balanced approach differ from traditional systems in that the competency development, accountability, and community protection objectives prescribe clear outcomes directed at the three primary clients of juvenile justice: offenders, victims, and the community. These outcomes in turn provide the basis for developing concrete performance measures for gauging the success of juvenile justice systems, agencies, and intervention. These may be evaluated in terms of whether offenders make measurable improvements in their ability to function as conventional, productive citizens; how well the public is protected during the time the offender is under court supervision; and whether victims are involved in the juvenile justice process as offenders learn to understand the harm they have caused and work to repay the victim and the community. By promoting development of consensus on these new performance-based objectives and the need for balance in allocating resources to achieve goals directed at each client, the balanced approach mission helps agencies transcend traditional, unproductive conflicts between crime control and treatment.

Figure 2: Balanced Approach Values, Clients, and Performance Objectives

---

Accountability. When an offense occurs, an obligation to the victim incurs. Victims and communities should have their losses restored by the actions of the offender making reparation, and victims should be empowered as active participants in the juvenile justice process.

Community protection. The public has a right to a safe and secure community and must be protected during the time the offender is under juvenile justice supervision. The juvenile justice system must provide a range of intervention alternatives geared to the varying risks presented by the offenders.

Competency development. Juvenile offenders who come within the jurisdiction of the court should leave the system capable of being productive and responsible in the community. Rather than simply receiving treatment and services aimed at suppressing problem behavior, offenders should make measurable improvements in their ability to function as productive, responsible citizens

Balance. Community, victim, and offender should receive balanced attention. All three should gain tangible benefits from their interactions with the juvenile justice system.

New priorities for intervention practices

Though closer to a conceptual framework than a prescriptive program, the balanced approach builds on more than a decade of research and practical experience with outcome-focused intervention strategies. This framework can best be described as a combined emphasis on three programming priorities.

Accountability. Restitution, community service, and victim offender mediation create an awareness in offenders of the harmful consequences of their actions for victims, require offenders to take action to make amends to victims and the community, and whenever possible, involve victims directly in the justice process.

Community protection. Intermediate, community-based surveillance and sanctioning systems channel the offender's time and energy into productive activities during nonschool working hours. A continuum of surveillance and sanctions provides a progression of consequences for noncompliance with supervision requirements and incentives that reinforce the youth's progress in meeting competency development and accountability objectives.

Competency development. Work experience, active learning, and service provide opportunities for offenders to develop skills, interact positively with conventional adults, earn money, and demonstrate publicly that they are capable of productive, competent behavior.

More important, any juvenile court disposition intended to achieve the objectives of the balanced approach in a given case must be individualized and based on the circumstances of the offense and the needs and risks presented by the offender. System balance is achieved when managers and policy makers carefully allocated resources giving equal priority to those programs and practices directed at achieving the three mission objectives. Each program or practice must in turn complement and reinforce other programs.

New roles for youth, juvenile justice professionals, and the community

* * * Attaining accountability requires an enhanced and expanded role for victims, and the restorative justice framework maximizes the involvement in all aspects of the juvenile justice process. * * * [T]he balanced approach [strongly relies] on local support and its implicit message to community organizations [is] that juvenile justice professionals cannot function alone. * * *

Attaining these objectives involves a key role for such socializing institutions as schools, employers, and advocacy and youth development groups. These institutions help young offenders and the justice system address the needs of victims and enhance the informal social control needed to protect the community. * * *

Ultimately, the balanced approach mission must be adaptable to the needs and resources of local communities. This implies sensitivity in adapting the model to local cultural strengths and diversities. In building community support, juvenile justice professionals should involve civic, employment, recreational, and other organizations whose members can serve as advocates for minority youth. Increasing cultural sensitivity and addressing the problems of disproportionate minority representation in the most restrictive end of the juvenile justice continuum should be a major priority.

Just as the public's perception may change when individual offenders take an active role in restoring losses caused by their offenses and demonstrating competency through productive work experience and service, juvenile justice systems that put forward concrete, objective, and consensus-based performance outcomes may upgrade their organizational image from tax liability to community asset. In sum, in its responsiveness to the needs of the community as a whole and to victims in particular, the balanced approach mission offers juvenile justice professionals a practical means of engaging their community institutions in a constructive partnership.

Restorative justice

Although restorative justice is an ancient concept, the restorative perspective gained impetus in the 1970's and 1980's from the victims' movement, from experiences with reparative sanctions and processes, and from the rise of informal neighborhood justice and dispute resolution programs. Restorative justice is based on the following values and assumptions:

> All parties should be included in the response to crime—offenders, victims, and the community.

> Government and local communities should play complementary roles in that response.

> Accountability is based on offenders understanding the harm caused by their offenses, accepting responsibility for that harm, and repairing it.

As a philosophy for the juvenile justice system, restorative justice guides professionals in the appropriate and equitable use of sanctions to ensure that offenders make amends to victims and the community. The restorative justice philosophy:

> Gives meaning to sanctions such as restitution and community service. Without a restorative understanding, these sanctions may be viewed as bureaucratic in nature and may be used for punitive purposes.

> Links disparate practices and programs such as restitution, victim services, community service, victim-offender mediation, and dispute resolution as part of a restorative agenda for juvenile justice.

While retributive justice is focused on public vengeance, deterrence, and punishment through an adversarial process, restorative justice is concerned with repairing the harm done to victims and the community through a process of negotiation, mediation, victim empowerment, and reparation. In contrast to the individual treatment approach, which focuses on providing limited services to offenders, restorative justice is concerned with the broader relationships among offenders, victims, and the community.

As a philosophical framework, restorative justice is neither punitive nor lenient in focus and provides a clear alternative to juvenile justice sanctioning and intervention based on retributive or traditional treatment assumptions. * * *

An integrated model

Through the restorative lens, the objectives of the balanced approach take on a particular meaning based on a set of core values defined by the new philosophical framework. For example, achieving accountability in sanctioning cannot be equated with punishment, but is instead linked to victim reparation. Likewise, rehabilitation is not understood to mean completing treatment programs and community protection is not equated with incarceration.

Ultimately, the balanced and restorative justice model provides the basis for reconciling the interests of victims, offenders, and the community through common programs and supervision practices that meet mutual needs. In these programs, competency development activities may reinforce community protection and accountability objectives. For example, programs that require young offenders to engage in meaningful, productive work and service in their communities (competency development) during free time under structured adult supervision (community protection) can also provide a source of funding for repayment of victims as well as opportunities for community service (accountability). Such restorative requirements must be based on consideration of the harm caused by the offender's willful action in the offense, consideration of a range of alternatives to meet the accountability obligation, attention to competency needs, and equal emphasis on how risk to the public can be minimized while the offender is sunder court supervision. * * *

Professor John Braithwaite is one of the leading scholars and proponents of restorative justice in the world. *See e.g.* John Braithwaite, *Crime, Shame and Reintegration* (1989); John Braithwaite, "Restorative Justice: Assessing Optimistic and Pessimistic Accounts," 25 *Crime and Justice* 1 (1999). The following excerpt, **John Braithwaite, "A Future Where Punishment is Marginalized: Realistic or Utopian?," 46** *U.C.L.A. L. Rev.* **1727, 1743–1450 (1999)**, summarizes the origins and characteristics of the restorative justice paradigm:

Restorative justice is a process of bringing together the individuals who have been affected by an offense and having them agree on how to repair the harm caused by the crime. The purpose is to restore victims, restore offenders, and restore communities in a way that all stakeholders can agree is just. One value of restorative justice is that we should be reluctant to resort to punishment. Punishment adds to the amount of hurt in the world, but justice has more meaning if it is about healing rather than hurting. * * *

The term "restorative justice" was first used in the late 1970s to describe victim-offender mediation programs of various kinds in North America and Europe. These mostly involved a meeting of a single offender with a single victim in the presence of a professional mediator. * * *

Restorative justice became a global social movement in the 1990s as a result of learning from indigenous practices of restorative justice the ways in which individualistic Western victim-offender mediation was impoverished. The most influential wisdom was from the oral justice traditions of the New Zealand Maori and North American native peoples. These restorative justice traditions were more radically communitarian. Instead of two individuals mediating a dispute across a table, members of two communities (one supporting a victim, another an offender, with other individuals supporting both) would come together as one community in a circle. This gave rise to the names "sentencing circle" or "healing circle" for the 1990s North American variants of restorative justice. The southern hemisphere variants were called "conferences." In both the Maori and North American traditions, the supporters in the circle were not limited to parents and siblings. * * *

The second big lesson we learned from indigenous practice was that material reparation was much less important than emotional or symbolic reparation. Victims often wanted an apology more than compensation. Forgiveness from their families was often more important to the restoration of offenders than anything else. The surprise was that talk about justice could sit so comfortably alongside talk about love. * * *

In a typical conference or circle, the consequences of the crime will first be discussed. Who has suffered as a result of the crime: the victim, the family of the offender? How have they suffered? Then the conference considers a plan of action to heal that suffering. Often the plan will include ways of making amends to the victim or the community that many will conceive as punishment. But it may also include apology, forgiveness, ways of helping victims to feel safer and preventing a recurrence of the crime. * * *

Proponents of restorative justice often represent it as an alternative model to the traditional justice system frameworks of punishment and treatment, retribution or rehabilitation, and crime control or due process. The following excerpt, **Kent Roach, "Four Models of the Criminal Process," 89 *J. Crim. L. & Criminology* 671, 692–695, 709–711, 712–13 (1999)**, suggests some of the ways in which a restorative justice perspective differs from more familiar justice system models:

* * * Griffiths presented a third "family" model that assumed that the state and the accused, like a parent and child, had common interests if only because they continued to live together after punishment. The needs of the accused were more important than his or her rights and the state was assumed to act in good faith. The closest example of this "family" model were juvenile delinquent acts which allowed the state to pursue the child's best interests in a parental manner. John Braithwaite has returned to Griffiths' family model as a source of inspiration for his influential model of re-integrative shaming through informal, non-punitive and non-adversarial interventions which shame offenders for their crimes, but offer support and re-integration through families and communities. * * * The family model of juvenile justice is now being re-invigorated through contemporary interest in family conferencing, restorative justice, and victim-offender reconciliation. * * *

Family models of justice and Aboriginal justice reveal Packer's assumptions of an adversarial criminal process and a liberal reactive state. New models might approach criminal justice with less emphasis on professional and adversarial conflict between the accused and the state and more emphasis on reconciling offenders, victims, their families, and their communities. * * *

Once a crime has been committed, the focus is on reducing the harm it causes through healing, compensation, and restorative justice. The circle can be closed without any outside intervention as crime victims take their own actions to heal and attempt to prevent the crime in the future. * * * [T]he circle can be represented by a process of restorative justice which allows the offender to take responsibility for the crime and attempt to repair the harm done to victims. This is often achieved through informal proceedings such as Aboriginal healing circles, family conferences, and victim-offender reconciliation programs in which all of the actors are seated in a circle. All of these interventions are united by their concern for the welfare of both offenders and victims, informal non-punitive approaches, and wide community participation. The key players in these circles should be the victim, the offender, and their families and supporters—not police, prosecutors, defense lawyers or judges who may appropriate their dispute. Victims play the most crucial role and this gives them some of the power and autonomy that was taken away by the crime. They have the power to decide whether to accept apologies and plans for reparation. In a punitive victims' rights approach, however, they can only make representations to legislators, judges, and administrators who retain the ultimate power to impose punishment.

Restorative justice focuses on factual guilt, but explores the reasons why the offender has committed the offense. * * * Restorative justice also marginalizes due process rights by encouraging the offender to accept responsibility for the offense rather than requiring the state to prove beyond a reasonable doubt that the offender committed the crime and that the state complied with the offender's legal rights. There is, however, no permanent opposition to due process and it is important that all participants be treated fairly and be allowed to speak. Restorative justice works best if offenders voluntarily participate and accept responsibility for the offense. Offenders already do this in many cases when they plead guilty, and they should be even more willing to do so in a less punitive system. The greater challenge will be persuading victims to participate because they may fear or disdain the offender or have unrealistic expectations about the benefits of a formal trial. Some offenders and/or victims will not participate and trials will be necessary. * * *

A non-punitive model of victims' rights may also address some concerns about the use of the term "victim." A focus on punishment tends to concentrate on what happened in the past and define a person by his or her past victimization. On the other hand, concerns about restoration and prevention look to the future and make room for healing, empowerment, forgiveness, and a richer and dynamic identity for crime victims that is not limited by being a victim who demands increased punishment. * * * Less punitive approaches can give those who have been victimized in the past more power and support than crime control measures which, while increasingly undertaken in the name of victims, often affirm the powers of criminal justice professionals and frequently collide with due process claims.

NOTES

1) Statutory Examples of Restorative Justice Programs. The statutes that follow provide examples of efforts to implement restorative justice programs. The various examples differ in their degree of program specificity, structure, and format. Consider, for example, in what ways Florida's "Neighborhood Restorative Justice" Act differ from the Washington and Minnesota diversion statutes, *supra*, at pp. 273–277 and 287–288.

Minn. Stat. § 611A.775 (1998). Restorative justice programs A community-based organization, in collaboration with a local governmental unit, may establish a restorative justice program. A restorative justice program is a program that provides forums where certain individuals charged with or petitioned for having committed an offense meet with the victim, if appropriate; the victim's family members or other supportive persons, if appropriate; the offender's family members or other supportive persons, if appropriate; a law enforcement official or prosecutor when appropriate; other criminal justice system professionals when appropriate; and members of the community, in order to:

(1) discuss the impact of the offense on the victim and the community;

(2) provide support to the victim and methods for reintegrating the victim into community life;

(3) assign an appropriate sanction to the offender; and

(4) provide methods for reintegrating the offender into community life.

Fla. Stat. § 985.303 (1998). Neighborhood Restorative Justice

(2) Neighborhood restorative justice center.—

(a) The state attorney may establish at least one Neighborhood Restorative Justice Center in designated geographical areas in the county for the purposes of operating a deferred prosecution program for first-time, nonviolent juvenile offenders.

(b) The state attorney may refer any first-time, nonviolent juvenile offender accused of committing a delinquent act to a Neighborhood Restorative Justice Center.

(3) Restorative Justice Board.—

(a) The state attorney may establish Restorative Justice Boards consisting of five volunteer members, of which: two are appointed by the state attorney; two are appointed by the public defender; and one is appointed by the chief judge of the circuit. The state attorney shall appoint a chair for each board.

(b) The board has jurisdiction to hear all matters involving first-time, nonviolent juvenile offenders who are alleged to have committed a delinquent act within the geographical area covered by the board.

(4) Deferred prosecution program; procedures.—

(a) The participation by a juvenile in the deferred prosecution program through a Neighborhood Restorative Justice Center is voluntary. To participate in the deferred prosecution program, the juvenile * * * must take responsibility for the actions which led to the current accusation. The juvenile and the juvenile's parent or legal guardian must waive the juvenile's right to a speedy trial and the right to be represented by a public defender while in the Neighborhood Restorative Justice program. This waiver and acknowledgment of responsibility shall not be construed as an admission of guilt in future proceedings. The board or the board's representative must inform the juvenile and the parent or legal guardian of the juvenile's legal rights prior to the signing of the waiver.

(b) If the state attorney refers a juvenile matter to a Neighborhood Restorative Justice Center, the board shall convene a meeting within 15 days after receiving the referral.

(c) The board shall require the parent or legal guardian of the juvenile who is referred to a Neighborhood Restorative Justice Center to appear with the juvenile before the board at the time set by the board. In scheduling board meetings, the board shall be cognizant of a parent's or legal guardian's other obligations. The failure of a parent or legal guardian to appear at the scheduled board meeting with his or her child or ward may be considered by the juvenile court as an act of child neglect * * * and the board may refer the matter to the Department of Children and Family Services for investigation * * *.

(d) The board shall serve notice of a board meeting on the juvenile referred to the Neighborhood Restorative Justice Center, the juvenile's parent or guardian, and the victim or family of the victim of the alleged offense. These persons and their representatives have the right to appear and participate in any meeting conducted by the board relative to the alleged offense in which they were the alleged juvenile offender or parent or guardian of the alleged juvenile offender, or victim or family of the victim of the alleged juvenile offender. The victim or a person representing the victim may vote with the board.

(5) Sanctions.—After holding a meeting pursuant to paragraph (4)(d), the board may impose any of the following sanctions alone or in any combination:

(a) Require the juvenile to make restitution to the victim.

(b) Require the juvenile to perform work for the victim.

(c) Require the juvenile to make restitution to the community.

(d) Require the juvenile to perform work for the community.

(e) Recommend that the juvenile participate in counseling, education, or treatment services that are coordinated by the state attorney.

(f) Require the juvenile to surrender the juvenile's driver's license and forward a copy of the board's resolution to the Department of Highway Safety and Motor Vehicles. The department * * * shall suspend the driving privileges of the juvenile, or the juvenile may be restricted to travel between the juvenile's home, school, and place of employment during specified periods of time according to the juvenile's school and employment schedule.

(g) Refer the matter to the state attorney for the filing of a petition with the juvenile court.

(h) Impose any other sanction except detention that the board determines is necessary to fully and fairly resolve the matter.

(6) Written contract.—

(a) The board, on behalf of the community, and the juvenile, the juvenile's parent or guardian, and the victim or representative of the victim, shall sign a written contract in which the parties agree to the board's resolution of the matter and in which the juvenile's parent or guardian agrees to ensure that the juvenile complies with the contract. The contract may provide that the parent or guardian shall post a bond payable to this state to secure the performance of any sanction imposed upon the juvenile. * * *

(b) A breach of the contract by any party may be sanctioned by the juvenile court as it deems appropriate upon motion by any party.

(c) If the juvenile disagrees with the resolution of the board, the juvenile may file a notice with the board within 3 working days after the board makes its resolution that the juvenile has rejected the board's resolution. After receiving notice of the juvenile's rejection, the state attorney shall file a petition in juvenile court.

(7) Completion of sanctions.—

(a) If the juvenile accepts the resolution of the board and successfully completes the sanctions imposed by the board, the state attorney shall not file a petition in juvenile court and the board's resolution shall not be used against the juvenile in any further proceeding and is not an adjudication of delinquency. The resolution of the board is not a conviction of a crime, does not impose any civil disabilities ordinarily resulting from a conviction, and does not disqualify the juvenile in any civil service application or appointment.

(b) If the juvenile accepts the resolution reached by the board but fails to successfully complete the sanctions imposed by it, the state attorney may file the matter with the juvenile court. * * *

2) Victim–Offender mediation as another example of Restorative Justice The following statutes and excerpt provide another version of a restorative justice resolution of a delinquency matter:

Del. Stat. Tit. 11 § 9501 (1998). Purpose.

(a) The General Assembly finds and declares that:

(1) The resolution of * * * juvenile delinquent disputes can be costly and complex in a judicial setting where the parties involved are necessarily in an adversary posture and subject to formalized procedures; and

(2) Victim-offender mediation programs can meet the needs of Delaware's citizens by providing forums in which persons may voluntarily participate in the resolution of certain criminal offenses in an informal and less adversarial atmosphere. * * *

Del. Stat. Tit. 11 § 9502 (1998) Program funding; operation; supervision.

(a) There is hereby established a Victim—Offender Mediation Committee to be composed of the Attorney General, Public Defender, Chief Magistrate, Chair of the Criminal Justice Council, Director of the Administrative Office of the Courts and the Chief Judge of Family Court or their designees to administer this chapter. * * *

(b) To be eligible for state funds, a program must do the following:

(1) Be operated by a 501(c)(3) organization in Delaware;

(2) Provide neutral mediators who have received training in conflict resolution techniques; * * *

(4) Provide victim-offender mediation in * * * juvenile delinquency cases without cost to the participants; and

(5) At the conclusion of the mediation process provide a written agreement or decision to the referral source setting forth the settlement of the issues and future responsibilities of each participant. * * *

Del. Stat. Tit. 11 § 9503 (1998). Confidentiality.

All memoranda, work notes or products, or case files or programs established under this chapter are confidential and privileged and are not subject to disclosure in any judicial or administrative proceeding unless the court or administrative tribunal determines that the materials were submitted by a participant to the program for the purpose of avoiding discovery of the material in a subsequent proceeding. * * * The foregoing privilege and limitation of evidentiary use does not apply to any communication of a threat that injury or damage may be inflicted on any person or on the property of a party to the dispute, to the extent the communication may be relevant evidence in a criminal matter. * * *

Del. Stat. Tit. 11 § 9504 (1998). Eligibility.

No offender shall be admitted to the program unless the Attorney General certifies that the offender is appropriate to the program, regardless of any criteria established under any program or this chapter.

Any person who voluntarily enters a mediation process at a victim-offender mediation program established under this chapter may revoke his or her consent, withdraw from mediation and seek judicial or administrative redress prior to reaching a written agreement. No legal penalty, sanction or restraint may be imposed upon the person for such withdrawal.

3) Efficacy of Victim—Offender Mediation The report by the National Academy of Science, **Joan McCord, Cathy Spatz Widom, and Nancy A. Crowell, Ed.,** *Juvenile Crime, Juvenile Justice* **175–176** (National Academy of Science, 2001), summarizes some of the research on victim-offender mediation and its role in the restorative justice movement:

> Victim-offender mediation is one increasingly popular form of diversion. * * * The vast majority of mediation cases are first-time offenders. Typically, mediation occurs prior to adjudication. Some pressure appears to be mounting to include more serious cases in mediation programs. Whether more serious or complicated cases can be handled through mediation remains to be seen.

> Studies have consistently shown that victims tend to be more satisfied with the process of mediation than with court processes. This may be because victims are included in the mediation process only if they volunteer to do so. * * * [F]or offenders, "participation in mediation appears to not have significantly increased their satisfaction with how the juvenile justice system handled their case." * * * [In one study], [o]ver 90 percent of mediations resulted in a restitution plan agreed to by both

victims and offenders and significantly more juvenile offenders completed the agreed-on restitution than did those whose restitution was ordered by the court.

Victim-offender mediation programs are one part of a larger diversion movement in juvenile justice that has been gaining attention world wide—the restorative justice model. Under a restorative justice model, victims are given the opportunity to come face to face with offenders to negotiate restitution. In addition, restorative justice programs keep youth in the community and maintain community safety by community-based surveillance practices designed to limit the opportunities for juveniles to reoffend and strengthen rather than sever their connections with the community. These practices include monitored school attendance, monitored employment attendance, monitored program attendance, supervised community work service, supervised recreation, adult mentors and supervisors, training offenders' families to provide appropriate monitoring and disciplinary practices, day reporting centers, electronic monitoring, house arrest, and random drug testing. * * *

C. FORMALIZING DIVERSION

Once states decide to divert youths from the juvenile court, how should they structure the diversion process? Should states vest diversionary authority in the judicial branch—juvenile court probation—or in the executive branch—the prosecutor? Which agency possesses greater institutional competency to make the screening decisions and according to what criteria—social welfare or social control considerations, characteristics of the offender or the nature of the offense? Depending upon the locus of decision-making, what procedural safeguards, if any, should states provide youths prior to the formal initiation of the justice process? What criteria should define juveniles' eligibility for diversion? What limitations, if any, should states place on the length or intensity of "informal" supervision or dispositions? To what types of programs should states divert youths? What consequences should follow and what processes should be used if a juvenile fails successfully to complete a diversion program or declines to participate in an appropriate one? If a youth later returns to juvenile court, what legal significance should a juvenile or criminal court judge attach to a youth's previous referral to and participation in or failure from a diversion program?

The materials in this section address these questions. They begin with examples of a state's efforts to structure the diversion process. How adequately do these various provisions answer the foregoing questions?

1. DIVERSION CONTRACTS

The State of Washington has one of the most elaborate statutes formalizing the diversion process. Moreover, because Washington adopted its' diversion statute in 1976, appellate courts have had the opportunity to answer several recurring legal and policy questions about the administration of diversion programs.

Washington Stat. § 13.40.070 (1998).

(1) Complaints referred to the juvenile court alleging the commission of an offense shall be referred directly to the prosecutor. The prosecutor, upon receipt of a complaint, shall screen the complaint to determine whether:

(a) The alleged facts bring the case within the jurisdiction of the court; and

(b) On a basis of available evidence there is probable cause to believe that the juvenile did commit the offense. * * *

(3) * * * [T]he prosecutor shall either file an information in juvenile court or divert the case. * * *

(4) An information shall be a plain, concise, and definite written statement of the essential facts constituting the offense charged. * * *

(5) Where a case is legally sufficient, the prosecutor shall file an information with the juvenile court if:

(a) An alleged offender is accused of a class A felony, a class B felony, an attempt to commit a class B felony, a class C felony * * *; or

(b) An alleged offender is accused of a felony and has a criminal history of any felony, or at least two gross misdemeanors, or at least two misdemeanors; or

(c) An alleged offender has previously been committed to the department; or

(d) An alleged offender has been referred by a diversion unit for prosecution or desires prosecution instead of diversion; or

(e) An alleged offender has two or more diversion contracts on the alleged offender's criminal history; or

(f) A special allegation has been filed that the offender or an accomplice was armed with a firearm when the offense was committed.

(6) Where a case is legally sufficient the prosecutor shall divert the case if the alleged offense is a misdemeanor or gross misdemeanor or violation and the alleged offense is the offender's first offense or violation. * * *

(7) Where a case is legally sufficient and falls into neither subsection (5) nor (6) of this section, it may be filed or diverted. In deciding whether to file or divert an offense under this section the prosecutor shall be guided only by the length, seriousness, and recency of the alleged offender's criminal history and the circumstances surrounding the commission of the alleged offense.

(8) Whenever a juvenile is placed in custody or, where not placed in custody, referred to a diversion interview, the parent or legal guardian of the juvenile shall be notified as soon as possible concerning the allegation

made against the juvenile and the current status of the juvenile. Where a case involves victims of crimes against persons or victims whose property has not been recovered at the time a juvenile is referred to a diversion unit, the victim shall be notified of the referral and informed how to contact the unit.

(9) The responsibilities of the prosecutor * * * may be performed by a juvenile court probation counselor for any complaint referred to the court alleging the commission of an offense which would not be a felony if committed by an adult, if the prosecutor has given sufficient written notice to the juvenile court that the prosecutor will not review such complaints.

(10) The prosecutor, juvenile court probation counselor, or diversion unit may * * * refer juveniles to mediation or victim offender reconciliation programs. Such mediation or victim offender reconciliation programs shall be voluntary for victims.

Washington Stat. § 13.40.080 (1997). Diversion agreement.

(1) A diversion agreement shall be a contract between a juvenile accused of an offense and a diversionary unit whereby the juvenile agrees to fulfill certain conditions in lieu of prosecution. Such agreements may be entered into only after the prosecutor, or probation counselor * * * has determined that probable cause exists to believe that a crime has been committed and that the juvenile committed it.

(2) A diversion agreement shall be limited to:

(a) Community service not to exceed one hundred fifty hours, not to be performed during school hours if the juvenile is attending school;

(b) Restitution limited to the amount of actual loss incurred by the victim, and to an amount the juvenile has the means or potential means to pay;

(c) Attendance at up to two hours of counseling and/or up to ten hours of educational or informational sessions at a community agency * * *; and

(d) A fine, not to exceed one hundred dollars * * * [and based only on] the juvenile's financial resources and whether the juvenile has the means to pay the fine. * * *

(3) In assessing periods of community service to be performed and restitution to be paid by a juvenile who has entered into a diversion agreement, the court officer to whom this task is assigned shall to the extent possible involve members of the community. Such members of the community shall meet with the juvenile and advise the court officer as to the terms of the diversion agreement and shall supervise the juvenile in carrying out its terms.

(4) A diversion agreement may not exceed a period of six months for a misdemeanor or gross misdemeanor or one year for a felony and may include a period extending beyond the eighteenth birthday of the divertee.

Any restitution assessed during its term may not exceed an amount which the juvenile could be reasonably expected to pay during this period. If additional time is necessary for the juvenile to complete restitution to the victim, the time period limitations of this subsection may be extended by an additional six months.

(5) The juvenile shall retain the right to be referred to the court at any time prior to the signing of the diversion agreement.

(6) Divertees and potential divertees shall be afforded due process in all contacts with a diversionary unit regardless of whether the juveniles are accepted for diversion or whether the diversion program is successfully completed. Such due process shall include, but not be limited to, the following:

(a) A written diversion agreement shall be executed stating all conditions in clearly understandable language;

(b) Violation of the terms of the agreement shall be the only grounds for termination;

(c) No divertee may be terminated from a diversion program without being given a court hearing, which hearing shall be preceded by:

(i) Written notice of alleged violations of the conditions of the diversion program; and

(ii) Disclosure of all evidence to be offered against the divertee;

(d) The hearing shall be conducted by the juvenile court and shall include:

(i) Opportunity to be heard in person and to present evidence;

(ii) The right to confront and cross-examine all adverse witnesses;

(iii) A written statement by the court as to the evidence relied on and the reasons for termination, should that be the decision; and

(iv) Demonstration by evidence that the divertee has substantially violated the terms of his or her diversion agreement.

(e) The prosecutor may file an information on the offense for which the divertee was diverted:

(i) In juvenile court if the divertee is under eighteen years of age; or

(ii) In superior court or the appropriate court of limited jurisdiction if the divertee is eighteen years of age or older.

(7) The diversion unit shall be responsible for advising a divertee of his or her rights as provided in this chapter.

(8) The right to counsel shall inure prior to the initial interview for purposes of advising the juvenile as to whether he or she desires to participate in the diversion process or to appear in the juvenile court. The juvenile may be represented by counsel at any critical stage of the

diversion process, including intake interviews and termination hearings. The juvenile shall be fully advised at the intake of his or her right to an attorney and of the relevant services an attorney can provide. * * *

The juvenile shall be advised that a diversion agreement shall constitute a part of the juvenile's criminal history. * * * A signed acknowledgment of such advisement shall be obtained from the juvenile, and the document shall be maintained by the diversionary unit together with the diversion agreement, and a copy of both documents shall be delivered to the prosecutor if requested by the prosecutor. * * *

(9) When a juvenile enters into a diversion agreement, the juvenile court may receive only the following information for dispositional purposes:

(a) The fact that a charge or charges were made;

(b) The fact that a diversion agreement was entered into;

(c) The juvenile's obligations under such agreement;

(d) Whether the alleged offender performed his or her obligations under such agreement; and

(e) The facts of the alleged offense.

(10) A diversionary unit may refuse to enter into a diversion agreement with a juvenile. It shall immediately refer such juvenile to the court for action and shall forward to the court the criminal complaint and a detailed statement of its reasons for refusing to enter into a diversion agreement. The diversionary unit shall also immediately refer the case to the prosecuting attorney for action if such juvenile violates the terms of the diversion agreement.

(11) A diversionary unit may, in instances where it determines that the act or omission of an act for which a juvenile has been referred to it involved no victim, or where it determines that the juvenile referred to it has no prior criminal history and is alleged to have committed an illegal act involving no threat of or instance of actual physical harm and involving not more than fifty dollars in property loss or damage and that there is no loss outstanding to the person or firm suffering such damage or loss, counsel and release or release such a juvenile without entering into a diversion agreement. * * *

NOTES

1) Does a Juvenile have a Statutory Right to be Diverted? Because Washington was among the first states to enact a diversion statute, it's courts have had several opportunities to consider many of the legal issues that arise when juvenile courts divert offenders. For example, the court in **State v. Chatham**, 28 Wash.App. 580, 624 P.2d 1180 (Wash.Ct.App. 1981), reviewed whether the diversion statute gave juveniles a right to be diverted in lieu of delinquency prosecution:

This appeal involves the juvenile's right to "diversion." * * * [The] Juvenile Justice Act of 1977 * * * established a comprehensive system for the disposition of complaints lodged against juveniles. One such disposition is a juvenile diversion program in which eligible juvenile offenders perform community services as an alternative to prosecution. The diversion unit is a community-based correctional unit where local citizens enter into contracts (diversion agreements) with eligible juveniles to pay restitution and perform community service in lieu of prosecution.

In diverting this juvenile's case, a member of the prosecuting attorney's staff phoned the chairperson of the local diversion unit, the Kent Conference Committee, and related the facts of the case as they appeared from the police reports. The chairperson thereupon declined to accept diversion of the juvenile's case because the serious nature of this case did not fall within the committee's eligibility standards for diversion.

The case then went before the juvenile court for an adjudicatory hearing and the defendant was found guilty of assault as charged. * * *

Although the juvenile did have a right to have his case referred to a diversionary unit, that unit also had the right to refuse to enter into a diversionary agreement with him. * * *

A juvenile's eligibility for diversion is determined by statute. Since the juvenile in this case was a first offender not charged with a felony, he had a right to have his case referred to a diversionary unit, RCW 13.40.070(5); and the prosecuting attorney's office, in turn, had the duty to so refer it, RCW 13.40.070(6). * * *

The juvenile's statutory right to have his or her case referred to a diversion unit does not guarantee that the unit will enter into a diversion agreement with the juvenile. Diversion is not always an appropriate disposition, even in first offender juvenile cases. * * *

The juvenile code grants diversion units the authority to exercise sound discretion and to reject a case referred to it for diversion [citing RCW 13.40.080 (10), *supra*]. By providing that the reasons for refusing to enter a diversion agreement be in writing, the statute assures fair and reasoned decisions for rejecting diversion and insures juvenile court control over the fairness of the procedure. * * *

The chairperson of the Kent Conference Committee testified at that hearing that in order to accommodate 300 to 350 diversions a year, the committee delegates to her the task of conducting a prescreening of diversion referrals to see that each one meets the committee's minimum standards of acceptance. These minimum standards excluded those cases involving serious injury or weapons from further consideration for diversion. * * *

Although the informal procedures followed in this case are not exemplary, the juvenile's case was referred to a diversionary unit, was considered by that unit through its authorized representative and was rejected for reasons that were neither arbitrary nor capricious. The juvenile court was satisfied that this juvenile's diversion was unacceptable to the diversion unit and that, therefore, no purpose would be served by sending the case back to perform some ritualistic paper work. We agree.

The prescreening procedure of the diversionary unit in this case is not prohibited by statute, and is contemplated by RCW 13.40.080(10). Because the rejection of this juvenile's referral was based on standardized safeguards properly adopted and reasonably applied to determine candidates with whom the committee would be likely to enter diversion agreements, it is not violative of due process. On these facts, exercise of some degree of informality in these preliminary proceedings did not deprive the defendant of a fair and reasoned decision or deny him his right to due process. * * *

2) Prosecutorial Determination of Eligibility for Diversion If the statute only grants a juvenile a right to be considered for diversion, but not necessarily to be accepted into the program, can the prosecutor, as matter of policy, decide that certain classes of cases are inappropriate for diversion? For example, in **State v. WS**, 40 Wash.App. 835, 700 P.2d 1192 (Wash.Ct.App. 1985), the prosecutor concluded that all prostitution cases required formal supervision and complied with the statutory diversion requirement by referring prostitution cases to the diversion unit with a rejection form attached:

A hearing was held on WS's motion for remand [for diversion]. During the hearing, the prosecution submitted an affidavit * * * [that] set forth the policy of the diversionary unit to reject all prostitution cases as well as the reasons therefore. Those reasons included the mobility of prostitutes, the repeated failure of those juveniles to appear for court, and the inadequacy of options under diversion to deter or impact further offensive behavior * * * [and the] need for ongoing supervision of such offenders which could best be provided by the courts by means of "stay out of areas of prostitution" (SOAP) orders. * * *

The question presented to this court is whether the rejection by the diversionary unit of referral of all prostitutes is arbitrary and capricious. We find that it is.

The categorical denial of all prostitutes is a usurpation of legislative authority and contrary to the intent of the Legislature in enacting the Juvenile Justice Act of 1977.

Statutes must be interpreted in accordance with the intent of the Legislature. * * * Indeed, the Juvenile Justice Act contemplates certain classes of crimes for which there need not even be a diversionary agreement. [See R.C.W. § 13.40.080(11), *supra* p. 392] * * *

Prostitution, as charged in this case, is an illegal act that involves "no threat of or instance of actual physical harm." Thus, the crime with which WS was charged was viewed by the Legislature as such a minor offense that it could be dismissed without even the necessity for a diversionary agreement.

Respondent argues that a diversionary unit has the authority to prescreen applicants and to set forth minimum standards for acceptance. * * * In *Chatham*, * * * the diversionary unit had a policy not to take cases involving serious injury. These minimum standards set by the unit were found to be well reasoned and the court held that nothing precluded a diversionary unit from setting such standards. * * * In *Chatham*, the diversionary unit's rejection was based upon certain behavior which can be present in different criminal acts. In the instant case, the diversionary unit is precluding from diversion an entire class of offenders regardless of the individual characteristics of the offender or his behavior. Such an exclusion is arbitrary. Our courts have defined arbitrary and capricious conduct as "willful and unreasoning action, without consideration and in disregard of facts or circumstances." The action taken by the diversionary unit disregards the particular circumstances of WS's case and denies her access to the unit without considering the particular facts of her case.

This is not to say that all prostitutes must be accepted by a diversionary unit or even that WS must necessarily be accepted by the diversionary unit but, rather, that a denial based on the crime itself is arbitrary when it is clear that the Legislature intended such crimes as appropriate for diversion. * * *

3) May a Prosecutor Charge a Juvenile Who Rejects a Diversion Program with a More Serious Offense? Suppose a juvenile refuses to enter into a diversion program on a complaint alleging a misdemeanor and the diversion unit refers her case back to the prosecutor to file a formal petition. May the prosecutor then charge the youth with a more-serious, felony level offense? May the juvenile court impose a more severe sentence than the disposition the youth would have received if she "voluntarily" had entered into a diversion agreement of community supervision? In **State v. McDowell**, 102 Wash.2d 341, 685 P.2d 595 (Wash. 1984), the Washington Supreme Court upheld the prosecutor's exercise of discretion and the more severe sentence imposed:

During the disposition hearing * * * McDowell argued that the sentencing court was limited by statute to a sentence no greater than what he could have received under the diversion program. * * * McDowell claims that * * * allowing the prosecutor to file a greater charge once a juvenile rejects diversion penalizes that juvenile for exercising his right to take his case to court. He relies on United States Supreme Court cases finding that "while an individual certainly may be penalized for violating the law, he just as certainly may not be punished for exercising a protected statutory or constitutional right."

In *Blackledge v. Perry*, the Court held that the prosecutor could not "up the ante" by filing felony charges against a defendant convicted of a misdemeanor, who chose to file for a trial de novo in a higher court. The Court opined that due process "is not offended by all possibilities of increased punishment upon retrial after appeal, but only by those that pose a realistic likelihood of 'vindictiveness.' " In order to free defendants from fearing a prosecutor's retaliatory motivations, the Court held that charging a more serious crime upon retrial raised a realistic likelihood of vindictiveness and justified a presumption of illegal motives. * * *

[A]ctual vindictiveness is required to invalidate the prosecutor's adversarial decisions made prior to trial. McDowell concedes that there is no evidence of actual vindictive motivation on the part of the prosecutor in this case. * * * Instead, he argues that the structure of the juvenile diversion system requires a presumption of illegal motives whenever the prosecutor, without justification, increases the charges against a juvenile who refuses diversion. He contends that, unlike other pretrial settings, the system presents a "realistic likelihood" of retaliatory motivation, because the safeguards of the adult criminal justice system are not present to ensure good faith behavior by the prosecutor.

We find no reason to presume that abuse of prosecutorial discretion is more likely when juveniles are brought to justice than when adults are prosecuted. Nor do we conclude that the statutory scheme of the juvenile diversion system presents any special potential for abuse. * * *

Before an information is filed, however, the prosecutor's statutory duty is simply to screen complaints for legal sufficiency. Complaints are then diverted to community programs or retained for further prosecutorial action depending on whether the complaint alleges a misdemeanor or felony, and on other statutory factors.

Once a legally sufficient complaint is determined to require filing, such as when the juvenile refuses the offer of diversion, the prosecutor's charging discretion must be exercised. Common sense dictates that the original complaint and screening procedure will be reviewed and evaluated before an information is filed. For any number of reasons, whether it be new evidence or new conclusions about the significance of the allegations in the complaint, the charge actually filed might differ from the offense alleged in the initial complaint. Nothing in this procedure suggests that retaliatory motivation on the part of the prosecutor will underlie the charging decision. * * * We have already determined that the Legislature contemplated prosecutorial discretion to charge a more serious crime in the information than was alleged in the original complaint. It is only reasonable to conclude that the Legislature intended the offender to be punished appropriately for the more serious offense. * * *

4) Does a Prosecutor's Decision to Divert or to Charge Violate Due Process, Equal Protection, or Separation of Powers? In State v. Tracy M., 43 Wash.App. 888, 720 P.2d 841 (Wash.Ct.App. 1986), the juvenile argued that allowing a prosecutor to make the final decision of whether to charge or to divert the case to a diversion unit violates the doctrine of separation of powers because diversion is a sentencing decision that the judiciary should make. The juvenile also challenged the prosecutor's authority to charge or divert without first conducting a hearing and the absence of standards to guide the prosecutor's decision. The Court of Appeals rejected these contentions:

> First, does RCW 13.40.070(7) constitute an unconstitutional delegation of judicial authority to the prosecutor? * * * [A] prosecutor's determination regarding an accused's eligibility for a diversion program may be upheld if it is "based on clear standards, and * * * subject to judicial review." * * * [T]he statute here does set out standards. RCW 13.40.070(7) states the prosecutor's decision to file or divert shall be "guided only by the length, seriousness, and recency of the alleged offender's criminal history and the circumstances surrounding the commission of the alleged offense." These standards protect against unfair and arbitrary decisions. * * *

Second, does the statute violate due process because the prosecutor makes the decision to file or divert without a hearing? * * * "The prosecutor's charging function under RCW 13.40.070 (3), (5)–(7) * * * does not alter the prosecutor's traditional discretion when making the charging decision." As the State points out, neither the filing of a criminal charge nor the decision to divert a juvenile's case affects his liberty interest. That interest is affected only if a judgment and sentence is obtained following a trial, or if community service is imposed following proceedings before a community diversion unit. A juvenile is accorded due process in both trial and diversion proceedings. Thus, we conclude the statute does not violate due process.

Third, does RCW 13.40.080(7) violate equal protection by making it possible for prosecutors to treat similarly situated juveniles differently? * * * "The failure to prosecute all other possible violators of the law is not, per se, contrary to the Equal Protection Clause of the Fourteenth Amendment." As noted above, the prosecutor's decision can be said to have been arbitrary only when his conduct was unreasonable and amounted to intentional or purposeful systematic discrimination in the enforcement of the law. * * *

5) May a juvenile court judge consider a youth's prior diversions to enhance a subsequent delinquency sentence? May a juvenile court judge take into account a youth's prior diversion and use it to enhance a subsequent delinquency disposition? If so, what procedural safeguards should youths receive at the time of their initial diversion to assure the validity of diversion agreements and the underlying conduct for purposes of increasing a subsequent delinquency sanction. The following two cases illustrate the range of practices. In **State v. Quiroz**, 107 Wash.2d 791, 733 P.2d 963 (Wash. 1987), the Washington Supreme Court upheld the use of prior diverted offenses to increase a juvenile's criminal history score:

The Juvenile Justice Act of 1977 * * * provides for very structured sentences, weighing both the severity of the offense as well as the juvenile's past criminal record. Quiroz' history consisted of two prior diverted misdemeanors. * * * These misdemeanors effectively increased Quiroz' sentence from a maximum of 20 to 40 days. * * * Quiroz asked the trial court to void the diversion agreement because at the time he was not informed of the nature of the charges against him * * * [and] that his right to counsel and trial was denied. * * *

The Supreme Court has promulgated a number of rules to control the procedure which the diversion unit and the juvenile must follow in order to enter into a diversion agreement. These rules are designed to protect the juvenile's constitutional and statutory rights while at the same time ensuring that the system functions efficiently and without the delays associated with formal hearings. JuvCR 6.2(a) ensures that a juvenile shall be told of his or her right to discuss with a lawyer whether or not to enter into a diversion agreement prior to the initial interview with the diversion unit. JuvCR 6.3 requires that a juvenile who has chosen to waive the right to counsel sign a written waiver form to that effect. JuvCR 6.4 and 6.5 require the juvenile to be read to, and to sign an advice form describing the diversion agreement. That advice form specifically includes the fact that the agreement becomes part of the juvenile's criminal history. * * *

In Quiroz' case, he arrived at the diversion unit prior to his appointment and was given a form entitled "Advice About Diversion." He read this form and then discussed it point by point with the probation officer who then entered into the diversion agreement with Quiroz. The advice agreement specifically stated:

You have the right to talk to a lawyer to help you decide whether or not you should enter into a Diversion Agreement or go to court. If you cannot afford a lawyer, the Court will appoint one at no cost. If you do not believe you committed this offense, you should talk to a lawyer.

The probation officer further testified that had Quiroz wanted a lawyer or a more detailed explanation of the charges against him or his possible options, she would have referred him to a lawyer. Quiroz then signed the diversion agreement and a waiver of counsel form * * *. * * *

Nevertheless, despite their signatures, the juveniles argue that they did not have an adequate opportunity to consult with counsel, and that any waiver of their rights could not be described as knowing, intelligent and voluntary. We agree that the short amount of time between the juveniles' receiving the forms and signing the diversion agreement, and the fact that the onus was placed on the juveniles to decide whether to ask for an attorney creates an issue of fact as to whether their waivers were completely voluntary. However, in hearings before two different judges, with testimony from both the juveniles and the probation officers, each court found that the juveniles made knowing and voluntary waivers of their right to counsel. Ample evidence supports the trial judge's conclusion. * * *

Nevertheless, to prevent this type of challenge to the diversion agreement, we believe the method described to us by the King County Juvenile Division is preferable. In King County advice to counsel forms are sent to the juvenile days prior to the initial diversion interview, giving the juvenile ample time to decide whether or not to seek the advice of counsel. Furthermore, JuvCR 6.3, 6.4 and 6.5 contemplate that different forms will be signed which advise the juveniles of their rights to counsel, of the diversion process and of the effect of a diversion agreement. While it is not fatal to the agreement that these forms be combined into one piece of paper given to the juvenile before the diversion agreement is signed, we believe it would be preferable to separate the forms and give the advice about counsel and the diversion process well prior to the initial interview. Finally, while the form prescribed by JuvCR 6.4 concerning the advice about diversion indicates that a juvenile has the option of entering the agreement or "going to court," the form does not list the rights which a juvenile has if he or she chooses to go to court and that the charges might be dismissed. A brief explanation of the right to cross-examine witnesses, the presumption of innocence, and the right against self-incrimination would prove useful at this point. While we explicitly hold that failure to advise the juvenile does not offend due process principles and that the overall process as it currently stands is constitutional, such additional language would save countless challenges to these arguments while not overly complicating the procedure. * * *

Both juveniles were notified of the charges against them in writing at the top of the diversion forms. They could have received a detailed explanation of the factual and legal explanations of the charges from lawyers had they chosen to do so. Furthermore, while this notice would not have been sufficient to uphold a criminal conviction by a guilty plea, the less formal nature of the diversion process, coupled with the fact that such an agreement is not the same as a conviction, justifies a less formal notice process. * * * In this case, we believe the written notice given to the juveniles prior to their signing the diversion agreement which indicated that they could consult with counsel meets our conceptions of fair play. The juveniles had adequate notice of the charges.

The juveniles also argue that the diversion process is tantamount to a conviction and does not safeguard basic constitutional rights such as: the right against self-incrimination, the right of confrontation and the right to trial. * * *

These arguments fail to recognize that a fundamental difference exists between a diversion agreement, which is essentially a contract between the juvenile and the diversion unit, and a guilty plea which results in a criminal conviction. A diversion agreement cannot result in a detention sentence, and requires at most that the juvenile pay a fine of $100 or less and attend community supervision and service activities for a short length of time. The procedure is designed to be informal * * *. We believe the less formal procedure used in this diversion context need not guarantee that the juvenile be informed of the panoply of constitutional rights which the juvenile would have if he or she were pleading guilty. A diversion agreement is not equivalent to a conviction, and there is no necessity to formalize this procedure by a lengthy recitation of rights which attach during criminal proceedings. * * *

[T]he diversion agreement plainly indicated that it could serve to enhance a future crime's penalty. The agreement warned the juveniles of its effect on their criminal histories, and therefore, the juveniles cannot complain that they were unaware of its consequences. Therefore, because the agreement warned about the possibility of its future use, and because the agreement itself was not the same as a conviction, its future use did not violate their constitutional rights. * * *

In contrast with the Washington Supreme Court's ruling in *Quiroz*, the Minnesota Court of Appeals in **In Re D.S.S.**, 506 N.W.2d 650 (Minn. Ct. Ap. 1993), barred the juvenile court judge from considering a juvenile's prior diverted offenses when it sentenced a youth in a subsequent delinquency proceeding:

D.S.S. first entered the * * * juvenile court system as a 14–year–old. At that time * * * [h]e and his parents received written notice of an appointment * * * [and the] reverse side of the notice provided a printed statement of rights, including the parents' and the child's rights to an attorney. The statement also noted that if the child admitted the delinquency alleged in the petition, the court would then have the power to transfer legal custody of the child.

Following receipt of these notices, D.S.S. and his parents attended meetings with a court services officer—[a social worker who is not an attorney—who] orally informed D.S.S. and his parents at these meetings of their right to counsel at any time. She also explained to D.S.S. that if he denied the charges, he had the right to a trial. It is undisputed that * * * D.S.S. expressly declined counsel and signed statements indicating he did not wish to speak to an attorney. * * *

This appeal arose following * * * petitions for which D.S.S. had obtained counsel. D.S.S. filed a motion * * * challenging the * * * proceedings in which he had not requested counsel. D.S.S. moved to vacate the prior uncounseled admissions * * * and urged the juvenile court to refrain from weighing the first * * * offenses in determining the disposition [on the current] petitions. * * *

D.S.S. contends the trial court erred in failing to withdraw his admissions. We agree. D.S.S. was not adequately advised of his right to counsel, did not voluntarily and intelligently waive his right to counsel and, as a result, suffered manifest injustice.

A juvenile has the right to counsel even though the juvenile justice system is a more informal system than the separate criminal justice system for adults. * * * Minnesota law reflects this concern in requiring that juveniles receive an on-the-record explanation of the right to counsel:

A child not represented by counsel shall be advised orally by counsel, who shall not be the county attorney, or orally by the court on the record of the right to counsel at or before any hearing on a petition.

The rule's requirement of an advisory by counsel (who is not the county attorney) or by the court assumes that an adequate explanation of the right to counsel can come only from a non-adversary attorney or the judge, both of whom must, of course, be trained in the law. * * *

D.S.S. * * * was not advised of his right to counsel orally by the court on the record or by counsel. Instead, D.S.S. received some notice of his right to counsel from a written statement of rights and from a social worker, who is not trained in the law. * * *

The social worker also failed to advise D.S.S. of the ramifications of admitting to the offenses, to wit, that a record would be kept of his offenses and that this record could be used to enhance the disposition of a later offense. * * *

A child's waiver of the right to counsel is valid only if made in a voluntary and intelligent manner. Before there can be an adequate waiver, however, the court or counsel, who is not the county attorney, is to inform the juvenile of the right to counsel. * * *

[E]ven if D.S.S. was in a "diversion" program, the informality of such a program does not justify the failure to follow procedures prescribed in the rules. The rules explicitly require an oral advisory of the right to counsel by an attorney or the court * * * and do not distinguish between informal or formal hearings. * * *

We hold that regardless of whether D.S.S. participated in a diversion program, he was entitled to a formal advisory of the right to counsel. * * *

D.S.S. testified that, after receiving some notice of his right to counsel by a social worker, he assumed that by admitting to the offenses and completing his contracts, there would be no record. From the ostensibly "informal" proceedings, he built up a lengthy record. * * * This record was included in a social history shown to the trial court, and the court referred to this record. * * * [T]he cumulative weight of D.S.S.'s record could not but affect the judgment in later petitions. * * *

NOTES

1) **Diversion Procedures—Another Alternative** Following *D.S.S.*, what should an intake worker do in order to be able to use prior diverted offenses to enhance a juvenile's subsequent delinquency sentence? Is the Washington practice or the Minnesota practice preferable for protecting the rights of juveniles? Which is better for preserving the informality of the diversion process?

Minnesota Statute § 388.24 (1997). Diversion

Subdivision 1. Definition. As used in this section:

(1) a child under the jurisdiction of the juvenile court is an "offender" if:

(i) the child is petitioned for, or probable cause exists to petition or take the child into custody for, a felony, gross misdemeanor, or misdemeanor offense, other than an offense against the person, but has not yet entered a plea in the proceedings; * * * [or the child has not previously been adjudicated for an offense against the person or participated in a diversion program];

(2) "pretrial diversion" means the decision of a prosecutor to refer an offender to a diversion program on condition that the delinquency petition against the offender will be dismissed or the petition will not be filed after a specified period of time if the offender successfully completes the program.

Subd. 2. Establishment of program. * * * [E]very county attorney shall establish a pretrial diversion program for offenders. * * * The program must be designed and operated to further the following goals:

(1) to provide eligible offenders with an alternative to adjudication that emphasizes restorative justice;

(2) to reduce the costs and caseload burdens on juvenile courts and the juvenile justice system;

(3) to minimize recidivism among diverted offenders;

(4) to promote the collection of restitution to the victim of the offender's crime;

(5) to develop responsible alternatives to the juvenile justice system for eligible offenders; and

(6) to develop collaborative use of demonstrated successful culturally specific programming, where appropriate.

Subd. 3. Program components. A diversion program * * * may:

(1) provide screening services to the court and the prosecuting authorities to help identify likely candidates for pretrial diversion;

(2) establish goals for diverted offenders and monitor performance of these goals;

(3) perform chemical dependency assessments of diverted offenders where indicated, make appropriate referrals for treatment, and monitor treatment and aftercare;

(4) provide individual, group, and family counseling services;

(5) oversee the payment of victim restitution by diverted offenders;

(6) assist diverted offenders in identifying and contacting appropriate community resources;

(7) provide educational services to diverted offenders to enable them to earn a high school diploma or GED; and

(8) provide accurate information on how diverted offenders perform in the program to the court, prosecutors, defense attorneys, and probation officers.

Subd. 4. Reporting of data to criminal justice information system (CJIS). * * * [E]very county attorney who establishes a diversion program * * * shall report to the bureau of criminal apprehension [the name and date of birth of each youth referred to a diversion program and whether and when the individual successfully completed the program or was removed from it]. * * * The superintendent shall cause the information described in this subdivision to be entered into and maintained in the criminal history file of the Minnesota criminal justice information system.

2) Diversion to What? Wash. Stat. § 13.40.080(2) and Minn. Stat. § 388.24 Subd. 3 describe some of the components of a diversion program. **Cheri Panzer, "Reducing Juvenile Recidivism Through Pre–Trial Diversion Programs: A Community's Involvement," 18 *J. Juv. L.* 186, 195–206 (1997),** describes some of the elements of California's diversion programs:

The common elements within each of the pre-trial diversionary programs are restitution, community service, parental involvement, continuing education, continuous monitoring and supervision, and counseling. These programs identify requirements which will provide accountability and responsibility for the offense by the juvenile and his parents. Section 652.5 of the California Welfare & Institutions Code provides that service programs include "constructive assignments that will help the minor learn to be responsible for his or her actions. The assignments may include, but are not be limited to, requiring the minor to repair damaged property or to make other appropriate restitution, or requiring the minor to participate in an educational or counseling program." The programs are designed to be completed within six months. * * *

A contract is generally signed by the juvenile, with his parents agreeing to certain terms such as restitution, community service, counseling and continuing education. The contract may stipulate a curfew, avoidance of certain associations (such as associating with known gang members), or other corrective actions deemed appropriate by the probation officer. The contract period is not to exceed six months. * * *

Restitution provides a method of reimbursing either the individual victim or the community for the pecuniary loss attributed to the juvenile's conduct. "Victim restitution is used to instill positive values and moral obligation through financial reimbursement to the victim by the child and parent. [T]he program also gives juveniles an opportunity to learn responsibility for their actions." * * *

California codes include restitution as an acceptable means of holding the juvenile offender accountable for his offenses. The California Supreme Court, in *Charles S.*, * * * held that "[r]estitution, then, can be a valuable tool of rehabilitation. As it is directly related to the crime, restitution can, if proper in the circumstances, lead the minor to realize the seriousness of his crime, and to accept the responsibility for it." * * *

Community service, similar to the principles of restitution, provides an opportunity for the juvenile offender to "pay back" the community for his offenses through the juvenile's personal time and effort. It allows the juvenile to realize that his offense has a negative impact on the community. Examples of effective community services have been repainting graffitied walls and trash removal in parks and other city properties. * * *

Parental involvement, with potential criminal and/or financial responsibility, is perhaps one of the most key and controversial elements. * * * Though the parents must consent to the participation in the program and co-sign the contract, little is done in the way of providing for parental guidance in dealing with their child. In many states, including California, parents are not just required to participate, but are being held criminally responsible for their children's delinquency. * * *

The Youth Accountability Board requires the juvenile offender to return to school if he has dropped out, or to maintain good grades if he is still in school. Some youths are required to attending specialized classes dealing with arson, drug addiction, petty theft, or other educational classes that inform the juveniles of the consequences of their conduct. Counseling may also be included in the contract if needed. These elements see to the special needs of the offenders. * * *

The Youth Accountability Board members not only attend the hearings, but they also provide supervision for the community service work. The social investigator or the associate probation officer checks up on compliance of the other contractual requirements regarding keeping up grades in school, curfews, etc. * * *

Pre-trial diversionary programs, both statutory and community based, allow the juvenile offender to avoid the stigma that is associated with the formal juvenile court system: being adjudicated "a ward of the state" or "juvenile delinquent." These programs "bridge the gap between parental sanctions which may be too lenient, and juvenile sanctions which may be too harsh for first-time offenders." * * *

D. PROCEDURAL SAFEGUARDS AT INTAKE

IN THE MATTER OF FRANK H.

71 Misc.2d 1042, 337 N.Y.S.2d 118 (N.Y.Fam.Ct.1972).

[At his first appearance before the family court, the judge assigned counsel for the juvenile.] When the assigned attorney appeared in this proceeding, he made a motion to vacate the petition and send the case back to intake for consideration *de novo* on the ground that the respondent had been denied his constitutional right to counsel at the intake stage of the Family Court proceeding. * * *

The sole question for determination is whether the initial intake conference is a critical stage in the proceedings within the meaning of the constitutional guarantee of the right to counsel thereby depriving the respondent of this right. This initial intake conference occurs before a petition is ordered drawn and prior to the holding of a Family Court hearing. * * *

The intake officer can adjust a case at intake where the accused youth denies his guilt of any offense. Intake process in juvenile courts is a specialized proceeding in the constellation of court services and procedures. There are more social than legal issues involved. Adjustment is not mandatory and the Rules specifically provide that the probation service may not prevent any person or complainant from having access to the court if he insists that a petition be filed. It permits informal adjustments to be made at intake but includes provisions designed to protect the rights of the parties in this process. No person can be compelled to appear at any conference, produce any papers or visit any place. * * *

Intake is not a legal term and with the exception of juvenile and family courts, is foreign to the court field. Its use in juvenile and family courts has no doubt been adopted from the field of social welfare. In the welfare field, the client has complete freedom of choice. He comes to the agency and he may or may not decide to accept the service if offered. * * *

The same is not true with court intake. The "client" defined as the person complained about or alleged to be in a situation necessitating action, has no freedom of choice. Here the request for action is initiated by someone other than the client. Whatever freedom of choice exists as to whether action will be taken rests in the court, not in the client. Unlike the private welfare agency, the court's authority to deny the right to file a petition is controlled by the nature of the case. Certainly giving the court this power can be justified and is fairly well established, at least by custom in delinquency cases.

Delinquency cases involve offenses which if committed by an adult would be a crime. Here the State is usually a party to the action. The decisions made at intake level, affect individual and community rights—the right of the child and family to personal freedom and privacy and at the same time the right of the child and family to receive the services of the State for care, protection and treatment. * * *

Section 241 of the Family Court Act provides: "that minors who are the subject of family court proceedings should be represented by counsel of their own choosing or by law guardians. This declaration is based on a finding that counsel is often indispensable to a practical realization of due process of law and may be helpful in making reasoned determinations of fact and proper orders of disposition." * * *

Gault is limited to adjudicatory hearings resulting in incarceration. The question then becomes whether right to counsel also exists at intake proceedings. No specific answers to whether the intake stage of a juvenile delinquency proceeding is a critical stage of the proceedings wherein the right to counsel attaches is supplied by Section 241 or the entire Family Court Act. * * *

The answer does however lie in Section 735 of the Family Court Act indicating strong legislative intent that no counsel is necessary at the intake stage of proceedings. This section provides that: "No statement made during a preliminary conference may be admitted into evidence at a fact-finding hearing or, if the proceeding is transferred to a criminal court, at any time prior to a conviction."

This section makes inadmissible at a fact-finding hearing any statement made during a preliminary conference carried on under probation service connected with the Family Court and does not refer to questioning by police and statements made to police which are not within the proscription of this section.

This preserves the spirit of cooperation which it is to be hoped prevails, at a preliminary conference such as intake and guards against self-incrimination, a prohibition in *Gault.* * * *

In other words, Section 735 accomplishes in effect what *Miranda* accomplishes: If the juvenile is to be encouraged to make admissions, despite the privilege against self-incrimination, he should be protected against the use of such admissions at ensuing proceedings. * * *

The threat of self-incrimination is mitigated by the exclusion provision of Section 735. Counsel for the respondent argues that the mere presence of counsel for the respondent at the intake level will prevent the issuance of a petition. This is not necessarily true and is a legal *non sequitur*. The fact that a petition may issue and a record created for the juvenile depends on what develops at the subsequent fact-finding hearing. * * * Is intake level to be designated a critical stage for the juvenile because it determines whether an official record of delinquency adjudication will become part of the child's dossier? Intake referral for petition per se would not create an institutional commitment. It may well be that the desired openness of the intake interview can be maintained with counsel present as well as absent at least where under Section 735 of the Family Court Act admissions made by the juvenile may not be used at the hearing.

To require counsel at intake would be an intolerable burden on an already overburdened court. The lack of manpower is both frightful and appalling. This is a valid argument entitled to great weight and has great relevancy. If there was no Section 735 * * * with its exclusionary rule, the argument would have no merit over the greater right to be represented at a critical stage of the proceeding, for it would then become truly a critical stage of the proceedings where counsel would be required.

In addition, it should be carefully noted that under Section 735 * * * there is an absolute prohibition of the use of any statements or confession made at the intake interview, even though voluntarily made and without coercion or undue influence or even where a waiver of that right was knowingly and intelligently made. Contrast this with admission statements and confessions voluntarily made after *Miranda* warning or waiver of such rights, intelligently and knowingly made, in adult criminal proceedings where such statements or confessions, voluntarily made can be used against the respondent or defendant. * * *

If intake proceedings are to be classified as critical stages of proceedings despite all the legal protections for the juveniles above enumerated as already in existing law, rules and procedures, then there would be no need for intake proceedings for accused juveniles in furtherance of Family Court policy of rehabilitation and not punishment for crime and petitions should be drawn automatically in all cases and set down for fact-finding hearings. * * *

NOTES

1) Does an intake conference constitute custodial interrogation for purposes of a *Miranda* warning? Consider the implications of **Minnesota v. Murphy**, 465 U.S. 420, 104 S.Ct. 1136, 79 L.Ed.2d 409 (1984), where the defendant—an adult probationer—met with his probation officer in her office as she had requested. The terms of his probation required Murphy to report to his probation officer periodically and to answer truthfully any questions the probation officer asked him. Although the probation officer suspected that Murphy's answers would incriminate him when she questioned him about an unrelated crime, the Supreme Court concluded that Murphy was not in custody when he made his incriminating responses and therefore his probation officer was not required to give him a *Miranda*:

> Custodial arrest is said to convey to the suspect a message that he has no choice but to submit to the officers' will and to confess. It is unlikely that a probation interview, arranged by appointment at a mutually convenient time, would give rise to a similar impression. Moreover, custodial arrest thrusts an individual [into] "an interrogation environ-

ment * * * created for no purpose other than to subjugate the individual to the will of his examiner." Many of the psychological ploys discussed in *Miranda* capitalize on the suspect's unfamiliarity with the officers and the environment. Murphy's regular meetings with his probation officer should have served to familiarize him with her and her office and to insulate him from psychological intimidation that might overbear his desire to claim the privilege. Finally, the coercion inherent in custodial interrogation derives in large measure from an interrogator's insinuations that the interrogation will continue until a confession is obtained. * * * [Because] Murphy was not physically restrained and could have left the office, any compulsion he might have felt from the possibility that terminating the meeting would have led to revocation of probation was not comparable to the pressure on a suspect who is painfully aware that he literally cannot escape a persistent custodial interrogation. * * *

2) *Miranda* Warning at Intake? In *Frank H.*, the statute provided juveniles with a form of use immunity for any incriminating statements that they made during their intake conference. By contrast, *Minnesota v. Murphy* declined to require a *Miranda* warning as a prerequisite to the admissibility of incriminating statements made during probation interviews. Is the custody situation in *Murphy* distinguishable from an intake conference? In any event, couldn't a state "have its cake and eat it too"—require a youth to attend an intake conference *and* use any incriminating statements made in subsequent delinquency proceedings—by the simple expedient of administering a *Miranda* warning. Consider, for example, the following juvenile court rule of procedure:

Tennessee Rules of Juvenile Court Procedure 12 (West 1998):

(c) **Intake Duties.** In addition to the duties otherwise provided by law, the designated court officer at the initial interview shall have the following duties in delinquent cases and cases in which an unruly child is alleged to have violated a valid court order:

(1) The officer shall immediately advise the child of the following rights:

(i) That the child has a right to an attorney;

(ii) That if the child is unable to hire an attorney and if the child's parent, guardian or legal custodian has not provided an attorney, one can be provided at no charge to the child;

(iii) That the child is not required to say anything and that anything the child says may be used against him or her; and

(iv) If the child's parent, guardian, legal custodian or attorney is not present, that the child has a right to communicate with them and that, if necessary, reasonable means will be provided to do so.

Wouldn't this alternative satisfy the court's concerns in *Frank H.* as to whether intake is a critical stage? As a matter of juvenile justice policy, do you consider the *Frank H.* or the Tennessee Rule 12 strategy preferable? Why? In **In re Wayne H.**, 24 Cal.3d 595, 596 P.2d 1, 156 Cal.Rptr. 344 (Cal. 1979), the juvenile appealed from a delinquency adjudication for armed robbery based, in part, on his incriminating statement made to a probation officer. Probation Officer Wright interviewed Wayne H. and gave him a *Miranda* warning prior to eliciting information to decide whether or not to recommend defendant's detention and a fitness proceeding. At the end of the interview, Wright told Wayne H. that he intended to recommend detention and a fitness hearing, and he replied, "I did this one." The California Supreme Court ruled that despite receiving a *Miranda* warning, the statement was inadmissible:

> Defendant contends that statements by a juvenile to a probation officer are inadmissible in any subsequent proceeding as confessions or admissions of guilt, or for purposes of impeachment. We agree that the statement in question should have been excluded. * * *

> Courts have recognized a number of situations in which the use of statements by adult defendants to a probation officer as admissions in a trial on the issue of guilt would be unfair. Thus, we have held that statements made to a probation officer in the hope that candor will induce a favorable sentencing report are inadmissible against the defendant in any retrial unless "volunteered" by the defendant under the guiding hand of counsel. Postconviction admissions to the adult criminal court made on a probation officer's advice in hope of lenient treatment are also excluded from use at any subsequent trial.

> Similar results have been reached under the Juvenile Court Law. Admissions by a juvenile to a probation officer for use in the preparation of the social study, and to the juvenile court itself in the course of a section 602 jurisdictional hearing, have both been excluded from subsequent adult criminal proceedings. Similarly, it has been held that, where a probation officer obtains damaging statements from a juvenile in the course of preparing the social study, without prior advice to the minor's counsel when the attorney's identity is known, the statements must be excluded from any subsequent juvenile adjudication proceeding.

> The cases have stressed the law's interest in encouraging complete candor between a defendant and his probation officer in the probation interview. The purpose of such an interview is not the marshalling of evidence on the issue of guilt, but rather the assembling of all available information relevant to an informed disposition of the case if guilt is established, or to assist in the evaluation of the minor's fitness for treatment as a juvenile. Such decisions, courts have uniformly concluded, should be based on the most complete knowledge of the defendant's background that is possible. His description and explanation of the circumstances of the alleged offense, and his acknowledgment of guilt and demonstration of remorse, may significantly affect decisions about punishment or transfer for adult proceedings. * * *

> The [intake and detention] interview required by a juvenile probation officer under section 628 is conducted in a nonaccusatorial setting. Contrary to the People's contention, the consultation is not analogous to police interrogation of an adult suspect. In fact, the section 628 interview has no counterpart in adult criminal proceedings in which the defendant confers with his probation officer only after conviction. The primary purpose of the section 628 interview * * * is not to elicit evidence of guilt—the function of police questioning—but to assist the probation officer in deciding at the outset of the case whether the minor need be further detained pending a court hearing. This approach thereby serves a

paramount concern of the Juvenile Court Law that a minor be treated in the least restrictive means feasible under the circumstances. * * *

[T]he minor's frank discussion of the offense may indicate that his involvement was innocent or secondary, or, more to the point, that he is cooperative and remorseful, and is therefore a good candidate for release pending further proceedings. Candor will assist the probation officer in discharging his statutory duty to determine the least restrictive feasible treatment of the minor. A free interchange between minor and officer should therefore be encouraged. * * *

We conclude that the subsequent use of statements made by a juvenile to a probation officer in a section 628 interview would frustrate important purposes of that statute, and of the Juvenile Court Law generally. We therefore hold that such statements are not admissible as substantive evidence, or for impeachment, in any subsequent proceeding to determine criminal guilt, whether juvenile or adult. Such statements may, of course, be admitted and considered in hearings on the issues of detention and fitness for juvenile treatment. * * *

3) Can police piggy-back on a probation summons to appear at intake? In **Deshawn E. v. Safir**, 156 F.3d 340 (2d Cir. 1998), a detective squad began to work in the Family Court building near the office of the Probation Department. The Squad's function was to "strengthen cases, pursue accomplices, apprehend persons selling guns to minors, conduct lineups, locate witnesses and complainants, and execute warrants." Detectives approached juveniles and their parent when they arrived at the Family Court for the preliminary intake conference with probation described in *Frank H.*, *supra*, p. 404. Police interrogated juveniles in an interview room decorated with police signs and notices and with the youths' parent present. Squad members questioned the child about the alleged crime and other unresolved crimes during interviews that typically lasted about 30 to 45 minutes. In cases in which the state filed delinquency petitions, it gave written notice of its intent to use statements made by the juveniles to the detectives in family court delinquency proceedings. Two juvenile plaintiffs, Deshawn E. and Anthony C., filed a § 1983 action, seeking declaratory and injunctive relief, claiming that the squad's interrogation practices violated the Fifth Amendment and that interrogation without the presence of counsel violated the Sixth Amendment. The Court of Appeals rejected their claims:

The Squad's failure to inform plaintiffs of their rights under *Miranda v. Arizona*, does not, without more, result in § 1983 liability. While a defendant has a constitutional right not to have a coerced statement used against him, a defendant does not have a constitutional right to receive *Miranda* warnings. The remedy for a violation of the right against self-incrimination is "the exclusion from evidence of any ensuing self-incriminating statements" and "not a § 1983 action." Although a juvenile's Fifth Amendment rights may be violated by the Squad's interrogations in an individual case, the appropriate remedy is suppression following a hearing * * * to determine the admissibility of a statement made by a criminal defendant, and not a § 1983 class action.

While plaintiffs cannot base a § 1983 claim solely on a law enforcement officer's failure to administer *Miranda* warnings, a § 1983 action may exist under the Fifth Amendment self-incrimination clause if coercion was applied to obtain a waiver of the plaintiffs' rights against self-incrimination and/or to obtain inculpatory statements, and the statements thereby obtained were used against the plaintiffs in a criminal proceeding. * * *

The key inquiry for Fifth Amendment purposes is whether the statement introduced in a judicial proceeding was obtained, not by failure to read a defendant the *Miranda* warnings, but by coercion—an inquiry determined by the totality of the circumstances.

Even if it can be shown that a statement was obtained by coercion, there can be no Fifth Amendment violation until that statement is introduced against the defendant in a criminal proceeding. * * * [T]o constitute a Fifth Amendment violation "use of the [coerced] statement at trial is not required," but that there must be some "use or derivative use of a compelled statement at any criminal proceeding against the declarant." * * *

[Although] the defendants have announced their intention to use the statements taken by the Squad at hearings in family court delinquency proceedings * * *[t]he planned future use of an allegedly coerced statement is simply too remote and attenuated to form the basis of a present constitutional claim. * * *

Plaintiffs also argue that even if the statements are not actually used at trial, they are used as an incentive in plea bargaining and to enhance cases. Specifically, plaintiffs contend that the *Miranda*-violating statements "provide[ ] an incentive for appellants to seek plea bargains" and "provide[ ] important ammunition in the prosecutorial arsenal." * * *

A showing that in some situations the Squad may coerce involuntary statements that are used against plaintiffs is insufficient to render the entire practice unconstitutional; they must establish that this necessarily happens in every case, and this they cannot do. Frequently, Squad interrogations are not followed by delinquency petitions at all. In other cases, the statements are not used against the declarant because they are exculpatory. Finally, we cannot conclude that there is no instance where a juvenile voluntarily waives his or her right against self-incrimination. * * *

While we agree that the Squad's interrogations are by their very nature deceptive, we do not find the circumstances of the interrogations to be so coercive as to amount to a constitutional violation. * * *

Plaintiffs argue that because the Squad's statements were intended to trick them into confessing, it is impossible to conclude that they voluntarily waived their rights. While the Squad's conduct may have caused some confusion, we do not believe it was so egregious as to result in a due process violation. Further, we do not find that the Squad's failure to explain every detail of the questioning amounts to affirmative deceit, particularly when the interviews are conducted in rooms that contain police signs, posters and notices. * * *

E.   WHETHER TO FILE A PETITION

A petition formally initiates the juvenile process and compares with the prosecutor's issuance of a complaint or information or a grand jury's indictment in the adult criminal process. The Court in *In re M.A.*, 310 N.W.2d 699, 701 (Minn. 1981) noted that "the right to counsel attaches at the time the formal petition is filed. At this point, there is a definite commencement of the adversary proceedings." Similarly, in *Deshawn E. v. Safir*, 156 F.3d 340 (2d Cir. 1998), *supra*, the Court of Appeals declined to extend the Sixth Amendment right to counsel to intake adjustment or preliminary investigation by police officers:

> The Sixth Amendment right to counsel attaches at "the time that adversary judicial proceedings have been initiated." We look to state law to determine when the adversarial process is commenced. * * * New York has held that a criminal proceeding, and with it the right to counsel, is initiated by the filing of an accusatory instrument.

> In a juvenile delinquency proceeding, the right to counsel attaches when "the respondent first appears before the court." Normally, a juvenile's first appearance before the court is upon a "prepetition hearing" application, or the initial appearance upon a petition. Of course, juveniles have a right to counsel in a juvenile delinquency proceeding. * * * The adjustment process takes place before any juvenile delinquency petition is filed. Adversarial judicial proceedings have not commenced and the right to counsel has not attached. As New York courts have determined, "the probation preliminary conference and the adjustment process are not critical stages of a juvenile delinquency proceeding," and thus a "juvenile is not entitled to counsel during the preliminary conference and the adjustment process." * * *

The relationship between the screening functions of a juvenile court's intake staff and the charging functions in the county attorney's office vary from state to state and often from county to county within a state. Should the prosecutor or juvenile court intake staff decide which youths appear in juvenile court and based on what criteria or factors?

IN THE MATTER OF APPEAL IN MARICOPA COUNTY

122 Ariz. 252, 594 P.2d 506 (1979).

HOLOHAN, JUSTICE. [Police arrested the juvenile for disturbing the peace after he released a German Shepherd dog to attack the police.]

A formal complaint was filed with the juvenile court describing the conduct of the juvenile. For reasons unexplained in the record, the juvenile probation officer to whom the case was referred decided to hold the complaint for possible adjustment. Subsequently the county attorney's office received a report from the police describing the incident, and a deputy county attorney filed a formal petition in juvenile court alleging that the juvenile, who was on probation at the time, had violated his probation by disturbing the peace.

Counsel for the juvenile moved to dismiss the petition, but the juvenile court judge denied the motion. * * * The issues presented may be stated as:

1. Does the juvenile probation officer, by choosing to "adjust" a juvenile matter pursuant to the Rules of Procedure for the Juvenile Court, preclude the county attorney from filing a juvenile petition? * * *

Counsel for the juvenile argues that the juvenile probation officer has the discretion to charge or not charge the juvenile with an act of delinquency or violation of probation. As authority he refers to the Rules of Procedure for the Juvenile Court. He points out that Rule 1 defines the word "adjusted" as meaning "the handling of a juvenile referral or complaint in a manner which obviates the necessity of filing a petition." Counsel also points out that Rule 2 provides in part:

> (b) The juvenile probation officer shall make a record of the complaint and investigate the matter to determine whether the facts, if true, are sufficient to bring the child within the court's jurisdiction, and whether they appear serious enough on their face to warrant some form of court action. If the facts are insufficient to meet the foregoing conditions, the complaint may be Adjusted.

> (c) If a child has acknowledged his responsibility for the delinquent act and the juvenile probation officer has found from his investigation of the child's total circumstances that court action is not necessary, the child may be referred to other agencies or to the parents, guardian or custodian for corrective action, and the complaint adjusted.

Finally, he points out that A.R.S. § 8–221 provides that the commencement of proceedings in juvenile court is accomplished by the filing of a petition in accordance with the Rules of Procedure for the Juvenile Court. * * *

[I]t is necessary to keep in mind that the rules for juvenile court were adopted prior to the revision of the juvenile code. Under the 1956 code the juvenile probation officer had the authority that counsel describes. The probation officer made investigations and filed petitions; he represented children and their interests in court; he was to be notified when a child was arrested and he would decide the disposition to be made of the child.

In 1967, modifications in Arizona's juvenile justice system were mandated by the United States Supreme Court in *Application of Gault*. * * *

This court promulgated the juvenile rules recognizing that due process required substantial changes in Arizona's procedure in juvenile court, but the legislature had not changed the juvenile code at the time the rules became effective. Subsequently the legislature made a comprehensive revision of the juvenile code.

Under the revised juvenile code the powers of the juvenile probation officer were significantly changed. * * * The code changed his role to that of an officer of the court charged with the responsibility of gathering and evaluating information for the court and supervising those children assigned to him by the juvenile court after an adjudication of delinquency or incorrigibility.

The new code provided that the probation officer would:

Receive and examine complaints involving an alleged delinquent or incorrigible child for the purpose of considering the commencement of proceedings under this chapter.

The new code did not, however, specifically authorize the probation officer to file petitions. It should be noted that there is a distinction between "complaints" and "petitions" in juvenile law. The complaint or referral is the written statement by an individual or agency setting forth facts describing the acts of a juvenile which may constitute delinquent conduct. The petition is the formal initiation of court action by a written instrument under oath filed with the juvenile court alleging an act of juvenile delinquency or incorrigibility. A complaint in juvenile law is somewhat similar to a complaint in criminal law, and the petition may, in a sense, be compared to an information or indictment.

The new juvenile code recognized that the adversary system had been introduced to juvenile law by *Gault*. Provision was made for the appointment of counsel for juveniles and the role of the prosecutor was defined under A.R.S. § 8–233 which provided:

A.   The county attorney shall:

1.   Direct such investigation he deems necessary of acts of alleged delinquent behavior;

2.   Cause petitions alleging delinquent behavior to be drafted and filed with the juvenile court as he deems necessary in the public interest; and

3.   Attend the juvenile court within his county and conduct on behalf of the state all contested hearings involving allegations of delinquent acts or incorrigibility. * * *

The authority to file petitions alleging delinquent behavior was granted to the county attorney. No restriction was placed on that authority. The code left the matter to the county attorney to file petitions as he deemed necessary in the public interest. * * * [W]e recognized the change which the juvenile code had made in the method of prosecuting juvenile cases, and we noted that the decision to file a delinquency petition in juvenile court was a matter exclusively for the prosecutor.

The position of counsel for the juvenile on the authority of the probation officer is a reversion to the pre-*Gault* era where the probation officer occupied too many roles. We do not propose to reinvest the probation officer with the role of prosecutor. At the complaint or referral stage in a juvenile case the probation officer may, as the statute provides, examine complaints "for the purpose of considering the commencement of proceedings * * *." The probation officer could decide that the matter should not be referred to the county attorney for the filing of a petition; that it be adjusted. The juvenile code, however, no longer leaves the decision solely to the probation officer. The decision to file a petition is now a function of the prosecutor. In his discretion the county attorney may, notwithstanding the opinion of the probation officer, deem it necessary in the public interest to file a petition alleging delinquent behavior. We believe this construction of the juvenile code and our rules is in harmony with due process and the changes in the juvenile system of justice. * * *

NOTES

1) H. Ted Rubin, "The Emerging Prosecutor Dominance of the Juvenile Court Intake Process," 26 *Crime and Delinquency* 299–301, 308, 310–11, 317 (1980), summarizes the changes in allocations of authority between probation staff and prosecutors reflected in the court's opinion in *Maricopa County*:

Discretionary processing decisions at the front end of the juvenile justice system, such as whether complained-against youths should or should not become subjects of formal delinquency petitions, have long been juvenile court hallmarks. Early juvenile codes provided that police or citizen complaints regarding youngsters should result in formal judicial hearings; however informal approaches were developed to interpose probation officer review to determine the need for official court processing. Over time, legislative enactments formalized these informal practices and specified that preliminary inquiries or intake investigations should be made to determine whether formal processing was consistent with the best interests of the child or of the community. The values of the juvenile court judge, often the employer of probation personnel, have influenced these decisions, as have the informal processing norms that have developed in different courts.

Beginning in the early 1970s, juvenile codes began adding an important new participant to the juvenile intake process, the prosecutor. Second-level prosecutor screening, with the referral flowing from police to intake officer to prosecutor, was adopted in a few jurisdictions and signaled a trend to require prosecutor signoff for each petition. * * * First-level prosecutor screening, the referral flowing from police to prosecutor, was adopted by other legislatures and represents the furthest evolution in prosecutor dominance of the intake system. * * *

Discretionary intake was consistent with a *parens patriae* juvenile court and its extensive informality, broadly defined jurisdiction, and largely unchecked authority. The awesome powers of the court did not need to be exercised with each child; informal probation officer advice or supervision, and the apparent acceptance of this counsel, was seen as a satisfactory end point. Formal petitions and formal hearings with the judge could be used later if the child did not respond to informal approaches. In earlier and simpler times, the court could engineer a working relationship with police agencies to accept the probation department's screening-out practices, at least with lesser offenders. And the mystique and authority of the court allowed probation officials to dominate conferences with parents complaining about their children's non-criminal misbehaviors and to work out a variety of informal approaches. * * *

This practice was also consistent with an individualized justice precept and a social casework model that emphasized the search for delinquency causation and a use of rehabilitation strategies. Juvenile courts, to a substantial degree, focused on the offender rather than the offense; since most juvenile referrals were for nonserious matters, and there was no prosecutorial involvement, the court for years was able to pick and choose the cases to be heard by the judge. * * *

The 1970 congressional act for the District of Columbia, a harbinger of things to come elsewhere, required that delinquency petitions be prepared by the corporation counsel. * * * The District of Columbia act set up a two-stage screening process for delinquency cases. The court's probation arm was mandated to conduct a preliminary inquiry. Where judicial action appeared warranted, a recommendation would be made to the corporation counsel to file the petition, but the latter official was required to make an independent inquiry into the facts and a determination of the legal basis for the petition. Intake's rejection of a formal petition was not reviewable by corporation counsel unless the complainant requested appeal. This two-step process has come to be known as second-level prosecutor screening. * * * First-level prosecutor screening, the referral flowing from police to prosecutor, was enacted in Colorado in 1973. Colorado prosecutors were furnished the option of requesting intake evaluations to expedite prosecutor determinations. Full intake authority over status offense referrals was retained with the probation office. Washington adopted first-level prosecutor screening in 1977 without authorizing intake officer assistance, although Washington prosecutors could delegate misdemeanor screening determinations to the intake office. * * *

These developments reflect the strongly increased prosecution role at the intake nexus. While in a number of states the juvenile prosecution role remains limited to trying contested cases and perhaps reviewing the accuracy of petitions before they are filed, such provisions are dwindling rapidly. The clear trend is toward the inclusion of the prosecutor in either first-or second-level screening functions or, at the least, toward agreements with intake officers that prosecution must be consulted regarding recommendations for informal disposition of certain more serious or repetitive offenders. Quite possibly, states that now use second-level prosecution screening will change this designation to the first-level approach. States where there is little prosecutor role at intake will move toward the second-level or directly to the first-level approach. * * *

Chapter 5

Pretrial Detention

■ ■ ■

If police take a juvenile into custody and do not immediately release him or her to a parent or guardian, then they must decide what should happen to the youth pending further investigation, intake screening, prosecutorial charging, and subsequent court proceedings. Several different juvenile justice system actors participate in the decision about a youth's interim status. Initially, a police officer decides whether or not to take a youth into custody. If the police bring a juvenile to the juvenile detention facility, then intake probation officers or social workers attempt to contact a parent and determine whether to release or detain the youth. If the detention facility staff decide to keep the juvenile in custody, then the prosecutor must file a petition. Finally, the juvenile court judge must decide whether or not to release the juvenile at a detention hearing. These different actors in the system must make these initial decisions within a 48 hour to 72 hour period. And, if a judge decides to detain a youth, the juvenile may spend a month or more in secure confinement pending a plea, adjudication, or other disposition.

Crucial differences in the detention processing of a youth hinge on the statutory grounds for pre-trial detention. For what purposes should states place youths in pretrial detention? How should legislatures define the criteria for detaining youths prior to trial? What procedures should the juvenile justice system provide youths to determine whether they meet the statutory criteria? What evidence should system actors consider and how promptly should they make these evaluations? How can states assure conditions of pretrial confinement that are consonant with juvenile courts' rehabilitative and social welfare missions?

Places For Detention Jurisdictions distinguish between placing a youth in "detention" and in "shelter care." Important differences in the handling of delinquents and status offenders hinge on the differences between these types of facilities. For example, as a result of recent reforms, states may not detain status offenders in secure detention facilities with delinquents. *E.g. In re Ronald S.*, 69 Cal.App.3d 866, 138 Cal.Rptr. 387 (1977). The following statutes illustrate the differences between "shelter care" and "secure juvenile detention" facilities:

Kan. Stat. Ann. § 38–1502. Definitions (1997):

(h) "Shelter facility" means any public or private facility or home other than a juvenile detention facility that may be used * * * for the purpose of providing either temporary placement for the care of children in need of care prior to the issuance of a dispositional order or longer term care under a dispositional order.

(i) "Juvenile detention facility" means any secure public or private facility used for the lawful custody of accused or adjudicated juvenile offenders which must not be a jail.

(k) "Secure facility" means a facility which is operated or structured so as to ensure that all entrances and exits from the facility are under the exclusive control of the staff of the facility, whether or not the person being detained has freedom of movement within the perimeters of the facility, or which relies on locked rooms and buildings, fences or physical restraint in order to control behavior of its residents. No secure facility shall be in a city or county jail.

New York Family Court Act § 301.2. Definitions (West 1999):

4. "Secure detention facility" means a facility characterized by physically restricting construction, hardware and procedures.

5. "Non-secure detention facility" means a facility characterized by the absence of physically restricting construction, hardware and procedures.

Grounds For Detention. The authority of police, probation staff, intake workers, and juvenile court judges to detain youths is based on the definition of juvenile courts' jurisdiction and the initial statutory authority to take juveniles into custody. Recall from Chapters Two and Three that statutes typically authorize police to take juveniles into custody for criminal law violations, for non-criminal status offenses, and when they find children in circumstances that endanger their health, safety, and welfare. Although states may want to give police broad authority initially to intervene, it does not necessarily follow that all youths taken into custody also should be detained pending further proceedings. Thus, states' detention statutes define with differing degrees of specificity the criteria and burden of proof for holding juveniles. How well do the statutes you encounter in this chapter define the reasons for detaining youths? Do some statutes exclude youths whom you believe should be detained? Should all youths who meet the detention criteria be held and, if not, who should decide which "eligible" juveniles should be released and on what bases?

Ga. Stat. § 15–11–18.1 (1998) When interim control or detention of accused juvenile permitted.

(a) As a matter of public policy, restraints on the freedom of accused juveniles prior to adjudication shall be imposed only when there is probable cause to believe that the accused juvenile did the act of which he is accused and there is clear and convincing evidence that the juvenile's freedom should be restrained.

(b) The imposition of interim control or detention on an accused juvenile may be considered for the purposes of:

(1) Protecting the jurisdiction and process of the court;

(2) Reducing the likelihood that the juvenile may inflict serious bodily harm on others during the interim period; or

(3) Protecting the accused juvenile from imminent bodily harm upon his or her request.

(c) Interim control or detention shall not be imposed on an accused juvenile:

(1) To punish, treat, or rehabilitate the juvenile;

(2) To allow parents to avoid their legal responsibilities;

(3) To satisfy demands by a victim, the police, or the community;

(4) To permit more convenient administrative access to the juvenile; or

(5) To facilitate further interrogation or investigation.

(d) Whenever an accused juvenile cannot be unconditionally released, conditional or supervised release that results in the least necessary interference with the liberty of the juvenile shall be favored over more intrusive alternatives. * * *

Iowa Code Ann. § 232.22 (West 1999). Placement in detention.

1. A child shall not be placed in detention unless one of the following conditions is met: * * *

d. There is probable cause to believe the child has committed a delinquent act, and one of the following conditions is met:

(1) There is a substantial probability that the child will run away or otherwise be unavailable for subsequent court appearance.

(2) There is a serious risk that the child if released may commit an act which would inflict serious bodily harm on the child or on another.

(3) There is a serious risk that the child if released may commit serious damage to the property of others. * * *

Who Gets Detained In light of the foregoing statutory criteria—juveniles who pose a danger to themselves, a danger to others, or who will fail to appear or frustrate court processes—which youths do states detain, under what conditions, and for how long? The following excerpt from **Howard Snyder and Melissa Sickmund,** *Juvenile Offenders and Victims: 2006 National Report* **168–170 (2006)** provides some data on the numbers and characteristics of juveniles held in detention pending adjudication:

When is secure detention used? A youth may be placed in a secure juvenile detention facility at various points during the processing of a case through the juvenile justice system. Although detention practices vary from jurisdiction to jurisdiction, a general model of detention practices is useful.

When a case is referred to juvenile court, intake staff may decide to hold the youth in a detention facility while the case is being processed. In general, the youth will be detained if there is reason to believe the youth is a threat to the community, will be at risk if returned to the community, or may fail to appear at an upcoming hearing. The youth may also be detained for diagnostic evaluation purposes. In most delinquency cases, however, the youth is not detained. * * *

The proportion of detained cases involving property offenses has declined Although property offense cases were the least likely to involve detention in 2002, they still accounted for the largest volume of cases involving detention because they represent the largest share of juvenile court caseloads. Property offense cases represented 32% of all detained delinquency cases in 2002, while person offenses accounted for 29% and public order cases 27%. Drug offense cases made up the smallest share of detained cases at 11%.

Compared with offense profile of detained cases in 1985, the 2002 detention caseload had a substantially smaller proportion of property offense cases. This was offset by a larger proportion of person offense cases.

Offense Profile of delinquency cases:

	All Cases		Detained Cases	
Offense	1985	2002	1985	2002
Delinquency	100%	100%	100%	100%
Person	16	24	19	29
Property	61	39	52	32
Drugs	7	12	7	11
Public Order	17	25	22	27

Note: Detail may not total 100% because of rounding

In 2002, the gender disparity in likelihood of detention was least for drug cases In 2002, the likelihood of detention in delinquency cases for male was 1.3 times the likelihood for females (22% vs. 17%). Males were more likely than females to be detained in each of the four general offense categories: 1.6 times more likely for property offenses, 1.3 times for public order offenses, 1.2 for person offenses, and 1.1 for drug offenses.

Percent of cases detained, 2002:

Offense	Male	Female
Delinquency	22%	17%
Person	26	22
Property	19	12
Drugs	20	18
Public Order	23	18

The degree of racial disparity in the likelihood of detention varied across offense In 2002, the likelihood of detention was greatest for black youth for all but public order offenses–youth of other races had a slightly greater percent of public order cases detained (24%) than black youth (23%). The overall percent of cases detained for blacks was 1.4 times that for whites and 1.2 that for other races. The greatest disparity between blacks and whites or other races was in the likelihood of detention in drug cases—the proportion of blacks was more than 2 times that for whites and nearly 2 times that for youth of other races.

Percent of cases detained, 2002:

Offense	White	Black	Other races
Delinquency	18%	25%	21%
Person	23	28	27
Property	15	22	17
Drugs	16	33	17
Public Order	21	23	24

The racial profile for detained delinquency cases was similar for males and females in 2002 In 2002, the black proportion of detained delinquency cases (36%) was substantially greater than the black proportion of the juvenile population (16%) and also greater than the black proportion of delinquency cases handled during the year (29%). The overrepresentation of black juveniles in the detention caseload was greater among person offenses (41%) than other offenses. The black proportion of detained person offense cases was similar among males (40%) and females (41%). Across offenses, for males and females, the black proportion of detained cases was in the 30%—40% range. The one exception was among detained females referred for drug offenses. Blacks accounted for just 19% of this group—close to their representation in the juvenile population (16%). * * *

The offense profile of detained cases varied by race and by gender in 2002 For males, the person offense share of delinquency cases was greater among detained cases involving black youth (31%) than among detained cases involving white youth (26%) or youth of other races (28%). For male youth of other races, drug offenses accounted for 8% of detained cases, compared with 12% for white males and 13% for black males.

Among females, blacks had a higher proportion of person offenses in the detention caseload (41%) than did either whites (31%) or youth of other races (27%). For white females, drug offense cases accounted for 11% of detained cases, compared with 5% for black females and 9% for females of other races. * * *

Another recent study documents racial disparities in juvenile justice processing. It reports differences in rates of detention for white juveniles and youths of color. **National Council on Crime and Delinquency, *And Justice For Some: Differential Treatment of Youth of Color* 11–12 (2007):**

> Some youth who are referred to juvenile court are held in detention as their case progresses, usually because of the seriousness of the crime or risk to the community or the youth. An estimated 331,779 delinquent youth were detained in 2003. With respect to their proportion of referrals, White youth were underrepresented while African American youth were overrepresented. While White youth made up 67% of juvenile referrals, they accounted for 60% of detentions. In contrast, African American youth made up 30% of referrals and 37% of detentions.

> This disparity remained when the referrals and detentions were separated according to offense categories. The pattern was most pronounced among drug cases. Drug offense cases involving White youth were 76% of those referred but only 62% of those detained. In contrast, drug offense cases involving African American youth were 22% of those referred but 36% of those detained. In every offense category, a substantially greater percentage of African American youth were detained than White youth. African American youth are more likely than White youth to be detained pretrial, even when charged within the same offense category.

> Overall, detention was used more often for referred African American youth (25%) and Asian and Pacific Islander youth (26%), than for referred White youth (18%). This was true among each of the four major offense categories as well. For youth charged with comparable offenses—whether person, property, drug, or public order offenses—youth of color, especially African Americans and Asian and Pacific Islanders, were locked up more often than White youth. Cases involving African American youth were more than twice as likely to be detained for a drug offense than White youth (31% and 15%, respectively).

A. RIGHT TO BAIL

The Eight Amendment to the Constitution provides, *inter alia*, that "Excessive bail shall not be required." The Supreme Court in *Stack v. Boyle*, 342 U.S. 1, 72 S.Ct. 1, 96 L.Ed. 3 (1951) held that "federal law has unequivocally provided that a person arrested for a non-capital offense *shall* be admitted to bail. This traditional right to freedom before conviction permits the unhampered preparation of a defense, and serves to prevent the infliction of punishment prior to conviction. * * * Unless this right to bail before trial is preserved, the presumption of innocence * * * would lose its meaning. The right to release before trial is condition upon the accused's giving adequate assurance that he will stand trial and submit to sentence if found guilty." For adults, "giving adequate assurance" may take the form of posting monetary bail or pledging other assets as collateral, paying a premium to a bail-bondsman who posts the bail, release on personal recognizance, supervised released, or release to a third-party. What justifies using a different system of pre-trial release and supervision for juveniles?

L. O. W. v. THE DISTRICT COURT
623 P.2d 1253 (Colo. 1981).

DUBOFSKY, JUSTICE. * * * [W]e issued a Rule to Show Cause why the respondent district court should not set bond for the petitioner. We now discharge the Rule.

Petitioner L. O. W., a child, was charged in a delinquency petition in Arapahoe County District Court with acts which would have constituted second-degree burglary, a class three felony, if the child had been an adult. At a detention hearing on October 23, 1980, the district court heard testimony from the investigating police officer and reviewed both a counselor's report and the petitioner's court history. The evidence disclosed that the petitioner twice had been adjudicated a delinquent child and was the subject of a reserved ruling in another case. He had previously failed to appear for a jury trial and revocation hearing in Arapahoe County and had missed a court appearance in Jefferson County. At the time of the detention hearing L. O. W. was on probation for carrying a concealed weapon. Delinquency petitions based on serious charges were pending against him in Denver and Jefferson Counties. He was also subject to probation revocation proceedings based on the allegations in this case.

The district court found that probable cause existed to believe that the petitioner had committed an act of delinquency and that it was in the best interests of the child and the community[2] for him to remain in detention[3] at the Arapahoe Youth Center. The trial court denied the petitioner's request that bond be set in a reasonable amount.[4]

---

2. "No child taken into custody pursuant to section 19–2–101(1)(a) * * * shall be held in a detention or shelter facility longer than forty-eight hours, excluding Saturdays, Sundays, and court holidays unless * * * the court determines that it would be contrary to the welfare of the child or of the community to release the child from detention. The juvenile court in each judicial district shall make provisions so that either the judge or commissioner is available to set bond seven days a week."

3. The Children's Code defines "detention" as the "temporary care of a child who requires secure custody in physically restricting facilities pending court disposition or an execution of a court order for placement or commitment."

4. The record of the detention hearing on October 23, 1980, includes the court's findings:

" * * * (T)he Court finds that the evidence is clear and convincing to this Court that the best interests of the child and the community would be served if the child was held in the Arapahoe County detention center without bond.

The petitioner contends that the trial court's refusal to set bond contravenes U.S. Const., Amend. VIII and Colo. Const., Art. II, Sec. 20 prohibiting excessive bail, and [state statutes]. We conclude that a child does not have an absolute constitutional or statutory right to bail pending adjudication of the charges filed against him in juvenile court. Because the respondent district court's findings in this case justified detention of L. O. W. without bail we discharge the Rule. * * *

The Eighth Amendment to the United States Constitution provides that "(e)xcessive bail shall not be required * * *." Beginning with the Judiciary Act of 1789, federal law has provided that, in all but capital cases, a person accused of a crime has an absolute right to be admitted to bail. The United States Supreme Court has interpreted the Eighth Amendment to require that bail be set because the

> " * * * traditional right to freedom before conviction permits the unhampered preparation of a defense and serves to prevent the infliction of punishment prior to conviction. * * * Unless this right to bail is preserved, the presumption of innocence, secured only after centuries of struggle, would lose its meaning."

The purpose of bail is to ensure the defendant's presence at trial and not to punish him before he has been convicted.

Rights provided to adult defendants in criminal proceedings, however, have not been made uniformly available to juveniles because the protective purposes of juvenile proceedings preponderate over their punitive function. Although early decisions held that "the juvenile is not entitled to bail, to indictment by grand jury, to a public trial or to trial by jury," the "applicable due process standard in juvenile proceedings, as (since) developed by *Gault* and (In re) *Winship*, is fundamental fairness."

The general thrust of these Supreme Court decisions has been to accommodate the goals and philosophies of the juvenile system within the due process framework of fundamental fairness. * * * To determine whether a juvenile has a constitutional right to bail, we first must inquire whether consistently with fundamental fairness " 'the juvenile court's assumed ability to function in a unique manner,' " justifies withholding from juveniles the constitutional right to bail. We must weigh the adverse impact of bail on informal pre-adjudication juvenile proceedings against the benefits to be anticipated from a right to bail. * * *

The use of bail in adult criminal proceedings has been criticized, particularly because it disadvantages indigent defendants. Observing that "to superimpose a provision for bail in the Juvenile Court would cause unexplored difficulties for most juveniles, particularly those who are indigent," the California Supreme Court declined to decide whether juve-

---

The Court finds from the evidence the child has been in possession of a deadly weapon; that he has committed offenses while on probation, that he is about to face another charge.

The Court finds from the foregoing that he is a danger to himself and he's a danger to others, and accordingly he's remanded to the detention center to be held without bond until further court proceedings."

niles have a constitutional right to bail. Instead the court ruled that the state's juvenile court law, which does not require that bond be posted, establishes an adequate system for the pre-hearing release of juveniles. Few children are financially independent and their parents may be unwilling or unable to post bail. At the same time, commercial surety may be unavailable because minors' contracts are voidable.

If children are detained too frequently, a right to bail will not remedy the practice. It is more likely that, were it recognized, a right to bail would become a substitute for other, more appropriate forms of release. * * *

Unlike bail setting proceedings, informal detention hearings afford a judge an opportunity to consider the child's needs and welfare. In some instances, the court may consider substitute care for the child if the parent is unwilling to have the child return home or the child does not wish to remain at home pending an adjudication hearing.

Bail does not necessarily result in a juvenile's release from detention. When a juvenile's bail is not posted, the setting of bail alone does not effectuate the presumption of innocence, aid the child's preparation of a defense, or assure the child's presence at future court proceedings. The presumption of innocence and the child's participation in preparation of his defense may, however, be effectuated by curtailing the use of pre-adjudication detention. And while monetary bail may, in some cases, provide an additional assurance of appearance if a child's inadequate ties to the community or record of past failures to appear militate against a personal recognizance bond, it is within the trial court's discretion to set bond for a child in such cases.

If the policy expressed in * * * the Children's Code disapproving the use of detention except in cases satisfying the demanding statutory standards is implemented, the need for bail will be minimized in juvenile proceedings. We therefore hold that there is no unqualified constitutional right to bail for a juvenile under the United States and Colorado Constitutions. However, a trial court may detain a juvenile without bail only after giving due weight to a presumption that a juvenile should be released pending a dispositional hearing except in narrowly defined circumstances where the state establishes that detention is necessary to protect the child from imminent harm or to protect others in the community from serious bodily harm which the child is likely to inflict.

The trial court in this case applied the Children's Code standards for detention: " * * * it would be contrary to the welfare of the child or of the community to release the child from detention." * * *

The transcript of the trial court's ruling includes specific findings that L. O. W. had avoided the jurisdiction and process of the court in the past and had been in possession of a deadly weapon. The court's findings and conclusions indicate that it gave due weight to the presumption that the petitioner should be released pending the dispositional hearing but found that there was a factual basis for detaining L. O. W. in order to protect others in the community from serious bodily harm which he was likely to inflict. The trial court's findings here were sufficient to detain the child without bail. * * *

Our opinion here should not be construed to negate the availability of bail to juveniles in appropriate situations. For example, bail may be appropriate if a juvenile is subject to detention solely because of danger that he will not appear for adjudication. In such situations bail should be considered as a viable, if not constitutionally mandated, alternative to detention. We recognize that the option of setting monetary bail in a juvenile proceeding does not preclude a trial court from considering conditions of release which will be in the child's best interests.

The trial judge here did not have a statutory or constitutional mandate to grant bail pending the juvenile delinquency adjudication. The court's reasons for detaining the petitioner justify denial of bail. * * *

NOTES

1) Is the following statute a preferable alternative to the court's decision in L.O.W.?

Ga. Stat. § 15–11–19 (1998) Procedure on taking child into custody; detention.

(d) Bail. All juveniles subject to the jurisdiction of the juvenile court and alleged to be delinquent or unruly, on application of the parent or guardian, shall have the same right to bail as adults; and the judge shall admit to bail all juveniles under his jurisdiction in the same manner and under the same circumstances and procedures as are applicable to adults accused of the commission of crimes.

The court in *State in Interest of Banks*, 402 So.2d 690 (La. 1981), found that "bail pending adjudication is necessary for the proceedings to conform to the fundamental fairness mandated by *Gault*. * * * Allowing the juvenile to be free pending adjudication preserves the presumption of innocence."

2) Undesirability of Importing Bail System into Juvenile Court Consider the arguments of **Robert O. Dawson, "The Future of Juvenile Justice: Is It Time to Abolish the System?," 81** *J. Crim. L. & Criminology* **136, 150–51 (1990)**, who concludes that:

Where bail bondsmen exist, they are extraordinarily powerful. They are likely to view adolescents as poor risks to appear for trial and are likely to be less willing to post bond for them than for an adult with a proven record of appearing for trial each time he or she is arrested. * * *

Bail has been handled in the juvenile system by pretending that it does not exist. The modern juvenile statute does not provide a right to bail and does not deny the right to bail. It simply ignores the subject entirely. Instead of providing by statute for a right to bond in juvenile proceedings, modern statutes typically provide for a prompt judicial detention hearing to be conducted under statutory release criteria. * * *

Since most adolescents involved in the juvenile process are totally dependent upon their families for money, whether they would be released on bond would depend not upon their resources, but upon those of parents and other relatives. Usually, that money could be better spent elsewhere, and the parents appreciate that fact. Further, they are very likely feeling quite hostile to their arrested child at that moment and, even if resources are available, may be unwilling to part with them for bail. * * *

3) Bail During Delinquency Proceedings In the cases of ordinary delinquents who remain within the juvenile justice system, most state courts that have considered whether bail is constitutionally required have concluded, like *L.O.W.*, that the juvenile detention statutes provide an "adequate alternative" to an adult's right to bail. *Doe v. State*, 487 P.2d 47 (Alaska 1971); *Fulwood v. Stone*, 394 F.2d 939 (D.C. Cir. 1967); *Pauley v. Gross*, 1 Kan. App.2d 736, 574 P.2d 234 (1977); Kathleen A. Baldi, "The Denial of a State Constitutional Right to Bail in Juvenile Proceedings: The Need for Reassessment in Washington State," 19 *Seattle U. L. Rev.* 573 (1996). Provisions for juvenile detention differ from the pre-trial custody and release bail decisions for adults. What is it about juvenile justice and/or juveniles that require these differences in handling of young offenders?

4) Bail Pending Waiver Proceedings The court in *In re K.G.*, 89 Ohio Misc.2d 16, 693 N.E.2d 1186, 1189 (Ohio Com. Pl. 1997) noted that "Legislatures throughout the various states have approached the juvenile-right-to-bail issue in three different manners: some allow bail as a discretionary matter, some deny any right to bail, and others have remained silent on the issue. Ohio's legislature has opted to remain silent on the issue of bail in preadjudicatory juvenile proceedings, and therefore, this court today holds that such a determination is within the discretion of the juvenile court." K.G.'s request for bail arose in the context of the state's petition to transfer the case to criminal court for prosecution as an adult. "K.G.'s petition for a commensurate increase in constitutional protections, i.e. bail, is consistent with the state's request to deprive K.G. of the rights attendant to juvenile proceedings, thereby exposing him to treatment as an adult." Other courts, by contrast, have denied juveniles a right to bail pending transfer to criminal court. "[W]hile the juvenile is before the juvenile court for such [transfer] determination and until the juvenile is bound over to district court on the criminal information, he or she is not a person actually 'charged with a crime' * * * and thus, denial of bail prior to bindover does not violate this [bail] provision." *State v. M.L.C.*, 933 P.2d 380, 384 (Utah 1997).

B. PRETRIAL PREVENTIVE DETENTION

SCHALL v. MARTIN

467 U.S. 253, 104 S.Ct. 2403, 81 L.Ed.2d 207 (1984).

JUSTICE REHNQUIST delivered the opinion of the Court.

Section 320.5(3)(b) of the New York Family Court Act authorizes pretrial detention of an accused juvenile delinquent based on a finding that there is a "serious risk" that the child "may before the return date commit an act which if committed by an adult would constitute a crime."[1]

---

1.   Section 320.5 of the Family Court Act (FCA) provides, in relevant part:

Appellees brought suit on behalf of a class of all juveniles detained pursuant to that provision. The district court struck down § 320.5(3)(b) as permitting detention without due process of law and ordered the immediate release of all class members. The Court of Appeals for the Second Circuit affirmed, holding the provision "unconstitutional as to all juveniles" because the statute is administered in such a way that "the detention period serves as punishment imposed without proof of guilt established according to the requisite constitutional standard." * * * We conclude that preventive detention under the Family Court Act serves a legitimate state objective, and that the procedural protections afforded pretrial detainees * * * satisfy the requirements of the Due Process Clause of the Fourteenth Amendment to the United States Constitution.

Appellee Gregory Martin was arrested on December 13, 1977, and charged with first-degree robbery, second-degree assault, and criminal possession of a weapon based on an incident in which he, with two others, allegedly hit a youth on the head with a loaded gun and stole his jacket and sneakers. Martin had possession of the gun when he was arrested. He was 14 years old at the time and, therefore, came within the jurisdiction of New York's Family Court. The incident occurred at 11:30 at night, and Martin lied to the police about where and with whom he lived. He was consequently detained overnight.[9] * * *

[Martin brought a habeas corpus class action on behalf of "those persons who are, or during the pendency of this action, will be preventively detained" and sought a declaratory judgment that § 320.5(3)(b) violates the Due Process and Equal Protection Clauses of the Fourteenth Amendment.] At trial, appellees offered in evidence the case histories of thirty-four members of the class, including the three named petitioners. Both parties presented some general statistics on the relation between pretrial detention and ultimate disposition. In addition, there was testimony

---

"1. At the initial appearance, the court in its discretion may release the respondent or direct his detention * * *.

3. The court shall not direct detention unless it finds and states the facts and reasons for so finding that unless the respondent is detained;

(a) there is a substantial probability that he will not appear in court on the return date; or

(b) there is a serious risk that he may before the return date commit an act which if committed by an adult would constitute a crime."

Appellees have only challenged pretrial detention under § 320.5(3)(b). Thus, the propriety of detention to ensure that a juvenile appears in court on the return date, pursuant to § 320.5(3)(a), is not before the Court.

9. Every accused juvenile is interviewed by a member of the staff of the probation department. This process is known as "probation intake." In the course of the interview, which lasts an average of 45 minutes, the probation officer will gather what information he can about the nature of the case, the attitudes of the parties involved, and the child's past history and current family circumstances. His sources of information are the child, his parent or guardian, the arresting officer and any records of past contacts between the child and the Family Court. On the basis of this interview, the probation officer may attempt to "adjust," or informally resolve, the case. Adjustment is a purely voluntary process in which the complaining witness agrees not to press the case further, while the juvenile is given a warning or agrees to counseling sessions or, referral to a community agency. In cases involving designated felonies or other serious crimes, adjustment is not permitted without written approval of the Family Court. If a case is not informally adjusted, it is referred to the "presentment agency."

concerning juvenile proceedings from a number of witnesses, including a legal aid attorney specializing in juvenile cases, a probation supervisor, a child psychologist, and a Family Court judge. On the basis of this evidence, the district court rejected the equal protection challenge as "insubstantial," but agreed with appellees that pretrial detention under the Family Court Act violates due process.[12] The court ordered that "all class members in custody pursuant to Family Court Act Section [320.5(3)(b)] shall be released forthwith."

The Court of Appeals affirmed. After reviewing the trial record, the court opined that "the vast majority of juveniles detained under [§ 320.5(3)(b)] either have their petitions dismissed before an adjudication of delinquency or are released after adjudication." The court concluded from that fact that § 320.5(3)(b) "is utilized principally, not for preventive purposes, but to impose punishment for unadjudicated criminal acts." The early release of so many of those detained contradicts any asserted need for pretrial confinement to protect the community. The court therefore concluded that § 320.5(3)(b) must be declared unconstitutional as to all juveniles. Individual litigation would be a practical impossibility because the periods of detention are so short that the litigation is mooted before the merits are determined.

There is no doubt that the Due Process Clause is applicable in juvenile proceedings. * * * We have held that certain basic constitutional protections enjoyed by adults accused of crimes also apply to juveniles. But the Constitution does not mandate elimination of all differences in the treatment of juveniles. The State has "a *parens patriae* interest in preserving and promoting the welfare of the child," which makes a juvenile proceeding fundamentally different from an adult criminal trial. We have tried, therefore, to strike a balance to respect the "informality" and "flexibility" that characterize juvenile proceedings, and yet to ensure that such proceedings comport with the "fundamental fairness" demanded by the Due Process Clause.

The statutory provision at issue in this case, § 320.5(3)(b), permits a brief pretrial detention based on a finding of a "serious risk" that an arrested juvenile may commit a crime before his return date. The question before us is whether preventive detention of juveniles pursuant to

12. The district court gave three reasons for this conclusion. First, under the FCA, a juvenile may be held in pretrial detention for up to five days without any judicial determination of probable cause. Relying on *Gerstein v. Pugh*, the district court concluded that pretrial detention without a prior adjudication of probable cause is, itself, a *per se* violation of due process. Second, after a review of the pertinent scholarly literature, the court noted that "no diagnostic tools have as yet been devised which enable even the most highly trained criminologists to predict reliably which juveniles will engage in violent crime." A fortiori, the court concluded, a Family Court judge cannot make a reliable prediction based on the limited information available to him at the initial appearance. Moreover, the court felt that the trial record was "replete" with examples of arbitrary and capricious detentions. Finally, the court concluded that preventive detention is merely a euphemism for punishment imposed without an adjudication of guilt. The alleged purpose of the detention—to protect society from the juvenile's criminal conduct—is indistinguishable from the purpose of post-trial detention. And given "the inability of trial judges to predict which juveniles will commit crimes," there is no rational connection between the decision to detain and the alleged purpose, even if that purpose were legitimate.

§ 320.5(3)(b) is compatible with the "fundamental fairness" required by due process. Two separate inquiries are necessary to answer this question. First, does preventive detention under the New York statute serve a legitimate state objective? And, second, are the procedural safeguards contained in the Family Court Act adequate to authorize the pretrial detention of at least some juveniles charged with crimes?

Preventive detention under the Family Court Act is purportedly designed to protect the child and society from the potential consequences of his criminal acts. When making any detention decision, the Family Court judge is specifically directed to consider the needs and best interests of the juvenile as well as the need for the protection of the community. In *Bell v. Wolfish*, we left open the question whether any governmental objective other than ensuring a detainee's presence at trial may constitutionally justify pretrial detention. As an initial matter, therefore, we must decide whether, in the context of the juvenile system, the combined interest in protecting both the community and the juvenile himself from the consequences of future criminal conduct is sufficient to justify such detention.

The "legitimate and compelling state interest" in protecting the community from crime cannot be doubted. We have stressed before that crime prevention is "a weighty social objective," and this interest persists undiluted in the juvenile context. The harm suffered by the victim of a crime is not dependent upon the age of the perpetrator.[14] And the harm to society generally may even be greater in this context given the high rate of recidivism among juveniles.

The juvenile's countervailing interest in freedom from institutional restraints, even for the brief time involved here, is undoubtedly substantial as well. But that interest must be qualified by the recognition that juveniles, unlike adults, are always in some form of custody. Children, by definition, are not assumed to have the capacity to take care of themselves. They are assumed to be subject to the control of their parents, and if parental control falters, the State must play its part as *parens patriae*. In this respect, the juvenile's liberty interest may, in appropriate circumstances, be subordinated to the State's "*parens patriae* interest in preserving and promoting the welfare of the child."

The New York Court of Appeals, in upholding the statute at issue here, stressed at some length "the desirability of protecting the juvenile from his own folly." *People ex rel. Wayburn v. Schupf* (1976).[15] Society has

---

14. In 1982, juveniles under 16 accounted for 7.5 percent of all arrests for violent crimes, 19.9 percent of all arrests for serious property crime, and 17.3 percent of all arrests for violent and serious property crimes combined. 1982 Crime in the United States 176–177 (United States Dept. of Justice) ("violent crimes" include murder, non-negligent manslaughter, forcible rape, robbery and aggravated assault; "serious property crimes" include burglary, larceny-theft, motor vehicle theft and arson).

15. "Our society recognizes that juveniles in general are in the earlier stages of their emotional growth, that their intellectual development is incomplete, that they have had only limited practical experience, and that their value systems have not yet been clearly identified or firmly adopted * * *."

a legitimate interest in protecting a juvenile from the consequences of his criminal activity—both from potential physical injury which may be suffered when a victim fights back or a policeman attempts to make an arrest and from the downward spiral of criminal activity into which peer pressure may lead the child.

The substantiality and legitimacy of the state interests underlying this statute are confirmed by the wide-spread use and judicial acceptance of preventive detention for juveniles. Every State, as well as the United States in the District of Columbia, permits preventive detention of juveniles accused of crime. A number of model juvenile justice acts also contain provisions permitting preventive detention. And the courts of eight States, including the New York Court of Appeals, have upheld their statutes with specific reference to protecting the juvenile and the community from harmful pretrial conduct, including pretrial crime. * * *

In light of the uniform legislative judgment that pretrial detention of juveniles properly promotes the interests both of society and the juvenile, we conclude that the practice serves a legitimate regulatory purpose compatible with the "fundamental fairness" demanded by the Due Process Clause in juvenile proceedings.[18]

Of course, the mere invocation of a legitimate purpose will not justify particular restrictions and conditions of confinement amounting to punishment. It is axiomatic that "[d]ue process requires that a pretrial detainee not be punished." Even given, therefore, that pretrial detention may serve legitimate regulatory purposes, it is still necessary to determine whether the terms and conditions of confinement under § 320.5(3)(b) are in fact compatible with those purposes. "A court must decide whether the disability is imposed for the purpose of punishment or whether it is but an incident of some other legitimate governmental purpose." Absent a showing of an express intent to punish on the part of the State, that determination generally will turn on "whether an alternative purpose to which [the

"For the same reasons that our society does not hold juveniles to an adult standard of responsibility for their conduct, our society may also conclude that there is a greater likelihood that a juvenile charged with delinquency, if released, will commit another criminal act than that an adult charged with crime will do so. To the extent that self-restraint may be expected to constrain adults, it may not be expected to operate with equal force as to juveniles. Because of the possibility of juvenile delinquency treatment and the absence of second-offender sentencing, there will not be the deterrent for the juvenile which confronts the adult. Perhaps more significant is the fact that in consequence of lack of experience and comprehension the juvenile does not view the commission of what are criminal acts in the same perspective as an adult * * *. There is the element of gamesmanship and the excitement of 'getting away' with something and the powerful inducement of peer pressures. All of these commonly acknowledged factors make the commission of criminal conduct on the part of juveniles in general more likely than in the case of adults." *People ex rel. Wayburn v. Schupf.*

18. Appellees argue that some limit must be placed on the categories of crimes that detained juveniles must be accused of having committed or being likely to commit. But the discretion to delimit the categories of crimes justifying detention, like the discretion to define criminal offenses and prescribe punishments, resides wholly with the state legislatures.

More fundamentally, this sort of attack on a criminal statute must be made on a case-by-case basis. The court will not sift through the entire class to determine whether the statute was constitutionally applied in each case. And, outside the limited First Amendment context, a criminal statute may not be attacked as overbroad.

restriction] may rationally be connected is assignable for it, and whether it appears excessive in relation to the alternative purpose assigned [to it.]'' There is no indication in the statute itself that preventive detention is used or intended as a punishment. First of all, the detention is strictly limited in time. If a juvenile is detained at his initial appearance and has denied the charges against him, he is entitled to a probable cause hearing to be held not more than three days after the conclusion of the initial appearance or four days after the filing of the petition, whichever is sooner. If the Family Court judge finds probable cause, he must also determine whether continued detention is necessary. * * *

Detained juveniles are also entitled to an expedited fact-finding hearing. If the juvenile is charged with one of a limited number of designated felonies, the fact-finding hearing must be scheduled to commence not more than fourteen days after the conclusion of the initial appearance. If the juvenile is charged with a lesser offense, then the fact-finding hearing must be held not more than three days after the initial appearance. In the latter case, since the time for the probable cause hearing and the fact-finding hearing coincide, the two hearings are merged.

Thus, the maximum possible detention under § 320.5(3)(b) of a youth accused of a serious crime, assuming a three-day extension of the fact-finding hearing for good cause shown, is seventeen days. The maximum detention for less serious crimes, again assuming a three-day extension for good cause shown, is six days. These time-frames seem suited to the limited purpose of providing the youth with a controlled environment and separating him from improper influences pending the speedy disposition of his case.

The conditions of confinement also appear to reflect the regulatory purposes relied upon by the State. When a juvenile is remanded after his initial appearance, he cannot, absent exceptional circumstances, be sent to a prison or lockup where he would be exposed to adult criminals. Instead, the child is screened by an ''assessment unit'' of the Department of Juvenile Justice. The assessment unit places the child in either nonsecure or secure detention. Nonsecure detention involves an open facility in the community, a sort of ''halfway house,'' without locks, bars or security officers where the child receives schooling and counseling and has access to recreational facilities. Secure detention is more restrictive, but it is still consistent with the regulatory and *parens patriae* objectives relied upon by the State. Children are assigned to separate dorms based on age, size and behavior. They wear street clothes provided by the institution and partake in educational and recreational programs and counseling sessions run by trained social workers. Misbehavior is punished by confinement to one's room. We cannot conclude from this record that the controlled environment briefly imposed by the State on juveniles in secure pretrial detention ''is imposed for the purpose of punishment'' rather than as ''an incident of some other legitimate government purpose.''

The Court of Appeals, of course, did conclude that the underlying purpose of § 320.5(3)(b) is punitive rather than regulatory. But the court did not dispute that preventive detention might serve legitimate regulatory purposes or that the terms and conditions of pretrial confinement in New York are compatible with those purposes. Rather, the court invalidated a significant aspect of New York's juvenile justice system based solely on some case histories and a statistical study which appeared to show that "the vast majority of juveniles detained under [§ 320.5(3)(b)] either have their petitions dismissed before an adjudication or are released after adjudication." The court assumed that dismissal of a petition or failure to confine a juvenile at the dispositional hearing belied the need to detain him prior to fact finding and that, therefore, the pretrial detention constituted punishment. Since punishment imposed without a prior adjudication of guilt is *per se* illegitimate, the Court of Appeals concluded that no juveniles could be held pursuant to § 320.5(3)(b).

There are some obvious flaws in the statistics and case histories relied upon by the lower court. But even assuming it to be the case that "by far the greater number of juveniles incarcerated under [§ 320.5(3)(b)] will never be confined as a consequence of a disposition imposed after an adjudication of delinquency," we find that to be an insufficient ground for upsetting the widely-shared legislative judgment that preventive detention serves an important and legitimate function in the juvenile justice system. We are unpersuaded by the Court of Appeals' rather cavalier equation of detentions that do not lead to continued confinement after an adjudication of guilt and "wrongful" or "punitive" pretrial detentions.

Pretrial detention need not be considered punitive merely because a juvenile is subsequently discharged subject to conditions or put on probation. In fact, such actions reinforce the original finding that close supervision of the juvenile is required. Lenient but supervised disposition is in keeping with the Act's purpose to promote the welfare and development of the child. * * *

Even when a case is terminated prior to fact finding, it does not follow that the decision to detain the juvenile pursuant to § 320.5(3)(b) amounted to a due process violation. A delinquency petition may be dismissed for any number of reasons collateral to its merits, such as the failure of a witness to testify. * * * Consequently, the final disposition of a case is "largely irrelevant" to the legality of a pretrial detention.

It may be, of course, that in some circumstances detention of a juvenile would not pass constitutional muster. But the validity of those detentions must be determined on a case-by-case basis. Section 320.5(3)(b) is not invalid "on its face" by reason of the ambiguous statistics and case histories relied upon by the court below. We find no justification for the conclusion that, contrary to the express language of the statute and the judgment of the highest state court, § 320.5(3)(b) is a punitive rather than a regulatory measure. Preventive detention under the Family Court Act serves the legitimate state objective, held in common with every State in the country, of protecting both the juvenile and society from the hazards of pretrial crime.

Given the legitimacy of the State's interest in preventive detention, and the nonpunitive nature of that detention, the remaining question is whether the procedures afforded juveniles detained prior to fact finding provide sufficient protection against erroneous and unnecessary deprivations of liberty. *See Mathews v. Eldridge* (1976). In *Gerstein v. Pugh* (1975), we held that a judicial determination of probable cause is a prerequisite to any extended restraint on the liberty of an adult accused of crime. We did not, however, mandate a specific time-table. Nor did we require the "full panoply of adversary safeguards—counsel, confrontation, cross-examination, and compulsory process of witnesses." Instead, we recognized "the desirability of flexibility and experimentation by the States." *Gerstein* arose under the Fourth Amendment, but the same concern with "flexibility" and "informality," while yet ensuring adequate predetention procedures, is present in this context.

In many respects, the Family Court Act provides far more predetention protection for juveniles than we found to be constitutionally required for a probable cause determination for adults in *Gerstein*. The initial appearance is informal, but the accused juvenile is given full notice of the charges against him and a complete stenographic record is kept of the hearing. The juvenile appears accompanied by his parent or guardian. He is first informed of his rights, including the right to remain silent and the right to be represented by counsel chosen by him or by a law guardian assigned by the court. The initial appearance may be adjourned for no longer than 72 hours or until the next court day, whichever is sooner, to enable an appointed law guardian or other counsel to appear before the court. When his counsel is present, the juvenile is informed of the charges against him and furnished with a copy of the delinquency petition. A representative from the presentment agency appears in support of the petition.

The nonhearsay allegations in the delinquency petition and supporting depositions must establish probable cause to believe the juvenile committed the offense. Although the Family Court judge is not required to make a finding of probable cause at the initial appearance, the youth may challenge the sufficiency of the petition on that ground. Thus, the juvenile may oppose any recommended detention by arguing that there is not probable cause to believe he committed the offense or offenses with which he is charged. If the petition is not dismissed, the juvenile is given an opportunity to admit or deny the charges.

At the conclusion of the initial appearance, the presentment agency makes a recommendation regarding detention. A probation officer reports on the juvenile's record, including other prior and current Family Court and probation contacts, as well as relevant information concerning home life, school attendance, and any special medical or developmental problems. He concludes by offering his agency's recommendation on detention.

Opposing counsel, the juvenile's parents, and the juvenile himself may all speak on his behalf and challenge any information or recommendation. If the judge does decide to detain the juvenile, he must state on the record the facts and reasons for the detention.

As noted, a detained juvenile is entitled to a formal, adversarial probable cause hearing within three days of his initial appearance, with one three-day extension possible for good cause shown.[28] The burden at this hearing is on the presentment agency to call witnesses and offer evidence in support of the charges. Testimony is under oath and subject to cross-examination. The accused juvenile may call witnesses and offer evidence in his own behalf. If the court finds probable cause, the court must again decide whether continued detention is necessary under § 320.5(3)(b). Again, the facts and reasons for the detention must be stated on the record.

In sum, notice, a hearing, and a statement of facts and reasons are given prior to any detention under § 320.5(3)(b). A formal probable cause hearing is then held within a short while thereafter, if the fact-finding hearing is not itself scheduled within three days. These flexible procedures have been found constitutionally adequate under the Fourth Amendment, and under the Due Process Clause. Appellees have failed to note any additional procedures that would significantly improve the accuracy of the determination without unduly impinging on the achievement of legitimate state purposes.

Appellees argue, however, that the risk of erroneous and unnecessary detentions is too high despite these procedures because the standard for detention is fatally vague. Detention under § 320.5(3)(b) is based on a finding that there is a "serious risk" that the juvenile, if released, would commit a crime prior to his next court appearance. We have already seen that detention of juveniles on that ground serves legitimate regulatory purposes. But appellees claim, and the district court agreed, that it is virtually impossible to predict future criminal conduct with any degree of accuracy. Moreover, they say, the statutory standard fails to channel the discretion of the Family Court judge by specifying the factors on which he should rely in making that prediction. The procedural protections noted above are thus, in their view, unavailing because the ultimate decision is intrinsically arbitrary and uncontrolled.

Our cases indicate, however, that from a legal point of view there is nothing inherently unattainable about a prediction of future criminal conduct. Such a judgment forms an important element in many decisions,[30] and we have specifically rejected the contention, based on the

---

28. The Court in *Gerstein* indicated approval of pretrial detention procedures that supplied a probable cause hearing within five days of the initial detention. The brief delay in the probable cause hearing may actually work to the advantage of the juvenile since it gives his counsel, usually appointed at the initial appearance, time to prepare.

30. See *Jurek v. Texas* (death sentence imposed by jury); *Greenholtz v. Nebraska Penal Inmates* (grant of parole); *Morrissey v. Brewer* (parole revocation). A prediction of future criminal conduct may also form the basis for an increased sentence under the "dangerous special offender"

same sort of sociological data relied upon by appellees and the district court, "that it is impossible to predict future behavior and that the question is so vague as to be meaningless."

We have also recognized that a prediction of future criminal conduct is "an experienced prediction based on a host of variables" which cannot be readily codified. Judge Quinones of the Family Court testified at trial that he and his colleagues make a determination under § 320.5(3)(b) based on numerous factors including the nature and seriousness of the charges; whether the charges are likely to be proved at trial; the juvenile's prior record; the adequacy and effectiveness of his home supervision; his school situation, if known; the time of day of the alleged crime as evidence of its seriousness and a possible lack of parental control; and any special circumstances that might be brought to his attention by the probation officer, the child's attorney, or any parents, relatives or other responsible persons accompanying the child. The decision is based on as much information as can reasonably be obtained at the initial appearance.

Given the right to a hearing, to counsel and to a statement of reasons, there is no reason that the specific factors upon which the Family Court judge might rely must be specified in the statute. * * *

The dissent would apparently have us strike down New York's preventive detention statute on two grounds: first, because the preventive detention of juveniles constitutes poor public policy, with the balance of harms outweighing any positive benefits either to society or to the juveniles themselves and, second, because the statute could have been better drafted to improve the quality of the decision-making process. But it is worth recalling that we are neither a legislature charged with formulating public policy nor an ABA committee charged with drafting a model statute. The question before us today is solely whether the preventive detention system chosen by the State of New York and applied by the New York Family Court comports with constitutional standards. Given the regulatory purpose for the detention and the procedural protections that precede its imposition, we conclude that § 320.5(3)(b) of the New York Family Court Act is not invalid under the Due Process Clause of the Fourteenth Amendment. The judgment of the Court of Appeals is

Reversed.

JUSTICE MARSHALL, with whom JUSTICE BRENNAN and JUSTICE STEVENS join, DISSENTING.

The New York Family Court Act * * * contains two provisions that authorize the detention of juveniles arrested for offenses covered by the Act for up to 17 days pending adjudication of their guilt. * * * Section 320.5(3)(b), the provision at issue in these cases, authorizes detention if

---

statute, 18 U.S.C. § 3575 (1976 & Supp. V 1981). Under § 3575(f), a "dangerous" offender is defined as an individual for whom "a period of confinement longer than that provided for such [underlying] felony is required for the protection of the public from further criminal conduct by the defendant." The statute has been challenged numerous times on the grounds that the standard is unconstitutionally vague. Every Court of Appeals considering the question has rejected that claim.

the judge finds "there is a serious risk [the juvenile] may before the return date commit an act which if committed by an adult would constitute a crime."

There are few limitations on § 320.5(3)(b). Detention need not be predicated on a finding that there is probable cause to believe the child committed the offense for which he was arrested. The provision applies to all juveniles, regardless of their prior records or the severity of the offenses of which they are accused. The provision is not limited to the prevention of dangerous crimes; a prediction that a juvenile if released may commit a minor misdemeanor is sufficient to justify his detention. Aside from the reference to "serious risk," the requisite likelihood that the juvenile will misbehave before his trial is not specified by the statute.

The Court today holds that preventive detention of a juvenile pursuant to § 320.5(3)(b) does not violate the Due Process Clause. Two rulings are essential to the Court's decision: that the provision promotes legitimate government objectives important enough to justify the abridgment of the detained juveniles' liberty interests; and that the provision incorporates procedural safeguards sufficient to prevent unnecessary or arbitrary impairment of constitutionally protected rights. Because I disagree with both of those rulings, I dissent. * * *

The first step in the process that leads to detention under § 320.5(3)(b) is known as "probation intake." A juvenile may arrive at intake by one of three routes: he may be brought there directly by an arresting officer; he may be detained for a brief period after his arrest and then taken to intake; he may be released upon arrest and directed to appear at a designated time. The heart of the intake procedure is a 10–to–40–minute interview of the juvenile, the arresting officer, and sometimes the juvenile's parent or guardian. The objectives of the probation officer conducting the interview are to determine the nature of the offense the child may have committed and to obtain some background information on him.

On the basis of the information derived from the interview and from an examination of the juvenile's record, the probation officer decides whether the case should be disposed of informally ("adjusted") or whether it should be referred to the Family Court. If the latter, the officer makes an additional recommendation regarding whether the juvenile should be detained. "There do not appear to be any governing criteria which must be followed by the probation officer in choosing between proposing detention and parole * * *."

The actual decision whether to detain a juvenile under § 320.5(3)(b) is made by a Family Court judge at what is called an "initial appearance"—a brief hearing resembling an arraignment. The information on which the judge makes his determination is very limited. He has before him a "petition for delinquency" prepared by a state agency, charging the juvenile with an offense, accompanied with one or more affidavits attesting to the juvenile's involvement. Ordinarily the judge has in addition the written report and recommendation of the probation officer. However, the probation officer who prepared the report rarely attends the hearing. Nor is the complainant likely to appear. Consequently, "[o]ften there is no one present with personal knowledge of what happened."

In the typical case, the judge appoints counsel for the juvenile at the time his case is called. Thus, the lawyer has no opportunity to make an independent inquiry into the juvenile's background or character, and has only a few minutes to prepare arguments on the child's behalf. The judge ordinarily does not interview the juvenile, makes no inquiry into the truth of allegations in the petition, and does not determine whether there is probable cause to believe the juvenile committed the offense.[6] The typical hearing lasts between 5 and 15 minutes, and the judge renders his decision immediately afterward.

Neither the statute nor any other body of rules guides the efforts of the judge to determine whether a given juvenile is likely to commit a crime before his trial. In making detention decisions, "each judge must rely on his own subjective judgment, based on the limited information available to him at court intake and whatever personal standards he himself has developed in exercising his discretionary authority under the statute." Family Court judges are not provided information regarding the behavior of juveniles over whose cases they have presided, so a judge has no way of refining the standards he employs in making detention decisions.

After examining a study of a sample of 34 cases in which juveniles were detained under § 320.5(3)(b) along with various statistical studies of pretrial detention of juveniles in New York, the District Court made findings regarding the circumstances in which the provision habitually is invoked. Three of those findings are especially germane to appellees' challenge to the statute. First, a substantial number of "first offenders" are detained pursuant to § 320.5(3)(b). For example, at least 5 of the 34 juveniles in the sample had no prior contact with the Family Court before being detained and at least 16 had no prior adjudications of delinquency. Second, many juveniles are released—for periods ranging from 5 days to several weeks—after their arrests and are then detained under § 320.5(3)(b), despite the absence of any evidence of misconduct during the time between their arrests and "initial appearances." Sixteen of the 34 cases in the sample fit this pattern. Third, "the overwhelming majori-

6. The majority admits that "the Family Court judge is not required to make a finding of probable cause at the initial appearance," but contends that the juvenile has the option to challenge the sufficiency of the petition for delinquency on the ground that it fails to establish probable cause. None of the courts that have considered the constitutionality of New York's preventive-detention system has suggested that a juvenile has a statutory right to a probable-cause determination before he is detained. The provisions cited by the majority for its novel reading of the statute provide only shaky support for its contention * * *. That counsel for a juvenile ordinarily is not even appointed until a few minutes prior to the initial appearance, confirms this interpretation. The lesson of this foray into the tangled provisions of the New York Family Court Act is that the majority ought to adhere to our usual policy of relying whenever possible for interpretation of a state statute upon courts better acquainted with its terms and applications.

ty" of the juveniles detained * * * are released either before or immediately after their trials, either unconditionally or on parole. At least 23 of the juveniles in the sample fell into this category.

Finally, the District Court made a few significant findings concerning the conditions associated with "secure detention" pursuant to § 320.5(3)(b). In a "secure facility," "[t]he juveniles are subjected to strip-searches, wear institutional clothing and follow institutional regimen. At Spofford [Juvenile Detention Center], which is a secure facility, some juveniles who have had dispositional determinations and were awaiting placement (long term care) commingle with those in pretrial detention (short term care)." * * *

To comport with "fundamental fairness," § 320.5(3)(b) must satisfy two requirements. First, it must advance goals commensurate with the burdens it imposes on constitutionally protected interests. Second, it must not punish the juveniles to whom it applies.

The majority only grudgingly and incompletely acknowledges the applicability of the first of these tests, but its grip on the cases before us is undeniable. It is manifest that § 320.5(3)(b) impinges upon fundamental rights. If the "liberty" protected by the Due Process Clause means anything, it means freedom from physical restraint. Only a very important government interest can justify deprivation of liberty in this basic sense.

The majority seeks to evade the force of this principle by discounting the impact on a child of incarceration pursuant to § 320.5(3)(b). The curtailment of liberty consequent upon detention of a juvenile, the majority contends, is mitigated by the fact that "juveniles, unlike adults, are always in some form of custody." In any event, the majority argues, the conditions of confinement associated with "secure detention" * * * are not unduly burdensome. These contentions enable the majority to suggest that § 320.5(3)(b) need only advance a "legitimate state objective" to satisfy the strictures of the Due Process Clause.

The majority's arguments do not survive scrutiny. Its characterization of preventive detention as merely a transfer of custody from a parent or guardian to the State is difficult to take seriously. Surely there is a qualitative difference between imprisonment and the condition of being subject to the supervision and control of an adult who has one's best interests at heart. And the majority's depiction of the nature of confinement under § 320.5(3)(b) is insupportable on this record. As noted above, the District Court found that secure detention entails incarceration in a facility closely resembling a jail and that pretrial detainees are sometimes mixed with juveniles who have been found to be delinquent. Evidence adduced at trial reinforces these findings. For example, Judge Quinones, a Family Court judge with 8 years of experience, described the conditions of detention as follows:

"Then again, Juvenile Center, as much as we might try, is not the most pleasant place in the world. If you put them in detention, you are liable to be exposing these youngsters to all sorts of things. They are liable to be exposed to assault, they are liable to be exposed to sexual assaults. You are taking the risk of putting them together with a youngster that might be much worse than they, possibly might be, and it might have a bad effect in that respect.''

Many other observers of the circumstances of juvenile detention in New York have come to similar conclusions.[13]

In short, fairly viewed, pretrial detention of a juvenile pursuant to § 320.5(3)(b) gives rise to injuries comparable to those associated with imprisonment of an adult. In both situations, the detainee suffers stigmatization and severe limitation of his freedom of movement. Indeed, the impressionability of juveniles may make the experience of incarceration more injurious to them than to adults; all too quickly juveniles subjected to preventive detention come to see society at large as hostile and oppressive and to regard themselves as irremediably "delinquent." Such serious injuries to presumptively innocent persons—encompassing the curtailment of their constitutional rights to liberty—can be justified only by a weighty public interest that is substantially advanced by the statute.
* * *

Appellants and the majority contend that § 320.5(3)(b) advances a pair of intertwined government objectives: "protecting the community from crime," and "protecting a juvenile from the consequences of his criminal activity." More specifically, the majority argues that detaining a juvenile for a period of up to 17 days prior to his trial has two desirable effects: it protects society at large from the crimes he might have committed during that period if released; and it protects the juvenile himself "both from potential physical injury which may be suffered when a victim fights back or a policeman attempts to make an arrest and from the downward spiral of criminal activity into which peer pressure may lead the child.''

Appellees and some *amici* argue that public purposes of this sort can never justify incarceration of a person who has not been adjudicated guilty of a crime, at least in the absence of a determination that there exists probable cause to believe he committed a criminal offense. We need not reach that categorical argument in these cases because, even if the purposes identified by the majority are conceded to be compelling, they are not sufficiently promoted by detention pursuant to § 320.5(3)(b) to justify the concomitant impairment of the juveniles' liberty interests. To state the case more precisely, two circumstances in combination render § 320.5(3)(b) invalid in toto: in the large majority of cases in which the provision is invoked, its asserted objectives are either not advanced at all or are only minimally promoted; and, as the provision is written and

13. All of the 34 juveniles in the sample were detained in Spofford Juvenile Center, the detention facility for New York City. Numerous studies of that facility have attested to its unsavory characteristics. Conditions in Spofford have been successfully challenged on constitutional grounds (by a group of inmates of a different type), see *Martarella v. Kelley* [Ed. *see infra* Note 446, p. 2], but nevertheless remain grim. Not surprisingly, a former New York City Deputy Mayor for Criminal Justice, has averred that "Spofford is, in many ways, indistinguishable from a prison.''

administered by the state courts, the cases in which its asserted ends are significantly advanced cannot practicably be distinguished from the cases in which they are not.

Both of the courts below concluded that only occasionally and accidentally does pretrial detention of a juvenile under § 320.5(3)(b) prevent the commission of a crime. Three subsidiary findings undergird that conclusion. First, Family Court judges are incapable of determining which of the juveniles who appear before them would commit offenses before their trials if left at large and which would not. In part, this incapacity derives from the limitations of current knowledge concerning the dynamics of human behavior. On the basis of evidence adduced at trial, supplemented by a thorough review of the secondary literature, the District Court found that "no diagnostic tools have as yet been devised which enable even the most highly trained criminologists to predict reliably which juveniles will engage in violent crime." The evidence supportive of this finding is overwhelming. An independent impediment to identification of the defendants who would misbehave if released is the paucity of data available at an initial appearance. The judge must make his decision whether to detain a juvenile on the basis of a set of allegations regarding the child's alleged offense, a cursory review of his background and criminal record, and the recommendation of a probation officer who, in the typical case, has seen the child only once. In view of this scarcity of relevant information, the District Court credited the testimony of appellees' expert witness, who "stated that he would be surprised if recommendations based on intake interviews were better than chance and assessed the judge's subjective prognosis about the probability of future crime as only 4% better than chance—virtually wholly unpredictable."[20]

Second, § 320.5(3)(b) is not limited to classes of juveniles whose past conduct suggests that they are substantially more likely than average juveniles to misbehave in the immediate future. The provision authorizes the detention of persons arrested for trivial offenses and persons without any prior contacts with juvenile court. Even a finding that there is probable cause to believe a juvenile committed the offense with which he was charged is not a prerequisite to his detention.

Third, the courts below concluded that circumstances surrounding most of the cases in which § 320.5(3)(b) has been invoked strongly suggest that the detainee would not have committed a crime during the period before his trial if he had been released. In a significant proportion of the

20. The majority brushes aside the District Court's findings on this issue with the remark that "a prediction of future criminal conduct * * * forms an important element in many decisions, and we have specifically rejected the contention * * * 'that it is impossible to predict future behavior and that the question is so vague as to be meaningless.' " Whatever the merits of the decisions upon which the majority relies, they do not control the problem before us. In each of the cases in which the Court has countenanced reliance upon a prediction of future conduct in a decision-making process impinging upon life or liberty, the affected person had already been convicted of a crime. *See Greenholtz v. Nebraska Penal Inmates* (grant of parole); *Jurek v. Texas* (death sentence); *Morrissey v. Brewer* (parole revocation). The constitutional limitations upon the kinds of factors that may be relied on in making such decisions are significantly looser than those upon decisionmaking processes that abridge the liberty of presumptively innocent persons. * * *

cases, the juvenile had been released after his arrest and had not committed any reported crimes while at large; it is not apparent why a juvenile would be more likely to misbehave between his initial appearance and his trial than between his arrest and initial appearance. Even more telling is the fact that "the vast majority" of persons detained under § 320.5(3)(b) are released either before or immediately after their trials. The inference is powerful that most detainees, when examined more carefully than at their initial appearances, are deemed insufficiently dangerous to warrant further incarceration. * * *

Most juveniles detained pursuant to the provision are not benefitted thereby, because they would not have committed crimes if left to their own devices (and thus would not have been exposed to the risk of physical injury or the perils of the cycle of recidivism). On the contrary, these juveniles suffer several serious harms: deprivation of liberty and stigmatization as "delinquent" or "dangerous," as well as impairment of their ability to prepare their legal defenses. * * *

Certainly the public reaps no benefit from incarceration of the majority of the detainees who would not have committed any crimes had they been released. Prevention of the minor offenses that would have been committed by a small proportion of the persons detained confers only a slight benefit on the community. Only in occasional cases does incarceration of a juvenile pending his trial serve to prevent a crime of violence and thereby significantly promote the public interest. Such an infrequent and haphazard gain is insufficient to justify curtailment of the liberty interests of all the presumptively innocent juveniles who would have obeyed the law pending their trials had they been given the chance.

The majority seeks to deflect appellees' attack on the constitutionality of § 320.5(3)(b) by contending that they have framed their argument too broadly. It is possible, the majority acknowledges, that "in some circumstances detention of a juvenile * * * would not pass constitutional muster. But the validity of those detentions must be determined on a case-by-case basis." The majority thus implies that, even if the Due Process Clause is violated by most detentions under § 320.5(3)(b) because those detainees would not have committed crimes if released, the statute nevertheless is not invalid "on its face" because detention of those persons who would have committed a serious crime comports with the Constitution. Separation of the properly detained juveniles from the improperly detained juveniles must be achieved through "case-by-case" adjudication.

There are some obvious practical impediments to adoption of the majority's proposal. Because a juvenile may not be incarcerated under § 320.5(3)(b) for more than 17 days, it would be impracticable for a particular detainee to secure his freedom by challenging the constitutional basis of his detention; by the time the suit could be considered, it would have been rendered moot by the juvenile's release or long-term detention pursuant to a delinquency adjudication. Nor could an individual detainee avoid the problem of mootness by filing a suit for damages or for

injunctive relief. This Court's declaration that § 320.5(3)(b) is not unconstitutional on its face would almost certainly preclude a finding that
detention of a juvenile pursuant to the statute violated any clearly
established constitutional rights. * * * And, under current doctrine pertaining to the standing of an individual victim of allegedly unconstitutional conduct to obtain an injunction against repetition of that behavior, it is
far from clear that an individual detainee would be able to obtain an
equitable remedy.

But even if these practical difficulties could be surmounted, the
majority's proposal would be inadequate. Precisely because of the unreliability of any determination whether a particular juvenile is likely to
commit a crime between his arrest and trial, no individual detainee would
be able to demonstrate that he would have abided by the law had he been
released. In other words, no configuration of circumstances would enable a
juvenile to establish that he fell into the category of persons unconstitutionally detained rather than the category constitutionally detained. Thus,
to protect the rights of the majority of juveniles whose incarceration
advances no legitimate state interest, § 320.5(3)(b) must be held unconstitutional "on its face."

The findings reviewed in the preceding section lend credence to the
conclusion reached by the courts below: § 320.5(3)(b) "is utilized principally, not for preventive purposes, but to impose punishment for unadjudicated criminal acts."

The majority contends that, of the many factors we have considered
in trying to determine whether a particular sanction constitutes "punishment," the most useful are "whether an alternative purpose to which [the
sanction] may rationally be connected is assignable for it, and whether it
appears excessive in relation to the alternative purpose assigned." * * *
The alternative purpose assigned by the State to § 320.5(3)(b) is the
prevention of crime by the detained juveniles. But, as has been shown,
that objective is advanced at best sporadically by the provision. Moreover,
§ 320.5(3)(b) frequently is invoked under circumstances in which it is
extremely unlikely that the juvenile in question would commit a crime
while awaiting trial. The most striking of these cases involve juveniles
who have been at large without mishap for a substantial period of time
prior to their initial appearances, and detainees who are adjudged delinquent and are nevertheless released into the community. In short,
§ 320.5(3)(b) as administered by the New York courts surely "appears
excessive in relation to" the putatively legitimate objectives assigned to it.

The inference that § 320.5(3)(b) is punitive in nature is supported by
additional materials in the record. For example, Judge Quinones and even
appellants' counsel acknowledged that one of the reasons juveniles detained pursuant to § 320.5(3)(b) usually are released after the determination of their guilt is that the judge decides that their pretrial detention
constitutes sufficient punishment. Another Family Court Judge admitted
using "preventive detention" to punish one of the juveniles in the sample.

In summary, application of the litmus test the Court recently has used to identify punitive sanctions supports the finding of the lower courts that preventive detention under § 320.5(3)(b) constitutes punishment. Because punishment of juveniles before adjudication of their guilt violates the Due Process Clause, the provision cannot stand.

If the record did not establish the impossibility, on the basis of the evidence available to a Family Court judge at a § 320.5(3)(b) hearing, of reliably predicting whether a given juvenile would commit a crime before his trial, and if the purposes relied upon by the State were promoted sufficiently to justify the deprivations of liberty effected by the provision, I would nevertheless still strike down § 320.5(3)(b) because of the absence of procedural safeguards in the provision. As Judge Newman, concurring in the Court of Appeals observed, "New York's statute is unconstitutional because it permits liberty to be denied, prior to adjudication of guilt, in the exercise of unfettered discretion as to an issue of considerable uncertainty—likelihood of future criminal behavior."

Appellees point out that § 320.5(3)(b) lacks two crucial procedural constraints. First, a New York Family Court judge is given no guidance regarding what kinds of evidence he should consider or what weight he should accord different sorts of material in deciding whether to detain a juvenile. For example, there is no requirement in the statute that the judge take into account the juvenile's background or current living situation. Nor is a judge obliged to attach significance to the nature of a juvenile's criminal record or the severity of the crime for which he was arrested. Second, § 320.5(3)(b) does not specify how likely it must be that a juvenile will commit a crime before his trial to warrant his detention. The provision indicates only that there must be a "serious risk" that he will commit an offense and does not prescribe the standard of proof that should govern the judge's determination of that issue.

Not surprisingly, in view of the lack of directions provided by the statute, different judges have adopted different ways of estimating the chances whether a juvenile will misbehave in the near future. "Each judge follows his own individual approach to [the detention] determination." This discretion exercised by Family Court judges in making detention decisions gives rise to two related constitutional problems. First, it creates an excessive risk that juveniles will be detained "erroneously"—*i.e.*, under circumstances in which no public interest would be served by their incarceration. Second, it fosters arbitrariness and inequality in a decision-making process that impinges upon fundamental rights.

One of the purposes of imposing procedural constraints on decisions affecting life, liberty, or property is to reduce the incidence of error. In *Mathews v. Eldridge*, the Court identified a complex of considerations that has proven helpful in determining what protections are constitutionally required in particular contexts to achieve that end:

> "[I]dentification of the specific dictates of due process generally requires consideration of three distinct factors: First, the private

interest that will be affected by the official action; second, the risk of an erroneous deprivation of such interest through the procedures used, and the probable value, if any, of additional or substitute procedural safeguards; and finally, the Government's interest, including the function involved and the fiscal and administrative burdens that the additional or substitute procedural requirement would entail."

As Judge Newman recognized, a review of these three factors in the context of New York's preventive detention scheme compels the conclusion that the Due Process Clause is violated by § 320.5(3)(b) in its present form. First, the private interest affected by a decision to detain a juvenile is personal liberty. Unnecessary abridgment of such a fundamental right, should be avoided if at all possible.

Second, there can be no dispute that there is a serious risk under the present statute that a juvenile will be detained erroneously—*i.e.*, despite the fact that he would not commit a crime if released. * * * Opportunities for improvement in the extant regime are apparent even to a casual observer. Most obviously, some measure of guidance to Family Court judges regarding the evidence they should consider and the standard of proof they should use in making their determinations would surely contribute to the quality of their detention determinations. * * *

Third and finally, the imposition of such constraints on the deliberations of the Family Court judges would have no adverse effect on the State's interest in detaining dangerous juveniles and would give rise to insubstantial administrative burdens. For example, a simple directive to Family Court judges to state on the record the significance they give to the seriousness of the offense of which a juvenile is accused and to the nature of the juvenile's background would contribute materially to the quality of the decisionmaking process without significantly increasing the duration of initial appearances. * * *

A principle underlying many of our prior decisions in various doctrinal settings is that government officials may not be accorded unfettered discretion in making decisions that impinge upon fundamental rights. Two concerns underlie this principle: excessive discretion fosters inequality in the distribution of entitlements and harms, inequality which is especially troublesome when those benefits and burdens are great; and discretion can mask the use by officials of illegitimate criteria in allocating important goods and rights.

So, in striking down on vagueness grounds a vagrancy ordinance, we emphasized the "unfettered discretion it places in the hands of the * * * police." Such flexibility was deemed constitutionally offensive because it "permits and encourages an arbitrary and discriminatory enforcement of the law." * * *

The concerns that powered these decisions are strongly implicated by New York's preventive-detention scheme. The effect of the lack of procedural safeguards constraining detention decisions under § 320.5(3)(b) is that the liberty of a juvenile arrested even for a petty crime is dependent upon the "caprice" of a Family Court judge. The absence of meaningful guidelines creates opportunities for judges to use illegitimate criteria when deciding whether juveniles should be incarcerated pending their trials— for example, to detain children for the express purpose of punishing them. Even the judges who strive conscientiously to apply the law have little choice but to assess juveniles' dangerousness on the basis of whatever standards they deem appropriate. The resultant variation in detention decisions gives rise to a level of inequality in the deprivation of a fundamental right too great to be countenanced under the Constitution.

The majority acknowledges—indeed, founds much of its argument upon—the principle that a State has both the power and the responsibility to protect the interests of the children within its jurisdiction. Yet the majority today upholds a statute whose net impact on the juveniles who come within its purview is overwhelmingly detrimental. Most persons detained under the provision reap no benefit and suffer serious injuries thereby. The welfare of only a minority of the detainees is even arguably enhanced. The inequity of this regime, combined with the arbitrariness with which it is administered, is bound to disillusion its victims regarding the virtues of our system of criminal justice. I can see—and the majority has pointed to—no public purpose advanced by the statute sufficient to justify the harm it works.

I respectfully dissent.

NOTES

1) Punishment vs. Treatment and Pretrial Detention Conditions of Confinement Both the majority and dissent in *Schall* referred to *Bell v. Wolfish*, 441 U.S. 520, 99 S.Ct. 1861, 60 L.Ed.2d 447 (1979), where the Supreme Court examined the conditions of confinement of adult pretrial detainees, all of whom remained in custody because they could not afford bail or qualify for other non-monetary conditions of release. The only justification for pretrial detention asserted by the Government in *Wolfish* was the need to ensure the detainees' presence at trial. The *Wolfish* Court adverted to its distinction between "punitive measures that may not constitutionally be imposed prior to a determination of guilt and regulatory restraints that may." The Court reiterated the test it had announced in *Kennedy v. Mendoza–Martinez*, 372 U.S. 144, 168–69, 83 S.Ct. 554, 9 L.Ed.2d 644 (1963), to determine whether a governmental imposition constituted punishment or "whether an alternative purpose to which [the restriction] may rationally be connected is assignable for it, and whether it appears excessive in relation to the alternative purpose * * *." The *Wolfish* Court concluded that because ensuring the defendant's presence at trial was a legitimate governmental objective, the detention of offenders pending trial was regulatory rather than penal. In *Wolfish*, however, the petitioners did not challenge the constitutionality of the initial decision to detain them, and the Court specifically reserved the question whether any governmental interest besides assuring the accused's presence at trial could justify pretrial detention in order to challenge the conditions of confinement. *Schall* provides an answer to this question, at least for juveniles.

In **A.J. v. Kierst**, 56 F.3d 849, 854 (8th Cir. 1995), a 16–year–old minor, filed a § 1983 class action on behalf of himself and others similarly situated juveniles to challenge the constitutionality of certain policies, practices, and conditions at the Jackson County Juvenile Justice Center ("JCJJC") in Missouri. The district court granted summary judgment to defendants on several claims involving overcrowding and conditions of confinement, plaintiffs appealed, and the 8th Circuit Court of Appeals, affirmed in part, and reversed and remanded in part:

> [T]he Due Process Clause of the Fourteenth Amendment, and not the Cruel and Unusual Punishments Clause of the Eighth Amendment, is the appropriate measuring stick for evaluating conditions in a juvenile facility. The due process standard was applied by the district court, which, quoting with approval Judge Ferguson's concurring opinion in *Gary H. v. Hegstrom*, noted that " '[t]he "evolving standards of decency" against which courts evaluate the constitutionality of . . . conditions certainly provide greater protection for juveniles than for adults.' " We note * * * that the Supreme Court has not yet articulated the appropriate federal standard by which to judge conditions in state juvenile facilities. * * * [B]y virtue of plaintiffs' status as pretrial detainees, the more protective Fourteenth Amendment, and not the Eighth Amendment, applies.
>
> In applying the due process standard to juveniles, we cannot ignore the reality that assessments of juvenile conditions of confinement are necessarily different from those relevant to assessments of adult conditions of confinement. Juveniles subject to pretrial detention have "not as yet had a 'judicial determination of probable cause which the Fourth Amendment requires as a prerequisite to extended restraint of liberty following arrest[,]' "; are, in some instances, before the court on charges in unverified petitions, *e.g.,* delinquency petitions filed on information and belief; and are in a system whose purpose is rehabilitative, not penal, in nature. In addition, juveniles are frequently detained for reasons entirely separate from those associated with adjudication of charges. Some are detained as a result of neglect or abusive home environments and are held in protective custody, *e.g.,* are "status offenders"; some are runaways; some are simply undisciplined. For these reasons, we conclude that, as a general matter, the due process standard applied to juvenile pretrial detainees should be more liberally construed than that applied to adult detainees. * * *

2) Conditions of Confinement at the Spofford facility The *Schall* majority found that the state did not detain juveniles for the purpose of punishment and therefore their pretrial detention did not violate due process. The Court observed that, "The conditions of confinement also appear to reflect the regulatory purposes relied upon by the State." How does a court know the purposes of confinement? How can the Justices assess the conditions of confinement to which a state subjects detained juveniles? The *Schall* Majority noted that the statute itself did not indicate "that preventive detention is used or intended as a punishment." Citing the time limits on such detention and the usual separation of juveniles from adults, the majority concluded that "[s]ecure detention is more restrictive, but it is still consistent with the regulatory and *parens patriae* objectives relied upon by the State." By contrast, the dissent quoted from testimony and studies revealing that the juvenile detention facility "is not the most pleasant place in the world."

New York detained the juveniles in *Schall* at the Spofford Detention Facility. Prior to and during the pendency of the *Schall* litigation, the Spofford facility was the subject of extensive litigation, judicial scrutiny, and critical reports, see Dissent, footnote 13, p. 439. *See, e.g., Martarella v. Kelley*, 349 F.Supp. 575 (S.D.N.Y. 1972), *enforced*, 359 F.Supp. 478 (S.D.N.Y. 1973). The *Martarella* court described Spofford as follows:

> The building is surrounded by a high wall. Although individual sleeping rooms are left open at night unless the particular child poses a risk to himself or others, the children (boys) are otherwise locked in their dormitories, recreation rooms or classrooms. * * * Each corridor of the building that leads to the dormitories, classrooms, dining halls or offices has metal doors at each end that are locked at all times. An electronically locked metal door controls movement in and out of the buildings. The windows are secured from inside by a screen made of institutional netting. * * *

> When boys arrive at Spofford their personal clothing is taken from them and they are issued uniforms of blue jeans and T-shirts on whose fronts is an institutional legend.* * *

> [T]he facility is "fraught with problems related both to architectural layout and to maintenance." For example, it is 1/7 of a mile from one end of the structure to the other; the building is "poorly designed for its functional purpose"; space for receiving children is inadequate so that searching is often conducted in the toilet facilities; there is lack of sufficient area for visitation; the school is divided among three separate floors, creating "traffic problems"; lighting is "generally inadequate," the rooms are often cold in winter.* * *

> In addition to being locked institutions (internally and externally) whose male "inmates" must wear uniform clothing, there are other characteristics which the centers share with penal institutions. * * * [C]hildren are required to walk in line from place to place without talking, and are "hit" or have a smoking break taken away if they get out of line. Knives are not generally furnished at meals. Homosexuality, both forced and consensual, exists in both boys' and girls' centers as what all parties appear to agree is an inevitable concomitant of incarceration. *Martarella v. Kelley*, 349 F.Supp. at 580–83.

Justice Rehnquist characterized the Spofford institution as the equivalent of parental supervision. Is this what he meant by the observation that "children are entitled not to liberty, but to custody"?

3) Conditions of Confinement in Detention Professor Michael J. Dale has litigated extensively juvenile detention conditions-of-confinement lawsuits. *See* Michael J. Dale and Carl Sanniti, "Litigation as an Instrument for Change in Juvenile Detention: A Case Study," 39 *Crime & Delinq.* 49

(1993). More recently, **Michael J. Dale, "Lawsuits and Public Policy: The Role of Litigation in Correcting Conditions in Juvenile Detention Centers," 32** *U.S.F. L. Rev.* **675–677, 696–698** (1998), analyzed the conditions in juvenile detention centers that prompted the litigation and observed that:

Conditions in many American juvenile detention centers are awful, and they have been for years. Reports by federal and state governmental agencies, private organizations, and accounts in newspapers and books attest to the endemic problems in America's juvenile detention centers. Many detention centers are currently overcrowded, and it appears that matters will get worse. The Justice Department recently reported that the population in detention centers continues to grow. Given the anticipated growth of the juvenile cohort in the population, further increases in youth crime with resultant rising rates of juvenile detention will inevitably take place. With so many children held each year in detention centers around the country, correcting conditions in these facilities and determining who should be placed in detention and for what reasons, have become important public policy issues. * * * The shortcomings are particularly obvious in the detention centers (the entry point for many children into the juvenile justice system). To make matters worse, the difficulty in maintaining safe detention centers has been exacerbated by the crushing public pressure to "get tough" with juvenile offenders. Legislators in various parts of the country have responded by increasing the rates of pretrial detention, using detention center placement to punish children, and approving placement in detention temporarily for those juveniles awaiting long-term placement. The legislatures have not responded by appropriating funds to ameliorate conditions in the centers. * * *

Two of the most successful ways to ameliorate conditions in juvenile detention centers are to develop intake criteria to narrow the permissible population housed in a facility, and to cap the population. Detention centers become difficult to govern when they are overcrowded with a heterogeneous adolescent population. * * *

The Annie E. Casey Foundation has sponsored efforts to reduce the use of detention and to improve conditions of confinement. Writing in the AECF *Pathways to Juvenile Detention Reform* series, Sue Burrell, **Improving Conditions of Confinement in Secure Juvenile Detention** 10–13 (http://www.aecf.org/upload/publicationfiles/improving% 20conditions.pdf), summarizes conditions of confinement in secure juvenile detention facilities:

On any given day, some 24,000 juveniles are incarcerated in public juvenile detention centers in this country. Figures for 1994 placed the annual number of admissions to public detention centers at 573,843. In 1995, 19 percent of youth undergoing formal delinquency proceedings were held in secure detention at some point between referral and disposition.

Many detained youth are held in facilities that fail to meet even minimum constitutional, statutory, and professional standards of care. In such conditions, some suffer terrible physical or emotional harm. Others are subjected to institutional indignities that damage already fragile self-images and that obliterate any lingering belief in fair treatment by the justice system.

The most comprehensive national study of detention conditions ever conducted, *Conditions of Confinement: Juvenile Detention and Corrections Facilities* (1994), found substantial deficiencies in living space, health care, security, and control of suicidal behavior. The study suggested other deficiencies in educational and treatment services; access to the community; and limits on staff discretion in such matters as the use of isolation, restraints, and searches.

At the time of the *Conditions of Confinement* study, 23 percent of detained juveniles were held in public facilities (including detention centers, ranches, and training schools) operating under a court order or consent decree. The dismal findings of the study are confirmed in the case files of dozens of lawsuits over conditions in juvenile detention centers. Such lawsuits have resulted in injunctions or consent decrees requiring changes in institutional conditions or practices. Others have resulted in damage awards to individual families for injuries suffered or the death of a child.

Issues in detention center lawsuits have ranged from deplorable physical conditions and inadequate programs to outright brutality. They have challenged inadequate living space, with youth sleeping on floors, in hallways, in day rooms, and in isolation rooms. They have decried deplorable sanitation, ventilation, fire-safety, and building maintenance, as well as appalling access to bathrooms, which causes youth to relieve themselves in their rooms or out the window. A number of lawsuits have complained that youth are forced to wear dirty clothes for long periods or that facilities do not have enough clothing or bed linens. Yet others have protested food shortages or practices that force youth to eat in unnatural settings.

Detention centers have repeatedly been sued for failure to provide legally required minimum education and/or special education programs to youth. Additional cases have dealt with a failure to provide minimum recreation and physical exercise—especially outdoor exercise. Some have addressed the failure to provide adequate counseling and programming to detained youth. Detention center cases have often challenged improper restrictions on visiting, correspondence, telephone use, and access to attorneys as well.

A number of cases have complained about the level of violence in detention centers, including the high incidence of sexual and physical assaults. Other cases have challenged the use of repressive discipline, citing inappropriate use of force, locked room time, and mechanical restraints. Cases have also challenged the inadequacies of due process and grievance systems for youth.

Lawsuits involving conditions in detention centers have frequently cited the failure to provide adequate medical and mental health care, including screening, emergency services, and ongoing services, as well as allegations of insufficient staffing, poor staff qualifications, and lack of training. A number of cases have also complained of inadequate protection for youth at risk of suicide.

Although inadequate conditions can occur in any detention center, many of the most abysmal conditions occur in facilities that are crowded. In 1991, as JDAI [Juvenile Detention and Alternatives to Institutions] was being conceptualized, 47 percent of detained juveniles were held in crowded public detention centers; by 1995, the percentage had risen to 62 percent. In 1994, some 319,806 youth were admitted to crowded facilities.

The *Conditions of Confinement* study found that crowding was associated with a range of unhealthy or dangerous conditions. For example, the rate of juvenile and staff injuries was higher in crowded facilities, and the rate of injuries to juveniles increased in large dormitories. High turnover rates (more common in crowded facilities) were also reflected in higher rates of suicidal behavior. The imposition of short-term isolation and incidence of searches of juveniles were higher in crowded facilities. Cases involving crowding in juvenile detention centers confirm the negative impact of crowding on every aspect of institutional life. Not surprisingly, the study found that in 53 percent of court cases involving detention centers, crowding was an issue.

Inadequate conditions are maintained at great financial cost to a jurisdiction. The expenses involved in defending against a conditions lawsuit can range from tens of thousands of dollars if the case is quickly settled to more than a million dollars if it is settled late in the proceedings or goes to trial. If damages are sought in connection with injury to or death of a child, the costs can be much greater. Inadequate conditions can also subject staff and administrators to unwanted, embarrassing publicity through reports from grand juries, advocacy groups, or the media.

Most importantly, inadequate conditions harm the very youth whose care is entrusted to the juvenile justice system. The fact that many of those subjected to such conditions are young, nonviolent, and overwhelmingly members of minority racial or ethnic groups exacts even greater costs upon already vulnerable youth. Holding them in dilapidated, crowded, inadequately staffed facilities may result in physical and emotional damage that leaves them worse off than before the system intervened. Conditions that interfere with family relations, education, jobs, and support programs may lead to future delinquency.

4) Strip Searches Prior to Admission to Juvenile Detention Facilities In **N.G. v. Connecticut**, 382 F.3d 225 (2nd Cir. 2004), parents of two female juveniles brought suit under § 1983 for damages and injunctive relief against the state and administrators of juvenile detention facilities (JDF) alleging that strip searches of the juveniles upon admission to JDF violated their Fourth Amendment rights. The girls were detained for status offenses under a statute authorizing detention of children in "families with service needs."[1] After police arrested one girl for running away from home in violation of a court order, a female staff member at the juvenile detention center followed a standard protocol to strip-search her.[2] The district court

---

1. Another frequent basis for detention arises from a designation known as "families with service needs." Conn. Gen.Stat. § 46b–120(8). "Families with service needs" means a family that includes a child who has acted in one of five ways: (1) run away from home without just cause, (2) become beyond the control of parents, (3) engaged in indecent or immoral conduct, (4) been a truant or overtly defied school rules, or (5) if thirteen years of age or older, has engaged in sexual intercourse with a person of similar age. * * * [D]etention can result upon a judge's finding that one of these five circumstances exists and that there is probable cause to believe that a delinquent act has been committed. Of these five categories, the most common are runaways and truants.

2. According to the NG court, "Strip search" is often used as an umbrella term that applies to all inspections of naked individuals. Various other phrases have been used depending on how the search is conducted. A "visual body-cavity search" usually means visual inspection of a naked

judge ruled that the strip searches were reasonable because "the history of both girls 'suggest[ed] prospective behavior which would predispose them to bringing various contraband into a JDC.' He found S.C. to be 'rebellious, defiant of authority, suicidal, belligerent, promiscuous, a drug user and dealer and mentally unstable.' Acknowledging that T.W.'s truancy was 'a quieter rejection of authority,' he nonetheless found that her bouts of depression and expression of regret at having been born created a risk of self-injury that rendered the strip searches reasonable." After the trial judge dismissed the complaint, the parents appealed. The 2nd Circuit Court of Appeals upheld the validity of suspicionless strip-searches upon entry to the juvenile detention facility. Newman, Circuit Judge:

> This appeal concerns the lawfulness of strip searches performed upon young girls in juvenile detention centers. * * * The Appellants contend that the searches were unlawful for lack of a reasonable basis to believe either that the juveniles had done anything that would be a crime if committed by an adult or had possessed weapons or other contraband. * * * We conclude that the searches conducted upon each initial entry into the custody of the State's juvenile authorities were lawful. * * *

> The Fourth Amendment prohibits "unreasonable" searches, a somewhat amorphous standard whose meaning varies with the context in which a search occurs and the circumstances of the search. * * * Outside the law enforcement context, "in the context of safety and administrative regulations, a search unsupported by probable cause may be reasonable when special needs, beyond the normal need for law enforcement, make the warrant and probable-cause requirement impracticable." * * * However, the "special needs" standard does not validate searches simply because a special need exists. Instead, what is required is "a fact-specific balancing of the intrusion . . . against the promotion of legitimate govern-

---

body, including genitals and anus, without any contact. A "manual body-cavity search" generally means an inspection of a naked body, including genitals and anus, by means of touching or probing with an instrument.

The protocol followed in *NG* described the following procedure to strip-search a new admittee to the juvenile detention center:

a.   Inform the detainee of the strip search and the purpose of the search.

b.   Check the detainee's ears, nose and mouth, including under the tongue.

c.   Have the detainee remove and step away from clothing and shoes and put on a JDC-issued robe.

d.   Have the detainee run his/her own hands through his/her hair.

e.   Check the bottom of detainee's feet.

f.   Have the detainee raise one arm of the robe to mid-biceps and examine top and bottom of arm and hand with fingers spread. Repeat the procedure with second arm and hand.

g.   Have the detainee raise the bottom of the robe to below the crotch to expose and inspect the front of the legs and feet.

h.   Have the detainee turn 180 degrees and drop the robe off the shoulders in order to inspect the upper back and shoulders.

i.   Have the detainee raise the bottom of the robe to above the waist in order to inspect the buttocks and legs.

j.   Have the detainee turn 180 degrees (facing staff), and drop the robe off the shoulders and open the front of the robe, exposing the entire front of the body, shoulders, and upper arms.

k.   Instruct the detainee to shower and dress immediately in a clean uniform.

l.   Search all clothing and personal items, and label and store them appropriately.

mental interests." This is simply an application of the overarching principle that "[t]he test of reasonableness under the Fourth Amendment . . . requires a balancing of the need for the particular search against the invasion of personal rights that the search entails."

These principles have been applied to permit reasonable searches, without warrants, in hospitals; schools; government agencies; and highly regulated industries. Pertinent to the pending case are decisions applying the "special needs" test to uphold suspicionless drug-testing (urinalysis) of middle and high school students participating in extracurricular activities, and students participating in school athletics.

Especially pertinent to the pending case, the "special needs" standard applies to searches in penal institutions. * * * Strip searches performed on those lawfully confined have provoked considerable litigation. * * * This Court has upheld routine random strip searches, including body-cavity inspections, performed on prison inmates. However, in several decisions, we have ruled that strip searches may not be performed upon adults confined after arrest for misdemeanors, in the absence of reasonable suspicion concerning possession of contraband. As far as we can tell, all the circuits to have considered the issue have reached the same conclusion with respect to strip searches of adults confined for minor offenses.

Strip searches of children pose the reasonableness inquiry in a context where both the interests supporting and opposing such searches appear to be greater than with searches of adults confined for minor offenses. Where the state is exercising some legitimate custodial authority over children, its responsibility to act in the place of parents (*in loco parentis*) obliges it to take special care to protect those in its charge, and that protection must be concerned with dangers from others and self-inflicted harm. * * *

In the pending case, neither side has called to our attention an appellate ruling on the reasonableness of strip searches of juveniles in lawful state custody, in the absence of individualized suspicion of possession of contraband. * * *

Connecticut acknowledges that its strip search policy "is not related to the investigation of criminal acts," and contends that the individualized suspicion requirement associated with criminal law enforcement is therefore not applicable. Instead, the State contends that the Policy comports with the "special needs" test of *Earls* and, alternatively, is reasonably related to legitimate penological interests * * *.

In determining whether the strip searches * * * violated the Fourth Amendment, * * * we first consider the nature of the intrusion upon the girls' privacy. A strip search with body-cavity inspection is the practice that "instinctively" has given the Supreme Court "the most pause." The Seventh Circuit has described strip searches as "demeaning," "dehumanizing," and "terrifying." The Tenth Circuit has called them "terrifying." The Eighth Circuit has called them "humiliating." And since "youth . . . is a . . . condition of life when a person may be most susceptible . . . to psychological damage," "[c]hildren are especially susceptible to possible traumas from strip searches." * * *

With respect to the searches performed upon the girls' initial admission to state custody, * * * S.C. and T.W. were confined in juvenile detention facilities. They had not been convicted of any crime, and were not confined awaiting trial on any criminal charges. On the other hand, contraband such as a knife or drugs can pose a hazard to the security of an institution and the safety of inmates whether the institution houses adults convicted of crimes or juveniles in detention centers. Yet before we can uphold a search as reasonably related to penological interests, there must be some justification for placing the person searched into the * * * institution. * * * S.C. was initially confined for violating a court order not to run away from home, and T.W. was initially confined for violating a court order to attend school. * * *

For several reasons, the State makes a more substantial contention in relying on the "special needs" standard of *Earls*. First, although the age of the children renders them especially vulnerable to the distressing effects of a strip search, it also provides the State with an enhanced responsibility to take reasonable action to protect them from hazards resulting from the presence of contraband where the children are confined. The State has temporarily become the *de facto* guardian of children lawfully removed from their home, and "when the government acts as guardian . . . the relevant question is whether the search is one that a reasonable guardian . . . might undertake." The State has a more pervasive responsibility for children in detention centers twenty-four hours a day than for the children in *Vernonia* and *Earls* who were under State authority for the few hours of the school day. Second, a strip search serves the protective function of locating and removing concealed items that could be used for self-mutilation or even suicide. Approximately one half of the girls admitted to JDCs showed signs of self-mutilation. * * * Third, a strip search will often disclose evidence of abuse that occurred in the home, and awareness of such abuse can assist juvenile authorities in structuring an appropriate plan of care. * * *

In the pending case, the evidence establishes the State's primary non-law enforcement purposes—to protect the children from harm inflicted by themselves or other inmates, and to protect the safety of the institution. With these valid purposes established, we think the additional purpose of detecting abuse may be weighed in the reasonableness assessment, even if it was not subjectively entertained by state officials. * * *

The facts of this case do not yield an obvious answer to the question whether it was constitutionally "reasonable" to perform strip searches upon S.C. and T.W. upon their initial admission to detention facilities. Assessing all of the circumstances—the risks to the psychological health of the children from performing the searches and the risks to their well-being and to institutional safety from not performing the searches, we conclude that the strip searches upon initial admission do not violate Fourth Amendment standards. * * *

SOTOMAYOR, Circuit Judge, concurring in part and dissenting in part.

* * * I dissent, however, from the Court's decision to uphold the * * * strip searches. * * * Our caselaw consistently has recognized the severely intrusive nature of strip searches and has placed strict limits on their use. The concerns animating our prior rulings in this area should be only heightened when the privacy interests of emotionally troubled children are at stake. Here, the government has failed to demonstrate that its special needs should overcome these concerns and allow for strip searches, in the absence of individualized suspicion, of adolescents who have never been charged with a crime. * * * I agree with the majority that the proper framework for analysis of the strip searches at issue is the "special needs" balancing test[, but] * * * the government has not demonstrated adequately that the highly invasive suspicionless strip searches bore a "close and substantial relationship to the government's special needs." * * *

The case before us presents facts that provoke all of our typical concerns about strip searches. The detention facility officers on numerous occasions ordered appellants—troubled adolescent girls facing no criminal charges—to remove all of their clothes and underwear. The officials inspected the girls' naked bodies front and back, and had them lift their breasts and spread out folds of fat. * * * The juvenile detention facilities perform similar searches on every girl who enters, notwithstanding the fact that many of them—indeed, most of them—have been victims of abuse or neglect, and may be more vulnerable mentally and emotionally than other youths their age.

Given the uniquely invasive and upsetting nature of strip searches, it is not surprising that with the exception of the prison setting, we have never found that a strip search in the absence of any individualized suspicion was reasonable. * * * The only exception to this principle that we thus far have recognized is an exception for prison inmates, which the plaintiffs—who have never faced any criminal charges—indisputably are not. Thus, to hold that the strip searches of the two girls in the instant appeal were reasonable is equivalent to saying that these girls are entitled to the same level of Fourth Amendment protection as prison inmates held on felony charges, and to decidedly less protection than people crossing the border, jail inmates detained on misdemeanor charges, prison corrections officers, or students in public school. * * *

I turn next to the government's concerns assertedly motivating the searches and the efficacy of the searches in meeting those concerns. The majority argues that the government's special needs are even more compelling in the context of juvenile detention facilities than they are in cases involving public schools or correctional facilities. I agree. However, it is not enough for the government simply to assert a compelling special need. Our special needs jurisprudence generally has also required that the search "seek a minimum of intrusiveness coupled with maximal effectiveness so that the search[ ] bear[s] a close and substantial relationship to the government's special needs." This is not to say that the Fourth

Amendment requires that only "least intrusive means" be used in order to effectuate the government's interests, but a "close and substantial relationship" between the intrusiveness and the need must be demonstrated nevertheless. The government bears the burden of demonstrating this nexus between the search and the asserted special need.

The government here has completely failed to demonstrate that the invasive strip searches bore a "close and substantial" relationship to any governmental need. This first becomes clear upon examining the thirty-four "event reports" for the years 1995 through 2000 * * * [that] describe the occasions on which officers discovered contraband in the possession of the detainees. Of the thirty-four reports of contraband violations, thirty-two describe contraband that either (1) was discovered through a search that was less intrusive than a full strip search; (2) could have been discovered through a search that was less intrusive than a full strip search; or (3) could have been discovered through a policy that allowed strip searches only in cases of individualized suspicion. * * * Thus, the detention centers' own documentation of contraband discoveries provides absolutely no evidence that suspicionless strip searches were necessary, or even helpful, in any case. * * *

The majority accepts the government's argument that strip searches serve the "special need" of deterring children from smuggling contraband. * * * While deterrence may be an important rationale for employees who know they will undergo drug tests, or for prisoners returning from contact visits with outsiders, it has little applicability to a person who does not expect to be detained and subjected to a search. * * * In Connecticut's juvenile detention centers, it is common for children to be arrested unexpectedly and confined immediately. In other cases the juveniles are brought first to their parents, who then must bring them to court. Even in those cases, however, the child does not necessarily expect to be detained, as prosecutors do not seek to have the child detained in all cases. * * *

In criticizing the government's evidence, I again emphasize that the question is not whether the government's concerns justify a potentially-invasive search of some kind—such as a frisk search or a thorough search of all of a detainee's clothes and possessions—in the absence of individualized suspicion. Nor is the question whether the government's concerns justify a full strip search when there is some reasonable suspicion that a particular juvenile possesses contraband. The question instead is whether the government's concerns are sufficiently credible and sufficiently weighty to justify a highly degrading, intrusive strip search absent any individualized suspicion that the particular young adolescents ordered by the state to disrobe possess contraband. * * *

In **Smook v. Minnehaha County Juvenile Detention Center**, 457 F.3d 806 (8th Cir. 2006), the court considered the constitutionality of the JDC policy of strip-searching all juveniles admitted to the facility regardless of the seriousness of charged offense or existence of individualized suspicion. Jodi Smook and her three companions were arrested for violating curfew while walking home after the car she was driving broke down. Although the district court found her suspicionless strip-search violated the Fourth Amendment, the 8th Circuit Court of Appeals upheld the searches based on *N.G., supra.*

Compare the *N.G.* and *Smook* courts' decisions here with the courts' greater concerns about strip-searching children in school settings. See *Doe v. Renfrow, supra* p. 216, and Notes 5 and 6, pp. 235–240, *supra.* In the school strip-searches, a dog-alert or informant's tip provided at least some individualized suspicion. What accounts for the differences in the courts' approval of these practices in detention facilities? Jessica R. Feierman and Riya S. Shah, "Protecting Personhood: Legal Strategies to Combat the Use of Strip Searches on Youth in Detention," 60 *Rut. L. Rev.* 67 (2007), strongly criticize the courts' reasoning in N.G. and Smook and propose a variety of litigation strategies to challenge suspicionless strip-searches of children.

5) Professional Reaction to *Schall* Most commentators criticized *Schall* on both substantive and procedural grounds. *See e.g.,* Irene Merker Rosenberg, "*Schall v. Martin*: A Child is a Child is a Child," 12 *Am. J. Crim. L.* 253, 277 (1984); Charles Patrick Ewing, "*Schall v. Martin*: Preventive Detention and Dangerousness Through the Looking Glass," 34 *Buff. L. Rev.* 173 (1985); Mary Jane Boswell, "Where Have All the Children Gone? The Supreme Court Finds Pretrial Detention of Minors Constitutional: *Schall v. Martin*," 34 *DePaul L. Rev.* 733 (1985); Barry C. Feld, "Criminalizing Juvenile Justice: Rules of Procedure for the Juvenile Court," 69 *Minn. L. Rev.* 141, 191–209 (1984). Later commentators contend that, as a result of *Schall*, "pretrial juvenile detention is overused by the juvenile justice system. The overuse of pretrial juvenile detention may actually create more problems for society than the crime itself. These potential problems include increased juvenile crime rates, increased juvenile recidivism and an increased alienation of the youth from societal guidelines." David A. Geller, "Putting the 'Parens' Back into Parens Patriae: Parental Custody of Juveniles as an Alternative to Pretrial Juvenile Detention," 21 *New Eng. J. on Crim. & Civ. Confinement* 509, 511 (1995).

Critics contend that *Schall*'s approval of detention decisions that used minimal procedures and lacked objective substantive criteria allows judges to detain too many and inappropriate youths which, in turn, exacerbates institutional overcrowding. **Bart Lubow and Joseph B. Tulman, "The Unnecessary Detention of Children in the District of Columbia," 3 *D.C. L. Rev.* IX (1995)**, note *Schall*'s contribution to overcrowding and inappropriate detention:

Despite the promise of juvenile justice reform occasioned by the passage of the federal Juvenile Justice and Delinquency Prevention Act of 1974, national data on juvenile detention depict a system that is overcrowded, expensive, inconsistent, and discriminatory. Since the early 1980s, the use of secure juvenile detention has significantly increased. The rate per 100,000 youths detained on a single day increased from 37 in 1979 to 70 in 1989, an increase of 89%. During the same period, detention admission rates rose from 1,574 per 100,000 to 1,959 per 100,000, an increase of 24%. The annual number of admissions is now approximately one-half million, an increase of 31% since 1982. A one-day census in 1979 showed 10,683 youths in secure detention facilities compared to 18,014 in 1989, an increase of 69%. These increases occurred despite the removal of many status offenders from juvenile detention and, significantly, at a time when juvenile arrests were decreasing. * * *

Several discrete factors contribute to the over-reliance on detention. First and foremost, decision-makers order detention without referring to statutory criteria and without accurate information about the individual arrestee. Many, and in some jurisdictions most, detention admissions are not justified in relation to detention's legitimate purposes of ensuring appearance in court and avoiding delinquency while cases are adjudicated. For example, some officials may use detention for punitive purposes, believing that a "taste of the system" can shock youths into better behavior. Because many detained youths lack effective legal representation, they have no one to advocate for their release and systemic misuses of detention go unchallenged.

Equally important, most jurisdictions do not utilize objective risk assessment approaches capable of accurately identifying the likelihood of court appearance or renewed delinquent behavior. Absent such information, the system relies on idiosyncratic decision-making (often reinforced by racial, ethnic and socio-economic stereotyping) that results in frequent mistakes and-as discussed above-the disproportionate detention of poor and minority youth.

Another basic reason for unnecessary utilization of secure detention is the dearth of effectively implemented programmatic alternatives. Few localities offer supervised release, home detention, non-secure residential facilities, or similar options for those youths who require more than mere release to a parent to ensure future court appearances and lawful behavior. Confronted with only two choices—outright release or secure confinement—the system frequently detains youths whose cases simply demand more appropriate, less costly options. * * *

Systemic inefficiencies also contribute to unnecessary detention. Petition screening often occurs after admission to detention, generating large numbers of short detention stays that end when charges are dismissed or cases are adjusted. Other youths remain confined despite speedy trial requirements. Defense lawyers are often assigned cases days after detention commences, limiting opportunities for effective advocacy. Dispositional report preparation may not be prioritized to ensure that detained cases are handled first. Waiting lists representing bureaucratic inefficiency and over-populated programs preclude timely post-adjudicatory placement. * * *

6) Adequacy of Procedural Safeguards at Detention Hearings
Both the majority and the dissent in *Schall* discuss "whether the procedures afforded juveniles detained prior to fact finding provide sufficient protection against erroneous and unnecessary deprivations of liberty." *Supra*, p. 433. The majority compared favorably the New York detention procedure with the Court's minimal Fourth Amendment safeguards approved in *Gerstein v. Pugh*. In addition to formal notice and a record, the Court emphasized that juveniles received the assistance of counsel. The dissent criticized the procedures because they lacked specific substantive criteria for detention or a standard of proof. Without those minimal procedures, even if a juvenile had an attorney, there would be very little an attorney could do. Unlike Rhenquist's assurances of the adequacy of the procedural "law on the books," the "law in action" of

juvenile detention hearings is quite different. Consider **Perry L. Moriearty, "Combating the Color–Coded Confinement of Kids: An Equal Protection Remedy," 32 N.Y.U. Rev. L & Social Change 285, 305 (2008)**, who describes the procedural safeguards many juveniles receive at a detention hearings:

> The pretrial detention hearing in juvenile court is often anything but [a hearing]. Apart from the comparative informality of most juvenile court proceedings, the arbitrary nature of many detention hearings can also be attributed to the absence of counsel. In fact, juvenile codes in certain states do not even require courts to appoint attorneys at the detention stage. Virginia law, for example, does not specifically provide for the right to counsel at arrest, intake, or the initial detention hearing. The absence of counsel, according to OJJDP, is one of the likely causes of "Virginia's high rate of detention (nearly twice the national average)." Other states have no uniform process to appoint public defenders for juvenile defendants at any point in the process and no eligibility criteria for indigency. Moreover, even when state law does afford juveniles the right to counsel at the pretrial detention hearing, juveniles frequently waive counsel's appearance. According to OJJDP, "[i]n some jurisdictions, as many as 80 to 90 percent of youth waive their right to an attorney because they do not know the meaning of the word 'waive' or understand its consequences." And finally, when attorneys do appear at detention hearings, they are frequently untrained in juvenile court procedures, inexperienced, and overburdened.

7) Substantive criteria to regularize detention decisions Justice Rehnquist, writing for the majority in *Schall*, asserted that "it is worth recalling that we are neither a legislature charged with formulating public policy nor an ABA committee charged with drafting a model statute. The question before us today is solely whether the preventive detention system * * * comports with constitutional standards." By contrast, in **Facilities Review Panel v. Coe**, 187 W.Va. 541, 420 S.E.2d 532 (W.Va.1992), the West Virginia Supreme Court modified and adopted the American Bar Association's *Juvenile Justice Standards Relating to Interim Status* (1980) to standardize judges' detention decisions and promulgated additional protective measures to regulate the uses of detention:

> With the implementation of tighter detention standards, it is hoped that the detention population would be significantly reduced. * * * [W]e adopt juvenile detention standards set forth in Appendices A. * * * We believe the use of these guidelines will discourage the vague and often subjective method of deciding whether to detain a juvenile. * * *

> Equally important are the accompanying recommendations, * * * which we adopt along with the Juvenile Detention Standards:

> 1. Before any juvenile can be sent to a detention facility, the arresting officer or the detention hearing officer must telephone the detention facility to determine whether there is a vacancy before the juvenile can be transported to that facility.

2. No facility can accept any juveniles beyond their licensed capacity and must immediately report any attempt to force them to do so to the Department of Human Services and the Juvenile Justice Committee.

3. A juvenile must remain in detention no longer than thirty days awaiting a dispositional hearing.

4. Following the dispositional hearing, a juvenile shall not remain in detention longer than fourteen days before moving the juvenile into an appropriate placement. Thus, the circuit courts must move swiftly and efficiently to avoid overcrowding.

5. In the event overcrowding occurs, the circuit courts must develop alternate methods of detention, such as in-home detention, electronic monitoring, and emergency shelters.

6. Within ten days after the end of each month, each detention facility must file a report with the Department of Human Services and the Juvenile Justice Committee which lists each new juvenile detained, the reason and charge, and the date the child enters and leaves the facility, including explanations of any interim absences. * * *

APPENDIX A

Standards Relating Interim Status: Secure Detention of Accused Juvenile Offenders Between Arrest and Disposition

Guidelines for status decision.

A. Mandatory release.—The intake official should release the accused juvenile unless the juvenile:

1. Is charged with a criminal-type delinquent behavior which in the case of an adult would be punishable by a sentence of not less than one year, and which if proven could result in commitment to a security institution, and one or more of the following additional factors is present:

a. The crime charged is a category one * * * juvenile offense [e.g. murder, rape, robbery].

b. The crime charged is a category two or four * * * juvenile offense [e.g. manslaughter, burglary, and other serious felonies] and there is a judicial finding that the juvenile presents a danger to the public if not securely detained, pursuant to an immediate full detention hearing in which the juvenile is represented by an attorney.

c. The crime charged is a category two, three, or four * * * juvenile offense and the juvenile is an escapee from detention or any commitment setting * * * or the juvenile has a recent record of willful failure to appear at juvenile court proceedings and no measure short of secure detention can be imposed to reasonably ensure appearance.

d. The crime charged is a violation of an alternative method of sentencing.

e. The juvenile is waiting adjudication or disposition for an offense which would be a felony under criminal jurisdiction or a category one, two, three, or four offense and is charged with committing another offense during the interim period which would be a felony or a category one, two, three, or four offense. Another less restrictive means of supervising the juvenile such as electronic monitoring, home detention, or shelter care must have been tried and failed.

f. The juvenile is awaiting adjudication or disposition for an offense which would be a felony under criminal jurisdiction or a category one, two, three, or four offense and is released on bond conditions but is found by a judicial authority to have committed a material violation of bond. * * * Another less restrictive means of supervising the juvenile, such as electronic monitoring, home detention, or shelter care must have been tried and failed.

2. The juvenile has been verified to be a fugitive from another jurisdiction, and an official of which has formally requested that the juvenile be placed in detention * * *.

B. Mandatory detention.—A juvenile who is excluded from mandatory release under subsection A is not, *pro tanto*, to be automatically detained. No category of alleged conduct in and of itself may justify a failure to exercise discretion to release in consideration of the needs of the juvenile and the community.

C. Discretionary situations.

1. Release vs. detention. In every situation in which the release of an arrested juvenile is not mandatory, the intake official should first consider and determine whether the juvenile qualifies for an available diversion program, or whether any form of control short of detention is available to reasonably reduce the risk of flight or misconduct. The official should explicitly state in writing the reasons for rejecting each of these forms of release.

2. Unconditional vs. conditional or supervised release. In order to minimize the imposition of release conditions on persons who would appear in court without them, and present no substantial risk in the interim, each jurisdiction should develop guidelines for the use of various forms of release based upon the resources and programs available, and analysis of the effectiveness of each form of release.

3. Secure vs. nonsecure detention. The intake official should consider nonsecure detention alternatives prior to committing a juvenile to a secure detention facility. * * *

F. Threatening Witnesses.

One additional ground for detention is a determination by a judicial authority that there exists a substantial probability of danger to witnesses should the applicant be granted bail.

A commentator noted the implications of the *Facilities Review* decision for reducing overcrowding in detention. **Elizabeth S. Lawton, "*Facilities Review Panel v. Coe*: The West Virginia Supreme Court of Appeals Adopts An Objective Approach to Deciding Pretrial Detention of Accused Juveniles," 95 *W. Va. L. Rev.* 505, 529–533 (1993):**

The most salient aspect of the court's decision in *Facilities Review* is the establishment of statewide objective standards upon which the decision to detain must be predicated. * * * [T]he court ultimately concluded that the use of such standards would "discourage the vague and often subjective method of deciding whether to detain a juvenile." * * * [T]he court articulated very specific, narrowly defined criteria upon which the detention decision must now be based. Although similar to those recommended by the IJA/ABA, the standards as adopted are "modified to fit the specialized needs of our juvenile system." These criteria constrain but do not abolish the use of detention. Specifically, they ensure release except in the most compelling circumstances, with the decision based on measurable and demonstrable determinants, while preserving the option to detain those who pose the greatest threat to the community.

A second important aspect of the *Facilities Review* decision is the adoption of realistic protective measures to ameliorate the overcrowding problem in some facilities. * * * The major focus of the measures set forth by the court is prevention of overcrowding. This is to be accomplished by requiring pre-commitment actions by the arresting or judicial officer to ascertain the availability of space for a child before attempting to place a child in a facility. The *Facilities Review* court also extended to facility personnel the authority to refuse commitments beyond their licensed capacity. Furthermore, the court set specific limits on the amount of time a juvenile may now be held in detention between adjudication, disposition, and placement, factors which were noticeably absent in the statutory provisions. * * *

The *Facilities Review* decision * * * provides clear and narrowly drawn standards upon which judges must base their decision to detain or release the accused juvenile. The factors to be evaluated are readily measurable and verifiable, and limit, but do not abolish, detention. However, the standards eliminate the overbroad judicial discretion embodied in the prior law which should result in a more uniform and consistent decision-making process statewide. Thus, application of these standards should effectively reduce the number of youths detained overall, and particularly the number held for vague or inappropriate reasons such as those detained out of unsubstantiated fear for public safety. At the same time, courts may detain those who pose a real threat to the community or the judicial process. Secondly, implementation of the procedural protective measures established by the court, and the use of the least restrictive alternative to detention, should ameliorate the problem of overcrowding of facilities. Additionally, the court's decision should bring about a reduction in the costs of detention borne by the taxpayers of the state. * * *

8) Predicting Dangerousness A crucial issue in *Schall* and one that underlies many juvenile and criminal justice system decisions is whether judges, clinicians, and social workers accurately can predict dangerousness or future criminal behavior. The district court decision in *Schall*, *United States ex rel. Martin v. Strasburg*, 513 F.Supp. 691 (S.D.N.Y. 1981), examined the research literature about prediction in considerable depth and concluded that the inability to predict dangerousness was the most pernicious defect of the entire New York preventive detention regime:

> The judge is empowered to make a prediction about the probability of an individual committing a crime if released. No guidelines for making that determination are set out in the statute, and none has been adopted by the court. The judge's determination is moored to no concrete or reasonably determinable yardsticks. * * * [E]ach judge utilizes his own personal standards. *Id.* at 707.

Following its review of the prediction literature and the expert testimony, the district court concluded that any effort to predict future dangerousness based on the present state of the art is necessarily doomed to failure.

Numerous commentators raise similar concerns about a court's ability accurately to predict human behavior, especially behavior that is unusual or violent. *See, e.g.,* John Monahan, *Predicting Violent Behavior* (1981); Norval Morris, *The Future of Imprisonment* 62–73 (1974); Ennis & Litwack, "Psychiatry and the Presumption of Expertise: Flipping Coins in the Courtroom," 62 *Calif. L. Rev.* 693, 711–16 (1974). Psychiatrists as well as lawyers have criticized the assumption of mental health professionals that they are able to predict dangerousness. One author, for example, observes that there is no empirical basis for the assumption that psychiatrists can predict dangerous behavior and that even with "the most careful, painstaking, laborious, and lengthy clinical approach to the prediction of dangerousness, false positives [or erroneous prediction] may be at a minimum of 60% to 70%." Rubin, "Prediction of Dangerousness in Mentally Ill Criminals," 27 *Archives Gen. Psychiatry* 397, 397–98 (1972). Among the many other studies reaching this conclusion are APA Task Force Report, Clinical Aspects of the Violent Individual 28 (1974) (90% error rate "[u]nfortunately * * * is the state of the art"); Henry Steadman and Joseph P. Morrissey, "The StatisticalPrediction of Violent Behavior," 5 *Law & Human Behavior* 263 (1981); George Dix, "Expert Prediction Testimony in Capital Sentencing: Evidentiary and Constitutional Considerations," 19 *Am. Crim. L. Rev.* 1 (1981); Joseph Cocozza & Henry J. Steadman, "Prediction in Psychiatry: An Example of Misplaced Confidence in Experts," 25 *Soc. Probs.* 265, 272–273 (1978); Henry Steadman & Joseph Cocozza, "Psychiatry, Dangerousness and the Repetitively Violent Offender," 69 *J. Crim. L. & Criminology* 226 (1978); Bernard L. Diamond, "The Psychiatric Prediction of Dangerousness," 123 *U. Pa. L. Rev.* 439 (1974).

In an *amicus* brief in **Barefoot v. Estelle**, 463 U.S. 880, 899–902, 103 S.Ct. 3383, 77 L.Ed.2d 1090 (1983), the American Psychiatric Association firmly rejected the notion that psychiatrists or other clinicians possess any special competence to predict violent behavior or to assist judges or juries attempting to predict the future dangerousness of a capital defendant. Despite the APA's disavowal of competence, the *Barefoot* majority allowed juries to consider psychiatric testimony to predict "future dangerousness." In dissent, Justices Blackmun, Brennan, and Marshall objected that such testimony is wrong two times out of three:

> The American Psychiatric Association (APA), participating in this case as *amicus curiae*, informs us that "[t]he unreliability of psychiatric predictions of long-term future dangerousness is by now an established fact within the profession." The APA's best estimate is that *two out of*

three predictions of long-term future violence made by psychiatrists are wrong. The Court does not dispute this proposition, and indeed it could not do so; the evidence is overwhelming. For example, the APA's Draft Report of the Task Force on the Role of Psychiatry in the Sentencing Process (1983) (Draft Report) states that "[c]onsiderable evidence has been accumulated by now to demonstrate that long-term prediction by psychiatrists of future violence is an extremely inaccurate process." John Monahan, recognized as "the leading thinker on this issue" even by the State's expert witness at Barefoot's federal habeas corpus hearing, concludes that "the 'best' clinical research currently in existence indicates that psychiatrists and psychologists are accurate in no more than one out of three predictions of violent behavior," even among populations of individuals who are mentally ill and have committed violence in the past. Another study has found it impossible to identify any subclass of offenders "whose members have a greater-than-even chance of engaging again in an assaultive act." Yet another commentator observes: "In general, mental health professionals * * * are more likely to be wrong than right when they predict legally relevant behavior. When predicting violence, dangerousness, and suicide, they are far more likely to be wrong than right." Neither the Court nor the State of Texas has cited a single reputable scientific source contradicting the unanimous conclusion of professionals in this field that psychiatric predictions of long-term future violence are wrong more often than they are right.

The APA also concludes, as do researchers that have studied the issue, that psychiatrists simply have no expertise in predicting long-term future dangerousness. A layman with access to relevant statistics can do at least as well and possibly better; psychiatric training is not relevant to the factors that validly can be employed to make such predictions, and psychiatrists consistently err on the side of overpredicting violence. * * *

That psychiatrists actually may be less accurate predictors of future violence than laymen, may be due to personal biases in favor of predicting violence arising from the fear of being responsible for the erroneous release of a violent individual. It also may be due to a tendency to generalize from experiences with past offenders on bases that have no empirical relationship to future violence. * * * Statistical prediction is clearly more reliable than clinical prediction, and prediction based on statistics alone may be done by anyone. * * *

Psychiatric predictions of future dangerousness *are not accurate*; wrong two times out of three, their probative value, and therefore any possible contribution they might make to the ascertainment of truth, is virtually nonexistent. Indeed, given a psychiatrist's prediction that an individual will be dangerous, it is more likely than not that the defendant will not commit further violence. It is difficult to understand how the admission of such predictions can be justified as advancing the search for truth, particularly in light of their clearly prejudicial effect. *Id*. at 920–928.

9) "From a legal point of view there is nothing inherently unattainable about a prediction of criminal conduct"—An Introduction to Predicting Dangerousness in *Schall* As the *Barefoot* dissenters indicate, the process of making predictions poses many methodological difficulties and moral dilemmas. Which predictive techniques—statistical versus clinical—should the justice system use, and what margins of error—false positives and false negatives—that result in the erroneous confinement of innocent people can a justice system tolerate? The following excerpt introduces some of these problems. **Jeffrey Fagan and Martin Guggenheim, "Preventive Detention and the Judicial Prediction of Dangerousness of Juveniles: A Natural Experiment," 86** *J. Crim. L. & Criminology* **415 (1996):**

Morris and Miller distinguish between three types of prediction: "anamnestic," "actuarial," and "clinical." It is not always clear which of these predictions best describes the judicial decisions in preventive detention. Although the predictions in *Schall* resembled clinical predictions made by judges, experts who looked at the New York scheme for assessing pretrial dangerousness criticized the predictions as more closely resembling "hunches" or "guesses."

Jurisdictions typically rely on three factors for determining pretrial dangerousness: prior criminal record, seriousness of the current offense, and judicial discretion. However, there is little empirical evidence that these charge-related bases for detention are good indicators of criminality during the pretrial period. Because judges must focus on the short-term danger posed by the defendant, they must rely on information about unproven prior acts and anticipated future conduct, as well as on subjective information of the personal restraints and social controls that will regulate the defendant's behavior if released. For this reason, juvenile court judges in *Schall* commonly considered such factors as the presence of family members at the detention hearing as an indication of the availability of familial controls during the pretrial period.

As applied, preventive detention reflects some combination of actuarial and clinical predictions. The actuarial component involves a complex framework of judicial experience and normative expectations derived from the accumulation of knowledge from decisions made over lengthy periods of pretrial decision-making. It also reflects a normative consensus among the court's everyday "working group" of decision-makers regarding particular individuals and types of cases. The clinical dimension of the preventive detention decision reflects the judges' professional opinion based on clinical elements that cannot be identified actuarially. These include judgments about the defendants' demeanor, dress, and perceptions of the quality of supervision from parents or caretakers. * * *

A crucial difference, of course, is that traditional clinical assessments by psychological professionals are rendered only after lengthy interviews and reviews of case records. Preventive detention decisions, by contrast, are made by judges often in a matter of minutes and frequently on the basis of unverified information. * * * What may we expect when judges are asked to make short-term predictions about a heterogeneous group of defendants where information is sketchy and unverified regarding the elements that comprise risk?

4. The Validity of Judicial Predictions of Dangerousness for Pretrial Defendants

* * * Efforts to predict both pretrial crime and those defendants who will commit such crimes run headlong into base rate problems. Base rate estimates of pretrial crime are generally low and are especially difficult to compute for juveniles. Indeed, the base rate of pretrial crime among juvenile defendants is unknown and estimates based upon adult pretrial crime rates are problematic as studies of pretrial crime among adults vary depending on the classification of pretrial crime. The rate of pretrial *violent* crime for adults appears to be particularly low, ranging from 3% to 7%. * * *

Base rates establish probabilities for defined groups, but the epistemology of prediction provides extremely weak grounds for making any prediction about a particular person, especially when the prediction is short-term. When base rates are low—as they appear to be for pretrial juvenile crime—the capacity to make accurate individual predictions of short-term criminality is particularly questionable. Several studies have estimated the accuracy of short-term predictions by using the statutory criteria for detention-eligible arrestees. These studies have concluded that the criteria for detention eligibility is a poor predictor of who will commit a crime during the pretrial period. There is general consensus that the capacity to predict pretrial crime on the basis of statutory standards for determining dangerousness is no better than one in three correct predictions.

The problems are different when base rates are high. In these circumstances, the difficulty involves developing bases to make predictions that improve on randomness. The difficulty of predicting events increases as the base rate falls below 50%. Because violent criminality is a rare event, the establishment of a valid base expectancy rate is critical. When the "true" rate of pretrial violence is one-in-ten, a one-in-three prediction is not a low rate of prediction. In fact, it would be quite high relative to the actual base rate. But a one-in-three prediction is poor relative to a 50% base rate. Even when the base rate is relatively high for a particular group, predicted future dangerousness will vary dramatically within the group. For this reason, the assignment of a threshold for an individual becomes a critical decision in determining which members of the group pose a sufficient risk to justify preventive detention. Given the low base rates of pretrial juvenile crime, the reduction in crime through preventive detention is likely to be quite low unless this threshold is set unreasonably low, close to the low base rate.

In general, predictions of pretrial failure invariably fail to improve on either chance or on the base rate. * * * These problems are even more acute for the short-term predictions inherent in preventive detention. Jackson's review of preventive detention notes that "[t]hree noteworthy findings emerge from studies: (1) arrests of pretrial releasees for serious crimes are relatively infrequent; (2) the ability to accurately predict pretrial crime, however measured, is very poor; and (3) the level of pretrial crimes correlates positively with time on release." * * *

5. The Problems of False Positives and False Negatives

Finally, the statutory authority for preventive detention in the *Schall* case empowered judges to detain defendants whenever the judge considered their risk of criminality to be high, recognizing that at least in some instances, the juvenile would not commit any crime. The assessment of these predictions is especially important because it provides an estimate of the number of persons detained unnecessarily in order to prevent crime. The threshold at which the number of needlessly detained individuals becomes *too* high is not reducible to a mathematical formula. But it may be useful to view *false positives* as individuals who are deprived of their liberty for utilitarian purposes unrelated to their own danger. Once these individuals are considered to be among a larger group of the "potentially dangerous," they are subject to loss of liberty not because their potential will be realized, but because an indeterminate number of the group will realize theirs.

Accordingly, unconvicted individuals are jailed not to stop them from any wrongdoing but in order to throw a wide enough net to cover others who, if not stopped, would endanger society. It is one thing, *after* conviction, to deprive someone who is no threat to society of his or her liberty for utilitarian purposes. In those circumstances, the convicted person has forfeited liberty based on his or her wrong doing. But *before* conviction, it is difficult to discern how the individual has forfeited anything. The only thing he or she has done, at this point in the criminal justice process, is get arrested.

The recurring errors in predictions must always be balanced by two additional considerations. First, does the cost of trying to prevent pretrial crime outweigh the benefits? Here, the problems of definition and prediction intersect. For these purposes, dangerousness is the product of the crime to be avoided and the predicted rate or odds of its occurrence. When base rates are low, so is the probability that the harm to be avoided would occur. Even within a group where base rates may be higher, the ceiling on predictions within those groups—for example, at one-in-three, as the Supreme Court suggested in *Barefoot v. Estelle*—indicates that the total harm is likely to be insubstantial. When the base rates are actually far lower * * * the total harm is extremely low, especially when the harm to be avoided is ill-defined and subject to overreach.

In the case of pretrial juvenile defendants, the costs both to the detained adolescent and to his or her community are quite high in terms of foreshadowing their eventual finding of delinquency and serious disposition. Detention causes considerable adverse impact on the detainee, including loss of employment or educational opportunities, separation from family, persistent future disadvantage in the workplace that results in poor job outcomes, and the ordinary inconveniences of being jailed. Pretrial detention of juveniles also has a negative impact on the outcome of the case in court. The conviction rate of detainees is higher, and because detainees are prevented from demonstrating improved behavior in the community, prison sentences are lengthier and more likely. Several studies have concluded that "detention *per se* exhibits an independent effect on dispositions* * *. In operation, detention almost randomly imposes punishment on some juveniles for no obvious reason and then punishes them again for having been punished before." * * *

10) The Accuracy of Judicial Predictions *Schall* created a unique opportunity to conduct "natural experiment" to assess the accuracy of judicial predictions. The district court in *Schall* held the statute unconstitutional and entered a restraining order to bar preventive detention. However, the judge entered the order against the Commissioner who administered the detention facility rather than the Family Court judges who committed youth to it. As a result, judges continued to predict youths' future dangerousness and to commit them, but the order prohibited the facility from detaining the youths. Judges and the Commissioner detained youths for reasons other than their "serious risk" of future crime, such as the danger they posed to themselves or their risk of flight. During the three years that the restraining order applied, judges predicted that seventy-four youths posed a "serious risk" of future crime as the sole grounds for detention and ordered them incarcerated, but the Commissioner released them. Thus, the judges made their predictions *and* the youths remained at liberty to validate their predictions. Researchers identified a sample of juveniles matched on the basis of age, demographic factors, offense, prior record, and the like whom judges predicted would not commit a crime and did not order detained. The researchers compared both "serious risk" and "safe" juveniles' criminal involvement during their pretrial liberty to assess the validity and accuracy of judges' predictions of dangerousness. In a multivariate evaluation of the accuracy of judges' predictions of dangerousness, **Jeffrey Fagan and Martin Guggenheim, "Preventive Detention and the Judicial Prediction of Dangerousness of Juveniles: A Natural Experiment," 86** *J. Crim. L. & Criminology* **415 (1996)**, controlled for the effects of legal and extra-legal variables and then compared the subsequent offenses of *Schall* cases—youths whom judges predicted would reoffend—and the matched sample of delinquents—youths whom judges predicted would not reoffend and did not order detained-during both ninety and 365 day intervals. They compared the two samples for re-arrests for any offense and for a violent offense:

The short-term, ninety day prediction model has direct relevance for assessing the efficacy of preventive decisions that concern the pretrial period. The model for rearrest for *any* crime is significant. Significant predictors * * * include age at first juvenile court contact (younger), and a current charge for a violent felony offense. * * * However, the model for rearrest for a *violent offense* is not significant, indicating that the model with predictors does not differ significantly from a model with no predictors. In other words, the prediction of pretrial rearrest for a violent crime using these variables is no better than chance. * * *

The accuracy of prediction of dangerousness during the pretrial period remains questionable. The prediction models are not significant for violent rearrests once we control prior and current dangerousness. While predictions of a broad range of pretrial crimes are efficient, the prediction of dangerousness is unreliable. Presumably, it is the protection from danger that justifies the false prediction and deprivation of liberty in over half of the *Schall* cases. Yet in using the statutory criteria and definitions for determining dangerousness, we are unable to estimate an efficient model for predicting such danger in the short term. The models were constructed so as to permit assessments of judicial predictions after controlling for the degree of risk or dangerousness in the population. The models fail to demonstrate such efficiency. Even the unmeasured factors inherent in the *Schall* prediction, those that would influence the coefficient after controls for legal and extra-legal factors, do not lead to an efficient prediction of pretrial danger. Whatever additional, un-measured risks influenced the *Schall* prediction, they were not sufficient to yield an efficient prediction model. * * *

Would an actuarial prediction improve predictive efficiency? When a particular defendant fits the statistical profile for a high base rate group, we could detain that individual based on an actuarial use of prediction with the same predictive validity and efficiency. In this study, that would mean if we detained all of the *Schall* youths without any benefit of a *clinical* assessment of dangerousness, one-out-of-six detainees would have committed a crime if released. The judges in the *Schall* study clearly improved on this actuarial prediction.

However, this improvement actually means that the judges detained 25% more juveniles who would have committed a crime if released than had the judges detained the entire group based on actuarial predictions. In other words, detaining the entire control group would result in the needless deten-tion of five youths to "catch" the sixth who would have recidivated within the pretrial period. Detaining the *Schall* group would result in the needless detention of six-youths-in-ten to "catch" the four who would have recidivated.

These differences are conservative estimates, since the comparisons were based on criteria that were limited to objective factors and did not include the social and behavioral cues that often guide detention decisions: demeanor, victim injury, parental involvement at the detention hearing, and details about current or past crimes. Had more detailed matching criteria been used, we would expect to narrow the gap in rearrest rates between *Schall* and any type of control group. * * *

When narrowed to violent crimes, the decision standard that guides preventive detention statutes in many state predictions are inefficient and the performance is unacceptable. Over 80% of the *Schall* juveniles were not rearrested for a violent offense within the normative pretrial confinement period. Such performance stands at odds with constitutional concerns over false imprisonment and equal protection. * * *

Given the adverse consequences for defendants, we should be quite sure that preventive detention will avoid the commission of a very serious crime. Detaining ten arrestees to prevent six from gambling in public, for example, ought clearly to be unacceptable. Yet, only 36.9% of the *Schall* youths were charged with a violent felony at the time of court appearance. More than six-out-of-ten of the *Schall* youths would have been ineligible for preventive detention under most adult preventive detention statutes. Limiting detention to those accused of violent offenses obviously is fairer to the defendant because this limitation precludes a large class of individuals from eligibility for preventive detention. However, * * * even this limitation on eligibility may be unrelated to the accuracy of the prediction of violence during the pretrial period.

It is difficult to assess this overinclusiveness. The statutes, narrowly interpreted, would suggest that the rate of false positives is unacceptable. It is only when we allow a wide, standardless definition of pretrial danger that the efficacy of the predictions even begins to make sense. In New York, the statute is so vague as to be meaningless with respect to what is being predicted: both petty and minor offenses would comprise the decision standard for dangerousness. This undifferentiated standard runs the risk of predicting everything and nothing at the same time. It is one thing to disadvantage the accused by detaining him or her to prevent violent felonies. It is quite another to disadvantage a detainee in the outcome of the pending charge. We suggest that this power should be sharply attenuated given the considerable adverse impact detention has on the detainee. Such detention amounts to unregulated punishment.

Ordinarily, the law will not tolerate deprivations of liberty for punitive purposes without a very high degree of certainty of guilt. The *Schall* cases emphasize the importance of this presumption. * * * There are reasonable and constitutional arguments to incapacitate a presumptively innocent individual when we are certain he or she is dangerous. But whenever a significant number of persons are preventively detained, many individuals will be deprived of their liberty even though they would not have endangered the community. In light of the great cost to defendants in terms of case outcomes and sanctions, and the marginal gains to society in crimes averted, preventive detention appears to be unjustified.* * *

11) Preventive Detention of Adults In *United States v. Salerno*, 481 U.S. 739, 107 S.Ct. 2095, 95 L.Ed.2d 697 (1987), the United States Supreme Court upheld the constitutionality of the Federal Bail Reform Act of 1984, 18 U.S.C. § 3141 et seq., which allows the federal government preventively to detain an arrestee pending trial if the government demonstrates by clear and convincing evidence after an adversary hearing that no release conditions "will reasonably assure * * * the safety of any other person and the community." Relying in part on *Schall v. Martin*, the *Salerno* majority concluded that "crime prevention" served a legitimate regulatory purpose and did not constitute pre-trial punishment. Unlike *Schall*, however, the Bail Reform Act provided for a full-blown adversary hearing, a standard of proof of "clear and convincing" evidence, and specified a narrow range of extremely serious crimes as the predicate offense for preventive detention. 18 U.S.C. § 3142(f). The Court relied on *Schall* as authority for the conclusion that "there is nothing inherently unattainable about a prediction of future criminal conduct."

12) Characteristics of Detained Youths In *Schall v. Martin*, the Court's description of the case histories of some of the thirty-four juveniles in the class of litigants implied that prosecutors charge most juveniles held in detention with serious offenses. While being charged with a serious offense increases a youth's probability of detention, most detention studies indicate that courts overuse detention facilities and that many, if not most, juveniles held in pre-trial custody are not charged with serious crimes. Recall the characteristics of detained juveniles reported in *Snyder and Sickmund, Juvenile Offenders and Victims*, supra p. 418. For what offenses did juvenile court judges detain the majority of juveniles? Which offenses accounted for the largest numbers of youths held in detention? *See also,* Ira M. Schwartz, et al., "Juvenile Detention: The Hidden Closets Revisited," 4 *Justice Q.* 219 (1987)(judges detained primarily property offenders); Belinda McCarthy, "Preventive Detention and Pretrial Custody in the Juvenile Court," 15 *J. Crim. Just.* 185 (1987) (judges detained predominantly non-violent offenders);

Charles Frazier and Donna M. Bishop, "The Pretrial Detention of Juveniles and Its Impact on Case Dispositions," 76 *J. Crim. L. & Criminology* 1132 (1985) (pretrial detention exerts independent effect on severity of sentences after controlling for offenses); Ira Schwartz and William Barton, *Reforming Juvenile Detention* (1994).

13) Detention of Racial Minorities—Disproportionate Minority Confinement (DMC) In his *Schall* dissent, Justice Marshall observed that "government officials may not be accorded unfettered discretion in making decisions that impinge upon fundamental rights. * * * [E]xcessive discretion fosters inequality in the distribution of entitlements and harms, inequality which is especially troublesome when those benefits and burdens are great; and discretion can mask the use by officials of illegitimate criteria in allocating important goods and rights." Empirical research raises concerns about both the racial and gender impact of discretionary preventive detention decisions. Without objective criteria or validated indicators, detention statutes remit speculative judgments about future behavior to each judge's discretion and foster seemingly random decisions. In addition to the dangers of erroneous predictions, unstructured discretion also fosters arbitrary, unequal, and discriminatory decisions. Recall the racial characteristics of detained juveniles reported in Snyder and Sickmund, *Juvenile Offenders and Victims*, supra p. 418.

Judges often apply vague and imprecise statutes in a discriminatory fashion. Juvenile justice entails a multi-stage decision-making process. Earlier discretionary rulings cumulate and affect later ones. Belinda McCarthy, "Preventive Detention and Pretrial Custody in the Juvenile Court." 15 *J. Crim. Just.* 185 (1987); Belinda McCarthy and Brent L. Smith, "The Conceptualization of Discrimination in the Juvenile Justice Process: The Impact of Administrative Factors and Screening Decisions on Juvenile Court Dispositions," 24 Criminology 41 (1986); Jeffrey Fagan, Ellen Slaughter, and Eliot Hartstone, "Blind Justice? The Impact of Race on the Juvenile Justice Process." 33 *Crime and Delinq.* 224 (1987). Although the relative impact of legal and socio-demographic factors on detention decisions varies, virtually every study reports that juvenile courts detain a disproportionately large number of minority offenders. After controlling for the present offense and prior records, a juvenile's race consistently exerts an independent effect on detention decisions. Carl Pope and William H. Feyerherm, "Minority Status and Juvenile Justice Processing: An Assessment of the Research Literature," 22 *Criminal Justice Abstracts* 327, 527 (1990); Carl Pope and William H. Feyerherm, *Minorities and the Juvenile Justice System* (1992); Ira Schwartz, et al., "Juvenile Detention: The Hidden Closets Revisited," 4 *Justice Quarterly* 221 (1987); Kimberly Kempf–Leonard, Carl Pope and William H. Feyerherm, eds., *Minorities in Juvenile Justice* (1995).

Between 1977 and 1982, the proportion of minority youths held in detention centers increased from 41% to 51%, a growth rate that did not reflect either racial demographic or arrest rate trends. Barry Krisberg, et al., "The Watershed of Juvenile Justice Reform." 32 *Crime & Delinq.* 5 (1986). Although juvenile courts detained about 20% of all referred youths, white juveniles experienced somewhat lower detention rates (18%) and black (25%) and other racial minority (22%) juveniles experienced somewhat higher rates.

See Jeffrey A. Butts, et al., *Juvenile Court Statistics 1994* (1995). After controlling for offense seriousness, black youths had higher rates of detention than whites in every offense category; the greatest racial disproportionality occurred in detention rates for drug referrals (26% white versus 47% black). *Id.* Recent disproportionate increases in minority admissions reflect judicial disparities in detaining black youths charged with drug possession or sale. Howard N. Snyder, *Growth in Minority Detentions Attributed to Drug Law Violators* (1990). Analyses of changes in racial disproportionality in juvenile justice processing between 1985 and 1989 report that the proportion of white youths detained actually *decreased* by 12.6% while that for non-white youths *increased* by 41.5%. *See* Edmund F. McGarrell, "Trends in Racial Disproportionality in Juvenile Court Processing: 1985–1989," 39 *Crime & Delinq.* 29 (1993). For youths referred for drug offenses, the white detention rate *decreased* 17.2% while non-white youths' detention rate *increased* 235.8%. A study of felony cases referred by police and detained by juvenile courts found that a youth's race affected both decision, even after controlling for weapons use, victim injury, and socio-economic and family structure. *See* Madeline Wordes, Timothy S. Bynum, and Charles J. Corley, "Locking up Youth: The Impact of Race on Detention Decisions," 31 *J. Res. Crime & Delinquency* 149 (1994).

Professor Donna Bishop, "The Role of Race and Ethnicity in Juvenile Justice Process," in Hawkins and Kempf–Leonard, ed., *Our Children, Their Children: Confronting Racial and Ethnic Differences in American Juvenile Justice* 23 (2005), provides a detailed analysis of the differential processing of youths by race at each stage of the juvenile justice system. She concludes that

> [f]ew features of the juvenile justice system are better documented than the long-standing and pronounced disparities in the processing of white and minority youths. Nationally, youths of color—especially African Americans and Hispanics—are arrested in numbers greatly disproportionate to their representation in the general population. They are over-represented among young people held in secure detention, petitioned to juvenile court, and adjudicated delinquent. Among those adjudicated delinquent, they are more often committed to the "deep end" of the juvenile system. When confined, they are more often housed in large public institutions rather than privately run group homes or specialized treatment facilities. And, at "the end of the line," prosecutors and judges are more apt to relinquish jurisdiction over them, transferring them to criminal court for prosecution and punishment as adults.

Analysts examine whether minority over-representation is the result of "differential offending"—racial or ethnic differences in the seriousness and persistence of delinquent involvement—or of "differential processing"—intentional or unintentional differences in juvenile justice personnel handling of similarly-situated offenders of different races or ethnicities. **Alex R. Piquero, "Disproportionate Minority Contact,"** 18 Future of Children 59 (2008), reviews the empirical research testing both explanations and reports that even after studies control for offense variables, differential processing persists.

[M]inority, especially black, youth and adults are over-represented at most stages of the system, beginning with the decisions by police agencies to target certain high-crime neighborhoods, which tend also to be high-minority neighborhoods, and to target certain crimes, both of which bring the police into more contact with minorities, especially blacks, than whites.* * * Several studies of the disposition and confinement process show that black youth in the system are given more restrictive dispositions than their white counterparts even when they have committed the same offense and have the same prior record—a finding that has also been made with respect to minorities, especially blacks, being sentenced more harshly than whites. Evidence also shows that black youth are more likely than white youth to be transferred to criminal court, regardless of offense type and age category * * *.

See also, National Council on Crime and Delinquency, *And Justice for Some: Differential Treatment of Youth of Color in the Juvenile Justice System* (2007); Kimberly Kempf–Leonard, "Minority Youths and Juvenile Justice: Disproportionate Minority Contact after Nearly 20 Years of Reform Efforts, 5 *Youth Violence & Juv. Just.* 71 (2007).

Perry L. Moriearty, "Combating the Color–Coded Confinement of Kids: An Equal Protection Remedy," 32 N.Y.U. Rev. L & Social Change 285, 312–313 (2008), summarizes the extensive research on DMC and the efforts of Office of Juvenile Justice and Delinquency Prevention, Department of Justice, to document and reduce it:

It has long been evident that the percentage of minority youth present in the United States justice system far exceeds their proportion in the general population. Over the last thirty years, multiple studies have shown that Disproportionate Minority Contact afflicts nearly every processing point in nearly every juvenile justice system in the country. * * *

Studies over the past thirty years, which have become increasingly sophisticated, demonstrate the strong likelihood that in many jurisdictions race plays an impermissible role in how children are treated in the juvenile courts. In 1990, in what is now considered a path-breaking meta-analysis, researchers Carl Pope and William Feyerherm concluded that, of the forty-six studies conducted between 1969 and 1989 regarding the relationship between race and processing in juvenile justice systems around the country, two-thirds found that race negatively affected outcomes for youth of color. In 2002, Pope repeated this analysis, this time focusing on studies completed between 1989 and 2001. Of the thirty-four studies reviewed, 80% of which employed multivariate analytic approaches, twenty-five reported "race effects" in the processing of youth, which resulted in poorer outcomes for youth of color; nine were inconclusive; and one found no race effects. Significantly, several of these studies have found that legal and social factors cannot by themselves account for the disparities observed in processing outcomes—in other words, but for the presence of race bias, overrepresentation would not exist to the same degree. * * *

One of the 1988 amendments to the JJDPA, known as the "DMC Mandate," required states receiving funding from the Title II, Part B, Formula Grants Program to investigate the problem of "disproportionate minority confinement" in secure facilities and to develop action plans to remedy the issues identified. Specifically, if the proportion of a given group of minority youth detained or confined in its secure detention facilities, secure correctional facilities, jails, and lockups exceeded the proportion that group represented in the general population, the state in question was required to develop and implement plans to reduce the disproportionate representation.

In 1992, presented with a series of new reports demonstrating that race played a role in juvenile justice processing (including Pope and Feyerherm's 1990 report), Congress made the DMC Mandate a core requirement of the JJDPA. Under the 1992 language, states were required to: (1) identify the extent to which DMC exists, (2) assess the reasons for its existence, and (3) develop intervention strategies to address the causes of DMC. * * *

In 2002, Congress again amended the JJDPA to require that states participating in the Formula Grants Program "address juvenile delinquency prevention efforts and system improvement efforts designed to reduce, without establishing or requiring numerical standards or quotas, the disproportionate number of juvenile members of minority groups, who come into contact with the juvenile justice system." This change broadened the concept of DMC from disproportionate minority "confinement" to disproportionate minority "contact" by requiring an examination of possible disproportionate representation of minority youth at all decision points along the juvenile justice system continuum. * * *

14) Preventive Detention and Gender Disparities Female juveniles also experience higher rates of pretrial detention than do male juveniles charged with similar, less-serious offenses. Male delinquents commit more than three times as many offenses as females overall and an even larger proportion of the serious and violent crimes. Howard Snyder and Melissa Sickmund, *Juvenile Offenders and Victims*, supra p. 418. Despite these differences in patterns of offending, however, juvenile court judges detain proportionately more female than male delinquents when prosecutors charge them with minor and status offenses. Meda Chesney–Lind and Randall G. Shelden, *Girls, Delinquency, and Juvenile Justice* (1992); Meda Chesney–Lind, "Girls and Status Offenses: Is Juvenile Justice Still Sexist?" 29 *Crim. Just. Abstracts* 144 (1988); Meda Chesney–Lind, "Judicial Paternalism and the Female Status Offender: Training Women to Know their Place," 23 *Crime & Delinq.* 121 (1977). For example, juvenile courts detained 44% of males for serious FBI Part I felony offenses, compared with only 23% of females. Conversely, judges detained 62% of females for Part II offenses and 15% for status offenses, compared with 53% of boys for Part II offenses and only 3% for status offenses. Ira Schwartz and William Barton, *Reforming Juvenile Detention 18* (1994). The disproportionate detention of females for minor offenses provided one impetus to de-institutionalize status offenders.

15) Sources of Racial and Gender Disparities in Detention Decisions Because the empirical studies reported in Notes 12 and 13 controlled for the seriousness of offenders' present offenses and prior records, what other factors might account for the apparent differences in rates of detention by race and by gender? How might living in an urban locale adversely affect black juveniles? Why might living in a suburban or rural locales adversely affect female offenders? What role might family composition or parental preferences play in the detention of minority and female offenders relative to white and male delinquents? How might "family sponsorship"—the ability and willingness of families to control their children—affect juvenile court judges' decisions to detain youths?

16) Risk Assessment Instruments—Reduce Institutional Populations, Improve Conditions of Confinement, Limit Inappropriate Detention, and Respond to Disproportionate Minority Confinement In Note 7, supra p. 458, Justice Rehnquist noted the Court only ruled on the constitutional minimum adequacy of the statute at issue in Schall. A state legislature could draft a more specific statute or juvenile justice administrators could develop more specific criteria or elaborate procedures to structure detention decision-making. Since 1992, the Annie E. Casey Foundation (http://www.aecf.org) has developed initiatives to reduce the use of pretrial detention. See http://www.aecf.org/Home/MajorInitiatives/JuvenileDetentionAlternatives Initiative.aspx The Casey Foundation has worked with local juvenile justice administrators to reduce reliance on secure confinement and to develop alternatives such as house arrest, electronic monitoring and the like. Local juvenile justice administrators develop Risk Assessment Instruments (RAI) or Detention Assessment Instruments (DAI) to provide more specific criteria to rationalize detention decision-making. The following excerpts describe the Casey Foundations Juvenile Detention Alternatives Initiative (JDAI) efforts and an example of a Risk Assessment Instrument:

National crowding crisis. A national crowding crisis in secure detention facilities has resulted from inappropriate and unnecessary confinement of youth. In the decade before JDAI was launched, detention populations increased by more than 70 percent, even though there was no corresponding increase in juvenile crime. By the beginning of the 1990's, two out of every three youth admitted to secure detention was entering a place that was crowded, that could not provide the kinds of custody and care that case law and professional standards require. Less than a third of youth in detention were charged with violent crimes. Indeed, as many youth were in detention for violating rules (e.g. technical probation violations) as were there for serious crimes. And, by 1995, almost two-thirds of detained youth were youth of color, a percentage that was disproportionate to both their percentage in the general population and their percentage of youth arrested.

Negative impact of secure detention. Research has shown that juvenile detention has critical, long-lasting consequences for court-involved youth. Youth who are detained are more likely than their counterparts to be formally charged, adjudicated and committed to an institution. Detention disrupts already tenuous connections in school, services and families. Over the long-haul, the detention experience negatively impacts educational and employment levels. JDAI believes that reforming detention use will also minimize the harmful, unintended effects.

Lack of public safety results. Despite its frequent use, detention is not improving public safety. In fact, detention is a stronger predictor of recidivism among juveniles than many well-known factors. Detention reform will help juvenile justice systems more accurately identify which youth really needed to be confined to minimize risks to the community. It will also hold the system accountable for public safety results.

High cost of detention. Detention is a growing expense in most jurisdictions. In some places, the average cost to operate a detention bed exceeds $70,000 annually, and experts estimate that the cost of building, financing and operating a single bed over 20 years is approximately $1.5 million. Crowded conditions force many communities to face huge new public expenditures for a detention center at a time when tax revenues are decreasing relative to need. * * *

JDAI focuses on the juvenile detention component of the juvenile justice system because youth are often unnecessarily or inappropriately detained at great expense, with long-lasting negative consequences for both public safety and youth development.

Under the Casey Foundation's auspices, JDAI sites use eight interrelated core strategies to reduce reliance on secure confinement; improve public safety; reduce racial disparities; reduce justice system expenditures; and stimulate overall juvenile justice reforms:

Collaboration between the major juvenile justice agencies, other governmental entities, and community organizations. * * *

Use of accurate data, both to diagnose the system's problems and proclivities and to assess the impact of various reforms, is critical. * * *

Objective admissions criteria and instruments must be developed to replace subjective decision making at all points where choices to place children in secure custody are made.

New or enhanced non-secure alternatives to detention must be implemented in order to increase the options available for arrested youth. These programs must be careful to target only youth who would otherwise be locked up. Whenever possible, they should be based in those neighborhoods where detention cases are concentrated and operated by local organizations.

Case processing reforms must be introduced to expedite the flow of cases through the system. These changes reduce lengths of stay in custody, expand the availability of non-secure program slots, and ensure that interventions with youth are timely and appropriate.

Special detention cases Youth in custody as a result of probation violations, writs and warrants, as well as those awaiting placement must be re-examined and new practices implemented to minimize their presence in the secure facility.

Reducing racial disparities requires specific strategies (in addition to those listed above) aimed at eliminating bias and ensuring a level playing field for youth of color. Change in this arena also requires persistent, determined leadership because the sensitive nature of these discussions and changes frequently provoke defensiveness and avoidance.

Improving conditions of confinement is most likely to occur when facilities are routinely inspected by knowledgeable individuals applying rigorous protocols and ambitious standards. Absent of this kind of consistent scrutiny, conditions in secure facilities are unlikely to improve and often will deteriorate.

In twenty-two states and more than one hundred sites, the Case Foundation has sponsored or provided technical assistance to local justice officials to develop RAI or DAI. These instruments provide justice system officials with more objective and easily administered tools to make detention decisions. The following is an example of an RAI used in Virginia:

VIRGINIA DEPARTMENT OF JUVENILE JUSTICE
DETENTION ASSESSMENT INSTRUMENT

Juvenile Name: _____ DOB: _____ / _____ / _____ Juvenile #: _____
_____ ICN# _____
Intake Date: _____ / _____ / _____ Time: ____ : ____ ☐AM ☐PM Worker Name: _____
_____ CSU #: _____
Completed as Part of Detention Decision: ☐   Completed as Follow-Up (On-Call Intake): ☐

Score

1. **Most Serious Alleged Offense** (see reverse for examples of offenses in each category)
   Category A: Felonies against persons. 15
   Category B: Felony weapons and felony narcotics distribution. 12
   Category C: Other felonies. 7
   Category D: Class 1 misdemeanors against persons. 5
   Category E: Other Class 1 misdemeanors. 3
   Category F: Violations of probation/parole 2   _____

2. **Additional Charges in this Referral**
   Two or more additional current felony offenses...3
   One additional current felony offense 2
   One or more additional misdemeanor OR violation of probation/parole offenses...........1
   One or more status offenses OR No additional current offenses 0   _____

3. **Prior Adjudications of Guilt** (includes continued adjudications with "evidence sufficient to finding of guilt")
   Two or more prior adjudications of guilt for felony offenses.............................6
   One prior adjudication of guilt for a felony offense...4
   Two or more prior adjudications of guilt for misdemeanor offenses 3
   Two or more prior adjudications of guilt for probation/parole violations 2
   One prior adjudication of guilt for any misdemeanor or status offense 1
   No prior adjudications of guilt 0   _____

4. **Petitions Pending Adjudication or Disposition** (exclude deferred adjudications)
   One or more pending petitions/dispositions for a felony offense......................8
   Two or more pending petitions/dispositions for other offenses 5
   One pending petition/disposition for an other offense 2
   No pending petitions/dispositions 0   _____

5. **Supervision Status**
   Parole 4
   Probation based on a Felony or Class 1 misdemeanor 3
   Probation based on other offenses OR CHINSup OR Deferred disposition with conditions 2
   Informal Supervision OR Intake Diversion 1
   None...0   _____

6. **History of Failure to Appear** (within past 12 months)
   Two or more petitions/warrants/detention orders for FTA in past 12 months...........3
   One petition/warrant/detention order for FTA in past 12 months 1
   No petition/warrant/detention order for FTA in past 12 months.......................0   _____

7. **History of Escape/ Runaways** (within past 12 months)
   One or more escapes from secure confinement or custody 4
   One or more instances of absconding from non-secure, court-ordered placements...........3
   One or more runaways from home 1
   No escapes or runaways w/in past 12 months 0   _____

8. **TOTAL SCORE**...   _____

Indicated Decision: ____ 0 - 9 Release   ____ 10 - 14 Detention Alternative   ____ 15+
Secure Detention

Mandatory Overrides: ☐ 1. Use of firearm in current offense

(must be detained)   ☐ 2. Escapee from a secure placement
                            ☐ 3. Local court policy (indicate applicable policy)

Discretionary Override: ☐ 1. Aggravating factors (override to more restrictive placement than indicated by guidelines)
                          ☐ 2. Mitigating factors (override to less restrictive placement than indicated by guidelines)
                          ☐ 3. Approved local graduated sanction for probation/parole violation

---

Actual Decision / Recommendation: _____ **Release** _____ **Alternative** _____
                                            Secure Detention

A number of examples of juvenile detention risk assessment instruments may be found at http://www.jdaihelpdesk.org/objective/Pages/Juvenile DetentionRiskAssessment.aspx.

C. DETENTION HEARING PROCEDURES

The Court in *Schall v. Martin* considered whether the procedures used to detain juveniles provided adequate "protection against erroneous and unnecessary deprivations of liberty" by comparing them with the Court's requirements for a probable cause determination for arrested adults established in *Gerstein v. Pugh*, 420 U.S. 103, 95 S.Ct. 854, 43 L.Ed.2d 54 (1975). *Gerstein* held that the constitution requires a judicial determination of probable cause before extended post-arrest restraints on liberty because prolonged detention entails a Fourth Amendment seizure of the person. The *Gerstein* Court also noted that all of the exigencies that justify arrests without a prior judicial determination of probable cause and a warrant dissipated once police take the defendant into custody:

> The consequences of prolonged detention may be more serious than the interference occasioned by arrest. Pretrial confinement may imperil the suspect's job, interrupt his source of income, and impair his family relationships. * * * Even pretrial release may be accompanied by burdensome conditions that effect a significant restraint of liberty. * * * When the stakes are this high, the detached judgment of a neutral magistrate is essential if the Fourth Amendment is to furnish meaningful protection from unfounded interference with liberty. Accordingly, we hold that the Fourth Amendment requires a judicial determination of probable cause as a prerequisite to extended restraint of liberty following arrest. *Id.* at 114

The *Gerstein* Court noted, however, that such a probable cause determination need not occur in an adversarial hearing. Because a judge made a probable cause determination in an *ex parte* proceeding if she initially issued a warrant to arrest, the court concluded that the Fourth Amendment did not require any more formal or adversarial proceeding when she made a probable cause determination following an offender's arrest.

The majority in *Schall* concluded that the New York procedures for juvenile preventive detention satisfied the *Gerstein* requirements because the juvenile received notice of the charges at an informal initial appearance, the court made a stenographic record of the appearance, a parent or guardian accompanied the juvenile, and the judge advised the juvenile of the right to remain silent and the right to counsel. The *Schall* majority implied that the juvenile court judge made a probable cause determination at the initial appearance, but it also noted that a petition stating probable cause had to be filed in any event and that a formal probable cause hearing was held within three days of the initial appearance. The dissent in *Schall* disputed the majority's conclusion that a probable cause determination occurred at the initial appearance. It pointed out that "[t]he judge ordinarily does not interview the juveniles, * * * makes no inquiry into the truth of allegations in the petition, * * * and does not determine whether there is probable cause to believe the juvenile committed the offense."

1. STATUTORY AND PROCEDURAL COMPARISON AND CONTRAST

What elements do the following states' statutes and rules of procedure have in common? How do they differ? What juvenile justice and crime control policies underlie the statutory and procedural differences?

Fla. Stat. § 985.213 (1998). Use of Detention

(2)(a) All determinations and court orders regarding placement of a child into detention care * * * shall be based on a risk assessment of the child. * * *

(b)1. The risk assessment instrument for detention care placement determinations and orders shall be developed by the Department of Juvenile Justice in agreement with representatives appointed by the [Associations of Circuit Judges, Prosecuting Attorneys, and Public Defenders who represent urban and rural areas]. * * * The risk assessment instrument shall take into consideration, but need not be limited to, prior history of failure to appear, prior offenses, offenses committed pending adjudication, any unlawful possession of a firearm, theft of a motor vehicle or possession of a stolen motor vehicle, and community control status at the time the child is taken into custody. The risk assessment instrument shall also take into consideration appropriate aggravating and mitigating circumstances, and shall be designed to target a narrower population of children than * * * [all of those eligible for detention]. The risk assessment instrument shall also include any information concerning the child's history of abuse and neglect. The risk assessment shall indicate whether detention care is warranted, and, if detention care is warranted, whether the child should be placed into secure, nonsecure, or home detention care.

Fla. Stat. Ann. § 985.215 (West 1999). Detention

* * * (2) [A] child taken into custody and placed into nonsecure or home detention care or detained in secure detention care prior to a detention hearing may continue to be detained by the court if: * * * [the child is alleged to be an escapee or an absconder from a commitment

program; the child is wanted in another jurisdiction for a felony offense; the child is charged with an offense and requests through counsel to be detained for protection; the child is charged with a domestic violence offense; the child is charged with a capital felony, a life felony, a felony of the first degree, or a felony of the second degree or a felony of the third degree that involves a firearm; or the child is charged with any second or third degree felony and the child has a record of failure to appear at court hearings, has a record of law violations prior to court hearings, has already been detained or released pending disposition of a case, has a record of violent conduct that resulted in physical injury or possessed a firearm.]

A child who meets any of these criteria and who is ordered to be detained pursuant to this subsection shall be given a hearing within 24 hours after being taken into custody. The purpose of the detention hearing is to determine the existence of probable cause that the child has committed the delinquent act or violation of law with which he or she is charged and the need for continued detention. * * * [T]he court shall utilize the results of the risk assessment performed by the juvenile probation officer and, based on the criteria in this subsection, shall determine the need for continued detention. * * * If the court orders a placement more restrictive than indicated by the results of the risk assessment instrument, the court shall state, in writing, clear and convincing reasons for such placement. * * *

(5)(a) A child may not be placed into or held in secure, nonsecure, or home detention care for longer than 24 hours unless the court orders such detention care. * * * The [detention] order shall be a final order, reviewable by appeal * * * and [a]ppeals of such orders shall take precedence over other appeals and other pending matters.

Fla. Rule Juv. Proc. 8.010. Detention Hearing

(a) When Required. No detention order * * * shall be entered without a hearing at which all parties shall have an opportunity to be heard on the necessity for the child's being held in detention, unless the court finds that the parent or custodian cannot be located or that the child's mental or physical condition is such that a court appearance is not in the child's best interest. * * *

(d) Notice. The intake officer shall make a diligent effort to notify the parent or custodian of the child of the time and place of the hearing. * * * Failure of notice to parents or custodians or their nonattendance at the hearing shall not invalidate the proceeding or the order of detention.

(e) Advice of Rights. At the detention hearing the persons present shall be advised of the purpose of the hearing and the child shall be advised of:

(1) the nature of the charge for which he or she was taken into custody;

(2) the right to be represented by counsel and if insolvent the right to appointed counsel;

(3) that the child is not required to say anything and that anything said may be used against him or her;

(4) if the child's parent, custodian, or counsel is not present, that he or she has a right to communicate with them and that, if necessary, reasonable means will be provided to do so; and

(5) the reason continued detention is requested.

(f) Issues. At this hearing the court shall determine the following:

(1) The existence of probable cause to believe the child has committed a delinquent act. This issue shall be determined in a nonadversary proceeding. The court shall apply the standard of proof necessary for an arrest warrant and its finding may be based upon a sworn complaint, affidavit, deposition under oath, or, if necessary, upon testimony under oath properly recorded.

(2) The need for detention according to the criteria provided by law. In making this determination in addition to the sworn testimony of available witnesses all relevant and material evidence helpful in determining the specific issue, including oral and written reports, may be relied upon to the extent of its probative value, even though it would not be competent at an adjudicatory hearing.

(g) Probable Cause. If the court finds that such probable cause exists, it shall enter an order making such a finding and may, if other statutory needs of detention exist, retain the child in detention. If the court finds that such probable cause does not exist, it shall forthwith release the child from detention. If the court finds that one or more of the statutory needs of detention exists, but is unable to make a finding on the existence of probable cause, it may retain the child in detention and continue the hearing for the purpose of determining the existence of probable cause to a time within 72 hours of the time the child was taken into custody. The court may, on a showing of good cause, continue the hearing a second time for not more than 24 hours beyond the 72–hour period. * * *

Minn. Stat. § 260.172 (1997). Detention hearing

Subdivision 1. (a) If a child was taken into custody [by court order] * * * the court shall hold a hearing within 72 hours of the time the child was taken into custody, excluding Saturdays, Sundays, and holidays, to determine whether the child should continue in custody.

(b) In all other cases, the court shall hold a detention hearing:

(1) within 36 hours of the time the child was taken into custody, excluding Saturdays, Sundays, and holidays, if the child is being held at a juvenile secure detention facility or shelter care facility; or

(2) within 24 hours of the time the child was taken into custody, excluding Saturdays, Sundays, and holidays, if the child is being held at an adult jail or municipal lockup.

(c) Unless there is reason to believe that the child would endanger self or others, not return for a court hearing, run away from the child's parent, guardian, or custodian or otherwise not remain in the care or control of the person to whose lawful custody the child is released, or that the child's health or welfare would be immediately endangered, the child shall be released to the custody of a parent, guardian, custodian, or other suitable person, subject to reasonable conditions of release including, but not limited to, a requirement that the child undergo a chemical use assessment. * * *

Minn. Rule Juv. Proc. 5.03 (1997). Detention Decision

Subd. 1. Presumption for Unconditional Release. The child shall be released unless:

(A) the child would endanger self or others; or

(B) the child would not appear for a court hearing; or

(C) the child would not remain in the care or control of the person into whose lawful custody the child is released; or

(D) the child's health or welfare would be immediately endangered.

There is a presumption that a child will not appear for a court hearing when the person to whom the child is to be released refuses to sign a written promise to bring the child to court.

Subd. 2. Detention Factors. The following non-exclusive factors may justify a decision to detain a child:

(A) the child is charged with the misdemeanor, gross misdemeanor or felony offense of arson, assault, prostitution or a criminal sexual offense;

(B) the child was taken into custody for an offense which would be a presumptive commitment to prison offense if committed by an adult, or a felony involving the use of a firearm;

(C) the child was taken into custody for additional felony charges while other delinquency charges are pending;

(D) the child was taken into custody for a felony and, as a result of prior delinquency adjudication(s), has received an out-of-home placement;

(E) the child was an escapee from an institution or other placement facility to which the court ordered the child;

(F) the child has a demonstrable recent record of willful failure to appear at juvenile proceedings;

(G) the child is a fugitive from another jurisdiction; or

(H) the above factors are not met but the detaining authority documents in writing, objective and articulable reasons why the child's welfare or public safety would be immediately endangered if the child were released.

Subd. 3. Discretion to Release Even if One or More Factors are Met. Even if a child meets one or more of the factors * * * the detaining authority has broad discretion to release that child before the detention hearing if other less restrictive measures would be adequate.

Subd. 4. Factors Which Can Not Support Detention Decision. In deciding whether detention is justified, the detaining authority shall not consider the child or the child's family's race, color, gender, sexual orientation, religion, national origin, economic or public assistance status, family structure or residential mobility.

Minn. Rule Juv. Proc. 5.04 (1997). Release or Continued Detention

Subd. 1. For Child Taken Into Custody Pursuant to Court Order or Warrant.

(A) *Detention Required.* Unless the court orders an earlier release, the child shall be detained for thirty-six (36) hours after being taken into custody, excluding Saturdays, Sundays and holidays. * * *

Subd. 4. Probable Cause Determination.

(A) *Time Limit.* The child shall be released no later than forty-eight (48) hours after being taken into custody without a court order or warrant signed by a judge, including the day the child was detained, Saturdays, Sundays and legal holidays, unless the court determines there is probable cause to believe the child committed the offense(s) alleged.

(B) *Application and Record.* The facts establishing probable cause to believe the offense(s) was committed and that the child committed the offense(s) shall be presented to the judge upon oath, either orally or in writing. Oral testimony shall be recorded and retained by the judge. Written facts may be presented to the judge by telephone, facsimile, video, or other similar device. * * * The judge shall be advised if a prior request for a probable cause determination was made and turned down relative to the same incident. * * *

Minn. Rule Juv. Proc. 5.07 (1997). Detention Hearing

Subd. 1. Time and Filing. The court shall commence a detention hearing within thirty-six (36) hours of the child being taken into custody. The following documents shall be filed with the court before the detention hearing:

(A) a report or reports that the child is being held in detention * * *; and

(B) a charging document with probable cause * * *.

Subd. 3. Advice of Rights. At the beginning of the detention hearing, the court shall advise all persons present of:

(A) the reasons why the child was taken into custody;

(B) the allegations of the charging document;

(C) the purpose and scope of the detention hearing;

(D) the right of the child to be represented by counsel at the detention hearing and at every other stage of the proceedings, and the right of a child alleged to be delinquent to counsel at public expense; and

(E) the right of the child to remain silent.

Subd. 4. Evidence. The court may admit any evidence including reliable hearsay and opinion evidence that is relevant to the decision whether to detain the child. The court may not admit evidence of privileged communications.

Subd. 5. Findings Necessary for Continued Detention. A court may detain a child beyond thirty-six (36) hours if, after a hearing, the court finds:

(A) probable cause to believe the child committed the offense(s) alleged * * *; and

(B) there is reason to believe that if the child were released, after consideration of the factors set forth [in Rules 5.03 Subd. 2], that:

(1) the child would endanger self or others; or

(2) the child would not appear for a court hearing; or

(3) the child would not remain in the care or control of the person into whose lawful custody the child is released; or

(4) the child's health or welfare would be immediately endangered.
* * *

2. TIME WITHIN WHICH TO HOLD DETENTION HEARING

ALFREDO A. v. SUPERIOR COURT OF LOS ANGELES COUNTY

6 Cal.4th 1212, 865 P.2d 56, 26 Cal.Rptr.2d 623 (Cal. 1994).

LUCAS, CHIEF JUSTICE. In *Gerstein v. Pugh*, (hereafter *Gerstein*), the United States Supreme Court held that the Fourth Amendment requires a prompt judicial determination of "probable cause to believe the suspect has committed a crime" as a prerequisite to an extended pretrial detention following a warrantless arrest. The court stopped short of mandating a specific timetable for making a "prompt" determination of probable cause.

In *County of Riverside v. McLaughlin*, (hereafter *McLaughlin*), the high court sought to further define the "promptness" requirement for making the probable cause determination mandated in *Gerstein*. The court held that, "Taking into account the competing interests articulated in *Gerstein*, we believe that a jurisdiction that provides judicial determinations of probable cause within 48 hours of arrest will, as a general matter, comply with the promptness requirement of *Gerstein*."

Neither *Gerstein* nor *McLaughlin* was a juvenile detention case. In contrast, the United States Supreme Court's decision in *Schall v. Martin*, (hereafter *Schall*) did directly address the constitutional parameters of a key provision of New York State's juvenile pretrial detention statute. * * * *Schall*, and other decisions of the high court, make it abundantly clear that Fourth Amendment and related due process claims pertaining to the pretrial detention of juveniles following warrantless arrests for criminal activity cannot be viewed in the same light as similar challenges to adult detentions. This is so because, in the words of the Supreme Court, juvenile proceedings are "fundamentally different" from adult criminal proceedings, requiring that a "balance" be struck between the "informality" and "flexibility" that must of necessity inhere in juvenile proceedings, and the further requirement that those proceedings comport with the juvenile's constitutional rights, and the " 'fundamental fairness' demanded by the Due Process Clause."

In July of 1991, the Los Angeles County Juvenile Court * * * adopted the "official position" that *McLaughlin*'s strict 48–hour rule does not apply in juvenile detention proceedings. We granted review in this case to determine whether that position passes constitutional muster, or whether *McLaughlin*'s 48–hour rule strictly applies to the pretrial detention of adults and juveniles alike following warrantless arrest for criminal activity. * * *

[W]e have concluded that the high court did not intend that the strict 48–hour rule subsequently announced in McLaughlin—a ruling handed down in a case involving the pretrial detention of adults—should automatically apply in the juvenile detention setting. To conclude otherwise we would have to ignore the fundamental differences between adult and juvenile proceedings recognized in all of the high court's cases that have specifically addressed juvenile detention issues.

As will be explained, California's juvenile detention statutes basically afford juvenile detainees who have been arrested without a warrant a formal, adversarial "detention hearing" within 72 hours of a warrantless arrest, which proceeding incorporates the "probable cause" determination mandated under *Gerstein*. * * * Given the fundamental difference in purpose and procedure between the treatment of adult and juvenile detainees, we have further concluded that juvenile detainees are constitutionally entitled to a judicial "probable cause" determination within 72 hours of arrest, consistent with the integrated provisions of our juvenile detention statutory scheme. * * *

In order to meaningfully examine and apply the controlling constitutional principles and case law, we need a brief overview of the relevant statutory provisions that govern juvenile detentions following warrantless arrests in California.

Under our juvenile criminal justice system, a peace officer can take a minor into temporary custody for violating a federal or state law, or a local ordinance. * * *

Various official functions must be performed at the time of the juvenile's arrest, and within the initial 24– to 48–hour period following the arrest—all patently designed to ensure that the detained minor is afforded every reasonable opportunity for his or her immediate release, preferably to a parent or guardian.

Hence, the arresting officer may release the minor outright, deliver him or her to a public or private shelter facility in contract with the city or county to provide shelter care, counseling, or diversion services to such minors, or release the minor on his or her written promise to appear before a county juvenile probation officer, or to a parent, guardian, or other responsible relative, who may also be required to execute a written promise to appear along with the minor. If the arresting officer elects instead to deliver custody of the minor directly to the county probation officer, the officer must prepare a concise, written statement of the probable cause for taking the minor into temporary custody, to be furnished along with custody of the minor to the juvenile probation officer within 24 hours of the initial detention following the arrest. The policy underlying this choice of dispositions provided for in section 626 is expressly set forth in the statute: "In determining which disposition of the minor to make, the officer shall prefer the alternative which least restricts the minor's freedom of movement, provided that alternative is compatible with the best interests of the minor and the community." * * *

Section 628 requires the juvenile probation officer to "immediately investigate the circumstances of the minor and the facts surrounding his being taken into custody," and further requires the officer to "immediately release the minor to the custody of his parent, guardian, or responsible relative unless one or more * * * [specified] conditions exist * * *." Like the arresting officer, the county juvenile probation officer is empowered with discretion at the intake-investigatory stage to "adjust the situation which brings the minor within the jurisdiction [or probable jurisdiction] of the court" by "delineat[ing] specific programs of supervision for the minor," or referring the case to another agency, arranging for informal supervision, or requesting the district attorney to prepare a wardship petition for filing.

A minor taken into custody must be released within 48 hours, excluding "nonjudicial days," unless a wardship petition is filed within that initial 48–hour period. If a section 602 petition is filed, the minor must be afforded a formal, adversarial "detention hearing" in juvenile court "as soon as possible but in any event [no later than] the expiration of the next judicial day after a petition to declare the minor a ward * * * has been filed"—i.e., 48 to 72 hours after arrest (excluding "nonjudicial days"). * * *

Most significantly, when a minor is detained on suspicion of criminal activity, in contrast to an adult detained under similar circumstances, the inquiry into the propriety of the extended detention is much broader in scope than a determination, in the strict Fourth Amendment sense, of whether "factual" probable cause exists to believe the minor committed the crime for which he was taken into custody. Section 628 lists seven "conditions," one or more of which must be found to exist in order to warrant detaining the minor and scheduling a detention hearing within 72 hours of his or her arrest (again, excluding "nonjudicial" days). These conditions include whether:

(1) The minor is in need of proper and effective parental care or control and has no parent, guardian, or responsible relative; or has no parent, guardian, or responsible relative willing to exercise or capable of exercising such care or control; or has no parent, guardian, or responsible relative actually exercising such care or control.

(2) The minor is destitute or is not provided with the necessities of life or is not provided with a home or suitable place of abode.

(3) The minor is provided with a home which is an unfit place for him by reason of neglect, cruelty, depravity or physical abuse of either of his parents, or of his guardian or other person in whose custody or care he is.

(4) Continued detention of the minor is a matter of immediate and urgent necessity for the protection of the minor or reasonably necessary for the protection of the person or property of another.

(5) The minor is likely to flee the jurisdiction of the court.

(6) The minor has violated an order of the juvenile court.

(7) The minor is physically dangerous to the public because of a mental or physical deficiency, disorder or abnormality.

Section 635 sets forth the factors to be considered by the juvenile court at the detention hearing, and the standard the court must apply, in evaluating the probation officer's findings pursuant to section 628 and determining whether to continue the minor's detention or order his or her release from custody. The section provides:

"The court will examine such minor, his parent, guardian, or other person having relevant knowledge, hear such relevant evidence as the minor, his parent or guardian or their counsel desires to present, and, unless it appears that such minor has violated an order of the juvenile court or has escaped from the commitment of the juvenile court or that it is a matter of immediate and urgent necessity for the protection of such minor or reasonably necessary for the protection of the person or property of another that he be detained or that such minor is likely to flee to avoid the jurisdiction of the court, the court shall make its order releasing such minor from custody. The circumstances and gravity of the alleged offense may be considered, in conjunction with other factors, to determine whether it is a matter of immediate and urgent necessity for the protection of the minor or reasonably necessary for the protection of the person or property of another that the minor be detained."

The minor and his or her parent or guardian have the right to be represented by counsel at every stage of the detention proceedings. If the minor or the parent or guardian is indigent or cannot otherwise afford an attorney, counsel will be appointed by the court. * * *

[T]he determination whether to detain a minor following a warrantless arrest for criminal activity is a complex one, requiring consideration of various factors personal to the minor and his family situation, and the application of several important statutory presumptions favoring the minor's early release to a parent, guardian or responsible relative, or, if extended detention is warranted, selection of the detention alternative most "compatible with the best interests of the minor * * *," and "which least restricts the minor's freedom of movement". These presumptions, and the policies they implement, are unique to juvenile detention proceedings and are not implicated when a judicial determination is made whether factual probable cause exists to extend the detention of an adult arrestee. Bearing these distinctions in mind, we turn next to the opinions in *Gerstein*, *Schall*, [and] *McLaughlin*, * * * to see if those decisions will support an inference that the high court intended the strict 48–hour rule announced in *McLaughlin* to apply in juvenile detention proceedings. * * *

In *Gerstein*, the United States Supreme Court held unconstitutional Florida procedures under which persons arrested without a warrant could be kept in police custody for 30 days or more without a probable cause determination. The court held that the Fourth Amendment requires a prompt judicial determination of "probable cause to believe the suspect has committed a crime" as a prerequisite to an extended pretrial detention following a warrantless arrest. * * *

In *Gerstein*, the court explained that the Fourth Amendment does not require that the arrestee be afforded the "full panoply of adversary safeguards—counsel, confrontation, cross-examination, and compulsory process for witnesses" in connection with a judicial determination of probable cause. The court delineated the scope of that determination as follows: "The sole issue is whether there is probable cause for detaining the arrested person pending further proceedings * * *. The standard is the same as that for arrest. That standard—probable cause to believe the suspect has committed a crime—traditionally has been decided by a magistrate in a nonadversary proceeding on hearsay and written testimony * * *."

In contrast, the constitutional parameters of *juvenile* detentions were directly at issue in *Schall*, a case decided nine years after *Gerstein*. In *Schall*, the court found the juvenile "preventive detention" provisions of the New York Family Court Act facially valid under the due process clause of the Fourteenth Amendment. The New York statute authorized the detention of a juvenile arrested for the commission of a crime when there is a "serious risk" the juvenile "may before the return date commit an act which if committed by an adult would constitute a crime."

Whereas the sole issue in *Gerstein* was whether there was factual probable cause to detain the adult arrestee pending further proceedings—i.e., the same standard as that for arrest: "probable cause to believe the suspect has committed a crime"—*Schall* makes it abundantly clear that, where *juvenile* detentions are concerned, such a factual probable cause determination *is but one component* of the broader inquiry implicated in the determination whether to extend the pretrial detention of a juvenile arrested without a warrant for criminal activity. * * *

The court ultimately concluded the procedural protections afforded postarrest juvenile detainees under the New York statute satisfied the requirements of the due process clause of the Fourteenth Amendment, and found the statutory scheme facially valid. * * *

Seven years after *Schall* was decided, the high court decided *McLaughlin*. The court set out in *McLaughlin* to further define the "promptness" requirement for making the Fourth Amendment probable cause determination required under *Gerstein*. The court concluded: "[A] jurisdiction that provides judicial determinations of probable cause within 48 hours of arrest will, as a general matter, comply with the promptness requirement of *Gerstein*." Unlike *Schall*, the facts in *McLaughlin* did not present the court with an opportunity to reach or discuss the Fourth Amendment probable cause requirement in the specific context of *juvenile* detention proceedings. Critically, the court had no occasion in *McLaughlin* to consider the fundamental necessity, in the administration of *juvenile* criminal justice systems, to "strike a balance * * * respect[ing] the 'informality' and 'flexibility' that characterize juvenile proceedings * * * [while ensuring] that such proceedings comport with the 'fundamental fairness' demanded by the Due Process Clause." * * *

[We conclude that] in the context of juvenile detention proceedings, the high court would not today find rigid application of the 48–hour rule of *McLaughlin*, compelled under a strict application of Fourth Amendment principles. We emphasize that we do not today suggest a juvenile arrestee facing postarrest detention has no Fourth Amendment liberty interest in a prompt determination of the legal cause for his or her extended detention. The Fourth Amendment principles at the core of the holding in *Gerstein*, apply to juveniles as well as adults. The high court expressly reaffirmed as much eight years ago in *Schall*. Indeed, although the court in *Schall* twice characterized its earlier holding in *Gerstein* to be "that a judicial determination of probable cause is a prerequisite to any extended restraint on the liberty of an adult accused of crime", we think that such characterization cannot, in reason or fairness, be understood as an attempt by the court to limit the fundamental principles announced in *Gerstein* solely to adult detentions. * * *

California's postarrest juvenile detention statutes are plainly designed to protect the arrested minor's Fourth Amendment rights. The arresting officer must, within 24 hours of the arrest, prepare a written summary of the probable cause for taking the minor into temporary custody. In contrast to adult criminal proceedings, the statutory presumptions require "immediate release" of the minor to the custody of his or her parents or legal guardian unless specific factors warranting extended detention are found to exist. Even when such factors supportive of further detention are found to exist, the juvenile arrestee must nonetheless be released within 48 hours unless a wardship petition is filed within that initial 48–hour period. And, if a wardship petition is filed, a formal, adversarial detention hearing, which incorporates a probable cause determination, and at which counsel is provided for both the minor and his parents or guardian, must be conducted "as soon as possible but in any event [no later than] the expiration of the next judicial day after a petition to declare the minor a ward * * * has been filed" (i.e., no later than 72 hours after arrest, excluding "nonjudicial days"). At that detention hearing, the juvenile court will consider "[t]he circumstances and gravity of the alleged offense" in determining whether extended pretrial detention is warranted under all the facts and circumstances.

In light of the foregoing, we therefore conclude that the United States Supreme Court's adoption of the strict 48–hour rule in *McLaughlin*, was neither foreseen nor intended by that court to be rigidly operable in juvenile postarrest detention proceedings. Given the fundamental differences between juvenile and adult detention proceedings recognized in a long line of that court's decisions, we will not infer otherwise, absent an express and definitive ruling from the high court to the contrary. * * *

Having examined the integrated components of California's juvenile detention statutes, we conclude that the Constitution, as interpreted by the United States Supreme Court's pertinent decisions reviewed herein, requires no more than that juvenile arrestees be afforded a judicial determination of "probable cause" for any postarrest detention extending beyond the 72–hour period immediately following a warrantless arrest.

In light of these conclusions, it follows that the formal detention hearing provided for in section 632, subdivision (a), may also serve to fulfill the constitutional requirement when the court at such a hearing, *where it is held within 72 hours of the juvenile's arrest*, makes a determination that sufficient probable cause exists for the extended postarrest detention of the juvenile. Consistent with our analysis and conclusions herein, if the 72–hour period immediately following arrest includes one or more "nonjudicial days," such that the juvenile court is unable or unwilling to provide a full statutory detention hearing within that period, then the Constitution independently requires that the juvenile be afforded a separate, timely judicial determination of probable cause for any extended period of detention beyond the 72 hours following arrest. * * *

MOSK, JUSTICE, dissenting.

* * * The question before the court is bipartite. Is *Gerstein*'s promptness requirement applicable to juveniles? If so, does *McLaughlin*'s definition of "promptness" operate in this setting? * * *

[T]he *Gerstein* court made plain that the prompt judicial probable cause determination mandated by the Fourth Amendment must be "prompt" in terms of the time that is required for the state "to take the administrative steps incident to arrest" as booking, photographing, and fingerprinting. * * *

In *McLaughlin*, the United States Supreme Court undertook to define "promptness" under *Gerstein*. The facts there are similar to those here. At issue was Riverside County's policy of combining judicial probable cause determinations with its arraignment procedures, which resulted in a delay of as many as seven days after a person's warrantless arrest. * * * The *McLaughlin* court adhered to, and indeed reaffirmed, the holding of *Gerstein* that the Fourth Amendment mandates a prompt judicial probable cause determination as a prerequisite to extended restraint of liberty following a warrantless arrest.

The *McLaughlin* court also remained faithful to *Gerstein*'s view that "promptness" must be measured in terms of the time that is required for the state "to take the administrative steps incident to arrest." * * *

As stated above, the question before this court is whether *Gerstein*'s promptness requirement is applicable to juveniles and, if so, whether *McLaughlin*'s definition of "promptness" operates in this setting.

The first issue is the applicability of *Gerstein*'s promptness requirement to juveniles. *Gerstein* declares, both expressly and impliedly, from beginning to end, that the Fourth Amendment's protection extends to "persons" or "individuals." It does not purport to limit the constitutional guaranty to adults or even to qualify its benefit to juveniles. * * *

To be sure, the particular commands and prohibitions of the Fourth Amendment may vary in some respects for adults and juveniles. The basic criterion of the constitutional provision is, of course, "reasonableness." * * * When probable cause is lacking, detention is unsupported as a matter of law. That proposition does not depend on how old the detainee is. The presence of youth does not make up for the absence of probable cause.

I recognize that the state, as *parens patriae*, may have a legitimate interest in detaining a juvenile for criminal activity prior to trial. That interest, however, is not served by holding *Gerstein*'s promptness requirement inapplicable. Without question, an adult arrested without probable cause must be released as soon as reasonably possible. The reason: grounds for detention are lacking. So too, a juvenile arrested without probable cause must be released as soon as reasonably possible. The reason is the same. Absent probable cause, the state's exercise of its power to preserve and promote the welfare of the child is without support. For juveniles as for adults, *Gerstein*'s promptness requirement operates to conserve and allocate resources by limiting the class of detainees to those who are properly subject to detention. * * *

The second issue is whether *McLaughlin*'s definition of "promptness" operates in the juvenile setting.

McLaughlin declares, both expressly and impliedly, from beginning to end, that its definition of "promptness" extends to "probable cause determinations" generally. It does not purport to limit its scope to adults or even to qualify its meaning for juveniles.

I do not see in *McLaughlin* itself any basis to restrict its definition of "promptness" against juveniles. * * * The reasoning of the *McLaughlin* court is premised on an assessment that the "undefined" promptness requirement of *Gerstein* is simply too "vague" a "standard." * * *

Neither do I discover any support outside *McLaughlin* to condition its definition of "promptness" against juveniles. * * * [U]nder the Fourth Amendment as construed by *Gerstein* and *McLaughlin*, a law-abiding person wrongfully arrested without a warrant is guaranteed his freedom within about 48 hours. It would be unreasonable to hold that when the person in question happens to be a juvenile, the guaranty is illusory.

In conducting my analysis, I have not overlooked *Schall v. Martin*. * * * After even brief consideration, it becomes plain that *Schall* does not affect the conclusion that *Gerstein*'s promptness requirement is indeed applicable to juveniles and that *McLaughlin*'s definition of "promptness" does in fact operate in this setting. * * *

To begin with, *Schall* is based on the Fourteenth Amendment's due process clause. *Gerstein* and *McLaughlin*, by contrast, rest on the Fourth Amendment. Indeed, the *Schall* court effectively declared that its reach did not extend to the Fourth Amendment question presented here when it expressly noted that it was solely concerned with "*judicially ordered* detention." Moreover, the *Schall* court referred only to formal, adversarial probable cause hearings, and not the informal, nonadversarial judicial probable cause determinations discussed in *Gerstein* and *McLaughlin*. Lastly, and perhaps most important, the *Schall* court dealt with a situation in which the juvenile was already detained pursuant to court order—unlike the situation here, where he was not. * * *

[T]he lead opinion sets out to answer the question posed—viz., whether the superior court's "official position" that *Gerstein*'s promptness requirement, at least as defined by *McLaughlin*, is not applicable to juveniles, is contrary to the Fourth Amendment as construed by those decisions—by addressing a question not posed—viz., whether the juvenile court law is compatible with "fundamental fairness" under the Fourteenth Amendment's due process clause as interpreted in *Schall*. The fatal flaw of such analysis is evident: it is altogether nonresponsive. The lead opinion may just as well have attempted to determine whether the superior court's "official position" is contrary to the Fourth Amendment by considering whether the juvenile court law violates the Eighth Amendment's prohibition against cruel and unusual punishments.* * *

Whenever the state predicates detention on criminal activity—in whatever proceeding, under whatever role, or for whatever objective—probable cause is crucial for Fourth Amendment purposes. And whenever probable cause is crucial, *Gerstein*'s promptness requirement, as defined by *McLaughlin*, is applicable. A prompt judicial probable cause determination generally within 48 hours of a juvenile's warrantless arrest—a determination that may be informal and nonadversarial—is altogether consistent with the juvenile court law, the goals of which include the expeditious resolution of issues in a relatively open and cooperative setting. * * *

The lead opinion also suggests that *Gerstein*'s promptness requirement, at least as defined by *McLaughlin*, is inapplicable to juveniles because their interest in freedom from restraint of liberty under the Fourth Amendment is assertedly less substantial than that of adults. But as stated, the basic * * * criterion of the constitutional provision is "reasonableness." Extended restraint for a criminal offense in the absence of probable cause is no more reasonable for juveniles than adults. * * *

Accordingly, I dissent.

NOTES

1) Academic Commentary Commentators have criticized *Alfredo A.* "By failing to extend equal Fourth Amendment protections to juveniles in the context of pretrial detainment, the California Supreme Court has marginalized juveniles' constitutional rights." Richard S. Baum, "Denial of Fourth Amendment Protections in the Pretrial Detention of Juveniles," 35 *Santa Clara L. Rev.* 689 (1995). Recall from Chapter 3, *Lanes v. State*, *supra* p. 170, required police to have probable cause when they took a youth into custody. Is the court's holding in *Alfredo A.* consistent with the court's reasoning in *Lanes*? Are the procedural contexts distinguishable?

2) Probable Cause and Petitions *Alfredo A.* involved the time within which to conduct a probable cause hearing. But, the filing of a delinquency petition constitutes a prerequisite to a probable cause determination, and state statutes typically require the prosecutor or presenting authority to file a petition within 36 to 48 hours of a youth being taken into custody. For example, in California, *Cal. Welf. & Inst.* § 631(a) provides that "whenever a minor is taken into custody by a peace officer or probation officer, * * * the minor shall be released within 48 hours after having been taken into custody, excluding nonjudicial days, unless within that period of time a petition to declare the minor a ward has been filed. * * * " Similarly, *Calif. R. Juv. Proc.* 1470(a) provides that "A child shall be released from custody within 48 hours, excluding nonjudicial days, after first being taken into custody unless a petition has been filed, either within that time, or prior to the time the child was first taken into custody." If the state fails to file the petition within the 48 hours required, the juvenile is entitled to be released. *See e.g., In re Robin*

M., 21 Cal.3d 337, 146 Cal.Rptr. 352, 579 P.2d 1 (1978); *In re Tan T.*, 55 Cal.App.4th 1398, 64 Cal.Rptr.2d 758 (1997).

3. SUBSTANTIVE GROUNDS FOR DETENTION

PEOPLE v. JUVENILE COURT, CITY AND COUNTY OF DENVER

893 P.2d 81 (Colo. 1995).

JUSTICE KIRSHBAUM delivered the Opinion of the Court. In this original proceeding * * * the People of the State of Colorado, challenges an order entered by the respondent, the Juvenile Court of the City and County of Denver, concluding that section 19–2–204(3)(a)(III), 8B C.R.S. (1994 Supp.) (the presumption statute), violates constitutional guarantees of substantive and procedural due process of law. * * * Having issued a rule to show cause why the relief requested should not be granted, we make the rule absolute. * * *

During that [1993] special session the General Assembly adopted several measures prohibiting the possession of handguns by juveniles, including the presumption statute.[2] That statute provides that a juvenile is presumed dangerous to himself or herself or the community and therefore may be ordered by a judicial officer to be detained if the juvenile is alleged to have committed a[n enumerated] crime * * *; to have committed a[n enumerated] felony offense * * *; to have used a firearm during the commission of a felony; or to have possessed a handgun in violation of the handgun statute.

[On Friday, October 8, 1993, police arrested F.N., a juvenile, for felony menacing, and unlawful possession of a handgun by a juvenile, in violation of the handgun statute, and immediately placed him in secure detention. On October 10, 1993, a magistrate found probable cause to detain F.N. for felony menacing and for violation of the handgun statute. On October 12, 1993, a hearing officer conducted a detention hearing at which F.N. was represented by a public defender. The prosecutor recommended continued detention of F.N. pending a priority filing of a delinquency petition.[6] The hearing officer found that F.N. had pointed a loaded

---

2. The presumption statute provides as follows: (III) With respect to this section, the court may further detain the juvenile if the court is satisfied from the information provided at the hearing that the juvenile is a danger to himself or herself or to the community. Any information having probative value shall be received regardless of its admissibility under the rules of evidence. In determining whether a child requires detention, the court shall consider any record of any prior adjudications of the juvenile. There shall be a rebuttable presumption that a juvenile is a danger to himself or herself or to the community if: (A) The juvenile is alleged to have committed a felony enumerated as a crime of violence, (B) The juvenile is alleged to have used, or possessed and threatened to use, a firearm during the commission of any felony offense against a person, (C) The juvenile is alleged to have committed possessing a dangerous or illegal weapon, [or carrying a concealed weapon]. * * *

6. In a priority filing, the district attorney must file a petition within 72 hours after the detention hearing, excluding Saturdays, Sundays, and legal holidays. The juvenile must then be tried on the charges on which bail is denied within 60 days after the entry of such order denying bail.

handgun at two people after making "some rather tasteless remarks" to them, concluded that he constituted a danger to himself and to the community, and ordered his continued detention. On October 14, 1993, the state filed a delinquency petition charging F.N. with the class 5 felony of felony menacing and the class 2 misdemeanor of illegal possession of a handgun by a juvenile, and he was transferred to the juvenile detention unit of the Arapahoe County Jail.]

F.N. filed a motion for release from custody, asserting as grounds therefor that the handgun statute creates a status offense and that detention for commission of a status offense violates the Colorado Children's Code, and the Juvenile Justice Delinquency and Prevention Act; that the detention of juveniles without bond at Gilliam and at the Arapahoe County Jail constitutes a violation of the Children's Code; and that the presumption statute, both facially and as applied to F.N., violates the due process and equal protection clauses of the * * * [United States and Colorado Constitutions].

A hearing on the motion was held, during which several witnesses testified with respect to conditions at Gilliam and the Arapahoe County Jail. At the conclusion of the hearing the juvenile court entered an order concluding in part that enactment of the handgun statute and the presumption statute "gives rise to a Constitutional right to bail for affected juveniles." The juvenile court found that Gilliam and the Arapahoe County Jail were overcrowded, unsanitary, and in many respects unsafe and that juveniles were not treated differently than adults at the Arapahoe County Jail. The juvenile court held that in light of these circumstances detention of juveniles in those two facilities constituted punishment and that no justification existed for denying to such juveniles the constitutional rights to bail enjoyed by adults. The juvenile court also determined that the presumption statute places the burden of persuasion on a detained juvenile to overcome the presumption of dangerousness and that a juvenile's constitutional right to refuse to make self-incriminating statements is impermissibly implicated by the presumption statute.

The juvenile court concluded that in combination the handgun statute and the presumption statute violate the Children's Code and the Juvenile Act and that the presumption statute violates constitutionally protected substantive and procedural due process rights of juveniles, facially and as applied to F.N. The juvenile court ordered F.N. released on bond and also entered an order prohibiting the state from detaining juvenile status offenders in secure facilities. Pursuant to the People's request, we have stayed that portion of the juvenile court's order purporting to prohibit the state from seeking secure detention of juveniles who allegedly have violated the handgun statute. * * *

It must first be observed that F.N. was initially detained on the basis of allegations that he committed the offense of felony menacing by use of a deadly weapon as well as the offense of possession of a handgun. The former offense is not a status offense. To the extent the juvenile court's analysis is focused exclusively on the assumption that F.N. was detained on the basis of an alleged status offense, the analysis is fundamentally flawed.

The juvenile court appropriately noted that the offense of possession of a handgun by a juvenile is a "status" offense—an offense consisting of conduct that would not constitute an offense if engaged in by an adult. The presumption statute establishes a presumption that any juvenile alleged to have committed one of several enumerated offenses will be presumed to be a danger to himself or herself or the community, warranting further detention. * * *

The juvenile court concluded that the detention in secured facilities of a juvenile for committing a status offense is prohibited. * * * It must again be noted that F.N. was arrested in part because he engaged in felony menacing with a deadly weapon—conduct which constitutes a felony offense if committed by an adult. The Juvenile Act does not prohibit detention in secured facilities of young persons who commit felonies. * * *

Because delinquency proceedings are fundamentally different from adult criminal proceedings, not all constitutional protections afforded to adult criminals have been extended to juveniles. In *L.O.W.*, [*supra* p. 422] we considered whether the Eighth Amendment to the United States Constitution or * * * the Colorado Constitution provide a juvenile with an unqualified right to release on bail. After weighing the adverse impact of the availability of bail on informal pre-adjudication juvenile proceedings against the benefits to be anticipated from extending the constitutional rights of adults to bail to affected juveniles, we held that "a child does not have an absolute constitutional or statutory right to bail pending adjudication of the charges filed against him in juvenile court." We also stated that a juvenile may be detained only after giving credence to a presumption of release "except in narrowly defined circumstances where the state establishes that detention is necessary to protect the child from imminent harm or to protect others in the community from serious bodily injury."

The juvenile court acknowledged our holding in *L.O.W.* However, it indicated that because the conditions at both Gilliam and the Arapahoe County Jail constituted punishment, F.N. and other juveniles placed in those two facilities were not being treated differently from adults and the "justification * * * for not extending the right to bail [articulated in *L.O.W.*] is no longer present." The juvenile court misconstrued *L.O.W.*

We did recognize in *L.O.W.* that the Children's Code establishes a presumption that juveniles awaiting dispositional hearings should be released. However, we also concluded that if in a particular case the state establishes that detention of a particular child is necessary for the protection of the child or the protection of other community members from bodily harm which the child is likely to inflict, the child may be detained. The inquiry concerning whether an exception to the presumption of bail for juveniles should be recognized focuses primarily on the circumstances surrounding the conduct and character of the juvenile rather than on the

nature of particular detention facilities. We reaffirm our decision in
L.O.W., and conclude that the juvenile court erred in suggesting that the
conditions of confinement at Gilliam and at the Arapahoe County Jail in
some fashion converted the statutory presumption of bail established by
the Children's Code into a constitutional requirement of release for F.N.
* * *

The juvenile court's conclusions are also based on its determination
that detention of juveniles at Gilliam and the Arapahoe County Jail
constitutes punishment. The juvenile court reasoned that punitive confinement of juveniles is "incompatible" with the legitimate governmental
interests underlying the presumption statute. We reject the juvenile
court's determination that the presumption statute violates constitutional
guarantees of due process of law.

A statute is facially unconstitutional only if no conceivable set of
circumstances exists under which it may be applied in a constitutionally
permissible manner. The presumption statute permits the release on bail
of juveniles who overcome the evidentiary presumption contained therein.
The fact that F.N. did not overcome such presumption in this case does
not establish that no juvenile ever will.

The juvenile court construed the presumption statute to in effect shift
the burden of proof from the state to the juvenile with respect to
establishing whether secure detention was warranted to protect the juvenile or society. We do not so construe the statute.

In L.O.W., we recognized a presumption that a juvenile should not be
confined pending a dispositional hearing "except in narrowly defined
circumstances where the state establishes that detention is necessary to
protect the child from imminent harm or to protect others in the community from serious bodily harm." The presumption statute defines one
narrow set of circumstances in which the presumption of release may
initially be overcome because of specific circumstances indicating that
detention is necessary for the protection of the juvenile or others: the
possession of a handgun by a juvenile. The statute does not shift the
burden of proof from the state, but merely requires a juvenile to introduce
some evidence to overcome the presumption of dangerousness created by
the statute. Furthermore, contrary to the view expressed by the juvenile
court, the evidence presented by the juvenile need not implicate constitutional protections against self-incrimination. Evidence that one does not
constitute a danger to himself, herself, or others need not focus on the
particular events giving rise to that person's detention. We reject the
juvenile court's conclusion that the presumption statute on its face violates F.N.'s constitutionally protected rights to procedural due process of
law. * * *

In order to determine whether preventive detention of juveniles in
secure facilities such as Gilliam and the Arapahoe County Jail constitutes
punishment for purposes of fundamental fairness analysis of the facial
validity of the presumption statute, we must consider the legislative

purposes giving rise to the statute, the relationship between the statute's substantive provisions and those purposes, and the procedures authorized by the statute.

We have previously recognized that preventive detention of juveniles pursuant to the Children's Code is designed to protect the juvenile from imminent harm or to protect others in the community from serious bodily harm. The state has a substantial and necessary interest in protecting all citizens from harm. As the Supreme Court observed in *Schall*, "[c]rime prevention is a 'weighty social objective'" and "this interest persists undiluted in the juvenile context." * * *

There is a relationship between possession of a deadly weapon by a juvenile and a risk of imminent and serious harm to the community or to the juvenile. In view of that relationship, detention of juveniles possessing deadly weapons prior to the conclusion of formal adjudicatory proceedings serves a legitimate state objective. * * *

The presumption statute provides that a juvenile is entitled to a hearing within forty-eight hours after his or her initial detention, excluding Saturdays, Sundays, and legal holidays, for a judicial determination of whether the juvenile should continue to be detained. The detention hearing is not a preliminary hearing. While evidence respecting the circumstances of the alleged conduct of the juvenile may be presented, the state need not at the detention hearing establish probable cause to believe the juvenile committed an offense. The evidence presented at a detention hearing must be relevant to the determination of whether the juvenile is dangerous to himself, herself, or others, thus requiring continued detention, and what terms of detention should be imposed if further detention is warranted.

The juvenile court concluded that the rebuttable presumption statute impermissibly restricts the right of a juvenile to refuse to make self-incriminating statements at a detention hearing. We do not agree.

Juveniles enjoy the privilege against self-incrimination guaranteed to adults by the Fifth and Fourteenth Amendments to the United States Constitution. Requiring a juvenile to present evidence that he or she does not constitute a danger to himself, herself, or the community implicates self-incrimination issues only if the juvenile elects to testify and subject himself or herself to cross-examination. Evidence other than testimony by the juvenile may be introduced by the juvenile to rebut the statutory presumption of dangerousness. Furthermore, trial courts may prevent the use at trial of testimony by a defendant that is necessary for the vindication of a constitutional right. * * * The presumption statute neither directly nor indirectly requires a juvenile to forego his or her right to refuse to present self-incriminating evidence at a detention hearing. * * *

Based on our conclusion that neither the presumption statute nor the rebuttable presumption of dangerousness established therein violates constitutional due process standards of fundamental fairness applicable to juveniles, we reverse that portion of the juvenile court's order.

NOTE

Many policy analysts and professional organizations recommend that states use offense criteria, risk assessment instruments, or other administrative guidelines to reduce excessive pre-trial detention, to reserve detention for high risk youths and to develop less restrictive alternatives for youths who pose minimal threat to public safety. Some recommend that judges detain only those youths whom prosecutor charged with a serious crime of violence which, if proven, would likely result in commitment to a secure facility; who escaped from an institution; or who would not appear at subsequent proceedings based on a demonstrated history of prior failures to appear. American Bar Association, *Juvenile Justice Standards Relating to Interim Status* (1980). Similarly, the National Criminal Justice Advisory Committee, *Task Force on Juvenile Justice and Delinquency Prevention* 390 (1976) recommended detention only "[t]o prevent the juvenile from inflicting bodily harm on others."

State laws could specify, like *Salerno, supra* Note 11 p. 469, explicit offense-based detention criteria or construct empirically validated risk assessment instruments to enumerate the categories of serious present offenses and prior records that provide compelling evidence of future "dangerousness." *See* Elizabeth Lawton, *"Facilities Review Panel v. Coe*: The West Virginia Supreme Court of Appeals Adopts an Objective Approach to Deciding Pretrial Detention of Accused Juveniles," 95 *W.Va. L. Rev.* 505 (1993). In addition, state laws could create a presumption to release all non-felony offenders and place a heavy burden on the prosecution to prove both a need for secure detention and exhaustion of all non-secure alternative placements. States could provide additional procedural safeguards and specify a higher standard of proof prior to making preventive detention decisions. Although states could promulgate substantive standards, apply the rule of law to the confinement decision that directly affects most delinquents' lives, and reduce the disparate and unequal incarceration of young offenders, most states decline to do so. Instead, they use less adequate procedures for juveniles than they require for adults, maximize judicial discretion and place juveniles at a comparative disadvantage in the justice system.

D.   DETAINING JUVENILES IN ADULT JAILS

The Federal Juvenile Justice and Delinquency Prevention Act (JJDP Act), 42 U.S.C. § 5602 (a)(9), (1998), declares, among its other purposes, "to assist State and local governments in removing juveniles from jails and lockups for adults." The JJDP Act further requires states to submit a plan for carrying out its purposes including annual performance reports that describe the implementation and compliance with the plan requirements. 42 U.S. C. § 5633 (1998). Among the other statutory requirements, the State plans shall:

(13) provide that juveniles alleged to be or found to be delinquent * * * shall not be detained or confined in any institution in which they have contact with adult persons incarcerated because they have been convicted of a crime or are awaiting trial on criminal charges or with the

part-time or full-time security staff (including management) or direct-care staff of a jail or lockup for adults;

(14) provide that no juvenile shall be detained or confined in any jail or lockup for adults, except that the Administrator shall * * * promulgate regulations which make exceptions with regard to the detention of juveniles accused of nonstatus offenses who are awaiting an initial court appearance pursuant to an enforceable State law requiring such appearances within twenty-four hours after being taken into custody (excluding weekends and holidays) * * * and—

(A)(i) are outside a Standard Metropolitan Statistical Area; and

(ii) have no existing acceptable alternative placement available;

(B) are located where conditions of distance to be traveled or the lack of highway, road, or other ground transportation do not allow for court appearances within 24 hours, so that a brief (not to exceed 48 hours) delay is excusable; or

(C) are located where conditions of safety exist (such as severely adverse, life-threatening weather conditions that do not allow for reasonably safe travel), in which case the time for an appearance may be delayed until 24 hours after the time that such conditions allow for reasonably safe travel;

(15) provide for an adequate system of monitoring jails, detention facilities, correctional facilities, and non-secure facilities. * * *

The following excerpt identifies some of the difficulties in achieving compliance with the JJDP Act mandate: **Ira M. Schwartz, Linda Harris, Laurie Levi, "The Jailing of Juveniles in Minnesota: A Case Study,"** 34 *Crime & Delinq.* 133 (1988)

* * * [T]he jailing of juveniles continues to be a major problem in the United States. In 1985, approximately 1,450 juveniles were confined in adult jails on any one given day. There is no credible evidence documenting the rehabilitative or deterrent effect of jailing juveniles. However, the adverse consequences of this practice have been well documented and include such things as bodily harm (e.g., sexual assaults, staff brutality, and physical abuse between inmates), psychological damage, and death.

In 1974, Congress enacted the Juvenile Justice and Delinquency Prevention Act. This legislation imposed important restrictions on the confinement of juveniles in adult jails and police lockups. The legislation mandated that young people housed in adult correctional facilities be kept completely separate from adult offenders in states participating in the federal juvenile justice program. Congress amended the federal Act in 1980 and required that participating states eliminate the jailing of juveniles altogether by 1985. Congress later extended the deadline to December 1988.

Twenty-two states were recently notified by the Office of Juvenile Justice and Delinquency Prevention that they have not been in compliance with the federal mandate in this area. Minnesota is one of the states that has yet to comply with this national objective. * * * [T]here are number of major obstacles that need to be overcome if the practice of jailing juveniles in Minnesota is to be brought to an end.

The most serious impediment cited is the lack of readily available alternatives. Law enforcement officials, probation workers, county board members, and others acknowledge that the incidence of juvenile jailing would drop substantially if such programs as 24–hour on-call crisis intervention and screening services, home detention, family operated shelter care, and staff operated shelter care were made available. Also, many counties are financially strapped and do not have the resources to develop such programs. Therefore, in all probability, state financing will have to be made available if these alternatives are to be put in place.

Transporting youth to community-based programs or to juvenile detention centers poses a major problem for law enforcement officials. Minnesota is a large state, most of which is rural. The juvenile detention centers are located in urban areas with the overwhelming majority of the beds being located in the Twin City metropolitan area. This means that law enforcement officials in many jurisdictions have to transport juveniles long distances in order to access appropriate services and facilities. This is a task they are often unable or unwilling to do.

Another reason why the movement to remove juveniles from adult facilities in Minnesota has stalled has to do with the attitudes and beliefs of some of the key actors in the juvenile justice policy arena. For example, many state and local juvenile justice and elected public officials do not feel that the jailing of juveniles is a serious problem. They point to the fact that only a small number of youth are incarcerated in adult jails and municipal lockups on any one given day. * * *

Some public officials and juvenile justice professionals argue that the jailing of juveniles is necessary to protect public safety. They feel this way despite the fact that this study as well as others indicates that only about 35% of the juveniles admitted to county jails and municipal lockups are confined for allegedly having committed a Part I offense. Also, there are some, particularly judges and probation and parole workers, who feel that the jailing of juveniles has a deterrent value or is an appropriate punishment for youth who violate the conditions of their probation or parole. * * *

[S]trategies need to be developed that will help to build the professional and political consensus needed to prohibit the confinement of youth in adult facilities under any circumstances.

In addressing this issue, policymakers, juvenile justice professionals, child advocates, public interest groups, and public opinion leaders should consider the following points.

(1) Legislation should be enacted prohibiting the confinement of juveniles in county jails and municipal lockups. * * *

(2) County board members and sheriffs need to be informed and educated about the risks and hazards of confining juveniles in adult facilities and about the potential liability exposure they face in the event of a tragedy and subsequent litigation. * * *

(3) The best available evidence suggests that six or, at most, eight strategically located secure detention beds would be needed to accommodate the number of youth requiring secure custody confinement pending disposition of their cases in court in counties that do not have access to juvenile detention facilities. * * *

(4) The legislature should appropriate the funds needed for the development of alternatives to the jailing of juveniles. The development of objective juvenile detention intake criteria * * *, 24–hour on-call detention screening and crisis intervention services, family shelter care, home detention, and staff operated shelter care would eliminate 80% to 90% of the juvenile jailing in the state without compromising public safety. As the data in this study indicate, more than 60% of the juveniles admitted to jails and lockups are confined for having committed minor and petty offenses and for exhibiting other types of relatively nonserious misbehavior. * * *

(5) This study includes the first examination of juvenile admissions to county jails and municipal lockups in Minnesota by race. The finding that minority youth, particularly Native Americans, are incarcerated for substantially longer periods of time than their white counterparts who are accused of similar offenses raises many serious questions that need to be addressed by policymakers and professionals. * * *

(6) Priority attention should be given to the development of alternatives to adult jails and municipal lockups for female juveniles. Females under the age of 18 make up nearly a quarter of all the youth admitted to adult facilities in 1986. The data indicate that the majority were confined for Part II crimes, status offenses, and probation and parole violations. In fact, less than one-third were accused of having committed a serious offense. Clearly, this population poses little or no threat to the community. This is a particularly pressing problem because jail staff report that it is extremely difficult to find adequate quarters for young females in jails, particularly when these facilities are overcrowded as is increasingly the case. * * *

Over a century ago, Progressive reformers created the juvenile court, in part, to remove youths from the criminal justice system and confinement with adults. The **Campaign for Youth Justice, *Jailing Juveniles: The Dangers of Incarcerating Youth in Adult Jails in America* 4, 6–7, 10, 13, 14, (2007)**, describes the prevalence of juveniles in adult jails and the dangers and problems that youths in adult facilities pose for juveniles and jail staff and administrators:

Every day in America, an average of 7,500 youth are incarcerated in adult jails. The annual number of youth who are placed in adult jails is even higher—ten or twenty times the daily average according to some researchers—to account for the "turnover rate" of youth entering and exiting adult jails. * * *

It is extremely difficult to keep youth safe in adult jails. When youth are placed with adults in jails, youth are at greater risk of physical and sexual assaults. For example, according to the U.S. Department of Justice Bureau of Justice Statistics (BJS) in 2005 and 2006, 21% and 13% respectively, of the victims of inmate-on-inmate sexual violence in jails were youth under the age of 18—a surprisingly high percentage of victims considering that only 1% of jail inmates are juveniles.

Recognizing the risks to youth in jails, some jailers separate youth from adult inmates. However, this is not an adequate solution either. Separating youth from adults in jail can reduce the physical or emotional harm that may result from contact with adult offenders, but unfortunately these youths are then often placed in isolation, a dangerous setting for youth. Youth in isolation are frequently locked down 23 hours a day in small cells with no natural light. Even limited exposure to such an environment can cause anxiety, paranoia, exacerbate existing mental disorders, and increase risk of suicide. In fact, youth have the highest suicide rate of all inmates in jails. Youth are 19 times more likely to commit suicide in jail than youth in the general population and 36 times more likely to commit suicide in an adult jail than in a juvenile detention facility. Jail staff are simply not equipped to protect youth from the dangers of adult jails.

Jails do not have the capacity to provide the necessary education and other programs crucial for the healthy development of adolescents. Even though legally required to, few jails provide appropriate education to youth. A BJS survey found that 40% of jails provided no educational services at all, only 11% of jails provided special education services, and only 7% provided vocational training. As many as one-half of all youth transferred to the adult system do not receive adult convictions, and are returned to the juvenile justice system or are not convicted at all. Many of these youths will have spent *at least one month* in and adult jail and one in five of these youths will have spent *over six months in an adult jail.* Without adequate education and other services, jails take youth off course. * * *

Adult jails are designed to house adults, whereas juvenile detention facilities are designed for youth. The result is that juvenile and adult detention facilities provide radically different services for the people in their facilities. From intake processes to meals to health care, adolescents have specific needs that jails are often ill-equipped to handle. For example, youth have different nutritional requirements because they are growing rapidly. * * * If youth do not receive appropriate physical and mental health care, their development can be compromises forever.

One main reason why juvenile detention facilities are better suited for adolescents is staffing. Jail staff who supervise youth are often put in awkward and dangerous positions because the "right way" to handle 99%

of the inmates in their facilities (the adults) is usually the "wrong way" for the remaining 1% (developing youth who happen to be inmates.) Juvenile detention facilities generally operate with higher levels of staffing (one staff person to eight youth) compared to jails (ratios can be as high as one staff person to 64 inmates). * * * Additional staffing is critical for engaging youth in exercise, education, and pro-social activities necessary for proper development. Juvenile detention facilities also find it easier to offer these activities because they usually have access to dayrooms, class-room spaces, or gyms, and are not as constrained by the physical limita-tions of many jails. Many jails are unable to offer these programs because youth need to be kept safe from the other adult inmates, and as a result are kept within cells or sections of jails.

The lack of education programs in jails has particularly serious consequences for youth who can be detained for several months pre-trial. Because of their age, most youth in jails have not completed their high school education and need classes to graduate or obtain a GED, or to acquire vocational skills to get a job. Without adequate schooling, too many youth are at risk of falling further and further behind academically even though they are legally entitled to an education. Many states have mandatory attendance laws requiring that children attend school unless they have obtained a diploma or a GED. The federal special education law, Individuals with Disabilities Education Act (IDEA), also requires jails to provide special education services for qualifying youth; however, jails frequently have difficulty meeting their legal obligations. * * * While juvenile detention centers often have full-time education staff, adult jails have weak educational programs and it is rare for jails to have classrooms for education. * * *

Another danger caused by housing youth within adult jails is that jails expose youth to "role models." By exposing juveniles to a criminal culture where inmates commit crimes against each other, adult institutions may socialize juveniles into become chronic offenders when they otherwise would not have. * * *

The Danger of Suicide According to the Surgeon General of the United States, youth suicide is a major public health problem: suicide is the third leading cause of death among 15- to 24-year-olds. * * * The best estimates reported by the CDC are from a 1978 study, which found that youth in adult jails were 36 times more likely to commit suicide in an adult jail than in a juvenile detention facility.

More recent estimates of youth suicide rates are available from the U.S. Department of Justice's Bureau of Justice Statistics. The findings are just as grim—jail inmates under 18 had the highest suicide rate of all inmates (101 per 100,000 during 2000–2002). By comparison, the suicide rate for 14- to 17-year-olds not in jail during the same time period was just 5.32 per 100,000. Youth in adult jails are 19 times more likely to commit suicide than are their counterparts in the general population. * * *

Youth held in jails for short periods of time are at great risk of suicide too. The Bureau of Justice Statistics found that suicides in jails were heavily concentrated in the first week spent in custody (48%), with almost a quarter of suicides taking place on the day of admission to jail (14%) or on the following day (9%). It appears that youth held in all jails, large and small, are at risk. Rates of inmate suicide were closely related to jail size, with the smallest facilities recording the highest suicide rates.

There are several reasons why suicide rates for incarcerated juveniles are so high. Experts have identified mental disorders, substance abuse, impulsive aggression, parental depression and substance abuse, family discord and abuse, and poor family support as risk factors for adolescent suicide in the general population. Many of these same risk factors are prevalent for youth held in jails. Experts surmise that juveniles in the adult system experience, similar, if not greater, rates of mental disorder and related problems compared with you in the juvenile justice system. * * *

Tragically, many adult jails are not equipped to identify and respond to the mental health needs of youth. Many jails lack appropriate screening and assessment tools to identify mental health problems in youth. * * *

The Danger of Rape and Sexual Assault Almost every jail and prison across America experiences problems with sexual violence. * * * [A]vailable data are likely to underestimate the true level of sexual violence currently occurring in adult jails.

The data do confirm that youth are at high risk of being sexually assaulted in jails. In 2005 and 2006, 21% and 13%, respectively, of all victims of substantiated incidents of inmate-on-inmate sexual violence in jails were juveniles under the age of 18—an extremely high proportion of victims given their relatively low numbers in jail populations (typically only 1% of all inmates are juveniles).

Even for youth not directly assault, the psychological effects of being in constant and legitimate fear of sexual assault, or of witnessing the sexual assault of others, can be devastating. * * * [M]any youth become disciplinary problems as a self-protective mechanism.

The Danger of Isolation Federal law requires states to keep youth who are under the jurisdiction of the juvenile court out of adult jail, but there is a loophole: the law does not apply to youth charged as adults. Most states permit the pre-trial detention of youth in jails, and only 20 states require that youth must be segregated from adult inmates. Regardless of the specific legal requirements, jail officials face a Catch–22: separating youth from adult inmates is beneficial in that it minimizes contact with people who can pose grave physical and emotional threats to youth, but when a youth is separated, he or she is often placed in isolation, which can exacerbate mental health issues and suicidal impulses.

When youth are segregated in jails, they often are placed in conditions that mimic the isolation or solitary confinement conditions in "supermax" facilities reserved for the most hardened adult offenders. Youth can be locked down 23 or 24 hours a day in small cells that may measure 48 to 80 square feet with no natural light, no control over the electric light in their cell, and no view outside of their cell. They have no contact with other prisons, even verbal contact, and no meaningful contact with staff. * * * Research shows that these periods of segregation are harmful to individuals and makes it more difficult to treat them successfully. * * * [T]he effects of isolation are profound and disabling because people lose their ability to test social reality.

CHAPTER 6

WAIVER OF JUVENILE COURT JURISDICTION

■ ■ ■

Beginning in the mid–1980s, politicians manipulated and exploited public frustration with crime, fear of increases in youth violence, homicide and offenses involving guns, and the racial characteristics of many violent young offenders, and adopted laws and policies to "get tough." Widespread misgivings about the ability of juvenile courts either to rehabilitate chronic and violent young offenders or simultaneously to protect public safety provide the impetus to "crack down" on youth crime and prosecute larger numbers of youths as adults. These initiatives either simplify the transfer of young offenders to criminal courts and expose waived youths to substantial sentences as adults or require juvenile court judges to impose determinate or mandatory minimum sentences on those youths who remain within the juvenile system. Both of these strategies de-emphasize rehabilitation and individualized consideration of the offender, stress personal and justice system accountability and punishment, and base decisions on the seriousness of the present offense and prior record.

Increasingly, people and politicians view juvenile courts' traditional commitment to rehabilitation as a bias toward leniency, often to the detriment of protecting the public or satisfying the victim. For more than two decades, conservatives have denounced juvenile courts for "coddling" young criminals and, more recently, states legislators have adopted more punitive policies toward young offenders in both the juvenile and criminal justice systems. Patricia Torbet, et al., *State Responses to Serious and Violent Juvenile Crime: Research Report* (1996). This Chapter examines the boundary of criminal "adulthood" and responsibility, the processes by which states determine whether to prosecute youths in juvenile or criminal courts, and the consequences for youths tried as adults. Specifically, how and why does the legal system decide which young offenders to prosecute as criminals or as delinquents, and what difference does it make for youths, for public safety, and for juvenile and criminal justice administration? **Jeffrey Fagan and Franklin E. Zimring, eds., *The Changing Borders of Juvenile Justice: Transfer of Adolescents to the Criminal Court* 408–410 (2000)**, describe the *ad hoc* nature and conceptual incoherence of the waiver policy debate:

Transfer of persons under maximum age of delinquency to the criminal courts has been an important issue for a century, yet there has been almost no thoughtful analysis of the transfer problem during this time. We suspect the reason for this is that all parties to the issue come with strong result preferences that have discouraged them from any interest in the principles that might inform transfer decisions.

Those who strongly support juvenile courts have approached the waiver issue by believing that youth welfare is always better served in juvenile courts than in criminal courts, so that the task of drafting standards or law is to hold the practice to an absolute minimum. * * *

For at least twenty years, there has been strong interest group support for substantial increases in the number of juveniles sent to criminal court. * * * The objective of these proposals is increasing the punishment for serious youth crime. This version of result orientation is the mirror image of those anti-transfer stalwarts who sought to minimize the number of criminal court cases in any event. The debate that is the product of these two preferences is only an exchange of preferred outcomes, with those who sought a minimum number of transfers being opposed by those who wish to encourage a maximum number of serious punishments. The difference of opinion is really just about the desirability of serious punishment for adolescent offenders, not about reasons for such outcomes. * * *

Two decades of debate and legislative activity on transfer have left almost no legacy of analysis and empirical data to inform future debate: the transfer question has generated no intellectual capital for all its years of high public importance. * * *

Unprincipled debate is a hard habit to break when both sides in a policy conflict are locked into positions that assign no importance to theory, fact, or analysis. It does not stretch matters much to suggest that this is the current condition of juvenile court transfer as an issue of political contention in the United States. * * *

Every state uses one or more statutory device to prosecute some youths below the maximum age of juvenile court jurisdiction as adults. The principal legal devices include judicial waiver, legislative exclusion of some offenses from juvenile court jurisdiction, and prosecutors' choices among concurrent juvenile and criminal court jurisdictions. In addition, some jurisdiction in which chronological juveniles' cases originate in criminal court have provisions by which a criminal court judge may "transfer back" the case to juvenile court. Each of these waiver strategies allocates to a different branch of government—judicial, legislative, or executive—the decision whether to prosecute a youth as a criminal or a delinquent. They reflect different ways of asking and answering similar questions: who are serious offenders; by what criteria should the state identify them; what characteristics of offenders and offenses should determine the outcome of the process; which branch of government can best make these decisions; and how should the juvenile or adult systems respond to them? All waiver strategies attempt to reconcile the rhetorical and cultural conceptions of children as immature and innocent with the frightening reality that some youths commit heinous, vicious, "adult-type" crimes. Violent or chronic young offenders highlight the contradiction between competing conceptions of children as dependent and vulnerable, and as autonomous and responsible. Waiver mechanisms choose between these conflicting constructions of young people, define the boundaries of criminal adulthood, and retrospectively ascribe criminal responsibility to some youths.

Because the Progressives situated the juvenile court on a number of cultural, legal, and criminological fault-lines, the "simple" question whether to try and sentence a young offender as a juvenile or as an adult poses many difficult theoretical and practical dilemmas. For example, until recent legislative amendments, judicial waiver laws typically required a judge to decide whether a youth was "amenable to treatment" or posed a threat to the public. Such laws presumed that juvenile courts can rehabilitate at least some youths, that judges possess diagnostic tools that enabled them to classify youths' treatment potentials, and that they could predict offenders' future dangerousness. Considered at another level, recent "get tough" changes in waiver legislation that emphasize characteristics of the offense rather than the offender represent a jurisprudential shift in emphasis from rehabilitation to retribution. Jurisdictional waiver policies that define the "boundary of adulthood" also implicate the relationship between juvenile and criminal court sentencing practices and highlight the need for a coherent sentencing policy to rationalize social control of career offenders on both sides of the juvenile-adult divide. Finally, trying and sentencing youths as adults reflects fundamental changes in cultural assumptions about adolescents' criminal responsibility, because waiver exposed at least some chronological juveniles to the death penalty and now to sentences of life without parole for crimes they committed as children.

During the late–1980s and early–1990s, the prevalence of guns in the hands of children, the apparent randomness of gang violence and drive-by shootings, the disproportional racial minority involvement in homicides, and media depictions of callous youths' gratuitous violence have inflamed public fear. Politicians have exploited these fears, decried a coming generation of "super-predators" suffering from "moral poverty," and demonized young people in order to muster support for policies to transfer youths to criminal court and to incarcerate them. See William Bennett, John DiIulio, and John Waters, *Body Count* (1996). Some analysts predicted a demographic "time-bomb" of youth crime in the near future to which minority juveniles will contribute disproportionally. *See* James Alan Fox, *Trends in Juvenile Violence: A Report to the United States Attorney General on Current and Future Rates of Juvenile Offending* (1996). However, the predicted adolescent "crime wave" never materialized, and serious youth violence has dropped steadily since 1994. *See* Howard Snyder and Melissa Sickmund, *Juvenile Offenders and Victims: A Nation-*

al Report (2006); Franklin Zimring, *American Youth Violence* (1998). Despite the recent diminution in youth homicide, the earlier increase in youth gun homicide provided a much broader political impetus to "crack down" on all young offenders in general and violent offenders in particular. *See generally*, Barry C. Feld, "Race, Politics and Juvenile Justice: The Warren Court and the Conservative 'Backlash,'" 87 *Minn. L. Rev.* 1447 (2003).

Recent changes in youth crime and violence and the "get tough" legislative responses they have engendered raise a host of complex juvenile and criminal policy issues. Can the current juvenile justice system adequately control chronic and violent young offenders? What alternative measures might better assure public safety? Do legislative changes in waiver statutes, youth sentencing policies, or rates of confinement have any appreciable impact on youth crime rates or public safety? How much more money should a state spend to increase rates or lengths of incarceration? What other social service, educational, or training programs that could prevent or reduce youth crime will receive less support as a result of expenditures on incarceration? Perversely, if states spend more to confine juveniles in prisons and reduce funds for crime prevention programs, will they exacerbate rather than ameliorate youth crime in the future? Legislators often allocate scarce resources and make value judgments about the impact or effectiveness of social and criminal justice policies based on their subjective perceptions, ideological preconceptions, political calculus, or wishful hopes rather than objective data and informed policy analyses. Political slogans, rather than empirical evidence or evaluation research, often guide efforts to formulate youth crime, juvenile court waiver and sentencing policies. *See* David Farrington, Lloyd E. Ohlin, and James Q. Wilson, *Understanding and Controlling Crime: Toward a New Research Strategy* (1986).

Transfer of juvenile offenders for adult prosecution provides the conceptual and administrative nexus between the more deterministic and rehabilitative predicates of the juvenile justice process and the free will and punishment assumption of the adult criminal justice system. Although juvenile courts theoretically attempt to rehabilitate all young offenders, a small but significant proportion of miscreant youths resist their efforts. These are typically either older delinquents nearing the maximum age of juvenile court jurisdiction, chronic recidivists who have not responded to prior intervention and for whom successful treatment may not be feasible during the time remaining to the juvenile court, or youths charged with a very serious violent crime like rape or murder. See Marcy Rasmussen Podkopacz and Barry C. Feld, "Judicial Waiver Policy and Practice: Persistence, Seriousness and Race." 14 *L. & Inequality J.* 73 (1995); Marcy Rasmussen Podkopacz and Barry C. Feld, "The End of the Line: An Empirical Study of Judicial Waiver." 86 *J. Crim. L. & Criminology* 449 (1996); United States General Accounting Office, *Juvenile Justice: Juveniles Processed in Criminal Court and Case Dispositions* (1995). Politicians and the public perceive these youths as mature and sophisticated criminal offenders. Moreover, these career offenders may account for a disproportionate amount of all juvenile crime. Highly visible, serious or chronic offenses evoke community outrage or fear which politicians believe only punitive adult sanctions can mollify. Mechanisms to prosecute some youths as adults provide an important safety valve; they permit the expiatory sacrifice of some youths to quiet political and public clamor, allow judges to demonstrate that they are not squeamish about protecting the public, and enable legislators to avoid otherwise irresistible pressures to lower the maximum age of juvenile court jurisdiction.

Jurisdictional waiver represents a type of *sentencing* decision. In response to the escalation of youth violence in the late–1980s, politicians, members of the public, juvenile justice professionals, and criminologist debated extensively the relative merits of different strategies to transfer some serious young offenders to criminal courts. Juvenile courts traditionally assigned primary importance to rehabilitation and individualized treatment. Criminal courts accorded greater significance to the seriousness of the offense committed and attempted to proportion punishment accordingly. Thus, all of the theoretical differences between juvenile and criminal courts' sentencing philosophies become visible in transfer proceedings and in legislative policy debates.

Transfer laws simultaneously attempt to resolve both fundamental crime control issues and the ambivalence embedded in our cultural construction of youth. The jurisprudential conflicts reflect many current sentencing policy debates: tensions between rehabilitation or incapacitation and retribution, between focusing on characteristics of the offender and the seriousness of the offense, between discretion and rules, and between indeterminacy and determinacy. Waiver laws also attempt to reconcile the contradictory impulses engendered when the child is a criminal and the criminal is a child. What processes best enable us to choose between competing conceptions of youths as responsible and culpable offenders and as immature and salvageable children? In the early stages of a criminal career and prospectively, what criteria best differentiate between adolescent-only offenders and life-course persistent offenders?

Although the technical and administrative details of states' transfer legislation vary considerably, judicial waiver, legislative offense exclusion, and prosecutorial choice of forum represent the three generic approaches employed. *See generally, United States General Accounting Office, Juvenile Justice: Juveniles Processed in Criminal Court and Case Dispositions (1995)*; Barry C. Feld, "Juvenile Court Meets the Principle of Offense: Legislative Changes in Juvenile Waiver Statutes," 78 *J. Crim. L. & Criminology* 471 (1987); Eric Fritsch and Craig Hemmens, "Juvenile Waiver in the United States 1979–1995: A Comparison and Analysis of State Waiver Statutes," 46 *Juv. & Fam. Ct. Judges* 17 (1995); Howard Snyder and Melissa Sickmund, *Juvenile Offenders and Victims: 2006 National Report* (2006); Ira Heilbrun, et al., "A National Survey of U.S. Statutes on Juvenile Transfer: Implications for Policy and Practice," 15 *Behav. Sci. Law* 125 (1997). These various legislative strategies balance sentencing policy values differently, rely on different organizational actors and administrative processes, and elicit different information to determine whether to try and sentence a particular young offender as an adult or as a juvenile.

Judicial waiver represents the most common transfer policy in virtually all states. A juvenile court judge may waive juvenile court jurisdiction on a discretionary basis after conducting a hearing to determine whether a youth is "amenable to treatment," poses a danger to "public safety," or simply whether "it would be contrary to the best interests of the juvenile or of the public to retain jurisdiction." These case-by-case clinical assessments reflect the traditional individualized sentencing discretion characteristic of juvenile courts.

Legislative offense exclusion frequently supplements judicial waiver provisions. This approach emphasizes the seriousness of the offense committed and reflects the retributive values of the criminal law. Because legislatures create juvenile courts, they possess considerable latitude to define their jurisdiction and to exclude youths from juvenile court based on their age and the seriousness of their offenses. A number of states, for example, exclude youths sixteen or older and charged with murder from juvenile court jurisdiction. *E.g.*, Joseph Sanborn, Jr., "Policies Regarding the Prosecution of Juvenile Murderers: Which System and Who Should Decide?" 18 *Law & Policy* 151 (1996). Others exclude even more extensive lists of offenses. Legislative line-drawing that sets the maximum age of juvenile court jurisdiction at fifteen or sixteen, below the general eighteen year old age of majority, results in the criminal prosecution of the largest numbers of chronological juveniles, for example, about 176,000 chronological juveniles in 1991. Howard Snyder and Melissa Sickmund, *Juvenile Offenders and Victims: 2006 National Report* (2006). Wisconsin and New Hampshire lowered their juvenile court jurisdictional age from seventeen to sixteen, and thereby criminalized large numbers of youth on a wholesale, rather than retail, basis.

About a dozen states use a third method—prosecutorial waiver or direct-file—to remove some young offenders from the juvenile justice system. With this strategy, juvenile and criminal courts share concurrent jurisdiction over certain ages and offenses, typically older youths and serious crimes. For example, prosecutors may exercise their discretion to select either a juvenile or criminal court forum in which to prosecute a youth sixteen or older and charged with murder. Because of the constitutional doctrine of separation of powers, courts ordinarily do not review discretionary executive decisions, and most judicial opinions characterize prosecutorial transfer as an ordinary charging decision. See Barry C. Feld, "Reference of Juvenile Offenders for Adult Prosecution: The Legislative Alternative to Asking Unanswerable Questions," 62 *Minn. L. Rev.* 515 (1978). To the extent that a prosecutor's decision to charge a case in criminal courts divests the juvenile court of jurisdiction, prosecutorial waiver constitutes another form of offense-based jurisdictional decision-making. Charles W. Thomas and Shay Bilchik, "Prosecuting Juveniles in

Criminal Courts: A Legal and Empirical Analysis," 76 *J. Crim. L. & Criminology* 439 (1985).

Each type of waiver strategy has supporters and critics. Proponents of judicial waiver endorse juvenile courts' rehabilitative philosophy and argue that individualized decisions provide an appropriate balance of flexibility and severity. *See* Franklin Zimring, "The Treatment of Hard Cases in American Juvenile Justice: In Defense of Discretionary Waiver," 5 *Notre Dame J. L., Ethics & Pub. Pol.* 267 (1991); Jeffrey Fagan, "Social and Legal Policy Dimensions of Violent Juvenile Crime," 17 *Crim. Just. & Behav.* 93 (1990). Critics object that judges lack valid or reliable clinical tools with which accurately to assess amenability to treatment or to predict dangerousness, and that their exercise of standardless discretion results in abuses and inequalities. See Jeffrey Fagan and Elizabeth Piper Deschenes, "Determinants of Judicial Waiver Decisions for Violent Juvenile Offenders," 81 *J. Crim. L. & Criminology* 314 (1990); Barry C. Feld, "Bad Law Makes Hard Cases: Reflections on Teen–Aged Axe–Murderers, Judicial Activism, and Legislative Default," 10 *J. Law & Inequality* 1 (1990).

Proponents of offense exclusion favor "just deserts" sentencing policies, advocate sanctions based on relatively objective factors such as offense seriousness, culpability, and criminal history, and value certainty, consistency, uniformity, and equality in the handling of similarly-situated offenders. Barry C. Feld, "Juvenile Court Legislative Reform and the Serious Young Offender: Dismantling the 'Rehabilitative Ideal'," 69 *Minn. L. Rev.* 141 (1981). Critics question whether legislators can remove discretion without making the process excessively rigid and over-inclusive, or simply delegating sentencing discretion to prosecutors in their charging decisions. Franklin Zimring, "Notes Toward a Jurisprudence of Waiver," In *John C. Hall, et al., Readings in Public Policy (1981)*; Barry C. Feld, "Legislative Exclusion of Offenses from Juvenile Court Jurisdiction: A History and Critique," in Franklin Zimring and Jeffrey Fagan, eds., *The Changing Borders of Juvenile Justice: Transfer of Adolescents to the Criminal Court* (2000).

Proponents of prosecutorial waiver claim that prosecutors can act as more neutral, balanced and objective gatekeepers than either "soft" judges or "get tough" legislators. Francis B. McCarthy, "The Serious Offender and Juvenile Court Reform: The Case for Prosecutorial Waiver of Juvenile Court Jurisdiction," 38 *St. Louis U. L.J.* 629 (1994). Critics observe that prosecutors succumb to political pressures and symbolically posture on crime issues, exercise their discretion just as subjectively and idiosyncratically as do judges, and introduce extensive geographic variability into the justice administration process. Donna Bishop and Charles Frazier, "Transfer of Juveniles To Criminal Court: A Case Study and Analysis of Prosecutorial Waiver," 5 *Notre Dame J. L., Ethics & Pub. Pol'y* 281 (1991).

Selecting a waiver strategy from among these competing and contradictory claims implicates many fundamental issues of sentencing policy. Defining the boundary between juvenile and criminal court depends, for example, on whether policy makers adopt a juvenile or criminal court's jurisprudential "point of view," and focus primarily on treatment and characteristics of the offender or on punishment and the seriousness of the offense. If policy makers endorse criminal laws' retributive values, then the present offense or prior record dominate and transfer decisions lend themselves to relatively mechanical rules, excluded offenses, or presumptive sentencing guidelines. If waiver policies reflect a commitment to offenders' rehabilitation, then judges must use more indeterminate and discretionary processes to make individualized assessments of youths' "amenability to treatment" or "dangerousness." Selecting between juvenile and criminal courts, treatment and punishment, and offender or offense creates a binary forced-choice when deciding whether to try and sentence a young offender as a criminal or as a child.

A. WAIVER POLICY ISSUES: WHAT TO DO WHEN THE KID IS A CRIMINAL AND THE CRIMINAL IS A KID

The following excerpt by **Barry C. Feld, "The Juvenile Court Meets the Principle of the Offense: Legislative Changes in Juvenile Waiver Statutes,"** 78 *J. Crim. L. & Criminology* 471, 488–89 **(1987),** briefly summarizes the policy conundrum presented by waiver:

Both judicial waiver and legislative offense exclusion statutes attempt to answer essentially the same questions: Who are the serious juvenile offenders? How are they identified? Which system will deal with them? Each type of waiver mechanism emphasizes different information in a determination of whether certain juvenile offenders should be handled as adults. * * * [E]ach mechanism has a different "framework of relevance."

The critical reassessment of individualized sentencing practices in adult courts raises troubling questions about the validity of the clinical diagnoses or predictions relied upon in waiver decisions and the propriety of delegating fundamental issues of sentencing policy to the discretionary judgments of social service personnel and judges. Proponents of just deserts in sentencing contend that there is no valid or reliable clinical basis upon which juvenile court judges can make accurate amenability or dangerousness determinations and that the standardless discretion afforded to judges results in inconsistent and discriminatory application. This critique of individualized sentencing in the waiver context has resulted in two types of legislation. One type defines youths below the maximum age of juvenile court jurisdiction as adults by automatically excluding from the juvenile justice system those persons who possess certain combinations of present offense and prior record; the other type of legislation places an increased emphasis on the significance of the offense as a dispositional criterion in a judicial waiver proceeding.

The analysis of waiver as a sentencing decision addresses two interrelated policy issues: the bases for sentencing practices within juvenile courts and the relationship between juvenile court and adult criminal court sentencing practices. The first issue implicates individualized sentencing decisions and the operational tension between discretion and the rule of law. The second issue focuses on rationalizing social control responses to serious or chronic offenders across the two systems. By constraining judicial sentencing discretion and improving the fit between waiver decisions and criminal court sentencing practices through the principle of offense, legislatures are increasingly using offense criteria to deal with both issues simultaneously.
* * *

NOTES

1) Conceptual, Analytical and Empirical Issues Embedded in Jurisdictional Transfer Decisions Waiver of juvenile offenders to criminal courts has intrigued legal scholars and criminologists for decades. Judicial waiver decisions only affect only about 1–2% of juveniles in most jurisdictions. *See* Barry C. Feld, "Bad Law Makes Hard Cases: Reflections on Teen–Aged Axe Murderers, Judicial Activism and Legislative Default," 8 *J. Law & Inequality* 1 (1990); Howard Snyder and Melissa Sickmund, *Juvenile Offenders and Victims: 2006 National Report* (2006). But, these difficult cases raise the fundamental choices between "child and adult" and "treatment and punishment" framed in the context of whether the state should prosecute a juvenile as an adult. Scholars and researchers find the study of waiver analytically irresistible because the process highlights the jurisprudential tensions between rehabilitation and retribution, the clinical effectiveness of treatment, the ability to predict dangerousness, the indeterminate versus determinate sentencing policy debates, the relationships between juvenile and criminal court sentencing practices, and ultimately, issues of life and death. As *Kent, infra* p. 523, *Breed, infra* p. 530, and *Roper, infra* p. 689, indicate, the United States Supreme Court has devoted more cases to the issues of waiver and the punishment of children than to any other aspect of juvenile justice administration. Similarly, because of the high stakes involved, state appellate courts probably review more juvenile court decisions involving waiver than any other issue.

Many scholars have analyzed various aspects of waiver decision-making. *See* Barry C. Feld, "Reference of Juvenile Offenders for Adult Prosecution: The Legislative Alternative to Asking Unanswerable Questions," 62 *Minn. L. Rev.* 515, 522 n. 21 (1978), citing more than 50 articles and books on the subject published prior to 1978. With increased public concern about youth crime and legislative efforts to "get tough," scholars continue to analyze statutory changes, their impact on juvenile and criminal courts, the sentences imposed on juveniles tried and convicted in criminal courts, and the sentencing policy issues that the transfer processes raise. You will find more recent reviews of the literature in: Barry C. Feld, "Juvenile Court Legislative Reform and the Serious Young Offender: Dismantling the 'Rehabilitative Ideal'," 65 *Minn. L. Rev.* 167 (1981); Barry C. Feld, "The Juvenile Court Meets the Principle of the Offense: Legislative Changes in Juvenile Waiver Statutes," 78 *J. Crim. L. & Criminology* 471 (1987); Barry C. Feld, "Bad Law Makes Hard Cases: Reflections on Teen–Aged Axe Murderers, Judicial Activism and Legislative Default," 8 *J. Law & Inequality* 1 (1990); and Barry C. Feld, "Juvenile and Criminal Justice Systems' Responses to Youth Violence," 24 *Crime and Justice* 189 (1998).

You will find extensive analyses of various aspects of waiver policy and practice in: Dean J. Champion and G. Larry Mays, *Transferring Juveniles to Criminal Courts: Trends and Implications for Criminal Justice* (1991); "Symposium on Serious Juvenile Crime," 5 *Notre Dame J. L., Ethics & Pub. Policy* 257–503 (1991) (9 articles); John Hall,, eds., *Readings in Public Policy 169–377* (1981) (10 articles); Donna Hamparian, et al., eds., *Youth in Adult Court: Between Two Worlds* (1982) (6 volume analyses of every juvenile waived to criminal court in 1978); Barry C. Feld and Simon Singer, co-eds., "Juveniles in Criminal Court," 18 *Law & Policy* 1 (1996) (8 articles); Jeffrey Fagan and Franklin Zimring, eds., *Changing Borders of Juvenile Justice: Transfer of Adolescents to the Criminal Court* (2000) (9 essays).

Which Juveniles Get Waived and Why Some research studies juvenile court decision-making processes and the characteristics of juveniles who get waived to criminal court. *See e.g.*, Jeffrey Fagan, Martin Forst, and T. Scott Vivona, "Racial Determinants of the Judicial Transfer Decision: Prosecuting Violent Youth in Criminal Court," 33 *Crime & Delinq.* 259 (1987); Jeffrey Fagan and Elizabeth Piper Deschenes, "Determinants of Judicial Waiver Decisions for Violent Juvenile Offenders," 81 *J. Crim. L. & Criminology* 314 (1990); Joel Peter Eigen, "Punishing Youth Homicide Offenders in Philadelphia," 72 *J. Crim.L. & Criminology* 1072 (1981); Marcy Rasmussen Podkopacz and Barry C. Feld, "Judicial Waiver Policy and Practice: Persistence, Seriousness and Race," 14 *J. Law & Inequality* 73 (1995); Marcy Rasmussen Podkopacz and Barry C. Feld, "The End of the Line: An Empirical Study of Judicial Waiver," 86 *J. Crim. L. & Criminology* 449 (1996).

Criminal Court Career of Waived Juveniles Other research examines the sentences that criminal court judges impose on transferred juveniles: *See e.g.* Peter W. Greenwood, "Differences in Criminal Behavior and Court Responses among Juveniles and Young Adult Defendants," 7 *Crime & Justice* 151 (1986); Cary Rudman, et al., "Violent Youth in Adult Court: Process and Punishment," 32 *Crime & Delinq.* 75 (1986); Marcy Rasmussen Podkopacz and Barry C. Feld, "Judicial Waiver Policy and Practice: Persistence, Seriousness and Race," 14 *J. Law. & Inequality* 73 (1995); Marcy Rasmussen Podkopacz and Barry C. Feld, "The End of the Line: An Empirical Study of Judicial Waiver," 86 *J. Crim. L. & Criminology* 449 (1996).

Waived versus Retained Juveniles Several studies examine differences in characteristics of juveniles whom judges do or do not transfer for adult prosecution: Robert O. Dawson, "An Empirical Study of *Kent* Style Juvenile Transfers to Criminal Court," 23 *St. Mary's L.J.* 975 (1992); Lee Ann Osbun and Peter A. Rode, "Prosecuting Juveniles as Adults: The Quest for 'Objective' Decisions," 22 *Criminology* 187 (1984); Marcy Rasmussen Podkopacz and Barry C. Feld, "Judicial Waiver Policy and Practice: Persistence, Seriousness and Race," 14 *J. Law & Inequality* 73 (1995); Marcy Rasmussen Podkopacz and Barry C. Feld, "The End of the Line: An Empirical Study of Judicial Waiver," 86 *J. Crim. L. & Criminology* 449 (1996).

Waiver Politics and Policies Still other analysts focus on changes in waiver legislation as an indicator of the reformulation of juvenile justice sentencing policy: Kathleen Ford Bay, "Juvenile Justice in California: Changing Concepts?," 7 *Am. J. Crim. L.* 171 (1979); National Council of Juvenile and Family Court Judges, *The Juvenile Court and Serious Offenders: 38 Recommendations* (1984); Alan B. Salazar, "The Expanding Scope of Prosecutorial Discretion in Charging Juveniles as Adults: A Critical Look at *People v. Thorpe*," 54 *U. Col. L. Rev.* 617 (1983); Gordon A. Martin, "The Delinquent and the Juvenile Court: Is There Still a Place for Rehabilitation," 25 *Conn. L. Rev.* 57 (1992); Donna M. Bishop and Charles E. Frazier, "Transfer of Juveniles To Criminal Court: A Case Study and Analysis of Prosecutorial Waiver," 5 *Notre Dame J. L. Ethics & Pub. Pol.* 281 (1991); Charles W Thomas and Shay Bilchik, "Prosecuting Juveniles in Criminal Courts: A Legal and Empirical Analysis," 76 *J. Crim. L. & Criminology* 439 (1985); Michael Norman and L. Kay Gillespie, "Changing Horses: Utah's Shift in Adjudicating Serious Juvenile Offenders," 12 *J. Contemp. L.* 85 (1986); Barry C. Feld, "Violent Youth and Public Policy: A Case Study of Juvenile Justice Law Reform," 79 *Minn. L. Rev.* 965 (1995); Patricia Torbet, et al., *State Responses to Serious and Violent Juvenile Crime: Research Report* (1996); Barry C. Feld, "Juvenile and Criminal Justice Systems' Responses to Youth Violence," 24 *Crime & Justice* 189 (1998); Barry C. Feld, "Race, Politics, and Juvenile Justice: The Warren Court and the Conservative 'Backlash'," 87 *Minn. L. Rev.* 1447 (2003).

The following excerpt, **Howard Snyder and Melissa Sickmund, *Juvenile Offenders and Victims: 2006 National Report* 110–116, 186–187 (2006)**, provides a brief overview of variations in waiver practices and summarizes some of the empirical research and data on the implementation of waiver laws:

Transferring juveniles to criminal court is not a new phenomenon Juvenile courts have always had mechanisms for removing the most serious offenders from the juvenile justice system. Traditional transfer laws establish provisions and criteria for trying certain youth of juvenile age in criminal court. Blended sentencing laws are also used to impose a combination of juvenile and adult criminal sanctions on some offenders of juvenile age.

Transfer laws address which court (juvenile or criminal) has jurisdiction over certain cases involving offenders of juvenile age. State transfer provisions are typically limited by age and offense criteria. Transfer mechanisms vary regarding where the responsibility for transfer decisionmaking lies. Transfer provisions fall into three general categories:

Judicial waiver: The juvenile court judge has the authority to waive juvenile court jurisdiction and transfer the case to criminal court. States may use terms other than judicial waiver. Some call the process *certification*, *remand*, or *bind over* for criminal prosecution. Others transfer or decline rather than waive jurisdiction.

Concurrent jurisdiction: Original jurisdiction for certain cases is shared by both criminal and juvenile courts, and the prosecutor has discretion to file such cases in either court. Transfer under concurrent jurisdiction provisions is also known as *prosecutorial waiver*, *prosecutor discretion*, or *direct file*.

Statutory exclusion: State statute excludes certain juvenile offenders from juvenile court jurisdiction. Under statutory exclusion provisions, cases originate in criminal rather than juvenile court. Statutory exclusion is also known as *legislative exclusion*.

In many states, criminal courts may send transferred cases to juvenile court Several states have provisions for sending transferred cases from criminal to juvenile court for adjudication under certain circumstances. This procedure, sometimes referred to as "reverse waiver," generally applies to cases initiated in criminal court under statutory exclusion or concurrent jurisdiction provisions. Of the 36 states with such provisions at the end of the 2004 legislative session, 22 also have provisions that allow certain transferred juveniles to petition for a "reverse." Reverse decision criteria often parallel a state's discretionary waiver criteria. In some states, transfer cases resulting in conviction in criminal court may be reversed to juvenile court for disposition.

Most states have "once an adult, always an adult" provisions. In 34 states, juveniles who have been tried as adults must be prosecuted in criminal court for any subsequent offenses. Nearly all of these "once an adult, always an adult" provisions require that the youth must have been convicted of the offenses that triggered the initial criminal prosecution.

Blended sentencing laws give courts flexibility in sanctioning Blended sentencing laws address the correctional system (juvenile or adult) in which certain offenders of juvenile age will be sanctioned. Blended sentencing statutes can be placed into two general categories:

Juvenile court blended sentencing: The juvenile court has the authority to impose adult criminal sanctions on certain juvenile offenders. The majority of these blended sentencing laws authorize the juvenile court to combine a juvenile disposition with a criminal sentence that is suspended. If the youth successfully completes the juvenile disposition and does not commit a new offense, the criminal sanction is not imposed. If, however, the youth does not cooperate or fails in the juvenile sanctioning system, the adult criminal sanction is imposed. Juvenile court blended sentencing gives the juvenile court the power to send uncooperative youth to adult prison—giving "teeth" to the typical array of juvenile court dispositional options.

Criminal court blended sentencing: Statutes allow criminal courts sentencing certain transferred juveniles to impose sanctions otherwise available only to offenders handled in juvenile court. As with juvenile court blended sentencing, the juvenile disposition may be conditional—the suspended criminal sentence is intended to ensure good behavior. Criminal court blended sentencing gives juveniles prosecuted in criminal court one last chance at a juvenile disposition, thus mitigating the effects of transfer laws (at least in individual cases).

In most states, age and offense criteria limit transfer provisions

Judicial waiver remains the most common transfer provision As of the end of the 2004 legislative session, in 45 states and the District of Columbia, juvenile court judges may waive jurisdiction over certain cases and transfer them to criminal court. Such action is usually in response to a request by the prosecutor; in several states, however, juveniles or their parents may request judicial waiver. In most states, laws limit waiver by age and offense.

Waiver provisions vary in terms of the degree of decisionmaking flexibility allowed. The decision may be entirely discretionary, there may be a rebuttable presumption in favor of waiver, or waiver may be mandatory. Some provisions mandate that waiver is required once the juvenile court judge determines that certain statutory criteria have been met. Mandatory waiver provisions differ from statutory exclusion provisions in that the case originates in juvenile rather than criminal court.

Some statutes establish waiver criteria other than age and offense In some states, waiver provisions target youth charged with offenses involving firearms or other weapons. Most state statutes also limit judicial waiver to juveniles who are "no longer amenable to treatment." The specific factors that determine lack of amenability vary, but they typically include the juvenile's offense history and previous dispositional outcomes. Such amenability criteria are generally not included in statutory exclusion or concurrent jurisdiction provisions.

Many statutes instruct juvenile courts to consider other factors when making waiver decisions, such as the availability of dispositional alternatives for treating the juvenile, the time available for sanctions, public safety, and the best interest of the child. The waiver process must also adhere to certain constitutional principles of due process.

States have slowed their expansion of transfer laws Traditionally, discretionary judicial waiver was the most common transfer mechanism. Beginning in the 1970s, however, state legislatures have changed laws to move juvenile offenders into criminal court based on age and/or offense seriousness without the case-specific consideration offered by the discretionary juvenile court judicial waiver process. State transfer provisions changed extensively in the 1990s. Since 1992, all states but Nebraska have changed their transfer statutes to make it easier for juveniles to be tried in criminal court. But the pace of such changes has slowed considerably. From 1992 through 1995, 40 states and the District of Columbia enacted or expanded transfer provisions. From 1998 through 2002, legislatures in 18 states enacted or expanded their transfer provisions. From 2003 through 2004, only 4 states made substantive changes in transfer provisions, and only 2 of those states expanded them.

Relatively few states allow prosecutorial discretion As of the end of the 2004 legislative session, 15 states have concurrent jurisdiction provisions, which give both juvenile court and criminal court original jurisdiction in certain cases. Under such provisions, prosecutors have discretion to file eligible cases in either court. Concurrent jurisdiction is typically limited by age and offense criteria. Often, concurrent jurisdiction is limited to cases involving violent or repeat crimes or offenses involving firearms or other weapons. (Juvenile and criminal courts often also share jurisdiction over minor offenses such as traffic, watercraft, or local ordinance violations.) No national data exist on the number of juvenile cases tried in criminal court under concurrent jurisdiction provisions. In Florida, which has a fairly broad concurrent jurisdiction provision, prosecutors sent more than 2,000 youth to criminal court in fiscal year 2001. In comparison, juvenile court judges nationwide waived fewer than 6,000 cases to criminal court in 2000.

State appellate courts have taken the view that prosecutorial discretion is equivalent to the routine charging decisions prosecutors make in criminal cases. Thus, prosecutorial transfer is considered an executive function, which is not subject to judicial review and is not required to meet the due process standards established by the U.S. Supreme Court. Some states, how ever, do have written guidelines for prosecutorial transfer.

Statutory exclusion accounts for the largest number of transfers Legislatures "transfer" large numbers of young offenders to criminal court by enacting statutes that exclude certain cases from juvenile court jurisdiction. As of the end of the 2004 legislative session, 29 states have statutory exclusion provisions. State laws typically set age and offense limits for excluded offenses. The offenses most often excluded are murder, capital crimes in general (offenses punishable by death or life imprisonment), and other serious offenses against persons. (Minor offenses such as traffic, watercraft, and wildlife violations are often excluded from juvenile court jurisdiction in states where they are not covered by concurrent jurisdiction provisions.)

Although not typically thought of as transfers, large numbers of youth younger than age 18 are tried in criminal court in the 13 states where the upper age of juvenile court jurisdiction is set at 15 or 16. Nearly 2 million 16– and 17–year–olds live in these 13 states. If these youth are referred to criminal court at the same rate that 16– and 17–year–olds elsewhere are referred to juvenile court, then a large number of youth younger than 18 face trial in criminal court because they are defined as adults under state laws. In fact, it is possible that more youth younger than 18 are tried in criminal court in this way than by all other transfer mechanisms combined.

Many states allow transfer of certain very young offenders In 23 states, no minimum age is specified in at least one judicial waiver, concurrent jurisdiction, or statutory exclusion provision for transferring juveniles to criminal court. For example, Pennsylvania's murder exclusion has no minimum age specified. Other transfer provisions in Pennsylvania have age minimums set at 14 or 15. Among states where statutes specify age limits for all transfer provisions, age 14 is the most common minimum age specified across provisions.

Minimum transfer age specified in statute, 2004:

Age	State
None	Alaska, Arizona, Delaware, District of Columbia, Florida, Georgia, Hawaii, Idaho, Indiana, Maine, Maryland, Nebraska, Nevada, Oklahoma, Oregon, Pennsylvania, Rhode Island, South Carolina, South Dakota, Tennessee, Washington, West Virginia, Wisconsin
10	Kansas, Vermont
12	Colorado, Missouri
13	Illinois, Mississippi, New Hampshire, New York, North Carolina, Wyoming
14	Alabama, Arkansas, California, Connecticut, Iowa, Kentucky, Louisiana, Massachusetts, Michigan, Minnesota, New Jersey, North Dakota, Ohio, Texas, Utah, Virginia
15	New Mexico

Like transfer laws, juvenile court blended sentencing allows imposition of adult sanctions on juveniles

Transfer laws and juvenile court blended sentencing laws have similar impact As of the end of the 2004 legislative session, 15 states have blended sentencing laws that enable juvenile courts to impose criminal sanctions on certain juvenile offenders. Although the impact of juvenile blended sentencing laws depends on the specific provisions (which vary from state to state), in general, juvenile court blended sentencing expands the sanctioning powers of the juvenile court such that juvenile offenders may face the same penalties faced by adult offenders. Thus, like transfer laws, juvenile court blended sentencing provisions define certain juvenile offenders as eligible to be handled in the same manner as adult offenders and expose those juvenile offenders to harsher penalties.

The most common type of juvenile court blended sentencing provision allows juvenile court judges to order both a juvenile disposition and a criminal (adult) sentence. The adult sentence is suspended on the condition that the juvenile offender successfully completes the terms of the juvenile disposition and refrains from committing any new offenses. The criminal sanction is intended to encourage cooperation and serve as a deterrent to future offending. This type of arrangement is known as an inclusive blend.

Most states with juvenile court blended sentencing have inclusive blends (11 of 15). Generally, statutes require courts to impose a combination of juvenile and adult sanctions in targeted cases. In Massachusetts and Michigan, though, the court is not required to order a combined sanction. The court has the option to order a juvenile disposition, a criminal sentence, or a combined sanction.

Among the four states that do not have inclusive juvenile court blended sentencing, three (Colorado, Rhode Island, and Texas) have some type of contiguous blended sentencing arrangement. Under the contiguous model, juvenile court judges can order a sentence that would extend beyond the state's age of extended jurisdiction. The initial commitment is to a juvenile facility, but later the offender may be transferred to an adult facility. The fourth state without an inclusive juvenile blend, New Mexico, simply gives the juvenile court the option of ordering an adult sentence instead of a juvenile disposition. This is referred to as an exclusive blend.

Reverse waiver laws and criminal court blended sentencing laws have similar impact Under criminal court blended sentencing, offenders of juvenile

age who have been convicted in criminal court can receive juvenile dispositions. Like reverse waiver laws, criminal court blended sentencing provisions
give defendants of juvenile age an opportunity to show that they belong in the
juvenile justice system. Criminal court blended sentencing laws have been
described as a "safety valve" or an "emergency exit" because they allow the
court to review the circumstances of a case and make an individualized
decision regarding the youth's suitability for juvenile or criminal treatment.
In this way, youth are given one last chance to receive a juvenile disposition.

Seventeen states allow criminal court blended sentencing. Of these states,
10 have exclusive blended sentencing arrangements: the criminal court has an
either/or choice between criminal and juvenile sanctions. Inclusive blend
models, in which juvenile offenders convicted in criminal court may receive a
combination sentence, exist in the remaining seven states with criminal court
blended sentencing. As with the juvenile court inclusive blend model, the
criminal court inclusive blend model allows the criminal court to suspend the
adult sanction on condition of the youth's good behavior.

Criminal court blended sentencing provisions, 2004:

Provision	State
Exclusive	California, Colorado, Illinois, Kentucky, Massachusetts, Nebraska, New Mexico, Oklahoma, West Virginia, Wisconsin
Inclusive	Arkansas, Florida, Idaho, Iowa, Michigan, Missouri, Virginia

As with transfer and juvenile court blended sentencing laws, the scope of
criminal court blended sentencing laws varies from state to state depending
on the specifics of the statutory provisions. Limitations typically stem from
the transfer provisions. The broadest criminal court blend statutes allow for
juvenile sanctions in any case involving a juvenile prosecuted in criminal
court (i.e., any transferred juvenile). Others exclude from blended sentencing
only those convicted of offenses that carry a mandatory life or death sentence.
The narrowest of the criminal court blend provisions limit the juvenile
disposition option to juvenile offenders who have been convicted of a lesser
offense that is not itself eligible for transfer and criminal prosecution. In still
other states, statutes require a "fitness hearing" to determine whether the
disposition for a lesser offense should be a juvenile sanction. At the hearing,
the court must base its decision on criteria similar to those used in juvenile
court discretionary waiver decisions.

**Courts waived fewer cases in 2002 than in 1985 — 2001 had the
fewest waivers of any year since 1985**

The profile of waived cases has changed In the late 1980s, property
cases accounted for at least half of all delinquency cases judicially waived from
juvenile court to criminal court. In the early 1990s, the property offense share
of waived cases diminished as the person offense share grew. By 1993, the
waiver caseload had a greater proportion of person offense cases than property cases (41% vs. 39%). Drug and public order cases made up smaller
proportions of waived cases across all years. For example, in 2002, 14% of
waived cases were drug offenses and 9% were public order cases. The
demographic characteristics of judicially waived cases have also changed since
the 1980s.

Demographic profiles of judicially waived delinquency cases:

Characteristic	1985	1994	2002
Gender			
Male	95%	95%	93%
Female	5	5	7
Race			
White	58	53	62
Black	41	43	35
Other races	2	4	3
Age			
15 or younger	6	12	13
16 or older	94	88	87

Although the proportions of judicially waived cases involving females and younger juveniles increased between 1985 and 2002, the vast majority of waived cases involved males age 16 or older. However, the proportion of males age 16 or older among judicially waived cases decreased somewhat, from 89% in 1985 to 80% in 2002.

    The likelihood of waiver varied across case characteristics In 2002, the proportion of cases waived was greater for males than for females. This was true in each of the four general offense categories. For example, males charged with person offenses were six times as likely as females charged with person offenses to have their cases waived to criminal court. However, this comparison does not control for differences in the seriousness of offenses or a juvenile's offense history.

Percent of petitioned cases judicially waived to criminal court, 2002:

Offense	Male	Female
Delinquency	0.9%	0.3%
Person	1.6	0.3
Property	0.9	0.3
Drugs	0.9	0.5
Public order	0.3	0.1

    In 2002, black youth were more likely than other youth to be waived for drug offenses. White youth were more likely than other youth to be waived for property offenses. Youth of other races were more likely than white youth or black youth to be waived for person offenses. Regardless of race, person offenses were more likely to be waived than cases involving other offenses.

Percent of petitioned cases judicially waived to criminal court, 2002:

Offense	White	Black	Other races
Delinquency	0.7%	0.8%	0.7%
Person	1.2	1.3	1.5
Property	0.8	0.6	0.6
Drug	0.7	1.2	0.7
Public Order	0.3	0.3	0.3

Cases involving younger juveniles were less likely to be waived than were cases involving older juveniles. This was true for each of the four general offense categories. For example, among person offense cases, youth age 16 or older were seven times more likely to be waived than youth age 15 or younger.

B. JUDICIAL WAIVER

KENT v. UNITED STATES

383 U.S. 541, 86 S.Ct. 1045, 16 L.Ed.2d 84 (1966).

MR. JUSTICE FORTAS delivered the opinion of the Court. This case is here on certiorari to the United States Court of Appeals for the District of Columbia Circuit. The facts and the contentions of counsel raise a number of disturbing questions concerning the administration by the police and the Juvenile Court authorities of the District of Columbia laws relating to juveniles. * * * Because we conclude that the Juvenile Court's order waiving jurisdiction of petitioner was entered without compliance with required procedures, we remand the case to the trial court.

Morris A. Kent, Jr., first came under the authority of the Juvenile Court of the District of Columbia in 1959. He was then aged 14. * * * On September 2, 1961, an intruder entered the apartment of a woman in the District of Columbia. He took her wallet. He raped her. The police found in the apartment latent fingerprints * * * [which] matched the fingerprints of Morris Kent, taken when he was 14 years old and under the jurisdiction of the Juvenile Court. At about 3 p.m. on September 5, 1961, Kent was taken into custody by the police. * * * Upon being apprehended, Kent was taken to police headquarters where he was interrogated by police officers. It appears that he admitted his involvement in the offense which led to his apprehension and volunteered information as to similar offenses involving housebreaking, robbery, and rape. His interrogation proceeded from about 3 p.m. to 10 p.m. the same evening. * * * [O]n September 6, 1961, the day following petitioner's apprehension, she [Kent's mother] retained counsel.

Counsel, together with petitioner's mother, promptly conferred with the Social Service Director of the Juvenile Court. In a brief interview, they discussed the possibility that the Juvenile Court might waive jurisdiction and remit Kent to trial by the District Court. Counsel made known his intention to oppose waiver.

Petitioner was detained at the Receiving Home for almost a week. There was no arraignment during this time, no determination by a judicial officer of probable cause for petitioner's apprehension.

During this period of detention and interrogation, petitioner's counsel arranged for examination of petitioner by two psychiatrists and a psychologist. He thereafter filed with the Juvenile Court a motion for a hearing on the question of waiver of Juvenile Court jurisdiction, together with an affidavit of a psychiatrist certifying that petitioner "is a victim of severe psycho-pathology'' and recommending hospitalization for psychiatric observation. Petitioner's counsel, in support of his motion to the effect that the Juvenile Court should retain jurisdiction of petitioner, offered to prove that if petitioner were given adequate treatment in a hospital under the aegis of the Juvenile Court, he would be a suitable subject for rehabilitation.

At the same time, petitioner's counsel moved that the Juvenile Court should give him access to the Social Service file relating to petitioner which had been accumulated by the staff of the Juvenile Court during petitioner's probation period, and which would be available to the Juvenile Court judge in considering the question whether it should retain or waive jurisdiction. Petitioner's counsel represented that access to this file was essential to his providing petitioner with effective assistance of counsel.

The Juvenile Court judge did not rule on these motions. He held no hearing. He did not confer with petitioner or petitioner's parents or petitioner's counsel. He entered an order reciting that after "full investigation, I do hereby waive" jurisdiction of petitioner and directing that he be "held for trial for (the alleged) offenses under the regular procedure of the U.S. District Court for the District of Columbia." He made no findings. He did not recite any reason for the waiver.[4] He made no reference to the motions filed by petitioner's counsel. We must assume that he denied, *sub silentio*, the motions for a hearing, the recommendation for hospitalization for psychiatric observation, the request for access to the Social Service file, and the offer to prove that petitioner was a fit subject for rehabilitation under the Juvenile Court's jurisdiction.

Presumably, prior to entry of his order, the Juvenile Court judge received and considered recommendations of the Juvenile Court staff, the Social Service file relating to petitioner, and a report dated September 8, 1961 (three days following petitioner's apprehension), submitted to him by the Juvenile Probation Section. The Social Service file and the September 8 report were later sent to the District Court and it appears that both of them referred to petitioner's mental condition. The September 8 report spoke of "a rapid deterioration of (petitioner's) personality structure and the possibility of mental illness." As stated, neither this report nor the Social Service file was made available to petitioner's counsel.

The provision of the Juvenile Court Act governing waiver expressly provides only for "full investigation." It states the circumstances in which jurisdiction may be waived and the child held for trial under adult procedures, but it does not state standards to govern the Juvenile Court's decision as to waiver. The provision reads as follows:

> "If a child sixteen years of age or older is charged with an offense which would amount to a felony in the case of an adult, or any child

---

4. At the time of these events, there was in effect Policy Memorandum No. 7 of November 30, 1959, promulgated by the judge of the Juvenile Court to set forth the criteria to govern disposition of waiver requests. It is set forth in the Appendix. This Memorandum has since been rescinded.

charged with an offense which if committed by an adult is punishable by death or life imprisonment, the judge may, after full investigation, waive jurisdiction and order such child held for trial under the regular procedure of the court which would have jurisdiction of such offense if committed by an adult; or such other court may exercise the powers conferred upon the juvenile court in this subchapter in conducting and disposing of such cases." * * *

It is to petitioner's arguments as to the infirmity of the proceedings by which the Juvenile Court waived its otherwise exclusive jurisdiction that we address our attention. Petitioner attacks the waiver of jurisdiction on a number of statutory and constitutional grounds. He contends that the waiver is defective because no hearing was held; because no findings were made by the Juvenile Court; because the Juvenile Court stated no reasons for waiver; and because counsel was denied access to the Social Service file which presumably was considered by the Juvenile Court in determining to waive jurisdiction. * * *

We agree with the Court of Appeals that the statute contemplates that the Juvenile Court should have considerable latitude within which to determine whether it should retain jurisdiction over a child or—subject to the statutory delimitation—should waive jurisdiction. But this latitude is not complete. At the outset, it assumes procedural regularity sufficient in the particular circumstances to satisfy the basic requirements of due process and fairness, as well as compliance with the statutory requirement of a "full investigation." The statute gives the Juvenile Court a substantial degree of discretion as to the factual considerations to be evaluated, the weight to be given them and the conclusion to be reached. It does not confer upon the Juvenile Court a license for arbitrary procedure. The statute does not permit the Juvenile Court to determine in isolation and without the participation or any representation of the child the "critically important" question whether a child will be deprived of the special protections and provisions of the Juvenile Court Act. It does not authorize the Juvenile Court, in total disregard of a motion for hearing filed by counsel, and without any hearing or statement or reasons, to decide—as in this case—that the child will be taken from the Receiving Home for Children and transferred to jail along with adults, and that he will be exposed to the possibility of a death sentence instead of treatment for a maximum, in Kent's case, of five years, until he is 21.

We do not consider whether, on the merits, Kent should have been transferred; but there is no place in our system of law for reaching a result of such tremendous consequences without ceremony—without hearing, without effective assistance of counsel, without a statement of reasons. It is inconceivable that a court of justice dealing with adults, with respect to a similar issue, would proceed in this manner. It would be extraordinary if society's special concern for children, as reflected in the District of Columbia's Juvenile Court Act, permitted this procedure. We hold that it does not. * * *

While there can be no doubt of the original laudable purpose of juvenile courts, studies and critiques in recent years raise serious questions as to whether actual performance measures well enough against theoretical purpose to make tolerable the immunity of the process from the reach of constitutional guaranties applicable to adults. There is much evidence that some juvenile courts, including that of the District of Columbia, lack the personnel, facilities and techniques to perform adequately as representatives of the State in a *parens patriae* capacity, at least with respect to children charged with law violation. There is evidence, in fact, that there may be grounds for concern that the child receives the worst of both worlds: that he gets neither the protections accorded to adults nor the solicitous care and regenerative treatment postulated for children. * * *

It is clear beyond dispute that the waiver of jurisdiction is a "critically important" action determining vitally important statutory rights of the juvenile. The statutory scheme makes this plain. The Juvenile Court is vested with "original and exclusive jurisdiction" of the child. This jurisdiction confers special rights and immunities. He is, as specified by the statute, shielded from publicity. He may be confined, but with rare exceptions he may not be jailed along with adults. He may be detained, but only until he is 21 years of age. The court is admonished by the statute to give preference to retaining the child in the custody of his parents "unless his welfare and the safety and protection of the public can not be adequately safeguarded without * * * removal." The child is protected against consequences of adult conviction such as the loss of civil rights, the use of adjudication against him in subsequent proceedings, and disqualification for public employment.

The net, therefore, is that petitioner—then a boy of 16—was by statute entitled to certain procedures and benefits as a consequence of his statutory right to the "exclusive" jurisdiction of the Juvenile Court. In these circumstances, considering particularly that decision as to waiver of jurisdiction and transfer of the matter to the District Court was potentially as important to petitioner as the difference between five years' confinement and a death sentence, we conclude that, as a condition to a valid waiver order, petitioner was entitled to a hearing, including access by his counsel to the social records and probation or similar reports which presumably are considered by the court, and to a statement of reasons for the Juvenile Court's decision. We believe that this result is required by the statute read in the context of constitutional principles relating to due process and the assistance of counsel. * * *

We are of the opinion that the Court of Appeals misconceived the basic issue and the underlying values in this case. * * * [T]he determination of whether to transfer a child from the statutory structure of the Juvenile Court to the criminal processes of the District Court is "critically important." We hold that it is, indeed, a "critically important" proceeding. The Juvenile Court Act confers upon the child a right to avail himself of that court's "exclusive" jurisdiction. As the Court of Appeals has said,

"(I)t is implicit in (the Juvenile Court) scheme that non-criminal treatment is to be the rule—and the adult criminal treatment, the exception which must be governed by the particular factors of individual cases."

Meaningful review requires that the reviewing court should review. It should not be remitted to assumptions. It must have before it a statement of the reasons motivating the waiver including, of course, a statement of the relevant facts. It may not "assume" that there are adequate reasons, nor may it merely assume that "full investigation" has been made. Accordingly, we hold that it is incumbent upon the Juvenile Court to accompany its waiver order with a statement of the reasons or considerations therefor. We do not read the statute as requiring that this statement must be formal or that it should necessarily include conventional findings of fact. But the statement should be sufficient to demonstrate that the statutory requirement of "full investigation" has been met; and that the question has received the careful consideration of the Juvenile Court; and it must set forth the basis for the order with sufficient specificity to permit meaningful review.

Correspondingly, we conclude that an opportunity for a hearing which may be informal, must be given the child prior to entry of a waiver order. * * * [T]he child is entitled to counsel in connection with a waiver proceeding, and * * * counsel is entitled to see the child's social records. These rights are meaningless—an illusion, a mockery—unless counsel is given an opportunity to function.

The right to representation by counsel is not a formality. It is not a grudging gesture to a ritualistic requirement. It is of the essence of justice. Appointment of counsel without affording an opportunity for hearing on a "critically important" decision is tantamount to denial of counsel. There is no justification for the failure of the Juvenile Court to rule on the motion for hearing filed by petitioner's counsel, and it was error to fail to grant a hearing.

We do not mean by this to indicate that the hearing to be held must conform with all of the requirements of a criminal trial or even of the usual administrative hearing; but we do hold that the hearing must measure up to the essentials of due process and fair treatment.

With respect to access by the child's counsel to the social records of the child, we deem it obvious that since these are to be considered by the Juvenile Court in making its decision to waive, they must be made available to the child's counsel. * * * We cannot agree with the Court of Appeals in the present case that the statute is "ambiguous." The statute expressly provides that the record *shall be* withheld from "indiscriminate" public inspection, "except that such records or parts thereof shall be made available by rule of court or special order of court to such persons * * * as have a *legitimate interest* in the protection* * * of the child * * *." counsel, therefore, have a "legitimate interest" in the protection of the child, and must be afforded access to these records.

We do not agree with the Court of Appeals' statement, attempting to justify denial of access to these records, that counsel's role is limited to presenting "to the court anything on behalf of the child which might help the court in arriving at a decision; it is not to denigrate the staff's submissions and recommendations." On the contrary, if the staff's submissions include materials which are susceptible to challenge or impeachment, it is precisely the role of counsel to "denigrate" such matter. There is no irrebuttable presumption of accuracy attached to staff reports. If a decision on waiver is "critically important" it is equally of "critical importance" that the material submitted to the judge—which is protected by the statute only against "indiscriminate" inspection—be subjected, within reasonable limits having regard to the theory of the Juvenile Court Act, to examination, criticism and refutation. While the Juvenile Court judge may, of course, receive *ex parte* analyses and recommendations from his staff, he may not, for purposes of a decision on waiver, receive and rely upon secret information, whether emanating from his staff or otherwise. The Juvenile Court is governed in this respect by the established principles which control courts and quasi-judicial agencies of the Government. * * *

Ordinarily we would reverse the Court of Appeals and direct the District Court to remand the case to the Juvenile Court for a new determination of waiver. If on remand the decision were against waiver, the indictment in the District Court would be dismissed. However, petitioner has now passed the age of 21 and the Juvenile Court can no longer exercise jurisdiction over him. In view of the unavailability of a redetermination of the waiver question by the Juvenile Court, it is urged by petitioner that the conviction should be vacated and the indictment dismissed. In the circumstances of this case, * * * we do not consider it appropriate to grant this drastic relief. Accordingly, we vacate the order of the Court of Appeals and the judgment of the District Court and remand the case to the District Court for a hearing de novo on waiver, consistent with this opinion. If that court finds that waiver was inappropriate, petitioner's conviction must be vacated. If, however, it finds that the waiver order was proper when originally made, the District Court may proceed, after consideration of such motions as counsel may make and such further proceedings, if any, as may be warranted, to enter an appropriate judgment.

Reversed and remanded.

Appendix to Opinion of the Court

Policy Memorandum No. 7, November 30, 1959.

* * * [The Statute] permits the Judge to waive jurisdiction "after full investigation" in the case of any child "sixteen years of age or older (who is) charged with an offense which would amount to a felony in the case of an adult, or any child charged with an offense which if committed by an adult is punishable by death or life imprisonment."

The statute sets forth no specific standards for the exercise of this important discretionary act, but leaves the formulation of such criteria to the Judge. * * *

Therefore, the Judge * * * has formulated the following criteria and principles concerning waiver of jurisdiction which are consistent with the basic aims and purpose of the Juvenile Court Act.

An offense falling within the statutory limitations (set forth above) will be waived if it has prosecutive merit and if it is heinous or of an aggravated character, or—even though less serious—if it represents a pattern of repeated offenses which indicate that the juvenile may be beyond rehabilitation under Juvenile Court procedures, or if the public needs the protection afforded by such action.

The determinative factors which will be considered by the Judge in deciding whether the Juvenile Court's jurisdiction over such offenses will be waived are the following:

1. The seriousness of the alleged offense to the community and whether the protection of the community requires waiver.

2. Whether the alleged offense was committed in an aggressive, violent, premeditated or willful manner.

3. Whether the alleged offense was against persons or against property, greater weight being given to offenses against persons especially if personal injury resulted.

4. The prosecutive merit of the complaint, i.e., whether there is evidence upon which a Grand Jury may be expected to return an indictment * * *.

5. The desirability of trial and disposition of the entire offense in one court when the juvenile's associates in the alleged offense are adults who will be charged with a crime * * *.

6. The sophistication and maturity of the juvenile as determined by consideration of his home, environmental situation, emotional attitude and pattern of living.

7. The record and previous history of the juvenile, including previous contacts with the Youth Aid Division, other law enforcement agencies, juvenile courts and other jurisdictions, prior periods of probation to this Court, or prior commitments to juvenile institutions.

8. The prospects for adequate protection of the public and the likelihood of reasonable rehabilitation of the juvenile (if he is found to have committed the alleged offense) by the use of procedures, services and facilities currently available to the Juvenile Court. * * *

MR. JUSTICE STEWART, with whom MR. JUSTICE BLACK, MR. JUSTICE HARLAN and MR. JUSTICE WHITE join, dissenting. This case involves the construction of a statute applicable only to the District of Columbia. Our general practice is to leave undisturbed decisions of the Court of Appeals for the District of Columbia Circuit concerning the import of legislation governing the affairs of the District. It appears, however, that two cases decided by the Court of Appeals subsequent to its decision in the present case may have considerably modified the court's construction of the statute. Therefore, I would vacate this judgment and remand the case to the Court of Appeals. * * *

NOTE

1) Kent's Appendix as Dicta Many states' waiver laws or judicial rulings adopted the Appendix in *Kent* as statutory criteria or judicial guidelines for waiver decisions. What is the constitutional status of the *Kent* Appendix? What was the status of the policy memorandum at the time the Supreme Court appended it? See, p. 524, n. 4.

BREED v. JONES

421 U.S. 519, 95 S.Ct. 1779, 44 L.Ed.2d 346 (1975).

MR. CHIEF JUSTICE BURGER delivered the opinion of the Court. We granted certiorari to decide whether the prosecution of respondent as an adult, after Juvenile Court proceedings which resulted in a finding that respondent had violated a criminal statute and a subsequent finding that he was unfit for treatment as a juvenile, violated the Fifth and Fourteenth Amendments to the United States Constitution.

On February 9, 1971, a petition was filed in the Superior Court of California, County of Los Angeles, Juvenile Court, alleging that respondent, then 17 years of age, was a [delinquent], in that, on or about February 8, while armed with a deadly weapon, he had committed acts which, if committed by an adult, would constitute the crime of robbery. * * *

The jurisdictional or adjudicatory hearing was conducted on March 1. * * * After taking testimony from two prosecution witnesses and respondent, the Juvenile Court found that the allegations in the petition were true and that respondent was a person described by § 602, and it sustained the petition. The proceedings were continued for a dispositional hearing, pending which the court ordered that respondent remain detained.

At a hearing conducted on March 15, the Juvenile Court indicated its intention to find respondent "not * * * amenable to the care, treatment and training program available through the facilities of the juvenile court."[5] Respondent's counsel orally moved "to continue the matter on

---

5. At the time, *Cal.Welf. & Inst. Code* § 707 (Supp. 1967) provided: "At any time during a hearing upon a petition alleging that a minor is, * * * a person described in Section 602, when substantial evidence has been adduced to support a finding that the minor was 16 years of age or older at the time of the alleged commission of such offense and that the minor would not be amenable to the care, treatment and training program available through the facilities of the juvenile court, * * * the court may make a finding * * * that the minor is not fit and proper subject to be dealt with under this chapter, and the court shall direct the district attorney or other appropriate prosecuting officer to prosecute the person under the applicable criminal

the ground of surprise," contending that respondent "was not informed that it was going to be a fitness hearing." The court continued the matter for one week, at which time, having considered the report of the probation officer assigned to the case and having heard her testimony, it declared respondent "unfit for treatment as a juvenile," and ordered that he be prosecuted as an adult. * * *

After a preliminary hearing respondent was ordered held for trial in Superior Court, where an information was subsequently filed accusing him of having committed robbery, while armed with a deadly weapon. * * * Respondent entered a plea of not guilty, and he also pleaded that he had "already been placed once in jeopardy and convicted of the offense charged, by the judgment of the Superior Court of the County of Los Angeles, Juvenile Court, rendered * * * on the 1st day of March, 1971." By stipulation, the case was submitted to the court on the transcript of the preliminary hearing. The court found respondent guilty of robbery in the first degree and ordered that he be committed to the California Youth Authority. No appeal was taken from the judgment of conviction.

On December 10, 1971, respondent * * * filed the instant petition for a writ of habeas corpus. * * * In his petition he alleged that his transfer to adult court and subsequent trial there "placed him in double jeopardy." The District Court denied the petition, rejecting respondent's contention that jeopardy attached at his adjudicatory hearing. It concluded that the "distinctions between the preliminary procedures and hearings provided by California law for juveniles and a criminal trial are many and apparent and the effort of (respondent) to relate them is unconvincing," and that "even assuming jeopardy attached during the preliminary juvenile proceedings * * * it is clear that no new jeopardy arose by the juvenile proceeding sending the case to the criminal court."

The Court of Appeals reversed, concluding that applying double jeopardy protection to juvenile proceedings would not "impede the juvenile courts in carrying out their basic goal of rehabilitating the erring youth," and that the contrary result might "do irreparable harm to or destroy their confidence in our judicial system." The court therefore held that the Double Jeopardy Clause "is fully applicable to juvenile court proceedings." * * *

We granted certiorari because of a conflict between Courts of Appeals and the highest courts of a number of States on the issue presented in this case and similar issues and because of the importance of final resolution of the issue to the administration of the juvenile-court system. * * *

[T]here is no dispute that the petition filed in Juvenile Court and the information filed in Superior Court related to the "same offence" within the meaning of the constitutional prohibition. The point of disagreement between the parties, and the question for our decision, is whether, by

statute or ordinance and thereafter dismiss the petition or, if a prosecution has been commenced in another court but has been suspended while juvenile court proceedings are held, shall dismiss the petition and issue its order directing that the other court proceedings resume. * * *"

reason of the proceedings in Juvenile Court, respondent was "twice put in jeopardy."

Jeopardy denotes risk. In the constitutional sense, jeopardy describes the risk that is traditionally associated with a criminal prosecution. Although the constitutional language, "jeopardy of life or limb," suggests proceedings in which only the most serious penalties can be imposed, the Clause has long been construed to mean something far broader than its literal language. At the same time, however, we have held that the risk to which the Clause refers is not present in proceedings that are not "essentially criminal."

Although the juvenile-court system had its genesis in the desire to provide a distinctive procedure and setting to deal with the problems of youth, including those manifested by antisocial conduct, our decisions in recent years have recognized that there is a gap between the originally benign conception of the system and its realities. With the exception of *McKeiver v. Pennsylvania*, the Court's response to that perception has been to make applicable in juvenile proceedings constitutional guarantees associated with traditional criminal prosecutions. *In re Gault*; *In re Winship*. In so doing the Court has evinced awareness of the threat which such a process represents to the efforts of the juvenile court system, functioning in a unique manner, to ameliorate the harshness of criminal justice when applied to youthful offenders. That the system has fallen short of the high expectations of its sponsors in no way detracts from the broad social benefits sought or from those benefits that can survive constitutional scrutiny.

We believe it is simply too late in the day to conclude, as did the District Court in this case, that a juvenile is not put in jeopardy at a proceeding whose object is to determine whether he has committed acts that violate a criminal law and whose potential consequences include both the stigma inherent in such a determination and the deprivation of liberty for many years. For it is clear under our cases that determining the relevance of constitutional policies, like determining the applicability of constitutional rights, in juvenile proceedings, requires that courts eschew the "civil label-of-convenience which has been attached to juvenile proceedings," and that "the juvenile process * * * be candidly appraised."

As we have observed, the risk to which the term jeopardy refers is that traditionally associated with "actions intended to authorize criminal punishment to vindicate public justice." Because of its purpose and potential consequences, and the nature and resources of the State, such a proceeding imposes heavy pressures and burdens—psychological, physical, and financial—on a person charged. The purpose of the Double Jeopardy Clause is to require that he be subject to the experience only once "for the same offence."

In *In re Gault*, this Court concluded that, for purposes of the right to counsel, a "proceeding where the issue is whether the child will be found to be 'delinquent' and subjected to the loss of his liberty for years is comparable in seriousness to a felony prosecution." The Court stated that the term "delinquent" had "come to involve only slightly less stigma than the term 'criminal' applied to adults," and that, for purposes of the privilege against self-incrimination, "commitment is a deprivation of liberty. It is incarceration against one's will, whether it is called 'criminal' or 'civil'."

Thus, in terms of potential consequences, there is little to distinguish an adjudicatory hearing such as was held in this case from a traditional criminal prosecution. For that reason, it engenders elements of "anxiety and insecurity" in a juvenile, and imposes a "heavy personal strain." And we can expect that, since our decisions implementing fundamental fairness in the juvenile court system, hearings have been prolonged, and some of the burdens incident to a juvenile's defense increased, as the system has assimilated the process thereby imposed.

We deal here, not with "the formalities of the criminal adjudicative process," but with an analysis of an aspect of the juvenile-court system in terms of the kind of risk to which jeopardy refers. Under our decisions we can find no persuasive distinction in that regard between the proceeding conducted in this case * * * and a criminal prosecution, each of which is designed "to vindicate (the) very vital interest in enforcement of criminal laws." We therefore conclude that respondent was put in jeopardy at the adjudicatory hearing. Jeopardy attached when respondent was "put to trial before the trier of the facts," that is, when the Juvenile Court, as the trier of the facts, began to hear evidence.

Petitioner argues that, even assuming jeopardy attached at respondent's adjudicatory hearing, the procedures by which he was transferred from Juvenile Court and tried on a felony information in Superior Court did not violate the Double Jeopardy Clause. The argument is supported by two distinct, but in this case overlapping, lines of analysis. First, petitioner reasons that the procedure violated none of the policies of the Double Jeopardy Clause. * * * Second, pointing to this Court's concern for "the juvenile court's assumed ability to function in a unique manner," petitioner urges that, should we conclude traditional principles "would otherwise bar a transfer to adult court after a delinquency adjudication," we should avoid that result here because it "would diminish the flexibility and informality of juvenile court proceedings without conferring any additional due process benefits upon juveniles charged with delinquent acts."

We cannot agree with petitioner that the trial of respondent in Superior Court on an information charging the same offense as that for which he had been tried in Juvenile Court violated none of the policies of the Double Jeopardy Clause. For, even accepting petitioner's premise that respondent "never faced the risk of more than one punishment," we have pointed out that "the Double Jeopardy Clause * * * is written in terms of potential or risk of trial and conviction, not punishment." * * *

Respondent was subjected to the burden of two trials for the same offense; he was twice put to the task of marshaling his resources against those of the State, twice subjected to the "heavy personal strain" which such an experience represents. We turn, therefore, to inquire whether either traditional principles or "the juvenile court's assumed ability to function in a unique manner," supports an exception to the "constitutional policy of finality" to which respondent would otherwise be entitled. * * *

The possibility of transfer from juvenile court to a court of general criminal jurisdiction is a matter of great significance to the juvenile. At the same time, there appears to be widely shared agreement that not all juveniles can benefit from the special features and programs of the juvenile-court system and that a procedure for transfer to an adult court should be available. This general agreement is reflected in the fact that an overwhelming majority of jurisdictions permits transfer in certain circumstances. As might be expected, the statutory provisions differ in numerous details. Whatever their differences, however, such transfer provisions represent an attempt to impart to the juvenile-court system the flexibility needed to deal with youthful offenders who cannot benefit from the specialized guidance and treatment contemplated by the system.

We do not agree with petitioner that giving respondent the constitutional protection against multiple trials in this context will diminish flexibility and informality to the extent that those qualities relate uniquely to the goals of the juvenile-court system. We agree that such a holding will require, in most cases, that the transfer decision be made prior to an adjudicatory hearing. To the extent that evidence concerning the alleged offense is considered relevant, it may be that, in those cases where transfer is considered and rejected, some added burden will be imposed on the juvenile courts by reason of duplicative proceedings. Finally, the nature of the evidence considered at a transfer hearing may in some States require that, if transfer is rejected, a different judge preside at the adjudicatory hearing.

A requirement that transfer hearings be held prior to adjudicatory hearings affects not at all the nature of the latter proceedings. More significantly, such a requirement need not affect the quality of decision-making at transfer hearings themselves. In *Kent v. United States*, the Court held that hearings under the statute there involved "must measure up to the essentials of due process and fair treatment." However, the Court has never attempted to prescribe criteria for, or the nature and quantum of evidence that must support, a decision to transfer a juvenile for trial in adult court. We require only that, whatever the relevant criteria, and whatever the evidence demanded, a State determine whether it wants to treat a juvenile within the juvenile-court system before entering upon a proceeding that may result in an adjudication that he has violated a criminal law and in a substantial deprivation of liberty, rather than subject him to the expense, delay, strain, and embarrassment of two such proceedings.

Moreover, we are not persuaded that the burdens petitioner envisions would pose a significant problem for the administration of the juvenile-court system. The large number of jurisdictions that presently require that the transfer decision be made prior to an adjudicatory hearing, and the absence of any indication that the juvenile courts in those jurisdictions have not been able to perform their task within that framework, suggest the contrary. The likelihood that in many cases the lack of need or basis for a transfer hearing can be recognized promptly reduces the number of cases in which a commitment of resources is necessary. In addition, we have no reason to believe that the resources available to those who recommend transfer or participate in the process leading to transfer decisions are inadequate to enable them to gather the information relevant to informed decision prior to an adjudicatory hearing.

To the extent that transfer hearings held prior to adjudication result in some duplication of evidence if transfer is rejected, the burden on juvenile courts will tend to be offset somewhat by the cases in which, because of transfer, no further proceedings in juvenile court are required. Moreover, when transfer has previously been rejected, juveniles may well be more likely to admit the commission of the offense charged, thereby obviating the need for adjudicatory hearings, than if transfer remains a possibility. Finally, we note that those States which presently require a different judge to preside at an adjudicatory hearing if transfer is rejected also permit waiver of that requirement. Where the requirement is not waived, it is difficult to see a substantial strain on judicial resources.

Quite apart from our conclusions with respect to the burdens on the juvenile court system envisioned by petitioner, we are persuaded that transfer hearings prior to adjudication will aid the objectives of that system. What concerns us here is the dilemma that the possibility of transfer after an adjudicatory hearing presents for a juvenile, a dilemma to which the Court of Appeals alluded. Because of that possibility, a juvenile, thought to be the beneficiary of special consideration, may in fact suffer substantial disadvantages. If he appears uncooperative, he runs the risk of an adverse adjudication, as well as of an unfavorable dispositional recommendation. If, on the other hand, he is cooperative, he runs the risk of prejudicing his chances in adult court if transfer is ordered. We regard a procedure that results in such a dilemma as at odds with the goal that, to the extent fundamental fairness permits, adjudicatory hearings be informal and nonadversary. Knowledge of the risk of transfer after an adjudicatory hearing can only undermine the potential for informality and cooperation which was intended to be the hallmark of the juvenile-court system. Rather than concerning themselves with the matter at hand, establishing innocence or seeking a disposition best suited to individual correctional needs, the juvenile and his attorney are pressed into a posture of adversary wariness that is conducive to neither.

We hold that the prosecution of respondent in Superior Court, after an adjudicatory proceeding in Juvenile Court, violated the Double Jeopardy Clause of the Fifth Amendment, as applied to the States through the

Fourteenth Amendment. The mandate of the Court of Appeals, which was stayed by that court pending our decision, directs the District Court "to issue a writ of habeas corpus directing the state court, within 60 days, to vacate the adult conviction of Jones and either set him free or remand him to the juvenile court for disposition." Since respondent is no longer subject to the jurisdiction of the California Juvenile Court, we vacate the judgment and remand the case to the Court of Appeals for such further proceedings consistent with this opinion as may be appropriate in the circumstances.

So ordered.

NOTES

1) "Full Investigation" of what? After *Kent* and *Breed*, what does a "full investigation" investigate? What does a judge actually decide in a judicial waiver hearing? How does she make that decision? What evidence should she consider? How should she weigh the evidence? What is the burden of proof? How should the statute allocate the burden of persuasion between a juvenile and the state? Who is "amenable to treatment"? How can a judge predict a youth's future "dangerousness"? Are the answers to these questions susceptible to judicial determination? *See generally*, Barry C. Feld, "Reference of Juvenile Offenders for Adult Prosecution: The Legislative Alternative to Asking Unanswerable Questions," 62 *Minn. L. Rev.* 151 (1978).

2) "Amenability to Treatment" in Theory and Practice *Kent* and *Breed* provide the formal procedural framework within which judges make waiver decisions. But the substantive bases of waiver decisions pose the principal difficulty. Despite recent legislative amendments, many states' waiver statutes allow juvenile court judges to transfer jurisdiction based on their discretionary assessment of subjective factors, such as youths' "amenability to treatment" or "dangerousness." *See* Barry C. Feld, "Violent Youth and Public Policy: A Case Study of Juvenile Justice Law Reform," 79 *Minn. L. Rev.* 965 (1995). Legislatures specify "amenability" criteria with varying degrees of precision and often adopt the general, contradictory list of factors appended in *Kent*. Although some states limit waiver to felony offenses and establish some minimum age for adult prosecutions, typically sixteen, fifteen, or fourteen, other provide neither offense nor minimum age restrictions.

In practice, judges appear to operationalize "amenability" and "dangerousness" criteria by considering three sets of variables. The first consists of a youth's age and the length of time remaining within juvenile court jurisdiction. Marcy Rasmussen Podkopacz and Barry C. Feld, "Judicial Waiver Policy and Practice: Persistence, Seriousness and Race." 14 *J. Law & Inequality* 73 (1995); Marcy Rasmussen Podkopacz and Barry C. Feld, "The End of the Line: An Empirical Study of Judicial Waiver." 86 *J. Crim. L. & Criminology* 449 (1996). Juvenile court judges waive older youths more readily than younger offenders. A youth's age in relation to the maximum dispositional jurisdiction restricts judges' sanctioning powers and provides an impetus to waive older juveniles or those whose offenses deserve a longer sentence than available in juvenile court. A youth's age may serve as a proxy for prior delinquency, since older juveniles have had a longer opportunity to acquire a prior record. Conversely, judges may view younger offenders as less blameworthy or responsible than their older and more culpable peers. Judges in states whose juvenile dispositions can continue until age twenty-one waive youths at about half the rate as do judges in states whose jurisdiction ends at ages eighteen or nineteen.

A second constellation of "amenability" factors include a youth's treatment prognosis as revealed in clinical evaluations and by prior correctional interventions. Once a juvenile exhausts the available treatment services and correctional resources, transfer becomes increasingly more likely. Marcy Rasmussen Podkopacz and Barry C. Feld, "Judicial Waiver Policy and Practice: Persistence, Seriousness and Race," 14 *J. Law & Inequality* 73 (1995); Marcy Rasmussen Podkopacz and Barry C. Feld, "The End of the Line: An Empirical Study of Judicial Waiver," 86 *J. Crim. L. & Criminology* 449 (1996).

Finally, judges pragmatically assess "dangerousness" and the threat a youth poses to others based on the present offense and the prior record. Dangerousness variables include the seriousness of the offense, whether the youth used a weapon, and the length of the prior record.

Despite the seeming rationality of focusing on factors like a youth's age, treatment prognosis, and offenses, judicial waiver criteria like "amenability" or "dangerousness" give judges broad, standardless discretion. Amorphous lists of contradictory factors, such as those appended in *Kent*, actually reinforce judges' discretion and allow them selectively to emphasize one element or another to justify any decision. Judicial waiver statutes and decisions share certain features with the standardless capital punishment statutes condemned by the Supreme Court in *Furman v. Georgia*, 408 U.S. 238, 92 S.Ct. 2726, 33 L.Ed.2d 346 (1972). Both "capital punishment in criminal justice and waiver in juvenile justice share four related characteristics: (1) low incidence, (2) prosecutorial and judicial discretion, (3) ultimacy, and (4) inconsistency with the premises that underlie the system's other interventions." Franklin Zimring, "Notes Toward a Jurisprudence of Waiver," in *John C. Hall, et al., Readings in Public Policy 195 (1981)*. In addition, waiver also exposes some transferred juveniles to the possibility of capital punishment. The subjective nature of waiver decisions, the absence of effective guidelines to structure outcomes, and the lack of objective indicators or scientific tools with which to classify youths allows judges to make unequal and disparate rulings without any effective procedural or appellate limitations.

The following excerpt summarizes some of the research findings about administration of judicial waiver statutes. **Barry C. Feld, "The Juvenile Court Meets the Principle of Offense: Legislative Changes in Juvenile Waiver Statutes," 78** *J. Crim. L. & Criminology* **471, 489–94 (1987)**:

[J]udicial waiver statutes that are couched in terms of amenability to treatment or dangerousness are simply broad, standardless grants of sentencing discretion characteristic of the individualized, offender-oriented dispositional statutes of the juvenile court. The addition of long lists of supposed substantive standards, such as that appended by the Supreme Court in *Kent*, does not provide objective indicators to guide discretion. "[T]he substantive standards are highly subjective, and the large number of factors that may be taken into consideration provides ample opportunity for selection and emphasis in discretionary decisions that shape the outcome of individual cases." Indeed, such catalogues of factors reinforce juvenile court judges' exercise of virtually unreviewable discretion by allowing selective emphasis of one set of factors or another to justify any disposition.

Like individualized sentencing statutes, the subjectivity inherent in waiver administration allows a variety of inequities and disparities to occur. The empirical reality is that judges cannot administer these discretionary statutes on a consistent, evenhanded basis. Within a single jurisdiction, waiver statutes are inconsistently interpreted and applied from county to county and from court to court. Hamparian's nationwide analysis of waiver in 1978 provides substantial evidence that judicial waiver practices are inherently arbitrary, capricious, and discriminatory. Among the states that rely on judicial waiver for the transfer decision, the rates of waiver vary from a high of 13.5 to a low of .07 per 10,000 youths at risk; youths in Oregon have nearly 200 times the probability of being waived for trial as adults as do youths in Montana. Fagan, Piper, and Forst analyzed waiver decisions involving a sample of violent youths in four different jurisdictions and concluded that there were no uniform criteria guiding the transfer decision.

> What we found was a rash of inconsistent judicial waiver decisions, both within and across sites. Inconsistent and standardless decisions for youth retained in juvenile court are not surprising in a judicial context which cherishes individualized justice. * * * But for youth who may be tried and convicted in criminal court and subjected to years of imprisonment in a secure institution, such subjective decision making is no longer justified.

Fagan and his colleagues * * * reported that "[n]either multivariate analysis nor simple explorations identified strong or consistent determinants of the judicial transfer decision. Except for a relationship between extensive prior offense history and the transfer decision, none of the identified variables could significantly describe differences between youths who were or were not transferred."

In addition to "justice by geography," there is evidence that a juvenile's race may influence the waiver decision. Hamparian reported that, nationally, 39% of all youths transferred in 1978 were Black and that, in eleven states, minority youths constituted the majority of juveniles waived. Eigen reported an interracial effect in transfers; black youths who murder white victims were significantly more at risk for waiver. In their study of transfer of violent youths, Fagan, Forst, and Vivona also found substantial disparities in the rates of minority and white offenders. * * *

Bortner concluded that a juvenile court's organizational and political considerations explain more about the waiver decision than does the inherent dangerousness or intractability of a youth.

> [P]olitical and organizational factors, rather than concern for public safety, account for the increasing rate of remand. In evidencing a willingness to relinquish jurisdiction over a small percentage of its clientele, and by portraying these juveniles as the most intractable and the greatest threat to public safety, the juvenile justice system not only creates an

effective symbolic gesture regarding protection of the public but it also advances its territorial interest in maintaining jurisdiction over the vast majority of juveniles and deflecting more encompassing criticisms of the entire system.

Idiosyncratic differences in judicial philosophies and the locale of a waiver hearing are far more significant for the ultimate adulthood decision than is any inherent quality of the criminal act or characteristic of the offending youth. The inconsistency in the interpretation and application of waiver statutes is hardly surprising in view of the inherent subjectivity of the dispositional issue, the lack of effective guidelines to structure the decision, and the latent as well as manifest functions the process serves. In short, judicial waiver statutes reveal all of the defects characteristic of individualized, discretionary sentencing schema. * * *

1. JUDICIAL WAIVER PROCEDURES AND EVIDENCE

The following materials illustrate legislative and judicial efforts to structure the judicial waiver decision-making process, to impart some procedural regularity to the decision, to refine the substantive criteria that judges apply, and to strike a balance between the "best interests" of the offender and considerations of "public safety." They illustrate the specificity of "amenability" criteria, the allocations of burdens of proof between the parties through the use of offense-based presumptions, the weight accorded various factors, and the evidence courts consider. They also reflect the "politics of crime" and the legislative changes in waiver laws over the past two decades.

A judicial waiver hearing typically involves two separate questions— whether there is probable cause to believe that the youth committed the crime, and whether or not the judge should transfer the juvenile based on the substantive waiver criteria. State waiver procedures typically treat the issues of probable cause and substantive waiver separately. *See e.g.* N. Car. Gen. Stat. §§ 7A–609; 7A–610 (West 1999) ("If probable cause is found * * * the prosecutor or the juvenile may move that the case be transferred to the superior court for trial as in the case of adults. The judge may proceed to determine whether the needs of the juvenile or the best interests of the State will be served by transfer of the case * * *.") States typically apply different evidentiary rule to the probable cause determination than to the substantive waiver hearing. Some waiver statutes employ presumptions depending upon the nature of the offense with which the state charges a juvenile. Thus, a probable cause determination constitutes a necessary prerequisite to determine the existence of a presumption or the allocation of a burden of proof.

Michigan Comp. Laws § 712A.4 (West 1999).

(1) If a juvenile 14 years of age or older is accused of an act that if committed by an adult would be a felony, the judge of the family division * * * may waive jurisdiction under this section upon motion of the

prosecuting attorney. After waiver, the juvenile may be tried in the court having general criminal jurisdiction of the offense.

(2) Before conducting a hearing on the motion to waive jurisdiction, the court shall give notice of the hearing in the manner provided by supreme court rule. * * *

(3) Before the court waives jurisdiction, the court shall determine on the record if there is probable cause to believe that an offense has been committed that if committed by an adult would be a felony and if there is probable cause to believe that the juvenile committed the offense. * * *

(4) Upon a showing of probable cause under subsection (3), the court shall conduct a hearing to determine if the best interests of the juvenile and the public would be served by granting a waiver of jurisdiction to the court of general criminal jurisdiction. In making its determination, the court shall consider all of the following criteria, giving greater weight to the seriousness of the alleged offense and the juvenile's prior record of delinquency than to the other criteria:

(a) The seriousness of the alleged offense in terms of community protection, including, but not limited to, the existence of any aggravating factors recognized by the sentencing guidelines, the use of a firearm or other dangerous weapon, and the impact on any victim.

(b) The culpability of the juvenile in committing the alleged offense, including, but not limited to, the level of the juvenile's participation in planning and carrying out the offense and the existence of any aggravating or mitigating factors recognized by the sentencing guidelines.

(c) The juvenile's prior record of delinquency including, but not limited to, any record of detention, any police record, any school record, or any other evidence indicating prior delinquent behavior.

(d) The juvenile's programming history, including, but not limited to, the juvenile's past willingness to participate meaningfully in available programming.

(e) The adequacy of the punishment or programming available in the juvenile justice system.

(f) The dispositional options available for the juvenile. * * *

(6) If legal counsel has not been retained or appointed to represent the juvenile, the court shall advise the juvenile and his or her parents, guardian, custodian, or guardian ad litem of the juvenile's right to representation and appoint legal counsel. * * *

(7) Legal counsel shall have access to records or reports provided and received by the judge as a basis for decision in proceedings for waiver of jurisdiction. A continuance shall be granted at legal counsel's request if any report, information, or recommendation not previously available is introduced or developed at the hearing and the interests of justice require a continuance.

(8) The court shall enter a written order either granting or denying the motion to waive jurisdiction and the court shall state on the record or in a written opinion the court's findings of fact and conclusions of law forming the basis for entering the order. If a juvenile is waived, a transcript of the court's findings or a copy of the written opinion shall be sent to the court of general criminal jurisdiction.

(9) If the court does not waive jurisdiction, a transcript of the court's findings or, if a written opinion is prepared, a copy of the written opinion shall be sent to the prosecuting attorney, juvenile, or juvenile's attorney upon request. * * *

Michigan Rules of Court—Probate Court 5.950 (West 1999)

(A) Motion by Prosecuting Attorney. A motion by the prosecuting attorney requesting that the juvenile court waive its jurisdiction to a court of general criminal jurisdiction must be in writing and must clearly indicate the charges and that if the motion is granted the juvenile will be prosecuted as though an adult. * * *

(B) Hearing Procedure. The waiver hearing shall consist of two phases. * * *

(1) First Phase. The first-phase hearing is to determine whether there is probable cause that an offense has been committed which if committed by an adult would be a felony, and that there is probable cause that the juvenile who is 14 years of age or older committed the offense. * * *

(b) At the hearing, the prosecuting attorney has the burden to present legally admissible evidence to establish each element of the offense and to establish probable cause that the juvenile committed the offense. * * *

(2) Second Phase. If the court finds the requisite probable cause at the first-phase hearing * * * the second-phase hearing shall be held to determine whether the interests of the juvenile and the public would best be served by granting the motion. * * *

(a) The Michigan Rules of Evidence, other than those with respect to privileges, do not apply to the second phase of the waiver hearing. * * *

(c) The prosecuting attorney has the burden of establishing by a preponderance of the evidence that the best interests of the juvenile and the public would be served by waiver.

(d) The court, in determining whether to waive the juvenile to the court having general criminal jurisdiction, shall consider and make findings on the following criteria, giving greater weight to the seriousness of the alleged offense and the juvenile's prior record of delinquency and to other criteria:

(i) the seriousness of the alleged offense in terms of community protection, including, but not limited to, the existence of any aggravating factors recognized by the sentencing guidelines, the use of a firearm or other dangerous weapon, and the effect on any victim;

(ii) the culpability of the juvenile in committing the alleged offense, including, but not limited to, the level of the juvenile's participation in planning and carrying out the offense and the existence of any aggravating or mitigating factors recognized by the sentencing guidelines;

(iii) the juvenile's prior record of delinquency including, but not limited to, any record of detention, any police record, any school record, or any other evidence indicating prior delinquent behavior;

(iv) the juvenile's programming history, including, but not limited to, the juvenile's past willingness to participate meaningfully in available programming;

(v) the adequacy of the punishment or programming available in the juvenile justice system;

(vi) the dispositional options available for the juvenile. * * *

(C) Grant of Waiver Motion.

(1) If the court determines that it is in the best interests of the juvenile and public to waive jurisdiction over the juvenile, the court must:

(a) enter a written order granting the motion to waive jurisdiction and transferring the matter to the appropriate court having general criminal jurisdiction for arraignment of the juvenile on an information.

(b) make findings of fact and conclusions of law forming the basis for entry of the waiver order. The findings and conclusions may be incorporated in a written opinion or stated on the record. * * *

(2) Upon the grant of a waiver motion, a juvenile shall be transferred to the adult criminal justice system and shall be subject to the same procedures used for adult criminal defendants. Juveniles waived pursuant to this rule are not required to be kept separate and apart from adult prisoners. * * *

(E) Psychiatric Testimony.

(1) A psychiatrist, psychologist, or certified social worker who conducts a court-ordered examination for purposes of a waiver hearing may not testify at a subsequent criminal proceeding involving the juvenile without the juvenile's written consent. * * *

PEOPLE v. HANA
443 Mich. 202, 504 N.W.2d 166 (Mich. 1993).

RILEY, JUSTICE. [Police arrested Hana in a drug raid and the state charged him with possession of 650 grams of cocaine. While in custody and being transported to the police station, officers repeatedly advised him of his *Miranda* rights and advised him to stop talking until he could speak with a parent or an attorney. Hana made incriminating statements to multiple officers and attempted to bribe one officer for his release.]

This case requires us to consider an intricate mix of factual and constitutional issues surrounding waiver procedures for juveniles pursuant to the provisions of the Probate Code and related Michigan Court Rules. The primary question is whether the full panoply of protections provided by the Fifth and Sixth Amendments of the United States Constitution apply to the dispositional phase, as well as to the adjudicative phase, of a juvenile waiver hearing. We hold that the legislative purpose and the underpinnings of the Probate Code mandate the conclusion that a probate court's discretion at the dispositional phase of a waiver hearing remains unfettered by certain evidentiary requirements recognized in criminal proceedings and already extended to the adjudicative phase of a waiver hearing. Accordingly, we reverse the decision of the Court of Appeals. * * *

Pursuant to the prosecutor's motion to waive jurisdiction over defendant for trial as an adult, the probate court conducted bifurcated hearings early in February and March of 1988. At the probable cause phase of the waiver hearing (phase I), * * * the probate court concluded that there was probable cause to believe that defendant committed the crimes charged. * * *

Several weeks later, the court conducted a hearing on the issue whether defendant should be treated as a juvenile or as an adult under the criteria set forth in M.C.L. § 712A.4(4) * * * and MCR 5.950(B)(2) (phase II). At the phase II hearing, the probate court permitted testimony of the probate court psychologist and [three police o]fficers * * * concerning statements allegedly made by defendant after his arrest. The court's basis for admissibility was "that we're in phase II here, to determine * * * [respondent's] pattern of living, his character, and that sort of thing" rather than in the phase I probable cause stage. * * * Defendant offered testimony of a character witness as well as the findings of his own psychologist. Following the phase II hearing, jurisdiction over defendant was waived.

Defendant appealed the waiver decision. * * * However, the Court of Appeals, relying on *In re Gault*, reversed, holding that the constitutional rights applicable in criminal proceedings extended to phase II, the dispositional phase of a waiver hearing. Moreover, the Court, drawing upon a trilogy of United States Supreme Court cases, concluded that a waiver of this nature is tantamount to an enhancement of defendant's sentence, and thus required application to a phase II waiver hearing of the same constitutional protections found in criminal trials. * * *

According to defendant, waiving probate jurisdiction over a minor is the harshest penalty that could be imposed on a juvenile, who could otherwise expect to be released at age nineteen, but for the waiver.

Defendant also notes that juvenile waiver procedures are a "critical phase" of the judicial process, so that certain rights, such as the right to counsel and the right against self-incrimination, must be recognized. Defendant then directs our attention to *Estelle v. Smith*, wherein the United States Supreme Court ruled that all Fifth and Sixth Amendment rights recognized in criminal trials applied to the sentencing phase of Texas' bifurcated trial procedure in capital punishment cases.

The Court of Appeals treated *Kent*, *Gault* and *Estelle* as dispositive. However, we conclude that the Court's analysis of these cases is flawed, and thus it erred in reversing the probate court's decision to waive jurisdiction over defendant. * * *

[I]t is clear that *Kent*, *Gault*, and *Estelle* are significantly distinguishable from the instant case and do not support the conclusion reached by the Court of Appeals in reversing the probate court's waiver decision. The *Kent* holding requires a degree of procedural regularity in juvenile waiver hearings that comports with "the basic requirements of due process and fairness" and "full investigation." Accordingly, juvenile courts are required to establish hearing procedures, afford the right to counsel, and set forth their findings to avoid arbitrariness and the inability to review waiver dispositions for lack of clear findings. *Gault* assured a juvenile the right to counsel at waiver proceedings, including the right to proper notification of this right and the right to appointment of counsel in appropriate circumstances. Neither *Kent* nor *Gault* extended these constitutional protections to the dispositional phase of the waiver hearing that focuses on balancing the interests of both the juvenile and the public.

In *Estelle*, the United States Supreme Court extended Fifth and Sixth Amendment rights to psychiatric examinations used at the penalty phase of a capital murder case to enhance the sentence *after* guilt had been established. In contrast, a juvenile waiver decision is distinguishable because it is a hearing to determine probable cause (phase I) and to determine whether the best interests of the public and the juvenile would be served by waiving jurisdiction of the juvenile to an adult court (phase II). Thus, the waiver hearing *precedes* any determination of guilt. Therefore, neither the *Estelle* holding nor the holdings of *Kent* and *Gault* mandate extending protections presently applicable to phase I hearings to phase II hearings.

Defendant argues that waiver is the harshest penalty that could be imposed on him. We disagree. In cases where a juvenile is waived to an adult criminal court, the juvenile is still afforded a right to jury trial and the presumption of innocence, and he is therefore not truly subjected to a harsher penalty *because guilt is not yet established*. Moreover, we are unaware of a constitutional right to be treated as a juvenile. Rather, and in derogation of the common law, juvenile justice procedures are governed by statutes and court rules that the probate courts are required to follow in the absence of constitutional infirmity. * * *

The statute and the court rule involved here both mandate a bifurcated waiver hearing to determine in separate proceedings whether probable cause to suspect a defendant exists, phase I, and whether waiver to an adult criminal court is appropriate, phase II. The evidentiary requirements for admissibility differ at each phase of a juvenile waiver hearing. Although the statute is silent on the matter, the court rule provides that only "legally admissible evidence" may be used to establish probable cause in phase I of a waiver hearing while "[t]he Michigan Rules of Evidence do not apply to * * * [phase II] of the waiver hearing."

In the recent past, this Court has adopted a number of significant revisions to the court rules for the purpose of clarifying juvenile court procedures. To aid the bench and bar, we have declared that these rules "are to be construed to secure fairness, flexibility, and simplicity" so that the rights and proper interests of *all* parties concerned are protected. The appropriate standard for purposes of a phase II hearing is "whether the interests of the juvenile *and the public* would best be served by granting the motion [for waiver]." * * * In short, we believe that the public policy underlying phase II hearings requires relaxed evidentiary standards so as to ensure a "full investigation." * * *

On the basis of the foregoing, we are persuaded that the Court of Appeals misconstrued the purpose of phase II of a waiver hearing and the underpinnings of the Juvenile Code. The requirements of a full investigation, protection of juveniles as well as the public, and the historic discretion afforded our probate courts in these matters convince us that the full panoply of constitutional rights was never intended to apply to the dispositional phase of a waiver hearing.

We conclude that the constitutional protections extended to juvenile proceedings in cases such as *Kent* and *Gault* apply in full force to the adjudicative phase of a juvenile waiver hearing. We also find that the statutes and court rules concerning phase I hearings, when properly applied, afford the appropriate protection. * * * We conclude further that the full panoply of constitutional rights asserted by defendant does not apply to the dispositional phase of a waiver hearing. The United States Supreme Court has confined its extension of Fifth and Sixth Amendment rights to the adjudicative and not the dispositional phase of waiver proceedings. Use of defendant's alleged statements to the police and the court psychologist at the phase II dispositional hearing, therefore, did not violate any constitutional provisions.

The historical and legislative directives are clear.[64] We therefore interpret the purpose behind the Probate Code and the court rules to

---

64. We disagree with the dissent's conclusion that our interpretation of the statutes and court rules does not comport with the " 'rehabilitative ideal.' " First, the dissent never addresses the concept of "protection of the public" as required by MCR 5.950(B)(2), nor does it reconcile its position with the historic "full investigation" required by court rule and case law.

Second, a clear purpose of the disposition hearing is to determine whether a juvenile is amenable to treatment in the juvenile justice system. If not, it is determined that the adult system is better equipped to rehabilitate; the determination is *not* to inflict a more severe

favor individualized tailoring of a juvenile's sentence with emphasis on both the child's and society's welfare. Such individualization would be seriously curtailed if the dispositional phase was restricted as defendant urges.

The decision of the Court of Appeals is reversed. * * *

MICHAEL F. CAVANAGH, CHIEF JUSTICE (dissenting). I respectfully dissent. The majority holds that "the legislative purpose and the underpinnings of the Probate Code mandate the conclusion that a probate court's discretion at the dispositional phase of a waiver hearing remains unfettered by certain evidentiary requirements recognized in criminal proceedings and already extended to the adjudicative phase of a waiver hearing." The decision to waive jurisdiction over a juvenile is not, however, consistent with the "rehabilitative ideal," underlying the creation of the juvenile courts. * * *

While there are no doubt instances where it is necessary to waive jurisdiction over certain juvenile offenders, the decision to waive cannot be characterized as being consistent with the philosophy underlying the juvenile court system. In reality, the decision to waive juvenile court jurisdiction is not a decision to rehabilitate, but, rather, a decision to punish the juvenile upon conviction. Thus, the juvenile should be afforded the traditional due process protections in judicial waiver proceedings enjoyed by adults accused of crime. * * *

Those jurisdictions that view the decision to waive juvenile court jurisdiction as being analogous to adult sentencing, generally rely on *Estelle v. Smith*, in finding that the privilege against compelled self-incrimination applies to juvenile waiver proceedings. In *Estelle*, the Supreme Court held that the Fifth Amendment protects against the use of testimonial disclosures that might subject a person to harsher punishment upon conviction. * * * The Court distinguished between the "limited, neutral purpose of determining his competency to stand trial," and the "plainly adverse" use of testimonial disclosures to enhance a defendant's punishment. * * *

The majority's reasoning to the contrary ignores reality. The waiver of juvenile court jurisdiction is "*a sentencing* decision that represents a choice between the punitive disposition of adult criminal court and the 'rehabilitative' disposition of the juvenile court." Given the substantial

---

punishment. In cases in which an appellate court is faced with facts that indicate a desire to punish, it is proper to search for error in the application of the waiver factors and not for error based on constitutional grounds. Moreover, there is no certainty of punishment where the juvenile is afforded the right to a jury trial. The possibility of acquittal or even probation in a criminal trial (contrasted to an indefinite term in a juvenile home, in some cases) is not properly characterized as "punishment."

Third, the authority cited in the dissent does not make the same clear distinction between the adjudicative and dispositional phases of a waiver hearing as we find in the relevant Michigan statutes and court rules. We would have to agree with the dissent's position were it the case that Michigan probate practice did not recognize rights afforded adult criminal defendants at some phase of a juvenile waiver hearing. However, these protections are recognized at the adjudicative or "probable cause" phase. * * *

interests at stake, there can be no question that waiver proceedings are adversarial. Indeed, this case demonstrates the adversarial nature of phase II waiver proceedings. The prosecution filed a petition for waiver of jurisdiction to the circuit court and presented evidence against the defendant, attempting to prove, as it must, that Kafan Hana, who had no prior juvenile record, was "beyond rehabilitation under existing juvenile programs and statutory procedures." * * *

There can also be no question regarding the punitive nature of the decision to waive juvenile jurisdiction over Kafan. Had Kafan been prosecuted as a juvenile, he would have faced a maximum of two and one half years (he was 16½) of confinement (until 19) in a juvenile reformatory. The decision to waive jurisdiction over Kafan, however, paved the way for the state to secure not only a conviction but also a life sentence in an adult prison. In my view, this case clearly demonstrates both the adversarial and punitive nature of juvenile waiver proceedings and compels the conclusion that *Estelle* requires the recognition of Fifth Amendment protections in such proceedings.

I also agree with the courts that find the rationale underlying the United States Supreme Court decision in *Gault* to compel the conclusion that the constitutional rights recognized in that case must apply in phase II proceedings. In my view, the rights affected by the decision to waive jurisdiction are equally, if not more important, than the rights affected in juvenile proceedings to determine delinquency, requiring equal, if not more protection. Further, * * * waiver of juvenile court jurisdiction deprives the juvenile of his statutory rights to the traditional benefits of the juvenile justice system. As recognized in both *Kent* and *Gault*, the justification for denying juveniles traditional due process rights is the benefits that juveniles purportedly derive from the juvenile justice system. Therefore, it seems to follow that traditional due process protections should be afforded to juveniles in any proceeding in which the state seeks to deprive a juvenile of those rights. * * *

For the foregoing reasons, I would remand this case to the juvenile court for a hearing to determine whether the statements and confessions introduced and considered at phase II of Kafan's juvenile waiver hearing were obtained in violation of his Fifth Amendment right to remain silent or his Sixth Amendment right to counsel. * * *

NOTES

1) Evidence in Waiver Hearings Recall that the United States Supreme Court in *Kent, supra* at p. 523, ruled that the child's counsel should have access to the child's social records if the juvenile court considers them as part of the evidence in deciding whether to waive jurisdiction. Following *Kent*, is hearsay testimony admissible—for example, comments of a juvenile's teacher or neighbor to a social worker—or must each witness testify and be cross-examined by defense counsel? *See* Note, "Juvenile Waiver Hearings and the Need for Reliable Evidence at the Critical Stage," 12 *Val. L. Rev.* 397 (1978).

In *Three Minors v. State*, 100 Nev. 414, 684 P.2d 1121 (Nev. 1984), the Court held that the hearing need not be adversarial and that the findings may be based on "informal but reliable evidence." *Id.* at 1124. Most states conclude that hearsay evidence is admissible in a juvenile transfer hearing. *Smith v. State*, 475 So.2d 633 (Ala. Cr. App. 1985); *United States v. H.S., Jr.*, 717 F.Supp. 911 (D.D.C. 1989); *State v. Wright*, 456 N.W.2d 661 (Iowa 1990). Courts typically characterize waiver hearings as dispositional or sentencing proceedings which do not follow rules of evidence as strictly as criminal trials. *See e.g. People v. Hana*, 443 Mich. 202, 504 N.W.2d 166 (1993); Minn. R. Juv. Proc. 18.04. Subd. 4 ("All evidence considered by the court on the certification question shall be made a part of the court record. The court may receive any information, except privileged communication, that is relevant to the certification issue, including reliable hearsay and opinions * * *.") In *In re T.D.S.*, 289 N.W.2d 137 (Minn.1980), the Court cited the A.B.A. *Juvenile Justice Standards Relating to Dispositional Procedures* § 2.5 which provide that "hearsay evidence is not objectionable where there are indicia of trustworthiness and where the evidence was not obtained in violation of the juvenile's constitutional rights." In *T.D.S.*, the Minnesota Supreme Court also held that "For purposes of the hearing, the charges are assumed to be true and the only issue for the court are public safety and the juvenile's amenability to treatment." 289 N.W.2d at 140. Is such a conclusive presumption constitutional?

2) Psychological and Psychiatric Evidence in Waiver Hearings Statutes and court rules authorize juvenile courts to obtain clinical evaluations and social reports to enable them to gain "clinical insight" to assess a child's "fitness" or "amenability to treatment." *See e.g.*, Minn. R. Juv. Proc. 18.03 Subd. 1. ("The court on its own motion or on the motion of the child's counsel or the prosecuting attorney, may order social, psychiatric, or psychological studies concerning the child who is the subject of the certification proceeding.") If the state requires psychological or psychiatric evidence either to prove that a youth is not "amenable to treatment" or to rebut clinical evidence of "fitness" offered by a juvenile, then allowing the state to obtain access for a clinical assessment may pose complex legal questions as well. In many respects, the clinical-legal conundrum of assessing "amenability to treatment" poses a problem akin to that which the state confronts when a defendant raises an insanity defense. For example, evaluations of a criminal defendant's competency to stand trial or sanity at the time of the offense may pose constitutional issues involving the Fifth Amendment privilege against self-incrimination.

In *Estelle v. Smith*, 451 U.S. 454, 101 S.Ct. 1866, 68 L.Ed.2d 359 (1981), the United States Supreme Court held that the privilege against self-incrimination applied to a court-ordered psychiatric examination conducted for purposes of a subsequent sentencing hearing and restricted psychiatrists' permissible access and disclosures. " '[T]he availability of the [Fifth Amendment] privilege does not turn upon the type of proceeding in which its protection is invoked, but upon the nature of the statement or admission and the exposure which it invites.' " *Id.* at 462 (quoting *In re Gault*, 387 U.S. 1, 49, 87 S.Ct. 1428, 18 L.Ed.2d 527 (1967) (Blackmun, J., plurality opinion)).

Since the Court decided *Estelle v. Smith*, some state courts have held that any court-ordered psychological evaluation of a youth to determine "amenability" violates the Fifth Amendment privilege against self-incrimination. *E.g., R.H. v. State,* 777 P.2d 204 (Alaska Ct. App. 1989). Other states require a youth's attorney to be present at the interview. *Christopher P. v. State,* 112 N.M. 416, 816 P.2d 485, 489 (N.M. 1991).

If, instead of disclosure in a court-ordered psychological evaluation, a juvenile testifies at a certification hearing about the alleged offense, then may a prosecutor introduce that testimony as evidence at a subsequent delinquency or criminal trial on the merits. *See e.g., Simmons v. United States,* 390 U.S. 377, 394, 88 S.Ct. 967, 19 L.Ed.2d 1247 (1968) (holding that a defendant's testimony in support of a motion to suppress evidence on Fourth Amendment grounds can not be used against him at trial); *State v. Christenson,* 371 N.W.2d 228, 232 (Minn. Ct. App. 1985) (same). In **Ramona R. v. Superior Court**, 37 Cal.3d 802, 210 Cal.Rptr. 204, 693 P.2d 789, 793–95 (Cal. 1985), the California Supreme Court held that any statements a juvenile gives during a certification hearing must receive use immunity, meaning that such statements can not be used in a subsequent delinquency or criminal trial. The court in *Ramona R.* analogized to the self-incrimination dangers posed for probationers in revocation hearings and reasoned that without a grant of use-immunity, a juvenile would be dissuaded from contesting a certification motion. Analogizing to the dangers of self-incrimination posed for a probationer in a revocation hearing, the court recognized that a juvenile at a certification hearing faced the cruel-trilemma of contempt, self-incrimination, or perjury:

> He might * * * seriously incriminate himself if he exercises his right to be heard, particularly where his testimony would consist of a truthful explanation of mitigating circumstances. * * * If he remains silent he not only loses his opportunity to present a conceivably convincing case against * * * [waiver] but also incurs the risk that notwithstanding the ideals of the Fifth Amendment * * * his silence will be taken as an indication that there are no valid reasons why * * * [he should not be tried as an adult]. To avoid the adverse effects of the foregoing alternatives, the * * * [juvenile] may be tempted to testify falsely in a manner which will not damage his defense at a subsequent criminal trial. *Id.* at 794.

Similarly, in *In re S.R.J.,* 293 N.W.2d 32 (Minn. 1980), the Minnesota Supreme Court analyzed how to obtain psychiatric evaluations and clinical evidence for certification hearings without violating the Fifth Amendment privilege against compelled self-incrimination. Because the Supreme Court in *Gault* extended the Fifth Amendment privilege against self-incrimination to juvenile court proceedings, *S.R.J.* attempted to resolve the dilemma of compelled self-incriminating testimony by providing a form of limited use-immunity to compel the interview but restrict its use. "Any matters disclosed by the juvenile to the doctor in the course of the examination may not be evidence or the source of evidence in any subsequent adjudicatory procedure against the accused." *S.R.J.,* 293 N.W.2d at 36. It can be difficult to conduct evaluations where clinicians cannot assure defendants confidentiality of communications. A juvenile may deny committing the alleged offense because of genuine non-participation, a strategic calculation of the affects of admitting it at trial, an avoidance or inability to acknowledge negative behavior, or repression, a dissociative reaction against the memory of the offense. Richard Barnum, "Self–Incrimination and Denial in the Juvenile Transfer Evaluation," 18 *Bull. Am. Acad. Psych.* L. 413, 419 (1990).

If a youth's attorney obtains a clinical evaluation to aid the defense in a waiver hearing, may the prosecution call the psychiatrist as a witness in the subsequent criminal prosecution? In *State v. Rhomberg*, 516 N.W.2d 803, 807 (Iowa 1994), defense counsel employed a psychiatrist to obtain evidence for the juvenile's waiver hearing. Although the psychiatrist did not testify on the juvenile's behalf, the state called him as a rebuttal witness at the youth's subsequent criminal prosecution. The court ruled that "the physician-patient privilege does not preclude the State from calling a psychiatrist * * * as a witness against [the] defendant" because the psychiatrist was retained not to aid in treatment but for litigation purposes. *Id.* at 808.

3) The Fifth Amendment and Procedural and Evidentiary Safeguards in Waiver Hearings In **R.H. v. State**, 777 P.2d 204 (Alaska Ct. App. 1989), the juvenile court judge ordered R.H. to submit to psychiatric evaluation. In order to safeguard R.H.'s privilege against self-incrimination, the judge directed R.H.'s attorney to be present during the examinations and prohibited the examiners from discussing their findings with the state. On appeal following his waiver, R.H. contended that the court-ordered evaluations violated his privilege against self-incrimination. The court of appeals agreed:

> In the present case, as in *Estelle v. Smith*, the prosecution was allowed to use a court-ordered psychiatric evaluation against the accused by relying on the evaluation to establish future dangerousness. The only significant distinction between the two cases is that Smith's statements to his examiner were used to influence the outcome of his sentencing hearing; R.H.'s statements to his examiner were used to influence the result of his waiver hearing.

> The state contends that this distinction is crucial. Emphasizing *Estelle v. Smith*'s conclusion that no fifth amendment violation occurs when a court-compelled psychiatric evaluation is used for the limited purpose of determining an accused's competency for trial, the state likens the determination of amenability to treatment in a juvenile waiver proceeding to the determination of competency in a criminal case. * * *

> We find the state's argument unpersuasive, for there are vast and fundamental differences between competency proceedings and juvenile waiver hearings. In holding that court-ordered psychiatric examinations are permissible for purposes of determining competency to proceed, the Court in *Estelle v. Smith* characterized such examinations as being conducted for "limited, neutral purposes." The Court distinguished the use of examinations for such purposes from their use in an "adversary system," by persons who are not "acting solely in [the] interest" of the accused.

> In contrast to competency proceedings, juvenile waiver hearings are hardly "neutral proceedings." Rather, they are fully adversary proceedings in which the burden of establishing a child's probable unamenability to treatment is formally allocated to the state. Similarly, a psychiatrist

conducting an examination at the request of the state for use in such cases is hardly a person "acting solely in the interest" of the child. To the contrary, the psychiatrist is directly involved in furthering the interests of the child's formal adversary.

Nor can juvenile waiver proceedings realistically be said to affect "only the forum where the issue of guilt will be adjudicated." A juvenile waiver proceeding is the only available avenue by which the state may seek to prosecute a child as an adult. * * * [T]he accused child's interest in the outcome of a juvenile waiver proceeding is important, because the waiver hearing can mean the difference between a limited period of confinement and a lengthy term of imprisonment. * * *

Just as the psychiatric evaluation in *Estelle v. Smith* enabled the prosecution to incriminate Smith by using his own statements to his disadvantage at sentencing, the court-compelled evaluations in the present case enabled the state to incriminate R.H. Admission of the psychiatric evidence against R.H. at the waiver hearing helped to pave the way for the state to prosecute R.H. as an adult, thereby exposing him to potential punishment far more severe than could otherwise have been visited upon him. * * *

The state expresses concern that a prohibition against court-compelled psychiatric evaluations would adversely impact the superior court's ability to reach an informed decision on the issue of amenability to treatment. * * * Although the Alaska Supreme Court has noted the possible desirability of psychiatric examinations in waiver proceedings, it has never suggested that an examination may be conducted against the wishes of a child, nor has it held that expert testimony is a necessary precondition of waiver. To the contrary, the Alaska Supreme Court has expressly recognized that the state need not present any psychiatric evidence to meet its burden of proving that a child is unamenable to treatment. Moreover, there appears to be good reason for caution to protect against excessive reliance on such evidence. * * *

Accordingly, we conclude that the superior court erred in compelling R.H. to submit to a psychiatric evaluation for the purpose of determining his amenability to treatment as a child.

We emphasize, however, that the same conclusion would not be warranted had R.H. sought to present psychiatric evidence in his own behalf at the waiver hearing or had he otherwise affirmatively placed his mental condition in issue. It is well established that, under those circumstances, the superior court could have properly found that R.H. waived his fifth amendment privilege, and that the state was entitled to an independent psychiatric evaluation for its own use. In the present case, it is sufficient to note that R.H. did not obtain a psychiatric evaluation for his own use in the waiver proceedings, and he disavowed any intent to affirmatively place his own mental condition in issue. * * *

The Court in *R.H.* emphasized that the juvenile had not sought to present psychiatric evidence on his own behalf or otherwise placed his mental condition at issue. May a juvenile court condition the juvenile's introduction of clinical evidence of her "amenability" on her submission to an examination by the state's psychologist? In **Commonwealth v. Wayne W.**, 414 Mass. 218, 228, 606 N.E.2d 1323 (1993), the defendant invoked the privilege against self-incrimination and refused to submit to court-ordered psychiatric examinations. The juvenile court judge then excluded the testimony of the defendants' psychiatric experts as a sanction for the defendants' failure to cooperate in the court-ordered examinations. The Supreme Judicial Court of Massachusetts concluded that the Fifth Amendment precludes a compelled psychological examination at the dispositional phase of a juvenile transfer proceeding unless the juvenile first offers psychiatric evidence. "We conclude that the privileges apply in these circumstances, but that the defendants, if they voluntarily choose to offer expert psychiatric evidence, can be ordered to participate in an examination by a Commonwealth expert." The court held that juveniles enjoyed a privilege against self-incrimination in waiver, or Part B, hearings, but also concluded that a juvenile who intends to offer evidence on his own behalf waives the privilege and may be examined by the state:

> [In *Estelle v. Smith*,] the Court reasoned that admission of the psychiatrist's evidence violated the defendant's privilege against self-incrimination because the testimony, based on the defendant's statements to the psychiatrist, was offered in a proceeding affecting the penalty to be imposed on the defendant. * * * In addition, *Estelle* clearly states that the privilege against self-incrimination is not confined to statements that reveal involvement in criminal activity, but extends to statements that reveal information about a defendant's mental and emotional state where that state is in issue in a proceeding affecting the criminal penalty that may be imposed.

> "[T]he civil-criminal distinction cannot be applied blindly to deny constitutional rights," to juveniles facing detention by the Commonwealth. It minimizes the importance, and the potential impact, of transfer hearings to characterize them as civil proceedings that merely determine the proper forum for an adjudication of guilt. Part B hearings are fully adversary—the Commonwealth seeks transfer; the juvenile seeks to remain in the juvenile justice system. In a murder case, the outcome of these proceedings will, in the event of conviction, usually mean the difference between a limited period of confinement in a treatment setting and a lengthy term of imprisonment. In such a context, a psychiatrist's role cannot be described as "neutral," where he testifies in support of the Commonwealth's goal of transfer. These characteristics of a Part B hearing lead us to conclude that the privileges against self-incrimination, protected by the Federal and State Constitutions, foreclose a compelled psychiatric examination, where the juvenile does not seek to introduce his own psychiatric evidence.

> In this case, however, both defendants sought to present psychiatric evidence on their own behalf, based on personal discussions with their expert witnesses. In effect, both defendants sought to introduce evidence at their Part B hearings which included statements made by them to their expert witnesses. It is a basic principle of constitutional law that a defendant who speaks on his own behalf thereby gives up his privilege of silence and may be compelled to respond to questions posed by the State on matters reasonably related to the subject matter of his own testimony.

In an analogous situation, Federal and State courts have concluded that a defendant who raises an insanity defense, and seeks to support it by the introduction of expert psychiatric testimony, can be compelled to submit to psychiatric examination at the request of the prosecution. At the core of the justifications supporting these decisions "is the unreasonable and debilitating effect it would have upon society's conduct of a fair inquiry," and the distorting effect on the fact finder's role, if only one party can introduce expert testimony on a crucial issue.

The defendants contend that their situation differs from that of a defendant raising an insanity defense at trial. * * * [A] Part B hearing focuses almost entirely on the juvenile's mental state, the statutory presumption places a burden of producing evidence on the juvenile, and among the factors the judge is required by statute to consider is "the success or lack of success of any past treatment efforts of the child." The defendants contend the statutory provisions compel the juvenile to offer psychiatric testimony to avoid transfer, and, therefore, the decision to do so cannot be considered a voluntary waiver of the privileges against self-incrimination.

We agree that a juvenile in a Part B hearing will often desire to present psychiatric evidence. The juvenile who does so has made a voluntary choice. There are other sources of probative evidence available to the juvenile, bearing on his dangerousness to the public and amenability to treatment, that may be introduced without implicating the privileges against self-incrimination. These include, but are not limited to, records of past treatment, school and probation records, Department of Youth Services records, Department of Social Services records, and testimony by a probation officer, Department of Social Services or Youth Services employees, teachers, friends, or family members. * * *

No examination may be ordered unless the Juvenile Court judge determines that the juvenile intends to offer at his Part B hearing psychiatric evidence based on his own statements or there is a reasonable likelihood that the juvenile will offer such evidence. The judge, on motion by the Commonwealth or by his own order, may direct the juvenile to disclose whether he intends to offer such evidence. Disclosure should be sufficiently in advance of the hearing to permit the Commonwealth to conduct its own examination. In addition, the order authorizing such an examination must contain limits on the use of such testimony required by State and Federal constitutional concerns. The juvenile's decision to introduce psychiatric evidence in a transfer hearing is limited to the Part B hearing. The substance of the juvenile's statements is not admissible at any proceeding adjudicating his guilt. * * *

In **State v. Davis**, 268 Kan. 661, 998 P.2d 1127 (Kan. 2000), the Kansas Supreme Court concluded that a juvenile has a Fifth Amendment right to refuse to participate in a court-ordered psychological examination in anticipation of a waiver hearing to determine whether the juvenile is to stand trial as an adult and that the fact of refusal may not be used against the juvenile. However, if the juvenile agrees to participate in the examination, the examiner is not required to advise the defendant of his *Miranda* rights as long as the information received during the examination is used solely in the juvenile waiver proceedings and is not introduced during trial or sentencing:

> Other courts have not been consistent in resolving the application of *Estelle* to evaluations for juvenile waiver proceedings. [The *Davis* court reviewed the courts' conflicting decisions in *R.H.*, *Wayne W.*, and *Hana*, *supra* p. 543] None of the above jurisdictions deal directly with the question raised by the defendant in this case, which is whether *Miranda* warnings are required to be given to a juvenile defendant during the court-ordered examination. The very nature of the court-ordered examination and a juvenile's participation in the examination does not easily lend itself to an application of *Miranda*. The purpose of the examination is to determine whether the juvenile should be afforded the protection of the juvenile justice system or instead be certified to stand trial as an adult. *Miranda* warnings would be particularly useless in this regard, as a juvenile's ability to pick and choose which questions to answer would frustrate the purpose of the evaluation. It seems to this court that the application of *Estelle* to an order for a psychological evaluation in a juvenile certification case involves the question of whether the juvenile must participate in the court-ordered evaluation rather than the question of whether the juvenile must be given warnings prior to and during participation. * * *

> The question of whether a juvenile should be required to participate in such psychological evaluation depends upon how one views the proceeding to determine whether the juvenile should be certified as an adult for purposes of trial. Kansas has recognized that certification proceedings are " 'comparable in seriousness to criminal prosecution' " and must comply with the essentials of due process and fair treatment. Thus, the process in Kansas is adversarial in nature, and the burden is on the State to show that the juvenile should be prosecuted as an adult. We * * * hold that a juvenile has the right under the Fifth Amendment of the United States Constitution to refuse to participate in a court-ordered psychological examination pursuant to a pending proceeding to determine whether the juvenile is to stand trial as an adult. The fact of refusal may not be admitted against the juvenile.

> However, under the facts of this case, the defendant was not compelled to participate in the psychological examination. Rather, the record establishes that the defendant's counsel approved the psychological evaluation in the hope that it would aid his client. Counsel for the defendant recognized that the psychological evaluation order would aid the court in its final decision on the question of certification. * * * [T]he defendant's participation in the evaluation itself was voluntary. Consistent with our holding today, once the choice was made to submit to the examination, and the results of the examination were to be used exclusively in the certification determination, there was no further need for *Miranda* warnings. It would be a different situation if the State had attempted to use statements made by the defendant during the evaluation at trial. In such a situation, consistent with *Estelle*, *Miranda* warnings would have been necessary to permit such statements to be admitted at trial. However, in this case the evaluation was used for its intended purpose. * * *

2. WAIVER IN MINNESOTA: FROM "AMENABILI-TY TO TREATMENT" TO "PUBLIC SAFETY"— A CASE–STUDY OF WAIVER REFORMS

Minnesota's reformulation of judicial waiver laws over two decades provides a microcosm and well-documented case-study of changes in waiver policies nationwide. *See* Barry Feld, "Reference of Juvenile Offenders for Adult Prosecution: The Legislative Alternative to Asking Unanswerable Questions," 62 *Minn. L. Rev.* 515 (1978) (criticizing "amenability to treatment" as an inherently subjective and amorphous criterion for making waiver decisions); Barry C. Feld, "Juvenile Court Legislative Reform and the Serious Young Offender: Dismantling the 'Rehabilitative Ideal'," 69 *Minn. L. Rev.* 141 (1981) (criticizing legislative revisions of juvenile waiver code, which created a rebuttable presumption for waiver but left the burden of proof on the state, for failing to eliminate "amenability to treatment" or to control judicial discretion); Barry C. Feld, "Bad Law Makes Hard Cases: Reflections on Teen–Aged Axe–Murderers, Judicial Activism, and Legislative Default," 8 *J. Law & Inequality* 1 (1990) (criticizing legislature for failing to remedy defects of "amenability to treatment" criterion and chiding Minnesota Supreme Court for abusing appellate court role in an effort to ameliorate law's short-comings); Barry C. Feld, "Violent Youth and Public Policy: A Case Study of Juvenile Justice Law Reform," 79 *Minn. L. Rev.* 965 (1995) (analyzing revisions of juvenile code and legislative policies in rejecting "amenability to treatment" in favor of "public safety" criteria, creating offense-based presumptions for waiver, and excluding 1st degree murder from juvenile court jurisdiction).

a. Amenability to Treatment

Before the 1995 revision of the Minnesota juvenile code, the Minnesota waiver statute and court rules provided the framework for a judge to certify a youth for criminal prosecution:

Minn. Stat. § 260.125(2)(d) (1992) Certification to District Court:

> [T]he juvenile court may order a reference only if: * * * The court finds that (1) there is probable cause * * * to believe the child committed the offense alleged by delinquency petition and (2) the prosecuting authority has demonstrated by clear and convincing evidence that the child is not suitable to treatment or that the public safety is not served under the provisions of laws relating to juvenile courts.

Minn. Rule Proc. Juv. Ct. 32.05(2) elaborated a nonexclusive list of the "totality of the circumstances" that a juvenile court could consider in determining a youth's dangerousness or amenability to treatment:

> (a) the seriousness of the offense in terms of community protection,

(b) the circumstances surrounding the offense,

(c) whether the offense was committed in an aggressive, violent, premeditated or willful manner,

(d) whether the offense was directed against persons or property, the greater weight being given to an offense against persons, especially if personal injury resulted,

(e) the reasonably foreseeable consequences of the act,

(f) the absence of adequate protective and security facilities available to the juvenile treatment system,

(g) the sophistication and maturity of the child as determined by consideration of the child's home, environmental situation, emotional attitude and pattern of living,

(h) the record and previous history of the child,

(i) whether the child acted with particular cruelty or disregard for the life or safety of another,

(j) whether the offense involved a high degree of sophistication or planning by the child, and

(k) whether there is sufficient time available before the child reaches age nineteen (19) to provide appropriate treatment and control.

The Minnesota Supreme Court derived those "amenability to treatment" criteria from the Supreme Court's Appendix in *Kent* and *State v. Hogan*, 297 Minn. 430, 438, 212 N.W.2d 664, 669–70 (1973).

Minnesota's judicial waiver statutes, criteria, and procedures typify the way most states decide to prosecute some chronological juveniles in criminal courts. Subject to the constitutional constraints of *Kent, supra* p. 523, and *Breed, supra* p. 530, Minn. Stat. § 260.125 and Juvenile Court Rule 32 govern the process of waiving juvenile court jurisdiction and prosecuting a young offender as an adult. The county attorney initiates a reference proceeding by filing a motion for adult prosecution. Following a finding of probable cause, the juvenile court may order a social study of the child and within thirty days of filing the motion must conduct a hearing to determine whether the youth meets the waiver criteria. The juvenile court may grant adult reference if it concludes that the child is "not suitable for treatment" or that "public safety is not served" by retaining the youth in juvenile court.

Prior to 1980, Minnesota's waiver law provided minimal guidance for juvenile courts trying to decide whether to certify a youth for criminal prosecution. In *In re Dahl*, 278 N.W.2d 316 (Minn. 1979), the Minnesota Supreme Court confronted some of the procedural and substantive problems in the juvenile waiver process. The court clearly indicated to the legislature that the waiver criteria needed modification and greater specificity, concluding that "re-evaluation of the existing certification process may be in order." The *Dahl* court observed that "the standards for referral adopted by present legislation are not very effective in making this important determination." *Id.* at 318. The court went on to note that "[d]ue to these difficulties in making the waiver decision, many juvenile court judges have tended to be overcautious, resulting in the referral of delinquent children for criminal prosecution on the erroneous, albeit good faith, belief that the juveniles pose a danger to the public." *Id.* at 319. The *Dahl* court held that "the existing statutory framework does not authorize referral based on the specific crime charged. * * * [T]his court did not intend * * * the referral of a juvenile solely because of the alleged offense." *Id.* at 321. The court went on to say that the offense charged was obviously "among the relevant factors to be considered" and "[t]he record must contain direct evidence that the juvenile endangers the public safety for the statutory reference standard to be satisfied." *Id.* at 321.

In 1980, the Minnesota legislature amended the certification process. The revised juvenile code retained, unchanged, the basic waiver criteria of amenability to treatment and dangerousness, and placed the burden of proof on the prosecution to establish by "clear and convincing evidence" that juvenile court jurisdiction should be waived. However, the legislature added a third subdivision to the certification statute to enable prosecutors to establish a prima facie case, or rebuttable presumption, of nonamenability and dangerousness by proving that a youth possessed various combinations of present offense and prior record. Under the amended statute, the prosecution can establish a prima facie case of nonamenability and dangerousness simply by proving that the juvenile is at least 16 years of age, that the present crime charged is one of the specified serious offenses, and that the combination of the present crime charged and the prior record brings the case within one of the subdivision's clauses. *See* Minn. Stat. § 260.125 (3) (1992); *see generally* Feld, *Dismantling the "Rehabilitative Ideal," supra,* at 194–95 n.96. Despite the legislative attempt to use offense criteria to rationalize waiver decisions, the rebuttable presumption strategy did not reduce judicial discretion.

The Minnesota law remitted the waiver decision to the trial judge's sound discretion. The prosecutor bore the burden of proof to demonstrate by "clear and convincing evidence" that a juvenile was not "amenable to treatment" or posed a threat to the public. Previous decisions emphasized the need for psychological data to support a finding that a juvenile was or was not suitable for treatment. *In re Dahl,* 278 N.W.2d 316, 319 (Minn. 1979) (requiring psychological data to support juvenile court's conclusion). In *In re R.D.W.,* 407 N.W.2d 113, 117 (Minn. Ct. App. 1987), the Court held that the determination that a juvenile is unsuitable for treatment "must be based on psychological data or a history of misconduct as well as the juvenile's age, level of maturity, and the seriousness of the offense."

The Minnesota waiver statute's emphasis on "amenability to treatment" encountered its most difficult test in the case of David F. Brom. The following synopsis of the waiver hearing testimony, psychiatric reports, and clinical evaluations presented in the waiver hearing of David F. Brom, *In re D.F.B.,* No. 88–J–0955 (Olmsted County, Minn. Dist. Ct. April 21, 1988), is adapted from **Barry C. Feld, "Bad Law Makes Hard**

Cases: Reflections on Teen–Aged Axe–Murderers, Judicial Activism, and Legislative Default," 8 *J. Law & Inequality* 54–59 (1990).
The narrative illustrates the nature of the evidence presented in a full-blown transfer hearing and the difficulty juvenile court judges encounter when they balance an offender's "amenability to treatment" and the seriousness of the offense:

IN RE D.F.B.: THE FACTS

Prior to February 18, 1988, no obvious signs indicated that sixteen-year-old David F. Brom was a seriously disturbed youth or a potential mass murderer. He was a high school sophomore, a B+ student, and regarded by his teachers as pleasant and cooperative. A counselor at Brom's high school testified, "David's attendance was excellent, his grades were good, his relationship with his teachers seemed very good. So there was nothing that would show that [there might be problems in the Brom household]." Brom's Spanish teacher testified, "David was an above average student. He got B's in my class. * * * He was pleasant, quiet, but we got along well." Brom's religion and home room teacher testified, "My relationship with David—first of all, I liked him very well and I think probably he felt the same way. His reactions in class were he was usually joking, usually laughing. He would say something clever and I would respond to it. * * * Yes, he was [a] cooperative [student]."

Dr. Carl Malmquist, the court-appointed psychiatrist who evaluated David Brom for the reference hearing, described him in his Psychiatric Evaluation Report as "a somewhat gangly boy, of 5′ 10″ 130 pounds, quite deferential, polite, compliant, and smiling. He was not muscular but appeared rather shy and withdrawn in some ways, yet he talked volubly and readily."

Although he appeared to his teachers and classmates to be a happy person, according to the clinicians who testified at his waiver hearing, he suffered from a progressive depression that emerged over a period of several years and which left him suicidal and ultimately caused him to slay his father, mother, and younger sister and brother with an axe. According to Dr. Carl Malmquist, a court-appointed psychiatrist:

> [H]e became progressively depressed and feeling life was not worth living going on this way. But his solution was to try to be happy and thinking that he could make everybody else happy. And this is how everybody got fooled. All the friends and people who knew him, and the peer group in the school, because they either saw him as a fool or a clown or a boy always jumping around or saying witty or entertaining things whereas, in fact, he was really a deeply depressed boy who from this past year, from last June on, was entertaining either suicide and at that point thoughts of homicide start to enter as well, from September on. * * *

At the reference hearing, Dr. Malmquist testified about Brom's suicide attempts:

Q: Were there any suicide attempts that you were aware of?

A: The first one that he mentioned to me was at the completion of ninth grade in June of 1987 and the second one was at the end of the summer in September, 1987.

In his report, Dr. Malmquist provided additional details of Brom's attempted suicide:

David then elaborated that he had made two suicide attempts earlier in the year which he had not told his parents about. * * * The first attempt was shortly after the conclusion of the academic year in June, 1987. Their home was near a forest area and he tried to hang himself in a tree with a rope noose. He tied the noose on a tree branch that was about 15–20 feet off the ground and was hanging there with the rope around his neck when he got the feeling that he did not want to die. He is not clear on details of how he got out of the noose but believes that he was not extended so far that he could not reach up and grab the sides of the tree arm by his arms and pull himself up again which was the way he was able to get out of the noose. Later that summer, shortly before the commencement of the school year, he stated he took an overdose of four to five pills. These were pills that a girl he knew took for a "sleeping disorder." He got sick and threw up at that time and his parents thought he had the flu. David stated he was also serious about committing suicide at that time and disappointed in the outcome.

Brom's depression, according to the clinicians, centered on his conflicted relationship with his family, particularly his father. These conflicts intensified after Brom's parents ejected his older brother, Joe, from the home because he adopted a "punk" style of dress. Apparently, Bernard and Paulette Brom imposed even stricter discipline on their other children to ensure that they would not follow Joe's pattern. David Brom's family was comfortably middle-class economically, imposed a strict discipline, subjected him to a tight curfew, required him to perform household chores, and slapped or grounded him if he failed to complete them promptly or satisfactorily.

One clinician testified that Brom wanted to be a dutiful son but found it impossible to please his father and, as a result, he developed an exaggerated fear of being punished:

[E]vents which happened to him, while unpleasant, had become greatly magnified in his own thinking. They had become overwhelming and seen as impossible to deal with. Hence, he described episodes where his father would slap him, usually only once at a time (although on rare occasions two-three times in succession), and with an open hand. David never described his father hitting him with a fist nor ever receiving any beatings. Yet to David the nature of the anticipation of being slapped in such a manner by his father was experienced as something he came to dread. It was experienced as one of the things he could not deal with, and from which he needed desperately to escape. * * * On these occasions, he would feel "terrified." * * * The striking thing is David's overreaction and sensitivity, his inability to deal with his father, and the persistent fear which did not leave.

David was unable to discuss his feelings with his father and confided to the psychiatrist that "his father and he rarely talked at all * * *."

David did not seek help with his fears from any teachers, counselors, or other adults because his parents were widely-respected in the community.

> In appearance the Broms were pillar-of-society material. Dad was an engineer at the IBM plant. Mom had run a preschool program at church, but had quit a couple of years before to spend more time with her own kids. She sewed at home. * * * Bernard, Paulette, Dave and the two younger kids attended mass every Sunday at Pax Christi Catholic Church. The parents were parish leaders and ardent participants in a variety of church activities. They hosted meetings at their house, and Bernard put his home computer to work for the parish. * * * The Broms were eulogized as a beautiful family. "Leaders of the church and very well-respected," the pastor called them. "There was not a clue that something was wrong," a neighbor woman said.

David told the clinicians that adults would neither believe nor appreciate the seriousness of his problems. Although Brom "defended psychologically," according to the experts, by pretending to be and attempting to make other people happy, maintaining this role became increasingly difficult as his depression deepened. Thoughts of suicide, he reported, mingled with thoughts of killing his family.

Brom shared his suicidal and homicidal thoughts with some young friends, albeit disguised in the form of a fantasy about a trip. One fifteen-year-old classmate testified that:

> [H]e said that this summer he wanted to go to Florida. He wanted to take the van and he said he wanted to kill his parents. * * * He said that he wanted to take a couple of other girls with him, but he didn't tell me who * * *. [H]e told me that he was going to kill them, too, but I didn't know if * * * I really didn't believe him when he told me. I mean I didn't think—It's not like you hear something like that every day. I didn't know what to think.

In one version of Brom's "fantasy," he would kill his family, steal the family van and money, and drive to Florida, where the three juveniles would "live it up" until their funds were exhausted, at which point Brom would kill himself. Another female classmate testified:

> A friend and me and Dave, we had a sort of vacation planned which seemed more like a story that we would add things into it to make it more exciting, add into the plot. Like saying [an ongoing] story. But not written. Just a conversation piece that we would have. * * * It involved me, Angie and Dave going to Florida this summer and how

we would live off the money we would have and just get an apartment and have fun. * * * We had to get a car to get down there and he said that the way we could do that was for him to get rid of his parents so that we could have the car. [He would] kill his family and call in to IBM and tell them that there had been a death in the family and so Mr. Brom would be taking off a few weeks and so therefore, no one would be looking for him. * * * I just thought it was a way to make the plot more exciting in our conversations. Like saying when I grow up I want to do this. Just making a story line and making everything more dramatic. But it wasn't like a big plan. It wasn't planned to happen February 18. * * * The whole thing was pretty much to live it up before—and Dave said he wanted to die—and me and Angie didn't want to die. Just when we talked to each other we always said when he does that, we'll just leave because we didn't want that. But it was still just a part of the story for me and Angie.

On the evening of February 17, 1988, according to the clinician who interviewed him, Brom's father threatened to take away David's extensive "heavy metal" music collection unless David's attitude changed. Bernard Brom then pushed David who fell backwards onto a table. Fearful that he would be struck again, David Brom fled the room. Later that evening, Brom called one of the friends with whom he shared the Florida-trip fantasy and asked her if she would skip school with him the next day if he killed his family that night.

Brom returned to his bedroom and listened to music. After brooding about his situation for hours, according to the experts, at about 3:00 a.m. he went to the garage and got a long-handled axe. Armed with the axe and a steak knife, he went into the bedroom where his parents were sleeping. Although he could not remember hitting anyone, he recalled that there was screaming and that he also cried and screamed. According to the psychiatric evaluation report:

> He recalled going to his parents' bedroom and opening the door. Their lights were out, and he recalled standing in the doorway with the axe. "When I think about it, I get kind of sick. What I remember is gross. I walk into my parents' room and they are asleep. I have the axe. There is a lot of screaming in there; I am screaming and they are. I was scared; I don't remember hitting anyone. I could hear the screaming though, and it went on and on. Then I remember being in my room and packing things like blankets. All the lights were on and I had to go into each room. My brother was in his bedroom and my mother and sister in the hall, and there was blood everywhere.

> I asked specifically if he could remember hitting anyone with the axe, and he could not nor could he remember entering any of the rooms specifically, but he remembered vividly hearing the constant screaming. The screaming was not only that of the victims, but he remembers himself screaming and believes he was crying at the time, as well. He does not know why he was screaming, but he remembered it

was not particularly any words, although he remembered screaming at the top of his voice.

Brom called a friend immediately after the slaying and confided the events to her. She repeated their conversation at the waiver hearing:

> [H]e went into his parents' room. And his mom started screaming and he went over to his dad and hit him in the head and knocked him over. And his dad tried to get up and so he hit him again * * * [with a]n axe. And he said that he had hit his dad several times because his dad kept trying to get up. And he walked out of the room and he didn't tell me what order after that, but he said that he got his mom and when he went into Rick's room, Rick screamed and so Dave screamed back. And he didn't say anything about hitting Rick. And he went out into the hall again and Diane was standing over her mom, just staring, and Diane screamed and so Dave, again, screamed back. And he didn't say anything about hitting Diane.

According to the testimony of the deputy county coroner, Bernard Brom received 22 axe wounds; Paulette Brom, 19; Diane Brom, 8; and Ricky Brom, 9. While in his room packing a duffel bag, Brom told the clinician evaluating him that he heard the sound of dripping blood. The first investigating officer on the scene testified, "We had never seen so much carnage in such a small area. I think we were both in a state of shock."

After the slayings, Brom called a friend at 3:30 a.m. but hung up when her father answered. Sometime thereafter, Brom drove the family van to a bank, withdrew money with his mother's cash card, and then purchased some cigarettes and snacks at a local supermarket. He then drove to an area overlooking a friend's house so that he could see her when she left for school. When he found his friend at school, he asked her to skip school with him, a not unusual request:

> I said, "So are we skipping school?" and he goes, "Yeah, you need a break." And so I was all happy and thinking that, "Okay, sure. Whatever." * * * I asked him if he had the car today, and he said, "Yeah." And I said, "Why? Did you have to work?" because usually when he worked he got to drive the car to school and he said, "No. I can get anything I want now. My parents are dead." * * * I didn't know if this was a way to make the cutting school more exciting, if we were going to add something into [the story] and make it exciting. And I said, "So, you did it?" and he said, "yep," and that's when we reached the car, the van.

After driving to a nearby park, and then withdrawing more money at a bank, they went to his friend's house where she attempted to shave the sides of Brom's head. After going to a K–Mart to obtain a razor, they returned to her home where she completed the "punk" haircut—"[h]e wanted the sides taken off and a design in the back with lines." When her mother returned home unexpectedly, Brom hid in her closet.

After his friend returned to school, Brom went to another high school where he met some friends for lunch. Brom then enlisted still another friend to dye his hair. After one unsuccessful attempt, Brom returned to his own home alone to try once again to dye his hair. He then returned a bookbag to a friend, acknowledged that he was in "deep trouble," and told his friend that he intended to sleep under a bridge and then walk to the Twin Cities in the morning. Brom spent the night after the murders in a culvert near his home and was taken into custody the following morning at the Rochester post office.

Other than the four brutal homicides alleged in the petition, the sixteen-year-old Brom had no prior history of illegal behavior, drug abuse, or aggressive behavior. The trial court's undisputed finding of fact was that "The Child has no history of illegal behavior, drug abuse, or aggressive behavior except for the incident alleged in this petition."

A psychiatrist diagnosed Brom as suffering from a major depressive disorder, but one that likely would respond to treatment. Gerard Ring, the juvenile court judge who presided at Brom's waiver hearing, reported in his findings of fact:

> Dr. Carl Malmquist, a psychiatrist with years of experience in criminal cases, examined the child. His report ran to 23 pages in an attempt to explain this child. In the end, his diagnosis was "major depressive episode." Dr. Malmquist testified that the child could be treated. He was reluctant to say how long it would take. He could not guarantee that the child could be treated in two-and-a-half years, but he did not say that the child could not be successfully treated in that time. The prosecution needed to prove that he could not be treated by clear and convincing evidence and needed testimony like that to carry that burden of proof. Dr. Gilbertson, on the other hand, said that two-and-a-half years would normally be a relatively long time for such treatment because it usually takes only a few weeks or months.

Three clinicians—Dr. Carl Malmquist, Dr. R. Owen Nelson, and Dr. James Gilbertson—provided written reports and oral testimony. Dr. Malmquist's testimony, bolstered by a 23–page report, concluded that Brom suffered from a "major depressive episode," but that "the child could be treated" and that he could not say that "the child could not be successfully treated" within the two-and-a-half years remaining under juvenile court jurisdiction. Dr. Malmquist emphasized that Brom needed long-term treatment, but "declined to say what period of time that would be, saying that you can never tell ahead of time how long treatment like this will take."

Dr. Gilbertson testified that "two-and-a-half years would normally be a relatively long time for such treatment because it usually takes only a few weeks or months,"and that "two-and-a-half years would be considered quite a long time for [treating] a problem such as we have here." Dr. Owen's psychometric assessments, relied upon by both clinicians in their evaluations of Brom, did not express an opinion as to the amount of time that treatment would take.

Dr. Carl Malmquist, a psychiatrist appointed by the court to evaluate Brom, testified that David's depression would require long-term treatment:

> I think somebody with the degree of depression David has had and which we know culminated in the acts that are a fact and his suicidal tendencies, you need some long-term treatment focused on his depressed state, which there are tendencies that he's had towards self-destruction as well as outbursts of violence this way and I think that's the kind of thing that would need addressing. * * * I couldn't [tell how long treatment would take], except I would say that I would presume it would take some time. The reason I can't ahead of time is that you can never tell ahead of time how long treatment like this is going to take and you have to monitor it just like with any other kind of medical condition. David was severely depressed, there's no doubt in my mind about that and in fact my concern about him at this point is David has always been a compliant boy, he doesn't know what to do with his aggression. It might seem paradoxical in view of the acts that have occurred, but that's exactly what I mean. And a whole reconstruction is needed in terms of how he deals with this problem within himself and the world, and something went awry there very deeply. That's where the problem is now. And so the concerns I'd have would be as much suicide as anything else now.

Dr. Malmquist was asked specifically whether he could assure the court that Brom could be successfully treated within the juvenile justice system before Brom's nineteenth birthday. While Dr. Malmquist could not guarantee a successful therapeutic intervention within that time, neither could he assert that such an intervention would not be successful:

> I'd have some real reservations if I was being asked to carry out the treatment, and I'm putting your question in those terms, that I could assure myself as well as David if he was my patient as well as the court that at 19 I could step back and say I'm totally assured in this matter to the degree of medical certainty, for example, that I don't have to worry about suicide or homicide for anybody. I say that on the basis that this is a whole unfolding personality which has emerged by 16 that needs reworking. David doesn't know what to do with his aggression. He smiles and is a nice kid, everybody likes him. That comes through in all the voluminous reports that everybody who has talked about David says. And he is likable. The problem is that he doesn't know what to do when other people or events in his life aren't likable and they're difficult, and that's the difficulty he ran into. He didn't know what to do about it. So is it possible by 19? Yeah, it's possible, but if I was going to weigh my bets on it I'd say I wouldn't be comfortable if somebody could say at 19 no matter what you do

we're done. That kind of either/all proposition for me would put me in a bind as a psychiatrist.

In his written report, Dr. Malmquist also expressed:

some serious reservations given my perspective on the boy's problems as a psychiatrist, whether he is going to be able to receive appropriate treatment and control to resolve the multiple problems he has been struggling with over many years by the time he reaches 19 years. Part of the answer to this question is related to what we mean by treatment * * *.

In contrast to Dr. Malmquist's somewhat guarded prognosis, Dr. James Gilbertson, who testified as an expert witness on Brom's behalf at the reference hearing, suggested several treatment programs that he believed would be appropriate for and successful with Brom.

Q. Imagine that you are to treat an individual who is a teen-age boy about 16 years of age who has committed such an act of explosive violence, who has no prior criminal history and no prior legal problems, no history of violence, who is seen as engaging and likeable and who does well in school, who has severe conflicts at home and who has been diagnosed as having a major depressive episode. First of all, is it possible to treat such an individual?

A. Yes. * * *

Q. So is the personality trait situation which we are discussing in our example treatable and able to be changed?

A. Given the diagnosis that Dr. Malmquist puts forward of a major depressive reaction or disorder, these typically are quite treatable, quite amenable to change.

Dr. Gilbertson went on to describe the type of treatment that Brom's disorder required:

Q. What kind of treatment would be used to change this personality?

A. Mind you, there are two facets to the personality we're talking about. One is the major depressive features which causes the negative thinking, the poor self esteem, the tendency to think that there are no other options other than to end his life or perhaps the life of others. And then there's this other feature, the over controlled part which gives the fuel, if you will, that is the triggering aspect of the depression. So if we're talking how does one treat that combination, first of all, depression is quite a treatable disorder, either through medication which often times is prescribed or through verbal psychotherapies or counseling, either individual or on a group basis. * * *

As far as the over controlled individual, * * * [o]ne of the things that we have to look at first is does the individual have some requisite skills to begin the process of therapy? Are they bright? Are they intelligent? Do they have verbal facility? Can they talk and label things? Can they form relationships with individuals? Is there a previous history of success in major institutions, school or church or family or other kinds of things? Given that, a good premorbid or pretrauma or preoffense history, there's a stronger likelihood that they'll respond to treatment.

The matter, as I see it with Mr. Brom, is that he was extremely over controlled, he collected injustices right and left. He saved up all the pressures and humiliations, real or imagined, experienced at his father or his family's hands. He had no way to bleed them off. He wouldn't share these with other individuals. He perhaps had a superficial relationship with some girlfriends, but it was only superficial and did not serve the process of venting or providing a catharsis or relief from his difficulties. He was not assertive in the family situation. He could not approach his father. He designed ways to avoid his father, to leave his father's presence, would not talk to his father in any fashion about the difficulties. So all of these things grew, simmered, increased in pressure and combined with his own personality, probably started the downslide into the depressive state Dr. Malmquist sets forward.

What would be needed with Mr. Brom is to teach him to come forward, to be more assertive, to learn to label his feelings, not to retreat from people if they hurt him, but to come up to them and share with them what they've done to him to help establish a dialogue on what hurts him or what doesn't hurt him, not to save them up quietly, not to retreat into rock music, not to avoid or evade, but to come forward. That could be done either individually [or] in a group process, and as I say, in combination with medication if it was deemed necessary by a physician to help calm his mood or reduce some of his fearfulness. I understand in reading Dr. Malmquist's report that he is an individual who is overly sensitive to things, becomes overly frightened of things that most people would not and sometimes calmative medication is helpful in the overall treatment plan.

The prosecutor asked Dr. Gilbertson whether Brom could be treated within less than three years, the time remaining within juvenile court jurisdiction, and he testified that successful treatment was likely within that time.

That's [time available] always a factor of the disorder and secondarily the program that the individual is in. I might say, however, that with * * * major depressive disorder as the working diagnosis, that typically that is a disorder that can be treated fairly rapidly as treatment programs are discussed. Depression typically is a discreet event. It has a beginning and an ending. For some it's longer, for some it's shorter. For some it ends in suicide. For some it may end in another cataclysmic event. In some cases it spontaneously remits or goes away. For some they get treatment, either medication or counseling and it goes away. If there's one good thing about depression, it's that it does have an ending, an end point. Certainly in this case the goal would be to intervene aggressively and to end the depression and to end the feelings of being trapped or that nothing counts and there is no way out. And I think that could be accomplished in an aggressive program that would follow an individual over the length of time at least available in this case.

On the ultimate question of "amenability to treatment" within the time remaining for juvenile court jurisdiction, Dr. Gilbertson's testimony was quite strong:

Q. So do you think an individual could successfully be treated in two-and-a-half years?

A. Yes, given cooperativeness, given aggressiveness and intensity of programming. Very definitely.

Dr. Gilbertson conceded, on cross-examination, that the success of a treatment program depended on the cooperation of the patient. On redirect, however, he opined there were no indications that Brom was averse to therapeutic intervention.

Q. Dr. Gilbertson, you were asked about whether or not the ability of the individual to accept his problem and to cooperate with treatment is an important factor. In reviewing Dr. Malmquist's report do you see anything in there that would indicate that David Brom is not—would not be cooperative or would not accept what his situation is?

A. I did not see in Dr. Malmquist's report that he was adverse to treatment or that he even knew what treatment meant or what he'd have to go about doing. I think Dr. Malmquist saw a young man who was naive, I guess would be the word, and just was certainly taken aback by what he had done, but probably had little notion, if I could read between the lines, of what to do about this, how this could be prevented. And given the fact that he has never been in counseling or treatment, I would expect him to be that non-knowledgeable about it. But I didn't read anything in Dr. Malmquist's report that's saying he was adverse against treatment, had taken a position not to change or in any way was oppositional toward treatment.

Finally, Brom's attorney asked Dr. Gilbertson whether Brom could be treated successfully within the time remaining under juvenile court jurisdiction, a period of two-and-a-half years. He responded:

Given the diagnosis of major depressive disorder and even with the over controlled nature, two-and-a-half years of availability of aggressive treatment is a luxury. To have sanctioned treatment for two-and-a-half years for most treatment folk is a luxury. Typically most depressive disorders are treated in a far shorter time. Most of them within ten days to two weeks in a hospital with follow-up. Some, four or five months if they're fairly untractable depressions that aren't yielding well to the combination of medication and talking therapies, if you will. Two-and-a-half years is quite a long time given the working diagnosis we have here.

On the basis of the clinical testimony and evaluation reports, Judge Ring's findings of fact concluded that "[t]he child has been diagnosed as having a major depressive disorder and it has not been shown that he cannot be successfully treated by his 19th birthday." Judge Ring also concluded, despite the extraordinary violence of Brom's crimes, that Brom did not pose a threat to public safety. In determining that Brom did not pose a threat to other members of the community, Judge Ring relied on the testimony of clinicians. "[Dr. Malmquist] found this child to be a quiet, compliant boy suffering from depression and did not see him as a significant threat to the community. Dr. Gilbertson said it [threat to the community] would be a factor only if untreated." Judge Ring further concluded that even though Minnesota does not have a secure juvenile treatment facility, that would not be a factor in evaluating Brom's threat to public safety:

> It does not appear to me that secure facilities is a major issue in this case. There is nothing about the child which has been presented to me which suggests a need for high security. He has been described by everyone as being polite, compliant, obedient, etc. * * * None of those who knew him and testified in court expressed major fear so long as he can be observed, counseled, etc. Again, this issue turns on whether he can be treated.

The testimony of Dr. Gilbertson supported Judge Ring's finding that Brom did not pose a threat to the public. Dr. Gilbertson testified that:

> Obviously, Mr. Brom was not an antisocial predatory type who fought and aggressed and lost his cool or exploded day after day, month after month. There did not appear to be intermittent explosive features to him, which often times you can see with this disorder. It appeared to be an explosive situation within the context of this family, an intimate grouping of individuals of which he was a member, with the pressures building up over time with the young man seeing at least no other option available. Re-offending for Mr. Brom, again, the prediction would be it would have to take those same concatenation of events. He'd have to be in an intimate grouping. He'd have to be in there long enough to feel bonded. He'd have to feel that there was no way to deal with the authority present. He would have to feel put down, rebuked, criticized, uncared for. Whether this was real or imagined, those series of events would have to all be occurring. And again, he'd have to be untreated. Namely, he'd still have this steel cap, if you will. What is so unusual in this case is the context of the acting out, the intimate grouping, if you will. It's the thing that makes it the wholesale tragedy that it is. He is not at risk to the general public. Untreated and were he not to change, the risk would probably be in the intimate grouping he would find himself later on in his life.

On the basis of the whole record and with "the focus on the child," Judge Ring concluded that the prosecution failed to prove by clear and convincing evidence either that Brom was not amenable to treatment or that he threatened public safety. "Since the evidence cannot be said to be clear and convincing proof that he cannot be treated, the petitioner [prosecutor] has failed to carry the burden of proof on this issue." Based on his findings of fact, Judge Ring's conclusion of law was that "the petitioner has failed to establish by clear and convincing evidence that the child is not suitable to treatment or that the public safety is not served under the provisions of law relating to the juvenile courts."

PROBLEM

On the basis of the foregoing record and the statute and court rule, if you were the trial judge, how would you rule on the state's motion to try Brom as an adult? Assume that you are an appellate court judge sworn faithfully to apply the waiver statute, *supra* at p. 555. Would you find that Judge Ring's findings of fact were "clearly erroneous" or an "abuse of discretion"? Does the record of the waiver hearing provide "substantial evidence" to support Judge Ring's decision about Brom's "amenability to treatment" or threat to the public? What is the significance of the allocation of the burden of proof in this case? Did the state demonstrate by "clear and convincing" evidence that Brom could not be successfully treated as a juvenile? If Judge Ring had reviewed the same record and written a somewhat different opinion, ruled for the prosecution, and waived Brom for adult criminal prosecution, would you conclude that his decision to waive jurisdiction was "clearly erroneous" or an "abuse of discretion"? Could a trial judge with this record err regardless of how she ruled?

Do you agree with Judge Ring's decision to retain juvenile court jurisdiction over David Brom? Why or why not? If you were an appellate court judge who did not like Judge Ring's decision to retain juvenile court jurisdiction with a maximum of two and a half year of intervention, what would you do? Do you think that the decisions of the Minnesota Court of Appeals, *In re D.F.B.*, *infra* p. 569, or the Minnesota Supreme Court, *In re D.F.B.*, *infra* p. 572, are any more correct in their application of the law to the facts of the case than was Judge Ring? Why? Based on what evidence on the record?

IN THE MATTER OF THE WELFARE OF D.F.B.
430 N.W.2d 475 (Minn. Ct. App. 1988).

HUSPENI, JUDGE. Appellant Olmsted County challenges the trial court's findings, conclusions and order denying the motion to refer respondent D.F.B. for adult prosecution. We reverse and remand for further proceedings consistent with this opinion. * * *

Did the juvenile court appropriately interpret the 1980 amendments to Chapter 260 in denying appellant's motion for reference?

In order to refer a child for adult prosecution, the trial court must find (1) probable cause "to believe the child committed the offenses alleged in the delinquency petition" and (2) a demonstration by "clear and convincing evidence that the child is not suitable to treatment or that the public safety is not served under the provisions of law relating to juvenile courts." The parties agree that probable cause was shown.

The parties also agree that as a result of certain 1980 amendments to Chapter 260, appellant has established a prima facie case for reference to stand trial as an adult. Section 260.125, subd. 3 provides in pertinent part:

> A prima facie case that the public safety is not served or that the child is not suitable for treatment shall have been established if the child was at least 16 years of age at the time of the alleged offense and:
> * * *
>
> (2) Is alleged by delinquency petition to have committed murder in the first degree; * * *.

D.F.B. is 16 years of age and is alleged to have committed the delinquent act of murder in the first degree.

The 1980 amendments were the legislative response to *In the Matter of the Welfare of Dahl*. In *Dahl*, a 17–year–old boy had been charged with delinquency for first degree murder. He had no history of prior delinquent acts. The supreme court vacated the trial court's reference order and remanded the matter observing:

> The legislature did not single out certain crimes for reference to adult prosecution, although it had that specific opportunity. The law does not say that all petitions filed in juvenile court alleging first degree murder are automatically subject to certification, nor does the statute provide that 17–year–old violators are automatically referred for adult prosecution. * * * [T]he existing statutory framework does not authorize referral based on the specific crime charged.

The 1980 legislative amendments provided that age and seriousness of the crime were, in fact, sufficient to create a prima facie showing that reference was appropriate. The legislature's response to the concerns expressed by the *Dahl* court regarding reference based solely on age and offense is unequivocal. * * *

In addition to addressing difficulties which had been encountered in applying criteria of unamenability to treatment and public safety interests, the 1980 amendments also reflect a shift in legislative attitude regarding punishment as a goal of juvenile courts. Prior to the amendments the stated purpose of those courts was to secure care and guidance, and to serve the welfare of the minor child. * * * Subsequent to the 1980 amendment [of] the "purpose" clause * * * [f]or youths charged with the commission of a crime, a more punitive approach is emphasized, and as to them the juvenile court operates to:

> promote the public safety and reduce juvenile delinquency by maintaining the integrity of the substantive law prohibiting certain behavior and by developing individual responsibility for lawful behavior.
> * * *

The trial court recognized that although the section 260.125, subd. 3 1980 amendatory language set forth the conditions under which a prima facie case for reference may be established, there was no amendatory language to guide the trial court when it determined that the prima facie case had been rebutted. At that point, pursuant to Rule 32.05, the state would once more be required to show by clear and convincing evidence that D.F.B. is not amenable to treatment or that the public safety is not served by retaining him in the juvenile court system.

If our search for legislative intent is limited to the amendatory language of section 260.125, subd. 3, we inevitably will be compelled to reach the conclusion reached by the trial court. * * * In addition, if we are permitted to look only to the amendatory language of section 260.125, subd. 3, and to the language of Rule 32.05, we will be compelled to echo the trial court's determination regarding the continued viability of *Dahl*; that upon rebuttal of the state's prima facie case *Dahl* is still good law, and that in the absence of supporting psychological data or a history of misconduct, the child's age, the serious nature of the offense charged, social adjustment and maturity level are insufficient to support a finding that D.F.B. could not be successfully treated within the juvenile court system. The trial court placed considerable reliance upon the similarity between *Dahl* and this case, particularly emphasizing the fact that neither youth had a history of violent acts aside from the offenses charged. Clearly, the trial court retained D.F.B. in the juvenile court system because it believed that neither the statute nor *Dahl* permitted reference.

We cannot criticize the trial court's application of section 260.125, subd. 3 and *Dahl* to the facts as it found them. We believe, however, that broader consideration of the 1980 amendments to Chapter 260 is not only warranted but is required. Such consideration irrevocably leads us, as we are certain it would have led the trial court, to a determination that D.F.B. must be referred to stand trial as an adult.

Section 260.011, subd. 2 as amended in 1980, provides in relevant part:

> The purpose of the laws relating to children alleged * * * to be delinquent is to promote the public safety * * * by maintaining the integrity of the substantive law prohibiting certain behavior and by developing individual responsibility for lawful behavior.

If the words "maintaining the integrity of the substantive law prohibiting certain behavior" are to have any meaning, trial courts must have the authority to look beyond the specific characteristics of the child and the child's behavioral history in its analysis of the totality of the circumstances. We are persuaded by the language of section 260.011 that the trial court, upon rebuttal of the prima facie case, must not be hobbled by the statutorily weakened analysis of *Dahl* and of Rule 32.05 * * * as the trial court here so clearly believed itself to be.

We are convinced that the legislature intended the language of section 260.011 to ensure that the criminal justice system would not be permitted to provide an excessively minimal response to an offense which had a major impact upon society. The brutal murders of these four family members has had a major impact on society. Retention of the alleged murderer within the criminal justice system for less than three years would constitute an excessively minimal response.

We conclude that the legislature intended to protect the strong and legitimate interest of the public in a fair response by the criminal justice system to a heinous crime. There can be no doubt that the offenses here are heinous and that the only fair response of the criminal justice system, as a matter of law, must be referral. The state's interest in the integrity of the substantive law, under the facts of this case, overcomes any consideration, however weighty, given by the trial court to the absence of anti-social or violent behavior in D.F.B.'s past. * * *

IN THE MATTER OF THE WELFARE OF D.F.B.

433 N.W.2d 79 (Minn. 1988).

AMDAHL, CHIEF JUSTICE. In *Matter of Welfare of D.F.B.*, the court of appeals reversed a decision of the district court denying a motion by the state * * * to refer D.F.B., a juvenile, for prosecution as an adult. We granted D.F.B's petition for review not because we disagree with the ultimate decision of the court of appeals but in order to provide a different analysis as to why reference is required. * * *

After thoughtful and careful consideration, the district court concluded that the facts were analogous to those in *Matter of Welfare of Dahl*, and that—given its conclusion that *Dahl* is still good law in a case such as this where the juvenile has produced substantial evidence of amenability to treatment in the juvenile court system consistent with the public safety—it had no choice but to deny the reference petition, much as it was otherwise inclined to grant the petition.

The court of appeals in a thoughtful opinion concluded that the district court misinterpreted the effect and the intent of the 1980 legislation enacted in response to our decision in *Dahl*. It concluded that keeping D.F.B. in the juvenile court system is inconsistent with the intent of the legislature expressed in those amendments and it therefore reversed the district court.

Our starting point is the *Dahl* case. * * * Although we vacated the reference order in *Dahl*, we did not hold, as it has been assumed, that the reference in that case was unjustified. Rather, we remanded for a further hearing for the purpose of considering all of the relevant factors—not just age or seriousness of the offense—to determine if the statutory test of reference had been met.

In 1980 the legislature did a number of significant things. One was to amend section 260.011, the statutory purpose section. * * * [F]or those charged with delinquent acts the legislature said that the purpose was "to promote the public safety and reduce juvenile delinquency by maintaining the integrity of the substantive law prohibiting certain behavior and by developing individual responsibility for lawful behavior." The legislature also amended section 260.125, changing it to provide not only that the state has the burden of proving the need for certification (something it had before) but that the state had to meet this burden by clear and convincing evidence (something that was not clear before). More significantly for our purposes, the legislature adopted a matrix, setting forth various ways that the state could establish a *prima facie* case for reference, one being the situation presented by this case, where the child was at least 16 at the time of the act and has been alleged to have committed first-degree murder.

We have decided a number of post-amendment reference cases. For example, we have made it clear that when the defendant produces "significant" or "substantial" evidence rebutting a prima facie case for reference under the statute, then the role for the juvenile court is to decide on the basis of the entire record, without reference to the *prima facie* case, whether the state has met its burden of proving by clear and convincing evidence that the juvenile is unamenable to treatment in the juvenile court system consistent with the public safety. * * *

In this case the juvenile, D.F.B., came forward with evidence bearing both on amenability to treatment and on public safety. At least, in our opinion, the clear implication of the testimony of the defense expert, Gilbertson, is that he was not just of the opinion that D.F.B. could be treated successfully but was also of the opinion that he could be treated in the juvenile court system consistent with the public safety.

The issue then becomes whether it can be said that the state met its burden of proof without regard to the presumption. In our view, once the district court concludes that the juvenile has rebutted the presumption, then the district court has to analyze the entire record, using the same basic multi-factor analysis discussed in *Dahl*, to see if it may be said that the state has proved by clear and convincing evidence that the juvenile is unamenable to treatment in the juvenile court system consistent with the public safety. Minn.R.Juv.Ct. 32.05, which sets forth the various circumstances that may be involved in the totality of the circumstances, supports this conclusion. Employing the multi-factor analysis in this case—which is what the trial court in *Dahl* was directed to do on remand—would justify a reference decision in this case even if the legislature's 1980 amendment of the purpose section was without significance. While we agree with the court of appeals' conclusion that the amendment of the purpose section makes it easier to conclude that reference is justified in this case, we do not agree with the implication that reference is justified any time a juvenile commits a heinous offense. Rather, reference in this case is justified because—bearing in mind the legislature's revised statement of purpose and looking at all the factors listed in R. 32.05, including the offense with which *D.F.B.* is charged, the manner in which he committed the offense, the interests of society in the outcome of this case, the testimony of Dr. Malmquist suggesting that treatment of D.F.B. might be unsuccessful, and the weakness of Dr. Gilbertson's testimony—the state met its burden of proving by clear and convincing evidence that D.F.B. is unamenable to treatment in the juvenile court system consistent with the public safety. * * * In summary, we affirm the decision of the court of appeals reversing the decision of the district court denying the motion to refer D.F.B. for prosecution as an adult.

NOTES

1) **Epilogue to *In re D.F.B.*** As a result of the Minnesota Supreme Court's decision to allow the state to try Brom as an adult, an Olmsted County Grand Jury indicted him on four counts of first degree murder. Brom's attorney filed notice of intent to raise an insanity defense. Under Minnesota procedure, an insanity defense entails a bifurcated hearing in which the jury first decides whether the defendant committed the crime and then decides in a separate proceeding whether the defendant lacked criminal responsibility. The guilt phase of Brom's trial required four days of testimony, following which the jury returned a verdict of guilty on October 3, 1989, Brom's 18th birthday. After the determination of guilt, Brom and the prosecution introduced evidence bearing on his mental illness. The jury of seven men and five women deliberated for 22 hours over three days before deciding that Brom was sane at the time he murdered his family. Under the Minnesota criminal law, a conviction of first degree murder carries an automatic sentence of life in prison. At the time of Brom's conviction, persons sentenced to life imprisonment for first degree murder must serve a minimum of 17½ years before they become eligible for parole release consideration. On October 16, 1989, the presiding criminal court judge criticized Minnesota's *M'Naghten* standard of criminal insanity as rigid and narrow as applied to a "mentally ill boy driven to despair by a pathetically sick mind." Despite the "emotional agony" she experienced, the judge sentenced Brom to three consecutive life sentences which require him to serve a minimum of 52½ years before he becomes eligible for parole release consideration. The criminal sentence imposed was about twenty times longer than the maximum sentence he could have received as a juvenile.

2) **Appellate Review of Trial Judges' Waiver Decisions** What approach did the Minnesota Court of Appeals use to reverse Judge Ring's decision to retain juvenile court jurisdiction over Brom? What approach did the Minnesota Supreme Court use to reverse Judge Ring's decision? Which strategy is more consistent with the role and function of an appellate court?

Transferred juveniles appeal juvenile court judges' waiver decisions while prosecutors file a smaller number of appeals in those instances in which the juvenile court judge declines to transfer the youth. Most states do not allow juveniles to appeal an order waiving juvenile court jurisdiction, but require a final judgment on the merits—a criminal conviction—before a youth can obtain appellate review of the initial transfer decision. *See e.g. People v. Browning*, 45 Cal.App.3d 125, 119 Cal.Rptr. 420 (1975); *In re Clay*, 246 N.W.2d 263 (Iowa 1976). Some states allow a juvenile to appeal a waiver decision because it terminates juvenile court jurisdiction and thus constitutes a final order. *See in re I.Q.S.*, 309 Minn. 78, 244 N.W.2d 30 (1976). While a juvenile may obtain appellate review of a waiver order following conviction in criminal court, *People v. Jiles*, 43 Ill.2d 145, 251 N.E.2d 529 (1969), most jurisdiction provide for immediate appeal by the prosecutor if the juvenile court judge declines to waive jurisdiction. *People v. Martin*, 67 Ill.2d 462, 10 Ill.Dec. 563, 367 N.E.2d 1329 (1977). Why would states treat appeals by juveniles and by the state differently? What bearing does *Breed v. Jones*, *supra* p. 530, have on a juvenile's and the state's right to appeal adverse waiver decisions?

Appellate courts occasionally reverse juvenile court judges if they fail to adhere to statutory procedures or fail to make the required findings. *See e.g.*, *Harden v. Commonwealth*, 885 S.W.2d 323, 325 (Ky. App. 1994) (stating that reasons for transfer "must be specific enough to permit meaningful review for the purpose of determining whether there has been compliance with the statute"); *State v. Collins*, 694 So.2d 624 (La. App. 1997) (holding that trial court must specifically address the transfer criteria); *State v. Sonja B.*, 183 W.Va. 380, 395 S.E.2d 803, 807 (W.V. 1990) (deciding that juvenile judge failed to review psychological evaluations or comply with statutory requirement to "make a careful, detailed analysis into the child's mental and physical condition, maturity, emotional attitude * * * and other similar personal factors"). Some appellate courts fault the juvenile court for failing to consider the juvenile's "amenability to treatment" and focusing solely on the seriousness of the alleged offense. *See e.g. In the Matter of J.D.W.*, 267 Mont. 87, 881 P.2d 1324 (Mont.1994); *In the Matter of J.K.C.*, 270 Mont. 342, 891 P.2d 1169 (Mont.1995).

Appellate courts are supposed to defer to trial judges' fact-finding decisions and application of substantive criteria to those facts either to retain or to waive jurisdiction. In part, the statutory criteria based on the *Kent* Appendix provide a broad, discretionary framework that appellate courts lack authority to review aggressively. The appellate standards of review—"substantial evidence," "clearly erroneous," and "abuse of discretion"—coupled with the deference appellate courts typically show the fact finder result in upholding the juvenile judge's decision, which in most appealed case is one to waive jurisdiction. *See e.g. Jeremiah B. v. State*, 107 Nev. 924, 823 P.2d 883 (Nev. 1991) (holding that whether vehicular homicide constituted sufficiently heinous crime within statutory criteria "seriousness of the charged offenses" rested with juvenile judge's discretion).

However, appellate courts do not always hew to their role only to review questions of law and not questions of fact. **In People v. Jones**, 958 P.2d 393, 18 Cal.4th 667, 76 Cal.Rptr.2d 641 (Cal. 1998), the California Supreme Court reviewed a Court of Appeals decision that reversed a finding by the juvenile court that two 15–year–olds who killed a store owner during a robbery were fit and proper subjects for treatment under the juvenile court law. The applicable waiver statute, Cal. Welf. & Inst. § 707(e), created a presumption that juveniles charged with murder should be tried as adult, but the minors could rebut the presumption if they established their fitness under each of five statutory criteria: (A) the degree of criminal sophistication exhibited by the minor; (B) whether the minor can be rehabilitated prior to the expiration of the juvenile court's jurisdiction; (C) the minor's previous delinquency history; (D) the success of previous attempts by the juvenile court to rehabilitate the minor; and (E) the circumstances and gravity of the offenses alleged to have been committed. The juvenile court made elaborate findings of fact, concluded that the minors rebutted the presumption for waiver, and retained jurisdiction. The Court of Appeal reversed, holding that the juvenile court abused its discretion in concluding that the minors were fit. The Supreme Court reviewed the facts, found that the juvenile court's findings of fitness under two statutory criteria—"the degree of criminal sophistication" and "the circumstances and gravity of the offenses alleged to have been committed"—were not supported by substantial evidence, and affirmed the judgment of the Court of Appeal. Compare the majority opinion, Mosk, J., with that of the dissent, Werdegar, J., regarding the role of appellate review of juvenile court judges' waiver decisions:

MOSK, J. The People conceded that the minors met several of the criteria for fitness—specifically that the minors could be rehabilitated prior to the expiration of the juvenile court's jurisdiction, had no previous delinquent history, and had been subject to no previous attempts by the juvenile court at rehabilitation—but contended that they were unfit under the criteria of the degree of criminal sophistication and the circumstances and gravity of the offenses alleged.

The juvenile court found the minors fit and proper subjects for treatment under the juvenile court law under each of the criteria. * * * It ruled that the minors carried their burden of establishing that they were fit subjects for treatment under the juvenile court law. * * * The trial court's ultimate finding of fitness or unfitness remains subject to review for error under an abuse of discretion standard. * * * The findings required under the criteria listed in [§ 707(e)], are evidently findings of fact.

Accordingly, the minor charged with an offense subject to that provision must carry the burden of rebutting the presumption of unfitness under each of the criteria "by a preponderance of the evidence." Evidence Code section 606 requires that "[t]he effect of a presumption affecting the burden of proof is to impose upon the party against whom it operates the burden of proof as to the nonexistence of the presumed fact." * * *

Findings of fact are reviewed under a "substantial evidence" standard. The standard is deferential: "When a trial court's factual determination is attacked on the ground that there is no substantial evidence to sustain it, the power of an appellate court begins and ends with the determination as to whether, on the entire record, there is substantial evidence, contradicted or uncontradicted, which will support the determination. * * * "

Because [§ 707(e)] requires a determination that the minor is unfit absent findings supporting fitness under each of the five factors, a determination of fitness resting on a finding unsupported by substantial evidence is necessarily an abuse of discretion. * * * First, "the minor shall be presumed to be not a fit and proper subject to be dealt with under the juvenile court law * * *." Second, the minor can rebut the presumption and be determined fit if the court concludes that he or she would be amenable to treatment under the juvenile court law "under each and every one" of the five criteria set forth above. Third, in making its determination of fitness, the juvenile court "may consider extenuating or mitigating circumstances" in evaluating each of the criteria. * * *

[T]he criteria used to determine fitness are based on the premise that the minor did, in fact, commit the offense. Instead, the minor may use the information contained in police reports, the probation report, expert evaluations, and other submissions to the court "to argue that his participation was not as grave or serious as the charge would initially lead a court to conclude." * * *

Applying the foregoing requirements to the matter before us, the juvenile court erred, under an abuse of discretion standard, in determining that the minors were fit and proper subjects for treatment under the juvenile court law. We so hold based on our conclusion that its findings that they were fit under the criteria of the degree of criminal sophistication and the circumstances and gravity of the offenses alleged were not supported by substantial evidence.

[The Supreme Court reviewed the facts on which the juvenile court judge based its decision that the juveniles had rebutted the presumption of unfitness. "It based its conclusion, inter alia, on the following considerations. The minors had no previous record of participation in any criminal offenses, gang activity, or mischievous conduct. Regarding the charged offense itself, the plan was uncomplicated and ineptly executed." By contrast, the Supreme Court found that "Although the minors apparently had no history of prior delinquency, and the offense was apparently "out of character," their planning and execution of the robbery involved a degree of criminal sophistication precluding a finding of fitness. The minors planned the offense in considerable detail. They obtained a gun, masks, and gloves. They selected as their target a neighborhood store, because they believed they could "get away with it." * * * In effect, the juvenile court improperly rewarded the minors for their miscalculations in carrying out a deliberate, well-planned robbery." In examining the circumstances surrounding the offense, the juvenile court judges found that "The minors were intoxicated at the time of the robbery, they did not intend to hurt or kill anyone, and they were inept in carrying out the offense, particularly in mishandling the gun. It also considered their subsequent remorse and their cooperative behavior in detention. Again, the Supreme Court found that "the finding was not supported by substantial evidence of any mitigating or extenuating circumstance."]

To overcome the presumption of unfitness under this criterion, the evidence supporting a juvenile court's findings must show that a minor's participation was not as grave or as serious as the charge itself would lead a court to believe. * * * Although some of the minors' blunders may have been "idiotic," the minors did not show that their participation was not as grave or serious as the charge would initially lead a court to conclude. Nor did the minors' subsequent remorse and good behavior, although clearly relevant to the question whether they could be rehabilitated prior to expiration of the juvenile court's jurisdiction, constitute extenuating or mitigating circumstances concerning the criterion at issue: the circumstances and gravity of the offenses alleged.

The Court of Appeal, in reversing the juvenile court finding, remanded with directions to set aside the finding of fitness and to instead find both minors unfit. We agree with that disposition. No juvenile court could reasonably conclude, based on all of the evidence presented, that these minors had overcome the presumption of unfitness under the criteria of criminal sophistication and circumstances and gravity of the offenses alleged.

WERDEGAR, JUSTICE, dissenting.

Clearly, on the facts of this case, one might disagree with the juvenile court that these minors were fit subjects for treatment in the juvenile justice system. Had I been the juvenile court judge, I might certainly have reached a different conclusion regarding their amenability to treatment and their fitness to remain in juvenile court. That, however, is not the question before this court. Instead, the question posed in this case is simply this: *Where does the primary responsibility for a juvenile fitness determination lie?* Is it in the trial court, in the exercise of its sound discretion based on substantial evidence, with deferential review by the appellate courts? Or is it in the trial court subject to independent review by the appellate courts?

Although the majority purports to follow the former, deferential standard of review, its actual resolution of the case cannot be reconciled with a deferential review standard. In holding the juvenile court's factual findings were unsupported by substantial evidence, the majority ignores contrary evidence in the record, fails to construe the record in a light most favorable to the party who prevailed below, and thereby deprives our trial judges of their traditional discretion to make a determination of suitability based on the facts and circumstances of each individual case, a determination trial judges, as experienced firsthand observers of the parties and all the circumstances, are best equipped to make. * * *

In evaluating the juvenile court's ruling for substantial evidence, we are required to view the evidence in a light most favorable to the minors, as the prevailing parties below. "When two or more inferences can reasonably be deduced from the facts, the reviewing court has no authority to substitute its decision for that of the trial court." We must assume the trial court resolved conflicts in the evidence in the minors' favor and accord the minors the benefit of all reasonable inferences raised by the evidence. * * *

The juvenile court assessed the minors' criminal sophistication, concluding their relative lack of criminal sophistication indicated they were amenable to the care and treatment of the juvenile court. The court explained this was a first offense for both minors and their lives showed no pattern of criminality. Although the crime was planned, the number of blunders the minors made in its execution indicated they did not really know what they were doing. * * * Of critical importance, the court found the minors *did not intend to kill* the victim. The court found that, after the minors were arrested, they were very frightened of the situation in which they found themselves. * * *

The juvenile court below concluded the minors' lack of any criminal record, blunders in the commission of the crime and evident lack of intent to kill indicated their relative degree of criminal sophistication was insufficient to indicate an unfitness to remain in juvenile court. In reaching that conclusion, the juvenile court did not, as the majority finds, rely on evidence so ephemeral or insubstantial that an appellate court should decline to accord the conclusion the traditional deference given to factual findings made by the trier of fact. * * *

Although the majority purports to apply the substantial evidence test, which is a deferential standard of appellate review, it instead merely substitutes its own view of the evidence. * * * [A]lthough we *say* appellate courts should show deference to a trial court's decision on a minor's fitness to remain in juvenile court, what we apparently mean is that appellate courts should reweigh the evidence, decline to construe the juvenile court's findings of fact in a light favorable to the party who prevailed below, make de novo credibility determinations based on the appellate record and reach an ultimate decision preferred by the appellate court. The majority's ad hoc approach is not only a departure from past practice, it also has the unfortunate by-product of encouraging unnecessary litigation, for without appellate deference to the trial court's factual decisions, a losing party has a much greater incentive to seek appellate review, seeking a second bite of the apple. Such a scheme ignores the basic function of our trial courts and the historic role of the appellate courts and threatens to add to an already overburdened appellate caseload.

Despite the principle of deference to trial judges' fact-finding, *People v. Jones* and *D.F.B.* illustrate that appellate courts may be more inclined to reverse a juvenile court judge's factual decision to retain jurisdiction over the juvenile than when they waive it. Not surprisingly, cases in which appellate courts order a juvenile transferred to criminal court typically involve youths charged with a very serious offense. *See e.g. People v. Fultz*, 453 Mich. 937, 554 N.W.2d 725 (Mich. 1996); *People in the Interest of Y.C.*, 581 N.W.2d 483, 489 (S.D. 1998) ("Society must be protected from violent crime and the agony of its effects * * *.") See generally, **Lynda E. Frost Clausel and Richard J. Bonnie, "Juvenile Justice on Appeal" in Jeffrey Fagan and Franklin E. Zimring, eds.,** ***The Changing Borders of Juvenile Justice: Transfer of Adolescents to the Criminal Court*** **184, 187 (2000),** who note that

Although decisions are occasionally reversed because the juvenile judge failed to adhere to the statutory procedures or failed to address some of the *Kent*-like criteria prescribed in the statute, appellate courts rarely reverse juvenile court judgments on substantive grounds. Appellate courts reviewing a juvenile judge's waiver decision typically examine the underlying findings of fact to see if any were clearly erroneous or lacked substantial evidence and to determine whether the trial judge abused his or her discretion. Perhaps because of this deferential standard of review, the vast majority of appellate rulings in all states uphold the juvenile judge's determination (which, in most appealed cases, is to waive jurisdiction). * * *

In sum, appellate courts reviewing judicial waiver decisions have been willing to specify procedural requirements for judicial decision making, but generally they have not been inclined to provide much substantive constraint on the exercise of juvenile judges' discretion. In the vast majority of appealed cases, state appellate courts have rejected claims that the juvenile judge abused his or her discretion in deciding the transfer issue. Overall, the courts tend to defer to juvenile judges' discretion either to retain or to transfer jurisdiction. Because the statutory criteria based on the *Kent* factors are generally viewed as broad guidelines, the appellate courts have not had the statutory leeway to provide more aggressive substantive review of judicial transfer decisions. * * * In recent cases, the most rigorous substantive review has occurred in instances in which the juvenile court retained jurisdiction and the prosecution challenged that determination. * * *

b. Presumptive Certification, Public Safety, and Excluded Offenses

In 1994, the Minnesota legislature substantially modified its juvenile court waiver processes. How do the statute and Juvenile Court Rule of Procedure below differ from their earlier iteration, *supra* p. 555? How would the juvenile justice system have treated David Brom's case under the new statute? *See* Barry C. Feld, "Violent Youth and Public Policy: A Case Study of Juvenile Justice Law Reform," 79 *Minn. L. Rev.* 965 (1995) (comprehensive analysis of the legislative process and substantive policies adopted).

Minn. Stat. § 260.125 (1995). Certification to district court

Subd. 1. When a child is alleged to have committed, after becoming 14 years of age, an offense that would be a felony if committed by an adult, the juvenile court may enter an order certifying the proceeding to the district court for action under the criminal laws.

Subd. 2. Order of certification; requirements. Except as provided in subdivision 3a or 3b, the juvenile court may order a certification to district court only if:

(1) a petition has been filed * * *.

(2) a motion for certification has been filed by the prosecuting authority;

(3) notice has been given * * *;

(4) a hearing has been held * * * within 30 days of the filing of the certification motion, unless good cause is shown by the prosecution or the child as to why the hearing should not be held within this period in which case the hearing shall be held within 90 days of the filing of the motion;

(5) the court finds that there is probable cause * * * to believe the child committed the offense alleged by delinquency petition; and

(6) the court finds either:

(i) that the presumption of certification created by subdivision 2a applies and the child has not rebutted the presumption by clear and convincing evidence demonstrating that retaining the proceeding in the juvenile court serves public safety; or

(ii) that the presumption of certification does not apply and the prosecuting authority has demonstrated by clear and convincing evidence that retaining the proceeding in the juvenile court does not serve public safety. If the court finds that the prosecutor has not demonstrated by clear and convincing evidence that retaining the proceeding in juvenile court does not serve public safety, the court shall retain the proceeding in juvenile court.

Subd. 2a. Presumption of certification. It is presumed that a proceeding involving an offense committed by a child will be certified to district court if:

(1) the child was 16 or 17 years old at the time of the offense; and

(2) the delinquency petition alleges that the child committed an offense that would result in a presumptive commitment to prison under the sentencing guidelines and applicable statutes, or that the child committed any felony offense while using, whether by brandishing, displaying, threatening with, or otherwise employing, a firearm.

If the court determines that probable cause exists to believe the child committed the alleged offense, the burden is on the child to rebut this presumption by demonstrating by clear and convincing evidence that retaining the proceeding in the juvenile court serves public safety. If the court finds that the child has not rebutted the presumption by clear and convincing evidence, the court shall certify the child to district court.

Subd. 2b. Public safety. In determining whether the public safety is served by certifying a child to district court, the court shall consider the following factors:

(1) the seriousness of the alleged offense in terms of community protection, including the existence of any aggravating factors recognized by the sentencing guidelines, the use of a firearm, and the impact on any victim;

(2) the culpability of the child in committing the alleged offense, including the level of the child's participation in planning and carrying out the offense and the existence of any mitigating factors recognized by the sentencing guidelines;

(3) the child's prior record of delinquency;

(4) the child's programming history, including the child's past willingness to participate meaningfully in available programming;

(5) the adequacy of the punishment or programming available in the juvenile justice system; and

(6) the dispositional options available for the child.

In considering these factors, the court shall give greater weight to the seriousness of the alleged offense and the child's prior record of delinquency than to the other factors listed in this subdivision * * *.

Subd. 5. Written Findings; Options. * * * If the juvenile court decides not to order certification in a case in which the presumption described in subdivision 2a applies, the court shall designate the proceeding an extended jurisdiction juvenile prosecution and include in its decision written findings of fact and conclusions of law as to why the retention of the proceeding in juvenile court serves public safety, with specific reference to the factors listed in subdivision 2b. If the court decides not to order certification in a case in which the presumption described in subdivision 2a does not apply, the court may designate the proceeding an extended jurisdiction juvenile prosecution.

Subd. 6. First-degree murder. When a motion for certification has been filed in a case in which the petition alleges that the child committed murder in the first degree, the prosecuting authority shall present the case to the grand jury for consideration of indictment * * * within 14 days after the petition was filed.

Subd. 7. Inapplicability to certain offenders. This section does not apply to a child excluded from the definition of delinquent child under section 260.015, subd. 5(b).

Minn. Stat. § 260.015 Subd. 5(b) (West 1999) The term delinquent child does not include a child alleged to have committed murder in the first degree after becoming 16 years of age, but the term delinquent child does include a child alleged to have committed attempted murder in the first degree.

Barry C. Feld, "Violent Youth and Public Policy: A Case Study of Juvenile Justice Law Reform," 79 *Minn. L. Rev.* **965 (1995),** describes the genesis and policies underlying the new waiver legislation:

The Task Force recommended a simplified certification procedure that linked the definition of serious juvenile offenders to the definition of serious offenses in the adult sentencing guidelines. * * * Under the Sentencing Guidelines, which apply to adult defendants, conviction for certain violent crimes creates a presumption that the offender should be committed to prison. The Task Force used the Sentencing Guidelines to structure juvenile court waiver and sentencing decisions. It proposed that older juveniles charged with presumptive-incarceration offenses be presumptively certified. * * * Thus, the Task Force used the Sentencing Guidelines' definition of serious offenses to make certification easier and more consistent, to integrate juvenile and criminal court sentencing practices, to emphasize public safety over treatment considerations, and to enhance the sentencing authority of juvenile courts.

The Task Force proposed, and the new legislation provides, that a prosecutor may file a motion to transfer only against juveniles charged with felony-level offenses. The new statute retains a revised version of the waiver process. For juveniles aged fourteen to seventeen and charged with any felony offense, the prosecutor must prove by "clear and convincing evidence" that protection of "public safety" requires the juvenile's transfer to criminal court.

For youths aged sixteen or seventeen at the time of offense who are charged with a crime requiring presumptive commitment to prison under the Minnesota Sentencing Guidelines, the Task Force recommended a *presumption* of transfer to criminal court. * * * While a prosecutor bears the burden of proof in an "ordinary" certification proceeding, the presumption shifts the burden of proof to older juveniles charged with serious offenses to show by "clear and convincing" evidence that retaining their case in juvenile court serves "public safety." * * * Under the new legislation, however, older juveniles charged with serious offenses bear the risk of non-persuasion. If a youth fails to meet that burden, waiver is nondiscretionary. * * *

Basing a presumption for waiver on an allegation of a serious crime and placing the burden upon the youth to prove why remaining in juvenile court serves public safety should significantly increase the number of youths certified to criminal court. To further expedite transfer to criminal court, the Task Force recommended a change in waiver criteria to give primacy to "public safety." Rather than asking unanswerable questions about a youth's "amenability to treatment" or "dangerousness," the Task Force proposed using more objective offense criteria to define "public safety." * * *

The Task Force's emphasis on "public safety" reflects the political reality that the public's fear of serious youth crime, rather than a child's responsiveness to treatment, is the real reason for waiver. * * * The legislative definition of "public safety" closely parallels the Task Force's recommendations and further links the definition of serious juvenile offenses to the adult sentencing guidelines. * * *

Legislatively linking presumptive certification with the Sentencing Guidelines also implicates many court decisions interpreting the Guidelines' policy and jurisprudence. For example, adult defendants may rebut the Sentencing Guidelines' presumption of commitment to prison by showing that they are "amenable to probation." * * * Thus, to the extent that the Sentencing Guidelines' rebuttable presumption jurisprudence shapes interpretation of the analogous presumptive-certification provisions, trial judges in certification hearings must still determine whether a youth is amenable to an EJJ probationary disposition. Despite the legislature's emphasis on "public safety" and "proportional sentencing," a substantial degree of individualized sentencing discretion remains inherent in presumptive certification. * * *

In the final analysis, a juvenile court judge who decides to certify a youth in the interest of "public safety" effectively must decide whether the youth's offense severity, criminal history, and "unamenability to probation" warrant adult imprisonment. * * *

NOTES

1) Offense Criteria, Statutory Presumptions, and the Burden of Persuasion In *People v. Jones*, supra Note 2, pp. 575–576, Cal. Welf. & Inst. § 707 (e) used offense criteria to create a presumption of unamenability and to shift the burden of persuasion to the youth to affirmatively demonstrate fitness for treatment within the juvenile justice system. Similarly, Minn. Stat. 260.125 Subd. 2(a), *supra*, creates a presumption for waiver for juveniles 16–years–of–age or older and charged with presumptive commitment to prison offenses. What justifies this common legislative strategy to use presumptions of unfitness based on the present offense or prior record to shift the burden of production and persuasion to the juvenile? *See e.g.*, Barry C. Feld, "Juvenile Court Legislative Reform and the Serious Young Offender: Dismantling the 'Rehabilitative Ideal'," 65 *Minn. L. Rev.* 167, 215 (1981), who observes that the use of presumptions and burden shifting reflects legislative policy to allocate the inevitable risks of error between the juvenile and the state in the face of the inherent uncertainty of clinical evaluations.

> Placing the burden of persuasion on a youth to prove amenability and nondangerousness would emphasize the policies of social defense and public safety in light of the uncertainty of the issues being determined. In many cases, a court cannot reliably determine whether a youth is amenable or dangerous. In these ambiguous cases the decision whether or not to waive is determined by which party bears the burden of persuasion. The legislative policies that justify creating a rebuttable presumption also justify placing the burden of persuasion on the juvenile rather than on the state.

Although many jurisdictions use offense criteria to create a presumption for certification, some courts have expressed reservations. The Court in **In the matter of William M.**, 124 Nev. 95, 196 P.3d 456 (Nev. 2008), considered the constitutionality of Nevada's certification statute. The law created a rebuttable presumption for waiver and placed the burden on the juvenile to rebut it with clear and convincing evidence that his criminal actions were substantially influenced by substance abuse or emotional or behavioral problems that may be appropriately treated within the jurisdiction of the juvenile court. The juveniles argued that the statute required them to admit to the charged, but unproven, criminal allegations and violated their Fifth Amendment privilege against self-incrimination. The court first held that *In re Gault* made the Fifth Amendment available to juveniles in certification proceedings. In a per curiam opinion, the court then considered whether the presumption statute violated juveniles' Fifth Amendment rights:

> We hold that, by requiring a juvenile to admit to the charged criminal conduct in order to overcome the presumption of adult certification, the presumptive certification statute violates the juvenile's Fifth Amendment right against self-incrimination. * * *
>
> Pursuant to NRS 62B.390, the State may move to certify a juvenile, over the age of 13, as an adult for the purpose of pursuing criminal proceedings against him or her on two bases: discretionary certification

and presumptive certification. * * * Presumptive certification applies if the juvenile is charged with either sexual assault involving the use or threatened use of force or violence or an offense involving the use or threatened use of a firearm and the juvenile was age 14 or older at the time the offense was committed. To rebut the presumption of certification, the juvenile must demonstrate by clear and convincing evidence that (1) he or she is developmentally or mentally incompetent to understand his or her situation and the proceedings of the court or to aid his or her attorney in those proceedings, or (2) that his or her actions were substantially the result of the substance abuse or emotional or behavioral problems of the child and the substance abuse or emotional or behavioral problems may be appropriately treated through the jurisdiction of the juvenile court. * * *

Appellants argue that Nevada's presumptive certification provisions violate their Fifth Amendment right against self-incrimination by requiring them to admit guilt to rebut the presumption of adult certification but failing to prohibit the admission of their incriminating statements in subsequent guilt-determination proceedings. * * *

[T]o rebut presumptive certification under the statute at issue here, the juvenile court must find by clear and convincing evidence that the juvenile's "actions ... were substantially the result of the substance abuse or emotional or behavioral problems." In *Anthony Lee R.*, this court recognized that while drugs and emotional or behavioral problems cannot be said to "cause" criminal conduct, they are often overwhelming factors that contribute to a juvenile's decision to commit a crime. Consequently, we interpreted * * * [the statute] as requiring the juvenile to rebut the presumption by establishing that substance abuse or emotional or behavioral problems had "substantially influenced or contributed to [the charged] criminal actions." Thus, under *Anthony Lee R.*'s interpretation of the rebuttal provision's operation, a juvenile must incriminate himself to rebut the certification presumption, as he must present clear and convincing evidence that due to a substance abuse, emotional, or behavioral problem, he committed the charged criminal actions. * * *

The juvenile court's current practice of requiring juveniles to establish a direct nexus between their substance abuse, emotional, or behavioral problems and the charged criminal conduct supports our conclusion that incriminating statements are required to rebut the certification presumption. * * * Thus, under *Anthony Lee R.*, NRS 62B.390(3)(b) appears to require the juvenile to make incriminating statements. * * *

Should the juvenile meet his burden under NRS 62B.390(3)(b) and *Anthony Lee R.*, the juvenile court may nonetheless certify the juvenile for criminal proceedings as an adult under the discretionary certification provision, NRS 62B.390(1). In determining whether to waive its jurisdiction under the discretionary certification provision, the juvenile court may consider the incriminating statements made by the juvenile in attempting to rebut the presumptive certification provision. Further, the juvenile's admission of the charged criminal conduct may ultimately be used against him in any adult criminal proceedings, if the statements are deemed to have been made voluntarily. And, although this court has not specifically addressed whether such statements may be admitted at a subsequent juvenile delinquency hearing, we have suggested that they could be admitted if made voluntarily, and nothing in the statute prohibits their admission. * * *

As a result, and because the statements arguably required under NRS 62B.390(3)(b) and *Anthony Lee R.* to rebut presumptive certification in juvenile proceedings are inculpatory in nature and invite exposure to commitment or imprisonment, since they may be used against the juveniles in subsequent delinquency and criminal proceedings that could directly result in a loss of liberty, the Fifth Amendment privilege against self-incrimination is available to juveniles in certification proceedings. * * *

The plain language of NRS 62B.390(3)(b) requires that a juvenile present clear and convincing evidence that his or her actions were substantially influenced by either substance abuse or emotional or behavioral problems. Clearly, the term "actions" refers to the charged criminal actions. Accordingly, a juvenile must present evidence that his substance abuse or emotional or behavioral problems substantially influenced his commission of the charged criminal actions. In other words, to rebut presumptive certification, the juvenile must incriminate himself. * * *

Even though presumptive certification is no longer available, the State may nonetheless petition for adult certification of juveniles who would have fallen under the presumptive certification provisions by seeking discretionary certification under NRS 62B.390(1). * * * Nothing in our decision today prevents the State from seeking certification of juveniles in appropriate cases under the discretionary certification provision. * * *

3. BLENDED JURISDICTION—AN INTEGRATED SENTENCING FRAMEWORK

Juvenile courts lose authority over young offenders when they attain the age of majority or some other statutory termination date. As a result, they cannot achieve proportionality when they sentence either older chronic juveniles or those youths convicted of very serious offenses. The jurisdictional limits heighten public and political perceptions that juvenile courts inadequately punish or control some youths and provide impetus either to to transfer more youths to criminal courts or further to increase juvenile courts' sanctioning powers.

Statutes that increase juvenile courts' punitive capacity to sentence violent and persistent young offenders provide some states with an alternative to waiving them to criminal court. These "blended" jurisdiction laws attempt to meld the rehabilitative sentencing authority of juvenile courts with the threat of criminal sanctions and to provide longer sentences for serious crimes than otherwise would be available to the juvenile court. These "blended" sentences provide juvenile courts with the option to punish as well as to treat youths of certain ages charged with serious or repeated offenses.

There are several variants of blended sentencing as Snyder and Sickmund, *National Report 2006*, briefly noted supra pp. 516–518. **Patricia Torbet, et al.,** ***State Responses to Serious and Violent Juvenile Crime* 11–15 (1996)** describes the forms that blended sentencing take and their relationship to waiver practices:

> Blended sentencing statutes represent a dramatic change in dispositional/sentencing options available to judges. Blended sentencing refers to the imposition of juvenile and/or adult correctional sanctions to cases involving serious and violent juvenile offenders who have been adjudicated in juvenile court or convicted in criminal court. Blended sentencing options are usually based on age or on a combination of age and offense. * * *

> Five basic model of blended sentencing have emerged in recent legislation. Each of the models applies to a subset of alleged juvenile offenders specified by State statute, usually defined by age and offense. In three of the models, the juvenile court retains responsibility for adjudicating the case. In the remaining models, the criminal court has jurisdiction for trying the case. Moreover, the models represent "exclusive" sanctioning (either juvenile or adult sanctions), "inclusive" sanctioning (both juvenile and adult sanctions), or "contiguous" sanctioning (first juvenile, then adult sanctions). The five models "blend" sentencing options in the following ways:

> *Juvenile–Exclusive Blend*: The juvenile court imposes a sanction involving either the juvenile correctional system or the adult correctional system.

> *Juvenile–Inclusive Blend*: The juvenile court simultaneously imposes both a juvenile correctional sanction and an adult correctional sanction, which is suspended pending a violation or revocation.

> *Juvenile–Contiguous*: The juvenile court imposes a juvenile correctional sanction that may remain in force beyond the age of its extended jurisdiction, at which point various procedures are invoked to transfer the case to the adult correctional system.

> *Criminal–Exclusive Blend*: The criminal court imposes either a juvenile or adult correctional sanction.

> *Criminal–Inclusive Blend*: The criminal court imposes both a juvenile and an adult correctional sanction and suspends the adult sentence pending a violation or re-offense.* * *

Juvenile blended sentencing laws begin with a youth's trial in juvenile court and then authorize the judge to impose enhanced sentences beyond those available for ordinary delinquents. Blended sentences in New Mexico, Minnesota, and Texas provide examples of three different versions of these enhanced sanctions for youths whom judges have not transferred to criminal court.

Juvenile–Exclusive Blend In 1993, New Mexico created a three-tier classification of "delinquent offender," "youthful offender," and "serious youthful offender." *N.M.Stat.Ann.* § 32A–2–3(C), (H), (I) (Michie 1993). The prosecutor selects which category to charge a young offender based on age and offense. A youth sixteen or seventeen years of age and charged with first degree murder constitutes a "serious youthful offender," and the court must sentence the youth as an adult. "Youthful offenders" consist of juveniles aged fifteen to seventeen years of age charged with legislatively designated aggravated or violent crimes, such as second degree murder, assault, rape, or robbery, or youths charged with any felony who have three prior felony adjudications within the previous two-year period. All "delinquents" and "youthful offenders" in New Mexico enjoy a statutory right to a jury trial in juvenile court, and the same judge may preside whether the case is tried as a juvenile or criminal proceeding. Following conviction as a "youthful offender," the juvenile court judge conducts a quasi-waiver sentencing hearing to decide whether to sentence the juvenile either as an adult or as a youthful offender. Depending upon the judge's assessment of a youth's "amenability to treatment or rehabilitation," *N.M.Stat.Ann.* § 32A–2–20(B)(1) (1998), the court may impose either an adult criminal sentence or a juvenile disposition with jurisdiction extended until age twenty-one. *N.M. Stat.Ann.* § 32A–2–20 (1993). Essentially, New Mexico tries youths in juvenile court with adult criminal procedural safeguards and then, after a finding of guilt, allows the judge either to impose an extended juvenile sentence or to sentence the youth as an adult.

Juvenile–Contiguous In 1987, Texas adopted a determinate sentencing law for juveniles convicted of certain violent crimes or as habitual offenders to provide an alternative to sentencing them either as ordinary delinquents or waiving them for adult prosecution. *Tex.Fam.Code Ann.* §§ 53.045, 54.04(d)(3) (Vernon Supp. 1988); Robert O. Dawson, "The Third Justice System: The New Juvenile Criminal System of Determinate Sentencing for the Youthful Violent Offender in Texas." 19 *St. Mary's Law J.* 943 (1988); Robert O. Dawson, "The Violent Juvenile Offender: An Empirical Study of Juvenile Determinate Sentencing Proceedings as an Alternative to Criminal Prosecution," 21 *Texas Tech L. Rev.* 1897 (1990); Eric Fritsch, Craig Hemmens, and Tory J. Caeti, "Violent Youth in Juvenile and Adult Court: An Assessment of Sentencing Strategies in Texas," 18 *Law & Pol'y* 115 (1996). To invoke the determinate sentencing law, the prosecutor must submit a petition to a grand jury and allege one of the enumerated violent or habitual crimes. If the indicted youth is convicted, "the court or jury may sentence the child to commitment to the Texas Youth Commission with a possible transfer to the institutional division or the pardons and paroles division of the Texas Department of Criminal Justice for a term of not more than" forty years for a capital or first degree felony, twenty years for a second degree felony, or ten years for a third degree felony. *Tex. Fam. Code Ann.* § 54.04(d)(3) (Vernon Supp. 1995). Juveniles receive the same procedural rights as do adult criminal defendants including the right to a jury trial. Juveniles begin their determinate sentences in juvenile facilities, and at age eighteen, a court conducts a sentencing review hearing, using *Kent*-like statutory criteria, to decide whether to retain them within the juvenile correctional system for the duration of their minority, until age twenty-one, or to complete their determinate sentence in the adult correction system. *Tex. Fam.Code Ann.* § 54.11(k) (Vernon 1995). The Texas law greatly increases the power of juvenile courts to impose substantial sentences on youths below fifteen years of age, the minimum age to transfer juveniles to criminal courts, as well as on older juveniles, and gives prosecutors a powerful plea bargaining tool and alternative to adult prosecution. In 1995, the Texas legislature increased from the original list of six to thirteen the number of offenses for which youths could receive determinate sentences, and increased the maximum length of determinate sentences from thirty to forty years. *Tex.Fam.Code Ann.* §§ 53.045, 54.04(d)(3) (Vernon 1995). Determinately sentenced youths served actual terms considerably longer than those of youths sentenced as ordinary delinquents. Fritch, Hemmens, and Caeti, *Violent Youth in Juvenile and Adult Court, supra*. A few other states, for example, Colorado and Massachusetts, have enacted provisions like Texas' that enable a juvenile court judge to impose a sentence on a youth convicted of a serious crime that extends beyond the maximum age of the juvenile court dispositional jurisdiction with completion of the sentence in adult correctional facilities. Patricia Torbet, et al., *State Responses to Serious and Violent Juvenile Crime: Research Report (1996)*.

Juvenile–Inclusive Blend In 1995, Minnesota created an intermediate category for serious young offenders called Extended Jurisdiction Juvenile (EJJ) prosecutions. *Minn.Stat.Ann.* § 260.126 (1995), *infra* at p. 590. The statutes restricts eligibility for EJJ prosecutions to youths sixteen years of age or older and charged with presumptive commitment to prison offenses like murder, rape, aggravated robbery, and assault, to youths whom judges decline to waive to criminal courts and sentence instead as EJJs, and to younger juveniles whom judges determine in an EJJ hearing meet offense-based "public safety" criteria. Juvenile courts try these EJJ youths in juvenile courts but provide them with all adult criminal procedural safeguards including the right to a jury trial. The right to a trial by jury constitutes an essential component of this quasi-adult status, because the judge imposes both a juvenile delinquency disposition and an adult criminal sentence, the execution of which is stayed, pending compliance with the juvenile sentence. *Minn. Stat. Ann.* § 260.126 (1995). Juvenile court dispositional jurisdiction continues until age twenty-one for EJJ youths rather than terminating at age nineteen as it does for ordinary delinquents. If the EJJ youth violates the conditions of the juvenile sentence, then the court may revoke the probation and execute the adult criminal sentence. Trying youths in juvenile courts with adult criminal procedural safeguards preserves access to juvenile correctional resources, provides longer periods of correctional supervision and control, and retains the possibility of adult incarceration if youths fail on probation or re-offend. Several other states have emulated this blended sentencing strategy.

Although the New Mexico, Minnesota, Texas, and other states' blended jurisdiction provisions differ in many details, they share several common features. Because the laws provide juvenile offenders with adult criminal procedural safeguards, they can acknowledge the reality of punishment in juvenile court. Once a state gives a juvenile the right to a jury trial and other criminal procedural safeguards, it retains the option to punish without apology, and thereby gains greater flexibility to treat a youth as well. These various enhanced sentencing strategies recognize that age jurisdictional limits of juvenile courts create binary forced-choices, either juvenile or adult, either treatment or punishment. By trying a juvenile with criminal procedural rights, these states preserve the option to extend jurisdiction for a period of several years or more beyond that available for ordinary delinquents. These "blended" provisions embody the procedural and substantive convergence between juvenile and criminal courts, provide a conceptual alternative to binary waiver statutes, and recognize that adolescence constitutes a developmental continuum that requires an increasing array of graduated sanctions. See e.g. Barry C. Feld, "Violent Youth and Public Policy: A Case Study of Juvenile Justice Law Reform," 79 *Minn. L. Rev.* 965 (1995); Mary E. Spring, "Extended Jurisdiction Juvenile Prosecution: A New Approach to the Problem of Juvenile Delinquency in Illinois," 31 *John Marshall L. Rev.* 1351 (1998); Randi–Lynn Smallheer, "Sentence Blending and the Promise of Rehabilitation: Bringing the Juvenile Justice System Full Circle," 28 *Hofstra L. Rev.* 259 (1999); Richard E. Redding and James C. Howell, "Blended Sentencing in American Juvenile Courts," in J. Fagan and F. Zimring, eds., *The Changing Border of Juvenile Justice 145* (2000); Patricia Torbet, et al., *Juveniles Facing Criminal Sanctions: Three States that Changed the Rules* (2000); Brandi Miles Moore, "Blended Sentencing for Juveniles: The Creation of a Third Criminal Justice System?", 22 *J. Juv. Law* 162 (2001); Christian Sullivan, "Juvenile Delinquency in the Twenty–First Century: Is Blended Sentencing the Middle–Road Solution for Violent Kids?," 21 *Northern Ill. U. L. Rev.* 483 (2001);

***Minn. Stat.* § 260.126 (1998). Extended jurisdiction juvenile prosecutions**

Subd. 1. Designation. A proceeding involving a child alleged to have committed a felony offense is an extended jurisdiction juvenile prosecution if:

(1) the child was 14 to 17 years old at the time of the alleged offense, a certification hearing was held, and the court designated the proceeding an extended jurisdiction juvenile prosecution;

(2) the child was 16 or 17 years old at the time of the alleged offense; the child is alleged to have committed an offense for which the sentencing guidelines and applicable statutes presume a commitment

to prison or to have committed any felony in which the child allegedly used a firearm; and the prosecutor designated in the delinquency petition that the proceeding is an extended jurisdiction juvenile prosecution; or

(3) the child was 14 to 17 years old at the time of the alleged offense, the prosecutor requested that the proceeding be designated an extended jurisdiction juvenile prosecution, a hearing was held on the issue of designation, and the court designated the proceeding an extended jurisdiction juvenile prosecution.

Subd. 2. Hearing on prosecutor's request. When a prosecutor requests that a proceeding be designated an extended jurisdiction juvenile prosecution, the court shall hold a hearing * * * to consider the request. * * * If the prosecutor shows by clear and convincing evidence that designating the proceeding an extended jurisdiction juvenile prosecution serves public safety, the court shall grant the request for designation. In determining whether public safety is served, the court shall consider the factors specified in section 260.125, subdivision 2b * * * [*supra* p. 580].

Subd. 3. Proceedings. A child who is the subject of an extended jurisdiction juvenile prosecution has the right to a trial by jury and to the effective assistance of counsel. * * *

Subd. 4. Disposition. (a) If an extended jurisdiction juvenile prosecution results in a guilty plea or finding of guilt, the court shall:

(1) impose one or more juvenile dispositions under section 260.185 [*infra* pp. 896–898]; and

(2) impose an adult criminal sentence, the execution of which shall be stayed on the condition that the offender not violate the provisions of the disposition order and not commit a new offense.

(b) If a child prosecuted as an extended jurisdiction juvenile after designation by the prosecutor in the delinquency petition is convicted of an offense after trial that is not an offense described in subdivision 1, clause (2), the court shall adjudicate the child delinquent and order a disposition under section 260.185. If the extended jurisdiction juvenile proceeding results in a guilty plea for an offense not described in subdivision 1, clause (2), the court may impose a disposition under paragraph (a) if the child consents.

Subd. 5. Execution of adult sentence. When it appears that a person convicted as an extended jurisdiction juvenile has violated the conditions of the stayed sentence, or is alleged to have committed a new offense, the court may, without notice, revoke the stay and probation and direct that the offender be taken into immediate custody. The court shall notify the offender in writing of the reasons alleged to exist for revocation of the stay of execution of the adult sentence. If the offender challenges the reasons, the court shall hold a summary hearing on the issue at which the offender is entitled to be heard and represented by counsel. After the hearing, if the court finds that reasons exist to revoke the stay of execution of sentence, the court shall treat the offender as an adult and order any of the adult sanctions authorized * * * If the offender was convicted of an offense described in subdivision 1, clause (2), and the court finds that reasons exist to revoke the stay, the court must order execution of the previously imposed sentence unless the court makes written findings regarding the mitigating factors that justify continuing the stay. * * *

IN THE MATTER OF L.J.S. AND J.T.K.

539 N.W.2d 408 (Minn. Ct. App. 1995).

LANSING, JUDGE. These consolidated certified questions raise constitutional challenges to the new extended jurisdiction juvenile statute and to the new presumption of certification applied in certain juvenile delinquency proceedings. See Minn. Stat. §§ 260.125, subd. 2a, 260.126, subd. 1(2). The trial court in each case denied defense challenges to the constitutionality of the statute, but certified the question as important and doubtful. We conclude that the statutes are constitutional and answer the consolidated certified questions in the negative.

In 1994 the legislature amended the laws pertaining to juveniles to provide extended jurisdiction that allows the juvenile court to retain jurisdiction until age twenty-one and to impose a juvenile disposition subject to a stayed adult penalty that can be imposed if the juvenile violates the conditions of his disposition or commits a new offense. * * *

Issues

The following issues are certified as important and doubtful:

I.   Is the provision in Minn.Stat. § 260.126, subd. 1(2) for prosecutor-designated extended jurisdiction juvenile proceedings unconstitutionally vague?

II.   Does the prosecutor-designated extended jurisdiction juvenile provision violate the separation of powers? * * *

Analysis

The section of Minn.Stat. § 260.126 at issue provides that a proceeding involving a child alleged to have committed a felony offense is an extended jurisdiction juvenile prosecution if: * * *

(2) the child was 16 or 17 years old at the time of the alleged offense; the child is alleged to have committed an offense for which the sentencing guidelines and applicable statutes presume a commitment to prison or to have committed any felony in which the child allegedly used a firearm; and the prosecutor designated in the delinquency petition that the proceeding is an extended jurisdiction juvenile prosecution. * * *.

J.T.K. asserts that this language is unconstitutionally vague and violates due process by creating the potential for arbitrary and discriminatory enforcement. * * *

A prosecutor can designate an extended jurisdiction juvenile proceeding only if the juvenile is sixteen or seventeen years old and only if the petition alleges an offense with a presumptively executed guidelines sentence or an offense involving use of a firearm. These criteria are very specific. They are neither vague nor conducive to arbitrary and discriminatory enforcement.

The Minnesota Supreme Court upheld the previous juvenile reference statute against a vagueness challenge when reference depended on suitability for juvenile treatment or whether public safety was served by proceeding in juvenile court. The criteria in the current statute for prosecutor-designated extended jurisdiction juvenile prosecutions are much more specific. The statute does not lack minimal guidelines for extended jurisdiction juvenile designation or give too much discretion to prosecutors in deciding what cases to designate. * * *

J.T.K. argues that the prosecutor's exclusive role in designating the extended jurisdiction juvenile proceedings under Minn.Stat. § 260.126, subd. 1(2) violates the separation of powers. He maintains that only the court can constitutionally designate a juvenile case as an extended jurisdiction juvenile proceeding because the designation sharply restricts the court's sentencing powers.

J.T.K. characterizes the prosecutor's designation of an extended jurisdiction juvenile prosecution as essentially a sentencing determination because it prevents the court from imposing a purely juvenile disposition. The state counters that the decision is merely a charging decision.

The Minnesota Supreme Court, in analyzing a similar issue, discounted the significance of the charging/sentencing distinction in juvenile proceedings * * *. The statute's provision for varying means of designation—by the court itself, by the court on the prosecutor's recommendation, or by the prosecutor based on the specific criteria—suggests that this decision is *sui generis*, with no analogue in criminal procedure. * * *

In analyzing a challenge to a similar federal statute, the D.C. Circuit Court of Appeals concluded that the statute did not violate due process or equal protection. *United States v. Bland*, [*infra* p. 601] (upholding statute allowing prosecutor to charge as adults, juveniles of a certain age who violate specified statutes). Although not directly addressing a separation-of-powers argument, *Bland* treated the prosecutor's discretion as merely a form of the charging discretion that had historically been accorded to the prosecutor. Courts in most other jurisdictions have followed the rationale of *Bland* and rejected separation-of-powers challenges to statutes giving a prosecutor absolute or conditional discretion to charge a juvenile as an adult. J.T.K. cites no contrary authority.

The U.S. Supreme Court has held that a juvenile is entitled to a hearing, the effective assistance of counsel, and a statement of reasons before the court can waive juvenile court jurisdiction. *Kent v. United States* (1966). But J.T.K. cites no authority holding that *Kent* prevents the legislature from giving the prosecutor sole discretion to decide that a juvenile should be prosecuted in adult court. Because the prosecutor's authority under Minn.Stat. § 260.126, subd. 1(2) is much more limited than that, and based on the persuasive authority from other jurisdictions, we conclude that the prosecutor-designated extended jurisdiction juvenile provision does not violate the separation of powers. * * *

The statutory provision for a prosecutor-designated extended jurisdiction juvenile proceeding is not unconstitutionally vague and does not violate the separation-of-powers doctrine. * * *

NOTES

1) Bases for EJJ Designation In **In the Matter of the Welfare of S.W.N.**, 541 N.W.2d 14 (Minn.Ct.App.1995), the Court of Appeals of Minnesota further clarified the EJJ legislation:

> If a child is 14 to 17 years old at the time of the charged offense, the prosecutor may move for an EJJ designation. A hearing is held, at which the prosecutor must show by clear and convincing evidence that "designating the proceeding an [EJJ] prosecution serves public safety." * * *

This is a case of first impression concerning the application of the new EJJ provisions. We apply the following standard of review in certification (formerly reference) cases: A juvenile court has considerable latitude in determining if certification for adult prosecution will be made. Its decision will not be upset unless its findings are clearly erroneous so as to constitute an abuse of discretion. In addition, for purposes of certification hearings, the charges against the juvenile are presumed to be true. We hold that these standards also govern this court's review of EJJ rulings.

Appellant argues that the EJJ designation was improperly based solely on his age and the seriousness of his offense. * * * The supreme court subsequently stated the rule as follows:

In order for the statutory reference standard to be satisfied, the record must contain direct evidence of dangerousness in addition to the inferences which may be drawn from the commission of the crime itself.

The rationale of this non-offense related evidence of dangerousness rule is that the legislature would have made reference as an adult mandatory for certain offenses had it intended that the seriousness of the offense alone would be sufficient to support reference.

We conclude that the same requirement of non-offense related evidence of dangerousness applies to motions for EJJ designation. The legislature may have intended that the EJJ classification serve as a middle ground appropriate for some juveniles who could not be certified for adult prosecution. Such an intent would accommodate threshold requirements somewhat more relaxed than those required for certification (formerly reference). A lower threshold does not necessarily mean, however, that EJJ designation should be permitted based solely on the charged offense because the legislature chose not to provide explicitly a list of offenses the seriousness of which required EJJ designation. The lower threshold for EJJ designation is demonstrated as follows: for certification, the prosecutor must show that retaining the child in the juvenile system does not serve public safety; for EJJ designation, on the other hand, the prosecutor need only show that such designation serves public safety. We hold that the prosecuting authority must submit non-offense related evidence of dangerousness to show that an EJJ designation serves public safety.

We disagree with appellant's contention that the "non-offense related evidence" requirement has not been met in the instant case. It is true that appellant had no prior record of delinquency and that the prosecutor presented no evidence that appellant has engaged in any harmful conduct other than the charged offenses. Evidence supporting EJJ designation of appellant is compelling, however, including appellant's diagnoses with a conduct disorder and explosive intermittent disorder, his lack of a conscience or any remorse, and his continuing inappropriate subjection to influences of his father, whose own violent crimes against appellant's mother inspired the charged offenses. Appellant's offenses are manifestations of appellant's emotional problems; the risk to public safety results from these problems. We conclude that the prosecuting authority satisfied its burden of presenting non-offense related evidence of the risk to public safety posed by appellant. * * *

2) Systemic Impact of Blended Sentencing Laws on Juvenile Justice Administration Analyses of blended sentencing provisions note that they have a number of systemic consequences. See e.g., **Patricia Torbet, et al.,** *Juveniles Facing Criminal Sanctions: Three States that Changed the Rules* 43–44 (2000), who report that blended sentencing encourages plea bargaining, gives prosecutors greater authority, and introduce geographic disparities in juvenile justice administration:

It is common practice in Minnesota for prosecutors to file a motion for criminal certification and then 'bargain down' to extended jurisdiction in juvenile court. As a result, first-time serious offenders in Minnesota, most of whom are unlikely to be certified, are being designated as EJJ cases. * * *

The authority to decide when juvenile offenders are beyond the rehabilitative reach of the juvenile justice system was once entrusted almost exclusively to juvenile court judges. In the first half of the 1990's, however, that changed considerably as more and more States passed laws excluding serious offenses from juvenile court jurisdiction or granting transfer authority to prosecutors. * * * New blended sentencing laws have also greatly expanded prosecutors' authority by entrusting them with broad discretion to decide when to seek special offender designations or criminal sentencing options. These decisions are generally not subject to formal guidelines or systematic reporting requirements. * * *

The case studies documented significant differences in the way local jurisdictions apply blended sentencing laws. * * * In Minnesota, data revealed considerable differences between urban and rural jurisdiction with regard to applying the extended jurisdiction designation to property offenders. Consideration should be given to setting meaningful guidelines for the exercise of both prosecutorial and judicial discretion in making designation, sentencing, and review decisions under the reforms to ensure fair and appropriate decisionmaking. * * *

Most commentators have written approvingly of blended sentencing "as a compromise protecting the safety of society and the needs of youthful offenders, by ensuring accountability and providing rehabilitation." Randi–Lynn Smallheer, "Sentencing Blending and the Promise of Rehabilitation: Bringing the Juvenile Justice System Full Circle," 28 *Hofstra L. Rev.* 259, 289 (1999). *See e.g.*, Brandi Miles Moore, "Blended Sentencing for Juveniles: The Creation of a Third Criminal Justice System," 22 *J. Juv. L.* 126 (2001); Christian Sullivan, "Juvenile Delinquency in the Twenty–First Century: Is Blended Sentencing the Middle–Road Solution for Violent Kids?,"21 *N. Ill. U. L. Rev.* 483 (2001); Kristin L. Caballero, "Blended Sentencing: A Good Idea for Juvenile Sex Offenders," 19 *St. J. J. L. C.* 379 (2005); Mary Spring, "Extended Jurisdiction Juvenile Prosecution: A New Approach to the Problem of Juvenile Delinquency in Illinois," 31 John Marshall L. Rev. 1351 (1998).

3) Net—Widening Impact of Blended Sentencing Several studies examined waiver practices in Hennepin County (Minneapolis), Minnesota, prior to and after the adoption of the EJJ provisions. *See* Marcy Rasmussen Podkopacz & Barry C. Feld, "Judicial Waiver Policy and Practice: Persistence, Seriousness, and Race," 14 *J. Law & Ineq.* 73 (1995); Marcy Rasmussen Podkopacz & Barry C. Feld, "The End of the Line: An Empirical Study of Judicial Waiver," 86 *J. Crim. L. & Criminology* 449 (1996). These studies provided a base-line against which to evaluate the effect of adopting the "blended sentencing" option in addition to the changes in waiver. *See e.g.*, Barry C. Feld, "Violent Youth and Public Policy: A Case Study of Juvenile Justice Law Reform," 79 *Minn. L. Rev.* 965 (1995). **Marcy Rasmussen Podkopacz and Barry C. Feld, "The Back–Door to Prison: Waiver Reform, 'Blended Sentencing,' and the Law of Unintended Consequences," 91 *J. Crim. L. & Criminology* 997, 1067–71 (2001)**, evaluated the impact of the new waiver and EJJ laws. They analyzed the 504 cases in which Hennepin County prosecutors filed either certification or EJJ motions or designations during the first three years of the new law's implementation, 1995–1997. They compared the characteristics of offenders and their subsequent sentences under the previous waiver legislation and under the new blended sentencing and certification laws. They reported significant "net-widening" effects with the adoption of the new juvenile sentencing option:

The youths against whom prosecutors filed waiver and EJJ motions under the new law differed significantly from those whom they previously sought to transfer. Under the presumptive certification and blended sentencing laws, prosecutors filed motions against a younger group of youths who began their delinquent careers somewhat later than our previous sample. They also filed motions against an even larger proportion of minority, almost exclusively African–American, and female youths than the previous practice.

Prosecutors and judges emphasized the seriousness of youths' offenses rather than their persistence of delinquency. Prosecutors charged a significantly larger proportion of these youths than in our previous study with presumptive commitment to prison offenses, and with the use of a weapon in the commission of their crimes. Although prosecutors charged the vast majority of these youths with violent crimes, they also filed fewer charges than under the previous practice. In short, one serious crime was sufficient to trigger the filing of a certification or EJJ motion. Because the prosecutors emphasized primarily serious, violent offenses, the youths against whom they filed certification and EJJ motions had significantly less extensive prior records than did the juveniles in our previous sample–fewer prior felony adjudications, fewer prior adjudications for felonies against the person or presumptive commitment to prison offenses, and correspondingly fewer prior out-of-home placements or other treatment interventions.

When we compared those youths against whom prosecutors filed certification motions versus EJJ motions, several similarities and differences emerged. The two groups did not differ significantly on the basis of race, gender, or age-of-onset of delinquency. Prosecutors differentiated somewhat between EJJ and certification youths on the basis of the seriousness of their present offenses with certification motions more likely against youths charged with felonies against the person, multiple felonies, the use of a weapon, and presumptive commitment to prison offenses. The two groups also differed significantly on the basis of age—prosecutors filed more certification motions against older youths and more EJJ motions against younger offenders. Arguably, this differentiation on the basis of age is consistent with the legislative intent, although one reason for extending juvenile courts' jurisdiction was to provide the option to treat older juveniles for a longer period of time. Although prosecutors filed more certification motions against older youths, the youths against whom they filed EJJ versus waiver motions did not differ significantly on the basis of their prior delinquency histories or treatment interventions. In short, age and the seriousness of the present offense provided the primary rationale to distinguish between these two groups of young offenders.

The apparent differences between the EJJ and certification youths also encouraged us to examine more closely the subsequent dispositions of these two categories. Clearly, the introduction of the EJJ law has widened the net of criminal social control. "Net widening" occurs when reformers introduce a new sanction intended to be used in lieu of another sanction which is more severe, in this instance, EJJ blended sentencing in lieu of certification and imprisonment as an adult. As an alternative to a system of binary sanctions such as presented by traditional waiver—either juvenile or adult, either treatment or punishment—judges more often impose Intermediate Sanctions not on those who previously would have been waived or punished, but rather on those who previously would have been treated less severely than the new sanction permits. * * * Analysts contend that public officials and practitioners often use intermediate sanctions for less serious offenders than those for whom the program initially was envisioned because they are risk averse and do not want to be held responsible for the new crimes some offenders inevitably will commit.

Prior to the adoption of the EJJ law, prosecutors filed an average over 47 transfer motions per year. Following the adoption of the presumptive waiver and EJJ statutes, prosecutors filed an average of 168 motions that exposed youths either to the immediate or secondary possibility of criminal sanctions. Judges previously transferred an average of 31 youths for criminal prosecution and subsequently transferred about 33 youths each year. Significantly, however, judges sentenced an average of 83 additional youths each year under the EJJ provisions, which included a stayed adult criminal sentence. These EJJ youths were considerably younger than those juveniles against whom prosecutors previously or presently filed waiver motions and appeared to be somewhat less serious offenders. Despite their relative lack of criminal maturity or seriousness, a sizeable proportion of these EJJ youths (35.3%) failed during their juvenile probationary period. And the majority of these failures (76.2%) consisted of probation violations rather than serious new offenses. This experience with EJJ is consistent with a substantial body of research on "intermediate sanctions" which also reports higher rates of violation of technical conditions of probation than for comparable offenders subject to ordinary probation or punishment. * * * And, when judges revoked these EJJ youths' probation, they sentenced substantial numbers of them to the workhouse and to prison for violations which ordinarily would not warrant certification or incarceration in the first instance. "If a new correctional program is justified and funded to serve as an alternative to incarceration and is instead used for people who would otherwise not have been incarcerated, patently, it has been misapplied." As a result, it appears that the blended sentencing law which the legislature hoped would give juveniles "one last chance" for treatment has instead become their "first and last chance" for treatment, widened the net of criminal social control, and moved larger numbers of younger and less serious or chronic youths into the adult correctional system indirectly through the "back door" of probation revocation proceedings rather than through certification hearings.

Although prosecutors charge most EJJ youths with serious offenses, prior to the enactment of the blended sentencing law, the juvenile justice system adequately dealt with most of these youths as ordinary delinquents. The adoption of the EJJ provisions and the creation of an intermediate sanction appears to sentence more severely offenders who otherwise would have been dealt with as ordinary delinquents rather than those who previously were bound for prison. And the new "back door" of revocation proceedings consigns to prison youths whom judges previously and currently would deem inappropriate for prison in the context of a certification hearing. * * *

C. LEGISLATIVE OFFENSE EXCLUSION AND PROSECUTORIAL DIRECT–FILE

The Minnesota legislature reacted to Judge Ring's decision to retain juvenile court jurisdiction by amending the definition of juvenile court jurisdiction to provide that "The term delinquent child does not include a child alleged to have committed murder in the first degree after becoming 16 years of age * * *." Minn. Stat. § 260.015 Subd. 5 (b) (West 1999).

Recall the excerpt by Howard Snyder and Melissa Sickmund, *Juvenile Offenders and Victims*, *supra* at p. 516, noted that many jurisdictions exclude certain categories of age and serious offenses from the jurisdiction of their juvenile courts.

Legislative offense exclusion removes from juvenile court jurisdiction youths charged with certain offenses or in conjunction with a prior record, and provides the primary conceptual alternative to judicial waiver. It bases a youth's delinquent or criminal status on the nature of the offense charged rather than an assessment of the youth's "amenability to treatment." Concurrent jurisdiction or direct-file laws grant to prosecutors the power to choose whether to charge a youth in juvenile or criminal court without justifying that decision in a judicial hearing or with a formal record. State legislatures create juvenile courts by statute and define their jurisdiction, powers, and purposes in many different ways. What they create, they also may modify or take away. For example, states currently set juvenile courts' maximum age jurisdiction at seventeen, sixteen, or fifteen years old as a matter of state policy and without any constitutional infirmity. If a legislature defines juvenile court jurisdiction to include only those persons below a jurisdictional age and whom prosecutors charge with a non-excluded offense, then, by statutory definition, all other chronological juveniles are "adult" criminal defendants.

Analysts long have criticized statutes that mandate adult prosecution on the basis of the offense charged rather than the characteristics of the offender or that give prosecutors authority to choose the jurisdictional forum without any judicial review because they conflict with the rehabilitative philosophy of the juvenile court. Wallace Mylniec, "Juvenile Delinquent or Adult Convict—Prosecutor's Choice," 14 *Am. Crim. L. Rev.* 29 (1976); Catherine R. Guttman, "Listen to the Children: The Decision to Transfer Juveniles to Adult Court." 30 *Harvard Civ. Rights—Civ. Lib. L. Rev.* 507 (1995); Eric K. Klein, "Dennis the Menace or Billy the Kid: An Analysis of the Role of Transfer to Criminal Court in Juvenile Justice." 35 *Am. Crim. L. Rev.* 371 (1998). Similarly, excluded youths tried in criminal courts have challenged their "automatic adulthood" as a denial of due process because they do not receive the procedural safeguards required by *Kent*, and contended that offense exclusion violates equal protection because basing their delinquent or criminal status on the alleged offense constitutes an arbitrary legislative classification. These youths direct their due process claims at the lack of judicial review of prosecutors' discretionary charging decisions that result in their removal to criminal court. Their equal protection claims question the rationality of the legislative decision to classify youths charged with certain offenses as adults rather than as juveniles.

1. EXCLUSION OF OFFENSES FROM JUVENILE COURT JURISDICTION

As you read the following statutes, note how they differ. How broad or narrow are the range of excluded offenses? What are the minimum ages at which the state may prosecute a juvenile in criminal court? What administrative or jurisprudential problems would you anticipate if the cases of 15 year old offenders originate in criminal court? Fourteen year old offenders? Thirteen year old offenders? Even younger offenders? What would be the appropriate disposition of a youth whom a criminal court convicts of a lesser included offense that the jurisdictional statute does not exclude?

Conn. Statute. § 46b–127 (West 1999)

(a) The court shall automatically transfer from the docket for juvenile matters to the regular criminal docket of the Superior Court the case of any child charged with the commission of a capital felony, a class A or B felony * * * provided such offense was committed after such child attained the age of fourteen years and counsel has been appointed for such child if such child is indigent. * * * The child shall be arraigned in the regular criminal docket of the Superior Court at the next court date following such transfer. * * *

(c) Upon the effectuation of the transfer, such child shall stand trial and be sentenced, if convicted, as if he were sixteen years of age [the age of criminal court jurisdiction]. * * * A child who has been transferred may enter a guilty plea to a lesser offense if the court finds that such plea is made knowingly and voluntarily. Any child transferred to the regular criminal docket who pleads guilty to a lesser offense shall not resume his status as a juvenile regarding said offense. If the action is dismissed or nolled or if such child is found not guilty of the charge for which he was transferred or of any lesser included offenses, the child shall resume his status as a juvenile until he attains the age of sixteen years. * * *

Under New York Criminal Procedure Law § 180.75 (West 1999), the state tries a "Juvenile Offender" in criminal court as contrasted with a "juvenile delinquent" over whom the family court has jurisdiction.

New York Criminal Procedure Law § 1.20 (West 1999) provides the following definition of a "Juvenile Offender":

(42) "Juvenile offender" means (1) a person, thirteen years old who is criminally responsible for acts constituting murder in the second degree * * * and (2) a person fourteen or fifteen years old who is criminally responsible for acts constituting the crimes defined in subdivisions one and two of section 125.25 (murder in the second degree) and in subdivision three of such section provided that the underlying crime for the murder charge is one for which such person is criminally responsible; * * * kidnapping in the first degree; * * * arson in the first degree; * * * assault in the first degree; * * * manslaughter in the first degree; * * * rape in the first degree; * * * sodomy in the first degree; * * * aggravated

sexual abuse; * * * burglary in the first degree; * * * burglary in the second degree; * * * arson in the second degree; * * * robbery in the first degree; * * * robbery in the second degree * * *; subdivision four of section 265.02 of the penal law, where such firearm is possessed on school grounds * * *; or section 265.03 of the penal law, where such machine gun or such firearm is possessed on school grounds * * *; or defined in the penal law as an attempt to commit murder in the second degree or kidnapping in the first degree.

Can a legislature exclude youths from juvenile court jurisdiction based on their age and offense without violating due process or equal protection? Should they exclude youths without any judicial review of the youth's "amenability to treatment" or evaluation of the validity of the prosecutor's charges? Why? If state legislatures can and should excise some youths from the jurisdiction of the juvenile court, who are appropriate candidates for exclusion? *See*, Barry C. Feld, "Legislative Exclusion of Offenses from Juvenile Court Jurisdiction: A History and Critique," in Jeffrey Fagan and Franklin E. Zimring, *The Changing Borders of Juvenile Justice: Transfer of Adolescents to the Criminal Court* (2000).

UNITED STATES v. BLAND

472 F.2d 1329 (D.C.Cir. 1972).

WILKEY, CIRCUIT JUDGE. The United States as statutory appellant seeks review of a memorandum opinion and order of the United States District Court for the District of Columbia, holding 16 D.C.Code § 2301(3)(A) unconstitutional as (1) an arbitrary legislative classification and (2) a negation of the presumption of innocence. Section 2301(3)(A) provides:

> The term "child" means an individual who is under 18 years of age, except that the term "child" does not include an individual who is sixteen years of age or older and—
>
> (A) charged by the United States Attorney with (i) murder, forcible rape, burglary in the first degree, robbery while armed, or assault with intent to commit any such offense, or (ii) an offense listed in clause (i) and any other offense properly joinable with such an offense. * * *

[Appellee was sixteen at the time of his arrest and indictment on charges of armed robbery of a post office and related offenses. He moved to dismiss the indictment for lack of jurisdiction and asserted the statute to prosecute him as an adult violated the constitution because it denied him procedural due process.] The District Court dismissed the indictment.

Congress, pursuant to its constitutional authority to exercise exclusive jurisdiction over the District of Columbia, created the Family Division of the Superior Court of the District of Columbia. In defining the jurisdiction of the Family Division, Congress conferred on it exclusive jurisdiction of "proceedings in which a child, as defined in section 16–2301, is alleged to be delinquent, neglected, or in need of supervision." Thus, the Family

Division's jurisdiction extends over a person—a child—alleged to have committed delinquent acts, a child being classified as a person not having yet reached the chronological age of 18 and not charged by the United States Attorney with certain specified crimes. As to any other individual, either one who has reached 18 or who has reached the age of 16 and has been charged by the United States Attorney with one or more of the enumerated felonies, he is not a child and is to be prosecuted in the regular adult court system, whether it be the D.C. Superior Court or the United States District Court.

The legislative history accompanying 16 D.C.Code § 2301 reveals Congress' intent in enacting this legislation: To improve the operation of the juvenile justice system in the District of Columbia by removing from its jurisdiction certain individuals between the ages of 16 and 18 whom Congress concluded (1) were beyond rehabilitation in the juvenile justice system, and (2) whose presence in that system served as a negative influence on other juveniles. This represents a policy judgment of Congress, after gathering extensive appropriate evidence, as to how persons should be classified as "adult" and "child" for the purposes of rehabilitation following the commission of a criminal offense. We note that the policy judgment was both negative and positive: some previously classified as juveniles were beyond rehabilitation; others of the same chronological age were susceptible to special juvenile treatment, and for any chance of success these latter should be protected against the hard-core repeat offenders of the same chronological age.

While Congress easily could have established 16 as the age cutoff date (it is not clear what constitutional infirmities our dissenting colleague would have found in that less sympathetic approach), it concluded that some within the 16–18 age bracket were susceptible of rehabilitation, and determined that those age 16 and 17 whose offenses charged were minor were to be included within the juvenile system. * * *

The Senate Committee on the District of Columbia, in revealing its rationale for excluding such persons from the jurisdiction of the Family Division, stated:

> The Committee has concluded that a juvenile can reliably be considered too well formed or sophisticated for, and beyond the reach of, mere juvenile therapy if the particular juvenile has already been exposed, in years of relative discretion, to the juvenile system and treated to the extent that his case required (as suggested by a prior finding of delinquency), and has nevertheless returned to serious misconduct (as suggested by a serious felony charge). * * *

The House Committee on the District of Columbia, * * * gave the following as the basis for its exclusion of those 16 years of age or older charged with a certain serious crime from the Family Division's jurisdiction:

> Because of the great increase in the number of serious felonies committed by juveniles and because of the substantial difficulties in

transferring juvenile offenders charged with serious felonies to the jurisdiction of the adult court under present law, provisions are made in this subchapter for a better mechanism for separation of the violent youthful offender and recidivist from the rest of the juvenile community.

As finally enacted, Section 2301 reflects a compromise between the initial Senate and House versions. It provides that the Family Division shall have jurisdiction over "persons under 18 except those 16 and older charged * * * with murder, forcible rape, robbery while armed, burglary in the first degree, or assault with intent to commit one of these offenses, or any such offense and a properly joinable offense." * * *

The District Court found Section 2301(3)(A) invalid as violative of due process of law:

> The determination that a child should be tried as an adult cannot be made without the safeguard of basic due process. Without a provision in the new statute that would require some determination, reached after a fair hearing, that an individual is beyond the help of the Family Division, that statute must fall as violative of due process. * * *

As the discussion on the legislative background * * * indicates, Congress was well acquainted with the problems confronting the juvenile justice system in the District of Columbia; logically its definition of the Family Division's jurisdiction reflects its particular concern with the rise in the number of serious crimes committed by those 16 years of age and over coupled with the growing recidivist rate among this group.

Secondly, legislative exclusion of individuals charged with certain specified crimes from the jurisdiction of the juvenile justice system is not unusual. * * * Several states have similarly excluded certain crimes in defining the jurisdiction of their respective systems of juvenile justice, while others vest concurrent jurisdiction over enumerated crimes in both their adult and juvenile courts. * * *

The disagreement of our dissenting colleague arises almost solely from his fundamental unwillingness to accept Congress' power to define what is a "child." The words "child," "infant," and "minor" from early times in various legal systems have been susceptible to definition by statute; the critical "age" for specified purposes has varied, and differed between male and female. Before 1970 the District of Columbia Code defined "child" as "a person under 18 years of age." Our dissenting colleague seems to consider this statute and its definition immutable, apparently because it was involved in *Kent v. United States*; we accept the fact that Congress has abolished this statutory definition and by statute substituted another, to which we simply give full effect. * * *

Believing that Congress has power to amend a statutory definition, we start with the definition of "child" currently on the statute books, and reach the legal conclusions set forth herein.

Similarly, the appellee's argument on an alleged "waiver" of the jurisdiction of the Family Court is based on the now outmoded definition. The District of Columbia Code states clearly that the jurisdiction of the Family Division of the Superior Court in delinquency cases is limited to those who come within the statutory definition of "child." * * * Until it is determined whether a person is a "child" within the statutory definition, there is no jurisdiction; therefore, *a fortiori* there can be no waiver of jurisdiction.

Nor is it true "a suspected juvenile remains a child until he is charged with an enumerated offense by the United States Attorney." There is just no classification of the person as a child or an adult until (1) his age is accurately ascertained, and (2) the decision on prosecution is made. Congress has incorporated more than one element in the definition of a "child." Until all the elements of the definition are ascertained, the status of the person is simply uncertain, just as under the 1967 definition the status of a person would be uncertain until his true age was established.

The District Court's finding in the case at bar, and appellee's assertion to the same effect—that the exercise of the discretion vested by Section 2301(3) (A) in the United States Attorney to charge a person 16 years of age or older with certain enumerated offenses, thereby initiating that person's prosecution as an adult, violates due process—ignores the long and widely accepted concept of prosecutorial discretion, which derives from the constitutional principle of separation of powers. The Fifth Circuit, in holding that a court had no power to compel a United States Attorney to sign an indictment, stated:

> Although as a member of the bar, the attorney for the United States is an officer of the court, he is nevertheless an executive official of the Government, and it is as an officer of the executive department that he exercises a discretion as to whether or not there shall be prosecution in a particular case. It follows, as an incident of the constitutional separation of powers, that the courts are not to interfere with the free exercise of the discretionary powers of the attorneys of the United States in their control over criminal prosecutions.

While there may be circumstances in which courts would be entitled to review the exercise of prosecutorial discretion, these circumstances would necessarily include the deliberate presence of such factors as "race, religion, or other arbitrary classification," not found in the case at bar.[24] For example, in the absence of such factors, this court has held that the exercise of prosecutorial discretion, even when it results in different treatment of codefendants originally charged in the same case with the same offense, does not violate due process or equal protection of the law.

---

24. As the Supreme Court suggested in *Oyler v. Boles*:

Moreover, the conscious exercise of some selectivity in enforcement is not in itself a federal constitutional violation. Even though the statistics in this case might imply a policy of selective enforcement, it is not stated that the selection was deliberately based upon an unjustifiable standard such as race, religion or other arbitrary classification. Therefore grounds supporting a finding of a denial of equal protection were not alleged.

The District Court and appellee in the case at bar point to the acknowledged significant effect of the United States Attorney's decision whether to charge an individual 16 years of age or older with certain enumerated offenses, and conclude that, in the absence of a hearing, due process is violated when such a decision is made. This, however, overlooks the significance of a variety of other common prosecutorial decisions, e.g., whether to charge one person but not another possible codefendant; whether to charge an individual with a misdemeanor or a felony; etc. Furthermore, the decision whether to charge an individual with a misdemeanor or a felony has long determined the court in which that person will be tried. We cannot accept the hitherto unaccepted argument that due process requires an adversary hearing before the prosecutor can exercise his age-old function of deciding what charge to bring against whom. Grave consequences have always flowed from this, but never has a hearing been required. * * *

[J]udicial consideration of the legitimate scope of prosecutorial discretion clearly encompasses the exercise of such discretion where it has the effect of determining whether a person will be charged as a juvenile or as an adult. In the absence of such "suspect" factors as "race, religion, or other arbitrary classification," the exercise of discretion by the United States Attorney in the case at bar involves no violation of due process or equal protection of the law.

The District Court and appellee assert that the exercise of discretion * * * violates due process in that it denies the individual charged the presumption of innocence. * * * The presumption of innocence, as the Supreme Court has long held, applies to the prosecution at trial and " * * * is a conclusion drawn by the law in favor of the citizen, by virtue whereof, when brought to trial upon a criminal charge, he must be acquitted, unless he is proven (beyond a reasonable doubt) to be guilty." * * * The United States Attorney's decision in the case at bar marks only the beginning of the process of adjudication of appellee's guilt, a process marked by the presence of all the traditional protections or procedural due process, followed by the extraordinarily liberal rehabilitation provisions of the Federal Youth Corrections Act.

For these reasons, the order of the District Court dismissing appellee's indictment, on the basis of its opinion holding 16 D.C.Code § 2301(3)(A) unconstitutional as an arbitrary legislative classification and as a negation of the presumption of innocence, is accordingly reversed and the case remanded for trial.

Reversed and remanded.

J. SKELLY WRIGHT, CIRCUIT JUDGE, dissenting. As a matter of abstract legal analysis, the opinion of my brethren might appear to some degree persuasive. But we do not sit to decide questions in the abstract, and we are not writing on a clean slate. In 1966 the Supreme Court spoke clearly and specifically about this area. *See Kent v. United States.* It held, in unmistakable terms, that before a child under 18 can be tried in adult court the Constitution requires a hearing "sufficient in the particular circumstances to satisfy the basic requirements of due process and fairness * * *." I had not supposed that it was within our power as a lower federal court to change this mandate. Nor had I imagined that Congress could "overrule" this constitutional decision by a simple statutory enactment. Yet the majority holds that whereas before passage of the Court Reform Act of 1970 the Constitution required a hearing, after its passage the Constitution requires no such thing. * * *

Before 1970 the District of Columbia Code defined "child" as "a person under 18 years of age" [and] granted "original and exclusive jurisdiction" to the Juvenile Court for the trial of children. * * * Thus initially any person under the age of 18 was to be tried in Juvenile Court. It did not necessarily follow, however, that such a trial always took place. * * * [T]he Juvenile Court was permitted to "waive" jurisdiction over a child 16 years of age or older who was charged with a felony or over any child charged with a crime punishable by death or life imprisonment [following a "full investigation."] * * *

Matters stood at this point when, in 1966, the Supreme Court considered the statute in its landmark *Kent* decision. The Court began its analysis by observing that the waiver decision was vitally important to the accused—that, indeed, it could potentially mean the difference between a few years confinement and a death penalty. * * * In light of the obviously crucial nature of these rights, the Court affirmed the * * * requirements of access to social records and assistance of counsel during waiver proceedings. But it also held that the statute, when "read in the context of constitutional principles relating to due process and the assistance of counsel," required more. Specifically, the juvenile was "entitled to a hearing * * * and to a statement of reasons for the Juvenile Court's decision."

Thus during the period immediately after *Kent* juveniles were afforded a wide range of procedural rights in connection with waiver proceedings. So matters stood until 1970 when, in conjunction with sweeping legislation to reform the District of Columbia judicial system, Congress made some innocuous sounding changes in the Juvenile Court's jurisdiction. The new legislation retained the basic waiver mechanism, although the statute now explicitly provided for a hearing and a statement of reasons and established some standards to guide the judge in making the waiver decision. Similarly, the new statute continued to grant "exclusive jurisdiction" to the Family Court for "proceedings in which a child, as defined in section 16–2301, is alleged to be delinquent * * *." But whereas previously a "child" had been defined to include all persons 18 years of age or younger, the new [Code] excepted from the definition "an individual who is sixteen years of age or older and * * * charged by the United States Attorney with (i) murder, forcible rape, burglary in the first degree, robbery while armed, or assault with intent to commit any such offense, or (ii) an offense listed in clause (i) and any other offense properly joinable with such an offense."

As a moment's reflection makes clear, this so-called "definition" in fact establishes a second, parallel waiver procedure whereby a juvenile can be transferred from the Family Division to adult court. If the Government chooses, it may institute waiver proceedings in Family Court and attempt to convince the judge that under the standards enunciated in the Act the child could more appropriately be tried in adult court. It would be surprising if this procedure were much utilized in cases covered by 16 D.C.Code § 2301(3)(A), however, since under it the Government must observe the procedural rules mandated by *Kent*. Moreover, there is always the possibility that the Government will not carry its burden before the Family Court judge, in which case the waiver attempt would fail.

These risks and inconveniences can be avoided by following the second alternative. If the prosecutor simply charges the juvenile with one of the enumerated offenses, the juvenile ceases to be a "child" * * * and, hence, the Family Court is automatically divested of jurisdiction. Thus if the prosecutor follows the second alternative the waiver decision becomes his alone, and he is permitted to make it without the encumbrance of a hearing, the requirement that he state reasons, the inconvenience of bearing the burden of proof, or the necessity of appointing counsel for the accused.

I think it obvious that this second procedure was written into the Act in order to countermand the Supreme Court's decision in *Kent*. * * * Indeed, the House Committee primarily responsible for drafting the provision virtually admitted as much. The Committee Report explains 16 D.C.Code § 2301(3)(A) as follows:

"Because of the great increase in the number of serious felonies committed by juveniles and because of the substantial difficulties in transferring juvenile offenders charged with serious felonies to the jurisdiction of the adult court under present law, provisions are made in this subchapter for a better mechanism for separation of the violent youthful offender and recidivist from the rest of the juvenile community."

While the surface veneer of legalese which encrusts this explanation need fool no one, a simultaneous translation into ordinary English might, perhaps, prove helpful. The "substantial difficulties * * * under present law" to which the Committee coyly refers are, of course, none other than the constitutional rights explicated in the *Kent* decision. And the "better mechanism" which the Committee proposes is a system for running roughshod over those rights in a manner which is unlikely to encourage those of us still committed to constitutionalism and the rule of law.

This blatant attempt to evade the force of the *Kent* decision should not be permitted to succeed. The result in *Kent* did not turn on the particular wording of the statute involved or on the particular waiver mechanism there employed. Rather, as the Court itself made clear, the rights expounded in *Kent* are fundamental and immutable. * * *

The issue in this case is not whether the prosecutor should be permitted to make waiver decisions, but rather how he should go about making those decisions. Put slightly differently, the question is whether the shift in decision making responsibility from the court to the prosecutor eliminates the need for the procedural rights expounded in *Kent*. I would, of course, answer that question "no." The transfer of the waiver decision from the neutral judge to the partisan prosecutor increases rather than diminishes the need for due process protection for the child. In answering the question "yes" the Government and the majority here rely on essentially three lines of argument. Although these contentions are interrelated, for purposes of analysis they are best addressed seriatim.

The Government first argues that the *Kent* decision should be limited to situations in which the Government attempts to retract some pre-existing right, and that this is not such a situation. * * * As the Government reads *Kent*, its holding is restricted to cases where the Family Court has exclusive jurisdiction *ab initio* and the prosecutor attempts to wrest this jurisdiction from it. After passage of the Court Reform Act, it is argued, the Family Court is no longer vested with exclusive jurisdiction over persons between 16 and 18 who are suspected of committing serious felonies. Rather, the Government contends, this jurisdiction is now concurrent, and the United States Attorney is vested with the authority to determine the forum in which to proceed. Since there is no longer a pre-existing right to juvenile treatment, there is no longer a necessity to observe the procedural formalities which, under *Kent*, must accompany divestiture of such a right.

Despite the superficial plausibility of this argument, I think it plainly fallacious. In the first place, I can find nothing in *Kent* which speaks to Platonic distinctions between divestiture of an existing right and failure to grant a right not already in existence. *Kent* rested, not on some fine point of metaphysics, but on the crucially important distinction between the treatment afforded children in an adult court and that granted them in Family Court. Of course, that distinction is just as important whether the selection of the adult forum is spoken of as the divestiture of an existing, exclusive juvenile jurisdiction or as the initial choice of a concurrent adult jurisdiction. In either case, the consequences to the child are precisely the same and, hence, the procedural protections should be identical.

Moreover, even if one excepts the dubious vestiture-divestiture distinction as relevant, the Government's argument simply does not fit the contours of the statute. It is not true that the United States Attorney's decision to proceed in adult court negates no pre-existing right or that the Family Court lacks exclusive jurisdiction *ab initio*. In fact, the basic jurisdictional statute remains, for our purposes, unchanged since the Supreme Court's decision in *Kent*. Now, as then, the Juvenile Court is in terms granted exclusive jurisdiction over all children as defined in 16 D.C.Code § 2301. True, the definition of child contained in 16 D.C.Code § 2301 has now been modified. But under the new definition, a suspected juvenile remains a child until he is charged with an enumerated offense by the United States Attorney. It follows that under 11 D.C.Code § 1101 the Family Court retains exclusive jurisdiction until the United States Attorney ends the defendant's status as a child by charging him with an enumerated crime. Thus the United States Attorney's charge acts to divest the Juvenile Court of its pre-existing exclusive jurisdiction in precisely the same manner as does the juvenile judge's waiver decision. Since the divestiture is the same, the procedural rights accompanying it should be the same, and we need look no farther than *Kent* to determine what those rights are.

The majority wisely eschews substantial reliance on the Government's divestiture argument to distinguish *Kent*. But in its stead my brethren adopt two other arguments which, to me at least, seem equally unconvincing. First, the majority seems to contend that *Kent* is inapposite because it applied to a judicial decision, whereas 16 D.C.Code § 2301 contemplates a prosecutorial decision. * * * The decision by a juvenile judge or by the United States Attorney to treat the child as an adult for prosecution purposes marks the beginning of precisely the same process of adjudication. And it cannot be doubted that the United States Attorney is certainly a less disinterested decision maker than the Juvenile Court judge. It would seem then that, in order to compensate for lack of neutrality, procedural niceties should be more rather than less carefully observed when the prosecutor is the decisionmaker.

It should be clear, then, that the test for when the Constitution demands a hearing depends not on which government official makes the decision, but rather on the importance of that decision to the individual affected. "The extent to which procedural due process must be afforded * * * is influenced by the extent to which (an individual) may be 'condemned to suffer grievous loss.'" The test is not a precise one, and reasonable men may differ as to its application in close cases, but at least the underlying requirement is clear. "Certain principles have remained relatively immutable in our jurisprudence. One of these is that where governmental action seriously injures an individual, and the reasonableness of the action depends on fact findings, the evidence used to prove the Government's case must be disclosed to the individual so that he has an opportunity to show that it is untrue." * * *

Finally, the Government argues that extension of *Kent* to prosecutorial waivers would abrogate the ancient doctrine of prosecutorial discretion. It is, of course, still widely believed that prosecutors have a broad, unreviewable discretion to determine which offenders to charge and what crimes to charge them with, although even this notion is now widely challenged by the leading scholars. But it should be readily apparent that usual notions of prosecutorial discretion have nothing to do with this case. The defendant does not ask us to review the substance of the prosecutor's charging decision or to place limits on the scope of his discretion. Bland directs his complaint to the procedures the prosecutor uses rather than to the merits of the decision ultimately reached. * * * I think it plain here that the prosecutor's broad authority to choose between juvenile and criminal procedures provides no argument for the power to exercise that authority in a manner which does not comport with procedural due process. * * *

My brothers point to "the significance of a variety of other common prosecutorial decisions, e.g., whether to charge one person but not another possible co-defendant; whether to charge an individual with a misdemeanor or a felony; etc. * * * Grave consequences have always flowed from this, but never has a hearing been required." * * * As the majority itself indicates, there are dramatically real differences between run-of-the-mill charging decisions and prosecutorial waiver of Family Court jurisdiction. A normal charging decision is "only the beginning of the process of adjudication of (defendant's) guilt, a process marked by the presence of all the traditional protections of procedural due process * * *." A defendant has the opportunity to show that he was improperly charged—that is, that he is not guilty—at the preliminary hearing, at the trial itself, and, if necessary, on appeal.

In contrast, the waiver decision marks not only the beginning but also the end of adjudication as to the child's suitability for juvenile treatment. It is well established that, barring equal protection problems, a guilty person has no right not to be charged with a criminal offense. But a "guilty" child may, under certain circumstances, have a right to be charged as a juvenile. The question of juvenile treatment turns not on the issue of guilt, but on such factors as the maturity of the child and his susceptibility to rehabilitation. These factors, unlike the question of guilt, drop out of the case once the initial waiver decision is made. Hence it is especially vital that the procedures be fair at the one point in the criminal process where these matters are considered. The very fact that the prosecutor's decision is largely unreviewable and therefore final argues for, rather than against, making certain that he has all the facts before him when he exercises his great responsibility. * * *

It trivializes the juvenile court system to suggest that it represents merely an alternative forum for the trial of criminal offenses. The Family Court is more than just another judicial body; it is another system of justice with different procedures, a different penalty structure, and a different philosophy of rehabilitation. We play a cruel joke on our children by arguing that the juvenile system is a nonadversary, noncriminal, beneficent instrument of rehabilitation when determination whether criminal procedures are to be required at trial, while at the same time maintaining that it is just another criminal court when determining the procedures which must accompany waiver.

It will not do to minimize or ignore the consequences of the decision reached today. * * * [A]fter our decision today there will be many impressionable 16– and 17–year–olds who will be packed off to adult prisons where they will serve their time with hardened criminals. These children will be sentenced, moreover, without any meaningful inquiry into the possibility of rehabilitation through humane juvenile disposition. * * *

Perhaps I should add that I harbor no illusions as to the efficacy of our juvenile court system. * * * Nor do I believe that a fair and constitutional waiver system would rescue from the clutches of adult punishment every juvenile capable of rehabilitation in a more beneficent environment. * * *

NOTES

1) Offender versus Offense Why does the majority in *Bland* conclude that he is not entitled to a hearing? What is the statutory waiver issue? Why is the exercise of prosecutorial discretion considered "non-reviewable"? In dissent, Judge J. Skelly Wright argues that the same consequences—criminal prosecution as an adult—require the same procedures. Why? What is the real difference between the majority and the dissent's analyses?

If you represented Bland, what would be your best "equal protection" argument? What would be your best "due process" argument? Juveniles tried as adults as a result of excluded offenses have claimed that automatic certification denies the procedural safeguards required by *Kent* and that exclusion on the basis of the offense alleged constitutes an arbitrary legislative classification. Courts have uniformly rejected these arguments. *See Woodard v. Wainwright*, 556 F.2d 781 (5th Cir. 1977); *Russell v. Parratt*, 543 F.2d 1214 (8th Cir. 1976); *Cox v. United States*, 473 F.2d 334 (4th Cir. 1973).

2) Judicial Reluctance to Review Prosecutors' Charging Decisions The *Bland* majority rejected Judge Wright's argument that the comparable consequences flowing from legislative or prosecutorial waivers necessitated procedural safeguards comparable to those provided in a judicial waiver hearing. The *Bland* majority relied on the well-established doctrine that judges do not review exercises of prosecutorial discretion except under manifestly discriminatory circumstances. In a similar challenge to a "pure" prosecutorial waiver statute, the court in *Cox v. United States*, 473 F.2d 334 (4th Cir. 1973), specifically rejected procedural safeguards as a precondition to the exercise of prosecutorial discretion:

> Judicial proceedings must be clothed in the raiment of due process, while the processes of prosecutorial decision-making wear very different garb. It is one thing to hold, as we have, that when a state makes waiver of a juvenile court's jurisdiction a judicial function, the judge must cast about the defendant all of the trappings of due process, but it does not necessarily follow that a state or the United States may not constitutionally treat the basic question as a prosecutorial function, making a highly placed, supervisory prosecutor responsible for deciding whether to proceed against a juvenile as an adult. If it does, as the United states has, the character of the proceeding, rather than its consequences to the accused, are largely determinative of his rights. *Id.* at 336.

Courts typically decline to review prosecutorial decisions because the constitutional doctrine of separation of powers denies the judicial branch the power to compel or control the executive branch in essentially discretionary matters. In the absence of invidious discrimination on the basis of race, religion, or the like, a prosecutor's decisions about whether and whom to charge and with what offense remain beyond judicial review. *See, e.g., Oyler v. Boles*, 368 U.S. 448, 82 S.Ct. 501, 7 L.Ed.2d 446 (1962); *Wayte v. United States*, 470 U.S. 598, 105 S.Ct. 1524, 84 L.Ed.2d 547 (1985); *United States v. Armstrong*, 517 U.S. 456, 116 S.Ct. 1480, 134 L.Ed.2d 687 (1996). Judicial reluctance to encumber prosecutors' discretion stems from a fear of intruding on sensitive legal and policy judgments. "Such factors as the strength of the case, the prosecution's general deterrence value, the Government's enforcement priorities, and the case's relationship to the Government's overall enforcement plan are not readily susceptible to the kind of analysis the courts are competent to undertake." *Wayte*, 470 U.S. at 607. Apart from separation of powers considerations, if judicial review entails the power to compel prosecutors to present or dismiss a case, then a judge could prevent prosecutors from maximizing enforcement effectiveness through selective prosecution and force them to misallocate resources. Courts also decline to review prosecutors' decisions because of the need to maintain secrecy during an investigation. A fitness hearing prior to the filing of charges could divulge confidential sources. Additionally, the factors that influence prosecutors' decisions—legal evaluations of evidence and guilt, resource allocation, and other law enforcement policies and priorities—seldom provide a written record in a form that permits meaningful pretrial judicial review.

The Supreme Court consistently reaffirms prosecutors' freedom from judicial review. In *Bordenkircher v. Hayes*, 434 U.S. 357, 98 S.Ct. 663, 54 L.Ed.2d 604 (1978), the Court noted that

> so long as the prosecutor has probable cause to believe that the accused committed an offense defined by statute, the decision whether or not to prosecute, and what charge to file or bring before a grand jury, generally rests entirely in his discretion. Within the limits set by the legislature's constitutionally valid definition of chargeable offenses, "the conscious exercise of some selectivity in enforcement is not in itself a federal constitutional violation" so long as "the selection was [not] deliberately based upon an unjustifiable standard such as race, religion, or other arbitrary classification." *Id.* at 364.

In *United States v. Armstrong*, 517 U.S. 456, 116 S.Ct. 1480, 134 L.Ed.2d 687 (1996), the Court reiterated that prosecutors possess "broad discretion" to enforce criminal laws, a strong "presumption of regularity supports their prosecutorial decisions," and the defendant bears the burden to rebut that strong presumption of administrative regularity. *Id.* at 464. Courts will review claims of selective or discriminatory enforcement decisions by prosecutors only when the defendant can present clear evidence of an equal protection violation, for example, selection of some defendants on the basis of their race and non-prosecution of other similarly-situated offenders of a different race. Even then, in order to prevail, the defendant must demonstrate both that the "prosecutorial policy had a discriminatory effect and that it was *motivated by a discriminatory purpose*." *Armstrong*, 517 U.S. at 465 (emphasis added). Thus, defendants must establish that charging decisions have an invidious impact *and* an improper motive. Under the rationale of *Armstrong*, a youth prosecuted in criminal court for an excluded offense would have to demonstrate that the prosecutor intentionally charged him *because* of his race and declined to prosecute as adults other youths of different races who committed the same offense, an almost insuperable burden in an individual case.

3) Excluded Offenses and Conviction of Lesser, Non–Excluded Crimes What happens if a prosecutor charges a youth with a crime that excludes her from juvenile court jurisdiction and a jury then convicts the youth of a lesser offense that would not have been excluded from juvenile court jurisdiction? Should the criminal court judge sentence the youth as an adult because the original charge divested the juvenile court of jurisdiction? Should the criminal court judge remand the youth to juvenile court for sentencing as a delinquent?

Consider the court's analysis in **State v. Morales**, 240 Conn. 727, 694 A.2d 758 (Conn. 1997), where a jury acquitted Morales of first-degree murder but convicted him of manslaughter in the first degree, an offense which the statute did not exclude from the juvenile court's jurisdiction. The trial court denied Morales' motion to return his case to the juvenile court for sentencing:

> The sole issue in this appeal is whether a child who has been transferred, pursuant to General Statutes § 46b–127 [*supra*, p. 600], from the docket for juvenile matters to the regular criminal docket of the Superior Court on a charge of murder must be returned to the docket for juvenile matters if he is acquitted of murder but convicted of the lesser included offense of manslaughter in the first degree. The defendant, David Morales, contends that allowing a child acquitted of murder but convicted of manslaughter to remain on the regular criminal docket for sentencing is contrary to both the language of § 46b–127 and the equal protection and due process provisions of the federal constitution. We disagree with the defendant's statutory and constitutional arguments and affirm the judgment of the Appellate Court, which affirmed the trial court's sentencing of the defendant for manslaughter as an adult. * * *

> In August, 1994, the defendant was tried by a jury. At the defendant's request, the trial court instructed the jury as to the lesser included offenses of manslaughter in the first and second degrees. The jury convicted the defendant of manslaughter in the first degree * * * and acquitted him of the charges of murder and conspiracy to commit murder.

> Thereafter, the defendant moved to have his case returned to the juvenile docket for further proceedings. The trial court denied the motion and sentenced the defendant to a term of incarceration. * * * [T]he Appellate Court * * * affirmed the judgment of the trial court. * * * We granted the defendant's petition for certification to determine: (1) whether, as a matter of statutory construction, a child who is transferred to the regular criminal docket pursuant to § 46b–127, on the basis of a finding of probable cause to believe that he has committed murder, must be transferred back to the juvenile docket if he is found guilty of the lesser included offense of manslaughter in the first degree; and (2) whether the statute, if construed not to require such a retransfer, violates the child's constitutional rights to equal protection and due process. We affirm the judgment of the Appellate Court.

> Section 46b–127 provides that the juvenile court must transfer to the regular criminal docket of the Superior Court all cases in which there has

been a finding of probable cause that a child has committed murder * * * and the alleged crime occurred after the child had attained fourteen years of age. Section 46b–127(c) also provides that "[u]pon the effectuation of the transfer, [the] child shall stand trial and be sentenced, if convicted, as if he were sixteen years of age. * * * Any child transferred to the regular criminal docket who pleads guilty to a lesser offense shall not resume his status as a juvenile regarding said offense. If the action is dismissed or nolled or if such child is found not guilty of the charge for which he was transferred, the child shall resume his status as a juvenile until he attains the age of sixteen years." We are asked to determine how the legislature intended this language to be applied where, as here, a child is properly transferred to the regular criminal docket on the basis of a finding of probable cause to believe that he has committed murder, but is later acquitted of murder by a jury and convicted of the lesser included offense of manslaughter. * * *

We first consider the language of § 46b–127(c), which provides that, "[u]pon the effectuation of the transfer, [the] child shall stand trial and be sentenced, if convicted, as if he were sixteen years of age. * * *" That language * * * dictates that children who are validly transferred from the juvenile docket to the regular criminal docket are to be prosecuted in all respects, including sentencing, as though they were adults. It is undisputed that an adult tried for murder may be convicted of any lesser included form of homicide. * * *

The defendant asks us to find such an exception in the last sentence of § 46b–127(c), which provides that "[i]f the action is dismissed or nolled or if such child is found not guilty of the charge for which he was transferred, the child shall resume his status as a juvenile until he attains the age of sixteen years." The defendant argues that murder is the only "charge for which he was transferred" and that, when the jury found him not guilty of that charge, the court was obligated to send his case back to the juvenile docket. We are not persuaded.

The defendant's interpretation of § 46b–127 would, within the context of cases transferred from the juvenile docket to the regular criminal docket, require a departure from our well established rules pertaining to lesser included offenses. Under the defendant's interpretation, in a transferred case a jury would never deliberate regarding a lesser included offense because the jury is routinely instructed, as the jury was in this case, that it may not begin to deliberate regarding any lesser included offense until it has concluded that the defendant is not guilty of the greater offense. Before it ever reached the lesser included offense, the jury would have had to conclude that the defendant was not guilty of the greater offense. Further deliberations regarding lesser included offenses would be meaningless under the defendant's construction of the statute and, therefore, trial courts presumably would be precluded from giving lesser included offense instructions. Forcing the jury to choose between murder and acquittal in a case where there is evidence of a less culpable state of mind "would limit the jury's function of determining questions of fact and undermine a defendant's right to a trial by jury." We are unable to find any indication that the legislature intended that the state and the child defendant engage in this version of Russian roulette.

Our interpretation finds further support in the provision of § 46b–127(d) that "[a]ny child transferred to the regular criminal docket who pleads guilty to a lesser offense shall not resume his status as a juvenile regarding said offense.* * *" It is clear that had the defendant pleaded guilty to manslaughter in the first degree, his case would have remained on the regular criminal docket and he would have been sentenced as an adult and subject to a maximum penalty of twenty years imprisonment. The defendant contends, however, that because he elected to go to trial and opted to request a lesser included offense instruction on manslaughter, he is subject to a maximum penalty in juvenile court, if it is assumed the court could penalize him at all, of only four years commitment to the department of children and families. * * * We do not believe that the legislature intended those child defendants who are transferred to the regular docket and subsequently are convicted of manslaughter in the first degree after a full trial to be afforded dramatically more lenient treatment than those juveniles who voluntarily plead guilty to manslaughter in the first degree. The defendant's proposed construction would provide transferred juvenile defendants with a significant disincentive to plead guilty. Such a construction is at odds with common sense and contradicts the policy encouraging plea bargaining. We conclude that § 46b–127 must be read to authorize the same sentences for those children convicted of lesser included offenses after a full trial as for those who plead guilty to lesser included offenses.

Only by interpreting the phrase "the charge for which he was transferred" in the last sentence of § 46b–127(c) to include not only the specific statutory offense for which the defendant was transferred but also any lesser included offenses, can we find internal harmony between that last sentence and the preceding sentences providing that a transferred child shall be treated the same as an adult defendant "if convicted" or if he pleads guilty to any lesser included offense. Once probable cause was found * * *, the defendant was on notice that he could be prosecuted for murder and for applicable lesser included offenses. * * *

Having rejected the defendant's statutory claim, we consider the defendant's alternative argument that the statute, as we have construed it, violates his federal constitutional rights to equal protection and due process. Although unclear, the defendant's equal protection argument appears to be that he is similarly situated to those children who are adjudged delinquent on the basis of findings in juvenile court that they have committed manslaughter in the first degree, and that there is no rational basis for subjecting him to more severe penalties than are imposed on those who are prosecuted in the juvenile court. We disagree. * * *

We conclude that there is a conceivable rational basis for treating differently those juveniles who are convicted by a jury of manslaughter after being transferred to the regular criminal docket to stand trial for murder and those who are adjudged delinquent on the basis of a court's initial finding that the juvenile has engaged in conduct amounting only to manslaughter. * * *

We conclude, however, that even if we assume that the two categories of offender identified by the defendant, i.e., children charged with murder and those charged only with manslaughter, are similarly situated with respect to the statute, there is more than an adequate rational basis for treating them differently. * * *

[T]he legislature has provided a variety of benefits to juvenile defendants. Some of the benefits exist before and during trial, while others exist after the merits of a defendant's case have been decided by a court. Regardless of the timing of the benefits, however, the legislature has chosen to bestow or withhold these benefits as a whole, rather than on a piecemeal basis. It is entirely possible that the legislature decided that, in the best interests of our open public court system, any defendant tried as an adult and exposed to the public for trial should be sentenced as an adult, regardless of the crimes of which he or she ultimately is convicted. The legislature could have reasoned that conferring postverdict benefits, such as more lenient sentencing and erasure of records, on a defendant who, in open court, had been tried as an adult and convicted of a serious crime would damage society's perception of the fair administration of justice. Because there exists a rational basis for this legislative scheme, we conclude that the legislature's decision to preclude a defendant from seeking the postverdict benefits of the juvenile statutes once validly transferred to the regular criminal docket does not violate the defendant's right to the equal protection of the laws. * * *

In **State v. Behl**, 564 N.W.2d 560 (Minn. 1997), the grand jury indicted sixteen-year old Behl for Murder 1 and related crimes, which resulted in his automatic prosecution as an adult on all charges, see *supra*, p. 582. A jury acquitted Behl of murder, but convicted him of manslaughter in the second degree and other offenses. After he was acquitted of the offense for which he was automatically certified as an adult, Behl argued that the trial court's refusal to return his case to juvenile court for sentencing violated due process and equal protection. A divided Minnesota Supreme Court rejected his argument:

We hold that no person, regardless of age, has a fundamental right to juvenile adjudication, which necessarily would include a juvenile disposition. Consequently, the statute's automatic imposition of a district court sentence on the basis of an enumerated charge would violate Behl's substantive due process rights only if it is not a reasonable means to a permissive object. * * *

It is clear that the portion of the automatic-certification statute that creates adult-court jurisdiction based upon age and offense criteria is rationally related to the legitimate government interests of serving public safety and determining if the defendant is amenable to juvenile rehabilitation. Behl is arguing that it is not rationally related to any legitimate government interest to subject two persons convicted of the same crime to completely different sentencing mechanisms simply because one person was indicted for first-degree murder and the other person was not. The state, on the other hand, argues only that such a distinction is rational because first-degree murder is the most serious criminal offense in Minnesota. Although this invariably is true, the fact remains that Behl did not commit such an offense. Consequently this issue will turn on whether it is reasonable to sentence a juvenile who is merely indicted for first-degree murder much more harshly than a similarly convicted (or adjudicated delinquent) juvenile who was not indicted for first-degree murder.

Although the state failed at oral argument to assert a rational basis upon which to base this different treatment, we conclude that the grand jury's finding of probable cause necessary to automatically certify a juvenile provides such a basis. * * * While it is true that an indictment does not prove the juvenile committed first-degree murder, the indictment is proof that a grand jury found facts sufficient to furnish probable cause that the juvenile has committed first-degree murder. * * * [W]e conclude that such a finding is at least a rational basis upon which to expose a juvenile who is within two years of becoming a legal adult to the more harsh sentences imposed in district court. * * *

KEITH, Chief Justice (dissenting), joined by GARDEBRING and STRINGER. * * * The statute states that juvenile courts "lack[ ] jurisdiction over proceedings concerning" children "alleged to have committed murder in the first degree after becoming 16 years of age." When an allegation of first-degree murder is made by the state, the district courts assume "original and exclusive jurisdiction."

The key term to be interpreted is "alleged." In my view, the best reading of the statute, in light of its underlying purposes, is that a juvenile offender is no longer "alleged" to have committed first-degree murder once he or she is actually acquitted by a jury in a district court. * * * There is no question that the state's allegation was sufficient to trigger adult-court jurisdiction. But after the jury rejected the state's allegation of first-degree murder, the statutory basis and rationale for adult-court jurisdiction was eliminated. * * *

The weakness of the majority's rationale would not be so troubling if the results seemed fair to juveniles like Behl. But the unavoidable consequence of the court's reasoning is that a child who is indicted but acquitted of the enumerated offense (first-degree murder) faces the harsher sentencing regime that the legislature crafted for adult perpetrators, while a child who was fortunate enough not to be indicted for first-degree murder in the first place is sentenced according to the juvenile court rules. This is not a result that the legislature envisioned. In my opinion, the automatic certification statute establishes a simple and legitimate policy: anyone over the age of 16 who commits first-degree murder will receive a life sentence. The statute does not say that certain juveniles should be treated "much more harshly," simply because they have been indicted, and despite exoneration by a jury. To do so, it seems, is to punish the juvenile for a crime he or she did not commit. * * *

If, as the majority concludes, the statute is silent and we must identify the legislature's intent, then I see no reason to prefer the more punitive result over a juvenile disposition. * * * This court has made clear that the ambit of an ambiguous criminal law should be construed narrowly according to the rule of lenity. * * * Thus, if there is to be a presumption about the legislature's intent regarding juvenile sentencing jurisdiction, the past interpretive practices of this court indicate that juvenile-court jurisdiction and its well-tailored dispositions should prevail. * * *

4) Legislative Checks on Prosecutorial Over–Charging Decisions like *Morales* and *Behl* invite prosecutors to over-charge youths in order to obtain longer sentences in criminal court. In light of the ease with which the state may establish probable cause of the more serious crime, is judicial review of probable cause in an *ex parte* proceeding or a grand jury indictment an adequate protection against the abuses of over-charging? One rationale of *Bland* was that a criminal jury trial provided the best evaluation of the prosecutor's offense-based evaluation. Conviction of a lesser, non-excluded offense constitutes a repudiation of the prosecutor's original evaluation of the seriousness of the crime that warranted adult prosecution. Moreover, the judicial policy reasons that militate against subjecting a prosecutor's charging decision to prior judicial review do not preclude re-examining it after the fact. The dangers of prosecutorial abuse via overcharging are substantial. The remedy is straightforward. *See* Barry C. Feld, "Reference of Juvenile Offenders for Adult Prosecution: The Legislative Alternative to Asking Unanswerable Questions," 62 *Minn. L. Rev.* 515 at 582 (1978):

> If the youth was acquitted or convicted of a lesser offense that would not exclude him as an adult under the legislative criteria, the jurisdiction of the juvenile court over the offender would be revived, and the case would be transferred back to the juvenile court for disposition. The provision for 'rejuvenating' young offenders not convicted of excluded offenses by basing dispositional jurisdiction on convictions rather than on initial charges provides an important additional check on the prosecutor's charging discretion. Transferring juveniles whose convictions do not fit the legislative criteria back to the juvenile court for disposition avoids one of the most serious potential abuses of present legislative waiver provisions.

5) Reverse Waiver Hearing One statutory method to check prosecutorial overcharging of excluded offenses would be a "reverse waiver" proceeding.

705 Ill. Comp. Stat. 405 § 5–130 (West 1999):

(1)(c)(ii) If after trial or plea the court finds that the minor committed an offense not covered * * * [by the excluded offense statute], that finding shall not invalidate the verdict or the prosecution of the minor under the criminal laws of the State; however, unless the State requests a hearing for the purpose of sentencing the minor under Chapter V of the Unified Code of Corrections, the Court must proceed under Sections 5–705 and 5–710 of this Article [the juvenile delinquency disposition provisions]. To request a hearing, the State must file a written motion within 10 days following the entry of a finding or the return of a verdict. * * * If the motion is made by the State, the court shall conduct a hearing to determine if the minor should be sentenced under Chapter V of the Unified Code of Corrections. In making its determination, the court shall consider among other matters: (a) whether there is evidence that the offense was committed in an aggressive and premeditated manner; (b) the age of the minor; (c) the previous history of the minor; (d) whether there are facilities particularly available to the Juvenile Court or the Department of Corrections, Juvenile Division, for the treatment and rehabilitation of the minor; (e) whether the security of the public requires sentencing under Chapter V of the Unified Code of Corrections; and (f) whether the minor possessed a deadly weapon when committing the offense. The rules of evidence shall be the same as if at trial. If after the hearing the court finds that the minor should be sentenced under Chapter V of the Unified Code of Corrections, then the court shall sentence the minor accordingly having available to it any or all dispositions so prescribed.

Automatic Rejuvenation If a jury convicts a youth of a lesser, non-excluded offense, what is the justification, as in the Illinois Statute, for conducting a "reverse waiver" hearing? Shouldn't a statute, consistently with the rationale of offense-exclusion, simply provide that "if a child is found not guilty of the charge for which he was transferred or of any lesser included but excluded offenses, then the child *shall* resume his status as a juvenile for purposes of disposition"? In **People v. A.T., Jr.**, 303 Ill.App.3d 531, 236 Ill.Dec. 943, 708 N.E.2d 529 (Ill.App. 2 Dist., 1999), the Illinois Court of Appeals noted that "when a minor who was charged with an offense that triggered the mandatory transfer provisions is convicted only of an offense or offenses that would not have triggered the mandatory transfer provision * * * the case should be transferred back to juvenile court. In such circumstances, if the State makes a timely request for a hearing for the purpose of sentencing the minor under the adult sentencing provisions, the trial court then conducts a hearing to determine if the request should be granted. * * * We believe that courts can best fulfill their duties with respect to minors if they are allowed to make a new determination of whether a minor's case should be returned to juvenile court for disposition or retained in criminal court for sentencing after a minor whose case has been transferred to criminal court * * * is found guilty only of an offense or offenses that are not predicate offenses."

2. CONCURRENT JURISDICTION OR PROSECUTORIAL DIRECT–FILE

Pure prosecutorial waiver statutes create concurrent jurisdiction in juvenile and criminal courts for certain offenses and give prosecutors discretion to direct-file or charge youths of certain ages with the same offense in either forum. Unlike offense-exclusion where charges only for certain offenses can result exclusively in criminal prosecution, direct-file legislation gives prosecutors greater discretionary authority to choose the forum. More than a dozen states have adopted some version of prosecutorial waiver statutes and allow prosecutors to charge youths of certain ages and offenses in either justice system. Francis Barry McCarthy, "The Serious Offender and Juvenile Court Reform: The Case for Prosecutorial Waiver of Juvenile Court Jurisdiction," 38 *St. L. U. L. J.* 629 (1994); U. S.

General Accounting Office, *Juvenile Justice: Juveniles Processed in Criminal Court and Case Dispositions (1995)*; Ark. Code Ann. § 9–27–318(b) (Michie 1997); Colo. Rev. Stat. Ann. § 19–2–518(2) (West 1997); Fla. Stat. Ann. § 985.226(2)(a)–(b) (West 1997); Ga. Code Ann. § 15–11–5(b) (1997); La. Child Code Ann. Art. 305(b)(3) (West Supp. 1997); Mich. Com. Laws Ann. § 600.606(1) (West 1997); Neb. Rev. Stat. § 43–247 (1997); Vt. Stat. Ann. Tit. 33, § 5505(c) (1997); Wyo. Stat. Ann. § 14–6–203 (1997). Unlike legislative offense-exclusion, in which the actual offense alleged determines juvenile or criminal jurisdiction, direct-file laws allow the prosecutor to select the forum without engaging in any charging subterfuges. In most pure or direct-file states, the statute provide no guidelines, standards, or criteria to control the prosecutors' choice of forum.

Florida Statute § 985.227 (West 1998).

(1) Discretionary direct file; criteria.—

(a) With respect to any child who was 14 or 15 years of age at the time the alleged offense was committed, the state attorney may file an information when in the state attorney's judgment and discretion the public interest requires that adult sanctions be considered or imposed and when the offense charged is:

> [1. Arson; 2. Sexual battery; 3. Robbery; 4. Kidnapping; 5. Aggravated child abuse; 6. Aggravated assault; 7. Aggravated stalking; 8. Murder; 9. Manslaughter; 10. Unlawful throwing, placing, or discharging of a destructive device or bomb; 11. Armed burglary * * * or specified burglary of a dwelling or structure * * *; 12. Aggravated battery; 13. Lewd or lascivious assault or act in the presence of a child; 14. Carrying, displaying, using, threatening, or attempting to use a weapon or firearm during the commission of a felony; or 15. Grand theft * * *.]

(b) With respect to any child who was 16 or 17 years of age at the time the alleged offense was committed, the state attorney may file an information when in the state attorney's judgment and discretion the public interest requires that adult sanctions be considered or imposed. However, the state attorney may not file an information on a child charged with a misdemeanor, unless the child has had at least two previous adjudications or adjudications withheld for delinquent acts, one of which involved an offense classified as a felony under state law.

(2) Mandatory direct file.—

(a) With respect to any child who was 16 or 17 years of age at the time the alleged offense was committed, the state attorney shall file an information if the child has been previously adjudicated delinquent for murder, sexual battery, armed or strong-armed robbery, carjacking, home-invasion robbery, aggravated battery, or aggravated assault, and is currently charged with a second or subsequent violent crime against a person.

(b) Notwithstanding subsection (1), regardless of the child's age at the time the alleged offense was committed, the state attorney must file an information with respect to any child who previously has been adjudicated for offenses which, if committed by an adult, would be felonies and such adjudications occurred at three or more separate delinquency adjudicatory hearings, and three of which resulted in residential commitments. * * *

(c) The state attorney must file an information if a child, regardless of the child's age at the time the alleged offense was committed, is alleged to have committed an act that would be a violation of law if the child were an adult, that involves stealing a motor vehicle, including, but not limited to, * * * carjacking, * * * [or] grand theft of a motor vehicle, and while the child was in possession of the stolen motor vehicle the child caused serious bodily injury to or the death of a person who was not involved in the underlying offense. For purposes of this section, the driver and all willing passengers in the stolen motor vehicle at the time such serious bodily injury or death is inflicted shall also be subject to mandatory transfer to adult court. * * *

(3) Effect of direct file.—

(a) Once a child has been transferred for criminal prosecution pursuant to information and has been found to have committed the presenting offense or a lesser included offense, the child shall be handled thereafter in every respect as if an adult for any subsequent violation of state law, unless the court imposes juvenile sanctions under § 985.233. * * *

(c) When a child has been transferred for criminal prosecution as an adult and has been found to have committed a violation of state law, the disposition of the case may be made under § 985.233 and may include the enforcement of any restitution ordered in any juvenile proceeding.

(4) Direct-file policies and guidelines.—Each state attorney shall develop and annually update written policies and guidelines to govern determinations for filing an information on a juvenile, to be submitted to the Executive Office of the Governor, the President of the Senate, the Speaker of the House of Representatives, and the Juvenile Justice Advisory Board not later than January 1 of each year.

Bases for Direct–File Decisions Essentially, in direct-file jurisdictions the prosecutor makes two types of decisions: whether probable cause exists to believe that the youth committed a particular offense and, if the youth's age and offense is one for which concurrent jurisdiction exists, whether to charge the youth in juvenile or criminal court. While prosecutors possess expertise to evaluate the sufficiency of evidence and to select charges, do they bring any unique professional insight to the forum selection decision whether to try a youth as a juvenile or as an adult? *See e.g.*, Stacey Sabo, "Rights of Passage: An Analysis of Waiver of Juvenile Court Jurisdiction," 64 *Fordham L. Rev.* 2425 at 2441 (1996), who notes that "Prosecutorial waiver does not require the prosecutor to petition the court for a waiver hearing, nor does it require her to consider the juvenile's best interests. The prosecutor herself determines the court in which to file the case. Although the choice of forum is 'critically important,' the prosecutor often has little statutory guidance regarding what criteria she should consider in making a waiver decision."

The Florida Statute permits the prosecutor to direct-file a juvenile as an adult "when in the state attorney's judgment and discretion the public interest requires that adult sanctions be considered or imposed * * *" and requires each state attorney to "develop and annually update written policies and guidelines" to govern direct-file decisions. Do those requirements provide any guidance to prosecutors' decision to select juvenile or criminal court jurisdiction. Does the requirement that each state's attorney develop written policies and guidelines assure any degree of consistency and uniformity in the application of the statute across the state?

Is the following prosecutorial direct-file provision an improvement on the Florida guidelines?

Neb. Rev. Stat. § 43–247 (1998):

The juvenile court shall have concurrent original jurisdiction with the district court as to any juvenile defined in subdivision (2) of this section. * * *

(2) Any juvenile who has committed an act which would constitute a felony under the laws of this state * * *.

Neb. Rev. Stat. § 43–276 (1998):

In cases coming within * * * subdivision (2) * * * of section 43–247, when the juvenile is under the age of sixteen years, the county attorney shall, in making the determination whether to file a criminal charge, juvenile court petition, or mediation referral, consider: (1) The type of treatment such juvenile would most likely be amenable to; (2) whether there is evidence that the alleged offense included violence or was committed in an aggressive and premeditated manner; (3) the motivation for the commission of the offense; (4) the age of the juvenile and the ages and circumstances of any others involved in the offense; (5) the previous history of the juvenile, including whether he or she had been convicted of any previous offenses or adjudicated in juvenile court, and, if so, whether such offenses were crimes against the person or relating to property, and other previous history of antisocial behavior, if any, including any patterns of physical violence; (6) the sophistication and maturity of the juvenile as determined by consideration of his or her home, school activities, emotional attitude and desire to be treated as an adult, pattern of living, and whether he or she has had previous contact with law enforcement agencies and courts and the nature thereof; (7) whether there are facilities particularly available to the juvenile court for treatment and rehabilitation of the juvenile; (8) whether the best interests of the juvenile and the security of the public may require that the juvenile continue in custody or under supervision for a period extending beyond his or her minority and, if so, the available alternatives best suited to this purpose; (9) whether the victim agrees to participate in mediation; and (10) such other matters as the county attorney deems relevant to his or her decision.

NOTES

1) Prosecutorial Direct–File and *Kent* Criteria Effectively, the Nebraska statute mandates a prosecutor to consider *Kent*-like criteria when
making the forum selection decisions for youths under the age of sixteen. Why
not for sixteen- and seventeen-year-old youths as well? Unlike a *Kent* judicial
waiver hearing, where clinicians and court services personnel can provide a
judge with information about a youth's maturity, sophistication, or "amenability to treatment" based on clinical evaluations, social service reports,
interviews, and the like, prosecutors typically lack access to such personal
information. Other than police reports about the current offense and the
juvenile's prior record, how would a prosecutor obtain information about the
other criteria—amenability, sophistication and maturity, or school activities—
listed in the statute? The prosecutor makes the initial forum determination in
her office, *ex parte*, and prior to the filing of a delinquency petition or criminal
complaint. Because the state has not yet charged the juvenile in either forum,
the youth will not be represented by counsel. What mechanisms exist to
assure the validity or reliability of the information on which the prosecutor
bases a forum selection decision?

Although most states' direct-file statutes do not provide any formal
criteria, prosecutors could adopt informal administrative guidelines. However,
interviews with Florida prosecutors revealed that relatively few did so, and
the "informal guidelines" of those who adopted them provided minimal
practical control over jurisdictional selection decisions. *See* Donna M. Bishop
and Charles S. Frazier, "Transfer of Juveniles To Criminal Court: A Case
Study and Analysis of Prosecutorial Waiver," 5 *Notre Dame J. Law, Ethics &
Pub. Policy* 281 (1991). For example, variations in prosecutors' juvenile justice
philosophy—just deserts, public safety, rehabilitation—had very little impact
on their charging or waiver practices; most youths whom they transferred
were not especially violent or dangerous. "[Y]ouths transferred via prosecutorial waiver are seldom the serious and chronic offenders for whom prosecution
and punishment in criminal court are arguably justified." *Id.* at 297. The
failure to provide any review procedures or to specify the waiver criteria
results almost inevitably in arbitrary, idiosyncratic, and inconsistent decisions.

**2) The Role of Guidelines to Control Prosecutors' Discretion to
Direct File** Although youths have challenged the validity of direct-file laws
that delegate to prosecutors untrammeled discretion to choose a youth's
juvenile or criminal status, appellate courts invoke the rationale of *Bland* and
reject their claims. In upholding Florida's direct-file law, for example, the
Florida Supreme Court noted that "prosecutorial discretion is itself an incident of the constitutional separation of powers, and that as a result the courts
are not to interfere with the free exercise of the discretionary powers of the
prosecutor in his control over criminal prosecutions." **State v. Cain**, 381
So.2d 1361 (Fla. Sup. Ct. 1980). The *Cain* court went on to explain:

> There was no common law right to be specially treated as a juvenile
> delinquent instead of a criminal offender. Nor is there any inherent or
> constitutional right to preferred treatment as a juvenile delinquent. * * *

Therefore, a child has the right to be treated as a juvenile delinquent only to the extent provided by our legislature. * * * The legislature has, however, provided for several exceptions to the juvenile court's otherwise exclusive jurisdiction over juveniles. * * * [T]he state attorney may, by filing an information, criminally prosecute a juvenile sixteen years of age or older when in his discretion the public interest requires that adult sanctions be imposed. * * *

It cannot be said that the legislature acted arbitrarily in providing for these statutory exceptions to juvenile treatment. The legislature could reasonably conclude based on circumstances such as age, seriousness of the offense and past record that certain juvenile offenders were not suitable candidates for the juvenile act's rehabilitative goals; consequently, the legislature could reasonably classify these offenders as persons against whom adult sanctions would be an alternative. * * *

[W]e have simply a traditional exercise of discretion within the executive branch, and while we recognize that the prosecutor's decision has a substantial impact on the course of subsequent proceedings, we cannot equate the prosecutorial decision with judicial proceedings, absent legislative direction.

It is also clear that the state attorney's decision to bring criminal charges against a juvenile does not involve an "adjudication." Rather, it is only the basis by which adjudication is initiated. * * * The juvenile who is charged with a criminal offense is afforded the same procedural and substantive rights as is any other person. Moreover, we disagree with defendants' threshold analysis that something is being "taken" from them as a result of their being prosecuted as adults rather than as juveniles. * * * [J]uveniles are given such immunity from criminal prosecution as is conferred on them under statute. * * * [W]hile exclusive jurisdiction over juveniles is initially vested in the juvenile division of the circuit court, this jurisdiction is expressly qualified * * *. Thus the statutory scheme * * * dispels any notion that a juvenile is guaranteed an absolute right to juvenile treatment. * * *

It is well established that the legislature may, within clearly defined limits, delegate to an administrative agency the authority to provide rules and regulations for the complete operation and enforcement of the law within its express purpose, but may not delegate the power to enact a law or to declare what the law shall be or to exercise an unrestricted discretion in applying the law. Here, however, we are dealing with the long-standing responsibility vested in a prosecutor, as a member of the executive branch, to enforce the criminal laws of the state. * * * [T]he discretion of a prosecutor in deciding whether and how to prosecute is absolute in our system of criminal justice. That [the statute] calls for the state attorney to exercise his discretion in the "public interest" merely states a truism, for that obligation is already ascribed to him. * * *

Based on *Bland*'s separation of powers rationale, courts uphold prosecutorial waiver statutes with virtual unanimity. *Walker v. State*, 309 Ark. 23, 827 S.W.2d 637 (Ark. 1992); *Chapman v. State*, 259 Ga. 592, 385 S.E.2d 661

(Ga. 1989); *Hansen v. State*, 904 P.2d 811 (Wyo.1995); *Myers v. District Court*, 184 Colo. 81, 518 P.2d 836 (Colo.1974).

3) Waiver in California Proposition 21, reviewed in *Manduley, infra,* converted some provisions of Cal. Welf. & Inst. § 707 traditional judicial waiver statute into a concurrent jurisdiction, prosecutorial direct file statute. As you read the latest iteration of Cal. Welf. & Inst. § 707, you will see the inter-mixture of legislative offense exclusion—§ 602(b)—the expansion of prosecutorial authority—§ 707(d)—and narrowing of judicial discretion to deal with less serious offenders. For youths with prior convictions or other special circumstances, the legislation also uses presumptions of unfitness to place the burden on the juvenile to demonstrate that she should be retained in juvenile court. See also, *People v. Jones*, Note 2, *supra* pp. 575–579. To further limit judicial discretion, if a judge retains juvenile court jurisdiction, then the statute limits judicial sentencing options to require some level of confinement:

Cal.Welf. & Inst.Code § 707 (2008)

(a)(1) In any case in which a minor is alleged to be a person described in subdivision (a) of Section 602[1] by reason of the violation, when he or she was 16 years of age or older, of any criminal statute or ordinance except those listed in subdivision (b), upon motion of the petitioner made prior to the attachment of jeopardy the court shall cause the probation officer to investigate and submit a report on the behavioral patterns and social history of the minor being considered for a determination of unfitness. Following submission and consideration of the report, and of any other relevant evidence that the petitioner or the minor may wish to submit, the juvenile court may find that the minor is not a fit and proper subject to be dealt with under the juvenile court law if it concludes that the minor would not be amenable to the care, treatment, and

---

1. Cal. Welf. & Inst. Code § 602 (2008) Minors violating laws defining crime; ward of court.

(a) Except as provided in subdivision (b), any person who is under the age of 18 years when he or she violates any law of this state or of the United States or any ordinance of any city or county of this state defining crime other than an ordinance establishing a curfew based solely on age, is within the jurisdiction of the juvenile court, which may adjudge such person to be a ward of the court.

(b) Any person who is alleged, when he or she was 14 years of age or older, to have committed one of the following offenses shall be prosecuted under the general law in a court of criminal jurisdiction:

(1) Murder * * * [if prosecutor alleges aggravating circumstances and that the minor personally killed the victim].

(2) The following sex offenses, if the prosecutor alleges that the minor personally committed the offense, and if the prosecutor alleges one of the circumstances enumerated in the One Strike law * * * applies:

(A) Rape * * *

(B) Spousal rape * * *

(C) Forcible sex offenses in concert with another * * *

(D) Forcible lewd and lascivious acts on a child under the age of 14 years * * *

(E) Forcible sexual penetration * * *

(F) Sodomy or oral copulation * * * by force, violence, duress, menace, or fear of immediate and unlawful bodily injury on the victim or another person.

(G) Lewd and lascivious acts on a child under the age of 14 years * * *

training program available through the facilities of the juvenile court, based upon an evaluation of the following criteria:

(A) The degree of criminal sophistication exhibited by the minor.

(B) Whether the minor can be rehabilitated prior to the expiration of the juvenile court's jurisdiction.

(C) The minor's previous delinquent history.

(D) Success of previous attempts by the juvenile court to rehabilitate the minor.

(E) The circumstances and gravity of the offense alleged in the petition to have been committed by the minor.

A determination that the minor is not a fit and proper subject to be dealt with under the juvenile court law may be based on any one or a combination of the factors set forth above, which shall be recited in the order of unfitness. In any case in which a hearing has been noticed pursuant to this section, the court shall postpone the taking of a plea to the petition until the conclusion of the fitness hearing, and no plea that may have been entered already shall constitute evidence at the hearing.

(2)(A) This paragraph shall apply to a minor alleged to be a person described in Section 602 by reason of the violation, when he or she has attained 16 years of age, of any felony offense when the minor has been declared to be a ward of the court pursuant to Section 602 on one or more prior occasions if both of the following apply:

(i) The minor has previously been found to have committed two or more felony offenses.

(ii) The offenses upon which the prior petition or petitions were based were committed when the minor had attained 14 years of age.

(B) Upon motion of the petitioner made prior to the attachment of jeopardy the court shall cause the probation officer to investigate and submit a report on the behavioral patterns and social history of the minor being considered for a determination of unfitness. Following submission and consideration of the report, and of any other relevant evidence that the petitioner or the minor may wish to submit, the minor shall be presumed to be not a fit and proper subject to be dealt with under the juvenile court law unless the juvenile court concludes, based upon evidence, which evidence may be of extenuating or mitigating circumstances, that the minor would be amenable to the care, treatment, and training program available through the facilities of the juvenile court based upon an evaluation of the following criteria [listed in § 707(a)(1)(A)–(E)]:

A determination that the minor is a fit and proper subject to be dealt with under the juvenile court law shall be based on a finding of amenability after consideration of the criteria set forth above, and findings therefore recited in the order as to each of the above criteria that the minor is fit and proper under each and every one of the above criteria. In making a finding of fitness, the court may consider extenuating and mitigating circumstances in evaluating each of the above criteria. In any case in which the hearing has been noticed pursuant to this section, the court shall postpone the taking of a plea to the petition until the conclusion of the fitness hearing and no plea which may have been entered already shall constitute evidence at the hearing. If the minor is found to be a fit and proper subject to be dealt with under the juvenile court law pursuant to this subdivision, the minor shall be committed to placement in a juvenile hall, ranch camp, forestry camp, boot camp, or secure juvenile home. * * *

(3) [If] the minor is found to be not a fit and proper subject for juvenile court treatment and is tried in a court of criminal jurisdiction and found guilty by the trier of fact, the judge may commit the minor to the Department of Corrections and Rehabilitation, Division of Juvenile Facilities, in lieu of sentencing the minor to the state prison. * * *

(b) Subdivision (c) shall be applicable in any case in which a minor is alleged to be a person described in Section 602 by reason of the violation of one of the following offenses:

[(1) Murder. (2) Arson * * *. (3) Robbery. (4) Rape with force or violence or threat of great bodily harm. (5) Sodomy by force, violence, duress, menace, or threat of great bodily harm. (6) Lewd or lascivious act * * *. (7) Oral copulation by force, violence, duress, menace, or threat of great bodily harm. * * * (9) Kidnapping for ransom. (10) Kidnapping * * *. (11) Kidnapping with bodily harm. (12) Attempted murder. (13) Assault with a firearm or destructive device. (14) Assault by any means of force likely to produce great bodily injury. (15) Discharge of a firearm into an inhabited or occupied building. * * * (18) A felony offense in which the minor personally used a weapon * * * (20) Manufacturing, compounding, or selling one-half ounce or more of any salt or solution of a controlled substance * * *. (22) Escape, by the use of force or violence, from any county juvenile hall, home, ranch, camp, or forestry camp * * * where great bodily injury is intentionally inflicted upon an employee of the juvenile facility during the commission of the escape. (23) Torture * * *. (24) Aggravated mayhem * * *. (25) Carjacking * * * while armed with a dangerous or deadly weapon. (26) Kidnapping * * *. (30) Voluntary manslaughter * * *.]

(c) With regard to a minor alleged to be a person described in Section 602 by reason of the violation, when he or she was 14 years of age or older, of any of the offenses listed in subdivision (b), upon motion of the petitioner made prior to the attachment of jeopardy the court shall cause the probation officer to investigate and submit a report on the behavioral patterns and social history of the minor being considered for a determination of unfitness. Following submission and consideration of the report, and of any other relevant evidence that the petitioner or the minor may wish to submit, the minor shall be presumed to be not a fit and proper subject to be dealt with under the juvenile court law unless the juvenile court concludes, based upon evidence, which evidence may be of extenuating or mitigating circumstances, that the minor would be amenable to the care, treatment, and training program available through the facilities of the juvenile court based upon an evaluation of each of the following criteria [listed in § 707(a)(1)(A)–(E):

A determination that the minor is a fit and proper subject to be dealt with under the juvenile court law shall be based on a finding of amenability after consideration of the criteria set forth above, and findings therefore recited in the order as to each of the above criteria that the minor is fit and proper under each and every one of the above criteria. In making a finding of fitness, the court may consider extenuating or mitigating circumstances in evaluating each of the above criteria. * * * [If] the minor is found to be not a fit and proper subject for juvenile court treatment and is tried in a court of criminal jurisdiction and found guilty by the trier of fact, the judge may commit the minor to the Department of Corrections and Rehabilitation, Division of Juvenile Facilities, in lieu of sentencing the minor to the state prison. * * *

(d)(1) Except as provided in subdivision (b) of Section 602, the district attorney or other appropriate prosecuting officer may file an accusatory pleading in a court of criminal jurisdiction against any minor 16 years of age or older who is accused of committing an offense enumerated in subdivision (b).

(2) Except as provided in subdivision (b) of Section 602, the district attorney or other appropriate prosecuting officer may file an accusatory pleading against a minor 14 years of age or older in a court of criminal jurisdiction in any case in which any one or more of the following circumstances apply:

(A) The minor is alleged to have committed an offense that if committed by an adult would be punishable by death or imprisonment in the state prison for life.

(B) The minor is alleged to have personally used a firearm during the commission or attempted commission of a felony, * * *.

(C) The minor is alleged to have committed an offense listed in subdivision (b) in which any one or more of the following circumstances apply:

(i) The minor has previously been found to be a person described in Section 602 by reason of the commission of an offense listed in subdivision (b).

(ii) The offense was committed for the benefit of, at the direction of, or in association with any criminal street gang * * * with the specific intent to promote, further, or assist in criminal conduct by gang members.

(iii) The offense was committed for the purpose of intimidating or interfering with any other person's free exercise or enjoyment of a right secured to him or her by the Constitution or laws of this state or by the Constitution or laws of the United States and because of the other person's race, color, religion, ancestry, national origin, disability, gender, or sexual orientation, or because the minor perceives that the other person has one or more of those characteristics * * *.

(iv) The victim of the offense was 65 years of age or older, or blind, deaf, quadriplegic, paraplegic, developmentally disabled, or confined to a wheelchair, and that disability was known or reasonably should have been known to the minor at the time of the commission of the offense.

(3) Except as provided in subdivision (b) of Section 602, the district attorney or other appropriate prosecuting officer may file an accusatory pleading in a court of criminal jurisdiction against any minor 16 years of age or older who is accused of committing one or more of the following offenses, if the minor has previously been found to be a person described in Section 602 by reason of the violation of a felony offense, when he or she was 14 years of age or older:

(A) A felony offense in which it is alleged that the victim of the offense was 65 years of age or older, or blind, deaf, quadriplegic, paraplegic, developmentally disabled, or confined to a wheelchair, and that disability was known or reasonably should have been known to the minor at the time of the commission of the offense.

(B) A felony offense committed for the purposes of intimidating or interfering with any other person's free exercise or enjoyment of a right secured to him or her by the Constitution or laws of this state or by the Constitution or laws of the United States and because of the other person's race, color, religion, ancestry, national origin, disability, gender, or sexual orientation, or because the minor perceived that the other person had one or more of those characteristics. * * *

(C) The offense was committed for the benefit of, at the direction of, or in association with any criminal street gang. * * *

(4) In any case in which the district attorney or other appropriate prosecuting officer has filed an accusatory pleading against a minor in a court of criminal jurisdiction pursuant to this subdivision, the case shall then proceed according to the laws applicable to a criminal case. In conjunction with the preliminary hearing, * * * the magistrate shall make a finding that reasonable cause exists to believe that the minor comes within this subdivision. If reasonable cause is not established, the criminal court shall transfer the case to the juvenile court having jurisdiction over the matter.

(5) For an offense for which the prosecutor may file the accusatory pleading in a court of criminal jurisdiction pursuant to this subdivision, but elects instead to file a petition in the juvenile court, if the minor is subsequently found to be a person described in subdivision (a) of Section 602, the minor shall be committed to placement in a juvenile hall, ranch camp, forestry camp, boot camp, or secure juvenile home. * * *

(6) If, pursuant to this subdivision, the minor is found to be not a fit and proper subject for juvenile court treatment and is tried in a court of criminal jurisdiction and found guilty by the trier of fact, the judge may commit the minor to the Department of Corrections and Rehabilitation, Division of Juvenile Facilities, in lieu of sentencing the minor to the state prison. * * *

In *Manduley*, the California Supreme Court reviewed the constitutionality of Proposition 21 shifting waiver and sentencing discretion from the judicial to the executive branch:

MANDULEY v. SUPERIOR COURT
OF SAN DIEGO COUNTY

27 Cal.4th 537, 117 Cal.Rptr.2d 168, 41 P.3d 3 (Cal. Sup. Ct. 2002).

GEORGE, C.J. Proposition 21, titled the "Gang Violence and Juvenile Crime Prevention Act of 1998" and approved by the voters at the March 7, 2000, Primary Election (Proposition 21), made a number of changes to laws applicable to minors accused of committing criminal offenses. As relevant here, the initiative measure broadened the circumstances in which prosecutors are authorized to file charges against minors 14 years of age and older in the criminal division of the superior court, rather than in the juvenile division of that court. Welfare and Institutions Code section 707, subdivision (d) (section 707(d)), confers upon prosecutors the discretion to bring specified charges against certain minors directly in criminal court, without a prior adjudication by the juvenile court that the minor is unfit for a disposition under the juvenile court law.

Petitioners are eight minors accused of committing various felony offenses. As authorized by section 707(d), the People filed charges against petitioners directly in criminal court. Petitioners demurred to the complaint, contending that section 707(d) is unconstitutional on several grounds. The superior court overruled the demurrers, but the Court of Appeal, Fourth Appellate District, issued a writ of mandate directing the superior court to vacate its ruling and to sustain the demurrers. The Court of Appeal (by a two-to-one vote) held that section 707(d) violates the separation of powers doctrine (Cal. Const., art. III, § 3) by allowing the prosecutor to interfere with the court's authority to choose a juvenile court disposition for minors found to have committed criminal offenses.

In considering the validity of the Court of Appeal's decision, we emphasize that this court is not confronted with any question regarding the wisdom of authorizing the prosecutor, rather than the court, to decide whether a minor accused of committing a crime should be treated as an adult and subjected to the criminal court system. In the present case, rather, we must decide whether section 707(d) satisfies minimum constitutional requirements; we are not called upon to resolve the competing public policies implicated by the measure, considered by the electorate when it voted upon Proposition 21, and discussed at length by numerous amici curiae who have filed briefs in support of petitioners or the People. As we shall explain, we conclude that a prosecutor's decision to file charges against a minor in criminal court pursuant to section 707(d) is well within the established charging authority of the executive branch. Our prior decisions instruct that the prosecutor's exercise of such charging discretion, before any judicial proceeding is commenced, does not usurp an exclusively judicial power, even though the prosecutor's decision effectively can preclude the court from selecting a particular sentencing alternative. Accordingly, we disagree with the Court of Appeal's conclusion that section 707(d) is unconstitutional under the separation of powers doctrine. * * *

As discussed below, we have reached the following conclusions with regard to these questions: (1) the absence of a provision requiring that a judicial fitness hearing take place before a minor can be charged in criminal court pursuant to section 707(d) does not deprive petitioners of due process of law; [and] (2) prosecutorial discretion to file charges against some minors in criminal court does not violate the equal protection clause. * * *

Petitioners demurred to the complaint, contending that section 707(d) is unconstitutional on a number of grounds. First, petitioners claimed that section 707(d) violates the separation of powers doctrine by vesting in the district attorney the discretion whether to file specified charges against minors 14 years of age and older in either the juvenile division or the criminal division of the superior court. Petitioners further contended that section 707(d) deprives them of due process of law because the statute does not provide for any hearing to determine whether they are fit for a disposition under the juvenile court law. Petitioners also claimed that section 707(d) violates their right to uniform operation of the laws and equal protection of the laws, because it permits two classes of minors charged with the same crime to be treated differently at the discretion of the prosecutor. * * *

The superior court overruled the demurrers. The court concluded that section 707(d) does not violate the separation of powers doctrine, because the decision whether to charge crimes lies within the traditional power and discretion of the prosecutor. The superior court also concluded that no due process right to a hearing exists in these circumstances, that the statute does not create any classes in which similarly situated individuals are treated disparately, that Proposition 21 does not violate the prohibitions against cruel and unusual punishment. * * *

In a divided decision, the Court of Appeal held that section 707(d) violates the separation of powers doctrine by conferring upon the prosecutor the discretion to determine which of two legislatively authorized sentencing schemes is available to the court. * * *

We begin our analysis of petitioners' challenge to section 707(d) by reviewing relevant provisions of the juvenile court law and then describing the pertinent changes effected by Proposition 21.

The law apart from the provisions of Proposition 21 provides that except as otherwise specified by statute, any individual less than 18 years of age who violates the criminal law comes within the jurisdiction of the juvenile court, which may adjudge such an individual a ward of the court. A minor accused of a crime is subject to the juvenile court system, rather than the criminal court system, unless the minor is determined to be unfit for treatment under the juvenile court law or is accused of certain serious crimes. For example, when a petition is filed alleging that a minor 16 years of age or older has violated the criminal law and should be adjudged a ward of the juvenile court, the minor generally is subject to the juvenile court law unless the court concludes, upon the motion of the prosecutor and after an investigation and report by a probation officer, that the minor would not be amenable to the care, treatment, and training program available through the facilities of the juvenile court. (§ 707 subd. (a)(1)) In assessing the minor's fitness for treatment under the juvenile court law, the court considers the minor's degree of criminal sophistication, whether the minor can be rehabilitated prior to the expiration of the juvenile court's jurisdiction, the minor's previous delinquent history, the success of previous attempts by the juvenile court to rehabilitate the minor, and the circumstances and gravity of the alleged offense.

A minor 14 years of age or older who is alleged to have committed one of the serious crimes specified in section 707, subdivision (b)—such as murder, robbery, or assault with a firearm—is presumed not to be a fit and proper subject for treatment under the juvenile court law. (§ 707, subds. (b), (c).) At the juvenile court hearing to determine the question of fitness for treatment, a minor accused of such a crime has the burden of rebutting this presumption of unfitness by a preponderance of the evidence. If a minor is declared not to be a fit and proper subject for treatment under the juvenile court law in accordance with the foregoing statutes, * * * the case then proceeds according to the laws applicable to a criminal proceeding. * * *

Proposition 21 revised the juvenile court law to broaden the circumstances in which minors 14 years of age and older can be prosecuted in the criminal division of the superior court, rather than in juvenile court. Section 707(d), as amended by the initiative, authorizes specified charges against certain minors to be filed directly in a court of criminal jurisdiction, without a judicial determination of unfitness under the juvenile court law. The statute sets forth three situations in which the prosecutor may choose to file an accusatory pleading against a minor in either juvenile court or criminal court: (1) a minor 16 years of age or older is accused of committing one of the violent or serious offenses enumerated in section 707, subdivision (b) (§ 707(d)(1)); (2) a minor 14 years of age or older is accused of committing certain serious offenses under specified circumstances (§ 707(d)(2)); and (3) a minor 16 years of age or older is accused of committing specified offenses, and the minor previously has been adjudged a ward of the court because of the commission of any felony offense when he or she was 14 years of age or older (§ 707(d)(3)). * * *

[P]etitioners challenge only the aspect of section 707(d) that confers upon the prosecutor the discretion to file certain charges against specified minors directly in criminal court, without any judicial determination that the minor is unfit for a juvenile court disposition. We proceed to consider petitioners' various constitutional claims that section 707(d) is invalid.

Petitioners first contend that section 707(d) violates the separation of powers doctrine by vesting in the prosecutor the authority to make a decision—whether to initiate a proceeding in criminal court or juvenile court—that ultimately dictates whether minors charged with certain offenses, upon conviction, shall be sentenced under the criminal law or receive a disposition under the juvenile court law. The exercise of such authority by the executive branch, petitioners contend, invades the exclusive power of the judiciary to determine the appropriate sentence for individuals who commit criminal offenses. * * *

We believe that the majority of the Court of Appeal adopted an unduly restrictive view of the scope of the executive power traditionally vested in prosecutors to decide what charges shall be alleged, and against whom charges shall be brought. This broad power to charge crimes extends to selecting the forum, among those designated by statute, in which charges shall be filed. Contrary to the majority of the Court of Appeal, the circumstance that such a charging decision may affect the sentencing alternatives available to the court does not establish that the court's power improperly has been usurped by the prosecutor. * * *

Petitioners contend that the legislative branch unconstitutionally has conferred upon the executive branch (that is, the prosecutor) an exclusively judicial function of choosing the appropriate dispositions for certain minors convicted of specified crimes. Several decisions of this court have addressed similar claims. As we shall explain, these decisions establish that the separation of powers doctrine prohibits the legislative branch from granting prosecutors the authority, *after* charges have been filed, to control the legislatively specified sentencing choices available to a court. A statute conferring upon prosecutors the discretion to make certain decisions *before* the filing of charges, on the other hand, is not invalid simply because the prosecutor's exercise of such charging discretion necessarily affects the dispositional options available to the court. Rather, such a result generally is merely incidental to the exercise of the executive function—the traditional power of the prosecutor to charge crimes. Because section 707(d) does not confer upon the prosecutor any authority to interfere with the court's choice of legislatively specified sentencing alternatives after an action has been commenced pursuant to that statute, we conclude that section 707(d) does not violate the separation of powers doctrine. * * *

"A prosecutor's charging decision may, for example, determine whether a defendant is convicted of an offense for which probation may not be granted, or for which a specific punishment is mandated. Those familiar consequences of the charging decision have, however, never been viewed as converting a prosecutor's exercise of his traditional charging discretion into a violation of the separation-of-powers doctrine." * * *

[W]e distinguished a line of decisions that invalidated statutory provisions purporting to give a prosecutor the right to veto decisions made by a court *after* criminal charges had been filed. Such decisions are based upon the principle that once the decision to prosecute has been made, the disposition of the matter is fundamentally judicial in nature. A judge wishing to exercise judicial power at the judicial stage of a proceeding never should be required to " 'bargain with the prosecutor' " before doing so. Charging decisions made before the jurisdiction of a court is invoked and before a judicial proceeding is initiated, on the other hand, involve purely prosecutorial functions and do not limit judicial power. * * *

Like the decision whether to charge a wobbler as a misdemeanor, considered in *Davis,* a prosecutor's decision pursuant to section 707(d) whether to file a wardship petition in juvenile court or an accusatory pleading in criminal court is made before the jurisdiction of the court is invoked. Although a decision to file charges directly in criminal court might preclude a juvenile court disposition, such a decision—like the prosecutor's decision in *Davis*—constitutes an aspect of traditional prosecutorial charging discretion and does not intrude upon the judicial function.

Petitioners concede that the legislative branch possesses the power to require that particular charges against certain minors always be initiated in criminal court, and to preclude juvenile dispositions for certain minors convicted of specified offenses. Petitioners assert, however, that where the juvenile court law provides for the *possibility* of a juvenile court disposition for a particular minor, the decision whether the minor ultimately receives such a disposition is exclusively a judicial function and cannot be made by the prosecutor.

A consideration of the statutory changes effected by Proposition 21, however, establishes that the legislative branch has eliminated the judicial power upon which petitioners base their claim. It is true that, prior to the enactment of section 707(d), section 707 provided that the juvenile court, after a hearing, made the decision whether certain minors charged with particular offenses were fit for treatment under the juvenile court law or instead could be charged and sentenced in criminal court. Now, however, with regard to minors within the scope of section 707(d), the statute confers upon the *prosecutor* the discretion to determine whether accusations of criminal conduct against the minor should be filed in the juvenile court or criminal court. If the prosecutor initiates a proceeding in criminal court, and the circumstances specified in section 707(d) are found to be true, the court generally is precluded by statute from ordering a juvenile disposition.

The prosecutor's discretionary charging decision pursuant to section 707(d), which thus can limit the dispositional alternatives available to the court, is no different from the numerous prefiling decisions made by prosecutors (e.g.), whether to charge a wobbler as a felony, or whether to charge a particular defendant with assault, assault with a deadly weapon, or another form of aggravated assault, or whether to charge manslaughter or murder, or whether to allege facts that would preclude probation eligibility that limit the dispositions available to the court after charges have been filed. Conferring such authority upon the prosecutor does not limit the judicial power, after charges have been filed, to choose among the dispositional alternatives specified by the legislative branch. The voters, through the enactment of Proposition 21, have determined that the judiciary shall not make the determination regarding a minor's fitness for a juvenile disposition where the prosecutor initiates a criminal action pursuant to section 707(d).

Contrary to the majority of the Court of Appeal, the circumstance that a fitness determination for minors accused of crimes within the scope of section 707(d) *formerly* was made by the court after a judicial hearing does not establish that granting the prosecutor discretion whether to file charges directly in criminal court invades the judicial prerogative. The Court of Appeal reasoned that, absent section 707(d), the determination of whether the juvenile or criminal sentencing scheme will apply "requires a particularized evidentiary hearing to adjudicate the individual juvenile's fitness or suitability for juvenile court treatment, and ... these adjudicatory functions are essentially judicial in nature." Therefore, the court determined, the decision regarding which dispositional scheme applies "is adjudicatory in nature, and ... section 707(d) allocates a judicial power and function to the district attorney in violation of separation of powers principles."

The Court of Appeal majority's analysis misapprehends the purpose and scope of the separation of powers doctrine. The charging authority implicated by section 707(d) constitutes an exclusive executive function, generally reviewable by the judicial branch only for certain constitutionally impermissible factors, such as discriminatory prosecution. * * *

The majority of the Court of Appeal also erred in equating the prosecutor's decision pursuant to section 707(d) with the fitness determination made by the juvenile court. In circumstances in which 707(d) applies, the statute dispenses with the requirement of "a particularized evidentiary hearing to adjudicate the individual juvenile's fitness or suitability for juvenile court treatment," which the Court of Appeal deemed to be an essential adjudicatory function that could not be delegated to the prosecutor. * * * [S]ection 707(d) grants the district attorney authority to establish and apply the criteria that guide his or her decision whether to file an accusatory pleading in criminal court. Such power is well within the district attorney's traditional executive authority. * * *

Petitioners further characterize the prosecutor's decision pursuant to section 707(d) as the selection of the "jurisdiction with the most 'appropriate' sentencing scheme" for a particular defendant, and they attempt to contrast such a decision with a prosecutor's well-established authority to select which crime to charge. As established above, however, the decision to charge a minor with a particular crime, like a decision pursuant to section 707(d) to file charges in criminal court, also can eliminate the juvenile court's jurisdiction over the matter and dictate the sentencing scheme that will apply upon conviction, and petitioners admit that the former decision properly can be exercised by the prosecutor. Inasmuch as petitioners concede that the Legislature possesses the authority to eliminate entirely the jurisdiction of the juvenile court and preclude juvenile court dispositions with regard to *all* minors who come within the scope of section 707(d), a statute conferring upon the prosecutor the discretion, before a judicial proceeding has been commenced, to charge *some* of these minors in criminal court does not usurp an exclusively judicial authority. * * * [M]ost prosecutorial charging decisions can circumscribe the sentencing options available to the court, and such decisions never have been considered to be analogous to fixing penalties for charged crimes or to require legislative guidelines governing the exercise of prosecutorial discretion. * * *

Petitioners further challenge section 707(d) on the ground that it deprives them of due process of law as guaranteed by the federal and California Constitutions. According to petitioners, a minor accused of criminal conduct possesses a statutory right to be subject to the jurisdiction of the juvenile court. Before a prosecutor may deprive a minor of that right by filing an action in criminal court pursuant to section 707(d), petitioners contend, the minor is entitled to a hearing to determine, pursuant to established criteria, whether he or she is amenable for a juvenile court disposition. Because section 707(d) neither provides for such a hearing nor sets forth criteria guiding the prosecutor's exercise of discretion, petitioners claim that the statute violates minimum constitutional standards of procedural fairness.

The premise of petitioners' claim is false, however, because minors who commit crimes under the circumstances set forth in section 707(d) do not possess any statutory right to be subject to the jurisdiction of the juvenile court. Although the juvenile court has jurisdiction over minors accused of most crimes, under the statutory provisions adopted by the enactment of Proposition 21, the criminal court also has jurisdiction over those minors who come within the scope of section 707(d), when the prosecutor files charges in that court. In these circumstances, when governing statutes provide that the juvenile court and the criminal court have concurrent jurisdiction, minors who come within the scope of section 707(d) do not possess any right to be placed under the jurisdiction of the juvenile court before the prosecutor initiates a proceeding accusing them of a crime. Thus, the asserted interest that petitioners seek to protect through a judicial hearing does not exist. * * *

Because petitioners do not possess a protected interest in being subject to the jurisdiction of the juvenile court, the authority upon which they rely in support of their claim is distinguishable. In *Kent v. United States,* the high court considered a statutory scheme conferring upon the juvenile court "original and exclusive" jurisdiction over a minor accused of committing various crimes. The law authorized the juvenile court to waive its jurisdiction and transfer the matter to criminal court after a "full investigation," but no statutory criteria or procedures governed the juvenile court's determination to waive jurisdiction. * * *

Unlike the statute considered in *Kent,* California's juvenile court law does not confer upon the juvenile court original and exclusive jurisdiction over minors accused of crimes under the circumstances set forth in section 707(d). Furthermore, pursuant to section 707(d), neither the juvenile court nor the criminal court renders a decision whether the minor is fit for a juvenile court disposition. Rather, as we have explained, the prosecutor's charging decision determines which court shall hear the matter. * * *

Kent held only that where a statute confers a right to a *judicial* determination of fitness for a juvenile court disposition, the due process clause requires that the determination be made in compliance with the basic procedural protections afforded to similar judicial determinations. A statute that authorizes discretionary direct filing in criminal court by the prosecutor, on the other hand, does not require similar procedural protections, because it does not involve a judicial determination but rather constitutes an executive charging function, which does not implicate the right to procedural due process and a hearing. * * *

[T]he legislative branch properly can delegate to the prosecutor—who traditionally has been entrusted with the charging decision—discretion whether to file charges against a minor directly in criminal court, and the Legislature also can eliminate a minor's statutory right to a judicial fitness hearing. Therefore, a prosecutor's decision pursuant to section 707(d) to file charges in criminal court does not implicate any protected interest of petitioners that gives rise to the requirements of procedural due process.

Petitioners next challenge section 707(d) on the ground that it violates their right to the equal protection of the laws, because the statute permits identically situated minors to be subject to different laws and disparate treatment at the discretion of the prosecutor. Petitioners assert that minors of the same age and charged with the same crime under the circumstances enumerated in section 707(d) are subject either to the juvenile court law or to the criminal justice system, based solely upon a prosecutorial decision that is unguided by any statutory standards. According to petitioners, the creation of two classes of minors pursuant to section 707(d) implicates fundamental liberty interests, and the disparity in treatment of minors falling within the scope of the statute is neither justified by a compelling state interest nor rationally related to a legitimate interest. Therefore, they contend, section 707(d) is unconstitutional on its face. We conclude that petitioners' equal protection claim lacks merit.

To succeed on their claim under the equal protection clause, petitioners first must show that the state has adopted a classification that affects two or more similarly situated groups in an unequal manner. Petitioners do not challenge the classification expressly set forth in section 707(d)—that is, they do not contend that the disparate treatment of minors who meet the criteria set forth in section 707(d), and of minors who do not meet such criteria, is impermissible. Instead they assert that section 707(d) authorizes *prosecutors* to create two classes of minors, both of which satisfy the criteria set forth in the statute. One class consists of those minors against whom prosecutors choose to file criminal charges in criminal court; the other consists of minors accused of having committed the same offenses, but against whom prosecutors choose to file wardship petitions in juvenile court. These two classes of minors are affected in an unequal manner, petitioners observe, because application of the juvenile court law or the criminal law can give rise to significantly different rights and penalties for similarly situated minors.

As petitioners implicitly concede, all minors who meet the criteria enumerated in section 707(d) equally are subject to the prosecutor's discretion whether to file charges in criminal court. Any unequal treatment of such minors who commit the same crime under similar circumstances results solely from the decisions of individual prosecutors whether to file against particular minors a petition in juvenile court or instead an accusatory pleading in criminal court. * * * Claims of unequal treatment by prosecutors in selecting particular classes of individuals for prosecution are evaluated according to ordinary equal protection standards. These standards require the defendant to show that he or she has been singled out deliberately for prosecution on the basis of some invidious criterion, and that the prosecution would not have been pursued except for the discriminatory purpose of the prosecuting authorities. "[A]n invidious purpose for prosecution is one that is arbitrary and thus unjustified because it bears no rational relationship to legitimate law enforcement interests...."

Section 707(d) contains no overtly discriminatory classification. In their challenge to section 707(d), petitioners do not contend that the district attorney filed charges against them in criminal court on the basis of some invidious criterion or for a discriminatory purpose, or that section 707(d) has had any discriminatory effect. Petitioners instead contend that section 707(d) *might* result in invidious discrimination because it contains no standards guiding the prosecutor's discretion whether to file charges in criminal court. * * *

[P]etitioners cannot establish a violation of their right to the equal protection of the laws by showing that other minors in circumstances similar to those of petitioners can be prosecuted under the juvenile court law. Section 707(d) limits the prosecutor's discretion to file charges in criminal court to minors of a specified age who commit enumerated crimes under certain circumstances, and at the preliminary hearing the magistrate must find reasonable cause to believe that the minor has committed such a crime under those circumstances. In addition, the prosecutor's decision is subject to constitutional constraints against invidious discrimination. Therefore, contrary to petitioners' contention, the prosecutor's decision is not unfettered or entirely without standards. The prosecutor's discretion to select those statutorily eligible cases in which to seek a criminal disposition against a minor—based upon permissible factors such as the circumstances of the crime, the background of the minor, or a desire to show leniency, for example—does not violate the equal protection clause. * * *

In support of their claim * * * petitioners rely upon a divided decision of the Utah Supreme Court—*State v. Mohi* [*see infra* Note 1, p. 641]— which invalidated a statute conferring upon prosecutors the discretion to file charges against minors directly in criminal court. The holding in *Mohi* was based exclusively upon a provision in the Utah Constitution. * * * As the plurality opinion in *Mohi* emphasized, however, Utah's constitutional provision concerning uniform operation of the laws established requirements different from those of the federal equal protection clause. * * *

In any event, we are not persuaded by the reasoning of the plurality opinion in *Mohi*. The opinion contrasted a prosecutor's traditional charging discretion with the prosecutor's assertedly arbitrary discretion to file charges against a minor directly in criminal court. According to the plurality opinion, traditional charging discretion concerned *which* law to apply to a single offender, whereas direct-filing discretion involved how to apply the *same* law to different offenders. Because the challenged statute permitted prosecutors to treat different offenders accused of the same criminal offense differently, without any statutory criteria to guide the prosecutors' decisions, the plurality opinion held that the law operated "nonuniformly on similarly situated juveniles" and thus violated the state constitutional requirement of uniform operation of the laws.

Contrary to the reasoning of the plurality opinion in *Mohi,* however, traditional prosecutorial charging discretion, which includes the discretion not to bring *any* charges against a particular offender, encompasses decisions how to apply the same law to different offenders, often without any express statutory criteria guiding such decisions. Thus, prosecutors properly may decide that some individuals who have engaged in criminal conduct proscribed by a particular penal statute should not be prosecuted at all. Prosecutors may charge some defendants with a misdemeanor violation of the statute, and others with a felony violation. With regard to some offenders, prosecutors may seek the maximum penalty authorized by the statute, while offering to recommend probation or diversion for other offenders. None of these prosecutorial decisions, unless based upon invidious discrimination or retaliatory motive, ever has been considered to be unconstitutionally arbitrary. Therefore, prosecutorial discretion resulting in the different application of the same law to different offenders does not necessarily violate the requirement of uniform operation of the laws. * * *

The judgment of the Court of Appeal is reversed.

Dissenting Opinion by KENNARD, J. Historically, in California the decision whether to grant a district attorney's request that a minor be prosecuted in adult court instead of juvenile court has been a function of the judiciary, a neutral body. In 2000, however, the voters of this state enacted Proposition 21, an initiative measure that among other matters grants a prosecutor arbitrary and virtually unlimited discretion to decide whether a minor should be tried in juvenile or adult court. There is no hearing, and no right to counsel. No standards guide the exercise of discretion. There is no judicial review. This last omission is fatal, for by depriving the judiciary of any role in making or reviewing the decision, this portion of Proposition 21 eliminates an essential check to arbitrary executive power, and thus offends the principle of separation of powers embodied in the California Constitution. * * *

Proposition 21 seeks to eliminate the required checks and balances. * * * But as to those minors who could be prosecuted in either adult court or juvenile court, it allows the prosecutor to make that decision unrestrained by any legislatively prescribed standards and without judicial review. If the decision is to prosecute in adult court, and it later appears that the juvenile court would have been more appropriate, the minor has no remedy because the judicial branch is excluded from the determination. This portion of Proposition 21, in my view, conflicts with the constitutional mandate.

The juvenile court system and the adult criminal courts serve fundamentally different goals. The punishment for serious crimes tried in the criminal courts is imprisonment, and "the purpose of imprisonment for crime is punishment." * * *

In contrast, the juvenile court system seeks not only to protect the public safety, but also the youthful offender. Section 202, subdivision (a), states that the purpose of the juvenile court system is "to provide for the protection and safety of the public and each minor under the jurisdiction of the juvenile court and to preserve and strengthen the minor's family ties whenever possible." * * *

The practical consequences are immense. An adult court may sentence a defendant to life imprisonment; a juvenile court cannot impose confinement beyond the age of 25. Adult convictions are public but juvenile commitments are sealed, a difference that affects future employability and many other matters. Adult convictions are criminal in character, and may deprive the person convicted of the right to vote, to serve on a jury, to carry firearms and to enter certain professions; juvenile convictions carry no such collateral consequences. Finally, by filing in adult court the prosecutor deprives the juvenile of the varied rehabilitative programs available in juvenile court. * * *

In my view, Proposition 21 unconstitutionally invaded a judicial function, for the following reasons:

First, almost from the inception of the juvenile court system in California, the decision whether a minor is unfit for juvenile court proceedings has been a judicial function. History alone may not be conclusive, but it is important, for the division of authority among the three co-equal branches of government is largely a product of history.

Second, the decision whether to prosecute in juvenile or adult court is critical, and thus deserving of the due process protections of a judicial proceeding. In *Kent v. United States*, * * * the high court repeatedly described the decision whether a minor should be tried as a juvenile or an adult as "critically important", one of "tremendous consequence", and thus deserving and requiring the protection of due process. * * *

These cases do not suggest that the critically important decision whether to try the minor in adult or juvenile court should receive due process protections only if it is made after charges have been filed. Yet if the same decision, equally important and consequential, is made before charges are filed, then, according to the majority, the prosecutor has unreviewable discretion, subject only to the most minimal of constitutional constraints prohibiting invidious discrimination or vindictive or retaliatory prosecution. There is no judicial review to correct erroneous decisions, inconsistent decisions, or decisions that certain classes of minors, or all minors, will always be prosecuted in adult court.

Third, at the time of filing charges, the district attorney's office has limited information—the details of the particular crime, and the minor's prior criminal history, if any. It may not know the minor's family, school, or community history, all matters that are important in deciding whether the minor is suitable for juvenile court treatment. It may not know the minor's view of the matter, and probably has not heard from the minor's counsel, who has yet to be appointed. There has been no hearing, no testimony, and no receipt of evidence. As a result, the prosecutor, acting with limited information, may err in the decision, and although an error in submitting the minor to juvenile court jurisdiction is correctable, one in assigning the minor to adult court is not. * * *

In conclusion, the validity of Proposition 21's provision giving the prosecutor power to decide whether to prosecute a minor in adult court or juvenile court turns not on the timing of the prosecutor's decision, but "the substance of the power and the effect of its exercise." The power, as I have explained, is unrestrained by legislative standards and susceptible to arbitrary exercise; the effect is profound, determining whether the minor will be prosecuted in a system that stresses punishment or one that stresses rehabilitation. In this setting, the absence of judicial review brings that portion of Proposition 21 into conflict with article III, section 3 of the California Constitution.

NOTES

1) Judicial Questioning of Standardless Prosecutorial Discretion The California court in *Manduley* distinguished **State v. Mohi**, 901 P.2d 991 (Utah 1995), which represents the singular deviation from uniform appellate approval of prosecutorial direct-file forum-selection statutes. Prosecutor charged Mohi in criminal court with intentional or reckless homicide with a firearm. The defendants in *Mohi* and in two companion cases argued that the direct-file law violated the Utah Constitution, which provides that "All laws of a general nature shall have uniform operation." Mohi argued that the direct-file provision to allow juvenile or criminal prosecution created a statutory scheme that treated one class of persons charged with a particular crime differently than another class of persons charged with the same crime. Mohi argued that the law allowed prosecutors to create an unreasonable and arbitrary classification because it did not provide any reasons to permit similarly-situated youths to receive such disparate consequences. The Utah Supreme Court construed the state constitutional provision for "uniform" application of laws to require treating similarly-situated offenders similarly, unless the differences in treatment reasonably furthered the statutory objectives. Because the direct-file statute contained no criteria or rationale, the court could find no reasons why prosecutors charged some youths as adults in criminal court while other youths of the same age and charged with the same offenses remained in juvenile court:

> Defendants contend that because they are being tried as adults for the same crimes that some of their peers will be tried for as juveniles, they are treated disparately. The State counters that being tried as a juvenile is not a "right" of anyone per se and that by bestowing a benefit on some juveniles but choosing not to bestow that same benefit on others, the legislature is not taking any rights away but merely giving benefits to appropriate persons. We are unable to reconcile this argument with the concept of uniform operation of laws because the selection process for beneficial treatment is arbitrary and standardless.

> We agree with defendants that the present Act treats a certain subclass of juveniles nonuniformly. Juveniles against whom indictments or informations are filed are statutorily indistinguishable from those who remain in juvenile jurisdiction. By the very terms of the statute, they are accused of the same offenses and fall into the same age ranges. There is absolutely nothing in the statute to identify the juveniles to be tried as adults; it describes no distinctive characteristics to set them apart from juveniles in the other statutory class who remain in juvenile jurisdiction. However, there are critically important differences in the treatment of those juveniles tried as adults compared to those left in the juvenile system. * * * Therefore, the statute permits two identically situated juveniles, even co-conspirators or co-participants in the same crime, to face radically different penalties and consequences without any statutory guidelines for distinguishing between them. This amounts to unequal treatment. * * *

> However, this finding alone does not invalidate the statute. The principle of uniform operation of laws requires invalidation of the statute only if defendants can demonstrate that this disparity is unreasonable in relation to the purpose of the statute. The final step in our analysis, therefore, is to determine whether there is a "reasonable relationship" between the purpose of the Act and the means adopted by the legislature to enact that purpose. * * * [T]he purpose of the Act is to promote public safety and individual accountability by the imposition of ["]appropriate sanctions on persons who have committed acts in violation of law [and] * * * consistent with the ends of justice, strive to act in the best interests of the children in all cases and attempt to preserve and strengthen family ties where possible.["] * * *

> The State argues that the direct-file provision of the Act is reasonably related to the statute's stated purpose because there is a legitimate

need to try certain violent juveniles as adults. We agree with the State's assertion of need but observe that the legislature has failed to specify which violent juveniles require such treatment, instead delegating that discretion to prosecutors who have no guidelines as to how it is to be exercised. Legitimacy of a goal cannot justify an arbitrary means. The State asserts that this problem is cured by the fact that prosecutors often have legitimate reasons for wanting to leave persons eligible for adult prosecution in juvenile court. But the statute does not require the prosecutor to have any reason, legitimate or otherwise, to support his or her decision of who stays in juvenile jurisdiction and who does not. Legitimacy in the purpose of the statute cannot make up for a deficiency in its design. Section 78–3a–25 is wholly without standards to guide or instruct prosecutors as to when they should or should not use such influential powers. The total absence of such standards makes the Utah statute unique among those of all other states employing any type of adult prosecution of juvenile offenders. It is ironic that the Act sets out in thirteen full paragraphs all of the factors that a court must consider to certify a juvenile into the adult system, but contains no guidelines for a prosecutor who may choose for any reason or no reason to place that juvenile into the adult system. * * *

There is no rational connection between the legislature's objective of balancing the needs of children with public protection and its decision to allow prosecutors total discretion in deciding which members of a potential class of juvenile offenders to single out for adult treatment. Such unguided discretion opens the door to abuse without any criteria for review or for insuring evenhanded decision making. * * *

Choosing which court to file charges in has significant consequences for the offender, and the statute does not indicate what characteristics of the offender mandate that choice. The scope for prosecutor stereotypes, prejudices, and biases of all kinds is simply too great. If it is the legislature's determination to have all members of a certain group of violent juveniles (such as repeat offenders, those who use guns, etc.) tried as adults, it is free to do so. However, the legislature may not create a scheme which permits the random and unsupervised separation of all such violent juveniles into a relatively privileged group on the one hand and a relatively burdened group on the other. * * *

The challenged statute permits prosecutors to treat different offenders accused of the same criminal offense differently. Thus, the same law operates disparately and nonuniformly on similarly situated juveniles. In a case where the prosecutor chooses to charge like-situated suspects with different crimes, the classic ''prosecutorial discretion'' question is which law to apply to an offender rather than how to apply the same law to different offenders. Once an offender is charged with a particular crime, that offender must be subjected to the same or substantially similar procedures and exposed to the same level of jeopardy as all other offenders so charged to satisfy the constitutional requirement of uniform operation of the laws.

We conclude that the provisions in section 78–3a–25 of the Code giving prosecutors undirected discretion to choose where to file charges against certain juvenile offenders are unconstitutional under article I, section 24 of the Utah Constitution. Therefore, * * * [the cases] are remanded to the appropriate juvenile jurisdictions for certification proceedings consistent with the requirements in section 78–3a–25.

3. TRANSFER BACK OR REVERSE CERTIFICATION

States made relatively limited use of offense-based strategies until *Kent* provided the impetus for offense exclusion and prosecutorial direct-file laws. A few states long had excluded from their juvenile courts older youths charged with capital offenses or crimes punishable by life imprisonment, such as murder. Some states also excluded youths charged with other serious crimes such as criminal sexual conduct or armed robbery, or those who had repeat offenses. But, reflecting the influences of "just deserts" jurisprudence, criminal career research, and "get tough" politics, two distinct legislative trends have emerged during the past quarter-century. First, more states have excluded at least some offenses from their juvenile courts' jurisdiction, lowered the ages of juveniles' eligibility for criminal prosecution, and increased the numbers of offenses for which states may prosecute youths as adults. Eric Fritsch and Craig Hemmens, "Juvenile Waiver in the United States 1979–1995: A Comparison and Analysis of State Waiver Statutes," 46 *Juv. & Fam. Ct. Judges J.* 17 (1995); Patricia Torbet, et al., *State Responses to Serious and Violent Juvenile Crime: Research Report* (1996). Second, the number of states that allow prosecutors, rather than judges, to make forum selection decisions via concurrent jurisdiction also has increased as has the range of offenses for which they may transfer youths. Howard N. Snyder and Melissa Sickmund, *Juvenile Offenders and Victims: 2006 National Report* (2006); United States General Accounting Office, *Juvenile Justice: Juveniles Processed in Criminal Court and Case Dispositions (1995).*

A compilation and analysis of states' waiver laws in 1986 reported that eighteen (18) states excluded at least some offenses from their juvenile courts' jurisdiction. Barry C. Feld, "Juvenile Court Meets the Principle of Offense: Legislative Changes in Juvenile Waiver Statutes." 78 *J. Crim. L. & Criminology* 471 (1987). Capital crimes or murder by youths sixteen or older constituted the most common form of excluded offense legislation, although a few states had adopted more extensive lists. One-third (6) of those states excluded youths on the basis of a prior felony conviction coupled with a serious present crime. Although six states had excluded capital- and life-sentence offenses for more than half a century, the other dozen states adopted or expanded their offense exclusion laws only in the decade after *Kent*. As we saw in *Bland*, in 1970 in response to *Kent*, Congress excluded murder, rape, and robbery by youths sixteen or older from the jurisdiction of the juvenile courts of the District of

Columbia. By 1975, four other states followed suit, and, by 1980, nine more states excluded some serious offenses from juvenile court jurisdiction. The legislative trend to excise the most serious young offenders from juvenile court jurisdiction that began in the 1970s accelerated during the 1980s.

One statutory compilation a decade later reported that twenty-six (26) states excluded some offenses from their juvenile courts' jurisdiction, a 45% increase in less than a decade. Snyder and Sickmund, *Juvenile Offenders and Victims, supra.* A second statutory compilation that also included judicially waived youths previously convicted as adults in its excluded offense classification reported that thirty-eight (38) states excluded at least some offenders from juvenile court jurisdiction. United States General Accounting Office, *Juvenile Justice: Juveniles Processed in Criminal Court and Case Dispositions, supra.* A third compilation that compared waiver statutes in 1979 with those in 1995 reported that during that period, one state repealed its offense exclusion provisions, while twenty-three states excluded some offenses, including eight additional states that joined the excluded-offense ranks during that period, a 35% increase. Fritsch and Hemmens, "Juvenile Waiver in the United States 1979–1995," *supra.* During the 1979–1995 period, almost half of the states also lowered the age of eligibility for adult prosecution, increased the catalogues of excluded offenses, or included provisions for exclusion on the basis of prior offenses. Still another statutory survey reported that simply between 1992 and 1995, twenty-four states added some crimes to their lists of excluded offenses and six states lowered the minimum ages for some or all of their excluded offenses. Torbet, et al., *State Responses to Serious and Violent Juvenile Crime, supra.* Thus, by any measure, the rate and scope of offense exclusion legislative amendments continued and expanded.

Oftentimes, a single highly-visible case inflames public fears and political passions, and provides the impetus to exclude offenses or to lower the age of eligibility for exclusion. The most dramatic example of a single case that produced an excluded offense law occurred in the state of New York. *See e.g.,* Fox Butterfield, *All God's Children: The Bosket Family and the American Tradition of Violence* (1995); Simon I. Singer, *Recriminalizing Delinquency: Violent Juvenile Crime and Juvenile Justice Reform* (1996). Prior to 1978, New York's family court jurisdiction ended at sixteen years of age and no method existed to transfer younger offenders to adult criminal court. Fifteen-year-old Willie Bosket robbed and murdered two subway passengers within months of his release from a secure juvenile facility. Even under a newly-strengthened 1976 Young Offender (YO) law for sentencing youths sixteen to eighteen years of age, the judge only could impose a maximum placement with the Division for Youth until Bosket's twenty-first birthday, i.e. a five year maximum sentence. Less than two weeks after the juvenile court judge sentenced Bosket, New York Governor Hugh Carey, a liberal democrat whom his opponent attacked as "soft on crime," called a special legislative session that quickly adopted the Juvenile Offender Act (JOA). The "Willie Bosket Law" excluded youths as young as thirteen years of age charged with murder and those fourteen years of age or older charged with rape, robbery, assault, and violent burglaries. *N.Y. Crim. Proc. Law* § 1.20(42) (McKinney 1992), *supra* p. 600. In Minnesota in 1988, the case of David Brom, *supra*, p. 558, provided the political impetus for the Minnesota legislature to exclude from juvenile court jurisdiction youths sixteen years of age or older whom prosecutors charged with first-degree murder. *Minn. Stat. Ann.* § 260.015 Subd. 5(b), *supra*, p. 582; Barry C. Feld, "Violent Youth and Public Policy: A Case Study of Juvenile Justice Law Reform," 79 *Minn. L. Rev.* 965 (1995).

State laws that exclude long lists of offenses from juvenile courts or that give prosecutors greater authority to direct-file charges in either juvenile or criminal court simply shift sentencing discretion from judges in a waiver hearing to prosecutors in their offices. Because offense categories are necessarily crude and imprecise indicators of the "real" seriousness of any particular offense, prosecutors inevitably exercise enormous sentencing discretion when they decide whether to charge a youth with an excluded offense rather than a lesser included offense, or to select the forum in a direct-file jurisdiction. Despite the extensive lists of excluded offenses and the ascendance of "get tough" policies, it seems unlikely that state legislators intend prosecutors to charge every theoretically eligible youth in criminal court. "Assaults and robberies vary tremendously in seriousness. These two offenses account for 94 percent of all youth violence arrests. Categorical generalizations are therefore a poor basis for policy in a great majority of cases." Franklin Zimring, "Toward a Jurisprudence of Youth Violence," 24 *Crime & Justice* 477, 494 (1998). Even among the serious crimes contained in most exclusion or direct file statutes, the heterogeneity of offenses within each category requires some decision maker, either a judge or a prosecutor, qualitatively to evaluate both the specific "seriousness" of that crime and the nature of the individual actor's participation. For example, aggravated assaults may range from a bloody nose to a severe beating to a grievous wounding with a firearm. "[U]ndifferentiated measures of aggravated assault will be rendered opaque by the mixture of serious and less serious events agglomerated in the overall pattern." Frank Zimring, "American Youth Violence: Issues and Trends." 1 *Crime & Justice* 67, 83 (1979). Similarly, armed robberies may run the gamut from appropriation of lunch money in a school yard while holding a screw-driver to dispossession at the point of a gun in a life-threatening confrontation.

Youths' degrees of participation in crimes vary as much as do offenses within the generic legal categories. Young offenders commit crimes in groups to a much greater extent than do adults. Franklin Zimring, "Kids, Groups, and Crime: Some Implications of a Well–Known Secret," 72 *J. Crim. L. & Criminology* 867 (1981); Franklin Zimring, *American Youth Violence* (1998); Snyder and Sickmund, *Juvenile Offenders and Victims*, *supra*. While the criminal law treats all participants as equally responsible

and may sentence principals and accessories alike, young people's susceptibility to peer group influences requires some individualized assessment
of their degree of participation, personal responsibility, and culpability.
The presence of a social audience of peers may induce youths to participate in criminal behavior that they would not engage in if alone. Although
the criminal law treats all accomplices as equally guilty as a matter of law,
they all may not be equally responsible for the actual harm inflicted.

Because of the heterogeneity of offenses and variations in degrees of
participation, some individualized differentiation necessarily and inevitably occurs in the course of charging and waiving young offenders. A study
of prosecutorial charging practices in filing judicial waiver motions in
Texas illustrates the magnitude of the discretionary selection process.
Robert O. Dawson, "An Empirical Study of *Kent*–Style Juvenile Transfers
to Criminal Court," 23 *St. Mary's L. J.* 975 (1992). Under the Texas law
applicable in 1988, juvenile court judges used *Kent* criteria to decide
whether to waive youths fifteen or sixteen years of age charged with *any
felony* and against whom prosecutors filed a waiver motion. During the
period of the study, juvenile courts received 14,150 felony referrals against
youths aged fifteen and sixteen, but prosecutors filed transfer motions
against only 112 youths. As would be expected, prosecutors focused on
more serious offenses, comparable to those listed in most excluded-offense
and direct-file statutes. Significantly, however, prosecutors filed transfer
motions against fewer than two percent of felony offenders, including only
31 percent of those eligible youths referred for homicide, only 3 percent of
those charged with sexual assault, only 6 percent of those charged with
robbery, and only .5 percent of those charged with aggravated assault. *Id.*
at 988. While prosecutors filed nearly two-thirds of all the waiver motions
they made against youths charged with murder, robbery, and rape, they
refrained from filing transfer motions against the vast majority of youths
referred to juvenile court for those offenses. This confirms that even
within most serious offense categories, prosecutors individualize and differentiate on some basis. Moreover, the study reported county-by-county
variations; geographic context also influenced the types of differentiation
that prosecutors made. *Id.* The heterogeneity of offenses, the variability of
youths' participation in crimes, and the idiosyncrasies of prosecutors have
important implications for the implementation of offense exclusion and
direct-file laws. Such statutes enable prosecutors covertly to manipulate
charges or to select a juvenile or criminal forum in a low visibility,
discretionary setting with minimal information or a record, and without
any form of legal accountability or review. As a matter of sentencing
policy, the question recurs whether prosecutors will make better informed
and more appropriate decisions under such circumstances than would
judges in an adversarial waiver hearing guided by appropriate waiver
criteria.

Progressive reformers created separate juvenile courts and correctional institutions in part to avoid confining vulnerable youths in prisons with
adults. Legislative policies to transfer more and younger juveniles to

criminal courts also expose more youths to adult correctional consequences. Because many excluded offenses also carry mandatory minimum
criminal sentences, juveniles charged and convicted as adults also face
greater prospects of incarceration. Barry C. Feld, "Juvenile and Criminal
Justice Systems' Responses to Youth Violence," 24 *Crime & Justice* 189
(1998). In order to restore some flexibility to a prosecutor-dominated
waiver process and to allow for judicial review and "more appropriate"
dispositions of some "amenable" younger offenders, many states allow
judges to "reverse waive" or "transfer back" to juvenile court cases that
originated in criminal court either as a result of excluded offense or
prosecutorial direct-file decisions. About half of the prosecutor "direct
file," and excluded offense jurisdictions allow a criminal court judge either
to return a youth to juvenile court for trial or sentencing, or to impose a
juvenile or youthful offender sentence in lieu of an adult criminal sentence. To which young offenders do "transfer back" laws apply? Who is
the decision maker—a juvenile court judge, a criminal court judge, or a
prosecutor? Who has the burden of proof? What standards and criteria
guide the "reverse waiver" or transfer back decision? Have we seen these
criteria previously? What evidence would the parties present to meet those
statutory criteria?

**Preserving Juvenile Court Sentencing Options for Youths
Convicted in Criminal Court** In Florida, prosecutors direct-file about
ten percent of juvenile offenders into criminal court for prosecution as
adults. Donna M. Bishop, et al., "Prosecutorial Waiver: Case Study of a
Questionable Reform," 35 *Crime & Delinq.* 179 (1989); Cynthia R. Noon,
" 'Waiving' Goodbye to Juvenile Defendants, Getting Smart vs. Getting
Tough," 49 *U. Miami L. Rev.* 431 (1994). Criminal court judges must
sentence juveniles convicted of offenses punishable by death or life imprisonment as adults. *Fla. Stat. Ann.* §§ 985.225; 985.233 (4)(a)(1) (West
1997). However, the following statute gives judges other sentencing options for youths tried and convicted in criminal court.

Florida Statute § 985.233 (West 1998):

(1) Powers of disposition.—

(a) A child who is found to have committed a violation of law may, as
an alternative to adult dispositions, be committed to the department for
treatment in an appropriate program for children outside the adult
correctional system or be placed in a community control program for
juveniles.

(b) In determining whether to impose juvenile sanctions instead of
adult sanctions, the court shall consider the following criteria:

1.   The seriousness of the offense to the community and whether the
community would best be protected by juvenile or adult sanctions.

2.   Whether the offense was committed in an aggressive, violent,
premeditated, or willful manner.

3. Whether the offense was against persons or against property, with greater weight being given to offenses against persons, especially if personal injury resulted.

4. The sophistication and maturity of the offender.

5. The record and previous history of the offender, including:

a. Previous contacts with the Department of Corrections, the Department of Juvenile Justice, * * * law enforcement agencies, and the courts.

b. Prior periods of probation or community control.

c. Prior adjudications that the offender committed a delinquent act or violation of law as a child.

d. Prior commitments to the Department of Juvenile Justice, * * * or other facilities or institutions.

6. The prospects for adequate protection of the public and the likelihood of deterrence and reasonable rehabilitation of the offender if assigned to services and facilities of the Department of Juvenile Justice.

7. Whether the Department of Juvenile Justice has appropriate programs, facilities, and services immediately available.

8. Whether adult sanctions would provide more appropriate punishment and deterrence to further violations of law than the imposition of juvenile sanctions.

(2) Presentence investigation report.—

(a) Upon a plea of guilty, the court may refer the case to the department for investigation and recommendation as to the suitability of its programs for the child. * * *

(3) Sentencing hearing.—

(a) At the sentencing hearing the court shall receive and consider a presentence investigation report by the Department of Corrections regarding the suitability of the offender for disposition as an adult or as a juvenile. * * *

(b) After considering the presentence investigation report, the court shall give all parties present at the hearing an opportunity to comment on the issue of sentence and any proposed rehabilitative plan. * * *

4) Sentencing alternatives.—

(a) Sentencing to adult sanctions.—

1. Cases prosecuted on indictment.—If the child is found to have committed the offense punishable by death or life imprisonment, the child shall be sentenced as an adult. If the juvenile is not found to have committed the indictable offense but is found to have committed a lesser included offense or any other offense for which he or she was indicted as a part of the criminal episode, the court may sentence as follows:

a. As an adult pursuant to this section;

b. Pursuant to chapter 958 [juvenile delinquency dispositions], notwithstanding any other provision of that chapter to the contrary; or

c. As a juvenile pursuant to this section.

2. Other cases.—If a child who has been transferred for criminal prosecution pursuant to information or waiver of juvenile court jurisdiction is found to have committed a violation of state law or a lesser included offense for which he or she was charged as a part of the criminal episode, the court may sentence as follows:

a. As an adult pursuant to this section;

b. Pursuant to chapter 958 [juvenile delinquency dispositions], notwithstanding any other provision of that chapter to the contrary; or

c. As a juvenile pursuant to this section.

3. Any sentence imposing adult sanctions is presumed appropriate, and the court is not required to set forth specific findings or enumerate the criteria in this subsection as any basis for its decision to impose adult sanctions. * * *

(b) Sentencing to juvenile sanctions.—In order to use this paragraph, the court shall stay adjudication of guilt and instead shall adjudge the child to have committed a delinquent act. Adjudication of delinquency shall not be deemed a conviction, nor shall it operate to impose any of the civil disabilities ordinarily resulting from a conviction. The court shall impose an adult sanction or a juvenile sanction and may not sentence the child to a combination of adult and juvenile punishments. * * *

In **Troutman v. State**, 630 So.2d 528, 531 (Fla. 1993), the Florida Supreme Court held that a juvenile convicted in criminal court may still receive special treatment as a juvenile and required sentencing judges specifically to decide a youth's suitability for juvenile or adult sanctions and provide written findings to support its conclusions. "[A] trial court must consider each of the criteria * * * before determining the suitability of adult sanctions. In so doing, the trial court must give an *individualized evaluation* of how a particular juvenile fits within the criteria. Mere conclusory language that tracks the statutory criteria is insufficient." Just as Judge J. Skelly Wright's dissent in *Bland* argued for an assessment of "the maturity of the child and his susceptibility to rehabilitation," *Troutman* emphasized that a criminal sentencing hearing provided the only opportunity to consider a youth's "suitability for treatment":

> Strict adherence to the [statutory] provisions * * * is especially important in cases involving the direct filing of criminal charges in adult court because the provisions provide the only formal means of ensuring that the juvenile is being properly treated as an adult. Unlike most situations in which a child is waived into adult court, direct file cases do not involve an initial hearing and determination by the trial judge that transfer of the case to adult court is appropriate. *Troutman*, 630 So.2d at 531 n. 5.

In *Walker v. State*, 304 Ark. 393, 803 S.W.2d 502 (Ark. 1991), the Arkansas Supreme Court held that a youth who sought to transfer the case from criminal to juvenile court was the moving party and bore the burden of proof. Moreover, as long as the trial court at least "considered" all of the statutory criteria, nothing required the judge to give equal weight to all factors. It would not constitute an "abuse of discretion" for a trial judge to place greater emphasis on the seriousness and violence of the offense than on the other "rehabilitation" factors, or to base its assessment of the nature of the offense primarily on the prosecutor's charging documents. *Id.* Because criminal court judges often may lack "knowledge of juvenile justice" and are predisposed "to the policies of retribution and punitive treatment," their decisions typically tend to ratify those of prosecutors. Allison Boyce, "Choosing the Forum: Prosecutorial Discretion and *Walker v. State*," 46 *Ark. L. Rev.* 985 at 1002 (1994). Analysts of judicial waiver practices have observed a similar proclivity of juvenile court judges to ratify prosecutors' transfer motions rather than to make independent evaluations of a case. Robert O. Dawson, "An Empirical Study of *Kent*–Style Juvenile Transfers to Criminal Court," 23 *St. Mary's L. J.* 975 (1992).

NOTES

1) Do Transfer Back Procedures Replicate *Kent* Procedures? As you read the Florida statute and the excerpts from the cases, does it seem to you that offense exclusion and direct-file waiver systems have shifted the "amenability" decision from an initial judicial determination of jurisdiction as in *Kent*, to a "reverse waiver" or post-conviction sentencing decision. The statutory criteria, procedural safeguards, and appellate review mirror the *Kent* judicial waiver process albeit at a different stage of the proceedings, in a different forum, and before a different judge.

2) Criminal Court Judge vs. Juvenile Court Judge Is there any reason to believe that criminal court judges possess any greater expertise with which to decide whether a youth is "suitable for treatment" as a juvenile than a juvenile court judge does to decide that a juvenile is not "amenable to treatment"? As a matter of institutional competencies, which judges do you believe are more likely to make appropriate "amenability" determinations and why?

An evaluation of Maryland juvenile and criminal court waiver decisions analyzed the factors that led juvenile court judges to relinquish jurisdiction over non-excluded youths and criminal court judges to remand to juvenile court those youths whose cases originated in criminal court. *See* Kristin Parsons Winokur, "Juvenile Jurisdictional Transfer: An Evaluation of the Judicial and Reverse Waiver Mechanisms," (1996), *cited* in Barry C. Feld, "Juvenile and Criminal Justice Systems' Responses to Youth Violence," 24 *Crime & Justice* 189 (1998). Criminal court judges granted nearly half (45%) of the excluded juveniles' "reverse waiver" motions, and "transferred back" significantly more younger offenders and those whom clinicians identified as "amenable to treatment." Within the group of serious excluded offenses, these "reverse waived" youths also had fewer prior convictions and less previous exposure to juvenile correctional services than did those youths over whom criminal court judges retained jurisdiction. These findings correspond to comparable research on judicial waiver decision making. Controlling for offense variables, juvenile court judges typically transferred older youths, those with prior juvenile correctional experiences, and those whom clinicians deemed "unamenable to treatment." Marcy Rasmussen Podkopacz and Barry C. Feld, "Judicial Waiver Policy and Practice: Persistence, Seriousness and Race," 14 *J. Law & Inquality* 73 (1995); Marcy Rasmussen Podkopacz and Barry C. Feld, "The End of the Line: An Empirical Study of Judicial Waiver," 86 *J. Crim. L. & Criminology* 449 (1996). In short, the limited evidence on "reverse waiver" practice suggests that it closely replicates juvenile court judicial waiver.

3) Convicted in Criminal Court and Sentenced as Youthful Offender For decades, states and the federal government have used a "youthful offender" status to preserve therapeutic sentencing options in criminal courts following the trial of young offenders as adults. A "youthful offender" status constitutes an intermediate category of chronological juveniles sentenced as adults as well as young adult offenders, typically sixteen to twenty-one years of age at the time of sentencing. Youthful offender laws separate this group by age, either in separate facilities or in age-segregated sections within adult facilities, limit the maximum penalty that criminal courts may impose to a period shorter than that authorized for adults, and provide for some relief from disabilities of conviction following successful completion of the sentence. Under the Federal Youth Corrections Act (FYCA), subsequently repealed with the adoption of the federal sentencing guidelines, federal judges had discretion to commit convicted offenders between the ages of sixteen and twenty-two to special facilities as youth offenders if they determined that the youth would "benefit" from treatment. 18 U.S.C. §§ 5005–5026 (1976). The California Youth Authority Act provides criminal court judges with the option of sentencing young adults and waived youths convicted as adults to the Youth Authority rather than to prison, for housing and programs, and the Authority's jurisdiction continues until age twenty-five. *Cal. Welf. & Inst. Code* § 1731.5 (West 1995). In New York, criminal court jurisdiction begins at age sixteen, but youths as young as thirteen years of age charged with murder, or youths fourteen- or fifteen-years-old charged with other violent crimes may be prosecuted as Juvenile Offenders (JO). Criminal courts may give youths sixteen- to nineteen-years-old a Youthful Offender (YO) status. Youths sentenced as JOs/YOs may receive a closed hearing, sealed record, or shorter sentence in a separate facility operated by the Division For Youth rather than a straight sentence to the Department of Corrections. Simon I. Singer, *Recriminalizing Delinquency: Violent Juvenile Crime and Juvenile Justice Reform* (1996). Similarly to New York, Connecticut's juvenile court jurisdiction ends at age fifteen but provides for youthful offender sentencing of youths sixteen or seventeen years of age convicted in criminal court. In *State v. Matos*, 240 Conn. 743, 694 A.2d 775 (Conn.1997), the Connecticut Supreme Court described the benefits a youth received when convicted in criminal court and sentenced as a youthful offender:

The youthful offender statutes confer certain benefits on those youths eligible to be adjudged youthful offenders. For instance, all proceedings, except the motion for investigation of eligibility, are private. If confined, a youth is segregated from other defendants over the age of eighteen years before and during trial and before sentencing. A youthful offender is also eligible to receive a more lenient sentence; is not disqualified from later holding public office, and does not forfeit any right or privilege to receive a license granted by a public authority. Moreover, a youthful offender is not considered a criminal, and a determination that a defendant is a youthful offender is not deemed a conviction. A youthful offender's records are kept confidential; and are automatically erased "when such person attains twenty-one years of age, provided such person has not subsequent to being adjudicated a youthful offender been convicted of a felony . . . prior to [having] attained such age." Id. at 780–81

Criminal sentencing laws in several other states also give judges the option to sentence youths convicted as adults to some type of youthful status rather than an adult prison commitment. Patricia Torbet, et al., *State Responses to Serious and Violent Juvenile Crime: Research Report* (1996).

D. CONSEQUENCES OF WAIVER: CRIMINAL COURT CAREERS OF TRANSFERRED JUVENILES

The recent changes in waiver laws increase the numbers of chronological juveniles charged, tried, and sentenced in criminal courts. Unfortunately, many states amended their waiver statutes without analyzing their systemic impacts on various components of the juvenile or criminal justice systems. Patricia Torbet, et al., *State Responses to Serious and Violent Juvenile Crime: Research Report* (1996). An influx of serious young offenders in criminal courts may impose greater demands on prosecutorial and judicial resources without corresponding increases in criminal justice personnel. In many states, waived juveniles' pretrial detention status remains ambiguous, and may result in lengthy confinement pending an appeal by the youth or by a prosecutor if a judge denies a waiver motion. Similarly, as criminal courts impose more severe sentences on young offenders, prison populations may increase without any corresponding increases in bed-space or age-appropriate programs.

Adult criminal courts sentence waived young offenders primarily on the basis of the seriousness of their present offense. The emphasis on the present offense reflects ordinary criminal sentencing practices as well as the failure to include juvenile convictions systematically in young adults' criminal histories. As a result, criminal courts often sentence violent and persistent young offenders significantly differently. The former may receive substantial sentences of imprisonment, including life without parole. Moreover, violent youths often receive these disparate consequences simply because judges or prosecutors idiosyncratically decided to try them as adults rather than as juveniles. Persistent property offenders, by contrast, often receive more lenient sentences as adult first-offenders than do their retained juvenile counterparts. Young property offenders sentenced in criminal court benefit from the comparative leniency accorded to property offenders generally, to younger offenders specifically, and to those without substantial adult prior criminal histories. As a result, chronic property offenders sentenced as juveniles often may receive longer sentences than did youths whom judges waived because they were not "amenable to treatment" or posed a threat to the community.

The following excerpt describes the numbers and types of youth judicial waived to criminal court and sentenced as adults. **National Council on Crime and Delinquency,** *And Justice for Some: Differential Treatment of Youth of Color in the Justice System* 16–19, 34–36 (2007):

Waiver to Adult Court

Some petitioned juveniles are processed in the adult system instead of the juvenile system, usually because of the seriousness of their crime and their arrest history. An estimated 6,735 petitioned delinquency cases were judicially waived from juvenile to adult court in 2003. This represents less than 1% of all petitioned cases. The racial proportions were fairly similar for petitioned and judicially waived cases. Overall, cases involving White youth represented a slightly smaller proportion of waived cases than of petitioned cases (61% vs. 63%), and cases involving African American youth represented a slightly larger proportion of waived cases than petitioned cases (35% vs. 34%). This pattern varied somewhat according to offense type. For drug offenses, White youth were 69% of the cases petitioned but only 58% of cases waived to adult court. African American youth charged with similar offenses were 29% of cases petitioned but 41% of cases waived to adult court. On the other hand, White youth represented 65% of property cases petitioned but 73% of property cases waived to adult court. African American youth charged with similar offenses were 31% of cases petitioned but 24% of cases waived to adult court.

The likelihood of waiver among petitioned delinquency cases was slightly greater for African American youth (0.8%) and youth of other races (0.9%) than for White youth (.7%). Again, the difference between White youth and African American youth is particularly noticeable for drug offenses. In 2003, 0.7% of the White youth charged with person offenses were waived to adult court, while 1.2% of the African American youth were waived.

Legislative changes in the past twenty years have enabled prosecutors and juvenile court judges to send more youth into the adult criminal justice system or to automatically exclude youth charged with certain offenses from the jurisdiction of the juvenile court. As a result, a significant number of youth are being sentenced to adult correctional facilities, such as state and federal prisons and county jails. While the "sight and sound separation" provisions of the Juvenile Justice and Delinquency Prevention Act prohibit youth under juvenile court jurisdiction from being within "sight or sound" of adult inmates, it does not cover youth under the jurisdiction of adult criminal court. Therefore, youth prosecuted as adults can be incarcerated with adult inmates in jails and prisons.

Nearly three out of four admitted to adult state prisons in 2002 were youth of color. An estimated 4,100 youth under the age of 18 were admitted to the nation's state prisons in 2002. The majority (73%) of these new commitments were youth of color; 58% were African American, 10% were Latino, and 5% were youth of other races. As such, African American, Latino, and Native American youth had significantly higher prison admissions rates than White youth. The prison admissions rates of Africa American, Latino, and Native American youth remained higher than the White youth rate throughout all offense types.

Differences in the rate of new commitments of youth to prison varied considerably among states. Nevertheless, African American youth had consistently higher rates of prison admissions than White youth. Other racial/ethnic group showed great overrepresentation in select states.

The following excerpt, **Howard Snyder and Melissa Sickmund, *Juvenile Offenders and Victims: 1999 National Report* 174–178 (1999)**, describes some of the differences in characteristics of juvenile and adult offenders entering prison:

Offense profiles of under–18 felons differed from those of older felons Person offenses were the conviction offense for a greater proportion of under–18 felons (40%) than of those age 18 or older (19%). This difference was attributable primarily to the robbery category: robbery was the conviction offense for 22% of under–18 felons, compared with 5% for felons 18 or older.

Drug offenses were the conviction offense for a greater proportion of felons age 18 or older (32%) than of those under 18 (19%). Among felons 18 or older, 3 were convicted of drug trafficking for every 2 convicted of drug possession. Among felons under 18, trafficking convictions outnumbered possession convictions nearly 3 to 1.

Half of convicted felons who were transferred juveniles were convicted of person offenses In most States, provisions for transferring juveniles to criminal court target the most serious offenses and offenders. The result is that, compared with youth under 18 who were adults by State definition, transferred juveniles had a greater proportion of person offense convictions and smaller proportions of property and drug convictions. * * *

Criminal courts sentenced juvenile transfers convicted of murder to longer prison terms than other convicted murderers The average maximum prison sentences imposed for felony murder and non-negligent manslaughter convictions were longer than sentences for other types of offenses. For those not sentenced to death or life in prison, *juvenile transfers convicted of murder received longer sentences than their adult counter parts.* [emphasis supplied] On average, the maximum prison sentence imposed on transferred juveniles convicted of murder in 1994 was 23 years 11 months. This was 2 years and 5 months longer than the average maximum prison sentence for adults age 18 or older, and 8 months longer than the average maximum sentence for under–18 adults convicted of murder. * * *

Iatrogenic Effects of Waiver—Increased Recidivism and No Deterrence Despite the dramatic increases in the numbers of youths tried and sentenced as adults, remarkably few studies have analyzed the relative efficacy of juvenile versus criminal processing on offender recidivism or for the youths themselves. *See generally*, Donna Bishop, et al., "The Transfer of Juveniles to Criminal Court: Does It Make a Difference?", 42 *Crime & Delinq.* 171 (1996); Donna Bishop, "Juvenile Offenders in the Adult Criminal Justice System," 27 *Crime & Justice* 81 (2000); Jodi Lane, et al., "Adult Versus Juvenile Sanctions: Voices of Incarcerated Youths," 48 *Crime & Delinq.* 431 (2002); Jeffrey A. Fagan, "Separating the Men from the Boys: The Comparative Advantage of Juvenile versus Criminal Court Sanctions on Recidivism among Adolescent Felony Offenders," in *Serious, Violent and Chronic Juvenile Offenders: A Sourcebook* (J. Howell, et al., eds. 1995); Jeffrey A. Fagan, "The Comparative Advantage of Juvenile versus Criminal Court Sanctions on Recidivism among Adolescent Felony Offenders", 18 *Law & Policy* 77 (1996). In an analytical review essay, **Donna Bishop, "Consequences of Transfer," in Jeffrey Fagan and Franklin E. Zimring, eds.,** *The Changing Borders of Juvenile Justice: Transfer of Adolescents to the Criminal Court* **246–48, 261 (2000),** summarizes the research findings of the Fagan and Bishop studies comparing juvenile and criminal court outcomes:

[Fagan] conducted a natural experiment to evaluate the effects of juvenile versus criminal justice processing. He identified two counties in New York and two in neighboring New Jersey that were very similar on important socio-economic, demographic, and crime indicators. New York and New Jersey also had very similar statutes for robbery and burglary. The key difference was that in New York fifteen-and sixteen-year-old robbers and burglars were automatically prosecuted in the criminal courts under that state's legislative exclusion statute [*see supra* p. 600], while in New Jersey, the juvenile courts retained jurisdiction over them. Fagan's samples consisted of four hundred robbery offenders and four hundred burglary offenders charged in 1981–82, who were randomly selected and evenly divided across the two states and four counties.

Postrelease recidivism was examined after a significant portion of the cohorts had completed their sentences and accumulated at least four years of time at risk. Several measures of recidivism were employed, including time to rearrest, prevalence of rearrest, prevalence of reincarceration, and frequency of rearrest adjusted for time at risk. While there were no significant differences in the effects of criminal versus juvenile court processing of burglary offenders, the findings for robbery offenders showed strong differences.

Transfer was associated with higher prevalence of rearrest: 76 percent of those processed in criminal court were rearrested, compared to 67 percent of those processed in juvenile court. An even greater effect was observed for the likelihood of reincarceration: 56 percent of the criminal court group were subsequently incarcerated, compared to 41 percent of the juvenile court group. Offenders prosecuted in criminal court also had higher rates of rearrest adjusted for time at risk (2.85 offenses) than those prosecuted in juvenile court (1.67 offenses), and they were rearrested more quickly (457 days compared to 553 for those processed in juvenile court). * * *

Subsequent studied conducted by * * * [Bishop and colleagues] reinforce Fagan's findings and conclusions. Our research was conducted in Florida, a state that uses prosecutorial waiver almost exclusively. In the course of other studies of prosecutorial waiver practices in the state, we had learned that, although thousands of juveniles are transferred each year, thousands of equally serious or even more serious offenders are not transferred. This finding provided the opportunity for a significant policy study similar to the one conducted by Fagan. Unlike Fagan's research, ours was carried out in a single state. To overcome the problem of selection bias, we used a matching procedure to pair each case transferred to criminal court with an equivalent case retained in the juvenile system. Each pair was matched on seven factors: the most serious offense charged, the number of counts charged, the number of prior delinquency referrals, the most serious prior offense, age, gender, and race. * * *

We assessed recidivism over the short and long terms. The short-term analysis followed cases for a maximum of twenty-four months, while the long-term follow-up tracked offenders for up to seven years. Both studies indicated that juveniles transferred to criminal court fared worse than those retained in the juvenile justice system. This was true over every comparison in the short term and over most comparisons in the long term study. * * *

From the studies that compared rates of recidivism among youths transferred to criminal court and youths retained in the juvenile system, there emerge three major findings. First, transfer appears to be counterproductive: transferred youths are more likely to reoffend, and to reoffend more quickly and more often, than those retained in the juvenile system. In addition, Fagan's research suggests that the differential effects of criminal and juvenile justice processing are not dependent on sentence type or sentence length. That is, the mere fact that juveniles have been convicted in criminal rather than juvenile court increases the likelihood that they will reoffend. Finally, the risk of reoffending is aggravated when a sentence of incarceration is imposed. * * *

Negative Effects of Transfer Several other reviews of juvenile transfer laws and policies sentencing juveniles as adult also report negative consequences. For example, Richard Redding, *Juvenile Transfer Laws: An Effective Deterrent to Delinquency* 8 (OJJPD, 2008) concludes that "The practice of transferring juveniles for trial and sentencing in adult criminal court has, however, produced the unintended effect of increasing recidivism, particularly in violent offenders, and thereby of promoting life-course criminality ... [T]he bulk of empirical evidence suggests that transfer laws as currently implement, probably have little general deterrent effect on would-be juveniles offenders." Benjamin Steiner and E. Wright, "Assessing the relative effects of state direct file waiver laws on juvenile crime: Deterrence or irrelevance," 96 *J. Crim. L. & Criminology* 1451 (2006), examined the effect of prosecutorial direct-file transfer laws, used time-series analyses of juvenile violent index crime arrest rates before and after the laws changed and in comparison control jurisdictions, and concluded that in 13 of the 14 states studied, juvenile crime before and after enactment of the transfer law either remained constant or increased. Donna M. Bishop, "Juvenile Offenders in the Adult Criminal Justice System, 27 *Crime & Justice* 81, 154–55 (2000), concludes that

> as a crime control policy, transfer tends to be counter-productive. * * * [The empirical studies] suggest that transfer is more likely to aggravate recidivism than to diminish it. The factors contributing to this effect are complex and include the sense of injustice young offenders associate with criminal court processing, the multiple criminogenic effects of incarceration in the adult system (e.g., exposure to negative shaming, opportunities for criminal socialization, modeling of violence), and the stigmatization and opportunity blockage that flow from a record of criminal conviction. Compared to the criminal justice system, the juvenile system seems to be more reintegrative in practice and effect.

A Report by the Task Force on Community Preventive Services, a standing committee of policy experts and advisors to the Center for Disease Control, reviewed seven studies of the deterrent effect of transfer laws on subsequent offending by juveniles tried as adults. See Task Force on Community Preventive Services, *Effects on Violence of Laws and Policies Facilitating the Transfer of Youth from the Juvenile to the Adult Justice System (2007)* (available at http://cdc.gov/mmwr/preview/mmwrhtml/rr 5609a1.htm), which concluded that youths transferred to criminal court subsequently commit violent crimes at higher rates than do those retained in juvenile court. It concluded that waiver exacerbates youths' subsequent offending and increases the risk to public safety. Finally, **Jeffrey Fagan, "Juvenile Crime and Criminal Justice: Resolving Border Disputes,"** 18 *Future of Children* 81, 105 (2008), provides a comprehensive review of all studies examining whether changes in transfer laws reduce subsequent criminality. He concludes that

> Without exception the research evidence shows that policies promoting transfer of adolescents from juvenile to criminal court fail to

deter crime among sanctioned juveniles and may even worsen public safety risks. The weight of empirical evidence strongly suggests that increasing the scope of transfer laws has no general deterrent effects on the incidence of serious juvenile crime or specific deterrent effects on the re-offending rates of transferred youth. In fact, compared with youth retained in juvenile court, youth prosecuted as adults had higher rates of rearrest for serious felony crimes such as robbery or assault. They were also rearrested more quickly and were more often returned to incarceration. Worse, the broad reach of new transfer laws and policies captures not only those youth whose crimes and reoffending risks may merit harsher punishment, but also many more who were neither chronic nor serious offenders, who pose little risk of future offending, and who seem to be damaged by their exposure to the adult court. Whatever the gains of short-term incapacitation, they are more than offset by the toxic effects of adult punishment for the larger group of adolescent offenders.

1. RECORDS OF JUVENILE CONVICTIONS TO ENHANCE ADULT SENTENCES

Criminal courts traditionally lacked access to the juvenile component of offenders' criminal histories because of the confidentiality of juvenile court records, the functional and physical separation of juvenile and criminal court staff who must collate and combine these records, sheer bureaucratic ineptitude, and the difficulty of maintaining an integrated system to track offenders and compile complete criminal histories across both systems. Juvenile courts' practices of sealing or purging records to avoid stigmatizing offenders impedes the use of juvenile court records to identify young career offenders and to enhance their subsequent sentences. "The prohibitions against merged juvenile and adult records, the failure to routinely include juvenile court data in police record systems, and the sealing and purging of juvenile records create a situation in most jurisdictions in which criminal justice authorities frequently make their decisions with no information about police contacts with juveniles." Alfred Blumstein, et al., *Criminal Careers and "Career Criminals" 193* (1986). Although extensive juvenile criminality provides the most reliable indicator of the onset of a criminal career, the failure to combine criminal histories across both systems creates a disjunction that "serious offenders can exploit to escape the control and punishment their chronic or violent offenses properly deserve." David Farrington, Lloyd E. Ohlin, and James Q. Wilson, *Understanding and Controlling Crime: Toward a New Research Strategy* 126 (1986).

Policies on access to juvenile records pose a conflict between the rehabilitative goals of the juvenile court and the public safety interests in identifying career criminals. Although juvenile courts restrict access to records in order to avoid stigmatizing youths for minor offenses or who desist from further offending, "the bifurcation does not seem reasonable for juveniles whose delinquency career are serious and who persist into serious adult offending. Thus, while juvenile records should continue to be protected from general public access, the adult criminal justice system should have access to juvenile records of at least those offenders arrested as adults on a felony charge." Alfred Blumstein, et al., *Criminal Careers and "Career Criminals"* 197 (1986). Access to juvenile records provides an important mechanism to coordinate juvenile and criminal court sentencing of career offenders. T. Markus Funk, "A Mere Youthful Indiscretion? Reexamining the Policy of Expunging Juvenile Delinquency Records," 29 *U. Mich. J. L. Reform* 885 (1996); T. Markus Funk and Daniel D. Polsby, "Distributional Consequences of Expunging Juvenile Delinquency Records: The Problem of Lemons," 52 *J. Urban and Contemp. L.* 161 (1997).

Despite the traditional confidentiality of and restricted access to juvenile courts records, states increasingly use prior juvenile convictions to enhance adult sentences. "Twenty-four States' laws provided for structured consideration of defendant's juvenile records in the setting of sentences. The most common structuring method is through inclusion of the juvenile record among the factors used in State sentencing guidelines (14 States). Typically the juvenile record is included in calculating a criminal history score." Neal Miller, State Laws on Prosecutors' and Judges' Use of Juvenile Records 3 (1995); Neal Miller, "National assessment of criminal court use of defendants' juvenile adjudication records," in *National Conference on Juvenile Justice Records: Appropriate Criminal and Noncriminal Justice Uses* (1997); Patricia Torbet, et al., *State Responses to Serious and Violent Juvenile Crime: Research Report* (1996); Daniel E. Feld, "Consideration of Accused's Juvenile Court Record in Sentencing for Offense Committed as Adult," 64 *A.L.R.3d* 1291 (1997).

A number of states' sentencing guidelines and the United States Sentencing Commission's guidelines include some juvenile prior convictions in an adult defendant's criminal history score. Is it permissible to equate juvenile and adult convictions for purposes of enhancing the sentences of adult offenders?

United States Sentencing Guidelines Manual § 4A1.2(1995):

(d) Offenses Committed Prior to Age Eighteen

(1) If the defendant was convicted as an adult and received a sentence of imprisonment exceeding one year and one month, add 3 points * * * for each sentence.

(2) In any other case

(A) add 2 points * * * for each adult or juvenile sentence to confinement of at least sixty days * * *;

(B) add 1 point * * * for each adult or juvenile sentence imposed within five years of the defendant's commencement of instant offense. * * *

UNITED STATES v. JOHNSON

28 F.3d 151, 307 U.S.App.D.C. 284 (U.S. Ct.Ap. D.C. Cir. 1994).

RANDOLPH, CIRCUIT JUDGE: Fulfilling his part of the bargain, Reco Vondell Johnson pled guilty to possession of 50 grams or more of cocaine base with intent to distribute. The statutory penalty for this crime, which Johnson committed when he was nineteen years old, is imprisonment for 120 months to life. Under the United States Sentencing Guidelines, Johnson fell into criminal history Category V. His base offense level amounted to 29. The lines on the sentencing table intersected at 140 to 175 months' imprisonment. In 1993, the district court sentenced Johnson to 140 months.

Before his eighteenth birthday, Johnson repeatedly violated the criminal laws of the District of Columbia. The presentence report, in compliance with U.S.S.G. § 4A1.2(d), relied on Johnson's extensive juvenile record to calculate his criminal history category. Nine of Johnson's ten criminal history points were for offenses he committed before his eighteenth birthday. In this appeal * * *, Johnson challenges the Sentencing Commission's authority to use juvenile records to determine a defendant's criminal history category. * * *

As Johnson sees it, U.S.S.G. § 4A1.2(d) exceeds the Commission's statutory authority. He asks how "criminal history" under § 994(d)(10) can include his juvenile offenses when D.C.Code Ann. § 16–2318 states that a juvenile adjudication "is not a conviction of a crime."

Juvenile justice systems, in theory, focus on treatment and rehabilitation. Juvenile crime is termed "delinquency" and those responsible for it are "youth offenders." Juvenile records are often sealed; juvenile convictions may later be set aside if the offender goes straight. * * * "[S]etting aside a conviction may allow a youth who has slipped to regain his footing by relieving him of the social and economic disabilities associated with a criminal record. * * * But if a juvenile offender turns into a recidivist, the case for conferring the benefit dissipates.* * * Society's stronger interest is in punishing appropriately an unrepentant criminal." Under the D.C.Code, therefore, a court may take into account the defendant's juvenile record in determining his sentence for crimes he committed as an adult. The practice of considering prior juvenile adjudications at sentencing * * * has long been accepted. A defendant with a juvenile record may not have been "convicted," but the defendant nevertheless "violated a provision of the criminal law," . The Sentencing Commission's mandate is to establish categories of defendants on the basis of factors bearing on punishment. It would be strange therefore if the Commission departed from the practice just described by ignoring a defendant's record of juvenile delinquency. Recidivism, so Congress and the Commission concluded, generally warrants increased punishment. * * * Since juvenile records are without doubt relevant, the Commission did not exceed its statutory authority in taking them into account when it established categories of defendants. * * *

Johnson also attacks U.S.S.G. § 4A1.2(d) on the ground that it unreasonably fails to differentiate between juvenile adjudications and adult criminal convictions. As the system now stands, a juvenile sixty-day sentence of confinement warrants the same number of points as an adult sentence of imprisonment for the same time. A juvenile sentence of less than sixty days is treated the same as an adult sentence of less than sixty days.

Juvenile delinquents achieve ignominy by committing crimes. Differences in society's response to youthful offenders and its response to adult offenders are not attributable to differences in the nature of their criminal acts. When yesterday's juvenile delinquent becomes today's adult criminal the reasons behind society's earlier forbearance disappear. The question before the sentencing court is what punishment to mete out to an adult criminal, not how to treat and rehabilitate a youthful offender. In light of the purposes of sentencing, the Commission's decision to give juvenile confinements or sentences the same weight as adult criminal imprisonments or sentences is not unreasonable. It is a method, rough to be sure, of measuring relative culpability among offenders and the likelihood of their engaging in future criminal behavior. * * *

Affirmed.

WALD, CIRCUIT JUDGE, dissenting: Although I agree with my colleagues' rejection of Johnson's constitutional claim, I cannot assent to their resolution of his challenge to the rationality of § 4A1.2(d)(2) of the Sentencing Guidelines. This case calls into question the Sentencing Commission's policy of treating adult sentences and periods of incarceration like juvenile sentences and periods of confinement for purposes of calculating a defendant's criminal history score. * * * I believe that the Commission's decision to treat juvenile sentences and confinement like adult sentences and incarceration for purposes of computing a criminal history score is a manifestly irrational exercise of its delegated discretion. * * *

As the majority recognizes, the Commission generally does not differentiate between juvenile and adult sentences or periods of juvenile confinement and adult incarceration. Both result in automatic, as opposed to discretionary, increases to the baseline criminal history score. In substantially equating the two, I believe that the Commission has irrationally treated very different things similarly for purposes of enhanced punishment. As such, the Commission has gone further than I think Congress would permit in exercising its admittedly considerable discretion under the SRA.

The modern juvenile justice system, which traces its origins to the turn-of-the-century Progressive reform movement, is premised on assumptions and goals that are profoundly different from those of the adult criminal system. Since its inception, the juvenile court system has rested on the *parens patriae* assumption that "the purpose of [confinement is] to serve the best interest of the child by meeting his or her need for regenerative care and supervision." Unlike criminal punishment, which might be imposed in pursuit of retributive as well as rehabilitative objectives, the focus of juvenile confinement traditionally has been primarily, or even exclusively, on reforming and treating the offender. Under this approach, "the actual crime or offense that the juvenile commits should not affect the severity or length of the court's intervention, because each individual child's needs are different and courts cannot determine those needs in advance merely by looking at the committed offense." * * *

Judges in most juvenile courts still enjoy a wide, virtually unchecked discretion over confinement decisions absent in the adult criminal context. Unlike the more rigid criminal model, "sentencing" in juvenile court varies from "open-ended, non-proportional and indeterminate, with the goal of rehabilitation or incapacitation," (two-thirds of states) to "determinate and proportional, with the objective of retribution or deterrence" (one-third). Most juvenile sentences remain indeterminate. Judges may choose among a wide variety of "sentencing" alternatives in these jurisdictions in response to the needs of particular defendants, including at-home probation, out-of-home placement in boarding schools, camps, group homes, or medical facilities, and institutional confinement. As Feld describes it, "[i]n the vast majority of indeterminate jurisdictions, the judge's sentencing power ends with a commitment to the state's juvenile correction agency. Thereafter, the juvenile correctional authority or a parole board determines when a youth should be released from custody."

Juvenile dispositions are made by a judge, rather than a jury. Juvenile confinement, unlike adult incarceration, is still largely imposed on the basis of characteristics of the offender, rather than characteristics of the offense. The imposition and duration of juvenile confinement may be set irrespective of proportionality; irrespective of the sentence ranges for adult offenders. It is therefore not instructive of criminal history at all, in the substantial majority of states and the District of Columbia, to reveal that the defendant, as a juvenile, spent sixty days or more in juvenile confinement. It may simply mean that the juvenile lacked an adequate home or that the community lacked adequate services. Even in the minority of states adhering to an expressly punitive model of juvenile confinement, juvenile sentences are inherently a less reliable indication of criminal disposition than periods of adult imprisonment given the untrammeled discretion of the sentencer and the absence of a jury trial.

In light of these differences, I believe the Sentencing Commission strayed beyond permissible boundaries of interpretation in treating juvenile sentences and periods of confinement like adult sentences and periods of incarceration for purposes of automatic increase to the defendant's criminal history category. * * * [T]he Commission's regulation, which mandates the addition of a specific number of points for all juvenile sentences, regardless of the juvenile's age or circumstances motivating the sentence, represents an inexcusable refusal to pursue different treatment where justice and reason require it. I do not believe this was the design of Congress, and accordingly must dissent.

N<small>OTES</small>

1) States' Use of Juvenile Prior Convictions to Enhance Adult Sentences Under California's "three-strikes" sentencing law, a juvenile adjudication qualifies as a prior felony conviction for purposes of sentence enhancements. *Cal. Penal Code* § 667 (d) (3) (1994) (stating that a prior juvenile adjudication shall constitute a prior felony conviction for purposes of sentence enhance if the juvenile was 16 years of age or older and convicted of one of 23 serious offenses enumerated in the California transfer statute, *supra* pp. 625–629); David C. Owen, "Striking Out Juveniles: A Re-examination of the Right to a Jury Trial in Light of California's 'Three Strikes' Legislation," 29 *Davis. L. Rev.* 437 (1996); Lise Forquer, "California's Three Strikes Law— Should a Juvenile Adjudication Be a Ball or a Strike?," 32 *San Diego L. Rev.* 1297 (1995). In *People v. Smith*, 110 Cal.App.4th 1072, 1 Cal.Rptr.3d 901 (Cal. Ct. App. 2003), the defendant acquired both of his two prior "strikes" from a single, jury-less delinquency adjudication for multiple counts arising out of the same transaction. As a result, upon his first adult conviction for burglary at age 19, the trial court sentenced him as a three-strike offender to a term of 30 years to life in prison. The court of appeals approved the use of delinquency convictions as "strikes." See Barry C. Feld, "The Constitutional Tension Between *Apprendi* and *McKeiver*: Sentence Enhancements Based on Delinquency Convictions and the Quality of Justice in Juvenile Courts," 38 *Wake Forest L. Rev.* 1111, 1208–1212 (2003) (analyzing California's approval of using juvenile delinquency adjudications as "strikes" for purposes of sentence enhancements).

A survey of state statutes reports that about half of states systematically consider juvenile records in setting adult sentences. Neal Miller, *State Laws on Prosecutors' and Judges' Use of Juvenile Records* (1995). Sentencing judges often assert the importance of access to defendants' prior records of juvenile convictions. *See e.g.*, *United States v. Davis*, 48 F.3d 277, 280 (7th Cir. 1995). Some states include the juvenile record as a discretionary "factor" to consider when available while others formally include some component of a juvenile record in calculating a youth's criminal history score. Most states' sentencing guidelines weight juvenile prior offenses less heavily than comparable adult convictions and include, for example, only juvenile felonies committed after age sixteen. However, a few states do not distinguish qualitatively between juvenile and adult prior convictions, and include both equally in an offender's criminal history score. *See e.g.*, *Kan.Stat.Ann.* § 21–4170(a) (1995).

2) Use of Juvenile Priors to Enhance Criminal Sentences in Light of Procedural Differences in How Convictions Originally Were Obtained States' expanded uses of juveniles' prior records to integrate the juvenile and criminal justice systems' responses to career offenders and to enhance the sentences of young adult offenders raise sometimes troubling issues in light of the quality of procedural justice by which juvenile courts obtain those original convictions. States use those delinquency convictions obtained with less stringent procedures to *treat* youths as juveniles in order subsequently to *punish* them more severely as adults. *United States v. Williams,* 891 F.2d 212 (9th Cir. 1989). The courts reason that the subsequent use for enhancement of a conviction valid at the time it was obtained does not violate due process. *Commonwealth v. Thomas,* 510 Pa. 106, 507 A.2d 57 (Pa. 1986). For example, in *Nichols v. United States,* 511 U.S. 738, 114 S.Ct. 1921, 128 L.Ed.2d 745 (1994), the Supreme Court held that an uncounseled conviction may be used to enhance a sentence as long as the conviction was valid at the time. In light of *Nichols,* there probably is no reason why states may not use a non-jury juvenile adjudication in the same way. However, it does seem contradictory to provide youths with fewer procedural rights in the name of rehabilitation and then to use those convictions to sentence them more severely as adults. Although rational sentencing policy supports systematic use of juvenile records of convictions, justice and fairness require adult criminal procedural safeguards to assure the quality and legitimacy of their use. David Dormont, "For the Good of the Adult: An Examination of the Constitutionality of Using Prior Juvenile Adjudications to Enhance Adult Sentences," 75 *Minn. L. Rev.* 1769, 1805 (1991) ("The collateral use of juvenile adjudications to enhance adult sentences demonstrates that the Supreme Court's 'fundamental fairness' standard has failed to protect the very persons it was meant to protect."); Deborah L. Mills, "*United States v. Johnson*: Acknowledging the Shift in the Juvenile Court System From Rehabilitation to Punishment," 45 *DePaul L. Rev.* 903 (1996).

3) Implications of *Apprendi v. New Jersey* for the Use of Juvenile Prior Convictions to Enhance Adult Sentences In *Apprendi v. New Jersey,* 530 U.S. 466, 120 S.Ct. 2348, 147 L.Ed.2d 435 (2000), the Supreme Court held that the constitution requires that any fact that increases the penalty of a crime beyond the prescribed statutory maximum, *other than the fact of a prior conviction,* must be submitted to a jury and proved beyond a reasonable doubt. In *Apprendi,* the Supreme Court, by a 5–4 vote, held that Fourteenth Amendment Due Process and the Sixth Amendment right to a jury trial entitled a criminal defendant to a jury determination that he is guilty of every element of the crime with which he is charged beyond a reasonable doubt. "The historic link between verdict and judgment and the consistent limitation on judges' discretion to operate within the limits of the legal penalties provided highlight the novelty of a scheme that removes the jury from the determination of a fact that, if found, exposes the criminal defendant to a penalty *exceeding* the maximum he would receive if punished according to the facts reflected in the jury verdict alone." *Id.* at 482–83.

Courts are divided on whether prior juvenile adjudications fall under the "prior conviction" exception in *Apprendi* and therefore do not need to be proved to a jury. The majority of jurisdictions that have considered this issue have held that delinquency adjudications fall under the prior conviction exception. *See, e.g., United States v. Jones,* 332 F.3d 688 (3d Cir. 2003) (juvenile proceedings provide sufficient procedural safeguards to qualify under the prior conviction exception); *United States v. Smalley,* 294 F.3d 1030 (8th Cir. 2002) (juvenile adjudications are prior convictions for *Apprendi* purposes); *United States v. Burge,* 407 F.3d 1183 (11th Cir. 2005) (holding, based on *Jones* and *Smalley,* that juvenile adjudications provide sufficient procedural safeguards to qualify as prior conviction); *People v. Superior Court,* 113 Ca.

App. 4th 817, 7 Cal.Rptr.3d 74 (2003) (juvenile adjudications may be used as a "strike" for the purposes of a "three strikes" law); *Nichols v. State*, 910 So.2d 863 (Fla. Dist. Ct. App. 2005) (juvenile adjudications may be included in a defendant's "scoresheet" unless he or she can prove they are "constitutionally infirm"); *State v. Hitt*, 273 Kan. 224, 42 P.3d 732 (2002) (juvenile adjudications "are included within the historical cloak of recidivism"); *Ryle v. Indiana*, 842 N.E.2d 320 (Ind. 2005) (juvenile adjudications may be used to enhance a sentence); *State v. Weber*, 159 Wash.2d 252, 149 P.3d 646 (WA 2006) (including juvenile prior adjudications within criminal history); State v. McFee, 721 N.W.2d 607 (Minn. 2006).

By contrast, several courts deem delinquency procedures inadequate to allow criminal courts to enhance sentences based on juvenile convictions. *See e.g., United States v. Tighe*, 266 F.3d 1187 (9th Cir. 2001); *State v. Brown*, 879 So.2d 1276 (LA 2004) (LA 2004) (holding that juvenile adjudications are not convictions for the purposes of the prior conviction exception); *State v. Harris*, 339 Or. 157, 118 P.3d 236 (2005) (holding that juvenile adjudications are not convictions under Oregon law and may not be used as sentence enhancement factors unless admitted by the defendant or proven to a jury).

In **State v. Brown,** 879 So.2d 1276 (LA 2004), the Louisiana Supreme Court considered whether it was constitutional to use a delinquency adjudication, for which the juvenile had not been afforded the right to a trial by jury, to enhance his sentence for a felony committed when he was an adult under the Louisiana's Habitual Offender Law. *Brown* provides a comprehensive analysis of the competing procedural and sentencing policy issues implicated by the majority and minority courts' interpretation of *Apprendi*'s "prior crimes" exception. After Brown was convicted of felonies as an adult, the State charged him as a habitual offender based on a juvenile adjudication. Defense counsel argued that the use of his delinquency adjudication to enhance his sentence violated *Apprendi,* because he did not have the right to a jury trial in the juvenile proceeding. The trial court rejected the motion, found Brown a second felony offender, and sentenced him to 198 years at hard labor without benefit of parole. The appellate court affirmed the conviction, but reversed the sentence as constitutionally excessive. The Court of Appeals noted the split in the federal circuit courts on the issue of whether prior juvenile adjudications obtained without right to a jury trial are constitutionally adequate under *Apprendi* for purposes of subsequent federal sentence enhancement. The Louisiana Supreme Court reviewed *Apprendi*, the federal circuit decisions, and its own juvenile jury decisions. The Court, per Knoll, J., explained:

> A proper discussion of the constitutional issue before us must commence with the United State's Supreme Court's decision in *Apprendi v. New Jersey.* The question before the Supreme Court was whether the Due Process Clause of the Fourteenth Amendment requires that a factual determination authorizing an increase in the maximum prison sentence be made by a jury on the basis of proof beyond a reasonable doubt. The catalyst for this issue was a New Jersey hate crime statute, which authorized a judge to increase a defendant's maximum prison sentence if the trial court found by a preponderance of the evidence that in committing the crime, the defendant acted with a purpose to intimidate an

individual or group of individuals because of race, color, gender, handicap, religion, sexual orientation or ethnicity. Charles Apprendi pleaded guilty to two counts of firearm possession for an unlawful purpose and one count of unlawful possession of an antipersonnel bomb. The trial judge imposed an enhanced sentence, finding by a preponderance of the evidence that Apprendi's actions were taken with a purpose to intimidate as provided by the statute. "The question of whether Apprendi had a constitutional right to have a jury find such bias on the basis of proof beyond a reasonable doubt [was] starkly presented." * * * The Court ruled "other than the fact of a prior conviction, any fact that increases the penalty for a crime beyond the prescribed statutory maximum must be submitted to a jury, and proved beyond a reasonable doubt." It reasoned due process required a jury to find the facts upon which a court based an enhanced sentence as an "element" of the offense at trial, rather than to allow a judge to find those facts by a preponderance of the evidence as a "sentencing factor" at a sentencing hearing. The Court exempted the fact of a prior conviction from its holding because defendants enjoyed criminal procedural safeguards, including the right to a jury trial and proof beyond a reasonable doubt, which assured the accuracy and reliability of the prior record.

After *Apprendi's* holding that "other than the fact of a prior conviction, any fact that increases the penalty for a crime beyond the prescribed statutory maximum must be submitted to a jury, and proved beyond a reasonable doubt," courts around the nation have been confronted with the question of whether a juvenile adjudication falls within the *Apprendi* exception for "prior convictions." The federal appellate courts have divided over the use of delinquency adjudications to enhance criminal sentences beyond the statutorily mandated maximum. The question that has divided the federal circuits is whether a prior juvenile adjudication, in which the juvenile does not have the right to a jury trial, qualifies as a "prior conviction" for purposes of the *Apprendi* exception. In each of these federal cases, the court reviewed the legality of using juvenile adjudications to enhance an adult sentence above a prescribed statutory maximum pursuant to the Armed Career Criminal Act (ACCA). Congress has characterized juvenile adjudications as prior convictions under the ACCA.

The Ninth Circuit Court of Appeals became the first court in *Apprendi's* wake to report a published decision on this issue. In *United States v. Tighe,* a divided panel held *Apprendi's* narrow "prior conviction" exception is limited to prior convictions resulting from proceedings that afforded the procedural necessities of a jury trial and proof beyond a reasonable doubt. In reaching this conclusion, the *Tighe* court noted the significant constitutional differences between adult convictions and juvenile adjudications, and inquired into the scope of the term "conviction" as used by the Supreme Court in *Apprendi,* and the cases leading up to *Apprendi.*

In examining the Supreme Court jurisprudence concerning the use of prior convictions as a sentencing factor, the *Tighe* court stated:

[I]n *Jones v. United States,* ... [t]he Court explained why the fact of prior convictions was constitutionally distinct from other sentence-enhancing facts, such that it was permissible, under *Almendarez–Torres,* to use prior convictions to increase the possible penalty for an offense without treating them as an element of the current offense: "One basis for that constitutional distinctiveness [of prior convictions] is not hard to see: unlike virtually any other consideration used to enlarge the possible penalty for an offense ... *a prior conviction must itself have been established through procedures satisfying the fair notice, reasonable doubt and jury trial guarantees.*" Thus, *Jones'* recognition of prior convictions as a constitutionally permissible sentencing factor was rooted in the concept that prior convictions have been, by their very nature, subject to the fundamental triumvirate of procedural protections intended to guarantee the reliability of criminal convictions: fair notice, reasonable doubt and the right to a jury trial.

One year later, in *Apprendi,* the ... Court explained that "the certainty that procedural safeguards attached to the 'fact' of prior conviction" was crucial to *Almendarez–Torres'* constitutional holding regarding prior convictions as sentencing factors..... "There is a vast difference between accepting the validity of a prior judgment of conviction entered in a proceeding in which the defendant had the right to a jury trial and the right to require the prosecutor to prove guilt beyond a reasonable doubt, and allowing the judge to find the required fact under a lesser standard of proof."

The *Tighe* court found the United States Supreme Court's continued acceptance of *Almendarez–Torres'* holding regarding prior convictions was premised on those convictions being the product of proceedings that afford crucial procedural protections, particularly the right to a jury trial and proof beyond a reasonable doubt. The court therefore reasoned the "prior conviction" exception to *Apprendi's* general rule must be limited to prior convictions that were themselves obtained through proceedings that included the right to a jury trial and proof beyond a reasonable doubt. The court held juvenile adjudications that do not afford these due process rights do not fall within *Apprendi's* "prior conviction" exception.

The Eighth Circuit disagreed with the Ninth Circuit's *Tighe* decision. In *United States v. Smalley,* the court held juvenile adjudications can count as prior convictions for *Apprendi* purposes. The *Smalley* court rejected *Tighe's* analysis, "conclud[ing] that the question of whether juvenile adjudications should be exempt from *Apprendi's* general rule should not turn on the narrow parsing of words, but on an examination of whether juvenile adjudications, like adult convictions, are so reliable that due process of law is not offended by such an exemption."

Noting that juvenile defendants have the right to notice, the right to counsel, the right to confront and cross-examine witnesses, the privilege against self incrimination, and that there must be a finding of guilt beyond a reasonable doubt, the court found these safeguards more than sufficient to ensure the reliability *Apprendi* requires. While *Apprendi* established what procedural safeguards were sufficient (a right to a jury trial and proof beyond a reasonable doubt), and what were not (judge-made findings under a lesser standard of proof), "the Court did not take a position on possibilities that lie in between these two poles." "[I]t is incorrect to assume that it is not only sufficient but necessary that the 'fundamental triumvirate of procedural protections,' as the Ninth Circuit put it, underly [sic] an adjudication before it can qualify for an *Apprendi* exception." The *Smalley* court recognized a jury does not have a role in trials for juvenile offenses, but did not think that fact undermines the reliability of such adjudications in any significant way because the use of a jury in the juvenile context would "not strengthen greatly, if at all, the fact-finding function" and is not constitutionally required.

The Third Circuit [in *United States v. Jones* (2004)] addressed this issue, considering both the *Tighe* and *Smalley* decisions. The *Jones* court, like the *Smalley* court, found nothing in *Apprendi* or *Jones v. United States,* that required holding prior nonjury juvenile adjudications, where all required due process safeguards were afforded, cannot be used to enhance a sentence under the ACCA. A prior nonjury juvenile adjudication that was afforded all constitutionally-required procedural safeguards can properly be characterized as a prior conviction for *Apprendi* purposes. The Supreme Court in *McKeiver* held due process does not require providing juveniles with the right to a jury trial. Therefore, the *Jones* court held when a juvenile is adjudicated guilty beyond a reasonable doubt in a bench trial that affords all the due process protections that are required, the adjudication should be counted as a conviction for purposes of subsequent sentencing.

Thus, as can be seen, following *Apprendi* there are two reasonable schools of thought on whether juvenile adjudications, in which the juvenile did not have the right to a jury, can properly be characterized as "prior convictions" for felony sentence enhancement purposes. The State, adopting the rationale of the *Smalley* and *United States v. Jones* decisions, argues the defendant was afforded all the safeguards that were constitutionally due in his juvenile proceedings. Therefore, the adjudication was reliable for purposes of the exception under *Apprendi,* and its use as a predicate crime * * * is proper. The defendant contends *Jones v. United States* and *Apprendi* foreclose the use of juvenile adjudications to enhance an adult sentence, where the juvenile did not have the right to a jury trial. In deciding this difficult question, we turn to our recent jurisprudence concerning the juvenile justice system and scholarly works addressing this issue to assist us.

A review of the history of juvenile courts illustrates why juvenile courts have fewer procedural safeguards. * * * Because of the rehabilitation rationale, the courts justified making the juvenile court less formal. * * * The purpose of sanctions would be for therapeutic and rehabilitative purposes, not for retribution or incapacitation.

In *In re C.B. et al.,* [*see* Note 4, p. 790], * * * we addressed the constitutionality of a statute that authorized the Department of Public Safety and Corrections to transfer juveniles who had been adjudicated delinquent to adult facilities upon reaching age seventeen, to be treated for punitive purposes the same as the convicted adult felons with whom they were confined. We found the statute unconstitutional * * * because they received a *de facto* criminal sentence to hard labor without being afforded the right to trial by jury as mandated by our state constitution.

In reaching this determination, we noted "the unique nature of the juvenile system is manifested in its non-criminal, or 'civil' nature, its focus on rehabilitation and individual treatment rather than retribution, and the state's role as *parens patriae* in managing the welfare of the juvenile in state custody." * * * Therefore when we were confronted with the constitutionality of the application of a statute that allowed adjudicated juveniles to be transferred to adult facilities, we found the statute unconstitutional as applied, holding the statute * * * had sufficiently tilted the scales away from a "civil" proceeding, with its focus on rehabilitation, to one purely criminal. Due process and fundamental fairness required that the juvenile have a jury trial if he or she was to be incarcerated at hard labor in an adult penal facility. The determination in *McKeiver* that a jury trial was not constitutionally required in juvenile adjudications was predicated upon the non-criminal treatment of the adjudicated delinquent.* * *

We recently had cause to re-visit the issue of the right to jury trials in our juvenile justice system in *State in the Interest of D.J.* [*see* p. 779] There we reaffirmed our holding in *State in the Interest of Dino,* denying juveniles a constitutional right to a jury trial in delinquency proceedings. The juveniles and the amici argued the policy-based analysis applied when *McKeiver* and *Dino* were decided was outdated. They contended, *inter alia,* the amendment to the Habitual Offender Law to allow use of juvenile adjudications to enhance subsequent adult felony offenses had torn down the remaining characteristics of what traditionally identified the juvenile system. * * *

Notwithstanding our finding in *State in the Interest of D.J.*, where we inferred the sentence enhancement statutes did not offend due process requirements to such an extent that a jury trial would be required in juvenile adjudicatory proceedings, we find because juveniles do not have a right to a jury trial in these proceedings, juvenile adjudications cannot be used to enhance adult felony convictions. * * * We have well established that juvenile adjudications in Louisiana are sufficiently reliable, even without a jury trial, to support dispositions within the juvenile justice system. However, *Apprendi* has raised the issue of whether these adjudications, rendered without the right to a jury trial, are sufficiently reliable to support enhanced sentencing for adults. For the reasons that follow, we find they are not.* * *

Because of the unique nature of the juvenile system manifested in its non-criminal or "civil" nature, its focus on rehabilitation and individual treatment rather than retribution, and the state's role as *parens patriae* in managing the welfare of the juvenile in its custody, the United States Supreme Court held, despite disappointments, failures and shortcomings in the juvenile court system, juveniles were not constitutionally entitled to jury trials.

Even though it was argued that because (1) the juvenile justice system had taken on more of the trappings of the criminal justice system; (2) the role of punishment had increased in the juvenile system; and (3) the legislative amendments opening the proceedings to the public and allowing juvenile adjudications to serve as predicate offenses for adult felony sentence enhancement, due process required juveniles receive a jury trial, we continued to uphold *Dino's* decree that [our state constitution] does not afford a juvenile the right to a jury trial in a juvenile proceeding. Among our reasons for our continued holding is that even with the changes in the juvenile justice system, "there remains a great disparity in the severity of penalties faced by a juvenile charged with delinquency and an adult defendant charged with the same crime." To allow these adjudications to serve as "prior convictions" for purposes of sentence enhancement for adult felony offenses would lessen this disparity and contribute to "blurr[ing] the distinction between juvenile and adult procedures."

We find there is a difference between a "prior conviction" and a prior juvenile adjudication, and we believe the *Tighe* decision more closely comports with the rationale for finding juveniles are not constitutionally entitled to a jury trial. * * * Our holdings that due process does not require juveniles be afforded *all* the guarantees afforded adult criminals under the constitution have been premised upon the "civil nature" of a juvenile adjudication, its focus on rehabilitation and the state's role as *parens patriae.* If a juvenile adjudication, with its lack of a right to a jury trial which is afforded to adult criminals, can then be counted as a predicate offense the same as a felony conviction for purposes of Louisiana's Habitual Offender Law, then "the entire claim of *parens patriae* becomes a hypocritical mockery."

A juvenile adjudication is not a conviction of any crime. Therefore, this adjudication should not be counted as a "prior conviction" for *Apprendi* purposes. The determination that a jury trial was not constitutionally required in juvenile adjudications was predicated upon the non-criminal treatment of the adjudicated juvenile delinquent. It would be incongruous and illogical to allow the non-criminal adjudication of a juvenile delinquent to serve as a criminal sentencing enhancer. To equate this adjudication with a conviction as a predicate offense for purposes of the Habitual Offender Law would subvert the civil trappings of the juvenile adjudication to an extent to make it fundamentally unfair and thus, violative of due process. In order to continue holding a trial by jury is not constitutionally required, we cannot allow these adjudications, with their civil trappings, to be treated as predicate offenses the same as felony convictions. It seems contradictory and fundamentally unfair to provide youths with fewer procedural safeguards in the name of rehabilitation and then to use adjudications obtained for treatment purposes to punish them more severely as adults. It is inconsistent to consider juvenile adjudications civil for one purpose and therefore not constitutionally entitled to a jury trial, but then to consider them criminal for the purpose of classifying them as "prior convictions," which can be counted as predicate offenses for purposes of the Habitual Offender Law.

We do not agree with the *Smalley* court and its progeny that because the procedures of juvenile adjudications are sufficiently reliable for juvenile dispositions, they are therefore reliable to "justify the much harsher consequences of their use as criminal sentence enhancements." We find, as did the *Tighe* court, the guidance from our United States Supreme Court indicates recidivism is distinct as a sentencing factor and therefore as an exception to the general rule that "any fact that increases the penalty for a crime beyond the prescribed statutory maximum must be submitted to a jury, and proved beyond a reasonable doubt[,]" because "unlike virtually any other consideration used to enlarge the possible penalty for an offense, ... a prior conviction must itself have been established through procedures satisfying the fair notice, reasonable doubt, *and jury trial guarantees.*" Because a juvenile adjudication is not established through a procedure guaranteeing a jury trial, it cannot be excepted from *Apprendi's* general rule; the use of these adjudications to increase the penalty beyond the statutory maximum violates the defendant's Due Process right guaranteed by the Fourteenth Amendment of the United States Constitution. * * *

In an extended analysis of the implications of *Apprendi* for enhancing adult criminal sentences by use of prior delinquency adjudications, **Barry C. Feld, "The Constitutional Tension Between *Apprendi* and *McKeiver*: Sentence Enhancements Based on Delinquency Convictions and the Quality of Justice in Juvenile Courts," 38 *Wake Forest L. Rev.* 1111, 1208–1212 (2003)**, concludes that:

The Supreme Court in *Apprendi* held that states must submit to a jury and prove beyond a reasonable doubt any fact that increased the penalty for a crime beyond the statutory maximum. To assure congruence between culpability and consequence, the Court reasoned that a jury must find the facts upon which a court based an enhanced sentence as an "element" of the offense to be proved at trial rather than as a judicial "sentencing factor."

[T]here is a vast difference between accepting the validity of a prior judgment of conviction entered in a proceeding in which the defendant had the right to a jury trial and the right to require the prosecutor to prove guilt beyond a reasonable doubt, and allowing the judge to find the required fact under a lesser standard of proof.

Apprendi exempted the *"fact of a prior conviction"* from its holding because defendants had the right to a jury trial and proof beyond a reasonable doubt at the time the state obtained the original conviction which assured its validity, accuracy, and reliability.

In delinquency proceedings, by contrast, *McKeiver* used a lower, "fundamental fairness" standard of procedural justice, rather than the Sixth Amendment rights it incorporated for adults, to deny a constitutional right to a jury trial. McKeiver used an outmoded analysis and uncritically accepted the rhetoric of juvenile justice in order to justify the result it reached. It did so because the Court envisioned delinquency proceedings as something more benevolent and therapeutic than criminal prosecutions. Although *Winship* requires States to prove delinquency beyond a reasonable doubt, the availability of a jury provides the prime checking mechanism to assure congruence of outcomes between trials and pleas. While *McKeiver* found non-jury delinquency procedures constitutionally adequate for rehabilitative dispositions, those standards clearly would not be adequate for an explicitly punitive disposition in the first instance.

Regardless of the unproven therapeutic character of delinquency dispositions three decades ago, juvenile courts today clearly punish young delinquents for crimes. Importantly, all of the courts that rely upon *McKeiver* to justify the use of delinquency convictions for sentence enhancements * * * fail to acknowledge or discuss *McKeiver*'s reasons for using less stringent procedural safeguards or the anomaly of using treatment dispositions for the purpose of extending subsequent punishment. Unfortunately, none of the cases that uphold the use of prior delinquency convictions for sentence enhancements adequately examine the differences in purposes for which the state initially obtained those convictions but mechanically rely on the idea that a conviction that is valid for one purpose therefore must be valid for all purposes. Moreover, none of them sufficiently evaluate the reliability and quality of those prior convictions compared with those of adult defendants. * * *

Every commentator who has considered the use of delinquency convictions obtained without the right to a jury trial to enhance adult criminal sentences has criticized the policy. *See e.g.*, Note, "Constitutional Law—Right to Jury Trial—Eighth Circuit Holds an Adjudication of Juvenile Delinquency to be a 'Prior Conviction' for the Purpose of Sentence Enhancement at a Subsequent Criminal Proceeding—*United States v. Smalley*, 294 F.3d 1030 (8th Cir. 2002)," 116 *Harv. L. Rev.* 705 (2002); Brian P. Thill, "Prior 'Convictions' under *Apprendi*: Why Juvenile Adjudications may not be used to increase an Offender's Sentence Exposure if they have not first been proven to a Jury Beyond a Reasonable Doubt," 87 *Marq. L. Rev.* 573 (2004); Stephen F. Donahoe, "The Problem with Forgiving (But Not Entirely Forgetting) the Crimes of our Nation's Youth: Exploring the Third Circuit's Unconstitutional use of Nonjury Juvenile Adjudications in Armed Career Criminal Sentencing, 66 *U. Pitt. L. Rev.* 887 (2005); Kimberly L. Johnson, "Should Juvenile Adjudications Count as Convictions for *Apprendi* Purposes?," 20 *Ga. St. U.L.Rev.* 791 (2004); Jeremy W. Hochberg, "Should Juvenile Adjudications Count as Prior Convictions for *Apprendi* Purposes?," 45 *Wm. & Mary L. Rev.* 1159 (2004). The only dissenting analysis is Daniel J. Kennedy, "Nonjury Juvenile Adjudications as Prior Convictions under *Apprendi*," 2004 *U. Ill. L. Rev.* 267 (2004).

2. SENTENCING JUVENILES AS ADULTS—PROPORTIONALITY AND PUNISHMENT

Waiver of youths to criminal courts for sentencing as adults implicates legal and cultural understandings of juveniles' criminal responsibility. For example, waiver legislation that excludes capital offenses from juvenile court jurisdiction exposes some youths to the possibility of execution for offenses they committed as juveniles. Transfer of young juveniles for very serious crimes exposes them to mandatory sentencing provisions that impose sentences of "life without parole" for crimes they committed at thirteen or fourteen years of age. Mandatory sentences of life imprisonment and the death penalty for the crimes committed as children challenge the social construction of adolescence and the idea that juveniles are less criminally responsible than adults. The materials in this section briefly explore criminal court sentences and correctional consequences for waived juveniles.

Questions about young people's criminal responsibility arise in the broader context of culpability and deserved punishments, the tension between retributive and utilitarian sentencing policies, and the social and legal construction of childhood. Laws that expose children to mandatory life terms or to the death penalty constitute a political and cultural judgment that young people may be just as blameworthy and culpable as their somewhat older counterparts. "Sound-bites" of contemporary politics—"adult crime, adult time," or "old enough to do the crime, old enough to do the time"—convey current youth sentencing policy. Many of the most serious crimes for which criminal courts convict youths carry substantial sentences, mandatory minima, or even life without parole. Exclusion statutes without minimum age restrictions expose even very young offenders to such harsh penalties. The following excerpt, **Wayne A. Logan, "Proportionality and Punishment: Imposing Life Without Parole on Juveniles," 33 *Wake Forest L. Rev.* 681 at 689–90, 692– 709 (1998),** summarizes the current status of "proportionality analysis" and its implications for the sentencing of juveniles tried as adults:

Once waived into adult court, a juvenile offender is deemed an adult, and therefore, the thinking goes, should be treated like one. For offenders who are at least sixteen years of age at the time of their crimes, this means that the death penalty might be in store. But even short of the death penalty, juvenile offenders increasingly risk being sentenced to society's penultimate punishment, LWOP [Life Without Parole].

Currently, the statutory law of only a handful of states expressly prohibits imposition of LWOP on those under age sixteen at the time of their offense, while the overwhelming majority of American jurisdictions appear to permit such sentences or even make LWOP mandatory upon conviction in adult court. As a result, in the State of Washington, for instance, offenders as young as eight years of age can be sentenced to LWOP, while in Vermont, ten-year-olds can draw such terms. * * *

It is a fundamental tenet of Anglo–American law that punishment must be proportional to the crime for which it is imposed. Since its landmark 1910 decision in *Weems v. United States*, the Supreme Court has recognized that a proportionality requirement inheres in the Eighth Amendment. Although initially the Court conceived the Eighth Amendment as barring only disproportionate physical punishment, in 1958 in *Trop v. Dulles* the Court expressly expanded Eighth Amendment protection to non-physical punishments. In subsequent opinions, * * * the Court expounded on the proportionality principle in the context of the death penalty. In the early 1980s, the Court was asked to address whether LWOP, a sentence enjoying renewed use in the wake of the Court's heightened procedural and substantive limits on capital sentences, satisfied Eighth Amendment proportionality requirements.

In its 1980 opinion *Rummel v. Estelle*, the Supreme Court issued its first modern pronouncement on proportionality with respect to sentence length.* * * The Court rejected Rummel's proportionality challenge, concluding that the Texas legislature knew best how to punish its recidivists, and that federal appellate courts were powerless to intervene. In due deference to this legislative wisdom, the Court reasoned, findings of excessiveness with respect to sentence length should be "exceedingly rare."

Three years later, in *Solem v. Helm*, the Court had before it a challenge to an actual LWOP sentence and reached a different result. * * * In striking down the sentence as disproportionate, Justice Powell flatly rejected the State's argument that proportionality analysis was inapplicable to terms of imprisonment. * * *

Justice Powell next articulated three "objective" factors that must inform proportionality analysis:

> First, we look to the gravity of the offense and the harshness of the penalty. * * * Of course, a court must consider the severity of the penalty in deciding whether it is disproportionate.

> Second, it may be helpful to compare the sentences imposed on other criminals in the same jurisdiction. If more serious crimes are subject to the same penalty, or to less serious penalties, that is some indication that the punishment at issue may be excessive. * * *

> Third, courts may find it useful to compare the sentences imposed for commission of the same crime in other jurisdictions. * * *

It was not until eight years later, in *Harmelin v. Michigan*, that the Court examined the question again, but provided little more in the way of clarity.

In *Harmelin*, the Court addressed whether a mandatory LWOP sentence imposed upon petitioner's conviction of possession of 672 grams of cocaine violated proportionality. Writing for an exceptionally fractured Court, Justice Scalia rejected the challenge, a result agreed with by four other members of the Court. According to Justice Scalia, mandatory punishment was not per se contrary to the Eighth Amendment. While arguably cruel, mandatory punishments were not "unusual" in constitutional terms. As a corollary, a defendant facing a mandatory non-capital sentence was not entitled to proffer or to have sentencing consideration given to mitigating factors. * * *

In the wake of *Harmelin*, state and lower federal courts have struggled mightily to assess the precise contours of proportionality analysis.

Despite its splintered rationale, however, *Harmelin* permits several basic teachings. First and foremost, seven members of the Court adhere to the historic view that the Eighth Amendment contains a proportionality requirement that extends to capital and non-capital sentences alike. Second, it appears that a majority of the Justices believe that a defendant facing a statutorily mandated minimum sentence, even LWOP, is not entitled to have possible mitigating factors considered by the sentencing authority. Finally, * * * only sentences raising an "inference of gross disproportionality" based on a "threshold comparison of the crime committed and the sentence imposed" trigger the inter-and intrajurisdictional analysis of the second and third parts of the three-part *Solem* test. * * *

Most courts have adopted a decidedly restrictive view of Justice Kennedy's comparison of "the crime committed and the sentence imposed." "Crime" is now typically conceived solely in terms of the relative seriousness of a given offense, to the exclusion of offender culpability.

By divorcing "crime" from offender culpability in proportionality analysis, these courts subscribe to an essentially circular inquiry: because murder, for instance, is a very "serious" crime in the eyes of the legislature, it can be met with a very "serious" statutory punishment. * * *

[M]ost American courts, especially federal courts, refuse to take account of such [culpability] considerations in proportionality analysis. This refusal * * * contravenes a core underpinning of proportionality, namely, that a sentence must correspond to the crime—not just to the harm caused by the offense, but also to the culpability of the offender. The upshot of the current jurisprudential approach is that state and federal legislatures can exercise virtually unfettered discretion in their formulation of sentences, as can prosecutors in their charging practices, unconstrained by the watchful eye of the judiciary and its constitutional duty of oversight. At present we are in the midst of a "race to the bottom" insofar as juvenile justice is concerned and the courts are virtually nowhere to be found as a buffer in this descent.

Although the Supreme Court has implied that the death penalty cannot, as a federal constitutional matter, be imposed on offenders who have not yet reached sixteen years of age at the time of their crime, and all death penalty states have specified sixteen as the minimum death-eligible age, the states are free to impose the "penultimate penalty" of LWOP on those under sixteen—and often in the form of a mandatory minimum sentence. As a result, youths waived to the adult system—unlike their chronological peers that remain in the juvenile system—can be required to spend the rest of their lives in an adult prison without a chance of meaningful appellate review of their sentences. And, from the perspective of a majority of American appellate courts, this mandatory decision is immune from review because, by definition, the sentence cannot as a threshold matter qualify as "grossly disproportionate." * * *

HARRIS v. WRIGHT

93 F.3d 581 (9th Cir. 1996).

KOZINSKI, CIRCUIT JUDGE. [Fifteen-year-old Harris and a thirteen-year-old co-defendant planned to rob a store. Harris gave his companion a gun. The two entered the store and the younger juvenile shot the storeowner and stabbed him to death. The two youths stole the money in the cash register, took assorted merchandise, and left. Police arrested Harris later that day and he confessed to participating in the robbery-murder. He was convicted of aggravated first-degree murder and sentenced to life imprisonment without parole. On appeal, Harris argued that the sentence was unconstitutionally "cruel and unusual" as applied to an offender less than sixteen years of age.]

The principal question presented is whether a fifteen-year-old murderer may be sentenced to mandatory life imprisonment without possibility of parole. * * *

Harris was convicted of aggravated first degree murder. The state didn't seek death and Harris received the only other sentence Washington law allows for his crime: life imprisonment without possibility of parole. * * *

Harris's petition raised the two constitutional challenges that are now before us: He claims that a mandatory sentence of life imprisonment without parole is unconstitutionally cruel and unusual as applied to punish an offense committed when the perpetrator was less than sixteen years of age. * * *

We first address Harris's Eighth Amendment challenge. The amendment has two possible applications here. A punishment is unconstitutional if the "evolving standards of decency that mark the progress of a maturing society" soundly reject it. The Eighth Amendment also bars, under certain circumstances, punishments that are grossly disproportionate to the crime being punished. *See Harmelin v. Michigan.*

To establish that evolving standards of decency preclude his punishment, Harris bears the "heavy burden," of showing that our culture and laws emphatically and well nigh universally reject it. The most important indicators of the nation's penal sentiments are the enactments of its elected legislatures.

At very least, then, Harris bears the burden of proving a strong legislative consensus against imposing mandatory life without parole on offenders who commit their crimes before the age of sixteen. Harris manages to cite two states whose laws explicitly preclude mandatory adult sentences in general or life without parole in particular for crimes committed below sixteen, two state high courts that prohibit mandatory life terms for such crimes, and twenty-six states that don't punish any crime with mandatory life without parole. On the other side, Harris admits there are at least twenty-one states that do impose mandatory life without parole on fifteen-year-old offenders. Whatever degree of consensus might be necessary before we could overturn the considered judgment of a state legislature, this doesn't come close.

An otherwise valid, if severe, punishment may nonetheless be unconstitutional when paired with a sufficiently minor crime. Disproportion analysis, however, is strictly circumscribed; we conduct a detailed analysis only in the "rare case in which a threshold comparison of the crime committed and the sentence imposed leads to an inference of gross disproportionality." * * *

Washington's legislature has decided that the appropriate punishment for anyone tried and convicted as an adult for aggravated murder is life in prison. The Constitution gives us no power to reverse its judgment.

Harris argues that, at very least, we must draw an inference of gross disproportionality when society imposes its "penultimate" punishment for a crime committed at fifteen. But, capital punishment aside, there's no constitutional (or rational) basis for classifying punishment in distinct, ordinal categories. As the Supreme Court noted in *Harmelin*, if we put mandatory life imprisonment without parole into a unique constitutional category, we'll be hard pressed to distinguish mandatory life with parole; the latter is nearly indistinguishable from a very long, mandatory term of years; and that, in turn, is hard to distinguish from shorter terms. Youth has no obvious bearing on this problem: If we can discern no clear line for adults, neither can we for youths. Accordingly, while capital punishment is unique and must be treated specially, mandatory life imprisonment without parole is, for young and old alike, only an outlying point on the continuum of prison sentences. Like any other prison sentence, it raises no inference of disproportionality when imposed on a murderer. * * *

Affirmed.

NAOVARATH v. STATE
105 Nev. 525, 779 P.2d 944 (Nev. 1989).

By the Court, SPRINGER, JUSTICE: We have before us a thirteen-year-old seventh grader who stands convicted of an unspecified degree of murder by reason of his plea of guilty to an amended information charging "murder." Rejecting a pre-sentence recommendation of life with possibility of parole, the trial court sentenced appellant Naovarath to imprisonment for the rest of his life without possibility of parole.

Before proceeding we pause first to contemplate the meaning of a sentence "without possibility of parole," especially as it bears upon a seventh grader. * * * Denial of this vital opportunity means denial of hope; it means that good behavior and character improvement are immaterial; it means that whatever the future might hold in store for the mind and spirit of Khamsone Kham Naovarath, he will remain in prison for the rest of his days. This is a severe penalty indeed to impose on a thirteen-year-old. The question is whether under the constitutions of Nevada and the United States this penalty is excessive, cruel or unusual. * * *

Let it not be thought that we are underestimating the gravity of this or other crimes committed by children. The undeniable increase in crimes by younger children has made it necessary for the criminal justice system to deal severely with young offenders. Our legislature has removed youthful murderers, whatever their age, from the grace of the juvenile court act, thus making the most severe adult penalties available, where appropriate, in the case of youthful murderers. Because, by statute, homicides committed by children even younger than Naovarath, for instance, ten or eleven year olds, are punishable by adult standards, careful judicial attention must be given to the subject of fair and constitutional treatment of children who find themselves caught up in the adult criminal justice system.

In deciding whether the sentence in this case exceeds constitutional bounds it is necessary to look at both the age of the convict and at his probable mental state at the time of the offense.

Certainly there must be some age at which a sentence of this severity must be judged to be unarguably cruel and unusual. Had Naovarath been only nine or ten years old, few would argue that this kind of sentence could be properly allowed. Most agree that it would be excessive to sentence a nine or ten year old to life imprisonment without possibility of parole. Children of this age simply cannot be said to *deserve* this kind of severe punishment, nor can it be said that a child of such tender years is so unalterably bad that no parole release should ever be considered.

When a child reaches twelve or thirteen, it may not be universally agreed that a life sentence without parole should never be imposed, but surely all agree that such a severe and hopeless sentence should be imposed on prepubescent children, if at all, only in the most exceptional of circumstances. Children are and should be judged by different standards from those imposed upon mature adults. To say that a thirteen-year-old deserves a fifty or sixty year long sentence, imprisonment until he dies, is a grave judgment indeed if not Draconian. To make the judgment that a thirteen-year-old must be punished with this severity and that he can never be reformed, is the kind of judgment that, if it can be made at all, must be made rarely and only on the surest and soundest of grounds. Looking at the case before us from this perspective, we conclude that the sentence of life imprisonment without possibility of parole imposed upon Naovarath was cruel and unusual under the Nevada Constitution and the United States Constitution. * * *

What constitutes cruel and unusual punishment for a child presents an especially difficult question. Under Nevada statutory law, since 1985, a child may be charged, convicted and sentenced for murder. For all other purposes the defendant in this case, a child, a seventh grader at the time of the incident, is almost entirely legally incapacitated. * * * If putting this child away until his death is not cruel, it is certainly unusual. To adjudicate a thirteen-year-old to be forever irredeemable and to subject a child of this age to hopeless, lifelong punishment and segregation is not a usual or acceptable response to childhood criminality, even when the criminality amounts to murder.

As said, hopelessness or near hopelessness is the hallmark of Naovarath's punishment. It is questionable as to whether a thirteen-year-old can even imagine or comprehend what it means to be imprisoned for sixty years or more. It is questionable whether a sentence of virtually hopeless lifetime incarceration for this seventh grader "measurably contributes" to the social purposes that are intended to be served by this next-to-maximum penalty.

Punishment by imprisonment is generally accepted as serving three moral and social purposes: retribution, deterrence of prospective offenders, and segregation of offenders from society.

Retribution has been characterized by the Supreme Court as being "an expression of society's outrage" at criminal conduct and as not being "inconsistent with our respect for the dignity of men." We do not question the right of society to some retribution against a child murderer, but given the undeniably lesser culpability of children for their bad actions, their capacity for growth and society's special obligation to children, almost anyone will be prompted to ask whether Naovarath *deserves* the degree of retribution represented by the hopelessness of a life sentence without possibility of parole, even for the crime of murder. * * *

Deterrence also has a rational and historically accepted legitimacy in determining the degree of punishment called for in a given criminal conviction. However, it is hard to claim that children of under fourteen years are really capable of being very much deterred by threatened punishment of this magnitude. Twelve and thirteen-year-olds just do not make the "kind of cost-benefit analysis that attaches any weight to the possibility" of future punishment. * * *

Naovarath's counsel is not here seeking a light sentence. His counsel stipulates that life imprisonment is the minimum punishment that can be imposed in this case if the appeal is granted. The only question is whether it is necessary in order to punish Naovarath enough * * * that he must be kept behind bars with no hope, never to be free again. * * *

[W]e conclude that the kind of penalty imposed in this case is cruel and unusual punishment for this mentally and emotionally disordered thirteen-year-old child. We therefore grant Naovarath's appeal and order that sentence be imposed against him for a term of life imprisonment with possibility of parole.

YOUNG, CHIEF JUSTICE, with whom STEFFEN, JUSTICE, agrees, Dissenting: * * * Naovarath argues that the sentence of life imprisonment without parole was disproportionate, and violated the Eighth Amendment's ban on cruel and unusual punishment. Again, we disagree.

Aside from capital cases, successful challenges to the proportionality of particular sentences are extremely rare. Reviewing courts should grant substantial deference to the broad authority that legislatures necessarily possess in determining the types and limits of punishments for crimes. Moreover, we owe the same deference to the discretion that trial courts possess in sentencing convicted criminals. * * *

Three basic tests exist for evaluating whether a punishment is cruel or unusual:

(1) In view of all the circumstances, is the punishment of such character as to shock the conscience and to violate principles of fundamental fairness? (2) Is the punishment greatly disproportionate to the offense? (3) Does the punishment go beyond what is necessary to achieve the aim of the public interest as expressed by the legislative act?

After consideration of all of the circumstances of this case, we do not find that the sentence imposed shocks the conscience or violates principles of fairness. * * *

In the instant case, the sentence of life imprisonment without possibility of parole was necessary to accomplish the objective of protecting society and to achieve the related goals of deterrence, rehabilitation and retribution. Thus, it was clearly within the purposes envisioned by the Nevada legislature.

The sentence imposed on Naovarath by the district court was within the statutory limits. Moreover, the penalty was not disproportionate to his offense, nor was it cruel and unusual punishment. Accordingly, we would affirm the decision of the district court.

NOTES

1) States' Response to Juveniles' Requests for Proportionality Analysis *Naovarath* represents an isolated exception to state courts' universal rejection of "proportionality" analysis in the sentencing of juveniles. In *State v. Massey*, 60 Wash.App. 131, 803 P.2d 340 (Wash. Ct. App. 1990), the thirteen-year-old juvenile who accompanied Harris, *see supra* p. 677, was waived to adult criminal court and convicted of aggravated murder. Massey argued that his sentence of mandatory life without possibility of parole constituted cruel and unusual punishment. The Washington court of appeals rejected his claim observing that:

The test is whether in view of contemporary standards of elemental decency, the punishment is of such disproportionate character to the offense as to shock the general conscience and violate principles of fundamental fairness. That test does not embody an element or consideration of the defendant's age, only a balance between the crime and the sentence imposed. Therefore, there is no cause to create a distinction between a juvenile and an adult who are sentenced to life without parole for first degree aggravated murder. Furthermore, the juvenile court's consideration at declination accounts for the disparity between juvenile and adult sentencing, and in this case the court elected for adult sentencing because the juvenile penalties were insufficient.

In *State v. Stinnett*, 129 N.C.App. 192, 497 S.E.2d 696 (1998), the North Carolina court of appeals rejected an Eighth Amendment challenge by a 15–year–old, waived to criminal court on a mere finding of probable cause that he committed a murder, and sentenced to mandatory LWOP upon being convicted. The court stated

> North Carolina courts have consistently held that when a punishment does not exceed the limits fixed by statute, the punishment cannot be classified as cruel and unusual in a constitutional sense. It is within the province of the General Assembly to enact a process for dealing with serious offenses committed by juveniles. The General Assembly has chosen a process that excludes juveniles accused of Class A felonies who are thirteen years of age or older from the preferred treatment of juvenile court disposition. Legislative bodies are free to make exceptions to the statutory rules that children are entitled to special treatment. The General Assembly has the constitutional authority to enact laws. Unless their enactments or the way they are applied offend our Constitution or the Constitution of the United States, we are bound by these enactments.

The Georgia Supreme Court in **Humphrey v. Wilson, 282 Ga. 520, 652 S.E.2d 501 (GA 2007)**, conducted a different type of proportionality analysis and mitigated the sentence imposed on a youth tried as an adult. Significantly, the adolescent's age played no direct role in the court's culpability or proportionality analyses. In February 2005, the criminal court found Wilson guilty of aggravated child molestation of T.C. Wilson was seventeen and the victim was fifteen years old years at the time of the crime. The sexual act involved the victim willingly performing oral sex on Wilson. At the time of Wilson's trial, the minimum sentence for aggravated child molestation was ten years in prison with no possibility of probation or parole; the maximum sentence was thirty years in prison. The trial court sentenced Wilson to ten years imprisonment and required him to register as a sex offender for the rest of his life. After 2006 legislative amendments made conduct such as his a misdemeanor and eliminated the requirements of the sex offender registration, Wilson filed for writ of habeas corpus. The Court, SEARS, Chief Justice, found his sentence disproportional:

> In determining whether a sentence set by the legislature is cruel and unusual, this Court has cited with approval Justice Kennedy's concurrence in *Harmelin v. Michigan*. Under Justice Kennedy's concurrence in *Harnelin,* as further developed in *Ewing v. California*, in order to determine if a sentence is grossly disproportionate, a court must first examine the "gravity of the offense compared to the harshness of the penalty" and determine whether a threshold inference of gross disproportionality is raised. * * * If this threshold analysis reveals an inference of gross disproportionality, a court must proceed to the second step and determine whether the initial judgment of disproportionality is confirmed by a comparison of the defendant's sentence to sentences imposed for other crimes within the jurisdiction and for the same crime in other jurisdictions. * * *

> We turn now to the threshold inquiry of disproportionality as developed in *Harmelin* and *Ewing*. In this regard, we conclude that * * *

considering the nature of Wilson's offense, his ten-year sentence does not further a legitimate penological goal and thus the threshold inquiry of gross disproportionality falls in Wilson's favor.

Here, the legislature has recently amended OCGA § 16–6–4 to substitute misdemeanor punishment for Wilson's conduct in place of the felony punishment of a minimum of ten years in prison (with the maximum being 30 years in prison) with no possibility of probation or parole. Moreover, the legislature has relieved such teenage offenders from registering as a sex offender. It is beyond dispute that these changes represent a seismic shift in the legislature's view of the gravity of oral sex between two willing teenage participants. * * * [W]e conclude that the amendments * * * reflect a decision by the people of this State that the severe felony punishment and sex offender registration imposed on Wilson make no measurable contribution to acceptable goals of punishment.

Stated in the language of *Ewing* and *Harmelin*, our legislature compared the gravity of the offense of teenagers who engage in oral sex but are within four years of age of each other and determined that a minimum ten-year sentence is grossly disproportionate for that crime. This conclusion appears to be a recognition by our General Assembly that teenagers are engaging in oral sex in large numbers; that teenagers should not be classified among the worst offenders because they do not have the maturity to appreciate the consequences of irresponsible sexual conduct and are readily subject to peer pressure; and that teenage sexual conduct does not usually involve violence and represents a significantly more benign situation than that of adults preying on children for sex. * * *

In addition to the extraordinary reduction in punishment for teenage oral sex reflected in the 2006 Amendment to OCGA § 16–6–4, the 2006 Amendment to that statute also provided for a large increase in the punishment for adults who engage in child molestation and aggravated child molestation. * * * The significant increase in punishment for adult offenders highlights the legislature's view that a teenager engaging in oral sex with a willing teenage partner is far from the worst offender and is, in fact, not deserving of similar punishment to an adult offender. * * *

Based on the foregoing factors and, in particular, based on the significance of the sea change in the General Assembly's view of the appropriate punishment for teenage oral sex, we could comfortably conclude that Wilson's punishment, as a matter of law, is grossly disproportionate to his crime without undertaking the further comparisons outlined in *Harmelin* and *Ewing*. However, we nevertheless will undertake those comparisons to complete our analysis.

A comparison of Wilson's sentence with sentences for other crimes in this State buttresses the threshold inference of gross disproportionality. * * * [The court describes examples of the crimes of voluntary manslaughter, involuntary manslaughter, aggravated assault and aggravated battery for which a defendant could receive a sentence of as little as one year in prison and no more than ten years.] There can be no legitimate dispute that the foregoing crimes are far more serious and disruptive of the social order than a teenager receiving oral sex from another willing teenager. * * *

Finally, we compare Wilson's sentence to sentences imposed in other states for the same conduct. A review of other jurisdictions reveals that most states either would not punish Wilson's conduct at all or would, like Georgia now, punish it as a misdemeanor. * * *

All of the foregoing considerations compel the conclusion that Wilson's sentence is grossly disproportionate to his crime and constitutes cruel and unusual punishment under both the Georgia and United States Constitutions. We emphasize that it is the "rare case [ ]" in which the threshold inference of gross disproportionality will be met and a rarer case still in which that threshold inference stands after further scrutiny. The present case, however, is one of those rare cases. * * *

2) Youthfulness as a Mitigating Factor in Sentencing Guidelines and Legislation The federal sentencing guidelines explicitly reject youthfulness as a justification to mitigate young offenders' sentences outside of the guidelines range. *See* U.S. Sentencing Guidelines Manual § 5H.1 (1995). Several states' laws recognize "youthfulness" as a mitigating factor. *See, e.g.,* Ariz. Rev. Stat. § 13–702(D)(1) (1996); Fla. Stat. § 921.0016(4)(k) (1996) ("the defendant was too young to appreciate the consequences of the offense"); La. Rev. Stat. Ann. § 905.5(f) (West 1997) ("the youth of the offender at the time of the offense"); N.C. Gen. Stat. § 15A–134.D.16 (e)(4) (1996) ("The defendant's age, immaturity, or limited mental capacity"). These statutes typically enumerate mitigating factors which include some recognition of youthfulness. Under such aggravating-mitigating sentencing laws, trial court judges regularly consider "youthfulness" both *de jure* and *de facto*; appellate courts remand them for resentencing if they do not. *See, e.g., State v. Adams*, 864 S.W.2d 31, 33 (Tenn.1993) ("courts should consider the concept of youth in context, i.e., the defendant's age, education, maturity, experience, mental capacity or development, and any other pertinent circumstance tending to demonstrate the defendant's ability or inability to appreciate the nature of his conduct."); *State v. Strunk*, 846 P.2d 1297, 1300–02 (Utah 1993) (noting that trial court's failure to consider defendant's youthful age as a mitigating factor warranted remand for resentencing). However, states that recognize youthfulness as a mitigating factor simply treat it as one element to weigh with other factors when sentencing. In most jurisdictions, whether a trial judge treats youthfulness as a mitigating factor rests within his or her sound discretion, and failure to exercise leniency does not constitute reversible error or an abuse of discretion. Appellate courts regularly affirm mandatory sentences of life without parole for thirteen-year-old juveniles convicted as adults and reject any special consideration of the youth's age. *See e.g., State v. Massey*, 60 Wash.App. 131, 803 P.2d 340 (1990); *State v. Green*, 124 N.C.App. 269, 284, 477 S.E.2d 182, 189 (1996) (approving mandatory "life without parole" and noting that "Defendant's age, mental capacity, and lack of a prior criminal record do not change this result.")

3) Correctional Consequences of Sentencing Youths as Adults Summarizing the correctional consequences of sentencing waived youths in criminal courts, **Barry C. Feld, "Juvenile and Criminal Justice Sys-**

tems' Responses to Youth Violence," 24 *Crime & Justice* 189, 218–220 (1998), observes:

As a result of recent changes in waiver laws, criminal courts sentence increasing numbers of youths to adult correctional facilities. Unfortunately, we lack reliable data on the number of incarcerated juveniles because most states do not classify young inmates on the basis of the process that brought them to prison. Many youths who committed their crimes as chronological juveniles may be adults by the time courts have waived, convicted, and sentenced them to prison. Because of the recency of many changes in waiver statutes, correctional administrators have not yet fully experienced the population or programming implications of these policy changes.

A 1991 survey of state correctional administrators reported that convicts aged seventeen or younger comprised less than one percent of 712,000 prisoners, but did not distinguish between waived or excluded youths and those in states in which juvenile court jurisdiction ended at fifteen or sixteen years of age. Another recent survey reported that offenders younger than eighteen years of age comprised about 2 percent of new court commitments to prisons in thirty-five states and the federal bureau of prisons, and that about three-quarters of those youths were seventeen at the time of their confinement. In 1993, criminal courts sentenced about 5,200 youths aged seventeen or younger to adult prisons.

Recall that criminal courts sentenced juveniles waived for property and for violent crimes differently as adults, and that recent waiver legislative amendments increasingly target violent youths. As a result, among persons sentenced to prison, a substantially larger proportion of younger offenders are committed for violent crimes than is true for adult prison commitments. For example, for violent crimes, of youths under age eighteen sentenced to prison, 50 percent had been convicted of violent crimes, compared with 29 percent of adults admitted to prison. The percentages of youths committed to prison who had been convicted of serious violent crimes exceeded the proportions for sentenced adults for murder (7 percent vs. 3 percent), for robbery (22 percent vs. 10 percent), and for assault (13 percent vs. 8 percent). Moreover, because of the disparities in rates of violent offending by race, criminal courts sentenced a majority of black youths (54 percent) to prison for violent offenses and a majority of white youths (57 percent) for property crimes. Because of the differences in lengths of sentences imposed for violent and property offenses, racial disparities in prison inmate populations will grow over time.

The infusion of juvenile offenders poses a challenge to corrections officials to develop more programming and age-appropriate conditions of confinement for young or more vulnerable inmates. Adult correctional administrators anticipate "increased pressure on an already burdened state corrections system." Half the agencies responding to a recent survey expect increases of ten percent or more and a quarter expected increases of more than 50 percent in their under-age–18 inmate population over the next five years.

Subject to variations in state laws and available facilities, correctional options for handling juveniles include straight adult incarceration with minimal differentiation between juveniles and adults other than routine classification of inmates by age, offense, size, or vulnerability; graduated incarceration in which youths begin their sentences in a juvenile or separate adult facility and then serve the remainder of their sentence in the adult facility; or age-segregated incarceration either in separate facilities within the prison or in separate youth facilities for younger adults. Recent analyses of correctional policies reported that nearly all states confine juveniles-sentenced-as-adults in adult correctional facilities either with younger adult offenders or in the general population if the juvenile is of a certain age, for example, sixteen. "In 1994, thirty-six states dispersed young inmates in housing with adult inmates (half as a general practice and half only in certain circumstances). Nine states housed young inmates with those aged eighteen to twenty-one, but not with older inmates. Only six states never housed young inmates with people eighteen and older; they either have transferred young inmates to their state juvenile training schools until they reached the age of majority or have housed them in segregated living units within an adult prison." Prison officials generally regarded juveniles convicted in criminal courts as adults and employed the same policies, programs, and conditions of confinement for waived youths as for other adult inmates. A few states house younger criminal offenders in facilities separately from adults. A one-day count on June 30, 1994, reported approximately 250 inmates aged thirteen–fifteen, and 3,100 aged sixteen–seventeen housed in separate adult correctional facilities.

The influx of younger offenders poses management, programming, and control challenges for correctional administrators. Young peoples' dietary and exercise needs differ from those of older inmates. Younger inmates may engage in more institutional misconduct, and management techniques appropriate for adults may be less effective when applied to juveniles. Evaluations of the prison adjustment of serious or violent youthful offenders are mixed. A few states report that young offenders pose special management problems or commit more disciplinary infractions than do older inmates, while other states report few differences. One systematic study of the prison adjustment of young offenders in Texas compared a sample of waived youths convicted of violent crimes committed before the age of seventeen with a matched sample of incarcerated inmates aged seventeen to twenty-one at the time of their offenses. The waived violent youths adapted less well, experienced more difficulty adjusting to institutional life, accumulated more extensive disciplinary histories, earned less good time, and received higher custody classifications. * * *

4) Adolescent Criminal Responsibility and Life Without Parole Sentences Consider the following excerpts from a recent report by **Human Rights Watch and Amnesty International,** *The Rest of Their Lives: Life Without Parole for Children Offenders in the United States* 25–44 (2004), reporting on the imposition of LWOP sentences on juveniles. After you read *Roper v. Simmons, infra,* p. 689, consider the implications of *Roper* for juvenile LWOPS. For ease of presentation, statistical tables are omitted. You may find the full report at http://hrw.org/reports/2005/us1005/.

Sentencing of Youth to Life without Parole Once children are prosecuted as adults, they become subject to the same prison sentences that can be imposed on adults, including in forty-two states, the sentence of life without parole. Only Kentucky, New York, Oregon, and the District of Columbia specifically exclude anyone under the age of eighteen who is tried as an adult from life without parole sentencing. In twenty-seven of the forty-two states in which youth can be sentenced to life without parole, the sentence is mandatory for anyone, child or adult, found guilty of certain enumerated crimes.

Age, Crime, and Gender As of 2004, there were at least 2,225 youth offenders serving life without parole in U.S prisons. Because of the absence of any national database tracking the sentencing of youth to life without parole (or indeed any data tracking the presence of child offenders in adult prisons), Human Rights Watch and Amnesty International compiled this figure from data obtained directly from individual state departments of corrections and other sources. * * *

[T]he youngest children (six in total) were thirteen years old at the time of offense, and the average age was sixteen. Sixteen percent were imprisoned for crimes committed when they were fifteen or younger. Applying this proportion to the total number of youth offenders serving life without parole suggests that some 354 youth offenders nationwide currently face a lifetime behind bars for crimes they committed before their sixteenth birthdays.

Life without parole is imposed for a variety of crimes. * * * However, it is most often imposed on child offenders who have been convicted of crimes of homicide. * * * Almost 93 percent of the youth sentenced to life without parole were convicted of homicide. It is a misconception, however, that the sentence is reserved only for the most calculated and heinous of murderers. As already emphasized, it is often imposed, for example, on children convicted of felony murder—that is, on teens who participated in a felony such as robbery during which another participant in the crime killed someone without the child offender having intended the murder to occur and sometimes without even knowing the other participant was armed. In the cases examined by Human Rights Watch and Amnesty International, many of these felony murder crimes were robberies that went awry, often involving a group of offenders, at least one of whom was an adult. Unfortunately, data are not available to enable us to determine the nationwide number of child offenders convicted of felony murder who are serving life without parole.

However, we do know that 26 percent, or 45 of the 172 youth offenders across the nation who self-reported to us on this question, were sentenced to life without parole for felony murder. We also know that 33 percent of the 24 youth offenders investigated in depth by Human Rights Watch in 2005 in Colorado are serving life without parole for felony murder offenses; and that nearly half of the 146 youth surveyed by the American Civil Liberties Union in Michigan in 2004 were sentenced to life without parole for felony murder or for "aiding and abetting" a murder in which another person pulled the trigger.

In terms of gender, all but a tiny fraction (2.6 percent) of the child offenders serving life without parole are male. This is not surprising considering both the marked differences in violent juvenile crime rates (especially homicide offenses) by gender and that boys are much more likely to be transferred to adult court than girls. * * *

The specter of "super predators" created much of the national furor over youth violence. Politicians and the public thought their communities were (or would be) besieged by vicious teenagers with long records of crime. Yet few of the child offenders sentenced to life without parole fit this super predator profile. Our research suggests that 59 percent of youth offenders received a life without parole sentence for their *first-ever* criminal conviction of any sort. These youth had neither an adult criminal record nor a juvenile adjudication. The other 39 percent had prior criminal records that ranged from convictions as adults for serious crimes such as robbery, to juvenile offenses such as getting into fights with other teenagers. * * *

Historical Trends in Sentencing to Life without Parole * * *[F]rom 1962 until 1981, an average of two youth offenders in the United States entered prison each year with life without parole sentences. Beginning in 1982, the number began to rise markedly, peaking at 152 youth in 1996. Although the number has declined since 1996, it has never returned to the much lower figures from the 1960s to mid–1980s.

While the absolute number of youth sentenced to life without parole has decreased since 1996, the nationwide proportion of youth sentenced to life without parole for murder has *increased* relative to the total number of youth arrested for or reliably implicated in murders nationwide ("known murder offenders").

Human Rights Watch and Amnesty International have compared the number of known murder offenders (including all degrees of murder and felony murder) who were below the age of eighteen for each year from 1980 through 2000, with the number of child offenders who entered prison during those same years with a life without parole sentence. * * * [T]he proportion of youth murder offenders who entered prison with life without parole sentences constituted an ever growing proportion of the number of known youth murder offenders. For example, the percentage going to prison with life without parole in 2000 was three times greater than the percentage in 1990. The data thus suggest an increasing punitiveness toward youth murder offenders.

Comparing the imposition of life without parole sentences on children and adults convicted of murder casts additional light on the increasing punitiveness toward child offenders. * * * [I]n eleven out of the seventeen years between 1985 and 2001, youth convicted of murder were *more likely* to enter prison with a life without parole sentence than adult murder offenders. Even when death sentences are included * * * in one quarter of the same seventeen years, child murder offenders were more likely to receive *either the death penalty or life without parole* than adults. In the remaining years, adults were only slightly more likely to enter prison with *either* life without parole or death sentences (between 1.3 and 0.1 percentage points)—a remarkable finding given that during most of the years studied, large numbers of states had abolished the juvenile death penalty. On its face, this data suggests that states have often been more punitive towards children who commit murder than adults. At the very least, it suggests age has not been much of a mitigating factor in the sentencing of youth convicted of murder. * * *

Race No examination of criminal justice in the United States is complete without a discussion of race. Therefore, we collected data on the total number of youth offenders in each racial group serving life without parole. Our data reveal that blacks constitute 60 percent of the youth offenders serving life without parole nationwide and whites constitute 29 percent. In addition, the data show that black youth nationwide are serving life without parole sentences at a rate that is ten times higher than white youth (the rate for black youth is 6.6 as compared with .6 for white youth). Neither the data we compiled nor other available sources answer the key question: are children from racial minorities sentenced to life without parole more frequently than white children convicted of similar crimes and with similar criminal histories?

As with the national totals given above, the percentage of minority youth serving life without parole are often very different from the percentage of white youth serving the sentence in a particular state. Again, while the differences are dramatic, we do not know the crime rates, criminal histories, or other race-neutral factors that would allow us to draw conclusions about racial disparities in the sentencing policies of states. However, research studies have found that minority youths receive harsher treatment than similarly situated white youths at every stage of the criminal justice system, from the point of arrest to sentencing. For example, Amnesty International's research indicates that one reason for the over-representation of black and other minority children in the criminal justice system is racial discrimination by law enforcement and justice authorities. * * *

3. DEATH PENALTY FOR JUVENILES

ROPER v. SIMMONS

543 U.S. 551, 125 S.Ct. 1183, 161 L.Ed.2d 1 (2005).

JUSTICE KENNEDY delivered the opinion of the Court.

This case requires us to address, for the second time in a decade and a half, whether it is permissible under the Eighth and Fourteenth Amendments to the Constitution of the United States to execute a juvenile offender who was older than 15 but younger than 18 when he committed a capital crime. In *Stanford v. Kentucky* (1989), a divided Court rejected the proposition that the Constitution bars capital punishment for juvenile offenders in this age group. We reconsider the question.

[Christopher Simmons was a 17 years old junior in high school when he committed the murder for which he was tried, convicted, and sentenced to death after he had turned 18. Simmons instigated the crime and told two friends that he wanted to murder someone. In chilling, callous terms, Simmons proposed to commit burglary and murder by breaking and entering, tying up a victim, and throwing the victim off a bridge. Simmons met with the other two boys at about 2 a.m. on the night of the murder, but one of the boys left before the other two set out. Simmons and another boy entered the home of the victim, Shirley Crook, through an open window and unlocked the back door. When Mrs. Crook awakened and called out, Simmons entered her bedroom. He recognized her from a car accident in which they both had been involved. The two youths used duct tape to cover her eyes and mouth and bind her hands, and drove her in her minivan to a state park. They tied her hands and feet together with electrical wire, wrapped her face in duct tape and threw her from a bridge into the Meramec River where she drowned. Fishermen recovered her body from the river the same afternoon. Simmons, meanwhile, bragged about the killing to friends. After receiving information of Simmons' involvement, police arrested him at his high school and took him to the police station. They read him his *Miranda* rights which he waived and after less than two hours of questioning, Simmons confessed to the murder and performed a videotaped reenactment at the crime scene. The State charged Simmons with burglary, kidnaping, and murder in the first degree. Because Simmons was 17 at the time of the crime, he was outside the age jurisdiction of the Missouri juvenile courts. He was tried as an adult and convicted of first degree murder. At the death penalty stage, the state proved three aggravating factors—he committed the murder to obtain money; he committed it to avoid or prevent his subsequent arrest; and he committed the murder in a cruel and depraved manner. In mitigation, Simmons showed that he had no prior delinquency charges or convictions. During closing arguments, both the prosecutor and defense counsel addressed Simmons' age, which the trial judge had instructed the jurors they could consider as a mitigating factor. Defense counsel argued that Simmons' age should make "a huge difference to [the jurors] in deciding just exactly what sort of punishment to make." In rebuttal, the prosecutor gave the following response: "Age, he says. Think about age. Seventeen years old. Isn't that scary? Doesn't that scare you? Mitigating? Quite the contrary I submit. Quite the contrary." The jury recommended the death penalty after it found that the State had proved each of the three aggravating factors submitted to it and the trial judge imposed the death penalty.

Simmons obtained new counsel, who moved to set aside the conviction and sentence contending that he had received ineffective assistance at trial. The trial court found no constitutional violations and denied the motion for post-conviction relief. The Missouri Supreme Court affirmed. After Simmons had exhausted his remedies, the United States Supreme Court in *Atkins v. Virginia* (2002) held that the Eighth and Fourteenth Amendments prohibit the execution of a mentally retarded person. Simmons filed a new petition for state post-conviction relief, arguing that the reasoning of *Atkins* established that the Constitution prohibits the execution of a juvenile who was under 18 when they committed their crime. The Missouri Supreme Court agreed and found that since *Stanford*, "a national consensus has developed against the execution of juvenile offenders . . . ." The Missouri Supreme Court set aside Simmons' death sentence and resentenced him to "life imprisonment without parole." The United States Supreme Court granted certiorari, and now affirmed the Missouri Court's ruling.]

The Eighth Amendment provides: "Excessive bail shall not be required, nor excessive fines imposed, nor cruel and unusual punishments inflicted." The provision is applicable to the States through the Fourteenth Amendment. As the Court explained in *Atkins*, the Eighth Amendment guarantees individuals the right not to be subjected to excessive sanctions. The right flows from the basic " 'precept of justice that punishment for crime should be graduated and proportioned to [the] offense.' " By protecting even those convicted of heinous crimes, the Eighth Amendment reaffirms the duty of the government to respect the dignity of all persons.

The prohibition against "cruel and unusual punishments," like other expansive language in the Constitution, must be interpreted according to its text, by considering history, tradition, and precedent, and with due regard for its purpose and function in the constitutional design. To implement this framework we have established the propriety and affirmed the necessity of referring to "the evolving standards of decency that mark the progress of a maturing society" to determine which punishments are so disproportionate as to be cruel and unusual.

In *Thompson v. Oklahoma* (1988), a plurality of the Court determined that our standards of decency do not permit the execution of any offender under the age of 16 at the time of the crime. The plurality opinion explained that no death penalty State that had given express consideration to a minimum age for the death penalty had set the age lower than 16. The plurality also observed that "[t]he conclusion that it would offend civilized standards of decency to execute a person who was less than 16 years old at the time of his or her offense is consistent with the views that have been expressed by respected professional organizations, by other nations that share our Anglo–American heritage, and by the leading members of the Western European community." The opinion further noted that juries imposed the death penalty on offenders under 16 with exceeding rarity; the last execution of an offender for a crime committed under the age of 16 had been carried out in 1948, 40 years prior.

Bringing its independent judgment to bear on the permissibility of the death penalty for a 15–year–old offender, the *Thompson* plurality stressed that "[t]he reasons why juveniles are not trusted with the privileges and responsibilities of an adult also explain why their irresponsible conduct is not as morally reprehensible as that of an adult." According to the plurality, the lesser culpability of offenders under 16 made the death penalty inappropriate as a form of retribution, while the low likelihood that offenders under 16 engaged in "the kind of cost-benefit analysis that attaches any weight to the possibility of execution" made the death penalty ineffective as a means of deterrence. With Justice O'Connor concurring in the judgment on narrower grounds, the Court set aside the death sentence that had been imposed on the 15–year–old offender.

The next year, in *Stanford v. Kentucky* (1989), the Court, over a dissenting opinion joined by four Justices, referred to contemporary standards of decency in this country and concluded the Eighth and Fourteenth Amendments did not proscribe the execution of juvenile offenders over 15 but under 18. The Court noted that 22 of the 37 death penalty States permitted the death penalty for 16–year–old offenders, and, among these

37 States, 25 permitted it for 17–year–old offenders. These numbers, in the Court's view, indicated there was no national consensus "sufficient to label a particular punishment cruel and unusual." A plurality of the Court also "emphatically reject [ed]" the suggestion that the Court should bring its own judgment to bear on the acceptability of the juvenile death penalty.

The same day the Court decided *Stanford*, it held that the Eighth Amendment did not mandate a categorical exemption from the death penalty for the mentally retarded. *Penry v. Lynaugh* (1989). In reaching this conclusion it stressed that only two States had enacted laws banning the imposition of the death penalty on a mentally retarded person convicted of a capital offense. According to the Court, "the two state statutes prohibiting execution of the mentally retarded, even when added to the 14 States that have rejected capital punishment completely, [did] not provide sufficient evidence at present of a national consensus."

Three Terms ago the subject was reconsidered in *Atkins* [*v. Virginia*]. We held that standards of decency have evolved since *Penry* and now demonstrate that the execution of the mentally retarded is cruel and unusual punishment. The Court noted objective indicia of society's standards, as expressed in legislative enactments and state practice with respect to executions of the mentally retarded. When *Atkins* was decided only a minority of States permitted the practice, and even in those States it was rare. On the basis of these indicia the Court determined that executing mentally retarded offenders "has become truly unusual, and it is fair to say that a national consensus has developed against it."

The inquiry into our society's evolving standards of decency did not end there. The *Atkins* Court neither repeated nor relied upon the statement in *Stanford* that the Court's independent judgment has no bearing on the acceptability of a particular punishment under the Eighth Amendment. Instead we returned to the rule, established in decisions predating *Stanford*, that " 'the Constitution contemplates that in the end our own judgment will be brought to bear on the question of the acceptability of the death penalty under the Eighth Amendment.' " Mental retardation, the Court said, diminishes personal culpability even if the offender can distinguish right from wrong. The impairments of mentally retarded offenders make it less defensible to impose the death penalty as retribution for past crimes and less likely that the death penalty will have a real deterrent effect. Based on these considerations and on the finding of national consensus against executing the mentally retarded, the Court ruled that the death penalty constitutes an excessive sanction for the entire category of mentally retarded offenders, and that the Eighth Amendment " 'places a substantive restriction on the State's power to take the life' of a mentally retarded offender."

Just as the *Atkins* Court reconsidered the issue decided in *Penry*, we now reconsider the issue decided in *Stanford*. The beginning point is a review of objective indicia of consensus, as expressed in particular by the enactments of legislatures that have addressed the question. This data gives us essential instruction. We then must determine, in the exercise of our own independent judgment, whether the death penalty is a disproportionate punishment for juveniles.

The evidence of national consensus against the death penalty for juveniles is similar, and in some respects parallel, to the evidence *Atkins* held sufficient to demonstrate a national consensus against the death penalty for the mentally retarded. When *Atkins* was decided, 30 States prohibited the death penalty for the mentally retarded. This number comprised 12 that had abandoned the death penalty altogether, and 18 that maintained it but excluded the mentally retarded from its reach. By a similar calculation in this case, 30 States prohibit the juvenile death penalty, comprising 12 that have rejected the death penalty altogether and 18 that maintain it but, by express provision or judicial interpretation, exclude juveniles from its reach. *Atkins* emphasized that even in the 20 States without formal prohibition, the practice of executing the mentally retarded was infrequent. Since *Penry* only five States had executed offenders known to have an IQ under 70. In the present case, too, even in the 20 States without a formal prohibition on executing juveniles, the practice is infrequent. Since *Stanford*, six States have executed prisoners for crimes committed as juveniles. In the past 10 years, only three have done so: Oklahoma, Texas, and Virginia. In December 2003 the Governor of Kentucky decided to spare the life of Kevin Stanford, and commuted his sentence to one of life imprisonment without parole, with the declaration that " '[w]e ought not be executing people who, legally, were children.' " By this act the Governor ensured Kentucky would not add itself to the list of States that have executed juveniles within the last 10 years even by the execution of the very defendant whose death sentence the Court had upheld in *Stanford v. Kentucky*.

There is, to be sure, at least one difference between the evidence of consensus in *Atkins* and in this case. Impressive in *Atkins* was the rate of abolition of the death penalty for the mentally retarded. Sixteen States that permitted the execution of the mentally retarded at the time of *Penry* had prohibited the practice by the time we heard *Atkins*. By contrast, the rate of change in reducing the incidence of the juvenile death penalty, or in taking specific steps to abolish it, has been slower. Five States that allowed the juvenile death penalty at the time of *Stanford* have abandoned it in the intervening 15 years—four through legislative enactments and one through judicial decision.

Though less dramatic than the change from *Penry* to *Atkins*, we still consider the change from *Stanford* to this case to be significant. As noted in *Atkins*, with respect to the States that had abandoned the death penalty for the mentally retarded since *Penry*, "[i]t is not so much the number of these States that is significant, but the consistency of the direction of change." In particular we found it significant that, in the wake of *Penry*, no State that had already prohibited the execution of the mentally retarded had passed legislation to reinstate the penalty. The number of

States that have abandoned capital punishment for juvenile offenders since *Stanford* is smaller than the number of States that abandoned capital punishment for the mentally retarded after *Penry*, yet we think the same consistency of direction of change has been demonstrated. Since *Stanford* no State that previously prohibited capital punishment for juveniles has reinstated it. This fact, coupled with the trend toward abolition of the juvenile death penalty, carries special force in light of the general popularity of anticrime legislation, and in light of the particular trend in recent years toward cracking down on juvenile crime in other respects. Any difference between this case and *Atkins* with respect to the pace of abolition is thus counterbalanced by the consistent direction of the change. * * *

As in *Atkins*, the objective indicia of consensus in this case—the rejection of the juvenile death penalty in the majority of States; the infrequency of its use even where it remains on the books; and the consistency in the trend toward abolition of the practice—provide sufficient evidence that today our society views juveniles, in the words *Atkins* used respecting the mentally retarded, as "categorically less culpable than the average criminal."

A majority of States have rejected the imposition of the death penalty on juvenile offenders under 18, and we now hold this is required by the Eighth Amendment.

Because the death penalty is the most severe punishment, the Eighth Amendment applies to it with special force. Capital punishment must be limited to those offenders who commit "a narrow category of the most serious crimes" and whose extreme culpability makes them "the most deserving of execution." This principle is implemented throughout the capital sentencing process. States must give narrow and precise definition to the aggravating factors that can result in a capital sentence. In any capital case a defendant has wide latitude to raise as a mitigating factor "any aspect of [his or her] character or record and any of the circumstances of the offense that the defendant proffers as a basis for a sentence less than death." There are a number of crimes that beyond question are severe in absolute terms, yet the death penalty may not be imposed for their commission. The death penalty may not be imposed on certain classes of offenders, such as juveniles under 16, the insane, and the mentally retarded, no matter how heinous the crime. These rules vindicate the underlying principle that the death penalty is reserved for a narrow category of crimes and offenders.

Three general differences between juveniles under 18 and adults demonstrate that juvenile offenders cannot with reliability be classified among the worst offenders. First, as any parent knows and as the scientific and sociological studies respondent and his *amici* cite tend to confirm, "[a] lack of maturity and an underdeveloped sense of responsibility are found in youth more often than in adults and are more understandable among the young. These qualities often result in impetuous and ill-considered actions and decisions." It has been noted that "adolescents are overrepresented statistically in virtually every category of reckless behavior." In recognition of the comparative immaturity and irresponsibility of juveniles, almost every State prohibits those under 18 years of age from voting, serving on juries, or marrying without parental consent.

The second area of difference is that juveniles are more vulnerable or susceptible to negative influences and outside pressures, including peer pressure. *Eddings, supra* ("[Y]outh is more than a chronological fact. It is a time and condition of life when a person may be most susceptible to influence and to psychological damage"). This is explained in part by the prevailing circumstance that juveniles have less control, or less experience with control, over their own environment.

The third broad difference is that the character of a juvenile is not as well formed as that of an adult. The personality traits of juveniles are more transitory, less fixed.

These differences render suspect any conclusion that a juvenile falls among the worst offenders. The susceptibility of juveniles to immature and irresponsible behavior means "their irresponsible conduct is not as morally reprehensible as that of an adult." Their own vulnerability and comparative lack of control over their immediate surroundings mean juveniles have a greater claim than adults to be forgiven for failing to escape negative influences in their whole environment. The reality that juveniles still struggle to define their identity means it is less supportable to conclude that even a heinous crime committed by a juvenile is evidence of irretrievably depraved character. From a moral standpoint it would be misguided to equate the failings of a minor with those of an adult, for a greater possibility exists that a minor's character deficiencies will be reformed. Indeed, "[t]he relevance of youth as a mitigating factor derives from the fact that the signature qualities of youth are transient; as individuals mature, the impetuousness and recklessness that may dominate in younger years can subside."

In *Thompson*, a plurality of the Court recognized the import of these characteristics with respect to juveniles under 16, and relied on them to hold that the Eighth Amendment prohibited the imposition of the death penalty on juveniles below that age. We conclude the same reasoning applies to all juvenile offenders under 18.

Once the diminished culpability of juveniles is recognized, it is evident that the penological justifications for the death penalty apply to them with lesser force than to adults. We have held there are two distinct social purposes served by the death penalty: " 'retribution and deterrence of capital crimes by prospective offenders.' " As for retribution, we remarked in *Atkins* that "[i]f the culpability of the average murderer is insufficient to justify the most extreme sanction available to the State, the lesser culpability of the mentally retarded offender surely does not merit that form of retribution." The same conclusions follow from the lesser culpability of the juvenile offender. Whether viewed as an attempt to express the community's moral outrage or as an attempt to right the balance for the wrong to the victim, the case for retribution is not as strong with a minor as with an adult. Retribution is not proportional if the law's most severe penalty is imposed on one whose culpability or blameworthiness is diminished, to a substantial degree, by reason of youth and immaturity.

As for deterrence, it is unclear whether the death penalty has a significant or even measurable deterrent effect on juveniles, as counsel for the petitioner acknowledged at oral argument. In general we leave to legislatures the assessment of the efficacy of various criminal penalty schemes, see *Harmelin v. Michigan* (1991). Here, however, the absence of evidence of deterrent effect is of special concern because the same characteristics that render juveniles less culpable than adults suggest as well that juveniles will be less susceptible to deterrence. In particular, as the plurality observed in *Thompson* "[t]he likelihood that the teenage offender has made the kind of cost-benefit analysis that attaches any weight to the possibility of execution is so remote as to be virtually nonexistent." To the extent the juvenile death penalty might have residual deterrent effect, it is worth noting that the punishment of life imprisonment without the possibility of parole is itself a severe sanction, in particular for a young person.

In concluding that neither retribution nor deterrence provides adequate justification for imposing the death penalty on juvenile offenders, we cannot deny or overlook the brutal crimes too many juvenile offenders have committed. Certainly it can be argued, although we by no means concede the point, that a rare case might arise in which a juvenile offender has sufficient psychological maturity, and at the same time demonstrates sufficient depravity, to merit a sentence of death. Indeed, this possibility is the linchpin of one contention pressed by petitioner and his *amici*. They assert that even assuming the truth of the observations we have made about juveniles' diminished culpability in general, jurors nonetheless should be allowed to consider mitigating arguments related to youth on a case-by-case basis, and in some cases to impose the death penalty if justified. A central feature of death penalty sentencing is a particular assessment of the circumstances of the crime and the characteristics of the offender. The system is designed to consider both aggravating and mitigating circumstances, including youth, in every case. Given this Court's own insistence on individualized consideration, petitioner maintains that it is both arbitrary and unnecessary to adopt a categorical rule barring imposition of the death penalty on any offender under 18 years of age.

We disagree. The differences between juvenile and adult offenders are too marked and well understood to risk allowing a youthful person to receive the death penalty despite insufficient culpability. An unacceptable likelihood exists that the brutality or cold-blooded nature of any particular crime would overpower mitigating arguments based on youth as a matter of course, even where the juvenile offender's objective immaturity, vulnerability, and lack of true depravity should require a sentence less severe than death. In some cases a defendant's youth may even be counted against him. In this very case, as we noted above, the prosecutor argued Simmons' youth was aggravating rather than mitigating. While this sort of overreaching could be corrected by a particular rule to ensure that the mitigating force of youth is not overlooked, that would not address our larger concerns.

It is difficult even for expert psychologists to differentiate between the juvenile offender whose crime reflects unfortunate yet transient immaturity, and the rare juvenile offender whose crime reflects irreparable corruption. As we understand it, this difficulty underlies the rule forbidding psychiatrists from diagnosing any patient under 18 as having antisocial personality disorder, a disorder also referred to as psychopathy or sociopathy, and which is characterized by callousness, cynicism, and contempt for the feelings, rights, and suffering of others. If trained psychiatrists with the advantage of clinical testing and observation refrain, despite diagnostic expertise, from assessing any juvenile under 18 as having antisocial personality disorder, we conclude that States should refrain from asking jurors to issue a far graver condemnation—that a juvenile offender merits the death penalty. When a juvenile offender commits a heinous crime, the State can exact forfeiture of some of the most basic liberties, but the State cannot extinguish his life and his potential to attain a mature understanding of his own humanity.

Drawing the line at 18 years of age is subject, of course, to the objections always raised against categorical rules. The qualities that distinguish juveniles from adults do not disappear when an individual turns 18. By the same token, some under 18 have already attained a level of maturity some adults will never reach. For the reasons we have discussed, however, a line must be drawn. The plurality opinion in *Thompson* drew the line at 16. In the intervening years the *Thompson* plurality's conclusion that offenders under 16 may not be executed has not been challenged. The logic of *Thompson* extends to those who are under 18. The age of 18 is the point where society draws the line for many purposes between childhood and adulthood. It is, we conclude, the age at which the line for death eligibility ought to rest.

These considerations mean *Stanford v. Kentucky* should be deemed no longer controlling on this issue. To the extent *Stanford* was based on review of the objective indicia of consensus that obtained in 1989, it suffices to note that those indicia have changed. It should be observed, furthermore, that the *Stanford* Court should have considered those States that had abandoned the death penalty altogether as part of the consensus against the juvenile death penalty, a State's decision to bar the death penalty altogether of necessity demonstrates a judgment that the death penalty is inappropriate for all offenders, including juveniles. Last, to the extent *Stanford* was based on a rejection of the idea that this Court is required to bring its independent judgment to bear on the proportionality of the death penalty for a particular class of crimes or offenders, it suffices to note that this rejection was inconsistent with prior Eighth Amendment decisions, . It is also inconsistent with the premises of our recent decision in *Atkins*. * * *

Our determination that the death penalty is disproportionate punishment for offenders under 18 finds confirmation in the stark reality that the United States is the only country in the world that continues to give official sanction to the juvenile death penalty. This reality does not become controlling, for the task of interpreting the Eighth Amendment remains our responsibility. Yet at least from the time of the Court's decision in *Trop*, the Court has referred to the laws of other countries and to international authorities as instructive for its interpretation of the Eighth Amendment's prohibition of "cruel and unusual punishments."

As respondent and a number of *amici* emphasize, Article 37 of the United Nations Convention on the Rights of the Child, which every country in the world has ratified save for the United States and Somalia, contains an express prohibition on capital punishment for crimes committed by juveniles under 18. No ratifying country has entered a reservation to the provision prohibiting the execution of juvenile offenders. Parallel prohibitions are contained in other significant international covenants.

Respondent and his *amici* have submitted, and petitioner does not contest, that only seven countries other than the United States have executed juvenile offenders since 1990: Iran, Pakistan, Saudi Arabia, Yemen, Nigeria, the Democratic Republic of Congo, and China. Since then each of these countries has either abolished capital punishment for juveniles or made public disavowal of the practice. In sum, it is fair to say that the United States now stands alone in a world that has turned its face against the juvenile death penalty. * * *

It is proper that we acknowledge the overwhelming weight of international opinion against the juvenile death penalty, resting in large part on the understanding that the instability and emotional imbalance of young people may often be a factor in the crime. The opinion of the world community, while not controlling our outcome, does provide respected and significant confirmation for our own conclusions. * * * It does not lessen our fidelity to the Constitution or our pride in its origins to acknowledge that the express affirmation of certain fundamental rights by other nations and peoples simply underscores the centrality of those same rights within our own heritage of freedom. * * *

The Eighth and Fourteenth Amendments forbid imposition of the death penalty on offenders who were under the age of 18 when their crimes were committed. The judgment of the Missouri Supreme Court setting aside the sentence of death imposed upon Christopher Simmons is affirmed.

It is so ordered.

[Appendices Omitted]

JUSTICE STEVENS with whom JUSTICE GINSBURG joins, concurring.

Perhaps even more important than our specific holding today is our reaffirmation of the basic principle that informs the Court's interpretation of the Eighth Amendment. If the meaning of that Amendment had been frozen when it was originally drafted, it would impose no impediment to the execution of 7–year–old children today. The evolving standards of decency that have driven our construction of this critically important part of the Bill of Rights foreclose any such reading of the Amendment. In the best tradition of the common law, the pace of that evolution is a matter for continuing debate; but that our understanding of the Constitution does change from time to time has been settled since John Marshall breathed life into its text. If great lawyers of his day—Alexander Hamilton, for example—were sitting with us today, I would expect them to join Justice Kennedy's opinion for the Court. In all events, I do so without hesitation.

JUSTICE O'CONNOR, dissenting.

The Court's decision today establishes a categorical rule forbidding the execution of any offender for any crime committed before his 18th birthday, no matter how deliberate, wanton, or cruel the offense. Neither the objective evidence of contemporary societal values, nor the Court's moral proportionality analysis, nor the two in tandem suffice to justify this ruling.

Although the Court finds support for its decision in the fact that a majority of the States now disallow capital punishment of 17–year–old offenders, it refrains from asserting that its holding is compelled by a genuine national consensus. Indeed, the evidence before us fails to demonstrate conclusively that any such consensus has emerged in the brief period since we upheld the constitutionality of this practice in *Stanford v. Kentucky*.

Instead, the rule decreed by the Court rests, ultimately, on its independent moral judgment that death is a disproportionately severe punishment for any 17–year–old offender. I do not subscribe to this judgment. Adolescents *as a class* are undoubtedly less mature, and therefore less culpable for their misconduct, than adults. But the Court has adduced no evidence impeaching the seemingly reasonable conclusion reached by many state legislatures: that at least *some* 17–year–old murderers are sufficiently mature to deserve the death penalty in an appropriate case. Nor has it been shown that capital sentencing juries are incapable of accurately assessing a youthful defendant's maturity or of giving due weight to the mitigating characteristics associated with youth.

On this record—and especially in light of the fact that so little has changed since our recent decision in *Stanford*—I would not substitute our judgment about the moral propriety of capital punishment for 17–year–old murderers for the judgments of the Nation's legislatures. Rather, I would demand a clearer showing that our society truly has set its face against this practice before reading the Eighth Amendment categorically to forbid it. * * *

It is by now beyond serious dispute that the Eighth Amendment's prohibition of "cruel and unusual punishments" is not a static command. Its mandate would be little more than a dead letter today if it barred only those sanctions—like the execution of children under the age of seven—that civilized society had already repudiated in 1791. Rather, because "[t]he basic concept underlying the Eighth Amendment is nothing less than the dignity of man," the Amendment "must draw its meaning from the evolving standards of decency that mark the progress of a maturing society." In discerning those standards, we look to "objective factors to the maximum possible extent." Laws enacted by the Nation's legislatures provide the "clearest and most reliable objective evidence of contemporary values." And data reflecting the actions of sentencing juries, where available, can also afford " 'a significant and reliable objective index' " of societal mores.

Although objective evidence of this nature is entitled to great weight, it does not end our inquiry. Rather, as the Court today reaffirms, "the Constitution contemplates that in the end our own judgment will be brought to bear on the question of the acceptability of the death penalty under the Eighth Amendment." "[P]roportionality—at least as regards capital punishment—not only requires an inquiry into contemporary standards as expressed by legislators and jurors, but also involves the notion that the magnitude of the punishment imposed must be related to the degree of the harm inflicted on the victim, as well as to the degree of the defendant's blameworthiness." We therefore have a "constitutional obligation" to judge for ourselves whether the death penalty is excessive punishment for a particular offense or class of offenders. * * *

By the time we heard *Atkins*, 30 States barred the death penalty for the mentally retarded, and even among those States theoretically permitting such punishment, very few had executed a mentally retarded offender in recent history. On the basis of this evidence, the Court determined that it was "fair to say that a national consensus ha[d] developed against" the practice.

But our decision in *Atkins* did not rest solely on this tentative conclusion. Rather, the Court's independent moral judgment was dispositive. The Court observed that mentally retarded persons suffer from major cognitive and behavioral deficits, *i.e.,* "subaverage intellectual functioning" and "significant limitations in adaptive skills such as communication, self-care, and self-direction that became manifest before age 18." "Because of their impairments, [such persons] by definition . . . have diminished capacities to understand and process information, to communicate, to abstract from mistakes and learn from experience, to engage in logical reasoning, to control impulses, and to understand the reactions of others." We concluded that these deficits called into serious doubt whether the execution of mentally retarded offenders would measurably contribute to the principal penological goals that capital punishment is intended to serve—retribution and deterrence. Mentally retarded offenders' impairments so diminish their personal moral culpability that it is highly unlikely that such offenders could ever deserve the ultimate punishment, even in cases of capital murder. And these same impairments made it very improbable that the threat of the death penalty would deter mentally retarded persons from committing capital crimes. Having concluded that capital punishment of the mentally retarded is inconsistent with the Eighth Amendment, the Court " 'le[ft] to the State[s] the task of developing appropriate ways to enforce the constitutional restriction upon [their] execution of sentences.' "

In determining whether the juvenile death penalty comports with contemporary standards of decency, our inquiry begins with the "clearest and most reliable objective evidence of contemporary values"—the actions of the Nation's legislatures. As the Court emphasizes, the overall number of jurisdictions that currently disallow the execution of under–18 offenders is the same as the number that forbade the execution of mentally retarded offenders when *Atkins* was decided. At present, 12 States and the District of Columbia do not have the death penalty, while an additional 18 States and the Federal Government authorize capital punishment but prohibit the execution of under–18 offenders. And here, as in *Atkins*, only a very small fraction of the States that permit capital punishment of offenders within the relevant class has actually carried out such an execution in recent history: Six States have executed under–18 offenders in the 16 years since *Stanford*, while five States had executed mentally retarded offenders in the 13 years prior to *Atkins*. In these respects, the objective evidence in this case is, indeed, "similar, and in some respects parallel to" the evidence upon which we relied in *Atkins*.

While the similarities between the two cases are undeniable, the objective evidence of national consensus is marginally weaker here. Most importantly, in *Atkins* there was significant evidence of *opposition* to the execution of the mentally retarded, but there was virtually no countervailing evidence of affirmative legislative *support* for this practice. The States that permitted such executions did so only because they had not enacted any prohibitory legislation. Here, by contrast, at least eight States have current statutes that specifically set 16 or 17 as the minimum age at which commission of a capital crime can expose the offender to the death penalty. Five of these eight States presently have one or more juvenile offenders on death row (six if respondent is included in the count), and four of them have executed at least one under–18 offender in the past 15 years. In all, there are currently over 70 juvenile offenders on death row in 12 different States (13 including respondent). This evidence suggests some measure of continuing public support for the availability of the death penalty for 17–year–old capital murderers.

Moreover, the Court in *Atkins* made clear that it was "not so much the number of [States forbidding execution of the mentally retarded] that [was] significant, but the consistency of the direction of change." In contrast to the trend in *Atkins*, the States have not moved uniformly towards abolishing the juvenile death penalty. Instead, since our decision in *Stanford*, two States have expressly reaffirmed their support for this practice by enacting statutes setting 16 as the minimum age for capital punishment. Furthermore, as the Court emphasized in *Atkins* itself, the pace of legislative action in this context has been considerably slower than it was with regard to capital punishment of the mentally retarded. In the 13 years between our decisions in *Penry* and *Atkins*, no fewer than 16 States banned the execution of mentally retarded offenders. By comparison, since our decision 16 years ago in *Stanford*, only four States that previously permitted the execution of under–18 offenders, plus the Federal Government, have legislatively reversed course, and one additional State's high court has construed the State's death penalty statute not to apply to under–18 offenders. The slower pace of change is no doubt partially attributable, as the Court says, to the fact that 11 States had already imposed a minimum age of 18 when *Stanford* was decided. Nevertheless, the extraordinary wave of legislative action leading up to our decision in *Atkins* provided strong evidence that the country truly had set itself against capital punishment of the mentally retarded. Here, by contrast, the halting pace of change gives reason for pause. * * *

Here, as in *Atkins*, the objective evidence of a national consensus is weaker than in most prior cases in which the Court has struck down a particular punishment under the Eighth Amendment. In my view, the objective evidence of national consensus, standing alone, was insufficient to dictate the Court's holding in *Atkins*. Rather, the compelling moral proportionality argument against capital punishment of mentally retarded offenders played a *decisive* role in persuading the Court that the practice was inconsistent with the Eighth Amendment. Indeed, the force of the proportionality argument in *Atkins* significantly bolstered the Court's confidence that the objective evidence in that case did, in fact, herald the emergence of a genuine national consensus. Here, by contrast, the proportionality argument against the juvenile death penalty is so flawed that it can be given little, if any, analytical weight—it proves too weak to resolve the lingering ambiguities in the objective evidence of legislative consensus or to justify the Court's categorical rule.

Seventeen-year-old murderers must be categorically exempted from capital punishment, the Court says, because they "cannot with reliability be classified among the worst offenders." That conclusion is premised on three perceived differences between "adults," who have already reached their 18th birthdays, and "juveniles," who have not. First, juveniles lack maturity and responsibility and are more reckless than adults. Second, juveniles are more vulnerable to outside influences because they have less control over their surroundings. And third, a juvenile's character is not as fully formed as that of an adult. Based on these characteristics, the Court determines that 17–year–old capital murderers are not as blameworthy as adults guilty of similar crimes; that 17–year–olds are less likely than adults to be deterred by the prospect of a death sentence; and that it is difficult to conclude that a 17–year–old who commits even the most heinous of crimes is "irretrievably depraved." The Court suggests that "a rare case might arise in which a juvenile offender has sufficient psychological maturity, and at the same time demonstrates sufficient depravity, to merit a sentence of death." However, the Court argues that a categorical age-based prohibition is justified as a prophylactic rule because "[t]he differences between juvenile and adult offenders are too marked and well understood to risk allowing a youthful person to receive the death penalty despite insufficient culpability."

It is beyond cavil that juveniles as a class are generally less mature, less responsible, and less fully formed than adults, and that these differences bear on juveniles' comparative moral culpability. But even accepting this premise, the Court's proportionality argument fails to support its categorical rule.

First, the Court adduces no evidence whatsoever in support of its sweeping conclusion, that it is only in "rare" cases, if ever, that 17–year-old murderers are sufficiently mature and act with sufficient depravity to warrant the death penalty. The fact that juveniles are generally *less* culpable for their misconduct than adults does not necessarily mean that a 17–year-old murderer cannot be *sufficiently* culpable to merit the death penalty. At most, the Court's argument suggests that the average 17–year-old murderer is not as culpable as the average adult murderer. But an especially depraved juvenile offender may nevertheless be just as culpable as many adult offenders considered bad enough to deserve the death penalty. Similarly, the fact that the availability of the death penalty may be *less* likely to deter a juvenile from committing a capital crime does not imply that this threat cannot *effectively* deter some 17–year-olds from such an act. Surely there is an age below which no offender, no matter what his crime, can be deemed to have the cognitive or emotional maturity necessary to warrant the death penalty. But at least at the margins between adolescence and adulthood—and especially for 17–year-olds such as respondent—the relevant differences between "adults" and "juveniles" appear to be a matter of degree, rather than of kind. It follows that a legislature may reasonably conclude that at least *some* 17–year-olds can act with sufficient moral culpability, and can be sufficiently deterred by the threat of execution, that capital punishment may be warranted in an appropriate case. * * *

The Court's proportionality argument suffers from a second and closely related defect: It fails to establish that the differences in maturity between 17–year-olds and young "adults" are both universal enough and significant enough to justify a bright-line prophylactic rule against capital punishment of the former. The Court's analysis is premised on differences *in the aggregate* between juveniles and adults, which frequently do not hold true when comparing individuals. Although it may be that many 17–year-old murderers lack sufficient maturity to deserve the death penalty, some juvenile murderers may be quite mature. Chronological age is not an unfailing measure of psychological development, and common experience suggests that many 17–year-olds are more mature than the average young "adult." In short, the class of offenders exempted from capital punishment by today's decision is too broad and too diverse to warrant a categorical prohibition. Indeed, the age-based line drawn by the Court is indefensibly arbitrary—it quite likely will protect a number of offenders who are mature enough to deserve the death penalty and may well leave vulnerable many who are not.

For purposes of proportionality analysis, 17–year–olds as a class are qualitatively and materially different from the mentally retarded. "Mentally retarded" offenders, as we understood that category in *Atkins*, are *defined* by precisely the characteristics which render death an excessive punishment. A mentally retarded person is, "by definition," one whose cognitive and behavioral capacities have been proven to fall below a certain minimum. Accordingly, for purposes of our decision in *Atkins*, the mentally retarded are not merely *less* blameworthy for their misconduct or *less* likely to be deterred by the death penalty than others. Rather, a mentally retarded offender is one whose demonstrated impairments make it so highly unlikely that he is culpable enough to deserve the death penalty or that he could have been deterred by the threat of death, that execution is not a defensible punishment. There is no such inherent or accurate fit between an offender's chronological age and the personal limitations which the Court believes make capital punishment excessive for 17–year–old murderers. Moreover, it defies common sense to suggest that 17–year–olds as a class are somehow equivalent to mentally retarded persons with regard to culpability or susceptibility to deterrence. Seventeen-year-olds may, on average, be less mature than adults, but that lesser maturity simply cannot be equated with the major, lifelong impairments suffered by the mentally retarded.

The proportionality issues raised by the Court clearly implicate Eighth Amendment concerns. But these concerns may properly be addressed not by means of an arbitrary, categorical age-based rule, but rather through individualized sentencing in which juries are required to give appropriate mitigating weight to the defendant's immaturity, his susceptibility to outside pressures, his cognizance of the consequences of his actions, and so forth. In that way the constitutional response can be tailored to the specific problem it is meant to remedy. * * *

The Court argues that sentencing juries cannot accurately evaluate a youthful offender's maturity or give appropriate weight to the mitigating characteristics related to youth. But, again, the Court presents no real evidence—and the record appears to contain none—supporting this claim. Perhaps more importantly, the Court fails to explain why this duty should be so different from, or so much more difficult than, that of assessing and giving proper effect to any other qualitative capital sentencing factor. I would not be so quick to conclude that the constitutional safeguards, the sentencing juries, and the trial judges upon which we place so much reliance in all capital cases are inadequate in this narrow context.

I turn, finally, to the Court's discussion of foreign and international law. Without question, there has been a global trend in recent years towards abolishing capital punishment for under–18 offenders. Very few, if any, countries other than the United States now permit this practice in law or in fact. While acknowledging that the actions and views of other countries do not dictate the outcome of our Eighth Amendment inquiry, the Court asserts that "the overwhelming weight of international opinion against the juvenile death penalty ... does provide respected and significant confirmation for [its] own conclusions." Because I do not believe that a genuine *national* consensus against the juvenile death penalty has yet developed, and because I do not believe the Court's moral proportionality argument justifies a categorical, age-based constitutional rule, I can assign no such *confirmatory* role to the international consensus described by the Court. In short, the evidence of an international consensus does not alter my determination that the Eighth Amendment does not, at this time, forbid capital punishment of 17–year–old murderers in all cases.

Nevertheless, I disagree with Justice Scalia's contention, that foreign and international law have no place in our Eighth Amendment jurisprudence. Over the course of nearly half a century, the Court has consistently referred to foreign and international law as relevant to its assessment of evolving standards of decency. * * * [T]he existence of an international consensus of this nature can serve to confirm the reasonableness of a consonant and genuine American consensus. The instant case presents no such domestic consensus, however, and the recent emergence of an otherwise global consensus does not alter that basic fact. * * *

In determining whether the Eighth Amendment permits capital punishment of a particular offense or class of offenders, we must look to whether such punishment is consistent with contemporary standards of decency. We are obligated to weigh both the objective evidence of societal values and our own judgment as to whether death is an excessive sanction in the context at hand. In the instant case, the objective evidence is inconclusive; standing alone, it does not demonstrate that our society has repudiated capital punishment of 17–year–old offenders in all cases. * * *

To be sure, the objective evidence supporting today's decision is similar to (though marginally weaker than) the evidence before the Court in *Atkins*. But *Atkins* could not have been decided as it was based solely on such evidence. Rather, the compelling proportionality argument against capital punishment of the mentally retarded played a decisive role in the Court's Eighth Amendment ruling. Moreover, the constitutional rule adopted in *Atkins* was tailored to this proportionality argument: It exempted from capital punishment a defined group of offenders whose proven impairments rendered it highly unlikely, and perhaps impossible, that they could act with the degree of culpability necessary to deserve death. And *Atkins* left to the States the development of mechanisms to determine which individual offenders fell within this class.

In the instant case, by contrast, the moral proportionality arguments against the juvenile death penalty fail to support the rule the Court adopts today. There is no question that "the chronological age of a minor is itself a relevant mitigating factor of great weight," and that sentencing juries must be given an opportunity carefully to consider a defendant's age and maturity in deciding whether to assess the death penalty. But the mitigating characteristics associated with youth do not justify an absolute age limit. A legislature can reasonably conclude, as many have, that some 17–year–old murderers are mature enough to deserve the death penalty in an appropriate case. And nothing in the record before us suggests that sentencing juries are so unable accurately to assess a 17–year–old defendant's maturity, or so incapable of giving proper weight to youth as a mitigating factor, that the Eighth Amendment requires the bright-line rule imposed today. In the end, the Court's flawed proportionality argument simply cannot bear the weight the Court would place upon it.

Reasonable minds can differ as to the minimum age at which commission of a serious crime should expose the defendant to the death penalty, if at all. Many jurisdictions have abolished capital punishment altogether, while many others have determined that even the most heinous crime, if committed before the age of 18, should not be punishable by death. Indeed, were my office that of a legislator, rather than a judge, then I, too, would be inclined to support legislation setting a minimum age of 18 in this context. But a significant number of States, including Missouri, have decided to make the death penalty potentially available for 17–year–old capital murderers such as respondent. Without a clearer showing that a genuine national consensus forbids the execution of such offenders, this Court should not substitute its own "inevitably subjective judgment" on how best to resolve this difficult moral question for the judgments of the Nation's democratically elected legislatures. I respectfully dissent.

JUSTICE SCALIA, with whom THE CHIEF JUSTICE and JUSTICE THOMAS join, dissenting.

* * * In determining that capital punishment of offenders who committed murder before age 18 is "cruel and unusual" under the Eighth Amendment, the Court first considers, in accordance with our modern (though in my view mistaken) jurisprudence, whether there is a "national consensus," that laws allowing such executions contravene our modern "standards of decency," We have held that this determination should be based on "objective indicia that reflect the public attitude toward a given sanction"—namely, "statutes passed by society's elected representatives." As in *Atkins*, the Court dutifully recites this test and claims halfheartedly that a national consensus has emerged since our decision in *Stanford*, because 18 States—or 47% of States that permit capital punishment—now have legislation prohibiting the execution of offenders under 18, and because all of four States have adopted such legislation since *Stanford*.

Words have no meaning if the views of less than 50% of death penalty States can constitute a national consensus. Our previous cases have required overwhelming opposition to a challenged practice, generally over a long period of time. * * *

In an attempt to keep afloat its implausible assertion of national consensus, the Court throws overboard a proposition well established in our Eighth Amendment jurisprudence. * * * *None* of our cases dealing with an alleged constitutional limitation upon the death penalty has counted, as States supporting a consensus in favor of that limitation, States that have eliminated the death penalty entirely. And with good reason. Consulting States that bar the death penalty concerning the necessity of making an exception to the penalty for offenders under 18 is rather like including old-order Amishmen in a consumer-preference poll on the electric car. Of *course* they don't like it, but that sheds no light whatever on the point at issue. That 12 States favor *no* executions says something about consensus against the death penalty, but nothing—absolutely nothing—about consensus that offenders under 18 deserve special immunity from such a penalty. In repealing the death penalty, those 12 States considered *none* of the factors that the Court puts forth as determinative of the issue before us today—lower culpability of the young, inherent recklessness, lack of capacity for considered judgment, etc. What might be relevant, perhaps, is how many of those States permit 16– and 17–year–old offenders to be treated as adults with respect to noncapital offenses. * * *

Recognizing that its national-consensus argument was weak compared with our earlier cases, the *Atkins* Court found additional support in the fact that 16 States had prohibited execution of mentally retarded individuals since *Penry v. Lynaugh* (1989). Indeed, the *Atkins* Court distinguished *Stanford* on that very ground, explaining that "[a]lthough we decided *Stanford* on the same day as *Penry*, apparently *only two* state legislatures have raised the threshold age for imposition of the death penalty." Now, the Court says a legislative change in four States is "significant" enough to trigger a constitutional prohibition. It is amazing to think that this subtle shift in numbers can take the issue entirely off the table for legislative debate. * * *

Relying on such narrow margins is especially inappropriate in light of the fact that a number of legislatures and voters have expressly affirmed their support for capital punishment of 16– and 17–year–old offenders since *Stanford*. Though the Court is correct that no State has lowered its death penalty age, both the Missouri and Virginia Legislatures—which, at the time of *Stanford*, had no minimum age requirement—expressly established 16 as the minimum. The people of Arizona and Florida have done the same by ballot initiative. Thus, even States that have not executed an under–18 offender in recent years unquestionably favor the possibility of capital punishment in some circumstances.

The Court's reliance on the infrequency of executions, for under–18 murderers, credits an argument that this Court considered and explicitly rejected in *Stanford*. That infrequency is explained, we accurately said, both by "the undisputed fact that a far smaller percentage of capital crimes are committed by persons under 18 than over 18," and by the fact that juries are required at sentencing to consider the offender's youth as a mitigating factor. Thus, "it is not only possible, but overwhelmingly probable, that the very considerations which induce [respondent] and [his] supporters to believe that death should *never* be imposed on offenders under 18 cause prosecutors and juries to believe that it should *rarely* be imposed.''

It is, furthermore, unclear that executions of the relevant age group have decreased since we decided *Stanford*. Between 1990 and 2003, 123 of 3,599 death sentences, or 3.4%, were given to individuals who committed crimes before reaching age 18. By contrast, only 2.1% of those sentenced to death between 1982 and 1988 committed the crimes when they were under 18. As for actual executions of under–18 offenders, they constituted 2.4% of the total executions since 1973. In *Stanford*, we noted that only 2% of the executions between 1642 and 1986 were of under–18 offenders and found that that lower number did not demonstrate a national consensus against the penalty. Thus, the numbers of under–18 offenders subjected to the death penalty, though low compared with adults, have either held steady or slightly increased since *Stanford*. These statistics in no way support the action the Court takes today. * * *

Today's opinion provides a perfect example of why judges are ill equipped to make the type of legislative judgments the Court insists on making here. To support its opinion that States should be prohibited from imposing the death penalty on anyone who committed murder before age 18, the Court looks to scientific and sociological studies, picking and choosing those that support its position. It never explains why those particular studies are methodologically sound; none was ever entered into evidence or tested in an adversarial proceeding. * * *

We need not look far to find studies contradicting the Court's conclusions. As petitioner points out, the American Psychological Association (APA), which claims in this case that scientific evidence shows persons under 18 lack the ability to take moral responsibility for their decisions, has previously taken precisely the opposite position before this very Court. In its brief in *Hodgson v. Minnesota* (1990), the APA found a ''rich body of research'' showing that juveniles are mature enough to decide whether to obtain an abortion without parental involvement. The APA brief, citing psychology treatises and studies too numerous to list here, asserted: ''[B]y middle adolescence (age 14–15) young people develop abilities similar to adults in reasoning about moral dilemmas, understanding social rules and laws, [and] reasoning about interpersonal relationships and interpersonal problems.'' Given the nuances of scientific methodology and conflicting views, courts—which can only consider the limited evidence on the record before them—are ill equipped to determine which view of science is the right one. Legislatures ''are better qualified to weigh and 'evaluate the results of statistical studies in terms of their own local conditions and with a flexibility of approach that is not available to the courts.' '' * * *

Moreover, the cited studies describe only adolescents who engage in risky or antisocial behavior, as many young people do. Murder, however, is more than just risky or antisocial behavior. It is entirely consistent to believe that young people often act impetuously and lack judgment, but, at the same time, to believe that those who commit premeditated murder are—at least sometimes—just as culpable as adults. * * * Though these cases are assuredly the exception rather than the rule, the studies the Court cites in no way justify a constitutional imperative that prevents legislatures and juries from treating exceptional cases in an exceptional way—by determining that some murders are not just the acts of happy-go-lucky teenagers, but heinous crimes deserving of death. * * *

Moreover, the age statutes the Court lists "set the appropriate ages for the operation of a system that makes its determinations in gross, and that does not conduct individualized maturity tests." The criminal justice system, by contrast, provides for individualized consideration of each defendant. In capital cases, this Court requires the sentencer to make an individualized determination, which includes weighing aggravating factors and mitigating factors, such as youth. In other contexts where individualized consideration is provided, we have recognized that at least some minors will be mature enough to make difficult decisions that involve moral considerations. For instance, we have struck down abortion statutes that do not allow minors deemed mature by courts to bypass parental notification provisions. It is hard to see why this context should be any different. Whether to obtain an abortion is surely a much more complex decision for a young person than whether to kill an innocent person in cold blood.

The Court concludes, however, that juries cannot be trusted with the delicate task of weighing a defendant's youth along with the other mitigating and aggravating factors of his crime. This startling conclusion undermines the very foundations of our capital sentencing system, which entrusts juries with "mak[ing] the difficult and uniquely human judgments that defy codification and that 'buil[d] discretion, equity, and flexibility into a legal system.'" The Court says that juries will be unable to appreciate the significance of a defendant's youth when faced with details of a brutal crime. This assertion is based on no evidence; to the contrary, the Court itself acknowledges that the execution of under–18 offenders is "infrequent" even in the States "without a formal prohibition on executing juveniles," suggesting that juries take seriously their responsibility to weigh youth as a mitigating factor. * * *

The Court's contention that the goals of retribution and deterrence are not served by executing murderers under 18 is also transparently false. The argument that "[r]etribution is not proportional if the law's most severe penalty is imposed on one whose culpability or blameworthiness is diminished," is simply an extension of the earlier, false generalization that youth *always* defeats culpability. The Court claims that "juveniles will be less susceptible to deterrence," because " '[t]he likelihood that the teenage offender has made the kind of cost-benefit analysis that attaches any weight to the possibility of execution is so remote as to be virtually nonexistent.'" The Court unsurprisingly finds no support for this astounding proposition, save its own case law. The facts of this very case show the proposition to be false. Before committing the crime,

Simmons encouraged his friends to join him by assuring them that they could "get away with it" because they were minors. This fact may have influenced the jury's decision to impose capital punishment despite Simmons' age. Because the Court refuses to entertain the possibility that its own unsubstantiated generalization about juveniles could be wrong, it ignores this evidence entirely.

Though the views of our own citizens are essentially irrelevant to the Court's decision today, the views of other countries and the so-called international community take center stage.

The Court begins by noting that "Article 37 of the United Nations Convention on the Rights of the Child, which every country in the world has ratified *save for the United States* and Somalia, contains an express prohibition on capital punishment for crimes committed by juveniles under 18." The Court also discusses the International Covenant on Civil and Political Rights (ICCPR), which the Senate ratified only subject to a reservation that reads:

"The United States reserves the right, subject to its Constitutional restraints, to impose capital punishment on any person (other than a pregnant woman) duly convicted under existing or future laws permitting the imposition of capital punishment, including such punishment for crime committed by persons below eighteen years of age."

Unless the Court has added to its arsenal the power to join and ratify treaties on behalf of the United States, I cannot see how this evidence favors, rather than refutes, its position. That the Senate and the President—those actors our Constitution empowers to enter into treaties—have declined to join and ratify treaties prohibiting execution of under–18 offenders can only suggest that *our country* has either not reached a national consensus on the question, or has reached a consensus contrary to what the Court announces. That the reservation to the ICCPR was made in 1992 does not suggest otherwise, since the reservation still remains in place today. It is also worth noting that, in addition to barring the execution of under–18 offenders, the United Nations Convention on the Rights of the Child prohibits punishing them with life in prison without the possibility of release. If we are truly going to get in line with the international community, then the Court's reassurance that the death penalty is really not needed, since "the punishment of life imprisonment without the possibility of parole is itself a severe sanction," gives little comfort. * * *

More fundamentally, however, the basic premise of the Court's argument—that American law should conform to the laws of the rest of the world—ought to be rejected out of hand. In fact the Court itself does not believe it. In many significant respects the laws of most other countries differ from our law—including not only such explicit provisions of our Constitution as the right to jury trial and grand jury indictment, but even many interpretations of the Constitution prescribed by this Court itself. The Court-pronounced exclusionary rule, for example, is distinctively

American. When we adopted that rule in *Mapp v. Ohio* (1961), it was "unique to American Jurisprudence." * * *

The Court responds that "[i]t does not lessen our fidelity to the Constitution or our pride in its origins to acknowledge that the express affirmation of certain fundamental rights by other nations and peoples simply underscores the centrality of those same rights within our own heritage of freedom." * * * What these foreign sources "affirm," rather than repudiate, is the Justices' own notion of how the world ought to be, and their diktat that it shall be so henceforth in America. The Court's parting attempt to downplay the significance of its extensive discussion of foreign law is unconvincing. "Acknowledgment" of foreign approval has no place in the legal opinion of this Court *unless it is part of the basis for the Court's judgment*—which is surely what it parades as today.

To add insult to injury, the Court affirms the Missouri Supreme Court without even admonishing that court for its flagrant disregard of our precedent in *Stanford*. Until today, we have always held that "it is this Court's prerogative alone to overrule one of its precedents." That has been true even where " 'changes in judicial doctrine' ha[ve] significantly undermined" our prior holding, and even where our prior holding "appears to rest on reasons rejected in some other line of decisions," Today, however, the Court silently approves a state-court decision that blatantly rejected controlling precedent.

One must admit that the Missouri Supreme Court's action, and this Court's indulgent reaction, are, in a way, understandable. In a system based upon constitutional and statutory text democratically adopted, the concept of "law" ordinarily signifies that particular words have a fixed meaning. Such law does not change, and this Court's pronouncement of it therefore remains authoritative until (confessing our prior error) we overrule. The Court has purported to make of the Eighth Amendment, however, a mirror of the passing and changing sentiment of American society regarding penology. The lower courts can look into that mirror as well as we can; and what we saw 15 years ago bears no necessary relationship to what they see today. Since they are not looking at the same text, but at a different scene, why should our earlier decision control their judgment?

However sound philosophically, this is no way to run a legal system. We must disregard the new reality that, to the extent our Eighth Amendment decisions constitute something more than a show of hands on the current Justices' current personal views about penology, they purport to be nothing more than a snapshot of American public opinion at a particular point in time (with the timeframes now shortened to a mere 15 years). We must treat these decisions just as though they represented *real* law, *real* prescriptions democratically adopted by the American people, as conclusively (rather than sequentially) construed by this Court. Allowing lower courts to reinterpret the Eighth Amendment whenever they decide enough time has passed for a new snapshot leaves this Court's decisions without any force—especially since the "evolution" of our Eighth Amendment is no longer determined by objective criteria. To allow lower courts to behave as we do, "updating" the Eighth Amendment as needed, destroys stability and makes our case law an unreliable basis for the designing of laws by citizens and their representatives, and for action by public officials. The result will be to crown arbitrariness with chaos.

NOTE

1) **The Implications of *Roper v. Simmons* for Recognition of Youthfulness as a Mitigating Factor in Sentencing Juveniles As Adults** Several commentators have noted the need formally to recognize youthfulness when sentencing younger offenders in criminal court. *See e.g.* Franklin Zimring, "Toward a Jurisprudence of Youth Violence," 24 *Crime & Justice* 477, 487 (1998) ("Even when sufficient cognitive capacity and emotional control is present to pass the threshold of criminal capacity, a significant deficit in the capacity to appreciate or control behavior would mean the forbidden conduct is not *as much* the offender's fault, and the quantum of appropriate punishment is less."); Katherine Hunt Federle, "Emancipation and Execution: Transferring Children to Criminal Court in Capital Cases," 1996 *Wis. L. Rev.* 447; Wayne Logan, "Proportionality and Punishment: Imposing Life Without Parole on Juveniles," 33 *Wake Forest L. Rev.* 681, 709 (1998) ("When juveniles are sentenced as adults, the judiciary should be especially sensitive to their relative youth, background and culpability. This necessity becomes even more vital when the inadequacies of the waiver procedures that usher a youth into the adult criminal system are taken into account.").

Recent research in adolescent developmental psychology has prompted an increasing number of legal scholars to develop rationale to sentence juveniles differently than adults and to formally recognize youthfulness as a mitigating factor in sentencing young offenders in criminal court. *See e.g.* Elizabeth S. Scott, "Judgment and Reasoning in Adolescent Decisionmaking," 37 *Vill. L. Rev.* 1607 (1992); Laurence Steinberg and Elizabeth Cauffman, "Maturity of Judgment in Adolescence: Psychosocial Factors in Adolescent Decision Making," 20 *Law & Hum. Behav.* 249 (1996); Elizabeth Cauffman and Laurence Steinberg, "The Cognitive and Affective Influence on Adolescent Decision–Making," 68 *Temp. L. Rev.* 1763 (1995); Steven J. Morse, "Immaturity and Irresponsibility," 88 *J. Crim. L. & Criminology* 15 (1997); Elizabeth S. Scott and Thomas Grisso, "The Evolution of Adolescence: A Developmental Perspective on Juvenile Justice Reform," 88 *J. Crim. L. & Criminology* 137, 160 (1997) Elizabeth S. Scott, "The Legal Construction of Adolescence," 29 *Hofstra L. Rev.* 547 (2000); Elizabeth S. Scott & Laurence Steinberg, "Blaming Youth," 81 *Tex. L. Rev.* 799 (2003); (*see* excerpt, Chapter 1, *supra* at pp. 46–48, summarizing developmental psychological research and its implications for adolescent criminal responsibility).

Following *Roper*, **Barry C. Feld, "A Slower Form of Death: Implications of *Roper v. Simons* for Juveniles Sentenced to Life Without Parole,"** 22 *Notre Dame J. Law, Ethics, & Pub. Pol'y* 9, 26–43, 55–64 (2008), builds on the Court's decision to propose a more complete rationale and administrative mechanism to formally recognize youthfulness as a mitigating factor when criminal courts sentence younger offenders:

Roper offered three reasons—immature judgment, susceptibility to negative peer and environmental influences, and transitional identities—to justify its conclusion that juveniles are less criminally responsible than adults. Although its conclusions about the differences between adolescents and adults seem intuitively obvious, the Court provided surprisingly little scientific evidence to support its assertions. * * * We know much more about adolescents' judgment, decision making, and self-control, and that research has important implications for understanding youths' criminal responsibility and formulating sentencing policy.

Retributive sentencing theory proportions punishment to the seriousness of the offense. Two separate elements—harm and culpability—define the seriousness of a crime and the punishment deserved. * * * An offender's age does not affect the amount of harm caused—a fifteen-year-old can inflict the same injuries as an adult. However, culpability subsumes an offender's ability to appreciate the wrongfulness of her actions and to control her behavior. Because youthfulness directly affects culpability, it necessarily influences assessments of blameworthiness and ultimately the seriousness of a crime. *Roper* emphasized that youthfulness affects judgment, reasoning ability, and self-control and reduces the culpability of juveniles who fail to exhibit adult-like qualities. Although states may hold youths accountable for the harms they cause, *Roper* explicitly limited the severity of the sentence a state could impose on them because of their diminished responsibility. Even after youths develop the nominal ability to distinguish right from wrong, their bad decisions lack the same degree of moral blameworthiness as those of adults and warrant less severe punishment.

For decades, developmental psychologists have studied how children's thinking and behaviors change as they mature. By mid-adolescence, most youths can distinguish right from wrong and reason similarly to adults. For example, youths and adults use comparable reasoning processes when they make informed consent medical decisions. But the ability to make good choices when provided with complete information under laboratory conditions differs from the ability to make good decisions under stressful conditions with incomplete information. Emotions play a significant role in decision making, and researchers distinguish between "cold cognition" and "hot cognition." For adolescents, in particular, mood volatility, an appetite for risk and excitement, and stress adversely affect the quality of decision making.

In the mid–1990s, the John D. and Catherine T. MacArthur Foundation sponsored a decade-long research network on Adolescent Development and Juvenile Justice (ADJJ) to study juveniles' decision making and judgment, adjudicative competence, and criminal culpability. * * * The ADJJ research reports a disjunction between youths' cognitive abilities and the quality of their judgment. Even though adolescents by age sixteen exhibit intellectual and cognitive abilities comparable with adults, they do not develop the psycho-social maturity, ability to exercise self-control, and competence to make adult-quality decisions until their early-twenties. The "Immaturity Gap" represents the sharp cleavage between adolescents' intellectual maturity, which reaches near-adult levels by age sixteen, and their psycho-social maturity of judgment that does not emerge for nearly another decade. This latter deficit provides the basis for finding the reduced criminal responsibility of youths.

Roper attributed youths' diminished culpability to a "lack of maturity and . . . underdeveloped sense of responsibility . . . [that] often result in impetuous and ill-considered actions and decisions." The Court focused on adolescents' immaturity of judgment to reduce culpability, rather than simple cognitive ability to distinguish right from wrong which is the typical criminal law inquiry. Youths' immature judgment manifests itself in several domains— perceptions of risk, appreciation of future consequences, capacity for self-management, and ability to make autonomous choices—that distinguishes them from adults. Because all youths' differences in knowledge and experience, short-term versus long-term time perspectives, attitude toward risk, and impulsivity are elements of normal development, their bad choices are categorically less blameworthy than those of adults. * * *

"As any parent knows," kids do stupid, dangerous, and destructive things. To exercise good judgment and self-control, a person must be able to think ahead, delay gratification, and restrain impulses. Adolescents act more impulsively, fail to consider long-term consequences, and engage in riskier behavior than adults. Their propensity to take risks is reflected in higher incidence of accidents, suicides, homicides, unsafe sexual practices, and the like.

To calculate risks, a person has to identify potential positive and negative outcomes, estimate their likelihood, and then apply value preferences to optimize outcomes. To a greater extent than adults, adolescents underestimate the amount and likelihood of risks, employ a shorter timeframe in their calculus, and focus on potential gains rather than losses. Juveniles fifteen years of age and younger act much more impulsively than do older adolescents, but even sixteen- and seventeen-year-old youths fail to exhibit adult levels of self-control. Because of their youth and inexperience, adolescents may possess less information or consider fewer options than adults when they make decisions. Similarly, youths and adults use about the same amount of time to solve simple problems, but the length of time used to solve complex problems increases with age.

The ADJJ Research Network studied juveniles' ability to delay gratification, to evaluate risks, and to exercise self-control. It reports that adolescents' risk perception actually declines during mid-adolescence and then gradually increases into adulthood—sixteen- and seventeen-year-old youths perceive fewer risks than do either younger or older research subjects. Mid-adolescents are the most "present-oriented" of all the age groups studied; future orientation gradually increases into the early twenties. Youths weigh costs and benefits differently than adults and give different subjective values to outcomes which affect their ultimate choices. A study of people's ability to delay gratification reported that adolescents more often opted for an immediate, but much smaller payout, whereas adults delayed a reward unless the immediate value was only slightly discounted. Youths also view not engaging in risky behaviors differently than adults, which also leads to riskier choices by adolescents.

Youths engage in risky behavior because it provides heightened sensations, excitement, and an "adrenaline rush." Their preferences for risk and sensation-seeking peak at sixteen and seventeen years of age and then sharply decline with adulthood. The widest divergence between the perception of and the preference for risk occurs during mid-adolescence when youths' criminal activity also increases. All of these risk proclivities are heightened by youths' feelings of "invulnerability" and "immortality."

Adolescents' and adults' differences in thinking and behavior reflect basic developmental differences in the human brain which does not fully mature until the early twenties. Adolescents simply do not have the physiological capacity of adults to exercise judgment or control impulses. The prefrontal cortex (PFC) of the frontal lobe of the brain operates as the "chief executive officer" to control advanced cerebral activities. Executive functions include reasoning, abstract thinking, planning, anticipating consequences, and impulse control. During adolescence and into the early twenties, increased myelination of the PFC improves cognitive function and reasoning ability. By contrast, the amygdale—the lymbic system located at the base of the brain—controls instinctual behavior, such as the "fight or flight" response. Adolescents rely more heavily on the amygdala and less heavily on the PFC than do adults when they experience stressful situations. Their impulsive behavior reflects a "gut reaction" rather than sober reflection. Novel circumstances and aroused emotions especially challenge youths' ability to exercise self-control and to resist impulsive decisions.

Neuroscience research provides a hard-science explanation for social scientists' observations about adolescents' behavior and self-control. Adolescents' immature brains do not provide a biological deterministic excuse for criminal behavior, however. Scientists have not established a direct link between immature adolescent brain structure and function and its impact on real-life decisions and behavior under stressful conditions or a basis on which to individualize among young offenders on the basis of brain development. Rather, the neuroscience research enhances our understanding of how and why juveniles think and behave differently from adults and furnishes a basis for mitigating punishment. * * *

Roper also ascribed juveniles' diminished responsibility to their greater susceptibility than adults to negative peer group influences. To a greater extent than do adults, juveniles commit their crimes in groups, and group offending increases youths' risks of accessorial criminal liability for serious crimes they did not necessarily intend or personally commit. Their susceptibility to peer influences interacts with their propensity to take risks, and they engage in riskier behavior when they are together than they would when they are alone. Youths' ability to resist peer influences only approaches adult levels of self-control in the late teens and early twenties. While failing to resist peer pressures does not excuse criminal liability, this normal developmental characteristic provides another basis on which to lessen their criminal responsibility compared with adults. Because youths disproportionately commit their crimes in groups, more juveniles may be prosecuted as accessories and states convict many youths serving LWOP sentences as accessories, rather than principals, to felony-murder.

The opportunity to learn positive behavior and to acquire self-control is socially constructed, and children's families, schools, and communities affect their developmental prospects, life chances, and risks of criminal involvement. Political economy and community structure contribute to higher crime rates in urban inner-cities, and subcultural norms expose some minority youths to far greater pressures to engage in criminal activity than most youths confront. *Roper* recognized that juveniles are unable to escape from these criminogenic environments as readily as adults because of their greater dependency.

In summary, *Roper* relied on intuition—"what any parent knows"— rather than the substantial body of recent developmental psychological research. However, the Court correctly identified the normal developmental characteristics of adolescents that impair their judgment, reduce their culpability, and diminish their criminal responsibility compared with adults. The Court recognized that youths are more impulsive, seek exciting and dangerous experiences, and prefer immediate rewards to delayed gratification. They misperceive and miscalculate risks and discount the likelihood of bad consequences. They succumb to negative peer and adverse environmental influences. All of these normal characteristics increase their likelihood of causing devastating injuries to themselves and to others. Although they are just as capable as adults of causing great harm, their immature judgment and lack of self-control reduces their culpability and warrants less-severe punishment. * * *

The Supreme Court's proportionality jurisprudence does not require states to enact, or courts to conduct, individualized culpability assessments, or to formally recognize youthfulness as a mitigating factor in sentencing. But, states should adopt and apply the principle of youthfulness as a mitigating factor as part of a just and fair sentencing policy. * * *

The principle of youthfulness as a mitigating factor should apply both to capital and non-capital sentences. It holds youths accountable and recognizes their diminished responsibility, without excusing their criminal conduct. Even when they produce the same harms, the crimes of children are not the moral equivalents of those of adults because of their reduced culpability. Sentencing policy can recognize this developmental reality and protect young people from the adult consequences of their immature decisions.

Roper opted to treat adolescents' diminished responsibility categorically rather than individually. Despite the Court's general preference for individualized culpability assessments, it adopted a categorical prohibition because "[t]he differences between juvenile and adult offenders are too well marked and well understood to risk allowing a youthful person to receive the death penalty despite insufficient culpability." The Court feared that a heinous crime would overwhelm a jury's ability to properly consider youthfulness as a mitigating factor. *Roper* concluded that neither clinicians nor jurors could accurately distinguish between the vast majority of immature juveniles, who deserve leniency, and the rare youth who might exhibit adult-like culpability.

Although some commentators advocate individualized culpability assessments prior to imposing an LWOP sentence on a juvenile, a bright-line rule like *Roper*'s that categorically treats youthfulness as a mitigating factor is preferable to a system of guided discretion. *Roper* endorsed a categorical bright-line even though it recognized individual variability in culpability. * * * Despite individual variability, the Court reasoned that a rule which occasionally "under-punishes the rare, fully-culpable adolescent still will produce less aggregate injustice than a discretionary system that improperly, harshly sentences many more undeserving youths."

Treating adolescents' reduced culpability categorically rests on *Roper*'s moral foundation of lesser blameworthiness and represents a normative judgment about deserved punishment. Because all adolescents share characteristics of immature judgment, impulsiveness, and lack of self-control that systematically reduce their culpability, all young offenders should receive categorical reductions of adult sentences. The principle of youthfulness as a mitigating factor represents a moral and criminal policy judgment that no child deserves to be sentenced as severely as an adult convicted of a comparable crime, that is, causing the same harm. "Even if there are a few juveniles who could be among the worst of society's offenders, jurors will make errors of unacceptable frequency and magnitude. For this reason, we cannot trust ourselves to decide that a child is culpable enough to be punished as an adult. . . ."

A categorical rule of mitigation is preferable to individualized sentencing discretion for two reasons. The first is our inability either to define or identify what constitutes adult-like culpability among offending youths. Development is highly variable—a few youths may be mature prior to becoming eighteen years of age, while many others may not attain maturity even as adults. Despite developmental differences, clinicians lack the tools with which to assess youths' impulsivity, foresight, or preference for risk in ways that relate to maturity of judgment and criminal responsibility. Because the vast majority of juveniles are less culpable than adults, the inability to define and measure immaturity or validly to identify the few responsible ones would introduce a systematic bias toward punishing less-culpable youths. A categorical approach reduces the risk of erroneous over-punishment of less blameworthy youths. Every other area of law uses categorical, age-based lines to approximate the level of maturity required for particular activities—e.g., voting, driving, and consuming alcohol—and restricts youths because of their immaturity and inability to make competent decisions.

The second reason to treat youthfulness categorically is the inability of judges or juries to fairly weigh an abstract consideration of youthfulness as a mitigating factor against the aggravating reality of a horrific crime. *Roper* recognized that "the brutality or cold-blooded nature of any particular crime would overpower mitigating arguments based on youth as a matter of course, even where the juvenile offender's objective immaturity, vulnerability, and lack of true depravity should require a sentence less severe than death." When assessing the seriousness of a crime—harm and culpability—the Court rightly feared that jurors could not adequately distinguish between the person's moral responsibility for causing the harm and the harm itself, and that they would not weigh diminished responsibility sufficiently. In surveys of jurors, the heinousness of a crime invariably trumped a youth's immaturity when deciding whether to impose the death penalty.

I long have advocated a categorical "youth discount" that provides adolescents with fractional reductions in sentence-lengths based on age as a proxy for culpability. In addition to recognizing youths' diminished responsibility, a "youth discount" recognizes that same-length sentences exact a greater "penal bite" from younger offenders than older ones. A judge would take the "youth discount" off of the appropriate sentence that she would impose on an adult offender. A youth would establish her eligibility for and the amount of discount only with a birth certificate. The "youth discount" includes a sliding scale of diminished responsibility and gives the largest sentence reductions to the youngest, least mature offenders. On a sliding scale of diminished responsibility that corresponds with developmental differences, a fourteen-year-old offender might receive a maximum sentence that is perhaps twenty-five percent of the sentence an adult would receive, and a sixteen-year-old defendant might receive a maximum sentence no more than half the adult length. The deeper discounts for younger offenders correspond with their greater developmental differences in maturity of judgment and self-control. By definition, a "youth discount" would preclude imposing LWOP and other "virtual life" sentences. Because the length of an LWOP is indeterminate, states can assume an actual sentence length of about forty years against which to apply a "youth discount" based on the average age at which adult murderers enter prison and their projected, often reduced, life expectancy. Apart from adolescents' diminished responsibility, the likelihood of recidivism decreases with age and the costs of confining geriatric inmates increase substantially. The specific amount by which to discount the sentences of young offenders is the proper subject of political and legislative debate. Although some legislators may find it difficult to resist the temptation to "get tough" and to engage in demagoguery, states can achieve all of their legitimate penal goals by sentencing youths to no more than twenty or thirty years for even the most serious crimes.

Roper also emphasized that because juveniles' personalities are more transitory and less-fixed, their crimes provide less reliable evidence of moral reprehensibility or "irretrievably depraved character," and that "a greater possibility exists that a minor's character deficiencies will be reformed." A "youth discount" enables young offenders to survive serious mistakes with a semblance of their life chances intact. We can hold juveniles accountable, manage the risks they pose to others, and provide them with "room to reform" without extinguishing their lives. Because young offenders eventually will return to the community, the state bears a responsibility to provide them with resources with which to reform as they mature.

CHAPTER 7

ADJUDICATION OF DELINQUENCY: PROCEDURAL RIGHTS AT TRIAL

■ ■ ■

Procedure and substance intertwine inextricably in juvenile courts. Progressive reformers envisioned an informal court that made decisions in the child's "best interests." The Supreme Court in *Gault* emphasized the disjunctions between rehabilitative rhetoric and punitive reality and required greater procedural safeguards in juvenile courts. Although *Gault* provided impetus for the procedural convergence between juvenile and criminal courts, a substantial gulf remains between theory and reality, between the "law on the books" and the "law in action." Theoretically, the U.S. Constitution and state laws entitle delinquents to formal trials and the assistance of counsel. In reality, juvenile courts try youths using procedures to which few adults facing the prospect of confinement would consent to be tried. More than three decades ago, the Supreme Court in *Kent v. United States* observed that "the child receives the *worst of both worlds*: he gets neither the protections accorded to adults nor the solicitous care and regenerative treatment postulated for children." In the "worst of both worlds" of contemporary juvenile justice, youths continue to receive neither therapy nor justice, but instead may experience punishment without the criminal procedural safeguards provided to adults.

Despite the increasing convergence of juvenile with criminal courts, most states provide neither special procedures to protect juveniles from their own immaturity nor the full panoply of adult procedural rights. In some instances, states treat delinquents just like adult criminal defendants when formal equality redounds to their disadvantage. In other cases, they use less adequate juvenile court safeguards when those deficient procedures provide a comparative advantage to the state. Legislators and judges manipulate the competing legal views of young people as autonomous and responsible, or as immature and incompetent to maximize social control, to reinforce legal paternalism, and to enhance adult authority.

As in Chapter 3, this Chapter does not propose to review every element of adults' criminal procedural trial rights and then compare and contrast the juvenile courts' analogues. Rather, it will examine how courts and legislators employ the fluid concepts of childhood or rehabilitation, for example, *McKeiver*'s denial of a constitutional right to a jury trial, to subordinate young peoples' legal claims to procedural parity with adult criminal defendants. Despite the theoretical and formal procedural convergence between juvenile and criminal courts, the question remains whether youths continue to receive the "worst of both worlds."

The legal construction of adolescence in the juvenile justice process contains an inherent, internal contradiction. As a matter of logic and consistency, either young offenders possess the competence of adults or they do not. If they do, then presumably they deserve the same legal rights as adults, for better or worse. If they do not, then they require special procedural protections that recognize their immaturity and developmental limitations and that protect them. In the "worst of both worlds" of juvenile justice, however, courts and legislators pick and choose between competing "liberationist" and "protectionist" policies in order to maximize the social control of young offenders. In some instances, as we saw in Chapter 3, for example, with waivers of *Miranda* rights and in *Fare v. Michael C.*, they treat youths like adults when juveniles manifestly do not function on a par. In other instances, as we saw in Chapter 5 and *Schall v. Martin*, states and the courts invoke imagery of childhood—a child's right to "custody not liberty"—to deny youths the procedural rights that adults enjoy.

As you read the materials in this chapter, consider how persuasive you find the justifications that courts and commentators provide for the procedural differences between juvenile and criminal courts. Do you feel that the processes of juvenile court provide "fundamental fairness"? If you were charged with criminal conduct and faced the prospect of a significant loss of liberty, would you deem adequate the procedures of the juvenile court? Do juveniles receive any off-setting benefits that compensate for those procedural differences?

A. CONSTITUTIONAL DOMESTICATION OF THE JUVENILE COURT

The United States Supreme Court undertook the "constitutional domestication of the juvenile court" in the 1960s during the Warren Court's "Due Process Revolution." During the 1960s, the Warren Court interpreted the Fourteenth Amendment of the Constitution and the Bill of Rights to restrict governmental intervention in citizens' lives, to extend equality to minorities and the disenfranchised, and to regularize administrative and criminal justice decision making. The Court's criminal procedure decisions followed closely upon its civil rights opinions because those accused of crimes consisted disproportionately of the poor, minorities, and the young. In the context of its criminal procedural reforms, the Supreme Court used three interrelated constitutional strategies to decide cases:

incorporation, reinterpretation, and equal protection. First, the Supreme Court incorporated many of the provisions of the Fourth, Fifth, and Sixth Amendments into the Fourteenth Amendment's due process clause and applied those provisions of the Bill of Rights to the states. Second, it reinterpreted those provisions, redefined and expanded the meanings of those constitutional rights, and exercised greater judicial oversight over local law enforcement officials. Finally, it expanded greatly the principles of equal protection of law and extended constitutional safeguards to administrative officials previously immune from judicial scrutiny.

The leading Supreme Court cases in this chapter—*Gault, Winship, McKeiver*—involve issues of constitutional methodology, federalism, and jurisprudence as well as the specific details of the procedural rights available to youths in juvenile courts. As you read the cases, consider the procedural rights the Court actually grants, the constitutional bases for the decisions, the processes of constitutional adjudication the various justices use, and the various factors that they balance in their decisions.

IN RE GAULT

387 U.S. 1, 87 S.Ct. 1428, 18 L.Ed.2d 527 (1967).

[Review *Gault, supra* p. 21]

MR. JUSTICE FORTAS delivered the opinion of the Court. This is an appeal * * * from a judgment of the Supreme Court of Arizona affirming the dismissal of a petition for a writ of habeas corpus. The petition sought the release of Gerald Francis Gault, appellants' 15–year–old son, who had been committed as a juvenile delinquent to the State Industrial School by the Juvenile Court of Gila County, Arizona. The Supreme Court of Arizona affirmed dismissal of the writ against various arguments which included an attack upon the constitutionality of the Arizona Juvenile Code because of its alleged denial of procedural due process rights to juveniles charged with being "delinquents." The court agreed that the constitutional guarantee of due process of law is applicable in such proceedings. It held that Arizona's Juvenile Code is to be read as "impliedly" implementing the "due process concept." It then proceeded to identify and describe "the particular elements which constitute due process in a juvenile hearing." It concluded that the proceedings ending in commitment of Gerald Gault did not offend those requirements. We do not agree, and we reverse. We begin with a statement of the facts.

On Monday, June 8, 1964, at about 10 a.m., Gerald Francis Gault and a friend, Ronald Lewis, were taken into custody by the Sheriff of Gila County. Gerald was then still subject to a six months' probation order * * * as a result of his having been in the company of another boy who had stolen a wallet from a lady's purse. The police action on June 8 was taken as the result of a verbal complaint by a neighbor of the boys, Mrs. Cook, about a telephone call made to her in which the caller or callers made lewd or indecent remarks. It will suffice for purposes of this opinion to say that the remarks or questions put to her were of the irritatingly offensive, adolescent, sex variety.

At the time Gerald was picked up, his mother and father were both at work. No notice that Gerald was being taken into custody was left at the home. No other steps were taken to advise them that their son had, in effect, been arrested. Gerald was taken to the Children's Detention Home. When his mother arrived home at about 6 o'clock, Gerald was not there. Gerald's older brother was sent to look for him at the trailer home of the Lewis family. He apparently learned then that Gerald was in custody. He so informed his mother. The two of them went to the Detention Home. The deputy probation officer, Flagg, who was also superintendent of the Detention Home, told Mrs. Gault "why Jerry was there" and said that a hearing would be held in Juvenile Court at 3 o'clock the following day, June 9.

Officer Flagg filed a petition with the court on the hearing day, June 9, 1964. It was not served on the Gaults. Indeed, none of them saw this petition until the habeas corpus hearing on August 17, 1964. The petition was entirely formal. It made no reference to any factual basis for the judicial action which it initiated. It recited only that "said minor is under the age of eighteen years, and is in need of the protection of this Honorable Court; (and that) said minor is a delinquent minor." It prayed for a hearing and an order regarding "the care and custody of said minor." Officer Flagg executed a formal affidavit in support of the petition.

On June 9, Gerald, his mother, his older brother, and Probation Officers Flagg and Henderson appeared before the Juvenile Judge in chambers. Gerald's father was not there. He was at work out of the city. Mrs. Cook, the complainant, was not there. No one was sworn at this hearing. No transcript or recording was made. No memorandum or record of the substance of the proceedings was prepared. Our information about the proceedings and the subsequent hearing on June 15, derives entirely from the testimony of the Juvenile Court Judge, Mr. and Mrs. Gault and Officer Flagg at the habeas corpus proceeding conducted two months later. From this, it appears that at the June 9 hearing Gerald was questioned by the judge about the telephone call. There was conflict as to what he said. His mother recalled that Gerald said he only dialed Mrs. Cook's number and handed the telephone to his friend, Ronald. Officer Flagg recalled that Gerald had admitted making the lewd remarks. Judge McGhee testified that Gerald "admitted making one of these (lewd) statements." At the conclusion of the hearing, the judge said he would "think about it." Gerald was taken back to the Detention Home. He was not sent to his own home with his parents. On June 11 or 12, after having been detained since June 8, Gerald was released and driven home. There is no explanation in the record as to why he was kept in the Detention Home or why he was released. At 5 p.m. on the day of Gerald's release, Mrs. Gault received a note signed by Officer Flagg. It was on plain paper, not letterhead. Its entire text was as follows:

"Mrs. Gault: 'Judge McGhee has set Monday June 15, 1964 at 11:00 A.M. as the date and time for further Hearings on Gerald's delinquency' /s/ Flagg"

At the appointed time on Monday, June 15, Gerald, his father and mother, Ronald Lewis and his father, and Officers Flagg and Henderson were present before Judge McGhee. Witnesses at the habeas corpus proceeding differed in their recollections of Gerald's testimony at the June 15 hearing. Mr. and Mrs. Gault recalled that Gerald again testified that he had only dialed the number and that the other boy had made the remarks. Officer Flagg agreed that at this hearing Gerald did not admit making the lewd remarks. But Judge McGhee recalled that "there was some admission again of some of the lewd statements. He—he didn't admit any of the more serious lewd statements." Again, the complainant, Mrs. Cook, was not present. Mrs. Gault asked that Mrs. Cook be present "so she could see which boy that done the talking, the dirty talking over the phone." The Juvenile Judge said "she didn't have to be present at that hearing." The judge did not speak to Mrs. Cook or communicate with her at any time. Probation Officer Flagg had talked to her once—over the telephone on June 9.

At this June 15 hearing a "referral report" made by the probation officers was filed with the court, although not disclosed to Gerald or his parents. This listed the charge as "Lewd Phone Calls." At the conclusion of the hearing, the judge committed Gerald as a juvenile delinquent to the State Industrial School "for the period of his minority (that is, until 21), unless sooner discharged by due process of law." An order to that effect was entered. It recites that "after a full hearing and due deliberation the Court finds that said minor is a delinquent child, and that said minor is of the age of 15 years."

No appeal is permitted by Arizona law in juvenile cases. On August 3, 1964, a petition for a writ of habeas corpus was filed with the Supreme Court of Arizona and referred by it to the Superior Court for hearing. At the habeas corpus hearing on August 17, Judge McGhee was vigorously cross-examined as to the basis for his actions. He testified that he had taken into account the fact that Gerald was on probation. He was asked "under what section of * * * the code you found the boy delinquent?"

His answer is set forth in the margin.[5] In substance, he concluded that Gerald came within ARS § 8–201, subsec. 6(a), which specifies that a "delinquent child" includes one "who has violated a law of the state or an ordinance or regulation * * *." The law which Gerald was found to have violated is ARS § 13–377. This section * * * provides that a person who

---

5. "Q. All right. Now, Judge, would you tell me under what section of the law or tell me under what section of—of the code you found the boy delinquent?

"A. Well, there is a—I think it amounts to disturbing the peace. I can't give you the section, but I can tell you the law, that when one person uses lewd language in the presence of another person, that it can amount to—and I consider that when a person makes it over the phone, that it is considered in the presence, I might be wrong, that is one section. The other section upon which I consider the boy delinquent is Section 8–201, Subsection (d), habitually involved in immoral matters."

"in the presence or hearing of any woman or child * * * uses vulgar, abusive or obscene language, is guilty of a misdemeanor * * *." The penalty specified in the Criminal Code, which would apply to an adult, is $5 to $50, or imprisonment for not more than two months. The judge also testified that he acted under ARS § 8–201, subsec. 6(d) which includes in the definition of a "delinquent child" one who, as the judge phrased it, is "habitually involved in immoral matters."[6]

Asked about the basis for his conclusion that Gerald was "habitually involved in immoral matters," the judge testified, somewhat vaguely, that two years earlier, on July 2, 1962, a "referral" was made concerning Gerald, "where the boy had stolen a baseball glove from another boy and lied to the Police Department about it." The judge said there was "no hearing," and "no accusation" relating to this incident, "because of lack of material foundation." But it seems to have remained in his mind as a relevant factor. The judge also testified that Gerald had admitted making other nuisance phone calls in the past which, as the judge recalled the boy's testimony, were "silly calls, or funny calls, or something like that."

The Superior Court dismissed the writ, and appellants sought review in the Arizona Supreme Court. That court stated that it considered appellants' assignments of error as urging (1) that the Juvenile Code * * * is unconstitutional because it does not require that parents and children be apprised of the specific charges, does not require proper notice of a hearing, and does not provide for an appeal; and (2) that the proceedings and order relating to Gerald constituted a denial of due process of law because of the absence of adequate notice of the charge and the hearing; failure to notify appellants of certain constitutional rights including the rights to counsel and to confrontation, and the privilege against self-incrimination; the use of unsworn hearsay testimony; and the failure to make a record of the proceedings. Appellants further asserted that it was error for the Juvenile Court to remove Gerald from the custody of his parents without a showing and finding of their unsuitability, and alleged a miscellany of other errors under state law.

The Supreme Court handed down an elaborate and wide-ranging opinion affirming dismissal of the writ and stating the court's conclusions as to the issues raised by appellants and other aspects of the juvenile process. In their jurisdictional statement and brief in this Court, appellants do not urge upon us all of the points passed upon by the Supreme Court of Arizona. They urge that we hold the Juvenile Code of Arizona

---

6. ARS § 8–201, subsec. 6, the section of the Arizona Juvenile Code which defines a delinquent child, reads:

"Delinquent child" includes:

"(a) A child who has violated a law of the state or an ordinance or regulation of a political subdivision thereof.

"(b) A child who, by reason of being incorrigible, wayward or habitually disobedient, is uncontrolled by his parent, guardian or custodian.

"(c) A child who is habitually truant from school or home.

"(d) A child who habitually so deports himself as to injure or endanger the morals or health of himself or others."

invalid on its face or as applied in this case because, contrary to the Due Process Clause of the Fourteenth Amendment, the juvenile is taken from the custody of his parents and committed to a state institution pursuant to proceedings in which the Juvenile Court has virtually unlimited discretion, and in which the following basic rights are denied:

1. Notice of the charges;
2. Right to counsel;
3. Right to confrontation and cross-examination;
4. Privilege against self-incrimination;
5. Right to a transcript of the proceedings; and
6. Right to appellate review.

We shall not consider other issues which were passed upon by the Supreme Court of Arizona. We emphasize that we indicate no opinion as to whether the decision of that court with respect to such other issues does or does not conflict with requirements of the Federal Constitution.

The Supreme Court of Arizona held that due process of law is requisite to the constitutional validity of proceedings in which a court reaches the conclusion that a juvenile has been at fault, has engaged in conduct prohibited by law, or has otherwise misbehaved with the consequence that he is committed to an institution in which his freedom is curtailed. This conclusion is in accord with the decisions of a number of courts under both federal and state constitutions.

This Court has not heretofore decided the precise question. In *Kent v. United States*, we considered the requirements for a valid waiver of the "exclusive" jurisdiction of the Juvenile Court of the District of Columbia so that a juvenile could be tried in the adult criminal court of the District. Although our decision turned upon the language of the statute, we emphasized the necessity that "the basic requirements of due process and fairness" be satisfied in such proceedings. * * * Accordingly, while these cases relate only to restricted aspects of the subject, they unmistakably indicate that, whatever may be their precise impact, neither the Fourteenth Amendment nor the Bill of Rights is for adults alone.

We do not in this opinion consider the impact of these constitutional provisions upon the totality of the relationship of the juvenile and the state. We do not even consider the entire process relating to juvenile "delinquents." For example, we are not here concerned with the procedures or constitutional rights applicable to the pre-judicial stages of the juvenile process, nor do we direct our attention to the post-adjudicative or dispositional process. * * * We consider only the problems presented to us by this case. These relate to the proceedings by which a determination is made as to whether a juvenile is a "delinquent" as a result of alleged misconduct on his part, with the consequence that he may be committed to a state institution. As to these proceedings, there appears to be little current dissent from the proposition that the Due Process Clause has a role to play. The problem is to ascertain the precise impact of the due process requirement upon such proceedings. * * *

We now turn to the specific issues which are presented to us in the present case.

Notice of Charges

Appellants allege that the Arizona Juvenile Code is unconstitutional or alternatively that the proceedings before the Juvenile Court were constitutionally defective because of failure to provide adequate notice of the hearings. No notice was given to Gerald's parents when he was taken into custody on Monday, June 8. * * * The only written notice Gerald's parents received at any time was a note on plain paper from Officer Flagg delivered on Thursday or Friday, June 11 or 12, to the effect that the judge had set Monday, June 15, "for further Hearings on Gerald's delinquency."

A "petition" was filed with the court on June 9 by Officer Flagg, reciting only that he was informed and believed that "said minor is a delinquent minor and that it is necessary that some order be made by the Honorable Court for said minor's welfare." The applicable Arizona statute provides for a petition to be filed in Juvenile Court, alleging in general terms that the child is "neglected, dependent or delinquent." The statute explicitly states that such a general allegation is sufficient, "without alleging the facts." There is no requirement that the petition be served and it was not served upon, given to, or shown to Gerald or his parents.

The Supreme Court of Arizona rejected appellants' claim that due process was denied because of inadequate notice. It stated that "Mrs. Gault knew the exact nature of the charge against Gerald from the day he was taken to the detention home." The court also pointed out that the Gaults appeared at the two hearings "without objection." The court held that because "the policy of the juvenile law is to hide youthful errors from the full gaze of the public and bury them in the graveyard of the forgotten past," advance notice of the specific charges or basis for taking the juvenile into custody and for the hearing is not necessary. It held that the appropriate rule is that "the infant and his parents or guardian will receive a petition only reciting a conclusion of delinquency. But no later than the initial hearing by the judge, they must be advised of the facts involved in the case. If the charges are denied, they must be given a reasonable period of time to prepare."

We cannot agree with the court's conclusion that adequate notice was given in this case. Notice, to comply with due process requirements, must be given sufficiently in advance of scheduled court proceedings so that reasonable opportunity to prepare will be afforded, and it must "set forth the alleged misconduct with particularity." It is obvious, as we have discussed above, that no purpose of shielding the child from the public stigma of knowledge of his having been taken into custody and scheduled for hearing is served by the procedure approved by the court below. The "initial hearing" in the present case was a hearing on the merits. Notice at that time is not timely; and even if there were a conceivable purpose served by the deferral proposed by the court below, it would have to yield to the requirements that the child and his parents or guardian be notified, in writing, of the specific charge or factual allegations to be considered at the hearing, and that such written notice be given at the earliest practicable time, and in any event sufficiently in advance of the hearing to permit preparation. Due process of law requires notice of the sort we have described—that is, notice which would be deemed constitutionally adequate in a civil or criminal proceeding. It does not allow a hearing to be held in which a youth's freedom and his parents' right to his custody are at stake without giving them timely notice, in advance of the hearing, of the specific issues that they must meet. Nor, in the circumstances of this case, can it reasonably be said that the requirement of notice was waived.[54]

Right to Counsel

Appellants charge that the Juvenile Court proceedings were fatally defective because the court did not advise Gerald or his parents of their right to counsel, and proceeded with the hearing, the adjudication of delinquency and the order of commitment in the absence of counsel for the child and his parents or an express waiver of the right thereto. The Supreme Court of Arizona pointed out that "(t)here is disagreement (among the various jurisdictions) as to whether the court must advise the infant that he has a right to counsel." * * * It referred to a provision of the Juvenile Code which it characterized as requiring "that the probation officer shall look after the interests of neglected, delinquent and dependent children," including representing their interests in court. The court argued that "The parent and the probation officer may be relied upon to protect the infant's interests." Accordingly it rejected the proposition that "due process requires that an infant have a right to counsel." It said that juvenile courts have the discretion, but not the duty, to allow such representation; it referred specifically to the situation in which the Juvenile Court discerns conflict between the child and his parents as an instance in which this discretion might be exercised. We do not agree. Probation officers, in the Arizona scheme, are also arresting officers. They initiate proceedings and file petitions which they verify, as here, alleging the delinquency of the child; and they testify, as here, against the child. And here the probation officer was also superintendent of the Detention Home. The probation officer cannot act as counsel for the child. His role

---

54. Mrs. Gault's 'knowledge' of the charge against Gerald, and/or the asserted failure to object, does not excuse the lack of adequate notice. Indeed, one of the purposes of notice is to clarify the issues to be considered, and as our discussion of the facts, supra, shows, even the Juvenile Court Judge was uncertain as to the precise issues determined at the two 'hearings.' Since the Gaults had no counsel and were not told of their right to counsel, we cannot consider their failure to object to the lack of constitutionally adequate notice as a waiver of their rights. Because of our conclusion that notice given only at the first hearing is inadequate, we need not reach the question whether the Gaults ever received adequately specific notice even at the June 9 hearing, in light of the fact they were never apprised of the charge of being habitually involved in immoral matters.

in the adjudicatory hearing, by statute and in fact, is as arresting officer and witness against the child. Nor can the judge represent the child. There is no material difference in this respect between adult and juvenile proceedings of the sort here involved. In adult proceedings, this contention has been foreclosed by decisions of this Court. A proceeding where the issue is whether the child will be found to be "delinquent" and subjected to the loss of his liberty for years is comparable in seriousness to a felony prosecution. The juvenile needs the assistance of counsel to cope with problems of law, to make skilled inquiry into the facts, to insist upon regularity of the proceedings, and to ascertain whether he has a defense and to prepare and submit it. The child "requires the guiding hand of counsel at every step in the proceedings against him." Just as in *Kent v. United States*, we indicated our agreement * * * that the assistance of counsel is essential for purposes of waiver proceedings, so we hold now that it is equally essential for the determination of delinquency, carrying with it the awesome prospect of incarceration in a state institution until the juvenile reaches the age of 21.

During the last decade, court decisions, experts, and legislatures[63] have demonstrated increasing recognition of this view. In at least one-third of the States, statutes now provide for the right of representation by retained counsel in juvenile delinquency proceedings, notice of the right, or assignment of counsel, or a combination of these. In other States, court rules have similar provisions.

The President's Crime Commission has recently recommended that in order to assure "procedural justice for the child," it is necessary that "Counsel * * * be appointed as a matter of course wherever coercive action is a possibility, without requiring any affirmative choice by child or parent."[65] As stated by the authoritative "Standards for Juvenile and

---

63. Only a few state statutes require advice of the right to counsel and to have counsel appointed. See N. Y. Family Court Act §§ 241, 249, 728, 741; Calif.Welf. & Inst'ns Code §§ 633, 634, 659, 700 (1966) (appointment is mandatory only if conduct would be a felony in the case of an adult); Minn. Stat.Ann. § 260.155(2) (1966 Supp.); District of Columbia Legal Aid Act, D.C.Code Ann. § 2–2202 (1961) (Legal Aid Agency "shall make attorneys available to represent indigents * * * in proceedings before the juvenile court * * *." See *Black v. United States*, (1965), construing this Act as providing a right to appointed counsel and to be informed of that right). Other state statutes allow appointment on request, or in some classes of cases, or in the discretion of the court, etc. * * *

65. *Nat'l Crime Comm'n Report*, pp. 86–87. The Commission's statement of its position is very forceful:

"The Commission believes that no single action holds more potential for achieving procedural justice for the child in the juvenile court than provision of counsel. The presence of an independent legal representative of the child, or of his parent, is the keystone of the whole structure of guarantees that a minimum system of procedural justice requires. The rights to confront one's accusers, to cross-examine witnesses, to present evidence and testimony of one's own, to be unaffected by prejudicial and unreliable evidence, to participate meaningfully in the dispositional decision, to take an appeal have substantial meaning for the overwhelming majority of persons brought before the juvenile court only if they are provided with competent lawyers who can invoke those rights effectively. The most informal and well-intentioned of judicial proceedings are technical; few adults without legal training can influence or even understand them; certainly children cannot. Papers are drawn and charges expressed in legal language. Events follow one another in a manner that appears arbitrary and confusing to the uninitiated. Decisions, unexplained, appear too official to challenge. But with lawyers come records of proceedings; records

Family Courts," published by the Children's Bureau of the United States Department of Health, Education, and Welfare:

> "As a component part of a fair hearing required by due process guaranteed under the 14th amendment, notice of the right to counsel should be required at all hearings and counsel provided upon request when the family is financially unable to employ counsel."

This statement was "reviewed" by the National Council of Juvenile Court Judges at its 1965 Convention and they "found no fault" with it. * * *

We conclude that the Due Process Clause of the Fourteenth Amendment requires that in respect of proceedings to determine delinquency which may result in commitment to an institution in which the juvenile's freedom is curtailed, the child and his parents must be notified of the child's right to be represented by counsel retained by them, or if they are unable to afford counsel, that counsel will be appointed to represent the child.

At the habeas corpus proceeding, Mrs. Gault testified that she knew that she could have appeared with counsel at the juvenile hearing. This knowledge is not a waiver of the right to counsel which she and her juvenile son had, as we have defined it. They had a right expressly to be advised that they might retain counsel and to be confronted with the need for specific consideration of whether they did or did not choose to waive the right. If they were unable to afford to employ counsel, they were entitled in view of the seriousness of the charge and the potential commitment, to appointed counsel, unless they chose waiver. Mrs. Gault's

---

make possible appeals which, even if they do not occur, impart by their possibility a healthy atmosphere of accountability.

"Fears have been expressed that lawyers would make juvenile court proceedings adversary. No doubt this is partly true, but it is partly desirable. Informality is often abused. The juvenile courts deal with cases in which facts are disputed and in which, therefore, rules of evidence, confrontation of witnesses, and other adversary procedures are called for. They deal with many cases involving conduct that can lead to incarceration or close supervision for long periods, and therefore juveniles often need the same safeguards that are granted to adults. And in all cases children need advocates to speak for them and guard their interests, particularly when disposition decisions are made. It is the disposition stage at which the opportunity arises to offer individualized treatment plans and in which the danger inheres that the court's coercive power will be applied without adequate knowledge of the circumstances.

"Fears also have been expressed that the formality lawyers would bring into juvenile court would defeat the therapeutic aims of the court. But informality has no necessary connection with therapy; it is a device that has been used to approach therapy, and it is not the only possible device. It is quite possible that in many instances lawyers, for all their commitment to formality, could do more to further therapy for their clients than can the small, overworked social staffs of the courts. * * *

"The Commission believes it is essential that counsel be appointed by the juvenile court for those who are unable to provide their own. Experience under the prevailing systems in which children are free to seek counsel of their choice reveals how empty of meaning the right is for those typically the subjects of juvenile court proceedings. Moreover, providing counsel only when the child is sophisticated enough to be aware of his need and to ask for one or when he fails to waive his announced right (is) not enough, as experience in numerous jurisdictions reveals.

"The Commission recommends:

"COUNSEL SHOULD BE APPOINTED AS A MATTER OF COURSE WHEREVER COERCIVE ACTION IS A POSSIBILITY, WITHOUT REQUIRING ANY AFFIRMATIVE CHOICE BY CHILD OR PARENT."

knowledge that she could employ counsel was not an "intentional relinquishment or abandonment" of a fully known right.

Confrontation, Self–Incrimination, Cross–Examination

Appellants urge that the writ of habeas corpus should have been granted because of the denial of the rights of confrontation and cross-examination in the Juvenile Court hearings, and because the privilege against self-incrimination was not observed. The Juvenile Court Judge testified at the habeas corpus hearing that he had proceeded on the basis of Gerald's admissions at the two hearings. Appellants attack this on the ground that the admissions were obtained in disregard of the privilege against self-incrimination. If the confession is disregarded, appellants argue that the delinquency conclusion, since it was fundamentally based on a finding that Gerald had made lewd remarks during the phone call to Mrs. Cook, is fatally defective for failure to accord the rights of confrontation and cross-examination which the Due Process Clause of the Fourteenth Amendment of the Federal Constitution guarantees in state proceedings generally. * * *

Mrs. Cook, the complainant, and the recipient of the alleged telephone call, was not called as a witness. * * * So far as appears, Mrs. Cook was spoken to only once, by Officer Flagg, and this was by telephone. * * * Gerald was also questioned by the Juvenile Court Judge at each of the two hearings. The judge testified in the habeas corpus proceeding that Gerald admitted making "some of the lewd statements * * * (but not) any of the more serious lewd statements." There was conflict and uncertainty among the witnesses at the habeas corpus proceeding—the Juvenile Court Judge, Mr. and Mrs. Gault, and the probation officer—as to what Gerald did or did not admit.

We shall assume that Gerald made admissions of the sort described by the Juvenile Court Judge, as quoted above. Neither Gerald nor his parents were advised that he did not have to testify or make a statement, or that an incriminating statement might result in his commitment as a "delinquent." The Arizona Supreme Court rejected appellants' contention that Gerald had a right to be advised that he need not incriminate himself. It said: "We think the necessary flexibility for individualized treatment will be enhanced by a rule which does not require the judge to advise the infant of a privilege against self-incrimination."

In reviewing this conclusion of Arizona's Supreme Court, we emphasize again that we are here concerned only with a proceeding to determine whether a minor is a "delinquent" and which may result in commitment to a state institution. Specifically, the question is whether, in such a proceeding, an admission by the juvenile may be used against him in the absence of clear and unequivocal evidence that the admission was made with knowledge that he was not obliged to speak and would not be penalized for remaining silent. In light of *Miranda v. State of Arizona*, we must also consider whether, if the privilege against self-incrimination is available, it can effectively be waived unless counsel is present or the right to counsel has been waived. * * *

The privilege against self-incrimination is, of course, related to the question of the safeguards necessary to assure that admissions or confessions are reasonably trustworthy, that they are not the mere fruits of fear or coercion, but are reliable expressions of the truth. The roots of the privilege are, however, far deeper. They tap the basic stream of religious and political principle because the privilege reflects the limits of the individual's attornment to the state and—in a philosophical sense—insists upon the equality of the individual and the state. In other words, the privilege has a broader and deeper thrust than the rule which prevents the use of confessions which are the product of coercion because coercion is thought to carry with it the danger of unreliability. One of its purposes is to prevent the state, whether by force or by psychological domination, from overcoming the mind and will of the person under investigation and depriving him of the freedom to decide whether to assist the state in securing his conviction.

It would indeed be surprising if the privilege against self-incrimination were available to hardened criminals but not to children. The language of the Fifth Amendment, applicable to the States by operation of the Fourteenth Amendment, is unequivocal and without exception. And the scope of the privilege is comprehensive. As Mr. Justice White, concurring, stated in *Murphy v. Waterfront Commission*:

> "The privilege can be claimed in *any proceeding*, be it criminal or civil, administrative or judicial, investigatory or adjudicatory. * * * It protects *any disclosures* which the witness may reasonably apprehend *could be used in a criminal prosecution or which could lead to other evidence that might be so used.*" (Emphasis added.) * * *

Against the application to juveniles of the right to silence, it is argued that juvenile proceedings are "civil" and not "criminal," and therefore the privilege should not apply. It is true that the statement of the privilege in the Fifth Amendment, which is applicable to the States by reason of the Fourteenth Amendment, is that no person "shall be compelled in any criminal case to be a witness against himself." However, it is also clear that the availability of the privilege does not turn upon the type of proceeding in which its protection is invoked, but upon the nature of the statement or admission and the exposure which it invites. The privilege may, for example, be claimed in a civil or administrative proceeding, if the statement is or may be inculpatory.

It would be entirely unrealistic to carve out of the Fifth Amendment all statements by juveniles on the ground that these cannot lead to "criminal" involvement. In the first place, juvenile proceedings to determine "delinquency," which may lead to commitment to a state institution, must be regarded as "criminal" for purposes of the privilege against self-incrimination. To hold otherwise would be to disregard substance because of the feeble enticement of the "civil" label-of-convenience which has been attached to juvenile proceedings. Indeed, in over half of the States, there is not even assurance that the juvenile will be kept in separate institutions, apart from adult "criminals." In those States juveniles may be placed in or transferred to adult penal institutions after having been found "delinquent" by a juvenile court. For this purpose, at least, commitment is a deprivation of liberty. It is incarceration against one's will, whether it is called "criminal" or "civil." And our Constitution guarantees that no person shall be "compelled" to be a witness against himself when he is threatened with deprivation of his liberty—a command which this Court has broadly applied and generously implemented in accordance with the teaching of the history of the privilege and its great office in mankind's battle for freedom.

In addition, apart from the equivalence for this purpose of exposure to commitment as a juvenile delinquent and exposure to imprisonment as an adult offender, the fact of the matter is that there is little or no assurance in Arizona, as in most if not all of the States, that a juvenile apprehended and interrogated by the police or even by the Juvenile Court itself will remain outside of the reach of adult courts as a consequence of the offense for which he has been taken into custody. In Arizona, as in other States, provision is made for Juvenile Courts to relinquish or waive jurisdiction to the ordinary criminal courts. * * *

It is also urged, as the Supreme Court of Arizona here asserted, that the juvenile and presumably his parents should not be advised of the juvenile's right to silence because confession is good for the child as the commencement of the assumed therapy of the juvenile court process, and he should be encouraged to assume an attitude of trust and confidence toward the officials of the juvenile process. This proposition has been subjected to widespread challenge on the basis of current reappraisals of the rhetoric and realities of the handling of juvenile offenders.

In fact, evidence is accumulating that confessions by juveniles do not aid in "individualized treatment," as the court below put it, and that compelling the child to answer questions, without warning or advice as to his right to remain silent, does not serve this or any other good purpose. In light of the observations of Wheeler and Cottrell, and others, it seems probable that where children are induced to confess by "paternal" urgings on the part of officials and the confession is then followed by disciplinary action, the child's reaction is likely to be hostile and adverse—the child may well feel that he has been led or tricked into confession and that despite his confession, he is being punished. * * *

We conclude that the constitutional privilege against self-incrimination is applicable in the case of juveniles as it is with respect to adults. We appreciate that special problems may arise with respect to waiver of the privilege by or on behalf of children, and that there may well be some differences in technique—but not in principle—depending upon the age of the child and the presence and competence of parents. The participation of counsel will, of course, assist the police, Juvenile Courts and appellate tribunals in administering the privilege. If counsel was not present for some permissible reason when an admission was obtained, the greatest care must be taken to assure that the admission was voluntary, in the sense not only that it was not coerced or suggested, but also that it was not the product of ignorance of rights or of adolescent fantasy, fright or despair.

The "confession" of Gerald Gault was first obtained by Officer Flagg, out of the presence of Gerald's parents, without counsel and without advising him of his right to silence, as far as appears. The judgment of the Juvenile Court was stated by the judge to be based on Gerald's admissions in court. Neither "admission" was reduced to writing, and, to say the least, the process by which the "admissions" were obtained and received must be characterized as lacking the certainty and order which are required of proceedings of such formidable consequences. Apart from the "admission," there was nothing upon which a judgment or finding might be based. There was no sworn testimony. Mrs. Cook, the complainant, was not present. The Arizona Supreme Court held that "sworn testimony must be required of all witnesses including police officers, probation officers and others who are part of or officially related to the juvenile court structure." We hold that this is not enough. No reason is suggested or appears for a different rule in respect of sworn testimony in juvenile courts than in adult tribunals. Absent a valid confession adequate to support the determination of the Juvenile Court, confrontation and sworn testimony by witnesses available for cross-examination were essential for a finding of "delinquency" and an order committing Gerald to a state institution for a maximum of six years. * * *

Appellate Review and Transcript of Proceedings

This Court has not held that a State is required by the Federal Constitution "to provide appellate courts or a right to appellate review at all." In view of the fact that we must reverse the Supreme Court of Arizona's affirmance of the dismissal of the writ of habeas corpus for other reasons, we need not rule on this question in the present case or upon the failure to provide a transcript or recording of the hearings—or, indeed, the failure of the Juvenile Judge to state the grounds for his conclusion. Cf. *Kent v. United States*, where we said, in the context of a decision of the juvenile court waiving jurisdiction to the adult court, which by local law, was permissible: " * * * it is incumbent upon the Juvenile Court to accompany its waiver order with a statement of the reasons or considerations therefor." As the present case illustrates, the consequences of failure to provide an appeal, to record the proceedings, or to make findings or state the grounds for the juvenile court's conclusion may be to throw a burden upon the machinery for habeas corpus, to saddle the reviewing process with the burden of attempting to reconstruct a record, and to impose upon the Juvenile Judge the unseemly duty of testifying under cross-examination as to the events that transpired in the hearings before him.

For the reasons stated, the judgment of the Supreme Court of Arizona is reversed and the cause remanded for further proceedings not inconsistent with this opinion. It is so ordered.

Mr. JUSTICE BLACK, concurring. The juvenile court laws of Arizona and other States, as the Court points out, are the result of plans promoted by humane and forward-looking people to provide a system of courts, procedures, and sanctions deemed to be less harmful and more lenient to children than to adults. For this reason such state laws generally provide less formal and less public methods for the trial of children. In line with this policy, both courts and legislators have shrunk back from labeling these laws as "criminal" and have preferred to call them "civil." This, in part, was to prevent the full application to juvenile court cases of the Bill of Rights safeguards, including notice as provided in the Sixth Amendment, the right to counsel guaranteed by the Sixth, the right against self-incrimination guaranteed by the Fifth, and the right to confrontation guaranteed by the Sixth. The Court here holds, however, that these four Bill of Rights safeguards apply to protect a juvenile accused in a juvenile court on a charge under which he can be imprisoned for a term of years. This holding strikes a well-nigh fatal blow to much that is unique about the juvenile courts in the Nation. For this reason, there is much to be said for the position of my Brother STEWART that we should not pass on all these issues until they are more squarely presented. But since the majority of the Court chooses to decide all of these questions, I must either do the same or leave my views unexpressed on the important issues determined. In these circumstances, I feel impelled to express my views. * * *

Young Gault was arrested and detained on a charge of violating an Arizona penal law by using vile and offensive language to a lady on the telephone. If an adult, he could only have been fined or imprisoned for two months for his conduct. As a juvenile, however, he was put through a more or less secret, informal hearing by the court, after which he was ordered, or more realistically, "sentenced," to confinement in Arizona's Industrial School until he reaches 21 years of age. Thus, in a juvenile system designed to lighten or avoid punishment for criminality, he was ordered by the State to six years' confinement in what is in all but name a penitentiary or jail. Where a person, infant or adult, can be seized by the State, charged, and convicted for violating a state criminal law, and then ordered by the State to be confined for six years, I think the Constitution requires that he be tried in accordance with the guarantees of all the provisions of the Bill of Rights made applicable to the States by the Fourteenth Amendment. Undoubtedly this would be true of an adult defendant, and it would be a plain denial of equal protection of the laws—an invidious discrimination—to hold that others subject to heavier punishments could, because they are children, be denied these same constitutional safeguards. I consequently agree with the Court that the Arizona law as applied here denied to the parents and their son the right of notice, right to counsel, right against self-incrimination, and right to confront the witnesses against young Gault. Appellants are entitled to these rights, not because "fairness, impartiality and orderliness—in short, the essentials of due process"—require them and not because they are "the procedural rules which have been fashioned from the generality of due process," but because they are specifically and unequivocally granted by provisions of the Fifth and Sixth Amendments which the Fourteenth Amendment makes applicable to the States. * * *

MR. JUSTICE HARLAN, concurring in part and dissenting in part. * * * I must first acknowledge that I am unable to determine with any certainty by what standards the Court decides that Arizona's juvenile courts do not satisfy the obligations of due process. The Court's premise, itself the product of reasoning which is not described, is that the "constitutional and theoretical basis" of state systems of juvenile and family courts is "debatable"; it buttresses these doubts by marshaling a body of opinion which suggests that the accomplishments of these courts have often fallen short of expectations. The Court does not indicate at what points or for what purposes such views, held either by it or by other observers, might be pertinent to the present issues. Its failure to provide any discernible standard for the measurement of due process in relation to juvenile proceedings unfortunately might be understood to mean that the Court is concerned principally with the wisdom of having such courts at all. * * *

The central issue here, and the principal one upon which I am divided from the Court, is the method by which the procedural requirements of due process should be measured. It must at the outset be emphasized that the protections necessary here cannot be determined by resort to any classification of juvenile proceedings either as criminal or as civil, whether made by the State or by this Court. Both formulae are simply too imprecise to permit reasoned analysis of these difficult constitutional issues. The Court should instead measure the requirements of due process by reference both to the problems which confront the State and to the actual character of the procedural system which the State has created. The Court has for such purposes chiefly examined three connected sources: first, the "settled usages and modes of proceeding," second, the "fundamental principles of liberty and justice which lie at the base of all our civil and political institutions" and third, the character and requirements of the circumstances presented in each situation. Each of these factors is relevant to the issues here, but it is the last which demands particular examination. * * *

It suffices for present purposes to summarize the factors which I believe to be pertinent. It must first be emphasized that the deference given to legislators upon substantive issues must realistically extend in part to ancillary procedural questions. Procedure at once reflects and creates substantive rights, and every effort of courts since the beginnings of the common law to separate the two has proved essentially futile. The distinction between them is particularly inadequate here, where the legislature's substantive preferences directly and unavoidably require judgments about procedural issues. The procedural framework is here a principal element of the substantive legislative system; meaningful defer-

ence to the latter must include a portion of deference to the former. The substantive-procedural dichotomy is, nonetheless, an indispensable tool of analysis, for it stems from fundamental limitations upon judicial authority under the Constitution. Its premise is ultimately that courts may not substitute for the judgments of legislators their own understanding of the public welfare, but must instead concern themselves with the validity under the Constitution of the methods which the legislature has selected.
* * *

The foregoing considerations, which I believe to be fair distillations of relevant judicial history, suggest three criteria by which the procedural requirements of due process should be measured here: first, no more restrictions should be imposed than are imperative to assure the proceedings' fundamental fairness; second, the restrictions which are imposed should be those which preserve, so far as possible, the essential elements of the State's purpose; and finally, restrictions should be chosen which will later permit the orderly selection of any additional protections which may ultimately prove necessary. In this way, the Court may guarantee the fundamental fairness of the proceeding, and yet permit the State to continue development of an effective response to the problems of juvenile crime.

Measured by these criteria, only three procedural requirements should, in my opinion, now be deemed required of state juvenile courts by the Due Process Clause of the Fourteenth Amendment: first, timely notice must be provided to parents and children of the nature and terms of any juvenile court proceeding in which a determination affecting their rights or interests may be made; second, unequivocal and timely notice must be given that counsel may appear in any such proceeding in behalf of the child and its parents, and that in cases in which the child may be confined in an institution, counsel may, in circumstances of indigency, be appointed for them; and third, the court must maintain a written record, or its equivalent, adequate to permit effective review on appeal or in collateral proceedings. These requirements would guarantee to juveniles the tools with which their rights could be fully vindicated, and yet permit the States to pursue without unnecessary hindrance the purposes which they believe imperative in this field. Further, their imposition now would later permit more intelligent assessment of the necessity under the Fourteenth Amendment of additional requirements, by creating suitable records from which the character and deficiencies of juvenile proceedings could be accurately judged. I turn to consider each of these three requirements.

The Court has consistently made plain that adequate and timely notice is the fulcrum of due process, whatever the purposes of the proceeding. Notice is ordinarily the prerequisite to effective assertion of any constitutional or other rights; without it, vindication of those rights must be essentially fortuitous. So fundamental a protection can neither be spared here nor left to the "favor or grace" of state authorities. Provision of counsel and of a record, like adequate notice, would permit the juvenile to assert very much more effectively his rights and defenses, both in the juvenile proceedings and upon direct or collateral review. The Court has frequently emphasized their importance in proceedings in which an individual may be deprived of his liberty, this reasoning must include with special force those who are * * * commonly inexperienced and immature. The facts of this case illustrate poignantly the difficulties of review without either an adequate record or the participation of counsel in the proceeding's initial stages. At the same time, these requirements should not cause any substantial modification in the character of juvenile court proceedings: counsel, although now present in only a small percentage of juvenile cases, have apparently already appeared without incident in virtually all juvenile courts; and the maintenance of a record should not appreciably alter the conduct of these proceedings.

The question remains whether certain additional requirements, among them the privilege against self-incrimination, confrontation, and cross-examination, must now, as the Court holds, also be imposed. * * * In my view, the Court should approach this question in terms of the criteria, described above, which emerge from the history of due process adjudication. Measured by them, there are compelling reasons at least to defer imposition of these additional requirements. First, quite unlike notice, counsel, and a record, these requirements might radically alter the character of juvenile court proceedings. The evidence from which the Court reasons that they would not is inconclusive, and other available evidence suggests that they very likely would. At the least, it is plain that these additional requirements would contribute materially to the creation in these proceedings of the atmosphere of an ordinary criminal trial, and would, even if they do no more, thereby largely frustrate a central purpose of these specialized courts. Further, these are restrictions intended to conform to the demands of an intensely adversary system of criminal justice; the broad purposes which they represent might be served in juvenile courts with equal effectiveness by procedural devices more consistent with the premises of proceedings in those courts. As the Court apparently acknowledges, the hazards of self-accusation, for example, might be avoided in juvenile proceedings without the imposition of all the requirements and limitations which surround the privilege against self-incrimination. The guarantee of adequate notice, counsel, and a record would create conditions in which suitable alternative procedures could be devised; but, unfortunately, the Court's haste to impose restrictions taken intact from criminal procedure may well seriously hamper the development of such alternatives. Surely this illustrates that prudence and the principles of the Fourteenth Amendment alike require that the Court should now impose no more procedural restrictions than are imperative to assure fundamental fairness, and that the States should instead be permitted additional opportunities to develop without unnecessary hindrance their systems of juvenile courts. * * *

MR. JUSTICE STEWART, dissenting. The Court today uses an obscure Arizona case as a vehicle to impose upon thousands of juvenile courts throughout the Nation restrictions that the Constitution made applicable to adversary criminal trials. I believe the Court's decision is wholly unsound as a matter of constitutional law, and sadly unwise as a matter of judicial policy.

Juvenile proceedings are not criminal trials. They are not civil trials. They are simply not adversary proceedings. Whether treating with a delinquent child, a neglected child, a defective child, or a dependent child, a juvenile proceeding's whole purpose and mission is the very opposite of the mission and purpose of a prosecution in a criminal court. The object of the one is correction of a condition. The object of the other is conviction and punishment for a criminal act. * * *

I possess neither the specialized experience nor the expert knowledge to predict with any certainty where may lie the brightest hope for progress in dealing with the serious problems of juvenile delinquency. But I am certain that the answer does not lie in the Court's opinion in this case, which serves to convert a juvenile proceeding into a criminal prosecution. The inflexible restrictions that the Constitution so wisely made applicable to adversary criminal trials have no inevitable place in the proceedings of those public social agencies known as juvenile or family courts. And to impose the Court's long catalog of requirements upon juvenile proceedings in every area of the country is to invite a long step backwards into the nineteenth century. In that era there were no juvenile proceedings, and a child was tried in a conventional criminal court will all the trappings of a conventional criminal trial. So it was that a 12–year–old boy named James Guild was tried in New Jersey for killing Catharine Beakes. A jury found him guilty of murder, and he was sentenced to death by hanging. The sentence was executed. It was all very constitutional. * * *

NOTES

1) Constitutional Methodology *Gault* and its progeny began the "constitutional domestication" of the juvenile court. What provisions of the Constitution provide the foundation for the Court's decision? How does the Court determine what procedural rights are "fundamental" and necessary to a fair proceeding in juvenile court? Is the sole function of the rights granted to determine the validity of the factual allegations in the petition? Why did the Court grant Gault the privilege against self-incrimination? What, if any, factors do Justices Fortas, Black, and Harlan balance in their constitutional calculus? What does *Gault* actually decide? Which youths are entitled to constitutional procedural safeguards? What are the implications of *Gault* for non-criminal status offenders?

2) Criticisms of Juvenile Courts' Traditional Procedural Informality Criticism of juvenile justice administration had been building for more than a decade prior to the *Gault* decision. *See, e.g.,* Monrad Paulsen, "Fairness to the Juvenile Offender," 41 *Minn. L. Rev.* 547 (1957); Joel Handler, "The Juvenile Court and the Adversary System: Problems of Function and Form," 1965 *Wis. L. Rev.* 7. The *Gault* Court relied heavily on the contemporaneous research findings of the President's Crime Commission, *The Chal-*

lenge of Crime in a Free Society (1967) and *Task Force Report: Juvenile Delinquency* (1967) to support its assessment of juvenile justice administration. During the 1960s, support for the "rehabilitative ideal" eroded as critics on the Left questioned the scientific underpinnings of treatment and challenged the inequalities that resulted from discretionary clinical decisions. *See, e.g.*, American Friends Service Committee, *Struggle for Justice* (1971), David Garland, *The Culture of Control* (2002). As the "baby boom" demographic bulge strained agencies of social control and increased urban crime rates, critics on the Right called for "law and order" and denounced juvenile courts for "coddling" young criminals. The issue of race provided the crucial link between the invidious consequences of discretionary decision-making, the increased concern about urban crime and violence, and the Warren Court's emphasis on procedural justice to enhance individual liberty and control agents of the state. *See* Gary A. Debele, "The Due Process Revolution and the Juvenile Court: The Matter of Race in the Historical Evolution of a Doctrine," 5 *J. Law & Inequality* 513 (1987); Barry C. Feld, "Race, Politics and Juvenile Justice: The Warren Court and the Conservative 'Backlash'," 87 Minn. L. Rev. 1447 (2003).

The *Task Force Report: Juvenile Delinquency* 7 (1967) reported disturbing findings about the qualifications of juvenile court judges at the time the Supreme Court decided *Gault*:

> In few jurisdictions, for example, does the juvenile court judgeship enjoy high status in the eyes of the bar. * * * One crucial presupposition of the juvenile court philosophy—a mature and sophisticated judge, wise and well-versed in law and the science of human behavior—has proved in fact too often unattainable. A recent study of juvenile court judges * * * revealed that half had not received undergraduate degrees; a fifth had received no college education at all; a fifth were not members of the bar. Almost three-quarters devote less than a quarter of their time to juvenile and family matters, and judicial hearings often are little more than attenuated interviews of 10 or 15 minutes' duration.

How would you expect the many juvenile court judges, who at the time were neither lawyers nor even college graduates, to react to *Gault*'s ruling to grant delinquents the right to counsel and other procedural safeguards?

3) The Social Context of *Gault* During the 1960s, the Warren Court's civil rights decisions, criminal due process rulings, and "constitutional domestication" of the juvenile court responded to broader structural and demographic changes taking place in America, particularly those associated with race and youth crime. *See generally* Barry Feld, *Bad Kids: Race and the Transformation of the Juvenile Court* (1999); Barry C. Feld, "Race, Politics and Juvenile Justice: The Warren Court and the Conservative 'Backlash'," 87 *Minn. L. Rev.* 1447 (2003). In the decades prior to and after World War II, Black migration from the rural south to the urban north increased minority concentrations in urban ghettos, made race a national rather than a regional issue, and provided the political and constitutional impetus for the Civil Rights movement. *See* Nicholas Lemann, *The Promised Land: The Great Black Migration and How it Changed America* (1993). The 1960s also witnessed the "baby boom" increases in youth crime that continued until the late–1970s. During the 1960s, the rise in youth crime and urban racial disorders provoked cries for "law and order" and provided the initial political impetus to "get tough." Republicans seized crime control and welfare as wedge issues with which to distinguish themselves from Democrats in order to woo white southern voters, and crime policies for the first time became a central issue in partisan politics. *See* Katherine Beckett, *Making Crime Pay* (1997). As a result of "sound-bite" politics, symbols and rhetoric began to shape penal policies more than criminological studies or substantive research. Since the 1960s, politicians' fear of being labeled "soft-on-crime" has led to a constant ratcheting-up of punitiveness. As we saw in Chapter 6, these racial, demographic, and political changes provided the impetus for the "get tough" juvenile justice policies of the 1980s and 1990s that promised to "crack down" on youth crime.

The Supreme Court's due process decisions responded to the macro-structural and demographic changes, and attempted to guarantee civil rights, to protect minority citizens, and to limit the authority of the state. *In re Gault* began to transform the juvenile court into a very different institution than the Progressives contemplated. *Gault* demonstrated the linkage between procedure and substance in the juvenile court, and engrafted some formal procedures at trial onto the individualized treatment schema. Although the Court did not intend its decisions to alter juvenile courts' therapeutic mission, in the aftermath of *Gault*, judicial, legislative, and administrative changes have fostered a procedural and substantive convergence with criminal courts. *Gault* shifted the focus of delinquency hearings from "real needs" to proof of legal guilt, and formalized the connection between criminal conduct and coercive intervention. Providing a modicum of procedural justice also may have legitimated greater punitiveness in juvenile courts.

4) Academic Commentary on *Gault* A number of commentators analyzed *Gault* and discussed its constitutional implications, its procedural implementation, and its limited scope. Read narrowly, *Gault* only decided procedural issues surrounding the adjudicatory hearing at which a youth charged with delinquency faced the prospect of institutional confinement. The most useful analyses of *Gault* and its implications for juvenile justice administration are: Monrad G. Paulsen, "The Constitutional Domestication of the Juvenile Court," 1967 *Sup. Ct. Rev.* 233 (1967); Irene M. Rosenberg, "The Constitutional Rights of Children Charged with Crime: Proposal for a Return to the Not So Distant Past," 27 *U.C.L.A. L. Rev.* 656 (1980); Francis Barry McCarthy, "Pre–Adjudicatory Rights in Juvenile Court: An Historical and Constitutional Analysis," 42 *U. Pitt. L. Rev.* 457 (1981); Barry C. Feld, "Criminalizing Juvenile Justice: Rules of Procedure for the Juvenile Court," 69 *Minn. L. Rev.* 141 (1984).

5) Treatment versus Punishment, the Fifth Amendment, and the Rationale of *Gault* In **Allen v. Illinois**, 478 U.S. 364, 106 S.Ct. 2988, 92 L.Ed.2d 296 (1986), the Supreme Court revisited the issue of the procedural safeguards necessary in avowedly non-criminal proceedings. *Allen* raised the question "whether the proceedings under the Illinois Sexually Dangerous Persons Act (Act), are 'criminal' within the meaning of the Fifth Amendment's guarantee against compulsory self-incrimination." The state charged Allen with sexual offenses and then filed a petition to "civilly" commit and treat him as a sexually dangerous person. The trial court ordered Allen to submit to psychiatric examinations and admitted the testimony of the examining psychiatrists in his sexually dangerous person commitment proceeding. The Illinois court of appeals relied on *Estelle v. Smith*, reversed the trial court, and held that the compelled psychiatric interviews violated Allen's privilege against self-incrimination. *See supra*, Notes 2 and 3 pp. 548–555 (analyzing the related Fifth Amendment *Estelle* issues in the context of waiver proceedings). The Illinois Supreme Court reversed the appellate court and reinstated the trial court's finding that Allen was a sexually dangerous person. It held that the privilege against self-incrimination was not available in sexually dangerous person proceedings because they are "essentially civil in nature," the aim of the statute being to provide "treatment, not punishment." The court observed that the State's interest in treating, and protecting the public from, sexually dangerous persons would be "almost totally thwarted" by allowing those persons to refuse to answer questions posed in psychiatric interviews and that "due process does not require the application of the privilege." Justice REHNQUIST delivered the opinion of the United States Supreme Court:

> This Court has long held that the privilege against self-incrimination "not only permits a person to refuse to testify against himself at a criminal trial in which he is a defendant, but also 'privileges him not to answer official questions put to him in any other proceeding, civil or criminal, formal or informal, where the answers might incriminate him in future criminal proceedings.'" In this case the Illinois Supreme Court ruled that a person whom the State attempts to commit under the Act is protected from use of his compelled answers in any subsequent criminal case in which he is the defendant. What we have here, then, is not a claim that petitioner's statements to the psychiatrists might be used to incriminate him in some future criminal proceeding, but instead his claim that because the sexually dangerous person proceeding is itself "criminal," he was entitled to refuse to answer any questions at all.

> The question whether a particular proceeding is criminal for the purposes of the Self–Incrimination Clause is first of all a question of statutory construction. Here, Illinois has expressly provided that proceedings under the Act "shall be civil in nature," indicating that when it files a petition against a person under the Act it intends to proceed in a nonpunitive, noncriminal manner, "without regard to the procedural protections and restrictions available in criminal prosecutions." As petitioner correctly points out, however, the civil label is not always dispositive. Where a defendant has provided "the clearest proof" that "the statutory scheme [is] so punitive either in purpose or effect as to negate [the State's] intention" that the proceeding be civil, it must be considered criminal and the privilege against self-incrimination must be applied. We think that petitioner has failed to provide such proof in this case.

> The Illinois Supreme Court reviewed the Act and its own case law and concluded that these proceedings, while similar to criminal proceedings in that they are accompanied by strict procedural safeguards, are essentially civil in nature. * * * Under the Act, the State has a statutory obligation to provide "care and treatment for [persons adjudged sexually

dangerous] designed to effect recovery," in a facility set aside to provide psychiatric care. And "[i]f the patient is found to be no longer dangerous, the court shall order that he be discharged." While the committed person has the burden of showing that he is no longer dangerous, he may apply for release at any time.

In short, the State has disavowed any interest in punishment, provided for the treatment of those it commits, and established a system under which committed persons may be released after the briefest time in confinement. The Act thus does not appear to promote either of "the traditional aims of punishment—retribution and deterrence." * * *

[T]he State has indicated quite clearly its intent that these commitment proceedings be civil in nature; its decision nevertheless to provide some of the safeguards applicable in criminal trials cannot itself turn these proceedings into criminal prosecutions requiring the full panoply of rights applicable there.

Relying chiefly on *In re Gault*, petitioner also urges that the proceedings in question are "criminal" because a person adjudged sexually dangerous under the Act is committed for an indeterminate period to the Menard Psychiatric Center, a maximum security institution that is run by the Illinois Department of Corrections and that houses convicts needing psychiatric care as well as sexually dangerous persons. Whatever its label and whatever the State's alleged purpose, petitioner argues, such commitment is the sort of punishment—total deprivation of liberty in a criminal setting—that *Gault* teaches cannot be imposed absent application of the privilege against self-incrimination. We believe that *Gault* is readily distinguishable.

First, *Gault*'s sweeping statement that "our Constitution guarantees that no person shall be 'compelled' to be a witness against himself when he is threatened with deprivation of his liberty," is plainly not good law. Although the fact that incarceration may result is relevant to the question whether the privilege against self-incrimination applies, *Addington* demonstrates that involuntary commitment does not itself trigger the entire range of criminal procedural protections. Indeed, petitioner apparently concedes that traditional civil commitment does not require application of the privilege. * * *

The Court in *Gault* was obviously persuaded that the State intended to *punish* its juvenile offenders, observing that in many States juveniles may be placed in "adult penal institutions" for conduct that if committed by an adult would be a crime. Here, by contrast, the State serves its purpose of *treating* rather than punishing sexually dangerous persons by committing them to an institution expressly designed to provide psychiatric care and treatment. That the Menard Psychiatric Center houses not only sexually dangerous persons but also prisoners from other institutions who are in need of psychiatric treatment does not transform the State's intent to treat into an intent to punish. * * *

Petitioner has not demonstrated, and the record does not suggest, that "sexually dangerous persons" in Illinois are confined under conditions incompatible with the State's asserted interest in treatment. Had petitioner shown, for example, that the confinement of such persons imposes on them a regimen which is essentially identical to that imposed upon felons with no need for psychiatric care, this might well be a different case. But the record here tells us little or nothing about the regimen at the psychiatric center, and it certainly does not show that there are no relevant differences between confinement there and confinement in the other parts of the maximum-security prison complex. Indeed, counsel for the State assures us that under Illinois law sexually dangerous persons must not be treated like ordinary prisoners. * * * We therefore cannot say that the conditions of petitioner's confinement themselves amount to "punishment" and thus render "criminal" the proceedings which led to confinement. * * *

[W]e conclude that the Illinois proceedings here considered were not "criminal" within the meaning of the Fifth Amendment to the United States Constitution, and that due process does not independently require application of the privilege. * * *

Justice STEVENS, with whom Justice BRENNAN, Justice MARSHALL, and Justice BLACKMUN join, dissenting. * * * When the criminal law casts so long a shadow on a putatively civil proceeding, I think it clear that the procedure must be deemed a "criminal case" within the meaning of the Fifth Amendment.

As the Court reaffirms today, the fact that a State attaches a "civil" label to a proceeding is not dispositive. Such a label cannot change the character of a criminal proceeding. *In re Gault* * * *.

A goal of treatment is not sufficient, in and of itself, to render inapplicable the Fifth Amendment, or to prevent a characterization of proceedings as "criminal." * * * In my opinion, permitting a State to create a shadow criminal law without the fundamental protection of the Fifth Amendment conflicts with the respect for liberty and individual dignity that has long characterized, and that continues to characterize, our free society. * * *

B. BURDEN OF PROOF

IN THE MATTER OF WINSHIP

397 U.S. 358, 90 S.Ct. 1068, 25 L.Ed.2d 368 (1970).

MR. JUSTICE BRENNAN delivered the opinion of the Court. Constitutional questions decided by this Court concerning the juvenile process have centered on the adjudicatory stage at "which a determination is made as to whether a juvenile is a 'delinquent' as a result of alleged misconduct on his part, with the consequence that he may be committed to a state institution." *In re Gault* decided that, although the Fourteenth Amendment does not require that the hearing at this stage conform with all the requirements of a criminal trial or even of the usual administrative proceeding, the Due Process Clause does require application during the adjudicatory hearing of "the essentials of due process and fair treatment."

This case presents the single, narrow question whether proof beyond a reasonable doubt is among the "essentials of due process and fair treatment" required during the adjudicatory stage when a juvenile is charged with an act which would constitute a crime if committed by an adult.

Section 712 of the New York Family Court Act defines a juvenile delinquent as "a person over seven and less than sixteen years of age who does any act which, if done by an adult, would constitute a crime." During a 1967 adjudicatory hearing, conducted pursuant to § 742 of the Act, a judge in New York Family Court found that appellant, then a 12–year–old boy, had entered a locker and stolen $112 from a woman's pocketbook. The petition which charged appellant with delinquency alleged that his act, "if done by an adult, would constitute the crime or crimes of Larceny." The judge acknowledged that the proof might not establish guilt beyond a reasonable doubt, but rejected appellant's contention that such proof was required by the Fourteenth Amendment. The judge relied instead on § 744(b) of the New York Family Court Act which provides that "(a)ny determination at the conclusion of (an adjudicatory) hearing that a (juvenile) did an act or acts must be based on a preponderance of the evidence."[2] During a subsequent dispositional hearing, appellant was ordered placed in a training school for an initial period of 18 months, subject to annual extensions of his commitment until his 18th birthday— six years in appellant's case. The Appellate Division of the New York Supreme Court affirmed without opinion. The New York Court of Appeals then affirmed by a four-to-three vote, expressly sustaining the constitutionality of § 744(b). * * * We reverse.

The requirement that guilt of a criminal charge be established by proof beyond a reasonable doubt dates at least from our early years as a Nation. The "demand for a higher degree of persuasion in criminal cases was recurrently expressed from ancient times, (though) its crystallization into the formula 'beyond a reasonable doubt' seems to have occurred as late as 1798. It is now accepted in common law jurisdictions as the measure of persuasion by which the prosecution must convince the trier of all the essential elements of guilt." Although virtually unanimous adherence to the reasonable-doubt standard in common-law jurisdictions may not conclusively establish it as a requirement of due process, such adherence does "reflect a profound judgment about the way in which law should be enforced and justice administered."

Expressions in many opinions of this Court indicate that it has long been assumed that proof of a criminal charge beyond a reasonable doubt is constitutionally required. Mr. Justice Frankfurter stated that "(i)t the duty of the Government to establish * * * guilt beyond a reasonable

---

2. The ruling appears in the following portion of the hearing transcript:

Counsel: "Your Honor is making a finding by the preponderance of the evidence."

Court: "Well, it convinces me."

Counsel: "It's not beyond a reasonable doubt, Your Honor."

Court: "That is true. * * * Our statute says a preponderance and a preponderance it is."

doubt. This notion—basic in our law and rightly one of the boasts of a free society—is a requirement and a safeguard of due process of law in the historic, procedural content of 'due process.'"

The reasonable-doubt standard plays a vital role in the American scheme of criminal procedure. It is a prime instrument for reducing the risk of convictions resting on factual error. The standard provides concrete substance for the presumption of innocence—that bedrock "axiomatic and elementary" principle whose "enforcement lies at the foundation of the administration of our criminal law." As the dissenters in the New York Court of Appeals observed, and we agree, "a person accused of a crime * * * would be at a severe disadvantage, a disadvantage amounting to a lack of fundamental fairness, if he could be adjudged guilty and imprisoned for years on the strength of the same evidence as would suffice in a civil case."

The requirement of proof beyond a reasonable doubt has this vital role in our criminal procedure for cogent reasons. The accused during a criminal prosecution has at stake interest of immense importance, both because of the possibility that he may lose his liberty upon conviction and because of the certainty that he would be stigmatized by the conviction. Accordingly, a society that values the good name and freedom of every individual should not condemn a man for commission of a crime when there is reasonable doubt about his guilt. * * * To this end, the reasonable-doubt standard is indispensable, for it "impresses on the trier of fact the necessity of reaching a subjective state of certitude of the facts in issue."

Moreover, use of the reasonable-doubt standard is indispensable to command the respect and confidence of the community in applications of the criminal law. It is critical that the moral force of the criminal law not be diluted by a standard of proof that leaves people in doubt whether innocent men are being condemned. It is also important in our free society that every individual going about his ordinary affairs have confidence that his government cannot adjudge him guilty of a criminal offense without convincing a proper factfinder of his guilt with utmost certainty.

Lest there remain any doubt about the constitutional stature of the reasonable-doubt standard, we explicitly hold that the Due Process Clause protects the accused against conviction except upon proof beyond a reasonable doubt of every fact necessary to constitute the crime with which he is charged.

We turn to the question whether juveniles, like adults, are constitutionally entitled to proof beyond a reasonable doubt when they are charged with violation of a criminal law. The same considerations that demand extreme caution in factfinding to protect the innocent adult apply as well to the innocent child. We do not find convincing the contrary arguments of the New York Court of Appeals, *Gault* rendered untenable much of the reasoning relied upon by that court to sustain the constitutionality of § 744(b). * * * In effect the Court of Appeals distinguished the proceedings in question here from a criminal prosecution by use of what *Gault* called the " 'civil' label-of-convenience which has been attached to juvenile proceedings." But *Gault* expressly rejected that distinction as a reason for holding the Due Process Clause inapplicable to a juvenile proceeding. The Court of Appeals also attempted to justify the preponderance standard on the related ground that juvenile proceedings are designed "not to punish, but to save the child." Again, however, *Gault* expressly rejected this justification. We made clear in that decision that civil labels and good intentions do not themselves obviate the need for criminal due process safeguards in juvenile courts, for "(a) proceeding where the issue is whether the child will be found to be 'delinquent' and subjected to the loss of his liberty for years is comparable in seriousness to a felony prosecution."

Nor do we perceive any merit in the argument that to afford juveniles the protection of proof beyond a reasonable doubt would risk destruction of beneficial aspects of the juvenile process. Use of the reasonable-doubt standard during the adjudicatory hearing will not disturb New York's policies that a finding that a child has violated a criminal law does not constitute a criminal conviction, that such a finding does not deprive the child of his civil rights, and that juvenile proceedings are confidential. Nor will there be any effect on the informality, flexibility, or speed of the hearing at which the factfinding takes place. And the opportunity during the post-adjudicatory or dispositional hearing for a wide-ranging review of the child's social history and for his individualized treatment will remain unimpaired. Similarly, there will be no effect on the procedures distinctive to juvenile proceedings that are employed prior to the adjudicatory hearing.

The Court of Appeals observed that "a child's best interest is not necessarily, or even probably, promoted if he wins in the particular inquiry which may bring him to the juvenile court." It is true, of course, that the juvenile may be engaging in a general course of conduct inimical to his welfare that calls for judicial intervention. But that intervention cannot take the form of subjecting the child to the stigma of a finding that he violated a criminal law and to the possibility of institutional confinement on proof insufficient to convict him were he an adult.

We conclude, as we concluded regarding the essential due process safeguards applied in *Gault*, that the observance of the standard of proof beyond a reasonable doubt "will not compel the States to abandon or displace any of the substantive benefits of the juvenile process." * * *

In sum, the constitutional safeguard of proof beyond a reasonable doubt is as much required during the adjudicatory stage of a delinquency proceeding as are those constitutional safeguards applied in *Gault*—notice of charges, right to counsel, the rights of confrontation and examination, and the privilege against self-incrimination. We therefore hold, in agreement with Chief Judge Fuld in dissent in the Court of Appeals, "that, where a 12–year–old child is charged with an act of stealing which renders him liable to confinement for as long as six years, then, as a matter of due process * * * the case against him must be proved beyond a reasonable doubt."

Reversed.

MR. JUSTICE HARLAN, concurring. * * * [W]e have before us a case where the choice of the standard of proof has made a difference: the juvenile court judge below forthrightly acknowledged that he believed by a preponderance of the evidence, but was not convinced beyond a reasonable doubt, that appellant stole $112 from the complainant's pocketbook. Moreover, even though the labels used for alternative standards of proof are vague and not a very sure guide to decisionmaking, the choice of the standard for a particular variety of adjudication does, I think, reflect a very fundamental assessment of the comparative social costs of erroneous factual determinations.

To explain why I think this so, I begin by stating two propositions, neither of which I believe can be fairly disputed. First, in a judicial proceeding in which there is a dispute about the facts of some earlier event, the factfinder cannot acquire unassailably accurate knowledge of what happened. Instead, all the fact-finder can acquire is a belief of what probably happened. The intensity of this belief—the degree to which a factfinder is convinced that a given act actually occurred—can, of course, vary. In this regard, a standard of proof represents an attempt to instruct the fact-finder concerning the degree of confidence our society thinks he should have in the correctness of factual conclusions for a particular type of adjudication. Although the phrases "preponderance of the evidence" and "proof beyond a reasonable doubt" are quantitatively imprecise, they do communicate to the finder of fact different notions concerning the degree of confidence he is expected to have in the correctness of his factual conclusions.

A second proposition, which is really nothing more than a corollary of the first, is that the trier of fact will sometimes, despite his best efforts, be wrong in his factual conclusions. In a lawsuit between two parties, a factual error can make a difference in one of two ways. First, it can result in a judgment in favor of the plaintiff when the true facts warrant a judgment for the defendant. The analogue in a criminal case would be the conviction of an innocent man. On the other hand, an erroneous factual determination can result in a judgment for the defendant when the true facts justify a judgment in plaintiff's favor. The criminal analogue would be the acquittal of a guilty man.

The standard of proof influences the relative frequency of these two types of erroneous outcomes. If, for example, the standard of proof for a criminal trial were a preponderance of the evidence rather than proof beyond a reasonable doubt, there would be a smaller risk of factual errors that result in freeing guilty persons, but a far greater risk of factual errors that result in convicting the innocent. Because the standard of proof affects the comparative frequency of these two types of erroneous outcomes, the choice of the standard to be applied in a particular kind of litigation should, in a rational world, reflect an assessment of the comparative social disutility of each.

When one makes such an assessment, the reason for different standards of proof in civil as opposed to criminal litigation becomes apparent. In a civil suit between two private parties for money damages, for example, we view it as no more serious in general for there to be an erroneous verdict in the defendant's favor than for there to be an erroneous verdict in the plaintiff's favor. A preponderance of the evidence standard therefore seems peculiarly appropriate for, as explained most sensibly, it simply requires the trier of fact "to believe that the existence of a fact is more probable than its nonexistence before (he) may find in favor of the party who has the burden to persuade the (judge) of the fact's existence."

In a criminal case, on the other hand, we do not view the social disutility of convicting an innocent man as equivalent to the disutility of acquitting someone who is guilty. As Mr. Justice Brennan wrote for the Court in *Speiser v. Randall*,

"There is always in litigation a margin of error, representing error in factfinding, which both parties must take into account. Where one party has at stake an interest of transcending value—as a criminal defendant his liberty—this margin of error is reduced as to him by the process of placing on the other party the burden * * * of persuading the fact-finder at the conclusion of the trial of his guilt beyond a reasonable doubt."

In this context, I view the requirement of proof beyond a reasonable doubt in a criminal case as bottomed on a fundamental value determination of our society that it is far worse to convict an innocent man than to let a guilty man go free. It is only because of the nearly complete and long-standing acceptance of the reasonable-doubt standard by the States in criminal trials that the Court has not before today had to hold explicitly that due process, as an expression of fundamental procedural fairness, requires a more stringent standard for criminal trials than for ordinary civil litigation.

When one assesses the consequences of an erroneous factual determination in a juvenile delinquency proceeding in which a youth is accused of a crime, I think it must be concluded that, while the consequences are not identical to those in a criminal case, the differences will not support a distinction in the standard of proof. First, and of paramount importance, a factual error here, as in a criminal case, exposes the accused to a complete loss of his personal liberty through a state-imposed confinement away from his home, family, and friends. And, second, a delinquency determination, to some extent at least, stigmatizes a youth in that it is by definition bottomed on a finding that the accused committed a crime. Although there are no doubt costs to society (and possibly even to the youth himself) in letting a guilty youth go free, I think here, as in a criminal case, it is far worse to declare an innocent youth a delinquent. I therefore agree that a juvenile court judge should be no less convinced of the factual conclusion that the accused committed the criminal act with which he is charged than would be required in a criminal trial. * * *

MR. CHIEF JUSTICE BURGER, with whom MR. JUSTICE STEWART joins, dissenting. The Court's opinion today rests entirely on the assumption that all juvenile proceedings are "criminal prosecutions," hence subject to constitutional limitations. This derives from earlier holdings, which, like today's holding, were steps eroding the differences between juvenile courts and traditional criminal courts. The original concept of the juvenile court system was to provide a benevolent and less formal means than criminal courts could provide for dealing with the special and often sensitive problems of youthful offenders. Since I see no constitutional requirement of due process sufficient to overcome the legislative judgment of the States in this area, I dissent from further strait-jacketing of an already overly restricted system. What the juvenile court system needs is not more but less of the trappings of legal procedure and judicial formalism; the juvenile court system requires breathing room and flexibility in order to survive, if it can survive the repeated assaults from this Court.

Much of the judicial attitude manifested by the Court's opinion today and earlier holdings in this field is really a protest against inadequate juvenile court staffs and facilities; we "burn down the stable to get rid of the mice." The lack of support and the distressing growth of juvenile crime have combined to make for a literal breakdown in many if not most juvenile courts. Constitutional problems were not seen while those courts functioned in an atmosphere where juvenile judges were not crushed with an avalanche of cases. My hope is that today's decision will not spell the end of a generously conceived program of compassionate treatment intended to mitigate the rigors and trauma of exposing youthful offenders to a traditional criminal court; each step we take turns the clock back to the pre-juvenile-court era. I cannot regard it as a manifestation of progress to transform juvenile courts into criminal courts, which is what we are well on the way to accomplishing. We can only hope the legislative response will not reflect our own by having these courts abolished.

NOTE

It is instructive to compare the *Winship* Court's treatment of the standard of proof in delinquency cases with the standard of proof required for involuntary civil commitment of the mentally ill, which requires only "clear and convincing" evidence. *See Addington v. Texas*, 441 U.S. 418, 433, 99 S.Ct. 1804, 60 L.Ed.2d 323 (1979). Even though civil commitment entails involuntary confinement, in *Addington*, Chief Justice Burger, who dissented in *Winship*, distinguished criminal and delinquency prosecutions from involuntary civil commitments and, in so doing, equated criminal trials and delinquency proceedings:

> The Court [in *Winship*] saw no controlling difference in loss of liberty and stigma between a conviction for an adult and a delinquency adjudication

for a juvenile. *Winship* recognized that the basic issue—whether the individual in fact committed a criminal act—was the same in both proceedings. There being no meaningful distinctions between the two proceedings, we required the state to prove the juvenile's act and intent beyond a reasonable doubt. * * * Unlike the delinquency proceeding in *Winship*, a civil commitment proceeding can in no sense be equated to a criminal prosecution. 441 U.S. at 427–28.

Chief Justice Burger also noted that proof "beyond a reasonable doubt" is a critical component of criminal cases because it helps to preserve the " 'moral force of the criminal law,' * * * and we should hesitate to apply it too broadly or casually in noncriminal cases." *Id.* at 428.

C. JURY TRIAL AND PUBLIC TRIAL

McKEIVER v. PENNSYLVANIA

403 U.S. 528, 91 S.Ct. 1976, 29 L.Ed.2d 647 (1971).

MR. JUSTICE BLACKMUN announced the judgments of the Court and an opinion in which THE CHIEF JUSTICE, MR. JUSTICE STEWART, and MR. JUSTICE WHITE join. These cases present the narrow but precise issue whether the Due Process Clause of the Fourteenth Amendment assures the right to trial by jury in the adjudicative phase of a state juvenile court delinquency proceeding.

The issue arises understandably, for the Court in a series of cases already has emphasized due process factors protective of the juvenile. * * * From these six cases–*Haley*, *Gallegos*, *Kent*, *Gault*, *DeBacker*, and *Winship*—it is apparent that:

1. Some of the constitutional requirements attendant upon the state criminal trial have equal application to that part of the state juvenile proceeding that is adjudicative in nature. Among these are the rights to appropriate notice, to counsel, to confrontation and to cross-examination, and the privilege against self-incrimination. Included, also, is the standard of proof beyond a reasonable doubt.

2. The Court, however, has not yet said that all rights constitutionally assured to an adult accused of crime also are to be enforced or made available to the juvenile in his delinquency proceeding. * * *

3. The Court, although recognizing the high hopes and aspirations of Judge Julian Mack, the leaders of the Jane Addams School and the other supporters of the juvenile court concept, has also noted the disappointments of the system's performance and experience and the resulting widespread disaffection. There have been, at one and the same time, both an appreciation for the juvenile court judge who is devoted, sympathetic, and conscientious, and a disturbed concern about the judge who is untrained and less than fully imbued with an understanding approach to the complex problems of childhood and adolescence. There has been praise for the system and its purposes, and there has been alarm over its defects.

4. The Court has insisted that these successive decisions do not spell the doom of the juvenile court system or even deprive it of its "informality, flexibility, or speed." On the other hand, a concern precisely to the opposite effect was expressed by two dissenters in *Winship*.

With this substantial background already developed, we turn to the facts of the present cases:

[Defendant, Joseph McKeiver, then age 16, was charged with robbery and at an] adjudication hearing [where] he was represented by counsel[2] * * * [h]is request for a jury trial was denied * * * [and] McKeiver was adjudged a delinquent. * * *

The Supreme Court of Pennsylvania granted leave to appeal. * * * The single question considered, as phrased by the court, was "whether there is a constitutional right to a jury trial in juvenile court." The answer, one justice dissenting, was in the negative. * * *

[In *In re Barbara Burrus*, highway patrolmen charged approximately 45 black children, ranging in age from 11 to 15 years, with misdemeanor offenses of "impeding traffic" arising out of a series of civil rights demonstrations in the county in late 1968 by black adults and children protesting school assignments and a school consolidation plan. Highway patrolmen testified that the juveniles sang, shouted, clapped, and refused to leave the paved portion of the highway, and thereby interfered with traffic. The juvenile court consolidated several groups of cases for hearing and appointed the same lawyer for all the juveniles. Over counsel's objection, the court excluded the general public and denied a request for a jury trial in each case. The juvenile court found the youths delinquent, committed them for placement in a suitable institution, but suspended these commitments and placed each juvenile on probation for either one or two years. The Supreme Court of North Carolina deleted that portion of the order in each case relating to commitment, and affirmed the delinquency adjudications.]

It is instructive to review * * * JUSTICE ROBERTS' opinion for the Pennsylvania court. He observes, that "(f)or over sixty-five years the Supreme Court gave no consideration at all to the constitutional problems involved in the juvenile court area"; that *Gault* "is somewhat of a paradox, being both broad and narrow at the same time"; that it "is broad in that it evidences a fundamental and far-reaching disillusionment with the anticipated benefits of the juvenile court system"; that it is narrow because the court enumerated four due process rights which it held applicable in juvenile proceedings, but declined to rule on two other claimed rights, that as a consequence the Pennsylvania court was "confronted with a sweeping rationale and a carefully tailored holding," that the procedural safeguards "*Gault* specifically made applicable to juvenile

---

2. At McKeiver's hearing his counsel advised the court that he had never seen McKeiver before and "was just in the middle of interviewing" him. The court allowed him five minutes for the interview. Counsel's office, Community Legal Services, however, had been appointed to represent McKeiver five months earlier.

courts have already caused a significant 'constitutional domestication' of juvenile court proceedings," that those safeguards and other rights, including the reasonable-doubt standard established by *Winship*, "insure that the juvenile court will operate in an atmosphere which is orderly enough to impress the juvenile with the gravity of the situation and the impartiality of the tribunal and at the same time informal enough to permit the benefits of the juvenile system to operate," that the "proper inquiry, then, is whether the right to a trial by jury is 'fundamental' within the meaning of *Duncan*, in the context of a juvenile court which operates with all of the above constitutional safeguards," and that his court's inquiry turned "upon whether there are elements in the juvenile process which render the right to a trial by jury less essential to the protection of an accused's rights in the juvenile system than in the normal criminal process." Justice Roberts then concluded that such factors do inhere in the Pennsylvania juvenile system: (1) Although realizing that "faith in the quality of the juvenile bench is not an entirely satisfactory substitute for due process," the judges in the juvenile courts "do take a different view of their role than that taken by their counterparts in the criminal courts." (2) While one regrets its inadequacies, "the juvenile system has available and utilizes much more fully various diagnostic and rehabilitative services" that are "far superior to those available in the regular criminal process." (3) Although conceding that the post-adjudication process "has in many respects fallen far short of its goals, and its reality is far harsher than its theory," the end result of a declaration of delinquency "is significantly different from and less onerous than a finding of criminal guilt" and "we are not yet convinced that the current practices do not contain the seeds from which a truly appropriate system can be brought forth." (4) Finally, "of all the possible due process rights which could be applied in the juvenile courts, the right to trial by jury is the one which would most likely be disruptive of the unique nature of the juvenile process." It is the jury trial that "would probably require substantial alteration of the traditional practices." The other procedural rights held applicable to the juvenile process "will give the juveniles sufficient protection" and the addition of the trial by jury "might well destroy the traditional character of juvenile proceedings." The court concluded, that it was confident "that a properly structured and fairly administered juvenile court system can serve our present societal needs without infringing on individual freedoms."

The right to an impartial jury "(i)n all criminal prosecutions" under federal law is guaranteed by the Sixth Amendment. Through the Fourteenth Amendment that requirement has now been imposed upon the States "in all criminal cases which—were they to be tried in a federal court—would come within the Sixth Amendment's guarantee." This is because the Court has said it believes "that trial by jury in criminal cases is fundamental to the American scheme of justice." *Duncan v. Louisiana*, (1968).

This, of course, does not automatically provide the answer to the present jury trial issue, if for no other reason than that the juvenile court proceeding has not yet been held to be a "criminal prosecution," within the meaning and reach of the Sixth Amendment, and also has not yet been regarded as devoid of criminal aspects merely because it usually has been given the civil label. * * *

All the litigants here agree that the applicable due process standard in juvenile proceedings, as developed by *Gault* and *Winship*, is fundamental fairness. As that standard was applied in those two cases, we have an emphasis on factfinding procedures. The requirements of notice, counsel, confrontation, cross-examination, and standard of proof naturally flowed from this emphasis. But one cannot say that in our legal system the jury is a necessary component of accurate factfinding. There is much to be said for it, to be sure, but we have been content to pursue other ways for determining facts. * * * In *Duncan* the Court stated, "We would not assert, however, that every criminal trial—or any particular trial—held before a judge alone is unfair or that a defendant may never be as fairly treated by a judge as he would be by a jury." * * *

We must recognize, as the Court has recognized before, that the fond and idealistic hopes of the juvenile court proponents and early reformers of three generations ago have not been realized. * * * Too often the juvenile court judge falls far short of that stalwart, protective, and communicating figure the system envisaged. The community's unwillingness to provide people and facilities and to be concerned, the insufficiency of time devoted, the scarcity of professional help, the inadequacy of dispositional alternatives, and our general lack of knowledge all contribute to dissatisfaction with the experiment.[5] * * *

Despite all these disappointments, all these failures, and all these shortcomings, we conclude that trial by jury in the juvenile court's adjudicative stage is not a constitutional requirement. We so conclude for a number of reasons:

1.   The Court has refrained, in the cases heretofore decided, from taking the easy way with a flat holding that all rights constitutionally

---

5. "What emerges, then, is this: In theory the juvenile court was to be helpful and rehabilitative rather than punitive. In fact the distinction often disappears, not only because of the absence of facilities and personnel but also because of the limits of knowledge and technique. In theory the court's action was to affix no stigmatizing label. In fact a delinquent is generally viewed by employers, schools, the armed services—by society generally—as a criminal. In theory the court was to treat children guilty of criminal acts in noncriminal ways. In fact it labels truants and runaways as junior criminals.

"In theory the court's operations could justifiably be informal, its findings and decisions made without observing ordinary procedural safeguards, because it would act only in the best interest of the child. In fact it frequently does nothing more nor less than deprive a child of liberty without due process of law—knowing not what else to do and needing, whether admittedly or not, to act in the community's interest even more imperatively than the child's. In theory it was to exercise its protective powers to bring an errant child back into the fold. In fact there is increasing reason to believe that its intervention reinforces the juvenile's unlawful impulses. In theory it was to concentrate on each case the best of current social science learning. In fact it has often become a vested interest in its turn, loathe to cooperate with innovative programs or avail itself of forward-looking methods." *Task Force Report* 9.

assured for the adult accused are to be imposed upon the state juvenile proceeding. * * *

2. There is a possibility, at least, that the jury trial, if required as a matter of constitutional precept, will remake the juvenile proceeding into a fully adversary process and will put an effective end to what has been the idealistic prospect of an intimate, informal protective proceeding.

3. The Task Force Report, although concededly pre-*Gault*, is notable for its not making any recommendation that the jury trial be imposed upon the juvenile court system. This is so despite its vivid description of the system's deficiencies and disappointments. Had the Commission deemed this vital to the integrity of the juvenile process, or to the handling of juveniles, surely a recommendation or suggestion to this effect would have appeared. The intimations, instead, are quite the other way. Further, it expressly recommends against abandonment of the system and against the return of the juvenile to the criminal courts.

4. The Court specifically has recognized by dictum that a jury is not a necessary part even of every criminal process that is fair and equitable.

5. The imposition of the jury trial on the juvenile court system would not strengthen greatly, if at all, the fact-finding function, and would, contrarily, provide an attrition of the juvenile court's assumed ability to function in a unique manner. It would not remedy the defects of the system. Meager as has been the hoped-for advance in the juvenile field, the alternative would be regressive, would lose what has been gained, and would tend once again to place the juvenile squarely in the routine of the criminal process.

6. The juvenile concept held high promise. We are reluctant to say that, despite disappointments of grave dimensions, it still does not hold promise, and we are particularly reluctant to say, as do the Pennsylvania appellants here, that the system cannot accomplish its rehabilitative goals. So much depends on the availability of resources, on the interest and commitment of the public, on willingness to learn, and on understanding as to cause and effect and cure. In this field, as in so many others, one perhaps learns best by doing. We are reluctant to disallow the States to experiment further and to seek in new and different ways the elusive answers to the problems of the young, and we feel that we would be impeding that experimentation by imposing the jury trial. The States, indeed, must go forward. If, in its wisdom, any State feels the jury trial is desirable in all cases, or in certain kinds, there appears to be no impediment to its installing a system embracing that feature. That, however, is the State's privilege and not its obligation.

7. Of course there have been abuses. * * * We refrain from saying at this point that those abuses are of constitutional dimension. They relate to the lack of resources and of dedication rather than to inherent unfairness.

8. There is, of course, nothing to prevent a juvenile court judge, in a particular case where he feels the need, or when the need is demonstrated, from using an advisory jury.

9.   "The fact that a practice is followed by a large number of states is not conclusive in a decision as to whether that practice accords with due process, but it is plainly worth considering in determining whether the practice 'offends some principle of justice so rooted in the traditions and conscience of our people as to be ranked as fundamental.'" It therefore is of more than passing interest that at least 29 States and the District of Columbia by statute deny the juvenile a right to a jury trial in cases such as these. The same result is achieved in other States by judicial decision. In 10 States statutes provide for a jury trial under certain circumstances.

10.   Since *Gault* and since *Duncan* the great majority of States, in addition to Pennsylvania and North Carolina, that have faced the issue have concluded that the considerations that led to the result in those two cases do not compel trial by jury in the juvenile court. * * *

11.   Stopping short of proposing the jury trial for juvenile proceedings are the Uniform Juvenile Court Act * * *; the Standard Juvenile Court Act * * * proposed by the National Council on Crime and Delinquency and the Legislative Guide for Drafting Family and Juvenile Court. * * *

12.   If the jury trial were to be injected into the juvenile court system as a matter of right, it would bring with it into that system the traditional delay, the formality, and the clamor of the adversary system and, possibly, the public trial. * * *

13.   Finally, the arguments advanced by the juveniles here are, of course, the identical arguments that underlie the demand for the jury trial for criminal proceedings. The arguments necessarily equate the juvenile proceeding—or at least the adjudicative phase of it—with the criminal trial. Whether they should be so equated is our issue. Concern about the inapplicability of exclusionary and other rules of evidence, about the juvenile court judge's possible awareness of the juvenile's prior record and of the contents of the social file; about repeated appearances of the same familiar witnesses in the persons of juvenile and probation officers and social workers—all to the effect that this will create the likelihood of prejudgment—chooses to ignore it seems to us, every aspect of fairness, of concern, of sympathy, and of paternal attention that the juvenile court system contemplates.

If the formalities of the criminal adjudicative process are to be superimposed upon the juvenile court system, there is little need for its separate existence. Perhaps that ultimate disillusionment will come one day, but for the moment we are disinclined to give impetus to it.

Affirmed.

MR. JUSTICE WHITE, concurring.

Although the function of the jury is to find facts, that body is not necessarily or even probably better at the job than the conscientious judge. Nevertheless, the consequences of criminal guilt are so severe that the Constitution mandates a jury to prevent abuses of official power by insuring, where demanded, community participation in imposing serious deprivations of liberty and to provide a hedge against corrupt, biased, or political justice. We have not, however, considered the juvenile case a criminal proceeding within the meaning of the Sixth Amendment and hence automatically subject to all of the restrictions normally applicable in criminal cases. * * *

The criminal law proceeds on the theory that defendants have a will and are responsible for their actions. A finding of guilt establishes that they have chosen to engage in conduct so reprehensible and injurious to others that they must be punished to deter them and others from crime. Guilty defendants are considered blameworthy; they are branded and treated as such, however much the State also pursues rehabilitative ends in the criminal justice system.

For the most part, the juvenile justice system rests on more deterministic assumptions. Reprehensible acts by juveniles are not deemed the consequence of mature and malevolent choice but of environmental pressures (or lack of them) or of other forces beyond their control. Hence the state legislative judgment not to stigmatize the juvenile delinquent by branding him a criminal; his conduct is not deemed so blameworthy that punishment is required to deter him or others. Coercive measures, where employed, are considered neither retribution nor punishment. Supervision or confinement is aimed at rehabilitation, not at convincing the juvenile of his error simply by imposing pains and penalties. Nor is the purpose to make the juvenile delinquent an object lesson for others, whatever his own merits or demerits may be. A typical disposition in the juvenile court where delinquency is established may authorize confinement until age 21, but it will last no longer and within that period will last only so long as his behavior demonstrates that he remains an unacceptable risk if returned to his family. Nor is the authorization for custody until 21 any measure of the seriousness of the particular act that the juvenile has performed. * * *

To the extent that the jury is a buffer to the corrupt or overzealous prosecutor in the criminal law system, the distinctive intake policies and procedures of the juvenile court system to a great extent obviate this important function of the jury. As for the necessity to guard against judicial bias, a system eschewing blameworthiness and punishment for evil choice is itself an operative force against prejudice and short-tempered justice. Nor where juveniles are involved is there the same opportunity for corruption to the juvenile's detriment or the same temptation to use the courts for political ends.

Not only are those risks that mandate juries in criminal cases of lesser magnitude in juvenile court adjudications, but the consequences of adjudication are less severe than those flowing from verdicts of criminal guilt. This is plainly so in theory, and in practice there remains a substantial gulf between criminal guilt and delinquency, whatever the failings of the juvenile court in practice may be. * * *

For me there remain differences of substance between criminal and juvenile courts. They are quite enough for me to hold that a jury is not required in the latter. Of course, there are strong arguments that juries are desirable when dealing with the young, and States are free to use juries if they choose. They are also free if they extend criminal court safeguards to juvenile court adjudications, frankly to embrace condemnation, punishment, and deterrence as permissible and desirable attributes of the juvenile justice system. But the Due Process Clause neither compels nor invites them to do so.

MR. JUSTICE BRENNAN, concurring in the judgment in No. 322 [*McKeiver v. Pennsylvania*] and dissenting in No. 128 [*Burrus v. North Carolina*]:

I agree with the plurality opinion's conclusion that the proceedings below in these cases were not "criminal prosecutions" within the meaning of the Sixth Amendment. For me, therefore, the question in these cases is whether jury trial is among the "essentials of due process and fair treatment." * * * The Due Process Clause commands not a particular procedure, but only a result: in my Brother BLACKMUN's words, "fundamental fairness * * * (in) factfinding." In the context of these and similar juvenile delinquency proceedings, what this means is that the States are not bound to provide jury trials on demand so long as some other aspect of the process adequately protects the interests that Sixth Amendment jury trials are intended to serve.

In my view, therefore, the due process question cannot be decided upon the basis of general characteristics of juvenile proceedings, but only in terms of the adequacy of a particular state procedure to "protect the (juvenile) from oppression by the Government,", and to protect him against "the compliant, biased, or eccentric judge."

Examined in this light, I find no defect in the Pennsylvania cases before us. The availability of trial by jury allows an accused to protect himself against possible oppression by what is in essence an appeal to the community conscience, as embodied in the jury that hears his case. To some extent, however, a similar protection may be obtained when an accused may in essence appeal to the community at large, by focusing public attention upon the facts of his trial, exposing improper judicial behavior to public view, and obtaining, if necessary, executive redress through the medium of public indignation. Of course, the Constitution, in the context of adult criminal trials, has rejected the notion that public trial is an adequate substitution for trial by jury in serious cases. But in the context of juvenile delinquency proceedings, I cannot say that it is beyond the competence of a State to conclude that juveniles who fear that delinquency proceedings will mask judicial oppression may obtain adequate protection by focusing community attention upon the trial of their cases. For, however much the juvenile system may have failed in practice, its very existence as an ostensibly beneficent and noncriminal process for the care and guidance of young persons demonstrates the existence of the community's sympathy and concern for the young. Juveniles able to bring the community's attention to bear upon their trials may therefore draw upon a reservoir of public concern unavailable to the adult criminal defendant. In the Pennsylvania cases before us, there appears to be no statutory ban upon admission of the public to juvenile trials. Appellants themselves, without contradiction, assert that "the press is generally admitted" to juvenile delinquency proceedings in Philadelphia. Most important, the record in these cases is bare of any indication that any person whom appellants sought to have admitted to the courtroom was excluded. In these circumstances, I agree that the judgment in [*McKeiver*] must be affirmed.

The North Carolina cases, however, present a different situation. North Carolina law either permits or requires exclusion of the general public from juvenile trials. In the cases before us, the trial judge "ordered the general public excluded from the hearing room and stated that only officers of the court, the juveniles, their parents or guardians, their attorney and witnesses would be present for the hearing," notwithstanding petitioners' repeated demand for a public hearing. The cases themselves, which arise out of a series of demonstrations by black adults and juveniles who believed that the * * * school system unlawfully discriminated against black schoolchildren, present a paradigm of the circumstances in which there may be a substantial "temptation to use the courts for political ends." And finally, neither the opinions supporting the judgment nor the respondent has pointed to any feature of North Carolina's juvenile proceedings that could substitute for public or jury trial in protecting the petitioners against misuse of the judicial process. Accordingly, I would reverse the judgment [in *Burrus*.]

Mr. Justice Douglas, with whom Mr. Justice Black and Mr. Justice Marshall concur, dissenting.

These cases from Pennsylvania and North Carolina present the issue of the right to a jury trial for offenders charged in juvenile court and facing a possible incarceration until they reach their majority. I believe the guarantees of the Bill of Rights, made applicable to the States by the Fourteenth Amendment, require a jury trial. * * *

Conviction of each of these crimes would subject a person, whether juvenile or adult, to imprisonment in a state institution. In the case of these students the possible term was six to 10 years; it would be computed for the period until an individual reached the age of 21. Each asked for a jury trial which was denied. The trial judge stated that the hearings were juvenile hearings, not criminal trials. But the issue in each case was whether they had violated a state criminal law. The trial judge found in each case that the juvenile had committed "an act for which an adult may be punished by law" and held in each case that the acts of the juvenile violated one of the criminal statutes cited above. The trial judge thereupon ordered each juvenile to be committed to the state institution for the care of delinquents and then placed each on probation for terms from 12 to 24 months.

We held in *In re Gault*, that "neither the Fourteenth Amendment nor the Bill of Rights is for adults alone." As we noted in that case, the Juvenile Court movement was designed to avoid procedures to ascertain whether the child was "guilty" or "innocent" but to bring to bear on these problems a "clinical" approach. It is, of course, not our task to determine as a matter of policy whether a "clinical" or "punitive" approach to these problems should be taken by the States. But where a State uses its juvenile court proceedings to prosecute a juvenile for a criminal act and to order "confinement" until the child reaches 21 years of age or where the child at the threshold of the proceedings faces that prospect, then he is entitled to the same procedural protection as an adult. * * *

Just as courts have sometimes confused delinquency with crime, so have law enforcement officials treated juveniles not as delinquents but as criminals. * * * Even when juveniles are not incarcerated with adults the situation may be no better. One Pennsylvania correctional institution for juveniles is a brick building with barred windows, locked steel doors, a cyclone fence topped with barbed wire, and guard towers. A former juvenile judge described it as "a maximum security prison for adjudged delinquents."

In the present cases imprisonment or confinement up to 10 years was possible for one child and each faced at least a possible five-year incarceration. No adult could be denied a jury trial in those circumstances. The Fourteenth Amendment, which makes trial by jury provided in the Sixth Amendment applicable to the States, speaks of denial of rights to "any person," not denial of rights to "any adult person"; and we have held indeed that where a juvenile is charged with an act that would constitute a crime if committed by an adult, he is entitled to be tried under a standard of proof beyond a reasonable doubt. * * *

Practical aspects of these problems are urged against allowing a jury trial in these cases.[6][*] They have been answered by Judge De Ciantis of

---

6. [*] The Public Defender Service for the District of Columbia and the Neighborhood Legal Services Program of Washington, D.C., have filed a brief *amicus* in which the results of a survey of jury trials in delinquency cases in the 10 States requiring jury trials plus the District of Columbia are set forth. The cities selected were mostly large metropolitan areas. Thirty juvenile courts processing about 75,000 juvenile cases a year were canvassed:

"(W)e discovered that during the past five and a half years, in 22 out of 26 courts surveyed, cumulative requests for jury trials totaled 15 or less. In the remaining five courts in our sample, statistics were unavailable. During the same period, in 26 out of 29 courts the cumulative number of jury trials actually held numbered 15 or less, with statistics unavailable for two courts in our sample. For example, in Tulsa, Oklahoma, counsel is present in 100% of delinquency cases, but only one jury trial has been requested and held during the past five and one-half years. In the Juvenile Court of Fort Worth, Texas, counsel is also present in 100% of the cases, and only two jury trials have been requested since 1967. The Juvenile Court in Detroit, Michigan, reports that counsel is appointed in 70—80% of its delinquency cases, but thus far in 1970, it has had only four requests for a jury. Between 1965 and 1969 requests for juries were reported as 'very few.'

"In only four juvenile courts in our sample has there clearly been a total during the past five and one-half years of more than 15 jury trial requests and/or more than 15 such trials held."

The four courts showing more than 15 requests for jury trials were Denver, Houston, Milwaukee, and Washington, D.C.

the Family Court of Providence, Rhode Island, in * * * an opinion, a part of which I have attached as an appendix to this dissent. He there concludes that "the real traumatic" experience of incarceration without due process is "the feeling of being deprived of basic rights." * * *

Judge De Ciantis goes on to say that "(t)rial by jury will provide the child with a safeguard against being prejudged" by a judge who may well be prejudiced by reports already submitted to him by the police or caseworkers in the case. * * *

These cases should be remanded for trial by jury on the criminal charges filed against these youngsters.

Appendix to Opinion of Douglas, J., dissenting

DE CIANTIS, J.

TRAUMA

* * * The fact is that the procedures which are now followed in juvenile cases are far more traumatic than the potential experience of a jury trial. Who can say that a boy who is arrested and handcuffed, placed in a lineup, transported in vehicles designed to convey dangerous criminals, placed in the same kind of a cell as an adult, deprived of his freedom by lodging him in an institution where he is subject to be transferred to the state's prison and in the "hole" has not undergone a traumatic experience?

The experience of a trial with or without a jury is meant to be impressive and meaningful. The fact that a juvenile realizes that his case will be decided by twelve objective citizens would allow the court to retain its meaningfulness without causing any more trauma than a trial before a judge who perhaps has heard other cases involving the same juvenile in the past and may be influenced by those prior contacts. To agree that a jury trial would expose a juvenile to a traumatic experience is to lose sight of the real traumatic experience of incarceration without due process. The real traumatic experience is the feeling of being deprived of basic rights. * * *

BACKLOG

An argument has been made that to allow jury trials would cause a great backlog of cases and, ultimately, would impair the functioning of the juvenile court. The fact however is that there is no meaningful evidence that granting the right to jury trials will impair the function of the court. Some states permit jury trials in *all* juvenile court cases; few juries have been demanded, and there is no suggestion from these courts that jury trials have impeded the system of juvenile justice. * * *

In fact the very argument of expediency, suggesting "supermarket" or "assembly line" justice is one of the most forceful arguments in favor of granting jury trials. By granting the juvenile the right to a jury trial, we would, in fact, be protecting the accused from the judge who is under pressure to move the cases, the judge with too many cases and not enough time. It will provide a safeguard against the judge who may be prejudiced against a minority group or who may be prejudiced against the juvenile brought before him because of some past occurrence which was heard by the same judge.

There have been criticisms that juvenile court judges, because of their hearing caseload, do not carefully weigh the evidence in the adjudicatory phase of the proceedings. * * * Granting the juvenile the right to demand that the facts be determined by a jury will strengthen the faith of all concerned parties in the juvenile system.

It is important to note, at this time, a definite side benefit of granting jury trials, *i.e.*, an aid to rehabilitation. The child who feels that he has been dealt with fairly and not merely expediently or as speedily as possible will be a better prospect for rehabilitation. Many of the children who come before the court come from broken homes, from the ghettos; they often suffer from low self-esteem; and their behavior is frequently a symptom of their own feelings of inadequacy. Traumatic experiences of denial of basic rights only accentuate the past deprivation and contribute to the problem. Thus, a general societal attitude of acceptance of the juvenile as a person entitled to the same protection as an adult may be the true beginning of the rehabilitative process.

PUBLIC TRIAL

Public trial in the judgment of this Court does not affect the juvenile court philosophy. (In) *In re Oliver*, MR. JUSTICE BLACK reviews the history of the public trial. * * * Among the benefits of a public trial are the following:

1. "Public trials come to the attention of key witnesses unknown to the parties. These witnesses may then voluntarily come forward and give important testimony."

2. "The spectators learn about their government and acquire confidence in their judicial remedies."

3. "The knowledge that every *criminal* trial is subject to contemporaneous review in the (forum) of public opinion is an effective restraint on possible abuse of judicial power."

JUSTICE BLACK has nothing to say on the question of whether a public trial acts as a deterrent to crime, but it is clear that he believes *publicity to improve the quality of criminal justice, both theoretically and practically.* * * *

In fact, the juvenile proceedings as presently conducted are far from secret. Witnesses for the prosecution and for the defense, social workers, court reporters, students, police trainees, probation counselors, and sheriffs are present in the courtroom. Police, the Armed Forces, the Federal Bureau of Investigation obtain information and have access to the police files. There seems no more reason to believe that a jury trial would destroy confidentiality than would witnesses summoned to testify. * * *

JUDGE'S EXPERTISE

The Court is also aware of the argument that the juvenile court was created to develop judges who were experts in sifting out the real problems behind a juvenile's breaking the law; therefore, to place the child's fate in the hands of a jury would defeat that purpose. This will, however, continue to leave the final decision of disposition solely with the judge. The role of the jury will be only to ascertain whether the facts, which give the court jurisdiction, have been established beyond a reasonable doubt. The jury will not be concerned with social and psychological factors. These factors, along with prior record, family and educational background, will be considered by the judge during the dispositional phase. * * *

Trial by jury will provide the child with a safeguard against being prejudged. The jury clearly will have no business in learning of the social report or any of the other extraneous matter unless properly introduced under the rules of evidence. Due process demands that the trier of facts should not be acquainted with any of the facts of the case or have knowledge of any of the circumstances, whether through officials in his own department or records in his possession. If the accused believes that the judge has read an account of the facts submitted by the police or any other report prior to the adjudicatory hearing and that this may prove prejudicial, he can demand a jury and insure against such knowledge on the part of the trier of the facts.

WAIVER OF JURY TRIAL

Counsel also questions whether a child can waive his right to a jury trial or, in fact, whether a parent or counsel may waive. * * *

Counsel is placed with the responsibility of explaining to the juvenile the significance of guilty and *nolo contendere* pleas, of instructing the juvenile on the prerogative to take the witness stand, and is expected to advise his client in the same manner as he would an adult about to stand trial. And now counsel suggests to the Court that counsel is not capable of explaining and waiving the right to a jury trial. The Court fails to see the distinction between this waiver and the absolute waiver, to wit, a guilty plea. * * *

JURY OF PEERS

* * * The word "peers" means nothing more than citizens. The phrase "judgment of his peers" means at common law, a trial by a jury of twelve men. "Judgment of his peers" is a term expressly borrowed from the Magna Charta, and it means a trial by jury. The Declaration of Independence also speaks of the equality of all men. Are we now to say that a juvenile is a second-class citizen, not equal to an adult? The Constitution has never been construed to say women must be tried by

their peers, to wit, by all-female juries, or Negroes by all-Negro juries. * * *

NOTES

1) Constitutional Conflict Between *McKeiver* and *Duncan v. Louisiana* In *McKeiver*, the Court adverted to the conflict between its holding in *Duncan v. Louisiana* that granted adult defendants a Sixth Amendment constitutional right to a jury trial in state criminal prosecutions and its denial of the same right to juveniles. The Court in *Duncan v. Louisiana*, 391 U.S. 145, 88 S.Ct. 1444, 20 L.Ed.2d 491 (1968), held that fundamental fairness in *adult* criminal proceedings requires both factual accuracy and protection against governmental oppression:

> Those who wrote our constitutions knew from history and experience that it was necessary to protect against unfounded criminal charges brought to eliminate enemies and against judges too responsive to the voice of higher authority. * * * Providing an accused with the right to be tried by a jury of his peers gave him an inestimable safeguard against the corrupt or overzealous prosecutor and against the compliant, biased, or eccentric judge. If the defendant preferred the common-sense judgment of a jury to the more tutored but perhaps less sympathetic reaction of the single judge, he was to have it. Beyond this, the jury trial provisions in the Federal and State Constitutions reflect a fundamental decision about the exercise of official power—a reluctance to entrust plenary powers over the life and liberty of the citizen to one judge or to a group of judges. Fear of unchecked power, so typical of our State and Federal Governments in other respects, found expression in the criminal law in this insistence upon community participation in the determination of guilt or innocence. *Id.* at 156.

As Justice White noted in Footnote 14 in *Duncan*:

> State criminal processes are not imaginary and theoretical schemes but actual systems bearing virtually every characteristic of the common-law system. * * * The question thus is whether given this kind of system a particular procedure is fundamental—whether, that is, a procedure is necessary to an Anglo–American regime of ordered liberty. * * * [T]he limitation in question is not necessarily fundamental to fairness in every criminal system that might be imagined but is fundamental in the context of the criminal processes maintained by the American States.

> When the inquiry is approached in this way the question whether the States can impose criminal punishment without granting a jury trial appears quite different from the way it appeared in the older cases opinion that States might abolish jury trial. A criminal process which was fair and equitable but used no juries is easy to imagine. It would make use of alternative guarantees and protections which would serve the purposes that the jury serves in the English and American systems. Yet no American State has undertaken to construct such a system.

In *McKeiver*, by contrast, the Court envisioned "alternative guarantees and protections" and noted that concerns about procedural safeguards, such as the jury trial, ignore "every aspect of fairness, of concern, of sympathy, and of paternal attention that the juvenile court system contemplates." 403 U.S. 528, 550, 91 S.Ct. 1976, 29 L.Ed.2d 647 (1971).

Many of the important procedural, evidentiary, and substantive differences between juvenile and criminal prosecutions hinge on the Court's decision in *McKeiver*. What reasons does Justice Blackmun provide for these differences? Adult versus child? Punishment versus treatment? Legal rules and formality versus flexibility and informality? Does the *McKeiver* plurality correctly analyze the requirements of "due process" and "fundamental fairness"? Is *McKeiver*'s mode of analysis consistent with that employed by the Court in *Gault*? What function(s) do constitutional procedures serve? Why did the Court in *Duncan v. Louisiana* provide jury trials for adults?

In **Baldwin v. New York**, 399 U.S. 66, 73–74, 90 S.Ct. 1886, 26 L.Ed.2d 437 (1970), the Court held that "no offense can be deemed 'petty' for purposes of the right to trial by jury where imprisonment of more than six months is authorized." Under *Baldwin*, the potential penalty authorized by statute, rather than the actual sentence imposed by a judge, determined whether the Sixth Amendment guaranteed a defendant the right to a jury trial. *Baldwin* has very important implications for the potential scope of the right to a jury in juvenile justice. Most states' juvenile court dispositional statutes authorize sentences much longer than six months, typically for the duration of minority, for a term of years, or even beyond the age of majority. *See e.g.*, Minn. Stat. § 260.191 (1997) (jurisdictional authority of juvenile court may last until juvenile reaches age of 19). Thus, if juveniles have a constitutional right to a jury trial at all, then no juvenile delinquency proceeding could be deemed "petty" under *Baldwin*.

2) Academic Criticism of *McKeiver* Virtually every commentator who analyzed *McKeiver*'s holding and rationales found them analytically flawed and unsupported by empirical evidence. *See* Comment, "Constitutional Law—Due Process: No Constitutional Right to Trial by Jury for Juveniles in Delinquency Proceedings," 56 *Minn. L. Rev.* 249 (1971); Comment, "Jury Trials in Juvenile Proceedings," 85 *Harv. L. Rev.* 113 (1971); Note, "*McKeiver v. Pennsylvania*: A Retreat in Juvenile Justice," 38 *Brooklyn L. Rev.* 650 (1971); W.J. Keegan, "Jury Trials for Juveniles: Rhetoric and Reality," 8 *Pac. L. J.* 811 (1977); Irene M. Rosenberg, "The Constitutional Rights of Children Charged with Crime: Proposal for a Return to the Not So Distant Past," 27 *U.C.L.A. L. Rev.* 656 (1980); Barry C. Feld, "Criminalizing Juvenile Justice: Rules of Procedure for the Juvenile Court," 69 *Minn. L. Rev.* 141 (1984); Joseph B. Sanborn, Jr., "Remnants of *Parens Patriae* in the Adjudicatory Hearing: is a Fair Trial Possible in Juvenile Court?," 40 *Crime & Delinq.* 599 (1994); Korine L. Larsen, "With Liberty and Juvenile Justice For All: Extending the Right to a Jury Trial to the Juvenile Courts," 20 *Wm. Mitchell L. Rev.* 835, 874 (1994) ("Because juvenile courts have shifted their focus so radically from rehabilitation toward retribution, due process protection is critical. Little justification remains for denying juvenile offenders the due process protections of jury trials when juvenile courts mirror criminal proceedings.").

Although Justice Blackmun expressed concern about the impact of jury trials on juvenile justice administration, the available research suggests that youths seldom avail themselves of the right to a jury even in those few jurisdiction that afford them in delinquency proceedings. *See* Patricia L. Shaughnessy, "The Right to a Jury Under the Juvenile Justice Act of 1977," 14 *Gonzaga L.Rev.* 401, 421 (1979), who reports that in those states that allow juries, the frequency of jury trials is very low: Alaska (0.36%); Colorado (3.2%); Michigan (1.8%); Massachusetts (1.7%); Oklahoma (0.56%); Texas (1.5%); Wyoming (1.0%). A more recent survey of jury trials in juvenile courts reported that delinquents used them in less than 1% of cases in Oklahoma and Texas and in less than 3% of cases in Wisconsin. Barry C. Feld, "Violent Youth and Public Policy: A Case Study of Juvenile Justice Law Reform," 79 *Minn. L. Rev.* 965, 1108 (1995).

3) Factual Accuracy and Preventing Governmental Oppression Is Justice Blackmun's assertion in *McKeiver* correct that *Gault* and *Winship* only concerned accurate "fact-finding procedures" to assure "fundamental fairness"? Is that all that *Gault* and *Winship* decided? Summarizing *Gault* and *Winship* and arguing that due process concerns only "factual accuracy," Justice Blackmun continued that "The requirements of notice, counsel, confrontation, cross-examination, and standard of proof naturally flowed from this emphasis [on fact-finding]." Which procedural right that *Gault* granted delinquents did Justice Blackmun omit from that list of rights in his *McKeiver* analysis? Why? What other values besides "accurate factfinding" do procedural safeguards advance? How does the one procedural safeguard that Justice Blackmun omitted from his description of *Gault* advance those values?

4) Reconciling *McKeiver* and *Winship*—The Jury and Accurate Fact-finding Even if we assume that the only function of constitutional procedural safeguards is to assure accurate "fact-finding procedures," is Justice Blackmun's assertion correct that "one cannot say that in our legal system the jury is a necessary component of accurate factfinding"? Can and do judges find facts as well as do juries? How and why might judges and juries differ? If the state charged you with a crime that could lead to your confinement, would you ask for a jury trial? Why or why not? Several analysts question *McKeiver*'s premise about the comparability of judicial and jury fact-finding and offer different explanations for the differences in outcomes.

Barry C. Feld, "The Constitutional Tension Between *Apprendi* and *McKeiver*: Sentence Enhancements Based on Delinquency Convictions and the Quality of Justice in Juvenile Courts," 38 *Wake Forest L. Rev.* 1111, 1161–69 (2003):

McKeiver's rejection of jury trials for juveniles, however, undermines factual accuracy and creates the strong probability that outcomes will differ in delinquency and criminal trials. Because there is no way to know the "correct" outcome or how an "ideal" decision-maker should resolve a factually disputed case, most research compares the decisions of jurors with those of judges, the only other decision-maker practically available. These comparisons indicate that juries serve special protective functions to assure the accuracy of factual determinations. Although judges and juries agree in their judgments of defendants' guilt or innocence in about four-fifths of cases, when they differ, juries are far more likely to acquit defendants than are judges given the same types of evidence.

Fact-finding by judges and juries is inherently different, because the former may preside over hundreds of cases annually while the latter may hear only one or two cases in a lifetime. As a result of routinely hearing many cases, judges sometimes become less meticulous in considering evidence, evaluate facts more casually, and apply less stringently the concepts of "reasonable doubt" and "presumption of innocence" than do jurors. Although the personal characteristics of judges differ from those of jurors, defendants have greater difficulty learning how those individual qualities might affect the decision in a case. Through voir dire, litigants may examine jurors about their attitudes, beliefs, and experiences to assess how they may affect the way they will decide the case, but defendants have no comparable opportunity to explore a judge's background to determine how her experiences might influence her decisions.

Juries and judges evaluate testimony differently. Juvenile court judges hear testimony from police and probation officers on a recurring basis and develop a settled opinion about their credibility. Similarly, as a result of hearing earlier charges against a juvenile or presiding over a detention hearing or pre-trial motion to suppress evidence, a judge already may have a pre-determined view about a youth's credibility and character or the merits of the case. Fact-finding by a judge differs from that by a jury because an individual fact-finder does not have to discuss either the law or the evidence with a group before reaching a conclusion. Indeed, Justice Blackmun, who wrote the *McKeiver* plurality opinion, later recognized the superiority of group decision-making over individual judgments in *Ballew v. Georgia*, which defined the constitutional minimum number of jurors whom a state must empanel. Some group members remember facts that others may forget, and the give-and-take of group deliberations promotes more accurate outcomes by airing competing points of view. Although a judge instructs a jury about the law to apply to the case, in a bench trial the judge does not explicitly state the law, and this makes it more difficult to know whether the judge correctly understood and applied it.

The youthfulness of a defendant is another factor that elicits jury sympathy and accounts for some of the differences between jury and judge trial outcomes. Consequently, it is easier to convict a youth in juvenile court without a jury than to convict a younger person in a criminal proceeding. Indeed, juvenile court judges may be more predisposed to find jurisdiction than criminal court judges or juries in order to "help" an errant youth. A comparison of the outcomes of cases in juvenile and adult courts with comparable evidence suggests that it is easier to convict a delinquent in juvenile court than a defendant in criminal court.

The greater flexibility and informality of non-jury, closed proceedings in juvenile court compounds the differences between judge and jury "reasonable doubt" and places delinquents at a further disadvantage. Juvenile court judges preside at detention hearings and receive prejudicial information about a youth's offense, criminal history, and social circumstances prior to trial. This increases the likelihood that a juvenile court will convict and subsequently institutionally confine her. The lack of a jury allows judges to conduct suppression hearings during the trial, exposes them to prejudicial information about the youth, and further increases the likelihood of erroneous conviction.

Criminal guilt does not involve just "factual guilt," but entails a complex assessment of moral culpability. The power of nullification provides the link between the legislature's original decision to criminalize conduct and the community's sense of justice when it applies the law to the facts of a particular case. Analysts attribute the differences in decision-making outcomes between juries and judges to various factors, including differences in jury-judge evaluations of evidence, jury sentiments about the "law" (jury equity), and jury sympathy for the defendant. Kalven and Zeisel attribute the substantial differences between judge and jury verdicts to the jury's use of a higher evidentiary threshold standard of "proof beyond a reasonable doubt." They conclude that "[i]f a society wishes to be serious about convicting only when the state has been put to proof beyond a reasonable doubt, it would be well advised to have a jury system." The factual and legal issues in delinquency hearings are exactly the same as those in criminal trials—has the state proven beyond a reasonable doubt that the defendant committed a crime? Given the importance of juries to answer this question, McKeiver's decision to dispense with juries in juvenile court makes it easier to convict a youth appearing before a judge in juvenile court than it would be to convict an adult criminal defendant, on the basis of the same evidence, before a jury of detached citizens. * * *

Janet E. Ainsworth, "Re–Imagining Childhood and Reconstructing the Legal Order: The Case for Abolishing the Juvenile Court," 69 N.Car.L.Rev. 1083, 1119 (1991):

* * * [T]he key factors contributing to a sense of procedural justice are consistency in the process, control of the process by the litigant, respectful treatment of the litigant, and ethicality of the fact-finder. Consistency in the process means both that the system always follows prescribed rules and that everyone is treated equally within the system. Process control is the litigant's ability to determine which issues will be contested and upon what basis the contest will proceed. Respectful treatment of the litigant connotes more than just courteous interchange; it also includes investing the litigant with the full complement of rights possessed by other actors in the system. Ethicality of the fact-finder entails a sense that the judge is honest, non-biased, forthright and non-arbitrary in adjudication.

Even in its current "constitutionally domesticated" version, juvenile court procedural practice cuts against these core notions of procedural justice. Treating juveniles differently from adults—by denying them jury trials, for example—violates the consistency norm of equal treatment for all and reminds the young that they do not have all of the rights assigned to full-fledged members of the society. Similarly, the paternalistic tendencies that juvenile court engenders in its functionaries undermines the norm of litigant process control. * * * Confidence in the ethicality of the fact-finder is undercut by the dual roles of the juvenile court judge as finder of fact and sentencing authority. Particularly for the repeat offender, the judge's knowledge of the accused's background and previous criminal record creates the unseemly appearance that guilt has been pre-judged. In the sentencing role, expressions by the judge of paternalistic concern for the juvenile accused coupled with stern judicial sanctioning likewise is inconsistent with the normative model of adjudicatorial behavior. All of these divergences from procedural justice norms strongly suggest that, in the eyes of juvenile respondents, the legitimacy of juvenile court is suspect. * * *

The value of the availability of jury trials for juveniles goes beyond curing the problems of biased judges or disadvantageous fact-finding, however. A jury trial requires the trial judge to articulate in detail the law to be applied in the case through the mechanism of jury instructions. Any error of law in the instructions is reviewable by an appellate court. If no jury instructions exist to make explicit the trial judge's understanding of the law, the reviewing court has no way of knowing whether the juvenile court judge misunderstood or misapplied the law to the juvenile's detriment. As a result, juveniles denied a jury trial lose out twice. They are more likely to be convicted in the first place, and are unlikely to be able to prove an error of law which would allow them to prevail on appeal. * * *

Martin Guggenheim and Randy Hertz, "Reflections on Judges, Juries, and Justice: Ensuring the Fairness of Juvenile Delinquency Trials," 33 *Wake Forest L. Rev.* 553, 556, 562–82 (1998):

* * * [A] review of appellate case law in bench trial cases raises troubling questions about the relative fairness and quality of judicial factfinding. The case law suggests that judges often convict on evidence so scant that only the most closed-minded or misguided juror could think the evidence satisfied the standard of proof beyond a reasonable doubt. * * * Because the American judicial system is structured to leave the assessment of guilt or innocence to the finder of fact at trial, an appellate court generally must reject an insufficiency claim unless the case for acquittal is so overwhelming that no "rational trier of fact could have found the essential elements of the crime beyond a reasonable doubt." * * *

It has been our experience that even fair-minded judges often convict alleged delinquents on obviously insufficient evidence. If, as we believe, the biased judge is the exception rather than the rule, then the problem of flawed factfinding cannot be rectified by simply rooting out and removing the biased judges.* * *

The first and most significant distorting influence in the bench trial context is that trial judges are often exposed to inadmissible, extra-record evidence. Such evidence often suggests, and sometimes virtually proves incontrovertibly, that the accused committed the crime(s) charged. For example, by presiding at a pretrial suppression hearing that results in the suppression of evidence (a statement of the accused, tangible evidence, or identification testimony), the judge will be apprised of highly incriminating evidence that is inadmissible at trial and would be kept from a jury. By presiding over the trial or a guilty plea of a co-respondent or adult co-perpetrator, the judge may hear another individual implicate the accused. In the course of encouraging the parties to settle the case with a guilty plea, the judge may learn from defense counsel that the accused admits guilt. Even in cases where the judge lacks such extra-record information about the accused's involvement in the charged crime, the judge may learn inadmissible information about the accused's prior record as a result of presiding over prior hearings in the case or while resolving evidentiary matters at trial. Finally, such information may reach the judge as a result of off-hand remarks by a clerk or bailiff in the judge's presence or as a result of the judge's review of the court file.

Appellate courts generally indulge in a fiction that a trial judge is capable of putting inadmissible information out of her mind and deciding a case solely on the basis of the evidence adduced at trial. However, * * * such highly prejudicial information inevitably affects a judge, even if only at a subconscious level. * * * Although judges undoubtedly are better than juries at ignoring or not acting upon inadmissible evidence, it strains the imagination to believe that a judge would not be affected by knowledge of a confession, if only at an unconscious level. * * *

Another distorting influence, and the one that helps explain judges' tendency to credit police officers even when their accounts seem highly dubious, is that judges who sit in a criminal or juvenile court for years come to know the police officers of the jurisdiction. If the judge knows that a particular officer is a "good cop" and particularly if the judge has found that the officer testified truthfully in previous cases, the natural tendency is to presume that the officer would not lie. As a result, the judge is less likely to subject the officer's testimony to the kind of critical evaluation that would expose untruths. * * *

In addition to subtly biasing a judge in favor of the prosecution's witnesses, a judge's experience in presiding over criminal and juvenile cases may make the judge unduly skeptical of the testimony of the accused. Judges who sit for years in a criminal or juvenile court tend to hear the same stories over and over. * * * A judge who has presided over numerous trials in which the accused invoked such a defense falsely (or, more precisely, in which the judge deemed the defense to be false) cannot help but be skeptical when yet another defendant or juvenile respondent comes forward with the same story. Accordingly, unlike a jury which would assess the accused's credibility with an open mind, a judge may start from the cynic's position that the story is false until proven otherwise * * *

The use of a jury also increases the likelihood that salient facts will not be overlooked or forgotten. * * * [M]embers of a group may remember testimony that other group members have forgotten. While trial judges generally have an advantage over jurors in this regard, in that judges can take notes of the testimony whereas most jurisdictions prohibit jurors from doing so, even the most assiduous note-taking judge may neglect to jot down an important response by a witness or argument of counsel because the judge failed to appreciate its significance at the time. Moreover, in her effort to take careful notes, the judge may fail to notice some meaningful aspect of a witness's demeanor or some highly salient gesture or meaningful glance by the witness while on the stand. Indeed, judges suffer from a particular disadvantage in this regard because, unlike jurors, their attention is constantly diverted by the need to resolve pending evidentiary matters, to control the courtroom, and to attend to a series of clerks and lawyers filing in and out of the courtroom.

A final advantage of group decisionmaking, and perhaps the most important one, is that the give-and-take of a discussion format promotes accuracy and good judgment by ensuring that competing viewpoints are aired and vetted. * * *

In addition to the differences in the ways in which juries and judges evaluate the evidence at the conclusion of a trial, there is also a subtle but important difference in the ways these two types of factfinders evaluate the evidence during trial. At the beginning of a jury trial, the lawyers for both sides commonly use opening statements to present the jury with their respective theories of the case. As social scientific studies have shown, opening statements serve a vital function of exposing the jurors to perspectives they might not otherwise have considered, as well as ensuring that the jurors appreciate the significance of apparently unimportant facts. In contrast, it is an almost universal convention that opening statements are waived in bench trials. Attorneys who insist upon "taking up the judge's time" by making an opening statement do so at the risk of irritating the factfinder. * * * By dispensing with opening statements, juvenile court judges deprive themselves of one of the few opportunities available in a bench trial for escaping the limitations of their own perspectives and preconceptions.

The problems caused by the absence of opening statements are exacerbated by the tendency of many juvenile court judges to evaluate witnesses' testimony as they hear it rather than withholding judgment until the conclusion of the trial. In jury trials, it is commonplace for judges to instruct jurors to refrain from making any judgments about the facts until they have heard all of the evidence and the lawyers' closing arguments. Yet, many juvenile court judges seem to assume that they are exempt from such a procedure when serving as finder of fact at a bench trial. Most lawyers who have practiced in juvenile court for an appreciable length of time have had the unsettling experience of delivering a closing argument to a judge who was neither taking notes nor even paying close attention and who immediately thereafter delivered the verdict by reading aloud from a piece of paper on which she had previously written her findings of fact and conclusions of law. Here again, judges' assumption of their innate ability to evaluate the facts deprives them of a critical opportunity to hear a perspective that they may have overlooked. * * *

1. THE RIGHT TO A JURY TRIAL IN THE STATES: AFTER "GET TOUGH" REFORMS, IS THE GLASS HALF–EMPTY OR HALF–FULL?

The following majority and dissenting opinions in *L.M.*, *D.J.*, and *Hezzie R.* debate whether juveniles should receive a federal or state constitutional right to a jury trial. They provide examples of how state courts analyze the impact of punitive, "get tough" changes in juvenile codes on juveniles' procedural rights and the analytical tools that they use to distinguish treatment from punishment. *See also, Allen v. Illinois, supra* Note 5, p. 740.

IN RE L.M.
286 Kan. 460, 186 P.3d 164 (Kan. 2008).

[The state prosecuted sixteen-year-old L.M. as a juvenile for the felony offense of aggravated sexual battery. L.M. requested a jury trial, which the district court denied. After a bench trial, the juvenile court judge found him guilty, sentenced him as a Serious Offender to a term of 18 months in a juvenile correctional facility, stayed his sentence, and placed him on probation until he was 20 years old. The court also ordered L.M. to complete sex offender treatment and to register as a sex offender. The Court of Appeals affirmed the district court's denial of a jury trial. The Kansas Supreme Court reviewed L.M.'s assertion that he had a constitutional right to a jury trial in a juvenile offender proceeding.] ROSEN, J., delivered the opinion of the court:

L.M.'s first argument relies on the Sixth Amendment [and Fourteenth Amendment] to the United States Constitution. * * * Kansas has previously resolved this issue against L.M.'s position. Twenty-four years ago, under the statutes then controlling the disposition of juvenile offender cases, this court held that juveniles do not have a constitutional right to a jury trial under either the federal or state constitutions. *Findlay v. State* (1984). Acknowledging that the Sixth Amendment applies only to criminal prosecutions, the *Findlay* court concluded that juvenile adjudications then were not criminal prosecutions. * * *

The *Findlay* court also adopted the United States Supreme Court's reasoning in *McKeiver v. Pennsylvania* where a plurality of the Court held that juveniles are not entitled to a jury trial under the Sixth and Fourteenth Amendments to the Constitution. * * * Although the resulting plurality opinion [in *McKeiver*] held that juveniles are not entitled to a jury trial under the federal constitution, the justices could not agree on the reasoning to support that holding. Four of the justices supported their decision with * * * 13 policy considerations and assumptions or speculations about the impact of jury trials on juvenile proceedings. * * *

L.M. recognizes the import of *Findlay* and *McKeiver* but asks us to overturn *Findlay*. L.M. raises three arguments to support his request. First, L.M. claims that the changes in the Revised Kansas Juvenile Justice Code (KJJC) have eroded the child-cognizant, paternal, and rehabilitative purposes of the juvenile offender process, thereby requiring us to recognize a juvenile's right to a jury trial under the federal Constitution. Second, L.M. argues that juveniles are entitled to a jury trial under the Kansas Constitution. Third, L.M. asserts that regardless of whether all juveniles are constitutionally entitled to a jury, he should have received one because he ran the risk of having to register as a sex offender.

We begin our analysis by noting that the Kansas Legislature has significantly changed the language of the Kansas Juvenile Offender Code (KJOC) since the *Findlay* court decided this issue 24 years ago. * * * L.M. asserts that these changes to the code negated the rehabilitative purpose set forth in the KJOC. According to L.M., the negating of the rehabilitative purpose is evidenced by the replacement of nonpunitive terminology with criminal terminology similar to the adult criminal code, the alignment of the KJJC sentencing provisions with the adult sentencing guidelines, and the removal of the protections that the *McKeiver* Court relied on to distinguish juvenile systems from the adult criminal systems.

One of the key changes in the KJJC is reflected in K.S.A.2006 Supp. 38–2301, which sets forth the purpose for the KJJC. * * * In 1982, the KJOC was focused on rehabilitation and the State's parental role in providing guidance, control, and discipline. However, under the KJJC, the focus has shifted to protecting the public, holding juveniles accountable for their behavior and choices, and making juveniles more productive and responsible members of society. These purposes are more aligned with the legislative intent for the adult sentencing statutes, which include protecting the public by incarcerating dangerous offenders for a long period of time, holding offenders accountable by prescribing appropriate consequences for their actions, and encouraging offenders to be more productive members of society by considering their individual characteristics, circumstances, needs, and potentialities in determining their sentences.

In addition to being more aligned with the purpose of the criminal sentencing statutes, the KJJC also incorporates language similar to that found in the Kansas Criminal Code and the Kansas Code of Criminal Procedure. Under the KJOC, juveniles were required to admit or deny the allegations against them or plead nolo contendere. Under the KJJC, a juvenile is required to plead guilty, not guilty, or nolo contendere like adults charged with a crime. Although both the KJOC and the KJJC refer to an adjudication rather than a conviction, a "dispositional proceeding" under the KJOC is now referred to as a "sentencing proceeding" in the KJJC. The "State youth center" referred to in the KJOC, is now called a "Juvenile correctional facility," which is more akin to an adult "correctional institution." Moreover, the KJJC emulates the language of the Kansas Criminal Code when it refers to the term of commitment to a juvenile correctional facility as a "term of incarceration." This conceptualization of juvenile offenders stresses the similarities between child and adult offenders far more than it does their differences.

The legislature also emulated the structure of the Kansas Sentencing Guidelines when it established a sentencing matrix for juveniles based on the level of the offense committed and, in some cases, the juvenile's history of juvenile adjudications. For example, a juvenile offender found guilty of committing an off-grid felony may be sentenced to "a juvenile correctional facility for a minimum term of 60 months and up to a maximum term of the offender reaching the age of 22 years, six months." A juvenile offender found guilty of committing a level 7, 8, 9, or 10 person felony with one prior felony adjudication may be sentenced to "a juvenile correctional facility for a minimum term of nine months and up to a maximum term of 18 months."

Like the adult sentencing guidelines, the KJJC allows the sentencing judge to depart from the juvenile placement matrix upon a motion by the State or the sentencing judge. The KJJC sentencing judge may consider the aggravating factors from [the Kansas adult sentencing guidelines.] If the sentencing judge departs from the presumptive sentence, he or she must state on the record the substantial and compelling reasons for the departure just as if he or she were sentencing an adult offender. Although any juvenile sentence within the presumptive sentencing range is not subject to appeal, juvenile departure sentences, like adult departure sentences, may be appealed. * * *

In addition to reflecting the provisions of the sentencing guidelines, the KJJC also establishes sentencing options that are similar to those available for adult offenders. Both adults and juveniles may be sentenced to probation; a community-based program; house arrest; a short-term behavior-modification program like a sanctions house or conservation camp; placement in an out-of-home facility; or incarceration in a correctional facility. The district court also has authority to order both adults and juveniles to attend counseling; drug and alcohol evaluations; mediation; or educational programs. In addition, the district court may require both adults and juveniles to perform charitable or community service; pay restitution; or pay a fine. Sentencing of juveniles has become much more congruent with the adult model.

Besides amending the 1982 version of the KJOC to reflect the purpose and provisions included in the adult criminal code, the legislature has removed some of the protective provisions that made the juvenile system more child-cognizant and confidential, a key consideration in the *McKeiver* plurality decision. In 1982, juvenile proceedings were confidential. The official court file and all police records of any juvenile under the age of 16 were not open to the public. Likewise, any hearing involving a juvenile under the age of 16 was confidential and the court could exclude anyone except the juvenile; his or her parents; the attorneys of any interested parties; officers of the court; and any testifying witness.

However, under the KJJC, the official file must be open to the public unless a judge orders it to be closed for juveniles under the age of 14 based on finding that it is in the best interests of the juvenile. Similarly, law enforcement records and municipal court records for any juvenile age 14 and over are subject to the same disclosure restrictions as the records for adults. Only juveniles under the age of 14 may have their law enforcement and municipal records kept confidential. * * *

These changes to the juvenile justice system have eroded the benevolent *parens patriae* character that distinguished it from the adult criminal system. The United States Supreme Court relied on the juvenile justice system's characteristics of fairness, concern, sympathy, and paternal attention in concluding that juveniles were not entitled to a jury trial. Likewise, this court relied on that parens patriae character in reaching its decision in *Findlay*. However, because the juvenile justice system is now patterned after the adult criminal system, we conclude that the changes have superseded the *McKeiver* and *Findlay* Courts' reasoning and those decisions are no longer binding precedent for us to follow. Based on our conclusion that the Kansas juvenile justice system has become more akin to an adult criminal prosecution, we hold that juveniles have a constitutional right to a jury trial under the Sixth and Fourteenth Amendments. As a result, K.S.A. 2006 Supp. 38–2344(d), which provides that a juvenile who pleads not guilty is entitled to a "trial to the court," and K.S.A.2006 Supp. 38–2357, which gives the district court discretion in determining whether a juvenile should be granted a jury trial, are unconstitutional.

In reaching this conclusion, we are mindful of decisions in other jurisdictions rejecting the argument that changes to the juvenile justice system have altered its *parens patriae* character. * * * We are also mindful that many of the state courts that have addressed this issue in one form or another have declined to extend the constitutional right to a jury trial to juveniles.

While there is wide variability in the juvenile offender laws throughout the country, it nevertheless seems apparent to us that the KJJC, in its tilt towards applying adult standards of criminal procedure and sentencing, removed the paternalistic protections previously accorded juveniles while continuing to deny those juveniles the constitutional right to a jury trial. Although we do not find total support from the courts in some of our sister states, we are undaunted in our belief that juveniles are entitled to the right to a jury trial guaranteed to all citizens under the Sixth and Fourteenth Amendments to the United States Constitution. * * *

Kansas Constitution

In addition to claiming a federal constitutional right to a jury trial, L.M. asserts that he has a right to a jury trial under the Kansas Constitution. L.M. relies on the Kansas Constitution Bill of Rights, Section 1, 5, and 10. * * * The plain language of § 10 extends the right to a jury trial to "all prosecutions." This court has previously interpreted the phrase "all prosecutions" to "mean all criminal prosecutions for violations of the laws of the state." * * *

The KJJC repeatedly refers to its proceedings as a prosecution. In addition, proceedings under the KJJC are based on allegations that juveniles have violated the criminal laws of this State. Because the KJJC has lost the parens patriae character of the former KJOC and has transformed into a system for prosecuting juveniles charged with committing crimes, we conclude that the proceedings under the KJJC fit within the meaning of the phrase "all prosecutions" as set forth in § 10, and juveniles have a right to a jury trial under the Kansas Constitution. Consequently, K.S.A.2006 Supp. 38–2344(d) and K.S.A.2006 Supp. 38–2357 are also unconstitutional under the Kansas Constitution. * * *

[W]e agree with L.M. that *Findlay* is no longer applicable because of the legislative overhaul to the juvenile justice code. The right to a jury trial in juvenile offender proceedings is a new rule of procedure; it does not operate retroactively. It does not create a new class of convicted persons, but merely raises " 'the possibility that someone convicted with use of the invalidated procedure might have been acquitted otherwise.' "

This right will apply only to cases pending on direct review or not yet final on the date of filing of this opinion. Because L.M. was tried without a jury, his adjudication is reversed and this matter is remanded to the district court for a new trial before a jury.

Reversed.

LUCKERT, J., concurring:

* * * In my view, the considerations relevant to the application of the Sixth Amendment and § 10 to juvenile proceedings vary depending upon the nature of the offense charged and the juvenile's prior adjudications. * * * Nevertheless, for a discrete population of juvenile offenders, the KJJC's procedural and substantive provisions do not differ from those for adult criminal prosecution in any material way. * * * [A] felony juvenile offender is confined to the custody of the state for significant periods of time—in some situations, for many years and for longer than some adults who receive a jury trial. Thus, for many juveniles in circumstances similar to L.M.'s, the denial of a jury trial is not constitutionally justified on due process grounds. * * * I would conclude that § 5 of the Kansas Constitution Bill of Rights grants a right to a trial by jury to all juveniles 14 years of age or older who are charged with a felony. Thus, 16–year–old L.M., who was charged with aggravated sexual battery, would be entitled to a trial by jury.

McFARLAND, C.J., dissenting:

I respectfully dissent from the majority's decision holding that changes to the juvenile offender system over the last couple of decades have eroded the protective, rehabilitative features of that system to the point that it has become akin to the adult criminal system and, therefore, juvenile offenders are now constitutionally entitled to a jury trial. * * *

Although it cannot be disputed that in the 20–plus years since *Findlay*, the juvenile system has become more punitive and has incorporated some of the terminology and mechanisms of the adult criminal system, the majority overstates and overemphasizes the changes while ignoring the many features of the current system that remain consistent with the benevolent, protective, rehabilitative, child-cognizant characteristics that distinguish the juvenile system from the criminal system. The protective, rehabilitative focus that has distinguished the juvenile system from the punitive, retributive adult criminal system is still very much alive.

The majority contends that the current juvenile system has changed to be more in line with the adult criminal system in four ways: (1) the policy goals of the juvenile system have shifted from rehabilitation to protection of the public and accountability, goals more akin to those underlying the criminal system; (2) the current juvenile code uses language similar to that used in the criminal codes; (3) juveniles are now subject to determinative sentencing that closely resembles the sentencing guidelines for adults, and the sentencing options available for juvenile offenders are analogous to those available in the adult sentencing system; and (4) some of the protective confidentiality features of the former juvenile system have been eliminated.

The Policy Goals

* * * The majority contends the amendments in the stated goals evidence a shift from rehabilitation and the State's parental role in providing care, custody, guidance, control, and discipline to protecting the public, holding juveniles accountable, and making juveniles more productive and responsible members of society. What the majority disregards, however, is that in 1982, protection of the public, along with rehabilitation, was an express goal of the juvenile system. * * * Similarly, protection of the public and rehabilitation remain primary goals of the juvenile justice system. * * *

Although the new statute is much more specific about how its goals will be accomplished, the basic goals of protecting the public and rehabilitating juvenile offenders, i.e., improving the ability of juveniles to live more productively and responsibly in the community, remain consistent.

Moreover, contrary to the majority's contention, these goals are nothing like those set out in the adult sentencing guidelines. * * * That statute makes it clear that in the adult sentencing system, the focus is on the protection of the public through long terms of confinement for dangerous offenders, with imposition of lesser sanctions only where consistent with public safety and the welfare of the offender. There is no language suggesting that rehabilitation is one of the goals of the adult sentencing system.

Language

The majority concludes that the current juvenile code incorporates language similar to that found in the adult system, thus stressing the similarities between juvenile and adult offenders over their differences. * * * Clearly some of the terminology has changed. And labels are important to some extent—hence the retention of the term adjudication instead of the term conviction. Nevertheless, form must not be placed over substance. If a change in terminology does not reflect any substantive change in the thing or process described, then too much emphasis should not be placed on that terminology. The facilities denominated as state youth centers, and now juvenile correctional facilities, are one and the same. Regardless of their names, these facilities have always been institutions where juvenile offenders are sent to serve a period of court-ordered confinement.

Sentencing

The majority contends that the sentencing scheme and the options available are now more like those in the adult criminal system. Specifically, the majority notes that juveniles now have determinate presumptive sentencing under a matrix that is based on the offense committed and the juvenile's unique adjudicatory history. And, the majority notes that, like the adult sentencing scheme under the guidelines grid, the current code allows the juvenile judge to depart upward from the presumptive matrix upon finding that substantial and compelling reasons support departure. In determining whether to depart, the court may consider the nonexclusive list of aggravating factors set forth in the adult guidelines.

Significant differences remain between the two systems that are overlooked by the majority. First, the majority's analysis fails to take into account the difference in the severity of the sentences juveniles face under the matrix for the same crime committed by an adult offender. * * *

Second, in contrast to the adult sentencing guidelines, the sentences provided under the juvenile sentencing matrix are not mandatory. Commitment to a juvenile correctional facility for a term under the matrix is only one of a number of sentencing alternatives available to a juvenile judge. Thus, the judge has discretion in deciding whether to sentence a juvenile to a juvenile correctional facility. If that option is chosen, however, the court must impose the applicable sentence specified in the matrix. * * *

Another compelling difference is the power given to the juvenile judge to modify the sentence after it has been imposed—a power that does not exist under the adult sentencing guidelines. * * * The discretionary sentencing provisions and the modification provisions are unique to the juvenile system and are a clear expression of the legislature's continued belief in the juvenile system as an individualized, protective, and rehabilitative process. * * *

Sentencing options

The majority contends that the sentencing options available to the juvenile judge are much more akin to those available for adult offenders. The court notes that juvenile offenders, like adult offenders, may be sentenced to probation; a community-based program; house arrest; a sanctions house, which the majority likens to conservation camps; placement in an out-of-home facility; and incarceration. In addition, the court may order both adults and juveniles to attend counseling; drug and alcohol evaluations; mediation; and educational programs. The court may also order both juveniles and adults to perform charitable or community service, pay restitution, and pay fines.

This broad overview overlooks the many unique features of the juvenile system that emphasize family and community involvement, early intervention diversionary procedures, flexibility to accommodate individualized needs of juveniles upon intake into the system, preference for noncustodial placements, graduated sanctions with preferences for the least-restrictive alternatives, and, above all, rehabilitation. * * *

A dispositional feature unique to the juvenile system is its preference for maintaining the family unit. Under the KJJC, the court must make specific findings that reasonable efforts were made to maintain the family unit or that an emergency exists before a juvenile may be removed from the home, whether for detention, placement in the custody of the commissioner, or commitment to a juvenile correctional facility. * * *

Additionally, and most importantly, the KJJC not only emphasizes, but requires, parental involvement in the entire process. Intake and assessment workers may require parents to participate in programs and services as a condition of the juvenile's release back home. * * * This emphasis on parental involvement is not merely incidental to the fact the juvenile offender is a child, but is, instead, part of the family and community centered approach to juvenile rehabilitation. * * *

Confidentiality and other protective provisions

The majority also contends that juvenile proceedings and records no longer have the confidentiality protections they did in 1982. The majority points to provisions concerning public access to juvenile court hearings and confidentiality of records. With respect to juvenile hearings, there is little practical difference between the KJOC provisions in 1982 and the current KJJC provisions. * * *

With respect to confidentiality of juvenile records, there are only two differences between the KJOC and the KJJC. First, the age of protection was lowered from 15 to 13. * * * Second, with respect to the official court file only, the file is now open for public inspection unless, in the case of a juvenile who is under age 14, the judge determines that public inspection is not in the juvenile's best interests. Previously, the official file of a juvenile under the age of 16 was privileged and not subject to disclosure to anyone other than the court, the parties and their attorneys, an agency or institution with custody of the juvenile, law enforcement, or upon court order.

The changes to the juvenile code cited by the majority have not so eroded the features of the juvenile system that distinguish it from the adult system that it can be said that the rationale underlying *McKeiver* and *Findlay* is no longer valid. The new system continues to further the goals that have always characterized the modern juvenile system: protection of the public and rehabilitation. * * * Given the fact that the juvenile system must deal with serious, violent, and habitual offenders, it is entirely appropriate that the juvenile system balance rehabilitation with protection of the public. * * *:

The incorporation of certain aspects of the adult sentencing scheme for the most violent and chronic juvenile offenders is a critical part of meeting the obligation to protect the community from these offenders. However, the legislature, in choosing to make sentencing under the matrix a discretionary sentencing option, kept in place the individualized sentencing flexibility that has always been characteristic of the juvenile system. In addition, in creating extended juvenile jurisdiction, the legislature extended the protective net of the juvenile system as a last-ditch effort for those juveniles who would otherwise be prosecuted and sentenced as adults. These key features demonstrate the legislature's effort to carefully balance protection of the public with the goal of rehabilitating youthful offenders.

The dual goals of the juvenile system that commanded its process in 1982 are very much alive and well. The juvenile system still retains significant individualized, protective, rehabilitative, child-cognizant features that distinguish it from the adult system and which allow it to operate toward achieving those goals. * * *

With no persuasive authority from other jurisdictions, and a less than comprehensive analysis of the current system, the majority concludes that the Kansas juvenile justice system is the essential equivalent of the adult criminal justice system and, thus, the right to trial by jury must be afforded. To what end? As the United States Supreme Court recognized in *McKeiver*, imposing the constitutional right to trial by jury on the juvenile court system would not greatly strengthen the fact-finding function, but would erode the juvenile court's ability to function in a unique manner, and "remake the juvenile proceeding into a fully adversary process and ... put an effective end to what has been the idealistic prospect of an intimate, informal protective proceeding." "If the formalities of the criminal adjudicative system are to be superimposed upon the juvenile court system, there is little need for its separate existence."

The experiment has not failed. The majority has overlooked the most significant features of the juvenile system that distinguish it from the adult system-features that promote protection of the public while not only preserving, but furthering, the individualized, protective, rehabilitative character unique to the juvenile system. To quote the Washington Supreme Court, the KJJA " 'has not utterly abandoned the rehabilitative ideal which impelled the juvenile justice system for decades. It does not embrace a purely punitive or retributive philosophy. Instead, it attempts to tread an equatorial line somewhere midway between the poles of rehabilitation and retribution.' "

For these reasons, I dissent.

STATE IN THE INTEREST OF D.J.

817 So.2d 26 (La. 2002).

[The state filed a delinquency petition charging thirteen-year-old D.J. and a companion with attempted second degree murder and carrying a firearm by a student on school property. D.J. filed a motion for a jury trial in juvenile court which the juvenile court granted. It found the statute which prohibited a trial by jury in serious delinquency proceedings unconstitutional. The State appealed to the Louisiana Supreme Court.]

VICTORY, J.

Both juveniles charged in this matter and numerous amici argue that recent developments in juvenile law have made the proceedings more criminal than civil in nature and as a result, due process requires that juveniles be afforded the right to elect a trial by jury. The state maintains otherwise, arguing that the rehabilitative focus of juvenile proceedings has not been undermined by recent legislative enactments to a degree requiring that the due process standard of "fundamental fairness" necessitates that juveniles be afforded the right to a trial by jury. * * *

[T]he Children's Code effectively prohibits jury trials in *all* juvenile court proceedings. Accordingly, the constitutionality of the absolute prohibition on jury trials in delinquency proceedings under the due process clauses of the Louisiana and United States Constitutions must be addressed on the merits and affords this Court an opportunity to revisit its holding in *State in Interest of Dino* (1978).

The juvenile justice system dates back to the early 1900s and was founded as a way to both nurture and rehabilitate youths. "[O]rdinary retributive punishment for the adolescent [was] inappropriate," in part, because "[j]uvenile court philosophy made no distinction between criminal and non-criminal behavior, as long as the behavior was considered deviant or inappropriate to the age of the juvenile." * * *

In *In re C.B.*, [*infra*, Note 4 p. 790] we noted that it is the above policy "that has guided this Court and others in determining which constitutional rights are guaranteed to juveniles under the dictates of fundamental fairness, inherent in the due process clause, beginning with the determination that the applicable due process standard in juvenile proceedings is fundamental fairness." "Because of the fundamental differences between the adult and juvenile systems, however, due process, and implicitly fundamental fairness, do not require that every constitutional right guaranteed to adults be automatically granted to juveniles."

The United States Supreme Court in *McKeiver v. Pennsylvania* held that the Due Process Clause of the Fourteenth Amendment does not impose the right to jury trial upon the states in juvenile delinquency proceedings. * * * [T]his Court in *Dino* tracked the holding of *McKeiver* and held that "[f]or reasons similar to those expressed in *McKeiver,* a majority of this Court has concluded that the Louisiana due process guaranty . . . does not afford a juvenile the right to a jury trial during the adjudication of a charge of delinquency based upon acts that would constitute a crime if engaged in by an adult."

In the present case, the juveniles and the amici strenuously argue that this policy-based analysis applied more than 20 years ago when *McKeiver* and *Dino* were decided is outdated and that recent changes in state law, as well as an ongoing national critique of the juvenile justice system, render the reasoning behind the two cases outdated and inapplicable to current conditions. The juveniles and their amici argue that since the *McKeiver* decision, the Louisiana juvenile system has taken on more trappings of the criminal justice system, so much so that the only substantial difference between the two is the right to a jury trial. They argue that not only do juvenile defendants have virtually all of the constitutional rights afforded to adult defendants (except the jury trial right), but that the following two recent legislative amendments have torn down the remaining characteristics of what traditionally identified the juvenile system.

First, in 1994, the legislature * * * open[ed] to the public all proceedings in juvenile delinquency cases involving crimes of violence * * * which includes attempted second degree murder (one of the instant crimes). They argue that this legislative action destroyed the confidentiality of certain juvenile proceedings which previously had been a hallmark of the juvenile system. * * *

Second, since 1994, the Habitual Offender Law has provided that juvenile adjudications for drug offenses or crimes of violence may be used to enhance a subsequent adult felony offense. Before this change, juvenile adjudications were sealed and did not follow an individual into adulthood.

With these changes taking place, the juveniles point out that many commentators are calling for states to give juvenile offenders the right to trial by jury. Further, thirteen states currently allow jury trials in juvenile delinquency adjudication proceedings as a matter of state law. Commentators note that the "increasing role of punishment in juvenile justice" makes the right to trial by jury that much more important.

However, in spite of these arguments, for the reasons stated below, we find that fundamental fairness does not require us to overrule *Dino*'s holding that due process does not afford a juvenile the right to a jury trial during the adjudication of a charge of delinquency in juvenile court. Since *Dino*, this Court had occasion to review the juvenile justice system in accordance with the fundamental fairness standard in *In re C.B.* In that case, this Court considered the constitutionality of a recently enacted statute which authorized the transfer of adjudicated juvenile delinquents to adult correctional facilities when the delinquents reached the age of 17. * * * [I]n considering whether the statute at issue was constitutional in *In re C.B.* [*see*, Note 4, *infra* p. 790], the Court stated that "the issue now becomes how much of the unique nature of the juvenile procedures can be eroded before due process requires that the juveniles be afforded all the guarantees afforded adult criminals under the constitution, including the right to trial by jury." Ultimately, we decided that confinement to hard labor at adult facilities would erode the unique nature of the juvenile procedure so far that due process required all the guarantees under the constitution; however, rather than require a jury trial, the Court declared the statute allowing the transfer to adult facilities to be unconstitutional under the due process clause. This holding is significant, because it infers that the Court determined that the other statutes that "blurred the distinction" between adult and juvenile proceedings, such as the public hearing and the sentence enhancement statutes, did not offend due process requirements to such an extent that a jury trial would be required.

In fact, in *McKeiver,* on which *Dino* was based, the United States Supreme Court "focused on the role of the jury as a 'factfinder,' . . . and noted that the imposition of a jury trial would not 'strengthen greatly, if at all, the factfinding function, and would, contrarily, provide an attrition of the juvenile court's assumed ability to function in a unique manner.' " Indeed, affording juvenile offenders the right to trial by jury would tend to destroy the flexibility of the juvenile judge as the trier of fact, which allows the judge to take into consideration social and psychological factors, family background, and education in order to shape the disposition in the best interest of both the child and society.

Further, notwithstanding the changes in the juvenile justice system discussed above, there remains a great disparity in the severity of penalties faced by a juvenile charged with delinquency and an adult defendant charged with the same crime. In fact, if the court adjudicated the juvenile in the instant case delinquent, he would face a maximum sentence of eight years detention while the court would retain the discretion to sentence him to a lighter term. An adult defendant convicted of the identical charge would face a maximum sentence of 55 years imprisonment at hard labor, 50 years without benefit of parole, probation or suspension of sentence. * * *

Further, despite the criticism of *McKeiver* by some commentators, the vast majority of the jurisdictions which have examined the issue have determined that such a right is not guaranteed by the Due Process Clause. Challenges, like the instant one, claiming that fundamental changes in the nature of the juvenile justice system have undermined the validity of the *McKeiver* Court's analysis have been routinely rejected.

In addition, attempts to recognize a state constitutional right to a jury trial in juvenile matters have been largely unsuccessful. Arguments claiming that particular statutory schemes are so punitive and have little or no rehabilitative focus so as to render *McKeiver* inapplicable have been similarly unavailing. Finally, arguments that other federal constitutional protections invoke a juvenile's right to a jury trial have failed. In fact, despite the variety of arguments on the issue, courts have almost universally rejected the claim that juveniles possess a constitutional right to a trial by jury.

Conclusion

Thus, we follow the rulings from the United States Supreme Court, this Court, and the vast majority of other jurisdictions on this issue, and hold that a trial by jury in a juvenile proceeding is not constitutionally required under the applicable due process standard in juvenile proceedings. While we recognize that the Louisiana juvenile justice system is far from perfect, we are "not yet ready to spell the doom of the juvenile court system by requiring jury trials in juvenile adjudications." * * *

Reversed and remanded.

JOHNSON, J., Dissenting.

The Louisiana juvenile system was founded upon the philosophy of nurturing and rehabilitating youths. Since the *McKeiver* decision, however, the Louisiana juvenile system has taken on more trappings of the criminal justice system, so much so that the only substantial difference between the two is the right to a jury trial. Not only do juvenile defendants have virtually all of the constitutional rights afforded to adult defendants (except the jury trial right), but two recent legislative amendments have torn down the remaining characteristics of what traditionally identified the juvenile system.

First, in 1994, the legislature * * * open[ed] to the public all proceedings in juvenile delinquency cases involving crimes of violence * * *. This legislative action destroyed the confidentiality of certain juvenile proceedings which previously had been a hallmark of the juvenile system. * * *

Second, the Habitual Offender Law provides that juvenile adjudications for drug offenses or crimes of violence may be used to enhance a subsequent adult felony offense. Before this change, juvenile adjudications were sealed and did not follow an individual into adulthood.

In addition, other amendments to the Children's Code further blur the distinction between juvenile and criminal courts. For example, the Children's Code calls for mandatory maximum sentencing in certain cases thus eliminating the traditional discretion of the juvenile court judge to mold a disposition to the needs of the juvenile. Furthermore, the four Louisiana Training Institutes, where most juvenile offenders are sent, are becoming increasingly more like adult prisons, providing less rehabilitation, education, etc. and are becoming more punishment oriented. "[T]he four Louisiana Training Institutes to which convicted juvenile offenders are sent are reportedly the scenes of the most violent and abusive practices of any children's prisons in the nation."

With these types of changes taking place, most commentators are calling for states to give juvenile offenders the right to trial by jury. Thirteen states currently allow jury trials in juvenile delinquency adjudication proceedings as a matter of state law. Commentators note that the "increasing role of punishment in juvenile justice" makes the right to trial by jury that much more important. They argue that because juveniles are facing mandatory sentences and juvenile adjudications are being used to enhance felony convictions, it is essential that the juvenile adjudication process be fair and accurate. * * *

Although we did not grant the juveniles the right to trial by jury in *In re C.B.,* we did note the increasing criminal focus on the punitive aspects of delinquency proceedings and suggested that there may come a time when the juvenile justice system is so far removed from its original purpose and character such that due process dictates the right to trial by jury, thereby rendering *McKeiver* and its rationale obsolete. * * *

I believe that our juvenile court system has evolved so drastically in nature that due process requires that juvenile offenders be afforded the right to elect to be tried by a jury. Even without the right to jury trial, all the elements necessary to make the juvenile process into an adversary process have already been injected into the juvenile system including the right to counsel, the privilege against self-incrimination, and the right to confront and cross-examine witnesses. * * *

I disagree with the State's argument that affording juvenile offenders the right to trial by jury would destroy the flexibility of the juvenile judge as the trier of fact. As in many other modern juvenile court statutes, the legislature has separated the proceedings into two phases: adjudicative and dispositional. While a jury would be the appropriate trier of fact at the adjudicative phase, the juvenile judge would retain flexibility in the dispositional phase of the proceeding. The judge would still be free to take into consideration social and psychological factors, family background, and education in order to shape the disposition in the best interest of both the child and society. In fact, if the court adjudicated the defendant in the instant case delinquent, he would face a maximum sentence of eight years detention while the court would retain the discretion to sentence him to a lighter term. An adult defendant convicted of the identical charge would face a maximum sentence of 55 years imprisonment at hard labor, 50 years without benefit of parole, probation or suspension of sentence. However, it should also be recognized that any adult charged with an offense punishable by more than six months imprisonment would be entitled to exercise the right to a trial by jury. This disparity between penalties meted out to the adult and juvenile offender apparently reflects the widely-held belief that juveniles who commit crimes are less culpable than their adult counterparts. It is clear that allowing the right to jury trial will not destroy this unique feature of the juvenile system. * * *

Although the trial court's decision was ultimately premised on fundamental fairness and due process, I also find that the provisions of the Louisiana Children's Code which deny juvenile offenders the right to trial by jury violate the Equal Protection Clause of the United States and Louisiana Constitutions.

Equal protection of the laws requires that, upon his request, a juvenile is entitled to receive the same mode of jury trial which is available to an adult charged with the same offense. Significantly, under the Habitual Offender Law, an adult defendant charged with a violent crime faces possible future enhancement of sentence but has the benefit of a jury trial, while a juvenile faced with these same possibilities is given less protection. What is the state's interest in this regard? The differential treatment of juveniles and adults cannot be justified on the theory that the denial of the jury trial to juveniles is essential to the preservation of the rehabilitative characteristics of the juvenile system. Nor can it be justified on the basis of the expedient nature of juvenile proceedings. * * *

Accordingly, I would affirm the trial court's granting of defendant's motion for jury trial and declaring [the statute barring a jury trial] unconstitutional in that it is in derogation of a juvenile offender's due process and equal protection rights.

NOTES

1) Federal vs. State Constitutional Adjudication Apart from the differences in their conclusions, in what way does the *L.M.* Court's analyses differ from *McKeiver*? Is it the difference between a federal and a state constitutional decision? How does the *D.J.* court's analyses differ from *L.M.*'s? Which opinions do you find more persuasive and why?

2) McKeiver and the Other Function of Constitutional Safeguards—"Preventing Governmental Oppression" Even if the court correctly decided *McKeiver* in 1971, is the rehabilitative juvenile justice system that the *McKeiver* plurality believed or hoped existed at that time still operative today? Did *McKeiver* adequately analyze the differences between treatment and punishment? Justice White's concurring opinion in *McKeiver* examined some of the differences between treatment as a juvenile and punishment as an adult that justified the procedural differences. "Whereas the criminal law punishes morally responsible actors for making blameworthy choices, the deterministic assumptions of the juvenile justice system regard juveniles as less culpable." Justice White observed that the indeterminate length of juvenile dispositions and the "eschewing [of] blameworthiness and punishment for evil choices" satisfied him that "there remained differences of substance between criminal and juvenile courts." What are those substantive differences? How might a juvenile court or appellate court judge assess those differences when a juvenile requests a jury trial? *See generally*, Barry C. Feld, "The Juvenile Court Meets the Principle of Offense: Punishment, Treatment, and the Difference it Makes," 68 *Boston U. L. Rev.* 821 (1988); Carol Berry, "A California Juvenile's Right to Trial by Jury: An Issue Now Overripe for Consideration," 24 *San Diego L. Rev.* 1223 (1987); Note, "A Recommendation for Juvenile Jury Trials in Minnesota," 10 *Wm. Mitchell L. Rev.* 587 (1984); Edward J. McLaughlin and Lucia Beadel Whisenand, "Jury Trial, Public Trial and Free Press in Juvenile Proceedings: An Analysis and Comparison of the IJA/ABA, Task Force and NAC Standards," 46 *Brooklyn L. Rev.* 1 (1979); Sara E. Kropf, "Overturning *McKeiver v. Pennsylvania*: The Unconstitutionality of Using Prior Convictions to Enhance Adult Sentences Under the Sentencing Guidelines," 87 *Geo. L.J.* 2149, 2170 (1999) ("[I]t is unlikely that the juveniles involved in the juvenile court system—brought before judges, held in prison cells prior to a judicial hearing, counseled by attorneys—view it as anything but formal and adversarial."). What factors might a court examine in deciding whether "treatment" as a juvenile differs sufficiently from "punishment" as an adult as to warrant the procedural differences between the two system? *See* Martin Gardner, "Punishment and Juvenile Justice: A Conceptual Framework for Assessing Constitutional Rights of Youthful Offenders," 35 *Vand. L. Rev.* 791 (1982); Andrew Walkover, "The Infancy Defense in the New Juvenile Court," 31 *U.C.L.A. L. Rev.* 503 (1984); Barry C. Feld, "The Juvenile Court Meets the Principle of Offense: Punishment, Treatment, and the Difference it Makes," 68 *B. U. L. Rev.* 821 (1988); Kerrin C. Wolf, "Justice By Any Other Name: The Right to a Jury Trial and the Criminal Nature of Juvenile Justice in Louisiana," 12 *Wm. & Mary Bill Rts. J.* 275 (2003) (criticizing Louisiana Court's decision in *D.J.* for failing to recognize punitive nature of delinquency proceedings). Recall the factors that the Supreme Court in *Allen v. Illinois, supra* at p. 740, considered when it decided that the state did not "punish" Allen and therefore could deny him the protections of the Fifth Amendment privilege against self-incrimination.

    3) The Continuing Vitality of *McKeiver* in the Aftermath of Legislative Amendments to "Get Tough" and "Crack Down" on Youth Crime—"Punishment" versus "Treatment" Revisited We will defer until Chapter 8 a full discussion of recent changes in juvenile court sentencing legislation and juvenile justice dispositional and correctional practices. Suffice it to say, the differences between punishment and treatment remain central and crucial to the contemporary vitality of the Supreme Court's rationale in *McKeiver*. During the 1990s, virtually every state has revised its juvenile code to make it easier to transfer some youths to criminal court for prosecution as adults and to enable juvenile court judges to impose longer and more restrictive sanctions on those delinquents who remain within the juvenile court's jurisdiction. *See e.g.* Patricia Torbet, et al., *State Responses to Serious and Violent Juvenile Crime: Research Report* (1996) (summarizing recent changes in juvenile justice sentencing laws). Other analysts offer rationale to reconcile the contradictions between punishment and treatment within the juvenile justice system. *See e.g.,* David M. Altschuler, "Tough and Smart Juvenile Incarceration: Reintegrating Punishment, Deterrence and Rehabilitation," 14 *St. Louis U. Pub. L. Rev.* 217 (1994); Julianne P. Sheffer, "Serious and Habitual Juvenile Offender Statutes: Reconciling Punishment and Rehabilitation within the Juvenile Justice System." 48 *Vand. L. Rev.* 479 (1995); Gordon A. Martin, "The Delinquent and the Juvenile Court: Is there Still a Place for Rehabilitation," 25 *Conn. L. Rev.* 57 (1992); Barry C. Feld, "Violent Youth and Public Policy: A Case Study of Juvenile Justice Law Reform," 79 *Minn. L. Rev.* 965 (1995). As states "get tough," juveniles' renewed requests for a constitutional right to a jury trial force state supreme courts to re-evaluate the distinctions between treatment as a juvenile and punishment as an adult.

    The Wisconsin Supreme Court in **State v. Hezzie R.,** 219 Wis.2d 848, 580 N.W.2d 660 (Wis. 1998), reviewed the "get tough" revisions of the Wisconsin juvenile code and revisited the continuing vitality of the rationale of *McKeiver.* Three juveniles—one aged 13 and two aged 14 and charged with sexual assaults—challenged the constitutionality of amendments to the Juvenile Justice Code (JJC) that increased the severity and consequences of delinquency adjudications *and* eliminated a previous statutory right to jury trial in delinquency cases. The juveniles argued that as a result of statutory changes in the Juvenile Justice Code (JJC),

> a juvenile is potentially subject to: (1) a possible lifetime commitment as a sexually violent individual * * *; (2) a possible need to register as a sex offender; (3) a possible lifetime ban on the possession of a firearm; (4) an adjudication of delinquency being considered in any future adult sentencing; (5) an adjudication of delinquency being considered for future impeachment proceedings and in future bail hearings; (6) the possibility of several years of placement in a juvenile secured correctional facility; and (7) a possible transfer from a juvenile secured correctional facility to an adult prison.

The trial court reviewed the 1995 amendments, determined that "[t]he procedures of the juvenile court have become more like criminal court proceedings" because of the severity of delinquency sanctions, and concluded that due process considerations entitled the juveniles to a jury trial. Despite the statutory changes, the Wisconsin Supreme Court affirmed the continuing vitality of *McKeiver* and a Wisconsin precedent that found no state constitutional right to a jury trial in light of the statutory amendments. While acknowledging the increased severity and collateral consequences of delinquency adjudications, Justice CROOKS, for the majority, emphasized that many features of which the juveniles complained did not come into play as a direct result of a delinquency conviction but only in subsequent proceedings, for example, in a later sexual civil commitment proceeding, or in a later delinquency or criminal proceeding:

> The juveniles maintain that the potential disposition of long periods of placement in a juvenile secured correctional facility imposes punishment equivalent to confinement under the criminal code, particularly under the SJOP [Serious Juvenile Offender Program] provisions in the JJC. The juveniles argue that they may be placed in a secured facility for several years, even until the age of 25. * * *

> Placement in a juvenile secured correctional facility is an option available to the juvenile court judge, subject to certain criteria. * * * [A]ny placement in a child caring institution, or a Type 1 or Type 2 secured correctional facility is placement in a facility that solely houses juveniles. The juveniles are not housed with adult criminals. The distinctions between juvenile placement and adult criminal placement are maintained, allowing the focus of juvenile treatment and rehabilitation to remain intact. * * * Placement in a juvenile facility is not criminal punishment and does not convert the JJC into a criminal code. * * *

> The legislative intent and purpose in enacting the JJC * * * reflect a desire to balance the rehabilitative needs for care and treatment of each juvenile, with holding the juvenile accountable for his or her acts, and protecting the public. This balanced approach was adopted with the best interests of the juvenile and of society as the foundation. * * *

> [W]e conclude that the JJC is not a criminal code. As such, the United States Supreme Court precedent in *McKeiver* * * * remain[s] controlling. * * * [J]uvenile delinquency proceedings are not criminal proceedings. * * * [W]e conclude there is no violation of Wis. Const. art. I, § 7, or the Sixth and Fourteenth Amendments, for failure to provide juveniles with a trial by jury. * * *

> The juveniles' final argument is that the denial of the right to a jury trial violates the equal protection clauses of the Wisconsin and United States Constitutions. * * * Equal protection requires that there exist reasonable and practical grounds for the classifications created by the legislature. * * * We conclude that a reasonable basis exists in this case.

> In enacting the JJC, the JJSC and the legislature expressed concerns about negating delays in the juvenile justice system. The JJSC recommended that "[t]he system should operate more efficiently through streamlining of processes and improved access to information by entities

that work with juvenile delinquents." * * * This desire for immediate intervention bears a "reasonable and practical" relationship to the legislature's desire to rehabilitate and treat juvenile offenders and protect the public. The distinct nature of juvenile delinquency proceedings and the objectives of the legislature evince that there is a "rational basis" for attempting to streamline the proceedings by not affording juveniles the right to a jury trial. * * *

In summary, * * * our conclusion that the remaining non-criminal portions of the JJC are constitutional even absent the right to a trial by jury is consistent with the United States Supreme Court's decision in *McKeiver* and * * * with a majority of the states in the union which have determined that juveniles do not have a state or federal constitutional right to a trial by jury in the adjudicative phase of a juvenile delinquency proceeding.

In a dissenting opinion, BRADLEY, Justice, conducted a thorough analysis of the changes in the Wisconsin Juvenile Justice Code to determine whether is purpose and effect were functionally criminal in nature so as to require the protections of state constitutional right to a jury trial:

After reviewing the JJC under art. I, § 7, I conclude that in moving the JJC from Chapter 48 (the Children's Code) to Chapter 938 (adjoining the criminal code), the legislature * * * signaled a change in direction from the unbalanced approach of the Children's Code, which has the paramount purpose of promoting the "best interests of the child" to a balanced approach akin to the criminal code, which balances rehabilitative interests along with protection of the public and accountability of the offender.* * *

In moving the juvenile delinquency provisions and changing the JJC's purposes, dispositions, and long-term consequences to more closely resemble the criminal code, while at the same time eliminating the right to a jury trial, I conclude that the legislature's enactment of the JJC crosses over the constitutional line. * * *

The operative philosophy of the juvenile justice system in Wisconsin has been modified in a substantial and material fashion since * * * *McKeiver* [was] decided. To blindly rely on those precedents, which go not to whether the JJC is sufficiently criminal to invoke the protections of the art. I, § 7 of the Wisconsin constitution, but rather to fundamental fairness challenges to *parens patriae* juvenile laws which no longer exist is to ignore the real constitutional challenge before the court. * * * [I]t is incumbent upon this court to examine the JJC from a perspective unjaundiced by prior constitutional conclusions derived from different juvenile codes. * * * [T]he inquiry is whether the proceedings at hand may be fairly characterized in purpose and effect as being "criminal" in nature. * * *

[T]o determine whether a statute is civil or punitive, the Wis. Const. art. I, § 7 inquiry has two prongs. First, the stated intention of the legislature must be examined. Second, a determination must be made as to whether the code's purposes and effects are so criminal in nature as to defeat the legislature's separation of the juvenile code from the protections inherent in the adult criminal code. Upon review of the structure, expressed purposes, and substantive provisions of the JJC, I conclude that not only has the JJC shifted treatment of juvenile offenders in Wisconsin "closer to" the criminal sphere, it has dramatically crossed the constitutional line invoking art. I, § 7 of the Wisconsin constitution.

In adopting a new juvenile code, the Juvenile Justice Code, the legislature intended a substantive reorientation of the law as it affects children who have committed acts which, if they were adults, would subject them to criminal sanction. This intention is readily apparent from the changes in placement and expressed legislative purpose accomplished through the enactment of the JJC. * * * Indeed, as the Study Committee indicated, the JJC has been rebalanced to address young "law violators who often are physically and mentally mature and who have demonstrated a willingness to engage in serious and even heinous acts." * * *

[I]t is apparent that the legislature intended to focus not primarily on rehabilitation, as in the old Children's Code, but also on punishment of the juvenile offender and protection of the community. Such a balance of purposes is inconsistent with the old *parens patriae* theory of juvenile justice. * * *

Such a balanced approach is, however, consistent with the approach of the adult criminal system, i.e. protection of the public, accountability for the offense, and the rehabilitative needs of the adult offender. Thus, while the JJC may retain some effort to rehabilitate the juvenile offender for the juvenile offender's sake, that goal combined with the explicit concentration on accountability for the offense and community protection in order to "attack the juvenile criminal problem" directly parallel the considerations behind the criminal code. * * *

Having considered the expressed purposes behind the JJC, I turn then to an examination of the substantive provisions of the new juvenile code. Accordingly, I examine the dispositions and potential long-term consequences of a delinquency adjudication to determine if the JJC "acts" criminal. * * *

[T]he circuit court may order the juvenile placed in, among others, a foster home, a "secure detention facility or juvenile portion of a county jail," a "secured correctional facility," or the Serious Juvenile Offender Program administered by the Department of Corrections (the "Department"). Many of these dispositions parallel those available to adult courts in sentencing.

Of particular concern is the ability of a juvenile court to place a juvenile in secure confinement. For instance, * * * a juvenile who commits an act for which an adult may spend six months or more in jail may be confined to a secured correctional facility for a two-year period, thereafter renewable on an annual basis up to age 18, so long as the court determines that the juvenile is a "danger to the public and in need of restrictive custodial treatment." Thus, for committing a crime for which an adult may only spend six months incarcerated, a juvenile may actually spend up to eight years in a secured correctional facility. * * *

The JJC also makes many juvenile offenders subject to several post-adjudication continuing sanctions that are imposed on adults convicted of committing the same acts.

Like adult felons, juveniles found delinquent for acts which would constitute a felony are subject to a lifetime ban on the possession of a firearm. Like adult convicts, who can be impeached at subsequent court proceedings by their prior criminal convictions, juvenile offenders can be impeached through the introduction of their delinquency adjudications. Like adult convicts, the juvenile delinquency adjudication can be used against the juvenile for sentencing purposes in subsequent criminal proceedings. Like adult convicts, in the event a juvenile commits a sex-related offense, the juvenile can be required to register as a sexual offender for 15 years. * * *

Wisconsin's juvenile code has dramatically shifted its focus. It has moved from providing paternalistic guidance to misguided youths to a broader balance of holding youthful offenders accountable for their criminal actions, protecting the public from juvenile crime, and making the offenders more productive members of society. This change and the tools used to implement that change lead me to conclude that the JJC is a criminal code in purpose and effect and cannot be deemed a civil code designed solely to rehabilitate the juvenile * * *. We must either restore the juvenile court's primary rehabilitative approach or restore the constitutional right of juveniles to trial by jury. Constitutionally, the court cannot have it both ways. * * *

What is "rehabilitation"? How does a court know? How are the analytical strategies of the courts in *McKeiver*, *L.M.*, *D.J.*, and *Hezzie R.* similar? How do they differ? Do they consider primarily the law-on-the-books or the law-in-action? Recall that *Gault* emphasized the disjunctions between juvenile justice rhetoric and reality? If rhetoric and reality or the law-on-the-books and the law-in-action differ, how might a court discover the reality of juvenile justice for purposes of ascertaining whether sanctions punish or treat young offenders? Are these cases in which the judges characterize the therapy-glass as "half-full" or "half-empty"?

4) McKeiver, Punishment versus Treatment, and Transfer of Adjudicated Delinquents to Adult Correctional Facilities One of the reasons that the Supreme Court in *Gault* granted juveniles the privilege against self-incrimination was the possibility of their confinement in an adult institution. "Indeed, in over half of the States, there is not even assurance that the juvenile will be kept in separate institutions, apart from adult 'criminals.' In those States juveniles may be placed in or transferred to adult penal institutions after having been found 'delinquent' by a juvenile court." *See also*, *Allen v. Illinois*, *supra* p. 740. Following *McKeiver*, may a state adjudicate a juvenile as a delinquent without a jury trial and then transfer the juvenile to an adult facility for the completion of his sentence after he or she attains the age of criminal responsibility, for example, age seventeen in Louisiana? In **In re C.B.,** 708 So.2d 391 (La. 1998), discussed in *D.J.*, *supra*, p. 779, the Louisiana Supreme Court held that such a statutory process violated fundamental fairness:

[T]he Legislature passed a statute authorizing the Department of Public Safety and Corrections to promulgate a regulation requiring juveniles who have been adjudicated delinquent (not convicted of a crime) to be transferred to adult facilities upon reaching the age of seventeen. During their confinement in the adult facility, they are * * * to be treated for punitive purposes the same as the convicted adult felons with whom they are confined. * * *

We hold that [the statute is unconstitutional as applied because it] denies the juveniles their constitutional right to due process, and fundamental fairness inherent therein * * * because they receive a *de facto* criminal sentence to hard labor without being afforded the right to trial by jury. * * * [T]here has been recognized in the juvenile system a "quid pro quo" under which juveniles who are placed in adult facilities without the safeguards of due process that are enjoyed by adults will receive in return rehabilitative treatment rather than mere punitive incarceration. * * *

The determination that a jury trial was not constitutionally required in juvenile adjudications was predicated upon the non-criminal treatment of the adjudicated juvenile delinquent. It therefore stands to reason that if the civil trappings of the juvenile adjudication are sufficiently subverted, then a proceeding without that safeguard is fundamentally unfair, and thus, violative of due process. With these legal principles established, we turn to the issue now confronting this Court, which is the constitutionality of transferring adjudicated juvenile delinquents to penal facilities, where they will be required to perform hard labor, without first affording them the opportunity to have a jury trial. * * *

[The new statute] transfers juveniles to adult facilities where they are to be treated no differently than the adult felons with whom they are confined. According to the regulation, they are to participate in all work programs on the same basis as the adult prisoners and will be subject to the same disciplinary procedures. * * * Hard labor is by its nature punitive. It is a punishment reserved for convicted felons. * * * Although there is no difference in treatment in the penal aspects of their confinement, the transferred juveniles differ from their fellow adult inmates in that they have been confined to a penal institution without the entitlement to a trial by jury. In effect, then, these transferred juveniles, who by virtue of their adjudication in juvenile court have not been convicted of any crime, are receiving a *de facto* sentence to hard labor; a criminal sentence heretofore reserved by law only for persons *convicted* of serious felony offenses. * * *

We therefore hold that the statute through its corresponding regulation has sufficiently tilted the scales away from a "civil" proceeding, with its focus on rehabilitation, to one purely criminal. Due process and fundamental fairness therefore require that the juvenile who is going to be incarcerated at hard labor in an adult penal facility must have been convicted of a crime by a criminal jury, not simply adjudicated a delinquent by a juvenile court judge. To deprive the juvenile of such an important procedural safeguard upsets the quid pro quo under which the juvenile system must operate. The hallmark of special juvenile procedures is their non-criminal nature. If, after adjudication in the juvenile court, the juvenile can be committed to a place of penal servitude and required to perform hard labor alongside convicted felons, then "the entire claim of parens patriae becomes a hypocritical mockery." * * *

Similarly, the Wisconsin Supreme Court in **State v. Hezzie R., et al.,** 219 Wis.2d 848, 580 N.W.2d 660 (Wis. 1998), struck down the provisions of the Juvenile Justice Code that allowed the state to transfer a juvenile as young as fifteen years of age to an adult correctional facility. The court held that laws "providing for transfer of juveniles to adult prisons, result in a 'de facto criminal sentence.' Juveniles transferred under these provisions are subject to placement in the exact environment to which adults with criminal convictions are subject. In addition, those juveniles are subject to being housed with the general population of criminally convicted adults. However, the juveniles subject to placement in adult prisons are not afforded the right to a trial by jury, unlike the adult offenders." Why are these easier cases for the courts to decide than the separate question of whether delinquents enjoy a constitutional right to a jury trial for their adjudication?

5) Delinquents' Right to Waive the Jurisdiction of Juvenile Court in Order to Obtain a Jury Trial Because the vast majority of states deny to juveniles the right to a jury trial in juvenile court, may a youth charged with a crime "waive" her right to juvenile court and insist that her case be tried in criminal court in order to obtain a jury trial? Suppose that a juvenile has a good factual "reasonable doubt" case, for example, one that a jury might decide differently than a judge and result in acquittal? Or, suppose that a juvenile, currently charged with a minor offense but with an extensive prior record of delinquencies, realistically concludes that the juvenile court judge is likely to impose a delinquency sentence considerably longer than she would receive if convicted as an adult first-offender? *Compare In re K.A.A.,* 397 N.W.2d 4 (Minn. Ct. Ap. 1986) ("A juvenile may waive his limited right to treatment as a juvenile and be tried and sentenced as an adult."), *with In re K.A.A.,* 410 N.W.2d 836 (1987) (reversing and holding that "The Legislature could, and apparently did, conclude that allowing a juvenile to waive juvenile court jurisdiction for some perceived short-term benefit ignores the best interests of the State in addressing juvenile problems as well as the overall interest of the juvenile.").

In *In re Anna Marie S.,* 99 Cal.App.3d 869, 872, 160 Cal.Rptr. 495, 497 (Cal. Ct. Ap. 1979), the California Court of Appeals ruled that "the state does have a compelling interest in seeing that all juveniles who are amenable to treatment under the juvenile court law, will be treated as juveniles. The Legislature has determined that juvenile offenders should in most instances be treated differently from adults; this policy would be thwarted by allowing the juvenile to select the forum for trial. * * * Since appellant has no constitutional right to a jury trial, she has not been deprived of a fundamental due process interest." *Accord, In re D.B.,* 187 Ga.App. 3, 4, 369 S.E.2d 498, 499 (Ga. Ct. Ap. 1988) ("[A]t least with regard to the issue of his transfer for treatment as an adult criminal defendant, a juvenile must abide by the determination of others as to what will be in his best interests. * * *

Accordingly, we hold that appellant has no absolute right to waive juvenile court jurisdiction * * *.'')

6) The Right to a Jury and Punishment in Juvenile Court Suppose a state gives delinquents the right to a jury trial in juvenile court. If it decided to "treat" a juvenile and the treatment proved unsuccessful, could it then punish the youth? *McKeiver*, *D.J.*, *Hezzie R.*, and the other state cases struggled with the differences between treatment and punishment because they deny delinquents the right to a jury. However, if a state grants juveniles all adult criminal procedural safeguards including the right to a jury, then it may punish the youth without apology. As we saw in Chapter 6, *supra* pp. 586–598, about a dozen states have adopted this strategy with the passage of several variants of "blended sentencing" laws. Although the statutory details vary, once states try a delinquent with a jury, they may impose both juvenile treatment and adult punishment sentences with the execution of the latter stayed pending successful completion of the juvenile disposition.

2. JUVENILES' RIGHT TO A PUBLIC TRIAL

McKeiver did not directly decide the issue of public trials in delinquency proceedings. However, one of Justice Blackmun's reasons for rejecting a constitutional right to a jury was the concern that "If the jury trial were to be injected into the juvenile court system as a matter of right, it would bring with it * * * the public trial." What reasons or analysis does Justice Blackmun advance for the undesirability of public trials? Are there any countervailing considerations? Do *L.M.* or *D.J.* adequately address them? Justice Brennan concurred and dissented in *McKeiver* because he concluded that a public trial provided a functionally equivalent protection against governmental oppression as a jury trial by assuring the visibility and accountability of the process. Although most states continue to exclude the general public from delinquency hearings, another consequence of "get tough" law reforms has been to erode the traditional confidentiality of juvenile court proceedings.

R.L.R. v. STATE

487 P.2d 27 (Alaska 1971).

RABINOWITZ, JUSTICE. This appeal raises significant issues regarding the constitutional rights of a child to a public jury trial. * * * [The court first found that juveniles enjoyed a state constitutional right to jury trial. The court rejected the premise that "the benevolent social theory supposedly underlying juvenile court acts justifies dispensing with constitutional safeguards. This theory, based on the assumption that the special features of juvenile court procedure lead to less recidivism than ordinary adult criminal proceedings, has not been supported with empirical evidence, but even if it is true, this theory does not justify deprivation of constitutional rights. * * * If an honest analysis of constitutional requirements leads us to believe that they apply to children, we lack authority to withhold their application in deference to a popular social theory. * * * Since we conclude that RLR was entitled to a public jury trial under Alaska's constitutional guarantee, we need not pass upon the federal constitutional question."]

PUBLIC TRIAL

The Federal and Alaska's Constitutions provide that "(i)n all criminal prosecutions, the accused shall enjoy ('have' in Alaska's Constitution) the right to a * * * public trial * * *." The sentence guaranteeing the right also guarantees the rights to speedy trial and an impartial jury. The leading case on public trial, *Re Oliver*, holds that the Due Process Clause of the Fourteenth Amendment prohibits secret trials in criminal proceedings. *Oliver* says that the traditional Anglo–American distrust for secret trials has been attributed to the despotism of the Spanish Inquisition, the English Court of Star Chamber, and the French lettre de cachet, and quotes Bentham's charge that secret proceedings produce "indolent and arbitrary" judges, unchecked no matter how "corrupt" by recordation and appeal. The court cites as values of a public trial that it safeguards against attempts to employ the courts as instruments of persecution, restrains abuse of judicial power, brings the proceedings to the attention of key witnesses not known to the parties, and teaches the spectators about their government and gives them confidence in their judicial remedies. * * *

Many authorities favor a policy in delinquency proceedings of avoiding total secrecy by admitting persons with a special interest in the case or the work of the court, including perhaps the press, but prohibiting disclosure of juveniles' names and excluding the general public. Various reasons are given for this policy. It is said that permitting an audience to attend the hearing would interfere with the "case work relationship" between the judge and the child. Publicity is condemned on the grounds that it is an additional and excessive punishment to that prescribed by the court, or in the alternative that it encourages delinquency by permitting a youngster to "flaunt his unregeneracy." Publication of names of juvenile delinquents is condemned on the ground that it confirms the child in his delinquent identity and impedes his integration into law-abiding society by reducing his ability to obtain legitimate employment, qualify for licenses and bonds, and join the armed services. * * * Some commentary favors open court proceedings for juveniles on the grounds that secrecy and the informality engendered thereby hinders rehabilitation partly by misleading juveniles and their parents into underestimating the seriousness of delinquency. Recent commentary tends to be critical of secrecy because it screens from public view arbitrariness and lawlessness by juvenile courts. * * *

The reasons for the constitutional guarantees of public trial apply as much to juvenile delinquency proceedings as to adult criminal proceedings. Delinquency proceedings as much as adult criminal prosecutions can be used as instruments of persecution, and may be subject to judicial abuse. The appellate process is not a sufficient check on juvenile courts, for problems of mootness and the cost of prosecuting an appeal screen most of what goes on from appellate court scrutiny. We cannot help but notice that the children's cases appealed to this court have often shown much more extensive and fundamental error than is generally found in adult criminal cases, and wonder whether secrecy is not fostering a judicial attitude of casualness toward the law in children's proceedings. * * *

Therefore, we hold that children are guaranteed the right to a public trial by the Alaska Constitution. * * *

NOTES

1) Constitutional differences between jury trial and public trial The Louisiana Supreme Court in *D.J.* reconsidered its earlier holding in **In re Dino**, 359 So.2d 586 (La. 1978), to deny juveniles of a constitutional right to a jury trial. Significantly, *Dino* did find that juveniles enjoyed a constitutional right to a public trial. According to Judge DENNIS in *Dino*:

> A judicial proceeding which may result in the removal of a child from the custody of his parents and in his confinement until the age of twenty-one years is not essentially different from a criminal trial. The purpose of the juvenile adjudicatory proceeding is to decide whether the accused is responsible for prohibited conduct and, when based on a criminal violation, the consequences may be in effect the same as in the case of an adult. Indeed, it is even possible that ultimately it could result in the juvenile being incarcerated in a penal institution with adult offenders. * * * Because the consequences which confront a child who is alleged to have committed a criminal offense are essentially the same as those faced by adult criminal defendants, the protections which may be afforded by a public trial in juvenile proceedings corresponding to criminal cases are of great importance. * * *

> Accordingly, the right to a public trial is one of the fundamental rights in the American scheme of justice and it is included in the constitutions of both the United States and the state of Louisiana because it works analogously to a jury trial to protect the accused from possible oppression by exposing improper judicial behavior to the indignation of the community at large. * * * We hold therefore that [the juvenile confidentiality statute] is unconstitutional insofar as it prohibits a juvenile from electing a public trial in adjudicatory proceedings based on criminal charges which would entitle an adult accused to have his trial conducted in public. * * *

Opening delinquency proceedings and sharing records with other agencies such as schools represent one of the recent areas of policy changes in juvenile justice administration. *See*, Patricia Torbet, et al., *State Responses to Serious and Violent Juvenile Crime* 36 (1996), who report that "Since 1992, State legislatures have increasingly called for a presumption of open proceedings and the release of juvenile offenders' names. * * * From 1992 through 1995, 10 States passed legislation that modified or created statutes that open juvenile proceedings. In all, 22 States require or permit open juvenile court hearings of cases involving either juveniles charged with violent or other serious offenses or juveniles who are repeat offenders."

R.L.R. questioned the validity of the "benevolent social theory" of juvenile courts that deny public hearings. What reasons did *R.L.R.* and *Dino* present to reject the conclusion in *McKeiver*? The American Bar Association, *Juvenile Justice Standards Relating to Adjudication Standard 4.1(a), commentary* at 54 (1980) recommend that juveniles should have a right to public trial. The Standards emphasize that the current practice of allowing attendance by students, social workers, lawyers, social scientists, and other observers of the court without any specific "interest" in the particular child or case already vitiates the promise of confidentiality without affording the benefits of a public hearing. The Standards also question whether traditional juvenile court practices have elevated the "benefits" of confidentiality over those of a public trial without adequately appraising the benefits of a public trial. What are the benefits of confidentiality? Does maintaining closed proceedings entail any off-setting costs for juveniles or the public? Is it important that "justice be seen to be done"? Does confidentiality benefit juveniles or does it hide judicial lawlessness? Does confidentiality erode public confidence that juvenile courts adequately control serious young offenders? *See* Eugene H. Czajkoski, "Why Confidentiality in Juvenile Justice?," 33 *Juv. & Fam. Ct. J.* 49 (1982).

2) Conflicting policies of public versus confidential delinquency proceedings If you were a legislator trying to decide whether to retain confidential hearings or to open juvenile court proceedings, what information would you need in order to answer these questions and make an informed policy judgment? An essay by **Judge Leonard P. Edwards, "Confidentiality and the Juvenile and Family Courts," 55 *Juv. & Fam. Ct. J.* 1, 3–6 (2004)**, summarizes the conflicting policy considerations involved in deciding whether to provide public and media access to juvenile and family court proceedings:

First, many in the public, including the media, regard court proceedings as public proceedings. They argue that the public has a right to know the details of court cases because they are public. * * *

Second, it is argued that openness will encourage all participants in the family court process to comply with the law and produce better, more timely decisions for families appearing in the courts. If the courts, attorneys, and the parties know the public is watching, they will improve their performance.

Third, many in the public also believe that openness in court proceedings is necessary to hold parties accountable for their actions. Public access fosters the appearance of fairness, thereby heightening public respect for the judicial process and for the law. * * *

Fourth, some argue that courts should be open because they are publicly funded and decide issues of public interest and concern. * * *

Fifth, many believe that opening proceedings to the public will bring more public attention to these cases and also may encourage more community support for the programs and resources to address the problems faced by the children and families appearing in the family court.

Sixth, some commentators have stated that protection of our most vulnerable citizens, our children, is public business and is of great public concern. * * *

Seventh, some claim that openness will educate the public on how the family court system handles cases. * * *

Eighth, many point out that openness will not involve a significant loss of privacy to the parties since few spectators will actually come to the court even if the courtrooms are open. The experience in several states seems to confirm this observation. Additionally, in smaller communities the names and facts of court cases are usually well known to the public anyway because of informal information exchanges.

Many others challenge the notion that all family court proceedings should be open to the public. * * * First, they argue that citizens have a right to privacy that the courts should uphold. They point out that court cases usually involve extraordinary accusations and facts potentially embarrassing to the parties. Many parties in those cases would prefer that the public not know about the sordid details of the legal actions they are involved in. * * *

Second, some confidentiality proponents claim that opening the courts will discourage citizens from turning to the courts. * * *

Third, many argue that some legal proceedings should not be public because public disclosure would harm the individuals in the case. The harm might be inflicted on parties and witnesses, but the most important interest is the right of children not to be * * * unfairly labeled and stigmatized within the community, and their names will remain forever in the public record * * *.

Fourth, confidentiality has been a hallmark of juvenile court proceedings since the first juvenile court was created in 1899. The juvenile court creators believed that by keeping juvenile court proceedings out of the public eye, children could better be rehabilitated without the stigma of public knowledge following them into adulthood. * * *

Fifth, some confidentiality proponents point out that confidentiality can facilitate settlement. * * *

Sixth, several appellate courts have stressed that the public policy of confidentiality is an integral part of the informal and non-adversarial nature of juvenile court hearings and that publicity can potentially endanger the fairness of the proceedings and disrupt the adjudication process.

Seventh, some commentators state that opening hearings will make no difference because neither the parties nor the courts will be more accountable to the public, and because more resources will not be allocated to the system. * * *

The law should declare that legal proceedings are to be held in open court unless the privacy rights of one of the participants outweigh the public interest in the proceedings. Thus, courtrooms should be open to the public, even in the family court. Opening courtrooms would immediately end the suspicion that the courts have something to hide, that courts are secreting something of importance from the public, or that those charged with public tasks are not discharging their duties. * * *

The public should be able to see how these courts operate. The judge should have authority to determine the number of people who may attend so that the proceedings can retain some intimacy and not be over-crowded. Further, the judge should be prepared to place conditions on public access depending on the case. For child protection or less serious juvenile delinquency cases, for example, one condition would be that any person attending the proceedings shall not reveal the parties' names or other identifying information about a particular case. This use of judicial discretion is not new because some state statutes already authorize this balancing process. * * *

When the court exercises its discretion to close a court proceedings, the statutory scheme should require the court to make a finding regarding the balance between the public's right to know and the parties' privacy interests. The balancing process should address the following factors: 1) the type of case; 2) the public interest in the particular case; 3) the potential harm that might be inflicted on any party to the legal action were identifying information released to the public; 4) any negative consequences public access may have on the integrity of the legal proceedings; and 5) the amount of information the public already has obtained about the particular case through other sources. * * *

Juvenile delinquency proceedings in which a youth is charged with serious delinquent behavior such as homicide would be open to the public in most cases. The public interest in the legal decisions that must be made is great and the impact on public life is significant. * * * The public needs to know how the accountability provided by the court system works. This balance in the weighing process will change depending on the nature of the hearing, the seriousness of the crime, and the age and sophistication of the youth. * * *

3) Closed and confidential delinquency proceedings—new lessons from history Although Judge Edwards asserts that juvenile court proceedings were closed from the inception of the Cook County juvenile court in 1899, recent research indicates that delinquency proceedings were open to the public for the first decade of the courts' existence. *See* David S. Tanenhaus, "The Evolution of Juvenile Courts in the Early Twentieth Century: Beyond the Myth of Immaculate Construction," in M. K. Rosenheim, F. E. Zimring, D. S. Tanenhaus, and B. Dorhn, eds., *A Century of Juvenile Justice* 43–44 (2002). Despite the Progressives' desire to shield children from the stigma of publicity, the initial open proceedings reflected Catholic immigrants' distrust of predominantly Protestant "private charity organizations" whom they feared would take their children. Because delinquency proceedings initially were open to the public, juvenile court supporters used them to educate the public about the juvenile court, to explain its rehabilitative mission, and to establish its legitimacy.

> Although the Progressives wanted to protect the privacy of the individual child in court, they also sought to publicize the plight of poor children in general. Case histories, which included a great deal of information about a child but not his or her actual name, served as one way of meeting the twin goals of educating the public about children through accounts of specific children who remained nameless. Id. at 63.

See also, David S. Tanenhaus, *Juvenile Justice in the Making* 25 (2004), who observes that "Most of the features that later became the hallmarks of progressive juvenile justice—private hearings, confidential records, a detention home, and a professional probation staff—were not present at creation. As a result, the world's first juvenile court opened with a public hearing and a public record. * * * "

4) Academic commentary on public delinquency proceedings Academic commentators divide more about the issue of public trial than they do about the desirability of a jury trial in delinquency proceedings. Proponents of openness contend that it provides a necessary check on the exercise of judicial discretion. *See* Note, "The Public Right of Access to Juvenile Delinquency Hearings," 81 *Mich. L. Rev.* 1540 at 1550–51 (1983), which asserts:

> [A]ccess to juvenile delinquency hearings would function as a check on the abuse of power by judges, probation officers, and other public officials. The nature of the juvenile justice system, even more than the criminal system, suggests a compelling need to check the exercise of government power. Juvenile court judges, for example, exercise more discretion than their criminal trial counterparts. * * * Such a system relies heavily on subjective judgments, making the "compliant, biased, or eccentric judge" a particular hazard. Juvenile court judges, moreover, are often less qualified and less competent than other judges. As a result, juvenile courts often commit "much more extensive and fundamental error than is generally found in adult criminal cases." Because juvenile cases are only rarely appealed, public scrutiny of the juvenile justice system takes on added importance as a check against official misconduct. Finally, judges, not juries, decide most delinquency cases. Thus, the juvenile is unable to appeal to the community conscience, as embodied in the jury, to protect against abuse of government power.

Others continue to subscribe to "benevolent social theory" and emphasize that "punishment" entails a ritual public ceremony of indignation and denunciation which is inappropriate to juvenile courts. *See* David Katz, "The Grim Reality of Open Juvenile Delinquency Hearings," 28 *N.Y. L. Sch. L. Rev.* 101 (1983). *See also*, David Howard, J. Thomas Grisso and Robert Neems, "Publicity and Juvenile Court Proceedings," *Clearinghouse Review* 203 (July 1977).

The issues of closed proceedings become even more complicated when they involve conflicts between juvenile "confidentiality" and the First Amendment and press access. Recall, *Smith v. Daily Mail, supra* p. 355. *See. e.g.*, Susan D. Cohen, "Reconciling Media Access with Confidentiality for the Individual in Juvenile Court," 20 *Santa Clara L. Rev.* 405 (1980); Stephen Jonas, "Press Access to the Juvenile Courtroom: Juvenile Anonymity and the First Amendment," 17 *Col. J. L. & Soc. Probs.* 287 (1982); D. Mark McIntyre, "Juvenile Court Proceedings: The Conflict Between Juvenile Anonymity and Freedom of the Press," 23 *S. Tex. L. J.* 383 (1982); Harry Todd, "The Right of Access and Juvenile Delinquency Hearings: The Future of Confidentiality," 16 *Ind. L.Rev.* 911 (1983); Allyson Dunn, "Juvenile Court Records: Confidentiality vs. The Public's Right to Know," 23 *Am. Crim. L. Rev.* 379 (1986); Jill K. McNulty, "First Amendment versus Sixth Amendment: A Constitutional Battle in the Juvenile Courts," 10 *N. Mex. L. Rev.* 311 (1980).

D. NOTICE OF CHARGES

The Supreme Court in *Gault* required that "the child and his parents or guardian be notified, in writing, of the specific charge or factual allegations to be considered at the hearing, and that such written notice be given at the earliest practicable time, and in any event sufficiently in advance of the hearing to permit preparation. Due process of law requires notice of the sort we have described—that is, notice which would be deemed constitutionally adequate in a civil or criminal proceeding. It does not allow a hearing to be held in which a youth's freedom and his parents' right to his custody are at stake without giving them timely notice, in advance of the hearing, of the specific issues that they must meet."

However, the *Gault* Court's reliance on the "due process" clause left unanswered a number of questions. Does the language "adequate in a civil or criminal proceeding" require the state to file a petition alleging probable cause as in a criminal charging document? Does the language that "the child and his parents or guardian [must] be notified" give parents a constitutional right to notice as well as the delinquent? What effect does the state's inability to locate or notify a parent have on the validity of a delinquency adjudication or transfer decision? May the state amend its petition during the trial if the facts and offense proven differ from those initially alleged?

N.Y. Fam. Ct. § 311.1 The petition; definition and contents (McKinney's 1999)

1. A petition originating a juvenile delinquency proceeding is a written accusation by an authorized presentment agency.

2. A petition shall charge at least one crime and may, in addition, charge in separate counts one or more other crimes. * * *

3. A petition must contain:

(a) the name of the family court in which it is filed;

(b) the title of the action;

(c) the fact that the respondent is a person under sixteen years of age at the time of the alleged act or acts;

(d) a separate accusation or count addressed to each crime charged, if there be more than one;

(e) the precise crime or crimes charged;

(f) a statement in each count that the crime charged was committed in a designated county;

(g) a statement in each count that the crime charged therein was committed on, or on or about, a designated date, or during a designated period of time;

(h) a plain and concise factual statement in each count which, without allegations of an evidentiary nature, asserts facts supporting every element of the crime charged and the respondent's commission thereof with sufficient precision to clearly apprise the respondent of the conduct which is the subject of the accusation;

(i) the name or names, if known, of other persons who are charged as co-respondents in the family court or as adults in a criminal court proceeding in the commission of the crime or crimes charged;

(j) a statement that the respondent requires supervision, treatment or confinement; and

(k) the signature of the appropriate presentment attorney. * * * * *

N.Y. Fam. Ct. § 311.2. Sufficiency of petition (McKinney's 1999)

A petition, or a count thereof, is sufficient on its face when: * * *

2. the allegations of the factual part of the petition, together with those of any supporting depositions which may accompany it, provide reasonable cause to believe that the respondent committed the crime or crimes charged; and

3. non-hearsay allegations of the factual part of the petition or of any supporting depositions establish, if true, every element of each crime charged and the respondent's commission thereof.

In *In the Matter of Jahron S.*, 79 N.Y.2d 632, 635, 584 N.Y.S.2d 748, 751, 595 N.E.2d 823, 826 (Ct. App. 1992), the Court of Appeals of New York elaborated on the contents of the petition:

> The phrasing of these statutes makes it clear that a juvenile delinquency petition may in actuality consist of two separate parts: the formal petition itself, which must conform to the requirements of Family Court Act § 311.1; and any supporting depositions that may be attached to and filed with the formal petition. Thus, where one or more supporting depositions accompany a petition, the petition and the depositions together must satisfy the facial sufficiency requirements of the Family Court Act. * * * A petition is 'the sole instrument for the commencement, prosecution, and adjudication of the juvenile delinquency proceeding'. In this, the petition is very similar to a criminal information, which is governed by the Criminal Procedure Law, not the Family Court Act, but which, like a Family Court petition, 'may serve as a basis both for the commencement of a criminal action and for the prosecution thereof,' and must contain '[n]on-hearsay allegations * * * [that] establish, if true, every element of the offense charged and the defendant's commission thereof,' * * * Family Court Act § 311.2 clearly contemplates * * * that supporting depositions may be filed in addition to petitions and that the sufficiency of the petition is to be measured by the factual allegations contained not only in the petition itself but also in any supporting depositions that may be attached to it. While no definition of the term 'supporting deposition' is contained in the Family Court Act, such a definition is contained at CPL 100.20, which provides that '[a] supporting deposition is a written instrument * * * containing

factual allegations of an evidentiary character, based either upon personal knowledge or upon information and belief, which supplement those of the accusatory instrument and support or tend to support the charge or charges contained therein.' Although Family Court Act § 303.1(1) provides that '[t]he provisions of the criminal procedure law shall not apply to proceedings under this article unless the applicability of such provisions are specifically prescribed by this act,' we believe that this section of the CPL is nonetheless instructive here in that supporting depositions serve the same function in Family Court petitions as they do in informations, simplified informations, misdemeanor complaints and felony complaints: they supplement the factual allegations contained in the petition and tend to support the charges.* * *

As we saw in Chapter Five, the Fourth Amendment requires a petition stating probable cause for juveniles held in pre-trial detention because of the "seizure" of the person. However, unlike the New York Family Court practice which contemplates a probable cause statement either as part of the allegations of the petition or by supplemental depositions that establish "reasonable cause," most states do not require a petition to allege probable cause that the child committed a crime, unless the youth is held in detention. *See e.g., Cal. Welf. & Inst. Code* § 656 (f) (1999) ("A concise statement of facts * * * to support the conclusion that the minor * * * is a person within the definition [of the jurisdiction of juvenile court]"); *Md. R. Proc. Juv. Causes* 11–103 (2)(c) (1998) ("The facts, in clear and simple language, on which the allegations are based"); *Minn. R. Juv. Proc.* 6.03 Subd. 3(A) and (B) (1999) ("a concise statement alleging the child is delinquent" and "a description of the alleged offense and reference to the statute or ordinance which was violated"). Typical of the statutes and court rules which do not require a full-blown probable cause statement is *North Carolina* § 7A–560 (1998) which provides that "A petition in which delinquency is alleged shall contain a plain and concise statement, without allegations of an evidentiary nature, asserting facts supporting every element of a criminal offense and the juvenile's commission thereof with sufficient precision clearly to apprise the juvenile of the conduct which is the subject of the accusation"; *In the Interest of A.W.*, 438 N.W.2d 557, 559 (S.D. 1989) ("We have never specifically explained the proper test for determining the sufficiency of a delinquency petition. Given the fact that it is similar in content to the necessary allegations of a criminal information, we hold that the test of the sufficiency of a petition of delinquency is whether it apprises a juvenile with reasonable certainty of the nature of the accusation against him so that he may prepare his defense and plead the judgment as a bar to any subsequent prosecution for the same offense.")

NOTES

1) Delinquency Petitions and Probable Cause To what extent do the notice and charging provisions for juveniles differ from those used for adult criminal defendants? Is "a plain and concise statement, without allegations of an evidentiary nature," the same as a statement of probable cause typically used in an adult criminal complaint or indictment? Recall from *Lanes v. State, supra* p. 170, the importance of probable cause to protect the individual against unjustified state intervention. Are there advantages for the juvenile and the state by requiring a statement of probable cause in every petition? *See* Barry C. Feld, "Criminalizing Juvenile Justice: Rules of Procedure for the Juvenile Court," 69 *Minn. L. Rev.* 141, 217–229 (1984):

> [P]robable cause serves a variety of salutary functions in the charging process. It strengthens the initial prosecutorial screening function by requiring a prompt evidentiary review of the underlying factual bases of an action to eliminate those cases that lack prosecutive merit, that may have insuperable evidentiary difficulties, or that may be motivated by malice or negligence. * * * A probable cause statement also supplies the notice required by *Gault* in juvenile cases by providing the fullest factual and legal notice of charges. A full notice requirement assists the state in framing the issues and aids the defense in preparing to respond to them. The factual information contained in the probable cause statement furnishes avenues for investigation and discovery that assure the fairest determination of ultimate questions of guilt or innocence. Finally, a probable cause requirement in the petition forces prosecutors to charge juveniles more realistically, in light of what the prosecutor can reasonably expect to prove, and provides a partial check on prosecutorial practices of overcharging as a prelude to plea bargaining. * * *

2) Failure to Notify a Juvenile's Parents as a Constitutional Violation or a Reversible Error Does the failure to notify a juvenile's parents constitute a basis to reverse a delinquency adjudication? The court in **United States v. Watts**, 513 F.2d 5 (10th Cir.1975) reasoned that:

> Although the express language in *Gault* requiring that notice be given to both the juvenile and his parents is unequivocal, we are not convinced that the failure of such notice to the parents must lead in all cases to the automatic reversal of the juvenile's adjudication as a delinquent.

> Our review of the decision in *Gault* and our search of other authorities does not convince us that there exists a separate and independent due process right to notice of delinquency proceedings belonging to the parents of the juvenile defendant. * * * However, because the parents are not parties to the present action we need not now decide whether such a right exists, and if so whether it has been violated. Further, we do not and need not decide what remedy may be available or appropriate.

> Instead, our concern on this appeal is solely with whether a violation of the standard established in *Gault* requiring that notice be given to a juvenile's parents constitutes such a deprivation of the juvenile's right to due process as to, *per se*, require a reversal of the determination of his delinquency. * * *

> [T]he purpose underlying statutes requiring notice to parents is to 'furnish a safeguard to minors accused of crimes by requiring that the opportunity be made available for consultation and advice with the

individuals, who, society must assume, are those most vitally concerned with the minor's best interests.' The basic right protected by such safeguards is that of the child to be made aware of the charges against him and to be assured a reasonable opportunity to prepare his defense. In this regard, the parents' function would seem to be similar to that of legal counsel. * * *

Where, as here, however, it is clear that the juvenile has not, in fact, been denied due process (even though there has been a technical violation of a prophylactic safeguard established to protect that right), we see no need for a *per se* rule requiring reversal. * * *

By contrast, other jurisdictions have construed statutes that require parental notification as a mandatory provision. Failure to comply with the statutory mandate requires reversal of a juvenile's adjudication or waiver to criminal court. *See e.g.*, *Karim v. Commonwealth*, 21 Va.App. 652, 466 S.E.2d 772 (Va. Ct. Ap. 1996): "A mandatory provision in a statute is one that connotes a command and the omission of 'which renders the proceeding to which it relates illegal and void, while a directory provision is one the observance of which is not necessary to the validity of the proceeding; and a statute may be mandatory in some respects, and directory in others.' * * * [W]e find that compliance with the Code sections at issue here, relating to procedures for instituting proceedings against juveniles and for transferring jurisdiction to a circuit court, are mandatory and jurisdictional. The failure to strictly follow the notice procedures contained in the Code denied appellant a substantive right and the constitutional guarantee of due process." *Accord*, *Baker v. Commonwealth*, 28 Va.App. 306, 504 S.E.2d 394 (Va. Ct. Ap. 1998): "A plain reading of [the Code] manifests legislative intent that both parents be notified and dispenses with this requirement only when the trial judge has certified on the record that the identity of a parent is not reasonably ascertainable. * * * At the least, the Commonwealth was required to make a reasonable inquiry as to the address of [the juvenile's father], and, if the address could not be ascertained '[a]fter reasonable effort,' to effect service of the summons by publication."

3) Refiling A Delinquency Petition In **In re Nan P.**, 230 Cal.App.3d 751, 281 Cal.Rptr. 468 (Cal. Ct. App. 1991), the California Court of Appeals considered whether a statute that prevents the state from recharging an adult offender once a court dismissed a misdemeanor charge also prohibited it from refiling a misdemeanor petition against a juvenile offender:

[T]he purpose of Penal Code section 1387 was to give the People only 'one bite at the apple' where the crime was less serious, causing a somewhat insignificant impact upon the general public. Such a differentiation between felonies and misdemeanors was irrelevant to the juvenile justice system's purpose, 'which is not protection of the public,' but the 'spiritual, emotional, mental, and physical welfare of the minor. * * * * ' "

The state's primary purpose in bringing juveniles who violate the criminal law into the juvenile court system is rehabilitation; with adults it is punishment. Penal Code section 1387 recognizes a dichotomy in adult cases between felonies and misdemeanors; the fact misdemeanors are generally less serious crimes, carrying less potential punishment, warrants the statutory policy of terminating such actions upon a single dismissal in adult cases. Since the primary purpose of the juvenile system is to rehabilitate a youthful offender, juvenile "misdemeanors" tend to follow the same procedure as juvenile "felonies." The focus is to find an effective rehabilitative means to modify the juvenile's behavior as soon as that behavior comes to the attention of the system. The state has a strong interest "in monitoring juvenile conduct in order to 'nip budding character defects before they blossom into adult criminal behavior.' " * * *

IN RE STEVEN G.

210 Conn. 435, 556 A.2d 131 (Conn.1989).

GLASS, ASSOCIATE JUSTICE. The state brought a petition to adjudicate the respondent, Steven G., a juvenile delinquent on the basis of a charge of criminal liability for robbery in the second degree. After the trial had commenced, the trial court permitted the state, pursuant to Practice Book § 1029,[3] to amend its petition to add four additional charges arising out of the same incident. Subsequently, the respondent was adjudicated a delinquent. On appeal, the Appellate Court upheld the trial court's allowance of the amendment on the ground that, in juvenile proceedings, a standard of "fundamental fairness" governs mid-trial amendments rather than the stricter provisions applicable to adult proceedings. We granted the respondent's petition for certification limited to the following issue: "In juvenile delinquency proceedings, what standard governs the authority of the state, after the commencement of trial, to amend the petition to include additional charges?" We conclude that the Appellate Court correctly applied the appropriate standard, and we therefore affirm its judgment. * * *

[On February 3, 1986, the state charged respondent with robbery in the second degree. On July 9, 1986, the trial commenced. The complainant testified that she was working alone in a natural food store in New Haven when two boys came into the store. One boy went to the rear of the store and engaged her in conversation while the other boy went to the front of the store, put his hand on the cash register, and pushed the buttons. When the complainant went to the front of the store, the boy ordered her to "open the drawer," which she did because she felt "threatened." While at the front of the store, the victim paid no attention to the boy at the back of the store, and could not testify about what he did. She could not identify the respondent "with certainty." After one of the boys took the money from the cash register, both boys "flew" out of the store. She did not see the boy at the back of the store take money from the register. The state then called the co-respondent, Ted F., as its next witness. Ted testified that he and respondent were walking around the State Street

---

3. Practice Book § 1029 provides: "A petition may be amended at any time by the court on its own motion or in response to the motion of any interested party prior to the final adjudication of delinquency or neglect. When an amendment has been so ordered, a continuance shall be granted whenever the court finds that the new allegations in the petition, as amended, justify the need for additional time to permit the parties to respond adequately to the additional or changed facts and circumstances."

area of New Haven "[planning] to go rob a store." When they came to the complainant's store, they decided to rob it. Ted testified that he and respondent entered the store, respondent went to the back of the store, and Ted went to the cash register and "tapped some buttons." Ted testified that the victim came to the front of the store and opened the cash register. He stated that respondent "snatched money first" from the register and that he then took the rest.]

Shortly after the beginning of the cross-examination of Ted, the respondent's counsel requested a recess, which the trial court granted. On the date that the trial resumed, July 16, 1986, the state filed a motion to amend the petition against the respondent to add four additional charges arising out of the same incident. The respondent and his mother were provided with notice of the amended petition on that date. The four additional charges in the amended petition were: (1) conspiracy to commit robbery in the second degree; (2) larceny in the sixth degree; (3) conspiracy to commit larceny in the sixth degree; and (4) criminal liability for larceny in the fifth degree. The respondent's counsel objected to the added charges claiming that they violated the respondent's right to notice of the charges against him, his right to counsel and to present a defense, and that the added charges prejudiced the respondent. The state argued that an amendment was proper under Practice Book § 1029, claiming that the additional charges were brought because it had been "surprised" by Ted's testimony. The trial court, pursuant to Practice Book § 1029, permitted the amended petition, and continued the case for one week until July 23, 1986, for completion of the trial. On July 21, 1986, the respondent filed a motion to dismiss the four additional charges. The trial court denied the motion on July 23, 1986. Thereafter, * * * the respondent entered a plea of nolo contendere to a reduced charge of conspiracy to commit robbery in the third degree. The respondent's plea was conditioned on his right to appeal the denial of his motion to dismiss. The respondent subsequently was adjudicated a delinquent child and was committed to the department of children and youth services for a period not to exceed two years.

The respondent argues that juveniles charged with delinquency offenses have a right to the same standard of fair and adequate notice of the charges against them in advance of trial as is constitutionally mandated for adult criminal defendants. He claims that the addition of four new and different charges against him after the commencement of trial * * * violated rights secured to him by the sixth and fourteenth amendments to the United States constitution and also article third, § 8 of the Connecticut constitution. In support of this claim the respondent relies principally on *In re Gault*, and Practice Book § 624.[6] * * *

---

6. Practice Book § 624 provides: "After commencement of the trial for good cause shown, the judicial authority may permit the prosecuting authority to amend the information or indictment at any time before a verdict or finding if no additional or different offense is charged and no substantive rights of the defendant would be prejudiced. An amendment may charge an additional or different offense with the express consent of the defendant."

Despite the state's assertions to the contrary, there can be no question that a mid-trial amendment to an information adding different charges in an adult criminal proceeding is violative of due process. "The state's right to amend must be limited to substitutions that do not charge the defendant with an additional or different offense because the defendant has a constitutional right to fair notice, prior to the commencement of trial, of the charges against which he must defend himself. *In re Gault*, however, did not address the issue of midtrial amendments to charges in juvenile delinquency proceedings. * * * "

Although some criminal trial standards have been implemented in juvenile delinquency proceedings, the public policy of Connecticut as expressed in the General Statutes contemplates a distinction between juvenile matters and criminal matters. * * * We note particularly that a juvenile delinquency hearing is circumscribed by Practice Book § 1034(1), which provides: "The hearing shall not be conducted as a criminal trial; the proceedings shall be at all times as informal as the requirements of due process and fairness permit."

In synthesizing the "fundamental fairness" analysis applicable to juvenile proceedings with the language of *In re Gault* pertinent to the sixth amendment right to notice, we conclude that the Appellate Court did not err in upholding the trial court's allowance of the amended petition.[9]

---

9. The respondent has cited a number of decisions from other jurisdictions to support his claim that a petition in a juvenile delinquency proceeding cannot be amended at midtrial to add different offenses under *In re Gault*. None of these cases, however, involved midtrial amendments. *See D.L., Jr. v. State* (Fla.App.1986) (no amendment issue); *D.P. v. State* (1973) (receiving stolen goods not lesser included offense of burglary; no amendment issue); *In re Interest of Bryant* (1974) (defective original petition); *Interest of Korkosz* (La.App.1980) (issue is whether state proved alleged offense beyond reasonable doubt).

The respondent also cites the Arizona Court of Appeal's opinion *In re Appeal in Maricopa County* (1974), which only addressed the issue whether trespass is a lesser included offense of burglary. In that case, the juvenile was charged with burglary. Based on the evidence at trial, however, the trial court found that the juvenile had committed a trespass, and entered an adjudication of delinquency. The court of appeals reversed the trial court's decision, on the basis that trespass was not a lesser included offense of burglary. That decision, however, was subsequently vacated by the Arizona Supreme Court. The court first determined that the court of appeals was correct in concluding that trespass was not a lesser included offense of burglary. The court, however, reversed the lower court upon the following ground: "Nevertheless the adjudication of delinquency may still be upheld. Rule 4(b), Rules of Procedure for the Juvenile Court provides that 'A petition may be amended by order of the court at any time on its own motion or in response to the motion of any interested party before an adjudication; provided the parties are notified and granted sufficient time to meet the new allegations.' * * * It is apparent from the foregoing that the court had in effect amended the petition alleging acts of delinquency on the part of the juvenile * * *. However it appears from the record that the court should have permitted the parties sufficient opportunity to meet the new allegations. Therefore it is necessary to remand the case to the juvenile court in order to permit the parties an opportunity to address themselves to the allegation that the juvenile had committed trespass."

A number of cases the respondent fails to cite, although arguably more on point, are ultimately distinguishable from the present case. In *In re Roy C.* (1985), the court held that the trial court erred in allowing the state, after it had rested its case, to amend the petition to include another offense that was not a lesser included offense of the original charge. In that case, however, "no continuance was offered to prevent prejudice to [the juvenile]." The court noted that, "given adequate time," the juvenile could have developed a defense to the new charge. See also *In Interest of Becker*, (1988) (holding that amendment at close of commonwealth's case alleging new charge violated due process; no discussion of effect of possible continuance); *In Interest of Bonner*

As we noted above, *In re Gault*, requires that "notice be given at the earliest practicable time, and in any event sufficiently in advance of the hearing to permit preparation." In the present case, the respondent, his attorney and his mother had known of the incident underlying the charges in both the original and the amended petitions since February 3, 1986. The state claims that Ted's "surprise" testimony on the first day of the hearing prompted it to add the additional charges. The respondent has not challenged the state's motives for adding the new charges, nor has he suggested that the additional charges resulted from bad faith on the part of the state. Further, the trial court continued the case for one week after allowing the amendment. Since the state had presented its witnesses' testimony and the respondent had begun his cross-examination of the co-respondent before the continuance, the continuance allowed the respondent to consider the scope of his further cross-examination of the co-respondent, and to investigate the new charges. Moreover, the continuance also allowed him to consider calling witnesses on his own behalf, and otherwise to challenge the evidence presented against him. The respondent has not claimed that the continuance did not provide adequate time to prepare a defense against the additional charges. * * *

Because Practice Book § 1029 requires a continuance if the new allegations justify additional time for preparation, and because the trial court ordered a continuance, we conclude that the respondent was given notice "at the earliest practicable time * * * sufficiently in advance of" the scheduled court proceedings. Nothing in *In re Gault* establishes a per se rule forbidding a midtrial amendment to a petition of delinquency adding substantively different charges arising out of the same incident. We conclude that the respondent's federal and state constitutional rights were not violated. It follows that the provisions of Practice Book § 624, which are inapplicable to juvenile delinquency proceedings, do not apply to the present case by reason of constitutional mandate.

We affirm the judgment of the Appellate Court.

NOTES

1) Limitations on Amendment of Petitions In **In re Roy C.**, 169 Cal.App.3d 912, 915 215 Cal.Rptr. 513, 515 (Cal. Ct. App. 1985), the state charged appellant with robbery and battery. At the conclusion of the People's case-in-chief, appellant moved to dismiss the robbery count for lack of sufficient evidence. The court denied the motion to dismiss and stated that it "would allow the prosecution to amend, to conform to the proof" an additional count alleging an assault. The state amended the petition over defense counsel's objection who stated that he was "not prepared to proceed" on the assault charge. Immediately thereafter, and without any discussion of a continuance, the court indicated to appellant's counsel that the defense should proceed. After appellant and another witness testified, the court sustained the allegation of assault against the minor:

(1982) (invalidating midtrial "amendment" naming new defendant); *cf. In re Man J.*, (1983) (upholding midtrial amendment supplementing factual allegations of original charge).

Our Supreme Court in *Robert G.* * * * held that a petition filed pursuant to Welfare and Institutions Code section 602 may not be sustained on findings that the minor had committed an offense or offenses other than those specifically alleged in the petition or necessarily included within an alleged offense, unless the minor consents to a finding on the substituted charge. * * *

It is fundamental that a defendant may rest his case without presenting evidence and move for an acquittal on grounds that the People had not presented sufficient evidence to sustain the charges filed. When the juvenile court denied the motion for an acquittal in the instant case and allowed the People to amend the petition to include an additional charge which was not necessarily included in the offenses contained in the petition, the appellant was faced with a Hobson's choice: (1) present no defense, risk being continued in custody at juvenile hall on a sustained petition and appeal the court's ruling based on the decision in *Robert G.* (which would have mandated certain reversal); or, (2) give up the right to a speedy trial, move for a continuance and prepare a defense to meet the new charges; or, (3) give up the due process right to receive adequate notice of the new charge filed, present whatever defense counsel could make given the time allowed and submit the matter to the court for decision. Given this dilemma, we cannot conclude that the minor's decision to proceed with the defense of the case could be construed as a waiver of his right to appeal the violation of his due process right to receive adequate notice of the amended charge. The holding in *Robert G.* mandates reversal because prejudice must be presumed since we cannot speculate what " 'defenses might have been asserted had defendant been given adequate and advance notice of the possible offenses for which he was criminally vulnerable.' "

2) Status Offense as a Lesser–Included of Delinquency In **In re Felton**, 124 Ohio App.3d 500, 706 N.E.2d 809 (Ohio Ct. App. 1997), the juvenile court judge allowed that state to amend the petition and adjudicated appellant "unruly" as a lesser included offense of charged delinquent conduct.

[A]ppellant was charged with delinquency by sexual imposition. * * * At the conclusion of the hearing, the court requested both parties to brief, *inter alia*, the issue of whether unruliness was a lessor included offense to the charge. * * * [T]he court further found that unruliness was a lessor included offense to the initial delinquency charge. * * * [A] trial court has the discretion to amend a complaint. Unless the juvenile court abuses its discretion in amending a complaint, we will not reverse that decision. * * * In the present case, appellant was originally charged with delinquency by sexual imposition. * * * A 'delinquent child' has been defined as a child whose conduct constitutes a violation of any criminal law statute. In contrast, an 'unruly child' is defined as including 'any child * * * [w]ho so deports himself as to injure or endanger the health or morals of himself or others.'

The record reflects that the underlying action on which appellant was tried was that of his allegedly grabbing the breast of a classmate. At appellant's hearing, * * * [t]hree of the witnesses testified as to appellant's allegedly grabbing the young woman's breast. * * * [W]e find that the record demonstrates that appellant's trial revolved around the issue of whether he grabbed a girl's breast. Moreover, the sole allegation in appellant's complaint was that he grabbed a girl's breast. The appellant had the opportunity to, and did, prepare and present a defense on this allegation. The same facts formed the basis for both the original charge of delinquency and the amended charge of unruliness. Therefore, we hold that the trial court did not err in amending the complaint. * * *

E. HEARINGS AND EVIDENCE

Following *Gault* and *Winship*, virtually all of the trial rights available to an adult criminal defendant, except for the right to a jury trial, *McKeiver*, also are available in delinquency hearings for juveniles. The Louisiana Statute succinctly expresses this procedural parity. "All rights guaranteed to criminal defendants by the Constitution of the United States or the Constitution of Louisiana, except the right to jury trial, shall be applicable in juvenile court proceedings brought under this Title." *La. Child. Code Art. 808* (West 1999). However, the right to a jury trial affects many other procedural and evidentiary aspects of a criminal or delinquency trial. States' statutes and juvenile court rules of procedure typically have separate provisions to deal with the conduct of trials, appointment of counsel, burdens of proof for delinquent and status offenders, admissibility of evidence, the presence of parents, and the like. The following provisions illustrate some of the variability of state procedures.

Cal. Welf. & Inst. Code § 701 (West 1999). At the hearing, the court shall first consider only the question whether the minor is a * * * [status offender, § 601, or delinquent, § 602]. The admission and exclusion of evidence shall be pursuant to the rules of evidence established by the Evidence Code and by judicial decision. Proof beyond a reasonable doubt supported by evidence, legally admissible in the trial of criminal cases, must be adduced to support a finding that the minor is a * * * [delinquent, Section 602], and a preponderance of evidence, legally admissible in the trial of civil cases must be adduced to support a finding that the minor is a * * * [status offender, Section 601]. * * * When it appears that the minor has made an extrajudicial admission or confession and denies the same at the hearing, the court may continue the hearing for not to exceed seven days to enable the prosecuting attorney to subpoena witnesses to attend the hearing to prove the allegations of the petition. If the minor is not represented by counsel at the hearing, it shall be deemed that objections that could have been made to the evidence were made.

Col. Rev. Stat. Ann. § 19–2–107 (West 1999). (1) In any action in delinquency in which a juvenile is alleged to be an aggravated juvenile offender * * * or is alleged to have committed an act that would constitute a crime of violence * * * if committed by an adult, the juvenile or the district attorney may demand a trial by a jury of not more than six persons * * * or the court, on its own motion, may order such a jury to try any case brought under this title. * * *

(2) The juvenile is not entitled to a trial by jury when the petition alleges a delinquent act which is a misdemeanor, a petty offense, a violation of a municipal or county ordinance, or a violation of a court order. * * *

Col. Rev. Stat. Ann. § 19–2–110 (West 1999). The general public shall not be excluded from hearings held under this article unless the court determines that it is in the best interest of the juvenile or of the community to exclude the general public, and, in such event, the court shall admit only such persons as have an interest in the case or work of the court, including persons whom the district attorney, the juvenile, or his or her parents or guardian wish to be present.

Minn. Stat. § 260.155 (1999). Subd. 1. (a) * * * [H]earings on any matter shall be without a jury and may be conducted in an informal manner, except that a child who is prosecuted as an extended jurisdiction juvenile has the right to a jury trial on the issue of guilt. The rules of evidence * * * and the law of evidence shall apply in adjudicatory proceedings * * * and [waiver] hearings * * * except to the extent that the rules themselves provide that they do not apply* * *

(c) * * * [T]he court shall exclude the general public from hearings under this chapter and shall admit only those persons who, in the discretion of the court, have a direct interest in the case or in the work of the court. The court shall open the hearings to the public in delinquency or extended jurisdiction juvenile proceedings where the child is alleged to have committed an offense or has been proven to have committed an offense that would be a felony if committed by an adult and the child was at least 16 years of age at the time of the offense, except that the court may exclude the public from portions of a certification hearing to discuss psychological material or other evidence that would not be accessible to the public in an adult proceeding. * * *

1. EVIDENCE

IN RE GLADYS R.

1 Cal.3d 855, 83 Cal.Rptr. 671, 464 P.2d 127 (Cal. 1970).

TOBRINER, JUSTICE. * * * The Santa Clara County Superior Court, sitting as a juvenile court, found that the appellant's conduct brought her within the terms of Welfare and Institutions Code section 602 [delinquent]. * * * Immediately after accepting factual allegations that the child committed acts which could invoke the jurisdiction of the court under section 602, the juvenile court proceeded: "Now, we come to the question of what action should be taken, and in this connection, the Court has been supplied with a special report called a social study, which is ordered admitted in evidence at this time and which has been thoroughly reviewed by the Court. The social study tells the Court whether the child has a prior record, where the child is now, what the child told the probation officer when interviewed, what the parents told the probation officer when interviewed, the child's school report, welfare report, juvenile hall report, psychological, psychiatric and medical reports, personal history and family backgrounds, and last of all the probation officer evaluates that information and data and makes a recommendation to the Court."

The quoted comments clearly indicate that the court examined the social study report prior to its determination of whether appellant had committed an act that would warrant the court's declaration of a wardship. The report contains matter not relevant to the jurisdiction of the court and therefore inadmissible at the hearing on that issue. * * *

The history of Welfare and Institutions Code sections 701, 702, and 706 clearly indicates that the Legislature intended to create a bifurcated juvenile court procedure in which the court would first determine whether the facts of the case would support the jurisdiction of the court in declaring a wardship and *thereafter* would consider the social study report at a hearing on the appropriate disposition of that ward.[5] This procedure affords a necessary protection against the premature resolution of the jurisdictional issue on the basis of legally incompetent material in the social report.

A prohibition of review of the social report before a determination of the jurisdictional issue does not hinder the creation of a court atmosphere conducive to a just consideration of the juvenile's case. We recognize that the juvenile court in this case acted entirely within its view of the best interest of the child. It undoubtedly believed that its perusal of the report prior to a decision on the jurisdictional issue would provide helpful background information. We hold, however, that Welfare and Institutions Code sections 701, 702, and 706 prohibit the judge from reading the social report before the jurisdictional hearing. * * *

We must hold that the court's review of the social study prior to the jurisdictional hearing constituted prejudicial error. Both *In re Corey* and

---

5. In 1959 the Governor of California appointed a Special Study Commission on Juvenile Justice to undertake a comprehensive study of the California Juvenile Court Law. The commission strongly criticized the juvenile courts because they "do not distinguish between the jurisdictional facts and the social data at the hearing. Consequently, wardship is sometimes decided on issues that evolve from a social investigation even though the jurisdictional facts have not been clearly substantiated.

In our opinion, a two-stage hearing procedure is essential. This will serve to differentiate more sharply between legal proof and treatment knowledge and will result in the application of each to the appropriate question for court decision.

We also realize that any increase in the number of hearings may further reduce the time available to hear such case. Therefore, we recommend that both hearings be permitted to be held on the same day, provided the probation report and treatment recommendations are available. The sequence, however, should be preserved in any event."

The commission thus recommended new statutory language which, with modifications not at issue in this case, the Legislature enacted as Welfare and Institutions Code sections 701, 702, and 706. *In re Corey*; quotes these passages from the commission's report in construing the Legislature's intent to foreclose the juvenile court from review of the social study report before determination of the jurisdictional issue.

In re Steven F., *state: "Where the commission of a crime is alleged as the jurisdictional fact and the allegation is disputed, the court's error in [reviewing] the social study before the jurisdictional hearing goes so directly to the fairness of the hearing that the resulting adjudication is not saved by article VI, section 13, of the California Constitution." The court's review of the social report in advance of the jurisdictional hearing would perhaps not require reversal in a case in which the contents of the social study entirely favored the minor and his home environment. But in the present case the social study showed some inquiry into appellant's intent * * * and some negative indications about appellant's home environment. Hence, the court's review of the social study prior to the jurisdictional hearing, at which the jurisdictional facts were far from conclusive, constituted prejudicial error. * * **

2. SUPPRESSION HEARING

The materials on jury trials, *supra* Note 4 at pp. 765–770, noted the tendency of judges to convict more readily than juries. One reason, emphasized in *Gladys R.*, resulted from judges' exposure to evidence not properly admitted at an adjudicatory hearing. Because judges conduct delinquency trials without a jury in most jurisdictions, many states conduct a suppression hearing in the midst of the trial on the merits and may co-mingle issues of evidentiary admissibility with questions of guilt or innocence at the adjudicatory proceeding. *See* Barry C. Feld, "Criminalizing Juvenile Justice: Rules of Procedure for the Juvenile Court," 69 *Minn. L. Rev.* 141, 229–243 (1984).

The United States Supreme Court in *Jackson v. Denno*, 378 U.S. 368 (1964), established the constitutional procedures for determining the admissibility of evidence at trial. *Jackson* rejected the practice of admitting a confession into evidence without any preliminary judicial determination of its voluntariness because an appellate court could not adequately determine from a general verdict of guilt whether the jury had properly disregarded a confession that it had found involuntary. The *Jackson* Court feared that a jury could not adequately compartmentalize the issue of the voluntariness and admissibility of the confession from the issue of the defendant's guilt. As a result, other evidence of guilt might influence the jury's determination of voluntariness, or a reliable but involuntary confession might provide a basis to convict. *Id.* at 383. The Court concluded that state procedures must provide a "reliable and clear-cut determination of the voluntariness of the confession. * * * Whether the trial judge, another judge or another jury, but not the convicting jury, fully resolves the issue of voluntariness is not a matter of concern here. * * * [T]he states are free to allocate functions between judge and jury as they see fit." *Id.* at 391, n. 19.

Unlike adult criminal proceedings, which require a constitutional determination of evidentiary admissibility prior to trial and out of the presence of the jury, many states' delinquency proceedings litigate suppression issues in the course of the trial itself rather than in a separate pretrial evidentiary hearing. The rationale for allowing judges, but not juries, to decide both admissibility and guilt in the course of the same proceeding is that judges, unlike juries, are by professional training, temperament, and experience, capable of compartmentalizing inadmissible evidence from admissible evidence in deciding a case. That presumption also underlies a host of interrelated evidentiary doctrines. Appellate courts regularly presume that inadmissible evidence that clearly would prejudice a jury does not improperly influence a trial judge exposed to the same evidence, even if the judge erroneously admitted it originally.

There are also practical and administrative considerations that lead courts to treat the impact of evidence differently when the state presents the evidence to a judge instead of a jury. It may be administratively inconvenient to require one judge to determine preliminary issues of evidentiary admissibility and another to sit as the ultimate trier of fact at the adjudication. Moreover, the suggestion that judges might be adversely influenced by evidence that they have heard but suppressed could jeopardize a number of other presumptions about the role of judges in bench trials. Indeed, some courts regard questioning the ability of trial judges to disregard the prejudicial impact of inadmissible evidence as an attack on the very foundation of the judicial trial process. *See* Feld, *Criminalizing Juvenile Justice, supra* at 233–34.

States can avoid the risk of "evidentiary contamination" for delinquents either by providing for jury trials or by requiring a different judge to rule on the admissibility of evidence prior to trial as is done in some jurisdictions. Conducting suppression hearings prior to the trial also protects the state's right to an interlocutory appeal. Once jeopardy has attached, a ruling that evidence is inadmissible may preclude either appellate review or retrial of the defendant. In addition, a pretrial suppression hearing assures that a juvenile defendant who wants to testify only on issues concerning the voluntariness of the confession or the admissibility of other evidence will be able to do so without prejudice. Finally, conducting the suppression hearing prior to the trial or before a different judge can minimize the possible confusion of the fact-finder by separating the defendant's testimony on the preliminary questions of admissibility from any subsequent testimony on the ultimate questions of guilt or innocence.

In **In the Matter of the Welfare of J.P.L.**, 359 N.W.2d 622 (Mn. Ct. Ap. 1984), the Minnesota Court of Appeals court noted that:

> The procedure used in this case, combining the constitutional question surrounding the admissibility of a statement along with the trial on the question of guilt or innocence, highlights the problem recognized by this court. * * * In any court trial, whether a juvenile matter or a criminal matter where the defendant has waived a jury, allowing the same judge who has considered a defendant's confession and then suppressed it to decide the defendant's guilt or innocence

requires the assumption that the contents of the confession do not lurk in the judge's subconscious. Such a rigid assumption is a legal fiction. To safeguard the integrity of a jury trial, the Minnesota Rules of Criminal Procedure jealously safeguard the right of a defendant to argue the suppression of his confession in a private pre-trial hearing apart from the jury.

If the confession is suppressed * * *, it is grounds for a reversal and/or mistrial for the prosecutor or the judge to bring it to the jury's attention, even inadvertently. The question is—why do we make exceptions for judges? Expecting a judge who is entitled to see and examine a confession before suppressing it on constitutional grounds to go on to decide the guilt or innocence of a defendant based solely on the state's other evidence without using that confession, subconsciously or consciously, to corroborate the state's other evidence, is unrealistic. Such an expectation asks for objectivity that logically cannot be delivered. * * *

The better procedure in juvenile cases would be to follow the procedure in criminal gross misdemeanor and felony cases—that is, have the suppression hearing separate and before trial. If the confession is ruled admissible, there is no harm in having that same judge hear the case on the merits, as the confession is now in. If the defendant feels he has been aggrieved on the suppression hearing, he has the right of appeal after conviction. If, however, the confession is suppressed, the adjudication hearing should be assigned to another juvenile judge to hear on the merits. * * *

NOTES

1) Separate Suppression Hearing How adequately does the following statute address the concerns of the court in *J.P.L.*? *Cal. Welf. & Inst.* § 700.1 (West 1999) provides that "Any motion to suppress as evidence any tangible or intangible thing obtained as a result of an unlawful search or seizure shall be heard prior to the attachment of jeopardy and shall be heard at least five judicial days after receipt of notice by the people unless the people are willing to waive a portion of this time."

Under California's adult criminal procedure, Penal Code § 1538.5 (West 1999), either the defendant or the state may obtain pretrial appellate review from an adverse ruling on a suppression motion. However, in **Abdullah B. v. Superior Court of Solano County**, 135 Cal.App.3d 838, 185 Cal.Rptr. 784 (Cal. Ct. App. 1982), the court endorsed a different procedure for review of judges' pretrial rulings on suppression motions brought by juveniles rather than adults:

It is readily apparent that the prior haphazard scheme for juvenile suppression hearings and review of rulings has been replaced by a statutory scheme which permits the juvenile to make a pretrial motion to suppress (and in limited circumstances to make a motion during the hearing) and permits review by appeal at the request of either the defendant or the prosecution. * * * The question arises whether equal protection principles permit the Legislature to authorize adult defendants to seek pretrial review of suppression rulings while relegating juveniles to review on appeal. * * *

Here, the consequence of a different procedure is that the juvenile is denied the opportunity to seek an appellate ruling before the evidence is introduced. This may mean that a juvenile whose jurisdictional ruling is eventually set aside will suffer the burden of a hearing and become a ward of the court under circumstances where with prehearing review neither would occur. It may also mean rehearing of juvenile court cases where with pretrial review erroneous introduction of evidence could be forestalled.

The deprivation is balanced by the favoritism given the juvenile in the appeal process. Adult criminal appeals receive priority because they are cases "in which the people of the state are parties." Juvenile appeals are given even higher priority by a sentence in Welfare and Institutions Code section 800, which provides that "[t]he appeal shall have precedence over all other cases in the court to which the appeal is taken." Thus, although a juvenile may not obtain pretrial review of the ruling on his suppression motion, his jurisdictional hearing will not be delayed by the writ procedure, and his appeal will be given preference over all adult appeals. The practical effect is that he may even obtain an appellate court ruling earlier than a similarly situated adult defendant seeking review by writ. In light of the fact that pretrial writ review is discretionary, and most adult defendants must await their appeals to obtain definitive rulings on their suppression issues, the juvenile's appeal preference more than compensates for the absence of pretrial review. Only a rare adult defendant would obtain an earlier appellate court ruling than a similarly situated juvenile. * * *

2) Remedies for Judicial Exposure to Inadmissible Evidence Recall that **Martin Guggenheim and Randy Hertz, "Reflections on Judges, Juries, and Justice: Ensuring the Fairness of Juvenile Delinquency Trials," 33 *Wake Forest L. Rev.* 553, 571 (1998),** attributed one source of judges' greater willingness to convict than juries to their "presiding at a pretrial suppression hearing that results in the suppression of evidence * * * [as a result of which] the judge will be apprised of highly incriminating evidence that is inadmissible at trial and would be kept from a jury." As a result, they propose judicial and legislative reforms to improve the fairness of fact-finding in delinquency adjudications:

What might such a model of a juvenile court bench trial look like? First, it would provide a mechanism for the resolution of pretrial suppression issues and other potentially prejudicial matters by a judge other than the one who will preside over the trial. * * *

In a number of jurisdictions, the state legislature or an administrative judge has taken steps to guard against a juvenile court judge's exposure to prejudicial information prior to conducting a bench trial. For example, in the District of Columbia, pursuant to statute, a juvenile court judge who presides over a pretrial detention hearing or transfer hearing (thereby learning of the respondent's prior record and possibly inadmissible information about the facts of the case) must recuse herself as the factfinder at trial if the defense so requests. In that same jurisdiction, a juvenile court administrative procedure provides for pretrial suppression motions to be heard by a judge other than the one who will preside over the trial.

Procedures such as these should be adopted by state legislatures and/or administrative judges in all jurisdictions that deny juveniles the right to a jury trial. There should be a rule that all pretrial matters, including detention pending trial, transfer to adult court, and suppression of evidence, be heard by a judge other than the one who will preside over the trial. Moreover, to guard against the danger of litigants tainting a bench trial factfinder by reciting prejudicial evidence in the course of arguing its admissibility, the burden should be upon litigants to raise close questions of admissibility prior to trial in motions *in limine*—with appropriate sanctions when a party willfully violates this procedure. To provide for the rare situation in which an issue of this sort arises at trial without either of the litigants having anticipated it, there should be a procedure for certifying the case temporarily to another judge to resolve the evidentiary matter without exposing the judicial trier of fact to a needless risk of prejudice.

It may seem impracticable to implement this proposal in jurisdictions that have only one juvenile court judge. Even in these jurisdictions, however, there is at least one other judge who is fully qualified to decide pretrial motions to suppress evidence or pretrial or mid-trial motions on evidentiary matters: the criminal court judge. The criminal court judge could hear motions, including evidentiary hearings on motions to suppress, and then remit the matter to the juvenile court judge for trial. Or, if the criminal court judge is unavailable for some reason, a civil court judge could substitute. Although the civil court judge may be unfamiliar with the applicable criminal and juvenile law and procedure, she can rely on the parties to inform her of the relevant authorities and procedures. Unlike the process of putting facts out of one's mind, the process of learning new law and legal procedures is one quite familiar to, and easily accomplished by, any reasonably competent judge.

Even in the absence of formal mechanisms for safeguarding trial court judges from exposure to prejudicial information, judges can accomplish the same goal themselves. Regardless of the standard a litigant must meet to require a judge to recuse herself, a judge may always grant a recusal motion or disqualify herself *sua sponte* if she is exposed to prejudicial information. Juvenile court judges should take such options seriously, keeping in mind the importance of avoiding any "appearance of impropriety." Judges also can, and should, structure pretrial hearings and trials so as to guard against exposure to prejudicial information. For example, confession suppression hearings can be conducted without the judge ever hearing the substance of the accused's statement. Similarly, evidentiary issues often can be resolved by the judge applying the law without hearing a proffer of the challenged evidence. *Id.* at 583–85.

3) Professional Responsibility and Suppression Hearings Richard Kay and Daniel Segal, "The Role of the Attorney in Juvenile Court Proceedings: A Non–Polar Approach," 61 *Geo. L. J.* 1401, 1412–1413 (1973), analyze issues of professional responsibility associated with practice in juvenile court. One arises in the context of the suppression hearing and concerns the moral message a lawyer conveys to a juvenile client when she files a motion to suppress evidence that the juvenile knows she possessed. "Should the juvenile's lawyer move to suppress such evidence? * * * First, such a strategy could encourage the child to lie and to conceal his activities, when the very purpose of the juvenile system is to teach the child moral values. Secondly, by attempting to suppress relevant evidence, the lawyer is blocking the presentation of complete and accurate information to the court. The decision whether to declare the child delinquent will be made more difficult, and the risk of an incorrect decision will be increased. * * * Concerned that a juvenile judge's distaste for adversary methods may have adverse effects on his client, a lawyer may properly believe that the child's best interest requires the presentation of his client's case without the aid of such tactics. By cooperating with the judge he can hope to earn a more desirable disposition for the child. When the lawyer feels that use of exclusionary tactics can block a justifiable finding of delinquency, it may well be appropriate for him to evaluate the child and the probability of various dispositions resulting from a finding of delinquency. * * * " On the other hand, why did *Gault* grant juveniles the right to counsel if it did not expect lawyers to acts as zealous advocates for their clients?

F. RIGHT TO COUNSEL

Procedural justice hinges on access to and effective assistance of counsel. *Gault* observed that juvenile courts' informality often resulted in arbitrary or erroneous decisions, and that benevolent discretion provided an inadequate substitute for fair procedures. 387 U.S. at 18. Recall *Gault* based juveniles' right to counsel on the Fourteenth Amendment due process clause rather than the Sixth Amendment's explicit provision of counsel in criminal proceedings. The Court asserted that as a matter of due process "the assistance of counsel is * * * essential for the determination of delinquency, carrying with it the awesome prospect of incarceration in a state institution." While *Gault* recognized that lawyers would make juvenile court proceedings more formal and adversarial, the Court asserted that their presence would impart "a healthy atmosphere of accountability." However, *Gault* did not require judges automatically to appoint counsel whenever delinquents appeared in juvenile court, but only held that "the child and his parents must be notified of the child's right to be represented by counsel retained by them, or if they are unable to afford counsel, that counsel will be appointed to represent the child."

When *Gault* granted juveniles the right to counsel, it reflected the Warren Court's beliefs that adversarial procedures protected constitutional rights, limited the coercive powers of the state, assured the regularity of law enforcement, and preserved individual liberty and autonomy. Several years prior to *Gault*, in *Gideon v. Wainwright,* 372 U.S. 335, 83 S.Ct. 792, 9 L.Ed.2d 799 (1963), the Court incorporated the Sixth Amendment's guarantee of counsel and required state judges to appoint counsel for indigent adult defendants in felony proceedings. "[I]n our adversary system of criminal justice, any person haled into court, who is too poor to hire a lawyer, cannot be assured a fair trial unless counsel is provided for him." *Gideon*, 372 U.S. at 344 (1963). Because *Gault* based its decision on the Fourteenth Amendment due process clause, rather than on the explicit provision of the Sixth Amendment and *Gideon*, some ambiguity remained about the scope of the right to appointed counsel in delinquency proceedings.

In *Argersinger v. Hamlin*, 407 U.S. 25, 92 S.Ct. 2006, 32 L.Ed.2d 530 (1972), the Court considered whether the Sixth Amendment required states to appoint counsel for indigent adult defendants charged with and imprisoned for a minor offense and held that "absent a knowing and intelligent waiver, no person may be imprisoned for any offense, whether classified as petty, misdemeanor or felony unless he was represented by counsel." 407 U.S. at 37. In *Scott v. Illinois*, 440 U.S. 367, 99 S.Ct. 1158, 59 L.Ed.2d 383 (1979), the Court clarified *Argersinger* and limited adult misdemeanants' constitutional right to court-appointed counsel to cases in which a judge actually sentenced a defendant to some form of incarceration. Recall from Chapter 2, prosecutors do not charge most delinquents with felony level offenses, and *Scott* limited misdemeanants' right to lawyers to cases of actual imprisonment. However, as a matter of due process, the "special circumstances" of youthfulness may require juvenile courts to appoint counsel even in less serious and non-incarceration cases if a child appears unable to prepare an adequate defense because of the inherent disabilities of youth, substandard intelligence, or the complexities of the case. *E.g. Betts v. Brady*, 316 U.S. 455, 62 S.Ct. 1252, 86 L.Ed. 1595 (1942). Most states' juvenile codes provide delinquents with a statutory right to court-appointed counsel even in misdemeanor cases that potentially could result in confinement. *See generally* Barry C. Feld, *Justice for Children: The Right to Counsel and Juvenile Courts* (1993); United States General Accounting Office, *Juvenile Justice: Representation Rates Varies As Did Counsel's Impact On Court Outcomes* (1995) (statutory summary in appendix).

1. THE DELIVERY AND QUALITY OF LEGAL SERVICES IN JUVENILE COURTS

In the immediate aftermath of *Gault*, a few studies evaluated the impact of the decision on the delivery of legal services and concluded that many juvenile court judges neither adequately advised juveniles of their right to counsel nor appointed lawyers for them. *See* Norman Lefstein, Vaughan Stapleton, and Lee Teitelbaum, "In Search of Juvenile Justice: *Gault* and Its Implementation," 3 *Law & Soc'y Rev.* 491 (1969); Sanford Fox, "Juvenile Justice Reform: An Historical Perspective," 22 *Stan. L. Rev.* 1187 (1970), W. Vaughan Stapleton and Lee E. Teitelbaum, *In Defense of Youth: A Study of the Role of Counsel in American Juvenile Courts* (1972). Beginning in the late–1980s, Professor Barry Feld conducted several empirical studies that examined the implementation of *Gault* and reported that two decades after *Gault*, the promise of counsel remained unfulfilled for many juveniles in many states. *See* Barry C. Feld, "*In re Gault* Revisited: A Cross–State Comparison of the Right to Counsel in Juvenile Court," 34 *Crime & Delinq.* 393 (1988); Barry C. Feld, "The Right to Counsel in Juvenile Court: An Empirical Study of When Lawyers Appear and the Difference They Make," 79 *J. Crim. L. & Criminology* 1185 (1989); Barry C. Feld, "Justice by Geography: Urban, Suburban, and Rural Variations in Juvenile Justice Administration," 82 *J. Crim. L. & Criminology* 156 (1991); Barry C. Feld, *Justice for Children: The Right to Counsel and Juvenile Courts* (1993). In 1992, Congress reauthorized the Juvenile Justice and Delinquency Prevention Act, 42 U.S.C.A. § 5601(a) (1994), and mandated the United States General Accounting Office to evaluate the delivery and effectiveness of counsel in juvenile court. The G.A.O. study, *Juvenile Justice: Representation Rates Varies As Did Counsel's Impact On Court Outcomes 15* (1995), replicated and corroborated many of Professor Feld's earlier research findings. "Our findings on the variability in representation rates across non-metropolitan and metropolitan court settings within states are consistent with Feld's study of representation in juvenile cases * * *."

Following the research by Feld and the G.A.O., the American Bar Association published two reports on the legal needs of young people. The American Bar Association, *America's Children at Risk 60* (1993), reported that "Many children go through the juvenile justice system without the benefit of legal counsel. Among those who do have counsel, some are represented by counsel who are untrained in the complexities of representing juveniles and fail to provide 'competent' representation." The A.B.A. concluded that providing competent counsel for every youth charged with a crime would alleviate some of the endemic problems of juvenile justice, overcrowded conditions of confinement, racial disparities in processing, and inappropriate adjudication or transfer of youths to adult courts. In a second study, the American Bar Association, *A Call for Justice* (1995), focused on the quality of lawyers in juvenile courts, surveyed public defender offices, court-appointed attorneys, law school clinics, and children's law centers, and observed attorney-client interviews and delinquency proceedings in urban, suburban and rural settings in ten jurisdictions. Although the A.B.A. commended those defense attorneys who represented their young clients vigorously and enthusiastically, it emphasized that they constituted the rare exception rather than the rule. Juvenile defenders reported that the conditions under which lawyers worked in juvenile courts often significantly compromised youths' interests and left many of them literally defenseless. Defense lawyer-respondents also reported that many youths waived counsel and appeared in juvenile courts without representation. Since the late—1990s, the American Bar Association has conducted a series of state-by-state assessments of juveniles' access to counsel and the quality of representation they receive. These studies consistently report that many, if not most, juveniles waive representation by counsel and that the lawyers who represent juveniles often provide substandard services. *See e.g.*, Gabriella Celese & Patricia Puritz, *The Children Left Behind: An Assessment of Access to Counsel and Quality of Representation in Delinquency Proceedings in Louisiana* 59–62 (2001) (observers in several parishes estimate 80% to 90% of delinquents waive right to counsel); Patricia Puritz & Kim Brooks, *Kentucky: Advancing Justice: An Assessment of Access to Counsel and Quality of Representation in Delinquency Proceedings* 29 (2002) (despite efforts to improve delivery of legal services, "it is clear that large numbers of youth are still waiving counsel. . . ."); Patricia Puritz et al., *Virginia: An Assessment of Access to Counsel and Quality of Representation in Delinquency Proceedings* 24–25 (2002) (estimating that 50% of juveniles waived their right to counsel, regardless of the seriousness of the charges); Kim Brooks and Darlene Kamine, *Justice Cut Short: An Assessment of Access to Counsel and Quality of Representation in Delinquency Proceedings in Ohio* 25 (2003) ("waiver of counsel was a common and pervasive practice, with as many as 80% of youth proceeding through the system without the benefit of counsel."). More than a dozen state reports currently are accessible at http://www.abanet.org/crimjust/juvjus/.

Delivering legal services in juvenile courts raise two constellations of issues. First, states must assure the availability and delivery of defense representation to youths in juvenile courts. Secondly, once states assure the presence of defense attorneys for juveniles, professionals and practitioners must define the appropriate role of defense counsel in juvenile courts. The following excerpt by **N. Lee Cooper, Patricia Puritz, and Wendy Shang, "Fulfilling the Promise of *In re Gault*: Advancing the Role of Lawyers for Children," 33 *Wake Forest L. Rev.* 651, 655–667 (1998),** examines some of the issues associated with the delivery and quality of legal services.

In the years that followed *In re Gault*, studies revealed that a child's right to counsel, as well as the right to effective representation in juvenile court, was, at best, implemented unevenly across the country. Some of the most extensive work on access to counsel has been conducted by Professor Barry Feld at the University of Minnesota. Professor Feld estimates that, prior to *In re Gault*, attorneys appeared on behalf of children in 5% of juvenile delinquency cases. Through an analysis of data from six states, gathered from the National Juvenile Court Data Archive, Professor Feld found that many jurisdictions still failed to appoint counsel in a majority of juvenile court cases. Large urban states were more successful at assuring juveniles the assistance of counsel, with rates of 85% to 95% representation, as opposed to 37.5% and 52.7% in Midwestern states. For example, New York State and the City of Philadelphia provided counsel in more than 95% of their cases, while North Dakota provided counsel in only 37.5% of cases.

In Professor Feld's analysis of other studies on access to counsel, he reported wildly varying representation rates in different parts of individual states. For example, lawyer appointment rates ranged from 19.3% to 94.5% in different counties of Minnesota. Professor Feld attributed the disparities, in part, to different appointment of counsel practices in urban, suburban and rural areas. Professor Feld has also noted that there is a positive correlation between the seriousness of the offense and the appointment of counsel. The fact remains, however, that serious offenses comprise only a small part of juvenile dockets. Thus, children accused of minor misbehavior are most likely to be incarcerated without the assistance of counsel. Studies from other jurisdictions confirm Professor Feld's findings that access to counsel remains a serious problem in many states.

In addition to the basic issue of whether children have *access* to legal representation, researchers have also questioned the quality of representation provided to juveniles. Richard A. Lawrence found that of the attorneys surveyed, 16.7% spent less than one hour, 44.4% spent one to two hours, 27.7% spent three to four hours, and 11.1% spent five or more hours preparing for a juvenile court case. Professor Lawrence urges earlier appointment of counsel in order to reduce the wide variation in the quality of legal counsel and to increase the amount of time attorneys spend in preparation of a juvenile court case.

A study of the New York Law Guardian Program also provides an insightful examination of the quality of representation received by children. The authors, Jane Knitzer and Merril Sobie, conducted surveys and site visits throughout New York State to analyze the characteristics of attorneys representing juveniles, the attorneys' caseloads, and the extent to which the attorneys specialized in juvenile law. The results showed, among other things, that over half of the lawyers reported that they had little interest in the substance of juvenile law.

Specifically, nearly 70% indicated that they had no special screening, orientation, or co-counsel experience prior to joining the panel, and 30% to 40% had no relevant clinical or academic experience. Furthermore, 42% of law guardians had no relevant training within the previous two years, with an even higher percentage of guardians in rural areas reporting no recent training. Site visits, reports from others in the system, and document analysis revealed that, using the most basic criteria of effectiveness, 45% of attorneys provided either seriously inadequate or marginally adequate representation. In 47% of observed cases, it appeared that the law guardian either had not prepared or had prepared minimally for the case. Moreover, almost 50% of the transcripts reviewed included appealable errors that went unchallenged. * * *

In the fall of 1993, the American Bar Association Juvenile Justice Center, * * * the Youth Law Center and Juvenile Law Center conducted a national assessment to examine the problems and issues relating to access to counsel and quality of representation for juveniles. The results were published in *A Call for Justice: An Assessment of Access to Counsel and Quality of Representation in Delinquency Proceedings. A Call for Justice* determined that while some attorneys were able to vigorously and enthusiastically represent their clients, many dedicated attorneys continued to labor under tremendous systemic burdens. Those burdens, in many cases, severely compromised the attorneys' abilities to provide effective legal services.

The study also found that large numbers of children appearing in court without an attorney are often induced to waive counsel by the suggestion "that lawyers are not needed because no serious dispositional consequences are anticipated," or by parental misperception that they will have to pay for legal services that are provided. One-third "of the public defender offices surveyed reported that some percentage of youth in the juvenile courts in which they work waive their right to counsel at the detention hearing." In addition, 45% of the public defenders said the waiver colloquy—a formal litany given by the judge of the consequences of pleading and an inquiry into whether the juvenile is entering the plea voluntarily—is only "sometimes" or "rarely" as thorough as that given to adult defendants. Concurring with Professor Feld's work, the study also found that youth waive their right to counsel more frequently in rural areas.

High caseloads were identified by defense attorneys as the single most important barrier to effective representation. The average caseload carried by a public defender often exceeded 500 cases per year, more than 300 of which were juvenile cases. This number almost doubles the caseload standard set out by the National Advisory Commission (NAC) on Criminal Justice Standards and Goals, which calls for attorneys to handle not more than 200 juvenile cases per year. In rural areas, where caseloads were sometimes lower, attorneys had other issues to contend with, including often driving long distances to represent a client at a brief hearing or providing coverage for multiple counties, thus hampering the investigative or dispositional process.

The ripple effect of high caseloads on the quality of representation was evident in other examinations of juvenile court practice. For example, 70% of the public defenders and private attorneys surveyed said they file pretrial motions "sometimes," "rarely," or "never," due to a lack of time and resources, as well as the vast majority of early plea bargains. At disposition hearings—the equivalent of sentencing hearings in the adult court—attorneys frequently did not have the ability to conduct adequate and individualized dispositional planning. In addition, most attorneys were not able to provide alternatives to the recommendations of the probation officers.

Policies and caseloads also prevented attorneys from conducting post-dispositional representation, such as appeals, dispositional reviews, or other collateral proceedings. In jurisdictions where caseloads are already overwhelming, the inability to handle post-dispositional issues may be, at least from a short-term point of view, a necessary arrangement; however, the lack of aggressive appellate advocacy is glaring and the consequences for children can be disastrous. One-third of the public defenders and one-quarter of the appointed counsel surveyed stated that they were not authorized to handle appeals. Of those who could handle appeals, 46% of public defenders and 79% of appointed lawyers said they took no appeals in the last year. Four out of five public defenders and two-thirds of appointed counsel "never" or "rarely" represented their clients in related non-delinquency proceedings, such as school discipline or special education hearings.

Attorneys representing children were also hampered by a lack of available training and resources which might be considered standard in other settings. Of the public defender offices surveyed, 78% did not have a budget for lawyers to attend training programs, 50% did not have a training program for new attorneys, 48% did not have an ongoing training program, 46% did not have a section in the office training manual for juvenile court lawyers, 35% did not include juvenile delinquency work in the general training program, 32% did not have any training manual, and 32% did not have a training unit. * * *

The alarming state of representation in the juvenile courts is attributable to many sources. Some legal commentators attribute the inadequacy of representation to a failure to clearly delineate the role of juvenile counsel. Professors Robert E. Shepherd, Jr., and Adrienne Volenik suggest that many attorneys who represent children do not understand their ethical obligations and, as a result, fail to zealously represent their young clients. The American Bar Association has clearly defined the responsibility of the juvenile defense attorney: the principal duty of the attorney "is the representation of the client's legitimate interests." * * *

Professor Feld points to a myriad of systemic issues when discussing the causes of inadequate representation: (1) insufficient public defender services in rural areas; (2) parental reluctance to retain an attorney; (3) judicial encouragement of defendants to waive the right to counsel in order to ease the administrative burdens of the court; (4) judicial hostility toward lawyers in traditional, treatment-oriented courts; (5) judicial predetermination not to appoint counsel in cases where probation is the anticipated outcome; and (6) cursory and misleading advisories of rights that inadequately convey the importance of the right to counsel and suggest that the waiver litany is simply a meaningless technicality. *A Call for Justice* and other reports have confirmed many of these findings. Attorneys in some areas reported that they felt a great deal of pressure not to file motions or advocate aggressively in court, lest they upset the "friendly" atmosphere in the courthouse. For attorneys who rely on the good graces of the court to receive appointments, upsetting the system is too great a risk to take on behalf of their clients.

The waiver of counsel by children is especially disturbing, and is often a common justification used by courts for not providing counsel to youth. Waiver of counsel has been strongly criticized as fundamentally unfair. As a result of immaturity or anxiety, a youth without a competent attorney may feel pressure to simply resolve the case quickly. A youth may not understand the possible consequences of admitting particular offenses, such as incarceration, waiver of the right to appeal, or sentencing penalties for future offenses. Even when a judge employs a colloquy, there are serious issues of whether a youth fully understands the terminology, the principles, or the impact of his/her decision to enter a plea. Studies of the waiver of *Miranda* rights by children strongly suggest that the majority of children in the juvenile system have difficulty understanding legal language and concepts to a satisfactory level, raising the issue of whether waiver of counsel by a child is ever able to meet the legal standard of "knowing and intelligent."

Other researchers have also examined the organizational and fiscal considerations that affect quality of representation for children. In the *IJA/ABA Juvenile Justice Standards*, Barbara Flicker recognized that many juvenile public defender systems suffer from under-funding, low morale, high turnover rates, lack of training, low status in "career ladders," political pressure and co-optation, low salaries, and huge caseloads. A poignant series of accounts from public defenders assigned to a juvenile court in one city confirmed much of what Flicker reported with respect to public defender offices; lawyers had fifteen cases set for trial on one day, or forty to fifty cases on calendar for a day.

High caseloads prevent attorneys from performing many of the tasks necessary for vigorous advocacy. The stress that caseloads put on the attorney/client relationship cannot be underestimated. Attorneys with heavy caseload burdens find it difficult to meet with their young clients, and explain the proceedings before the clients appear at their detention hearings. Attorneys with high caseloads do not have time to discover the individual strengths and needs of their clients, which would allow them to make arguments against detention and/or for specialized services. Attorneys who can barely keep up with their day-to-day caseloads are unable to follow up with clients during dispositional reviews, or monitor placement problems which may arise. Their relationship with the client becomes increasingly attenuated.

These systemic stresses frequently lead to children trying to navigate a chaotic and complicated system on their own. Children often meet their lawyers for the first time as they are sitting down at counsel table for the detention hearing. Many youths are often unable to identify who, among the many adults in the room, is their lawyer. Probation officers report that in many cases, juveniles do not know who their lawyers are, and do not understand the charges lodged against them. The absence of a relationship with an attorney, as well as an inability to understand the system they find themselves in, renders children passive and distrustful of their lawyers. This distrust, in some instances, leads children to withhold important information and engenders a belief by the children that their lawyers do not care.

The cumulative effect of these factors is a derogation of juvenile court practice itself. According to *A Call for Justice*, public defenders spent only 24 months in juvenile court. In many offices, the low status of juvenile defense attorneys becomes a self-fulfilling prophecy: the juvenile court is viewed as a training ground for beginners, and few attorneys stay on to advise and mentor other attorneys and improve the level of practice. In some instances, the starting salaries for defense attorneys were as low as $15,000, and lawyers had to transfer to other divisions in order to be promoted. Other attorneys simply burned out under the stress of huge caseloads with little support, or became disenchanted with an atmosphere that consistently works against them. * * *

2. APPOINTMENT AND WAIVER OF COUNSEL

The following statutes and court rules provide examples of the variability of states' strategies to deliver legal services in juvenile courts' adjudicatory hearings. How do these provisions differ in assuring the presence of counsel to represent delinquents? The cases that follow these statutes suggest the strategies that appellate courts employ to assure the validity of juveniles' waivers of the right to counsel.

Fla. Stat. Ann. § 985.203 (1) (West 1998):

A child is entitled to representation by legal counsel at all stages of any proceedings under this part. If the child and the parents or other legal guardian are indigent and unable to employ counsel for the child, the court shall appoint counsel. * * * Legal counsel representing a child who exercises the right to counsel shall be allowed to provide advice and counsel to the child at any time subsequent to the child's arrest, including prior to a detention hearing while in secure detention care. A child shall be represented by legal counsel at all stages of all court proceedings unless the right to counsel is freely, knowingly, and intelligently waived by the child. If the child appears without counsel, the court shall advise the child of his or her rights with respect to representation of court-appointed counsel. * * *

Fla. R. Juv. Proc. 8.165 (a) The court shall advise the child of the child's right to counsel. The court shall appoint counsel as provided by law unless waived by the child at each stage of the proceeding. This waiver shall be in writing if made at the time of a plea of guilty or no contest or at the adjudicatory hearing.

(b) Waiver of Counsel * * *

(2) A child shall not be deemed to have waived the assistance of counsel until the entire process of offering counsel has been completed and a thorough inquiry into the child's comprehension of that offer and the capacity to make that choice intelligently and understandingly has been made.

(3) No waiver shall be accepted where it appears that the party is unable to make an intelligent and understanding choice because of mental condition, age, education, experience, the nature or complexity of the case, or other factors.

(4) If a waiver is accepted at any stage of the proceedings, the offer of assistance of counsel shall be renewed by the court at each subsequent stage of the proceedings at which the party appears without counsel.

Minn. Stat. § 260.155 Subd. 2. Appointment of counsel. (a) The child, parent, guardian or custodian has the right to effective assistance of counsel in connection with a proceeding in juvenile court. * * *

(b) The court shall appoint counsel, or stand-by counsel if the child waives the right to counsel, for a child who is:

(1) charged by delinquency petition with a gross misdemeanor or felony offense; or

(2) the subject of a delinquency proceeding in which out-of-home placement has been proposed.

(c) If they desire counsel but are unable to employ it, the court shall appoint counsel to represent the child or the parents or guardian in any case in which it feels that such an appointment is appropriate * * *.

Minn. Juv. Proc. Rule 3.02 Subd. 1. Felonies and Gross Misdemeanors (1999). In any proceeding in which the child is charged with a felony or gross misdemeanor, the court shall appoint counsel at public expense to represent the child, if the child can not afford counsel and private counsel has not been retained to represent the child. If the child waives the right to counsel, the court shall appoint stand-by counsel to be available to assist and consult with the child at all stages of the proceedings.

Subd. 2. Misdemeanors. In any proceeding in which the child is charged with a misdemeanor, the court shall appoint counsel at public expense to represent the child if the child can not afford counsel and private counsel has not been retained to represent the child, and the child has not waived the right to counsel. If the child waives the right to counsel, the court may appoint stand-by counsel to be available to assist and consult with the child at all stages of the proceedings.

Subd. 3. Out-of-Home Placement. In any proceeding in which out-of-home placement is proposed, the court shall appoint counsel at public expense to represent the child, if the child cannot afford counsel and private counsel has not been retained to represent the child. If the child waives the right to counsel, the court shall appoint stand-by counsel to be available to assist and consult with the child. No out-of-home placement may be made in disposition proceedings, in violation proceedings, or in subsequent related violation proceedings or in subsequent contempt proceedings, if the child was not initially represented by counsel or stand-by counsel. If out-of-home placement is based on a plea or adjudication obtained without assistance of counsel, the child has an absolute right to withdraw that plea or obtain a new trial. * * *

Rule 3.04 Subd. 1. * * * Any waiver of counsel must be made knowingly, intelligently, and voluntarily. Any waiver shall be in writing and on the record. The child must be fully and effectively informed of the child's right to counsel and the disadvantages of self-representation by an in-person consultation with an attorney, and counsel shall appear with the child in court and inform the court that such consultation has occurred. In determining whether a child has knowingly, voluntarily, and intelligently waived the right to counsel, the court shall look to the totality of the circumstances including, but not limited to: the child's age, maturity, intelligence, education, experience, ability to comprehend, and the presence of the child's parents, legal guardian, legal custodian or guardian ad litem. The court shall inquire to determine if the child has met privately with the attorney, and if the child understands the charges and proceedings, including the possible disposition, any collateral consequences, and any additional facts essential to a broad understanding of the case. * * *

N.Y. Fam. Ct. Act § 249–a (McKinney's 1999). A minor who is a subject of a juvenile delinquency or person in need of supervision proceeding shall be presumed to lack the requisite knowledge and maturity to waive the appointment of a law guardian. This presumption may be rebutted only after a law guardian has been appointed and the court determines after a hearing at which the law guardian appears and participates and upon clear and convincing evidence that (a) the minor understands the nature of the charges, the possible dispositional alternatives and the possible defenses to the charges, (b) the minor possesses the maturity, knowledge and intelligence necessary to conduct his own defense, and (c) waiver is in the best interest of the minor.

NOTE

In **Faretta v. California**, 422 U.S. 806, 95 S.Ct. 2525, 45 L.Ed.2d 562 (1975), the Supreme Court held that the Sixth Amendment guarantees that a defendant in a state criminal trial has an independent constitutional right of self-representation and that he may proceed to defend himself without counsel when he voluntarily and intelligently elects to do so.

> The Sixth Amendment does not provide merely that a defense shall be made for the accused; it grants to the accused personally the right to make his defense. It is the accused, not counsel, who must be 'informed of the nature and cause of the accusation,' who must be 'confronted with the witnesses against him,' and who must be accorded 'compulsory process for obtaining witnesses in his favor.' Although not stated in the Amendment in so many words, the right to self-representation—to make one's own defense personally—is thus necessarily implied by the structure of the Amendment. The right to defend is given directly to the accused; for it is he who suffers the consequences if the defense fails. The counsel provision supplements this design. It speaks of the 'assistance' of counsel, and an assistant, however expert, is still an assistant. The language and spirit of the Sixth Amendment contemplate that counsel, like the other defense tools guaranteed by the Amendment, shall be an aid to a willing defendant—not an organ of the State interposed between an unwilling defendant and his right to defend himself personally. To thrust counsel upon the accused, against his considered wish, thus

violates the logic of the Amendment. In such a case, counsel is not an assistant, but a master; and the right to make a defense is stripped of the personal character upon which the Amendment insists. *Id.* at 819–20.

The *Faretta* majority recognized that a constitutional right to self-representation "seems to cut against the grain" of cases like *Gideon v. Wainwright* which assumed that "the help of a lawyer is essential to assure the defendant a fair trial." *Id.* at 832. But the Court insisted that respect for individual dignity, autonomy, and self-determination required it to allow self-representation.

> It is undeniable that in most criminal prosecutions defendants could better defend with counsel's guidance than by their own unskilled efforts. But where the defendant will not voluntarily accept representation by counsel, the potential advantage of a lawyer's training and experience can be realized, if at all, only imperfectly. To force a lawyer on a defendant can only lead him to believe that the law contrives against him. Moreover, it is not inconceivable that in some rare instances, the defendant might in fact present his case more effectively by conducting his own defense. Personal liberties are not rooted in the law of averages. The right to defend is personal. The defendant, and not his lawyer or the State, will bear the personal consequences of a conviction. It is the defendant, therefore, who must be free personally to decide whether in his particular case counsel is to his advantage. And although he may conduct his own defense ultimately to his own detriment, his choice must be honored out of 'that respect for the individual which is the lifeblood of the law.' *Id.* at 834.

In order to exercise the constitutional right to proceed *pro se*, the defendant must waive her Sixth Amendment right to counsel. "[T]he accused must 'knowingly and intelligently' forgo those relinquished benefits. Although a defendant need not himself have the skill and experience of a lawyer in order competently and intelligently to choose self-representation, he should be made aware of the dangers and disadvantages of self-representation, so that the record will establish that 'he knows what he is doing and his choice is made with eyes open'." *Id.* at 835.

Faretta relied upon its earlier decision in *Von Moltke v. Gillies*, 332 U.S. 708, 68 S.Ct. 316, 92 L.Ed. 309 (1948), in which the Court described the "thorough inquiry" a trial judge must undertake in order to ensure that a defendant has made an informed waiver decision:

> This protecting duty imposes the serious and weighty responsibility upon the trial judge of determining whether there is an intelligent and competent waiver by the accused. To discharge this duty properly in light of the strong presumption against waiver, a judge must investigate as long and as thoroughly as the circumstances of the case before him demand. * * * To be valid such waiver [of counsel] must be made with an apprehension of the nature of the charges, the statutory offenses included within them, the range of allowable punishments thereunder, possible defenses to the charges and circumstances in mitigation thereof, and all other facts essential to a broad understanding of the whole matter. A judge can make certain that an accused's professed waiver of counsel is understandingly

and wisely made only from a penetrating and comprehensive examination of all the circumstances.

IN RE MANUEL R.

207 Conn. 725, 543 A.2d 719 (Conn. 1988).

PETERS, CHIEF JUSTICE. The right to legal representation is guaranteed by statute to any child charged with delinquency. The question in this case is whether, and under what circumstances, that right to counsel can be waived by the child. The respondent, Manuel R., appeals from the disposition of the Superior Court committing him to the department of children and youth services (DCYS) for placement at Long Lane School. We find error and remand for a new dispositional hearing. [The juvenile court placed Manuel R. on probation for one year on a burglary charge. Several months later, his probation officer filed a petition alleging that Manuel violated the terms of the court's probation order. The probation officer also filed an application for Manuel's detention pending the proceeding.]

A hearing on the application for detention was held on April 22, 1987. According to the transcript of this hearing, the probation department sought to detain Manuel not on the basis of his alleged probation violations but rather because he had allegedly committed a third degree assault on his mother. The court declined to place Manuel in the only then available group home and instead continued the detention review hearing until the following week to allow a further exploration of residential placement possibilities. At this hearing, and at all subsequent detention and adjudicatory hearings, Manuel was represented by Attorney George Oleyer of the office of the public defender. * * * At the close of the hearing, Manuel's mother, Carmen R., stated that, while she had confidence in Manuel and hoped that the detention would help him, she was "not going to keep letting him pull me down 'cuz I still have a life to lead, too. And he fails to realize that I'm punished for every time he does something."

The adjudicative phase of the proceeding took place two weeks later. After a colloquy following Manuel's admission that he had violated the terms of his probation, the trial court, *Barnett, J.,* accepted the plea of admission and adjudicated Manuel a delinquent child. * * * Manuel next appeared before the Superior Court, so far as the record discloses, on August 17, 1987, at proceedings that, although docketed as relating to the entry of pleas on new charges, quickly evolved into a disposition of the previously adjudicated probation violations. These are the proceedings whose validity is presently at issue in this appeal. * * *

Before commencing the plea hearing, the trial court * * * summoned Attorney Oleyer to the courtroom, having been told by the probation officer that Oleyer represented Manuel. Oleyer appeared on the scene within a few moments and asked the court, "Can we pass this? I haven't seen him. I didn't know [Manuel and his mother] were here." Manuel's mother objected to a continuance in the following manner: "Excuse me, but I don't want—I don't want—if I have to go without an attorney I'll go without an attorney because Mr. Oleyer's going to force this thing into where Manuel's going back home and Manuel's going to do the same thing again. I'm going to miss more time from work and I'm going to lose my job, and I'm not going for it. If I have to represent my son I'll represent him."

In order to allow for further consultation between the parties, the trial court called a five minute recess. Upon its expiration, the hearing resumed when all parties, except Oleyer, reentered the courtroom. Thereafter the following exchange took place:

"Mrs. [R]: I don't want Mr. Oleyer for my son's attorney.

"The Court: Well, we have nobody else here.

"Mrs. [R]: Well, I'll represent him myself then. He tells me—he tells us five minutes then he goes out there and he's calling everybody else into the office sitting there with him. I mean, I have to go to work 'cuz I got other kids I gotta support."

The trial court then moved ahead with the plea hearing by informing Manuel of three new charges against him. * * * Having described the charges, the court expressed its reluctance to proceed any further without representation for Manuel, to which Mrs. R. responded: "Yeah, but Mr. Oleyer—he thinks that he's gonna come in here and sit here and have Manuel sent home again today, or whatever, and just keep sending him back and forth, back and forth." Before Mrs. R. could complete her objections to a continuance on the entry of the pleas, Elizabeth Gleason, the state's advocate, brought to the court's attention, for the first time, Manuel's outstanding adjudication of delinquency and asked the court to enter a disposition in accordance with the recommendation of the probation officer, "which the state strongly supports." Mrs. R. then commented that if Manuel were sent home again and "he goes and gets in trouble again then I gotta miss work again." The probation officer informed the court that three residential facilities had rejected Manuel and that the only option was placement at the state training school (Long Lane). In answer to the trial court's question, "Is this for disposition today?" the probation officer replied, "Well, yes, I was going to ask that it go for disposition because of problems in the home." After again being told that Manuel had already been adjudicated delinquent for probation violations, the trial court initiated the following discussion between all present:

"The Court: Okay. You want to get rid of those other two files [the probation violations] that he has against him?

"Mrs. [R]: Yes, sir.

"The Court: All right, and you're waiving on behalf of your son the attorney that would be sitting here? That's Mr. Oleyer because he was involved in these files.

"Mrs. [R]: Yes, sir.

"Mr. Carlos [the probation officer]: Your Honor, would you like me to get another attorney?

"The Court: No. The mother has indicated that she doesn't want it—it's for disposition—a replacement. And it's recommendation by you is to place him in Mead Hall until other placement is found?

"Mr. Carlos: Oh, well, no, your Honor. My recommendation today is Long Lane. That's why I was concerned about him not being represented.

"The Court: Do you understand what that recommendation is?

"Mrs. [R]: Yes, I do.

"The Court: And you still don't want him to be represented?

"Mrs. [R]: Yes.

"Mr. Carlos: I've also explained it to the youngster, your Honor. He might have different feelings about it. But I did explain to him what I was recommending.

"Mrs. [R]: Do you want an attorney?

"The Respondent [Manuel]: No.

"The Court: You don't?

"Mrs. [R]: You sure?

"The Respondent: (Nods no.)

"The Court: You understand that the recommendation is for you to be committed to Long Lane?

"The Respondent: Yes."

The court thereafter ordered Manuel committed to the custody of the DCYS for a period of two years with placement at Long Lane. Manuel appealed from the disposition to the Appellate Court and we transferred his appeal here pursuant to Practice Book § 4023. We conclude that the record in this case fails to establish that Manuel knowingly and voluntarily waived the assistance of counsel during the dispositional stage of his delinquency proceeding. Accordingly, we find error and remand for a new hearing.

Any child in Connecticut is guaranteed the right to assistance of counsel in the defense of a delinquency petition by virtue of General Statutes § 46b–135(a), which provides that, "[a]t the commencement of any proceeding" involving his or her delinquency, a child "shall have the right to counsel" and, if necessary because of indigency, the state shall incur the cost. Under Connecticut law, a delinquency proceeding is bifurcated into adjudicatory and dispositional phases. The express language of § 46b–135(a) is without limitation and therefore encompasses both phases of the proceeding. This statutory right to counsel comports with governing constitutional requirements.

The sole issue in this case, then, is whether a valid waiver of the respondent's right to counsel took place during the dispositional hearing. The respondent makes a two-fold attack on the validity of the waiver, claiming (1) that a child's right to counsel during a delinquency proceeding is nonwaivable as a matter of law, and (2) that, even if the right to counsel is waivable, the record in this case fails to establish a knowing and voluntary relinquishment of legal representation. While we disagree with the first of these claims, we agree with the second. We conclude that, in the circumstances of this case, the child did not effectively waive his right to counsel and that his mother, given her primary concern for a speedy resolution of the case, had such a conflict of interest that she lacked authority to do so on his behalf.

The respondent first urges us to adopt a per se rule declaring that children under the age of sixteen are legally incompetent to waive the assistance of counsel under any circumstance. In support of this claim, the respondent cites empirical research that suggests a definite correlation between youth and lack of comprehension of constitutional rights. This research has special relevance, according to the respondent, because in Connecticut the only persons who are subject to the delinquency jurisdiction of the Superior Court are below the age of sixteen. In light of empirical findings that persons of such tender years are, as a class, prone to misunderstanding legal rights, the respondent argues that a per se rule is justified.

We are not persuaded, however, that a per se rule based on the age of the child is an appropriate response to the admittedly delicate issue of juveniles' waiver of rights. The empirical evidence to date suggests that age, by itself, is not a reliable touchstone for determining a juvenile's capacity to exercise fundamental rights. A major study concluded that "age itself is quite limited in its effectiveness as a guide for weighing decisions about juveniles' understanding." It is true that, for all children below the age of fourteen, the available evidence suggests that comprehension of legal rights is elusive. With regard to children between the ages of fourteen and sixteen, however, general intelligence level, as well as socio-economic status and prior court experience, become increasingly significant factors in a child's ability to grasp and exercise legal rights. The empirical literature therefore fails definitively to identify age as a surrogate for incapacity for children below the age of sixteen. * * *

Furthermore, a per se rule of nonwaivability might actually frustrate a principal goal of juvenile law of encouraging children to accept responsibility for their transgressions and take an active role in their rehabilitation. Juvenile law embodies goals of control and treatment that are often difficult to reconcile. On the one hand, protecting society from disruptive and dangerous children often requires that courts control and incarcerate children in prison-like institutions. On the other hand, nurturing children into productive and responsible adults requires that persistent efforts be made toward individualized treatment and rehabilitation. Without minimizing the significance of this inevitable tension, we are persuaded that allowing a child to make an informed and deliberate choice about legal representation, if properly supervised by the trial court, can advance both the goal of control and that of treatment.

In juvenile proceedings, counsel for the child plays an important role in ensuring the reliability of adjudications underlying disposition and in developing alternative placement plans thereafter. To mandate the presence of counsel, however, might serve to reduce the child's own sense of involvement and might enhance his perception of his own role as merely that of spectator. The difficulty of engaging children meaningfully in their own cases has been recognized as a major challenge: "Courtroom deliberations often make the delinquent highly aware of his own irrelevance and inability to affect the course of the proceeding. Many decisions are reached, for example, without consulting the youth and in ways that suggest his complete incompetence to determine his own future." For those concerned with intervening successfully in the lives of troubled young persons, there is an increasing awareness that the procedures followed by the court can have a lasting impact on the child's development. In light of these principles, we believe that the waiver of counsel decision, *in itself*, can be a significant rehabilitative moment for the child. We accordingly reject the respondent's invitation to impose a per se rule of incompetency on all children.

We now turn to the central question of this appeal: what standards are to guide the trial court in its determination of whether to find that a child has validly waived his or her right to counsel. As the present proceedings poignantly demonstrate, those standards must take into account the possibility of a conflict of interest when a parent or guardian advocates a waiver on behalf of the child.

We begin our analysis with a reiteration of the standards for the waiver of counsel by adult defendants. A valid waiver is defined, in accordance with the well known test of *Johnson v. Zerbst*, as the intentional relinquishment or abandonment of a known right or privilege. The United States Supreme Court has emphasized, subsequent to *Zerbst*, that a proper waiver of counsel must be intelligent and voluntary and that its basis, having been "clearly determined" by the trial court, should appear on the record.

In like fashion, Practice Book § 961 mandates a "thorough inquiry" into specific factors about which the court must be "satisfied" before the accused "shall be permitted" to forego counsel. In particular, § 961 establishes four criteria for an effective waiver: (1) clear advisement of the right to counsel; (2) possession of sufficient intelligence and capacity to appreciate the consequences of self-representation; (3) comprehension of the charges and proceeding, the permissible punishment exposure and any additional facts essential to a broad understanding of the case; and (4) awareness of the dangers and disadvantages of self-representation.

We conclude that these constitutional and procedural guidelines apply with equal, if not greater, force in the context of a delinquency proceeding.

It is now commonly recognized that courts should take "special care" in scrutinizing a purported confession or waiver by a child. As the United States Supreme Court acknowledged in *In re Gault*, "special problems may arise with respect to waiver of the privilege by or on behalf of children and * * * there may well be some differences in technique—but not in principle—depending upon the age of the child and the presence and competence of parents."

These judicial pronouncements embody the common sense notion that the validity of a child's waiver of counsel depends upon furnishing the child full information not only about the child's own legal rights but also about the overall nature of the proceeding against him or her. The need for broad-gauged advice is underscored by recent empirical studies demonstrating that significant numbers of children erroneously believe that lawyers are responsible for deciding issues of guilt and punishment, that defense lawyers will not advocate the interests of a juvenile who admits to the violation and that defense lawyers have a duty to report to the court any evidence of the juvenile client's culpability. Only a full colloquy between the court and the child can avoid such misperceptions and provide a solid basis for the intelligent exercise or waiver of the right to counsel. Only a full colloquy will permit the court to make an accurate determination of whether a child who professes to wish to proceed pro se, without counsel, has the developmental and cognitive ability to undertake a realistic assessment of the consequences of such an action. For all these reasons, our general policy of indulging every presumption against the waiver of fundamental rights has special application in the context of juvenile waiver.

The fact that, at juvenile proceedings, a child is often accompanied by a parent or guardian does not diminish judicial responsibility for a searching inquiry into the validity of a potential waiver of the right to counsel. At a minimum, the presence of a lay parent or guardian, with no training in law, is no guarantee that a child will be fully informed or meaningfully represented. Moreover, as judicial and scholarly authorities attest, parents may, for their own reasons, exert pressure on children to confess to alleged offenses and to waive the assistance of counsel. The potential for undue parental influence is greatly increased in the event of a specific conflict of interest between parent and child. Such a potential conflict may arise, for example, when the parent bears fiscal responsibility for the cost of retained counsel, or acts as the complaining witness in the delinquency petition, or harbors anger and resentment about the child's misbehavior. Recognizing the possibility of such conflicts of interest between parent and child, Practice Book § 1045(2)(b) expressly provides that the court "shall appoint * * * counsel for the child, whether a request is made or not * * * if in the opinion of the court the interests of the child and his parents conflict * * *." Similarly, once a conflict of interest becomes apparent, the court may not permit a parent to waive counsel for a child.

Applying these standards for the validity of a child's waiver of the right to counsel to the facts of this case, we conclude that the record fails to establish that Manuel knowingly and voluntarily waived his right to legal representation at his dispositional hearing. The record manifests minimal participation by Manuel himself and substantial deference to the conflicting interests of his mother in immediate disposition of the charges against her son. Our statute and § 961 of our rules of practice require more of the court.

The first of the four inquiries that a court must make, under § 961, before it accepts a waiver of the right to counsel, is whether the defendant, in this case the child, has been advised of his right to counsel. Concededly, that advice was given to the respondent in this case.

The second inquiry that § 961 requires concerns the child's intelligence and capacity to appreciate the consequence of the decision to represent himself. On this question, the trial court record is sparse at best. The court made no effort to address the respondent directly to determine whether he possessed the qualities described by the rule. In fact, the transcript reveals that Manuel uttered only five words throughout the hearing: the answer "Yes" or "No" on five separate occasions. Of these five monosyllabic answers, two were in response to the questions whether he understood his right to counsel and his right to remain silent and three were in response to the following questions from the bench: (1) "Do you want an attorney?"; (2) "You don't?"; and (3) "You understand you are going up to Long Lane for a period of time?" * * * We note in addition that the trial court did not preside over the detention and adjudicatory phases of this case and therefore had no prior opportunity on this record to observe the respondent and form a judgment about his mental capacity. * * * Accordingly, the record falls short of "*affirmatively* show[ing] that [the respondent] was literate, competent and understanding, and that he voluntarily exercised his informed free will."

The third requirement of § 961 is that the court satisfy itself that the child comprehends the "charges and proceedings, the range of permissible punishments, and any additional facts essential to a broad understanding of the case." The record in this regard raises the contrary inference, that the respondent did *not* understand the proceeding or the range of potential dispositions. * * *

Finally, it is apparent that the respondent was not "made aware of the dangers and disadvantages of self-representation" as required by the fourth element of § 961. Counsel can perform a variety of useful functions during the dispositional phase of a delinquency proceeding. In particular, the child might be informed that a primary obligation of defense counsel is to augment and investigate the placement recommendation of the state so that the ultimate disposition is tailored to the child's individual needs. Additionally, counsel can exercise the rights of confrontation and cross-examination, subpoena witnesses, ensure adherence to procedural regularity and assist the child and the family in securing important state services.

On the record before us, there was no effort whatsoever to inform the respondent and his mother of the risks of self-representation.

In its totality, this record manifests a canvass that fails to comport with well established rules concerning waiver of the right to counsel. Without a compliance with Practice Book § 961, and in the absence of other evidence sufficient to establish the respondent's knowing and voluntary waiver of his statutory right to counsel, it was error to order his commitment to the department of children and youth services with placement at the state training school. * * *

NOTES

1) Factors courts consider to assess validity of juveniles' waiver of counsel—The Law-on-the-Books In **In re Christopher H.**, 259 S.C. 161, 596 S.E.2d 500 (App. 2004), the South Carolina Court of Appeals reviewed the sufficiency of a juvenile's waiver of counsel and described the factors the trial court must consider prior to accepting a waiver:

> A valid waiver of counsel, either by affirmative, verbal request or by conduct, requires compliance with *Faretta*. *Faretta* allows an accused to waive his right to counsel if he is (1) advised of his right to counsel, and (2) adequately warned of the dangers of self-representation. Furthermore, "[i]n the absence of a specific inquiry by the trial judge addressing the disadvantages of a *pro se* defense as required by the second *Faretta* prong, [the appellate court] will look to the record to determine whether petitioner had sufficient background or was apprised of his rights by some other source." To determine if an accused has sufficient background to comprehend the dangers of self-representation, courts consider a variety of factors including:

> (1) the accused's age, educational background, and physical and mental health;

> (2) whether the accused was previously involved in criminal trials;

> (3) whether the accused knew the nature of the charge(s) and of the possible penalties;

> (4) whether the accused was represented by counsel before trial and whether that attorney explained to him the dangers of self-representation;

> (5) whether the accused was attempting to delay or manipulate the proceedings;

> (6) whether the court appointed stand-by counsel;

> (7) whether the accused knew he would be required to comply with the rules of procedure at trial;

> (8) whether the accused knew of the legal challenges he could raise in defense to the charge(s) against him;

> (9) whether the exchange between the accused and the court consisted merely of *pro forma* answers to *pro forma* questions; and

(10) whether the accused's waiver resulted from either coercion or mistreatment.

The record in this case reveals that neither the judge at the adjudicatory hearing nor the judge at the dispositional hearing complied with the procedures in *Faretta*. * * * Christopher was never adequately warned of the dangers of self-representation. In addition, the record reflects that Christopher has an insufficient background to comprehend the dangers of self-representation: * * * (1) Christopher was sixteen years old at the time of the proceedings, but his psychosocial report states that he "appears emotionally and physically younger than his stated age." Christopher has a full scale IQ of seventy-four (borderline range) and his last year in school was the tenth grade. (2) It appears from the record that Christopher had been to family court before, but it is unclear as to the nature of his family court experience. (3) Nothing in the record indicates that Christopher had any knowledge of the nature of the charges or the possible penalties. Instead, Christopher merely indicated his willingness to accept responsibility for certain acts he had committed. (4) Christopher never appeared represented by counsel. * * * (6) The court did not appoint stand-by counsel. (7) The record does not indicate Christopher had any knowledge that he needed to comply with any rules of procedure or (8) any of the legal challenges he could raise in his defense. (9) The exchange between Christopher and the family court judges amounted to little more than *pro forma* questions and answers. * * *

We find the record in this case does not show that Christopher knowingly and intelligently waived his right to counsel. * * * Because we find the record clearly reflects that the family court failed to adequately advise Christopher of the right to counsel, failed to make a specific inquiry as to Christopher's knowledge of the dangers of self-representation, and demonstrated that Christopher has an insufficient background to comprehend the dangers of self-representation, * * * we reverse and remand for a new trial.

2) Juveniles' Waiver of the Right To Counsel—The Law-in-Action In a study the ninety-nine post-*Gault* cases in which juveniles appealed and challenged the validity of their waivers of counsel, **Mary Berkheiser, "The Fiction of Juvenile Right to Counsel: Waiver in the Juvenile Courts," 54 *Fla. L. Rev.* 577, 609–619, 633 (2002)**, reports that although appellate courts ultimately reversed the vast majority of counsel waivers, the cases demonstrate juvenile court judges' routine failure to comply with the legal requirements for a valid waiver:

Reported decisions in appeals challenging a juvenile's waiver of counsel are as unsettling as the studies discussed above [reporting low rates of attorney representation of juveniles]. Research for this Article revealed ninety-nine post-*Gault* appellate decisions that addressed the validity of a juvenile's waiver of right to counsel after a delinquency petition had been filed. In an overwhelming majority of the cases, eighty of the ninety-nine, the waivers were overturned on appeal. In those cases, children as young as nine had been permitted to waive right to counsel, while a waiver by an eleven–year–old boy was among those upheld on appeal.

Analysis of the cases showed that in all but two of the nineteen in which the waivers were upheld, the accused child had admitted the charges after waiving counsel. Similarly, fifty-one of the eighty juveniles whose waivers were overturned on appeal had entered admissions or pleas of nolo contendere. More often than not, the delinquency petitions alleged serious felony charges. Only a handful were status offenses (runaways, truancies, curfew violations), and all were in cases overturned on appeal. Most of the juveniles whose waivers were upheld were committed to the custody of the state agency responsible for delinquent youth; the remaining youths were put on intensive probation. Nearly three-quarters of the juveniles in the overturned cases had been committed to state custody. The courts had specifically ordered most of those children to be confined in a state "training school" or other institution, many for an indefinite period of time, others ranging from five months to a maximum of eight years.

Juvenile court judges' advisories to accused juveniles concerning their right to counsel were consistent with the results of the studies reported above concerning judicial noncompliance with *Gault*. Over thirty percent of the juveniles were not advised at all. In several cases, the juvenile court record was silent regarding the rights advisories or waiver proceedings. In others, the docket sheet or court minutes reflected only that the juvenile had been informed of his right to counsel and had waived it. In many cases, the judge informed the accused of his right to counsel and then simply asked if he wanted a lawyer. In three other cases, the judge merged the right to counsel inquiry with the entry of a plea.

In the few cases in which the explanation of rights was relatively complete, the courts conducted no waiver colloquy, simply concluding that the waiver was valid from the juvenile's indication that he understood his rights. Other cases so clearly reveal the involuntariness of the juvenile's waiver that the judge's acceptance of it is shocking. * * * [T]he cases, viewed together, present a bleak picture of juveniles' access to counsel. Many juvenile courts do little, if anything, to assure that juveniles waiving their right to counsel understand what they are doing. More specifically, the cases compel two deeply disturbing conclusions: neither the presumption against waiver nor the enactment of detailed statutory waiver procedures have been effective constraints against juvenile court judges' continued exercise of their "discretion" to deny juveniles their right to counsel.

The Supreme Court has often warned that trial court judges should indulge "every reasonable presumption" against waiver of constitutional rights by criminal defendants. Yet juvenile court practices as revealed in the reported cases demonstrate a total disregard for the presumption. Not a single court in nearly one hundred waiver cases conducted a thorough inquiry into the circumstances to determine whether the juvenile's waiver was knowing, voluntary and intelligent, and few courts acknowledged that they were bound by a legal standard. Most courts either said nothing or simply recited the adult waiver standard. Only a handful of cases went further, some suggesting that the standard for juvenile waiver was "at least equal to" that accorded adults, and others stating that the court needed to be even more careful or "particularly solicitous" of the juvenile's rights. * * *

Even in juvenile courts which did not so blatantly disregard juveniles' right to counsel, the waiver proceedings did not reflect the thorough-going inquiry contemplated by the "knowing, voluntary and intelligent" standard and the "totality of the circumstances" test. That test, first articulated by the United States Supreme Court in *Johnson v. Zerbst*, requires an examination of a multiplicity of factors to determine the validity of a waiver, including the person's age, intellectual ability, educational level, emotional or mental problems, and prior experience with the court system.

Few of the waiver decisions discussed any of those factors. The courts did not generally consider age to be a factor affecting the validity of the waiver decision, even when the child was as young as nine. Only seven cases discussed more than one factor, and in three cases, the juvenile's prior experience with the court appeared to trump evidence concerning his mental, emotional or medical problems. In the remaining four cases, the judges concluded that the juvenile's waiver was valid despite evidence of the child's educational deficiencies or emotional and behavioral problems.

Even in the most extreme cases, the totality of the circumstances test did not protect the child from an ill-advised waiver. * * * In a method apparently favored by some judges in Orange County, Florida, the judge spoke to all the juveniles in the courtroom at once, lecturing them *en masse* about their right to counsel (court-appointed if they were financially eligible), their other constitutional rights, procedures for waiving and entering pleas, and other details. * * *

Similarly, cases in which the juvenile's waiver was upheld showed little attention to the circumstances under which the waiver was made, and none conducted a thorough analysis of the "totality" factors. Only four of the nineteen cases considered two or more factors. Like the cases overturning waiver, prior juvenile court experience appeared to be the most significant factor in determining the validity of waiver, as reflected in four cases. * * *

The decisions in more than two-thirds of the collected cases were based in whole or in part on juvenile court judges' failure to follow the mandates of state statutes or court rules. In sixty-six of the eighty cases overturning waivers, the reviewing courts cited such noncompliance by the lower courts. The ineffectiveness of duly enacted statutes and court rules in ensuring the validity of juvenile waivers demonstrates the resistance of juvenile court judges to externally imposed limits on their discretion. Even in states with the most specific and detailed directives for the acceptance of juvenile waiver, judges often fail to provide juveniles with the most basic reading of their rights. * * *

Because few cases contain a well-developed record of the proceedings below, reversal often was based on the insufficiency of the record to support the juvenile court's acceptance of waiver. * * *

For juveniles, as for adults, right to counsel is the key to their ability to receive a fair trial that accords them their due process rights. When the juvenile court permits a juvenile to waive right to counsel without establishing that the waiver was knowing, voluntary, and intelligent, the juvenile is deprived of his right to counsel. That deprivation so contaminates the entire trial process that it can never constitute harmless error. Instead, as in adult waiver cases, the juvenile court's acceptance of an invalid waiver is a structural error that requires automatic reversal without a showing of prejudice.

However, correction at the appellate level provides faint hope for most juveniles who waive their right to counsel. The sheer enormity of the problem is reflected in the low appeal rate for juvenile adjudications and dispositions. A 1996 study by the ABA Juvenile Justice Center found that the practice of taking appeals in juvenile court is "lacking in most jurisdictions." Nearly one-half of juvenile public defenders and more than three quarters of appointed lawyers authorized to file appeals reported that they had taken no appeals in the preceding year. [Ed. *See* Note 9, *infra* pp. 848–851] Add to those numbers the one-third of public defenders and one-quarter of appointed lawyers who were not authorized to appeal, and the prospects for review of a juvenile court's decision are dim, even for those who were provided counsel in the first instance. For all those who waived their right to counsel, the opportunities are rare indeed. Relying on the wisdom of the appellate courts to remedy the injustice visited upon youth by the juvenile court's acquiescence in invalid waivers of right to counsel, therefore, is an inadequate remedy for such a significant problem. * * *

3) Juveniles' competence and waivers of the right to counsel Reconsider *Fare v. Michael C.* and the materials on juveniles' adjudicative competence, *supra* pp. 109–112, and their capacity to waive *Miranda* rights, *supra* at pp. 295–297. Should different legal policies govern juveniles' waivers of *Miranda* rights and waivers of the right to counsel after the formal initiation of delinquency proceedings? To what extent are the policy options considered respecting juveniles' waivers of *Miranda* rights applicable to waivers of counsel? Did *Gault* require appointment of counsel or only advice of a right to counsel? To what extent do the various states' statutes and rules of juvenile procedure respond to the empirical research on juveniles' competence to waive legal rights? Does the court's analysis in *Manuel R.* respond adequately to the issues of adolescents' compromised competence to make waiver decisions? See Donna Bishop and Hillary B. Farber, "Joining the Legal Significance of Adolescent Developmental Capacities with the Legal Rights Provided in In re Gault," 60 *Rut. L. Rev.* 125, 149—160 (2007) (arguing that the same cognitive and behavioral deficits that informed the Court's decision in *Roper v. Simmons* also limit juveniles' ability to make valid waiver decisions).

4) Consultation With Counsel Prior to Waiver In **D.R. v. Commonwealth**, 64 S.W.3d 292 (Ky. Ct. App. 2001), the Kentucky Court of Appeals construed two provisions of KRS 610.060 which provide, in relevant part, that when a child is brought before the court, the court shall:

(a) Explain to the child and his parents, guardian, or person exercising custodial control their respective rights to counsel and, if the child and his parents, guardian, or person exercising custodial control are unable to obtain counsel, shall appoint counsel for the child, * * * [and]

(e) Advise the child that these rights belong to him and may not be waived by his parents, guardian, or person exercising custodial control.

The juvenile argued that the use of "shall" in subsection (a) prohibited a juvenile's waiver of counsel and the Commonwealth contended that subsection (e) permits a child to waive the right to counsel afforded under subsection (a). The Court of Appeals reconciled the statutory conflict by requiring mandatory consultation with counsel prior to any waiver of counsel:

> We view subsections (a) and (e) to be ambiguous and to be in apparent conflict with each other. In subsection (a), the legislature *explicitly* signaled its intent that a child "shall" be appointed counsel; however, in subsection (e), the legislature *implicitly* signaled its intent that a child may waive any of the rights set out in subsections (a) through (d). * * *

> [W]e construe subsection (a) as mandating the district court to initially appoint the child counsel; after appointment and consultation with counsel, the child then may waive the right to counsel under subsection (e). Simply stated, we think a child may waive the right to counsel *only if* that child has first been appointed, and consulted with, counsel concerning the waiver. We perceive such construction as consistent with the intent of the legislature as expressly provided in subsection (a), and as implicitly provided in subsection (e). * * *

The court in **State ex rel. J.M., G.E., and A.H. v. Taylor**, 166 W.Va. 511, 276 S.E.2d 199 (W.Va. 1981), also found authority in its juvenile waiver statute to require a juvenile to consult with an attorney prior to any relinquishment of the right to counsel:

> In its *Standards Relating to Adjudication*, the Juvenile Justice Standards Project has drafted Rule 1.2:

> 1.2 Attorneys for respondent and the government.

>> The juvenile court should not begin adjudication proceedings unless the respondent is represented by an attorney who is present in court and the government is represented by an attorney who is present in court.

> A commentary teaches that the juvenile right to counsel should be non-waivable.

> We admire this rule, but are confronted with a suggestion that our Legislature intended that there could be knowing waiver of counsel. Our statute about the preliminary hearing stage of juvenile proceedings provides that a court or juvenile referee shall:

> (2) Appoint counsel by order entered of record, if counsel has not already been retained, appointed or *knowingly waived*. (Emphasis added.).

> Juvenile waiver of constitutional rights obviously must be more carefully proscribed than adult waiver because of the unrebuttable presumption, long memorialized by courts and legislatures, that juveniles lack the capacity to make legally binding decisions. No juvenile legal status is treated the same as that of an adult, to our knowledge. * * *

> We therefore recognize that juvenile waiver has been contemplated by our Legislature; but must also observe that it seems to be a contradiction that an infant might waive his constitutional right to counsel in proceedings wherein his very liberty is threatened, but not do so if

someone is about to force sale of a piece of land in which he owns even a $1.00 interest.

We will, therefore, accommodate the statutory implication that he can waive his right to counsel, by requiring that he can do so, but only upon advice of counsel. Only then can there be knowing waiver. * * *

5) Policy Options for the Appointment of Counsel The various statutes, rules of procedure, and court opinions represent a continuum of options for the delivery of legal services. Despite the variability in state laws, **Marsha Levick and Neha Desai, "Still Waiting: The Elusive Quest to Ensure Juveniles a Constitutional Right to Counsel at All Stages of the Juvenile Court Process,"** 60 Rut. L. Rev. 175 at 178, (2007), argue that

> juveniles charged as delinquents must be provided with legal representation throughout the course of their involvement with the juvenile justice system. This comprehensive view of juveniles' right to counsel includes proceedings or hearings that precede or follow the adjudicatory hearing itself, the primary focus of the *Gault* decision. * * *

[J]uveniles need assistance of counsel for three fundamental reasons. First, juveniles need lawyers precisely because they are juveniles. Because of their developmental characteristics, juveniles as a class are ill-equipped to understand, manage, or navigate the complexities of the modern juvenile (or adult) justice system on their own. Second, juveniles need lawyers to keep the rehabilitative component of juvenile court in focus and to make sure that they have access to programs, services, and other opportunities designed to meet their individual needs for treatment and rehabilitation. Third, juveniles need lawyers to help blunt the increasingly punitive edge of the juvenile justice system, which threatens to obscure its rehabilitative purpose, and to ensure that their release or discharge from the juvenile justice system occurs in a timely and appropriate manner.

Consider the analyses of **Barry C. Feld, "The Right to Counsel in Juvenile Court: An Empirical Study of When Lawyers Appear and the Difference They Make," 79** *J. Crim. L. & Crim.* **1185, 1187–1209; 1317–1337 (1989)**, who examines the policy alternatives to allowing juveniles to waive their right to counsel:

Legislation or judicial rules of procedure mandating the automatic and non-waivable appointment of counsel at the earliest stage in a delinquency proceeding is necessary. As long as it is possible for a juvenile to waive the right to counsel, juvenile court judges will continue to find such waivers on a discretionary basis under the "totality of the circumstances." The very fact that it is legally possible for a juvenile to waive counsel itself may discourage some youths from exercising their right if asserting it may be construed as an affront to the presiding judge. The A.B.A.–I.J.A. Juvenile Justice Standards recommend that "[t]he right to counsel should attach as soon as the juvenile is taken into custody, * * * when a petition is filed * * * or when the juvenile appears personally at an intake conference, whichever occurs first." In addition, "[the juvenile] should have the 'effective assistance of counsel at all stages of the proceeding,' " and this right to counsel is mandatory and non-waivable. * * *

The systematic introduction of defense counsel would provide the mechanism for creating trial records which could be used on appeal and which could provide an additional safeguard to assure that juvenile court judges adhere more closely to the formal procedures that are now required. Moreover, eliminating waivers of counsel would lead to greater numbers of public defenders in juvenile justice cases. An increased cadre of juvenile defenders would get education, support, and encouragement from statewide association with one another similar to the post-*Gideon* revolution in criminal justice that resulted from the creation of statewide defender systems.

More fundamentally, however, since the *Gault* decision, the juvenile court is first and foremost a legal entity engaged in social control and not simply a social welfare agency. As a legal institution exercising substantial coercive powers over young people and their families, safeguards against state intervention and mechanisms to implement those safeguards are necessary. The *Gault* Court was unwilling to rely solely upon the benevolence of juvenile court judges or social workers to safeguard the interests of young people. Instead, it imposed the familiar adversarial model of proof which recognizes the likely conflict of interests between the juvenile and the state. Further, in an adversarial process, only lawyers can effectively invoke the procedural safeguards that are the right of every citizen, including children, as a condition precedent to unsolicited state intervention.

A rule mandating non-waivable assistance of counsel for juveniles appearing in juvenile court might impose substantial burdens on the delivery of legal services in rural areas. * * * Presumably, however, those counties already are providing adult defendants with representation and standby counsel in criminal proceedings so the organizational mechanisms already exist. Moreover, despite any possible fiscal or administrative concerns, every juvenile is already entitled by *Gault* to the assistance of counsel at every critical stage in the process and only an attorney can redress the imbalance between a vulnerable youth and the state. As the Supreme Court said in *Gault*, "the condition of being a boy does not justify a kangaroo court," especially if the justification proffered for such a proceeding is simply the state's fiscal convenience. The issue is not one of entitlement, because all are entitled to representation, but rather the ease or difficulty with which waivers of counsel are found, which in turn has enormous implications for the entire administration of juvenile justice.

Short of mandatory and non-waivable counsel, a prohibition on waivers of counsel without prior consultation and the concurrence of counsel would provide greater assurance than the current practice that any eventual waiver was truly "knowing, intelligent, and voluntary." Because waivers of rights, including the right to counsel, involve legal and strategic considerations as well as knowledge and understanding of rights and an appreciation of consequences, it is difficult to see how any less stringent alternative could be as effective. A per se requirement of consultation with counsel prior to a waiver takes into account the immaturity of youths and their lack of experience in law enforcement situations. In addition, it recognizes that only attorneys possess the skills and training necessary to assist the child in the adversarial process. Moreover, a requirement of consultation with counsel prior to waiver would assure the development of legal services delivery systems that would then facilitate the more routine representation of juveniles.

At the very least, court rules or legislation should prohibit the removal from home or incarceration of any juvenile who was neither represented by counsel nor provided with standby counsel. Such a limitation on disposition is already the law for adult criminal defendants, for juveniles in some jurisdictions, and the operational practice in jurisdictions such as New York and Pennsylvania, where virtually no unrepresented juveniles are removed or confined. * * *

6) Negative impact of representation on juveniles' dispositions

Although providing a lawyer in juvenile court remains problematic in many jurisdictions, the role an attorney adopts is also fraught with difficulties. Whether or not an attorney simply adopts the traditional role of defense counsel established in adult criminal courts and applies it in juvenile proceedings may be complicated by the perceived differences in sentencing policies, the more therapeutic orientation of juvenile courts, and the greater dependency of child-clients. See e.g., Abbe Smith, " 'I Ain't Takin' No Plea': The Challenges in Counseling Youth People Facing Serious Time," 60 Rut. L. Rev. 11 (2007) (describing how young peoples' developmental limitations effect their ability to make significant decisions and complicate the role of the lawyer advising them). In addition, empirical research suggests that a lawyer's adversarial stance may adversely affect the interests of the juvenile client. **Barry C. Feld, "The Right to Counsel in Juvenile Court: An Empirical Study of When Lawyers Appear and the Difference They Make," 79 *J. Crim. L. & Crim.* 1185, 1187–1209; 1317–1337 (1989):**

> Even when juveniles are represented, attorneys may not be capable of or committed to representing their juvenile clients in an effective adversarial manner. Organizational pressures to cooperate, judicial hostility toward adversarial litigants, role ambiguity created by the dual goals of rehabilitation and punishment, reluctance to help juveniles "beat a case," or an internalization of a court's treatment philosophy may compromise the role of counsel in juvenile court. Institutional pressures to maintain stable, cooperative working relations with other personnel in the system may be inconsistent with effective adversarial advocacy. Several studies have questioned whether lawyers can actually perform as advocates in a system rooted in parens patriae and benevolent rehabilitation. Indeed, there are some indications that lawyers representing juveniles in more traditional "therapeutic" juvenile courts may actually disadvantage their clients in adjudications or dispositions. [Five studies] all reported that juveniles with counsel are more likely to be incarcerated than juveniles without counsel. * * * Feld's evaluation of the impact of counsel in six states' delinquency proceedings reported that:

> > it appears that in virtually every jurisdiction, representation by counsel is an aggravating factor in a juvenile's disposition. * * * In short, while the legal variables [of seriousness of present offense, prior record, and pretrial detention status] enhance the probabilities of representation, the

fact of representation appears to exert an independent effect on the severity of dispositions. * * *

Although other studies have alluded to this phenomenon, this research provides strong and consistent evidence that representation by counsel redounds to the disadvantage of a juvenile. One possible explanation is that the lawyers who appear in juvenile courts are incompetent and prejudice their clients' cases. While systematic qualitative evaluations of the actual performance of counsel in juvenile courts are lacking, the available evidence suggests that even in jurisdictions where counsel are routinely appointed, there are grounds for concern about their effectiveness. Public defender offices in many jurisdictions often assign their least capable lawyers or newest staff attorneys to juvenile courts to get trial experience and these neophytes may receive less adequate supervision than their prosecutorial counterparts. Similarly, court appointed counsel may be beholden to the judges who select them and more concerned with maintaining an ongoing relationship with the court than vigorously protecting the interests of their frequently changing clients. * * *

Perhaps, however, the relationship between the presence of counsel and the increased severity of disposition is spurious. * * * It may be that early in a proceeding, a juvenile court judge's familiarity with a case alerts him or her to the eventual disposition that will be imposed if the child is convicted and counsel may be appointed in anticipation of more severe consequences. In many states and counties, the same judge who presides at a youth's arraignment and detention hearing will later decide the case on the merits and then impose a sentence. Perhaps the initial decision to appoint counsel is based upon the evidence developed at those earlier stages which also influences later dispositions. * * *

Another possible explanation for the aggravating effect of lawyers on sentences is that juvenile court judges may treat more formally and severely juveniles who appear with counsel than those who do not. Within statutory limits, judges may feel less constrained when sentencing a youth who is represented. Adherence to formal due process may insulate sentences from appellate reversal. Such may be the price of formal procedures. While not necessarily punishing juveniles who are represented because they appear with counsel, judges may be more lenient toward those youths who appear unaided and "throw themselves on the mercy of the court." While such an interpretation is consistent with this data, it raises in a different guise the question of judicial hostility toward adversarial litigants. Why should the fact that a youth avails himself of an elementary, constitutional procedural safeguards result in an aggravated sentence compared to that of an unrepresented juvenile? * * *

7) Another Explanation of the Negative Impact of Lawyers in Juvenile Court Janet E. Ainsworth, "Re–Imagining Childhood and Reconstructing the Legal Order: The Case for Abolishing the Juvenile Court," 69 *N. C. L. Rev.* **1083, 1126–30 (1991),** summarizes some of the research on the quality of lawyers' performance in juvenile courts:

[S]tudies have shown that juveniles with lawyers fare worse in juvenile court than those proceeding without counsel, being more likely to be incarcerated and jailed for longer periods than if represented pro se. * * *

As is demonstrated in two in-depth examinations of juvenile court procedures, trials in juvenile court are frequently "only marginally contested," marked by "lackadaisical defense efforts." Defense counsel generally make few objections, and seldom move to exclude evidence on constitutional grounds. Defense witnesses rarely are called, and the cross-examination of prosecution witnesses is "frequently perfunctory and reveals no design or rationale on the part of the defense attorney." Closing arguments are sketchy when they are made at all. Watching these trials, one gets the overall impression that defense counsel prepare minimally or not at all. The New York State Bar Association study estimated that in forty-five percent of all juvenile trials, counsel was "seriously inadequate"; in only five percent could the performance of defense counsel be considered "effective representation."

One explanation for the abysmal performance of defense counsel is that lawyers in juvenile court are all too frequently both inexperienced and overworked. Particularly in jurisdictions where juveniles have no right to jury trial, public defender offices often assign their greenest attorneys to juvenile court to season them. Supervision from senior attorneys is not always what might be desired, and caseloads in these high volume courts are crushing. Moreover, in a forum without jury trials, there is a tendency for lawyers to cut corners in these cases of comparatively low public visibility, a tendency often tacitly encouraged by judges anxious to process cases as expeditiously as possible. Under these circumstances, it is no wonder that juvenile bench trials are seldom models of zealous defense advocacy.

In addition, defense lawyers who routinely practice in juvenile court face tremendous institutional pressures to cooperate in maintaining a smoothly functioning court system. The defense lawyer who is seen as obstreperous in her advocacy will be reminded subtly, or overtly if necessary, that excessive zeal in representing her juvenile clients is inappropriate and counter-productive. If she ignores these signals to temper her advocacy, the appointed defense lawyer is vulnerable to direct attacks, such as having her fees slashed or being excluded from the panel of lawyers from which the court makes indigent appointments. Seldom are such crude measures necessary, however. For most defense lawyers, withstanding the psychological debilitation attendant upon being the sustained focus of judicial and prosecutorial disapproval is hopeless.

Perhaps the most pervasive and insidious reason for less than zealous defense advocacy is the ambiguity felt by many juvenile court lawyers concerning their proper role. The legacy of decades of paternalistic parens patriae ideology is still evident in the attitudes of many defense lawyers, who cannot help thinking of themselves as charged, at least in part, with a responsibility to act in their clients' long term best interests rather than scrupulously to safeguard their legal rights. Despite the clear ethical mandate to represent juveniles on the same terms and with the same zeal as they would adults, many defenders nevertheless find themselves deeply torn between their professional obligation to press their clients' legitimate legal claims and their paternalistic inclination to help the court address their clients' often desperate social needs. Even lawyers who have not internalized this role conflict may face external pressure from judges and probation officers to conform to a guardian-like role. * * *

8) Juveniles' right to appeal The Supreme Court in *Gault* did not reach the question whether the Constitution requires States "to provide appellate courts or a right to appellate review at all." *Supra*, p. 733. However, the Court noted that "the consequences of failure to provide an appeal, to record the proceedings, or to make findings or state the grounds for the juvenile court's conclusion" posed numerous problems for appellate courts and sometimes required remand for new hearings in their absence. State statutes routinely provide for the creation of a record of judicial proceedings "by stenographic notes or by electronic, mechanical, or other appropriate means." Tex. Fam. Code Ann. § 54.09 (Vernon 2000); Wash. R. Juv. Ct. 10.2 (delinquency proceedings "shall be recorded verbatim by means which provide an accurate record and which can be subsequently reduced to written form"). At the conclusion of the fact finding hearing, the trial court must make written findings of fact and give conclusions of law relating to the allegations of the petition. E.g. Wash. Rev. Code. § 13.34.110 (2000); Wis. Stat. § 938.31 (2000).

State laws differ on the scope and timing of appellate review. Some states have enacted comprehensive appellate legislation while others provide little statutory or case law guidance for appeals from juvenile court. Appellate statutes generally restrict juveniles' appeals to review of a "final order" or "final judgment." E.g. Colo. Rev. Stat. Ann. § 19–1–109 (2008)(an appeal "may be taken from any order, decree or judgment."). To avoid interlocutory, partial reviews, and delays in the disposition of a case, most states do not allow a juvenile to appeal from an adjudication of delinquency but only after the court imposes a final sentence. E.g. B.F. v. State, 550 P.2d 991 (Okla. Crim.App.1976). Statutes or case law define what constitutes a final order and as a result, juvenile court decisions to place youths on informal supervision or to defer judgment are not appealable. Ricki J. v. Superior Court, 128 Cal. App.4th 783, 27 Cal.Rptr.3d 494 (2005). State appeals statutes often give juveniles priority on the appellate docket and expedited review. For example, cases of California juveniles appealing from a final order as delinquents or status offenders "shall have precedence over all other cases in the court to which the appeal is taken." Cal. Welf. & Inst. Code § 800(a)(2008). Others provide that juveniles' appeals "shall take precedence over all other business of the court to which the appeal is taken." Ala. Code 1975 § 12–15–120(a)(2008). Even with expedited review, appeals by many delinquents may fail because their cases become moot when dispositional orders expire or they are released from custody. E.g. A.M. v. State, 653 P.2d 346 (AK. Ct. App. 1982). Other courts hear juveniles' appeals regardless of mootness. E.g. In re Jeremy M. 918 A.2d 944 (Conn. App. Ct. 2007) (delinquent's discharge "from further accountability to the court was not rendered moot on ground that no practical relief could be afforded to juvenile.")

9) The Right to Counsel on Appeal and Appellate Lawyers as a Force for Law Reform Despite *Gault*'s reluctance to create a constitutional right to appellate review and a record of proceedings, every state grants juveniles a statutory right to appeal. However, a right appellate review may be of limited utility without the assistance of counsel to raise the appeal. **Donald J. Harris, "Due Process vs. Helping Kids in Trouble: Implementing the Right to Appeal From Adjudications of Delinquency in**

Pennsylvania," 98 *Dick. L. Rev.* 209, 220–230 (1994), analyzes the availability and impact of juvenile appellate defense counsel and accounts for differences between juvenile and adults rates of appeals:

Most juvenile appeals, like adult criminal appeals, are brought through the county public defender's office or its equivalent. Thus, it bears inquiry why the same organization of lawyers that files appeals in large numbers for its adult clients rarely does so for juveniles. * * * [T]he state totals are stable and reveal that the adult appeal rate is at least ten times greater than the juvenile appeal rate. Recall that the issues raised on appeal could account, by our best judgment, for just one fifth of this disparity.

The propensity for filing more adult appeals does not seem to depend on the type of underlying offense. * * * [T]he appeal rates are considerably greater for adults than for juveniles for each offense type * * *.

[T]he statistical data * * * document a strikingly large difference between juvenile and adult appeal rates, but for the most part they are silent as to the reasons this disparity exists. One explanation might be that adult defendants place greater store than juveniles in the notion of legal guilt (was every element of the offense proved beyond a reasonable doubt?) as opposed to factual guilt (did the accused commit the crime?) such that adverse rulings of the trial court may occasion more dissatisfaction with adults. Another explanation might be that adults face longer prison terms than minors and are more prone to appeal on that account. Still another might be that adolescents recognize that placement may serve a constructive purpose in their lives, where adults see incarceration more in terms of punishment. * * *

One of the more direct ways to research the question of why juvenile appeals are hardly ever filed is to ask the public and private defenders handling juvenile delinquency cases to describe their participation in the decision-making process. Accordingly, I interviewed chief public defenders, supervisors and staff attorneys in the county public defender offices, and several private attorneys who practice criminal law and who occasionally represent children. * * *

The defenders' interview responses quickly revealed an important aspect of the values and perspectives of the juvenile court community. While a few defenders view their roles as advocates whose sole job is to protect the child's legal rights, many see their roles in multi-dimensional terms. Concern with the long-term developmental needs of the child and with legal advocacy prompts some attorneys to see appeals as an obstacle to getting the child back on track. They fear that the taking of an appeal merely encourages the child to hold a cynical view. * * *

Almost all of the defenders, in describing the decision not to take an appeal, omit any reference to the child or the parents or guardian as participants in the process. More typical is the total absence of any decision-making process at all. This is especially true in busy court systems where defenders have so little time between cases that the thought of an appeal often never even arises. Follow-up questions reveal, with only a few exceptions, that neither the juvenile nor the parents or guardians are advised of the right to appeal.

The defenders proffered several justifications for this practice. Some said that the likelihood of success on appeal is slim because the superior and supreme courts try very hard to affirm the trial judge. Others suggest that appeals are futile because children get short sentences and it takes months to decide an appeal. Several defenders spoke of the chronic underfunding of their offices such that they simply don't have the resources to file juvenile appeals. * * *

Additionally, all of the defenders said that the trial court does not inform the juveniles of their appellate rights, and there is no legal obligation to do so. * * *

Defenders are subject to a variety of cross-pressures. They are legal advocates, yet they take on the role of "guardian ad litem" or substitute decision-maker when they decide not to inform juvenile defendants of their appellate rights. They are part of a "courtroom work group" which tries to guide children into a positive future, although they recognize that a juvenile record could be used by the adult sentencing court. They serve as a liaison between the court and the family, an important role as the family's and child's acceptance of the treatment plan is crucial to its success, yet they must seek and be guided by the client's wishes. Also, in comparison with their counterparts in the prosecutor's office, they frequently struggle with higher attorney caseloads, fewer investigative resources and weaker political support. * * *

Apparently, part of the reluctance to advise juveniles of their appellate rights stems from the immaturity of the youngsters. Many attorneys feel that adolescents, particularly delinquent adolescents, have not reached the age of discretion and therefore lack the capacity to intelligently discern their own best interests. * * *

In Pennsylvania there exists among juvenile court practitioners a generally shared set of values, a juvenile court subculture, which, in the tradition of *parens patriae*, effectively nullifies the autonomy of juveniles and their parents to decide whether or not to challenge the legality of their adjudication or commitment. By the same process, the state juvenile court system bypasses appellate review and the accountability that review brings to judicial tribunals which function, in deference to the welfare of the affected party, without public access or citizen juries. * * *

Judge Gary L. Crippen, "Can the Courts Fairly Account for the Diminished Competence and Culpability of Juveniles?", in T. Grisso and R. Schwartz, eds., ***Youth on Trial: A Developmental Perspective on Juvenile Justice*** **409–411, 414 (2000)**, examines the dearth of appellate cases and the importance of effective appellate review as a source of juvenile law reform. Only by providing counsel for appeals can appellate counsel require trial judge to comply with procedural and substantive limitations on juvenile court judges' exercises of discretion:

Special attention should be given to the matter of counsel for appeals. The importance of this law improvement is revealed by noting the rare occurrence of juvenile court appeals in jurisdictions where the justice system does not provide a positive guarantee of effective counsel to assist juveniles for this purpose. * * * I have examined the historic incidence of appeals that challenge juvenile court dispositions in all fifty states. The findings are alarming.

In the history of the nation's juvenile courts, only seven delinquency dispositions, three of them in Minnesota since 1985, have been reversed outright on grounds that they offended governing dispositional standards. Aside from these reversals, there have only been approximately twenty additional instances, seven of them in Minnesota, where appeals courts reviewed application of dispositional standards. In many of these cases, dispositions were reversed due to deficient or misdirected trial-court findings of fact, but with remand that permitted unfettered reconsideration of the case by the trial court. Since 1995, the juvenile court segment of Minnesota appellate law has greatly expanded because of legislation that charges the office of the state public defender with responsibility to represent juveniles on appeal. * * *

To make any dispositional law effective, the services of counsel * * * must be sufficient to create a meaningful right of appeal. Without a healthy juvenile court appellate practice, legal rights are often illusory—and given their limited competence, adolescent offenders should be protected by the rule of law with at least the same consistency as that provided adults. * * *

Because of the exaggerated importance of time for children and the rapid changes in their developmental circumstances, the appellate-court process must move swiftly to be meaningful.

An awareness of the developmental incapacity of adolescents should lead to an anticipation that they will not commonly understand why they might exercise their right to appeal. To be meaningful, the right must be supported by the services of competence counsel, who would give the child information on an appeal and respond to the child's interest in this process. * * *

3. THE ROLE OF THE JUVENILE DEFENSE LAWYER—EFFECTIVE ASSISTANCE OF COUNSEL

Representation by counsel in juvenile court is a two-step process. The first is simply to assure that attorneys actually appear and competently represent youths in delinquency proceedings. As the preceding section indicates, the delivery of legal services remains an issue in many jurisdictions. The second step of the process concerns the appropriate role of counsel in juvenile court. Should an attorney in juvenile court simply replicate the traditional adversarial role of the criminal defense lawyer? To what extent do the rehabilitative goals of juvenile justice require a modification of the adversarial role developed for an explicitly punitive justice system? To what extent do the more discretionary procedures of juvenile justice militate against an adversarial role? Even assuming that an attorney wants to play an adversarial role, does she need to modify that stance because the client is a child rather than a presumptively competent adult? Is the model of client-control an appropriate one for dealing with youngsters? Can children know their own "best interests" and direct counsel accordingly? What if the child's preference is inconsistent with an attorney's perception of an appropriate legal position, whose views should prevail? Because a child's parents actually may retain defense counsel's services and the lawyer necessarily will require their cooperation in many decisions and dispositions, how should a lawyer accommodate the respective preferences of the juvenile and her parents?

Since the Supreme Court decided *Gault*, legal scholars, judges, and practicing lawyers have struggled to resolve the conflicts embedded in juvenile justice—treatment versus punishment, child versus adult, and discretion versus rules—and to define an appropriate role for defense counsel that reconciles these polarities. *See e.g.*, Theodore McMillian and Dorothy McMurtry, "The Role of the Defense Lawyer in the Juvenile Court—Advocate or Social Worker?," 14 *St. Louis U. L.J.* 561 (1970); Elyce Ferster, Thomas Courtless and Edith Snethen, "The Juvenile Justice System: In Search of the Role of Counsel," 39 *Fordham L. Rev.* 375, 410–11 (1971); American Bar Association—Institute of Judicial Administration, *Juvenile Justice Standards Relating to Counsel for Private Parties* (1980); Ketherine Hunt Federle, "The Ethics of Empowerment: Rethinking the Role of Lawyers in Interviewing and Counseling the Child Client," 64 *Fordham L. Rev.* 1655 (1996); Ellen Marrus, "Best Interests Equals Zealous Advocacy: A Not So Radical View of Holistic Representation for Children Accused of Crime", 62 *Md. L. Rev.* 288 (2003). Although beyond the scope of this Chapter, attorneys who represent dependent, neglected, abused, or very young children experience even greater difficulty defining their roles. *See e.g.*, Emily Buss, "You're My What?—The Problem of Children's Misperceptions of Their Lawyers' Roles," 64 *Fordham L. Rev.* 1699 (1996); Martin Guggenheim, "The Right to Be Represented but Not Heard: Reflections on Legal Representation for Children," 59 *N.Y.U. L. Rev.* 76 (1984); Jerry R. Foxhoven, "Effective Assistance of Counsel: Quality of Representation for Juveniles is Still Illusory," 9 *Barry L. Rev.* 99 (2007) (summarizing assessments of delivery and quality of legal services in several states). Because the function of counsel may differ at different stages of proceeding—intake, detention, waiver, adjudication, disposition, post-conviction relief—scholars have focused on how different contexts affect the appropriate attorney role. *See e.g.*, Marsha Levick and Neha Desai, "Still Waiting: The Elusive Quest to Ensure Juveniles a Constitutional Right to Counsel at All Stages of the Juvenile Court Process," 60 *Rut. L. Rev.* 175 (2007); Sandra Simkins, "Out of Sight, Out of Mind: How the Lack of Postdispositional Advocacy in Juvenile Court Increases the Risk of Recidivism and Institutional Abuse," 60 *Rut. L. Rev.* 207 (2007); National Juvenile Defender Center, *Ten Principles for Providing Effective Defense Advocacy at Juvenile Detention Hearings* (2008).

a. Juvenile's Attorney as Guardian ad Litem or Zealous Advocate

Consider the following positions suggested by various commentators and professional organizations on the appropriate role for counsel in delinquency proceedings and the competing interests that attorneys attempt to accommodate.

Richard Kay and Daniel Segal, "The Role of the Attorney in Juvenile Court Proceedings: A Non–Polar Approach," 61 *Geo. L. J.* 1401, 1404, 1410–1411, 1414, 1415, 1417 (1973), analyze the competing perspectives on the role of counsel in delinquency matters:

At one pole is the view that the juvenile attorney should adopt a single-minded adversary stance, indistinguishable from the criminal attorney. This role demands that the attorney do anything within ethical bounds to achieve an adjudication of no delinquency for his client or, should that prove impossible, to attain that disposition for the client which imposes the least restraints on him. The opposite pole, reflecting the unique features of juvenile proceedings, represents the view that the juvenile attorney's role should be that of a participant in a non-adversary, open, and conciliatory activity. This role calls on a lawyer to focus not so much on verdicts of no delinquency or on lenient dispositions as on achieving a resolution which is in a more general and less restricted sense in the "best interests of the child." * * * However, the steps that occur between a juvenile's arrest and the termination of judicial supervision over him are so varied, that it may be that a type of middle ground is called for, one which argues that an adversary role is appropriate at some stages and a non-adversary role is at others. * * *

The nature of the lawyer's professional responsibility in the adjudicatory stage of juvenile proceedings becomes more clouded as it begins to manifest a basic conflict between the adversary tradition and the juvenile court system itself: to what extent should the lawyer act in a traditional adversary role in an attempt to prevent the adjudication of his client as a delinquent child? * * * The role difference between the two contexts is explained by the fundamentally different character of both the court proceedings and the clients involved. An adult criminal trial is a means of ascertaining the facts about the alleged criminal conduct of the defendant. The adversary process is firmly established as the preferred factfinding system in ordinary criminal courts. This system of factfinding, however, has been expressly rejected as the optimum method in the case of juvenile offenders; there, cooperation, consultation and investigation have been deemed the most sensible ways of arriving at the truth. * * * The nature of the client also radically affects the lawyer's professional responsibility in a juvenile adjudication proceeding. An adult defendant is presumably capable of determining his own interest; an attorney who represents him should work on behalf of that interest. While conclusive weight may be given to an adult's decision that it is not in his best interest to be convicted, it is not surprising that such weight might not be given to a similar decision by a juvenile. * * * As distinguished from the adult situation, the juvenile attorney may feel permitted—indeed obligated—to act on a conviction that non-criminal sanctions and parental guidance are the best thing for the child he is representing. * * *

If the lawyer has good reason to believe that the juvenile court often makes the wrong determination and that the treatment it prescribes is often harmful, then abandonment of the adversary role in every case would be directly counter to the child's welfare. Similarly when the attorney believes that by a full presentation of the facts his client is likely to receive treatment which would be in the child's best interests, it would certainly be improper to deprive the child of that benefit by use of strict adversary tactics. So long as the juvenile court fails to function completely along the lines of the rehabilitation model which it was designed to approximate, an attorney has no choice but to make the difficult evaluations suggested. * * *

The arguments for an attorney's abandoning the adversary role in favor of concentrating on what will serve the best interests of the child are strongest with regard to the dispositional phase of a formal juvenile proceeding. * * * First, in juvenile proceedings, far more than in adult proceedings, it may not be at all clear what the most lenient disposition is. * * * A second distinction between the adult and juvenile situations is that the alternative dispositions potentially available for a juvenile offender may be more numerous than for an adult offender. * * * Once the range of dispositional alternatives is expanded, however, the identity between leniency, narrowly construed, and what is best for the child may be destroyed. In an adversary framework, the task of expanding alternatives might not be see as the job of the child's attorney. However, in the framework of a role not narrowly adversary in nature, it becomes appropriate, perhaps critical, for the attorney actively to search out and recommend to the court dispositional alternatives. * * *

In its introduction, **American Bar Association—Institute of Judicial Administration,** *Juvenile Justice Standards Relating to Counsel for Private Parties* **5–7 (1980)** provides the rationale for the adversarial role of counsel that it subsequently proposes in the Standards and Commentary:

> [T]he traditional juvenile court view claiming identify of interest between the state and the accused juvenile has been rejected in favor of recognition of a privilege in juvenile respondents to withhold cooperation in proceedings that may affect their liberties. In this connection, it is important that the Supreme Court, in extending the privilege against self-incrimination to delinquency proceedings, did so not only out of concern for untrustworthy confessions, but also because children, like adults, may claim a measure of distance from the state in actions which may result, however benevolent the motivation, in a substantial restriction of freedom. * * * Once the traditional premise of identity of interests between the state and the juvenile in delinquency proceedings is impeached, the related notion—that adversarial procedures ought to be avoided in a noncontentious forum—becomes flawed as well. * * *

Juvenile Justice Standards Relating to Counsel for Private Parties, Standard **3.1 (1980)**: "(a) * * * [T]he lawyer's principal duty is the representation of the client's legitimate interests. Considerations of personal and professional advantage or convenience should not influence counsel's advice or performance.

(b)(i) In general, determination of the client's interest in the proceedings, and hence the plea to be entered, is ultimately the responsibility of the client after full consultation with the attorney.

(ii)[a] Counsel for the respondent in a delinquency or in need of supervision proceeding should ordinarily be bound by the client's definition of his or her interests with respect to admission or denial of the facts or conditions alleged. It is appropriate and desirable for counsel to advise the client concerning the probable success and consequences of adopting any posture with respect to those proceedings. * * * "

Katherine Hunt Federle, "The Ethics of Empowerment: Rethinking the Role of Lawyers in Interviewing and Counseling the Child Client," 64 *Fordham L. Rev.* **1655, 1671–1679 (1996)**:

[T]he traditional lawyer's role, with its emphasis on the zealous protection of individual rights, seemed peculiarly unsuitable to the unique goals of the juvenile justice system. The lawyer was not a vigorous advocate of civil and constitutional rights and * * * her role was that of guardian and officer of the court. The lawyer was to interpret the philosophy of the juvenile justice system to the child and to assist in the minor's rehabilitation by insuring the child's cooperation with the court's orders. * * *

Several commentators have subsequently interpreted *Gault* to require zealous advocacy from the child's attorney in delinquency proceedings. Noting the *Gault* Court's recognition of the similarities between delinquency and criminal cases, the legal system's commitment to adversarial proceedings, and doubts about the lawyer's ability to make therapeutic judgments in the child's best interests, these scholars have suggested that the lawyer has an ethical obligation to assume a more traditional role in juvenile court. Thus, the child's lawyer is a partisan advocate at all stages of the proceeding who has a duty to present the best possible case for her client. The lawyer should treat all communications with the child as confidential and should vigorously protect the child's privilege against self-incrimination. Furthermore, the lawyer should not hesitate to put the state to its burden of proof, even if that may mean the client's release.

This vision of the child's lawyer as zealous advocate is consistent with the client autonomy paradigm of lawyering. The parallels between delinquency and criminal proceedings suggest that the justification for adversariness is equally applicable to all cases in which the state seeks to limit the freedom of the individual. Because freedom is a central value, the erroneous deprivation of individual liberty is intolerable even when the person whose freedom is constrained is a child. * * *

Furthermore, this approach to lawyering accords the child client considerable autonomy. Some commentators have indicated that the lawyer is obligated to seek those results desired by the child client and to represent the child's expressed preferences. Such an approach comports with traditional ethical rules governing the attorney's behavior while promoting certain goals of the legal system. The lawyer's failure to act upon the client's objectives, however, would prevent the child from presenting certain legal claims to the court for consideration and adjudication. The adversarial approach is also likely to encourage respect for the courts if the child, as a participant, believes she has had a full and fair opportunity to present her case through loyal counsel.

The client autonomy model, however, does assume a competent client. Therefore, several proponents of the adversarial approach to lawyering for the child have suggested that, in most instances, the child client is capable of making decisions about her case. They argue that the assumption of incompetency often is based on a definition of capacity that few adult clients could meet: to require more of the child client merely because of her age would be illegitimate. Furthermore, the child's prosecution for a delinquent act reflects a legislative determination that the child is of sufficient maturity to be held accountable for her actions if she is adjudicated. Thus, fairness mandates that any individual held morally responsible for her actions should be given the autonomy to seek the outcome she desires.

Although proponents of the client autonomy model note that the child often is competent to instruct the attorney, they also concede that the young child may be incompetent to make certain decisions. Consequently, the lawyer must make an initial assessment of the minor's decision-making capacity. Under certain circumstances, if the attorney determines that the child is incapable of making reasoned choices, the attorney may make decisions on behalf of her client. Such decisions should be made only after the lawyer has conducted a thorough investigation and considered the child's wishes and interests. The lawyer, too, should argue for the least intrusive disposition that may be justified under the circumstances.

Assessments of client competence, however, provide significant opportunities for unwarranted infringements upon client autonomy. The lawyer's belief in the foolishness of the choice may convince the lawyer that the child is not capable of considered judgment. Furthermore, even within the client autonomy paradigm, there continues to be some recognition of the need to preserve the client's future autonomy. Thus, the minor's attorney may have a special role in juvenile court given the needs and possibilities of the child. The lawyer may counsel the juvenile about the importance of accepting responsibility for her wrongful acts and explain the limits of her advocacy. * * *

For critics of an adversarial role, systemic concerns for the minor's welfare and rehabilitation appropriately limit the adversarial behavior of lawyers. During the dispositional phase of a delinquency proceeding, a systemic concern for the child's well-being suggests that the judge should consider a range of dispositional alternatives. But adversariness would impede the court's search for an appropriate disposition, redounding to the child's disadvantage if the judge were to impose a more restrictive disposition out of ignorance of the available alternatives. According to these critics, the child's attorney, should adopt a nonadversarial posture to insure that the court consider a broader range of alternative proposals for disposition. The result may be a more positive disposition that proves less restrictive for the child.

These critics also argue that the attorney's nonadversarial role at disposition serves an additional systemic interest in uncovering the truth. Certainly, assisting the court in searching for the truth does sacrifice some of the client's rights; the child, however, may be advantaged by her lawyer's nonadversarial approach. By presenting the court with information about the child, rather than simply the offense, the attorney may help structure a less punitive disposition. * * *

From this perspective, the justification for adversarial behavior has little persuasive moral force. It is the lawyer's nonadversarial behavior that promotes the child's rehabilitation during the dispositional phase of a delinquency proceeding. In this sense, it can be said that the lawyer engages in a positive moral act that benefits the child by espousing the child's right to rehabilitation and treatment. Similarly, the lawyer's duty to convince the minor that the court's disposition is fair is morally obligatory because by securing the child's compliance with the court's orders, the lawyer facilitates the child's rehabilitation. By counseling the client to accept responsibility for her actions, the lawyer also promotes the client's goodness. * * *

Martin Guggenheim, "The Right to be Represented But Not Heard: Reflections on Legal Representation For Children," 59 N.Y.U. L. Rev. 76, 83–89 (1984):

My central concern in this Part is, once again, with client control: Should an attorney be ethically bound to follow the directions of an older child client, or should the attorney be allowed to decide for himself, perhaps in consultation with the parents, what is in the child's best interests? For example, should counsel for an adolescent charged with delinquency be allowed to refuse to mount a defense because he believes his client's interests would be served best by sending him to a state institution, even though the client vigorously opposes such a course of action? * * * [T]he client's power to control his own attorney reflects, in large measure, the rights-based nature of our legal system. It also noted that client control is consonant with our system's commitment to personal autonomy and decisionmaking. Resolving the question at what age children should be accorded the power to control their own attorneys therefore depends on the answers to two more fundamental questions: At what age should society first accord a child particular legal rights? At what age should society recognize a child to be autonomous for the purpose of making certain kinds of legal decisions?

Clearly, to answer these questions, we would have to look both to the conclusions of modern social science and to the teachings of moral philosophy. * * * Today, most people would recognize that, at some point before they reach the age of majority, children are entitled to make certain kinds of decisions about their own lives. Furthermore, our legal system confers on older children a variety of rights and powers. Thus, children below the age of eighteen are granted legal authority to make such decisions as whether to go to school, work, drive a car, or obtain an abortion. Similarly, children also have important rights against the state, including the rights of privacy and of free speech. * * *

In the context of delinquency proceedings, a strong argument can be made that attorneys should always be bound by their young clients' instructions. Since in most jurisdictions, a child under the age of seven cannot be prosecuted for delinquency, this view would generally accord children seven years of age and older the power to direct their own counsel in delinquency proceedings.

To develop this argument, we must look to the Supreme Court's opinion in *In re Gault*. In addition to the right to counsel, *Gault* gave the juvenile accused of delinquency other important rights, including the rights to remain silent, to confront and cross-examine witnesses, and to notice of the charges. These rights would be rendered illusory if the child were not given the power to direct his own counsel. If the child were not given this power, for example, the attorney who believed that his young client was guilty and that incarceration would benefit the child would be able to hasten the process of rehabilitation by waiving the child's right to remain silent. * * *

The fact that the state may have acted in the child's best interests was thus insufficient to deny Gerald Gault his right to due process. Yet those commentators who would deny juveniles the power to instruct counsel are in effect asserting the very same theory that was rejected in *Gault*. They argue, in essence, that the child is either incapable of knowing his own best interests or is not entitled to determine for himself where those interests lie; as a result, they reason, the child must be denied an active hand in the litigation in order to assure the outcome most beneficial to himself. Thus, they would simply replace the paternalism of the state with the paternalism of the lawyer. Nothing could be further from the spirit of *Gault*, especially when the state appoints the child's counsel.

Finally, consistency and equity demand that the child be allowed to direct his own counsel in delinquency proceedings. The decision to prosecute children seven years of age and older for acts of delinquency reflects a legislative judgment that these children are mature enough and autonomous enough to be held responsible for their own actions. It would be both inconsistent and unfair to treat the child as a morally responsible actor who must suffer the legal consequences of his own delinquent acts and yet, at the same time, deny that he is autonomous enough to be capable or entitled to instruct counsel in the adjudication of those same acts. * * *

Ellen Marrus, "Best Interests Equals Zealous Advocacy: A Not So Radical View of Holistic Representation for Children Accused of Crime", 62 *Md. L. Rev.* 288, 326–327, 334–338, 340–343 (2003):

Many attorneys practicing in juvenile court view their role in representing minors in delinquency cases more as guardian ad litems who seek the child's best interests, than as zealous advocates for the child-client. The attorneys who see themselves as guardian ad litems are often passive and somewhat uncomfortable dealing with "criminal matters" in the juvenile court atmosphere. Conflict is seen not only as unnecessary, but harmful. To such attorneys, serving the best interests of the child-client usually means following the disposition recommended by the probation department, even if it is incarceration, and even though one might argue that the best interests of the child-client would be better served by keeping the child out of prison-like detention facilities. The term "kiddie court" is a revealing aphorism denoting informality, the absence of traditional lawyering, social work attitudes, and either the dispensing of slaps on the wrist punishment or therapeutic treatment. * * *

The model of holistic lawyering that I propose permits, and indeed requires the lawyer to act as a lawyer. While zealous advocacy informs the entire model, the attorney also is associated with other professionals in a team. The combined skills of each team member contribute to the kind of advocacy that truly ensures the best interests of the child. This model requires money, access to professionals in other disciplines, a keen appreciation of the dangers of the juvenile court system, attitudinal changes regarding the attorney child-client relationship, the necessity for adversarial representation, and expertise in child development and criminal, juvenile, and civil court law and practice. Even attorneys with limited means can employ aspects of this model. The differences between the ideal and real worlds are more in degree than in kind, and, as with most things, ultimately rest on the extent of available resources.

Simply stated, my proposal of ideal holistic lawyering for minors charged with juvenile delinquency encompasses a team approach. The team should include attorneys who specialize in juvenile law, social workers, educators, therapists, psychologists, psychiatrists, investigators, and criminal and civil law attorneys who work together to provide high quality representation for the child-client. * * *

Juvenile court procedures are usually termed civil matters; that requires the attorney to know civil law—how to preserve the record, motions, discovery, rules of appellate practice, etc. The reality, however, is that the child is charged with committing a penal offense, and therefore the attorney must know both substantive criminal law and criminal procedure. But that is not enough. The attorney must also know juvenile law and practice, which may differ from both civil and criminal law. If the child is found guilty, dispositional alternatives become critical. The attorney cannot rely on an overworked probation officer to explore all possibilities. The attorney needs a social worker who is experienced in such matters and knows of private treatment facilities that are specially geared for the child's particular problem and that are less prison-like. Psychiatrists and psychologists will provide necessary information on the particular child's intelligence and emotional state, the differences in child development, and how to communicate effectively with minor children. Educational specialists can determine why the child hates school and is doing poorly there. While some such services are provided by the juvenile courts, there is often a long waiting period to receive them, and these professionals, paid by the state, are not always sympathetic to the child's perspective. Furthermore, they are not available on a day to day basis to assist the attorney and child in communicating. * * *

Children in juvenile court often do not understand what is happening to them, what the possible consequences are, or how selecting different choices can affect their lives. At the very least, children in juvenile court have to be kept informed. Many children will ultimately ask the lawyer to make the decision, particularly when the juvenile is very young. That is fine, because the child is deciding to let the lawyer decide. What is important is that the child knows he or she has a say in the outcome. Of course, the older the child, the greater the likelihood that the child, after being informed, will elect to make the ultimate decision. Realistically, however, based on my experience, almost all children, even older adolescents, will elect to follow their attorney's recommendation. That too is fine, because the child is still the decisionmaker.

However, if the attorney agrees with this view of lawyering in the juvenile court, he or she must be careful not to unduly influence the client. Children naturally look to authority figures to make decisions for them. If the attorney under the guise of providing information overwhelms the child, he or she implicitly becomes a guardian rather than a lawyer. * * *

b. The Attorney and the Parents

Because children live with and are dependent upon their families, the presence and preferences of parents may complicate an attorney's role when she represents a juvenile. **Richard Kay and Daniel Segal, "The Role of the Attorney in Juvenile Court Proceedings: A Non–Polar Approach," 61** *Geo. L. J.* **1401 at 1420–21 (1973):**

Most juveniles come to juvenile proceedings with their parents. Whom does the attorney represent, the parents or the child? Potential conflicts between the juvenile and his parents can be classified into two categories. A "conflict of desires" may occur when parent and child disagree as to the most desirable adjudication or disposition. The parents may disbelieve the juvenile's protestation of innocence or may feel that a strong admonition or a period of probation may be the best thing for a difficult child. Some parents simply may welcome the opportunity to get a troublesome son or daughter out of the home. In other situations an attorney may believe that the home environment is such that custody by the state is in the child's best interests, while an adjudication which might lead to this result would be resisted ardently by the parents.

A second category of conflicts, a "conflicts of interests," presents even more serious difficulties in terms of the attorney's representation of both child and parents. Two common situations typify this conflict between parent and child. First, the parents themselves may institute proceedings against a child for waywardness or as an unsupervisable child. * * * In other instances * * *, an attorney may have to demonstrate facts and circumstances which would lead to criminal charges against the parents. * * *

Deciding if and when a conflict of desires exists and how to deal with it presents serious issues, especially when viewed against the legal and social background of parental control over almost every facet of a child's life. The tradition of parental control is based at least partially upon the sound assumption that normally the parent knows the child best. The attorney, therefore, should give heavy weight to the parents' desires in choosing his goals in both the adjudicatory and dispositional phases of the juvenile process. Even when the parents' decision appears to the attorney to have been based on faulty perceptions of either the child's behavior or the juvenile justice and treatment systems, meetings in which both lawyer and parents contribute their unique knowledge and experience usually will lead to a strategy satisfactory to all parties. In cases including blatant conflict of interests * * *, the problem of the norm of parental control is minimal. In those cases a determination has already been made that the interests of parents and child may be contradictory; the legal representative of the juvenile clearly must advocate only one of those interests. * * *

Another commentator also notes the complexity of representing children when their parents also demand a role in the proceedings. **Ellen Marrus, "Best Interests Equals Zealous Advocacy: A Not So Radical View of Holistic Representation for Children Accused of Crime", 62** *Md. L. Rev.* **288, 320–323, 325 (2003):**

An attorney representing adults in criminal court usually has to deal only with her client. In juvenile court there is an added wrinkle—the parents. In *Gault*, Justice Fortas recognized the parental interest in delinquency cases and required that both the child and parent be notified of the right to counsel. However, he also made clear that counsel was to be appointed to "represent the child." Many parents find it difficult to believe that the child is the client and, therefore, the one who makes the ultimate decisions. They feel entitled to sit in on attorney-client interviews and to determine the direction of the representation. In doing so, parents often clash with the attorney on what should be done. Additionally, parents will often try to subvert their children's decision-making power by telling them they must do what they (the parents) want. Furthermore, some parents will provide information to the probation department which is then used against the child, and indeed, parental complaints are the basis for many petitions for violation of probation.

In the criminal courts, relatives and friends are under no illusion as to the consequences of the criminal proceeding. Therefore, they tend to look to the attorney as the expert who can shield the defendant from criminal sanctions. On the other hand, parents do not always understand what can happen to their children in juvenile court, because they may view it as a therapeutic institution. In such cases, the parents see the attorney as an intruder who may stand in the way of what is beneficial to the child.

One way to resolve conflicts between parents, children, and attorneys is to make clear to the parents the consequences of different choices. * * *

Sometimes clients will divulge confidential information that they do not want their parents to know. * * *

In sum, parents of children alleged to be delinquents can be an impediment to zealous advocacy by insisting on sitting in on attorney-client interviews, demanding that their children plead guilty, testifying against their children, or trying to hide neglectful behavior including their own complicity in the crime. Not all parents present such problems and it is helpful when parents are on the child's side. The attorney, however, must be aware at all times that the child, not the parent, is the client. If there is a clash between parent and child, the child must come first. * * *

How successfully does the following Juvenile Court Rule and Commentary address the issues raised by Marrus and by Kay and Segal? **Minn. R. Proc. Juv. Ct. 3.01** (West 1999): "The child has the right to be represented by an attorney. * * * The attorney shall initially consult with the child privately, outside of the presence of the child's parent(s), legal guardian or legal custodian. The attorney shall act solely as the counsel for the child."

COMMENT TO RULE 3

Whether counsel is appointed by the court or retained by the child or the child's parents, the attorney must act solely as counsel for the child. American Bar Association, *Juvenile Justice Standards Relating to Counsel for Private Parties* (1980). While it is certainly appropriate for an attorney representing a child to consult with the parents whose custodial interest in the child potentially may be affected by court intervention, it is essential that counsel conduct an initial interview with the child privately and outside of the presence of the parents. Following the initial private consultation, if the child affirmatively wants his or her parent(s) to be present, they may be present. The attorney may then consult with such other persons as the attorney deems necessary or appropriate. However, the child retains a right to consult privately with the attorney at any time, and either the child or the attorney may excuse the parents in order to speak privately and confidentially.* * *

PROBLEM

How should a lawyer balance the conflicting tensions between acting as an advocate, a social worker, or a *guardian ad litem* and at different stages of a delinquency proceeding? How should a lawyer resolve the tensions between treatment and punishment? How should a lawyer balance the competing preferences of the parents and the child? What should a lawyer do when the child-client's preferences either are unrealistic, immature, or very likely to be rejected by the juvenile court judge as contrary to the youth's "best interest"?

Consider, for example, a situation in which an attorney represents a 14–year–old youth taken into custody for possession and use of drugs—alcohol, marijuana, cocaine, or heroin. Would the type of drug make a difference in your advocacy strategy? The youth's parent and the juvenile court's chemical dependency evaluator tell you that the child abuses illegal substances. The chemical dependency counselor also tells you that good treatment programs exist in the jurisdiction, but that the juvenile court and county only could pay for the costs of treatment if the judge adjudicates the youth delinquent and commits her to the program. Would it make a difference in your advocacy strategy if the program entailed out-patient treatment, a community residential facility, or an intensive drug-treatment program located in the state juvenile correctional institution? Assume that the police officer's arrest and seizure of the youth's drugs occurred under questionable Fourth Amendment circumstances. Would you make a motion to suppress the evidence if prevailing would preclude the juvenile court from exercising jurisdiction? If you prevail on the suppression motion, what is the moral message that you give to the youth who knows she possessed drugs illegally? What would you tell her parent when she insists that her daughter in fact possessed the drugs? What would you tell the parent who wants her daughter to receive treatment and who lacks medical insurance to pay for such services if they are not ordered by the court? Suppose that the juvenile court adjudicates the youth a delinquent. The court social worker recommends that the judge commit the youth to a chemical dependency treatment program and the parents agree. Suppose that your client informs you that she wants to go home and get "high" with her boy-friend. What information would you give the court and what disposition would you advocate at the dispositional hearing?

G. PROCEDURAL RIGHTS AND THE ADJUDICATION OF STATUS OFFENDERS

The narrow reading of the Supreme Court's holding in *Gault* is that the Constitution only requires procedural safeguards in delinquency proceedings, i.e. when the state charges a youth with conduct that would be criminal for an adult and the child could be confined in an institution. In response to *Gault*, many jurisdictions relabeled non-criminal status offenses as Persons in Need of Supervision (PINS) or Children in Need of Protection and Services (CHIPS) rather than delinquency. As a result, states neither charge such youths with crimes nor label them as delinquents. The 1974 Juvenile Justice and Delinquency Prevention Act offered the states federal fiscal incentives to deinstitutionalize status offenders and to not place them in detention facilities or institutions with youths charged or adjudicated delinquent for criminal behavior. 42 *U.S.C.* §§ 5601–39 (1982). As we will see in Chapter 8, states also adopted policies to prohibit institutional confinement of status offenders in institution with delinquents. *See e.g.*, *State ex rel. Harris v. Calendine*, 160 W.Va. 172, 233 S.E.2d 318 (W. Va. 1977); Rayna Hardee Bomar, "The Incarceration of the Status Offender," 18 *Memphis St. U. L. Rev.* 713 (1988); Jan Costello and Nancy Worthington, "Incarcerating Status Offenders: Attempts to Circumvent the Juvenile Justice and Delinquency Prevention Act," 16 *Harv. Civ. Rights–Civ. Lib. L. Rev.* 41 (1981).

Because of the holding in *Gault* and the formal legal differences between delinquency and status proceedings—criminal versus non-criminal conduct as the underlying basis for jurisdiction and restrictions on secure institutional confinement with delinquents adjudicated for crimes—are status offenders entitled to the same procedural rights at their adjudicatory hearings as are delinquent offenders? *See e.g.*, Erin M. Smith, "In a Child's Best Interests: Juvenile Status Offenders Deserve Procedural Due Process," 10 *J. Law & Inequality* 253 (1992) (analysis of the procedural differences between the safeguards accorded to delinquents and status offenders).

1. PRIVILEGE AGAINST SELF–INCRIMINATION

IN THE MATTER OF SPALDING

273 Md. 690, 332 A.2d 246 (Md. Ct. App. 1975).

LEVINE, JUDGE. In the landmark decision of *In re Gault*, the Supreme Court held, for the first time, that various of the federal constitutional guarantees accompanying ordinary criminal proceedings are applicable, in certain instances, to state juvenile delinquency cases. * * * Appellant seeks to extend that holding—with specific reference to self-incrimination—to another area of juvenile court jurisdiction in Maryland, known as "Children in Need of Supervision" (CINS).

The Court of Special Appeals * * * upheld the decision of the Circuit Court for Baltimore County sitting as a Juvenile Court rejecting appellant's claim. We granted certiorari to consider whether statements made to the police by appellant—then 13 years of age—should have been suppressed; whether she was denied her constitutional right to refuse to testify; and whether she should have been permitted to cross-examine a police officer with regard to both voluntariness of the statements made to him and the warnings mandated by *Miranda v. Arizona*.

In the early morning hours of January 31, 1973, Officer Joseph W. Price * * * responded to a call from City Hospital to investigate a possible rape and overdose of narcotics. There, he was met by a Mr. Carter, who advised him that his daughter, age 11, had taken a white tablet which had impaired her speech, had caused a loss of equilibrium and had dilated her pupils. She had also admitted to her parents that she had engaged in sexual intercourse with an adult male on January 29 in an apartment immediately below that occupied by her family. * * *

Later that morning, at approximately 6:30 A.M., Officer Price again met with the Carter family at the Dundalk police station. Also there in response to a phone call from the officer were appellant and her mother. The minister of the church attended by both families was also present. Officer Price and one of his superiors then proceeded to interrogate both girls under somewhat disorganized conditions. Much of this appears to have resulted from interference by both the minister, who exercised considerable influence over the girls, and the parents. Ultimately, with permission of the latter, Officer Price obtained written statements from both girls. * * *

In her oral and written statements to the police that morning * * * appellant admitted her participation in the events of the 29th * * * supplied the names of all those who had been in attendance on that occasion. She also recounted additional episodes of similar sexual activity in the basement of her home with male boarders residing there; and at a number of other "parties" in the apartment below that occupied by the Carters. She was able to attend these early-morning functions amounting to nothing less than orgies at which adults and juveniles were in heavy attendance, by placing a sleeping pill in her mother's coffee. * * *

After the police had struggled through their various interrogation procedures on the 31st, they took the girls to the Parkville police station * * * where they were detained overnight. * * * The official report filed by the police specified "protective custody" as the reason for the detention. Once the police had completed the interviews, they immediately sought arrest warrants for the large number of adults identified by the girls. The men in this group were charged with "statutory rape" and the women with "unnatural and perverted sexual practices." In both instances, the two girls were listed as victims.

On the following morning, February 1, 1973, both girls were brought before Juvenile Master Kahl pursuant to petitions * * * which charged each with being a "delinquent child" and "in need of supervision,"[6] within the meaning and intent of Section 70–2 of Article 26 of the Annotated Code of Maryland. The Master found both girls to be in need of care and treatment, but, significantly, did not find them to be "delinquent."[4] * * * During the ensuing month, extensive psychiatric and family studies were conducted at the Maryland Children's Center.

---

6. The reasons assigned for these allegations are:

" * * * investigation by the Baltimore County Police Department revealed that the respondent had consumed controlled and prohibitive (sic) narcotics and engaged in acts of sexual intercourse and sexual perversion with an unknown number of male and female adults for a period of more than one year. The respondent is ungovernable and beyond the control of her parent, deports herself in such a manner as to be a danger to herself and others and is in need of care and treatment."

4. In fact, the petition previously referred to above appears to contain the only official suggestion of delinquency in the record. Ironically, the "complaint" form of the Department of

On March 7, 1973, immediately upon their return from the Children's Center, the girls attended a hearing before Juvenile Master Peach. Armed with the thorough reports and comprehensive recommendation of the Children's Center, he adjudicated each girl to be "a child in need of supervision" and "in need of care and treatment." He therefore "committed both of them to the Department of Juvenile Services for placement and planning so that they can receive some therapy to help them cope with the problems which I am sure lie ahead for both of them." Exceptions to the findings and recommendations of the Master were duly noted on behalf of each juvenile, accompanied by a request for a de novo hearing before the court.

Pursuant to the exceptions and requests, the cases came on for trial on May 3, 1973, before the Circuit Court for Baltimore County sitting as a Juvenile Court (Jenifer, J.), where extensive testimony and argument ensued. * * * Shortly before the trial commenced, a written motion was filed on behalf of appellant aimed at suppressing the statements made by her to the police, to the Juvenile Service workers and to the staff of the Children's Center. At the outset of the trial, the court announced that it would reserve its ruling on that motion. During the course of the trial, objections to the admissibility of those statements were renewed on the grounds that the fourfold *Miranda* warnings had not been given by any of the interrogating officers prior to or during any questioning. Officer Price, however, had announced to all those assembled at the police station that "anything they said could be used against them in a court of law if they were charged." This colloquy also appears in the testimony:

> "MR. MEOLA: Your Honor, I would like to question the officer about what warning he did give these children.
>
> "THE COURT: I don't think he has to give any warning. They were not in custody for the commission of a crime or for a delinquency petition at this time. They were volunteered statements given with the consent at the insistence of the parents. The *Miranda* warning doesn't apply to these statements, gentlemen."

It is this refusal that laid the groundwork for one of the three questions framed by the Writ of Certiorari.

Later in the trial, when asked by the court to describe how he elicited the statements from the girls, Officer Price stated "They volunteered all of this information to begin with, and it was to bizarre I started asking questions to try to pinpoint dates and time and individuals." The confusion which reigned at the police station and the abbreviated warning announced by Officer Price are demonstrated in this excerpt from his testimony:

> "Q. Okay, you stated earlier the parents were shouting at the girls?

Juvenile Services, apparently completed on either the 31st or 1st, lists "child in need of supervision" as the sole "offense description."

"A. Everybody was yelling at each other trying to get information, specifically from Elaine (Carter), because she was still under the influence of drugs, trying to get through to her. The parents were upset.

"Q. You stated earlier the girls were crying?

"A. Yes, I did, from the yelling of the parents.

"Q. Whom did you make the statement to the statement they made would be used against them, to whom did you make that statement?

"A. I made it to everyone in the room there, anything they said could be used against them in a court of law.

"THE COURT: Did you go any further?

"A. Yes, sir, if they were charged with a crime, named offense.

"Q. Was this while they were quiet or were they still yelling?

"A. Everybody was milling around. I had a little bit of trouble with Reverend Gatling there. I had to threaten to arrest him just to keep him quiet.

"Q. Do you know for certain that the parents heard that statement?

"A. I cannot be certain anybody heard anything."

In the course of their testimony, Officer Price * * * state[d] what the girls had said during the various interviews. Then, an announcement by the prosecuting attorney that he proposed to call appellant to the stand as a witness drew a vigorous objection from counsel on the ground of self-incrimination. Prior to any definitive ruling by the court, however, she was shown her written statement given to Officer Price on January 31, and confirmed the truth of its contents. * * * When asked by her own counsel whether anyone at the police station had informed her that she was not required to make any statements, she replied:

"A. Well, we more or less made it on our own. We figured we could save some more kids, but they gave us no rights or anything.

"THE COURT: Give you what?

"A. Any kind of rights, we thought we were doing the State a favor.

"THE COURT: Well, as I understand that you said you made the statement on your own?

"A. Yes."

At the conclusion of the trial, the court rendered its decision orally, finding that the evidence overwhelmingly had established the girls to be in need of supervision because they had "deported themselves so as to injure or endanger themselves or others" and therefore required "guidance, treatment, or rehabilitation." These findings were incorporated into written orders, which also committed the girls to the jurisdiction of the Department of Juvenile Services for placement in foster homes with prescribed visitation rights granted to their parents. It is from those orders that the appeal was taken to the Court of Special Appeals.

The contentions that the statements made to the police should have been suppressed at the court hearing and that cross-examination of the police officer should have been permitted regarding the voluntariness of those statements and the *Miranda* warnings were rejected by the Court of Special Appeals on the basis that the questioning of the police at the hospital and at the police station was not custodial interrogation within the meaning of *Miranda*.

In holding that appellant's compelled testimony did not violate her privilege against self-incrimination, the court of Special Appeals carefully traced the enactment of the jurisdictional category, "Child in Need of Supervision," created by Chapter 432 of the Laws of 1969. As Judge Moore noted for the court, such a child refers to one who is:

> "(1) Subject to compulsory school attendance who is habitually and without justification truant from school;
>
> (2) Without substantial fault on the part of his parents, guardian, or other custodian, who is habitually disobedient, ungovernable, and beyond their control;
>
> (3) Who so deports himself as to injure or endanger himself or others; or
>
> (4) Who has committed an offense applicable only to children; and
>
> (5) Requires guidance, treatment or rehabilitation."

This classification, therefore, stands in marked contrast to a "Delinquent child," defined as one "who commits a delinquent act and who requires supervision, treatment or rehabilitation." * * *

Essentially, then, the Court of Special Appeals stressed the basic statutory distinctions between the delinquency and CINS categories, taking particular care to emphasize the differences in disposition which are prescribed for each. For example, Code Art. 26, § 70–19, applicable at all times material to these proceedings, provided:

> "(a) If a child is found to be neglected, delinquent, in need of supervision, mentally handicapped, or dependent, the court may make disposition as most suited to the physical, mental, and moral welfare of the child; but no child (except a delinquent child) may be confined in an institution or other facility designed or operated for the benefit of delinquent children." * * *

The Court of Special Appeals summed it all up in stating:

> "It is evident, we think, that an important purpose of the legislative revision of the juvenile code was to insulate certain forms of juvenile misconduct from the consequences of an adjudication of delinquency as described in *Gault*. The creation of the category of CINS reflects a studied design of the legislature to insure that treatment of children guilty of misconduct peculiarly reflecting the propensities and suscep-

tibilities of youth, will acquire none of the institutional, quasi-penal features of treatment that in *Gault*'s view had been the main difference between the theory and the practice of the juvenile court system." * * *

Thus, it "decline(d) to go further and hold that in a proceeding upon a CINS petition due process requires that the child be permitted, on Fifth Amendment grounds, to have relevant evidence excluded and to refuse to testify."

We shall affirm, finding it necessary, however, to decide only that the Fifth Amendment privilege against self-incrimination is inapplicable to this proceeding. Because we so hold, the related questions of *Miranda* warnings and voluntariness are subsumed within that holding. * * *

Since this case derives its impetus from *Gault*, we pause for a careful examination of the relevant facts on which that decision is bottomed. * * *

Gault was predicated on alleged admissions made in response to questions propounded by the juvenile court judge. Since the complainant did not appear, the adjudication of delinquency appears to have rested solely on those admissions. Neither Gault nor his parents were advised that he was not required to testify or make a statement, or that an incriminating statement might result in his commitment as a "delinquent." As we have already intimated, Gault was not represented by counsel. * * *

Turning to the issue of self-incrimination, the Court again emphasized that it was " * * * concerned only with a proceeding to determine whether a minor is a 'delinquent' and which may result in commitment to a state institution." This same emphasis was repeated in even stronger terms when the Court said that " * * * juvenile proceedings to determine 'delinquency,' which may lead to commitment to a state institution, must be regarded as 'criminal' for purposes of the privilege against self-incrimination." Thus, the scope of *Gault* is clear. When the Supreme Court " * * * conclude(d) that the constitutional privilege against self-incrimination is applicable in the case of juveniles as it is with respect to adults,", it was referring to a proceeding to determine "delinquency," viz., " * * * an act which would be a crime if done by a person who is not a child," which is the statutory definition in Maryland. The test enunciated in *Gault*, however, is two-pronged. In addition, the "delinquency" must be such that it may result in commitment to a state institution. * * *

Whatever else is established by *Gault*, it is clear that labels are not controlling in determining the applicability of the Due Process Clause to juvenile proceedings. In regard to the first "prong" of the test, for example, it is doubtful that the *Gault* result would have been different had merely the title of the proceedings been changed from "delinquency" to "CINS," and all else had remained the same. The essential element is that the juvenile be charged with an act which would be a crime if committed by an adult. * * *

Labels are equally unimportant in terms of the second "prong," confinement in a state institution. As the Court said: * * * "For this purpose, at least, commitment is a deprivation of liberty. It is incarceration against one's will, whether it be called 'criminal' or 'civil.' "

In sum, then, Due Process requires that various of the federal constitutional guarantees accompanying ordinary criminal proceedings, specifically including the privilege against self-incrimination, be made applicable at the adjudicatory stage of those juvenile proceedings in which the act charged would constitute a crime if committed by an adult and which may result in confinement of the child to a state institution.

We turn then to Cindy Ann Spalding. The state contends that the *Gault* rights do not apply to CINS because of the significant differences between those proceedings and delinquency cases. It cites these dissimilarities: CINS children may not be confined in institutions designed or operated for the benefit of delinquent children; CINS children may not be placed in detention; and CINS children may not be waived to adult criminal courts. Also, in the teeth of the *Gault* teaching that labels are of little consequence, the State nevertheless argues that the label "CINS" bears significantly less stigma than "delinquent." Finally, the State claims that, having been placed in a foster home, appellant was not committed to a "state institution" because shelter care and foster homes are not in that category.

Understandably enough, appellant maintains that "CINS" children, though treated differently in certain respects, are the same as "delinquent" children for the purpose of applying *Gault* rights. She emphasizes that at the time of her hearing, she conceivably could have been confined with delinquent children; that she could have been committed to a "state institution," and thus compelled to leave her home with a resulting curtailment of her freedom; that she is now one step closer to incarceration; and that she was charged with violating a criminal statute. Although there is much to commend these arguments, we need not decide whether the second prong of the *Gault* test, i.e., potential confinement of the child to a state institution, mandated an application of the privilege against self-incrimination in this case. We reach this conclusion because, in any event, we think that appellant was not charged in this proceeding with an act which would constitute a crime if committed by an adult.

As we noted earlier, the petition filed on February 1, 1973, did allege that appellant was both a "delinquent child" and a "child in need of supervision." The reasons assigned for these allegations were the consumption of narcotics, the acts of sexual intercourse and perversion practiced upon her, and her ungovernability. But, in the context of all the material events, which ensued during the critical period, since she was, in fact, a victim, the charge of "delinquency" in the petition must be regarded as simply an unexplained anomaly. * * *

[W]e do not find it necessary to rest our decision on the second prong of the test laid down by *Gault*, pertaining to possible confinement in a "state institution." It is sufficient to hold that since appellant was not charged with an act which, in the circumstances of this case, would constitute a crime if committed by an adult, the privilege against self-incrimination is not applicable to these proceedings. * * *

ELDRIDGE, JUDGE (dissenting): The majority's decision in this case cannot be reconciled with *In re Gault*, and later Supreme Court cases dealing with the constitutional rights to be accorded accused children in juvenile proceedings.

The majority opinion, in my view, correctly construes *Gault*, and the subsequent Supreme Court cases, as setting forth a two-pronged test for determining whether the Fifth Amendment privilege against self-incrimination is applicable to a juvenile proceeding. The test is: (1) whether the juvenile "is charged with an act that would constitute a crime if committed by an adult,"; and (2) whether the child may be "subjected to the loss of his liberty," or whether the proceedings "may result in commitment to a state institution."

Moreover, as the majority opinion in this case seems initially to acknowledge, labels are not controlling as to either aspect of the test. It does not matter whether the name of the proceedings is "delinquency" or "child in need of supervision" ("CINS"), or whether the loss of liberty may be commitment to an "industrial school" or a "receiving home." The child's entitlement to the protection of the privilege against self-incrimination depends upon the substance of the matter, namely whether he or she is charged with an act that would be a crime if committed by an adult and whether the proceedings could result in a deprivation of liberty. * * *

At the juvenile court trial itself, testimony offered by the prosecution to sustain the charge of "child in need of supervision" largely related to the girls' use of narcotics, to petitioner's having "drugged" her mother, and to the "sex orgies." The trial judge, in his opinion delivered at the end of the trial adjudicating petitioner and her co-defendant to be "children in need of supervision," found as a fact that the girls "have been associated in immoral sexual activities" and have "indulged" in the taking of "drugs of a narcotic nature." * * *

The majority opinion states that there is a "marked contrast" between the "delinquent" classification and the "CINS" or "child in need of supervision" classification. However, as this case illustrates, criminal conduct may furnish the factual basis for the "CINS" adjudication. * * * Of course, a child who commits criminal acts such as using narcotic drugs or "drugging" someone else, is deporting herself "so as to injure or endanger" herself or others. This is why "labels" should not be, and under the Supreme Court's decisions are not, controlling.

While not dealt with in the majority opinion, the other "prong" or requirement of the *Gault* test was also met in this case. While petitioner was in fact committed to a "foster home" instead of an "institution," forced living for a period of years in a "foster home" and away from one's own home and family is a "loss of his liberty." Moreover, even if commitment to a foster home, and against the will of the child and her parents, would not be deemed to meet the second requirement of the *Gault* test, petitioner was subjected to the possibility of commitment to an institution. * * * [A] juvenile court judge [may] commit a "CINS" child "to any public or private institution * * *." As to limitations upon this authority, the pertinent statute in effect at the time of petitioner's trial, authorized confinement of a "CINS" child in an institution provided that the institution were not designed or operated for the benefit of delinquent children. * * * The present statute, adds the further limitation to the authority to commit "CINS" children to institutions, requiring that such institutions may not be juvenile training schools or something similar to juvenile training schools. Limitations upon the nature of the institutions to which "CINS" children may be committed do not change the fact that under Maryland law, a child adjudicated to be in need of supervision may be committed to "an institution of confinement in which the child is incarcerated for a greater or lesser time."

The two-pronged test of *Gault* was therefore met in this case. Petitioner was charged with acts that would be crimes if committed by adults, and petitioner was subjected to the prospect of a loss of liberty or confinement in an institution. Consequently, under *Gault*, the Fifth Amendment privilege against self-incrimination was fully applicable to this proceeding. * * *

Finally, wholly apart from the matter of *Miranda* warnings, petitioner's Fifth Amendment rights were violated when at the trial she was compelled, over her attorney's objection, to take the witness stand and testify against herself. * * *

NOTE

In *In re Henderson*, 199 N.W.2d 111 (Iowa 1972), the Iowa Supreme Court rejected the "unruly" child's objections to being questioned by a probation officer in derogation of the privilege against self-incrimination:

> We have already observed the purpose of juvenile proceedings is to help and assist the child, not to punish. The constitutional safeguard of 'fundamental fairness' must be preserved in that setting. However, where there is no public offense charged we believe the requirement of advising the juvenile and his parents of his right to remain silent would frustrate the very purpose of the juvenile proceeding. Admittedly, upon the findings of the trial court the child may have to spend some time away from his home but such time will not be spent in a completely institutionalized setting. The record establishes visitation rights are lenient, and that the average stay for a child at the Home is about one year.

> We conclude, therefore, that in a juvenile proceeding where no public offense is charged, the question of self-incrimination is not presented. * * *

2. RIGHT TO COUNSEL

IN RE WALKER

282 N.C. 28, 191 S.E.2d 702 (N.C. 1972).

On 2 August 1971 Mrs. Katherine Walker, mother of Valerie Lenise Walker, filed a petition in the district court alleging in pertinent part [that] * * *

> 3. Said child is an undisciplined child as defined by G.S. 7A–278 in that she has been regularly disobedient to her parents during the last six months; that the said child will not mind and obey; that the child goes and comes as she pleases and keeps late hours; that the child associates with persons of questionable character and frequents places not approved by the parents; further, that the child is almost beyond the control of her parents. * * *

The matter came on for hearing before Judge Gentry on 17 August 1971. Valerie was present with her mother and the court counselor, Mrs. Ann M. Jones. Valerie was not represented by an attorney at this hearing. Judge Gentry heard evidence and found * * * that Valerie has been regularly disobedient to her parents in that she goes and comes without permission, keeps late hours, associates with persons that her parents object to, and goes to places where her parents tell her not to go; and that Valerie is an undisciplined child and in need of the discipline and supervision of the State. * * *

Based on the foregoing findings, it was ordered, adjudged and decreed that Valerie was an undisciplined child within the meaning of the law. She was placed on probation subject to the following conditions:

> 1. That she be of good behavior and conduct herself in a law-abiding manner;

> 2. That she mind and obey her parents and not leave home without permission and then to go only to places that she has permission to go and return as directed;

> 3. That she attend school regularly during the school year and obey the school rules and regulations; * * *

Thereafter, on 21 September 1971, Ann M. Jones, Court Counselor, filed a verified petition and motion in the cause for further consideration and review of the case, alleging:

> "That the said child is a delinquent child as defined by G.S. § 7A—278(2) in that the said child has violated Conditions No. 1, 2, and 3 of the probation order dated August 19, 1971, in that the said child continuously disobeys her parents in that she goes and comes as she pleases; keeps late hours; and frequents places not approved by her parents; further, the said child refuses to obey school rules and regulations in that she misbehaves in the classroom and is disrespect-

ful to school officials; further, the said child is beyond the control of her parents." * * *

Prior to the hearing the public defender * * * was appointed to represent Valerie, and the matter came on for hearing before Judge Gentry on 15 October 1971. At that time Valerie was present with her mother and was represented by Wallace C. Harrelson and J. Dale Shepherd, Public Defenders. Present representing the State was Thaddeus A. Adams, III, Assistant Solicitor.

Prior to the introduction of evidence, Valerie's counsel moved to vacate the order dated 19 August 1971 finding that Valerie was an undisciplined child and placing her on probation for that she was not represented by counsel at that time and was unable to defend herself on the charge that she was an undisciplined child, resulting in a denial of due process. * * *

[Katherine Walker, Valerie's mother, testified that Valerie disobeyed her instructions, kept late hours and sometimes remained out until twelve, one and two o'clock at night, and frequented a bar that had a bad reputation and despite the fact that she was a fourteen-year-old girl. The Assistant Principal at her junior high school testified that he saw Valerie in his office many times on referral from teachers for disrupting classes.]

The respondent elected to offer no evidence and moved to dismiss the proceeding at the close of all the evidence. The motion was denied, and under date of 27 October 1971 Judge Gentry signed an order providing in pertinent part as follows:

"The court finds, upon hearing evidence, that the child was before the court on August 17, 1971 and that she was adjudged to be an undisciplined child and placed on probation. * * * The court finds that these acts of the child constitute a violation of the conditions of probation and that she is a delinquent child for having violated the conditions of probation and that she is in need of the discipline and supervision of the state. * * * The court finds that she is in need of more discipline and supervision than can be provided for her within Guilford County.

IT IS NOW THEREFORE ORDERED, ADJUDGED AND DECREED THAT Valerie Walker, having been found to be a delinquent child, that the said child is hereby committed to the North Carolina Board of Juvenile Correction and is to be in the custody and under the control and supervision of the officials thereof until discharged, in keeping with the requirements of law. That she is to remain in the temporary custody of the court until she can be delivered to the designated correction school by Court Counselor Mrs. Jones.

This the 27th day of October, 1971.

B.   GORDON GENTRY

JUDGE PRESIDING"

From the foregoing order respondent appealed to the Court of Appeals which found no error. Respondent thereupon appealed to the Supreme Court, allegedly as of right, asserting involvement of substantial constitutional questions arising under the Constitution of the United States and of this State.

HUSKINS, JUSTICE: Appellant Valerie Walker contends that she had a constitutional right to counsel at the hearing on the initial petition alleging her to be an Undisciplined child. We first consider whether the Constitution affords her such right.

In *In re Gault*, the United States Supreme Court held that "the Due Process Clause of the Fourteenth Amendment requires that in respect of proceedings to determine delinquency which may result in commitment to an institution in which the juvenile's freedom is curtailed, the child and his parents must be notified of the child's right to be represented by counsel retained by them, or if they are unable to afford counsel, that counsel will be appointed to represent the child." A similar statutory right to counsel for indigent juveniles at a hearing which could result in commitment to an institution is afforded by G.S. § 7A–451(a)(8).

The initial petition alleging that Valerie was an Undisciplined child was heard on August 17, 1971. * * * Despite the somewhat awkward structure of G.S. § 7A—286 (1969), it is clear that under its terms no judge exercising juvenile jurisdiction had any authority upon finding the child to be Undisciplined to commit such child to the Board of Juvenile Correction for assignment to a State facility in which the juvenile's freedom is curtailed.[5] The statute permitted incarceration of Delinquent children only. * * *

Therefore, we hold that neither *Gault*, nor G.S. § 7A–451(a)(8) afforded Valerie Walker the right to counsel at the hearing on the initial petition alleging her to be an undisciplined child, for under the wording of G.S. § 7A–286(4) (1969) that hearing could not result in her commitment to an institution in which her freedom would be curtailed. * * *

Appellant would have this Court go further than *Gault* requires. She argues for the right to counsel at the hearing of an Undisciplined child petition on the theory that such a hearing is a critical stage in the juvenile process since it subjects the child to the risk of probation and since a violation of probation means that the child is Delinquent and subject to commitment. In such fashion appellant seeks to engraft upon the juvenile process the "critical stage" test used by the United States Supreme Court in determining the scope of the Sixth Amendment right to counsel in Criminal prosecutions. We find no authority for such engraftment. Whatever may be the proper classification for a juvenile proceeding in which

---

5. G.S. § 7A–286 (1969), after requiring the judge to select the disposition which provides for the protection, treatment, rehabilitation or correction of the child, as may be appropriate in each case, makes the following alternatives available to any judge exercising juvenile jurisdiction: "(4) In the case of any child who is delinquent or undisciplined, the court may: a. Place the child on probation* * *; or b. Continue the case* * *; or, If the child is delinquent, the court may c. Commit the child to the care of the North Carolina Board of Juvenile Correction* * *."

the child is alleged to be undisciplined, it certainly is not a criminal prosecution within the meaning of the Sixth Amendment which guarantees the assistance of counsel "in all criminal prosecutions."

The right to counsel delineated in *Gault* has not been extended to other procedural steps in juvenile proceedings. Neither this Court nor the United States Supreme Court has ever applied the 'critical stage' test to the juvenile process. Accordingly, we hold that counsel is not constitutionally required at the hearing on an Undisciplined child petition. See *In re Gault*, in which it is stated: "(W)hat we hold in this opinion with regard to the procedural requirements at the adjudicatory stage has no necessary applicability to other steps of the juvenile process."

The fact that a child initially has been found to be undisciplined and placed on probation is merely incidental to a later petition and motion alleging delinquency based on violation of the terms of probation. The initial finding can never legally result in commitment to an institution in which the juvenile's freedom is curtailed. It is only the latter petition and motion, and the finding that the child is a Delinquent child by reason of its conduct since the initial hearing, they may result in the child's commitment. * * *

Finally, appellant urges that the trial judge's failure to state in his order that he found "beyond a reasonable doubt" that appellant had violated the conditions of her probation was constitutional error under *In re Winship*. In *Winship*, * * * the Court held that the Due Process Clause requires proof beyond a reasonable doubt in delinquency proceedings wherein the child is charged with an act that would constitute a crime if committed by an adult. Here, Valerie Walker was charged with delinquency by reason of probation violations, none of which violations amounted to a crime. Therefore, *Winship* does not apply to these findings, and is not authority for the argument that the findings here must be made upon proof beyond a reasonable doubt. * * *

Affirmed.

BOBBITT, CHIEF JUSTICE (dissenting). Valerie Lenise Walker * * * appeals from an order entered October 27, 1971, which, based on a finding that Valerie was a "delinquent" child, committed her to the North Carolina Board of Juvenile Correction, to be and remain in the custody and under the control and supervision of the officials thereof until discharged in accordance with law. The basis for the finding that Valerie was a delinquent child was that she had violated the conditions of probation set forth in an order of August 19, 1971, which adjudged that Valerie was an "undisciplined child." * * *

Valerie was found delinquent and committed solely on the ground she had violated certain of the probation conditions imposed when she was adjudicated an "undisciplined child" on August 19th. The adjudication that she was an undisciplined child was absolutely essential to a valid commitment for violation of probation conditions. The Court holds that she was entitled to assigned counsel *only at the final hearing* to determine whether the probation conditions had been violated. In my opinion, she was equally entitled to assigned counsel at the earlier hearing to determine whether she should be adjudged an "undisciplined child." * * *

NOTES

1) "Bootstrapping" as a "Critical Stage" in the Proceedings In contrast to the reasoning in *Walker*, the Florida Supreme Court in *In re Hutchins*, 345 So.2d 703, 706 (Fla.1977), ruled in a factual situation similar to *Walker*, that a youth charged with "ungovernability" enjoyed the right to counsel at the initial proceeding:

> The parties agree that, at a second or subsequent adjudicatory hearing on ungovernability, the juvenile has the right to counsel since the adjudication may result in the child being defined and treated as a delinquent. But, it is argued, the first adjudication may only result in dependency status, and therefore, the right to counsel need not be accorded at that time. * * *

> [T]he status of dependency may be established by a preponderance of evidence, the powers of the court and the Division of Family Services are limited, and only delinquent children may be committed to the Division of Youth Services for custody, care, training and treatment.

> The first hearing on ungovernability is not necessarily a first step in the adjudication of delinquency. The hearing and the resulting care, custody or supervision by the Division of Family Services may correct any existing problems the child may have and be the last of the child's experiences with the juvenile authorities. In such cases, the constitutional right to counsel is not mandatory.

> If, however, the first ungovernability adjudication is to be used in a subsequent proceeding in which the child's status may change from dependency to delinquency because of two or more adjudications of ungovernability, the first such adjudicatory hearing is a critical first step in the delinquency determination and the child is entitled to all due process rights at each step in the procedure. * * *

> We conclude that it is constitutionally impermissible to base an adjudication of ungovernability for the second time on a previously conducted hearing in which the child was not instructed as to his right to counsel or provided counsel if an indigent.

> We reject the argument that such a requirement will convert all of the proceedings to determine ungovernability into criminal type proceedings with both state attorney and defense counsel present in an adversary atmosphere. If the appropriate authority believes that the ungovernability hearing will suffice, there is no reason why it cannot be held as any other dependency proceeding. But if the conduct of a child is such that there is doubt about the effectiveness of the proceeding and that such proceeding will likely mature into a delinquency proceeding, the child must be given the opportunity to have counsel. If this right is not

afforded the juvenile, the first adjudication may not be used in the delinquency hearing. * * *

2) "Bootstrapping" Status Offenders into Delinquents Without Due Process *Walker* provides an example of the consequences that follow from providing status offenders with fewer procedural safeguards than delinquents. Amendments to the Juvenile Justice and Delinquency Prevention Act, 42 U.S.C. 5601 at § 223(a)(12)(A) provide that juvenile court judges may find status offenders in contempt of court for violating a valid court order, for example, a condition of probation, and place them in secure detention facilities. This enables juvenile courts to use their contempt power to incarcerate repeat status offenders as delinquents. *See* Donna M. Bishop and Charles Frazier, "Gender Bias in Juvenile Justice Processing: The Implications of the JJDP Act," 82 *J. Crim. L. & Criminology* 1162, 1185 (1992). "Our findings point to the conclusion that the traditional sexual double standard continues to operate. * * * Historical patterns of gender bias continue. * * * It is important to highlight the fact that, had we not introduced contempt status as a variable in our analyses and looked for interaction effects, our findings would have suggested that gender bias in juvenile justice processing had diminished considerably. * * * Future research should pay special attention to the contempt power as a mechanism for enabling justice officials to act upon perceptions that males and females require or deserve different sorts of responses form the juvenile justice system."

3) The Use of Uncounseled Convictions to Enhance Subsequent Sentences In **Nichols v. United States**, 511 U.S. 738, 114 S.Ct. 1921, 1927, 128 L.Ed.2d 745 (1994), the Supreme Court held that trial judges could use a prior uncounseled misdemeanor conviction to enhance a defendant's subsequent sentences. The original, uncounseled convictions was constitutionally valid under *Scott v. Illinois* because the court did not order imprisonment at the time of the original conviction. "[A]n uncounseled conviction valid under *Scott* may be relied upon to enhance the sentence for a subsequent offense, even though that sentence entails imprisonment. Enhancement statutes * * * do not change the penalty imposed for the earlier conviction." *See* Lily Fu, "High Crimes from Misdemeanors: The Collateral Use of Prior, Uncounseled Misdemeanors Under the Sixth Amendment, *Baldasar* and the Federal Sentencing Guidelines, 77 *Minn. L. Rev.* 165, 194 (1992).

The dissent in *Nichols* objected to using collaterally a conviction that could not support incarceration initially to extend a period of imprisonment. See *Nichols*, 114 S. Ct. at 1931–37, Blackmun, J., dissenting. As a result of *Nichols*, under the Constitution, trial court judges may deny counsel to misdemeanor defendants, even if they request a lawyer, as long as they do not incarcerate them at that time. Trial court judges may then use those convictions to increase substantially a defendant's subsequent sentence.

4) Burden of Proof What is the burden of proof that the state must satisfy in a status offense proceeding? Recall that the court in *Walker* rejected *Winship* and the standard of proof "beyond a reasonable doubt" for a juvenile whom the state did not charge with a crime. Recall, too, *Cal. Welf. & Inst. Code* § 701 (West 1999), which provides that "Proof beyond a reasonable doubt supported by evidence, legally admissible in the trial of criminal cases, must be adduced to support a finding that the minor is a * * * [delinquent, Section 602], and a preponderance of evidence, legally admissible in the trial of civil cases must be adduced to support a finding that the minor is a * * * [status offender Section 601]."

On the other hand, the Iowa Supreme Court in *In re Henderson*, 199 N.W.2d 111 at 120 (Iowa 1972), rejected appellant's request for proof beyond a reasonable doubt. "The Code, only requires the evidence to be 'clear and convincing', and does not require the facts to be established beyond a reasonable doubt. * * * The facts upon which *Winship* was based are distinguishable from our case. In *Winship* the accused was charged with stealing (a public offense) and was subject to confinement in a penal institution for a term of up to six year. The very holding in *Winship* is bottomed on the fact the basis of the delinquency proceedings was a commission of a public offense.

Here, the basis of the delinquency proceedings is only that John Henderson was uncontrolled. He was not charged with the commission of a public offense, nor did the State seek to prove or even assert that he had committed a crime. * * *

We have observed above the standard of due process in juvenile courts is 'fundamental fairness.' There is, to us, no departure from such standard when we use the 'clear and convincing' requirement of proof as opposed to the 'beyond reasonable doubt' standard when the basis of the proceedings is not the commission of a public offense."

Finally, the Family Court in *In the Matter of Karen Price*, 94 Misc.2d 345, 404 N.Y.S.2d 821 (Fam. Ct. 1978), dismissed a PINS petition charging the juvenile with a status offense because "the Respondent has not been proved, beyond a reasonable doubt, to be a person 'habitually disobedient' and 'beyond the lawful control' of her mother * * *." *See also, In re Henderson*, 199 N.W.2d 111 at 123 (Iowa 1972) MCCORMICK, JUSTICE (concurring specially), who argued that "The Code is unconstitutional because it permits delinquency adjudication upon clear and convincing evidence rather than proof beyond a reasonable doubt. * * * The majority seeks to save the lesser standard where delinquency is predicated upon a claim the child is 'uncontrolled' or 'habitually disobedient' * * *. There is no rational basis for distinction. We cannot abdicate our responsibility to apply due process standards simply because the United States Supreme Court has not previously decided a case on exactly the same facts.

Winship did not reach the issue of constitutionality of New York procedures governing a 'person in need of supervision.' * * * Since *Winship*, New York has required proof beyond a reasonable doubt both in delinquency and 'person in need of supervision' hearings finding no real adjudicatory distinction between them. We should now say with New York. ' * * * (W)e do not see how we can give some children less rights than others. Would this not be the case of saying that you have more rights when it is alleged that you have perpetrated more of a wrong?' "

If you were a state legislator prescribing the standard of proof for noncriminal status offenses, as a matter of juvenile justice policy, what burden of proof would you require the state to meet and why?

CHAPTER 8

DISPOSITION DECISION: WHAT TO DO WITH THE JUVENILE?

■ ■ ■

Many juvenile justice personnel make decisions concerning the welfare, legal status, and custody of a youth. "Disposition" refers to the process by which the various actors decide what to do with a child-offender who falls within the juvenile court's jurisdiction. As we saw in Chapters 3 and 4, police officers may refer a case to intake for formal processing, adjust it informally on the street or at the station-house, or divert it. Intake social workers or probation staff, in turn, may refer a youth to the juvenile court for formal adjudication or dispose of the case through informal supervision or diversion. Finally, even after formal adjudication, the juvenile court judge may choose from a wide array of dispositional alternatives—dismissal, continuing a case without a finding of delinquency, probation, out of home placement, or commitment to a state training school.

Research indicates that dispositional decisions cumulate—decisions made by the initial participants, for example, police or intake workers, affect the decisions made by subsequent participants. *See, e.g.*, Donna Bishop and Charles Frazier, "The Influence of Race in Juvenile Justice Processing," 25 *J. Res. Crime & Delinquency* 242 (1988); Belinda McCarthy & Brent L. Smith, "The Conceptualization of Discrimination in the Juvenile Justice Process: The Impact of Administrative Factors and Screening Decisions on Juvenile Court Dispositions," 24 *Criminology* 41 (1986); Jeffrey Fagan, Ellen Slaughter, and Elliot Hartstone, "Blind Justice? The Impact of Race on the Juvenile Justice Process," 33 *Crime & Delinquency* 224 (1987). Evaluating judicial sentencing decision requires an appreciation of the decisions made by other juvenile justice actors who winnow the cases ultimately presented to the court. If police refer a case to juvenile court, as we saw in Chapter 4, typically an intake probation officer will screen it to decide whether to process the case formally or informally. About half of the cases referred to intake are closed or informally adjusted. Some research suggests that a child's social characteristics, demeanor, or race, rather than the referral offenses, influence intake decision-making, thereby amplifying racial and class disparities in processing youths referred to juvenile court. *See* Bell & Lang, "The Intake

Dispositions of Juvenile Offenders," 22 *J. Res. Crime & Delinquency* 309 (1985); Fagan, Slaughter & Hartstone, *supra*; Donna M. Bishop and Charles Frazier, "Race Effects in Juvenile Justice Decision–Making: Findings of a Statewide Analysis." 86 *J. Crim. L. and Criminology* 392 (1996).

Following a formal determination of delinquency, state statutes and rules typically offer a range of sentencing alternatives—dismissal, continuance without a finding of delinquency, restitution, probation with or without additional conditions or supervision, out-of-home placement, or institutional confinement—and give the juvenile court judge broad discretion to impose an appropriate disposition. Because the juvenile court adjudicates virtually all juveniles against whom the state files delinquency petitions delinquent, the dispositional decision becomes the crucial one in the process. As Judge Mack observed in Chapter 1, *supra*, pp. 8–12, the primary focus of juvenile justice remains "what to do with this child?"

STATE EX REL. D. D. H. v. DOSTERT

165 W.Va. 448, 269 S.E.2d 401 (W.Va.1980).

NEELY, CHIEF JUSTICE: In this case we shall endeavor, with some apprehension, to clarify the proper procedures at the dispositional stage of a juvenile proceeding. The facts of these three consolidated cases provide an excellent opportunity to explore the nature of the juvenile disposition. Indeed this particular child's journey into the juvenile justice system constitutes a veritable primer on how a juvenile should not be handled.
* * *

Historically, protecting society from juvenile delinquency and helping juvenile offenders modify their behavior have been seen as complementary goals of the juvenile law; however, it is now generally recognized that caring for the juvenile and controlling the juvenile are often quite contradictory processes. Much of our juvenile law at the moment is predicated upon a healthy skepticism about the capacity of the State and its agents to help children when they are incarcerated in one of the juvenile detention facilities. Thus, the control of juveniles and the treatment of juveniles (if that expression can be used without conjuring Kafkaesque images) are frequently irreconcilable goals. Furthermore, children can be dangerous, destructive, abusive, and otherwise thoroughly anti-social, which prompts an entirely understandable expectation in society of protection, even if we have matured beyond expecting retribution.

The dispositional stage of a juvenile proceeding is designed to do something which is almost impossible, namely, to reconcile: (1) society's interest in being protected from dangerous and disruptive children; (2) society's interest in nurturing its children in such a way that they will be productive and successful adults; (3) society's interest in providing a deterrent to other children who, but for the specter of the juvenile law, would themselves become disruptive and unamenable to adult control; (4) the citizens' demand that children be responsible for invasion of personal rights; and, (5) the setting of an example of care, love, and forgiveness by the engines of the state in the hope that such qualities will be emulated by the subject children. While retribution is considered an unhealthy instinct and, conceivably, an immoral instinct in an enlightened society, nonetheless, State imposed retribution has historically been the quid pro quo of the State's monopoly of force and its proscription of individual retribution. Retribution is merely another way of saying that children are to be treated as responsible moral agents.

It is possible to make the dispositional stage of a juvenile proceeding so burdensome in requiring exhaustive examination of all "less restrictive alternatives," no matter how speculative, that we, in effect, direct lower courts to abandon all hope of confining a child. That is not the clear purport, however, of W.Va. Code, 49–5–13(b) (1978) which says:

> In disposition the court shall not be limited to the relief sought in the petition and shall give precedence to the least restrictive of the following alternatives consistent with the best interests and welfare of the public and the child. * * *

W.Va. Code 49–5–13(b)(5) (1978) says:

> Upon a finding that no less restrictive alternative would accomplish the requisite rehabilitation of the child, and upon an adjudication of delinquency, * * * commit the child to an industrial home or correctional institution for children. Commitments shall not exceed the maximum term for which an adult could have been sentenced for the same offense, with discretion as to discharge to rest with the director of the institution, who may release the child and return him to the court for further disposition. * * *

[I]t is important to explain exactly what the elaborate procedure at the dispositional stage is designed to do. Unless there are clear, understandable standards, procedure becomes confounding at best and disguised legislation at worst.

Chapter 49 of the W.Va. Code covering child welfare is clearly committed to the rehabilitative model. As we noted in *State ex rel. Harris v. Calendine,*

> The Legislature could choose to punish children guilty of criminal conduct in the same manner as it punishes adults, but as a matter of public policy the Legislature provided instead for a comprehensive system of child welfare. The aim of this system is to protect and rehabilitate children, not to punish them.

The rehabilitative model requires a great deal of information about the child at the dispositional hearing. Much of that information must necessarily focus on the critical issue of whether it is possible for the State or other social service agencies to help the child. Although helping the child is the first concern of the juvenile law, it is not the only concern, since at the operational rather than theoretical level, the rehabilitative approach has dramatic limitations, preeminent among which is that it interferes both with the deterrence of other children and the protection of society.

* * * [W]e have not yet refined an approach which intelligently uses procedure to arrive at sufficient information to permit a balancing of the child's liberty interest with society's need for protection and deterrence.

There is no alternative in our efforts to reconcile the competing goals of the juvenile justice system but to enter reluctantly into a brief discussion of the age-old philosophical controversy about free will and determinism. Neither this Court nor anyone else in the world will ever definitively answer the question of whether mankind is determined or is possessed of free will. The philosophy of the law has generally accepted that at times people are determined while at other times they have free will. Pragmatically our legal tradition has answered the question by rules which recognize that men are guided entirely neither by external forces nor by free will; every person is influenced by both but is never totally controlled by either.

As perplexing as the philosophical argument over free will versus determinism may be, no single concept is as critical to the dispositional stage of a juvenile proceeding. The facts of the case before us clearly show a child whose sorrows are largely the result of external forces. That she is difficult, ungovernable, and unmanageable is not disputed in the elaborate record before us, yet she was to the social forces around her the "wingless fly in the hands of small boys." On the other hand, hypothetically, we can envisage a child from a perfect middle class background, selling drugs to other children for no apparent reason other than the allure of enormous profits. To speculate that deep inside that child's psyche there is some hidden, predetermining factor is not adequate for the "deterrent" or "responsibility" purposes of the juvenile law. Furthermore, it is a negation of our entire tradition to say that every social transgression is the result of "illness." Many a very sane and well adjusted person has found the allure of illegal profits compelling. Children can, and often do, engage in delinquent conduct for no better reason than that they prefer having money to not having money.

Some things we have enough knowledge to treat and other things we do not have enough knowledge to treat. Broken homes, uncaring parents, learning disabilities, Dickensian poverty, parental abuse, and an unhealthy environment are all things which the State, "solicitous of the welfare of its children but also mindful of other demands upon the State budget for humanitarian purposes," can begin to cure. Where, however, no factor or factors can be isolated which we can treat, or which our over-all view of the State's role in providing social justice deems not worthy of a treatment approach, we must, for want of any other reasonable alternative, accept the free will model, the goals of which are deterrence and juvenile responsibility.

At the dispositional stage of the juvenile proceeding there are a number of actors whose roles have been established by statute. The first major actor is obviously the judge who, is entitled to request the juvenile probation officer or State department worker to make an investigation of the environment of the child and the alternative dispositions possible. The second actor is the probation officer or State department worker who must fulfill this obligation, and the third actor is the counsel for the petitioner who is entitled to review any report made by the probation officer or welfare worker seventy-two hours before the dispositional hearing. In addition there is the child and his parents, guardian, or adult relatives, and the representatives of any social service agencies, including the schools, which have been involved in the case. Since the threshold question at any dispositional hearing is whether the child is delinquent because of his own free will or for environmental reasons which society can attack directly, all of the actors in the dispositional drama should concentrate their attention initially on that one subject. Obviously this is a question which the trial judge has always answered in his own mind. However, the thrust of the formal procedural model which has been evolving is that this question be developed on the record and reasons for determining a particular disposition be articulated for appellate review. We shall now focus on the role of each major actor.

The Role of Court Appointed Counsel:

The dispositional stage of any juvenile proceeding may be the most important stage in the entire process; therefore, it is the obligation of any court appointed or retained counsel to continue active and vigorous representation of the child through that stage. We have already held that counsel has a duty to investigate all resources available to find the least restrictive alternative, and here we confirm that holding. Court appointed counsel must make an independent investigation of the child's background. Counsel should present to the court any facts which could lead the court to conclude that the child's environment is a major contributing factor to his misbehavior. In this regard counsel should investigate the child's performance in school, his family background, the level of concern and leadership on the part of his parents, the physical conditions under which the child is living, and any health problems. Counsel must also inform himself in detail about the facilities both inside and outside the State of West Virginia which are able to help children.

Armed with adequate information, counsel can then present the court with all reasonable alternative dispositions to incarceration and should have taken the initial steps to secure the tentative acceptance of the child into those facilities. It is not sufficient to suggest upon the record as an abstract proposition that there are alternatives; it is the affirmative obligation of counsel to advise the court of the exact terms, conditions, and costs of such alternatives, whether the Department of Welfare or any other source can pay for such alternative, and under what conditions any alternative facilities would be willing to accept the child.

The faithful discharge of these duties requires substantial industry; however, appointed counsel is entitled to be compensated for his time up to the statutory limit set for the criminal charges fund. Furthermore, energetic advocacy implies that the court must accommodate an adversarial proceeding at the disposition stage. In the case at bar, the court reacted to the legitimate efforts of the appointed attorney to arrange an alternative disposition by finding him in contempt and removing him from his appointment. Such practices are obviously condemned since it is envisaged that the child shall have an advocate who will make a record. * * *

The Role of the Probation Officer or Welfare Worker:

The probation officer or welfare worker when requested by the judge is also responsible for discovering whether there are forces which are at work upon the child which either the Department of Welfare or other social service agencies can correct. In the case before us it is obvious that the petitioner had no adult supervision whatsoever and that she was left to fend for herself in the back streets. Obviously, before incarcerating a first offender like the petitioner it would have been incumbent upon the Department of Welfare to find a suitable environment for her. The record amply demonstrates from the history of the petitioner after this Court released her from the industrial school, that the petitioner is a somewhat unmanageable and ungovernable child who, at the time, would not remain in a juvenile refuge. Nonetheless, absent at least one predisposition incidence of flight from a reasonable alternative, it was quite improper for the court to place her in the first instance in the industrial school. Upon remand the court must focus on her level of cooperation at the time she is again considered for disposition at the remand. * * *

The Role of the Court:

It is the obligation of the court to hear all witnesses who might shed light upon the proper disposition of a child and before incarcerating a child, to find facts upon the record which would lead a reasonable appellate court to conclude in the words of the statute, either that "no less restrictive alternative would accomplish the requisite rehabilitation of the child * * * " or "the welfare of the public" requires incarceration. Where the court directs incarceration, he should affirmatively find upon the record either that the child's behavioral problem is not the result of social conditions beyond the child's control, but rather of an intentional failure on the part of the child to conform his actions to the law, or that the child will be dangerous if any other disposition is used, or that the child will not cooperate with any rehabilitative program absent physical restraint. Where the court concludes that simple punishment will be a more effective rehabilitative device than anything else, the conclusion is certainly legitimate and within the discretion of the trial court; nonetheless, the trial court must elaborate on the record his reasons for that conclusion.

If the proceeding is merely the last in a long series involving the same child, the court should set forth any "less restrictive alternatives" which have already been tried and the actions of the child after those alternatives were implemented. Even when the child's behavior results from environmental factors, the court may find the child to pose an imminent danger to society because he will flee from all but secure facilities and, therefore, conclude that incarceration is the only reasonable alternative.

The court has a duty to insure that the child's social history is reviewed intelligently so that an individualized treatment plan may be designed when appropriate. * * * The effectiveness of treatment is disputed to say the least, and this is particularly true whenever commitment to an institution is involved. Therefore, the judge making the dispositional determination should not place a child who is not dangerous and who can be accommodated elsewhere in an institution under the guise of "treating" the child. * * *

The Role of the Child:

* * * [T]here is an affirmative obligation on the part of the child to cooperate. Certainly one instance of a child failing to follow some Rhadamanthine ruling of a circuit court does not justify instant removal to an industrial school, but a consistent course of noncooperation, particularly when combined with a predilection to commit dangerous or destructive acts does justify the court in resorting to commitment.[17] This rule must be tempered, however, by the conclusion that where the agents of the State are gross incompetents and where the treatment and rehabilitative programs prescribed for the child are unreasonable, this Court will not permit incarceration where the true fault lies with the State and not with the child.

When however, there is a consistent pattern of noncooperation which makes alternative rehabilitative programs impossible, the court should set forth the facts upon the record so that this Court will understand why the trial court concludes that there are no alternatives to placement in an institution.

In reaching the conclusion that rehabilitation alone does not exhaust the goals of a juvenile disposition, and that responsibility and deterrence are also important elements in our juvenile philosophy, we have not simply embraced a conservative theory that juvenile delinquents need to be punished. Liberals and conservatives alike may find solace in this opinion because we acknowledge what has been an unspoken conclusion: our treatment looks a lot like punishment. At first glance an agreement among commentators at both philosophical poles may appear strange; however, both share the conclusion that treatment is often disguised punishment. Liberals are pleased that juvenile courts must exercise restraint in resorting to questionable "treatments" at the dispositional stage and conservatives are pleased that it has been admitted that punishment can be a viable goal of any given juvenile disposition.

---

17. Certain individuals must be punished and it is folly to think that judgments of juveniles do not serve as deterrents to at least a portion of juvenile society, not because juveniles fear rehabilitation, but because they fear punishment and incarceration. Despite all protestations to the contrary the label "juvenile delinquent" does carry stigma, and it is not always confidential. * * *

While the conservatives talk about punishment as "retribution" and the cornerstone of "responsibility," the liberal, child advocates speak in terms of the "right to punishment." Once the rehabilitative model is accepted, the next fight is always to show that "treatment" is often a caricature something worthy of a story of Kafka or a Soviet mental hospital. Therefore, while the conservatives throw up their hands because they believe punishment works better than treatment, the juvenile advocates return increasingly to punishment on the grounds that punishment is much less punishing than "treatment." Therefore, while our opinion in this case is hardly definitive, it is designed to give guidance concerning the factors to be developed in the record. In the final analysis, since we are dealing with a love of things irreconcilable, the successful implementation of the juvenile law must rest in the sound discretion of the trial court. A record which discloses conclusively that the trial court has considered all relevant factual material and dispositional theories will permit us to make an intelligent review, keeping in mind that discretionary, dispositional decisions of the trial courts should only be reversed where they are not supported by the evidence or are wrong as a matter of law. * * *

A. INDETERMINATE AND NON–PROPORTIONAL DELINQUENCY DISPOSITIONS—INDIVIDUALIZED TREATMENT IN THE CHILD'S "BEST INTERESTS"

Historically, juvenile court judges imposed indeterminate and non-proportional dispositions in the "best interests" of the child-offender. Recall from Chapter One, Judge Mack's assertion that

> The problem for determination by the judge is not, Has this boy or girl committed a specific wrong, but What is he, how has he become what he is, and what had best be done in his interest and in the interests of the state to save him from a downward career. It is apparent at once that the ordinary legal evidence in a criminal court is not the sort of evidence to be heard in such a proceeding.

According to the theory of the "Rehabilitative Ideal," the judicial inquiry does not focus on a youth's prior misconduct but rather on the development of a program to alleviate the conditions that caused the youth's delinquency. A delinquency disposition assumes that judges and clinicians can identify the antecedent causes of the "delinquency," make a prognosis about its likely course if left untreated, develop and deliver appropriate forms of intervention to alter those causal conditions, and make a judgement about the ultimate prospects of success. In short, it requires diagnosis, classification, prescription, and prognosis. Because one cannot predict accurately the length of rehabilitative therapy necessary to ensure success, juvenile courts traditionally imposed indeterminate and non-proportional sentences. The offense that brought a child before the court did not circumscribe either the intensity or the duration of intervention.

Contemporary juvenile sentencing provisions reflect their Progressive origins. *See e.g.*, Barry C. Feld, "The Juvenile Court Meets the Principle of Offense: Punishment, Treatment, and the Difference it Makes," 68 *B. U. L. Rev.* 821 (1988); Julianne P. Sheffer, "Serious and Habitual Juvenile Offender Statutes: Reconciling Punishment and Rehabilitation within the Juvenile Justice System," 48 *Vand. L. Rev.* 479 (1995). In most states, following an adjudication of delinquency, statutes typically authorize a range of sentencing alternatives-dismissal, probation, out-of-home place-ment, or institutional confinement-and give the juvenile court judge broad discretion to impose an appropriate disposition and to modify a youth's disposition depending upon her responsiveness to earlier intervention. Some legislatures instruct the court to consider the "least restrictive alternative" when choosing among dispositional options in the child's "best interests."

Most juvenile sentences are indeterminate; confinement may range from one day to a period of years or until the offender reaches the age of majority. In *Gault*, for example, the judge committed fifteen-year-old Gerald Gault to the State Industrial School "for the period of his minority [that is, until age 21], unless sooner discharged by due process of law" for making "lewd phone calls" even though an adult convicted of the same offense would face a fine of fifty dollars or imprisonment for a maximum of two months. Most states' indeterminate juvenile sentencing statutes authorize disposition that continue for the duration of minority or some other maximum termination age. Other states prescribe a statutory maxi-mum sentencing period for juvenile offenders, typically two years with judicial authority to extend a disposition for an additional two years or more following a review hearing. Within the broad range of sentences authorized by the juvenile statutes, the judge's authority is virtually unrestricted.

NOTES

1) Judicial Discretion and Individualized Dispositions The follow-ing statutes and cases provide examples of the broad discretion and range options available to judges when they decide "what to do with this child."

Cal. Welf. & Inst. Code § 727 (1999).

(a) When a minor is adjudged a ward of the court * * * [as a delinquent] the court may make any and all reasonable orders for the care, supervision, custody, conduct, maintenance, and support of the minor, including medical treatment, subject to further order of the court. * * *

In the discretion of the court, a ward may be ordered to be on probation without supervision of the probation officer. The court, in so ordering, may impose on the ward any and all reasonable conditions of behavior as may be appropriate under this disposition. A minor who has been adjudged a ward of the court on the basis of the commission of any of the offenses described in [§ 707(b), *supra* pp. 627–628] * * * shall not be eligible for probation without supervision of the probation officer. A minor who has been adjudged a ward of the court on the basis of the commission of any offense involving the sale or possession for sale of a controlled substance, except misdemeanor offenses involving marijuana, * * * shall be eligible for probation without supervision of the probation officer only when the court determines that the interests of justice would best be served and states reasons on the record for that determination.

In all other cases, the court shall order the care, custody, and control of the minor to be under the supervision of the probation officer who may place the minor in any of the following:

(1) The home of a relative. When a decision has been made to place the minor in the home of a relative, the court may authorize the relative to give legal consent for the minor's medical, surgical, and dental care and education as if the relative caretaker were the custodial parent of the minor.

(2) A suitable licensed community care facility.

(3) With a foster family agency to be placed in a suitable licensed foster family home or certified family home which has been certified by the agency as meeting licensing standards.

(b) Where the court has ordered a specific minor placed under the supervision of the probation officer and the probation officer has found that the needs of the child cannot be met in any available licensed or exempt facility, including emergency shelter, the minor may be placed in a suitable family home that has filed a license application with the State Department of Social Services. * * *

When a minor has been adjudged a ward of the court * * * and when the court orders that a parent or guardian shall retain custody of that minor * * *, the parent or guardian may be required to participate with that minor in a counseling or education program including, but not limited to, parent education and parenting programs operated by community colleges, school districts, or other appropriate agencies designated by the court. * * *

Cal. Welf. & Inst. § 730 (1999).

(a) When a minor is adjudged a ward of the court on the ground that he or she is [delinquent] * * * the court may order any of the types of treatment referred to in Section 727, and as an additional alternative, may commit the minor to a juvenile home, ranch, camp, or forestry camp. If there is no county juvenile home, ranch, camp, or forestry camp within the county, the court may commit the minor to the county juvenile hall.

(b) When a ward described in subdivision (a) is placed under the supervision of the probation officer or committed to the care, custody, and control of the probation officer, the court may make any and all reasonable orders for the conduct of the ward including the requirement that the ward go to work and earn money * * * and apply these earnings as directed by the court. The court may impose and require any and all reasonable conditions that it may determine fitting and proper to the end that justice may be done and the reformation and rehabilitation of the ward enhanced.

(c) When a ward described in subdivision (a) is placed under the supervision of the probation officer * * * and is required as a condition of probation to participate in community service or graffiti cleanup, the court may impose a condition that if the minor unreasonably fails to attend or unreasonably leaves prior to completing the assigned daily hours of community service or graffiti cleanup, a law enforcement officer may take the minor into custody for the purpose of returning the minor to the site of the community service or graffiti cleanup.

Cal. Welf. & Inst. § 731 (1999).

When a minor is adjudged a ward of the court on the ground that he or she is a [delinquent] * * *, the court may order any of the types of treatment referred to in Sections 727 and 730 and, in addition, may order the ward to make restitution, to pay a fine up to the amount of two hundred fifty dollars ($250) * * * if the court finds that the minor has the financial ability to pay the fine, or to participate in uncompensated work programs or the court may commit the ward to a shelter-care facility or may order that the ward and his or her family or guardian participate in a program of professional counseling as arranged and directed by the probation officer as a condition of continued custody of such minor or may commit the minor to the Department of the Youth Authority.

A minor committed to the Department of the Youth Authority may not be held in physical confinement for a period of time in excess of the maximum period of imprisonment which could be imposed upon an adult convicted of the offense or offenses which brought or continued the minor under the jurisdiction of the juvenile court. * * *

2) Individualized and Particularized Dispositional Assessments In **In re Ronnie P.**, 10 Cal.App.4th 1079, 12 Cal.Rptr.2d 875 (Cal. Ct. App. 2d Div. 1992), the California court of appeals held that juvenile court judges must make particularized dispositional decisions and may not simply execute delinquency sanctions previously "stayed":

> First we note the complete absence of authority for an order imposing a "suspended" or "stayed" Youth Authority commitment. Courts have permitted the imposition of a brief juvenile hall detention stayed on condition that other dispositional orders be performed. This practice has been codified * * * [and] permits the court to enforce, upon a violation of "a condition or conditions of probation," a "stayed" order for confinement in a county institution for up to 30 days. * * *

> Nor do we find anything suggesting that the court may forego a thorough review of dispositional considerations in favor of a previously "stayed" Youth Authority commitment. Such a notion runs contrary to the basic purposes, principles, and procedures of juvenile law. The stated central objective of the law with respect to delinquent children is to provide the "care, treatment and guidance which is consistent with their best interest, which holds them accountable for their behavior, and which is appropriate for their circumstances." To determine what is appropriate under a given set of circumstances, a court must review those circumstances every time the minor appears for a dispositional hearing. Thus, "[j]uvenile courts * * * shall consider the safety and protection of the

public and the best interests of the minor in all deliberations pursuant to this chapter." "Each time a ward comes before the court * * *, the goal of any resulting dispositional order is to rehabilitate the minor." A lockstep escalation of dispositions "falls short of the particularized consideration which underlies the entire juvenile court system." * * *

[T]he court is required to examine the entire dispositional picture whenever the minor comes before the court for disposition. It cannot treat an earlier order as "self-executing" or "automatic."

Nor could the court properly impose a "stayed" Youth Authority commitment by analogy to criminal law. It is commonplace to grant probation to an adult offender subject to a stayed or suspended sentence which may be executed more-or-less automatically if the conditions of probation are violated. However, a dispositional hearing on a supplemental juvenile court petition "is only superficially analogous to an adult probation revocation hearing because neither the purposes nor the consequences of these proceedings are the same. * * * [J]uvenile probation is not, as with an adult, an act of leniency in lieu of statutory punishment; it is an ingredient of a final order for the minor's reformation and rehabilitation. A grant of juvenile probation is not revoked upon sustaining a supplemental petition; rather, the entire underlying order is subject to modification 'as the judge deems meet and proper.' "

In making a dispositional order, of course, the juvenile court can not only direct an appropriate placement but may also issue orders concerning the minor's conduct. In content these orders are often comparable to adult probation conditions, and regrettably the similarities have led both legislators and courts to refer to them as "conditions of probation." They differ, however, in the critical respect that with narrow statutory exceptions, violation of such an order cannot lead automatically to imposition of some reserved measure, but requires a complete review of the order and such amendments as the court finds "meet and proper" under the governing statutory criteria.

This brings us to respondent's assertion that appellant "squandered his chances at a lesser alternative." Underlying this argument is the concept of retributive justice which is explicitly incorporated in adult penal law and just as explicitly excluded from the Juvenile Court Law. A juvenile disposition is not an act of graceful abstention by the state, the benefits of which the minor forfeits by misconduct. The significance of subsequent misconduct in juvenile cases is that it may reveal the ineffectiveness of a current disposition in achieving the statutory objectives of rehabilitating the minor and protecting the public.

A "stayed" Youth Authority commitment has no place in this scheme.[8] The law presumes that at a given point in time the statutory

---

8. Of course, the threat of Youth Authority commitment may have a salutary effect on a particular minor's attitude, and nothing said here should be understood to restrict the court's ability to employ such a threat to encourage the minor's reform. Further, a minor's failure to heed such a warning may be taken as some evidence of resistance to rehabilitation. Aside from these purposes and effects, however, such a warning can have no legal bearing on a subsequent dispositional proceeding. Certainly it cannot operate to foreclose the imposition or continuation of a less restrictive placement.

criteria are best satisfied by one dispositional alternative. If commitment appears to be that alternative, then the minor should be committed. If some lesser alternative appears preferable, the court should choose the alternative. The court cannot determine in advance that if the lesser alternative fails, commitment will become the optimal disposition. Instead a failure of the lesser disposition calls for a complete reassessment of dispositional issues in light of then-prevailing circumstances.

By relying on the "stayed" commitment, the court here failed to "consider" the dispositional evidence, including the social study. This inference is reinforced by the fact that * * * [the judge refused] to consider the facts noted in the report, or any other facts tending to support a disposition less restrictive than Youth Authority. By failing to consider any of the prescribed dispositional factors the court also failed to make a finding on critical ultimate issues and failed to exercise a discretion conferred and compelled by law. Such error constituted the denial of a fair hearing and deprivation of fundamental procedural rights compelling reversal. * * *

3) Probationary Dispositions The California Court of Appeals in **In re Kazuo G.**, 22 Cal.App.4th 1, 8–9, 27 Cal.Rptr.2d 155, 159–160 (Cal. Ct. App. 1st Dist., 1994), discussed the alternatives to institutionalization available to a juvenile court judge:

When a minor is adjudged a ward of the court under section 602, the juvenile court has various dispositional alternatives, including supervised or unsupervised probation. Juvenile probation has long been recognized as an alternative to the more serious measure of commitment to a county juvenile institution or to the Youth Authority. Indeed probation is the statutorily preferred alternative. Before a minor is removed from the physical custody of a parent the minor must ordinarily have been tried on probation.

"Probation" is nowhere defined in the Juvenile Court Law, but there is little doubt that a grant of juvenile probation is an order of release into the community. That is, a minor placed on probation ordinarily remains in physical custody of the parent. Upon the grant of juvenile probation, the juvenile court may impose and require "any and all reasonable conditions that it may determine fitting and proper to the end that justice may be done and the reformation and rehabilitation of the ward enhanced." * * *

[S]ection 730 authorizes confinement to juvenile hall as a condition of probation: "Its purpose is to demonstrate to the minor the road to which continuation of delinquency will lead * * *." For the same reason, the Supreme Court has upheld a stay of juvenile hall commitment as a condition of probation: "[T]he court could reasonably conclude that * * * the threat of further confinement if he again violated the conditions of probation would serve as a deterrent to delinquent behavior."

4) Findings of Fact and Reasons for Juvenile Court Judge's Dispositional Decision In **In re Interest of J.A.**, 244 Neb. 919, 923–925, 510 N.W.2d 68 (Neb. 1994), the juvenile challenged the juvenile court judge's commitment of her to the Geneva Training School without explicitly providing findings of fact or reasons for her commitment:

> Appellant contends that the juvenile court violated § 43–286(4)(f) by committing her to Geneva without articulating any reason why she should be so committed. We disagree. * * *

> Under § 43–286, a juvenile court has broad discretion as to the disposition of a delinquent juvenile. Specifically, § 43–286 provides that a juvenile court may continue the dispositional portion of the juvenile's hearing from time to time under such terms and conditions as the court may prescribe, may place the juvenile on probation, or may place the juvenile in a family home or institution. A juvenile court may also commit a juvenile to Geneva.

> Under § 43–286(4), a juvenile court also has the power to change the juvenile's disposition. Section 43–286(4) provides, in relevant part:

>> When a juvenile is placed on probation or under the supervision of the court * * * and it is alleged that the juvenile has violated a term of probation or supervision or that the juvenile has violated an order of the court, a motion to revoke probation or supervision or to change the disposition may be filed and proceedings held as follows: * * *

>> (f) In cases when the court revokes probation, it shall enter a written statement as to the evidence relied on and the reasons for revocation.

> In other words, subsection (4) outlines the procedures which must be followed when a court revokes probation, revokes supervision, or otherwise changes the juvenile's disposition. Subsection (4)(f) describes more particularly the procedures which must be followed when a court revokes probation.

> In the instant case, the juvenile court continued the dispositional portion of appellant's hearing several times. At one point, as described above, the court imposed terms and conditions upon appellant. When appellant violated one of the terms set forth by the court, the court ordered her committed to Geneva. The court indisputably possessed the statutory authority, under § 43–286, to take each of these actions.

> Appellant contends that although the court had the power to act as it did, the court was required, by virtue of § 43–286(4)(f), to give a reason why she should be committed to Geneva. This contention is without merit. Section 43–286(4)(f), by its terms, applies only when a juvenile court revokes probation. The court never placed appellant on probation. The court therefore had no obligation, under § 43–286(4)(f), to provide reasons on the record for committing her to Geneva. * * *

5) Scope of appellate review of disposition orders—De Novo Review *See e.g. In re B.B.*, 516 N.W.2d 874, 877 (Iowa 1994), where the Iowa Supreme Court noted that "Our scope of review of juvenile court proceedings is de novo. We review both questions of law and fact."

In **In the Interest of S. J.**, 304 N.W.2d 685, 686–687 (N.D.1981), the juvenile appealed from her commitment to the State Industrial School until she attained the age of eighteen. The North Dakota Supreme Court stated the standard of appellate review of juvenile court dispositions:

> We have previously stated that our scope of review * * * is equivalent to the former procedure of trial de novo. Thus, we are not bound by the "clearly erroneous" rule * * *. Despite the fact that we are not bound by the clearly erroneous rule, we ascribe appreciable weight to the juvenile court's findings of fact. * * * After a careful examination of the facts in the instant case, we conclude that the order of disposition of the juvenile court was proper. * * *

> In arriving at an order of disposition of a delinquent child, the best interests of the child and the State of North Dakota must be considered. S. J. asserts that a stay of the order of disposition would be proper because the delinquent child who accompanied her in the robbery received a stay despite the fact that such child was sixteen years of age. S. J. argues that the denial of the motion for a stay results in a form of retribution or punishment contrary to one of the purposes of the Uniform Juvenile Court Act, which purpose is to remove from children committing delinquent acts the taint of criminality and the consequences of criminal behavior and to substitute a program of treatment, training, and rehabilitation. * * *

> The juvenile court considered and rejected this proposal [to return S.J. to the family home while under the custody of the State Youth Authority] as an ineffective method of disposition because S. J.'s past history indicated that she had difficulty adjusting to restrictions imposed at her family home. S. J. had lived by herself and with relatives and, in each case, her living arrangements were unsuccessful. In addition, S. J. had not attended school for some time. These facts lead us to conclude that the district court's order of disposition was proper because the structured environment of the State Industrial School accounts for S. J.'s best interests in view of her past behavior. By placing her in the care, custody, and control of the Superintendent of the State Industrial School, the juvenile court has provided the means by which S. J. may receive the necessary treatment, rehabilitation, and correction.

Abuse of Discretion. In other jurisdictions, appellate court review of juvenile court dispositional orders typically employ the "abuse of discretion" standard and defer to trial judge's findings of fact and discretionary dispositional decisions. *See e.g. In re J.M.*, 546 N.W.2d 383, 386 (S.D.1996), "In reviewing a court's order of disposition in a delinquency proceeding, we consider whether or not the trial court abused its discretion or otherwise committed an error of law requiring reversal."

As a practical matter, how significantly will the standard of review affect the ability of appellate courts to supervise and oversee the discretionary sentencing decisions of trial judges who provide an adequate factual record for their decision?

6) Extension or Modification of Order of Disposition In **In re T. B.**, 268 Ga. 149, 486 S.E.2d 177 (Ga.1997), the delinquent challenged the juvenile court judge's decision to extend the juvenile's custody for an additional period of two years from the date of original commitment as a violation of the constitutional prohibition against double jeopardy. The statute provided that:

> Except as otherwise provided by law, any other order of disposition in a proceeding involving delinquency, unruliness, or deprivation * * * continues in force for not more than two years. The court may sooner terminate its order or extend its duration for further periods. An order of extension may be made if:
>
> (1) A hearing is held prior to the expiration of the order upon motion of a party or on the court's own motion;
>
> (2) Reasonable notice of the factual basis of the motion and of the hearing and opportunity to be heard are given to the parties affected;
>
> (3) The court finds that the extension is necessary to accomplish the purposes of the order extended; and
>
> (4) The extension does not exceed two years from the expiration of the prior order. OCGA § 15–11–41(g) (1996).

The juvenile court judge adjudicated T.B. delinquent and committed him to the Department of Children and Youth Services for a period of two years. Near the end of that time, DCYS moved for an extension of custody. The juvenile court conducted a hearing at which T.B. was represented by an attorney who argued that the statute violated the substantive due process and double jeopardy provisions of the State and Federal Constitutions. The juvenile court judge found that T.B. was in need of continuing treatment, that a continuation of commitment to DCYS would be in T. B.'s best interest, and entered an order extending T.B.'s custody for an additional period of two years. The Georgia Supreme Court rejected T.B.'s double jeopardy claim and approved the extension of disposition:

> T.B. urges that the juvenile court erred in refusing to find the statutory provision violative of federal and state constitutional protections against double jeopardy because it permits the juvenile court to increase the sentence for a delinquent act after the juvenile has begun serving the sentence. However, the argument miscasts an extension of custody under the statutory scheme as a sentence of punishment and ignores the very purpose of Chapter 11 and Title 15. The express purpose of the Juvenile Court Code is to assist, protect, and restore children whose well-being as secure members of society is threatened. In furtherance of that goal, the Legislature created a comprehensive civil forum for the treatment and protection of juveniles. The statutory scheme is "replete with distinctions between criminal matters and matters concerning juveniles alleged delinquent. * * * The juvenile code is concerned with the care, guidance, and well-being of children * * *, [and] [j]uveniles are declared delinquent because they need treatment and rehabilitation."

It is certainly true that "constitutional considerations must necessarily transcend even the most admirable legislative purposes." However, here there is no conflict. An order of extension * * * operates to further the accomplishment of the juvenile's treatment and rehabilitation, and thus, does not run afoul of the constitutional prohibitions against double jeopardy.

7) Appellate control of trial court decisions under a typical disposition statute Consider the range of dispositional options available to a trial judge. If a judge makes the procedural findings—"why the best interests of the child are served by the disposition" and "what alternative dispositions" the court considered and rejected—can an appellate court control judges sentencing discretion? What is the court's role in *In re L.K.W.*, *infra*, p. 898? Why does Judge Crippen dissent from the application of the statute in *In re D.S.F.*, *infra*, p. 906?

Minn. Stat. § 260.185 (1997). Dispositions; delinquent child

Subdivision 1. Court order, findings, remedies, treatment. If the court finds that the child is delinquent, it shall enter an order making any of the following dispositions of the case which are deemed necessary to the rehabilitation of the child:

(a) Counsel the child or the parents, guardian, or custodian;

(b) Place the child under the supervision of a probation officer or other suitable person in the child's own home under conditions prescribed by the court including reasonable rules for the child's conduct and the conduct of the child's parents, guardian, or custodian, designed for the physical, mental, and moral well-being and behavior of the child, or with the consent of the commissioner of corrections, in a group foster care facility which is under the management and supervision of said commissioner;

(c) Subject to the supervision of the court, transfer legal custody of the child to one of the following:

　　(1) a child-placing agency; or

　　(2) the local social services agency; or

　　(3) a reputable individual of good moral character * * *; or

　　(4) a county home school, if the county maintains a home school or enters into an agreement with a county home school; or

　　(5) a county probation officer for placement in a group foster home * * *;

(d) Transfer legal custody by commitment to the commissioner of corrections;

(e) If the child is found to have violated a state or local law or ordinance which has resulted in damage to the person or property of another, the court may order the child to make reasonable restitution for such damage;

(f) Require the child to pay a fine of up to $700; the court shall order payment of the fine in accordance with a time payment schedule which shall not impose an undue financial hardship on the child;

(g) If the child is in need of special treatment and care for reasons of physical or mental health, the court may order the child's parent, guardian, or custodian to provide it. If the parent, guardian, or custodian fails to provide this treatment or care, the court may order it provided;

(h) If the court believes that it is in the best interests of the child and of public safety that the driver's license of the child be canceled until the child's 18th birthday, the court may recommend to the commissioner of public safety the cancellation of the child's license for any period up to the child's 18th birthday, and the commissioner is hereby authorized to cancel such license without a hearing. * * *

(i) If the court believes that it is in the best interest of the child and of public safety that the child is enrolled in school, the court may require the child to remain enrolled in a public school until the child reaches the age of 18 or completes all requirements needed to graduate from high school. * * *

If the child is petitioned and found by the court to have committed a controlled substance offense * * *, the court shall determine whether the child unlawfully possessed or sold the controlled substance while driving a motor vehicle. If so, the court shall notify the commissioner of public safety of its determination and order the commissioner to revoke the child's driver's license. * * *

If the child is petitioned and found by the court to have committed or attempted to commit an act [of criminal sexual conduct] * * * the court shall order an independent professional assessment of the child's need for sex offender treatment. * * * If the assessment indicates that the child is in need of and amenable to sex offender treatment, the court shall include in its disposition order a requirement that the child undergo treatment. * * *

Any order for a disposition authorized under this section shall contain written findings of fact to support the disposition ordered, and shall also set forth in writing the following information:

(a) why the best interests of the child are served by the disposition ordered; and

(b) what alternative dispositions were considered by the court and why such dispositions were not appropriate in the instant case.

Subd. 1a. Possession of firearm or dangerous weapon. If * * * the court also finds that the child was in possession of a firearm at the time of the offense, in addition to any other disposition the court shall order that the firearm be immediately seized and shall order that the child be required to serve at least 100 hours of community work service unless the child is placed in a residential treatment program or a juvenile correctional facility. * * *

Subd. 1b. Commitment to secure facility; length of stay; transfers. An adjudicated juvenile may not be placed in a * * * secure treatment facility unless the placement is approved by the juvenile court. However, the program administrator may determine the juvenile's length of stay in the secure portion of the facility. The administrator shall notify the court of any movement of juveniles from secure portions of facilities. However, the court may, in its discretion, order that the juveniles be moved back to secure portions of the facility.

Subd. 1c. Placement of juveniles in secure facilities; requirements. Before a postadjudication placement of a juvenile in a secure treatment facility * * * the court may:

(1) consider whether the juvenile has been adjudicated for a felony offense against the person or that in addition to the current adjudication, the juvenile has failed to appear in court on one or more occasions or has run away from home on one or more occasions;

(2) conduct a subjective assessment to determine whether the child is a danger to self or others or would abscond from a nonsecure facility or if the child's health or welfare would be endangered if not placed in a secure facility;

(3) conduct a culturally appropriate psychological evaluation which includes a functional assessment of anger and abuse issues; and

(4) conduct an educational and physical assessment of the juvenile.

In determining whether to order secure placement, the court shall consider the necessity of:

(1) protecting the public;

(2) protecting program residents and staff; and

(3) preventing juveniles with histories of absconding from leaving treatment programs * * *

Subd. 3. Continuance. When it is in the best interests of the child to do so and when the child has admitted the allegations contained in the petition before the judge or referee, or * * * the allegations contained in the petition have been duly proven but, in either case, before a finding of delinquency has been entered, the court may continue the case for a period not to exceed 90 days on any one order. Such a continuance may be extended for one additional successive period not to exceed 90 days * * * During this continuance the court may enter an order in accordance with the provisions of subdivision 1, clause (a) or (b) or enter an order to hold the child in detention for a period not to exceed 15 days. * * *

Subd. 4. All orders for supervision under subdivision 1, clause (b) shall be for an indeterminate period unless otherwise specified by the court, and shall be reviewed by the court at least annually. All orders under subdivision 1, clause (c) shall be for a specified length of time set by the court. * * *

IN THE MATTER OF L.K.W.

372 N.W.2d 392 (Minn. Ct. App. 1985).

CRIPPEN, JUDGE. [In May 1984, L.K.W., then aged 16, admitted to a misdemeanor violation of the shoplifting statute and the juvenile court adjudicated her delinquent. Following a series of disposition orders, the juvenile court removed her from her home and placed her in a private residential facility 150 miles away for a stay of 90 to 100 days at a cost of $6,500. L.K.W. remained in the placement for 66 days, until the court stayed the order and returned her to the custody of her parents.]

Innumerable delinquency dispositions have been determined since the legislature first established juvenile courts eighty years ago. Remarkably, however, the topic has not been previously addressed in a published Minnesota appellate decision. We approach the subject with recognition of the broad discretion of the trial court. * * * [W]e will affirm so long as the trial court determination is not arbitrary. Trial court dispositional findings of fact will be accepted unless clearly erroneous.

Dispositional choices are enumerated in Minn.Stat. § 260.185, subd. 1 (1984). The juvenile court is directed to use the choice of disposition judged "necessary to the rehabilitation of the child."

In 1976, the Minnesota Legislature added a standard, a demand that the order for a disposition state "why the best interests of the child are served by the disposition ordered." Findings must also note alternative dispositions considered by the court and reasons "why such dispositions were not appropriate in the instant case."

1. The least drastic step necessary to restore law-abiding conduct

The aim in delinquency dispositions is "rehabilitation," restoration of lawful conduct. The juvenile court act is aimed at instilling a capacity for lawfulness, "developing individual responsibility for lawful behavior."

It is reversible error, both arbitrary and unjust, to impose a disposition without evidence that it is "necessary" for the declared statutory purpose of restoring law-abiding conduct. * * *

To measure what is necessary, a trial court must assess two factors, the severity of the child's delinquency, and the severity of the proposed remedy. When the severity of intervention is disproportionate to the severity of the problem, the intervention is not necessary and cannot lawfully occur. The court must take the least drastic necessary step.

The Minnesota "necessary" standard coincides with principles stated by other authorities. The supreme court of a neighbor state calls for approaching the determination of a delinquency disposition "in a spirit of optimism," with recognition and favor for less "drastic" steps that still permit a "reasonable hope" for equal success. Recently promulgated standards state this spirit in the form of a preference for the least restrictive action consistent with the child's problem.[7]

We find no evidence at all showing rehabilitation needs of L.K.W. in April 1985 such as to call for a severe corrections disposition, confinement to a residential facility to instill obedience.

Prior violations of law enlarge the need for rehabilitation. The child here had none.

---

7. National standards provide:

  In determining the type of sanction to be imposed following adjudication of a delinquency petition and the duration of that sanction within the statutorily prescribed maximum, the family court should select the least restrictive category and time period consistent with the seriousness of the offense, the juvenile's role in that offense, and the juvenile's age and prior record.

  Standards for the Administration of Juvenile Justice § 3.182, National Advisory Committee for Juvenile Justice and Delinquency Prevention (1980). See also *Juvenile Justice Standards: Standards Relating to Dispositions* § 2.1, A.B.A., Inst. of Judicial Administration (1979).

Need is measured in part by the seriousness of the offense. The child admitted a misdemeanor theft.

Rehabilitation may require restitution. The child completed restitution before the first disposition was determined in July 1984.

The need for rehabilitation is enlarged by repetition of unlawful conduct. There is no evidence of any public offense by the child since her only delinquent act.

Rehabilitation needs may be indicated by violations of conditions of probationary supervision. During ten months of supervision beginning July 1984, the juvenile followed 21 child behavior conditions. * * *

Finally, the showing of need must be considered alongside the facts on the severity of the disposition. Here the child was confined to a residential facility. Reason does not permit a distinction between punitive incarceration and a so-called "placement" to "teach you discipline," a disposition explained as the end of personal choice and as a consequence of breaking rules. The placement took the child from her home, her school, and her job, and 150 miles from her family and friends. It extended the trial court's use of authority to at least the 18th month after a misdemeanor violation. * * *

2.   Special regard for valuable family relationships.
Suitable for the child's needs

A delinquency disposition must also serve the child's best interests. * * *

The best interests standard adds at least two requirements in any case where a residential placement is considered. First, there must be evidence that aims of the law cannot be realized without removal of the child from her home.

The preference against removal has been legislated in Minnesota and independently recognized by the supreme court. Juvenile care and guidance that serves the interests of the child and the state will "preferably" be in the child's own home. * * *

What is the significance of the preference against removal in a delinquency case? If a child has valuable home relationships, they cannot be taken away without evidence of unusually severe needs of the child for rehabilitation. * * *

Second, there must be evidence that the placement being considered is suitable for the needs of the child.

If a placement is not suited to actual needs of the child, it cannot serve the child's best interests. * * *

There is no evidence to describe the staff or program. * * * The probation officer testified that the program was "excellent" and "meaningful;" he explained that he was well-acquainted with "the people that run the program," and that the facility had been "successful" in one or two cases handled by another officer. These observations fail to show the nature of the program or a reliable basis for evaluating its services.

The probation officer reported to the court that the * * * program would be an "excellent mechanism" to teach the child "limits" and elevate her "self-esteem." The record does not indicate the child has self-esteem problems. Her acceptance of limits was not currently discussed and had never been even partly detailed. * * *

3.   Findings on rehabilitation needs and family relationships. Findings on suitability of a residential program

Dispositional findings are mandated by the legislature and the supreme court. These must address the dispositional choices "considered by the court" and reasons "why" one is preferred. They must address the interests and the needs of the child.

These requirements for findings are among others in family law cases which are designed to guarantee that the trial courts consider vital standards. The findings also enable the parties to understand the decisions of the court. Finally, they are necessary for meaningful review. Because the findings serve these important purposes, it is reversible error to omit them. * * *

4.   Control over the choice to remove children

In one sense, the law of the case is uncomplicated. The juvenile court act demands restraint of juvenile justice personnel. More particularly, the statutes compel control over the choice to remove children from their own home, a determination to avoid unnecessary or harmful placements.

On the other hand, the language employed in this field of law can easily obfuscate the issue. Several observations must be made to avoid this hazard.

a.   The issue is not a creature of modern due process law. Instead, the issue is one of legal standards, and the issue has been recognized for at least a half century. * * *

b.   The rule of law on restraint toward placements does not erode the *parens patriae* role of the juvenile court. To the contrary, it gives integrity to the guardianship of the court for the welfare of the child.

c.   Similarly, the discipline of restraint does not conflict with notions of individualized justice. That concept does not license public authorities to do whatever they wish, to act on their individualized views. Rather, it involves a primary demand that nothing be done which is not necessary and suitable for the individual.

d.   The standard of restraint toward placements cannot be compromised due to policy concerns for public safety, for the protection of children from abuse, or for residential programs designed to treat children or to positively modify their behavior. * * *

The three month confinement of L.K.W. 150 miles from her home, summarily ordered, for no lawful cause, was singularly harsh and unjust. * * * The events here sharply contrast with practice and procedure L.K.W. would have encountered in adult court. With restitution already completed, an adult in a comparable case could anticipate a moderate fine. If other penalties were imposed, they would likely be suspended on the sole condition that no other offenses occur. Some courts would suspend all or part of the fine. Some courts or prosecutors would withhold the record of conviction for a first offense of the kind. Ironically, adult process includes a right to trial by jury that is extended to the case because of the possibility of incarceration.

In sum, the record here demonstrates public action which is alarmingly arbitrary. * * * We have searched the record to find cause for the trial court's decision, but none has been found. We are bound by the record, as is the trial court, and we are not permitted to speculate about the knowledge or motives of officials that might further explain what happened here. * * *

NOTES

1) **Least Restrictive Alternative as a Principle of Delinquency Dispositions** In **In the Interest of B.B.**, 516 N.W.2d 874, 878–80 (Iowa 1994), the Iowa Supreme Court heard a juvenile's appeal from a delinquency adjudication and commitment to the state training school. B.B. contended that his commitment to the institution was dictated by fiscal considerations and a state limit on the number of youths who could be placed in group homes rather than his need for more secure confinement and violated his statutory and constitutional right to a "least restrictive placement":

B.B. contends that Iowa Code § 232.143, which establishes a cap on the number of children in group foster care, violates his substantive due process rights. He asserts that the State's interest in the public fisc should not outweigh his interest in being placed in the least restrictive setting, here, group foster care. * * *

The right asserted by B.B. here is the right to the least restrictive placement. B.B. argues that his liberty is less restricted in group foster care than it would be at the State Training School. We accept this premise * * *. The question then becomes whether B.B. has an absolute right to the least restrictive placement. In other words, is B.B. entitled to a placement that is less restrictive than the placement ordered even though the less restrictive placement is not authorized by the legislature or is otherwise unavailable? We think neither state law nor the constitution gives him this right.

A. *State law.* Iowa law requires the juvenile court to enter "the least restrictive dispositional order appropriate in view of the seriousness of the delinquent act, the child's culpability * * *, the age of the child and the child's prior record." In the same statute, the legislature provides that the court cannot order group foster care placement if the placement is not in accordance with the regional plan established pursuant to [the statute]. * * *

Certainly the legislature did not intend to give a juvenile the right to be placed in the least restrictive setting despite the unavailability of a less restrictive placement when in the same statute purportedly giving such a right the legislature limits the number of group foster care placements. We conclude that in deciding which disposition is the least restrictive, the juvenile court is confined to consideration of those facilities which have a bed available and in which the juvenile can be legally placed. Since B.B. could not legally be placed in group foster care, he had no right under state law to such a placement, although it might be less restrictive than assignment to the State Training School.

B. Constitutional right. We must now consider whether the liberty interest protected by the Due Process Clause entitles B.B. to the least restrictive placement. * * * [In *Reno v. Flores*, 507 U.S. 292, 113 S.Ct. 1439, 123 L.Ed.2d 1 (1993)] [t]he Court held that if institutional custody is constitutional, it does not become unconstitutional just because there may be a more desirable form of child care for the juvenile. The Court stated:

"The best interests of the child" is likewise not an absolute and exclusive constitutional criterion for the government's exercise of the custodial responsibilities that it undertakes, which must be reconciled with many other responsibilities. Thus, child-care institutions operated by the state in the exercise of its *parens patriae* authority * * * are not constitutionally required to be funded at such a level as to provide the best schooling or the best health care available; nor does the Constitution require them to substitute, wherever possible, private nonadoptive custody for institutional care. * * * Minimum standards must be met, and the child's fundamental rights must not be impaired; but the decision to go beyond those requirements—to give one or another of the child's additional interests priority over other concerns that compete for public funds and administrative attention—is a policy judgment rather than a constitutional imperative. * * *

Here, B.B. does not claim that institutional custody of him is unconstitutional. Therefore, we start with the basic premise that placement of B.B. in some form of child care institution does not violate his constitutional rights. We must then consider B.B.'s claim that he is entitled to a particular form of institutional custody—the least restrictive placement. * * * [W]e hold that a juvenile has no constitutional right to the least restrictive form of institutional placement.

Even if such a right did exist, it is not a "fundamental" right. Therefore, substantive due process demands, at the most, that there be a reasonable fit between the governmental purpose and the means chosen to advance that purpose. Here the state's goals are to reduce spending on group foster care and to encourage the development of alternatives to group foster care placements. Limitations on the number of placements in group foster care "reasonably fit" these goals. Indeed, it is difficult to imagine a more direct manner in which to control spending and reallocate limited resources. * * *

The United States and Iowa Constitutions guarantee the equal protection of the laws to all persons. B.B. claims that [the statute] violates his right of equal protection because it serves to treat him differently than similarly situated juveniles who require group foster care merely because he falls within the class of juveniles referred at a time when the caps have been reached. B.B. argues the statute unreasonably allocates group foster care among children needing such care on a first-come-first-served basis rather than based on need. * * *

The statute challenged here is state social legislation which is entitled to broad deference. Therefore, the rational basis test is applicable. * * *

We believe the statute is not unreasonable in allocating the limited group foster care available on a first-come-first-served basis. B.B. argues that group foster care should be assigned on the basis of need. Allocating this type of placement based on need would be impracticable, expensive, and adversely affect the stability of group foster care placements.

The amount of time and resources that would be required to compare the relative needs of all juveniles for whom group foster care is the least restrictive form of placement would be substantial. Additionally, a recomparison of these juveniles would theoretically be necessary every time the juvenile court recommends group foster care for another juvenile. Allocating group foster care based on relative need would also result in the disruption of placements. A juvenile placed in group foster care could conceivably be taken out of a group foster care facility later because a newly adjudicated juvenile's need for group foster care is identified as greater. The very real practical difficulties in allocating group foster care on the basis of relative need demonstrate the reasonableness of the system of priority chosen by the legislature. * * *

In contrast with *B.B.*, in **State ex rel. S. J. C. v. Fox**, 165 W.Va. 314, 319–20, 268 S.E.2d 56, 60–1 (W.Va.1980), the West Virginia Supreme Court elaborated on the role of the "least restrictive alternative" as a dispositional principle in the rehabilitation of the juvenile:

First, we think the fact that relator's three codefendants were incarcerated was not material to the determination that relator's rehabilitation could not be accomplished by a less restrictive means than incarceration. Whether the rehabilitation of a child adjudged delinquent can be accomplished by any less restrictive means than incarceration is a determination which requires an inquiry into the individual needs and circumstances of the child and is not dependent on an automatic standard of comparative justice. This is only in keeping with the purpose of our juvenile law which is to promote the rehabilitation of troubled children rather than to punish them. This purpose is expressed with regard to dispositions in the requirement that the juvenile court arrive at a disposition which will effect the rehabilitation of the child in the least restrictive manner concomitant with the best interests of the child and of the public. In view of the rehabilitative purpose of our juvenile law and its emphasis on individualized assessment and treatment, we must conclude that the sentence imposed on a juvenile's codefendants is neither a material nor permissible factor for the juvenile court to consider in determining the final disposition of a juvenile case and does not justify the commitment of a child to a juvenile correctional facility. * * *

This Court has already stated that the gravity of the offense and previous acts of delinquency, their frequency, seriousness and relationship to the present charge are relevant considerations in determining the rehabilitative prospects of the juvenile. We have also held that the nature of the offense is not alone sufficient to warrant transfer of juvenile proceedings to the criminal jurisdiction of the circuit court. As we stated there,

> All persons who commit violent crimes are not alike in their prospects for rehabilitation. Some violent offenders can be rehabilitated, others can not be. Placing undue weight on the nature of the crime and excluding other factors assures that no distinction is made between these groups.

This reasoning appears equally applicable to the determination of which of the statutorily enumerated dispositions will accomplish the rehabilitation of the child. * * *

In view of the evidence adduced at the dispositional hearings we think that the respondent placed undue emphasis on the prior acts of the juvenile and on the nature of the offense. While prior delinquent acts of the child and the nature of the offense may figure prominently in the dispositional stage of a juvenile case, so too must consideration be given to the fact that children, as they grow older, may recognize the wrongfulness of their prior conduct and attempt to change. The conduct of the child during a period of observation serves as an indication of the possibility of rehabilitation at the time of the dispositional hearing and reflects possible changes in his behavior and temperament which may preclude the harsh necessity of incarcerating him in a correctional facility to achieve that goal. In considering the least restrictive dispositional alternative for sentencing a juvenile, a juvenile court must consider the reasonable prospects for rehabilitation of the child as they appear at the time of the dispositional hearing, with due weight given to any improvement in the child's behavior between the time the offense was committed and the time sentence is passed. * * *

In **State ex rel. R. S. v. Trent**, 169 W.Va. 493, 289 S.E.2d 166 (W.Va.1982), the juvenile challenged his commitment to the Industrial School. The West Virginia Supreme Court emphasized the primacy of the "least restrictive alternative" as a principle in delinquency dispositions. The statute "requires the juvenile court at the dispositional stage of delinquency proceedings to" "give precedence to the least restrictive" of the enumerated dispositional alternatives "consistent with the best interests and welfare of the public and the child." Moreover, juveniles are constitutionally entitled to the least restrictive treatment that is consistent with the purpose of their custody. A juvenile against whom delinquency proceedings are brought as the result of the child's commission of an act which would be a crime if committed by an adult may be committed to an industrial home or correctional facility "[u]pon a finding that no less restrictive alternative would accomplish the requisite rehabilitation of the child * * *." * * *

[T]he court's decision to commit the juvenile to an industrial school or correctional facility must be grounded on a number of factors indicating that incarceration is the appropriate disposition.

> In this regard the court should specifically address the following: (1) the danger which the child poses to society; (2) all other less restrictive alternatives which have been tried either by the court or by other agencies to whom the child was previously directed to avoid formal juvenile proceedings; (3) the child's background with particular regard to whether there are pre-determining factors such as acute poverty, parental abuse, learning disabilities, physical impairments, or any other discrete, causative factors which can be corrected by the State or other social service agencies in an environment less restrictive than an industrial school; (4) whether the child is amenable to rehabilitation outside an industrial school, and if not, why not; (5) whether the dual goals of deterrence and juvenile responsibility can be achieved in some setting less restrictive than an industrial school and if not, why not; (6) whether the child is suffering from no recognizable, treatable determining force and therefore is entitled to punishment; (7) whether the child appears willing to cooperate with the suggested program of rehabilitation; and, (8) whether the child is so uncooperative or so ungovernable that no program of rehabilitation will be successful without the coercion inherent in a secure facility.

Before ordering the incarceration of the child, the juvenile court is required to set forth upon the record the facts which lead to the conclusion that no less restrictive alternative is appropriate. The record must affirmatively show

> that the child's behavioral problem is not the result of social conditions beyond the child's control, but rather of an intentional failure on the part of the child to conform his actions to the law, or that the child will be dangerous if any other disposition is used, or that the child will not cooperate with any rehabilitative program absent physical restraint. * * *

Since we have no record which would enable us to determine the factors that led to the conclusion that incarceration was the least restrictive appropriate alternative and to decide whether that conclusion was justified, we award a writ of habeas corpus * * * and order the petitioner discharged from the custody of the Superintendent of the Industrial School." * * *

IN THE MATTER OF D.S.F.

416 N.W.2d 772 (Minn. Ct. App. 1987).

LANSING, JUDGE. [D.S.F., 17 years old, went to the high school he previously attended to pick up his girlfriend. When a hall monitor asked

D.S.F. to leave, he became upset, struck a locker with his fist, and, when he encountered three students walking in the opposite direction, he grabbed one by the arm and hit him in the lower jaw with his closed fist. The injured student required three hours of emergency surgery to wire together his jaw which D.S.F.'s blow had broken in four places. The juvenile court adjudicated D.S.F. delinquent for an act of third-degree assault, ordered him committed to the County Home School for 90 days, followed by a term of probation, and ordered restitution of $581.13 for the victim's out-of-pocket expenses.]

The goal of disposition in a delinquency case is to rehabilitate the child, and the court's decision must be necessary to achieve that goal. In determining what is necessary, the court must consider the severity of both the act and the proposed disposition.

The transcript of the disposition hearing reveals that the trial court in this case considered both of these factors. The court noted that physical violence against a person is more serious than a property offense, which might not require confinement. * * * D.S.F. launched an unprovoked, vicious and unjustified attack. The court evaluated the offense as severe.

In evaluating the effect of the disposition on D.S.F., the court found that 90 days would not substantially disrupt D.S.F.'s life and that a disposition which involved only counseling would not be sufficient to trigger rehabilitation—that a specific consequence was necessary to impress upon D.S.F. the seriousness of his behavior. * * * In addition, the court considered the importance of maintaining the integrity of the substantive law and developing individual responsibility.

Although the dissent characterizes this disposition as "punitive," the trial court's statements indicate that it was concerned with rehabilitating, rather than punishing, D.S.F.

> [I]f the Court overlooks the behavior because of your past and because * * * this is a single incident, you are likely to reach a conclusion that you don't have to face the consequences of your acts. And the reality of that in the Court's opinion is going to be more helpful than counseling or anything of that kind. Counselors don't have any miracle method of changing people's behavior. Oftentimes the reality of what occurs can have a much greater effect. * * *

D.S.F. asserts that absent a specific finding that his home life is inadequate, he should not be removed from his home.

The disposition is well within the broad discretion permitted the trial court in delinquency cases. The disposition is not arbitrary or disproportionate to the offense, and it is supported by reasonable rehabilitative considerations. We find no abuse of discretion in the court's refusal to impose a less restrictive disposition. * * *

Affirmed.

CRIPPEN, J., dissents. I concur in the decision that the punishment of D.S.F. fits his crime. * * *

For criminal justice purposes, little more needs to be said.[1] The juvenile's wrongdoing, although an unexpected single offense, provokes a temptation to affirm a straight-forward sentencing decision. The record, however, shows a definite abandonment of primary precepts of juvenile law. An affirmance signals the demise of an 80–year–old Minnesota experiment to deal with juvenile delinquency, a system which sacrifices procedural safeguards but pretends to offset this unprecedented lapse in American jurisprudence by making dispositions which respond to an offender's individual needs, not just his offense.

We are confronted here with a purely offense-based determinate sentence of incarceration as a largely predetermined consequence for a serious assault. Unquestionably, D.S.F. has received a determinate sentence. In addition, the sentence was chosen based solely on the occurrence of a serious offense; this opinion reports the personal circumstances of D.S.F., the absence of steps to identify problems leading to his out-of-character act in 1986, and acceptance by the trial court of a settled local court sentencing practice. In sum, the trial court's disposition raises questions going to the very core of Minnesota juvenile court law. Can American law suffer criminal justice sentencing in a court which denies criminal law safeguards for the accused? * * *

Deliberate acceptance of offense-based determinate sentencing categorically belies the promises which are the foundation for the 1971 due process analysis of the United States Supreme Court [in *McKeiver*]. Appellate affirmation of criminal justice sentencing in the juvenile court unravels the rationale underlying the equal protection analysis of the Minnesota Supreme Court. A system already on the brink of its demise is pushed still closer to a long postponed day of reckoning.

b. Options

There are three plausible choices for a response to punitive dispositional practices of the juvenile court in serious delinquency cases:

1. As Justice Harlan suggested in *McKeiver*, the juvenile delinquency systems could be "restructured to fit their original purpose." The appellate courts in Minnesota can be a tool in this restructuring by insisting upon careful adherence to demands of the legislature that juvenile dispositions be designed to serve the individual interests of children and the special interests of their families, not just the public's demands for punishment. * * *

---

1. Remarkably, however, under Minnesota's criminal justice standards, the 90–day sentence of D.S.F. would be appropriate only as a case out of the ordinary, one of a "small number of cases" where sentencing guidelines are ignored because of substantial and compelling aggravating factors. Minnesota Sentencing Guidelines, Comment to § II.D (comment). This offender, who had a criminal history score of zero, would be presumptively entitled to a stayed 12–month sentence. Id. II.C. See id. IV (sentencing guidelines grid), and V (designating assault in the third degree as a severity level IV offense). Even with a criminal history score of three, the offender in the adult system would be entitled to a presumptive stay of sentence. Id. The fact that D.S.F. is particularly amenable to probationary supervision would be a consideration in determining his sentence in criminal justice proceedings.

2. Alternatively, we can follow the prescription stated by Justice White in *McKeiver*, embracing punitive dispositions as an acceptable and inherent part of delinquency proceedings, but calling upon the Minnesota Legislature and the Minnesota Supreme Court to extend to accused juveniles all procedural safeguards guaranteed for adults in criminal cases. Most critically, we could assert the demonstrated need for jury trials in accusatory proceedings where juveniles may be incarcerated, and the additional need for representation by competent counsel in every case where a juvenile is faced with incarceration. * * *

3. Finally, we can confess the "ultimate disillusionment" the United States Supreme Court thought might one day occur. Thus, we could call for dismantling a system that openly exacts from our younger citizens a sacrifice of liberties and gives in return a false promise to serve the best interests of those who come before it. The federal and state constitutions do not permit a criminal justice system without criminal justice safeguards. Many who address these issues, including the author of this opinion, are reluctant to support this step, hoping still that the system can discipline itself to be faithful to its purposes and promises. That reluctance is not an option in light of the decision to affirm the disposition of this case.

Is there another option? Can we accept as merely unfortunate a system meting out punishment without fundamental constitutional safeguards? There is no such option, unless we are to count merely unfortunate the repeated, deliberate choice to deny citizenship and personhood to a major class of American people, all of those who are under the age of majority. * * *

The first of the three options is available to us, and it should be conscientiously pursued. The trial court has not utilized standards mandated by existing statutes. We should remand these proceedings for a disposition crafted so as to take careful account of the legislative purpose to recognize the unique characteristics and needs of D.S.F. and provide for services or supervision, beneficial to the juvenile and his family, that enhance his personal and social growth.

It is imaginable, of course, that a disposition under governing juvenile laws would lead to involvement of D.S.F. in a residential treatment program. Such a decision, however, would follow identification of pertinent needs of the juvenile, determination that a particular program would be suitable for response to those needs and beneficial for the juvenile and his family, and a considered decision that this step had more advantages than nonresidential supervision. * * *

The trial court concluded that it would be appropriate to impose an offense-based determinate sentence. * * * Making the issue here even more serious, it is evident that a determinate sentence of incarceration imposed by the trial court was prompted by unpublished sentencing guidelines, based singularly on the offense committed, and not by the spontaneous exercise of discretion by the presiding judge. The trial court rejected arguments which would lead to departure from an established policy to incarcerate youths for serious offenses. * * *

Inescapably, it must be concluded that we are dealing here with a criminal justice sentence, not a juvenile court disposition aimed at doing what is best for the individual. The juvenile has been ordered incarcerated for a definite term as part of a predetermined sentencing practice. * * *

Of course, it may be asserted that a punitive sentence is in the best interests of D.S.F., that it is for his own good. A probation officer expressed her hope that the recommended disposition would help appellant recognize what triggers his anger and to learn what he could do to avoid any similar misconduct. The trial court observed that facing consequences would be "more helpful to D.S.F. than counseling." * * * Although there is deceit in systematically pursuing care with tools of punishment, it cannot be disputed that there may be therapeutic aims in a purely punitive sentence. That fact, however, makes the disposition no less punitive. * * *

I respectfully dissent.

NOTES

1) Principles of "Rehabilitative Sentencing" in Juvenile Court. Judge Gary Crippen, in a special concurrence in **In the Matter of the Welfare of J.A.J.**, 545 N.W.2d 412 (Minn. Ct. Ap. 1996), identified several substantive principles governing the sentencing of juveniles in a rehabilitative juvenile justice system:

I concur in the conclusions that state law did not permit the residential confinement of J.A.J. because (a) the trial court failed to find that this disposition was "necessary to the rehabilitation of the child" and (b) the record does not contain facts that would support such a finding. But we have a duty to catalogue the disregard in this case for several additional juvenile court rubrics on out-of-home placements of children. And we have a larger responsibility to examine a more vital issue, one that makes the welfare of J.A.J. a matter of remarkable importance. The disposition in this case offends fundamental, minimum standards of substantive due process.

Because of the inattention to the constitution and other basic standards that is evident in this case, the disposition is singularly unacceptable. The issue is not about technical rights of the child, asserted to trump vital functions of government. Rather, the case involves essential liberty, the freedom against being taken from your home, incarcerated, and then confined * * * for an indeterminate term, all without a showing of cause. And the case does not speak alone to risks connected with decisions to take action. When "doing good" replaces meaningful standards and good process in a caring system, there are equal risks that nothing is done in cases where remedial steps are both critical and justified.

There is also an issue here that is larger than the freedom of J.A.J. The case reveals or at least suggests a dangerous legal culture in the juvenile justice system. The illegal taking of J.A.J.'s liberty should prompt, at a minimum, strict scrutiny of the system that produced it. * * *

In committing J.A.J. [for 12 to 18 months to a residential treatment facility] on a parole officer's recommendation of this "help" to the child, the juvenile court proceeded in conflict with explicit United States Supreme Court holdings that confinement for mental health therapy is a "massive curtailment of liberty" under the Fifth Amendment. * * * None of our decisions holds that conviction for a crime entitles a State not only to confine the convicted person but also to determine that he has a mental illness and to subject him involuntarily to institutional care in a mental hospital.

J.A.J. was indeterminately committed to a psychiatric treatment facility. The record includes only a sparse report on the characteristics of care, treatment, or discipline at [the treatment center]. * * * The probation officer did not address the restrictiveness of the facility. * * * Weeks after the confinement order, the facility sought and obtained unrestricted authority to administer psychotropic medications to J.A.J. * * *

This case, illustrating the failure of thorough procedure to secure a just result, presents compelling justification for reform of the substantive workings of juvenile courts in the same vein as hallmark cases *Kent* and *Gault* reformed the procedural juvenile processes. The juvenile system as founded celebrated being (a) beneficial and (b) informal. Informality yielded to stricter procedural requirements. This case should signal the arrival of a time for scrutinizing what the juvenile justice system finds "beneficial" to the juvenile. * * * Dispositional standards in human welfare cases—in juvenile, domestic, and hospitalization cases—are often very general, creating immense discretion for judges and others. The most illustrative of these general standards is the notion of doing what is "best." But there have been a number of achievements in developing more useable standards, and that is especially true for juvenile court dispositions.

Seven meaningful points of law were implicated in the trial court decisions now before us:

a.   For a lawful disposition, there must be a record that the choice of action is necessary, not merely that it is best.

b.   The law prefers, when determining what is best, to leave children in their own home.

c.   When a child is placed out of the home, the record must show a correlation between the child's needs and the residential services proscribed.

d.   Treatment recommendations must be premised on a fact-based assessment, not on assumptions.

e.   When choosing an out-of-home placement, the prospective duration of care must be determined.

f. Rigid statutory proscriptions govern the choice to place a child in secure detention.

g. Findings of fact must be sufficiently particularized to fairly disclose the reasons for a juvenile court disposition.

The disposition in the matter of the welfare of J.A.J. transgressed each of these matters of law on juvenile court dispositions. * * *

The juvenile code invites attention to the child's best interests in a delinquency disposition. The code requires that the juvenile court's dispositional findings show "why the best interests of the child are served by the disposition ordered." * * * [P]recisely because of the statutory reference to the child's best interests, * * * a residential treatment placement is appropriate only when the needs of the child cannot be met at home. * * *

The legal preference against out-of-home placements is an historic cornerstone of the juvenile court. * * *

a. The purpose clause on delinquency cases continues to insist that public safety concerns be pursued through fair and just means that respect the needs and opportunities of children.

b. The statutory requirement of findings on a child's best interests puts a burden on the juvenile court in delinquency cases to explain why a placement is made and why the child is not kept in the home.

c. The preference for a home placement is compelled in part by the statutory standard permitting only what disposition is "necessary," which, in turn, protects the present circumstances of a child who poses no threat to public safety.

d. The preference for non-removal coincides precisely with the related family law concept that child custody will ordinarily not be changed absent a showing of danger in the child's current placement.

e. The preference for non-removal, a public policy view that "the best interests of the child are normally served by parental custody," is a settled, historic principal in the traditions of Minnesota law, not rooted alone in declarations of aims by the legislature. * * *

The preference for non-removal may give way in appropriate cases to public safety concerns. But public safety, if generally of some weight, has no effect at all on the juvenile court's * * * disposition in this case. The juvenile court's action, although in a delinquency case, was not based on the delinquency of J.A.J. or on any evidence of public safety hazards. Rather, the court acted on purported treatment needs of the child, for the child's best interests. In the circumstances of this case, a respect for the child's home placement is a showing of due regard for the stated legislative aim in child protection cases, which continues to state the historic preference for non-removal. * * *

The most effective form of monitoring juvenile court dispositions is likely through the scrutiny of a lawyer for the child who is experienced in juvenile justice and appellate jurisprudence and who is obligated to consider a child's appellate remedies. It is significant that this case was appealed in October 1995, about 18 months after an amendment changing Minnesota law to permit the services of the state public defender for appeals in juvenile delinquency cases. This appeal was initiated by an assistant state public defender and is evidently one of the first juvenile court dispositional appeals handled by that office. The surfacing of this case for appellate scrutiny, in this substantive and procedural condition, is testimony to the remarkable juvenile court reform that may be achieved in Minnesota by the simple choice to guarantee qualified and committed counsel to effect the right of appeal. * * *

1. DISPOSITIONAL ALTERNATIVES—PROBATION

As the foregoing statutes and cases indicate, juvenile court judges may impose a variety of dispositions that do not affect a youth's legal custody or residential status, including probation, restitution, and community service. When a judge imposes such a disposition, as the court in *In re Kazuo G.*, *supra* Note 3, p. 892, emphasized, the crucial issue is that the judge's order seeks to rehabilitate rather than simply to punish the offending youth. Probation represented the most commonly imposed disposition in delinquency cases and enables a juvenile to remain within the family home subject to appropriate limitations. Judicial orders may specify conditions of probation, tailored to fit the needs of the child, to enable probation officers to monitor the child, to impose structure on the child's life, and to foster the delinquent's long-term prospects. Appellate courts routinely uphold conditions of probation that require a juvenile to attend school regularly, *In re Gerald B.*, 105 Cal.App.3d 119, 164 Cal.Rptr. 193 (Cal.Ct.App.1980), to earn passing grades, *In re Angel J.*, 9 Cal.App.4th 1096, 11 Cal.Rptr.2d 776 (Cal. Ct. App. 1992), and to obey all laws including curfews.

In *In re Frank V.*, 233 Cal.App.3d 1232, 285 Cal.Rptr. 16, 21 (Cal.Ct.App.1991), the California court of appeals articulated the criteria for review of juvenile court judges' probationary dispositions:

> A probation condition will not be held invalid unless is 1) has no relationship to the crime of which the offender was convicted, 2) related to conduct which is not in itself criminal, and 3) requires or forbids conduct which is not reasonable related to future criminality. All three requirements must be met before the condition is invalidated."

The following materials reflect the scope of judicial authority to impose non-residential sanctions.

In **In the Matter of the Interests of A.L.J. v. State**, 836 P.2d 307 (Wyo.1992), the Wyoming Supreme Court reviewed the validity of several conditions of probation that the juvenile court judge imposed on a juvenile adjudicated delinquent for "reckless endangerment" for pointing a .25 caliber semi-automatic pistol at several others youths attending a "drinking" party at a gravel pit:

Appellant's probationary conditions, among others, were that (1) Appellant would submit to random chemical testing for the presence of alcohol; (2) Appellant's driving privileges would be temporarily revoked with further revocation to be automatic if Appellant violated any probation condition or was arrested or ticketed for a traffic violation; (3) Appellant's parents would cooperate in residential checks at the probation officer's discretion; and (4) Appellant would reimburse the Wyoming public defender for the cost of his defense. * * *

Appellant claims that the probation condition requiring him to submit to random chemical testing for the presence of alcohol violates his right to be free from unreasonable searches and seizures * * *. However, the Fourth Amendment protections which apply to adult probationers do not necessarily apply to juvenile probationers. The dispositional phase of juvenile proceedings requires broad judicial discretion to accommodate the unique rehabilitative needs of juveniles. We hold that it is within the court's discretion to allow a probation officer to search a juvenile without reasonably suspecting that a probation violation exists. * * *

This difference between the adjudicative and dispositional phases reflects the broad discretion judges need for making an appropriate disposition. Wyoming requires that, when entering an order of disposition, the court must do what is best suited for the public safety, the preservation of families, and the physical, mental, and moral welfare of the child. To fulfill this mandate and to address the rehabilitative needs of juveniles, the court must have flexibility when it is formulating the probation conditions. * * * In this case, alcohol was being consumed at the party. Appellant's background showed that he had previously been involved in an alcohol-related incident. The testing-for-alcohol condition was designed to avoid any future problems involving alcohol. We believe that, under these circumstances, the chemical-testing condition was appropriate.

Appellant next contests probation condition (n) which states, "Said minor's parents shall cooperate in all respects with said minor's probation officer and allow residential checks at the discretion of said officer." * * * Our constitutional analysis regarding chemical testing is applicable to the probation condition requiring residential checks. Appellant's Fourth Amendment rights were not violated by the court allowing the probation officer to make residential checks without reasonably suspecting the existence of a probation violation. The condition was clearly within the court's discretion. Residential checks are an appropriate probation condition because they allow the probation officer to verify that the minor is not consuming alcohol or otherwise violating his probation conditions. * * *

Appellant contends that this condition [of probation to temporarily revoke his driver's license] is beyond the court's statutory authority. * * *[T]he court may "[r]estrict or restrain the child's driving privileges for a period of time the court deems appropriate, and if necessary to enforce the restrictions the court may take possession of the child's driver's license." Appellant objects to the court using the word "revoke" as opposed to using the words "restrict or restrain." In the context of condition (1), we see no discernible difference between "revoking" and "restraining or restricting" the child's driving privileges. By revoking the child's driving privileges, the court is not revoking the child's driver's license.

Appellant's probation condition (p) requires him to reimburse the public defender for the cost of his defense. Appellant claims that the trial court must inquire into his ability to reimburse the public defender before it can order reimbursement. We agree. * * *

We hold that the court must inquire and find that the juvenile has the ability to pay before the court can order reimbursement of attorney fees, and we vacate that probation condition requiring Appellant to reimburse the public defender.

Appellant argues that his three-year probation term violates the Equal Protection Clauses of the Wyoming and United States Constitutions. He [argues] * * * that a probation term cannot exceed the maximum imprisonment term. Since the maximum sentence for reckless endangerment is one year, Appellant claims that his three-year probation term denies him equal protection under the law. * * *

By enacting a juvenile code separate from the criminal code, Wyoming's legislature has recognized that juveniles and adults are not similarly situated. Juvenile proceedings are designed to rehabilitate and protect the juvenile, not to punish him. These goals of rehabilitation and protection are reflected throughout the juvenile code. Proceedings in juvenile court are equitable as opposed to being criminal. Juveniles are not convicted; they are merely adjudicated delinquents. By treating juveniles more gently than it treats adults, the legislature is compensating for juveniles' inherent lack of experience and maturity.

Since juvenile probations and adult probations are not similarly situated, Appellant suffered no denial of his right to equal protection under the law. * * *

In **In the Interest of James P. (State v. James P.)**, 180 Wis.2d 677, 510 N.W.2d 730 (Wis. Ct. App. 1993), considered whether the juvenile court judge could impose a condition of probation on a juvenile unrelated to the offense for which it adjudicated him delinquent. Although the court adjudicated James P. delinquent for possessing a firearm, because the judge intended to order home placement, it directed a blood test conducted to determine whether James P. or James' father had fathered the child of James P.'s eleven year old sister:

At a continued dispositional hearing the court stated its reasons for the condition. The court noted that a court report recommended home placement during the probationary period. The sister also lived in the home. The court commented that it is in James' best interest to resolve the issue of his paternity now rather than wait until his sister becomes older, more sophisticated and perhaps disposed to prefer criminal charges against him after he becomes an adult. The court also reasoned that if the test establishes that James is not the father of the child, that test result will remove a cloud from James' head and will facilitate living with his sister and her child. Further, the trial court explained that if his paternity is established he may be provided advice and treatment to avoid similar situations. The court concluded that the condition was reasonable and was in James' best interest.* * *

Disposition of a child's delinquency adjudication lies in the sound discretion of the court. A court has broad discretion in imposing conditions of probation, and is limited only by the exercise of reasonableness and propriety. The exercise of discretion requires judicial application of relevant law to the facts of record to reach a rational conclusion. * * *

The Children's Code does not explicitly or implicitly require a child's disposition to be related to the violation that resulted in the delinquency. * * * While a court determining disposition must focus on the offender, and while the court also may consider the gravity of the offense, the court is not required to focus on the nature of the offense except as mandated by statute. * * *

Once the delinquency finding is made, the children's court has an obligation to fashion a program of care, protection and rehabilitation of the child within the scope of the Children's Code regardless of the nature of the child's offense. * * *

Courts have approved numerous ancillary conditions of probation. See e.g., *In re L.R.*, 382 N.J.Super. 605, 890 A.2d 343 (N.J. Super. A.D. 2006) (requiring juvenile adjudicated delinquent for criminal mischief to provide DNA sample to DNA Database); In re. J.B., 172 N.C.App. 747, 616 S.E.2d 385 (N.C.App. 2005) (requiring juvenile adjudicated delinquent for manslaughter as a condition of probation to wear a necklace with a picture of the victim and to visit victim's grave with flowers twice a year).

NOTES

1) Probation Revocation. Juvenile court judges may revoke a delinquent's probation and impose different conditions of probation or institutionalize a juvenile either for new criminal conduct or for a violation of the previous conditions of probation. Probation officers often initiate revocation proceedings when they have probable cause to believe a probationer has violated conditions of probation. Because a probation revocation proceeding affects a youth's liberty interests, basic due process protections apply such as the requirement of a revocation hearing. Some states use the same procedures applicable to adult probation revocation proceedings for juveniles.

Minn. R. Juv. Proc. 15.07 (1999). Probation Violation

Subd. 1. Commencement of Proceedings. Proceedings for revocation of probation may be commenced based upon a written report showing probable cause to believe the juvenile has violated any conditions of probation. Based upon the report, the court may issue a warrant * * * or the court may schedule a review hearing and provide notice of the hearing * * *. If the juvenile fails to appear in response to a summons, the court may issue a warrant.

(A) Contents of Probation Violation Report. The probation violation report and supporting affidavits, if any, shall include: * * *

(3) a description of the surrounding facts and circumstances upon which the request for revocation is based. * * *

Subd. 3. Admit/Deny Hearing. The child shall either admit or deny the allegations of the probation violation report at the admit/deny hearing. * * *

(C) Denial. If the child denies the allegations, the matter shall be set for a revocation hearing * * *.

Subd. 4. Revocation Hearing.

(A) Generally. At the hearing, both the prosecuting attorney and the child shall have the right to offer evidence, present arguments, subpoena witnesses, and call and cross-examine witnesses, provided, however, that the child may be denied confrontation by the court when good cause is shown that a substantial risk of serious harm to others would exist if it were allowed. Additionally, the child shall have the right at the hearing to present mitigating circumstances or other reasons why the violation, if proved, should not result in revocation.

(B) Timing. The revocation hearing shall be held within seven (7) days after the child is taken into custody or, if the child is not in custody, within a reasonable time after the filing of the denial. If the child has allegedly committed a new offense, the court may postpone the revocation hearing pending disposition of the new offense whether or not the child is in custody.

(C) Violation Not Proved. If the court finds that a violation of the dispositional order has not been established by clear and convincing evidence, the revocation proceedings shall be dismissed, and the child shall continue under the dispositional order previously ordered by the court.

(D) Violation Proved. * * * If the court finds by clear and convincing evidence, or the child admits violating the terms of the dispositional order, the court may proceed as follows:

(1) order a disposition * * *; or

(2) for a child who was previously granted a continuance without adjudication * * *, adjudicate the child and order a disposition * * *.

2) Burden of Proof in Probation Revocation Proceedings The Colorado Supreme Court in **In the Interest of C. B.**, 196 Colo. 362, 585 P.2d

281 (Colo. 1978), addressed the burden of proof in juvenile probation revocation proceedings:

> From its inception the juvenile court system has permitted wide differences in the treatment of children and adults who have violated the law. The juvenile court system was created to ensure the care and guidance for the errant child that will ultimately "best serve his welfare and the interests of society." These purposes of the juvenile justice system will not be served by affording juveniles lesser procedural protections than adults against the revocation of probation for allegedly criminal conduct. The same considerations that motivated the General Assembly to require a high degree of caution in findings of fact for the protection of adults apply as well to the child.

> The stigma that attaches to a juvenile upon the finding that he has committed acts which would constitute a criminal offense if done by an adult is not always less than that imposed on an adult when he is convicted of a crime. * * *

> Upon revocation of probation, a juvenile and an adult face the same potential consequence: incarceration. Both the juvenile probationer and the adult probationer are subject to the punishment that originally could have been imposed. For a juvenile this punishment potentially involves no less a restraint of liberty than it does for an adult. * * *

> The fact that the purpose of the commitment of a juvenile delinquent is rehabilitative and not punitive does not change the nature of the commitment. * * *

> We find no basis for depriving juveniles of the burden of proof protections afforded adults in probation revocation proceedings. Children and adults facing revocation of probation are in legally and practically indistinguishable positions. The integrity of the factfinding process is equally at stake whether the probationer is over or under eighteen years of age. Neither the flexibility nor the efficiency of the juvenile court system will be disrupted by requiring proof "beyond a reasonable doubt" of juvenile probation violations based upon alleged acts which would constitute crimes if done by adults. In our view minimal due process guarantees of fundamentally fair procedures require no less. * * *

In contrast to Colorado's requirement of proof "beyond a reasonable doubt," the standard of proof for probation revocation under Minnesota's Rule of Juvenile Procedure 15.07 Subd. 4 (D) is "clear and convincing evidence." And, in **People v. Belcher**, 143 Mich.App. 68, 371 N.W.2d 474 (Mich.Ct.App.1985), the Michigan court of appeals held that

> a probation violation hearing is dispositional rather than adjudicative, because the original decision to place the child on probation rather than to impose some other sanction was dispositional rather than adjudicative. * * * [A] finding that the child violated the conditions of probation carried different consequences than a finding of guilt on a substantive charge. * * *

> Although proceedings in juvenile court need not conform with all the requirements of a criminal trial, essential requirements of due process

and fair treatment must be met. Proof beyond a reasonable doubt is an essential requirement of due process and fair treatment in the adjudicative phase of a proceeding in which a juvenile is charged with an act which would be a crime if committed by an adult and faces possible confinement in a state institution.

In *Gagnon v. Scarpelli*, however, the court explained that, although an adult probationer is entitled to a hearing at which certain minimum requirements of due process are observed before probation is revoked, a probationer is not entitled to all of the protections of a criminal trial, because the probationer has already been convicted of a crime. It is well settled in Michigan that the standard of proof in adult probation revocation proceedings is proof by a preponderance of the evidence. The status of a juvenile probationer is analogous to that of an adult probationer, and we see no reason to impose a higher burden of proof in juvenile probation revocation proceedings than in adult probation revocation proceedings. * * *

2.   DISPOSITIONAL ALTERNATIVES— COMMUNITY SERVICE

Juvenile court judges commonly impose "community service" orders as part of a juvenile's conditions of probation. Judges may impose community service requirements in the exercise of their "broad discretion" to tailor appropriate dispositions. Judges typically impose community service orders to benefit the community, to enable juveniles to accept responsibility for their actions, and to provide them with work experience. Community service work orders may vary from cleaning parks or public grounds, performing maintenance or clerical work for public agencies, or helping in recreational programs for younger children under the supervision of probation officers or regular agency personnel. In *In re T.S.*, 144 Vt. 592, 481 A.2d 21 (Vt. 1984), the Vermont Supreme Court approved a juvenile court dispositional order that required T.S. to complete 45 hours of community service as a condition of probation:

T.S. contends that the probation condition requiring 45 hours of community service was improper because the State made no showing that the condition was reasonably related to rehabilitation.

In imposing the condition, the trial court stated:

One of the preparations for future life is responsibility and accountability. And we see that as our responsibility as a Court. * * * And we see accountability and responsibility as a part of his rehabilitation. * * * And we feel that it's important that he be made to understand that he has to be responsible for that act, and he is accountable for having done it. * * *

The statutes also provide that the juvenile court, in fulfilling its statutory duty to make a disposition "most suited to [the delinquent child's] treatment, rehabilitation, and welfare," may, among other alternatives, "[p]lace the child on probation under such conditions and limitations as the court may prescribe." The juvenile court thus has been granted broad discretion in establishing the terms and conditions of probation. Absent an abuse of discretion, its order must stand. * * *

The trial court properly focused on accountability and responsibility in making its disposition order, settling on community service after finding the juvenile had no ability to make restitution. There has been no showing of an abuse of discretion. * * *

In *In re Shannon A.*, 60 Md.App. 399, 483 A.2d 363 (Md. Ct. Sp. App. 1984), the Maryland Court of Appeals upheld, as a special condition of probation, a requirement that Shannon perform 1000 hours of community service, under the supervision of Juvenile Services, by working with a brain-damaged child. "[W]e find that the 1000 hours of community service imposed on Shannon * * * certainly may be viewed as 'rehabilitative services that are in the best interest of the child. . . .' The comments of the trial judge clearly indicate that he imposed the condition for its rehabilitative effect, not as punishment. Accordingly, we affirm the disposition order."

3. DISPOSITIONAL ALTERNATIVES— RESTITUTION

As with other conditions of probation, the crucial question is whether a court imposes a sanction to rehabilitate or to punish a delinquent. In the absence of express statutory authority to impose a fine, for example, most courts have little difficulty characterizing a fine payable to the state as a penal imposition. In *In re Gardini*, 243 Pa.Super. 338, 365 A.2d 1252 (Pa. Sup. Ct. 1976), the Pennsylvania Superior Court vacated the juvenile court's dispositional order that imposed a $200 fine on the juvenile and held that "There can be no doubt that the lower court sought to punish the appellant for his actions by fining him. 'A fine is a pecuniary punishment imposed by a court for an offense.' We find the penal directive of the lower court to be contrary to the protective procedures prescribed by the Juvenile Act."

On the other hand, with appropriate statutory authorization, juvenile court judges frequently order delinquents to pay restitution to the victims of their crimes for the personal injury or property damages they inflicted.

In **State v. Kristopher G.**, 201 W.Va. 703, 500 S.E.2d 519 (W.Va. Ct. App. 1997), the juvenile court judge ordered three young delinquents to pay restitution of $7,947.52 for the damages they caused to a mobile home. The West Virginia court of appeals instructed the juvenile court judge how to calculate the "reasonable amount" of a restitution order on remand:

A trial judge may order restitution as part of a "program of treatment or therapy" designed to aid in the rehabilitation of the child in a juvenile case when probation is granted. * * * Such order, however, must be reasonable in its terms and within the child's ability to perform. * * * An order imposing conditions of probation that are unreasonable or beyond the ability of the child to perform, is not an order of probation at all but rather a disguised order of commitment. The frustration that would arise from the child's inherent inability to comply with an unreasonable condition of probation would negate the purpose of the statutory scheme of rehabilitation. * * *

[W]e must first decide if the amount ordered was part of a program of treatment or therapy. The record does not disclose any particular program of treatment or therapy as being prescribed for these juveniles, other than general supervised and unsupervised probation. It is to be hoped that their act of vandalism was an isolated incident, the sort in which many children may become involved. We accept that the circuit judge in the instant case ordered restitution to be paid for therapeutic and rehabilitative purposes, and thus this order of restitution would meet the treatment or therapy program test. * * *

In the instant case, there does not appear to be record evidence indicating that there "is a reasonable chance that the [juveniles] may be able to pay the restitution amount in question." Jobs available to nine and eleven year old children—or ten, or thirteen, or fourteen, or fifteen-year olds—are rare, and rarer still would be jobs which would enable these children to pay a debt of $7,947.52 (at ten percent interest)—assuming they were allowed to keep at least some of the money they made, which is a principle we have recognized in our adult restitution cases.

The primary aim of [the restitution statute] * * * is to require restitution based on the fair market value of damaged or destroyed property, either when it was destroyed or damaged, or on the date of sentencing. This section does not contemplate restitution based on repair or replacement cost. If the restitution statutes for adults do not call for restitution based upon repair or replacement cost, it would be manifestly unreasonable to require a child to be bound by the stricter standard. * * *

In **State v. Fambrough**, 66 Wash.App. 223, 831 P.2d 789 (Wash. Ct. App. 1992), the juvenile court judge ordered the juvenile to pay restitution in amount of $946.78 for damages to a motor scooter based on a written estimate submitted by the victim. The Washington court of appeals affirmed the restitution order and held that:

Once the fact of damage is established, the precise amount does not have to be shown with mathematical certainty. "Evidence of damage is sufficient if it affords a reasonable basis for estimating loss and does not subject the trier of fact to mere speculation or conjecture." If the amount of damages is established by "substantial credible evidence" at the restitution hearing, no abuse of discretion will be found. * * *

[T]he statute does not require a court to hold a special restitution hearing, although courts usually do. It requires only that the court hold a disposition hearing where it shall, among other things, determine the amount of restitution. More importantly, * * * because restitution involves neither sentence enhancement nor a sentence outside the standard range, the amount of loss need not be proven beyond a reasonable doubt or by clear and convincing evidence. RCW 13.40.020(17), which requires the loss to be "easily ascertainable", does not limit the amount of restitution only to an undisputed amount. * * * The *Smith* court concluded

that proof of loss for imposing restitution under the juvenile justice act requires a standard similar to that required to prove damages in a tort context, evidence sufficient to afford a reasonable basis for estimating the loss.

We base this conclusion on a number of considerations. * * * [I]f restitution was limited to the amount the offenders indicated, the effectiveness of the restitution provisions would be greatly weakened. Additionally, requiring evidence sufficient to afford a reasonable basis for the loss is consistent with the language of the act and purposes underlying the restitution provisions. The act grants the hearing judge the right to determine the "amount, terms, and conditions of the restitution." * * *

In **D.J.W. v. State**, 705 So.2d 521 (Ala. Ct. Crim. App. 1996), the Alabama court of criminal appeals emphasized that the amount of restitution that a juvenile is ordered to pay must be based not only on an amount that compensates the victim but must also take into account the ability of the juvenile to "reasonably" meet the obligation:

"The goal of juvenile restitution * * * is primarily 'rehabilita[tion]'—not compensation of the victim." In pursuing that rehabilitative remedy, the juvenile court must take into account what a child can reasonably be expected to pay: "It is an abuse of discretion to fail to take the following into consideration when fashioning a restitution order in a juvenile court case: 1) The financial resources and obligations of the juvenile; 2) the burden that payment of restitution will impose; 3) the juvenile's age, education, background, and all other relevant factors; and 4) the rehabilitative effect of the restitution order".

B. FROM OFFENDER TO OFFENSE: TREATMENT VERSUS PUNISHMENT AND JUVENILE COURT DISPOSITIONS

Since *Gault* and *McKeiver*, judicial, legislative, and administrative changes have eroded the original rehabilitative premises of juvenile justice sentencing. In part, the appropriate disposition of a youth hinges on jurispruden-tial considerations. What are the goals of delinquency dispositions? For what purposes should courts employ coercive sanctions? Historically, the "rehabilitative ideal" and its focus on the "best interests" of the child provided a ready answer. However, with the erosion of public and political support for penal rehabilitation, the juvenile court has become an institu-tion in search of a rationale. *See* Francis Allen, *The Decline of the Rehabilitative Ideal* (1981); Barry C. Feld, *Bad Kids: Race and the Transformation of the Juvenile Court* (1999); David Garland, *The Culture of Control* (2001).

What are the justifications for intervention in the lives of young people who violate the criminal law in a separate juvenile justice system? Rehabilitation? Retribution? General or specific deterrence? Selective inca-pacitation? Mitigating the severity of adult sanctions for younger offend-ers? Insulating youths from the collateral consequences of criminal convic-tions? Because juvenile courts pursue multiple goals—the "best interests" of the child and the "protection of the community"—how should state sentencing laws and juvenile court judges balance these competing pur-poses when they conflict. *See generally*, Franklin E. Zimring, *American Youth Violence* (1998); Franklin E. Zimring, "The Common Thread: Diversion in the Jurisprudence of Juvenile Courts," in M. Rosenheim, et al., eds, *A Century of Juvenile Justice 142 (2002).*

The juvenile court's retreat from an unqualified and exclusive com-mitment to the "Rehabilitative Ideal" is based, in part, on evaluations of the effectiveness of treatment. *See* pp. 998–1001, *infra.* Earlier empirical evaluation research studies often provided only negative or guarded an-swers to the question of "what works." However, more recent research identifies effective or promising programs to reduce the likelihood of recidivism. The critique of rehabilitation focuses in part on the exercise of discretion by juvenile court judges and the search for some limiting principles to guide their decisions. As Judge Crippen noted in *J.A.J.*, *supra*, pp. 910–913, developing substantive juvenile sentencing policies implicates fundamental value choices about State coercion and the uses and abuses of power. As a result of empirical evaluation studies, practical short-comings, and changing penal policies, states' commitment to rehabil-itative sentencing began to decline in the 1970s and 1980s. As the preceding section suggests, however, rehabilitation remains the dominant rationale for delinquency sentences. Moreover, there is no evidence that indicates that any of the other justifications for punishment-retribution, deterrence, and incapacitation—are any more effective in reducing recidi-vism or improving the life-chances of young offenders. But, reducing recidivism may not be the only reason for juvenile courts to intervene? Since the late–1980s, "get tough" politicians have proposed to "crack down" on youth crime, greatly have increased the sanctioning powers of juvenile courts, and have fostered a jurisprudential and substantive con-vergence with criminal court sentencing practices. *See generally*, Barry C.

Feld, "Race, Politics, and Juvenile Justice: The Warren Court and the Conservative 'Backlash'," 87 *Minn. L. Rev.* 1447 (2003).

Many commentators have described and analyzed the changing jurisprudence of the juvenile court and its implications for procedural and substantive juvenile justice. *See e.g.* Martin R. Gardner, "Punitive Juvenile Justice: Some Observations on a Recent Trend," 10 *Int. J. L. and Psych.* 129 (1987); Martin R. Gardner, "The Right of Juvenile Offenders to be Punished: Some Implications of Treating Kids as Persons," 68 *Neb. L. Rev. 182* (1989); Gary B. Melton, "Taking *Gault* Seriously: Toward a New Juvenile Court," 68 *Neb. L. Rev.* 146 (1989); Michael J. Dale, "Children Before the Supreme Court: In Whose Best Interests?," 53 *Alb. L. Rev.* 513 (1989); Stephen Wizner and Mary F. Keller, "The Penal Model of Juvenile Justice: Is Juvenile Court Delinquency Jurisdiction Obsolete?," 52 *N.Y.U. L. Rev.* 1120 (1977); Barry C. Feld, "Juvenile Court Legislative Reform and the Serious Young Offender: Dismantling the "Rehabilitative Ideal"," 65 *Minn. L. Rev.* 167 (1980); Barry C. Feld, "The Juvenile Court Meets the Principle of Offense: Punishment, Treatment, and the Difference It Makes," 68 *B. U. L. Rev.* 821 (1988); Janet E. Ainsworth, "Re–Imagining Childhood and Reconstructing the Legal Order: The Case for Abolishing the Juvenile Court," 69 *N. C. L. Rev.* 1083 (1991); Julianne Sheffer, "Serious and Habitual Juvenile Offender Statutes: Reconciling Punishment and Rehabilitation within the Juvenile Justice System." 48 *Vand. L. Rev.* 479 (1995). These various commentators identify and analyze the jurisprudential shift from treatment to punishment, from rehabilitation to retribution, from sentences based on considerations of the offender to those that focus on the offense, and from concern about a youth's future welfare to penalties based on past crimes. Because the "Rehabilitative Ideal" provides the foundation for a separate juvenile justice system with fewer criminal procedural safeguards than those afforded adult criminal defendants, the Court in *Allen v. Illinois*, *supra* p. 740, and *McKeiver v. Pennsylvania*, *supra* p. 750, and commentators suggest several indicators to probe the similarities and differences between the two systems of justice and social control.

1. THE PURPOSE OF DELINQUENCY SANCTIONS

The Supreme Court in *McKeiver v. Pennsylvania* posited treatment as a juvenile rather than punishment as an adult as the justification to deny delinquents a constitutional right to a jury trial. In deciding whether juveniles enjoyed a state constitutional right to a jury trial—L.M., D.J., and State v. Hezzie R.—the state Supreme Court justices looked to legislative changes in the juvenile code purpose clauses as guides to the state's policy. When analysts attempt to identify the elements of delinquency dispositions that distinguish them from criminal sanctions, changes in legislative purpose clauses provide one indicator of the changing jurisprudence of juvenile justice. In the following excerpt, **Barry C. Feld, "The Juvenile Court Meets the Principle of Offense: Punish-**

ment, Treatment, and the Difference It Makes," 68 *B.U. L. Rev.* **821, 839–842 (1988)**, analyzes changes in statutory purposes at the beginning of the "get tough" era:

Even when a State incarcerates on the basis of underlying conduct that is criminal, however, the Court must still determine whether the purpose of the confinement is penal. In *Allen v. Illinois,* [*supra* p. 740] the Supreme Court considered the distinctions between "punishment" and "treatment' "in deciding whether a person incarcerated under a "Sexually Dangerous Persons Act" "was entitled to invoke the fifth amendment privilege against self-incrimination. * * * While acknowledging that a "civil label is not * * * dispositive," "the Court concluded that because the statutory purpose was to provide 'care and treatment' " and commitment was indeterminate,

> the State has disavowed any interest in punishment, provided for the treatment of those it commits, and established a system under which committed persons may be released after the briefest time in confinement. The Act thus does not appear to promote either of "the traditional aims of punishment—retribution and deterrence." * * *

Finally, the Court concluded that Allen had failed to negate the State's claim of "treatment" "by failing to show that the nature of his confinement was 'essentially identical to that imposed upon felons with no need for psychiatric care. * * * ' " The Court acknowledged, however, "that the conditions of * * * confinement [could] amount to 'punishment' and thus render 'criminal' the proceedings which led to confinement." * * *

Despite lingering rhetoric of rehabilitation as an "alternative purpose," "the contemporary juvenile court system increasingly and explicitly resembles a punitive institution."

Most states' juvenile court statutes contain a "purpose clause" "or preamble, a statement of the underlying rationale of the legislation intended to aid the courts in interpreting the statute. Thus, examining a juvenile code's purpose clause provides one insight into the goal of juvenile court intervention. Since the creation of the original juvenile court in Cook County, Illinois, in 1899, the historical purpose of juvenile court law has been

> to secure for each minor subject hereto such care and guidance, preferably in his own home, as will serve the moral, emotional, mental, and physical welfare of the minor and the best interests of the community; to preserve and strengthen the minor's family ties whenever possible, removing him from the custody of his parents only when his welfare or safety or the protection of the public cannot be adequately safeguarded without removal; and, when the minor is removed from his own family, to secure for him custody, care, and discipline as nearly as possible equivalent to that which should be given by his parents. * * *

Many states included this statement of purpose from the original Illinois juvenile court act in the preamble to their juvenile codes. Some states provided the additional purpose of "remov[ing] from a minor committing a delinquency offense the taint of criminality and the penal consequences of criminal behavior, by substituting therefore an individual program of counseling, supervision, treatment, and rehabilitation."

Forty-two of the states' juvenile codes contain a statement of legislative purpose or similar preamble. Within the past decade, however, ten state legislatures—almost one-quarter of states with a legislative purpose statement or preamble in their juvenile law statutes—have redefined the purpose of their juvenile courts. These recent amendments of juvenile code purpose clauses downplay the role of rehabilitation in the child's "best interest" and acknowledge the importance of public safety, punishment, and individual accountability in the juvenile justice system. One of the distinguishing characteristics of the "new" juvenile law is that "in many jurisdictions accountability and punishment have emerged among the express purposes of juvenile justice statutes." * * *

NOTES

1) Linda F. Giardino, "Statutory Rhetoric: The Reality Behind Juvenile Justice Policies in America," 5 *J.L. & Pol'y* 223, 275–276 (1996), analyzes changes in juvenile code purpose clauses and waiver statutes and concludes that "statutory rhetoric" reflects the ascendance of "get tough" juvenile sentencing policies:

[S]everal jurisdictions have explicitly shifted away from juvenile justice systems based on rehabilitation and moved toward more punitive policies. For other jurisdictions, the shift away from rehabilitation cannot be masked by drafting benevolent, yet rhetorical, statutory purposes. However consummate such draftsmanship may appear, it does not evince the true policy behind a state's juvenile justice system. Rather, the actual purpose behind a state's juvenile justice system is evinced by analysis of both the judicial treatment of its laws and its subsequent legislative provisions.

Nonetheless, considerations of the best interests of the child still permeate most areas of the law that affect children, including areas beyond the scope of this analysis. Throughout virtually all areas of juvenile law, the welfare and interests of the child have been balanced against the interests and desire for protection of the public. It is this contradiction, the state serving as both protector and prosecutor of the child, that makes the emerging trends in the juvenile justice system inconsistent and questionable. Contrasting statutory goals serve as a means to justify any dispositional decision a state chooses to apply to its juvenile offenders, whether it be the rehabilitation or the punishment of such children. * * *

2) Legislative changes in juvenile court purpose In deciding whether delinquency dispositions "treat" or "punish" youths, consider the following statutory statements of purpose contained in states' juvenile codes:

Cal. Welf. & Inst. Code § 202 (West Group 1999).

(a) The purpose of this chapter is to provide for the protection and safety of the public and each minor under the jurisdiction of the juvenile court and to preserve and strengthen the minor's family ties whenever possible, removing the minor from the custody of his or her parents only when necessary for his or her welfare or for the safety and protection of the public. When removal of a minor is determined by the juvenile court to be necessary, reunification of the minor with his or her family shall be a primary objective. When the minor is removed from his or her own family, it is the purpose of this chapter to secure for the minor custody, care, and discipline as nearly as possible equivalent to that which should have been given by his or her parents. This chapter shall be liberally construed to carry out these purposes.

(b) * * * Minors under the jurisdiction of the juvenile court as a consequence of delinquent conduct shall, in conformity with the interests of public safety and protection, receive care, treatment and guidance which is consistent with their best interest, which holds them accountable for their behavior, and which is appropriate for their circumstances. This guidance may include punishment that is consistent with the rehabilitative objectives of this chapter. If a minor has been removed from the custody of his or her parents, family preservation and family reunification are appropriate goals for the juvenile court to consider when determining the disposition of a minor under the jurisdiction of the juvenile court as a consequence of delinquent conduct when those goals are consistent with his or her best interests and the best interests of the public. When the minor is no longer a ward of the juvenile court, the guidance he or she received should enable him or her to be a law-abiding and productive member of his or her family and the community. * * *

(e) As used in this chapter, "punishment" means the imposition of sanctions which include the following:

(1) Payment of a fine by the minor.

(2) Rendering of compulsory service without compensation performed for the benefit of the community by the minor.

(3) Limitations on the minor's liberty imposed as a condition of probation or parole.

(4) Commitment of the minor to a local detention or treatment facility, such as a juvenile hall, camp, or ranch.

(5) Commitment of the minor to the Department of the Youth Authority.

"Punishment," for the purposes of this chapter, does not include retribution. * * *

Tex. Fam. Code § 51.01 (1997).

This title shall be construed to effectuate the following public purposes:

(1) to provide for the protection of the public and public safety;

(2) consistent with the protection of the public and public safety:

(A) to promote the concept of punishment for criminal acts;

(B) to remove, where appropriate, the taint of criminality from children committing certain unlawful acts; and

(C) to provide treatment, training, and rehabilitation that emphasizes the accountability and responsibility of both the parent and the child for the child's conduct;

(3) to provide for the care, the protection, and the wholesome moral, mental, and physical development of children coming within its provisions;

(4) to protect the welfare of the community and to control the commission of unlawful acts by children;

(5) to achieve the foregoing purposes in a family environment whenever possible, separating the child from the child's parents only when necessary for the child's welfare or in the interest of public safety and when a child is removed from the child's family, to give the child the care that should be provided by parents; and

(6) to provide a simple judicial procedure through which the provisions of this title are executed and enforced and in which the parties are assured a fair hearing and their constitutional and other legal rights recognized and enforced.

3) Reconciling changes in legislative purpose with the traditional conception of the juvenile court In the following two case excerpts, different branches of the California Court of Appeals ascribe different significance to the legislative changes in the state's juvenile code, *supra* Note 2. In **In re Charles C.**, 232 Cal.App.3d 952, 960–961 284 Cal.Rptr. 4, 8–9 (Cal. Ct. Ap. 5th Dist., 1991), the court of appeals considered and rejected a juvenile's request for a jury trial because the juvenile court judge committed him to the California Youth Authority until age 25, a term of nine years. The court assayed the implications of the legislative changes in the purpose clause:

While the aim of adult incarceration is punishment, a juvenile commitment is geared toward treatment and rehabilitation with the state providing substitute parental care for wayward youths during their minority. However, in 1982, the Legislature enacted provisions allowing minors to be held to age 25 for their juvenile offenses. * * *

Despite the legislative changes extending juvenile court jurisdiction over certain committed wards until the age of 25, the reasoning of the *McKeiver* Court remains persuasive. Neither the extension of juvenile court jurisdiction nor the addition of punishment as an expressed purpose of the Juvenile Court Law changes the overriding purpose or design of the juvenile justice system warranting the imposition of a jury trial requirement. * * *

"The fundamental * * * purpose of the juvenile justice system in this state is the treatment and rehabilitation of youths. Reason and common experience tell us the prime necessity to achieve this goal is a system as flexible as financial means and constitutional restraints allow.* * * [T]ime requirements necessary to effect rehabilitation by their very nature demand flexibility. Punishment can be meted out in precise time units but modification of behavior is not a task subject to similar quantification." * * *

Thus, case law tells us the justification for a juvenile commitment which extends into adulthood lies in the rehabilitative function of the juvenile court system. Implicit in the authority for commitments beyond minority is the belief that rehabilitation may not be possible if an older minor—16 or 17 years of age—cannot remain under the jurisdiction of the juvenile court for an adequate period of time to complete the necessary rehabilitative programs available at CYA. However, the fact that a minor may be confined into adulthood for his juvenile offenses does not compel a jury trial. * * * Further, since the minor is actually sentenced to an indeterminate term, he is not similarly situated to the adult who faces a determinate term of six months or more. Thus, the fact that a juvenile offender may be committed to CYA for a term extending into his adulthood does not warrant a jury trial in the adjudicative phase of the proceedings.

In 1984, the Legislature amended the purpose of the Juvenile Court Law and put an increased emphasis on punishment. However, the reference to punishment did not alter the overall rehabilitative aspect of the juvenile justice system. In fact, the new language only reinforces the different purposes underlying the juvenile and adult procedures:

> Minors under the jurisdiction of the juvenile court as a consequence of delinquent conduct shall, in conformity with the interests of public safety and protection, receive care, treatment and guidance which is consistent with their best interest, which holds them accountable for their behavior, and which is appropriate for their circumstances. This guidance may include punishment that is consistent with the rehabilitative objectives of this chapter.

> The state's punishment of minors is a "rehabilitative tool", distinguishable from the criminal justice system for adults which has a purely punitive purpose separate from its rehabilitative goals. Thus, even though punishment is now an express purpose of the Juvenile Court Law, the underlying purpose of the juvenile system remains sufficiently distinct from the adult criminal system to support confinement at CYA rehabilitative programs into adulthood for juvenile offenses without a jury trial.
> * * *

By contrast, the California court of appeals **In re Javier A.**, 159 Cal.App.3d 913, 206 Cal.Rptr. 386 (Cal. Ct. App. 1984), analyzed the changes in purpose and administration of California's juvenile justice system in connection with a youth's request for a jury trial. Although the court in *Javier A.* reached a different conclusion about the purpose of delinquency proceedings, the court found itself bound by *stare decisis* to follow the California Supreme Court's decision in *In re Daedler* (1924) which denied juveniles a state constitutional right to a jury trial:

> In 1924, the California Supreme Court was able to distinguish juvenile courts from adult criminal proceedings in glowing terms which spoke of benevolent purposes and minimal consequences. * * * Now 60 years later we find the Legislature has redefined the purposes of the juvenile process to make them more punitive. Those same 60 years have brought dramatic changes in the procedures followed in juvenile courts

causing them to become trials in the full sense of the word—formal, adversarial and public. Finally, the consequences of a finding the accused juvenile committed the charged crime now closely resemble what would follow conviction in adult criminal court. * * *

The differences between the 1924 and 1984 juvenile justice systems are symbolized by the captions affixed to juvenile delinquency proceedings in the two eras. In 1924 it was *"In re Daedler"*; in 1984 it is *"The People of the State of California versus Javier A."* The change in caption is consistent with a change in motive. In 1924 the proceedings focused on protecting the child from unwholesome environmental influences. In 1984 the emphasis is on protecting the citizens of the state of California from the child. * * *

At the time of the *Daedler* opinion and for decades thereafter, the stated purpose of the juvenile court act was to serve "the spiritual, emotional, mental and physical welfare of the minor" and "to secure for him custody, care, and discipline as nearly as possible equivalent to that which should have been given by his parents." But in 1975 the Legislature added a new and second purpose to the generally beneficent language of the original statement in the Juvenile Court Law. This additional goal was placed in a completely separate subsection which reads: [The purpose of this chapter] * * * also "(b) * * * includes the protection of the public from the consequences of criminal activity, and to such purpose probation officers, peace officers, and juvenile courts shall take into account such protection of the public in their determinations under this chapter." Not satisfied, in 1977 the Legislature also inserted a new clause in the first paragraph of the section. This further refinement reads: "to protect the public from criminal conduct by minors; to impose on the minor a sense of responsibility for his own acts * * *."

The courts have not been blind to the shifting goals of the juvenile courts. Even before the California Legislature enacted this express language emphasizing protection of the public, the United States Supreme Court had recognized the actual purposes already were similar to those of the adult criminal system. Writing for a unanimous court in a case arising out of a California juvenile delinquency proceeding, Chief Justice Burger held: "Although the juvenile-court system had its genesis in the desire to provide a distinctive procedure and setting to deal with the problems of youth, including those manifested by anti-social conduct, our decisions in recent years have recognized that there is a gap between the originally benign conception of the system and its realities. * * * "

By 1980, Division Two of this court was acknowledging the continuing evolution of California juvenile courts toward the goals of the adult criminal courts. "In [*County of Alameda v. Espinoza*] the court acknowledged the existence, but rejected the validity, of a widely held belief that * * * current practices juvenile court proceedings * * * are in reality criminal proceedings and the claim that such proceedings are 'for the protection of the minor' is pure fiction. * * * Whatever the validity of that belief in 1966 when the *Espinoza* opinion was filed, it is certainly true today." In 1984, the California Supreme Court while admitting "section 602 proceedings are not technically criminal" cited with approval Division Two's characterization they are "in reality criminal proceedings" and the claim they are for the protection of the minor is "pure fiction." * * *

[A] juvenile delinquency proceeding in 1984 asks a court to decide whether a child has violated a specified criminal law and whether this violation is a felony or misdemeanor. If the court decides beyond a reasonable doubt the child did commit the crime, it can, in order to "protect the public from criminal conduct," deprive the child of his liberty for the same period of time an adult would lose his liberty for violating the same criminal law. * * *

4) Judicial Approval of Punishment in the Name of Treatment
Some courts acknowledge that the changes in juvenile code purpose clauses signal basic changes in philosophical direction, but assert that "punishment" constitutes an acceptable purpose of juvenile courts' "therapeutic" dispositions. In *State v. Lawley*, 91 Wash.2d at 656–57, 591 P.2d at 773 (1979), the Washington Supreme Court reasoned that "sometimes punishment is treatment," and upheld the legislature's conclusion that "accountability for criminal behavior, the prior criminal activity and punishment commensurate with age, crime, and criminal history does as much to rehabilitate, correct, and direct an errant youth as does the prior philosophy of focusing upon the particular characteristics of the individual juvenile." Similarly, in *In re Seven Minors*, 99 Nev. at 432, 664 P.2d at 950 (1983), the Nevada Supreme Court endorsed punishment as an appropriate function of juvenile courts. "By formally recognizing the legitimacy of punitive and deterrent sanctions for criminal offenses juvenile courts will be properly and somewhat belatedly expressing society's firm disapproval of juvenile crime and will be clearly issuing a threat of punishment for criminal acts to the juvenile population."

2. INDETERMINATE vs. DETERMINATE SENTENCING STATUTES

The Supreme Court in *McKeiver v. Pennsylvania* denied juveniles a constitutional right to a jury trial based on the purported differences between punishment and treatment. Juveniles typically request a jury trial as a legal strategy to challenge punitive juvenile court sentencing laws and practices. Similarly, the Court in *Allen v. Illinois* identified Allen's indeterminate commitment as one indicator of the state's "therapeutic" purpose of confinement. Juveniles typically request a jury trial when the state's sentencing laws allow or require judges to impose determinate or mandatory minimum sentences based on the seriousness of a youth's offense and argue that such provisions punish rather than treat them. Consider the following courts' analyses of the differences between indeterminate and determinate sentences for the rehabilitative rationale of the juvenile court.

IN THE MATTER OF FELDER

93 Misc.2d 369, 402 N.Y.S.2d 528 (Fam. Ct. 1978).

McLAUGHLIN, JUDGE. This juvenile delinquency proceeding involves a designated felony pursuant to the Juvenile Justice Reform Act of 1976. It presents a case of first impression for this court. Respondent, a boy of fifteen, allegedly committed a robbery in the first degree, a designated felony. When the case came before the Court, the Respondent moved for a jury trial, asserting that under *Baldwin v. New York*, (1970) [*supra* Note 1, pp. 763–764], an individual charged with a crime where the penalty could exceed six months imprisonment is entitled to a jury trial. The respondent alleged that since he can be confined in a secure facility for a period of time up to twelve months, * * * he is entitled to a trial by jury. On the other hand, the petitioner alleged that the United States Supreme Court decision in *McKeiver v. Pennsylvania*, is controlling. *McKeiver* holds that a juvenile charged with a delinquency * * * does not have a due process right to a jury trial. * * * The issue before the court, then, is whether the instant proceeding is controlled by *McKeiver* or by *Baldwin*. Specifically, the question turns on whether this is a juvenile proceeding within the meaning of *McKeiver*, or, whether so many of the attributes of a juvenile proceeding have been discarded that the proceeding is in effect "criminal" in nature and thus within the ambit of *Baldwin*. * * *

The fundamental substantive distinction between a juvenile proceeding and a criminal proceeding is that a juvenile disposition is limited to treatment, while a criminal proceeding may impose punishment regardless of whether the punishment results in retribution and, or, deterrence. The view that the difference between criminal and juvenile proceedings is the difference between retribution and deterrence, on the one hand, and treatment, on the other, is confirmed by an examination of the history of the juvenile court system. This examination will also show that a denial of a juvenile's full exercise of his constitutional rights can only be predicated upon the presence of the treatment principle of the juvenile justice system. * * *

[W]hen the juvenile proceeding was primarily for retributive and deterrent purposes, it was considered criminal in nature, and hence subject to all of the limitations of a regular criminal proceeding. Sometimes referred to as the "exchange principle of juvenile law", the trading of the constitutional protections of a criminal proceeding for rehabilitation still remains today the *sine qua non* of juvenile proceedings. * * *

The determination in *McKeiver* that in a juvenile proceeding a jury trial is not required, is, therefore, necessarily limited to those proceedings that are juvenile in nature. Thus, there is no requirement of a jury trial in family court where the disposition is rehabilitative and non-penal. When, however, the protections provided to the juvenile criminal offender have been so eroded away that what is actually a punishment is characterized as a treatment, an abuse of constitutional dimension has occurred, and, a jury trial is required before punishment, although appropriate, may be inflicted.

In response to the reported increase in the frequency and severity of crimes committed by juveniles, the Legislature in the 1976 session enacted the Juvenile Justice Reform Act. * * * The express purpose of Article 7 was redefined to include, for the first time, consideration of the needs of the community: "In any juvenile procedure under this article, the court shall consider the needs and best interests of the respondent as well as the need for protection of the community." To this end, the Legislature created restrictive placement. Rejecting proposals to transfer seriously violent juveniles to the adult criminal system, the Legislature adopted restrictive placement as a method of dealing with the juveniles within the juvenile system.

The amendments to Article 7 define four new terms: designated felony act,[4] designated Class A felony act, secure facility,[6] and restrictive placement. Further, the amendments allow the County Attorney to be assisted by members of the District Attorney's staff, provides that the probation service may not attempt to adjust some cases without the prior written approval of a judge, requires that, with a few exceptions, the judge presiding at the fact finding hearing shall preside at the dispositional hearing, and, eliminates in designated felony cases the judge's discretionary right to prevent disclosure of portions of the juvenile's reports and histories to either the respondent or the petitioner.

A significant change made by the Juvenile Justice Reform Act is the requirement that restrictive placement may be ordered for a juvenile found to have committed a designated felony, when the court determines that a juvenile requires such restrictive placement. Once restrictive placement is ordered by the court, the delinquent must remain in the placement for twelve months, if the placement results from an adjudication on a Class A designated felony, or for six months, if the placement results from the adjudication of any designated felony. Further, during the period of restrictive placement, the right to petition the court to stay the execution, to set aside, modify, or vacate the disposition is suspended. * * * Thus, the Legislature has created a definite sentence of placement nearly indistinguishable from definite sentences imposed upon adults under * * * the Penal Law.

Further, in mandating the minimum period of restrictive placement, when restrictive placement has been found to be needed at all, the

---

4. F C A § 712(h) "Designated felony act." An act committed by a person fourteen or fifteen years of age which, if done by an adult, would be [murder in the first degree; murder in the second degree; kidnapping in the first degree; arson in the first degree; assault in the first degree; manslaughter in the first degree; rape in the first degree; sodomy in the first degree; kidnapping in the second degree, but only where the abduction involved the use or threat of use of deadly force; arson in the second degree; robbery in the first degree; or an attempt to commit murder in the first or second degree or kidnapping in the first degree].

6. F C A § 712(j) "Secure facility." A residential facility in which the juvenile delinquent may be placed under this article, which is characterized by physically restricting construction, hardware and procedures, and is designated a secure facility by the division for youth.

Legislature has introduced two other concepts of the criminal justice process previously unknown in the juvenile system. First, the length of the commitment is determined by the act committed rather than by the needs of the child, and second, the sentence is mandatory. In effect, the Legislature has determined that a child who at the time of his dispositional hearing requires restrictive placement will continue to require restrictive placement for the entire period of the minimum sentence. Prior to the enactment of this statute, the court was only required to determine that at the time of the dispositional hearing the needs of the child were for placement in an institution and that at any time during that initial period, if the child was successfully rehabilitated, he was entitled to release. Consistent with this philosophy of treatment was the provision that if at the end of the initial placement the child was not successfully rehabilitated, then, the period of placement could be extended. In effect, once the court makes a finding that restrictive placement is needed at the time of the disposition, the act then mandates a minimum sentence, a result which is more harsh on the juvenile than is the criminal procedure for the adult who is entitled to an indeterminate sentence in nearly all cases.

The distinction between indeterminate and determinate sentencing is not semantic, but indicates fundamentally different public policies. Indeterminate sentencing is based upon notions of rehabilitation, while determinate sentencing is based upon a desire for retribution or punishment. * * *

The thinly disguised intent of the Legislature [is] to punish an adjudicated designated felon, based upon the criminal act and upon the characteristics of the victim of the criminal act, as opposed to rehabilitating and treating a juvenile offender. * * *

This court does not deny that punishment may be appropriate for certain designated felons. This court does insist, however, that deprivation of liberty for purposes of punishment based on the nature of criminal acts committed must be surrounded by constitutional protections not now available in family court proceedings.

The very heart of the rehabilitative nature of the juvenile justice system in New York is the array of remedies * * * that have protected the right of a juvenile to an indeterminate sentence. It is the indeterminate quality of a juvenile disposition that makes the disposition rehabilitative. To refuse to allow a [court] to modify or to terminate a placement gives the disposition clearly criminal characteristics.

The Juvenile Justice Reform Act requires that treatment be available at restrictive placement facilities. The availability and quality of treatment available to the respondent is not at issue here. What is at issue is the mandatory time period required for treatment. * * *

Clearly, treatment may result in a cure in six days, or in six weeks, or in six months, or in one year, or never! By setting a mandatory minimum time period for restrictive placement, treatment becomes indistinguishable from punishment. * * *

The revision of the Family Court Act by the Juvenile Justice Reform Act of 1976 transformed a purely rehabilitative juvenile statute into a statute that mirrors a retributive criminal statute, but fails to reflect the constitutional protections presumed to apply to such statutes. This transformation is most particularly evidenced by the requirement of restrictive placement in a secure facility for a definite period of time for a person found to have committed a designated felony and to be in need of restrictive placement with no provision for changing the placement if rehabilitation of the juvenile offender is found to have occurred. Other aspects of the revision also indicate that the designated felony proceeding is in its very essence a criminal proceeding, although labeled a juvenile proceeding. Since it is essentially a criminal proceeding, it is required that all the safeguards mandated by the United States Constitution be afforded the accused.

The particular constitutional safeguard now before the court is the Sixth Amendment right to a trial by jury. * * * [T]he respondent is entitled to a trial by jury for a criminal prosecution. * * *

Unfortunately, it is not possible for this court to have the facts determined by a jury, since the law in this state is clear that no court may conduct a trial by jury unless such proceeding is authorized by statute.

The quandary thus created for the court is, may it proceed in this case given its inability to extend a right to a trial by jury? And further, if it may so proceed, how does it protect the rights of the respondent and the rights of society?

It is the determination of this court that it is entitled to proceed to the fact finding hearing on this alleged act of delinquency without a jury, provided that prior to the taking of any testimony the court advises the respondent that regardless of the outcome, this court will not order restrictive placement, and this it now does. If the alleged facts are proven, thereby giving this court jurisdiction to make a disposition, and if at that dispositional hearing it is determined that placement is necessary, such disposition will be ordered and the respondent may be placed for an initial period of eighteen months. If the treatment is not completed at the end of such time, placement will be extended within the provisions of the law and, accordingly, the right of society to be protected from further depredations will be as effectively insured as if a restrictive placement were ordered, and at the same time the right of the respondent to modification of that disposition as soon as he responds to treatment will be preserved.

Accordingly, motion for trial by jury is denied.

NOTES

1) New York's Juvenile Offender and Designated Felony Law
Prior to the New York legislature's adoption of the Juvenile Offender law in 1976 and the Young Offender law in 1978, New York's juvenile court jurisdiction ended at age 16 for all offenses and contained no waiver provision.

Fifteen-year-old Willie Boskett committed several subway murders, but the family court judge could impose only a juvenile court disposition. In response, the New York legislature excluded youths as young as thirteen years of age charged with murder and many additional violent crimes by fourteen-and-fifteen year old juveniles from family court jurisdiction and expanded the youthful sentencing alternatives to adult criminal sentences. The Juvenile Offender and Young Offender laws then provided a non-adult sentencing option to the Family Courts that tried these youths. *See,* Simon Singer, *Recriminalizing Delinquency: Violent Juvenile Crime and Juvenile Justice Reform* (1996); Fox Butterfield, *All God's Children* (1995).

2) Treatment and Punishment—Future Welfare and Past Offense
In *In re M.D.N.*, 493 N.W.2d 680, 682–83 (N.Dak. 1992), the North Dakota Supreme Court also adverted to the jurisprudential framework that distinguishes treatment as a juvenile from punishment as an adult. Although *M.D.N.* involved a waiver hearing, the court's jurisprudential analysis applies to delinquency sentences as well:

> Whether violent young offenders should be tried and, if found guilty, should be sentenced as juveniles or as adults poses difficult practical and theoretical problems. Relinquishing juvenile court jurisdiction over young offenders to an adult criminal court represents a choice between sentencing in rehabilitative juvenile courts or sentencing in essentially punitive adult criminal courts. Conceptually, rehabilitation and punishment may be mutually exclusive penal goals. Punishment is retrospective and imposes harsh consequences for past offenses. It has a goal of proportional punishment which accords great significance to the seriousness of the offense. Rehabilitation, however, is prospective and tries to improve the offender's future welfare. Rehabilitation assigns primary importance to the individual as its sentences are nonproportional and indeterminate.

> But punishment and rehabilitation are not the only concern. In recent years, society has demanded more incarcerations of criminals, and many states have responded by diluting the rehabilitative philosophy of juvenile court. It is difficult to embrace a rehabilitative stance toward juveniles who have committed particularly heinous or serious violent crimes which provoke strong emotions and fear for safety of the public.* * *

3) Determinate Sentences with a Rehabilitative Purpose In **Ex Parte R.E.C.**, 678 So.2d 1041 (Ala.1995), the Alabama Supreme Court considered whether a juvenile court judge could impose a determinate sentence on a delinquent without adjudicating him and sentencing him under a separate "serious juvenile offender" statute which includes a mandatory minimum commitment of one year. Ala. Code § 12–15–71.1(a) and (b) (1994), *infra* at p. 798. The applicable delinquency sentencing statute authorized the juvenile court to "Make any other order as the court in its discretion shall deem to be for the welfare and best interests of the child, including random drug screens, assessment of fines not to exceed $250, and restitution against the parent, guardian, or child, as the court deems appropriate * * * ", Ala. Code § 12–15–71(c)(4). R.E.C. objected that the statute did not confer on the juvenile court discretionary power to order a determinate commitment as part of a delinquency disposition:

> Drawing a distinction between "punishment" and "rehabilitation," R.E.C. contends that the focus of the Act is rehabilitative, not retributive, and that a determinative commitment like the one ordered in his case is "essentially a punitive sentence," which, he insists, with the exception of the sections specifically applicable to "serious juvenile offenders," the Act "[does] not authorize." The State, by contrast, construes § 12–15–71(c)(4) broadly enough to authorize the juvenile court to "provide for some measure of punishment in fashioning its [commitment] order."

> In our view, R.E.C. places too much emphasis on the distinction he perceives between "rehabilitation" and "punishment." To be sure, this Court has * * * stated that "the intent of the Juvenile Justice Act is not punitive but rehabilitative." However, that case does not stand for the proposition that a determinate sentence is inimical to the concept of rehabilitation. * * *

> We agree that the Act aims to rehabilitate, but we assign particular significance to its two-fold statement of purpose, one of which "is to facilitate the care, protection and discipline of children who come within the jurisdiction of the juvenile court." " 'Discipline' (as a noun) signifies 'punishment; * * * retribution for an offense, especially in a subordinate; * * * control gained by enforcing obedience or order.' As a verb, it means 'to chastise, to impose a penalty upon.' " Moreover, rehabilitation is one of the goals of punishment. To effectuate this goal, the legislature expressly authorized the juvenile court "[t]o hold a child found to be delinquent accountable for his or her actions to the extent of the child's age, * * * background and all other relevant factors and to provide a program of supervision, care, and rehabilitation, including rehabilitative restitution by the child to the victim of [the child's] delinquent acts." Indeed, the Act uses such "rehabilitative" terms virtually interchangeably with "punitive" or "disciplinary" terms. We conclude, therefore, that the legislature did not intend to restrict the juvenile court exclusively to courses of action devoid of an arguably punitive flavor. * * *

> Significant also in this connection is the second prong of the stated purpose of the Juvenile Justice Act, which recognizes that it is "the responsibility of the juvenile court to preserve the public peace and security." No one in this case contends that the juvenile court's authority to order a determinate commitment would not facilitate this goal. Logic and experience suggest that such authority would, indeed, promote public safety. * * *

> Thus, we conclude that, provided certain criteria are met, a determinate commitment is appropriately rehabilitative within the context of the Juvenile Justice Act, even if the juvenile has not been adjudicated a "serious juvenile offender." * * * [A]n order of commitment for a definite period does not offend the Act, even though the juvenile has not been adjudicated a serious juvenile offender, provided that the order is accompanied by specific findings of fact and a reasoned analysis as to how the determinate period is calculated to benefit the juvenile or to further his or

her rehabilitation; and provided, further, that the court's intent to incorporate its order into the Plan plainly appears in the order. * * *

4) Mandatory Minimum Juvenile Sentences and Equal Protection In **State v. J. K. and R. T.**, 383 A.2d 283 (Del.1977), the juvenile court adjudicated R.T. delinquent for committing two separate felony offenses, and adjudicated J.K. delinquent for burglary and he had a prior record.[7] The State contended that both should be sentenced under the Juvenile Mandatory Commitment Act. The juvenile court held the Act unconstitutional and refused to sentence them under its terms. The Delaware Supreme Court upheld the mandatory sentences against the juveniles' equal protection argument that the Act subjected them to mandatory sentences as juveniles but they would be eligible for probation sentences if, following transfer, a criminal court convicted them of the same offenses as adults:

> As we understand its ruling, the Family Court determined that the Act denied equal protection to juveniles found to be "amenable," and hence subject to mandatory commitment, because non-amenable juveniles bound over for the Superior Court [for prosecution as adults] might be placed on probation for committing the same acts. * * *

> The classification of minors for adult and/or juvenile disposition, based upon the amenability tests discussed herein, does not involve "inherently suspect" distinctions * * *. Hence, the traditional principles of equal protection apply, requiring a reasonable basis for the classification.

> We emphasize that the classes under review here are not those of children and adults. The classifications are those of minors only, that is, between minors who are amenable to the Family Court rehabilitative processes and those who are not. We recognize that there is not in this lawsuit a direct attack on such classifications, but that is what underlays the surface criticism of possible difference in consequences for a minor who remains in the Family Court, and one who is bound over for Superior Court for engaging in the same conduct.

> The non-amenability classification of a child is made by judicial decision under the statutory guidelines. * * * Clearly, the object of the classification is to sort out any minors who, because of their personal characteristics and prior criminal conduct, and considering the allegations as to death or serious personal injuries to anyone during commission of the offense, and other relevant factors, are not judged suitable for the rehabilitative processes available in the Family Court. * * * Only after it clearly appears to the Court that a reasonable difference exists between

7. [Ed.] See 10 Del.C. § 937(c)(1) (1976) which provides:

Subject to the provisions governing amenability pursuant to § 938 of this title, the Court shall commit a delinquent child to the custody of the Department of Correction under such circumstances and for such periods of time as hereinafter provided:

(1) Where he has been once or more than once adjudicated delinquent for committing separate and distinct acts or courses of conduct, not arising from the same transaction or occurrence, committed within any 1–year period, which said acts, when aggregated, and were he an adult and tried as such, would constitute 2 offenses designated as felonies, * * * then custody shall be awarded for 1 year;(.)

two juveniles so as to classify one as amenable and one as non-amendable, may the Court bind each of them over to different treatment.

We find the classifications drawn by the amenability process to be reasonable, and we also find that they rest upon a basis of difference bearing a fair and substantial relation to legitimate goals. In this respect, we note that the object of the legislation, rehabilitation, particularly as to youthful offenders, is a compelling State interest. * * * The legislative judgment is that an attempt to salvage something in a juvenile who has committed the equivalent of two separate felonies in one year, should begin with a mandatory commitment for a six-month minimum. * * *

The Delaware scheme creates a classifying technique, the amenability process, which results from the outset in treating two classes of juveniles differently, processing one through the Family Court as a juvenile, and one through the criminal courts as an adult. The plan contemplates different treatment for amenable and non-amenable juveniles, respectively, not merely at the sentencing stage, but from the very early stages of a juvenile's encounter with the State.* * *

The final question certified is whether the Act denies a juvenile sentenced under it the Sixth Amendment right to a jury trial. However, counsel for the juveniles did not brief this question nor did the Family Court decide it. For this reason we do not regard the jury trial issue as before us in this case.[15] * * *

Is the *J.K.* Court's reference to *McKeiver* in its footnote 15 apt? How might the court justify its dicta that a juvenile is not entitled to a jury trial as a prerequisite to imposing a mandatory sentence based on the offense?

5) The Jurisprudence of Sentencing Juveniles *Felder*, *State v. J.K.*, and the note cases provide some conceptual tools with which to analyze juvenile court sentencing laws. **Barry C. Feld, "The Juvenile Court Meets the Principle of Offense: Punishment, Treatment, and the Difference It Makes," 68** *B. U. L. Rev.* **821, 835–915 (1988)** suggests a conceptual framework with which to analyze the differences between punishment and treatment in juvenile courts' sentencing legislation and practices:

The fundamental justification for denying jury trials in delinquency proceedings and, more basically, for maintaining a juvenile justice system separate from the adult one is based on the differences between punishment and treatment. Yet, part of the *McKeiver* Court's failure to distinguish between punishment and treatment in the contemporary juvenile justice system stems from a lack of analytical clarity about the conceptual differences between the two justifications for intervention. Punishment involves the imposition by the State, for purposes of retribution or deterrence, of burdens on an individual who has violated legal prohibitions. Treatment, by contrast, focuses on the mental health, status, and future welfare of the individual rather than on the commission of prohibited acts.

Conceptually, punishment and treatment are mutually exclusive penal goals. Both make markedly different assumptions about the sources of crimi-

---

15. We think it desirable, however, to invite the attention of the Trial Courts to *McKeiver v. Pennsylvania.*

nal or delinquent behavior. Punishment assumes that responsible, free-will moral actors make blameworthy choices and deserve to suffer the prescribed consequences for their acts. Punishment imposes unpleasant consequences because of an offender's past offenses. By contrast, most forms of rehabilitative treatment, including the rehabilitative ideal of the juvenile court, assume some degree of determinism. Whether grounded in psychological or sociological processes, treatment assumes that certain antecedent factors cause the individual's undesirable conditions or behavior. Treatment and therapy, therefore, seek to alleviate undesirable conditions in order to improve the offender's future welfare.

In analyzing juvenile court sentencing practices, it is useful to examine whether the sentencing decision is based upon considerations of the past offense or the future welfare of the offender. When a sentence is based on the characteristics of the offense, it is typically determinate and proportional with the objective of retribution or deterrence. The decision is based upon a assessment of past conduct—the present offense and any prior criminal record. When a sentence is based upon characteristics of the offender, however, it is typically open-ended, non-proportional and indeterminate with the goal of rehabilitation or incapacitation. The decision is based upon a diagnosis or prediction about the effects of intervention on an offender' future course of conduct. * * *

In the adult dispositional framework, determinate sentences based on the offense increasingly supersede indeterminate sentences as "just deserts" displaces rehabilitation as the underlying sentencing rationale. The Progressives' optimistic assumptions about human malleability are challenged daily by the observation that rehabilitation programs fail to consistently rehabilitate and by volumes of empirical evaluations that question both the effectiveness of treatment programs and the "scientific" underpinnings of those who administer the enterprise.

Proponents of "just deserts" reject rehabilitation as a justification for intervention for a number of reasons. First, they argue that an indeterminate sentencing scheme vests too much discretionary power in presumed experts. Second, they point to the inability of such clinical experts to justify their differential treatment of similarly situated offenders based on validated classification schemes with objective indicators. Finally, opponents of rehabilitation emphasize the inequalities, disparities, and injustices that result from therapeutically individualized sentences. "Just deserts" sentencing, with its strong retributive foundation, punishes offenders according to their past behavior rather than on the basis of who they are or who they may become. Similarly situated offenders are defined and sanctioned equally on the basis of relatively objective and legally relevant characteristics such as seriousness of offense, culpability, or criminal history.

The same changes in sentencing philosophy are appearing in the juvenile process as well. However, "just deserts" sentences for juveniles have important implications for *McKeiver*'s therapeutic rationale and procedural implementations. The inability of proponents of juvenile rehabilitation to demonstrate the effectiveness of *parens patriae* intervention has led an increasing number of states to incorporate "just deserts" sentencing principles into their juvenile justice systems. The underlying premises of "just deserts" are that a juvenile's personal characteristics or social circumstances do not provide a principled basis for determining the length or intensity of coercive intervention and that "only a principle of proportionality (or "deserts") provides a logical, fair, and humane hinge between conduct and an official, coercive response." * * *

6) Professional Impetus For Determinacy and Proportionality In the late–1970s, the American Bar Association and the Institute of Judicial Administration promulgated 23 volumes of standards issued by a joint commission and covering the entire field of juvenile justice administration. The Standards were intended as guidelines for action by legislators, judges, administrators, public and private agencies and civic groups responsible for the handling of youths. The volumes ultimately were approved by the ABA House of Delegates for dissemination and to provide the basis for law reform. Two volumes, American Bar Association, *Juvenile Justice Standards Relating to Dispositions* (1980) and *Juvenile Justice Standards Relating to Delinquency and Sanctions* (1980), provided a conceptual impetus for the changing jurisprudence of juvenile justice. The ***Juvenile Justice Standards Relating to Delinquency and Sanctions § 4.1*** (1980) recommended the adoption of determinate and proportional sentences in juvenile courts:

> This move toward determinacy is consistent with the direction of recent statutory changes and with model legislation recently proposed. Determinacy of delinquency sanctions, moreover, is demanded by the logic of the principle of limited intervention. It would make little sense to restrict the occasions for government intervention in the lives of juveniles if any such occasion, however minor, might yield relatively unlimited sanctioning authority." *Id.* at 37. Proposing a ranking of offenses and a corresponding hierarchy of sanctions, "the standard is designed to assure that juvenile court delinquency sanctions that abridge freedom be proportional to the offense committed and determinate in the type and duration of sanction imposed. *Id.* at 39.

The American Bar Association implemented these principles of determinacy and proportional in ***Juvenile Justice Standards Relating to Dispositions*** (1980):

PART I: General Purposes and Limitations

§ 1.1 Purpose:

The purpose of the juvenile correctional system is to reduce juvenile crime by maintaining the integrity of the substantive law proscribing certain behavior and by developing individual responsibility for lawful behavior. This purpose should be pursued through means that are fair and just, that recognize the unique characteristics and needs of juveniles, and that give juveniles access to opportunities for personal and social growth.

Commentary

This standard is based on the premise that we know little about the specific causes of crime and delinquency. The past fifty years have seen the flowering—and the waning—of the conviction that, given adequate research, behavioral and social scientists eventually might pinpoint the causes of delinquency and shape public policy to remove them. Instead, the efforts of science to date have served to illuminate the complexity and virtual insolubility of the problems of the causation and prevention of delinquent behavior. Indeed, if—as social scientists long have maintained—the roots causes of delinquency lie in poverty, racial discrimination, and the breakdown of family structure and values, there may be little that a correctional system can do to reduce crime. * * *

Of the recognized purposes of corrections, none recently has been subject to such relentless attack as rehabilitation. Mounting evidence indicates that the juvenile correctional system does not help young people and may even harm them. Beginning with Professor Allen's critique in the early 1960s, a steadily growing number of social and behavioral scientists have questioned the effectiveness and, indeed, the appropriateness of the "rehabilitative ideal." * * *

In the face of critical research findings, supporters of rehabilitation have argued that the failure to date does not compel abandonment of the ideal, but rather the development of new and better attempts. The standard does not disagree with this position. * * *

The standards are intended to encourage the development of more meaningful ways of providing rehabilitative programs. The standards do reflect, however, the fact that we currently do not possess sufficient knowledge to make rehabilitation the exclusive—or even the fundamental—purpose of corrections. Thus, the standard is intended to serve as a limiting principle designed to narrow the aims of the correctional system to a more modest perspective. * * *

In searching for the limiting principle made necessary by the failure of empirical science to provide the data on which to base a unitary, coherent approach to correctional policy, the standard returns to some of the basic elements of Anglo–American law. One important function of the sanctions provided for in the juvenile criminal code and the correctional system that implements it is to ensure that the code's substantive provisions are observed by making the strictures of the code credible. Thus, according to H.L.A. Hart, certain actions are forbidden by law and designated as offenses "to announce to society that these actions are not to be done and to secure that fewer of them are done."

More important in the framing of a limiting principle is the fundamental legal concept that confines the application of criminal law to past misconduct. * * *

This does not mean that the correctional system must look only to the past. The standard, which recognizes that a correctional system for juveniles also should contain prospective elements, attempts to promote the development of individual responsibility for lawful behavior on the part of offenders by providing opportunities for personal and social growth. The importance of this prospective element reflects the traditional legal perception of the physical dependence of the very young and the slow process of intellectual and emotional maturation during adolescence.[5]

In this view of corrections as one component in a broader system of preventing antisocial behavior, the role of the juvenile correctional system is modest. The system represents one way—and one way only—of dealing with juvenile crime. This attempt to limit the goals, as well as the claims of corrections does not preclude either the obligation of the state to provide a full range of services for juveniles subject to the correctional system (see Part IV of these standards) or broader efforts outside of the correctional system to provide services aimed at improving their social and economic situation to all juveniles. Especially in view of the large number of juveniles who commit delinquent acts but entirely escape the juvenile justice system, no persuasive reason exists for making the correctional system the primary provider of services to juveniles who have broken the law. * * *

DISSENTING VIEWS

Statement of Hon. Justice Wise Polier

* * * The proposed standards invite an abandonment of the goal and raison d'etre of the juvenile court system: the recognition that children should be treated differently from adults and are entitled to receive care and treatment in accordance with their individual needs. They fail to establish or support entitlements for children directed to providing unique benefits under law.

Statement of Commissioner Patricia M. Wald

* * * My view of what should and should not be changed in our juvenile justice system are, at points, sharply divergent.

I would, first of all, reaffirm the bedrock objective of juvenile justice to provide individualized attention to the needs of the juveniles—medical, educational, social, and psychological—insofar as they can reasonably be ascertained and satisfied. Yet the volume nowhere acknowledges the legitimacy of rehabilitation as a goal of the system. Abandonment of this rationale could seriously undermine the constitutional basis for a separate system of juvenile justice. See J. White in *McKeiver v. Pennsylvania*; and J. Harlan in *In re Gault* * * *

In short, I am not yet willing to give up on the concept of rehabilitating juveniles—however unfashionable that idea may currently seem. We are not yet omniscient enough to be sure such attempts will fail, and I hope we are not so cynical as to build a juvenile justice system on the tarnished "just deserts" model of the adult penal system. I agree with the volume that efforts at rehabilitation so far do not justify indefinite sentences or compulsory treatment, but I would continue the legal obligation of judges and correctional

---

5. "Juveniles may be viewed as incomplete adults, lacking in full moral and experiential development, extended unique jural status in other contexts, and deserving of the social moratorium extended by this and all other societies of which I am aware. Thus, removal of the treatment rationale does not destroy the rationale for a separate system or for the utilization of an ameliorative approach; it does, however, require a different rationale." Cohen, Position Paper (Juvenile Justice Standards Project, no. 18, 1974).

personnel to make bona fide attempts at meeting individual juvenile needs in the sentencing and correctional processes.

7) Changes in Juvenile Sentencing Laws to "Crack Down" on Youth Crime In response to increases in youth violence and homicide in the late–1980s and early–1990s, many state legislatures amended their juvenile codes to "get tough" and increase the sentencing powers of juvenile courts. The following excerpt summarizes these recent changes in juvenile justice sentencing policy and practices. **Barry C. Feld, "Juvenile and Criminal Justice Systems' Responses to Youth Violence," 24 *Crime and Justice* 189, 223–228 (1998)**:

1. *Juvenile Court Sentencing Statutes and Dispositional Practices.* Originally, juvenile courts fashioned indeterminate and nonproportional sentences to meet the child's "real needs." In principle, a youth's offense constituted only a diagnostic "symptom" and treatment personnel released the offender once they determined that rehabilitation had occurred. By contrast, when courts punish offenders, they typically impose determinate or mandatory sentences based on the gravity of the past offense. Contrasting indeterminate, nonproportional and offender-oriented dispositions with determinate, proportional, and offense-based sentences provides another indicator of juvenile courts' increasing reliance on punishment as a response to delinquency.

a. *Indeterminate and Determinate Sentences.* Most states' juvenile codes authorized courts to impose indeterminate sentences because penal therapists cannot predict in advance the course or duration of treatment necessary to attain success. While some statutes instruct judges to consider the "least restrictive alternative," most allow the court to confine a delinquent within a range for a period of years or until the offender reaches the age of majority or some other statutory limit. Traditionally, juvenile court judges exercised virtually unrestricted discretion to dismiss, place on probation, remove from home, or institutionalize a youth.

In many states, once a judge sentences a youth to the state's juvenile correctional agency, the judge loses authority over the youth and the correctional authority or parole board determines when to release the juvenile. Indeterminate sentencing statutes typically provide for an unspecified period of confinement and a wide range between the minimum and maximum terms available. Corrections officials base their release decisions, in part, on youths' behavior during confinement and progress toward rehabilitative goals rather than on formal standards or the committing offense.

By contrast, when judges sentence juveniles under a determinate or presumptive sentencing framework, they typically impose proportional sanctions within a relatively narrow dispositional range based on the seriousness of the offense, offense history, and age. In several states, courts impose mandatory minimum sentences based on the offense for which they convicted the youth. In other states, correctional administrators determine youths' presumptive length of institutional stay or eligibility for parole shortly after their commitment based on formal standards that prescribe terms proportional to the seriousness of the offense or prior record.

Currently, nearly half of the states use some type of determinate or mandatory minimum offense-based sentencing provisions to regulate aspects of juvenile dispositions, institutional commitment, or release. As with legislative changes in waiver statutes, amendments to juvenile court sentencing statutes allocate to the judicial, legislative, and executive branches the power to make institutional commitment and release decisions. Determinate sentencing provisions restrict judicial sentencing discretion, mandatory minimum statutes reflect legislative sentencing decisions, and correctional or parole release guidelines enable the executive branch to determine lengths of confinement. And, as with waiver, these provisions use offense criteria to rationalize sentencing decisions, to increase the penal bite of juvenile court sanctions, and to enable legislators symbolically to demonstrate their "toughness" regardless of the impact on juvenile crime rates. It is difficult to attribute the various statutory responses exclusively to youth violence, but rather to the political "felt-need" to punish serious and persistent offenders.

b. *Determinate Sentences in Juvenile Courts.* In 1977, the state of Washington departed dramatically from traditional rehabilitative dispositions, revised its juvenile code to emphasize "just deserts," and became the first state to enact a determinate sentencing statute for delinquents. The Washington law used presumptive sentencing guidelines to achieve offender and system accountability, and based youths' sentences on the seriousness and persistence of their offending rather than their "real needs." * * *

Other jurisdictions also employ offense-based sentencing principles in juvenile courts. In New Jersey, juvenile court judges consider offense, criminal history and statutory "aggravating" and "mitigating" factors to sentence juveniles. Recently, Oklahoma adopted a "serious and habitual juvenile offender" law that targets violent youths and those persistent offenders with three separate felony adjudications and creates a mechanism to develop determinate sentencing guidelines. * * * In 1996, Texas adopted "progressive sanctions guidelines" to "ensure * * * uniform and consistent consequences and punishments that correspond to the seriousness of each offender's current offense, prior delinquent history * * * [and] balance public protection and rehabilitation while holding juvenile offenders accountable." The Texas guidelines assign a youth to one of seven "sanction levels" based on the seriousness of the offense and attach dispositional consequences to each severity level. * * *

c. *Legislative Sentencing Decisions—Mandatory Minimum Terms of Confinement.* Nearly half (twenty-two) of the states use some type of offense-based guidelines to regulate judicial sentencing discretion. These statutes typically include age and offense criteria to define serious or persistent offenders and prescribe their sentences. Juvenile codes in a number of states allow or require judges to impose mandatory minimum sentences for certain serious crimes or "designated felonies." Under some laws, judges retain discretion whether or not to impose the mandated sanctions, whereas others require a judge to commit a youths convicted of defined offense for the mandatory minimum period. * * *

While states' nomenclatures differ, these mandatory minimum sentencing laws typically apply to "violent and repeat offenders," "mandatory sentence offenders," "aggravated juvenile offenders," "habitual offenders," "serious juvenile offenders," or "designated felons." The statutory criteria target those violent and persistent juvenile offenders over whom juvenile courts do not waive jurisdiction either because of their youthfulness or lesser culpability. * * * "Since 1992, fifteen states and the District of Columbia have added or modified statutes that provide for a mandatory minimum period of incarceration of juveniles committing certain violent or other serious crimes."

Most of these mandatory minimum sentencing statutes target youths similar to or only somewhat less serious or younger than those considered eligible for waiver or exclusion to criminal court. In the event that juvenile courts retain jurisdiction over serious young offenders, legislators use mandatory minimum sentences to assure that judges and corrections officials confine these youths for significant terms. For youths convicted of these serious offenses, the statutes prescribe mandatory minimum terms of confinement that range from twelve to eighteen months, to age twenty-one, or to the adult limit for the same offense. * * * Regardless of the statutory details, mandatory minimum sentences based on youths' serious or persistent offending preclude individualized consideration of their "real needs." Moreover, mandating extended minimum terms of confinement for serious offenders increases the average length of stay, and institutional populations, and exacerbates overcrowding.

     d. *Executive Sentencing Decisions—Correctional or Parole Release Guidelines.* A number of states' departments of corrections have adopted administrative security classification and release guidelines that use offense criteria to specify proportional or mandatory minimum terms of institutional confinement. These guidelines constitute still another form of offense-based sentencing. Unlike presumptive or mandatory sentencing statutes that attempt to regulate judicial sentencing discretion, administrative or parole guidelines affect only those youths whom judges commit to states' correctional agencies. Except when constrained by presumptive or mandatory minimum sentencing statutes, judges in most states retain discretion over the "in-out" decision whether to commit a youth. * * *

     All of these *de jure* sentencing provisions—determinate and mandatory minimum laws, and correctional and parole release guidelines—share the common feature of offense-based dispositions. They represent different strategies to relate the duration and intensity of a youth's sentence to the seriousness of the offense and prior record.

     8) States' Serious and Habitual Juvenile Offender Statutes The following statutes provide examples of states' responses to serious youth violence. Consider how these statutes differ in their definitions of "serious juvenile offenders" and how they sentence "serious juvenile offenders." Within the framework of indeterminate and determinate sentences and treatment versus punishment, how might a youth challenge the sentences imposed?

     Alabama Code § 12–15–71.1 (1998).

     (a) The juvenile court may find a child to be a serious juvenile offender if:

     (1) The child is adjudicated delinquent and the delinquent act or acts charged in the petition would constitute any of the following if committed by an adult:

    a. Class A felony;

    b. A felony resulting in serious physical injury * * *;

    c. A felony involving physical force * * *, or a deadly weapon * * *, or a dangerous instrument * * *; or

(2) The child has been adjudicated delinquent for an act which would constitute a Class A or B felony or burglary in the third degree involving a residence and the child has previously been adjudicated delinquent of two previous acts which would have been a Class A or B felony or burglary in the third degree involving a residence if such acts had been committed by an adult.

(b) A child found to be a serious juvenile offender shall be committed to the custody of the Alabama Department of Youth Services, where he shall remain for a minimum of one year.

(c) A serious juvenile offender review panel shall be created by the Board of the Alabama Department of Youth Services. The serious juvenile offender review panel shall review quarterly the progress of each serious juvenile offender and determine at the end of the one year term served by each child, further treatment plan for that child. The panel may extend the commitment, order alternative treatment or release the child. The serious juvenile offender review panel must provide the court with all reports and recommendations, and notify the judge in writing of the decision to release the child at least 30 days in advance of said release.

(d) The Alabama Department of Youth Services shall maintain and staff a separate, secure facility and implement programs for serious juvenile offenders. The minimum one year term required by this section shall be served at said facility and the review panel may extend the period of confinement in said facility as determined necessary. * * *

Louisiana Children's Code Art. 897.1 (1999). Disposition after adjudication of certain felony-grade delinquent acts

A. Notwithstanding any other provision of law to the contrary, after adjudication of a felony-grade delinquent act based upon * * * first degree murder; * * * second degree murder; * * * aggravated rape; * * * aggravated kidnapping; * * * armed robbery; * * * treason; the court shall commit the child to the custody of the Department of Public Safety and Corrections to be placed within a secure detention facility until the child attains the age of twenty-one years without benefit of parole, probation, suspension of imposition or execution of sentence, modification, or furlough.

B. Notwithstanding any other provision of law to the contrary, after adjudication of a felony-grade delinquent act based upon * * * armed robbery, the court shall commit the child to the custody of the Department of Public Safety and Corrections to be placed within a secure detention facility for the length of the term imposed by the court at the disposition hearing without benefit of parole, probation, suspension of imposition or execution of sentence, modification, or furlough.

9) Analysis of Serious and Habitual Juvenile Offender Statutes
Although many legislatures opt primarily for "get tough" provisions rather

than for treatment programs with a secure component, **Julianne P. Sheffer, "Serious and Habitual Juvenile Offender Statutes: Reconciling Punishment and Rehabilitation Within the Juvenile Justice System," 48** *Vand. L. Rev.* **479, 489–493, 496–499, 502–504 (1995),** argues that state sentencing policies can reconcile punitive and therapeutic purposes in their juvenile sentencing laws:

At least sixteen states have enacted statutes specifically addressing the problem of sentencing serious and habitual juvenile offenders. Some of these statutes set forth special sentencing criteria for a specific list of particularly severe or violent crimes. Other statutes set forth a definition of a "serious or habitual juvenile offender" and combine this with a section or provision for the disposition of juveniles who satisfy the criteria. Generally, only children above a certain minimum age are subject to the terms of a serious and habitual juvenile offender statute, but this limitation is by no means universal.

Despite differences in form, all serious and habitual juvenile offender statutes are, to a degree, punitive. Their punitive nature can be seen in two ways. First, some statutes expressly acknowledge their punitive purposes. Second, all serious and habitual juvenile offender statutes impose particular sentences, or give the court authority to impose tougher sentences, based on the offense a juvenile commits. Statutes which set forth a sentence or disposition based on the crime committed (as opposed to focusing on individual characteristics of the juvenile offender) are, according to current theory, primarily designed to punish rather than to rehabilitate.

Serious and habitual juvenile offender statutes do, however, vary in the means chosen to achieve their punitive goals. * * * [T]he typical approaches fall into two major categories: (1) "get tough" reforms; and (2) integrated serious and habitual juvenile offender programs.

The phrase "get tough" refers to those statutory reforms which are primarily designed to impose harsher or more certain punishments on juveniles. Generally, such statutes minimize or eliminate specific attempts at rehabilitating or treating delinquent youth. Typical get tough approaches include: (1) imposing mandatory minimum sentences or sentencing ranges for listed offenses; (2) authorizing the juvenile court to impose a determinate sentence for specified offenses, rather than the traditional indeterminate period used for the majority of delinquent acts; (3) authorizing the juvenile court to impose a longer period of incarceration, up to a statutory maximum, for certain serious offenses; (4) authorizing the juvenile court to impose harsher sentences, at the discretion of the juvenile judge, on youths who commit certain listed crimes; (5) extending the juvenile court's jurisdiction over serious juvenile offenders to a later age than is allowed for non-serious juvenile delinquents; (6) giving the juvenile court discretion to place the serious or habitual offender in an adult facility; and (7) authorizing the court to place serious or habitual juvenile offenders in juvenile boot camps. * * *

The second type of statute implements integrated serious and habitual juvenile offender programs. In contrast to "get tough" statutes, these programs attempt to combine punishment and rehabilitation in a single, comprehensive plan. To the extent they succeed, integrated serious and habitual juvenile offender ("SHJO") statutes demonstrate that rehabilitation and punishment are compatible, both in theory and in practice. These comprehensive programs * * * thereby support the claim that punitive reforms can be reconciled with—and perhaps improve upon—the juvenile court's traditionally rehabilitative focus.

Integrated programs for serious and habitual juvenile offenders exist in approximately one-third to one-half of all U.S. jurisdictions. The characteristics of these programs vary considerably from state to state, and therefore any attempt to evaluate such programs inevitably involves some degree of generalization. * * * The phrase "integrated serious and habitual juvenile offender (SHJO) program," * * * refers to such a model approach, although the names (and details) of such programs vary in practice.

The very design of most integrated SHJO programs demonstrates a continued commitment to achieving both punishment and rehabilitation. The common characteristics of SHJO programs include: an initial period of incarceration or detention; the use of small facilities; an emphasis on accountability; intensive supervision throughout the program; and a substantial offering of rehabilitation services.

For example, most integrated SHJO programs involve an initial period of incarceration in a secure facility or in the home, using house arrest or daily contacts with the probation officer. This initial period of incarceration or in-home confinement is clearly designed to fulfill punitive objectives: community protection through deterrence and incarceration, as well as, to a certain extent, retribution. Overwhelmingly, such programs require or emphasize detention in small, non-institutional settings. Integrated SHJO programs also emphasize accountability, both through the detention period, and by requiring victim restitution.

In addition, integrated SHJO programs generally require intensive supervision for a relatively lengthy period of time after the initial period of full confinement. Such periods of frequent and highly-structured supervision are designed to satisfy two goals. One is continued punishment (both social control and retribution). A second is ensuring continued contact with the offender so that rehabilitative services may be delivered effectively.

Indeed, a hallmark of integrated SHJO programs is that they provide a wide array of rehabilitation services, which frequently continue for substantial lengths of time after the initial period of incarceration is complete. For many programs, a primary rationale for such services, and the principal focus of their delivery, is to increase the likelihood of the juvenile's successful reintegration into society.

Integrated serious and habitual juvenile offender programs, emphasizing initial detention, accountability, and treatment and reintegration services, are plainly designed to achieve a workable balance between the rehabilitative and punitive goals of the juvenile justice system. * * *

3. THE JUSTICE MODEL OF JUVENILE JUSTICE—THE WASHINGTON CASE-STUDY

For most of the twentieth century, theories of positivism prevailed and juvenile court judges based sentencing practices on utilitarian, preventive, or rehabilitative purposes. *See e.g.*, David Garland, *Culture of Control* (2002). Indeterminate sentences were the norm to treat rather than to punish youths and the duration of confinement was supposed to relate to the juvenile's need for rehabilitation. The most dramatic departure from traditional *parens patriae* juvenile rehabilitation occurred in 1977, when the State of Washington enacted "just deserts" sentencing principles for its juvenile justice system. The primary goals of the new legislation were to assure individual and systemic accountability through presumptive sentencing guidelines. The legislation created a juvenile sentencing guidelines commission to emphasize uniformity, consistency, proportionality, equality and accountability. Under these guidelines, presumptive sentences—standard range—are determinate and proportional to the age of the offender, the seriousness of the offense, and the juvenile's prior record. Over the past three decades, the guidelines have evolved to give judges greater discretion to depart from the presumptive guidelines and to use chemical dependency, mental health, or sex offender disposition alternatives. Judges may also impose upward departures from the presumptive guidelines if the guideline sentence would constitute a "manifest injustice." The statutes also allow juveniles to appeal from departures from the standard range and Washington's appellate courts have addressed a number of sentencing policy issues. The following statutes and cases provide a detailed case study of one of the most significant departures from traditional juvenile court sentencing policy and practice.

Rev. Code of Washington § 13.40.010 (2004):

(2) It is the intent of the legislature that a system capable of having primary responsibility for, being accountable for, and responding to the needs of youthful offenders, as defined by this chapter, be established. It is the further intent of the legislature that youth, in turn, be held accountable for their offenses and that both communities and the juvenile courts carry out their functions consistent with this intent. To effectuate these policies, it shall be the purpose of this chapter to:

(a) Protect the citizenry from criminal behavior;

(b) Provide for determining whether accused juveniles have committed offenses as defined by this chapter;

(c) Make the juvenile offender accountable for his or her criminal behavior;

(d) Provide for punishment commensurate with the age, crime, and criminal history of the juvenile offender;

(e) Provide due process for juveniles alleged to have committed an offense;

(f) Provide necessary treatment, supervision, and custody for juvenile offenders;

(g) Provide for the handling of juvenile offenders by communities whenever consistent with public safety;

(h) Provide for restitution to victims of crime;

(i) Develop effective standards and goals for the operation, funding, and evaluation of all components of the juvenile justice system and related services at the state and local levels;

(j) Provide for a clear policy to determine what types of offenders shall receive punishment, treatment, or both, and to determine the jurisdictional limitations of the courts, institutions, and community services;

(k) Provide opportunities for victim participation in juvenile justice process, including court hearings on juvenile offender matters, and ensure that * * * the victim bill of rights is fully observed; and

(*l*) Encourage the parents, guardian, or custodian of the juvenile to actively participate in the juvenile justice process.

Rev. Code of Washington § 13.40.020 (2004).

For the purposes of this chapter:

(1) "Community-based rehabilitation" means one or more of the following: Employment; attendance of information classes; literacy classes; counseling, outpatient substance abuse treatment programs, outpatient mental health programs, anger management classes, education or outpatient treatment programs to prevent animal cruelty, or other services; or attendance at school or other educational programs appropriate for the juvenile as determined by the school district. Placement in community-based rehabilitation programs is subject to available funds;

(2) Community-based sanctions may include one or more of the following:

(a) A fine, not to exceed five hundred dollars;

(b) Community service not to exceed one hundred fifty hours of service;

(3) "Community restitution" means compulsory service, without compensation, performed for the benefit of the community by the offender as punishment for committing an offense. Community service may be performed through public or private organizations or through work crews;

(4) "Community supervision" means an order of disposition by the court of an adjudicated youth not committed to the department or an order granting a deferred disposition. A community supervision order for a single offense may be for a period of up to two years for a sex offense * * * and up to one year for other offenses. As a mandatory condition of

any term of community supervision, the court shall order the juvenile to refrain from committing new offenses. As a mandatory condition of community supervision, the court shall order the juvenile to comply with the mandatory school attendance provisions * * * and to inform the school of the existence of this requirement. Community supervision is an individualized program comprised of one or more of the following:

(a) Community-based sanctions;

(b) Community-based rehabilitation;

(c) Monitoring and reporting requirements;

(d) Posting of a probation bond;

(5) "Confinement" means physical custody by the department of social and health services in a facility operated by or pursuant to a contract with the state, or physical custody in a detention facility operated by or pursuant to a contract with any county. * * * Pretrial confinement or confinement of less than thirty-one days imposed as part of a disposition or modification order may be served consecutively or intermittently, in the discretion of the court; * * *

(15) "Juvenile offender" means any juvenile who has been found by the juvenile court to have committed an offense, including a person eighteen years of age or older over whom jurisdiction has been extended under RCW 13.40.300;

(16) "Local sanctions" means one or more of the following: (a) 0–30 days of confinement; (b) 0–12 months of community supervision; (c) 0–150 hours of community service; or (d) $0–$500 fine;

(17) "Manifest injustice" means a disposition that would either impose an excessive penalty on the juvenile or would impose a serious, and clear danger to society in light of the purposes of this chapter; * * *.

Rev. Code Washington § 13.40.030 (2003).

(1) The secretary shall submit guidelines pertaining to the nature of the security to be imposed on youth placed in his or her custody based on the age, offense(s), and criminal history of the juvenile offender. * * *

(2) The permissible ranges of confinement resulting from a finding of manifest injustice under RCW 13.40.0357 are subject to the following limitations:

(a) Where the maximum term in the range is ninety days or less, the minimum term in the range may be no less than fifty percent of the maximum term in the range;

(b) Where the maximum term in the range is greater than ninety days but not greater than one year, the minimum term in the range may be no less than seventy-five percent of the maximum term in the range; and

(c) Where the maximum term in the range is more than one year, the minimum term in the range may be no less than eighty percent of the maximum term in the range.

Rev. Code Washington § 13.40.150 (2004). Disposition hearing—Scope—Factors to be considered prior to entry of dispositional order

(1) In disposition hearings all relevant and material evidence, including oral and written reports, may be received by the court and may be relied upon to the extent of its probative value, even though such evidence may not be admissible in a hearing on the information. The youth or the youth's counsel and the prosecuting attorney shall be afforded an opportunity to examine and controvert written reports so received and to cross-examine individuals making reports when such individuals are reasonably available, but sources of confidential information need not be disclosed. The prosecutor and counsel for the juvenile may submit recommendations for disposition. * * *

(3) Before entering a dispositional order as to a respondent found to have committed an offense, the court shall hold a disposition hearing, at which the court shall: * * *

(a) Consider the facts supporting the allegations of criminal conduct by the respondent;

(b) Consider information and arguments offered by parties and their counsel;

(c) Consider any predisposition reports;

(d) Consult with the respondent's parent, guardian, or custodian on the appropriateness of dispositional options under consideration and afford the respondent and the respondent's parent, guardian, or custodian an opportunity to speak in the respondent's behalf;

(e) Allow the victim or a representative of the victim and an investigative law enforcement officer to speak;

(f) Determine the amount of restitution owing to the victim, if any, or set a hearing for a later date not to exceed one hundred eighty days from the date of the disposition hearing to determine the amount, except that the court may continue the hearing beyond the one hundred eighty days for good cause;

(g) Determine the respondent's offender score;

(h) Consider whether or not any of the following mitigating factors exist:

(i) The respondent's conduct neither caused nor threatened serious bodily injury or the respondent did not contemplate that his or her conduct would cause or threaten serious bodily injury;

(ii) The respondent acted under strong and immediate provocation;

(iii) The respondent was suffering from a mental or physical condition that significantly reduced his or her culpability for the offense though failing to establish a defense;

(iv) Prior to his or her detection, the respondent compensated or made a good faith attempt to compensate the victim for the injury or loss sustained; and

(v) There has been at least one year between the respondent's current offense and any prior criminal offense;

(i) Consider whether or not any of the following aggravating factors exist:

(i) In the commission of the offense, or in flight therefrom, the respondent inflicted or attempted to inflict serious bodily injury to another;

(ii) The offense was committed in an especially heinous, cruel, or depraved manner;

(iii) The victim or victims were particularly vulnerable;

(iv) The respondent has a recent criminal history or has failed to comply with conditions of a recent dispositional order or diversion agreement;

(v) The current offense included a finding of sexual motivation * * *;

(vi) The respondent was the leader of a criminal enterprise involving several persons;

(vii) There are other complaints which have resulted in diversion or a finding or plea of guilty but which are not included as criminal history; and

(viii) The standard range disposition is clearly too lenient considering the seriousness of the juvenile's prior adjudications.

Rev. Code Washington § 13.40.160 (2004). Disposition order

(1) The standard range disposition for a juvenile adjudicated of an offense is determined according to RCW 13.40.0357.

(a) When the court sentences an offender to a local sanction as provided in RCW 13.40.0357 option A, the court shall impose a determinate disposition within the standard ranges, except as provided in subsections (2), (3), (4), (5), or (6) of this section. The disposition may be comprised of one or more local sanctions.

(b) When the court sentences an offender to a standard range as provided in RCW 13.40.0357 option A that includes a term of confinement exceeding thirty days, commitment shall be to the department for the standard range of confinement, except as provided in subsections (2), (3), (4), (5), or (6) of this section.

(2) If the court concludes, and enters reasons for its conclusion, that disposition within the standard range would effectuate a manifest injus-

tice the court shall impose a disposition outside the standard range, as indicated in option C of RCW 13.40.0357. The court's finding of manifest injustice shall be supported by clear and convincing evidence.

A disposition outside the standard range shall be determinate and shall be comprised of confinement or community supervision, or a combination thereof. When a judge finds a manifest injustice and imposes a sentence of confinement exceeding thirty days, the court shall sentence the juvenile to a maximum term, and the provisions of RCW 13.40.030(2) shall be used to determine the range. A disposition outside the standard range is appealable * * * by the state or the respondent. A disposition within the standard range is not appealable * * *.

(3) When a juvenile offender is found to have committed a sex offense, other than a sex offense that is also a serious violent offense* * * and has no history of a prior sex offense, the court, on its own motion or the motion of the state or the respondent, may order an examination to determine whether the respondent is amenable to treatment. * * *

After receipt of reports of the examination, the court shall then consider whether the offender and the community will benefit from use of this special sex offender disposition alternative and consider the victim's opinion whether the offender should receive a treatment disposition under this section. If the court determines that this special sex offender disposition alternative is appropriate, then the court shall impose a determinate disposition within the standard range for the offense, or if the court concludes, and enters reasons for its conclusions, that such disposition would cause a manifest injustice, the court shall impose a disposition under option D, and the court may suspend the execution of the disposition and place the offender on community supervision for at least two years. As a condition of the suspended disposition, the court may impose the conditions of community supervision and other conditions, including up to thirty days of confinement and requirements that the offender [receive out-patient or in-patient sex offender treatment and comply with other conditions of probation] * * *

A disposition entered under this subsection (3) is not appealable * * *.

(11) In no case shall the term of confinement imposed by the court at disposition exceed that to which an adult could be subjected for the same offense.

Rev. Code of Washington § 13.40.165 (2004). Chemical dependency disposition alternative

(1) The purpose of this disposition alternative is to ensure that successful treatment options to reduce recidivism are available to eligible youth. * * * The court must consider eligibility for the chemical dependency disposition alternative when a juvenile offender is subject to a standard range disposition of local sanctions or 15 to 36 weeks of confinement and has not committed an A− or B+ offense, other than a first time

B+ offense. * * * The court, on its own motion or the motion of the state or the respondent if the evidence shows that the offender may be chemically dependent or substance abusing, may order an examination by a chemical dependency counselor from a chemical dependency treatment facility * * * to determine if the youth is chemically dependent or substance abusing. The offender shall pay the cost of any examination ordered under this subsection unless the court finds that the offender is indigent and no third party insurance coverage is available, in which case the state shall pay the cost. * * *

(5) (b) If the court determines that this chemical dependency disposition alternative is appropriate, then the court shall impose the standard range for the offense, or if the court concludes, and enters reasons for its conclusion, that such disposition would effectuate a manifest injustice, the court shall impose a disposition above the standard range as indicated in option D of RCW 13.40.0357 if the disposition is an increase from the standard range and the confinement of the offender does not exceed a maximum of fifty-two weeks, suspend execution of the disposition, and place the offender on community supervision for up to one year. As a condition of the suspended disposition, the court shall require the offender to undergo available outpatient drug/alcohol treatment and/or inpatient drug/alcohol treatment. For purposes of this section, inpatient treatment may not exceed ninety days. As a condition of the suspended disposition, the court may impose conditions of community supervision and other sanctions, including up to thirty days of confinement, one hundred fifty hours of community restitution, and payment of legal financial obligations and restitution. * * *

Determining a Youth's Sentence. Washington's juvenile justice sentencing standards base a juvenile's disposition on the seriousness of the offense and the prior record. The Offense Category table below provides examples of the classification of offense seriousness. The sentencing grid that follows illustrate how a judge arrives at a youth's disposition based on the nature of the present offense and prior record, any aggravating or mitigating factors proved at the dispositional hearing, and the youth's need for treatment as well as punishment.

Rev. Code of Washington § 13.40.0357 (1998). Juvenile offender sentencing standards

Description and Offense Category

Juvenile Disposition Offense Category	Description (RCW Citation)	Juvenile Disposition Category for Attempt, Bailjump, Conspiracy, or Solicitation
	Arson and Malicious Mischief	
A	Arson 1 (9A.48.020)	B+
B	Arson 2 (9A.48.030)	C
C	Reckless Burning 1 (9A.48.040)	D
B	Malicious Mischief 1 (9A.48.070)	C

* * *

Juvenile Disposition Offense Category	Description (RCW Citation)	Juvenile Disposition Category for Attempt, Bailjump, Conspiracy, or Solicitation
	Assault and Other Crimes Involving Physical Harm	
A	Assault 1 (9A.36.011)	B+
B+	Assault 2 (9A.36.021)	C+
C+	Assault 3 (9A.36.031)	D+
D+	Assault 4 (9A.36.041)	E
	* * *	
	Burglary and Trespass	
B+	Burglary 1 (9A.52.020)	C+
B	Residential Burglary (9A.52.025)	C
B	Burglary 2 (9A.52.030)	C
	* * *	
	Drugs	
E	Possession/Consumption of Alcohol	E
C	Illegally Obtaining Legend Drug	D
C+	Sale, Delivery, Possession of Legend Drug with Intent to Sell	D+
E	Possession of Legend Drug	E
	* * *	
	Firearms and Weapons	
B	Theft of Firearm (9A.56.300)	C
B	Possession of Stolen Firearm (9A.56.310)	C
E	Carrying Loaded Pistol Without Permit	E
C	Possession of Firearms by Minor (<18)	C
	* * *	
	Homicide	
A+	Murder 1 (9A.32.030)	A
A+	Murder 2 (9A.32.050)	B+
B+	Manslaughter 1 (9A.32.060)	C+
C+	Manslaughter 2 (9A.32.070)	D+
B+	Vehicular Homicide (46.61.520)	C+
	* * *	
	Kidnapping	
A	Kidnap 1 (9A.40.020)	B+
B+	Kidnap 2 (9A.40.030)	C+
C+	Unlawful Imprisonment (9A.40.040)	D+
	* * *	

Juvenile Disposition Offense Category	Description (RCW Citation)	Juvenile Disposition Category for Attempt, Bailjump, Conspiracy, or Solicitation
	Sex Crimes	
A	Rape 1 (9A.44.040)	B+
A–	Rape 2 (9A.44.050)	B+
C+	Rape 3 (9A.44.060)	D+
	* * *	
	Theft, Robbery, Extortion, and Forgery	
B	Theft 1 (9A.56.030)	C
C	Theft 2 (9A.56.040)	D
D	Theft 3 (9A.56.050)	E
	* * *	
	Other	
A	Other Offense Equivalent to an Adult Class A Felony	B+
B	Other Offense Equivalent to an Adult Class B Felony	C
C	Other Offense Equivalent to an Adult Class C Felony	D
D	Other Offense Equivalent to an Adult Gross Misdemeanor	E
E	Other Offense Equivalent to an Adult Misdemeanor	E
V	Violation of Order of Restitution, Community Supervision or Confinement (13.40.200)[1]	V

Juvenile Sentencing Standards

This schedule must be used for juvenile offenders. The court may select sentencing option A, B, C, D, or RCW 13.40.167 [Mental health disposition alternative]

---

1. If the court finds that a respondent has violated terms of an order, it may impose a penalty of up to 30 days of confinement

STANDARD RANGE

CURRENT OFFENSE CATEGORY	0	1	2	3	4 or more
A+	180 weeks to age 21 for all category A+ offenses				
A	103 - 129 weeks for all category A offenses				
A-	15 - 36 weeks Except 30 – 40 weeks for 15 to 17 year olds	52 - 65 weeks	80 - 100 weeks	103 - 129 weeks	103 - 129 weeks
B+	15 - 36 weeks	15 – 36 weeks	52 - 65 weeks	80 - 100 weeks	103 - 129 weeks
B	LS	LS	15 - 36 weeks	15 - 36 weeks	52 - 65 weeks
C+	LS	LS	LS	15 - 36 weeks	15 - 36 weeks
C	LS	LS	LS	LS	15 - 36 weeks
D+	LS	LS	LS	LS	LS
D	LS	LS	LS	LS	LS
E	LS	LS	LS	LS	LS

PRIOR ADJUDICATIONS

Option A

Juvenile Offender Sentencing Grid Standard Range

NOTE: References in the grid to days or weeks mean periods of confinement.

(1) The vertical axis of the grid is the current offense category. The current offense category is determined by the offense of adjudication.

(2) The horizontal axis of the grid is the number of prior adjudications included in the juvenile's criminal history. Each prior felony adjudication shall count as one point. Each prior violation, misdemeanor, and gross misdemeanor adjudication shall count as 1/4 point. Fractional points shall be rounded down.

(3) The standard range disposition for each offense is determined by the intersection of the column defined by the prior adjudications and the row defined by the current offense category.

(4) RCW 13.40.180 applies if the offender is being sentenced for more than one offense.

(5) A current offense that is a violation is equivalent to an offense category of E. However, a disposition for a violation shall not include confinement.

OR

OPTION B

SUSPENDED DISPOSITION ALTERNATIVE

(1) If the offender is subject to a standard range disposition involving confinement by the department, the court may impose the standard range and suspend the disposition on condition that the offender comply with one or more local sanctions and any educational or treatment requirement. The treatment programs provided to the offender must be either research-based best practice programs as identified by the Washington state institute for public policy or the joint legislative audit and review committee, or for chemical dependency treatment programs or services, they must be evidence-based or research-based best practice programs. For the purposes of this subsection:

(a) "Evidence-based" means a program or practice that has had multiple site random controlled trials across heterogeneous populations demonstrating that the program or practice is effective for the population; and

(b) "Research-based" means a program or practice that has some research demonstrating effectiveness, but that does not yet meet the standard of evidence-based practices.

(2) If the offender fails to comply with the suspended disposition, the court may impose sanctions pursuant to RCW 13.40.200 or may revoke the suspended disposition and order the disposition's execution.

(3) An offender is ineligible for the suspended disposition option under this section if the offender is:

(a) Adjudicated of an A+ offense;

(b) Fourteen years of age or older and is adjudicated of one or more of the following offenses:

(i) A class A offense, or an attempt, conspiracy, or solicitation to commit a class A offense;

(ii) Manslaughter in the first degree; or

(iii) Assault in the second degree, extortion in the first degree, kidnapping in the second degree, robbery in the second degree, residential burglary, burglary in the second degree, drive-by shooting, vehicular homicide, hit and run death, intimidating a witness, violation of the uniform controlled substances act, or manslaughter 2, when the offense includes infliction of bodily harm upon another or when during the commission or immediate withdrawal from the offense the respondent was armed with a deadly weapon;

(c) Ordered to serve a disposition for a firearm violation * * *; or

(d) Adjudicated of a sex offense * * *.

OR

OPTION C

CHEMICAL DEPENDENCY DISPOSITION ALTERNATIVE

If the juvenile offender is subject to a standard range disposition of local sanctions or 15 to 36 weeks of confinement and has not committed an A– or B+ offense, the court may impose a disposition under * * * RCW 13.40.165 [Chemical dependency disposition alternative]

OR

OPTION D

MANIFEST INJUSTICE

If the court determines that a disposition under option A, B, or C would effectuate a manifest injustice, the court shall impose a disposition outside the standard range under RCW 13.40.160(2).

STATE v. RICE

98 Wash.2d 384, 655 P.2d 1145 (1982).

PEARSON, JUSTICE. [The juvenile court adjudicated Daniel Rice guilty of attempted criminal trespass, a misdemeanor. Monte Sanchez pleaded guilty to a misdemeanor assault. Both defendants] appeal the length of terms of confinement in disposition orders issued by the juvenile division of the Superior Court. The issues raised on appeal are twofold: first, whether the legislature intended that juvenile dispositions under RCW 13.40 may include terms of confinement which exceed the maximum sentences allowed by RCW 9A.20.020; second, if the legislature so intended, whether confining juveniles for periods longer than the maximum allowed for adults violates the equal protection clauses of the United States and Washington constitutions. We hold that the legislature did not intend RCW 9A.20.020 to apply to juvenile dispositions, and that imposing longer terms of confinement on juveniles than on adults does not violate the requirement of equal protection.

At the disposition hearing * * * Rice's parole officer recommended a 52–65 week commitment. Rice had a history of prior offenses. * * * Rice's counsel conceded at the disposition hearing that the standard range disposition of 20–35 hours of community service or 3 months of community supervision was inadequate in light of the parole officer's report. However, he argued that Rice's sentence should be limited to the 90–day maximum allowed under RCW 9A.20.020 for an adult convicted of a misdemeanor. The court found a manifest injustice on Rice's recent criminal history, violations of the terms of prior dispositions, refusal to submit to supervision, and the other aggravating factors in the file. Rice was committed to the Department of Institutions for a period of 52 weeks. * * *

The juvenile parole officer recommended a manifest injustice sentence and commitment to the Department of Institutions. Sanchez had a prior criminal history. * * * The court found that the limits established by the category of offender disposition of 10–20 days' detention, 80–110 hours' community service, and 1 year community supervision was insufficient for the defendant. It ordered a manifest injustice sentence of 52 weeks' confinement; this was based on the short time since Sanchez' prior offense and his being still under community supervision at the time of the present offense, the lack of parental control, his failure to comply with a prior diversion agreement, and the fact that community supervision would not provide the structure necessary for his rehabilitation and correction.

Defendants argue that their terms of commitment on a finding of manifest injustice cannot exceed the maximum terms laid down in RCW 9A.20.020. This section sets out maximum sentences which may be imposed on persons convicted of offenses. The maximum sentence for a misdemeanor is 90 days' imprisonment or $1,000 fine or both. Defendants argue that this section applies to dispositions under the Juvenile Justice Act of 1977, (hereinafter JJA), as well as to adult criminal sentences. They argue that the legislature intended that RCW 9A.20.020 apply to all sentences, including juvenile dispositions. They argue further that the legislature could not have legislated otherwise because to impose longer terms of confinement on children than on adults would violate the equal protection clauses of the United States and Washington constitutions. We disagree. We hold that the legislature did not intend RCW 9A.20.020 to apply to juvenile dispositions. And equal protection does not preclude the legislature's mandating longer terms of confinement for children than for adults.

We begin our analysis with a very brief review of the history of our juvenile justice system, so as to place the present legislation in a historical perspective. * * * The Juvenile Justice Act of 1977 is clearly an effort to overcome the inadequacies of the juvenile justice system. In this effort the legislature has departed from wholehearted acceptance of the philosophy which impelled the old system. * * *

However, it would be a mistake to assume that the new legislation has turned completely from the ideal of rehabilitating juvenile offenders. The new legislation clearly does not set up a rigidly punitive system which mirrors in every respect the adult criminal justice system. This is particularly true in the matter under consideration in this appeal, the disposition of the juvenile offender. The purposes underlying the juvenile system and the procedures designed to effect those purposes are significantly different from the purposes and procedures of the adult system. * * *

The purposes and policies underlying the JJA are rather more complex than these sentencing purposes in the adult criminal justice system. The formal statement of the intent of the legislature in enacting the JJA is found in RCW 13.40.010(2). This provision states first, the policies of the Act, and second, the purposes of the Act. The policies are twofold: to establish a system of having primary responsibility for, being accountable for, and responding to the needs of youthful offenders; and to hold juveniles accountable for their offenses.

The critical distinction here is that nowhere in RCW 9.94A.010, or anywhere else in the adult criminal justice system, is there expressed a policy of "responding to the needs" of offenders. Much less is such a policy stated as the first of the two policies underlying the whole system. This legislative directive that the juvenile system respond to the needs of the offender is therefore one of considerable significance. It clearly indicates that the juvenile system is to some extent geared to respond to the needs of the child. Thus, while some of the ten policies of the JJA are similar to the purposes of the adult system, others go beyond anything provided in the adult system. In particular, RCW 13.40.010(2)(f) and (j) both provide for treatment of juvenile offenders. Such "treatment" may be given in lieu of or in addition to punishment. Nowhere in the statute is "treatment" defined; it is not limited to any particular kind of "treatment." The provision of "treatment" appears to be one way in which the system can respond to the needs of the juvenile offender, and the appropriate treatment would be determined by the nature of those needs.

Thus, while the JJA shares with the adult system the purposes of rendering a child accountable for his acts, punishing him and exacting retribution from him, such purposes are tempered by, and in some cases must give way to, purposes of responding to the needs of the child. In other words, the JJA has not utterly abandoned the rehabilitative ideal which impelled the juvenile justice system for decades. It does not embrace a purely punitive or retributive philosophy. Instead, it attempts to tread an equatorial line somewhere midway between the poles of rehabilitation and retribution. * * *

We have previously recognized the dichotomy of purpose in the JJA. We noted in *In re Smiley*, that the JJA had replaced *parens patriae* as the single guiding principle of juvenile justice, with twin principles of rehabilitation and punishment. Therefore, in resolving any issue which turns on the legislative purpose of this Act, we must ensure that our decision effectuates to the fullest possible extent both the purpose of rehabilitation and the purpose of punishment.

With this in mind, we turn to consider the provisions of the JJA which deal with the disposition of juvenile offenders. Any juvenile offender over whom jurisdiction is not declined or who is not diverted from prosecution is subject to the juvenile court procedures. After a plea of guilty or a finding by the court that the prosecution has proved the allegations of the information beyond a reasonable doubt a disposition hearing is held. For the purposes of disposition, the court may consider a wide variety of matters including aggravating and mitigating factors. In most cases the court is required to order a disposition within the standard range for the offense. The disposition standards are established by the juvenile disposition standards committee. * * * The standards establish ranges which may include either confinement or community supervision, or both, on the basis of a youth's age, the instant offense, and the history and seriousness of previous offenses. The statute provides both upper and lower limits on the standard range. Upper limits may not exceed that to which an adult may be subjected for the same offense. And the minimum term may not be less than 50 percent of the maximum where the maximum is 90 days or less, 75 percent of the maximum where the maximum is 90 days to 1 year, and 80 percent of the maximum where the maximum is more than 1 year. In no event may the juvenile be committed by the juvenile court beyond his twenty-first birthday.

The court must in each case order a disposition within the standard range unless to do so would effectuate a "manifest injustice." A manifest injustice is defined in [as]: "a disposition that would impose an excessive penalty on the juvenile or a clear danger to society in light of the purposes of this chapter." It is this concept of manifest injustice which is central to the issues before us. The statute clearly requires * * * that the standard range of disposition may not exceed the adult maximum specified. * * * But the court may exceed the standard range maximum where necessary to avoid "a clear danger to society in light of the purposes of" the JJA. The issue is, therefore, whether the adult maximum of RCW 9A.20.020 applies to the manifest injustice disposition as well as to the disposition standards.

The legislature has manifested its intent that RCW 9A.20.020 should not apply to manifest injustice juvenile dispositions. RCW 13.04.450 provides

> The provisions of chapters 13.04 and 13.40 RCW, as now or hereafter amended, shall be the exclusive authority for the adjudication and disposition of juvenile offenders except where otherwise expressly provided.

* * * There being no express provision that RCW 9A.20.020 apply to dispositions outside the standard range, RCW 13.04.450 clearly requires that RCW 13.40 be the exclusive authority for the disposition of juvenile offenders. And RCW 13.40 does not provide that "manifest injustice" dispositions outside the standard range be limited to the terms provided by RCW 9A.20.020. The plain meaning of RCW 13.04.450 and RCW 13.40 is therefore that RCW 9A.20.020 does not apply to juvenile dispositions.

This result is consistent with the legislative intent that underlies RCW 13.40. As we have discussed, rehabilitation is one of the purposes of the JJA, and in certain cases commitments in excess of the maximum provided for adults may be necessary to respond to the needs of the juvenile offender. * * *

If we were to apply the adult maximum to the disposition provisions of the JJA, we would leave the juvenile courts without a means of responding to the obvious needs of juveniles like the defendants. It would be, in effect, telling the juvenile court to ignore the needs of the juvenile until he is convicted of committing an even more serious offense. Such an approach is necessary under the adult system in which punishment is the paramount purpose and where the punishment must fit the crime. But it is inimical to the rehabilitative purpose of the juvenile justice system. It would destroy the flexibility the legislature built into the system to allow the court, in appropriate cases, to fit the disposition to the offender, rather than to the offense.

Accordingly, we conclude that both the language and the purpose of the JJA require that the adult maximum sentence does not apply to juvenile dispositions under the manifest injustice provisions. * * *

We turn now to consider the second issue raised on this appeal, whether confining juveniles for longer than the maximum sentence provided for adults violates state or federal requirements of equal protection. Essentially, defendants argue that by subjecting juveniles to periods of confinement longer than those provided for adults for the same offense, the JJA denies juveniles the equal protection guaranteed by the fourteenth amendment to the United States Constitution and article 1, section 12 of the state constitution. * * *

[A]ge discriminations are not inherently "suspect," and therefore the legislature's differential treatment of juveniles does not in this case create a suspect class so as to require strict scrutiny of the classification. However, the interest involved in the classification is one which is fundamental. It is nothing less than the juveniles' right to liberty. This is a right which is explicitly preserved in both the fourteenth amendment to the United States Constitution and the constitution of this state. * * *

Therefore, the appropriate standard of review to be applied in this case is the strict scrutiny test. We have recently stated this test as follows:

> The enactment will not be upheld unless the state establishes a compelling interest. And, to do so, the state must show its purpose or interest in the enactment is both constitutionally permissible and substantial, and that use of the classification is necessary to the accomplishment of its interest.

We find that the State has satisfied this test.

The state's purpose and interest in the confinement of juvenile offenders is at least in part to achieve some measure of rehabilitation. This is clearly constitutionally permissible. *McKeiver v. Pennsylvania.* It is also a substantial interest. * * *

We have discussed earlier in this opinion the reason we consider that, in certain cases, confinement in excess of the adult maximum is necessary to achieve the state's substantial purpose of rehabilitating juvenile offenders. Therefore, we find that the State has satisfied the strict scrutiny test. The provision for confinement of juveniles in excess of the maximum terms for adults does not violate the state or federal equal protection clauses.

* * * Accordingly, we affirm the disposition orders of the Superior Court.

DORE, JUDGE (dissenting). * * * If the juveniles had been adults, the maximum sentence they could have received would have been 90 days. Because they were juveniles, however, the court sentenced them to confinement in a correctional institution for 1 year. The majority, by its opinion, sanctions this unconstitutional sentence. I would remand, with instructions to reduce the sentence to 90 days.

Traditional rules of statutory construction require that the court ascertain and give effect to the intent and purpose of the Legislature as expressed in the act. * * * Among the enumerated statements of legislative purpose, RCW 13.40.010(2)(d) emphasizes that the act is designed to "[p]rovide for punishment commensurate with the age, crime, and criminal history of the juvenile offender". This expression of legislative purpose certainly does not contemplate a statutory scheme of punishment which would allow incarceration of a 15–year–old juvenile offender until his 21st birthday for the offense of attempted criminal trespass in the first degree, while a similarly situated 18–year–old codefendant would be subjected only to a maximum penalty of 90 days in jail. Such an incongruous scenario is possible if RCW 9A.20.020 does not set the maximum sentence for a juvenile offender. * * *

Juveniles are entitled to equal protection of the laws with regard to sentencing. The new Juvenile Justice Act shifts policy considerations from an emphasis on rehabilitation to an emphasis on accountability, punishment, and the protection of society.[2] Consequently, juvenile offenders, especially those sentenced under a declaration of manifest injustice, are similarly situated to their adult counterparts for purposes of sentencing.

Allowing juveniles sentenced under the Juvenile Justice Act to receive longer terms of incarceration than could be imposed on adults for the same offense does not promote a compelling state interest and is, therefore, in violation of Const. art. 1, s 12.

Assuming the right involved is not fundamental, in order to satisfy minimal scrutiny under the equal protection clause, a statutory classification must at the very least rationally promote a valid government purpose. The purposes of the Juvenile Justice Act are many and varied and arguably very similar to the purposes of sentencing adults in this state. The obvious purpose of the manifest injustice exception, however, is the protection of society. While this is certainly a valid government objective, there is no rational reason for sentencing juvenile offenders to longer terms of incarceration than could be imposed on adults convicted of the same offense, unless the basic theory of the Act in general and the manifest injustice exception in particular is rehabilitative. If the objective of the sentencing is accountability, and punishment commensurate with the offense and the protection of society, there is no rational basis for

---

2. The majority in *State v. Lawley*, although denying juveniles the right to a jury trial, recognized the shift, as did the dissent in that case. *State v. Rhodes*, clearly recognizes this shift. In *In re Erickson*, the Court of Appeals found RCW 13.40 to be so similar to adult criminal statutes as to constitute punishment for crime sufficient to fall within the constitutional exception to involuntary servitude. * * *

determining that a juvenile, simply by reason of his age, should be subject to a term of incarceration longer than the adult maximum for the same offense. * * *

Even assuming that the state provides substantial "treatment" benefits to juveniles, the Washington court has rejected the proposition that these benefits sufficiently compensate a juvenile for the loss of liberty to dispense with the need for strict scrutiny. A juvenile still shares with an adult offender the one feature that overwhelms the differences between their circumstances—they are both incarcerated against their will. * * *

I would reverse and remand to the trial court and sentence each defendant to not more than 90 days confinement.

NOTES

1) Juvenile Justice Jurisprudence in Washington Significantly, because the Juvenile Justice Act provides for appellate review of juveniles' sentences that depart from the presumptive sentence within the standard range, the Washington appellate courts have considered many appeals and developed a substantial body of case law to govern the sentencing of juveniles. The Washington courts have insisted that juvenile dispositions are not the equivalent of adult criminal sentences, but sometimes have experienced considerable difficulty treading the fine line between the "twin principles of rehabilitation and punishment." In *In re Erickson*, 24 Wash.App. 808, 604 P.2d 513 (1979), the court of appeals held that juvenile sentences, like adult criminal sentences, constitute punishment for crimes sufficient to fall within the constitutional exception to involuntary servitude. In *In re Trambitas*, 96 Wash.2d 329, 635 P.2d 122 (Wa.1981), the supreme court held that the time that juveniles spent in pre-adjudication detention must be credited against their eventual sentences. In *State v. Bourgeois*, 72 Wash.App. 650, 658, 866 P.2d 43, 47 (Wash. Ct. App. 1994), the Washington court of appeals concluded that "a juvenile court may enter a disposition setting a maximum term of confinement beyond the offender's twenty-first birthday."

In *State v. Hartke*, 89 Wash.App. 143, 948 P.2d 402 (Wash. Ct. App. 1997), the court of appeals considered "whether extending juvenile jurisdiction retroactively to collect restitution violates the ex post facto prohibition of the federal and state constitutions. Juvenile restitution is imposed for the primary purposes of compensating victims, juvenile accountability, and juvenile rehabilitation. Because restitution is not punishment, we conclude there has been no violation of the ex post facto clause. The ex post facto prohibition applies only if restitution is punishment. * * * Restitution is the "financial reimbursement by the offender to the victim. * * * " The purpose of juvenile restitution is to compensate the victim and impose accountability on the juvenile. * * * Because restitution is not punitive, the ex post facto doctrine is not implicated. The fact that a sanction, including imprisonment, might later be imposed for willfully violating a restitution order does not change the remedial nature of the restitution."

2) Scope of Review and "Manifest Injustice" In *State v. T.E.H.*, 91 Wash.App. 908, 960 P.2d 441 (Wash. Ct. App. 1998), the court of appeals granted trial judges enormous latitude to impose a "manifest injustice" disposition. " 'Once a juvenile court has concluded that a disposition within the standard range would effectuate a manifest injustice, the court is vested with broad discretion in determining the appropriate sentence to impose.' This court will find a sentence excessive only when it cannot be justified by any reasonable view of the record."

       3) **Aggravating and Mitigating Sentencing Factors** In *State v. S.H.*, 75 Wash.App. 1, 9, 20, 877 P.2d 205, 210, 216 (Wash. Ct. App. 1994), the court of appeals considered the aggravating and mitigating factors, Rev. Code of Washington § 13.40.150 (3)(h) and (i), that justified a departure from the standard range. "S.H. contends several aggravating factors relied on by the trial court are not supported by the record or do not support the manifest injustice disposition. The court's findings of fact are reviewed under a clearly erroneous standard and will be reversed only if 'no substantial evidence supports its conclusion.' 'Whether an aggravating factor justifies a departure from the standard range is a question of law.' "

> An aggravating factor is legally adequate to justify a sentence outside of the standard range as long as the aggravating factor was not necessarily considered by the Legislature in establishing the standard range, and as long as the asserted aggravating factor is "sufficiently substantial and compelling to distinguish the crime in question from others in the same category." * * *

[W]e conclude that due process and the JJA require that juveniles serving a manifest injustice disposition the length of which is based on a need for treatment, must receive adequate, individualized treatment provided by qualified persons, and the treatment must continue and be beneficial to the juvenile for the length of the disposition. * * *

4. EMPIRICAL EVALUATIONS OF JUVENILE COURT SENTENCING PRACTICES: THE PRINCIPLE OF OFFENSE AND RACE

       Changes in legislative purposes clauses and sentencing statutes provide one indicator of the jurisprudential shift in juvenile court sentencing policies from focusing on the offender to emphasizing the seriousness of the offense. Another indicator of therapeutic or punitive purposes may be found in judicial sentencing practices. Despite sometimes discrepant findings, two general conclusions emerge clearly from the research evaluating juvenile court sentencing practices. First, the Principle of Offense—present offense and prior record—accounts for most of the variance in juvenile delinquency sentences that can be explained. *See e.g.*, Belinda McCarthy and Brent L. Smith, "The Conceptualization of Discrimination in the Juvenile Justice Process: The Impact of Administrative Factors and Screening Decisions on Juvenile Court Dispositions," 24 *Criminology* 41 (1986). Every methodologically rigorous study of juvenile court sentencing practices reports that judges focus primarily on the seriousness of the present offense and the prior record when they sentence delinquents. The legal and offense variables typically account for about 25 to 30 percent of the total variance in sentencing and explain most of that variance. *See e.g.*, Stevens H. Clarke and Gary G. Koch, "Juvenile Court: Therapy or Crime Control, and Do Lawyers Make a Difference?" 14 *Law & Soc'y Rev.* 263 (1980); McCarthy and Smith, *supra*; Jeffrey Fagan, Ellen Slaughter, and Elliot Hartstone, "Blind Justice? The Impact of Race on the Juvenile Justice Process," 33 *Crime & Delinq.* 224 (1987). In short, juvenile court judges attend primarily to the same offense factors as do criminal court judges when they sentence delinquents.

Second, after controlling for offense variables, the individualized justice of juvenile courts often produces racial disparities in the sentencing of minority offenders. Other than the principle of offense and a youth's age, gender, and detention status, race appears as a significant factor in most multivariate sentencing studies. These studies indicate that juvenile court judges disproportionately sentence minority youths more severely than they do white juveniles with similar offenses and prior records. Carl E. Pope and William H. Feyerherm, *Minorities and the Juvenile Justice System* (1992); Kimberly Kempf–Leonard, Carl Pope, and William Feyerherm, *Minorities in Juvenile Justice* (1995); Fagan, Slaughter, and Hartstone, "Blind Justice?", *supra*; Barry Feld, *Bad Kids: Race and the Transformation of the Juvenile Court* (1999), Joan McCord, et al., *Juvenile Crime, Juvenile Justice* (2001).

The following excerpt from **Donna M. Bishop and Charles E. Frazier, "Race Effects in Juvenile Justice Decision–Making: Findings of a Statewide Analysis," 86 *J. Crim L. & Criminology* 392 (1996)**, constitutes one of the most sophisticated and comprehensive studies of juvenile justice dispositional decision-making. Professors Bishop and Frazier analyzed the case processing of 137,028 youths referred to Florida's juvenile courts for delinquent acts between January 1, 1985 and December 31, 1987. In addition to their quantitative statistical analyses, Bishop and Frazier also interviewed a sample of intake supervisors, prosecutors and public defenders, and juvenile court judges from each judicial circuit to determine how those officials perceived and interpreted the effects of offenses and race on dispositional decision making:

Over-representation of minorities in the juvenile justice system is well-established. On a national level, minority youths are arrested in numbers greatly disproportionate to their numbers in the general population. While black youths comprise approximately 15% of the ten to seventeen year old population at risk for delinquency, recent figures indicate that they constitute approximately 28% of youths arrested. Further, according to the Office of Juvenile Justice and Delinquency Prevention's (OJJDP) "Children in Custody" census, minority over-representation increases dramatically as one moves beyond arrest to later stages in processing. For example, minorities constitute approximately 62% of youths held in short-term detention facilities, and approximately 60% of those committed to "deep end" long-term institutional programs.

Quite apart from issues related either to the extent or causes of differential minority involvement in crime, a number of researchers have expressed concern about whether the juvenile justice system operates with a selection bias that differentially disadvantages minority youths. * * *

Because the juvenile justice system consists of multiple decision points, it is essential that researchers track cases from arrest to final disposition through as many stages as possible. * * *

In the analyses that follow, the juvenile justice system is viewed as a series of decision points, each of which is simplified to represent a dichotomous contrast. Four stages are involved in delinquency case processing [— intake screening, detention, prosecutorial referral, and judicial disposition]. * * *

[I]t is important to note that nonwhites comprise 21% of the population at risk (ages ten to seventeen) and 29% of the group referred to delinquency intake * * *.

[A]mong those referred for delinquent acts, a greater proportion of nonwhites than whites received the more severe disposition at each successive stage in processing. Racial disparities are most pronounced at intake screening and judicial disposition. For example, 53% of nonwhite youths referred to intake are recommended for referral to court, compared to 42% of white youths. At judicial disposition, 31% of nonwhite youths are incarcerated or transferred, compared to 18% of white youths. The cumulative effect of these decisions is that the racial composition of the cohort becomes increasingly nonwhite as it moves through the system: while nonwhites make up 21% of the population at risk (ages ten to seventeen) and 29% of the cohort referred to delinquency intake, they make up 44% of the cohort incarcerated or transferred. * * *

[F]or judicial disposition [t]he * * * severity of the current offense and prior record each have significant, though fairly modest, effects on dispositional outcomes. Juveniles who are detained are also more likely to receive dispositions of incarceration. Once again, race, operating through detention status, indirectly affects disposition. * * * At this final stage in processing, each of the sociodemographic characteristics has a significant effect on case outcomes, the effect of race being relatively strong. The typical white delinquent has a 9% probability of being committed or transferred, compared to a 16% probability for nonwhites. * * *

Our analysis points to clear disadvantages for nonwhites at multiple stages in delinquency case processing. While the magnitude of the race effect varies from stage to stage, there is a consistent pattern of unequal treatment. Nonwhite youths referred for delinquent acts are more likely than comparable white youths to be recommended for petition to court, to be held in preadjudicatory detention, to be formally processed in juvenile court, and to receive the most formal or the most restrictive judicial dispositions. * * *

A majority of the juvenile justice officials whom we interviewed were quick to indicate that our findings of racial disparities in processing were consistent with their experiences and observations. * * * Some respondents, for example, believed the main problem was individuals who held and applied prejudicial attitudes. Many more saw the problem as endemic to the system, the consequence of well-intended policies and practices that impact differentially on whites and nonwhites.

This latter group of respondents suggested that racial disparities in delinquency case processing are in part a result of agency policies and practices that focus on family support and family cooperation as considerations for diversion, for detention, and for final disposition. They noted that, in some instances, these considerations are incorporated into formalized agency decision criteria.

For example, DHRS policy renders youths referred for delinquent acts ineligible for diversion programs if their parents or guardians (a) cannot be contacted, (b) are contacted but are unable to be present for an intake interview, or (c) exhibit attitudes and styles of behavior that are perceived as uncooperative to intake staff. It is important to note that availability of a telephone and access both to transportation to DHRS offices and child care for young children who must remain at home are all taken for granted in this diversion policy.

DHRS intake supervisors reported that minority parents often are single working mothers or single mothers on welfare with other young children at home. If employed, they are often employed in low-paying, low-status occupations * * * [and] often lack the flexibility to take time from work to be interviewed. * * *

Many respondents also reported that juvenile justice decisions in delinquency cases are affected by differentials in access to retained counsel and private treatment resources, differentials that impact negatively on low-income—especially minority—clients. Especially in later stages of delinquency processing, respondents observed that the system emphasizes treatments (e.g., psychological counseling, drug treatment) that are often best obtained through private agencies. Youths from affluent families may take advantage of these treatment options and avoid formal processing. Minority youths who are less affluent can only obtain comparable services by being adjudicated delinquent and then committed to residential facilities. As one of the judges in our sample observed:

> Minorities and low income kids get more [juvenile justice system] resources. If parents can afford [an expensive private treatment facility], the child gets probation. If not, he gets committed. Income is significant in that a lot of early interventions are directed to middle income groups. If a child needs constructive activity, a middle class family can afford it. Maybe there is institutional bias.

As might be expected, some respondents were very critical of practices which resulted in minorities receiving harsher treatment by justice officials. Others argued that these practices were quite defensible. In their view, justice officials were merely trying to provide needed services to the disadvantaged that wealthy families could purchase on their own. To become eligible for these services, however, youths had to be formally processed—e.g., referred to court, adjudicated delinquent, and placed on formal probation or committed to residential programs. Only then could these services be provided at state expense. Moreover, this sort of policy negatively impacts on nonwhites anytime they come back to the system on a subsequent charge. A juvenile's prior record and prior disposition history are primary predictors of (and primary justifications for) formal processing and more severe sanctions. What may begin with good intentions at an earlier stage ultimately becomes a self-fulfilling prophecy. The influence of race is obscured as decisions to formally prosecute and detain in the past are used to justify more severe sanctions for youths returning to the system.

In addition, many respondents indicated that juvenile justice officials make decisions influenced in part by perceptions (or misperceptions) of youths' family backgrounds and circumstances. Respondents frequently reported that delinquent youths from single-parent families and those from families incapable of (or perceived to be incapable of) providing good parental supervision are more likely to be referred to court and placed under state control. In other words, when justice officials perceive that there is family strength and support, they are more likely to select less intrusive treatments and sanctions. For the most part, our respondents believed that these distinctions were fair and appropriate. They also indicated that, at least in delinquency cases, black family systems generally tend to be perceived in a more negative light, that pre-disposition reports give disproportionate attention to assessments of family situations, and that judges rely heavily on pre-disposition reports in reaching dispositional decisions. * * *

Our qualitative findings support several interpretations. Intentional race discrimination does not appear to play a major role in accounting for racial disparities in processing. Although some officials whom we interviewed believed that some justice officials were motivated by prejudicial attitudes, few recounted specific instances of racially motivated actions. Without question, there are some justice officials who hold and act upon racially prejudicial attitudes. * * * However, we are not inclined to conclude that the disparities we observed are largely attributable to intentional race discrimination.

Instead, we see much evidence of institutional racism. This is evident both in criteria for diversion and pre-trial release that focus on family support and cooperation, and in efforts to provide the economically disadvantaged with resources at state expense that the more affluent can purchase on their own. Obtaining these resources exacts a price in terms of adjudications of delinquency and sentences to confinement. * * *

a. The Principle of Offense

Juvenile court judges answer the question "what should be done with this child?" in part, by reference to explicit statutory mandates. Sentencing guidelines and presumptive and mandatory sentencing provisions operate formally to restrict judges' broad discretion. Despite the recent statutory changes, however, juvenile court judges exercise far greater sentencing discretion than do their criminal court counterparts because of the presumed need in juvenile proceedings to look beyond the present offense to the "best interests of the child" and because of paternalistic assumptions about children and the state's ability to rehabilitate them. Even in jurisdictions like Washington, with its formalized sentencing framework, the juvenile justice system differs significantly from its adult counterpart and incorporates more flexible processing of delinquents because the beliefs in rehabilitation and "childhood" foster greater informality and discretion.

While sentencing laws constrain the discretionary powers of judges somewhat, practical and bureaucratic considerations also restrict judges' dispositional latitude and encourage them to emphasize the seriousness of the present offense and prior record when they sentence delinquents. Barry C. Feld, "The Juvenile Court Meets the Principle of Offense: Punishment, Treatment and the Difference it Makes," 68 *B.U.L.Rev.* 821 (1988). Despite the "rhetoric of rehabilitation," some analysts attribute judges' reliance on traditional criminal sentencing criteria to juvenile courts' bureaucratic imperatives—the desire of justice agencies to avoid scandal and unfavorable political and media attention. *See e.g.* M.A. Bortner, *Inside a Juvenile Court: The Tarnished Ideal of Individualized Justice* (1982); Aaron Cicourel, *The Social Organization of Juvenile Justice* (1968); Robert Emerson, *Judging Delinquents: Context and Process in Juvenile Courts* (1969); David Matza, *Delinquency and Drift* (1964). The fear of scandal and adverse political repercussions inhibit juvenile courts' dispositional latitude. One sociological observer of juvenile court sentencing practices reported that

> juvenile court decision-making comes to be pervaded by a sense of vulnerability to adverse public reaction for failing to control or restrain delinquent offenders. * * * [Fear of scrutiny and criticism increases pressures] to impose maximum restraints on the offender— in most instances incarceration. Anything less risks immediate criticism. But more than this, it also exposes the court to the possibility of even stronger reaction in the future. For given any recurrence of serious illegal activity, former decisions that can be interpreted as "lenient" become difficult to defend. Robert Emerson, "Role Determinants in Juvenile Court," in *Handbook of Criminology 624* (D. Glaser ed. 1974).

David Matza, *Delinquency and Drift* 122 (1964), also notes that the juvenile court judge is

> ultimately responsible to the public. He will have to explain * * * why the 17–year–old murderer of an innocent matron was allowed to roam the streets, on probation, when just last year he was booked for mugging. This is no easy question to answer. Somehow, an invoking of the principle of individualized justice and a justification of mercy on the basis of accredited social-work theory hardly seems appropriate on these occasions.

Concerns about avoiding scandals encourage judges to impose more formal and restrictive responses on those delinquents who commit more serious offenses or who have more extensive prior records. "[W]hether a juvenile goes to some manner of prison or is put on some manner of probation * * * depends first, on a traditional rule-of-thumb assessment of the total risk of danger and thus scandal evident in the juvenile's current offense and prior record of offenses." *Matza, Delinquency and Drift* 125.

Internal and external organizational factors also restrain judicial sentencing autonomy. The bureaucratic setting within which judges exercise their discretion restrict their theoretical latitude. Juvenile court judges have more responsibilities than do criminal court judges to administer their court, maintain public relations and internal harmony, and efficiently manage their docket. Judges experience contradictory pressures from internal bureaucratic and external political and public constituencies. "[I]n every case he is subjected to the remaining cross-pressures; one calling for severity, the other for mercy; one emanating from far-off and occasional critics, the other from nearby and ever-present underlings with whom he must work; one irrelevant to the day-to-day administration of an efficient court, the other crucially relevant; but one representing what he takes to be public opinion, the other what he takes to be professional opinion; and one holding the sanction of public scandal, the other of professional criticism." *Matza, Delinquency and Drift* at 122–23.

Juvenile courts develop bureaucratic strategies to reconcile their mandates to individualize dispositions in the child's "best interests" with their other, often contradictory, purposes like "protecting public safety," "punishing consistently with rehabilitative objectives," and "controlling the commission of unlawful acts by children." Juvenile court personnel develop administrative criteria that enable them to categorize youths quickly, simply, and efficiently. The types of information that juvenile courts routinely collect provide the bases for classifying and sentencing youths and for defending those decisions subsequently, if necessary. Because juvenile courts routinely collect information about youths' present offense and prior delinquency record, these factors readily lend themselves to decisional rules. For example, a survey of juvenile sentencing practices in California reported that juvenile dispositions appear to be based primarily on the youth's present offense and prior record. The study concluded that

> comparisons of juvenile and adult sentencing practices suggest that juvenile and criminal courts in California are much more alike than statutory language would suggest, in the degree to which they focus on aggravating circumstances of the charged offense and the defendant's prior record in determining the degree of confinement that will be imposed. Peter Greenwood, et al., *Youth Crime and Juvenile Justice in California* 51 (1983).

In short, the principle of offense predominates at dispositions because of the penal basis of juvenile courts' delinquency jurisdiction and the courts' bureaucratic and administrative concerns.

b. Racial Disparities in Sentencing Delinquents

Within the flexible juvenile justice dispositional process, minority youths are disproportionately over-represented at every stage. An analytic review of the juvenile court sentencing research literature concluded that "there are race effects in operation within the juvenile justice system, both direct and indirect in nature." *Pope and Feyerherm, Minorities in Juvenile Justice, supra* at 41 (1992). Studies consistently report racial disparities in case processing after controls for offense variables, that inequalities occur at various stages of the process in different jurisdictions, and that discriminatory decisions amplify minority over-representation as youths proceed through the system. Carl E. Pope, Rick Lovell, and Heidi M. Hsia, *Disproportionate Minority Confinement: A Review of the Research Literature from 1989–2001* (OJJDP 2002); Jessica Short and Christy Sharp, *Disproportionate Minority Contact in the Juvenile Justice System* (Child Welfare League 2005); Donna M. Bishop, "The Role of Race and Ethnicity in Juvenile Justice Processing," in *Our Children, Their Children: Confronting Racial and Ethnic Differences in American Juvenile Justice* (2006); Alex R. Piquero, "Disproportionate Minority Contact," 18 *Future of Children* 59 (2008).

The discretion inherent in a *parens patriae* system raises concerns that the cumulative impact of individualized decisions contributes to the substantial over-representation of minority youths. Quite apart from overt discrimination, juvenile justice personnel may view black youths as more threatening or likely to recidivate than white youths and process them differently. *See e.g.*, Robert J. Sampson and John H. Laub, "Structural Variations in Juvenile Court Processing: Inequality, the Underclass, and Social Control," 27 *Law & Soc'y Rev.* 285 (1993); George Bridges and Sara S. Steen, "Racial Disparities in Official Assessments of Juvenile Offenders: Attributional Stereotypes as Mediating Mechanisms," 63 Am. Soc. Rev. 554 (1998); Sara Steen, et al., "Explaining Assessments of Future Risk: Race and Attributes of Juvenile Offenders in Presentencing Reports," in *Our Children, Their Children: Confronting Racial and Ethnic Differences in American Juvenile Justice* (2006). More benignly, if juvenile courts sentence youths on the basis of social circumstances that indirectly mirror socioeconomic status or race, then minority youths may receive more severe dispositions than white youths because of their personal characteristics, social characteristics, or "real needs." Minority youth over-representation may also reflect racial group differences in involvement in criminal activity. If court personnel and judges base their screening decisions and youths' sentences on the seriousness of juveniles' offenses and criminal history, then minority over-representation may result from real differences in the incidence and prevalence of offending by race. Or, the social structural context of juvenile justice decision-making may redound to the detriment of minority juveniles. For example, urban courts tend to be more formal and to sentence all juveniles more severely than do suburban or rural courts. Barry C. Feld, *Justice For Children: The Right To Counsel and Juvenile Courts* (1993). Urban courts also have greater access to detention facilities, and youths held in pretrial detention typically receive more severe sentences than do those who remain at liberty. *See,* Bishop and Frazier, "Race Effects in Juvenile Justice Decision–Making," *supra* 969, and Chapter 5, *supra* pp. 470–473. A larger proportion of minority youths reside in urban than in rural settings, and police disproportionately arrest and detain minority juveniles for violent and drug crimes. Thus crime patterns, urbanism, "underclass threat," and race may interact to produce minority over-representation in detention facilities and institutions.

The disproportionate over-representation of minority youths in juvenile detention and correctional institutions prompted the United States Congress to amend the Juvenile Justice and Delinquency Prevention Act in 1988 to require states receiving federal funds for juvenile justice programs to assure equitable treatment on the basis, *inter alia*, of race, and to assess the sources of minority over-representation in juvenile detention facilities and correctional institutions. 42 U.S.C. § 5633(a)(16) (1993 Supp.). In response to this federal mandate, a number of states examined and found racial disparities in their juvenile justice systems. *See e.g.,* Bishop and Frazier, "Race Effects in Juvenile Justice Decision–Making," *supra,* p. 969; Pope and Feyerherm, *Minorities and the Juvenile Justice System, supra;* Kempf–Leonard, Pope, and Feyerherm, *Minorities in Juvenile Justice, supra.* These evaluation studies reported that, after controlling for legal variables like the present offense and prior record, forty-one of forty-two states found minority youths over-represented in secure pre-adjudication detention facilities, and all thirteen of thirteen states that analyzed other phases of juvenile justice decision-making found evidence of minority over-representation.

Howard Snyder and Melissa Sickmund, *Juvenile Offenders and Victims: 1999 National Report* **193–194 (1999)** summarize research on disproportionate minority confinement:

There is substantial evidence of widespread disparity in juvenile case processing While research findings are not completely consistent, data available for most jurisdictions across the country show that minority (especially black) youth are over represented within the juvenile justice system, particularly in secure facilities. These data further suggest that minority youth are more likely to be placed in public secure facilities, while white youth are more likely to be housed in private facilities or diverted from the juvenile justice system. Some research also suggests that differences in the offending rates of white and minority youth cannot explain the minority overrepresentation in arrest, conviction, and incarceration counts.

Further, there is substantial evidence that minority youth are often treated differently from majority youth within the juvenile justice system. In a review by Pope and Feyerherm of existing research literature, approximately two-thirds of the studies examined showed that racial and/or ethnic status did influence decision making within the juvenile justice system. Since that review, a rather large body of research has accumulated across numerous geographic regions that reinforces these earlier findings. Thus, existing research suggests that race/ethnicity does make a difference in juvenile justice decisions in some jurisdictions at least some of the time.

Because juvenile justice systems are fragmented and administered at the local level, racial/ethnic differences exist in some jurisdictions but not in others. One would not expect research findings to be consistent, given variation across time frames and regions.

Racial/ethnic differences occur at various decision points within the juvenile justice system Pope and Feyerherm found that when racial/ethnic effects do occur, they can be found at any stage of processing within the juvenile justice system. Across numerous jurisdictions, however, a substantial body of research suggests that disparity is most pronounced at the beginning stages. The greatest disparity between majority and minority youth court processing outcomes occurs at intake and detention decision points. Existing research also suggests that when racial/ethnic differences are found, they tend to accumulate as youth are processed through the justice system.

Pope and Feyerherm found that research reveals substantial variation across rural, suburban, and urban areas. Correspondingly, the concept of "Justice by geography" introduced by Feld suggests that there are marked differences in outcome depending on the jurisdiction in which the youth is processed. For example, cases in urban jurisdictions are more likely to receive severe outcomes at various stages of processing than are cases in non-urban areas. Because minority populations are concentrated in urban areas, this effect may work to the disadvantage of minority youth and result in greater over representation.

More than 6 in 10 juveniles in residential placement were minority youth In 1997, two-thirds of all juveniles in custody in public facilities were minorities as were just over half of all juveniles in private facilities.

Race/Ethnicity	In Population in 1997	Residential Placement October 29, 1997
Total	100%	100%
White	66	37
Minority	34	63
African American	15	40
Latino	15	18
Native American	1	2
Asian	4	2

In another study using OJJDP data, **Eileen Poe–Yamagata and Michael A. Jones, *And Justice for Some* 2, 18–21 (2000)** (available at http://www.buildingblocksforyouth.org/justiceforsome/jfs.html) report juvenile court sentencing practices and patterns of confinement for youth of different racial backgrounds:

Disposition

African American youth were overrepresented among cases receiving a disposition of out-of-home placement (e.g., commitment to a locked

978   DISPOSITION DECISION   CH. 8

institution). This was true in all offense categories and was most pro-nounced among drug offense cases.

In every offense category, minority youth were more likely than White youth to be placed out-of-home.

Conversely, among all offense categories, White youth were more likely than minority youth to be placed on probation.

Incarceration in Juvenile Facilities

Although minority youth are one-third of the adolescent population in the United States, minority youth are two-thirds of the over 100,000 youth confined in local detention and state correctional systems.

Minority youth are overrepresented in residential placement facilities for all offense categories. In fact, minority youth were at least one-half of all youth in residential placement among each of the non-status offense categories.

Minorities comprise the majority of youth held in both public and private facilities. Minority youth, especially Latino youth, are a much larger proportion of youth in public than private facilities.

Minority youth were confined behind locked doors twice as often as White youth. African American youth represent the largest racial/ethnic proportion of youth held behind locked doors.

In 1993, when controlling for current offense and prior admissions, incarceration rates to state public facilities were higher for African American and Latino youth than White youth.

When White youth and minority youth were charged with the same offenses, African American youth with no prior admissions were six times more likely to be incarcerated in public facilities than White youth with the same background. Latino youth were three times more likely than White youth to be incarcerated.

Admission rates to public facilities were seven times greater among African American youth with one-to-two prior admissions than for White youth in 1993. Admission rates for Latino youth were twice the rate of White youth.

In 1993, African American youth were confined on average for 61 days more than White youth, and Latino youth were confined 112 days more than White youth.

While representing just 34% of the U.S. population in 1997, minority youth represented 62% of youth in detention, 67% of youth committed to public facilities, and 55% of youth committed to private facilities.

Nationwide, minority youth were overrepresented in the detained population at 1.8 times their rate in the general population, among commitments to public facilities at 2.0 times their rate, and among private commitments at 1.6 times their rate in the population.

Nationally, custody rates were five times greater for African American youth than for White youth. Custody rates for Latino and Native American youth were 2.5 times the custody rate of White youth. * * *

Juvenile Corrections

1. The National Perspective

A 1999 study from OJJDP reported that on October 29, 1997 there were 105,790 youth in juvenile detention facilities prior to adjudication or committed to state juvenile correctional facilities following adjudication. Minority youth represented almost two-thirds (63%) of detained or committed youth although they represent only about one-third (34%) of the total adolescent population in the country.

Minority youth were overrepresented in residential placement for all offense types. In fact, minority youth were at least one-half of all youth in residential placement among each of the major offense categories. Further, with the exception of status offenses, African American youth were almost 1/3 or more of all youth in residential placement among each of the major offense categories.

Public juvenile facilities are typically locked local detention facilities or locked state correctional institutions. Private juvenile facilities are often less restrictive and less prison-like. Minorities represented a greater proportion of youth in public (66%) than private (54%) facilities, and the minority proportion of youth in public facilities was almost twice the White proportion (66% vs. 34%). Among Latinos, the proportion of detained and committed youth in public facilities was almost double the proportion in private facilities (21% vs. 11%).

While most youth confined by both locked and staff-secured arrangements were minorities, the minority proportion of youth confined by locked doors exceeded the proportion staff secured (66% vs. 54%). In fact, the number of minority youth held behind locked doors was almost twice the number of White youth similarly confined (66% vs. 34%).

Admission rates to state public facilities were much higher for African American youth and Latino youth with no prior admissions than for comparable White youth. This was also true for youth with one-to-two prior admissions, in all offense categories.

Overall, the admissions rate to state public facilities for youth with no prior admissions was six times higher for African American than White youth (373 and 59) and 3 times higher among Latino than White youth (166 and 59) in 1993. Among youth with one-to-two prior admissions, the overall admissions rate for African American youth exceeded the White rate by a factor of 7 (96 and 14) and the admissions rate for Latino youth was twice the rate of White youth (28 and 14).

In 1993, Latino youth were in custody on average 112 days more than White youth. African American youth were in custody on average 61 days more than White youth. While the average lengths of stay in public facilities were higher for minority youth than White youth across all offenses, it was particularly dramatic for drug offenses. On average, the length of stay for Latino youth admitted for a drug offense was double the length of stay of White youth (306 days vs. 144 days). Similarly, African American youth admitted for a drug offense were held longer than White youth, on average (235 days vs. 144).

In addition, the range in the length of stay above the median was also greater for non-Whites than Whites. For example, among the top 25th percentile of cases involving a violent offense and no prior admissions, the length of stay for Latino youth ranged from 625 to over 1,400 days compared to between 400 and 900 days for White youth. Among the top 25th percentile of cases involving a drug offense and no prior admissions, the length of stay for Latino youth was between 500 and 1,100 days compared to between 200 and 400 days for White youth. * * *

The Report by the National Academy of Science identifies one source of the differential processing. **Joan McCord et al, *Juvenile Crime, Juvenile Justice* 251–252 (2001)** emphasizes that discretionary decisions at various stages of the justice process amplify racial disparities as minority youths proceed through the system and result in more severe dispositions than for comparable white youths. Initial screening decisions affect the populations of juveniles whom juvenile courts ultimately try and sentence. One source of disparity in juvenile justice processing is that among decision-makers,

> minorities are perceived differently from whites, despite having similar offense histories and characteristics, and often are seen as threatening and dangerous. The first question Bridges and Steen asked is whether court officials perceived and judged minority offenders differently from whites with similar characteristics. They also asked whether officials perceive minorities as more likely than white youths to commit future crimes. If court officials perceive minorities as more threatening, then they will be more likely to recommend greater punishment and control.

> Bridges and Steen found pronounced differences in [probation] officers' attributions about the causes of crime committed by white and minority youth. For black children, crime was attributed to negative attitudinal traits and personality defects. Among white children, their offenses were thought to be primarily caused by external environmental factors (e.g., family dysfunction, drug abuse, negative peer influence). Furthermore, they found that these differences contributed significantly to differential assessment of the risk of reoffending and to sentence recommendations, even after adjusting for legally relevant case and offender characteristics. These differences tended to shape the probation officers' evaluations of how likely the child would be to commit crime in the future and how amenable the child would be to treatment. * * *

> Bridges and Steen found that race indirectly influenced decisions to detain through factors like performance in school and family

situation. This was the case regardless of the nature and severity of the offense. When school performance and family were viewed as positive and stable, juveniles were more likely to be viewed as amenable to the court's influence and control. The perceived ability of the family to supervise the juvenile may affect the court's decision about whether or not to detain. Black juveniles are more likely than whites or Hispanics to live in single-parent family (62 percent, 27 percent, and 36 percent, respectively). To the extent that court decision makers believe that single-parent families provide less supervision of youngster than two-parent families, black juveniles are at higher risk of being detained. Being detained before adjudication negatively affects sentencing outcomes (e.g., whether or not to incarcerate as well as the length of a sentence). * * *

The research by Bishop and Frazier, Pope and Feyerherm, Snyder and Sickmund, and The National Academy of Science all emphasize the importance of analyzing juvenile justice decision-making as a multi-stage process rather than focusing solely on the final dispositional decision. For example, dramatic increases in referral rates of minority youths to juvenile courts in seventeen states result in corresponding increases in detention and institutional placement. Edmund F. McGarrell, "Trends in Racial Disproportionality in Juvenile Court Processing: 1985–1989," 39 *Crime and Delinquency* 29 (1993). Juvenile courts detain black youths at higher rates than they do white youths charged with similar offenses, and detained youths typically receive more severe sentences. A national study of incarceration trends reported confinement rates for minority youths three to four times greater than those of similarly-situated white juveniles, and that judges sentenced proportionally more minority youths to public secure facilities and committed more white youths to private facilities. Barry Krisberg, Ira Schwartz, Gideon Fishman, Zvi Eisikovits, Edna Guttman, and Karen Joe, "The Incarceration of Minority Youth," 33 *Crime and Delinquency* 173 (1987). By 1991, juvenile courts confined less than one-third (31 percent) of non-Hispanic white juveniles in public long-term facilities; minority youths comprised more two-thirds (69 percent) of confined youths. Howard Snyder and Melissa Sickmund, *Juvenile Offenders and Victims, supra*.

PROBLEM

Based on the foregoing empirical evaluations and analyses of juvenile court sentencing practices, what, if any, recommendations would you make to state legislators, juvenile court intake staff and judges, prosecutors and defense attorneys, and departments of corrections to avoid racial disparities in dispositional decision-making and to reduce disproportionate over-confinement?

C. CONDITIONS OF CONFINEMENT AND REHABILITATIVE JURISPRUDENCE

The Supreme Court in *Gault* characterized juveniles incarceration as a severe penalty, a substantial deprivation of autonomy, and a continual reminder of one's delinquent status, all of which constitute elements of punishment. 387 U.S. at 26–27. The contradictions between the rhetoric of rehabilitation and the reality of institutional conditions of confinement motivated the *Gault* Court to grant juveniles some procedural safeguards.

Evaluations of juvenile correctional facilities in the decades following *Gault* reveal a continuing gap between the rhetoric of rehabilitation and a more custodial and punitive reality. Kenneth Wooden, *Weeping in the Playtime of Others: America's Incarcerated Children* (1976); Clements Bartollas, Walter Miller, and Simon Dinitz, *Juvenile Victimization: The Institutional Paradox* (1976); Barry C. Feld, *Neutralizing Inmate Violence: Juvenile Offenders in Institutions* (1977); Steven Lerner, *Bodily Harm* (1986). Research in Massachusetts described violent and punitive facilities in which staff physically punished inmates, and frequently failed to prevent inmates' physical abuse and homosexual rape by other inmates. Feld, *Neutralizing Inmate Violence*, *supra*. A study in Ohio revealed a similarly violent and oppressive institutional environment for "treating" young delinquents. Bartollas et al., *Juvenile Victimization*, *supra*. Although the California Youth Authority (CYA) aspired to realize the juvenile court's "rehabilitative ideal," Barry Krisberg and James Austin, *Reinventing Juvenile Justice* (1993), by the 1980s youths committed to CYA institutions clearly experienced punishment rather than treatment in overcrowded and dangerous youth prisons. Lerner, *Bodily Harm*, *supra*. An evaluation of the Louisiana training schools described institutions populated predominantly by black juveniles whom guards regularly physically abused, kept in isolation for long periods of time, restrained with handcuffs, and confined in punitive facilities surrounded by high chain-link fences topped with coiled razor wire. Human Rights Watch, *Children in Confinement in Louisiana* (1995).

A study, sponsored by the Office of Juvenile Justice and Delinquency Prevention (OJJDP), Dale G. Parent, et al., *Conditions of Confinement: Juvenile Detention and Corrections Facilities* (1994), used nationally recognized professional standards to assess the quality of 984 juvenile detention centers and training schools that housed more than two-thirds (69 percent) of all the confined delinquents in the nation. It reported endemic institutional overcrowding. In 1991, almost half (44 percent) of all long-term public institutions operated above their design capacity, as did more than three-quarters (79 percent) of the largest facilities, those which housed more than 350 inmates. Nearly two-thirds (62 percent) of all delinquent inmates resided in overcrowded facilities operating well above their design capacity. As states sentenced more youths to juvenile institutions, they increased their prison-like character, relied more extensively on fences and walls to maintain perimeter security, and used surveillance equipment to provide internal security. The OJJDP evaluation classified nearly half (46 percent) the training schools as medium or maximum security facilities with perimeter fences, locked internal security, or both.

The recent changes in juvenile court sentencing legislation exacerbate the deleterious side effects associated with institutional overcrowding. Youths confined under "get tough" sentencing laws to long terms often comprise the most serious and chronic delinquent population. Yet the institutions that house them often suffer from over-crowding, limited physical mobility, and inadequate program resources. Overcrowding also contributes to higher rates of inmate violence and suicide. *Parent, Conditions of Confinement, supra.* These juvenile correctional "warehouses" exhibit many negative features associated with adult prisons and sometimes function as little more than youth prisons in which inmates "do time." Peter Greenwood and Franklin Zimring, *One More Chance: The Pursuit of Promising Intervention Strategies for Chronic Juvenile Offenders* (1985). The large custodial institutions enable politicians to demonstrate their toughness, provide the public with a false sense of security, afford employment for correctional personnel, and minimize the demands placed on custodial staff to maintain institutional order, but do little to improve the life-chances of troubled youths.

Howard Snyder and Melissa Sickmund, *Juvenile Offenders and Victims: 1999 National Report* **205–206 (1999)** describe some of the conditions under which states confine juveniles in detention and correctional facilities:

National accreditation standards for juvenile facilities express a preference for relying on staff, rather than on hardware, to provide security. The guiding principle is to house juveniles in the "least restrictive placement alternative." Staff security measures include periodically taking counts of the youth in custody, using classification and separation procedures, and maintaining an adequate ratio of security staff to juveniles.

For each juvenile reported to the CJRP (Census of Juveniles in Residential Placements), respondents were asked about the "locked doors and/or gates [that] confined THIS young person within the facility and its grounds during the after school, day-time hours on October 29, 1997." Overall, facilities reported that 7 in 10 juveniles in residential placement were confined during after school hours by at least one locked door or gate. The vast majority of juveniles in residential placement in public facilities were confined under locked arrangements. For juveniles in private facilities, the reverse was true. Nearly 4 in 10 committed juveniles and nearly 1 in 10 detained juveniles were confined by means of staff security only. The use of locked doors or gates varied by offense category. Juveniles held for Violent Crime Index offenses and technical violations were the most likely to be held behind locked doors. Unlike juveniles held for delinquency offenses, those in residential placement for status offenses were more likely to be confined under staff-secure than under locked arrangements.

Minority juveniles were more likely than nonminority juveniles to be confined behind locked doors. Among minorities, black and Hispanic juveniles were more likely to be confined behind locked doors than were other minorities. There was less overrepresentation of minorities among the population of juveniles who were confined under staff-secure arrangements than among those who were locked in. * * *

Crowding in juvenile facilities has increased as the juvenile custody population has grown. Since the vast majority of juveniles in custody are held in secure public facilities, such as detention centers and training schools, even small increases in crowding in these facilities affect a large number of juveniles.

In 1995, half of all public *detention centers* were operating above their design capacity. These crowded facilities held nearly three-quarters of residents in public detention centers. In comparison, one-third of detention centers were crowded in 1991, and they held about half of detention center residents that year. The increase in the number of over-capacity public detention facilities meant that there were 7,400 more residents in crowded detention centers in 1995 than in 1991—a rise of nearly 75%.

The situation was much the same in public *institutional facilities* for long-term placements (such as training schools). Although the proportion of such facilities that were operating above their design capacity stayed constant (about 45% in 1991 and 1995), the number of residents held in crowded facilities increased substantially. Public long-term institutional facilities that were over capacity held more than 70% of public long-term institutional residents in 1995, compared with 62% in 1991.

There were 10,000 more residents in overcapacity training schools and other public long-term institutional facilities in 1995 than in 1991—an increase of more than 55%. * * *

In addition to the studies conducted by OJJDP, Amnesty International and Human Rights Watch have conducted studies of conditions of confinement in several states around the country. These studies report excessive use of confinement for minor offenders, staff misuse of force and restraints, excessive reliance on solitary confinement, and inadequate provision of treatment services. Amnesty International, Betraying the Youth: Children in the US Justice System (1998). In a study of juvenile correctional facilities in Georgia, **Human Rights Watch, *Modern Capital of Human Rights? Abuses in the State of Georgia* 120 (1996)**, concluded that

> Many children are confined in shamefully overcrowded, squalid and unsanitary institutions with inadequate programming. As a result of the overcrowding, institutions can be dangerous places for weaker children who are preyed upon by older, tougher juvenile offenders; in some of the facilities, four boys share housing space intended for one.

Moreover, we found disciplinary measures that are inappropriate and excessive. These included an overuse of isolation (sixty-three days in one case) land locking children in their cells for long periods of time. In addition, four-point restraints, with children bound to a bed at wrists and ankles, are used as disciplinary measures. * * * Correctional officers have also used pepper gas to restrain children. Children with psychological disorders have been punished or ignored instead of being treated by medical personnel.

Another evaluation by Human Rights Watch, *Children in Confinement in Louisiana* 1 (1995) found that "substantial numbers of children in the state training institutions are regularly physically abused by guards, are kept in isolation for long periods of time, and are improperly restrained in handcuffs." In another report, Human Rights Watch, *High Country Lockup: Children in Confinement in Colorado* (1997), reported shameful crowding at almost every institution, disproportionate over representation of minority children in confinement, excessive use of restraints and isolation, and lack of educational opportunities and psychological treatment. In a very thorough compilation and analysis, Douglas E. Abrams, "Reforming Juvenile Delinquency Treatment to Enhance Rehabilitation, Personal Accountability, and Public Safety," 84 *Ore. L. Rev.* 1001 (2005), collects and analyzes media reports of institutional abuses and lawsuits initiated by the US Department of Justice under the authority of Civil Rights of Institutionalized Persons Act (CRIPA), 42 U.S.C. §§ 1997–1997j (2006). The next section of materials provides one type of litigation strategy to improve conditions of confinement.

1. THE "RIGHT TO TREATMENT"

NELSON v. HEYNE

491 F.2d 352 (U.S. Ct. App., 7th Cir. 1974).

KILEY, JUDGE. The district court in this class civil rights action enjoined defendants from implementing alleged unconstitutional practices and policies in conducting the Indiana Boys School under their administration; and declared the practices and policies unconstitutional * * *. We affirm.

The School, located in Plainfield, Indiana, is a medium security state correctional institution for boys twelve to eighteen years of age, an estimated one-third of whom are non-criminal offenders. The boys reside in about sixteen cottages. The School also has academic and vocational school buildings, a gymnasium and an administrative building. The average length of a juvenile's stay at the School is about six and one-half months. Although the School's maximum capacity is less than 300 juveniles, its population is generally maintained at 400. The counseling staff of twenty individuals includes three psychologists with undergraduate academic degrees, and one part-time psychiatrist who spends four hours a week at the institution. The medical staff includes one part-time physician, one registered nurse, and one licensed practical nurse. * * *

The court found that it had jurisdiction and that the corporal punishment and the method of administering tranquilizing drugs by defendants constituted cruel and unusual punishment in violation of plaintiffs' 8th and 14th Amendment rights. The judgment restraining the challenged practices followed. The court thereafter, in a separate judgment, declared plaintiffs had the right to adequate rehabilitative treatment.

I—Cruel and Unusual Punishment

It is not disputed that the juveniles who were returned from escapes or who were accused of assaults on other students or staff members were beaten routinely by guards under defendants' supervision. There is no proof of formal procedures that governed the beatings which were administered after decision by two or more staff members. Two staff members were required to observe the beatings.

In beating the juveniles, a 'fraternity paddle' between 1/2' and 2' thick, 12' long, with a narrow handle, was used. There is testimony that juveniles weighing about 160 pounds were struck five blows on the clothed buttocks, often by a staff member weighing 285 pounds. The beatings caused painful injuries. The district court found that this disciplinary practice violated the plaintiffs' 8th and 14th Amendment rights, and ordered it stopped immediately. We recognize that the School is a correctional, as well as an academic, institution. No case precisely in point has been cited or found which decided whether supervised beatings in a juvenile reformatory violated the 'cruel and unusual' clause of the 8th Amendment. * * * Expert evidence adduced at the trial unanimously condemned the beatings. The uncontradicted authoritative evidence indicates that the practice does not serve as useful punishment or as treatment, and it actually breeds counter-hostility resulting in greater aggression by a child. For these reasons we find the beatings presently administered are unnecessary and therefore excessive. * * * [T]he district court did not err in deciding that the disciplinary beatings shown by this record constituted cruel and unusual punishment.[6]

The 8th Amendment prohibition against cruel and unusual punishment is binding on the states through the 14th Amendment. The meaning of cruel and unusual punishment in law has varied through the course of history, and as the Court observed in *Trop v. Dulles*:

> The (8th Amendment) must draw its meaning from the evolving standards of decency that mark the progress of a maturing society.

The district court's decision meets tests that have been applied in decisions to determine whether the standards of decency in a maturing society have been met, i.e.: whether the punishment is disproportionate to the offense; and whether the severity or harshness of the punishment offends "broad and idealistic concepts of dignity, civilized standards, humanity, and decency.". The record before us discloses that the beatings employed

---

6. We do not hold that all corporal punishment in juvenile institutions or reformatories is per se cruel and unusual.

by defendants are disproportionate to the offenses for which they are used, and do not measure up to contemporary standards of decency in our contemporary society.

There is nothing in the record to show that a less severe punishment would not have accomplished the disciplinary aim. And it is likely that the beatings have aroused animosity toward the School and substantially frustrated its rehabilitative purpose. We find in the record before us, to support our holding, general considerations similar to those the court in *Jackson* found relevant: (1) corporal punishment is easily subject to abuse in the hands of the sadistic and unscrupulous, and control of the punishment is inadequate; (2) formalized School procedures governing the infliction of the corporal punishment are at a minimum; (3) the infliction of such severe punishment frustrates correctional and rehabilitative goals; and (4) the current sociological trend is toward the elimination of all corporal punishment in all correctional institutions* * *.

Witnesses for both the School and the juveniles testified at trial that tranquilizing drugs, specifically Sparine and Thorazine, were occasionally administered to the juveniles, not as part of an ongoing psychotherapeutic program, but for the purpose of controlling excited behavior. The registered nurse and licensed practical nurse prescribed intramuscular dosages of the drugs upon recommendation of the custodial staff under standing orders by the physician. Neither before nor after injections were the juveniles examined by medically competent staff members to determine their tolerances.

The district court also found this practice to be cruel and unusual punishment. Accordingly the court ordered the practice stopped immediately, and further ordered that no drug could be administered intramuscularly unless specifically authorized or directed by a physician in each case, and unless oral medication was first tried, except where the staff was directed otherwise by a physician in each case. * * *

We are not persuaded by defendants' argument that the use of tranquilizing drugs is not "punishment." Experts testified that the tranquilizing drugs administered to the juveniles can cause: the collapse of the cardiovascular system, the closing of a patient's throat with consequent asphyxiation, a depressant effect on the production of bone marrow, jaundice from an affected liver, and drowsiness, hematological disorders, sore throat and ocular changes. * * *

We hold today only that the use of disciplinary beatings and tranquilizing drugs in the circumstances shown by this record violates plaintiffs' 14th Amendment right protecting them from cruel and unusual punishment. We do not intend that penal and reform institutional physicians cannot prescribe necessary tranquilizing drugs in appropriate cases. Our concern is with actual and potential abuses under policies where juveniles are beaten with an instrument causing serious injuries, and drugs are administered to juveniles intramuscularly by staff, without trying medication short of drugs and without adequate medical guidance and prescription.

II—The Right to Rehabilitative Treatment

The School staff-to-juvenile ratio for purposes of treatment is approximately one to thirty. The sixteen counselors are responsible for developing and implementing individualized treatment programs at the institution, but the counselors need have no specialized training or experience. Administrative tasks ("paper work") occupy more than half of the counselors' time. The duties of the staff psychiatrist are limited to crises. He has no opportunity to develop and manage individual psychotherapy programs. The three staff psychologists do not hold graduate degrees and are not certified by Indiana. They render, principally, diagnostic services, mostly directed toward supervising in-take behavior classifications. * * *

The district court decided that both Indiana law and the federal Constitution secure for juvenile offenders a "right to treatment," and that the School failed to provide minimal rehabilitative treatment. * * * We hold, with the district court, that juveniles have a right to rehabilitative treatment.

The right to rehabilitative treatment for juvenile offenders has roots in the general social reform of the late nineteenth century, was nurtured by court decisions throughout the first half of this century, and has been established in state and federal courts in recent years. * * *

The United States Supreme Court has never definitively decided that a youth confined under the jurisdiction of a juvenile court has a constitutionally guaranteed right to treatment. But the Court has assumed, in passing on the validity of juvenile proceedings, that a state must provide treatment for juveniles. * * * [S]everal recent state and federal cases, out of concern—based upon the *parens patriae* doctrine underlying the juvenile justice system—that rehabilitative treatment was not generally accorded in the juvenile reform process, have decided that juvenile inmates have a constitutional right to that treatment.

In [*Martarella v. Kelley*, 349 F.Supp. 575 (S.D.N.Y.1972)] the court found a clear constitutional right to treatment for juveniles based on the 8th and 14th Amendments:

> What we have said, although the record would justify more, is sufficient to establish that, however benign the purposes for which members of the plaintiff class are held in custody, and whatever the sad necessities which prompt their detention, they are held in penal condition. Where the State, as *parens patriae*, imposes such detention, it can meet the Constitution's requirement of due process and prohibition of cruel and unusual punishment if, and only if, it furnishes adequate treatment to the detainee.

After an historical analysis of the development of the right, the court concluded:

In sum, the law has developed to a point which justifies the assertion that: "A new concept of substantive due process is evolving in the therapeutic realm. This concept is founded upon a recognition of the concurrency between the state's exercise of sanctioning powers and its assumption of the duties of social responsibility. Its implication is that effective treatment must be the quid pro quo for society's right to exercise its parens patriae controls. Whether specifically recognized by statutory enactment or implicitly derived from the constitutional requirements of due process, the right to treatment exists."

In a most recent case, *Morales v. Turman* (E.D.Tex.1973), a federal district court specifically found that juveniles at Texas' six juvenile training schools have both a statutory and constitutional right to treatment.

We hold that on the record before us the district court did not err in deciding that the plaintiff juveniles have the right under the 14th Amendment due process clause to rehabilitative treatment.[12]

III—Adequacy of Treatment

* * * We leave to the competent district court the decision: what is the minimal treatment required to provide constitutional due process, having in mind that the juvenile process has elements of both the criminal and mental health processes.

In our view the "right to treatment" includes the right to minimum acceptable standards of care and treatment for juveniles and the right to individualized care and treatment. Because children differ in their need for rehabilitation, individual need for treatment will differ. When a state assumes the place of a juvenile's parents, it assumes as well the parental duties, and its treatment of its juveniles should, so far as can be reasonably required, be what proper parental care would provide. Without a program of individual treatment the result may be that the juveniles will not be rehabilitated, but warehoused, and that at the termination of detention they will likely be incapable of taking their proper places in free society; their interests and those of the state and the school thereby being defeated.

We therefore affirm the judgment of the district court in each appeal, and remand only for the limited purpose of further proceedings in No. 73–1446 with respect to the right to rehabilitative treatment.

NOTES

1) **The "Right to Treatment"** What protection does the *Nelson* Court's Eighth Amendment "cruel and unusual punishment" analysis provide for

---

12. We note that the district court additionally determined that a right to treatment in this case has a statutory basis in view of the 'custody, care, and discipline' language of the Indiana Juvenile Court Act, Burns Ind.Stat.Ann. 9–3201, IC 1971, 31–5–7–1. We agree with this conclusion. Since we have today determined that the federal Constitution affords juveniles a right to treatment, any interpretation of the Indiana Act which would find no such right to exist would itself be unconstitutional.

juveniles? What tests do the Court use to determine if conditions of confinement constitute "cruel and unusual" punishment?

Where does the *Nelson* Court find the "right to treatment"? What does the "right to treatment" entail? Must a state treat a youth successfully in order to satisfy his or her "right" to treatment? If the "right" only means a "right" to have the institution try to "treat" a youth, what efforts are necessary? Does "milieu therapy," in which the entire institutional environment constitutes the treatment program, satisfy the right to treatment? How does a court know? If the "real" reason for inadequate institutional conditions is simply lack of resources, how can a Court, or more properly, the state department of corrections, obtain the necessary funding? Is it appropriate for the judicial branch to make resource allocation decisions that normally fall within the legislative or executive purview? What can a court do if the legislature fails to appropriate resources to implement the "right" to treatment?

Lower federal courts differ on the appropriate standard: some, like *Nelson v. Heyne*, apply the eighth amendment to prohibit guards' beatings of juveniles. Other courts apply the Fourteenth Amendment due process clause to prohibit abusive institutional practices. E.g., *H.C. by Hewett v. Jarrard*, 786 F.2d 1080 (11th Cir.1986) (applying due process clause to conditions of confinement of a juvenile confined pending trial on delinquency charges); *Santana v. Collazo*, 714 F.2d 1172, 1179 (1st Cir.1983) (using eighth amendment standards as constitutional minimum, but applying due process clause to juveniles confined for status and minor offenses), cert. denied, 466 U.S. 974, 104 S.Ct. 2352, 80 L.Ed.2d 825 (1984); *Milonas v. Williams*, 691 F.2d 931, 942 & n. 10 (10th Cir.1982) (applying due process clause to conditions involving juveniles confined for discipline problems and crimes), cert. denied, 460 U.S. 1069, 103 S.Ct. 1524, 75 L.Ed.2d 947 (1983).

Unlike the situations in *In re C.B.* and *Hezzie R.*, *supra*, pp. 790–792 where the states confined delinquents in adult prisons under identical conditions with criminals, courts confront greater difficulties assessing the differences between treatment and punishment when states house delinquents in separate juvenile correctional facilities and provide somewhat different correctional regimes. If the procedural differences between juvenile and criminal courts, such as the right to a jury trial, hinge on the distinctions between treatment and punishment, then courts must determine how juveniles' conditions of confinement differ from criminals' or what affirmative benefits juveniles must receive that adults do not to justify those differences.

2) Rationale of the Right to Treatment The right to treatment follows from a state's invocation of its *parens patriae* power to intervene for the benefit of the individual. In a variety of institutional settings other than juvenile correctional facilities, such as involuntary commitment of the mentally ill or mentally retarded, states confine individuals without affording them the procedural safeguards associated with criminal incarceration for punishment. In all of these settings, the promise of benefit provides the justification for the less stringent procedural safeguards. A failure to deliver the promised treatment as a compensatory trade-off for the less stringent procedures may constitute a denial of due process. *See e.g., Donaldson v. O'Connor*, 493 F.2d

507, 513 (5th Cir.1974), *vacated on other grounds*, 422 U.S. 563, 577, 95 S.Ct. 2486, 45 L.Ed.2d 396 (1975); *Rouse v. Cameron*, 373 F.2d 451, 461 (D.C.Cir. 1966); *Wyatt v. Stickney*, 325 F.Supp. 781, 786 (M.D.Ala.1971), *aff'd in part, rev'd in part sub nom. Wyatt v. Aderholt*, 503 F.2d 1305, 1319 (5th Cir.1974). For commentary on these mental health "right to treatment" cases, *see* Birnbaum, "The Right to Treatment," 46 *A.B.A. J.* 499 (1960); "The Right to Treatment," 57 *Geo.L.J.* 673 (1969) (symposium); "Developments in the Law– Civil Commitment of the Mentally Ill," 87 *Harv.L.Rev.* 1190, 1316–57 (1974).

Delinquents incarcerated in state training schools have invoked the constitutional "quid pro quo" rationale of the civil commitment cases in order to obtain positive treatment rather than simple custodial confinement. *See, e.g., Pena v. New York State Div. for Youth*, 419 F.Supp. 203 (S.D.N.Y.1976); *Morales v. Turman*, 383 F.Supp. 53 (E.D.Tex.1974), *rev'd on other grounds*, 535 F.2d 864 (5th Cir.1976); *Martarella v. Kelley*, 349 F.Supp. 575 (S.D.N.Y. 1972); *Inmates of Boys' Training School v. Affleck*, 346 F.Supp. 1354 (D.R.I. 1972); *Baker v. Hamilton*, 345 F.Supp. 345 (W.D.Ky.1972); *Lollis v. New York State Dep't of Social Serv.*, 322 F.Supp. 473 (S.D.N.Y.1970). Juveniles success- fully have invoked the right to treatment against juvenile institutions when they demonstrated either that the state did not provide minimally adequate rehabilitative services or subjected them to custodial warehousing or punitive practices. *See, e.g., In re Elmore*, 382 F.2d 125 (D.C.Cir.1967); *Creek v. Stone*, 379 F.2d 106 (D.C.Cir.1967). For commentary on these and other related cases, Patricia Wald and Larry Schwartz, "Trying a Juvenile Right to Treat- ment Suit: Pointers and Pitfalls for Plaintiffs," 12 *Am.Crim.L.Rev.* 125 (1974); Note, "The Courts, The Constitution and Juvenile Institutional Re- form," 52 *B.U.L. Rev.* 33 (1972); Note, "Judicial Recognition and Implementa- tion of a Right to Treatment for Institutionalized Juveniles," 49 *Notre Dame Law.* 1051 (1974); "Constitutional Right to Treatment for Juveniles Adjudi- cated to be Delinquent—*Nelson v. Heyne*," 12 *Am. Crim. L. Rev.* 209 (1974); "Limits on Punishment and Entitlement to Rehabilitative Treatment of Institutionalized Juveniles: Nelson v. *Heyne*," 60 *Va.L.Rev.* 864 (1974); Mi- chael J. Dale, "Lawsuits and Public Policy: The Role of Litigation in Correct- ing Conditions in Juvenile Detention Centers," 32 U.S.F.L.Rev. 675 (1998) (Survey and analysis of litigation challenging conditions of confinement in juvenile detention and correctional institutions).

3) Judicial Disagreement About the Existence and Scope of a Juvenile's Constitutional "Right to Treatment" In **Santana v. Colla- zo**, 714 F.2d 1172, 1177 (1st Cir.1983), the First Circuit Court of Appeals concluded that adjudicated delinquents did not enjoy a constitutional right to treatment:

> A number of courts have found that juveniles involuntarily incarcer- ated have a right to rehabilitative treatment. The reasoning of these courts is two-fold. First, relying on the Supreme Court's insistence * * * that "the nature and duration of commitment must bear some reasonable relation to the purpose for which the individual is committed", courts have reasoned that because the state's authority over delinquent juveniles derives from its *parens patriae* interest in their welfare, due process requires that juveniles confined under that authority be given treatment consistent with the beneficent purpose of their confinement. Second,

courts have relied on the fact that the juvenile justice system denies certain due process safeguards, which denials have been found constitutionally acceptable because the purpose of incarceration is rehabilitation, not punishment.

As the district court in this case recognized, both of the theoretical bases for the claimed right to rehabilitative treatment are questionable. Although states have asserted their *parens patriae* authority in exercising control over problem juveniles, they may legitimately confine individuals solely to protect society from them. In addition, even without treatment, simply removing a juvenile from a dangerous or unhealthy environment may be a legitimate exercise of the state's *parens patriae* authority. In short, since rehabilitative treatment is not the only legitimate purpose of juvenile confinement, the Supreme Court's insistence that the nature of confinement must bear a reasonable relationship to the purpose of that confinement gains plaintiffs little ground in their effort to establish a right to rehabilitative treatment.

The second aspect of the quid pro quo theory has even less merit. The procedural protections accorded juvenile offenders may differ from those accorded criminal defendants, because the demands of due process differ according to the interests of the individual and of society in the given situation. The Supreme Court has found certain distinctions between the protections accorded juveniles and those accorded criminal defendants constitutionally acceptable. Were that not the case, no amount of treatment would make up for the denial of due process along the way.

In short, there is no legally cognizable quo to trigger a compensatory quid. We therefore agree with the district court that although rehabilitative training is no doubt desirable and sound as a matter of policy and, perhaps, of state law, plaintiffs have no constitutional right to that rehabilitative training. * * *

Even more important than Eighth Amendment concerns for our purposes, juveniles like plaintiffs, who have not been convicted of crimes, have a due process interest in freedom from unnecessary bodily restraint which entitles them to closer scrutiny of their conditions of confinement than that accorded convicted criminals. * * *

The Supreme Court has recognized that the deprivation of liberty and conditions of confinement of both juvenile detention and involuntary confinement of the mentally ill may be sufficiently analogous to criminal punishment to warrant the protection of the Eighth Amendment. The possibility of Eighth Amendment protection, however, does not mean that the state may assert punishment as a legitimate goal of incarceration. Thus, because the state has no legitimate interest in punishment, the conditions of juvenile confinement, like those of confinement of the mentally ill, are subject to more exacting scrutiny than conditions imposed on convicted criminals.

The distinction between conditions imposed for the legitimate purpose of maintaining institutional order and safety and those that amount to retribution is a fine one. Certainly, administrators of a juvenile home must be free to discipline the home's residents. And, in doing so, the state of course inflicts punishment for offending behavior. The distinction, however, is not an entirely meaningless one. In a case such as this, it may simply be a matter of the closeness with which courts should be willing to scrutinize the state's asserted interest in imposing burdensome conditions of confinement. When the conditions are imposed on convicted criminals, the Supreme Court has deferred to the judgment of prison administrators unless the conditions are cruel and unusual, because "[t]o the extent that such conditions are restrictive and even harsh, they are part of the penalty that criminal offenders pay for their offenses against society." For an individual not convicted of a crime, however, restrictions on his liberty beyond his initial incarceration must be reasonably related to some legitimate government objective—of rehabilitation, safety or internal order and security.

The district court * * * made no findings regarding the legitimacy and weight of the state's interest in confining the juveniles in isolation. Were there nothing of concern in the record, we might be inclined to assume that the state's interest, presumably in protecting the juveniles from harm, in discouraging offending behavior and in preventing escapes, was sufficient to justify the deprivations imposed. A number of experts testified, however, that isolation for longer than a few hours serves no legitimate therapeutic or disciplinary purpose and is unnecessary to prevent harm unless a juvenile is severely emotionally disturbed. In addition, the experts testified, extended isolation can be psychologically damaging and * * * may be physically harmful. The district court recognized that "[i]solation as a disciplinary measure, under the circumstances present in this case, entails a substantial curtailment of a juvenile's freedom." We agree and are satisfied that the curtailment is substantial enough to warrant further examination of the necessity for and conditions of this confinement. * * *

The court **Alexander S. v. Boyd**, 876 F.Supp. 773 (D.S.C.1995), found that the incarcerated juveniles established that the conditions of confinement violated their constitutional and statutory rights to adequate treatment but declined to prescribe a specific remedy:

Courts around the country are not in agreement as to the appropriate federal standard by which to judge state juvenile detention facility conditions. * * *

After reviewing these authorities, the court has determined that the Due Process Clause of the Fourteenth Amendment, which implicitly encompasses the protections of the Eighth Amendment, is the appropriate standard for reviewing the conditions at the DJJ facilities. Adoption of the more stringent Due Process Clause is appropriate in this case because the juveniles incarcerated at DJJ facilities have, with few exceptions, not been convicted of a crime; rather, they have merely been adjudicated to be juvenile delinquents. * * *

In *Jackson v. Indiana*, the Supreme Court held that, in the noncriminal setting, there must be a relationship between the purpose for which an individual's liberty is taken and the treatment provided to that person. In *Jackson*, a case involving a mentally retarded individual, the Court stated: "At the least, due process requires that the nature and duration of commitment bear some reasonable relation to the purpose for which the individual is committed."

Numerous district courts have relied upon the rationale employed by the Supreme Court in *Jackson* to hold that where, as in South Carolina, the purpose of incarcerating juveniles in a state training school is treatment and rehabilitation, the Due Process Clause "requires that the conditions and programs at the school must be reasonably related to that purpose."

In addition, the Due Process Clause guarantees to juveniles who are incarcerated the right to reasonably safe conditions of confinement, freedom from unreasonable bodily restraint, and minimally adequate training to protect those interests.

Safety, in the context of this case, encompasses the Plaintiffs' right to reasonable protection from the aggression of others, whether "others" be juveniles or staff.

The interest in freedom from unreasonable bodily restraint includes freedom from unnecessary bodily restraint through mechanical devices as well as unreasonably restrictive conditions of confinement. Unreasonably restrictive conditions of confinement are those which unduly restrict the juveniles' freedom of action and are not reasonably related to legitimate security or safety needs of the institution.

The right to minimally adequate training is more difficult to define. As noted by the Supreme Court in *Youngberg* [*v. Romeo*]:

> It is not feasible * * * to define or identify the type of training that may be required in every case. A court properly may start with the generalization that there is a right to minimally adequate training. The basic requirement of adequacy, in terms more familiar to courts, may be stated as that training which is reasonable in light of identifiable liberty interests and the circumstances of the case.

Additionally, as noted by the *Youngberg* court, when a court is called upon to decide what is reasonable under the circumstances presented, the court

> must show deference to the judgment exercised by a qualified professional. * * * [T]he decision, if made by a professional, is presumptively valid; liability may be imposed only when the decision by the professional is such a substantial departure from accepted professional judgment, practice, or standards as to demonstrate that the person responsible actually did not base the decision on such a judgment.

The court must emphasize that its role in this litigation is to identify minimally acceptable standards for treatment and rehabilitation. In other words, it is not necessary that the state provide the best possible services and training available to the Plaintiffs. The test in this case is whether the state is providing minimally adequate or reasonable services and training necessary to ensure the protected interests of the Plaintiffs. It is not appropriate that the state be held to a standard which imposes an affirmative duty to succeed in the purpose of correcting the juveniles' behavior. Although such a standard may be desirable, it is not constitutionally mandated. All that is required is that the juveniles be housed under conditions that provide them with a reasonable opportunity to correct their behavior. Obviously, this standard incorporates the security, program, and service functions that are basic to juvenile corrections. These basic services include sufficient numbers of adequately trained staff so that the purpose of the confinement may be advanced, minimal levels of programming reasonably geared toward aiding juveniles to correct their behavior, and other services that are minimally necessary to give the Plaintiffs a reasonable opportunity to accomplish the purpose of the confinement while protecting the other recognized interests in safety and reasonable restraint.

In deciding minimum constitutional requirements for the institutions under challenge here, this court is not bound by standards promulgated by organizations such as the American Correctional Association. * * *

Having determined that certain constitutional and statutory deficiencies exist at facilities operated by DJJ, the court must determine an appropriate method for devising and implementing a remedial plan. The Plaintiffs have invited the court to devise and impose a judicially created plan based on the record before it. The court has concluded, however, that it must first afford the state of South Carolina the opportunity to correct the deficiencies that have been brought to light by this litigation and identified in this order.

It is well settled that under principles of comity and federalism, this court must decline the Plaintiffs' invitation to impose a broad and sweeping remedy upon the Defendants, but must instead allow the Defendants an opportunity to devise a plan of their own for remedying the constitutional violations. * * *

4) Analysis of Legal Developments in the Right to Treatment In an article analyzing the evolution and limitations of the "right to treatment" as a strategy to improve the quality of services available to institutionalized youths, **Paul Holland and Wallace J. Mlyniec, "Whatever Happened to the Right to Treatment?: The Modern Quest of a Historical Promise," 68** *Temp. L. Rev.* **1791 (1995)**, the doctrinal developments and constitutional limits:

Right to treatment cases were of two types. The first type involved basic concepts of human decency. For example, the cases of *Nelson v. Heyne*, *Morgan v. Sproat*, *Pena v. Division of Youth*, and *Morales v. Turman* involved challenges to institutional conditions such as the use of corporal punishment, disciplinary isolation, mechanical restraints, tranquilizers and tear gas, in addition to inadequate medical and dental care, invidious discrimination based on race and national origin, and overcrowding. The second type of claim challenged the failure of the juvenile justice system's treatment regimen to live up to its quasi-medical pretensions. Plaintiffs attacked the lack of services, such as psychiatric and psychological treatment, group and individual counseling, health care, and education, that would be required in an effective rehabilitation program. * * *

Several legal sources were cited to support the children's claims for relief. For example, judges ruling in early cases like *Creek v. Stone*, *In re Elmore* and *Nelson v. Heyne* found support for the right to treatment in the state juvenile court statutes. The guarantee of the right to treatment was also found in both the Eighth and Fourteenth Amendments to the Constitution. Two views of the Eighth Amendment prevailed. Some courts, like that in *Martarella*, believed that a right to treatment existed within the Eighth Amendment. Others, like the court in *Affleck*, found no right to treatment in the Eighth Amendment but, instead, held that the challenged conditions violated the state constitution's cruel and unusual punishment clause.

The Fourteenth Amendment Due Process Clause also provided two bases for the right to treatment. The first, known as the "quid pro quo" theory, was endorsed by the courts in *Morales, Nelson*, and *Sproat*. This theory states that a juvenile must receive rehabilitative treatment in exchange for receiving fewer procedural protections at a delinquency trial than would an adult in a criminal trial. The other Fourteenth Amendment theory used to support a right to treatment was the right to substantive due process. In *Jackson v. Indiana*, the United States Supreme Court stated that "[a]t the least, due process requires that the nature and duration of commitment bear some reasonable relation to the purpose for which the individual is committed." From this language, the courts in *Sproat, Morales*, and other cases declared that treatment—the announced purpose of state custody—must be provided lest that custody devolve into a purely arbitrary exercise of governmental authority over an involuntarily committed juvenile delinquent.

The relief requested in these cases was extensive. Not only did the plaintiffs seek to enjoin abusive practices and control overcrowding, but they sought to tell juvenile corrections officials how to operate viable treatment programs. In many cases, experts in mental health care, drug treatment, medicine, education, architecture, crime prevention, rehabilitation programming, and accreditation testified not only about the shortcomings of the institutions but about the need to provide specific rehabilitative programs. The testimony concerning the physical dangers in the facilities and their lack of rehabilitative programming shocked the judges, who responded by issuing sweeping remedial orders. Monitors were appointed to make independent assessments of agency activities; buildings were closed; baseline conditions of confinement were established; disciplinary codes were imposed; diagnostic and evaluation procedures were required and individualized treatment plans were created; staff-inmate ratios were imposed and staff training was required; the hiring of new medical, mental health, and drug counsellors was ordered; and educational and vocational training was required. Agencies were ordered to go to their legislatures to request more money.

The courts continued to monitor these cases for many years, involving themselves in the day-to-day operations of the facilities. * * * Thus, the constitutional right to treatment appeared to provide not only a sufficient legal theory for challenging conditions, but a potent weapon for revamping the entire juvenile justice system. * * *

The demise of the right to treatment as a basis for improving conditions in juvenile treatment centers came not from a direct assault on the doctrine but from a convergence of judicial resistance to attacks on other systems. In *Youngberg v. Romeo*, the United States Supreme Court delineated the substantive due process rights that were retained by a profoundly mentally retarded adult who had been involuntarily committed. Romeo had claimed a right to safe conditions, freedom from bodily restraints, and minimally adequate habilitation. Habilitation was defined as training and development of needed skills. The Court easily acceded to Romeo's first two claims, but it ruled narrowly on the issue of his right to training. Recognizing that Romeo's condition precluded release, the Court acknowledged his right to be trained but endorsed it only as it related to his safety and to his freedom from restraint within the institution. The Court further limited relief to minimally adequate training and ordered that the lower courts defer to the judgments of the professionals about what kind of training was necessary. Finally, the Court saw no need to rule on whether a person involuntarily committed to a state institution had some general constitutional right to training per se* * *.

Although the *Youngberg* ruling has slowed the filing of right to treatment suits, it has provided some protection to incarcerated children. For example, in *Santana v. Collazo*, the court required the territory of Puerto Rico to provide minimally adequate training to avoid the use of unnecessary bodily restraints. The *Santana* court also used the *Youngberg* Court's concern for a safe environment as the basis for removing fire hazards. Some courts have used the rationale of *Youngberg* to rule that children are entitled to minimum care and other courts have ruled that the Eighth Amendment concern for humane care is subsumed into the Fourteenth Amendment by virtue of *Youngberg*'s right to safe care and freedom from restraint. * * *

In light of *Youngberg* and recent Eighth Amendment jurisprudence, the constitutional right to treatment for confined juveniles has lost much of its doctrinal foundation. As currently understood, the Fourteenth and Eighth Amendments require only freedom from unnecessary restraint and minimally humane conditions of confinement. Food, clothing, shelter and medical care must only be adequate enough to avoid harm. In the main, treatment or training is directed at little more than preserving the peace within the training school. * * *

5) Prison Litigation Reform Act In 1996, Congress passed the Prison Litigation Reform Act (PLRA) which restricts the powers of state and federal courts to order prospective relief from conditions of confinement based on violations of federal rights. The PLRA applies to juvenile detention facilities and correctional institutions as well as to adult jails and prisons. 18 *U.S.C.A.* § 3626 (1999). Appropriate remedies with respect to prison conditions

(a) Requirements for relief.—

(1) Prospective relief.—(A) Prospective relief in any civil action with respect to prison conditions shall extend no further than necessary to correct the violation of the Federal right of a particular plaintiff or plaintiffs. The court shall not grant or approve any prospective relief unless the court finds that such relief is narrowly drawn, extends no further than necessary to correct the violation of the Federal right, and is the least intrusive means necessary to correct the violation of the Federal right. The court shall give substantial weight to any adverse impact on

public safety or the operation of a criminal justice system caused by the relief. * * *

In light of the uncertainty about a Federal "right to treatment," what are the implications of the PRLA for juveniles confined in state correctional institutions?

2. THE EFFECTIVENESS OF TREATMENT IN DELINQUENCY INSTITUTIONS

Progressive reformers expressed considerable optimism that delinquents' youthfulness and greater malleability would enable them to respond more readily to treatment. By contrast, a comprehensive assessment of rehabilitation research conducted by the National Academy of Sciences questioned both the efficacy of juvenile justice interventions and the assumption that youths manifest greater treatment responsiveness. Lee B. Sechrest, White, and Brown, *The Rehabilitation of Criminal Offenders* 102 (1979). "The current research literature provides no basis for positive recommendations about techniques to rehabilitate criminal offenders. The literature does afford occasional hints of intervention that may have promise, but to recommend widespread implementation of those measures would be irresponsible. Many of them would probably be wasteful, and some would do more harm than good in the long run."

Evaluations of juvenile institutional programs provide mixed evidence that they effectively treat youths or reduce their recidivism rates. Steven P. Lab and John T. Whitehead, "An Analysis of Juvenile Correctional Treatment." 34 *Crime and Delinquency* 60 (1988); Steven P. Lab and John T. Whitehead, "From 'Nothing Works' to 'The Appropriate Works': The Latest Stop on the Search for the Secular Grail," 28 *Criminology* 405 (1990). Evaluations of training schools, the most common form of institutional "treatment" for the largest numbers of serious and chronic delinquents, consistently report negative findings. Most state training schools "fail to reform * * * [and] make no appreciable reductions in the very high recidivism rates, on the order to 70 to 80 percent, that are expected for chronic offenders." Peter Greenwood and Franklin Zimring, *One Last Chance: The Pursuit of Promising Intervention Strategies for Chronic Juvenile Offenders* 40 (1985). An analysis in Minnesota of recidivism rates of youths released from state correctional and private facilities in 1985 and 1991 found that between 53 percent and 77 percent continued their criminal careers into adulthood. Minnesota Legislative Auditor, *Residential Facilities for Juvenile Offenders* (1995). Analyses of recidivism among 926 males released from Washington state's residential facilities in 1982 reported that over half (58.8%) reoffended within one year and more than two-thirds (67.9%) reoffended within two years. John C. Steiger and Cary Dizon, *Rehabilitation, Release, and Reoffending: A Report on the Criminal Careers of the Division of Juvenile Rehabilitation "Class of 1982"* (1991). A study of 527 males released from ten residential facilities in Pennsylvania in 1984 reported that police rearrested more than half (57%) and courts recommitted to residential facilities or prisons about one-quarter (23%) within two years. Lynn Goodstein and Henry Sontheimer, *A Study of the Impact of 10 Pennsylvania Residential Placements on Juvenile Recidivism* (1987).

Despite these earlier negative results, more recent evaluation studies report more promising findings of the effects of rehabilitative interventions. One methodological strategy to identify "what works" entails meta-analyses or studies of studies. By coding each evaluation study on a number of variables (e.g., characteristics of the research design, subjects studied, type of treatment applied, and outcome measures), and combining and reanalyzing the studies, meta-analyses attempt to separate treatment effects from differences due to uncontrolled characteristics of the subjects or other limitations of research design. Proponents of treatment reject the suggestion that "nothing works," Robert Martinson, "What Works?: Questions and Answers About Prison Reform," *Public Interest* 25 (Spring 1974), and offer literature reviews, meta-analyses, or program descriptions that report that some interventions may produce positive effects on selected clients under certain conditions. Proponents of juvenile rehabilitation strenuously resist the general conclusion that "nothing works" in juvenile or adult corrections. *See e.g.* Greenwood and Zimring, *One Last Chance, supra* at 70, ("we consider the 'nothing works' conclusion to be simplistic overreaction to the empirical evidence"); Mark W. Lipsey, "Juvenile Delinquent Treatment: A Meta–Analytic Inquiry into the Variability of Effects," in *Meta–Analysis for Explanation: A Casebook* 97–98 (1992) (positive treatment effects typically occur in small, experimental programs that provide an intensive and integrated response to the multiplicity of problems that delinquent youths present); Albert R. Roberts and Michael J. Camasso, "The Effects of Juvenile Offender Treatment Programs on Recidivism: A Meta–Analysis of 46 Studies," 5 *Notre Dame J.L. Ethics & Pub. Pol'y* 421, 437 (1991) (family therapy produced positive effects); D.A. Andrews et al., "Does Correctional Treatment Work?: A Clinically Relevant and Psychologically Informed Meta–Analysis," 28 *Criminology* 369, 384 (1990) (meta-analysis reported positive effects when offenders received clinically appropriate psychological treatments "according to the principles of risk, need, and responsivity"); Jeffrey Fagan, "Social and Legal Policy Dimensions of Violent Juvenile Crime," 17 *Crim. Just. & Behav.* 93 (1990) ("the conclusion that 'nothing works' may be based more on the absence of empirical evidence that treatment is effective than on conclusive evidence that treatment does not work"); Rhena L. Izzo & Robert R. Ross, "Meta–Analysis of Rehabilitation Programs for Juvenile Delinquents," 17 *Crim. Just. & Behav.* 134, 141 (1990) (treatment strategies that developed juvenile offenders' cognitive skills appeared to show positive effects); Paul Gendreau & Bob Ross, "Revivification of Rehabilitation: Evidence from the 1980s," 4 *Just. Q.* 349, 395 (1987) ("it is downright ridiculous to say '[n]othing works' "); Carol J. Garrett, "Effects of Residential Treatment on Adjudicated Delinquents: A Meta–Analysis," 22 *J. Res. Crime & Delinq.* 287, 306 (1985) (meta-analysis of delinquency in residential treatment concluded that some programs produce positive results).

A recent and comprehensive meta-analyses of treatment interventions for delinquents by **Mark W. Lipsey and David B. Wilson, "Effective Intervention for Serious Juvenile Offenders: A Synthesis of Research," in Rolf Loeber and David P. Farrington, eds.,** *Serious and Violent Juvenile Offenders: Risk Factors and Successful Interventions* **313, 329–330, 338 (1998)**, summarizes the evaluations of juvenile correctional interventions for serious young offenders:

The meta-analysis reported in this chapter reviewed the statistical findings of 200 experimental or quasi-experimental studies of the effects of intervention with serious juvenile offenders and attempted to answer two questions: (a) Can intervention programs reduce the reoffending rates of serious delinquents? And (b) if so, what programs are most effective?

The first of these questions can be answered rather easily and convincingly, even though the answer is not very informative. The studies examined in this meta-analysis represented a large portion, if not virtually all, of the interventions with serious delinquents that have been studied with methods that yield some assessment of their impact on recidivism. The average intervention effect for these studies was positive, statistically significant, and equivalent to a recidivism reduction of about 6 percentage points, for example, from 50% to 44% (mean effect size = .12). The variation around this overall mean, however was considerable. Some studies and groups of studies reported effects much larger than this, and others reported effects very much smaller. The average effect, therefore does not provide a good summary of what can be expected from intervention with this juvenile population. The interesting question, then, is the second one above: Given a range of results from very bad to very good, what types of programs are the best for reducing recidivism? * * *

The first finding has to do with the differentiation of those intervention programs administered to offenders who were institutionalized and those administered to offenders in the community, that is, those not institutionalized. The former were primarily incarcerated in juvenile justice facilities, and the latter were mostly on probation or parole. * * * For noninstitutional intervention, effects were most strongly related to the characteristics of the juveniles, especially their prior offense histories. The influence of treatment type and amount was intermediate, and general program characteristics were only weakly related to effect size. For intervention with institutionalized juveniles, however, this ordering was reversed. General program characteristics showed the strongest relationship to the size of the intervention effects, especially the age of the program and whether service was administered by mental health or juvenile justice personnel. The type and amount of treatment displayed moderate relationships to the size of the intervention effects, and the characteristics of the juveniles were not especially important. * * *

Effective intervention, therefore, requires more than a "magic bullet" program concept—it also depends on a good match between program concept, host organization, and the clientele targeted. * * *

Andrews et al. (1990) described the "risk principle" as one of the elements of effective therapeutic intervention with juvenile delinquents. According to the risk principle, treatment for delinquent behavior is most effective when the juveniles to whom the treatment is administered have appreciable risk of actually reoffending. This principle reflects, in part, the truism that there must be potential for bad behavior before bad behavior can be inhibited. The contrary view is often expressed—that it is the more serious "hardened" cases that will be least amenable to treatment. The 200 studies of intervention with serious offenders in this meta-analysis supported the risk principle over the view that serious delinquents cannot be helped to reduce their offending. For both institutionalized and non-institutionalized offenders, the "average" intervention program represented in the research literature produced positive, statistically significant effects equivalent to about a 12% reduction in subsequent reoffense rates. The effects of the average program, however, were not representative of the impact achieved by the best programs. These were capable of reducing recidivism rates by as much as 40%, an accomplishment of considerable practical value in terms of the expense and social damage associated with the delinquent behavior of these juveniles. On the other hand, the "below average" programs generally had negligible effects on recidivism, indicated that success is not ensured in this domain. * * *

Doris Layton MacKenzie, *What Works in Corrections: Reducing the Criminal Activities of Offenders and Delinquents* 168 (2006), provides a rigorous assessment of the effectiveness of different types of correctional interventions. Several types of programs—including some of the institutional programs reviewed by Lipsey and Wilson and Multi–Systemic Therapy—reduced rates of recidivism for youths exposed to the treatment compared with control groups. A variety of preventive interventions also reduce the rate of offending by "at-risk" youth. See e.g. Peter W. Greenwood, *Changing Lives* (2006); David P. Farrington and Brandon C. Welsh, *Saving Children from a Life of Crime: Early Risk Factors and Effective Interventions* (2007).

NOTES

Lipsey and Wilson's analysis of successful program characteristics reports that positive treatment effects typically occur in smaller programs that provide an intensive and integrated response to the multiplicity of problems—educational deficits, family dysfunction, inadequate social and vocational skills, and poverty—that delinquent youths present. Generally, positive treatment effects occur only under optimal conditions, such as high treatment integrity in an established program with services provided by non-juvenile justice personnel. Research on the elements of effective correctional programs suggest some "promising directions" either to provide more humane short-term correctional experiences or to improve youths' long-term life chances. To what extent do the institutions described in this section meet Lipsey and Wilson's criteria for effective intervention?

D. DISPOSITION OF NON–CRIMINAL STATUS OFFENDERS

As juvenile courts' delinquency dispositions became more punitive during the 1970s and 1980s, analysts, policy makers, and courts questioned the appropriateness of committing non-criminal status offenders to delinquency institutions and pondered the alternatives available.

HARRIS v. CALENDINE

160 W.Va. 172, 233 S.E.2d 318 (W.Va.1977).

NEELEY, JUSTICE. * * * The primary question presented by this proceeding is whether W. Va. Code, 49–1–4 (1941) and W. Va. Code, 49–5–11 (1975) establish methods for handling juvenile offenders which are inherently unconstitutional. These West Virginia statutes, which indiscriminately combine status offenders with criminal offenders, present an enormous potential for abuse and unconstitutional application. * * *

The statutes under consideration, in the absence of guidelines for their application, fail to meet the equal protection, substantive due process, and the cruel and unusual punishment standards because they permit the classification and treatment of status offenders in the same manner as criminal offenders. * * *

We are * * * concerned with a child who is incorrigible, ungovernable, habitually disobedient and beyond the control of his parents, truant, repeatedly deserts his home or place of abode, engages in an occupation which is in violation of law, or frequents a place the existence of which is in violation of law. The Legislature has vested the juvenile court with jurisdiction over children who commit these status offenses so that the court may enforce order, safety, morality, and family discipline within the community. The intention of the law is laudable; however, the means employed to accomplish these ends are unconstitutional insofar as they result in the commitment of status offenders to secure, prison-like facilities which also house children guilty of criminal conduct, or needlessly subject status offenders to the degradation and physical abuse of incarceration.

At the outset the Court should make clear that we are not impressed with euphemistic titles used to disguise what are in fact secure, prison-like facilities. We define a secure, prison-like facility, regardless of whether it be called a "home for girls," "industrial school," "forestry camp," "children's shelter," "orphanage," or other imaginative name, as a place which relies for control of children upon locked rooms, locked buildings, guards, physical restraint, regimentation, and corporal punishment. * * *

We find that with regard to the status offender the procedure for disposition * * * can be applied in a manner repugnant to the basic principles of equal protection because it discriminates invidiously against children based upon social class, sex, and geographic location. It is obvious that a child from a family with financial resources will have an opportunity to use private institutional facilities which are far less restrictive, less dangerous, and less degrading than public correctional institutions. * * *

Furthermore, the status offender is inherently in a different class from the criminal offender. The Legislature could choose to punish children guilty of criminal conduct in the same manner as it punishes adults, but as a matter of public policy the Legislature provided instead for a comprehensive system of child welfare. The aim of this system is to protect and rehabilitate children, not to punish them. It has always been assumed that the Legislature can at any time withdraw some or all the benefits of this system from children guilty of criminal conduct. There is no such prospect for status offenders, however, since without the child welfare legislation they are guilty of no crimes cognizable and punishable by courts. This explains why status offenders have a special position within the current system, despite the fact that technically they are not distinguished from children guilty of actual criminal conduct. Since the class to which status offenders belong has been created under authority of the State's inherent and sovereign *parens patriae* power, and not under the plenary powers of the State to control criminal activity and punish criminals, status offenders must be treated in a fashion consistent with the *parens patriae* power, namely, they must be helped and not punished, otherwise their classification becomes invidious, and accordingly, unconstitutional.

Finally, it should be noted that status offender legislation discriminates invidiously against females. It is apparent that status offense petitions can easily be used to bring under control young women suspected by their parents or by other authorities of promiscuous behavior. Our society tends to condemn female promiscuity more severely than male promiscuity, and this tendency may explain why females often are unfairly classified and treated as status offenders. This Court offers no explanation for this phenomenon, nor do we make any normative judgments regarding the wisdom of such a distinction; however, we recognize its existence and its discriminatory effect on female status offenders. The control of sexual behavior may be accomplished by other means.

Furthermore the Court finds no rational connection between the legitimate legislative purposes of enforcing family discipline, protecting children, and protecting society from uncontrolled children, and the means by which the State is permitted to accomplish these purposes, namely incarceration of children in secure, prison-like facilities.

It is generally recognized that the greatest colleges for crime are prisons and reform schools. The most egregious punishment inflicted upon a child incarcerated in a West Virginia penal institution is not the deprivation of his liberty but rather his forced association with reprehensible persons. Prisons, by whatsoever name they may be known, are inherently dangerous places. Sexual assaults, physical violence, psychological abuse and total degradation are the likely consequences of incarceration. * * *

In view of the foregoing, and in view of the fact that there are numerous alternatives to incarceration for status offenders we hold that the State must exhaust every reasonable alternative to incarceration before committing a status offender to a secure, prison-like facility. Furthermore, for those extreme cases in which commitment of status offenders to a secure, prison-like facility cannot be avoided, the receiving facility must be devoted solely to the custody and rehabilitation of status offenders. In this manner status offenders can be spared contact under degrading and harmful conditions with delinquents who are guilty of criminal conduct and experienced in the ways of crime.

However, this does not limit the authority of the juvenile court to house and educate status offenders and criminal offenders together in shelter homes, residential treatment centers, and other modern facilities staffed by well trained, attentive, and dedicated people, where the atmosphere is characterized by love and concern rather than physical violence, corporal punishment and physical restraint of liberty, provided the court determines there is no danger to the physical safety or emotional health of the status offender. * * *

At the outset this Court acknowledges that the cruel and unusual punishment standard cannot easily be defined and certainly is not fixed; consequently, we feel the standard tends to broaden as society becomes more enlightened and humane. The standard ought to be especially broad in its application to status offenders, whom the State has pledged not to punish at all, but rather, to protect and rehabilitate. Furthermore, status offenders are not guilty of the criminal conduct which ordinarily serves to make society's exercise of the penal sanction legitimate. * * *

As the preceding sections of this opinion have made clear, this Court is concerned with the class of offenders known as status offenders. By definition, the nature of the class of offenses committed by status offenders is non-criminal. Accordingly, the status offender is located on the extreme end of a spectrum of juvenile misconduct running from most serious to least serious offenses. The nature of their offenses thus tends to indicate that status offenders incarcerated in secure, prison-like facilities, along with children guilty of criminal conduct, are suffering a constitutionally disproportionate penalty. * * *

Accordingly, we hold that a status offender may still be adjudged delinquent under W. Va. Code, 49-1-4 (1941); however, before he may be committed to a penal institution pursuant to the provisions of W. Va. Code, 49-5-11(4) (1975), there must be evidence on the record which clearly supports the conclusion, and the juvenile court must specifically find as a matter of fact, that no other reasonable alternative either is available or could with due diligence and financial commitment on the part of the State be made available to help the child, and that the child is so totally unmanageable, ungovernable, and anti-social that he or she is amenable to no treatment or restraint short of incarceration in a secure, prison-like facility. Furthermore, to reiterate in this context what we said above, no status offender in any event, regardless of incorrigibility, may be incarcerated in a secure, prison-like facility which is not devoted exclusively to the custody and rehabilitation of status offenders. We emphasize here that State parsimony is no defense to an allegation of deprivation of constitutional rights. The State may not punish a person not deserving of punishment merely because such action serves the State's interest in convenience of frugality.

Consequently, the standard which the juvenile court must apply is not a standard of what facilities are actually available in the State of West Virginia for the treatment of juvenile status offenders, but rather a standard which looks to what facilities could reasonably be made available in an enlightened and humane state solicitous of the welfare of its children but also mindful of other demands upon the State budget for humanitarian purposes. We recognize that problems may arise, as for example, when a court is located in a rural part of West Virginia which lacks child-care facilities, and the court has no place to send a status offender except a correctional facility. Nevertheless, in such cases, if rehabilitation of the status offender could be accomplished by his commitment to a well-run, centralized state residential treatment center, or a local shelter facility where a small number of children live with professionally trained house parents, or by any other reasonable method, then the juvenile judge, as a matter of state constitutional law, must make a disposition * * * which does not involve commitment to a secure, prison-like facility, or he must discharge the defendant. * * *

NOTES

1) Juvenile Justice and Delinquency Prevention Act In 1974, Congress passed the Juvenile justice and Delinquency Prevention Act of 1974, 42 U.S.C.A. §§ 5601, et seq., (1992), which mandated the deinstitutionalization of status and non-criminal offenders. The Federal sanction for a state's failure to achieve compliance with the JJDP de-institutionalization mandate is the termination of state eligibility to receive funds under the Juvenile Justice and Delinquency Prevention program. 42 U.S.C.A. § 5633 (c). The act discouraged the institutional co-mingling of status offenders and delinquents; encouraged the diversion of status offenders from the juvenile court whenever possible; and encouraged alternatives to juvenile detention and correctional facilities. In order for states to be eligible to receive Federal funds, the act also required states to remove all status offenders from secure institutions:

42 U.S.C.A. § 5603. Definitions (1999)

For purposes of this chapter—

(1) the term "community based" facility, program, or service means a small, open group home or other suitable place located near the juvenile's

home or family and programs of community supervision and service which maintain community and consumer participation in the planning operation, and evaluation of their programs which may include, but are not limited to, medical, educational, vocational, social, and psychological guidance, training, special education, counseling, alcoholism treatment, drug treatment, and other rehabilitative services; * * *

(12) the term "secure detention facility" means any public or private residential facility which—

(A) includes construction fixtures designed to physically restrict the movements and activities of juveniles or other individuals held in lawful custody in such facility; and

(B) is used for the temporary placement of any juvenile who is accused of having committed an offense, of any nonoffender, or of any other individual accused of having committed a criminal offense;

(13) the term "secure correctional facility" means any public or private residential facility which—

(A) includes construction fixtures designed to physically restrict the movements and activities of juveniles or other individuals held in lawful custody in such facility; and

(B) is used for the placement, after adjudication and disposition, of any juvenile who has been adjudicated as having committed an offense, any nonoffender, or any other individual convicted of a criminal offense;

(16) the term "valid court order" means a court order given by a juvenile court judge to a juvenile—

(A) who was brought before the court and made subject to such order;

(B) who received, before the issuance of such order, the full due process rights guaranteed to such juvenile by the Constitution of the United States;

(C) with respect to whom an appropriate public agency (other than a court or law enforcement agency), before the issuance of such order—

(i) reviewed the behavior of such juvenile and the circumstances under which such juvenile was brought before the court and made subject to such order;

(ii) determined the reasons for the behavior that caused such juvenile to be brought before the court and made subject to such order;

(iii) determined that all dispositions (including treatment), other than placement in a secure detention facility or a secure correctional facility, have been exhausted or are clearly inappropriate; and

(iv) submitted to the court a written report stating the results of the review conducted under clause (i) and the determinations made under clauses (ii) and (iii); * * *.

42 U.S.C.A. § 5633 (a) (1999):

(a) Requirements

In order to receive formula grants under this part, a State shall submit a plan for carrying out its purposes applicable to a 3–year period. Such plan

shall be amended annually to include new programs and challenge activities
* * *. The State shall submit annual performance reports to the Administrator which shall describe progress in implementing programs contained in the
original plan, and shall describe the status of compliance with State plan
requirements. In accordance with regulations which the Administrator shall
prescribe, such plan shall—* * *

(12)(A) provide within three years after submission of the initial plan that
juveniles who are charged with or who have committed offenses that would
not be criminal if committed by an adult or offenses (other than an offense
that constitutes a violation of a valid court order * * *), or alien juveniles in
custody, or such nonoffenders as dependent or neglected children, shall not be
placed in secure detention facilities or secure correctional facilities; and

(B) provide that the State shall submit annual reports to the Administrator containing a review of the progress made by the State to achieve the
deinstitutionalization of juveniles described in subparagraph (A) and a review
of the progress made by the State to provide that such juveniles, if placed in
facilities, are placed in facilities which (i) are the least restrictive alternatives
appropriate to the needs of the child and the community; (ii) are in reasonable
proximity to the family and the home communities of such juveniles; and (iii)
provide the services described in section 5603(1) of this title; * * *

2) Bootstrapping Status Offenders into Delinquents The following
excerpt describes the process of "bootstrapping" contained in the provisions
of the Juvenile Justice and Delinquency Prevention Act that prohibits institutionalization of status offenders for non-criminal behavior "other than an
offense that constitutes a violation of a valid court order." **Harry J.
Rothgerber, Jr., "The Bootstrapping of Status Offenders: A Vicious
Practice,"** 1 *J U L Ky. Children's Rts. J.* 1 (1991):

* * * [B]oth on the national and state levels, it has become public policy
to closely restrict the placement of status offenders. On the federal level, the
Juvenile Justice and Delinquency Prevention Act of 1974 (JJDPA) mandates
the deinstitutionalization of status offenders in all states receiving formula
grants under the legislation. The JJDPA requires that all participating states
cease placing juvenile status offenders in secure detention or secure correctional facilities except in very limited circumstances in which the due process
rights of the juvenile must be protected and effectuated. The underlying
theory is that "an outright ban on institutionalizing status offenders would do
more good for the great majority of status offenders who do not need
institutions than harm for the very few who do." The acceptance of federal
dollars by a state constitutes the sole basis of the federal right to require
compliance. Indeed, the acceptance of the principles and spirit of the JJDPA
by a majority of the states has had a stimulating effect on state juvenile
justice legislation in the area of deinstitutionalization. * * *

Efforts to deinstitutionalize status offenders and to separate them from
delinquents create difficult problems for judges, especially with the dispositional aspects of a juvenile case. Since the juvenile court judge's options
concerning status offenders are limited, the court may attempt to re-label or
transform the status offender into a delinquent, in order to provide more
placement possibilities, by the unconscionable practice of "bootstrapping".

Bootstrapping is the process whereby a juvenile court, either through its contempt power or by means of an escape petition, elevates a status offender to a public offender ("delinquent") for the same noncriminal misbehavior which brought the child before the Court in the first place. Bootstrapping occurs in the following situation: A child runs away from home and is adjudicated a status offender; the same child then runs away from the group home and becomes a public offender escapee. The child's behavior did not change. Yet the court's adjudication of the child's case was entirely different insofar as what had previously constituted a status offense was now treated as a public offense. * * *

[F]ederal and state policies mandate that status offenders be treated differently than public offenders (delinquents); and, it is violative of those policies to elevate a status offender into a public offender for the same noncriminal misbehavior which brought the child before the court in the first place.* * *

3) Courts' Authority to Enforce Orders What are the implications of these Federal provisions for state juvenile justice administration? What dispositions remain available to a state juvenile court judge who commits a status offender to a non-secure facility and from which the child then runs away? May a judge commit a status offender to an institution as a delinquent for contempt of court for violating a "valid court order" which requires the youth to attend school regularly or to remain in a non-secure placement and not run away? Is it appropriate to commit a youth who never committed a "real" crime to a delinquency institution for repeated status offenses? What can a state or the court do to protect its authority and to help problem juveniles?

In **In the Interests of J.E.S.**, 817 P.2d 508 (Colo.1991), the Colorado Supreme Court considered the validity of legislative restrictions on juvenile courts' authority to impose secure confinement sanctions on status offenders for contempt of court. In *J.E.S.*, the juvenile court sentenced J.E.S., a chronic truant, to forty-five days in Zebulon Pike Detention Center, instructing that twenty days be served immediately and twenty-five days be suspended, for contempt of a court order to attend school:

> The issue we must determine on appeal is whether the amended section 22–33–108(7), 9 C.R.S. (1990 Supp.), which precludes a court from incarcerating a child in a secure facility as a sanction for contempt in a compulsory school attendance case, violates the separation of powers doctrine of the Colorado Constitution by impermissibly abrogating the judiciary's power to incarcerate juveniles for contempt of court orders. * * *

Effective April 20, 1990, the language that is the subject of the present controversy was added. It states:

> The court may not impose any sanction of incarceration to a jail, lockup, other place used for the confinement of adult offenders, or any juvenile detention facility operated by or under contract with the department of institutions.

The district court concluded that, as amended, section 22–33–108(7) was an unconstitutional legislative abrogation of the judiciary's inherent contempt power. We agree. * * *

Contemnors who disregard the authority of the judiciary by refusing to obey valid court orders impair the efficient operation of the courts in fulfilling their judicial duties. Punishment for contemptuous conduct by fine or imprisonment, "is designed to vindicate the dignity and authority of a court when its orders have been flouted," and is thus meant to safeguard "the administration of the law, a function residing in the courts, rather than the operation of the law."

The judiciary's authority to punish for contempt of court has long been recognized as an inherent power essential to the effective administration of justice. * * *

The inherent and indispensable nature of the courts' right to punish contemptuous conduct necessarily shields this judicial power from legislative control under the separation of powers doctrine. * * * [W]hile the legislature may reasonably regulate the procedures the judiciary employs when exercising the contempt power, it may not unduly limit the sanctions for contemptuous conduct so as to seriously impair or destroy the courts' contempt power. * * *

[W]e believe that by prohibiting courts from incarcerating juveniles who repeatedly act in contempt of a court order, the amended section 22–33–108(7) unreasonably limits the courts' inherent contempt power in violation of the separation of powers doctrine.

Of those states that have confronted the problem of status offenders who disobey court orders, most have affirmed the courts' inherent right to order the secure detention of contemptuous status offenders despite a legislative ban or expression of legislative intent against such detention. Those cases holding otherwise are distinguishable in that they disapproved in particular of a practice not employed in the case before us, and that is the practice of bootstrapping where a child is adjudicated a delinquent for contemptuous conduct and then the child's delinquency status is used to justify secure detention. * * *

[B]y prohibiting "any sanction of incarceration to a jail, lockup, other place used for the confinement of adult offenders, or any juvenile detention facility operated by or under contract with the department of institutions," the Colorado General Assembly's enactment of section 22–33–108(7), 9 C.R.S. (1990 Supp.), effectively abolished incarceration as an available punishment for contemptuous truants since no other type of secure facility presently exists. J.E.S. argues that removing incarceration as an alternative was a reasonable restriction on the juvenile courts' contempt power because lesser sanctions such as community service remained viable options. We agree with the School District, however, that it is the threat of incarceration that allows the lesser sanctions to work.

In our view, the legislature's enactment of the amended section 22–33–108(7) has so deprived those courts having jurisdiction over truants of their inherent contempt power as to render them unable to preserve the dignity of the court and to administer their judicial functions in an effective manner. If responsibility for the enforcement of compulsory school attendance is to remain in the courts, the judiciary's power to enforce its orders must remain intact. We therefore hold that the legislature's amendment to section 22–33–108(7) usurps the courts' inherent contempt power so as to violate the separation of powers doctrine preserved by article III of the Colorado Constitution. * * *

MICHAEL G. v. SUPERIOR COURT

44 Cal.3d 283, 747 P.2d 1152, 243 Cal.Rptr. 224 (Cal. 1988).

ARGUELLES, JUSTICE. In this case we decide whether a minor made a ward of the court pursuant to Welfare and Institutions Code section 601, subdivision (b) as a result of his truancy, and later found in contempt of court for wilfully disobeying a juvenile court order to attend school, may be punished with confinement in a secure facility during nonschool hours, or whether sections 601, subdivision (b) and 207 prohibit such a disposition. Like the majority of other state courts which have addressed similar statutory schemes, we conclude that a juvenile court retains the authority, pursuant to its contempt power, to order the secure, nonschool-hours confinement of a contemptuous section 601 ward. At the same time, in order to harmonize the juvenile court's exercise of its contempt power with the legislative determination that status offenders, including truants,[2] should not ordinarily be confined in secure facilities, we conclude—again following the lead of a number of out-of-state decisions—that before a juvenile court orders such incarceration pursuant to its contempt authority, it should make a number of specified findings establishing the necessity of such a course of action.

Petitioner Michael G., a minor, was adjudged a ward of the Fresno County Superior Court, Juvenile Division, pursuant to section 601, subdivision (b)—truancy. As a condition of probation he was ordered, *inter alia*, to "attend school regularly and not be tardy or absent." Following numerous unexcused absences from school, the court ordered petitioner to show cause why he should not be held in contempt of court. * * * [T]he juvenile court concluded petitioner wilfully disobeyed the order of the court to attend school regularly and not be tardy or absent. * * * [T]he court ordered petitioner be delivered to the custody of the Director of Institutions of the Fresno County Probation Department for confinement for a 48–hour period. The court also ordered petitioner be held out of sight and hearing of any section 602 wards and that the 48–hour period would

---

2. "The status offender is a statutory creation, who occupies a unique position in the juvenile justice system. In contrast to the neglected, dependent or abused child, the status offender comes within the jurisdiction of the juvenile court because of his or her behavior, rather than on a finding of improper parental care or guidance. Unlike children charged with or found guilty of delinquency, alleged or adjudicated status offenders have not committed acts which would be considered criminal if done by an adult. When status offenders are incarcerated, therefore, it is not for any violation of the penal code, but for behavior which is considered unacceptable solely because of their age." In California, juvenile court jurisdiction over status offenders is conferred by section 601. This opinion will use the terms "status offender" and "section 601 ward" interchangeably.

commence on Friday at 6 p.m., and end at 6 p.m., the following Sunday.
* * *

In finding petitioner in contempt for violating a valid court order, the juvenile court exercised the traditional power inherent in judicial officials. "We start with the premise that the right of courts to conduct their business in an untrammeled way lies at the foundation of our system of government and that courts necessarily must possess the means of punishing for contempt when conduct tends directly to prevent the discharge of their functions." * * * The contempt power thus exists independent from legislative sanction although in this case the Legislature has specifically recognized that the juvenile court retains the ordinary contempt powers. (§ 213.)[3]

Although petitioner concedes that the juvenile court in general retains authority to hold wards who disobey its orders in contempt, he argues that, with respect to truants and other status offenders, the Legislature has specifically proscribed the incarceration of such juveniles even as a sanction for contempt. He relies on sections 601, subdivision (b) and 207. * * * [W]e conclude that the applicable statutes can and should be harmonized to both preserve the trial court's contempt authority and at the same time give recognition to the legislative policy reflected in sections 601, subdivision (b) and 207.

We begin with the actual language of those sections. The relevant portion of section 601, subdivision (b) states "it is the intent of the Legislature that no minor who is adjudged a ward of the court pursuant solely to this subdivision shall be removed from the custody of the parent or guardian except during school hours." Section 207, subdivision (a) states in pertinent part: "[n]o minor shall be detained in any jail, lockup, juvenile hall, or other secure facility who is taken into custody solely upon the ground that he or she is a person described in Section 601 or adjudged to be such or made a ward of the juvenile court solely upon that ground * * *."

While the language of the statutes clearly indicates that the Legislature has determined that no juvenile is to be detained in jail or juvenile hall "solely upon the ground that he or she is a person described in section 601," neither statute expressly indicates that it was intended to apply to the contempt setting. * * *

The history of section 207 and its prohibition on secure detention for status offenders also fails to inform us whether the Legislature intended to affect the juvenile court's contempt power. Section 207 was first added to the code as part of the Arnold–Kennick Juvenile Court Law in 1976, and was a mirror image of former section 507, added to the code in 1961.

---

3. Section 213 states "[a]ny willful disobedience or interference with any lawful order of the juvenile court or of a judge or referee thereof constitutes a contempt of court." While no case has yet construed the scope of this section, the penalties for violation of section 213 are apparently those set forth in Code of Civil Procedure section 1218 for contempts generally: a fine of up to $1,000, imprisonment of up to five days, or both.

This initial version of section 207 permitted the secure detention of status offenders if no other option was available. However, the Legislature amended the statute the next year to prohibit such detention of status offenders. * * *

Little more than one year prior to the enactment of the section 207 exceptions, a court confronted the instant statutory scheme for the first time. In *In re Ronald S.* (1977), a minor was adjudged a section 601 ward and sent to a nonsecure crisis center, from which he promptly walked away. A section 602 petition was thereafter filed, alleging the minor had violated Penal Code section 166 subd. 4, making it a misdemeanor to wilfully disobey "any process or order lawfully issued by any Court." The petition was sustained and he was ordered detained in juvenile hall, a secure facility.

The minor's petition for a writ of habeas corpus was granted. * * * The court noted that under prior law, a juvenile could become a section 602 ward by failing to obey a lawful order of the juvenile court. Thus, by walking out of a foster home or failing to attend school, a section 601 ward was transformed into a section 602 ward, i.e., a juvenile delinquent. Observing that such express "bootstrapping" was eliminated by a 1976 amendment deleting failure to obey a court order as a basis for sustaining a section 602 petition, the court reasoned that resort to Penal Code section 166 subd. 4 to sustain a section 602 petition and thereby justify secure incarceration was contrary to legislative intent. To permit such a procedure, the court noted, would render the "deletion of language in section 602 * * * meaningless and we would simply revert to the boot-strapping operation again. The court would be doing by indirection that which cannot be done directly. As the law now stands, the Legislature has said that if a [section] 601 [ward] wants to run, let him run. While this may be maddening, baffling and annoying to the juvenile court judge, ours is not to question the wisdom of the Legislature." Thus, after *Ronald S.*, it was clear that the secure detention of a status offender could not be justified by converting him into a section 602 ward via a criminal contempt citation.

Because the section 207 exceptions were enacted just over a year later, those provisions may have been a response to the *Ronald S.* decision. However, since none of the exceptions in section 207 * * * embrace the juvenile contemner situation, we can initially infer the Legislature intended to preserve the *Ronald S.* holding. " 'Where a statute has been construed by judicial decision, and that construction is not altered by subsequent legislation, it must be presumed that the Legislature is aware of the judicial construction and approves of it.' "

Although *Ronald S.* involved a contemptuous status offender, it also involved elevating a section 601 ward to delinquency status as a result of the contempt, something not done in petitioner's case. Thus, even assuming we can infer that the Legislature intended to preserve the *Ronald S.* holding (i.e., that a contempt conviction pursuant to Penal Code section

166 subd. 4 is impermissible to justify secure confinement via a section 602 wardship proceeding), that decision does not answer the question of whether a juvenile court is prohibited * * * from ordering the secure, nonschool-hours detention of a contemptuous status offender without converting the youth into a section 602 ward. * * *

Viewing the statutory scheme as a whole, we thus conclude that while the legislative history demonstrates an intent to prohibit the juvenile court from relying on a ward's violation of a court order as a justification for elevating a section 601 ward to a delinquent, there is nothing in that history which specifically indicates that the Legislature intended to prohibit a juvenile court from enforcing obedience to a court order through a contempt sanction that does not alter the status of the ward. * * *

By so concluding we avoid deciding whether the Legislature could constitutionally override the inherent contempt power of the courts. * * *

Although we conclude the limitations as stated in sections 207 and 601, subdivision (b) were not intended to affect the juvenile court's power to punish a contemptuous section 601 ward with secure detention during nonschool hours, we need not ignore the Legislature's general intent to deinstitutionalize status offenders. " '[E]very statute should be construed with reference to the whole system of law of which it is a part so that all may be harmonized and have effect.' " Thus, although the Legislature's general prohibition on the secure detention during nonschool hours for section 601 wards does not apply to contemners, respect for the intent of our coequal branch of government demands that courts exercise caution when imposing such sanctions against contemptuous status offenders.

In mandating that courts exercise caution before ordering a status offender into secure custody for a contemptuous act, we do not paint on a wholly blank canvas. In 1974, Congress passed the Juvenile Justice and Delinquency Prevention Act (hereafter the Act) (42 U.S.C. §§ 5601–5639 (1976) & Supp.III 1979, as amended by Juvenile Justice Amendments of 1980, Pub.L. No. 96–509, 94 Stat. 2750), conditioning block grants to the states on compliance with the Act's requirement of the deinstitutionalization of status offenders.[11] As a result, nearly every state in the union passed a statute similar to section 207.

Thus, many of our sister states have already confronted the problem of how juvenile courts can effectively deal with status offenders who continually disobey the court's orders if secure incarceration is not an

---

11. Interestingly, the Act initially prohibited incarcerating a status offender after elevating him to delinquency status due to his failure to comply with a court order. (Legal Opinion No. 77–25—Classification of Juveniles as Status Offenders (Mar. 15, 1977) [from the Office of the General Counsel of the Law Enforcement Assistance Administration].) However, section 5633, subdivision (a)(12)(A) of title 42 of the United States Code was amended in 1980 and now requires the states to file a plan to achieve the goal, within three years, "that juveniles who are charged with or who have committed offenses that would not be criminal if committed by an adult or offenses which do not constitute violations of valid court orders ... shall not be placed in secure detention facilities or secure correctional facilities." The amended Act would now apparently except juvenile contemners from its general requirement of abolishing the secure confinement of status offenders.

available option. Most states have affirmed their courts' use of the contempt power to order the secure detention of contemptuous status offenders despite an expression of legislative intent generally banning such detention * * *

Accordingly, we determine that a status offender may be found in contempt and incarcerated, but with the following limitations: (1) the juvenile is given sufficient notice to comply with the order and understands its provisions; (2) the violation of the court order is egregious; (3) less restrictive alternatives were considered and found to be ineffective; and (4) special confinement conditions are arranged consistent with * * * [the statutory provisions barring intermingling with delinquents]."

These four qualifications are sound and we hold California courts should adhere to them. Imposition of these qualifications on a juvenile court's contempt power achieves the twin goals of vindicating the inherent power of the courts while giving practical effect to the Legislature's express intent to deinstitutionalize status offenders in general. The necessity of the first requirement is self-evident; due process concerns would be implicated if the juvenile who lacked notice of the court's orders was held in contempt for violating those orders.

The requirement of an egregious violation ensures that secure incarceration will not become a commonplace sanction in contravention of the Legislature's intent to comply with the federal mandate to deinstitutionalize status offenders. The reservation of the nonschool hours, secure-detention sanction for the most severe cases will require the juvenile court to decide whether, based on the entire record, imposition of this harsh penalty is justified because no other sanction will suffice. Moreover, this requirement has the additional benefit of ensuring our juvenile courts will exercise this facet of their inherent contempt power to the least extent possible so as to give maximum effect to the Legislature's avowed intent to house status offenders in nonsecure surroundings.

The third requirement—consideration and rejection of less restrictive sanctions—is closely akin to the second requirement that the violation of the court's order be egregious since it too has its genesis in the idea that incarceration should be the exception, not the rule. While the court need not necessarily have attempted lesser penalties before imposing secure confinement, the record should indicate that lesser alternatives were considered by the juvenile court before ordering incarceration.

By requiring the juvenile court to memorialize its findings on the record, we again ensure the court is aware that, by ordering the secure confinement of a juvenile who has not committed a criminal offense, it is taking the extraordinary step of acting contrary to the wishes of the Legislature but is justified in doing so because it is convinced there is no other alternative which will adequately serve the purpose of the contempt citation. * * *

Finally, the juvenile court ordering the incarceration of a status offender should also prohibit the minor from coming in contact with those minors confined due to their commission of a crime, i.e., section 602 wards. * * *

We realize our decision permits the contemptuous status offender to suffer the major disadvantage heretofore reserved for section 602 wards: secure confinement during nonschool hours. However, the nature of the confinement suffered by the contemptuous status offender differs in at least one substantial respect: he cannot come in contact with other section 602 wards who may be confined in the same facility. This limitation, as recognized by the juvenile court below, is important to ensure the status offender's problems, noncriminal at that time, are not exacerbated by mingling with delinquents. We thus avoid the unsavory situation whereby "the youngster whose only offense against society was that he could not get along with his parents, found himself cheek by jowl with the underage rapist, robber or heroin peddler." * * *

BROUSSARD, JUSTICE, dissenting. I dissent. The Legislature has made it clear that juvenile status offenders are not to be incarcerated. The majority hold that the status offender who disobeys a court order to attend school can be incarcerated, despite the fact that there is no statutory language, case law, or evidence of legislative intent to support such a conclusion. The majority ignore the Legislature's considered judgment that the harm which incarceration causes a status offender is too great to be permitted, even when the status offender fails to obey court orders. Instead the majority exalt the dignity of the court issuing the order over the best interest of the minor. Neither logic nor compassion can countenance such a result. * * *

Legislative authority for jailing truants for contempt of a section 601 order simply does not exist. I also see no constitutional infirmity in a system which prohibits incarceration of habitual truants. Though a court has the inherent power to punish contempt, the Legislature may place reasonable limitations on this power. A statute that took away all contempt power from the court or fixed a "wholly inadequate" penalty for a class of contempts would be an unconstitutional invasion of the court's power. But as long as the courts retain the power to "vindicate their authority and maintain the dignity and respect due to them," the legislative regulation of the contempt power is considered within constitutional bounds.

The juvenile court can punish the repeat truant for contempt, staying within the bounds of the section 601 wardship, by imposing fines, compulsory service to the community, or detention in nonsecure facilities during school hours. Under present law, * * * the juvenile court cannot incarcerate a minor made a ward of the court as a result of his truancy for willfully failing to obey the court's order to attend school. In holding otherwise, the majority reach too far.

Notes

1) Contempt and Confinement of Status Offenders States have struggled with the issue of secure detention and post-conviction dispositions of non-criminal youths, and most have affirmed their juvenile courts' use of the contempt power to order the secure detention of contemptuous status offenders despite an expression of legislative intent generally banning such detention. *In the Interest of D.L.D.*, 110 Wis.2d 168, 327 N.W.2d 682 (1983); *Interest of Darlene C.*, 278 S.C. 664, 301 S.E.2d 136 (1983); *State v. Norlund*, 31 Wash.App. 725, 644 P.2d 724 (1982); *In re G.B.*, 88 Ill.2d 36, 58 Ill.Dec. 845, 430 N.E.2d 1096 (1981), cert. den. 456 U.S. 963, 102 S.Ct. 2041, 72 L.Ed.2d 487; *State ex rel. L.E.A. v. Hammergren*, 294 N.W.2d 705 (Minn. 1980). A minority of states have disapproved the practice of using the contempt power to place a status offender in a secure facility. *W.M. v. State of Indiana*, 437 N.E.2d 1028 (Ind.App.1982); *Interest of Tasseing H.*, 281 Pa.Super. 400, 422 A.2d 530 (1980). *See also*, Rayna Hardee Bomar, "The Incarceration of the Status Offender," 18 *Memphis St. U. L. Rev.* 713 (1988); Evelyn C. Knauerhase, "The Federal Circle Game: The Precarious Constitutional Status of Status Offenders," 7 *Cooley L. Rev.* 31 (1990).

Why are these non-criminal youths such a problem? Too much autonomy or not enough? What can be done with youths who are simply "out of control" and who won't respond to parents or official authority?

In **In Interest of D.L.D.**, 110 Wis.2d 168, 327 N.W.2d 682, the trial court found the status offender in contempt of court for not following the court's previously ordered conditions of supervision, and ordered the minor to serve 20 days in secure detention. The Wisconsin Supreme Court reasoned that although the Wisconsin Children's Code generally prohibited the secure incarceration of status offenders with some exceptions, the statutory limitation cannot operate to deprive the court of its inherent contempt powers to enforce its orders:

> [T]wo policy decisions made by the legislature when revising the Children's Code become apparent. First, treatment and services for status offenders are to be emphasized in dispositional orders. And, second, secure detention for juveniles is to be discouraged and is appropriate only in a few limited situations. The question in this case then becomes whether a trial judge can rely on his contempt powers * * * and incarcerate a truant, notwithstanding the above legislative policy decisions present in the Children's Code. * * *

> The contempt order here appears to have both a remedial purpose and a punitive purpose. The contempt order was entered partially to uphold the court's authority, but at the same time, the order was remedial in that its purpose was to coerce D.L.D. into complying with the court's order. We hold the primary purpose of the contempt order was to force D.L.D. to attend school. The goal of a juvenile court judge is a protective one, not a punitive one. While we recognize that compliance with the order does vindicate the court's authority, this effect is only secondary. * * *

Where a court is granted jurisdiction over subject matters, it is implicit in that grant of jurisdiction that a court can use the contempt power to effectively carry out the functions ordered by the legislature. * * * Once jurisdiction has been granted to a court, it must have the requisite power to enforce its orders. Indeed, it is the court's duty to insure that its orders are obeyed by invoking the appropriate remedial sanctions. * * *

In **L.E.A. et al. v. Hammergren**, 294 N.W.2d 705 (1980), the Minnesota Supreme Court held that:

Juvenile courts have the authority to find a juvenile in contempt of court and to impose appropriate sanctions. But, given the Legislature's expressed disapproval of the practice of confining status offender juveniles in secure facilities, juvenile courts should not direct such confinement for contempt of court unless they first find specifically that there is no less restrictive alternative which could accomplish the court's purpose. * * *

Minnesota, in adopting the federal policy of deinstitutionalization of status offenders, is moving in the direction adopted by the ABA Juvenile Justice Standards Project, *Standards Relating to Noncriminal Misbehavior*. The ABA Standards, and their Commentary, conclude that runaway youth, truant youth, and otherwise "incorrigible" or "wayward" youth are best served outside the juvenile court system and outside juvenile detention facilities. * * * The Legislature may well have determined that removing status offenders from facilities designed for and used for law violators would result in better treatment, better programs, and better services for the child and that child's family. In addition, we interpret the amendment as reflecting the Legislature's concern with the effects of commingling disobedient or wayward children with juveniles who have allegedly committed more serious crimes.

In light of the foregoing, we hold that only under the most egregious circumstances should the juvenile courts exercise their contempt power in such a manner that a status offender will be incarcerated in a secure facility. If such action is necessary, the record must show that all less restrictive alternatives have failed in the past.

Before a party may be held in criminal or civil contempt for failure to abide by a court order, certain elements must be established: (1) the existence of a valid order directing the alleged contemnor to do or refrain from doing something and the court's jurisdiction to enter that order; (2) the contemnor's notice of the order within sufficient time to comply with it; and in most cases, (3) the contemnor's ability to comply with the order; and (4) the contemnor's willful failure to comply with the order.

In order for the juvenile court to find a "willful failure to comply" which warrants a holding of contempt, the record from the previous hearing must show that the child understood that disobedience would result in incarceration in a secure facility. A child too young to comprehend the warning cannot be found in contempt of court. With these limitations, the juvenile court can resort to the use of the secure facility if absolutely necessary.

Finally, if it is necessary to rely on the use of a secure facility, the order must include instructions to the administrator of the institution that the disobedient child's contact with the more committed juvenile be kept to a minimum. * * *

2) Status Offenders, Contempt of Court, and Continuing Sources of Gender Bias An evaluation of the use of juvenile court's contempt power revealed a continuing source of gender bias in dealing with status offenders. **Donna M. Bishop and Charles E. Frazier, "Gender Bias in Juvenile Justice Processing: Implications of the JJDP Act," 82 *J. Crim. L. & Criminology* 1162, 1182–86 (1992)** analyzed the case-processing delinquent and status offenders in the Florida juvenile justice system. Their analyses focused, in part, on the impact of the JJDP Act prohibitions of confinement of status offenders on the case-processing of male and female status offenders. The following excerpt summarizes their findings:

Our analyses of status offense cases, on the other hand, detected little evidence of gender bias. Youths referred to the justice system for status offenses tend to be younger than the average delinquency referral, and they are typically first-time offenders. The decision to refer these youths to court, as well as the decision to place them in foster care or group homes or to return them to their natural homes, was unaffected, for the most part, by the variables included in our models. Females were somewhat more likely than males to be referred to court for status offenses, but they had approximately the same probability as males of being adjudicated dependent and returned to their natural homes.

The finding that female status offenders do not receive harsher treatment than comparable males may be a result of the restrictions imposed by the JJDP Act. * * * Like most other states participating in programs under the JJDP Act, Florida has enacted laws prohibiting the secure detention and institutionalization in training schools of status offenders. Our findings are consistent with the notion that, at least insofar as first-time status offenders are concerned, this prohibition may have had a salutary impact upon females.

Finally and importantly, our analyses of contempt cases demonstrate that considerable gender bias remains in the handling of repeat status offenders. We found that females referred for contempt are more likely to be petitioned to court than females referred for other criminal-type offenses, and are substantially more likely to be petitioned to court than males referred for contempt. Moreover, females found in contempt are much more likely than their male counterparts to be sentenced to a period of up to six months' incarceration in secure detention facilities. These differences in the treatment of male and female offenders are striking and dramatic.

Our findings point to the conclusion that the traditional sexual double standard continues to operate. Neither cultural changes, such as those associated with the feminist movement, nor changes in the law, illustrated by the JJDP Act's mandate to deinstitutionalize status offenders, have brought about legal equality between young men and women in the juvenile justice system. Historical patterns of gender bias continue: Both female status offenders and male delinquents are differentially disadvantaged in the juvenile justice system. This state of affairs appears to reflect the continuation of protectionist policies toward female status offenders, as well as an attitude toward non-status offenders (delinquents) that sanctions differentially harsher penalties for males and more leniency toward females.

It is important to highlight the fact that, had we not introduced contempt status as a variable in our analyses and looked for interaction effects, our findings would have suggested that gender bias in juvenile justice processing had diminished considerably. This conclusion certainly does not fit our findings, but it is one that has been drawn in several recent studies that did not explore possible methods by which the JJDP Act's mandate to deinstitutionalize status offenders might be circumvented. Future research should pay special attention to the contempt power as a mechanism for enabling justice officials to act upon perceptions that males and females require or deserve different sorts of responses from the juvenile justice system.

1. ALTERNATIVE DISPOSITIONS OF "TROUBLESOME" YOUTHS—THE "HIDDEN SYSTEM"

As Federal and state laws make it increasingly difficult to institutionally confine non-criminal youths, other mechanisms of social control have emerged, such as commitment to private psychiatric hospitals or chemical dependency treatment facilities. *See e.g.* Paul Lerman, "Child Welfare, the Private Sector, and Community–Based Corrections," 30 *Crime & Delinquency* 5 (1984); Marilyn Jackson–Beeck, Ira M. Schwartz, and Andrew Rutherford, "Trends and Issues in Juvenile Confinement for Psychiatric and Chemical Dependency Treatment," 10 *J. L. and Psych.* 153 (1987). A number of commentators have noted the expansion of the "hidden system" of social control of chemical dependency facilities and secure mental hospitals as alternative mechanisms to confine "problematic" but non-criminal youths in conflict with their families as juvenile justice reforms eliminate traditional institutional placements. *See e.g.* Beverly Balos and Ira Schwartz, "Psychiatric and Chemical Dependency Treatment of Minors: The Myth of Voluntary Treatment and the Capacity to Consent," 92 *Dickinson L. Rev.* 631 (1988); Marc N. Sperber, "Short–Sheeting the Psychiatric Bed: State–Level Strategies to Curtail the Unnecessary Hospitalization of Adolescents in For–Profit Mental Health Facilities," 18 *Am. J. Law & Med* 251 (1992); Sandra A. Garcia, Eric Drogin, Robert Batey, and Richard E. Spana, "Institutionalized Delinquents and Maladjusted Juveniles: A Psycholegal Systems Analysis," 68 *Neb. L. Rev.* 261 (1989).

In examining alternative social control in the "hidden system", it is useful to contrast the legal regulations to which "voluntary civil commitment" institutions are subject with those of the juvenile justice process. Compare the procedural safeguards granted to delinquents in *Gault* with those afforded to youths in *Parham*.

PARHAM v. J. R.

442 U.S. 584, 99 S.Ct. 2493, 61 L.Ed.2d 101 (1979).

Mr. Chief Justice Burger delivered the opinion of the Court. The question presented in this appeal is what process is constitutionally due a minor child whose parents or guardian seek state administered institutional mental health care for the child and specifically whether an adversary proceeding is required prior to or after the commitment. * * *

After considering expert and lay testimony and extensive exhibits and after visiting two of the State's regional mental health hospitals, the District Court held that Georgia's statutory scheme was unconstitutional because it failed to protect adequately the appellees' due process rights. To remedy this violation, the court enjoined future commitments based on the procedures in the Georgia statute. It also commanded Georgia to appropriate and expend whatever amount was "reasonably necessary" to provide nonhospital facilities deemed by the appellant state officials to be the most appropriate for the treatment of those members of plaintiffs' class * * * who could be treated in a less drastic, nonhospital environment. * * *

Georgia Code § 88–503.1 (1975) provides for the voluntary admission to a state regional hospital of children such as J. L. and J. R. Under that provision, admission begins with an application for hospitalization signed by a "parent or guardian." Upon application, the superintendent of each hospital is given the power to admit temporarily any child for "observation and diagnosis." If, after observation, the superintendent finds "evidence of mental illness" and that the child is "suitable for treatment" in the hospital, then the child may be admitted "for such period and under such conditions as may be authorized by law."

Georgia's mental health statute also provides for the discharge of voluntary patients. Any child who has been hospitalized for more than five days may be discharged at the request of a parent or guardian. Even without a request for discharge, however, the superintendent of each regional hospital has an affirmative duty to release any child "who has recovered from his mental illness or who has sufficiently improved that the superintendent determines that hospitalization of the patient is no longer desirable." * * *

In holding unconstitutional Georgia's statutory procedure for voluntary commitment of juveniles, the District Court first determined that commitment to any of the eight regional hospitals constitutes a severe deprivation of a child's liberty. The court defined this liberty interest in terms of both freedom from bodily restraint and freedom from the "emotional and psychic harm" caused by the institutionalization.[7] Having

---

7. In both respects, the District Court found strong support for its holding in this Court's decision in *In re Gault*, (1967). In that decision, we held that a state cannot institutionalize a juvenile delinquent without first providing certain due process protections.

determined that a liberty interest is implicated by a child's admission to a mental hospital, the court considered what process is required to protect that interest. It held that the process due "includes at least the right after notice to be heard before an impartial tribunal."

In requiring the prescribed hearing, the court rejected Georgia's argument that no adversary-type hearing was required since the State was merely assisting parents who could not afford private care by making available treatment similar to that offered in private hospitals and by private physicians. The court acknowledged that most parents who seek to have their children admitted to a state mental hospital do so in good faith. It, however, relied on one of appellees' witnesses who expressed an opinion that "some still look upon mental hospitals as a 'dumping ground.'" No specific evidence of such "dumping," however, can be found in the record.

The District Court also rejected the argument that review by the superintendents of the hospitals and their staffs was sufficient to protect the child's liberty interest. The court held that the inexactness of psychiatry, coupled with the possibility that the sources of information used to make the commitment decision may not always be reliable, made the superintendent's decision too arbitrary to satisfy due process. * * *

The parties agree that our prior holdings have set out a general approach for testing challenged state procedures under a due process claim. Assuming the existence of a protectible property or liberty interest, the Court has required a balancing of a number of factors:

> "First, the private interest that will be affected by the official action; second, the risk of an erroneous deprivation of such interest through the procedures used, and the probable value, if any, of additional or substitute procedural safeguards; and finally, the Government's interest, including the function involved and the fiscal and administrative burdens that the additional or substitute procedural requirement would entail." *Mathews v. Eldridge* (1976).

In applying these criteria, we must consider first the child's interest in not being committed. Normally, however, since this interest is inextricably linked with the parents' interest in and obligation for the welfare and health of the child, the private interest at stake is a combination of the child's and parents' concerns. Next, we must examine the State's interest in the procedures it has adopted for commitment and treatment of children. Finally, we must consider how well Georgia's procedures protect against arbitrariness in the decision to commit a child to a state mental hospital.

It is not disputed that a child, in common with adults, has a substantial liberty interest in not being confined unnecessarily for medical treatment and that the state's involvement in the commitment decision constitutes state action under the Fourteenth Amendment. We also recognize that commitment sometimes produces adverse social consequences for the child because of the reaction of some to the discovery that the child has received psychiatric care.

This reaction, however, need not be equated with the community response resulting from being labeled by the state as delinquent, criminal, or mentally ill and possibly dangerous. The state through its voluntary commitment procedures does not "label" the child; it provides a diagnosis and treatment that medical specialists conclude the child requires. In terms of public reaction, the child who exhibits abnormal behavior may be seriously injured by an erroneous decision not to commit. Appellees overlook a significant source of the public reaction to the mentally ill, for what is truly "stigmatizing" is the symptomatology of a mental or emotional illness. * * *

For purposes of this decision, we assume that a child has a protectible interest not only in being free of unnecessary bodily restraints but also in not being labeled erroneously by some persons because of an improper decision by the state hospital superintendent.

We next deal with the interests of the parents who have decided, on the basis of their observations and independent professional recommendations, that their child needs institutional care. Appellees argue that the constitutional rights of the child are of such magnitude and the likelihood of parental abuse is so great that the parents' traditional interests in and responsibility for the upbringing of their child must be subordinated at least to the extent of providing a formal adversary hearing prior to a voluntary commitment.

Our jurisprudence historically has reflected Western civilization concepts of the family as a unit with broad parental authority over minor children. Our cases have consistently followed that course; our constitutional system long ago rejected any notion that a child is "the mere creature of the State" and, on the contrary, asserted that parents generally "have the right, coupled with the high duty, to recognize and prepare [their children] for additional obligations." Surely, this includes a "high duty" to recognize symptoms of illness and to seek and follow medical advice. The law's concept of the family rests on a presumption that parents possess what a child lacks in maturity, experience, and capacity for judgment required for making life's difficult decisions. More important, historically it has recognized that natural bonds of affection lead parents to act in the best interests of their children. * * *

Simply because the decision of a parent is not agreeable to a child or because it involves risks does not automatically transfer the power to make that decision from the parents to some agency or officer of the state. The same characterizations can be made for a tonsillectomy, appendectomy, or other medical procedure. Most children, even in adolescence, simply are not able to make sound judgments concerning many decisions, including their need for medical care or treatment. Parents can and must make those judgments. * * * The fact that a child may balk at hospitalization or complain about a parental refusal to provide cosmetic surgery does not diminish the parents' authority to decide what is best for the child.

Neither state officials nor federal courts are equipped to review such parental decisions. * * *

In defining the respective rights and prerogatives of the child and parent in the voluntary commitment setting, we conclude that our precedents permit the parents to retain a substantial, if not the dominant, role in the decision, absent a finding of neglect or abuse, and that the traditional presumption that the parents act in the best interests of their child should apply. We also conclude, however, that the child's rights and the nature of the commitment decision are such that parents cannot always have absolute and unreviewable discretion to decide whether to have a child institutionalized. They, of course, retain plenary authority to seek such care for their children, subject to a physician's independent examination and medical judgment.

The State obviously has a significant interest in confining the use of its costly mental health facilities to cases of genuine need. The Georgia program seeks first to determine whether the patient seeking admission has an illness that calls for inpatient treatment. * * *

The State in performing its voluntarily assumed mission also has a significant interest in not imposing unnecessary procedural obstacles that may discourage the mentally ill or their families from seeking needed psychiatric assistance. The *parens patriae* interest in helping parents care for the mental health of their children cannot be fulfilled if the parents are unwilling to take advantage of the opportunities because the admission process is too onerous, too embarrassing, or too contentious. * * *

The State also has a genuine interest in allocating priority to the diagnosis and treatment of patients as soon as they are admitted to a hospital rather than to time-consuming procedural minuets before the admission. One factor that must be considered is the utilization of the time of psychiatrists, psychologists, and other behavioral specialists in preparing for and participating in hearings rather than performing the task for which their special training has fitted them. Behavioral experts in courtrooms and hearings are of little help to patients. * * *

We now turn to consideration of what process protects adequately the child's constitutional rights by reducing risks of error without unduly trenching on traditional parental authority and without undercutting "efforts to further the legitimate interests of both the state and the patient that are served by" voluntary commitments. We conclude that the risk of error inherent in the parental decision to have a child institutionalized for mental health care is sufficiently great that some kind of inquiry should be made by a "neutral factfinder" to determine whether the statutory requirements for admission are satisfied. That inquiry must carefully probe the child's background using all available sources, including, but not limited to, parents, schools, and other social agencies. Of course, the review must also include an interview with the child. It is necessary that the decisionmaker have the authority to refuse to admit any child who does not satisfy the medical standards for admission.

Finally, it is necessary that the child's continuing need for commitment be reviewed periodically by a similarly independent procedure. * * *

Due process has never been thought to require that the neutral and detached trier of fact be law trained or a judicial or administrative officer. Surely, this is the case as to medical decisions, for "neither judges nor administrative hearing officers are better qualified than psychiatrists to render psychiatric judgments." Thus, a staff physician will suffice, so long as he or she is free to evaluate independently the child's mental and emotional condition and need for treatment.

It is not necessary that the deciding physician conduct a formal or quasi-formal, hearing. A state is free to require such a hearing, but due process is not violated by use of informal traditional medical investigative techniques. Since well-established medical procedures already exist, we do not undertake to outline with specificity precisely what this investigation must involve. The mode and procedure of medical diagnostic procedures is not the business of judges. What is best for a child is an individual medical decision that must be left to the judgment of physicians in each case. We do no more than emphasize that the decision should represent an independent judgment of what the child requires and that all sources of information that are traditionally relied on by physicians and behavioral specialists should be consulted. * * *

Here, the questions are essentially medical in character: whether the child is mentally or emotionally ill and whether he can benefit from the treatment that is provided by the state. While facts are plainly necessary for a proper resolution of those questions, they are only a first step in the process. In an opinion for a unanimous Court, we recently stated in *Addington v. Texas*, that the determination of "whether [a person] is mentally ill turns on the meaning of the facts which must be interpreted by expert psychiatrists and psychologists."

Although we acknowledge the fallibility of medical and psychiatric diagnosis, we do not accept the notion that the shortcomings of specialists can always be avoided by shifting the "decision from a trained specialist using the traditional tools of medical science to an untrained judge or administrative hearing officer after a judicial-type hearing. Even after a hearing, the nonspecialist decisionmaker must make a medical-psychiatric decision." * * *

Another problem with requiring a formalized, factfinding hearing lies in the danger it poses for significant intrusion into the parent-child relationship. Pitting the parents and child as adversaries often will be at odds with the presumption that parents act in the best interests of their child. It is one thing to require a neutral physician to make a careful review of the parents' decision in order to make sure it is proper from a medical standpoint; it is a wholly different matter to employ an adversary contest to ascertain whether the parents' motivation is consistent with the child's interests.

Moreover, it is appropriate to inquire into how such a hearing would contribute to the successful long-range treatment of the patient. Surely, there is a risk that it would exacerbate whatever tensions already exist between the child and the parents. Since the parents can and usually do play a significant role in the treatment while the child is hospitalized and even more so after release, there is a serious risk that an adversary confrontation will adversely affect the ability of the parents to assist the child while in the hospital. Moreover, it will make his subsequent return home more difficult. These unfortunate results are especially critical with an emotionally disturbed child; they seem likely to occur in the context of an adversary hearing in which the parents testify. A confrontation over such intimate family relationships would distress the normal adult parents and the impact on a disturbed child almost certainly would be significantly greater.

It has been suggested that a hearing conducted by someone other than the admitting physician is necessary in order to detect instances where parents are "guilty of railroading their children into asylums" or are using "voluntary commitment procedures in order to sanction behavior of which they disapprov[e]." Curiously, it seems to be taken for granted that parents who seek to "dump" their children on the state will inevitably be able to conceal their motives and thus deceive the admitting psychiatrists and the other mental health professionals who make and review the admission decision. It is elementary that one early diagnostic inquiry into the cause of an emotional disturbance of a child is an examination into the environment of the child. It is unlikely, if not inconceivable, that a decision to abandon an emotionally normal, healthy child and thrust him into an institution will be a discrete act leaving no trail of circumstances. Evidence of such conflicts will emerge either in the interviews or from secondary sources. * * *

By expressing some confidence in the medical decisionmaking process, we are by no means suggesting it is error free. On occasion, parents may initially mislead an admitting physician or a physician may erroneously diagnose the child as needing institutional care either because of negligence or an overabundance of caution. That there may be risks of error in the process affords no rational predicate for holding unconstitutional an entire statutory and administrative scheme that is generally followed in more than 30 states. "[P]rocedural due process rules are shaped by the risk of error inherent in the truthfinding process as applied to the generality of cases, not the rare exceptions." In general, we are satisfied that an independent medical decisionmaking process, which includes the thorough psychiatric investigation described earlier, followed by additional periodic review of a child's condition, will protect children who should not be admitted; we do not believe the risks of error in that process would be significantly reduced by a more formal, judicial-type hearing. * * *

Some members of appellees' class, including J. R., were wards of the State of Georgia at the time of their admission. Obviously their situation differs from those members of the class who have natural parents. While the determination of what process is due varies somewhat when the state, rather than a natural parent, makes the request for commitment, we conclude that the differences in the two situations do not justify requiring different procedures at the time of the child's initial admission to the hospital.

For a ward of the state, there may well be no adult who knows him thoroughly and who cares for him deeply. Unlike with natural parents where there is a presumed natural affection to guide their action, the presumption that the state will protect a child's general welfare stems from a specific state statute. * * * [W]e cannot assume that when the State of Georgia has custody of a child it acts so differently from a natural parent in seeking medical assistance for the child. * * * There is no evidence that the State, acting as guardian, attempted to admit any child for reasons unrelated to the child's need for treatment. * * *

On this record, we are satisfied that Georgia's medical factfinding processes are reasonable and consistent with constitutional guarantees. Accordingly, it was error to hold unconstitutional the State's procedures for admitting a child for treatment to a state mental hospital. The judgment is therefore reversed, and the case is remanded to the District Court for further proceedings consistent with this opinion.

Reversed and remanded. * * *

MR. JUSTICE BRENNAN, with whom MR. JUSTICE MARSHALL and MR. JUSTICE STEVENS join, concurring in part and dissenting in part. I agree with the Court that the commitment of juveniles to state mental hospitals by their parents or by state officials acting *in loco parentis* involves state action that impacts upon constitutionally protected interests and therefore must be accomplished through procedures consistent with the constitutional mandate of due process of law. I agree also that the District Court erred in interpreting the Due Process clause to require preconfinement commitment hearings in all cases in which parents wish to hospitalize their children. I disagree, however, with the Court's decision to pretermit questions concerning the postadmission procedures due Georgia's institutionalized juveniles. While the question of the frequency of postadmission review hearings may properly be deferred, the right to at least one postadmission hearing can and should be affirmed now. I also disagree with the Court's conclusion concerning the procedures due juvenile wards of the State of Georgia. I believe that the Georgia statute is unconstitutional in that it fails to accord preconfinement hearings to juvenile wards of the State committed by the State acting *in loco parentis*. * * *

Georgia denies hearings to juveniles institutionalized at the behest of their parents. Georgia rationalizes this practice on the theory that parents act in their children's best interests and therefore may waive their children's due process rights. Children incarcerated because their parents wish them confined, Georgia contends, are really voluntary patients. I cannot accept this argument.

In our society, parental rights are limited by the legitimate rights and interests of their children. * * * This principle is reflected in the variety of statutes and cases that authorize state intervention on behalf of neglected or abused children and that, *inter alia*, curtail parental authority to alienate their children's property, to withhold necessary medical treatment, and to deny children exposure to ideas and experiences they may later need as independent and autonomous adults. * * *

The presumption that parents act in their children's best interests, while applicable to most child-rearing decisions, is not applicable in the commitment context. Numerous studies reveal that parental decisions to institutionalize their children often are the results of dislocation in the family unrelated to the children's mental condition. Moreover, even well-meaning parents lack the expertise necessary to evaluate the relative advantages and disadvantages of inpatient as opposed to outpatient psychiatric treatment. Parental decisions to waive hearings in which such questions could be explored, therefore, cannot be conclusively deemed either informed or intelligent. In these circumstances, I respectfully suggest, it ignores reality to assume blindly that parents act in their children's best interests when making commitment decisions and when waiving their children's due process rights.

This does not mean States are obliged to treat children who are committed at the behest of their parents in precisely the same manner as other persons who are involuntarily committed. The demands of due process are flexible and the parental commitment decision carries with it practical implications that States may legitimately take into account. While as a general rule due process requires that commitment hearings precede involuntary hospitalization, when parents seek to hospitalize their children special considerations militate in favor of postponement of formal commitment proceedings and against mandatory adversary preconfinement commitment hearings.

First, the prospect of an adversary hearing prior to admission might deter parents from seeking needed medical attention for their children. Second, the hearings themselves might delay treatment of children whose home life has become impossible and who require some form of immediate state care. Furthermore, because adversary hearings at this juncture would necessarily involve direct challenges to parental authority, judgment, or veracity, preadmission hearings may well result in pitting the child and his advocate against the parents. This, in turn, might traumatize both parent and child and make the child's eventual return to his family more difficult.

Because of these special considerations, I believe that States may legitimately postpone formal commitment proceedings when parents seek inpatient psychiatric treatment for their children. Such children may be admitted, for a limited period, without prior hearing, so long as the admitting psychiatrist first interviews parent and child and concludes that short-term inpatient treatment would be appropriate. * * *

Although Georgia may postpone formal commitment hearings, when parents seek to commit their children, the State cannot dispense with such hearings altogether. * * * Whenever prior hearings are impracticable, States must provide reasonably prompt postdeprivation hearings. * * *

The special considerations that militate against preadmission commitment hearings when parents seek to hospitalize their children do not militate against reasonably prompt postadmission commitment hearings. In the first place, postadmission hearings would not delay the commencement of needed treatment. Children could be cared for by the State pending the disposition decision.

Second, the interest in avoiding family discord would be less significant at this stage since the family autonomy already will have been fractured by the institutionalization of the child. In any event, postadmission hearings are unlikely to disrupt family relationships. At later hearings, the case for and against commitment would be based upon the observations of the hospital staff and the judgments of the staff psychiatrists, rather than upon parental observations and recommendations. The doctors urging commitment, and not the parents, would stand as the child's adversaries. * * *

Georgia does not accord prior hearings to juvenile wards of the State of Georgia committed by state social workers acting *in loco parentis*. The Court dismisses a challenge to this practice on the grounds that state social workers are obliged by statute to act in the children's best interest. * * *

The social worker-child relationship is not deserving of the special protection and deference accorded to the parent-child relationship, and state officials acting *in loco parentis* cannot be equated with parents.

Second, the special considerations that justify postponement of formal commitment proceedings whenever parents seek to hospitalize their children are absent when the children are wards of the State and are being committed upon the recommendations of their social workers. The prospect of preadmission hearings is not likely to deter state social workers from discharging their duties and securing psychiatric attention for their disturbed clients. Moreover, since the children will already be in some form of state custody as wards of the State, prehospitalization hearings will not prevent needy children from receiving state care during the pendency of the commitment proceedings. Finally, hearings in which the decisions of state social workers are reviewed by other state officials are not likely to traumatize the children or to hinder their eventual recovery. * * *

Children incarcerated in public mental institutions are constitutionally entitled to a fair opportunity to contest the legitimacy of their confinement. They are entitled to some champion who can speak on their behalf and who stands ready to oppose a wrongful commitment. Georgia should not be permitted to deny that opportunity and that champion simply because the children's parents or guardians wish them to be confined without a hearing. The risk of erroneous commitment is simply too great unless there is some form of adversary review. And fairness demands that children abandoned by their supposed protectors to the rigors of institutional confinement be given the help of some separate voice.

NOTES

1) *Parham* and "Normal" Family Functioning How does the Court in *Parham* "know" about the functioning of families and the "neutrality" of physicians-as-factfinders in the commitment process? Should the Court have any concerns about the financial needs of private hospitals for new patients? How might fiscal considerations affect a physician's evaluation of an "acting out" youth? *See e.g.* Donald H. Stone, "The Civil Commitment Process for Juveniles: An Empirical Study," 65 *U.Det. L. Rev.* 679 (1988).

Most commentators' analyses of *Parham* conclude that it was insufficiently sensitive to the possible conflicts between youth's liberty interests, parental frustration with problematic adolescents, and hospital decision-makers' fiscal considerations. *See e.g.* Sidney S. Hollar, "The Never–Never Land of Mental Health Law: A Review of the Legal Rights of Youth Committed by Their Parents to Psychiatric Facilities in California," *Berkeley Women's L. J.* 300 (1978); Lee E. Teitelbaum and James W. Ellis, "The Liberty Interests of Children: Due Process Rights and Their Application," 12 *Fam. L. Q.* 153 (1978); Allen E. Shoenberger, " 'Voluntary' Commitment of Mentally Ill or Retarded Children: Child Abuse by the Supreme Court," 7 *U. Dayton L. Rev.* 1 (1981); Note, "The Mental Hospitalization of Children and the Limits of Parental Authority," 88 *Yale L.J.* 186 (1978); Carol K. Dillon, Margaret R. Roisman, Joel S. Sander, Betsy B. Adler, "*In re Roger S.*: The Impact of a Child's Due Process Victory on the California Mental Health System," 70 *Cal. L. Rev.* 373 (1982); Susan Turner, "*Parham v. J.R.*: Civil Psychiatric Commitment of Minors," 5 *J. Contemp. Health L. & Policy* 263 (1989); Willis J. Spaulding, "Post–*Parham* Remedies: The Involuntary Commitment of Minors in Virginia After *Parham v. J.R.*," 13 *U. Rich. L. Rev.* 695 (1979).

2) "Trans-institutionalization" and the "Hidden System" Dr. **Lois Weithorn, "Mental Hospitalization of Troublesome Youth: An Analysis of Skyrocketing Admission Rates," 40 *Stanford L. Rev.* 773 (1988)**, provides the definitive analysis of the "trans-institutionalization" of non-criminal youths into the "hidden system." She explores some of the legal and policy issues created by the Court's decision in *Parham* to allow parents "voluntarily" to institutionalize their children and to eschew post-commitment review of that decision:

Growing concerns in the 1960s and 1970s about the unchecked discretion of courts and mental health professionals to restrict the liberty of persons through incarceration in mental institutions led to judicial reforms, such as procedural protections and substantive standards, to guard against improper involuntary hospitalization. But these reforms typically did not extend to juvenile hospitalization procedures. Indeed, through the mid–1970s, most states still permitted parents or guardians to admit children in their custody to inpatient mental health facilities without any form of judicial oversight.

This lack of scrutiny of parental decisions is consistent with the traditional view that parents should have the power to consent to health care services for their minor children. Thus, minors admitted to psychiatric facilities based upon parental consent were regarded as "voluntary" admittees, even if they were unwilling patients. * * * In *Parham v. J.R* * * * the Court held that parental discretion, reinforced by the judgment of admitting staff that inpatient treatment was medically necessary, was adequate to protect minors' constitutional interests. Formal due process protections and strict substantive standards of the type required for the civil commitment of adults were deemed unnecessary.

Parham left the door open for states to provide protections to minors beyond the articulated constitutional minimum. Presently, state statutes vary in the protections they afford minors for whom mental hospitalization is sought. These statutes range from those that apply virtually the same procedural protections and substantive commitment criteria to minors as to adults to those that require little more than the *Parham* minimum. The dimensions on which state laws vary include: the extent to which they require *any* type of review prior to the admission of a minor beyond that performed by admitting staff; the timing of such review; whether such review is mandatory or triggered by petition; the form and process of such review and the concomitant rights of prospective patients (such as right to counsel); the substantive standards applied in such review; the role, if any, minors of various ages are given in choosing or refusing admission and in triggering any review process; and the extent to which admissions to private facilities are governed by statute. In general, however, minors are significantly less able than are adults to resist mental hospitalization sought for them by others. * * *

National data reveal that, between 1971 and 1980, admission rates for children and adolescents continued to rise, although most notable was the shift in the *location* of hospitalization from public to private facilities. Thus, whereas in 1971 private hospital admissions accounted for 37 percent of juvenile mental hospitalizations, in 1980 the proportion had risen to 61 percent. * * * [D]ata reveal a four and one-half fold increase in national juvenile admissions to private psychiatric hospitals between 1980 and 1984. The available statistics on psychiatric admissions to private *general* hospitals during that period also indicate striking upsurges, as high as a tripling of rates in one state. * * * [T]he private sector of the mental health industry is the fastest growing system of juvenile institutional care or control in the United States.

Some have argued that the recent dramatic increases in admissions of minors for inpatient mental health treatment reflect an appropriate societal response to allegedly increasing levels of serious emotional disorder experienced by America's youth, while others have concluded that a sizable proportion of recent juvenile admissions are inappropriate. * * * But even assuming arguendo that the frequency and magnitude of psychological distress experienced by children and adolescents have increased in recent years, the existence of such phenomena does not necessarily support the position that increased use of mental hospitalization for these juveniles is an appropriate societal response to such a problem. * * *

There exist no criteria, commonly accepted or applied within the fields of child and adolescent psychiatry and psychology, to guide decisions about juvenile mental hospital admissions. Various professional and licensing/accreditation organizations have promulgated sets of standards, but neither the American Psychological Association nor the American Psychiatric Association has developed formal criteria.

In the absence of professional guidance in the form of standards, certain rather vague and overly broad criteria have been promulgated. * * * The National Association of Private Psychiatric Hospitals ("NAPPH"), an organization whose members may have a financial interest in high admission rates, publishes criteria that could be used to justify the hospitalization of most troublesome, and many not-so-troublesome, juveniles. Not only do these criteria cite "sexual promiscuity" as an example of "self-defeating" and/or "self-destructive" behavior necessitating "immediate acute-care hospitalization [as] the only reasonable intervention," but they fail to define what type of sexual activity constitutes "promiscuity." Such a standard allows anyone using the guidelines to apply personal moral standards in making admission decisions. * * * The NAPPH criteria mention as another justification for hospitalization "inability to function" in one of the following areas: family life, vocational pursuits, and "choice of community resources." The commentary accompanying the criteria implies that a teenager who prefers certain nonfavored social activities (such as listening to punk rock music) over attending scout or church youth group meetings may be making a sufficiently poor "choice of community resources" to justify his hospitalization.

Of currently existing standards, the most useful are those developed by the American Academy of Child and Adolescent Psychiatry ("AACAP") because of their relative specificity and congruence with more general legal and clinical principles. Basically, these standards reflect the perspective that inpatient treatment should be recommended only when "less-intensive" alternatives, such as outpatient and other community treatments, have been shown to be inadequate. * * * The doctrine of the "least restrictive alternative" reflects the legal policy that interference with the liberty of those experiencing psychological problems should be permitted only when no less restrictive or intrusive alternatives exist. * * *

The AACAP recommends that hospitalization for children and adolescents, even for a period of time as brief as two weeks, be used only when children are having *severe* problems that are primarily attributable to a "psychiatric disease." Criteria justifying hospitalization include, for example: (a) "acute disabling symptoms or mental illness such as impaired reality testing, disordered or bizarre behavior, psychotic organic brain symptoms * * *," (b) "acute danger to property or self or others * * * attributable to primary psychiatric disease * * *," and (c) "*severely* impaired social or family or educational or vocational or developmental functioning." Lengthier hospitalizations require stronger justification that twenty-four hour care is in fact needed. Such justification may include establishing that patients continue to be dangerous to themselves or others, or that the home environments to which they would be returned are inadequate or problematic (as where parents may be actively mentally ill or abusing drugs or alcohol). * * *

[A]lthough many seriously emotionally disturbed adolescents benefit from the intensive and structured care of an inpatient treatment setting, a large proportion (perhaps as great as one-half to two-thirds) of recent juvenile admissions to psychiatric facilities are inappropriate. First, many adolescents admitted to psychiatric facilities in recent years did not have severe or acute mental illnesses, nor did their behavior require an inpatient environment in order to protect them or others from their potentially dangerous conduct. Second, in many cases psychiatric hospitalization provides less effective treatment than do outpatient alternatives. * * * Third, psychiatric hospitalization inherently restricts liberty and invades privacy, rendering it less desirable than community-based treatment. * * * Whereas these disadvantages of hospital-based psychiatric treatment may be justified when children require institutional restraint in order to protect them and others from their behavior, it clearly does not appear justified when other, less restrictive and equally effective options are available. * * *

Fewer than one-third of those juveniles admitted for inpatient mental health treatment in recent years were diagnosed as having severe or acute mental disorders of the type typically associated with such admissions (such as psychotic, serious depressive, or organic disorders). By contrast, about one-half to two-thirds of adults admitted for inpatient mental health treatment were diagnosed as having such serious disorders. Yet, once hospitalized, juvenile psychiatric patients remain in the hospital approximately twice as long as do adults. And, children hospitalized in *private* facilities are both more likely to have longer stays and less likely to be severely disturbed than are children in public facilities.

About two-thirds of juvenile inpatients receive initial diagnoses of conduct disorder, personality or childhood disorder, or transitional disorder. An examination of the various "symptoms" that characterize each type of disorder reveals that, in general, these categories describe troublemakers, children with relatively mild psychological problems, and children who do not appear to suffer from anything more serious than normal developmental changes.

For example, in order to assign a conduct disorder diagnosis, a clinician must note a persistent pattern of antisocial conduct for at least six months. Depending upon which of the enumerated behavioral problems a child exhibits, a clinician might diagnose the child as demonstrating a more "aggressive" versus "nonaggressive" conduct disorder, or a more socially oriented (such as gang-directed) or "solitary" conduct disorder. The more aggressive constellations of behavior may manifest as physical violence against persons or property, or thefts involving personal confrontation. As such, this "disorder" may mirror the type of behavior that could lead to an adjudication of delinquency in the juvenile justice system. The nonaggressive manifestations of this behavior problem include chronic violations of rules at home or at school, truancy, running away, persistent lying, or stealing not involving personal confrontation. Thus, the conduct required for this category is virtually parallel to conduct that could lead a judge to find that a minor is a status offender. These parallels have not escaped researchers, who have studied the similarities among juveniles in psychiatric and correctional facilities. Several have posited that rising rates of juvenile psychiatric admission result from the transinstitutionalization of children from the juvenile justice to the mental health system.

A second class of diagnoses frequently assigned to adolescent inpatients is that of the "personality disorders." This category includes the "oppositional disorder," the "identity disorder," and the "avoidant disorder." Children exhibiting the behavior required for a diagnosis of one of these disorders also are unlikely to be seriously mentally ill. For example, the oppositional disorder diagnosis requires a six month pattern of behavior such as stubbornness, violations of minor rules, argumentativeness, and temper tantrums. Yet developmental researchers often regard such nondangerous expressions of oppositional behavior as a normal aspect of the transition from childhood to adolescence. Similar claims as to the nonpathological nature of the identity disorder and avoidant disorder can be made. An identity disorder is defined by a pattern of "severe subjective distress regarding uncertainty about a variety of issues relating to identity" (such as long-term goals, career choice, and friendship patterns). Many psychologists, however, view an "identity crisis" as an essential step on the path to healthy psychological development. Finally, although the excessive shyness that characterizes an avoidant disorder can interfere with social functioning, it also may represent one end of a continuum of normal behavior. Research suggests that in a large percentage of cases, the presence of such behavior in childhood is transitory.

The symptoms associated with "adjustment disorders" also do not suggest the presence of a serious mental disorder. Adjustment disorders, also called "transitional disorders" or "situational disorders," are characterized by an "overreaction" of some sort to identifiable social stressors (such as parental fighting), leading to impairment in social or occupational functioning. Incorporated into the formal definition of these disorders, however, is a recognition that "the disturbance will eventually remit after the stressor ceases or, if the stressor persists, when a new level of adaptation is achieved." This acknowledgment directly contradicts the notion that the disorders in this category represent serious mental illnesses. Nonetheless, in 1975 they accounted for more than 30 percent of all juvenile admissions to public and private psychiatric hospitals, and to psychiatric units of private general hospitals. * * *

In sum, the behaviors that characterize about half of the patients in juvenile psychiatric units do not reflect severe or acute mental illness. Despite the very real psychological pain that children assigned one of the diagnoses described in this section may experience, most do not require the intensive intervention of a mental hospital. Although some proportion of juveniles in such hospitals are psychotic or seriously emotionally disturbed, many more appear to be troublemakers, children reacting to disturbed or inadequate family situations, or adolescents experiencing nonpathological turmoil, rebellion, or identity crisis. If an emotionally disturbed adolescent is imminently dangerous to herself or to others, many argue that it is appropriate to restrain that individual in a mental institution until such time as she can be rendered nondangerous. But most children undergoing inpatient mental health treatment are not dangerous. * * *

Studies that have examined the comparative efficacy of psychiatric hospitalization and alternative treatments consistently reveal that community-based alternatives are more effective than is institutional treatment. * * * In general, the findings of these studies suggest that intensive home and community-based services for emotionally disturbed and troublesome adolescents are extremely promising alternatives to institutional and residential placements. Furthermore, the studies reveal that these noninstitutional services can be provided at lower costs than can institutional services. * * *

In summary, it is clear that mental hospitalization *generally* is not more effective than are community-based methods for adult psychiatric patients. And, the limited number of studies that have compared inpatient and outpatient services for children reached similar conclusions. Finally, initial empirical results suggest that recent innovations in home-and community-based programs for families with difficult children may be more effective than is institutional care. * * *

Changes in the American family structure, particularly increases in the rates of divorce and in the prevalence of single-parent households, have made it more likely that youth will experience adjustment difficulties *and* that their parents will be unable to cope effectively with those difficulties or other behavioral problems within the family unit. In the absence of intrafamilial resources adequate to handle troublesome youth, families and community agencies, such as schools and police departments, seek assistance from sources external to the family, most frequently the mental health or juvenile justice systems. Although the community-based interventions described above might adequately meet family and community needs, unavailability and lack of insurance coverage reduce the likelihood that families will have access to such programs. Thus, institutional solutions for problematic juvenile behavior are typically sought.

Whereas in prior years, the juvenile justice system institutionalized troublemaking youth as status offenders, recent legal reforms have closed the doors of juvenile justice institutions to a sizable population of difficult children. Families and community agencies seeking intensive intervention have turned increasingly to mental hospitals: the only institutional alternative that is available, provides easy access, and is adequately funded by third-party payment. * * *

[T]he juvenile correctional system experienced steady increases in the numbers of residents in its short-term detention and long-term facilities until the 1970s. * * * The growing push for deinstitutionalization of youth in juvenile justice facilities prompted Congress to pass the Juvenile Justice and Delinquency Prevention Act ("JJDPA") in 1974. Supporters of the JJDPA had hoped that the Act would condition state receipt of federal juvenile justice funds upon removal of all but the most serious offenders from juvenile correctional facilities. The legislation Congress eventually passed, however, mandated only the deinstitutionalization of nonoffenders (that is, dependent and neglected youth) and status offenders.

The effect of the JJDPA on the dispositions of status offenders was dramatic. From 1974 to 1979, the arrest rate of status offenders decreased by about 16 percent; from 1975 to 1979, the rate of status offense cases processed by juvenile courts dropped more than 21 percent; and, most dramatically, from 1975 to 1979, the rate at which juvenile courts referred offenders to detention facilities decreased by 68 percent. Thus, not only has the number of status offenders processed by the juvenile justice system decreased, but those identified as status offenders are less likely to be sent to juvenile justice institutions. These data suggest that states successfully implemented Congress' mandate to deinstitutionalize status offenders. However, a more cautious interpretation of these results is in order in light of the recent increases in rates of admission to psychiatric facilities and the discussion below. * * *

The available data for the late 1970s reveal reductions in juvenile court processing and incarceration of status offenders that may have been offset by increases in admissions to mental hospitals. If this in fact occurred, many youth are not being deinstitutionalized, as policymakers intended, but are being "transinstitutionalized." The term "transinstitutionalization" refers to the transfer of a population from one institutional system to another as an inadvertent consequence of policies intended to deinstitutionalize the target population. * * *

There is no way to be certain that shifting rates of institutionalization among the child care and control systems are, in fact, some form of transinstitutionalization. Yet, several factors support such a conclusion. First, studies conducted with reference to populations other than youth strongly support the argument that the transinstitutionalization phenomenon may be an artifact of deinstitutionalization programs more generally. Second, as described above, institutions for the care and control of children historically have handled a somewhat interchangeable population. Recent intersystem shifts thus may represent simply a new manifestation of a familiar phenomenon. Third, the diagnoses given to a substantial proportion of children now in psychiatric facilities indicate that a label of status offender or juvenile delinquent could be just as easily applied to them as to those actually assigned such labels in the juvenile justice system. Fourth, the "case histories" of many minors admitted to psychiatric facilities reveal either that they personally have been transferred from one institutional system to another, or that they could have been processed in the juvenile justice or child welfare system, given the behaviors and situations leading to their hospitalization. Finally, some juvenile court and social welfare practitioners specifically have acknowledged trying to "get around" mandates not to institutionalize status offenders by having minors before them diagnosed as mentally ill so that they may be hospitalized in psychiatric facilities. * * *

The search for an institutional means to handle troublesome youth is a search for some social mechanism to control these youth. And, as argued above with specific reference to the three primary juvenile care and control systems, mechanisms of social control are interdependent in this country. That is, when access to one social control system is blocked, persons who might have been handled within that system are managed through remaining social control mechanisms. If a new legal label is required to allow access to the available system of social control, society may assign a new designation to the troublesome behavior, as when adolescents who might have been called status offenders in prior years are diagnosed as having conduct disorders. The different labels merely represent "alternative rationales for containment and control" of the same persons. Shifts from system to system, and the use of whatever labels are appropriate to the available system, permit the retention of social control in the face of legal reforms designed to counteract that control. In short, whatever social control mechanism "works" or is most convenient at a given point in time and in a given legal, economic, and sociocultural context may be the designation of choice. * * *

As the doors to juvenile justice institutions began to close to minors who did not commit criminal acts, and the doors to child welfare facilities remained barely ajar, the doors to psychiatric hospitals were swung wide open by the United States Supreme Court. In 1979, in *Parham v. J.R.,* a divided Court declined to require states to take meaningful steps to prevent inappropriate use of juvenile psychiatric facilities. The Court essentially endorsed unbridled discretion for parents (or state guardians) and admitting staffs in decisions concerning juvenile admissions to such facilities. * * *

Another, and perhaps the most disturbing, assumption the Court made in *Parham* is that hospital staff are able to serve as "neutral factfinders." The Court relied on this assumption in concluding that staff findings provide an adequate due process check on the discretion of parents or state custodians seeking to hospitalize a child. * * * Assuming that the staff have no vested interest in higher admission rates, substantial questions remain about the adequacy of present-day methods for determining when a child or adolescent requires inpatient psychiatric treatment. Given the paucity of useful scientific guidance and the confused state of mental health practice regarding this subject, the Court's sole reliance on the expertise of mental health practitioners clearly seems misplaced.

Moreover, the emergence and gradual domination of for-profit psychiatric hospital services for children and adolescents undermines the Court's crucial assumption that admitting staff are impartial decisionmakers. The fact that these facilities' profits increase when beds are filled raises serious doubts about the ability of their staffs to function as "neutral factfinders." Thus, even if the Court were correct in its assessment of how state facility staff function in this protective role, the world has changed since *Parham* was decided. Psychiatric hospitalization of juveniles no longer occurs primarily in state-run and non-profit settings. The admission of juveniles for inpatient mental health treatment is now "big business." Private hospital admissions account for the large majority of juvenile psychiatric admissions, and the numbers continue to rise. This shift in the locus of care seriously erodes the validity of the *Parham* Court's critical assumption that hospital staff will make disinterested admission decisions. * * *

In the absence of meaningful scrutiny of juvenile mental hospital admissions, there are few obstacles to using mental hospitals to deal with society's demand that something be done with or for troublesome youths. Most ironic about this scenario is that the individuals whose judgment the Supreme Court substituted for impartial judicial oversight—the hospital admitting staff—

increasingly have become those with the most to gain from rising admission rates. * * *

The Supreme Court's decision in *Parham* has perpetuated a situation in which many juvenile admissions are only minimally scrutinized. But the permissive legal context is only part of the reason why juvenile mental hospital admissions have increased so dramatically. Perhaps the most powerful factor encouraging the overuse of mental health hospital services is that private and government funding of mental health services strongly favors inpatient over outpatient treatment. * * *

Considering the dilemmas of families with problem children, one can understand why even those families who prefer to keep their children at home may choose inpatient mental health services, despite the existence of community-based alternatives that may be more effective and less expensive: Inpatient treatment may be the only option adequately covered by their insurance. Thus, a more effective option is not really an option if the absence of any reimbursement or the presence of high deductibles and copayment requirements makes access impossible. Although community-based services may be less expensive than inpatient services *to provide,* they are not less expensive *to the consumer* if the consumer can obtain 100 percent coverage for inpatient services and significantly less coverage for community-based services. * * *

Further complicating the reimbursement picture is the fact that consumer-oriented mental health advocacy groups have often lobbied for greater parity in insurance coverage between mental and physical health services. Partially as a result of such lobbying, some state legislatures have enacted policies requiring private insurance companies to provide certain minimum inpatient and outpatient mental health benefits. * * *

The proprietary hospital movement is increasingly dominated by large enterprises owning several institutions. Businesspeople * * * rather than physicians or hospital administrators, often direct these enterprises. The business of for-profit health care has proven financially profitable for investors, and all indications suggest that corporate domination of health care resources will continue to expand. * * *

Perhaps the most problematic aspect of the increasing for-profit control of juvenile psychiatric facilities is the potential conflict of interests experienced by referring professionals who have financial interests in the facilities to which they refer prospective patients.

The interchangeability of the social and legal labels defining "bad" behavior (actions suitable for control in the criminal or juvenile justice systems) and "sick" behavior (actions suitable for control in the mental health system) has been the subject of much scholarship. Researchers have coined the phrase, "the medicalization of deviance," to describe society's redesignation of certain behaviors (previously considered to be "bad" or "sinful") as "sick." * * * Shifts in deviance designations may represent "alternative rationales for containment and control" of the same persons, and the labels may change to accommodate the inaccessibility of a former social control mechanism and the availability of an alternative. * * *

Shifts in deviance designations also may have "symbolic" implications for society. Our society's emphasis on humanitarian values, such as benevolent care for those in distress, together with the "optimism of science," may support trends toward medicalization. When medical terminology characterizes the nature of and interventions imposed on deviant behavior, we feel better about our treatment of deviants than we would if we thought we were "punishing" them or that they were "hopeless." The characterization of a category of "deviants" as having medical (and, preferably, biologically-based) disorders, rather than as simply being "bad," may be especially appealing to parents of the "deviant" persons. The "illness" designation makes parents the objects of sympathy and compassion, rather than the objects of blame as allegedly inadequate parents. * * *

Medicalization of certain behavioral forms, such as troublesome juvenile conduct, is aided by the fact that formal psychiatric diagnostic categories are sufficiently manipulable to facilitate redesignation. These categories also command the social respect necessary to make the shift believable and acceptable to the public. Thus, extremely malleable categories of psychiatric diagnosis serve to facilitate sociological processes of shifting deviance designations. * * * In sum, traditional psychiatric diagnoses are quite malleable. Their reach may be extended to label as "sick" many forms of behavior that, albeit troublesome, are relatively normative and not in need of intensive intervention.

A combination of factors, including laissez-faire judicial policies, insurance coverage favoring inpatient treatment, the rise of corporate medicine, a mental health establishment willing to assume control over troublesome youth, and the symbolic appeal of a medical perspective on deviance appear to have converged to promote the inappropriate use of inpatient mental health services for the management of difficult children and adolescents. * * *

INDEX

References are to Pages

References are to Pages

†